Criminal Defense Tools and Techniques

by Thomas J. Farrell

HIGHLIGHTS

The 2017 edition of *Criminal Defense Tools and Techniques* overflows with new and updated legal analysis and practical advice to help you protect your clients' rights. You receive **five new forms**, plus **expanded coverage of a broad range of topics** throughout the book, including:

ENTERING THE CASE
- Protecting the confidentiality of attorney-client communications when your client calls from jail
- Impact of joint representation on the confidentiality of attorney-client communications

BAIL AND PRETRIAL RELEASE
- Use of Detention Risk Assessment Instruments
- Impact of immigration detainers

EXPERTS AND INVESTIGATORS
- Minimum requirements established by the constitutional rule of *Ake*, as outlined by the Supreme court in *McWilliams v. Dunn*, 137 S.Ct. 1790 (2017)
- Precautions you must take when interviewing your client's employees

SEARCH AND SEIZURE
- Relationship between "overbreadth" and "particularity" requirements in a warrant
- Does the Confrontation Clause require witnesses to testimonial hearsay to appear and face cross-examination at pretrial suppression hearings?
- What happens when a lawful search yields evidence the government has no right to review (e.g., privileged communications)?

IDENTIFICATION PROCEDURES
- Updated case law reflecting the trend to allow trial judges discretion to admit expert testimony on the weaknesses of eyewitness identification

FORFEITURE
- "Substitute assets" theory under which a prosecutor can seek forfeiture
- Arguments in support of defendant's claim that forfeiture is disproportionate to the offense

GRAND JURY PRACTICE
- Arguing the full breadth of the Fifth Amendment privilege against self-incrimination
- Steps to take when the prosecutor subpoenas a defense attorney

TRIAL
- Prosecution motions *in limine* to preclude a defense
- Voir dire – how to deal with bad evidence you know the jury will hear
- Tips for preparing your client to testify

NEW FORMS
- Motion to Compel Return of Property
- Motion to Impound Privileged Documents for In Camera or Special Master Review
- Letter Asserting Privilege to Former Attorney's Counsel
- Letter to Grand Jury Judge Asking to be Heard Before Attorney Testifies
- Civil Proffer Agreement

 James Publishing

We Welcome Your Feeback

Our most useful source of improvements is comments from our subscribers, so if you have any comments, we would love to hear from you.

Revision Editor
James Publishing, Inc.
3505 Cadillac Avenue, Suite P-101
Costa Mesa, California 92626

Visit us on the Internet at www.JamesPublishing.com.

How To Access Your Digital Forms

Included with your copy of this book is access to all its forms in digital format. So you can easily open and modify the forms, **we have replaced our jamesforms.com website and our old CDs with a convenient ZIP file of Word documents.**

Access is easy.
If you purchased this title on jamespublishing.com, a link to download the ZIP file should have already been delivered to your email inbox. Be sure to add customer-service@jamespublishing.com to your safe sender list so this message doesn't land in a spam folder. You can also access the download link at any time by **logging in at jamespublishing.com and clicking My Account** in the upper right-hand corner.

No account yet? No problem.
If you do not yet have a jamespublishing.com account, or you are having trouble, please contact customer support at **1-866-725-2637** or customer-service@jamespublishing.com. We will get you setup right away.

How to unzip the file:
Once you download the ZIP file, you need to extract the files onto your system. Typically, files are downloaded into your Downloads folder unless another directory was specified. Follow these steps to unzip:

1. **Double-click the ZIP file**. In Windows XP or newer and Mac OS X, you can double-click the ZIP file and it will open in a new window. You can then copy the contents to another folder. OS X will create a new folder next to the ZIP file when you double-click it, but may not open it automatically.

2. **Right-click the ZIP file**. In Windows you can right-click the ZIP file and select *Extract All...* or *Extract Here*. Extract All will allow you to set a path for the extracted folder to go, and Extract Here will decompress the folder and leave it in the same location as the ZIP file.

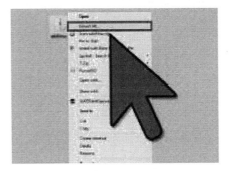

Can I share my digital forms with others?
No. Our forms are copyrighted, and they are licensed to a single individual book purchaser for his or her use only. It is unfair to our book authors if their forms are freely distributed, so please honor their hard work by not sharing their forms. Thank you for understanding.

(This page intentionally left blank.)

Thomas J. Farrell

Criminal Defense
Tools and Techniques

Contact us at (866) 72-JAMES (866-725-2637) or visit www.jamespublishing.com

James Publishing
Copyright © 2017
James Publishing, Inc.
ISBN: 978-1-945421-67-9

Related Titles

Federal Criminal Practice
Relentless Criminal Cross-Examination
Texas Criminal Lawyer's Handbook
Texas Criminal Forms

We view the publication of this work as the beginning of a dialogue with our readers. Periodic revisions to it will give us the opportunity to incorporate your suggested changes. Call us at (866) 72-JAMES or send your comments to:

Revision Editor
James Publishing
3505 Cadillac Ave., Suite P-101
Costa Mesa, CA 92626

PUBLISHER'S STAFF

Managing Editor: Lisa Dunne
Typesetter: Alexandru Oprescu

First Edition, 12/08
Revision 1, 12/09
Revision 2, 12/10
Revision 3, 4/12
Revision 4, 4/13
Revision 5, 3/14
Revision 6, 5/15
Revision 7, 10/17

ABOUT THE AUTHOR

Thomas J. Farrell's practice focuses on criminal defense, ranging from pre-indictment investigations and negotiations and the representation of witnesses and victims, to appeals and post-conviction petitions; from white collar matters such as health care fraud, tax evasion, complex securities frauds, and environmental crimes, to capital murder. His cases have included such high profile matters as the representation of New York Yankees pitcher Andy Pettitte before Congress; the largest Clean Water Act recovery from a citizen's suit in the state of Pennsylvania; the only False Claims Act whistleblower suit in the for-profit education sector to merit intervention by the U.S. Department of Justice; defense of the largest fraud case ever prosecuted in the Western District of Pennsylvania; and defense of the Penn State perjury case. He also teaches as an adjunct professor at Duquesne Law School and the University of Pittsburgh School of Law. He is a partner with Farrell & Reisinger, LLC, in Pittsburgh, PA (www.farrellreisinger.com).

Mr. Farrell was selected as one of The Best Lawyers in America from 2006 to 2013 for white collar and non-white collar criminal defense. He is AV-rated by Martindale-Hubbell.

Mr. Farrell has been in private practice since 2000. From 1995 to 2000, he was an Assistant United States Attorney in the Western District of Pennsylvania, where he prosecuted financial crimes, including health care fraud, government contracting fraud, tax evasion, bank fraud, and public corruption. The Executive Office for United States Attorneys awarded him the Director's Award for Exceptional Performance by an Assistant United States Attorney for his work in prosecuting corrupt public officials. Before his term as an AUSA, Mr. Farrell was an Assistant Federal Public Defender in New York City, where he tried cases ranging from robbery and check theft to organized crime and public corruption. He started his legal career as law clerk to U.S. District Court Judge Gustave Diamond of the Western District of Pennsylvania.

EDITORIAL ADVISORY BOARD

The following individuals have assisted in this book by providing editorial feedback on one or more of the chapters.

SUMMARY TABLE OF CONTENTS

TABLE OF CONTENTS

Chapter 1

ENTERING THE CASE

Chapter 2

THE REPRESENTATION AGREEMENT

Chapter 3

ARREST & INITIAL APPEARANCE

Chapter 4

BAIL & PRE-TRIAL RELEASE

Chapter 5

EXTRADITION

Chapter 6

EXPERTS & INVESTIGATORS

Chapter 7

SEARCH & SEIZURE

Chapter 8

INTERROGATIONS, CONFESSIONS AND OTHER STATEMENTS

Chapter 9

IDENTIFICATION PROCEDURES

Chapter 10

PRELIMINARY HEARINGS

Chapter 11

FORFEITURE

Chapter 12

GRAND JURY PRACTICE

Chapter 13

MENTAL HEALTH ISSUES

Chapter 14

DISCOVERY

Chapter 15

MOTION PRACTICE

Chapter 16

[RESERVED]

Chapter 17

PLEA BARGAINING

Chapter 18

REPRESENTING VICTIMS AND WITNESSES

Chapter 19

RELATED CIVIL LITIGATION

Chapter 20

TRIAL

Chapter 21

POST-TRIAL MOTIONS

Chapter 22

SENTENCING

Chapter 23

PROBATION, PAROLE & OTHER POST-RELEASE SUPERVISION

Chapter 24

APPEALS

INDEX

Chapter 1

ENTERING THE CASE

I.   THE FIRST STEPS

§1:01   Getting the Case

The criminal matter can come to practitioners in many forms and ways:
- Someone may call from jail or the stationhouse.
- The court may appoint you to a client already indicted.
- A civil attorney may call you because his client has received a grand jury subpoena or because the authorities are at the client's business or home with a search warrant.
- A school principal may find a child's e-mails to classmates disturbing, and the parents and child show up at your office to determine if they should worry about more than the child's academic record.
- An ex-client may contact you because a brother has been arrested.

While clients come with differing exigencies and personalities, taking the following steps before you meet the client should insure that the relationship starts well:
- Learn how to contact the client. [See §1:02.]
- Tell authorities that you represent the defendant. [See §1:03.]
- Learn where the client stands in the criminal process. [See §1:04.]
- Learn the positions of the police and prosecutor on bail. [See Chapter 4, Bail & Pre-Trial Release.]
- Tell the client to not speak to anyone about the offense. [See §1:05.]

Exercise caution with potential clients who are shopping for attorneys. If a person discusses with you the possibility of entering into an attorney-client relationship, you are obligated to maintain the confidentiality of any information learned from the potential client, even if he does not retain you. [Rule of Professional Conduct 1.18; *see generally*, Peter A. Joy and Kevin C. McMunigal, "Client or Prospective Client: What's the Difference?," 27 CRIMINAL JUSTICE 51 (Fall 2012).] The brief relationship also may bar you from representing someone else in the same or a substantially related matter if you "received information from the prospective client that could be significantly harmful to that person in the matter." [Mode Rule of Professional Conduct 1.18(c).] You can avoid this future disqualification by conditioning your "conversations with a prospective client on the person's informed consent that no information disclosed during the consultation will prohibit the lawyer from representing a different client in the matter." [Model Rule 1.18, Comment 5.] At least one commentator suggests the use of non-engagement letters which "should explicitly state that the lawyer did not provide any advice to the prospective client and that the lawyer does not plan to provide any legal service to the prospective client." [Joy & McMunigal, *supra*, 27 CRIMINAL JUSTICE at 54.] You might add to the letter as well the ex-prospective client's consent to your representation of other clients in the same matter.

§1:02   Find the Client

Find out where the client is, and obtain the information necessary to contact him:
- Address.
- Phone number.
- Driving directions.
- Name by which the client is known.

If the client is under arrest, find out where he is detained (i.e., which jail or stationhouse). Ask for his inmate number and the floor on which he resides.

§1:03   Tell Authorities That You Represent the Defendant

Tell the authorities that you represent the defendant and that they are not to question him about the offense in your absence.

If your client is in police custody, call the police officer in charge of the investigation immediately and inform him of your representation and instruct him not to speak to your client. You should also tell the police to inform your client that (1) an attorney is available to represent him; (2) you want to speak to your client; (3) the attorney said not to talk to the police; and (4) you will be at the station shortly. [*Commonwealth v. Rivera*, 464 Mass. 56, 66, 981 N.E.2d 171, 181-82 (2013) (holding that police are obligated to convey the above to the arrestee, but the police are not obligated to follow an instruction *to them* (as opposed to the above advice *to the client*) that they are not to talk to the arrestee).]

The United States Supreme Court has held that the U.S. Constitution does not require the police to honor such demands and that the police can interrogate until the client initiates a demand for counsel. [*Moran v. Burbine*, 475 U.S. 412 (1986).] Nevertheless, many state courts have rejected *Moran* on state law grounds and ruled that upon a request from counsel, the police must stop interrogation and grant the arrestee access to counsel, or, at minimum, inform the arrestee that counsel is trying to contact him. [See *State v. McAdams*, 193 So. 3d 824, 832 (Fla. 2016) ("we now hold that when an individual is being questioned in a non-public area, and an attorney retained on his or her behalf arrives at the location, the Due Process Clause of the Florida Constitution requires that the police notify the individual of the attorney's presence and purpose. Pursuant to this holding, a person can no longer be deprived of the critical information that an attorney is present and available to provide legal advice based on pure police conjecture that the individual is not in custody. We also cannot allow law enforcement to refuse to interrupt an interview, as occurred here. Under the interpretation of the Due Process Clause of the Florida Constitution that we adopt today, it is the individual, rather than law enforcement, who is given the knowledge and power to decide whether to take advantage of the attorney's services."); *People v. Grice*, 100 N.Y.2d 318, 794 N.E.2d 9, 763 N.Y.S.2d 227 (2003) (New York prohibits police questioning when an attorney or his associate notifies police that the arrestee is represented, but not when the arrestee's father tells the police that an attorney is coming to the police station to represent the arrestee); *Commonwealth v. Mavredakis*, 430 Mass. 848, 725 N.E.2d 169, 176 & n.13 (Mass. 2000) (finding a similar right under Massachusetts law and collecting cases from other jurisdictions that reject *Moran*'s limitations).]

If a prosecuting attorney is involved, you should contact him or her and invoke the rules of professional conduct, which prohibit an attorney or agent from communicating directly with a represented party. [See ABA Model Rules of Professional Conduct, MR 4.2, 5.3(c)(1); 28 U.S.C. §530B (state rules of ethics apply to federal prosecutors).]

Whether or not your client is in custody, as soon as possible, send a letter to the prosecutor memorializing your representation.

Form:
• **Form 1-1** Representation Letter

§1:04   Learn Where the Client Is in the Process

Ask the arresting officers or prosecuting authority where the client stands in the criminal process.

If the client has not been arrested, is he the "target" of an investigation? Is the client a "subject" or just a witness?

The terms "target," "witness," and "subject" are formally defined in the United States Attorney's Manual [US Att Manual, 9-11.151], but all law enforcement officials use equivalent categories to classify persons under investigation:
• Targets are those the prosecution intends to charge.
• Witnesses are those who have useful information but will not be charged.
• Subjects are those who can go either way.

If the client has been charged or arrested, ask for a copy of the charging document, such as the complaint, arrest warrant, search warrant, affidavit of probable cause, or indictment. Also ask the authorities to describe the evidence against him.

The authorities may not identify witnesses, but they likely will disclose whether there was a search, what was seized, and whether the client made any incriminating statement.

Usually, you may discover more by asking the police first and then the prosecutor.

§1:05   Warn the Client Not to Talk About the Offense

Tell your client not to speak to anyone about the offense. This includes the police, friends, family and cellmates.

Tell the client not to consent to any searches, and to demand to see any warrant if the police try to search his home or place of business.

§1:06   Dealing With Pressure to Cooperate

Prosecutors and police might insist that your client decide immediately whether to cooperate with their investigation and might threaten that should your client decline, all deals will be "off."

In most instances, ignore this threat. If your client has valuable information, it usually will retain its value after you have had time to interview your client and investigate his situation.

Prosecutors and the police routinely overstate the need for an immediate decision. Consider three criteria before counseling immediate cooperation:

- Is the crime in progress, so that the opportunity to cooperate will pass quickly? Drug deals and bank robberies are such situations. Long-term crimes, such as bribery schemes, may not be.
- Is the evidence against your client overwhelming? For example, if he is caught with a substantial amount of cocaine in his car, and he confesses to knowing it was there, there may be meritorious legal challenges to how the drugs were found and the confession elicited, but those challenges do not often succeed.
- Does your client have an opportunity to provide undercover cooperation in an ongoing investigation, and will that opportunity pass if word spreads that your client has been arrested?

If you decide to counsel in favor of cooperation, insist on dealing with a prosecutor rather than just the police, because the police cannot make promises that bind the prosecutor's office.

§1:07   Meeting the Client

Common sense and courtesy hold many of the answers as to how to introduce yourself to a new client.

Greet him warmly and politely. If he is older than you, ask permission before using his first name.

If you meet in your office, begin by offering water, coffee or tea. Try to sit around a conference table rather than across a desk from your client. Instruct your secretary to hold your calls and turn off your cell phone. If you must take a call during the meeting, or if you must end the meeting early, advise your client in advance and apologize.

Clients are not "problems." Avoid that word. Instead, ask, "What brings you here?" "How can I help you?" Or even, "So, what's up?"

Comfort and reassure the client, but at the same time avoid raising unrealistic expectations.

You may need to impress on some clients the seriousness of the matter. In white collar criminal investigations, business people sometimes think they can treat a criminal investigation like they have treated civil litigation: hide documents and lean on employees to slant their stories to the employer's benefit. In the initial interview and later, remind the client of sophisticated defendants, such as former President Nixon, the accounting firm of Arthur Anderson, and media maven Martha Stewart, who brought about their own demise by tampering with evidence or lying to the authorities.

Start with introductions and background information. Give your client your card and some way to contact you after hours: a cell phone or home phone number. You can warn your client that you may not be able to talk much at night because you have other obligations, but at least you are available in case of emergency.

Get background information first. While you and your client might be tempted to rush to the heart of the matter, you need to obtain information that you may need to contact the client. You may forget to ask background questions once you become preoccupied with your client's story of his arrest and defense. Further, answering background questions affords your client an opportunity to relax and you a chance to evaluate your client's articulateness, intelligence, personality and even mental stability.

§1:08   Consultations

Potential clients who are shopping around can consume a great deal of your time. You should charge them a flat fee for an initial consultation, equal to an hour or two of your time.

Such prospective clients often will seek your opinion about other attorneys they have consulted. Never badmouth another attorney. Slander always finds its mark. Speak highly of your peers, and they will return the favor. Most clients will be impressed by your magnanimity. It projects self-confidence.

If potential clients seek your comment on advice they have obtained from other lawyers, caution that you may not know all the facts and any assessment of the case depends on all the circumstances. Be honest. Do not contradict another lawyer's advice solely for the sake of showing you can do better. You may land the client and find that you advise an identical course, disappointing the client and dismaying your peers. Likewise, do not be afraid to agree with the advice if it seems correct to you. Again, your self-assurance will elicit business, in future cases if not this one.

[§1:09 Reserved]

II.   INTERVIEWING THE CLIENT

A.   General Points

§1:10   Interview Style

One show of competence is to conduct a disciplined, searching initial interview.

Empathize

Now is not the time to judge, confront or impeach. The victim and police may have been right, but defending them disappoints your client. You do not need to encourage fantasies that some police peccadillo, such as failing to read the *Miranda* warnings when there was no questioning or bursting in on the client and spouse in their underwear, will result in a dismissal, but your client needs allies and support.

You can validate your client's feelings without endorsing his legal analysis. For example, you might say, "Your poor wife. I'm sure the arrest was very upsetting. The police never think of how a person's wife and children will feel."

Eye contact, nodding, and saying "Uh-huh" or "Hmm" all show you are listening.

Follow up on sources of evidence and witnesses

Ask how your client knows what he says or how might the witnesses know what the police attribute to them:
*   Were the witnesses present at the scene?
*   Did they hear about the crime from someone else?
*   Did the client speak to them about it?

Whenever your client mentions a possible witness, ask for the name, contact information and your client's relationship to the witness.

Once you get the story, go through it again, repeating it to your client, asking him to fill in gaps, and covering whatever was unclear.

Take notes

Some attorneys prefer to listen without writing. However, most attorneys need to take notes to remind themselves of what was said. Taking notes rarely disturbs the rapport with a client; rather, it demonstrates interest.

If you can, dictate a file memo as soon afterwards as possible.

Do not record the interview

Recordings make people uneasy. You probably will not have an opportunity to listen to it anyway.

Your objective in an initial interview is to obtain facts, form an impression of your client, and establish a relationship, not to tie him down to a story.

§1:11   Questioning Techniques

The same questioning techniques work for many areas:
*   Background.
*   The day of the arrest or search.
*   Your client's knowledge of the charges.
*   Your client's knowledge of the witnesses.

Use these techniques in your questioning:
*   Unless you need a specific answer to a narrow question, ask open-ended, non-leading questions.
*   Let your client give a complete answer and tell his story without interruption.
*   Exhaust each topic and area of inquiry before moving on to the next. Ask at the end of each topic, something along the lines of, "Is there anything else (I should know about)/(you want to tell me about) (what the police said to you)/(what happened after the victim entered your room)?"
*   Listen and observe. Note which questions your client answers directly and which he evades. Answers like, "I would not be so stupid as to..." or "I would never..." or "How could I ever get away with..." are not forthright answers. While you should not jump to conclusions, such answers indicate that either the question or its answer

makes your client very uncomfortable. Take note. Observe, too, at which questions your client changes his demeanor or gesticulations. Fidgeting does not necessarily signify anxiety for the naturally fidgety, but when the fidgety become still or the still fidgety, something has disturbed them.

§1:12   Goals of the Initial Interview

There are four goals for the initial interview of the client. In ideal situations, you would take substantial steps toward achieving all in the initial interview.

Depending on the situation, the goals may complement each other, and in achieving one goal you may serve others. Sometimes, however, you must choose among them. Prioritize them in the following order:

- Obtain information necessary for the immediate tasks. [See §1:13.]
- Impart to the client an understanding of his legal rights and how to avoid waiving or undermining them. [See §1:14.]
- Obtain all the facts to prepare for long term obligations in the case. [See §1:15.]
- Instill in the client confidence and trust in you. [See §1:16.]

§1:13   Goal #1: Immediately Necessary Information

This includes background and contact information, as well as information necessary for the most pressing task at the start of a criminal case: getting the client out of jail.

Cover the following topics:

- Full name, including middle name, nicknames, maiden names and any other names used.
- Home and work addresses and phone numbers.
- Cell phone or pager number.
- E-mail address.
- Date and place of birth.
- If your client was not born in the United States, immigration status.
- Social Security number.
- Arrest record and the outcome of those arrests. Even older, respectable clients with responsible jobs may have an arrest record for drunk driving, college fights, domestic assaults or the like. Ask "What happened with the case?" "Did you plead guilty or go to trial?" "Did you spend any time in jail?" Do not ask, "What was the disposition?" Many clients consider a release from jail a dismissal even if they were convicted and sentenced to time served, probation or a fine. Specifically, ask if the client was put on probation, was ordered to pay a fine or restitution or received time served.
- Education, whether completed or not, from high school to any professional education.
- Military service (including length and type of service and discharge, special training, combat exposure, commendations, and health and mental health services). Not only may military service speak well of the client's character, but the trauma of combat may explain some of the client's issues.
- Work history and current work phone number.
- Marital status, ages of children and whether the client supports them.
- Recent hospitalizations.
- Medications and other medical needs. Have the client sign releases to begin the process of obtaining records from health care and mental health providers.
- History of psychiatric treatment or counseling. Unless your client's disorder is obvious, you may wish to postpone this discussion for later interviews when you have developed more of a relationship, or the client's relatives and friends have divulged such an issue to you.

Many defendants have pressing medical needs. They may have been injured in the arrest, or they may take prescription medications. Ask, and inform the court, police and jail that the client needs his medication and medical attention.

Form:
- **Form 1-2** Medical and Mental Health Release for Records

§1:14   Goal #2: The Client's Understanding of His Legal Rights

Even the most sophisticated client needs constant education and reminding about his legal rights and what he must do to avoid waiving or undermining them.

The Right to Remain Silent

Merely telling the client that everything he says will be used against him is insufficient. Emphasize to the client the importance of speaking to no one about the charges. Spell out to whom the client cannot talk and why.

Friends, co-workers, employees, cellmates and accomplices will be pressured to turn state's evidence with threats of prosecution and severe penalties, or they already may be informants. Family members can be subpoenaed and forced on penalty of contempt to testify to what the client told them. With the limited exception of the marital privilege, there is no intra-family privilege. Best to tell the client that the only privilege on which he can rely is the attorney-client privilege.

Repeat these warnings frequently and whenever you hear some hint that your client discussed his case with others, because you must appreciate that this advice is difficult to follow. You are telling your client to remain silent on the matter that occupies his waking hours and haunts his sleep. You are telling him to forsake those to whom he always turned for advice in the past.

Even if your client does not articulate the thought, he may fear that if he says nothing to friends and family, if he does not explain his version of the facts, they will believe he is hiding his guilt. To address this concern:

- Tell your client to blame you: "My lawyer told me that I can't talk about the case."
- Explain to the client that confiding in friends and family may harm them by making them targets of the prosecution's inquiry: "My lawyer said that if I talk to you, the prosecutor might subpoena you to find out what I said."
- Tell your client to have his friends and family direct inquiries to you. When they call, you can pacify them with assurances that you are investigating the case thoroughly and intend to defend it vigorously.

The Attorney-Client Privilege

Explain the attorney-client privilege, and perhaps more importantly, some of its limitations.

Most important, the privilege does not apply to communications attended by third parties or which the client can expect others to overhear.

Jails typically inform inmates that all calls are recorded; unless the inmate calls on a line reserved for confidential attorney-client conversations, even a call to his attorney can be used against him. [See *United States v. Noriega*, 917 F.2d 1543, 1551 (11th Cir. 1990) (where an inmate signed a release acknowledging that all his calls would be monitored, even his calls to his attorney would not be privileged).] Further, jail phones often stand out in the open, where other inmates can overhear calls.

Searches

Clients who are not in custody, especially those not yet charged with a crime, may find the police at their homes or places of business attempting to search for evidence. If the police have a warrant, the client must let them search.

However, the client should be instructed that he never should consent to a search. If the police ask to search, he should demand to see a warrant and call counsel immediately. [For more on searches, see Chapter 7, Search & Seizure.]

§1:15   Goal #3: Obtain All the Facts

It is important to learn everything in order to prepare for the longer-term tasks, including preparing suppression motions, preparing for trial, negotiating a plea or other favorable disposition, and preparing for sentencing.

You want to find out the client's version of events and the story of his life not just because you are after the truth, but because this information will assist in your client's defense. Much as lawyers like to believe they can control what is presented in court, reality (i.e., what really happened on the day of the crime) often dictates what the evidence will be.

Since the facts usually will out and refute a false story, you must seek the honest truth from your client. [See ABA Standards for Criminal Justice, The Defense Function, 4-3.2 (attorney should not attempt to maintain "intentional ignorance" about the client's version of events).]

Still, you should explain to your client the legal rules that govern the offense and possible defenses, as well as the rules concerning the validity of searches or interrogations. This demonstrates your knowledge and competence, educates the client as to the purpose of your questions, and equips him to focus his answers appropriately.

The events on the day of your client's arrest are a good starting point. These events will provide insight on the focus of the police investigation and will also begin to reveal the client's story.

If your client spoke with the police, explore the discussion in great detail. Do not use terms such as "statement" or "confession." The answer to "Did you give the police a statement (or confession)?" is always "No," even if you later find that your client discussed the case for hours. Ask:

- How long did you talk to the police? (Clients invariably claim they told the police nothing. The interview's duration will tend to prove whether that claim is accurate.)

- Was anyone else there (*e.g.,* a friend or spouse)?
- Did the police take notes?
- Did they record the interview?
- Did you sign anything? What did it say?
- What did they ask you and what did you say?
- Did you talk to them about anything else?

Generally, an initial interview is not the time to confront the client with what you perceive to be his untruths in an effort to break him down. You should ask for explanations and for the client to fill in gaps in the story, but gently.

§1:16   Goal #4: Instill Trust and Confidence

Criminal clients can be a distrustful lot. Furthermore, you enter their lives at a stressful time, fraught with threatening possibilities. Gaining their trust can be difficult, especially if a court, not the client, has chosen you to represent them. Forget salesmanship or self-promotion.

To gain trust, you must:
- Work hard and competently.
- Keep your word.

Achieving the following goals will help gain trust:
- Protecting the client from further police interrogation.
- Putting the client at ease in your office.
- Visiting the client in jail.
- Locating the client and securing his release.
- Seeing to the client's medical needs.
- Informing the client of his rights.
- Delving into the client's version of events.

In addition, learn as much about the case as possible before the initial interview. Speak with the prosecutor, the arresting officer, and your client's family. Demonstrate your competence by explaining to the client the elements of the charges, the possible penalties, any applicable sentencing guidelines, and any other possible charges. Describe the way and pace at which criminal investigations and prosecutions are handled in your jurisdiction. With respect to federal investigations and charges, you can consult the United States Attorney Manual and the IRS Criminal Tax Manual.

Keeping your word can be more difficult than it sounds. You have many other cases and many other business and personal obligations. But if you tell a client you will do something, you must do it. If you say you will visit him at the jail on Monday, be there, or else don't promise it.

[§§1:17-1:19 Reserved]

B. Specific Cases

§1:20   Misdemeanor Charges

You should begin immediately talking of dispositions:
- Alternatives to prosecution, such as a deferred prosecution program or its local equivalent. [*See* Chapter 17, Plea Bargaining.]
- Mediation.
- Drug or mental health treatment.

§1:21   Murder Charges

Most clients do not need to be reminded of the seriousness of a murder prosecution.

However, with this charge more than any, the prosecution will continue to build its case even after arrest. Caution your client in the strongest terms that he cannot speak to anyone about the case because the prosecution will try to turn everyone state's evidence. All calls from jail will be recorded, and the police will study them to find something incriminating. Even without police encouragement, fellow inmates realize that eliciting incriminating statements from a murder suspect can be their ticket out of jail. Therefore, your client cannot confide in anyone.

§1:22   Theft Charges

In nonviolent theft cases (*e.g.*, bad checks and embezzlements), many jurisdictions will consider dismissal of the charges in return for full restitution. [*E.g.*, Pa. R.Crim.P. 586 (dismissal permitted if the prosecutor consents, the public interest will not be adversely affected, and satisfaction has been made or there is an agreement that satisfaction will be made to the victim).] Start exploring that option immediately with your client. Encourage him to borrow the money from a friend or relative; better in debt to a friend than to the court.

§1:23   Motor Vehicle Accidents

If your client is charged with an assault or homicide arising from a motor vehicle accident, it is imperative that you elicit immediately from your client a description of how the accident occurred so you can have an investigator begin to gather evidence from the scene. Skid and yaw marks and debris disappear quickly. Your investigator needs to visit and photograph and even videotape the scene immediately.

§1:24   Fraud and Business Crime Charges

Begin to learn your client's business. Often, the prosecution's Achilles Heel is that they do not understand your client's business, and what they perceive to be unusual or fraudulent is standard and legitimate business practice. Your client can educate you to this. Further, the more your client can show that he provides a legitimate service to the public, the less eager a prosecutor will be to shut him down.

Prepare your client for the long haul. The more complex the alleged offense, the longer the investigation will endure before it results in charges or a declination.

[§§1:25-1:29 Reserved]

III.   COMMUNICATING IN SPECIAL ENVIRONMENTS

§1:30   Preserving Confidentiality

Any communications with your client that occur in the presence of third parties are not confidential, unless the third party is an agent of the lawyer present to facilitate the representation. [See Restatement (Third) of the Law Governing Lawyers (2000) §71 (communications between attorney and client are privileged only if communicating person "reasonably believes that no one will learn the contents of the communication") and §70 (privilege extends to agents).]

Individuals whose presence may destroy the privilege include your client's friends, spouse, paramours, siblings and parents. [*See, e.g., State v. Gordon*, 197 Conn. 413, 504 A.2d 1020, 1025-26 (Conn. 1985) (discussions of trial strategy in presence of client's wife not privileged).]

Whether communications in the presence of a spouse benefit from the spousal privilege is unclear, so avoid them. [See generally Michael G. Walsh, Applicability of Attorney-Client Privilege to Communications Made in Presence of or Solely to or By Third Person, 14 A.L.R.4th 594 (1985).]

This does not mean that you must exclude your client's nearest and dearest from all discussions. Especially when it comes time to make decisions, such as whether to retain you or whether to plead guilty, clients may benefit from the presence of those whom they have always relied on for advice. Nevertheless, avoid revealing your client's version of events to these individuals. Relationships deteriorate; even close friends speak carelessly and may betray confidences, willfully or inadvertently.

§1:31   Going to Jail

Unfortunately, many initial meetings in criminal cases occur at jails. Merely displaying a bar card does not guarantee that the visit will go without a hitch.

Most jail and prison rules are now available on the internet. For example:
- Pennsylvania: www.cor.state.pa.us
- California: www.cdcr.ca.gov/Divisions_Boards/CSA

- New York City: www.nyc.gov/html/doc/html/how/how_do_i.shtml
- Cook County, Illinois: www.cookcountysheriff.org/doc
- Clay County, Florida: www.claysheriff.com
- Orange County, Florida: www.orangecountyfl.net/cms/DEPT/correct/default.htm
- Wayne County, Michigan (Detroit): www.waynecounty.com/sheriff/jails.html
- Federal: www.bop.gov

However, a telephone call might obtain quicker answers. Call ahead to check the visiting hours and rules:

- Can you give your client legal papers?
- Must your client put you on a visiting list, or do you need to bring a copy of your notice of appearance or the court order appointing you?
- Do you need special approval to bring an interpreter, law student, paralegal or investigator?
- Can you put money in your client's account?
- Can you bring change and buy your client a soft drink or snack during the visit?

You usually should ask for a "contact" visit–one in which you can shake hands and talk face-to-face, without a screen or glass between you. You can review documents together and develop more of a rapport.

Most jails have private rooms in the visiting area where an attorney can meet with the client in privacy. Some, however, have a single open room where attorneys and clients sit at tables in earshot of each other. You can try to maintain confidentiality by speaking sotto voce, or you can go early in the morning when few attorneys will have arrived, but if you need to discuss particularly sensitive matters, like the facts of a sex offense or high profile crime, or the client's possible cooperation against other defendants, you should insist on privacy. This may mean choosing a non-contact booth where the two of you can speak privately, even if through a glass or screen.

PRACTICE TIPS:

- Security is tight for all jail visitors, even attorneys, so check carefully what you carry: no knives, razors or weapons. Do not try to bring your client food or cigarettes without prior permission. To avoid metal detector embarrassments, do not wear steel shank shoes, underwire bras or body piercings. Many jails scan or vacuum visitors for drug residue. Some jails randomly search visitors' cars in the parking lot, so you may want to clean out the car after your teenager returns it and before jail visits.
- Treat guards respectfully and patiently. Do not ask them to bend the rules, for jail rules seldom have flexibility. Instead, learn the rules beforehand and follow them. If you believe you are not being treated appropriately, explain how you called ahead to inquire about the rules, what you were told, and what you need. Politely ask to speak with a supervisor.
- Some jails permit you to use change or to purchase tokens to use in visiting room vending machines. Bring money for this; your client will appreciate a snack or soft drink.

§1:32   Telephone Conversations

Try to avoid discussing confidential matters with a client over the telephone. Although wiretaps are rare, and law enforcement officials have an obligation to "minimize" their surveillance to avoid intercepting attorney-client communications, phone calls still hold many dangers. You do not know who is in the room or on the street with your client as he talks. Calls made in the presence of third parties are not protected by the privilege. [See *People v. Harris*, 57 N.Y.2d 335, 442 N.E.2d 1205, 456 N.Y.S.2d 694 (1982) (defendant's call to attorney not privileged when she spoke before police officer who gave her phone could leave the room).]

However, there are times when your client has an immediate concern, or you need an immediate answer, or your client is in a distant jail, and the phone is the only practical means of communication. To safeguard confidentiality, ask your client who is present on his end of the line. If he is at a stationhouse, ask if the officer who gave him the phone is there or is listening on another line. If he calls from a jail, ask if he is calling on a line reserved for confidential attorney-client communications, or if he made a request that the call be a confidential attorney call.

Even attorney phone conversations with inmates carry risks. Rules on phone use and their application to attorney-client conversations vary from state to state and even jail to jail. Nearly all detention facilities notify inmates of a policy of recording all telephone calls, and prosecutors often subpoena those conversations and use them as damning evidence. Most jurisdictions have rules that exempt attorney calls from recording and monitoring. [28 C.F.R. §540.102 (U.S. Bureau of Prisons); 40 Rules of the City of New York 1-10(h)(" Telephone calls to the Board of Correction, Inspector General and other monitoring bodies, as well as to treating physicians and clinicians, attorneys and clergy shall not be listened to or monitored.")] Some caselaw supports the argument that the opportunity for privileged attorney calls is necessary to effectuate inmates' right to the assistance of counsel. [*Murphy v. Walker*, 51 F.3d 714, 718 (7th Cir. 1995); *see also People v. Johnson*, 51 N.E.3d 545, 552-53 (NY 2016) (Pigott, C.J., concurring)(notes that calls to family members as well might be necessary for a detained defendant to prepare an adequate defense, and wholesale recording should be evaluated carefully).] Recently, however, it came to light that some privately-run jails recorded attorney calls and even surreptitiously video-recorded attorney-client meetings. [Jordan Smith, Micah Lee, The Intercept, "Not So Securus: Massive Hack of 70 Million Prisoner Phone Calls Indicates Violations of Attorney-Client Privilege" (Nov. 11, 2015) (theintercept.com; last visited Sept. 16, 2016); Dahlia Lithwick, "Leavenworth's Spygate" (Aug. 23, 2016) (slate.com; last visited Sept. 16, 2016).]

To minimize these risks, you should:

1. Instruct your client to request of the jail staff that he be permitted to make an attorney call, often on a designated phone line. At the beginning of any call you receive from a jail, you should ask your client if he explicitly requested of jail staff an attorney-client call.
2. Some jails request that attorneys provide their phone numbers to the jail so that the call is not automatically recorded. Make sure your number is registered with the jail according to the policy.
3. Some jails place a time limit on calls and require that the attorney make a written request to extend the duration. [*E.g.*, Connecticut Department of Corrections, Directive Number 10-7, Section 5.F (2012) (available at http://www.ct.gov/doc/LIB/doc/PDF/AD/ad1007.pdf) (last visited Sept. 15, 2016).]
4. Do not allow your client to put you on a third-party forwarded call. Clients not infrequently will call a friend and have the friend forward the call to the attorney. The privilege will not protect such calls, and they often violate jail rules and could result in loss of your client's phone privileges. [28 C.F.R. §541.13, Code 297; U.S. BOP Policy Statement 5264.08, p.12 (2008); Connecticut Department of Corrections, Directive Number 10-7, Section 5.]

§1:33   E-Mail, Voicemail and Text Message Communication

E-mails and text messages have the same status under the wiretapping laws as phone calls. That is, law enforcement cannot intercept the contents of the message without a court order. [*See* 18 U.S.C. §§2510 et seq. (court order required for real-time monitoring and interception of electronic communications; 18 U.S.C. §2703 (search warrant required for retrieval of stored electronic communications). *But see United States v. Guerrero*, 768 F.3d 351, 358 (5th Cir. 2014) (suppression is not a remedy for violations of the Stored Communications Act); *United States v. Perrine*, 518 F.3d 1196, 1202 (10th Cir. 2008) (under the Electronic Communications Privacy Act, suppression of evidence is not a remedy for non-constitutional statutory violations; statute limits remedies to damages and administrative discipline; surveys cases); *United States v. Clenney*, 631 F.3d 658, 667 (4th Cir. 2011) (same).] Most jurisdictions permit confidential communications over e-mail. [*See* ABA Formal Opinion 99-413 (1999) (lawyers and clients may reasonably expect unencrypted e-mail to have the same privacy as telephone calls and regular mail).] Some jurisdictions-the Missouri bar, for example-do not consider unencrypted e-mail sufficient protection of client confidences and require lawyers to notify all recipients of e-mail that (1) e-mail communication is not a secure method of communication; (2) any e-mail that is sent may be copied and held by various computers it passes through; and (3) persons not participating in a communication may intercept it by improperly accessing a computer through which e-mail has passed.

E-mail presents a great risk of inadvertent disclosure. Your client probably is not the only person with access to his computer; friends and family may use it as well. Either you or the client may mistakenly include others in the "To" line of an e-mail.

Text messages may be less accessible to others than email. However, many businesses have an electronic communications policy that puts employees on notice that e-mails and texts transmitted over work-issue computers and cell phones belong to the business, and they cannot expect anything they send to remain confidential. [*See, e.g., City of Ontario v. Quon*, 560 U.S. 746 (2010); *United States v. Angevine*, 281 F.3d 1130, 1134-35 (10th Cir. 2002); *Holmes v. Petrovich Development Co.*, 191 Cal. App. 4th 1047, 1068-69, 119 Cal. Rptr. 3d 878, 896 (2011) (plaintiff's emails from her work computer and work e-mail account to her attorney were discoverable and admissible because the employer had a no-personal-use policy that allowed for employer monitoring of all e-mail).]

The sweep of these policies may be broader than you and your client suspect. Communications on a work email address (e.g., jdoe_employee@workplaceinc.com) usually go through a company server; most clients will understand the insecurity of those communications. The same lack of privacy may apply to texts on a work-issued phone. Communications through a personal email account (e.g., jdoe@gmail.com) conducted on a work computer also may be subject to employer review. Some employers have a "bring your own device" ("BYOD") practice for smartphones, in which employees buy and use a personally-owned device for work mobile calls, texts and emails, but the employer compensates some part of that cost. Whether employers can search those devices is an unanswered question. [See *United States v. Barrows*, 481 F.3d 1246 (10th Cir. 2007) (employee did not have a reasonable expectation of privacy in a personally-owned laptop computer that he brought to work and used for work purposes, that he left running at all times, and that he failed to password-protect); Julie Chow, Note, "Bring Your Own Devices": A Cautionary Tale for Public Employees During Investigatory Searches, 41 Hastings Const. L.Q. 623 (2014).]

Many business phone systems now convert voicemail messages to text or audio files and automatically email them to the employee. Thus, the confidentiality of voice mail messages left on a client's work phone may fall victim to the same electronic communications policies that beset e-mail communications. To be safe, do not leave confidential information in voicemail messages, both because of this and the risk that your client may play the message in the open, in the hearing of others.

Some courts have held that even absent such a policy, employees have no expectation of privacy in communications over workplace e-mail. [See *Smythe v. Pillsbury*, 914 F.Supp. 97, 100-01 (E.D.Pa 1996); *Garrity v. John Hancock Mut. Life Ins. Co.*, 2002 U.S. Dist LEXIS 8343, 2002 WL 974676 (D.Mass. 2002); *but see Quon*, 560 U.S. 746 (assuming without deciding that employees retained a constitutionally-recognized privacy expectation in personal text messages transmitted over a work-issue phone); *United States v. Ziegler*, 474 F.3d 1184, 1189-90 (9th Cir. 2007) (where employee used a password for his computer and kept his private office locked, he had an objectively reasonable expectation of privacy in his computer).] Even where the employee's use of passwords entitles him to a reasonable expectation of privacy in his work computer, workplace policies that afford the employer the right to inspect the computer to ensure that it is used consistent with office policies and procedures may authorize the employer to consent to a police search of the computer. [*United States v. Zhu*, 23 F. Supp.3d 234, 238-41 (S.D.N.Y. 2014).]

Most dangerously, e-mail has a permanence which the oral word does not. The police routinely include computers in search warrants, and civil litigators always demand electronic records in discovery. A pure attorney-client communication will remain protected, but once it is seized, you must defend it against all the exceptions to it, such as the crime-fraud exception. The crime-fraud exception strips the privilege from any communication that is designed to assist in planning or committing a crime. The client's intent as to the communication's improper purpose controls, even if the attorney had honest intentions. [*In re: Grand Jury Proceedings*, 604 F.2d 798, 802 (3d Cir. 1979); *United States v. Cohn*, 303 F. Supp. 2d 672, 682 (D.Md. 2003) (collecting cases).]

Furthermore, you cannot shake the suspicion that an officer has reviewed privileged communications and now knows some of the defense strategy, but will not admit having seen the communication.

Text messages may be more or less secure than emails, depending on your client's device and his practices. If your client does not password-protect his phone and it falls into other hands–an informant, spouse, employer, friend–they might be able to examine the message. [*See State v. Roden*, 279 P.3d 461, 466 (Wash. Ct. App. 2012) (finding that the defendant "impliedly consented" to a law enforcement officer's interception of his text messages because "as a user of text message technology," the defendant necessarily "understood that [his drug dealer's cell phone] would record and store the text messages that he sent"), *rev'd on state law grounds*, 321 P.3d 1183 (Wash. Sup.Ct. 2014).] On the other hand, some smartphone systems – notably, Apple iPhones – employ sophisticated encryption technology that renders locked phones impervious to government searches. [*See* Devlin Barrett, et al., "Apple and Others Encrypt Phones, Fueling Government Standoff," Wall Street Journal, Nov. 18, 2014 (available at http://online.wsj.com/articles/apple-and-others-encrypt-phones-fueling-government-standoff-1416367801).]

The American Bar Association recently issued a formal opinion on some aspects of this topic, Formal Opinion 11-459, "Duty to Protect the Confidentiality of E-mail Communications with One's Client" (August 4, 2011). The opinion covers text messages and other electronic communications on employer devices and accounts as well as emails. The opinion warns, "Unless a lawyer has reason to believe otherwise, a lawyer ordinarily should assume that an employer's internal policy allows for access to the employee's e-mails sent to or from a workplace device or system." Thus, "as soon as practical after a client-lawyer relationship is established, a lawyer typically should instruct the employee-client to avoid using a workplace device or system for sensitive or substantive communications, and perhaps for any attorney-client communications, because even seemingly ministerial communications involving matters such as scheduling can have substantive ramifications." Besides the duty to warn the client, the lawyer has an obligation to take protective measures, and "[p]rotective measures would include the lawyer refraining from sending e-mails to the client's workplace, as distinct from personal, e-mail address, and cautioning the client against using a business e-mail account or using a personal e-mail account on a workplace computer or device at least for substantive e-mails with counsel."

It would seem needless to remind lawyers that they must not communicate or post client secrets, confidences and private information on Facebook, Twitter and the like, but lawyers do it with disastrous results for their careers and their clients' cases. [*E.g.,* John G. Browning, Symposium on Legal Ethics for the Transactional Lawyer: Facebook, Twitter, and LinkedIn–Oh My! *40 N. Ky. L. Rev.* 255, 263-68 (2013) (giving examples of ethical violations); *United States v. Bowen,* 969 F.Supp.2d 546 (E.D. La. 2013) (conviction reversed for prosecutor's pseudonymous comments about a case on the local newspaper's website), *aff'd* 799 F.3d 336 (5th Cir. 2015).] Thus, a reminder: privileged communications are only the start of the duty of nondisclosure; "[a] lawyer shall not reveal *information relating to the representation of a client* unless the client gives informed consent." [Model Rules of Professional Conduct, Rule 1.6(a) (emphasis added).] This obligation extends beyond privileged information "to all information relating to the representation, whatever its source." [*Id.* at Comment [3].]

§1:34   Dealing With the Media

Most of the time, little good can result from you or your client speaking to the media. Being associated with a notorious crime harms your client. The more you say, the more coverage and reports there will be, and those stories will live forever in internet searches, even after an acquittal or a declination to prosecute. The news cycle and the media's attention are very brief; if you say nothing, often there will be no story or only a brief one–buried in the back pages–or preempted on television by the star quarterback's pulled groin. Reporters frequently use the tactic of floating a rumor, which lacks the substance or support to report. Your denial and explanation then create a story where none would have run, accompanied and lengthened by rebuttal from prosecutors and pundits. The news is like a fire, and information is its fuel. Starve it of its fuel, and the fire will extinguish.

The media, and the reading or viewing or surfing public, crave melodrama when it comes to crime: the bloodied victim, the grieving parents, the betrayed and defrauded investors. Your story–mistaken identification, reasonable doubt, lack of intent–does not sell newspapers. Comments like, "We look forward to our day in court" or "We are confident that a jury will acquit" sound like evasive lawyer-talk or just plain ridiculous. [*E.g.,* Mike Lupica, "Roger Clemens Claims Andy Pettitte 'Misremembers' But Rocket May Want to After Prosecution," New York Daily News August 22, 2010) (available at http://www.nydailynews.com/sports/baseball/yankees/2010/08/22/2010-08-22_roger_clemens_claims_andy_pettitte_misremembers_but_rocket_may_want_to_after_pro.html) (mocking pitcher Rogers Clemens' attorneys' comments that they relished his indictment and eagerly anticipate his trial).]

Do not believe that any reporters are friendly. You will find all of them try to take your remarks out of context to capture a "gotcha" quote, and they will respond to your more fact-specific explanations by investigating and refuting them publicly, thereby providing leads to the prosecution. They will report all your slips of the tongue, all your mistaken factual allegations; begging or calling on friendship will not help you. Only one currency will buy a reporter's temporary silence, and that is the promise of future leaks and stories. Make that deal, and the reporter owns you; break it, and the reporter will ruin you. [In words attributed to H. L. Mencken, "Don't pick a fight with someone who buys ink by the barrel."]

Trying to reach and influence potential jurors with your own media campaign is hazardous. Even in the most newsworthy cases, the public loses attention, and the jury pool consists of people who have heard nothing about the case.

Nonetheless, if the publicity will not go away, you might attempt to generate a theme that journalists, bloggers or frequent internet commentators on media websites pick up and recycle. These might become part of the public mindset that jurors carry into deliberations. Discussions of the evidence hold risk; you may not know what the evidence will be, and arguments about the evidence may send the prosecutors out to investigate and create rebuttal evidence. Themes like prosecutor misconduct, a government conspiracy, or a star witness' dishonesty or special bias, on the other hand, resound with the public.

However, efforts to generate the kind of intense publicity that might reach the jurors or change the zeitgeist could run afoul of the disciplinary rules. [*United States v. Wecht,* 484 F.3d 194 (3d Cir. 2007) (courts may prohibit attorney comments that are substantially likely to materially prejudice the jury venire)]. Judges and prosecutors will also notice and remember your remarks and try to punish you for trying your case in the media. In addition, prospective jurors who admit following the case intensely or commenting on blogs or the like might be removed for cause.

Some defendants, such as athletes, publicly traded corporations, entertainers, and politicians, may depend on their public images for their livelihoods. Even these clients benefit more from having someone other than their criminal defense attorney as their media spokesperson. The public views you as the hired gun, the one who crafts a defense based on what the public perceives are technicalities.

Your statements as media spokesperson may create damaging evidence against the client. An attorney's statements on his client's behalf constitute agent-admissions, admissible at trial against the client. [See FRE 801(d)(2)(E).] Statements made early in a representation which you believe to be exculpatory may later prove admissible as a false exculpatory statement if the defense evolves into one arguably inconsistent with your statements. False exculpatory statements, even by an agent, tend to show, in an especially harmful way, the client's consciousness of his own guilt. [*United States v. Reyes*, 660 F.3d 454 (9th Cir. 2011) (attorney's press release to the effect that the defendant did not backdate stock options was admitted at trial to contradict defense, which admitted that defendant did backdate options, but without fraudulent intent, and as evidence of defendant's "guilty state of mind")].

Clients of means should hire media consultants. Respected surrogates, like community leaders, sympathetic friends or family–or the media consultant, if necessary–should do the talking. Ideally, it should take place after the criminal case ends.

One potential benefit too often motivates criminal defense lawyers to speak to the media: free advertising for their practices. Sacrificing your client's interests to advance your business is unethical. Don't do it. And in the long run, it will lose you the more substantial clients, the ones who want the case to go away with a minimum of publicity.

What to do then, in most cases: Walk through throngs of reporters and cameras without stopping to answer questions, eyes straight ahead, face uncovered and expressionless. Meet comments with a "Good morning, good afternoon, have a good day," and nothing else. When contacted one-on-one, listen, because sometimes reporters will reveal rumors and investigative leads they've heard from the prosecutor, but refuse comment with an explanation that your silence is a principled position, not one tied to the weakness of your case: "I don't comment / talk to the media about an ongoing case/ about one of my cases." "No, we won't have anything to say about the case."

[§§1:35-1:39 Reserved]

IV. JOINT AGREEMENTS AND APPEARANCES

§1:40 Joint Representation

Generally, you should not represent more than one defendant or target of an investigation in a single investigation or prosecution. [ABA Standards for Criminal Justice, The Defense Function, Standard 4-3.5.] Lawyers in the same firm cannot represent co-defendants. This arrangement frequently leads to disqualification of the whole firm and all its lawyers; withdrawal of one lawyer does not cure the problem, at least where there is "a serious potential for conflict." [*United States v. Self*, 681 F.3d 190, 198 (3d Cir. 2012) (disqualifying both attorneys).]

Unlike in civil cases, liability in criminal cases is nearly always individual, not joint and several. Therefore, much of effective criminal defense consists of assigning blame to others. Joint representation limits counsel's ability to employ that tactic.

The exceptions are usually at the pre-charging stage or early phases of a prosecution [see Standard 4-3.5(c)] or where there is a familial or business relationship among the clients, such as among spouses, siblings, and small business corporations and their sole owners. Counsel should be skeptical, though, of conflict waivers where the defendants are family members because familial loyalty, rather than the defendants' self-interest, may drive their decision. [*United States v. Self*, 681 F.3d 190, 198 (3d Cir. 2012) (disqualifying both attorneys from representing brothers in a drug conspiracy case even where one attorney withdrew, and the defendants agreed that there was no conflict), *aff'g* 2009 U.S. Dist. LEXIS 121386 (E.D.Pa. Dec. 30, 2009)(emphasizing the distorting effect of family loyalty).]

If you represent more than one client in the same matter, you must understand and explain to your clients the impact joint representation has on the confidentiality of attorney-client communications. First, your obligation to each client requires that you fully share with all clients relevant information received from any client, even if imparted in confidence:

> As to the duty of confidentiality, continued common representation will almost certainly be inadequate if one client asks the lawyer not to disclose to the other client information relevant to the common representation. This is so because the lawyer has an equal duty of loyalty to each client, and each client has the right to be informed of anything bearing on the representation that might affect that client's interests and the right to expect that the lawyer will use that information to that client's benefit. See Rule 1.4. The lawyer should, at the outset of the common representation and as part of the process of obtaining each client's informed consent, advise each client that information will be shared and that the lawyer will have to withdraw if one client decides that some matter material to the representation should be kept from the other.

[Model Rules of Professional Conduct, Rule 1.7, cmt. 31. *See also* Restatement (Third) of the Law Governing Lawyers, § 75, cmt. d,] This obligation distinguishes joint or co-client representation from joint defense agreements, also known as common interest or information sharing agreements. [*See* §1:41, *infra*.] There, each client has a separate attorney, and each attorney owes an obligation of loyalty, and its concomitant requirement of information sharing, only to her individual client, not to other clients in the joint defense or common interest group. [*See In re Teleglobe*, 493 F.3d 345, 363 n.18 (3d Cir. 2007).]

Second, unlike the usual situation, in which a client's expectation that attorney communications will be conveyed to third parties eliminates the privileged nature of the communications, the sharing of confidential communications among co-clients does not destroy the privilege. [*Commonwealth v. Schultz*, 133 A.3d 294, 324 (Pa. Super. Ct. 2016).] This enables you to share information among co-clients for their mutual benefit, but it has an important and sometimes confounding corollary: No co-client can unilaterally waive another co-client's privilege. [*In re Teleglobe*, 493 F.3d at 379; Restatement, *supra*, § 75, cmt. e; ("One co-client does not have authority to waive the privilege with respect to another co-client's communications to their common lawyer.").] Thus, while you might be compelled to share with client A client B's statements exculpating him, client A cannot use those statements without client B's consent.

You may represent co-defendants at the initial appearance or bail hearings. [ABA Standards for the Defense Function §4-3.5.] However, if you do, avoid eliciting confidential communications from the clients because having such confidential information may later lead to your disqualification from representing either defendant.

PRACTICE TIP:

Investigating and clearing such potential conflicts may provide an opportunity to mine the prosecutor or investigating officer for information about the case. Ask if your potential client is a target of the investigation, a subject (or possible target), or a pure witness.

While the more prudent course may seem to be to retain separate counsel for each individual involved in a criminal investigation, costs may dictate otherwise. A single person or entity, such as the head of household or the firm owner, may be paying all counsel. You may represent several witnesses in a single investigation or prosecution as long as none are targets of the investigation, and they do not accuse each other of criminal wrongdoing. [See *In re Abrams*, 62 N.Y.2d 183, 465 N.E.2d 1, 476 N.Y.S.2d 494 (1984) (attorney could not be prevented from representing multiple grand jury witnesses on the grounds that he was asserting the privilege on behalf of all and insisting on immunity for each).]

CAUTION:

When you undertake the representation of several witnesses or defendants in the same matter, you must meet the prerequisites of Rule 1.7(b) of the Model Rules of Professional Conduct:
- You must reasonably believe that the representation of each will not be adversely affected by the representation of another.
- You must advise each client of the advantages and risks of joint representation and obtain their explicit consent to the joint representation.

[For more on joint representation, see Chapter 2, The Representation Agreement.]

§1:41   Joint Defense Agreements

A joint defense agreement ("JDA") is an agreement to share confidential information among counsel and their respective clients when they share a common legal position and interest. [*See, e.g., United States v. Schwimmer*, 892 F.2d 237 (2d Cir. 1989); *National Med. Enterprises, Inc. v. Godbey*, 924 S.W.2d 123 (Tex. 1996).]

NOTE:

This type of agreement may also be called an information sharing agreement ("ISA") or a common interest agreement ("CIA"). Some lawyers feel that these terms describe the arrangement's purpose more specifically and accurately and minimize subsequent attempts to disqualify attorneys if one defendant breaks rank and cooperates with the government.

With a joint defense agreement, each attorney retains his duty of loyalty solely to his client, but assumes an obligation to maintain the confidentiality of information obtained through the joint defense. By encouraging and protecting the voluntary exchange of information, the joint defense agreement facilitates the coordination of the defense and the pooling of resources. [See *Lugosch v. Congel*, 219 F.R.D. 220, 238 (N.D.N.Y. 2003) (discussing advantages of joint defense agreements).]

The joint defense or common interest privilege protects the sharing of work product among the parties as well as attorney-client communications. [*Am. Eagle Outfitters, Inc. v. Payless Shoesource, Inc.*, 2009 U.S. Dist. LEXIS 105608, *7 (E.D.N.Y. Nov. 12, 2009.)]

However, a joint defense agreement does not forbid defendants from later turning on each other, nor from using against each other information obtained outside the joint defense arrangement. [See Restatement (Third) of the Law Governing Lawyers, §69, Comment d.]

Joint defense agreements can be oral or written. [*United States v. Almeida*, 341 F.3d 1318, 1320 (11th Cir. 2003) (construing oral agreement).] However, if the information sharing will be more than sporadic, it is best to commit the agreement to writing to withstand any later attempts by the prosecution to pierce the privilege. The privilege's claimant has the burden of proving its existence, and memories might differ as to when the interests were common and when they diverged. [See *United States v. Weissman*, 195 F.3d 96, 98-99 (2d Cir. 1999) (attorneys forced to testify about whether joint defense privilege applied; court held that it did not, and defendant convicted on damaging admissions made in meeting with his employer-corporation's attorneys); *Lugosch*, 219 F.R.D. at 237 (N.D.N.Y. 1993) (discussing problems that arise with oral agreements).]

A joint defense agreement does not prohibit a defendant from testifying to facts he knew before he entered the joint defense. If the agreement is written, draft it carefully so that counsel will not be disqualified if his client leaves the joint defense agreement and offers to testify against the other defendants.

If the agreement is oral, specify in your notes of each meeting that the discussion occurred under an oral joint defense agreement.

Although joint defense agreements are legal and ethical, prosecutors tend to view them as conspiracies to obstruct justice. While it disavows such a judgment in its latest version of the "Principles of Federal Prosecution of Business Organizations," the Department of Justice warns, in a section entitled "Obstructing the Investigation," that joint defense agreements may prevent a corporation from receiving credit for cooperating with an investigation by impeding its ability to share information with the government. [USAM 9-28.730.]

PRACTICE TIP:

Consider a joint defense agreement when the defendants share a consistent defense. For example, in a fraud or regulatory prosecution, the defendants may deny that any crime took place, or, in a conspiracy case, they may all share an interest in attacking the government's cooperating witnesses where those witnesses implicate all defendants. By coordinating efforts and resources, defendants can allocate tasks without duplication, save time and money and avoid inadvertently harming each other. Access to other defendants' information may not only strengthen the defense, but it may educate the defense as to the strengths of the prosecution's case, perhaps persuading the defense that a negotiated plea is the wiser course.

CAUTION:

Joint defense agreements generally benefit most the more culpable defendants. The agreement enables those defendants to learn what the lesser defendants, the ones the government is likely to approach as possible cooperating witnesses, have to say, and it tips off the more culpable when the less culpable begin to cooperate. Once a defendant or his lawyer stops attending joint defense meetings, you can conclude that he has decided to plead guilty and cooperate. Consequently, the defendant alleged to be most culpable should try to rally the troops and assemble them all into a joint defense, offering the benefit of his counsel's expertise and work product to the other defendants and their counsel. The less culpable defendants should approach the agreement cautiously, for it may limit their ability to cooperate against the more culpable and to earn themselves a lenient sentence.

Form:
•   **Form 1-3** Joint Defense Agreement

§1:42   Entering Your Appearance

Once charges are filed, you must formally enter your appearance in the court where charges lie.

In some courts, particularly local magistrates, merely giving your name and address or handing your card to the judge's clerk suffices. However, in most courts, you must present to the judge or clerk a simple "Notice of Appearance" form. Usually, you can hand this to the clerk at the first court appearance.

Filing this notice, simple as it is, has momentous consequences. After filing it, you cannot withdraw from the representation without leave of court. [See Pa.R.Cr.P. 120(C); Local Rules of Court, United States District Court for the Western District of Pennsylvania, LR 83.2.2 (D).] Therefore, before you file the notice, you should guarantee that your fee arrangement is in place. [For fee arrangements, see Chapter 2, The Representation Agreement.]

Forms:
- **Form 1-4** Notice of Appearance–State
- **Form 1-5** Notice of Appearance–Federal

V.   FORMS

Form 1-1   Representation Letter

COMMENT:

When you begin representation of a client, especially in a matter which has not yet been filed in court, you should notify the prosecutor of your representation and memorialize that notification to protect your client from being contacted directly by the prosecutor, law enforcement officials or informants working for the government.

After charges are filed, the Sixth Amendment prohibits the government or its agents from questioning a represented defendant. [*Maine v. Moulton*, 474 U.S. 159 (1985) (Sixth Amendment violated when prosecution had cooperating co-defendant meet and discuss pending charges with defendant).]

Before charges are filed, the only prohibition lies in the Rules of Professional Conduct, which bar attorneys from communicating directly with represented parties [ABA Model Rule of Professional Conduct 4.2], or from using their agents to do so [Model Rule 5.3(c)(1)], or, if the charges are brought by the state, in state law.

Since the ethical prohibition runs against the lawyer for the government, send the letter to the prosecutor. The government remains free, however, to record surreptitious conversations with your client to prevent him from obstructing justice or committing new crimes. [*Moulton*, 474 U.S. at 179-80.]

Via Facsimile (412) xxx-xxxx and First Class Mail

Assistant United States Attorney
United States Attorney's Office
400 U.S. Post Office & Courthouse
Pittsburgh, PA 15219

RE: Louis Client Investigation

Dear Mr. _____:

I write to inform you that I represent Louis Client with respect to this investigation. I ask that you direct all communications regarding this matter to me.

I hope to talk to you more about the investigation in the future. Of course, I trust that you will instruct your agents that they should have no direct communications with Louis Client.

Sincerely,

_____

Thomas J. Farrell

cc: Louis Client

Form 1-2   Medical and Mental Health Release for Records

COMMENT:

Send this release as soon as possible.

Since the enactment of HIPAA, many health care providers have created their own releases and will respond to your release by demanding that you use their particular version.

AUTHORIZATION FOR RELEASE OF MEDICAL RECORDS

TO: _____
                        [Health care provider]

FROM: _____
                        [Client name]

I, _____, (date of birth), (Social Security number), hereby authorize you and your agents to release all medical records in your possession to any duly designated representative of Farrell Law Offices, 000 Seventh Avenue, Pittsburgh, PA 15000 for the purpose of legal representation.

Disclosure should include, but is not limited to, admission and discharge summaries, ambulance records, emergency room reports, nursing notes, physician notes and orders, progress notes, discharge instructions, laboratory reports and records, radiology reports, medication and prescription records, medical, social and mental health histories recorded by your staff in relation to my treatment, and mental health evaluations.

In addition, I authorize any physician, psychologist, social worker, nurse, aide or other personnel active in or familiar with my treatment to communicate orally or in writing to the above designated representative concerning my history, treatment, prognosis and/or other topics of which treatment personnel may have knowledge.

In authorizing this disclosure, I explicitly waive any and all rights I may have as to the confidential maintenance of these records, including any such rights that exist under local, state and federal statutory and/or constitutional law, rule or order, including those contained in the Pennsylvania Mental Health Procedures Act, 1976, and the Pennsylvania Drug and Alcohol Abuse Control Act, 1972, and the federal Standards for Privacy of Individually Identifiable Health Information ("the Privacy Rule") promulgated pursuant to the Health Insurance Portability and Accountability Act of 1996 ("HIPAA").

This authorization is valid until revoked by me in writing. You may accept a photocopy of this authorization.

_____
        [client signature]

Form 1-3   Joint Defense Agreement

COMMENT:

This agreement includes language which has been recommended by courts to avoid the disqualification of remaining counsel when one defendant breaks ranks and testifies against the others. [*United States v. Stepney*, 246 F.Supp.2d 1069, 1085 (N.D.Cal. 2003); *United States v. Almeida*, 341 F.3d 1318, 1326-27 (11th Cir. 2003).]

Remaining counsel may possess confidential information disclosed by the testifying defendant pursuant to the joint defense agreement. Absent such language, the testifying defendant or the prosecution can seek either to disqualify remaining counsel or to prevent them from using confidential information on cross-examination. [See *United States v. Henke*, 222 F.3d 633 (9th Cir. 2000) (where cooperating co-defendant did not waive the joint defense privilege, the duty of confidentiality prevented counsel from impeaching the former co-defendant with statements made in confidence and required counsel's disqualification).]

JOINT DEFENSE AND CONFIDENTIALITY AGREEMENT

This Agreement among the undersigned parties ("the clients") and their counsel ("counsel") memorializes understandings reached among counsel. The understandings concern the common defense of the clients in the matter of an investigation involving possible criminal, civil or administrative proceedings, which have been or may be initiated by the Department of Justice or any other investigative agency investigating possible violations of law which are being alleged against the clients.

Counsel believes that there is a common legal interest in a joint defense and representation of their respective clients in these proceedings. In this regard, the Defense Group wishes to continue to pursue separate but common interests and avoid any claim or suggestion of waiver of the clients' privileges. Accordingly, it is our intention and understanding that the communications among the clients and counsel are confidential and are protected from disclosure to any third party by the clients' attorney-client and attorney work product privileges.

The undersigned believe that such disclosures are matters of common legal interest and concern essential to the effective representation of our respective clients and, therefore, that such disclosures are covered by the joint defense doctrine recognized and explained at length in *In Re: Grand Jury Subpoenas 89-3, 89-4, John Doe 89-129*, 902 F.2d 244 (4th Cir. 1990); *United States v. Schwimmer*, 892 F.2d 237 (2d Cir. 1989); *United States v. McPartlin*, 595 F.2d 1321, 1336-37 (7th Cir. 1979); *Eisenberg v. Gagnon*, 766 F.2d 770, 787-88 (3rd Cir. 1985).

In order to accomplish the objectives of this Agreement, the undersigned agree that any and all of the following, no matter how disclosed to one another or to our respective clients, shall be covered by this Agreement: (a) witness interviews and statements, (b) memoranda of law, (c) briefing and debriefing memoranda, (d) summaries, (e) transcripts, (f) documents or conversations containing plans or theories for mutual, separate, or joint defense and representation, and (g) any documents or information which would otherwise be protected from disclosure to third parties under any theory.

No information obtained by any counsel to this Agreement as a result of this Agreement shall be disclosed to any third party without the express consent of the parties to this Agreement. Each party to this Agreement retains the right to determine what information in its possession it shall disclose to the other parties to this Agreement.

The parties agree that if any attempt is made by any third party to secure or obtain information covered by this Agreement, the other parties to this Agreement shall be promptly notified and shall be given copies of any writings or documents, including subpoenas, summonses and the like, which relate to the attempt by the third party to obtain the information.

It is further understood that all documents and information disclosed by and between the undersigned and their clients shall be treated as if protected by the attorney-client and attorney work product privileges, whether or not so identified or marked. The parties agree on behalf of their clients not to enter into any settlement with a third party which would require or result in disclosure of material covered by this Agreement.

If any party to this Agreement enters into negotiations with any third party for the purpose of resolving any or all of a client's potential liability, that client and his/her attorney agree (a) to inform all the other signatories to this Agreement of that fact; (b) to disclose the terms of any final settlement of the client's liability, including, but not limited to, the content of proffers and statements made by the client; and (c) to keep confidential and not disclose any information covered by this Agreement.

Upon final settlement of any client's potential liability, the member of the Defense Group representing that client shall disclose the terms of that settlement to the other members of the Defense Group and thereafter withdraw from the Defense Group, as provided below, if asked to do so by the other members.

Any member of the Defense Group may, on behalf of his client, withdraw from this Agreement at any time by giving written notice, hand delivered or by certified mail, upon all other members of the Defense Group, in which case this Agreement shall no longer be operative as to the withdrawing party, but shall continue to protect all communications and information covered by the Agreement and disclosed to the withdrawing party prior to the withdrawing party's notification of intent to withdraw. Immediately upon demand by any member of the Group, the withdrawing party and his counsel shall return all joint defense materials and copies thereof.

Each party waives the right to object to the continued retention by any other party of counsel or to seek the counsel's disqualification, on the ground that: (a) the counsel had access to the Joint Litigation Information pursuant to this Agreement; or (b) the counsel has a conflict of interest by reason of participation in joint litigation efforts under this Agreement. Each party waives any right to take testimony from counsel for another party based on that counsel's participation in joint litigation efforts.

Nothing contained herein shall be deemed to create an attorney-client relationship between any attorney and anyone other than the client of that attorney, and the fact that any attorney has entered this Agreement shall not be used as a basis for seeking to disqualify any counsel from representing any other party in this or any other proceeding; and no attorney who has entered into this Agreement shall be disqualified from examining or cross-examining any client who testifies at any proceeding, whether under a grant of immunity or otherwise, because of such attorney's participation in this Agreement; and the signatories and their clients further agree that a signatory attorney examining or cross-examining any client who testifies at any proceeding, whether under a grant of immunity or otherwise, may use any Defense Material or other information contributed by such client during the joint defense; and it is herein represented that each undersigned counsel to this Agreement has specifically advised his or her respective client of this clause and that such client has agreed to its provisions.

It is further understood and agreed that, to the extent that the parties have already been in communication with one another prior to the execution of this Agreement in relation to Joint Defense Matters, all previous privileged communications and all materials and information exchanged are subject to this Agreement.

This Agreement may be modified only in a writing signed by all parties. By signing this Agreement each attorney certifies that s/he has explained the contents of this joint defense agreement to his/her client and that each of us agree to abide by the understandings contained herein.

This Agreement shall remain in effect and be binding upon successor counsel in accordance with its terms and may be terminated by successor counsel only in accordance with its terms.

_____   Dated:
Defendant One

_____
Attorney for Defendant One

_____   Dated:
Defendant Two

_____
Attorney for Defendant Two

Form 1-4   Notice of Appearance–State

IN THE COURT OF COMMON PLEAS OF _____ COUNTY, _____

COMMONWEALTH OF _____
v.   No. #### CR ###
LOUIS CLIENT

NOTICE OF APPEARANCE

TO THE CLERK OF COURT OF _____ COUNTY:
Kindly enter the undersigned's appearance as counsel of record for Defendant Louis Client.
Respectfully submitted,
Dated: _____   _____
                       Thomas J. Farrell, Esquire
                       000 Seventh Avenue
                       Pittsburgh, PA 15000
                       (412) 555-5555
Pa. I.D. #00000

Form 1-5 Notice of Appearance–Federal

UNITED STATES DISTRICT COURT
DISTRICT OF _____

APPEARANCE
Case Number:

To the Clerk of this court and all parties of record:
    Enter my appearance as counsel in this case for _____.
    I certify that I am admitted to practice in this court.

Date: _____

_____
Signature
Print Name   Bar Number
Address
City, State, Zip Code
Phone   Fax Number

Chapter 2

THE REPRESENTATION AGREEMENT

I. GENERAL POINTS

II. FEE ARRANGEMENTS AND BILLING

III. FORMS

(This page intentionally left blank.)

I.   GENERAL POINTS

§2:01   The Representation Agreement

Except for court-appointed cases, always commit your agreement to represent a client to writing. [See Model Rules of Professional Conduct, MR 1.5(b) (fee arrangements should be communicated in writing unless you regularly represent this particular client).]

In court appointed cases, court rules and statutes will define the scope of your representation and the terms of your compensation. Several state bars publish sample fee agreements on the internet:

- Massachusetts: www.massbar.org/pdf/lawhelp/legal_info/criminal_mfa.pdf
- Ohio: www.cbalaw.org/formsdocuments/modelBody.asp
- New Hampshire: www.nhbar.org/pdfs/crimdef.pdf

Forms:
- **Form 2-1** Engagement Letter–Hourly Billing
- **Form 2-2** Engagement Letter–Flat Fee
- **Form 2-3** Engagement Letter–Evergreen Retainer
- **Form 2-4** Engagement Letter–Multiple Clients

§2:02   Defining the Scope of the Representation

Define the scope of your representation carefully.

Once you enter an appearance in a court of record, the court may force you to remain in a case from initial appearance to appeal if the engagement agreement does not say otherwise–and sometimes even if it does. [*Compare Commonwealth v. Librizzi*, 2002 Pa. Super. 343, 810 A.2d 692 (Pa. Super. 2002) (petition to withdraw after trial denied where no written fee agreement) *with Commonwealth v. Sweeney*, 368 Pa. Super. 33, 533 A.2d 473 (Pa. Super. 1987) (lower court reversed for abuse of discretion in denying petition for withdrawal where the fee agreement limited representation to the trial level). *See also* Local Appellate Rules, United States Court of Appeals for the Third Circuit, LAR Misc. 109.1 ("Trial counsel in criminal cases, whether retained or appointed, are expected to continue on appeal absent extraordinary circumstances."); Eleventh Cir. Rule 46-1(g)(1) (Retained counsel must continue on appeal until successor counsel is appointed and cannot withdraw absent order of court).]

Therefore, if you are representing the client before an information or indictment has been filed, you should specify that once charges are filed the client must provide an additional retainer before you will file a notice of appearance.

Explain in writing that you represent the client only through trial and sentencing. Appeals and re-trials require a new fee and engagement agreement.

Specify whether you represent the client in related proceedings, such as civil lawsuits, forfeiture proceedings and licensing hearings. While you may be inclined to file an appearance in such matters to protect your client from incriminating himself, you may find yourself stuck in a lengthy and time-consuming case.

§2:03   The Scope of the Representation in Court Appointed Cases

Generally, a court appointment encompasses only the pending criminal case on which the defendant has a constitutional right to counsel.

Counsel appointed to a federal criminal case under the Criminal Justice Act [18 U.S.C. §3006A] may be able to represent a client in "ancillary matters appropriate to the proceedings." These may include appearing for a client in related civil litigation to claim the Fifth Amendment privilege against self-incrimination and representing a client on the merits in a related civil forfeiture case, but little more. [*See Guidelines for the Administration of the Criminal Justice Act and Related Statutes*, §2.01.F(5) & (6) (available at www.fd.org).]

The Guidelines authorize you to seek an *ex parte* ruling in advance from the Court as to whether it will compensate you for the ancillary representation. You may also call the district's federal public defender or the court's financial administrator with further questions.

Local jurisdictions may lack such written guidelines. Call the chambers of the judge who appointed you or the office which approves appointments and vouchers and ask.

[§§2:04-2:09 Reserved]

II.   FEE ARRANGEMENTS AND BILLING

§2:10   Types of Fee Arrangements; Retainers

Two types of fee arrangements predominate in criminal cases:
- Flat, nonrefundable fees.
- Hourly fees.

Contingent fees are unethical in criminal cases. [Model Rule 1.5(d)(2).]

Even when charging on an hourly basis, you should obtain a retainer that approximates the total amount you anticipate charging on the case, or at least what you will need until you reach a stage in the representation at which you can demand that the retainer be replenished (i.e., when charges are filed or after the preliminary hearing and before entering an appearance in the court of record). Shortly before trial is not an optimum time to seek additional money because the judge is not likely to allow you to withdraw at that late stage.

Retainers are necessary because the fact of a prosecution, even apart from the resulting incarceration, often severely hampers the client's earning ability. Once convicted, clients have little incentive or ability to pay outstanding legal bills, and perhaps even less incentive if acquitted.

§2:11   Refundable Retainers

If the retainer is refundable, you must deposit it in a client trust account, because the money is the client's until you earn it by providing legal services. [*See, e.g., Iowa Sup. Ct. Bd. of Professional Ethics and Conduct v. Frericks*, 671 N.W.2d 470 (Iowa, 2003) (retainers must be maintained in trust account and may not be withdrawn until earned).]

The rules require that you maintain accurate records of the money in the account and its disposition. [*See, e.g.*, MR 1.15; Rules of Prof. Conduct of State Bar of Calif. R. 4-100 (detailing attorney's accounting duties to include, among others, maintaining a written record of all client deposits and the date, amount and purpose of each disbursement); *Iowa Sup. Ct. Attorney Disciplinary Board v. Piazza*, 756 N.W2d 690 (2008) (imposing public reprimand for attorney's failure to provide contemporaneous accounting to client of the services provided and the fees earned when advance fee was transferred into general office account).]

§2:12   Estimating the Retainer

If you are retained before charges are filed, estimating an appropriate retainer may be difficult because the case's demands will be unpredictable:
- The prosecution may drop the matter without much work on your part.
- You may engage in extensive research, investigation, and negotiation that result in a pre-charging resolution.
- The pre-charging work may be but a prelude to defending the charges once filed.

The client reasonably may not want to commit to a large retainer at the outset.

You might consider an "evergreen" retainer. These take several forms:
- You may preserve the retainer in your trust account to use for the final bills and have the client pay current bills monthly.
- You may draw on the retainer to pay your bills for monthly services, but demand that it be replenished once it drops below a specific amount.
- You may charge the monthly bills against it and require that the client restore it to full value monthly.

The evergreen retainer can serve as an early warning that the client has payment problems while ensuring that you will get paid for work toward the end of the representation, a time when many clients believe they no longer need counsel.

[For several versions of evergreen retainers, see Form 2-3.]

§2:13   Nonrefundable Retainers

Check the ethics rulings in your particular jurisdiction to determine whether nonrefundable retainers are permissible.

The majority of jurisdictions forbid such fees. [*See, e.g., In re Hawver*, 339 P.3d 573, 585 (Kan. 2014) (Charging a flat attorney fee in a capital murder defense was unreasonable and created a conflict of interest. "The ABA Guidelines 'unequivocally disapprove of flat fees in death penalty cases precisely because such fee arrangements pit the client's interests against the lawyer's interest in doing no "more than what is minimally necessary to qualify for the flat payment."'"); *In re O'Farrell*, 942 N.E.2d 799, 807 (Ind. 2011); *Iowa Supreme Court Board of Professional Ethics and*

Conduct v. Apland, 577 N.W.2d 50 (Iowa 1998) (non-refundable fee for specific services to be performed in the future is unethical); *In re Cooperman*, 83 N.Y.2d 465, 611 N.Y.S.2d 465, 633 N.E.2d 1069 (1994) (non-refundable retainers are unenforceable and unethical because they conflict with the client's right to terminate the relationship at any time); *In re Roman*, 601 F.3d 189, 207 (2d Cir. 2009) ("It is now well-established that non-refundable retainer agreements constitute per se violations of the Disciplinary Rules of New York's Code of Professional Responsibility.")]

Other jurisdictions permit nonrefundable retainers. [*See, e.g., Diaz v. Paul J. Kennedy Law Firm*, 289 F.3d 671, 675 (10th Cir. 2002) (attorneys could keep whole of flat fee if client discharged them early in representation; applying New Mexico law); *Ryan v. Butera, Beausang, Cohen & Brennan*, 193 F.3d 210 (3d Cir. 1999) (applying Pennsylvania law); Rules Regulating Fla. Bar, R. 4-1.5, 1.16; *see generally McQueen, Rains & Tresch, LLP v. Citgo Petroleum Corp.*, 195 P.3d 35, 44-45 & nn.21-30 (OK 2008); Theresa M. Costonis, Construction and Operation of Attorney's General or Classic Retainer Fee or Salary Contract Under State Law, 102 A.L.R.5th 253 (extensive surveys of various types of retainers–advance, special and general, refundable and nonrefundable–and the positions of various jurisdictions on their legality).]

In any jurisdiction, the amount of the fee must be reasonable. [*See, e.g., Matter of Hirschfeld*, 192 Ariz. 40, 960 P.2d 640 (1998) (flat fee must be evaluated carefully against extent of services ultimately rendered); *Bunker v. Meshbesher*, 147 F.3d 691, 695 (8th Cir. 1998) (applying Minnesota law); *Ryan*, 193 F.3d at 214.] Even where a written fee agreement calls the fee "non-refundable," some jurisdictions will force the attorney to return that portion which has not been earned by work if the attorney is discharged early. [*State ex rel. Counsel for Discipline of Nebraska Supreme Court v. Wintroub*, 277 Neb. 787, 765 N.W.2d 482 (2009) (disciplining attorney for failure to return portion of $1,500 nonrefundable flat fee after client discharged him two weeks into the representation).]

Hostility to nonrefundable retainers seems to be growing. [*See In re Miles*, 335 S.C. 242, 247 n.2, 516 S.E.2d 661, 664 n.2 (S.C. 1999) (noting the trend against them).]

Even if you do not face a disciplinary action for charging a nonrefundable retainer in a jurisdiction hostile to such arrangements, charging the wrong kind of fee can bring other inconveniences:

- If the client discharges you before you have performed substantial services and earned the fee, your client may sue for the return of monies you already spent.
- A bankruptcy court may rule that the fee payment was a fraudulent conveyance, and the money must be returned. [*See, e.g., In re Bressman*, 214 B.R. 131 (Bankr. D.N.J. 1997).]
- If the disciplinary board treats the fee as an advance or retainer to be earned by future work, the money belongs to the client until earned and should be maintained in your trust account until earned. [See Model Rule 1.15(d).] You can be held in violation of the strict rules against commingling client funds with your own and face the strict disciplinary penalties commingling usually brings. [E.g., *Att. Griev. Comm'n of MD v. Stinson*, 429 Md. 147 (2012) (despite language in engagement letter that $5,000 of the engagement fee was nonrefundable, it should have been deposited into a client trust account. Distinguishes nonrefundable fees such as this from general retainers or "availability fees," which are earned upon receipt because it is paid to secure an attorney's availability over a given period of time and to foreclose attorney from appearing for an adverse party); *In re Mance*, 980 A.2d 1196 (D.C. 2009) (holding that flat fees remain client's property until earned and disciplining attorney for failing to deposit $7,500 flat fee for a homicide representation in his client trust account).]

For these reasons and to budget your practice, you should track your time by month even in flat fee cases. [*See also* §2:16.] You also may want to bill and draw against a retainer, even a nonrefundable one, on a monthly basis rather than spending it all when received. You should document the nonrefundable fee in a written engagement letter that justifies the fee by explaining that acceptance of the representation caused you to make time commitments and assumed potential conflict of interest positions that prevented you from taking clients and cases.

A prohibition against flat, nonrefundable fees in your jurisdiction does not limit you to charging hourly fees, however. You can structure your fee agreement to deem the fees earned on the passage of certain milestones, such as the stage of a case (e.g., 60 days before trial), or the accomplishment of certain tasks: the preliminary hearing, filing of motions, at a certain time before trial. [*See In re Mance*, 980 A.2d at 1204 (approving of milestone structure); Douglas R. Richmond, *Understanding Retainers and Flat Fees*, 34 J.Legal Prof. 113, 142 (2009) (same; good survey of types of retainers, ethical issues, and the positions of various jurisdictions).]

[For a flat fee engagement letter, *see* Form 2-4A.]

However, if the fee truly is nonrefundable and fully earned when paid, the Internal Revenue Service will consider it taxable in the year and quarter when paid, not when you draw on it.

Forms:
- **Form 2-4A** Engagement Letter–Flat Fee in Stages

§2:14   Accepting Cash

There is nothing wrong with accepting cash as long as a few rules are obeyed.

You have no obligation to inquire where your client obtained the money except where circumstances raise undeniable suspicion. [*See, e.g., United States v. Saccoccia*, 165 F.Supp.2d 103 (D.R.I. 2001) (district court ordered forfeiture of post-trial fees, where attorneys paid by "covert deliveries of large quantities of cash, made by anonymous intermediaries"; defendant had no legitimate source of income and just had been convicted of racketeering), *rev'd, United States v. Saccoccia*, 354 F.3d 9 (1st Cir. 2003) (reversing because forfeiture laws do not allow recovery of substitute assets for criminal proceeds when those assets are held by a third party, here, the attorneys).]

If a client suspected of bank robbery offers cash in bank wrappers, ask for a check. Follow these rules:

- Record all fees received and report them to the taxing authorities.
- When you receive an amount of cash in excess of $10,000 you must file a Form 8300 with the IRS. [*See* 26 U.S.C. §6050I.] "Cash" means currency (domestic or foreign), but not personal checks. Violations of §6050I carry a fine of up to $100,000. Cashier's checks, bank drafts, traveler's checks and money orders are considered reportable cash or currency only if "the recipient knows that such instrument is being used in an attempt to avoid the currency reporting requirement." [31 CFR §103.30 (c)]
- Do not break a cash fee of $10,000 or more into several payments for the purpose of avoiding the reporting requirement. This is the felony offense of structuring currency transactions in order to avoid the reporting requirement. [31 U.S.C. §5324.]
- Confirm payments with your clients. Provide a receipt for flat fee payments. If you bill by the hour, bill every month and note on the statement how much remains in escrow. Clients who pay two thousand dollars a month for a year without complaint often will balk at a single annual bill for $10,000.

If you file a Form 8300 and fail to identify the source of the money, you will receive a form letter from the IRS [*see* Form 2-6] urging you to supplement your Form 8300 filing before the IRS commences enforcement action against you.

Generally, fee arrangements and client or payor identities are not privileged. [*Lefcourt v. United States*, 125 F.3d 79 (2d Cir. 1997); *United States v. Blackman*, 72 F.3d 1418 (9th Cir. 1995).] However, there is an exception in special circumstances, where the disclosure of client identity and fee information would necessarily disclose confidential communications or implicate the client in the very criminal activity for which advice was sought. [*See United States v. Sindel*, 53 F.3d 874, 876 (8th Cir. 1995) (describing various doctrines which might justify nondisclosure); *Ralls v. United States*, 52 F.3d 223, 225-26 (9th Cir. 1995) (assertion of the privilege valid where party paying attorney's fee to represent the defendant had consulted attorney concerning his culpability in the very transaction for which defendant was charged.]

Form 8300 is available at IRS offices or can be downloaded from its website, www.irs.gov, as a fill-in form.

Forms:
- **Form 2-5** IRS Form 8300
- **Form 2-6** IRS Demand for Supplementation of Form 8300

§2:15   Third-Party Payors

Clients frequently depend on the kindness of friends, relatives, and employers for the payment of attorneys' fees. [*See United States v. Stein*, 435 F.Supp. 2d 330, 335, 354-55 (S.D.N.Y 2006) (describing prevalence of practice of corporations advancing attorneys' fees for officers and employees under investigation), *aff'd*, 541 F.3d 130 (2nd Cir. 2008).]

Accepting payment from such sources is ethical as long as you guarantee all parties that your allegiance and duty of confidentiality run to the client, not the payor, and you advise your client of any potential conflicts and the client consents. [*See United States v. Corona*, 108 F.3d 565, 575 (5th Cir. 1997) (third party's payment of fees did not raise conflict of interest); MR 1.7(b), 1.8(f), 5.4(c) ("A lawyer shall not permit a person who recommends, employs, or pays the lawyer to render legal services for another to direct or regulate the lawyer's professional judgment in rendering such legal services.")]

A more acute ethical problem arises where the target of an investigation *selects and retains* counsel to represent a lawyer to represent witnesses against it and the lawyer relies on the target for the payment of legal fees, as often is the case when a business entity is under investigation. The entity frequently selects and pays for counsel for its employees who may well be witnesses against the entity and its higher management. Many corporations have bylaws requiring that it advance counsel fees in such situations.

At least one state's highest court has imposed several stringent conditions on such arrangements:
(1) The informed consent of the client is secured, meaning that the client is informed of the risks of the arrangement and his ability to secure other counsel.
(2) "The third-party payer is prohibited from, in any way, directing, regulating or interfering with the lawyer's professional judgment in representing his client."
(3) "There cannot be any current attorney-client relationship between the lawyer and the third-party payer."
(4) "The lawyer is prohibited from communicating with the third-party payer concerning the substance of the representation of his client. The breadth of this prohibition includes, but is not limited to, the careful and conscientious redaction of all detail from any billings submitted to the third-party payer."
(5) The third-party must pay as quickly and regularly as it pays its own counsel.
(6) The payer cannot be relieved of its continuing obligation to pay without leave of court.
[*In the Matter of the State Grand Jury Investigation*, 208 N.J. 481, 495-96, 983 A.2d 1097, 1105-06 (NJ 2009).]
[For a fee agreement with language concerning third-party payors, see Form 2-1.]

CAUTION:

In certain situations, such as organized crime cases or large-scale drug conspiracies, the kingpins may offer to pay fees to buy a defendant's silence or to be forewarned of his intent to cooperate against them. Accepting representation under such circumstances may endanger your license, liberty and life. [*See Quintero v. United States*, 33 F.3d 1133, 1134 (9th Cir. 1994) (trial judges in drug cases should determine whether third parties are paying the fees of retained counsel when a defendant is indigent, and, if so, whether the defendant understands the potential conflict of interest and voluntarily waives the conflict); *United States v. Locasio*, 6 F.3d 924, 933 (2d Cir. 1993) (Mafia "house counsel's" representation of underlings was part of the racketeering enterprise); *United States v. Coiro*, 922 F.2d 1008 (2d Cir. 1991) (upholding obstruction of justice conviction of defense attorney for counseling subpoenaed witnesses to testify falsely in the grand jury).]

§2:16   Billing

Whether the case is retained or appointed, you must keep accurate time records. Record your time immediately after an event; it is the only way to ensure your time is accurate. Nothing sours the relationship with a client like an accusation that you have overcharged for meetings and calls in which you both participated.

You should keep track of your time in flat fee cases as well for a number of reasons:
- If you must withdraw at an early stage, you may be obligated to return part of the fee. Even in those jurisdictions which permit nonrefundable retainers, bankruptcy law might force return of any portion that has not been earned through services provided. [*In re Bressman*, 214 B.R. 131 (Bankr. D.N.J. 1997) (nonrefundable retainers are not "reasonable" under Bankruptcy Code §328(a)).]
- Tracking your time might help salvage at least part of your fee from a forfeiture proceeding. [*See United States v. McCorkle*, 321 F.3d 1292, 1295 n. 4 (11th Cir., 2003) (only that portion of fee representing payment for services provided before the attorney learns that the client's money is derived from an illegal source may resist forfeiture).]
- Contemporaneous records of the time the matter consumed may be necessary to establish how much of the fee you deserve to keep if the attorney-client relationship is terminated before your services are completed. [*Wong v. Michael Kennedy, P.C.*, 853 F.Supp. 73 (E.D.N.Y. 1994) (to meet his burden of showing entitlement to portion of the retainer under a quantum meruit theory, attorney must present contemporaneous records detailing the dates of services, hours expended and nature of the work performed).]

Additionally, at the end of the representation, you can tally the time and determine if you priced the case accurately.

Bill clients monthly and promptly, not only to maintain your cash flow and to detect quickly if a client has payment problems, but also so that the client has a detailed description of what you did for him that month.

§2:17   Adjusting the Fee Arrangement According to the Case

You may adjust your fee arrangements according to the seriousness of the case, the impact of a prosecution on your client, and the amount of work the case may demand.

Misdemeanors or felony charges that are likely to be reduced often will be resolved at the initial appearance or preliminary hearing. A flat fee works best for that type of case. The fee can be calculated based on an estimate of the time the appearance and any preparation will take and the market rate for those types of hearings. Since the case and your client's need for you will end quickly, you do not want to bill and chase the client for an hourly fee. Build into your flat fee any amounts needed for investigators, court reporters, and interpreters.

In deciding how much of your fee to demand up front, evaluate not only your client's income and assets, but the impact the prosecution will have on his earnings:

• Is he likely to be detained without bail and lose his job?
• If the charge or investigation arises from his business, can he continue to operate it profitably?
• Does the charge carry such infamy that it will cause loss of employment or business?

If your client has not been charged yet, remember that you will have another chance to request a hefty retainer if charges are filed. If your client refuses the increase, you can withdraw easily because you have not entered an appearance in any court. While you need enough money to start work with confidence, you do not want to demand such a high retainer as to scare away the client.

III. FORMS

Form 2-1   Engagement Letter–Hourly Billing

[Date]

RE: COMMONWEALTH V. _____

Dear Mr.:

This letter confirms that the law firm of Thomas Farrell & Associates has agreed to represent you in connection with your prosecution by the District Attorney's office for Allegheny County at the above case number. Consistent with our ethical obligations and what we have found to be sound practice, this letter will define our mutual responsibilities during the course of the representation.

SCOPE OF REPRESENTATION

We have agreed to represent you in the defense of the criminal prosecution at Cr. No. 04-000 through trial and sentencing.

It is understood and agreed that this agreement does not cover any appeals which you may wish to undertake. Any appeals would only be undertaken upon execution of a mutually satisfactory appellate representation agreement. It is further understood that in the event this matter is pursued through trial, this representation agreement does not cover re-trials or new trials and such re-trials and new trials will be undertaken only upon a mutually agreeable representation arrangement.

Thomas Farrell & Associates does not represent you in connection with any other matter, civil, criminal, or administrative. Any such additional representation will be the subject of a separate engagement letter.

It is understood and agreed that Thomas Farrell and Associates has made no promise or guarantee as to the eventual outcome of the criminal charges, and that this agreement is not based upon any such promises or anticipated results.

CASE MANAGEMENT AND FEES

It has been agreed that we will use our best professional efforts to obtain a resolution satisfactory to you. In return, you have agreed to pay an initial retainer in the amount of $10,000. The retainer will be refunded, to the extent it has not been utilized in fees and costs related to your representation, upon resolution of this matter. We have informed you that, by law, all interest earned on this retainer will be paid automatically to the IOLTA program of Pennsylvania.

I will be the attorney responsible for this matter and it has been explained that we will bill our normal hourly rates of $250, against the retainer. In addition, my associate, John Doe, may work on this case at the rate of $175 per hour, and we may also use the services of paralegals at the rate of $100 per hour. These rates may increase from time to time but only to the extent of periodic increases for all similar clients.

[*Where a third party pays the fee:* We understand that your parents/employer may pay your attorneys' fees in this matter. However, our ethical obligation and duty of loyalty and confidentiality are to you; you are our client.]

[*Referral fees:* We may pay a referral fee to _____, the attorney who referred you to our office. This does not affect the fees that you will be charged.]

We also require that the client pay certain expenses, such as long distance telephone, printing, postage, witness fees, mileage or other travel, lodging, photocopying and computerized legal research. If there is any other unusually large expense, we may ask you to pay that amount directly to the person or entity providing the service or to prepay for the contemplated expenditure. No significant cost will be incurred without your prior approval.

TERMS AND CONDITIONS OF PAYMENT

At the beginning of each month, an invoice will be sent detailing the services which were performed on your behalf in the month just ended. The invoice will show the date, hours spent, itemized description of the service rendered and any expenses incurred during the billing period and the total fees and expenses charged during the billing period.

TERMINATION OF SERVICES

Under our agreement, you have the right to terminate our services for any reason upon written notice at any time. We retain the right to terminate services: 1) upon your failure to cooperate in any reasonable request; 2) upon failure to pay fees and expenses as they come due; or 3) upon determination that continued representation violates the Rules of Professional Conduct. The termination of services, whether by you or by Thomas Farrell & Associates, will not relieve you of the obligation to pay any outstanding amounts due for our services and expenses through the date of termination.

ACCEPTANCE

If these terms are acceptable to you, please sign this letter in the space indicated below and return a signed original along with your retainer check to me. A duplicate original has been enclosed for your records. If you have any questions about the terms of this letter, please feel free to call me.

MISCELLANEOUS

If there are any special instructions that you have relating to your invoice or any other matter relating to this representation, please let me know and I will try to accommodate you. If I am unavailable, my office manager, Linda Loe, will usually know status information. At this time I want to thank you for selecting our law firm to represent you in this matter and we look forward to working with you.

Sincerely,
Thomas Farrell & Associates

_____

Thomas J. Farrell

Enclosure

AGREED AND ACCEPTED:

DATED:

Form 2-2   Engagement Letter–Flat Fee

[Date]

RE: COMMONWEALTH V. _____

Dear Mr.:

This letter confirms that the law firm of Thomas Farrell & Associates has agreed to represent you in connection with your prosecution by the District Attorney's office for Allegheny County at the above case number. Consistent with our ethical obligations and what we have found to be sound practice, this letter will define our mutual responsibilities during the course of the representation.

SCOPE OF REPRESENTATION

We have agreed to represent you in the defense of the criminal prosecution at Cr. No. 04-000 through trial and sentencing.

It is understood and agreed that this agreement does not cover any appeals which you may wish to undertake. Any appeals would only be undertaken upon execution of a mutually satisfactory appellate representation agreement. It is further understood that in the event this matter is pursued through trial, this representation agreement does not cover re-trials or new trials and such re-trials and new trials will be undertaken only upon a mutually agreeable representation arrangement.

Thomas Farrell & Associates does not represent you in connection with any other matter, civil, criminal, or administrative. Any such additional representation will be the subject of a separate engagement letter.

It is understood and agreed that Thomas Farrell & Associates has made no promise or guarantee as to the eventual outcome of the criminal charges, and that this agreement is not based upon any such promises or anticipated results.

CASE MANAGEMENT AND FEES

It has been agreed that we will use our best professional efforts to obtain a resolution satisfactory to you. In return, you have agreed to pay a flat fee of $50,000. This fee becomes the property of the firm upon payment. This fee is based upon accepting your case and undertaking your legal representation, which precludes us from employment in other matters. In addition, you have agreed to pay into our escrow account an additional sum of $15,000, which, it is anticipated, will be sufficient to cover further work by our investigators and to retain an expert witness. However, it is understood that the expenses of the investigators, an expert witness, and local counsel cannot be determined with certainty at this point and therefore are not subject to the flat fee arrangement.

To date, you have paid $10,000 toward our flat fee of $50,000. If the remaining $40,000 is not paid prior to our entering our appearance in the Court of Common Pleas after the preliminary hearing, we are not obligated to enter an appearance or to further continue our representation. In such a case, the $10,000 is our nonrefundable fee for the representation to that point. Once we have entered our appearance in the Court of Common Pleas, the $50,000 flat fee becomes nonrefundable.

[*Where a third party pays the fee:* We understand that your parents/employer may pay your attorneys' fees in this matter. However, our ethical obligations and duties of loyalty and confidentiality are to you; you are our client.]

We also require that the client pay certain expenses, such as long distance telephone, printing, postage, witness fees, mileage or other travel, lodging, photocopying and computerized legal research. If there is any other unusually large expense, we may ask you to pay that amount directly to the person or entity providing the service or to prepay for the contemplated expenditure. No significant cost will be incurred without your prior approval.

TERMINATION OF SERVICES

Under our agreement, you have the right to terminate our services for any reason upon written notice at any time. We retain the right to terminate services: 1) upon your failure to cooperate in any reasonable request; 2) upon failure to pay fees and expenses as they come due; or 3) upon determination that continued representation violates the Rules of Professional Conduct. The termination of services, whether by you or by Thomas Farrell & Associates, will not relieve you of the obligation to pay any outstanding amounts due for our services and expenses through the date of termination.

ACCEPTANCE

If these terms are acceptable to you, please sign this letter in the space indicated below and return a signed original along with your retainer check to me. A duplicate original has been enclosed for your records. If you have any questions about the terms of this letter, please feel free to call me.

MISCELLANEOUS

If there are any special instructions that you have relating to your invoice or any other matter relating to this representation, please let me know and I will try to accommodate you. If I am unavailable, my office manager, Louisa Loe, will usually know status information. At this time I want to thank you for selecting our law firm to represent you in this matter and we look forward to working with you.

Sincerely,
Thomas Farrell & Associates

_____

Thomas J. Farrell

Enclosure

AGREED AND ACCEPTED:

DATED:

Form 2-3   Engagement Letter–Evergreen Retainer

[Date]

RE: COMMONWEALTH V. _____

Dear Mr.:

This letter confirms that the law firm of Thomas Farrell & Associates has agreed to represent you in connection with your prosecution by the District Attorney's office for Allegheny County at the above case number. Consistent with our ethical obligations and what we have found to be sound practice, this letter will define our mutual responsibilities during the course of the representation.

SCOPE OF REPRESENTATION

We have agreed to represent you in the defense of the criminal prosecution at Cr. No. 04-000 through trial and sentencing.

It is understood and agreed that this agreement does not cover any appeals which you may wish to undertake. Any appeals would only be undertaken upon execution of a mutually satisfactory appellate representation agreement. It is further understood that in the event this matter is pursued through trial, this representation agreement does not cover re-trials or new trials and such re-trials and new trials will be undertaken only upon a mutually agreeable representation arrangement.

Thomas Farrell & Associates does not represent you in connection with any other matter, civil, criminal, or administrative. Any such additional representation will be the subject of a separate engagement letter.

It is understood and agreed that Thomas Farrell & Associates has made no promise or guarantee as to the eventual outcome of the criminal charges, and that this agreement is not based upon any such promises or anticipated results.

CASE MANAGEMENT AND FEES

[*Replenish below specific amount:* It has been agreed that we will use our best professional efforts to obtain a resolution satisfactory to you. In return, you have agreed to pay an initial retainer in the amount of $10,000. The retainer will be refunded, to the extent it has not been utilized in fees and costs related to your representation, upon resolution of this matter. We have informed you that, by law, all interest earned on this retainer will be paid automatically to the IOLTA program of Pennsylvania. Should the retainer drop below $5,000, you agree to replenish it to $10,000 within two weeks of notice from us.]

[*Bills paid from retainer that is replenished monthly:* It has been agreed that we will use our best professional efforts to obtain a resolution satisfactory to you. In return, you have agreed to pay an initial retainer in the amount of $10,000. When we render monthly bills to you, we will use the retainer account to pay those bills and when you send your payment to us it will be used to restore the retainer account back to its original amount. Upon completion of the work, any unused retainer will be refunded to you. We have informed you that, by law, all interest earned on this retainer will be paid automatically to the IOLTA program of Pennsylvania.]

[*Retainer applied to final bills:* It has been agreed that we will use our best professional efforts to obtain a resolution satisfactory to you. You have agreed to pay an initial retainer of $20,000. We will apply the first $10,000 of this retainer to our initial bills for services. The remaining $10,000 will be held in a trust account on your behalf. At the conclusion of this matter, the remaining retainer will be applied to your last monthly bill and any excess remaining, to the extent it has not been utilized in fees and costs related to your representation, upon resolution of this matter. We have informed you that, by law, all interest earned on this retainer will be paid automatically to the IOLTA program of Pennsylvania.]

I will be the attorney responsible for this matter and it has been explained that we will bill our normal hourly rates of $250, against the retainer. In addition, my associate, John Doe, may work on this case at the rate of $175 per hour, and we may also use the services of paralegals at the rate of $100 per hour. These rates may increase from time to time but only to the extent of periodic increases for all similar clients.

[*Where a third party pays the fee:* We understand that your parents/employer, may pay your attorneys' fees in this matter. However, our ethical obligation and duty of loyalty and confidentiality are to you; you are our client.]

[*Referral fees:* We may pay a referral fee to _____, the attorney who referred you to our office. This does not affect the fees that you will be charged.]

We also require that the client pay certain expenses, such as long distance telephone, printing, postage, witness fees, mileage or other travel, lodging, photocopying and computerized legal research. If there is any other unusually large expense, we may ask you to pay that amount directly to the person or entity providing the service or to prepay for the contemplated expenditure. No significant cost will be incurred without your prior approval.

TERMS AND CONDITIONS OF PAYMENT

At the beginning of each month, an invoice will be sent detailing the services which were performed on your behalf in the month just ended. The invoice will show the date, hours spent, itemized description of the service rendered and any expenses incurred during the billing period and the total fees and expenses charged during the billing period.

TERMINATION OF SERVICES

Under our agreement, you have the right to terminate our services for any reason upon written notice at any time. We retain the right to terminate services: 1) upon your failure to cooperate in any reasonable request; 2) upon failure to pay fees and expenses as they come due; or 3) upon determination that continued representation violates the Rules of Professional Conduct. The termination of services, whether by you or by Thomas Farrell & Associates, will not relieve you of the obligation to pay any outstanding amounts due for our services and expenses through the date of termination.

ACCEPTANCE

If these terms are acceptable to you, please sign this letter in the space indicated below and return a signed original along with your retainer check to me. A duplicate original has been enclosed for your records. If you have any questions about the terms of this letter, please feel free to call me.

MISCELLANEOUS

If there are any special instructions that you have relating to your invoice or any other matter relating to this representation, please let me know and I will try to accommodate you. If I am unavailable, my office manager, Louisa Loe, will usually know status information. At this time I want to thank you for selecting our law firm to represent you in this matter and we look forward to working with you.

Sincerely,
Thomas Farrell & Associates

_____
Thomas J. Farrell

Enclosure

AGREED AND ACCEPTED:

DATED:

Form 2-4   Engagement Letter–Multiple Clients

[Date]

RE: _____ GRAND JURY INVESTIGATION.

Dear Ladies and Gentlemen:

This letter confirms that the law firm of Thomas Farrell & Associates has agreed to represent you in connection with the federal grand jury investigation into _____ Family Auto Salvage Yard being conducted by the Federal Bureau of Investigation, the Criminal Investigation Division of the Internal Revenue Service and the United States Attorney's Office for the District of New Jersey. Consistent with our ethical obligations and what we have found to be sound practice, this letter will define our mutual responsibilities during the course of the representation.

SCOPE OF REPRESENTATION

We have agreed to represent you in the investigation described above. Should charges result against any of you, representation in the defense of those charges would be the subject of a separate representation agreement. Thomas Farrell & Associates does not represent you in connection with any other matter, civil, criminal, or administrative. Any such additional representation will be the subject of a separate engagement letter.

It has been agreed that we will use our best professional efforts to obtain a resolution satisfactory to each of you. In return, you have agreed to pay an initial retainer in the amount of $10,000. The retainer will be refunded, to the extent it has not been utilized in fees and costs related to your representation, upon resolution of this matter. We have informed you that, by law, all interest earned on this retainer will be paid automatically to the IOLTA program of Pennsylvania.

I will be the attorney responsible for this matter and it has been explained that we will bill our normal hourly rates of $250, against the retainer. In addition, my associate, John Doe, may work on this case at the rate of $175 per hour, and we may also use the services of paralegals at the rate of $100 per hour. These rates may increase from time to time but only to the extent of periodic increases for all similar clients.

[*Where a third party pays the fee:* We understand that your parents/employer, may pay your attorneys' fees in this matter. However, our ethical obligation and duty of loyalty and confidentiality are to you; you are our client.]

[*Referral fees:* We may pay a referral fee to _____, the attorney who referred you to our office. This does not affect the fees that you will be charged.]

We also require that the client pay certain expenses, such as long distance telephone, printing, postage, witness fees, mileage or other travel, lodging, photocopying and computerized legal research. If there is any other unusually large expense, we may ask you to pay that amount directly to the person or entity providing the service or to prepay for the contemplated expenditure. No significant cost will be incurred without your prior approval.

POTENTIAL CONFLICT OF INTEREST

The representation of more than one client in the same matter ("joint representation") provides cost savings over the cost that otherwise would be incurred were each client to retain separate counsel, but it also presents special ethical considerations. We may undertake your joint representation if you agree in writing after consultation with us about the risks of joint representation. You also may consult with legal counsel other than us regarding this representation.

A potential exists that conflicts of interest could arise with respect to the subject matter of our representation. Based on the information now available to us, we are not aware of any actual conflicts among you in this matter. If you become aware of anything you believe might suggest an actual conflict of interest, please bring it to our attention immediately. In addition, if you become aware of any strategic or other considerations that in your opinion are such as to prevent us from continuing to represent you (or any of you) jointly, we ask that you promptly call such matters to our attention.

If circumstances arise during the course of this matter that require or make it desirable that any of the clients obtain separate legal representation in this matter, our firm would be free to continue to represent the remaining members of the client group in this matter. By signing this engagement letter and accepting our joint representation, you agree that, if it becomes necessary or desirable for any of you to retain other counsel, you will not seek to disqualify our firm from continuing to represent the remaining members of the group or any of them.

In addition, in an ordinary attorney-client relationship, information given to counsel by the client in confidence as part of the representation may be considered privileged, and the attorney may not disclose that information to any third person without the client's consent. By agreeing to this joint representation, each and every client we represent in the client group is authorizing the disclosure of any information and confidences we learn to all of our clients in the client group. However, the privilege protects the confidences of the group and each and every member of the group from disclosure to any person who is not a member of the group.

TERMS AND CONDITIONS OF PAYMENT

At the beginning of each month, an invoice will be sent detailing the services which were performed on your behalf in the month just ended. The invoice will show the date, hours spent, itemized description of the service rendered and any expenses incurred during the billing period and the total fees and expenses charged during the billing period.

TERMINATION OF SERVICES

Under our agreement, you have the right to terminate our services for any reason upon written notice at any time. We retain the right to terminate services: 1) upon your failure to cooperate in any reasonable request; 2) upon failure to pay fees and expenses as they come due; or 3) upon determination that continued representation violates the Rules of Professional Conduct. The termination of services, whether by you or by Thomas Farrell & Associates, will not relieve you of the obligation to pay any outstanding amounts due for our services and expenses through the date of termination.

ACCEPTANCE

If these terms are acceptable to you, please sign this letter in the space indicated below and return a signed original along with your retainer check to me. A duplicate original has been enclosed for your records. If you have any questions about the terms of this letter, please feel free to call me.

MISCELLANEOUS

If there are any special instructions that you have relating to your invoice or any other matter relating to this representation, please let me know and I will try to accommodate you. If I am unavailable, my office manager, Linda Loe, will usually know status information. At this time I want to thank you for selecting our law firm to represent you in this matter and we look forward to working with you.

Sincerely,
Thomas Farrell & Associates

_____

Thomas J. Farrell

Enclosure

AGREED AND ACCEPTED:

Client One	Client Three
DATED:	DATED:
Client Two	Client Four
DATED:	DATED:

Form 2-4A   Engagement Letter–Flat Fee in Stages

Re: Fee Agreement

Dear Client:

This correspondence represents and confirms our agreement concerning the Fees to be charged by Thomas J. Farrell, Esquire, for undertaking representation in the following matter:

1. Name: Investigation into mortgage fraud at A-1 Realty by United States Attorney ("A-1 Realty Investigation").
2. Procedural Level: Initial Contact with U.S. Attorney through Trial.

You seek to retain me to represent you in the ongoing investigation by the United States Attorney into alleged mortgage fraud at A-1 Realty. I am requesting a **non-refundable $25,000.00** retainer. This requested non-refundable retainer will be applied as my fee to the initial investigation and contact and negotiations with the United States Attorney in any Queen for a Day or proffer proceeding, plus any Grand Jury proceeding and any other criminal proceeding (related to the A-1 Realty matter) prior to indictment, should an indictment be filed.

If an indictment is filed against you and the matter must be taken to trial, then trial of the matter will require you to pay a flat Fee of **$150,000.00 (less** the retainer paid). This Fee will cover the investigation, filing of any pretrial motions, trial preparation, trial and sentencing, but excludes costs and expenses.

This fee agreement does not include any appellate matters, including a direct appeal subsequent to trial. This retainer quoted herein must be paid within fifteen (15) days after execution of this Fee Agreement. This Fee Agreement is provided to you in order to comply with the Rules of Professional Conduct adopted by order of the Supreme Court of Pennsylvania, and to avoid any misunderstanding regarding the fees charged and the services which I have agreed to perform.

Request for Services. Client has requested Attorney to represent the client's interest with respect to the matter more fully described above. In order to comply with the Rules of Professional Conduct of the Supreme Court of Pennsylvania and to avoid any misunderstandings, I will confirm all Retainer and Fee arrangements in writing.

Case Evaluation. Attorney has evaluated the facts known to the attorney at this time as a result of disclosure by the client prior to execution of this Fee Agreement. In setting the retainer and fee, he has considered the time and labor required to provide a defense, the novelty and difficulty of the legal questions involved in the case, and the skill required to perform these services properly, as well as his experience, reputation and ability, among other considerations.

Retainer. A retainer is a fee which is paid to retain a lawyer to act on behalf of a client. Payment of a retainer engages the legal services of the lawyer, prohibits him from representing anyone else involved in the same case or related cases, and is charged, in part, because acceptance of the representation of an individual in any given case requires the lawyer to set aside other cases or to forego accepting other cases. A non refundable retainer is the minimum amount of money that a lawyer charges in order to be involved in a case. In this case a non refundable retainer of Twenty-five Thousand Dollars (**$25,000.00**) is requested. Non-refundable retainers are earned when they are paid and are deposited into the general operating account of the firm. The retainer is due, in two installments of **$12,500.00**, within fifteen (15) and thirty (30) days of the signing of the Fee Agreement between the parties.

Legal Fees. It is understood that Attorney and Client are entering into a contract for the payment of legal fees. The fee quoted is a flat fee for services provided from the initial contact, pre-indictment period through trial, if required. If the matter proceeds beyond indictment to trial, the fee in this matter will be One Hundred Fifty Thousand Dollars (**$150,000.00**), less any retainer paid. The Fee must be paid in **full** at least thirty (30) days prior to trial. If the matter proceeds past indictment but results in the entry of a negotiated plea, then the fee in this matter will be Seventy five Thousand Dollars (**$75,000.00**).

Costs and Expenses. Costs and expenses are in addition to attorneys' fees. These costs and expenses can include, for example, fees for investigators, expert witnesses, researchers, couriers, travel expenses, long distance phone calls, costs for copying and transcripts, filing fees, exhibits, etc. You agree to cover the cost of any expenses as they are incurred. If the matter proceeds to trial, I will provide you with an estimate of costs and expenses as required. In this case it is anticipated that a forensic accountant will be necessary. Other experts may also be required. It is agreed that, if any costs must be advanced by the Law Offices of Thomas J. Farrell, these costs will be billed to you and payable immediately. If, at the conclusion of these proceedings, all of the monies you have advanced for costs have not been expended, they will be refunded to you. However, in the event you have an outstanding bill for legal services, then you agree that any unexpended costs that have been escrowed may be applied to any fees due and owing at that time.

Client Responsibility. It is the client's responsibility and obligation to appear at proceedings or Court when required. It is also the client's responsibility to disclose, consult and cooperate with counsel and to consider and follow the advice given. Failure to do so and/or failure to appear as required may result in the termination of legal services.

No Guarantee of Outcome. It is understood that the attorney has made no promises or guarantees regarding the outcome of this case.

Attorney's Right to Withdraw/Termination of Services. If you do not fulfill your obligations under this agreement, Attorney reserves the right to withdraw from your case.

File Retention. Contents of a client's file are owned by the law office and shall remain the property of the law firm after the conclusion of the case. You will always be provided a copy of any documents and/or pleadings in the file. Files are normally destroyed five (5) years after the completion of the case.

Acceptance. By payment of the retainer quoted herein and the return of the enclosed copy of this letter, you agree to the terms and conditions set forth herein. Unless the retainer is paid and the copy of this letter is signed and returned, the firm will not undertake any aspect of legal representation on your behalf. The terms and provisions of this agreement expire and are withdrawn if this agreement is not accepted by you by the payment of a retainer and the return of the enclosed copy of this letter by [date]. If you have any questions regarding these terms or any issue with respect to fees, please contact this office immediately so that we may resolve them prior to you paying the retainer specified herein and returning a signed copy of this letter.

Sincerely,
Thomas Farrell & Associates

_____
Thomas J. Farrell

Form 2-5   IRS Form 8300

IRS Form **8300**	Report of Cash Payments Over $10,000 Received in a Trade or Business	FinCEN Form **8300**
(Rev. December 2004)	▶ See instructions for definition of cash.	(Rev. December 2004)
OMB No. 1545-0892 Department of the Treasury Internal Revenue Service	▶ Use this form for transactions occurring after December 31, 2004. Do not use prior versions after this date. For Privacy Act and Paperwork Reduction Act Notice, see page 5.	OMB No. 1506-0018 Department of the Treasury Financial Crimes Enforcement Network

1 Check appropriate box(es) if: **a** ☐ Amends prior report;   **b** ☐ Suspicious transaction.

Part I   **Identity of Individual From Whom the Cash Was Received**

2 If more than one individual is involved, check here and see instructions . . . . ▶ ☐

3 Last name	**4** First name	**5** M.I.	**6** Taxpayer identification number

7 Address (number, street, and apt. or suite no.)	**8** Date of birth . ▶ (see instructions)	M M D D Y Y Y Y

9 City	**10** State	**11** ZIP code	**12** Country (if not U.S.)	**13** Occupation, profession, or business

14 Identifying document (ID)	**a** Describe ID ▶	**b** Issued by ▶ ....
	c Number ▶	

Part II   **Person on Whose Behalf This Transaction Was Conducted**

15 If this transaction was conducted on behalf of more than one person, check here and see instructions . . . . . ▶ ☐

16 Individual's last name or Organization's name	**17** First name	**18** M.I.	**19** Taxpayer identification number

20 Doing business as (DBA) name (see instructions)	Employer identification number

21 Address (number, street, and apt. or suite no.)	**22** Occupation, profession, or business

23 City	**24** State	**25** ZIP code	**26** Country (if not U.S.)

27 Alien identification (ID)	**a** Describe ID ▶	**b** Issued by ▶ ....
	c Number ▶	

Part III   **Description of Transaction and Method of Payment**

28 Date cash received M M D D Y Y Y Y	**29** Total cash received $ .00	**30** If cash was received in more than one payment, check here . . . . . ▶ ☐	**31** Total price if different from item 29 $ .00

32 Amount of cash received (in U.S. dollar equivalent) (must equal item 29) (see instructions):

a U.S. currency $ _____ .00   (Amount in $100 bills or higher $ _____ .00)
b Foreign currency $ _____ .00   (Country ▶ _____)
c Cashier's check(s) $ _____ .00 ⎫ Issuer's name(s) and serial number(s) of the monetary instrument(s) ▶
d Money order(s) $ _____ .00 ⎬ ....
e Bank draft(s) $ _____ .00 ⎭ ....
f Traveler's check(s) $ _____ .00

33 Type of transaction		**34** Specific description of property or service shown in 33. Give serial or registration number, address, docket number, etc. ▶
a ☐ Personal property purchased	**f** ☐ Debt obligations paid	
b ☐ Real property purchased	**g** ☐ Exchange of cash	....
c ☐ Personal services provided	**h** ☐ Escrow or trust funds	....
d ☐ Business services provided	**i** ☐ Bail received by court clerks	....
e ☐ Intangible property purchased	**j** ☐ Other (specify in item 34) ▶	

Part IV   **Business That Received Cash**

35 Name of business that received cash	**36** Employer identification number

37 Address (number, street, and apt. or suite no.)	Social security number

38 City	**39** State	**40** ZIP code	**41** Nature of your business

42 Under penalties of perjury, I declare that to the best of my knowledge the information I have furnished above is true, correct, and complete.

Signature ▶ _____   Title ▶ _____
          Authorized official

43 Date of signature	M M D D Y Y Y Y	**44** Type or print name of contact person	**45** Contact telephone number ( )

IRS Form **8300** (Rev. 12-2004)   Cat. No. 62133S   FinCEN Form **8300** (Rev. 12-2004)

IRS Form 8300 (Rev. 12-2004)   Page **2**   **FinCEN Form 8300** (Rev. 12-2004)

Multiple Parties
(Complete applicable parts below if box 2 or 15 on page 1 is checked)

Part I   Continued—Complete if box 2 on page 1 is checked

3 Last name	4 First name	5 M.I.	6 Taxpayer identification number

7 Address (number, street, and apt. or suite no.)	8 Date of birth ► (see instructions)	M M D D Y Y Y Y

9 City	10 State	11 ZIP code	12 Country (if not U.S.)	13 Occupation, profession, or business

14 Identifying document (ID)	a Describe ID ►	b Issued by ► ....
	c Number ►	

3 Last name	4 First name	5 M.I.	6 Taxpayer identification number

7 Address (number, street, and apt. or suite no.)	8 Date of birth ► (see instructions)	M M D D Y Y Y Y

9 City	10 State	11 ZIP code	12 Country (if not U.S.)	13 Occupation, profession, or business

14 Identifying document (ID)	a Describe ID ►	b Issued by ► ....
	c Number ►	

Part II   Continued—Complete if box 15 on page 1 is checked

16 Individual's last name or Organization's name	17 First name	18 M.I.	19 Taxpayer identification number

20 Doing business as (DBA) name (see instructions)	Employer identification number

21 Address (number, street, and apt. or suite no.)	22 Occupation, profession, or business

23 City	24 State	25 ZIP code	26 Country (if not U.S.)

27 Alien identification (ID)	a Describe ID ►	b Issued by ► ....
	c Number ►	

16 Individual's last name or Organization's name	17 First name	18 M.I.	19 Taxpayer identification number

20 Doing business as (DBA) name (see instructions)	Employer identification number

21 Address (number, street, and apt. or suite no.)	22 Occupation, profession, or business

23 City	24 State	25 ZIP code	26 Country (if not U.S.)

27 Alien identification (ID)	a Describe ID ►	b Issued by ► ....
	c Number ►	

Comments – Please use the lines provided below to comment on or clarify any information you entered on any line in Parts I, II, III, and IV

_____

_____

_____

_____

IRS Form 8300 (Rev. 12-2004)   **FinCEN Form 8300** (Rev. 12-2004)

IRS Form 8300 (Rev. 12-2004)   Page **3**   **FinCEN Form 8300** (Rev. 12-2004)

Section references are to the Internal Revenue Code unless otherwise noted.

Important Reminders

● Section 6050I (26 United States Code (U.S.C.) 6050I) and 31 U.S.C. 5331 require that certain information be reported to the IRS and the Financial Crimes Enforcement Network (FinCEN). This information must be reported on IRS/FinCEN Form 8300.

● Item 33 box i is to be checked only by clerks of the court; box d is to be checked by bail bondsmen. See the instructions on page 5.

● For purposes of section 6050I and 31 U.S.C. 5331, the word "cash" and "currency" have the same meaning. See *Cash* under *Definitions* on page 4.

General Instructions

Who must file. Each person engaged in a trade or business who, in the course of that trade or business, receives more than $10,000 in cash in one transaction or in two or more related transactions, must file Form 8300. Any transactions conducted between a payer (or its agent) and the recipient in a 24-hour period are related transactions. Transactions are considered related even if they occur over a period of more than 24 hours if the recipient knows, or has reason to know, that each transaction is one of a series of connected transactions.

Keep a copy of each Form 8300 for 5 years from the date you file it.

Clerks of Federal or State courts must file Form 8300 if more than $10,000 in cash is received as bail for an individual(s) charged with certain criminal offenses. For these purposes, a clerk includes the clerk's office or any other office, department, division, branch, or unit of the court that is authorized to receive bail. If a person receives bail on behalf of a clerk, the clerk is treated as receiving the bail. See the instructions for Item 33 on page 5.

If multiple payments are made in cash to satisfy bail and the initial payment does not exceed $10,000, the initial payment and subsequent payments must be aggregated and the information return must be filed by the 15th day after receipt of the payment that causes the aggregate amount to exceed $10,000 in cash. In such cases, the reporting requirement can be satisfied either by sending a single written statement with an aggregate amount listed or by furnishing a copy of each Form 8300 relating to that payer. Payments made to satisfy separate bail requirements are not required to be aggregated. See Treasury Regulations section 1.6050I-2.

Casinos must file Form 8300 for nongaming activities (restaurants, shops, etc.).

Voluntary use of Form 8300. Form 8300 may be filed voluntarily for any suspicious transaction (see *Definitions*) for use by the IRS, even if the total amount does not exceed $10,000.

Exceptions. Cash is not required to be reported if it is received:

● By a financial institution required to file Form 104, Currency Transaction Report.

● By a casino required to file (or exempt from filing) Form 103, Currency Transaction Report by Casinos, if the cash is received as part of its gaming business.

● By an agent who receives the cash from a principal, if the agent uses all of the cash within 15 days in a second transaction that is reportable on Form 8300 or on Form 104, and discloses all the information necessary to complete Part II of Form 8300 or Form 104 to the recipient of the cash in the second transaction.

● In a transaction occurring entirely outside the United States. See Publication 1544, Reporting Cash Payments Over $10,000 (Received in a Trade or Business), regarding transactions occurring in Puerto Rico, the Virgin Islands, and territories and possessions of the United States.

● In a transaction that is not in the course of a person's trade or business.

When to file. File Form 8300 by the 15th day after the date the cash was received. If that date falls on a Saturday, Sunday, or legal holiday, file the form on the next business day.

Where to file. File the form with the Internal Revenue Service, Detroit Computing Center, P.O. Box 32621, Detroit, MI 48232.

Statement to be provided. You must give a written or electronic statement to each person named on a required Form 8300 on or before January 31 of the year following the calendar year in which the cash is received. The statement must show the name, telephone number, and address of the information contact for the business, the aggregate amount of reportable cash received, and that the information was furnished to the IRS. Keep a copy of the statement for your records.

Multiple payments. If you receive more than one cash payment for a single transaction or for related transactions, you must report the multiple payments any time you receive a total amount that exceeds $10,000 within any 12-month period. Submit the report within 15 days of the date you receive the payment that

causes the total amount to exceed $10,000. If more than one report is required within 15 days, you may file a combined report. File the combined report no later than the date the earliest report, if filed separately, would have to be filed.

Taxpayer identification number (TIN). You must furnish the correct TIN of the person or persons from whom you receive the cash and, if applicable, the person or persons on whose behalf the transaction is being conducted. You may be subject to penalties for an incorrect or missing TIN.

The TIN for an individual (including a sole proprietorship) is the individual's social security number (SSN). For certain resident aliens who are not eligible to get an SSN and nonresident aliens who are required to file tax returns, it is an IRS Individual Taxpayer Identification Number (ITIN). For other persons, including corporations, partnerships, and estates, it is the employer identification number (EIN).

If you have requested but are not able to get a TIN for one or more of the parties to a transaction within 15 days following the transaction, file the report and attach a statement explaining why the TIN is not included.

Exception: *You are not required to provide the TIN of a person who is a nonresident alien individual or a foreign organization if that person does not have income effectively connected with the conduct of a U.S. trade or business and does not have an office or place of business, or fiscal or paying agent, in the United States. See* Publication 1544 *for more information.*

Penalties. You may be subject to penalties if you fail to file a correct and complete Form 8300 on time and you cannot show that the failure was due to reasonable cause. You may also be subject to penalties if you fail to furnish timely a correct and complete statement to each person named in a required report. A minimum penalty of $25,000 may be imposed if the failure is due to an intentional or willful disregard of the cash reporting requirements.

Penalties may also be imposed for causing, or attempting to cause, a trade or business to fail to file a required report; for causing, or attempting to cause, a trade or business to file a required report containing a material omission or misstatement of fact; or for structuring, or attempting to structure, transactions to avoid the reporting requirements. These violations may also be subject to criminal prosecution which, upon conviction, may result in imprisonment of up to 5 years or fines of up to $250,000 for individuals and $500,000 for corporations or both.

IRS Form 8300 (Rev. 12-2004)   Page **4**   FinCEN Form 8300 (Rev. 12-2004)

Definitions

Cash. The term "cash" means the following:

• U.S. and foreign coin and currency received in any transaction.

• A cashier's check, money order, bank draft, or traveler's check having a face amount of $10,000 or less that is received in a designated reporting transaction (defined below), or that is received in any transaction in which the recipient knows that the instrument is being used in an attempt to avoid the reporting of the transaction under either section 6050I or 31 U.S.C. 5331.

Note. Cash does not include a check drawn on the payer's own account, such as a personal check, regardless of the amount.

Designated reporting transaction. A retail sale (or the receipt of funds by a broker or other intermediary in connection with a retail sale) of a consumer durable, a collectible, or a travel or entertainment activity.

Retail sale. Any sale (whether or not the sale is for resale or for any other purpose) made in the course of a trade or business if that trade or business principally consists of making sales to ultimate consumers.

Consumer durable. An item of tangible personal property of a type that, under ordinary usage, can reasonably be expected to remain useful for at least 1 year, and that has a sales price of more than $10,000.

Collectible. Any work of art, rug, antique, metal, gem, stamp, coin, etc.

Travel or entertainment activity. An item of travel or entertainment that pertains to a single trip or event if the combined sales price of the item and all other items relating to the same trip or event that are sold in the same transaction (or related transactions) exceeds $10,000.

Exceptions. A cashier's check, money order, bank draft, or traveler's check is not considered received in a designated reporting transaction if it constitutes the proceeds of a bank loan or if it is received as a payment on certain promissory notes, installment sales contracts, or down payment plans. See Publication 1544 for more information.

Person. An individual, corporation, partnership, trust, estate, association, or company.

Recipient. The person receiving the cash. Each branch or other unit of a person's trade or business is considered a separate recipient unless the branch receiving the cash (or a central office linking the branches), knows or has reason to know the identity of payers making cash payments to other branches.

Transaction. Includes the purchase of property or services, the payment of debt, the exchange of a negotiable instrument for cash, and the receipt of cash to be held in escrow or trust. A single transaction may not be broken into multiple transactions to avoid reporting.

Suspicious transaction. A transaction in which it appears that a person is attempting to cause Form 8300 not to be filed, or to file a false or incomplete form. The term also includes any transaction in which there is an indication of possible illegal activity.

Specific Instructions

You must complete all parts. However, you may skip Part II if the individual named in Part I is conducting the transaction on his or her behalf only. For voluntary reporting of suspicious transactions, see Item 1 below.

Item 1. If you are amending a prior report, check box 1a. Complete the appropriate items with the correct or amended information only. Complete all of Part IV. Staple a copy of the original report to the amended report.

To voluntarily report a suspicious transaction (see *Definitions*), check box 1b. You may also telephone your local IRS Criminal Investigation Division or call 1-800-800-2877.

Part I

Item 2. If two or more individuals conducted the transaction you are reporting, check the box and complete Part I for any one of the individuals. Provide the same information for the other individual(s) on the back of the form. If more than three individuals are involved, provide the same information on additional sheets of paper and attach them to this form.

Item 6. Enter the taxpayer identification number (TIN) of the individual named. See *Taxpayer identification number (TIN)* on page 3 for more information.

Item 8. Enter eight numerals for the date of birth of the individual named. For example, if the individual's birth date is July 6, 1960, enter 07 06 1960.

Item 13. Fully describe the nature of the occupation, profession, or business (for example, "plumber," "attorney," or "automobile dealer"). Do not use general or nondescriptive terms such as "businessman" or "self-employed."

Item 14. You must verify the name and address of the named individual(s). Verification must be made by examination of a document normally accepted as a means of identification when cashing checks (for example, a driver's license, passport, alien registration card, or other official

document). In item 14a, enter the type of document examined. In item 14b, identify the issuer of the document. In item 14c, enter the document's number. For example, if the individual has a Utah driver's license, enter "driver's license" in item 14a, "Utah" in item 14b, and the number appearing on the license in item 14c.

Note. You must complete all three items (a, b, and c) in this line to make sure that Form 8300 will be processed correctly.

Part II

Item 15. If the transaction is being conducted on behalf of more than one person (including husband and wife or parent and child), check the box and complete Part II for any one of the persons. Provide the same information for the other person(s) on the back of the form. If more than three persons are involved, provide the same information on additional sheets of paper and attach them to this form.

Items 16 through 19. If the person on whose behalf the transaction is being conducted is an individual, complete items 16, 17, and 18. Enter his or her TIN in item 19. If the individual is a sole proprietor and has an employer identification number (EIN), you must enter both the SSN and EIN in item 19. If the person is an organization, put its name as shown on required tax filings in item 16 and its EIN in item 19.

Item 20. If a sole proprietor or organization named in items 16 through 18 is doing business under a name other than that entered in item 16 (e.g., a "trade" or "doing business as (DBA)" name), enter it here.

Item 27. If the person is not required to furnish a TIN, complete this item. See *Taxpayer Identification Number (TIN)* on page 3. Enter a description of the type of official document issued to that person in item 27a (for example, "passport"), the country that issued the document's number in item 27c.

Note. You must complete all three items (a, b, and c) in this line to make sure that Form 8300 will be processed correctly.

Part III

Item 28. Enter the date you received the cash. If you received the cash in more than one payment, enter the date you received the payment that caused the combined amount to exceed $10,000. See *Multiple payments* under *General Instructions* for more information.

Item 30. Check this box if the amount shown in item 29 was received in more than one payment (for example, as installment payments or payments on related transactions).

Item 31. Enter the total price of the property, services, amount of cash exchanged, etc. (for example, the total cost of a vehicle purchased, cost of catering service, exchange of currency) if different from the amount shown in item 29.

Item 32. Enter the dollar amount of each form of cash received. Show foreign currency amounts in U.S. dollar equivalent at a fair market rate of exchange available to the public. The sum of the amounts must equal item 29. For cashier's check, money order, bank draft, or traveler's check, provide the name of the issuer and the serial number of each instrument. Names of all issuers and all serial numbers involved must be provided. If necessary, provide this information on additional sheets of paper and attach them to this form.

Item 33. Check the appropriate box(es) that describe the transaction. If the transaction is not specified in boxes a–i, check box j and briefly describe the transaction (for example, "car lease," "boat lease," "house lease," or "aircraft rental"). If the transaction relates to the receipt of bail by a court clerk, check box i, "Bail received by court clerks." This box is only for use by court clerks. If the transaction relates to cash received by a bail bondsman, check box d, "Business services provided."

Part IV

Item 36. If you are a sole proprietorship, you must enter your SSN. If your business also has an EIN, you must provide the EIN as well. All other business entities must enter an EIN.

Item 41. Fully describe the nature of your business, for example, "attorney" or "jewelry dealer." Do not use general or nondescriptive terms such as "business" or "store."

Item 42. This form must be signed by an individual who has been authorized to do so for the business that received the cash.

Comments

Use this section to comment on or clarify anything you may have entered on any line in Parts I, II, III, and IV. For example, if you checked box b (Suspicious transaction) in line 1 above Part I, you may want to explain why you think that the cash transaction you are reporting on Form 8300 may be suspicious.

Privacy Act and Paperwork Reduction Act Notice. Except as otherwise noted, the information solicited on this form is required by the Internal Revenue Service (IRS) and the Financial Crimes Enforcement Network (FinCEN) in order to carry out the laws and regulations of the United States Department of the Treasury. Trades or businesses, except for clerks of criminal courts, are required to provide the information to the IRS and FinCEN under both section 6050I and 31 U.S.C. 5331. Clerks of criminal courts are required to provide the information to the IRS under section 6050I. Section 6109 and 31 U.S.C. 5331 require that you provide your social security number in order to adequately identify you and process your return and other papers. The principal purpose for collecting the information on this form is to maintain reports or records which have a high degree of usefulness in criminal, tax, or regulatory investigations or proceedings, or in the conduct of intelligence or counterintelligence activities, by directing the Federal Government's attention to unusual or questionable transactions.

You are not required to provide information as to whether the reported transaction is deemed suspicious. Failure to provide all other requested information, or providing fraudulent information, may result in criminal prosecution and other penalties under Title 26 and Title 31 of the United States Code.

Generally, tax returns and return information are confidential, as stated in section 6103. However, section 6103 allows or requires the IRS to disclose or give the information requested on this form to others as described in the Code. For example, we may disclose your tax information to the Department of Justice, to enforce the tax laws, both civil and criminal, and to cities, states, the District of Columbia, to carry out their tax laws. We may disclose this information to other persons as necessary to obtain information which we cannot get in any other way. We may disclose this information to Federal, state, and local child support agencies; and to other Federal agencies for the purposes of determining entitlement for benefits or the eligibility for and the repayment of loans. We may also provide the records to appropriate state, local, and foreign criminal law enforcement and regulatory personnel in the performance of their official duties. We may also disclose this information to other countries under a tax treaty, or to Federal and state agencies to enforce Federal nontax criminal laws and to combat terrorism.

The IRS authority to disclose information to combat terrorism expired on December 31, 2003. Legislation is pending that would reinstate this authority. "In addition, FinCEN may provide the information to those officials if they are conducting intelligence or counter-intelligence activities to protect against international terrorism."

You are not required to provide the information requested on a form that is subject to the Paperwork Reduction Act unless the form displays a valid OMB control number. Books or records relating to a form or its instructions must be retained as long as their contents may become material in the administration of any law under Title 26 or Title 31.

The time needed to complete this form will vary depending on individual circumstances. The estimated average time is 21 minutes. If you have comments concerning the accuracy of this time estimate or suggestions for making this form simpler, you can write to the Tax Products Coordinating Committee, Western Area Distribution Center, Rancho Cordova, CA 95743-0001. Do not send this form to this office. Instead, see *Where To File* on page 3.

Form 2-6 IRS Demand for Supplementation of Form 8300

DEPARTMENT OF THE TREASURY
IRS, Detroit Computing Center
P.O. Box 33104
Detroit, Michigan 48232-0104

Document Control No
(DCN:)
Taxpayer ID No (TIN):

_____

Date of This Notice:

Questions regarding this letter
Refer to the above DCN
Call: (313) 234-1651
Hours 7:30 am–2:30 pm EST

Dear Sir or Madam:

Our review of the attached Form 8300 (Report of Cash Payment Over $10,000 Received in a Trade or Business) filed by you or your firm indicates it was either incomplete, incorrect, or illegible. Section 6050I and the respective regulations require the filing of form 8300 by all trades and businesses, including attorneys. See Treas. Reg. S 1.6050I-1 (c) (7) (iii) Ex. 2 (requiring attorneys who represent clients for cash fees in excess of $10,000 to comply with section 6050I). Four federal circuits have held that the identification on Form 8300 of clients who make substantial cash fee payments is not a disclosure of privileged or confidential information. *See United States v. Goldberger & Dubin, P.C.,* 935 F.2d 501 (2d Cir. 1991) (rejecting Fourth, Fifth, and Sixth Amendment, attorney-client privilege, and confidentiality challenges to section 6050I); *United States v. Leventhal,* 961 F.2d 936 (11th Cir. 1992) (following *Goldberger* and rejecting the position that information may be withheld absent a court order); *United States v. Ritchie,* 15 F.3d 592 (6th Cir. 1994) (following *Goldberger* and rejecting the "last link" doctrine); *United States v. Blackman,* 72 F.3d 1418 (9th Cir. 1995) (holding that the attorney-client privilege did not protect the clients' identities and that the Service was not required to follow John Doe summons procedures).

We would appreciate your providing the missing information needed to complete the form, specified on the attachment, to the Detroit Computing Center within 30 days of the date of this letter. For this purpose, please use the attached facsimile of Form 8300; do not send a new Form 8300.

You should be aware that the failure to comply with cash reporting requirements may result in the imposition of civil penalties and the issuance of a summons. Section 6721 (a) provides an assessable penalty of $50 for each Form 8300 which is not timely filed, or which fails to include correct or complete information. Section 6721 (e) provides that those who intentionally disregard the cash reporting requirements may be assessed a penalty equal to the greater of $25,000 or the amount of cash required to be reported up to $100,000 per Form 8300. *See Goldberger*, 935 F.2d at 506.

If you have any questions concerning this matter, you may contact the Compliance Review Group at (313) 234-1613. Please refer to the DCN noted above.

Sincerely yours,
/s/ Cecil K. Marshall
Department Manager
Edit and Error Resolution

****
PLEASE RETURN ALL MATERIAL
SENT WITH YOUR REPLY
RETURN ADDRESS MUST SHOW
THROUGH WINDOW
****

DEPARTMENT OF THE TREASURY
IRS, Detroit Computing Center
P.O. Box 33104

Enclosures: 2881–259N
Facsimile of Form 8300
Return Envelope
***** N O T E: ********

(This page intentionally left blank.)

Chapter 3

ARREST & INITIAL APPEARANCE

(This page intentionally left blank.)

I.   THE ARREST

§3:01   The Defendant's Journey

Most criminal cases begin with:
- An arrest.
- The filing of a complaint or other charging document.
- An initial appearance before a member of the minor judiciary (*e.g.,* a magistrate, district justice or justice of the peace).

Usually, the arrest and the first call to counsel come without warning. However, you may occasionally represent the defendant during a lengthy investigation prior to these steps; white collar criminal investigations and vehicular homicides are common examples.

The client's journey from arrest to initial appearance in court can be tortuous. From the place of arrest, the arrestee is transported to the local precinct or stationhouse. The arrestee is "booked" either at that location or at some central holding facility.

"Booking" involves steps to identify the arrestee and record the arrest, such as photographing and fingerprinting, asking him pedigree questions and searching databases for his criminal record. Pedigree questioning gathers information about identity, residence, nationality and immigration status, health, employment and associates. During this time, either the arresting officer or a prosecutor will draft the charging documents.

Unless the police release the arrestee on stationhouse bail or with a summons, they will take him/her to the courthouse where a bail agency, which operates as an arm of the court, may interview the defendant and assess whether he has sufficient community ties to recommend release. [See §3:02 for stationhouse bails.]

§3:02   Minor Offenses

For minor offenses, the police have discretion to issue a citation, summons or appearance ticket instead of putting the arrestee through the full arrest and booking process. [*See, e.g.,* NY Crim. Pro. Law 150.10, 150.20 (desk appearance tickets for misdemeanors and low level felonies); Pa. R. Crim. P. 403 (citation), 509 (summons where maximum punishment is not more than one year.)]

Some jurisdictions permit the police to set bail at the stationhouse and release the defendant before he is taken to court. [*See, e.g.,* NY CPL 140.20 [2] (for less than Class D felonies).]

The decision to release the arrestee with a summons or on stationhouse bail lies within the arresting officer's unreviewable discretion. Arresting and booking an individual even for a minor fine-only offense does not violate the Fourth Amendment. [*Atwater v. City of Lago Vista*, 532 U.S. 318 (2001) (rejecting Fourth Amendment claim of mother who was arrested and taken from her three- and five-year-old children for the offense of not wearing a seatbelt, punishable by a $25 to $50 fine).]

However, several state courts have rejected Atwater on state court grounds. They subject the officer's decision to arrest or detain a person for a minor offense to a test of reasonableness **or prohibit arrest for minor misdemeanors absent special circumstances**. [*State v. Askerooth*, 681 N.W.2d 353, 363 (Minn. 2004); *State v. Brown*, 99 Ohio St.3d 323, 792 N.E.2d 175, 178–79 (2003) (applying the Ohio Constitution, which provided greater protection than the Fourth Amendment, and holding that arrest of jaywalker violated the constitutional provision against unreasonable seizures where the arresting officer violated a state statute) *State v. Bayard*, 119 Nev. 241, 247, 71 P.3d 498, 502 (Nev. 2003) (special circumstances required for arrest); *State v. Bauer*, 307 Mont. 105, 111-12, 36 P.3d 892, 897 (2001) (under the Montana Constitution, a person stopped for a non-jailable offense should not be subject to arrest absent special circumstances such as a concern for the safety of the offender or the public).]

§3:03   Finding Your Client After Arrest

During the time from arrest to initial court appearance, your client may lack access to a phone, and his family may look anxiously to you to locate him and assure them of his well-being.

Typically, arrestees go from the stationhouse to the county jail and then court, perhaps with a stop at some central booking facility along the way, depending on the jurisdiction. The route may vary not only from state to state, but from precinct to precinct. A different routine may prevail at night-time and on weekends.

Because of the variations, call rather than guess.

If you know which agency or officer arrested your client, call them first and ask for your client's whereabouts, and estimated time of arrival at court.

If the arresting authority is unknown, work your way backwards: court, the jail, central booking and, if any of the previous entities can tell you in which precinct or district your client was arrested, the stationhouse.

When you find your client, ask the facility:

- How long will your client be there?
- Can he be bailed and released from that facility?
- Can you and/or family visit?

§3:04   Consequences of an Illegal Arrest

An illegal arrest does not terminate the prosecution. [*See United States v. Crews*, 445 U.S. 463, 474 & n.20 (1980) (defendant could be prosecuted for robbery even though illegal arrest gave victim opportunity to identify him); *Frisbie v. Collins*, 342 U.S. 519 (1952) (defendant can be prosecuted even when he was illegally abducted to bring him within court's jurisdiction).]

Arrest of a defendant within his home requires probable cause and a search warrant, unless exigent circumstances justify dispensing with a warrant. [*Payton v. New York*, 445 U.S. 573 (1980).] "[W]here law enforcement officers summon a suspect to the door of his home and place him under arrest while he remains within his home, in the absence of exigent circumstances, *Payton* is violated regardless of whether the officers physically cross the threshold." [*United States v. Allen*, 813 F.3d 76,88-89 (2d Cir. 2016) (suppressing evidence found in home when officers, standing outside the threshold, summoned defendant to the door and informed him that he was under arrest and then searched the house and found a weapon).]

Even where the arrest lacks probable cause, if the prosecution can develop sufficient evidence of probable cause between the arrest and the initial appearance, the prosecution can continue to detain the defendant.

Two consequences follow from an illegal arrest:

- If the illegality lies in the lack of probable cause, and that deficiency continues at the initial appearance, the defendant must be released.
- Any physical evidence gained from the illegal arrest and any statements the defendant made following the arrest must be suppressed.

If, however, the police discover an outstanding warrant for the defendant between his stop or arrest and the search, the search is considered sufficiently attenuated so that the exclusionary remedy does not apply and the results are admissible. [*Utah v. Strieff*, 136 S.Ct. 2056 (2016).]

[§§3:05-3:09 Reserved]

II.   POLICE POST-ARREST INVESTIGATION

§3:10   Authorized Procedures

The police may use their access to the arrestee to undertake further investigation. They may:
- Place the arrestee in a line-up.
- Take fingerprints, handwriting samples and voice exemplars.
- Seek consent to search his property.
- Interrogate him.

With a court order or warrant, the police may clip hair or collect saliva for testing.

After a drunk-driving arrest, the police have authority to request that the driver submit to both a breathalyzer and the drawing of blood for blood alcohol analysis.

§3:11   Refusal to Cooperate With Investigation

With the exception of interrogation or consent to searches, an arrestee does not have the right to refuse any of the authorized post-arrest investigation procedures.

However, the police usually will not try to wrestle the defendant into a line-up or forcefully bleed him, and the laws of many states prohibit the use of force to draw blood. [*See* Note, *Shed Thou No Blood: The Forcible Removal of Blood Samples from Drunk Driving Suspects*, 60 So.Cal.L.Rev. 1115, 1117 (1987); *but see Hammer v. Gross*, 884 F.2d 1200 (9th Cir. 1989), on reh'g, 932 F.2d 842 (9th Cir. 1991) (actions of three officers in holding arrestee down to draw blood held not to be unreasonable).] A blood draw requires a warrant unless the case-specific exigencies justify dispensing with one. [*Missouri v. McNeely*, 133 S.Ct. 1552 (2013).] In *McNeely*, the Supreme Court held that the natural metabolization of alcohol in the bloodstream does not present a per se exigency that would justify an across-the-board exception to the warrant requirement.

Instead, the defendant's refusal may be used at trial as evidence of consciousness of guilt. [*South Dakota v. Neville*, 459 U.S. 553, 560-562 (1983) (refusal to take blood alcohol test); *People v. Clark*, 5 Cal.4th 950, 1003, 22 Cal.Rptr.2d 689, 857 P.2d 1099 (1993) (refusal to provide handwriting exemplar); *United States v. Terry*, 702 F.2d 299, 314 (2d Cir. 1983) (refusal to supply palm prints); *but see State v. Jones*, 234 Conn. 324, 662 A.2d 1199, 1216 (1995) (where the defendant, rather than merely refusing, litigates legality of order to produce hair and blood on religious grounds and loses, improper to give consciousness of guilt charge or to admit the evidence of the refusal).]

If an arrestee disobeys a court order commanding submission to such testing, he faces contempt proceedings and incarceration.

In drunk driving arrests, the statutes authorizing breathalyzers and blood tests provide for license suspension upon refusal, and refusal may enhance the sentence upon conviction. [*E.g.*, 75 Pa.C.S. §1547(b).] *McNeely* did not undermine state implied consent laws that impose a license suspension and allow an adverse inference to be drawn as consequence of a motorist's refusal to permit a blood alcohol test. [*McNeely*, 133 S.Ct. at 1566.] In *Birchfield v. North Dakota*, 136 S.Ct. 2160 (2016), the Supreme Court held that the Fourth Amendment requires warrants for blood tests, and the Court invalidated statutes that implied consent to blood tests on penalty of criminal prosecution for the refusal. *Birchfield* may be used to invalidate sentence enhancements flowing from a refusal to consent [*Commonwealth v. Giron*, 155 A.3d 635, 640 (Pa. Super. 2017)], but it seems to leave intact civil penalties, such as license suspension [*see Birchfield*, 136 S.Ct. at 2185; *Boseman v. Department of Transportation*, 157 A.3d 10 (Pa.Cmwlth. 2017)], as well as evidentiary consequences, such as use of the refusal as evidence of consciousness of guilt [*Birchfield*, 136 S.Ct. at 2185]. Most jurisdictions do not recognize a right to counsel for an arrestee prior to submitting to a DUI chemical test, but some do, principally under statute or state constitution. [*See Commonwealth v. McCoy*, 975 A.2d 586, 590 n.7 (Pa. Sup. Ct. 2009) (surveying states; refuses to recognize Sixth Amendment right to counsel prior to submitting to a chemical test).]

§3:12   Attorney's Role in the Police Investigation

Accompany your client during as many of the investigative procedures as you can (or have an associate, paralegal or investigator do so).

With pedigree questions and bail interviews, your role is primarily to counsel your client to be truthful and to avoid misunderstandings. However, even these questions may elicit incriminating information:
- Stating your client's true name may reveal his identification documents to be fraudulent or that his immigration status is not only unlawful, but criminal. [*See* 8 U.S.C. §1326(b)(2) (illegal re-entry after deportation for an aggravated felony is a felony punishable by up to 20 years).]
- Acknowledging his place of work may implicate him in criminal activity if, for example, it is a known chop shop or front for money-laundering.
- A lack of legal income may raise suspicions that his ability to retain a high-priced lawyer or post substantial bail come from illegal sources.

Unless you know that the answer will provide incriminating information that otherwise will not be discovered, your client should answer. The authorities will learn the true answers to most of these questions on their own soon enough. Refusing to answer guarantees that your client will not be released on bail.

With investigative procedures, your role is to see that no interrogation occurs. Tell the police not to ask your client any questions, and instruct your client not to answer anything or consent to any requests to search. Never consent to an interview or search on your client's behalf.

With other authorized police investigative steps (*i.e.*, handwriting exemplars, line-ups, blood-drawing) your role is three-fold:
- Try to shape the investigation to be less intrusive to your client and less likely to yield incriminating evidence. You have the most leeway in this respect with regard to line-ups. [For more on line-ups, *see* Chapter 9, Pre-Trial Identifications.]
- See that your client avoids incriminating himself, either by blurting out admissions or attempting to falsify or destroy evidence. This occurs most frequently during handwriting exemplars, when your client might be tempted to comment on why he is being asked to write certain words or might attempt to disguise his handwriting. [*See, e.g., United States v. Jacobowitz*, 877 F.2d 162 (2d Cir. 1989) (defendant's efforts to disguise handwriting and his statement during uncounseled giving of exemplars that he was unable to write suspected false name could be used against him).]
- Be a witness to deter and report any police abuses.

§3:13 Collection of DNA

Federal law and statutes in 30 states authorize collection of arrestees' DNA without particularized suspicion or a warrant. [42 U.S.C. §14135a; 38 C.F.R. §28.12; Ariz. Rev. Stat. Ann. §13-610; Minn. Stat. §299C.155. *See generally* Jesika S. Wehunt, Drawing the Line: DNA Databasing at Arrest and Sample Expungement, 29 Ga. St. U. L. Rev. 1063 (2013); www.ncsl.org/Documents/cj/ArresteeDNALaws.pdfwww.ncsl.org, "DNA Arrestee Laws" (last visited August 6, 2017).] In *Maryland v. King*, the Supreme Court upheld Maryland's statute: "When officers make an arrest supported by probable cause to hold for a serious offense and bring the suspect to the station to be detained in custody, taking and analyzing a cheek swab of the arrestee's DNA is, like fingerprinting and photographing, a legitimate police booking procedure that is reasonable under the Fourth Amendment." [133 S.Ct. 1958, 1980 (2013). *See also State v. Johnson*, 813 N.W.2d 1, 12 (Minn. 2012) (upholding Minnesota's DNA collection statute). *But see State v. Medina*, 102 A.3d 6611 (VT 2014) (striking down arrestee DNA collection statute under the Vermont state constitution).]

Nonetheless, issues remain. Many statutes authorize expungement should the charge be dismissed; insist on it, because often it is not automatic. [*See* http://www.ncsl.org/Documents/cj/ArresteeDNALaws.pdf (sixteen states provide for expungement, but only thirteen automatically)] Some statutes provide that an identification using a sample that should have been expunged still is admissible in court. [Cal. Penal Code §299(d) ("Any identification, warrant, probable cause to arrest, or arrest based upon a data bank or database match is not invalidated due to a failure to expunge or a delay in expunging records"); Haw. Rev. Stat. §844D-72(d) ("Any identification, warrant, probable cause to arrest, or arrest based upon a data bank match shall not be invalidated due to a failure to expunge or a delay in expunging records").] Most statutes restrict the collection to arrests for certain serious offenses, such as homicide, sex offenses, and burglary. Finally, most challenges have been facial ones; you might still have an argument that your client's offense is such–minor and non-violent–that there is insufficient government interest to justify collection of DNA in your particular case.

[§§3:14-3:19 Reserved]

III. THE APPEARANCE

A. Procedure

§3:20 Initial Appearance Procedures

After arrest and processing, the defendant is taken to an inferior court (a magistrate, district justice, or justice of the peace) for an initial appearance.

At this time, the judge will review the charges to determine whether probable cause exists to hold the defendant. In addition to the probable cause determination, a defendant is entitled to the following:

- Notice and explanation of the charges.
- A copy of the charges.
- Notice of rights, especially the right to remain silent and the right to counsel.
- Representation by counsel or appointment of counsel. [*Hamilton v. Alabama*, 368 U.S. 52 (1961); *Rothgery v. Gillespie County*, 554 U.S. 191 (2008).]
- A bail determination.
- Setting of a preliminary hearing date. [NY CPL170.10, 180.10; Pa. R. Crim. P. 540; Fed. R. Cr. P. 5(d).]

§3:21 Distinction Between Initial Appearance and Arraignment

The initial appearance is not the same as an arraignment.

"Arraignment" refers to the first appearance at which the defendant must enter a plea to the charge. [*See, e.g.,* Fed. R. Crim. P. 10; C.J.S., *Criminal Law*, §362; *State v. Cadorette*, 826 A.2d 101 (Vt 2003) (explaining arraignment process; reversing conviction where as a result of the failure to be arraigned, defendant did not have adequate notice of the charges and an opportunity to defend against them).]

In many jurisdictions, neither a prosecutor nor defense counsel attends the initial appearance, although defense counsel is entitled to attend (if counsel has been retained). While the initial appearance can proceed without defense counsel, it marks the point at which the Sixth Amendment right to counsel attaches, and the Court must appoint counsel within a reasonable time. [*Rothgery v. Gillespie County*, 554 U.S. 191 (2008). *But see People v. Hurt*, 2013 WL 2120275 (Mich. App. 2013) (unpublished) (whether the right to counsel has attached is distinct from whether a defendant has been denied his right to counsel at a critical stage in the proceeding; arraignment on a warrant was not a critical stage requiring representation).] With the attachment of that right come limitations on police ability to elicit statements and conduct lineups in the absence of counsel. [*See Massiah v. United States*, 377 U.S. 201 (1964); *United States v. Wade*, 388 U.S. 218 (1967).]

However, defendants have a constitutional right to representation by counsel at arraignment. [*Hamilton v. Alabama*, 368 U.S. 52 (1961).]

In most jurisdictions, the inferior court (which handles the initial appearance) cannot accept anything but a not-guilty plea to felony offenses. Therefore, strictly speaking, the arraignment occurs when the defendant appears before the superior court or court of general jurisdiction on the formal charges, such as the information or indictment.

§3:22   Counsel's Function at the Initial Appearance or Arraignment

Despite its limited function, the initial appearance presents opportunities to begin advocating for your client:
- Study the accusatory instrument and challenge its sufficiency if it fails to establish probable cause. Do not forget to consider whether your client is the person named in the charges.
- Seek your client's release on bail. A bail argument also may compel the prosecution to disclose some additional facts on the record to justify its request for a high bail.

In many jurisdictions, the arraignment is the time when the prosecution and defense exchange notice of the intent to offer certain evidence or to exercise certain rights. At this time:
- The prosecution:
  - Offers statements of the accused or evidence of a pre-trial identification. [*See, e.g.,* NY CPL 710.30.]
  - Demands alibi notice. [*See, e.g.,* NY CPL 250.20.]
- The defense:
  - Requests a preliminary hearing.
  - Demands that the defendant have an opportunity to testify in the grand jury. [*See, e.g.,* NY CPL 190.50.]

Generally, the defendant has some time period after the arraignment to file such notices, but the arraignment often is the most convenient time to do so for all concerned, and doing so at the arraignment prevents waiver by inadvertent omission.

Forms:
- **Form 3-1** Notice of Intent to Testify Before the Grand Jury (New York Statute)
- **Form 3-2** Checklist for Initial Appearance or Arraignment

[§§3:23-3:29 Reserved]

B. Plea Bargaining

§3:30   Plea Bargaining at Initial Appearance

There are practical and legal obstacles to disposing of a case through a guilty plea at the initial appearance.

The magistrate has limited jurisdiction and cannot enter a plea of guilty to a felony or serious misdemeanor. [*See, e.g.,* NY CPL 10.20, 10.30 (local criminal court cannot accept a guilty plea to a felony); NY CPL 220.10[5] (placing limits on how much a prosecutor may reduce a felony charge for a post-indictment plea).]

Further, at this early stage, the parties have limited knowledge about the seriousness of the case and the possible defenses.

§3:31   Plea Bargaining at Arraignment

Sometimes plea bargaining starts at the arraignment because of:
- The great pressure to dispose of cases quickly with the minimum use of court and prosecutorial resources.
- The defendant's inability to make bail.
- A statute or unwavering prosecutorial policy that prohibits pleas to lesser charges once an indictment or felony information is filed. [*See, e.g.,* NY CPL 220.10[5].]

A most difficult choice arises where a plea could result in a defendant's immediate release on probation whereas a not-guilty plea means that the defendant will stay in jail. Accepting probation may mean a plea to a more serious charge that the defendant would face later. For many defendants, especially the transient ones who cannot make bail, being on probation almost guarantees more serious problems. Probation creates obligations these defendants are unlikely to fulfill, and once violated they likely will receive a stiff jail sentence.

Likewise, many defendants are tempted by the offer of a more serious charge but with a guarantee of relatively little jail time even when they are likely to see the charges reduced to a summary offense and face either a small fine or a sentence of time served at the next court appearance. The more serious charge creates a more serious criminal history that could haunt the defendant on a future arrest. It also may carry collateral consequences. For example:

- A plea to a state misdemeanor that has a maximum possible sentence of more than two years imprisonment forever disqualifies him from possessing a firearm. [18 U.S.C. §921(a)(20), 922(g)(1).]
- A plea to a drug offense, either delivery or simple possession, prevents him from obtaining any federal student aid for at least one year, including federally guaranteed student loans. [34 C.F.R. §668.40.]

PRACTICE TIPS:

- Enter into a plea only with great caution. A prosecutor's generosity early in the process may reflect an undisclosed weakness in the case. If you see serious weaknesses in the prosecution's evidence, advise your client to hold out for a better deal later. Sometimes, the prosecutor will see that the bluff has been called and make a second, more acceptable offer at the arraignment.
- Consult with public defenders or others who appear regularly in the local criminal court and know the value of particular kinds of cases.
- Learn as much about the case as you can from your client and the prosecutor and police.
- Advise your client that as unbearable as jail may seem, he will have to live with the consequences of a plea for the rest of his life. A conviction exposes him to greater punishment upon later prosecutions and may stymie his job prospects forever.

§3:32   Pre-Trial Diversion

In many jurisdictions, the prosecutor may offer some sort of pre-trial diversion on minor charges. [*See, e.g.,* NY CPL 170.55, 170.56 (adjournment in contemplation of dismissal); S.C. Code Ann. §17-22-60 (pre-trial intervention).]

Generally, under these programs, if the defendant agrees to an adjournment of a year or so and stays out of trouble or completes other conditions, such as a drug or alcohol rehabilitation program or the payment of restitution, the charge will be dismissed and the record expunged. Some programs require that the defendant enter a guilty plea before he may be admitted into the program, and upon unsuccessful discharge from the diversion program, he is subject to sentencing in accordance with his guilty plea–with the added strike that he botched one chance at leniency. [*See, e.g., Williams v. Commonwealth,* 354 S.W.3d 158 (KY Court of Appeals 2011) (construing KY Revised Statutes §§533.250, 533.256).]

While pre-trial diversion usually is a good deal, it is not always appropriate. Defendants usually have only one chance at pre-trial diversion, so accepting the program on this arrest disqualifies them from diversion for a subsequent arrest.

Evaluate your client and the strength of the prosecution's case. If your client is likely to be arrested again (*e.g.,* a driver with a drinking problem, a serious marijuana smoker, a dedicated political protestor) and the case is weak, he might be better served by fighting this case in the hope that victory will save the diversion for a future arrest on stronger charges.

Some defendants, perhaps with the self-knowledge that they cannot stay out of trouble, would rather be done with the case with a fine or a brief jail sentence.

[§§3:33-3:39 Reserved]

C. Special Situations

§3:40   Mental Evaluation

If your client appears mentally unstable and the charge is a very serious one, request an evaluation for mental competence. [*See, e.g.,* NY CPL 730.]

However, do this only if your client faces lengthy incarceration. The risks of seeking a mental evaluation are:

- The client will be committed to custody for several months to undergo an evaluation.
- If found incompetent, the client might face institutionalization in a mental facility for longer than the sentence he might have received if the charge is a relatively minor one.

[For more on mental competence, see Chapter 13, Mental Health Issues.]

§3:41 Medical Needs

Ask the court to address your client's medical needs.

You have the opportunity to begin to make a record that the police mistreated your client, a record that might pressure the prosecution to offer a dismissal or lenient plea to dispose of the case and any possible suit against the government.

If your client will not be released on bail, try to bring copies of his prescriptions or labeled pill bottles to read the precise prescription to the court. Or, you might give prescriptions to the marshal or sheriff or jail so they know exactly what he needs.

§3:42 The Media

Shield your client from the media.

Above everything else, instruct your client not to say anything in response to any questions.

He should walk straight ahead, at a steady pace, but not at a run. He should not cover his face, wave, smirk, smile or sneer.

If you can, walk out of court with a decoy while your client escapes through some other exit.

If the media are present in or immediately outside the courtroom, inform them that you and your client will not be making any comment; this may deter some of them from asking. Some may ask anyway to capture for the evening news the film of the reporter valiantly thrusting the microphone at the fleeing defendant. You should do one of the following:

- Say nothing.
- Say, "We have no comment at this time." (A complete sentence is better than grunting, "No comment.")
- Make some statement demonstrating your belief that the legal system will vindicate your client, such as: "We look forward to answering these charges in court/at trial."

§3:43 Prosecution Witnesses

If prosecution witnesses attend, you might introduce yourself.

If you do not have an opportunity to interview them at the appearance, explain politely that you may wish to do so later. Your courtesy may open doors. Further, talking to the witnesses may yield an initial feel for how hostile, articulate or unstable they are.

[§§3:44-3:49 Reserved]

D. Delay in Initial Appearance

§3:50 Right to Prompt Determination

Both the Fourth Amendment to the U.S. Constitution and state laws mandate that an arrestee have a prompt determination of probable cause. [*County of Riverside v. McLaughlin*, 500 U.S. 44, 56-57 (1991).]

The Fourth Amendment requires some probable cause determination within 48 hours. [*County of Riverside v. McLaughlin*, 500 U.S. 44, 56-57 (1991) (an arrested person must receive a probable cause determination within forty-eight hours unless the prosecution establishes a "bona fide emergency or other extraordinary circumstance").]

The determination can be made *ex parte* and upon a mere review of papers without an evidentiary hearing. [*Gerstein v. Pugh*, 420 U.S. 103, 120-21 (1975).] If the arrest was pursuant to a warrant, a magistrate already made the probable cause determination upon issuing the warrant, and no more process is required. [*Gerstein v. Pugh*, 420 U.S. at 117 n. 18; *Michigan v. Doran*, 439 U.S. 282, 285 n.3 (1979).]

State law may impose more stringent demands. Most states require an appearance well before 48 hours. [*See, e.g., People ex re. Maxian v. Brown*, 77 N.Y.2d 422, 568 N.Y.S.2d 575, 570 N.E.2d 223 (1991) (24 hours). See NY CPL 140.20[1] (arrestee must be brought before local criminal court "without unnecessary delay"); Pa.R.Cr.P. 519(A)(1) (defendant arrested without warrant must have preliminary arraignment "without unnecessary delay"). *See also, Riverside*, 500 U.S. at 69-70. (Scalia, J., dissenting) (most states require arrestee's presentment or arraignment within 24 hours).]

Local law may require the defendant's appearance in court even if a warrant has issued. [NY CPL 120.10[1], 120.90[1]; FL Rule 3.130.]

### §3:51	Remedy for Excessive Delay

If the defendant has not had a probable cause review within the prescribed time, you may seek release by filing a writ of habeas corpus with the court or judge assigned to hear miscellaneous motions. [*People ex rel. Maxian v. Brown*, 77 N.Y.2d 422, 568 N.Y.S.2d 575, 570 N.E.2d 223 (1991).]

However, filing a writ takes time on your part and time to schedule the hearing, by the end of which your client might have been arraigned. Therefore, start with telephone calls, going up the chain of command: to the arresting officer or his commander, to a responsible assistant district attorney, to the supervising prosecutor in charge of preliminary proceedings, and then to the motions part judge. Make the last call for the putative purpose of scheduling the presentation of the habeas petition, but be sure to explain the situation to the judge or clerk. The explanation, and the judge's desire to avoid unnecessary litigation, may prompt the judge to make a call and to get your client arraigned sooner, and with less expense, than later.

You might also consider threatening a federal civil rights action against the officers, sheriff and prosecuting office. Request a preliminary injunction ordering that your client be brought before a magistrate consistent with his Fourth Amendment rights. [*See Gerstein v. Pugh*, 420 U.S. 103, 107 n.6 (Federal civil rights action was appropriate because defendants only requested hearings, not release).]

The threat of such an action should bring immediate relief, because if you bring such an action and prevail, the defendants must pay your attorneys' fees. [*See* 42 U.S.C. §§1983, 1988(b) (reasonable attorneys' fees should be awarded to prevailing party).]

If you are not retained in time to take action, the defendant's undue wait for an arraignment is not grounds for dismissing the charge, but it may justify suppression of any statements elicited during the delay. [For the effect of delay, see §3:52.]

Also, you can include the delay in your argument for bail. Judges sometimes will punish the state for its abusive conduct by releasing the defendant.

Form:
- **Form 3-3** Petition for a Writ of Habeas Corpus for Delay in Initial Appearance

### §3:52	Effect of Delay on Statements

Sometimes delay occurs because the police are busy extracting a confession from the defendant.

Undue delay in presenting the defendant to a magistrate for an initial appearance and probable cause determination may support suppression of the statements under the following arguments:

- Delay in excess of the constitutionally mandated 48 hours is a Fourth Amendment violation, and the statements may be suppressible as the fruits of that violation. [*See, e.g., People v. Jenkins*, 122 Cal. App. 4th 1160, 1176-77, 19 Cal. Rptr. 3d 386, 398-99 (Cal. App. 1st Dist. 2004) (Fourth Amendment violation required suppression regardless of voluntariness of the statements); *State v. Huddleston*, 924 S.W. 2d 666, 673 (Tenn. 1996) (same). *See generally*, 3 Wayne R. LaFave, *Search and Seizure*, §5.1 & n.315 (2007) (surveying split in decisions in various jurisdictions).]
- Delay may be one factor to consider in determining if the statement was involuntary and suppressible under the Fifth Amendment. [*People v. Willis*, 215 Ill. 2d 517, 831 N. E. 2d 531 (Ill. 2005); *Commonwealth v. Bryant*, 67 A.3d 716, 724 (Pa. 2013) (The test for determining voluntariness, and thus the admissibility of an accused's statement, is the totality of the circumstances test); *People v. Ramos*, 99 N.Y.2d 27, 780 N.E.2d 506, 750 N.Y.S.2d 821 (2002).]
- Suppression may be necessary to remedy and deter violations of a prompt presentment rule or statute. [*Corley v. United States*, 556 U.S. 303 (2009) (since Fed. R. Crim. P. 5(a) requires that an arrestee be arraigned before a judicial officer as quickly as possible, any unreasonable or unnecessary delay beyond six hours in arraigning the defendant is grounds for suppression of a confession obtained beyond that six hour period).]

IV. FORMS

Form 3-1   Notice of Intent to Testify Before the Grand Jury (New York Statute)

People of the State of New York	)	
	)	
v.	)	No. _____
	)	
John Doe,	)	
	)	
Defendant	)	

DEFENDANT'S GRAND JURY NOTICE PURSUANT TO NY CPL 190.50

PLEASE TAKE NOTICE that having been arraigned on a felony complaint, defendant, John Doe, hereby requests an opportunity to testify before the grand jury pursuant to NY CPL 190.50.

Respectfully submitted,

_____
Thomas J. Farrell, Esquire
Counsel for Defendant
436 Seventh Avenue
Brooklyn, NY
(718) 555-1212

Form 3-2   Checklist for Initial Appearance or Arraignment

Consider the following tasks for an initial appearance or arraignment:
- Request on the record or in writing that the prosecution preserve certain evidence that might be destroyed (*e.g.*, 911 tapes, calls to the victim's voicemail, numbers called to the victim's cell phone or to your client's–if the phone was seized, emails, blood samples).
- Serve a discovery request. [For more on discovery, see Chapter 14, Discovery.]
- Give notice of your client's intent to testify in the grand jury, if required by local rules.
- Speak with or obtain the names of any prosecution witnesses in attendance.
- Start to build a relationship with the arresting or prosecuting officer: ask his opinion or your client's cooperativeness or the victim's credibility and his amenability to favorable dispositions, such as pre-trial diversion or dismissal in return for restitution.
- If your client claims that the police beat him, document his injuries: have a witness other than yourself (so the witness later can testify as to when the observations were made) photograph and describe them; inform the court of the need for medical treatment if your client is in custody; get your client medical treatment yourself if he is free on bail.

Form 3-3   Petition for a Writ of Habeas Corpus for Delay in Initial Appearance

Commonwealth	)	
	)	
v.	)	No. _____
	)	
John Doe,	)	
	)	
Defendant	)	

PETITION FOR WRIT OF HABEAS CORPUS
ON BEHALF OF DEFENDANT, JOHN DOE

And now comes Defendant, John Doe, by his counsel Thomas J. Farrell, Esquire, and files this Petition for a Writ of Habeas Corpus:

1. On March 1, 2007, at approximately 9:15 a.m., City of Pittsburgh Police Officers arrested defendant in front of his home at 100 1st Way, Pittsburgh, PA. The Police did not have a warrant for his arrest.
2. The police detained and continue to detain defendant at the Zone 1 police station.
3. Undersigned counsel called Zone 1 on March 1 (twice), March 2 (twice) and March 3 (three times) to ask when Mr. Doe would be brought to Municipal Court for his initial appearance. The Police repeatedly said "in a few hours," but to this date, Mr. Doe remains in custody without having seen a judicial officer.
4. The officers at Zone 1 inform me that Mr. Doe was arrested for simple assault, which is a misdemeanor of the second degree. 18 Pa.C.S.A. §2701.
5. Pa.R.Cr.P. 519(A)(1) requires that a defendant arrested without a warrant be produced for an initial arraignment "without unnecessary delay." The Fourth Amendment to the U.S. Constitution requires that a defendant have a probable cause determination within 48 hours of his arrest. The police have violated and continue to violate both provisions.

WHEREFORE, defendant requests that a writ of habeas corpus issue to order his immediate release from custody.

Respectfully submitted,

_____

Thomas J. Farrell, Esquire
Counsel for Defendant
436 Seventh Avenue
Brooklyn, NY
(718) 555-1212

Chapter 4

BAIL & PRE-TRIAL RELEASE

V.   CONDITIONS OF RELEASE

VI.   SPECIFIC CASES

VII. POST HEARING OR TRIAL PROCEEDINGS

VIII. FORMS

I. GENERAL POINTS

§4:01   Bail Is a Release on Conditions

After arrest and at or immediately after the defendant's initial appearance, the court must set bail.

"Bail" is the defendant's release on conditions. The conditions may include the posting of collateral and the promise to obey court-ordered restrictions on the defendant's liberty.

§4:02   The Importance of Bail and Release

Getting your client out of jail is a principal goal of your representation. Not only does success in bailing out your client gain his confidence, but it facilitates your work and improves your chances of success on the merits.

An incarcerated client loses leverage in plea bargaining, especially if the sentence he is offered approaches the time he has already served.

Furthermore, consulting with an incarcerated client is difficult:
*   You will expend considerable time in traveling to the jail and awaiting your client's delivery to an interview room.
*   The rooms in many jails lack privacy; often, conference tables sit side-by-side enabling other inmates and lawyers to overhear your conversations.
*   Reviewing documents and other physical evidence, especially audio and video tapes, is awkward.
*   Your client will not have free access to the phone.
*   The likelihood of an informant repeating your client's words increases enormously in a jail setting. After all, the other inmates also want out, and many realize that the most effective form of self-help is to turn state's evidence, especially in a serious or high-profile case.

In contrast, a client who is free on bail can assist in trial preparation. He can visit the scene with you and help you find witnesses.

§4:03   Stationhouse Bail

The arresting officer may have discretion under the law to set a minimal bail and release the arrestee from the stationhouse for minor offenses. [See NY Crim. Pro. L. §150.30.]

There is no right to such bail, and the decision to defer the setting of bail from the stationhouse to court is unreviewable. [*Legal Aid Society v. City of Syracuse,* 89 Misc.2d 394, 391 N.Y.S.2d 787 (NY Sup. Ct. 1977).]

[For more on stationhouse bail, see Chapter 3, Arrest and Initial Appearance.]

§4:04   Bail Bond Agencies

Licensed bonding companies may be willing to post a cash bail for your client upon payment of a fee.

The bonding company becomes the suretor on the bail bond. Bonding companies usually are conversant with the system, and once paid, can obtain your client's release rather quickly.

However, bail bond agencies hold several risks. If your client deposits money with the court to satisfy a ten percent or straight cash bail, the money will be refunded on completion of the case. When using a bonding agency, the agency posts that money out of its own funds, but the fee to the company (which can be substantial) is not refundable.

Also, using a bonding agency exposes your client to the risk that a bounty hunter may one day attempt to "arrest" him for non-appearance. The common law authorizes a suretor to arrest the absconding defendant without process and return him to the jurisdiction without any court hearing or protection–what otherwise would be a gunpoint kidnapping and detention. Bounty hunters lack the professional training and accountability of the police, and one still hears of bounty hunters harming or even killing their prey.

§4:05   Detention Risk Assessment Instruments

Many counties have begun to employ Detention Risk Assessment instruments, especially in juvenile cases. The instrument aims to be an objective, evidence-based checklist for the pretrial services or bail agency to use to evaluate the defendant's risk of noncompliance with bail conditions. Evidence-based risk factors include the seriousness of the current offense and of prior offenses; history of warrants; current supervision status; employment status and education; and residential stability. A point total yields recommendations for release, release with conditions, house arrest, or detention. [For a general description of these instruments, see Bechtel, Kristin and Holsinger, Alexander and Lowenkamp, Christopher T and Warren, Madeline, A Meta-Analytic Review of Pretrial Research: Risk Assessment, Bond Type, and Interventions (March 3, 2016)(Available at SSRN: https://ssrn.com/abstract=2741635 or http://dx.doi.org/10.2139/ssrn.2741635); National Center for Juvenile Justice, Charles Puzzanchera, Crystal Knoll, Benjamin Adams, and Melissa Sickmund, *Allegheny County Detention Screening Study* (February 2012) (available at http://www.ncjj.org/pdf/MFC/FINAL_Allegheny%20Detention%20Assessment.pdf).]

Commendable goals lie behind these instruments: uniform release decisions; elimination of racial and ethnic bias; decrease in the use of cash bail; and reduction in pre-trial detention, in part by resort to alternatives to cash bail. Concerns exist, however, that factors such as employment history or residential stability may result in racial and class discrimination. The prevailing trend is that while such instruments should be consulted in reaching a bail or detention decision, they should not be the sole factor a court considers in deciding upon release, bail, and conditions of release. [*E.g.*, Pa. R. Cr. P. 523, Comment ("Nothing in this rule prohibits the use of a pretrial risk assessment tool as one of the means of evaluating the factors to be considered under paragraph (A). However, a risk assessment tool must not be the only means of reaching the bail determination.").]

[§§4:06-4:09 Reserved]

II.   CONSTITUTIONAL LIMITS

§4:10   Excessive Bail Shall Not Be Required

The Eighth Amendment to the United States Constitution states, "Excessive bail shall not be required..."

Most state constitutions contain similar language, though many have been amended to allow for preventive pre-trial detention. [*See, e.g.,* Penn. Const. Art. I, §14 ("All prisoners shall be bailable by sufficient sureties, unless for capital offenses or for offenses for which the maximum sentence is life imprisonment or unless no condition or combination of conditions other than imprisonment will reasonably assure the safety of any person and the community when the proof is evident or presumption great...").]

Courts and legislators are becoming receptive to arguments that cash bail set in an amount a defendant cannot make is unconstitutional and bad policy. [*See, e.g.,* Brief of the United States as *Amicus Curiae in Walker v. City of Calhoun, GA*, No. 16-10521-HH (11th Cir. Court of Appeals) (filed Aug. 18, 2016, available at https://www.justice.gov/crt/file/887436/download); General Order No. 18.8A. In the Circuit Court of Cook County, IL (July 17, 2017) (available at www.cookcountycourt.org)(a judge must ensure that "the defendant has the present ability to pay the amount necessary to secure his or her release on bail." Bail must be set in an amount that a defendant can afford to pay at the time of the bail hearing.)]

State law may be more helpful than arguments under the Eighth Amendment. Statutes and rules may command the court to consider a number of factors in addition to the severity of the charge and to make an individualized decision. [*See New Mexico v. Brown*, 2014 NMSC 38 (New Mexico S. Ct. Nov. 6, 2014)(striking down reliance on bail schedules tied solely to the severity of the crime as contrary to New Mexico's bail rules).]

§4:11   Preventive Detention

Notwithstanding the apparently clear language of the Eighth Amendment, the Supreme Court has upheld preventive detention statutes under which defendants can be denied bail for serious offenses if the court finds that no combination of conditions will assure the defendant's appearance or the community's safety. [*United States v. Salerno*, 481 U.S. 739 (1987).]

§4:12   Bail Can Be Beyond Defendant's Means

Even in situations in which preventive detention and the denial of bail are not justified, a bail is not considered excessive merely because it is in an amount that the defendant cannot post. What the Eighth Amendment dictates is that bail cannot be set at a figure higher than an amount reasonably calculated either to:
*   Assure the presence of the defendant in court. [*Stack v. Boyle*, 342 U.S. 1 (1951).

- Achieve the other purposes of the bail statute, such as protection of the victim. [See *Galen v. County of Los Angeles*, 477 F.3d 652, 660 (9th Cir. 2007).]

Thus, most courts have held that the Constitution is not offended if that amount lies beyond the defendant's means. However, setting a bail beyond the defendant's ability to post where the amount set is not reasonably calculated to assure the defendant's appearance does violate the Eighth Amendment's Excessiveness clause. [*Wagenmann v. Adams*, 829 F.2d 196, 213-14 (1st Cir. 1987) (upholding civil rights damages verdict against police for setting excessive bail).]

Recently, however, the New Mexico Supreme Court ruled that unless the trial court decides that bail must be denied entirely because the defendant is a risk of flight or violence, the court must set bail in an amount the defendant can make. [*New Mexico v. Brown*, 2014 NMSC 38 (New Mexico S.Ct. Nov. 6, 2014).] There seems to be renewed receptivity to the argument that unless the defendant is a risk of danger or flight, bail should be set in an amount that he can make. [*See* §4:10, *supra.*]

On the other hand, bail set at an amount higher than necessary to assure the defendant's appearance might be unconstitutionally excessive even if the defendant can make it. [*Galen*, 477 F.3d at 661-62; *Wagenmann*, 829 F.2d at 213.]

§4:13   Due Process Arguments

A constitutional argument that may have more success in limited circumstances is that an unduly lengthy pre-trial detention violates Due Process and requires release of the defendant. [*United States v. Ojeda-Rios*, 846 F.2d 167 (2d Cir. 1988) (release ordered where defendant had been jailed for 32 months and trial still months away).]

When a detained defendant faces such delay, the court should expedite his trial. [*United States v. Jackson*, 823 F.2d 4, 8 (2d Cir. 1987).]

If a co-defendant's motion practice or continuance requests cause the delay, you might use this to justify a severance of your client.

[§§4:14-4:19 Reserved]

III.   TYPES OF BAIL

§4:20   Unsecured Bonds

A defendant may be released either:
- "On his own recognizance" (an "OR" bond)
- On a bond with a face amount but requiring no cash deposit and no collateral except for the defendant's own signature. If the defendant fails to appear or otherwise violates his bail conditions, he is liable to the court for the amount of the bond.

Even with an OR bond, a defendant faces serious consequences if he fails to appear. Not only may the court refuse to re-release him, but failure to appear is a separate crime with its own penalties. [*See, e.g.,* 18 U.S.C. §3146 (failure to appear punishable by up to ten years imprisonment).]

Further, even if the defendant is not prosecuted separately for the failure to appear, the court is sure to add that factor into the sentence for the underlying offense. [*See, e.g.,* USSG §3C1.1, comment, n.4(e) (failure to appear merits a two-point, or twenty-five percent, increase under the federal sentencing guidelines).]

§4:21   Cash Bonds

Courts may require the deposit of cash as collateral to secure the defendant's release.

The court will announce whether the bail is "straight" (requiring deposit of the whole amount) or whether a deposit of some percentage (typically ten percent) will suffice.

Even on a ten percent bond, if the defendant fails to appear, he is liable for the full amount of the bond.

Statutes and local rules and practices define what will be accepted as cash other than United States currency. Typically, checks are unsatisfactory. However, most states do permit the deposit of United States Treasury bonds or state government bonds. [*See, e.g.,* Cal. Penal Code §1298 (court may accept United States or California government bonds in addition to cash); Pa. R. Crim. P. (D)(2) (Pennsylvania accepts U.S. or Pennsylvania bonds, or bonds of any political subdivision of Pennsylvania).]

A bond has the advantage that it will continue to accrue interest during the defendant's release. Courts do not pay interest on cash deposited to secure release.

If the defendant's sentence includes a fine or restitution, and the cash posted was the defendant's rather than a third party's, the court may order that the cash bond be applied to the fine or restitution. [28 U.S.C. §2044.]

§4:22   Surety Bonds

The Court may demand that a third-party sign the bond as surety and perhaps post collateral to secure the defendant's release.

The suretor may be a friend or relative, or it may be a bonding company.

There may be statutory qualifications for suretors. [*See, e.g.,* Cal. Penal Code §1279 (suretor must be a resident of the state and must have a net worth equal to the amount of the undertaking).]

§4:23   Real Property Bonds

A common form of collateral is real estate, either the defendant's or a friend or relative's home.

This is an attractive form of collateral for several reasons:

- It permits the defendant and his family to reserve their cash to pay living expenses and counsel.
- The suretor does not lose the interest that could have been earned on cash and does not expend the interest cost of using the house to obtain a mortgage or home equity loan to fund the bail.
- Posting a home strengthens the argument for release because if the defendant fails to appear, either he or a loved one will lose their home. [See *United States v. Carbone*, 793 F.2d 559 (3d Cir. 1986) (the willingness of friends and family to post property rebutted the presumption that the defendant posed a danger to the community).] The suretor thereby demonstrates great confidence in the defendant's reliability, and you can argue that the defendant thus has a strong incentive to appear.

To post property, you must either obtain an appraisal to prove to the court the amount of equity in the property or use the county's assessed value for real estate tax purposes. [See Cal Penal Code §1298 (requiring that the equity in the real property be twice the amount of the bond ordered); 725 Illinois C.S.A. 110-8(2) (Illinois; same); Pa. R. Crim. P. 528 (D)(3) (real property's value net of encumbrances must equal at least the full amount of the monetary condition of release); U.S. District Court for the W.D.Pa, L.Cr. R. 46.1.B (a defendant who claims a value higher than the assessed value must present a current appraisal from a licensed real estate appraiser).]

In addition, you may be required to produce certified copies of the deed and any mortgages or liens. [W.D.Pa. L.Cr.R. 46.1.B.] Unfortunately, obtaining certified copies of these documents may delay your client's release. If the court is willing to accept it, as an alternative, you can present the settlement papers for the purchase of the house and any statement from the lender that shows the amount of principal remaining on the loan to prove how much has been paid on the principal and the equity in the property.

The court may demand that you file a lien against the property to prevent its sale during the pendency of the case. If this requirement is imposed, try to have your client released first, with a promise that you will have a copy of the lien filing for the court within the next day or promptly thereafter.

The bond may specify that should the defendant violate the bond's conditions, the property will be forfeited. If possible, restrict the forfeiture condition to non-appearance rather than violation of any of the other many conditions often imposed on pre-trial release. If the bond is unclear, have the magistrate state on the record which conditions would warrant forfeiture.

For sample appearance bonds, see www.uscourts.gov/forms/uscforms.cfm (Forms AO 098 and 098A).

§4:24   Using Your Money to Post Bail for Your Client

Don't. It creates a conflict of interest between you and your client. [See Model Rules of Professional Conduct 1.8(e), 1.7; John Wesley Hall, PROFESSIONAL RESPONSIBILITY IN CRIMINAL DEFENSE PRACTICE §13:23 (2013).] Ethical rulings and statutes and rules in some states explicitly forbid it. [Wisc. Stat. §757.34; Mich. C.L. 600.2665; Pa. R. Crim. P. 531(B); N.C. Bar Op'n 173 (1994) (prohibiting lawyers from posting bail for clients); Oregon Bar Op'n 04-431 (discouraging lawyers from posting bail for clients).]

[§§4:25-4:29 Reserved]

IV. PREPARING FOR THE HEARING

A. Determining the Amount

§4:30   Relevant Factors

Courts consider the following factors when setting bail:
- The seriousness of the offense and the likely penalties.
- The strength of the case against the defendant.
- The defendant's criminal history and his history of honoring release and probation or parole conditions.
- The defendant's community ties, including family ties and other community roots.
- The defendant's employment history.
- The defendant's financial assets.
- The defendant's use of false identities.

[*See, e.g.,* 18 U.S.C. 3142(g); Pa. R. Crim. P. 523(A).]
The overarching questions in a judge's mind are whether the defendant can be trusted to:
- Return to court, even when faced with the near certainty of conviction and incarceration.
- Refrain from further criminal activity.
- Leave the witnesses alone.

Courts usually emphasize the first factor, the seriousness of the offense. They do this because the more heinous the crime, the more likely that the penalty will be severe and the incentive to flee great, and the more likely that the defendant might pose a danger to the community by repeating conduct of the same sort or by tampering with witnesses.

PRACTICE TIP:
> The attorney's role is to do one or more of the following:
> - Make the crime appear less serious.
> - Make the likelihood of conviction seem less certain.
> - Shift the court's focus to other factors by providing the court with verifiable information about the defendant's reliability and community ties.

§4:31   Bail Agency Evaluations

In many jurisdictions, an independent agency or a division of the courts will conduct an investigation and make a recommendation as to the defendant's bail-worthiness.

While these agencies consider the seriousness of the offense, they do not weigh it as heavily as the police, the prosecutor or perhaps the magistrate might.

Your client and his family should cooperate fully with these agencies because the agency's recommendation may either doom or redeem a bail application. If the agency confirms that your client, his friends, family and employers are reputable and supportive, it is likely to recommend a bail that the defendant can make. On the other hand, if no one cooperates, or if your client and his cohorts mislead the bail agency, release on bail might be nearly impossible.

Statutes may prohibit the prosecution from using the bail interview to prove its direct case. [*See, e.g.,* 18 U.S.C. §3153(c)(3); Pa. R. Crim. 530(C).] However, your client's statements might be usable to impeach him if he testifies otherwise at trial. [*See* Pa. R. Crim. P. 530(C); *People v. Brown,* 109 Misc.2d 366, 438 N.Y.S.2d 955 (N.Y. Co. Sup. Ct. 1981).]

Furthermore, lying to the bail agency might constitute a separate crime, or the court might consider it at sentencing to increase your client's sentence. Courts take special umbrage at lies to their own agencies. [See *United States v. Restrepo,* 53 F.3d 396 (1st Cir. 1995) (providing false name to pre-trial services agency constitutes obstruction of justice and warrants a lengthier sentence); *United States v. Harrison,* 42 F.3d 427, 430-31 (7th Cir. 1994) (defendant's false statement to magistrate that he was no longer on parole justified increased sentence for obstruction of justice even though it did not result in defendant's release).]

§4:32   The Attorney's Role With the Bail Agency

You usually will not have an opportunity to be present while the bail agency conducts its interviews, even of your client. However, you should develop a helpful attitude toward the bail agency.

Gather as much information as you can about your client's community ties and provide it to the bail agency. This can consist of:

- Corroborating documents (*e.g.,* pay stubs, deeds, and real estate appraisals).
- Information necessary for the agency to do its own investigation (*e.g.,* the names, phone numbers, addresses and best times to call family, friends and employers).

Background information itself may be incriminating, depending upon the nature of the crime. For example, your client may have been reporting fictitious employment to conceal the illegal source of his income.

Interview your client as thoroughly as you can about the sorts of questions the bail agency will cover: age, nationality, education, employment, residence, family ties and criminal history. Instruct your client to answer honestly. If you detect an area where an honest answer will hurt your client (*e.g.,* no one has discovered yet that your client has used a false name to re-enter the country after a previous deportation), you may have to choose to forego the interview.

Criminal history may pose especially sensitive concerns:

- First, make sure that your client understands what is being asked. Many individuals believe that they were not convicted if their arrest did not result in jail time or if they were released with a sentence of time served. Ask specifically: Did you have to pay a fine or restitution? Did the judge say he was giving you time served?
- Second, consider advising your client that he not be interviewed or that he refuse to answer criminal history questions under circumstances where the government might not discover the convictions on its own (i.e., where your client has out of state or foreign convictions, especially if they were under a different name).

[§§4:33-4:39 Reserved]

B. Bail and Source Hearings

§4:40   Preparation for the Bail Hearing

Bail hearings take place early in the criminal process, when both the prosecutor and judge have little in the way of accurate information about your client's employment, personal history and family and community ties.

The prosecutor, judge and even the bail agency usually base their recommendations and decisions on the seriousness of the current charge, prior criminal record, past failures to appear, parole/probation status, and whether there are pending charges; after all, the system has the most information about these facts.

Misunderstandings are the rule, and good lawyering can bear excellent results. Bail hearings are won not by constitutional arguments or statutory parsing, but by the presentation of accurate and corroborated facts.

Investigate your client's criminal record thoroughly. For example:

- What was that dismissed rape charge really about? It may have been a false accusation made for leverage in a custody proceeding.
- Was your client previously released on bail and did he make all his court appearances?
- If he is on probation or parole, contact the supervising officer and elicit his opinion about your client's reliability.

Verify everything your client tells you. However, you do not need to go to primary sources. For example, often you will not want to inform your client's employer of his arrest. Speak instead to a reliable relative who can confirm what your client says.

Use a form questionnaire to be sure that you cover all the topics.

Form:
- **Form 4-1** Bail Questionnaire

§4:41   The Presentation at the Hearing

Often, bail hearings consist largely of proffers from counsel, not the presentation of witness testimony.

Explain your client's employment history: job position, responsibilities, duration of the employment, his family's need for the income and health benefits and the likelihood that he will lose the job if imprisoned for any length of time.

Present family ties. Portray them not as a plea for sympathy but as a web of support and responsibilities that ensure your client's return to court. State your client's monthly rent or mortgage and explain that should he be incarcerated or fail to return to court, his family's homelessness is a certain consequence. If siblings and parents live nearby and see your client often, explain that. If they have the means and the inclination, explain that they are willing to stake their financial futures on your client's release by posting cash bail or signing a property bond.

Bailing your client can be a challenge, especially when the charges are serious. You may need to describe defenses and mitigating factors about the offense. Work from evidence the prosecution has disclosed or issues that appear on the face of any charging documents. For example, you may want to emphasize that the reports may show a strong suppression issue, or that the alleged victim is a domestic partner who has made allegations in the past that he or she did not pursue. You generally should not present defenses that you have not yet had time to develop fully, such as an alibi defense. They may fall apart, either at the bail hearing or later, after the prosecution, once informed, has had opportunity to investigate and refute them.

§4:42   Dealing With a Past Failure

A bail hearing is particularly challenging if your client has failed to appear, either on the present charge or a previous one.

If your client eventually showed of his own volition, he has demonstrated some reliability and willingness to meet his obligations. However, if only a new arrest brought him to court, your task will be difficult.

Explore whether there is some plausible explanation for the nonappearance:
- Did your client move and fail to receive a court notice?
- Did counsel fail to inform him of the court date?

Even with an explanation, a judge will be curious as to why your client did not make an effort to contact the court or counsel and resolve the charges. Explain that your client had and met other pressing obligations during the period of his absence. For example, he worked and supported his family.

You want to show that the defendant did not shirk all his responsibilities to society. Try to present the information as explanations rather than as excuses.

§4:43   Having the Defendant Testify

The defendant who testifies at a bail hearing does so at his peril.

Generally, a defendant's testimony at a bail hearing can be used against him without violating either his Eighth Amendment right to bail or his Fifth Amendment privilege against self-incrimination. [E.g., *Cowards v. State*, 266 Ga. 191, 193, 465 S.E.2d 677, 679 (1996); *People v. Atencia*, 113 Ill. App.3d 247, 252-53, 446 N.E.2d 1243, 1246-47 (Ill. App. 1983); *United States v. Dohm*, 618 F.2d 1169, 1173 (5th Cir. 1980); *United States v. Miller*, 589 F.2d 1117, 1135 (1st Cir. 1978).]

Some courts nonetheless have used their supervisory power to create a limited form of use immunity for a defendant's bail hearing testimony. [See *United States v. Perry*, 788 F.2d 100, 115-16 (3d Cir. 1986) (granting use immunity for defendant's testimony at bail hearing based upon analogy to *Simmons v. United States*, 390 U.S. 377, 393-94 (1968) (defendant's testimony in support of a fourth amendment suppression claim may not be used at trial)); *Dohm*, 618 F.2d at 1176-77 (Tate, J., concurring in part and dissenting in part) (recommending such use of supervisory power).]

You also might request that the court preclude cross-examination of your client's statement, but such testimony might carry little weight. [See *United States v. Shakur*, 817 F.2d 189, 200 (2d Cir. 1987) (while noting that district court did not err in prohibiting cross-examination of defendant at bail hearing in order to protect his privilege against self-incrimination, appellate court overturned findings based on defendant's credibility, reasoning that such findings are of limited value absent cross-examination).]

Consider carefully whether your client's testimony adds any fact that cannot be elicited from another witness. Merely to express his earnestness in promising to appear is not worth the risk of testifying.

If your client must testify, object frequently to the prosecutor's cross-examination to avoid a fishing expedition for impeaching material.

§4:44   "Source" Hearings

When cash bail is posted, courts may hold a hearing into the source of the funds, upon a showing of reasonable cause to believe that the money constitutes the fruits of unlawful conduct. [*State v. Donahoe ex rel. County of Maricopa*, 220 Ariz. 126, 203 P.3d 1186 (Ariz. App. Div. 2009); *Matter of Johnson v. Crane*, 171 A.D.2d 537, 568 N.Y.S.2d 22 (1st Dept. 1991) (relying on NY CPL 520.30[1]); *United States v. Nebbia*, 357 F.2d 303 (2d Cir. 1966); 18 U.S.C. §3142(g)(4).]

The prosecution may call and examine witnesses at this hearing.

Source hearings are most likely in drug-trafficking cases, where your client does not appear to have legitimate employment. You must prepare for such an eventuality by questioning those who post the bail on the source of the money and assuring yourself that they can show a trail from a legitimate source into a bank account and then to the court.

[§§4:45-4:49 Reserved]

V.   CONDITIONS OF RELEASE

§4:50   General Points

You need to be conversant with possible conditions of release both to prepare your client for what to expect during release, and to devise creative bail packages when the court seems reluctant to release your client or when money and suretors are scarce.

A combination of restrictive conditions may satisfy a judge's concern about your client's possible flight or risk to the community.

§4:51   Travel Restrictions

Restriction to the state or federal judicial district is routine.

Check with your client whether he needs to travel regularly for business. For travel needs that arise, such as family events or business trips, seek consent and file a motion to travel.

Form:
*   **Form 4-2** Motion to Modify Bail Conditions to Permit Travel

§4:52   Waiver of Extradition

A defendant may be required to waive in advance the right to an extradition hearing in the event of a violation of probation or parole. [*State v. Arundell*, 278 NJ Super. 202, 207, 650 A.2d 845, 848 (NJ Super. 1994). *See, e.g.,* 42 Pa.C.S.A. §9146.1 (recognizing validity of waivers of interstate extradition which are pre-signed as a condition of bail).]

§4:53   Curfew and Notification of Contact Changes

Release conditions may include:
*   A curfew.
*   A requirement that the defendant immediately notify the court of any change in address or phone number.

§4:54   Drug and Alcohol Use

Release conditions may include prohibitions against drug and alcohol use. [*See, e.g.,* D.C. Stat. 23-1321 (c)(1) (B)(ix)("refrain from excessive use of alcohol, or any use of a narcotic drug or other controlled substance without a prescription by a licensed medical practitioner..."); 15 Maine Rev. Stat. Ann. §1026(3)(A)(9).]

Some courts have technology to enforce this condition through a device that straps onto your client's ankle and takes periodic readings through the skin of blood alcohol levels, a "SCRAM" (Secure Continuous Remote Alcohol Monitor).

Be sure either to specify which prescription drugs your client takes or to obtain the court's consent that he may take prescribed drugs. Otherwise, your client innocently may test positive for controlled substances.

Do not make a knee-jerk objection to a condition prohibiting drug or alcohol use. If the magistrate suggests it and your client rejects it, the magistrate likely will detain your client or set an unattainable bail or even more onerous conditions, such as house arrest. [*See In re York*, 9 Cal.4th 1133, 40 Cal. Rptr.2d 308, 892 P.2d 804, 812 n.9 (1995) ("if we interpreted section 1318, subdivision (a)(2), to *preclude* a court or magistrate from conditioning OR release upon a defendant's promise to fulfill requirements unrelated to ensuring his or her appearance at future court proceedings, or upon the waiver of a constitutional right, a court or magistrate in many instances would be *less* likely to grant the request for OR release, concluding that the defendant was an inappropriate candidate for release prior to judgment in the absence of specified, reasonable conditions").]

Furthermore, if your client has an evident drug problem that makes the magistrate reluctant to grant bail, you may need to suggest drug-testing, and perhaps even submission to searches, to obtain your client's release.

§4:55   Consent to Searches

Release conditions may include consent to random, warrantless searches of the defendant's home and person.

Search conditions pose more risk that drug-testing. Drug-testing will reveal only if your client is using drugs, not any other criminal activity. A search of his/her house may uncover countless other contraband, such as guns or pornography, or may expose other criminal activity.

Also, a search will be disruptive to your client's family and certainly will capture neighbors' notice.

§4:56   Psychiatric Evaluation or Treatment

Some jurisdictions require that before a defendant charged with certain types of offenses may be released, he must undergo a psychiatric evaluation to ensure that he is not a danger to the community. [E.g., PA Allegheny Cty. Crim. LR 300.29 (homicide, arson, kidnapping, crimes against children and sex offenses).]

If your client is charged with such an offense, his release will be delayed until the interview is completed. There is nothing you can do in such a case except warn and prepare your client for the delay.

Furthermore, release conditions may include psychiatric treatment, including drug and alcohol dependency treatment. [*See, e.g.,* D.C. Stat. 23-1321(c)(1)(B)(x).]

§4:57   Prohibitions Against Certain Contacts

Release conditions may include prohibitions against contact with witnesses or the alleged victim.

No-contact provisions require case-by-case consideration. Generally, you share the court's interest that your client not contact witnesses. Contact carries the risk that your client will say something that may be construed as witness tampering or as an admission.

However, sometimes it is impractical to require the defendant to have no contact with the purported victim, or at least witnesses. They may be your client's employees, co-workers, or family.

A prohibition against contact with certain people is generally understood to permit defense counsel and investigators working for the defense to contact the victim and witnesses. However, be sure to clarify this on the record. Having the judge state in open court that such contact is permissible may open the door to later interviews. You can assure witnesses that in trying to interview them, you are just doing your job, and that the judge granted permission for you to speak to them. A judicial bar against defense team contact would violate the defendant's Sixth Amendment right to the effective assistance of counsel. [*Martell v. County Court of County of Summit*, 854 P.2d 1327 (Colo. App. 1992).]

§4:58   Third Party Custodians

Release conditions may include a requirement that the defendant must reside with a third party custodian, and the custodian assumes the obligation to monitor the defendant's compliance with any bail conditions and to inform the court of any violations. [*See, e.g.,* 15 Maine Rev. Stat. Ann. §1026(3)(A)(1).]

§4:59   Electronic Monitoring

Release conditions may include electronic monitoring.

There are two principal kinds of electronic monitoring:
- For house arrest, a transmitting device restricts the defendant to a radius from the device.
- For travel restrictions, some courts have begun to use global positioning ("GPS") devices to monitor a defendant's location. These permit the defendant to leave the home, but monitor his obedience to travel restrictions.

If your client has the means, the court will make him pay for the monitoring.

[§§4:60-4:69 Reserved]

VI.   SPECIFIC CASES

§4:70   Violent Crimes

Faced with a charge entailing serious violence, a judge will want to protect the community and victims. The easiest way is to detain your client, either through a preventive detention statute allowing detention for risk to the community, or by setting a high bail your client cannot make.

Suggest conditions that will address the judge's concerns:
- Home detention with a monitoring device.
- A curfew.

•   A prohibition against contacting witnesses and victims.

Many judges think, without voicing the thought, that detention does little harm because your client will serve substantial time. Rebutting this assumption may require you, even at this early stage, to challenge the prosecution's case on guilt. Do not lay out an affirmative defense at this early juncture because doing so gives the prosecution an opportunity to elicit and note the details and then work to investigate and rebut the defense later. Rather, attack weaknesses apparent on the face of the charging documents, such as a reliance on stranger identifications or informants who stand to gain from their testimony.

§4:71   Drug Offenses

Agreement to a high monetary bail may backfire in a drug trafficking case, especially if your client lacks a high-paying legitimate job. Your client's wealth almost proves the charge, and the prosecutor may seek a source hearing. [See §4:44.]

The better approach is to post real property or to bring forward a number of suretors who are willing to stake their own financial well-being on your client (so long as they are not themselves suspected coconspirators). Suggest non-monetary conditions of release if necessary:

•   Frequent in-person reporting to the pre-trial services agency.
•   GPS monitoring.
•   Home confinement.

§4:72   Fraud Offenses

Defendants charged with white collar crimes and other fraud offenses (*e.g.,* bad checks) usually are released without much struggle, particularly if they have legitimate jobs and roots in the community.

Aim low. That is, do not propose much in the way of collateral or conditions until you hear the prosecution's proposal, because often it will be OR or an unsecured bond. Victim and witness safety are rarely concerns.

An important goal is avoiding conditions that might impair your client's ability to continue his business or livelihood. You would rather have a high monetary bail than a home detention restriction. Check with your client whether he needs to travel outside the jurisdiction and see if the judge will agree to relax the geographical restrictions. Even if he will not, the judge's statement that you can file a motion when travel is necessary suggests to the prosecutor and the next judge to handle the case that such a motion should be granted.

Where restitution is possible, you also should argue that your client should be free to work for the victims' eventual recovery.

§4:73   Minor Offenses

Most defendants charged with misdemeanors will obtain release on an OR bond or a modest cash bail.

However, a vexing problem arises when the client has a history of nonappearance or transience. The judge likely will impose a bail your client cannot make, which creates tremendous incentive for your client to plead guilty at the earliest time possible and reduce his jail time. Sometimes that is the right choice, such as when your client's guilt is obvious and the prosecutor or judge offers to reduce the charges or penalty.

If the plea offer's terms are too harsh or issues exists as to your client's guilt, explore whether a relative might act as third-party custodian or whether social services are available and can be combined with pre-trial reporting requirements to create an acceptable bail package. This may entail finding your client a place to live or gaining his admission into an inpatient drug treatment program and making continued residence at that address or in the program conditions of release. Some pre-trial services or bail agency officers are helpful in this regard; others do not want the bother; and in many jurisdictions, the resources just do not exist.

You might also try making a strong argument as to your client's innocence or the success of a particular defense at an initial appearance or bail hearing. In this kind of case, laying out a defense before you have all the facts carries less risk than in a more serious case. The prosecution and police are unlikely to invest the time and resources to investigate. Everyone expects such a case to be resolved sooner or later by a plea or dismissal, so neither the judge nor the prosecutor will attend to representations made at early appearances in order to use them against the defense later. Your presentation might convince the judge that your (perhaps innocent) client's continued incarceration is unjust, and the judge might find a way to dismiss the charge, or might pressure the prosecutor to offer a lenient plea, or might release your client. Remember, your argument, at least aloud, is not that since the charge will not stick, who cares if your client fails to appear; rather, your client knows he will be cleared; therefore, he has strong incentive to return to court.

§4:74 Immigration Detainers

The local jurisdiction's compliance with an immigration detainer is discretionary, not mandatory. Many jurisdictions, especially larger cities, have refused to honor these detainers. Further, the jail can hold someone otherwise entitled to release for only 48 hours on an immigration detainer. [*See generally Orellana v. Nobles County*, 230 F.Supp.3d 934 (D.Minn. 2017) (County subject to civil rights liability under Fourth Amendment for policy of continuing to detain individuals beyond when they are eligible for release solely because of ICE detainers); ICE Policy Number 10074.2 (Eff. April 2, 2017)(available at www.ice.gov)]

Detainers are often issued in error, such as against first-generation citizens. Defense attorneys can call ICE to request that detainers be lifted. ICE says that it will pay special attention to cases where people allege that they are lawful permanent residents or US citizens. [ICE Directive 16001.2, available at www.ice.gov/detainer-policy]. A hotline exists for detained citizens: (855) 448-6903. [*See generally* www.immdefense.org; https://www.americanimmigrationcouncil.org/research/immigration-detainers-overview (last visited Aug. 18, 2017)]

[§§4:75-4:79 Reserved]

VII. POST HEARING OR TRIAL PROCEEDINGS

§4:80 Appealing the Bail Decision

The procedure for appealing a bail determination and the likelihood of success vary by jurisdiction and with local practice.

Usually bail was set by a magistrate or justice of the peace in a court of limited jurisdiction. In that situation, the first appeal is to the court of general jurisdiction.

This initial appeal of a bail decision does not require the procedural formalities of a post-conviction appeal. It may be accomplished by calling the duty judge's clerk and scheduling a bail application or hearing as soon as possible. Some jurisdictions may require the filing of a petition for a writ of habeas corpus with the court of general jurisdiction.

The scope of review is de novo. However, as a practical matter the reviewing court may defer to the original judge, depending on the circumstances and the judge's reputation. In many jurisdictions, bail is set with inadequate information or even without counsel being present and having an opportunity to be heard. The reviewing judge may know these conditions well, but if the judge is not aware of them, point them out.

If you fail in the court of general jurisdiction you may consider an appeal to the intermediate appellate court. However, such appeals rarely succeed. The appeals court will defer considerably to the lower courts' discretion. Bail appeals rarely present legal issues that merit more searching review.

§4:81 Bail Forfeiture and Remission

Violation of any condition of release may result in the revocation of release and the forfeiture of the bail posted. [*Commonwealth v. Mayfield*, 2003 PA Super 213, 827 A.2d 462 (Pa. Super. 2003) (re-arrest on other charges); *United States v. Gigante*, 85 F.3d 83, 85 (2d Cir.1996) ("[A] bail bond and its collateral may be forfeited not only for the defendant's failure to appear, but also for other violations of bond conditions, including the defendant's commission of a crime"); *United States v. Terrell*, 983 F.2d 653, 654 (5th Cir.1993) (holding that forfeiture was appropriate when defendant violated court condition of "travel restriction and his promise not to possess marijuana and drug paraphernalia"). See generally *State v. Korecky*, 169 N.J. 364, 373-75, 777 A.2d 927, 933-34 (N.J. 2001) (surveying cases and finding that majority rule is to permit forfeiture for violation of conditions other than nonappearance). *But see State v. Cardinal*, 147 Vt. 461, 520 A.2d 984, 987 (Vt. 1986) (bail forfeiture not permitted except for nonappearance; court should address violation of other conditions by imposing more stringent release conditions or revoking bail).]

After forfeiture, either the defendant or the suretor may petition the court for remission of the forfeiture. [*United States v. Ciotti*, 579 F.Supp. 276 (W.D.Pa. 1984).]

Whether to permit remission lies in the court's discretion, applying an interests-of-justice standard. Many courts guide their discretion by a three-part test:

- The willfulness of the defendant's breach of the bond.
- The cost, inconvenience and prejudice suffered by the government.
- Any explanation or mitigating factors.

[*Ciotti*, 579 F.Supp. at 278. See also *Mayfield*, 827 A.2d at 467-68 (applying same factors).]

PRACTICE TIP:

In a petition for remission, emphasize the lack of prejudice to the government. Since this factor does not focus on the defendant, it relieves him from offering a detailed explanation, which may be proven untrue and reflect badly on his character. Finding and re-arresting a defendant often does not entail substantial investigation and cost. Most defendants are found at home or upon re-arrest for another offense–so the prejudice usually will be minimal. [See *Mayfield*, 827 A.2d at 468 (ordering remission because the prosecution failed to show prejudice).]

§4:82   Readmission to Bail

Do not abandon all hope if your client violates his bail.

A violation of conditions does not prohibit admission to bail; it merely informs the court that greater restrictions are necessary.

You still may obtain your client's release, but you must develop a realistic plan.

- First, if you can, offer a plausible explanation for the violation of the release conditions. Confessing confusion about court dates or bail restrictions (either on your part or your client's) will elicit a tongue-lashing. However, it may be the price to pay for readmission to bail.
- Second, suggest more restrictive conditions that will meet the court's concerns about your client's specific violation of his bail conditions. These conditions might be electronic monitoring under home confinement, a curfew, a third-party custodian, or regular reporting to a pre-trial services officer.

§4:83   Credit for Time Spent in Pre-Trial or Pre-Sentence Custody

Most states and the federal government have statutes crediting time served in pre-trial custody towards a defendant's sentence, even though the Constitution may not require such credit, [*Martin v. Pennsylvania Bd. of Probation and Parole*, 576 Pa. 588, 840 A.2d 299, 303 (Pa. 2003)].

However, if incarceration results from a defendant's financial inability to post bond, the Fourteenth Amendment Equal Protection clause requires that credit be given for all custody that results from indigency. [*State v. Sorenson*, 2000 SD 127, 617 N.W.2d 146, 149 (S.D. 2000). See also *Faye v. Gray*, 541 F.2d 665, 667 (7th Cir. 1976) (defendant must be given credit for pre-sentence custody if he could not make bail and the sum of the time spent in pre-sentence custody and the court's sentence would exceed the statutory maximum).]

Most credit statutes have been interpreted so as not to award credit for pre-trial or presentence time spent in a halfway house, under house arrest or on electronic monitoring. [See Wade R. Habeeb, Right to Credit for Time Spent in Custody Prior to Trial or Sentence, 77 A.L.R.3d 182, §16. *See, e.g., Commonwealth v. Kyle*, 582 Pa. 624, 874 A.2d 12 (2005) (forbidding credit spent on bail under home electronic monitoring).]

Always try for bail, even under house arrest, before conviction. Pre-trial detention facilities are always miserable; incarceration is never certain before conviction; and your client will be better able to assist in his defense and wind down his business and personal affairs if released, even under home confinement. The calculation changes considerably with conviction, especially if incarceration seems certain. In that circumstance, you may advise your client to forego a request for house arrest as a condition of bail pending appeal.

§4:84   Credit in Two-Jurisdiction Situations

If your client has a detainer or pending charges in another jurisdiction, you face special challenges in guaranteeing that his time in custody counts toward his sentence. Pre-trial time in custody counts only toward the sentence imposed by the jurisdiction responsible for the pre-trial custody. [*See, e.g.,* 18 U.S.C. §3585(b).]

Furthermore, if your client was in another jurisdiction's custody and has been brought to your jurisdiction for trial and sentencing, then as soon as those proceedings are completed he will be returned to the first jurisdiction. In this situation, any sentence imposed in your jurisdiction will not start to run until the first jurisdiction finishes its proceedings and sentence because the second jurisdiction most likely "borrowed" the defendant under a writ of habeas corpus ad prosequendum rather than taking custody of him. [See *Ruggiano v. Reish*, 307 F.3d 121, 125 n.1 (3d Cir. 2002) (explaining interplay between the writ and sentence credit for time in custody).]

[For more, see Chapter 22, Sentencing.]

Your task, then, is to determine where your client would prefer to apply the credit and serve his time and coordinate the bail determinations in the respective jurisdiction so that he is released to the custody of the jurisdiction he prefers.

The client will usually prefer to apply any credit to the jurisdiction where the likely sentence is lengthier because (1) he will need the credit for the lengthier sentence, and (2) the sentencing judge in the jurisdiction of the less serious charges is likely to run that sentence concurrent to the lengthier sentence.

If the sentences are likely to be similar, the choice may ride on where your client prefers to serve his time. Usually, federal institutions are less threatening. However, do not assume that your client wants to go to a "Club Fed." There are fewer Federal institutions, so placement in one may make family visits more difficult. Also, your client may have friends and associates in local and state institutions that would make his transition to incarceration less onerous. Raise all of these factors and let your client choose.

§4:85   Bail Pending Sentencing and Appeal

While there is no constitutional right to bail after conviction, statutes often provide for it. Furthermore, courts have held that once a state makes provision for such bail, the Eighth and Fourteenth Amendments require that it not be denied arbitrarily or unreasonably. [*Marks v. Zelinski*, 604 F.Supp. 1211, 1213 (D.N.J. 1985); *see also Finetti v. Harris*, 609 F.2d 594, 599 (2d Cir. 1979); *United States ex rep. Rainwater v. Morris*, 411 F. Supp. 1252 (N.D. Ill. 1967) (due process violated by denial of bail to defendant pending appeal where he had no prior criminal record, he made all court appearances, and his appeal had merit).]

With conviction, your client sheds the presumption of innocence, and incarceration becomes likely. These factors militate in favor of detention. On the other hand, by the time of conviction your client has established a track record of showing up and meeting his other release obligations. This track record may be especially compelling if your client knowingly pleaded guilty under a plea agreement that guaranteed some period of imprisonment.

If the case is appealed, even if the appeal seems pointless to you, you should generally seek your client's release. Reversals on appeal are relatively rare, but the unexpected does happen.

The following strategies are possible approaches in arguing for your client's continued release:

- Obtain the prosecutor's agreement. This may be indispensable where a statute makes bail revocation mandatory upon conviction of certain offenses. [E.g. 18 U.S.C. §3143(a)(2) (revocation mandatory on conviction of nearly any drug felony).] Prosecutors sometimes soften after a conviction, particularly if there was a plea showing that the defendant has accepted responsibility and recognized the system's authority. Many judges will not insist on detention if the prosecutor remains silent on the issue.
- Point out your client's good behavior and reliability on pre-trial release. Your client has proven that he will make his appearance perhaps over years of pre-trial release conditions, leave the witnesses alone and not commit other crimes.
- Ask to let the client have just a few weeks or months to put his affairs in order. For this argument to have traction, you should detail what your client must do to wrap up his affairs (*e.g.,* complete projects at work, sell off properties or businesses, or see his child off to college).
- Propose even more restrictive release conditions. If your client has been unrestrained, suggest electronic monitoring or the posting of property.
- Convince the court that an appeal has a substantial likelihood of success that will result either in reversal of the conviction or a substantial reduction in sentence.
- If you had partial success at trial, argue that your client has been convicted of lesser charges carrying a lesser penalty than he anticipated before trial. Therefore, he presents a better bail risk after conviction than before.

§4:86   Self-Reporting to Prison

If the jurisdiction permits self-reporting to the designated prison (*e.g.,* the federal system), seek self-reporting. There are two substantial benefits to self-reporting:

- Your client may avoid being transported from one holding facility to another. The trips often are extremely uncomfortable and the jails unsafe. During the trips, your client must either leave behind personal belongings and legal papers or risk their loss or theft. If he self-reports, he may be able to go directly to his final place of incarceration with his papers and belongings and money to deposit in his prison account.
- Self-surrender bespeaks reliability and often helps earn a lower security classification and designation to a less secure and less oppressive correctional institution.

Federal judges limit the time to self-report to the time it takes the Bureau of Prisons to designate the defendant to an appropriate institution, a period of no more than four to six weeks, depending on the federal district.

VIII. FORMS

Form 4-1   Bail Questionnaire

<u>Residential Information</u>
- Where do you live?
- How long have you lived there?
- Do you rent or own?
- If rent, who is the landlord and what is the rent? Do you have a written lease? How can the lawyer get his hands on it as soon as possible?
- If you own your home, in whose name[s] is the deed?
- How much equity does the house have: when was it purchased, for how much down, and what is the balance on the mortgage?
- Who else lives there, and what is their relationship to you?
- If you cannot return to your home, where can you live? With whom? What is their relationship to you and their contact information?

<u>Employment Information</u>
- Where do you work, and for how long have you worked there?
- What are the hours?
- What is your job title?
- Who is your immediate supervisor, and how can he be contacted to confirm employment?
- If the job is recent, where did you work before?
- If bailed, will you be able to return to the job?

<u>Who Does the Client Support?</u>
- Remember to ask about not only spouse and children, but extended family–grandparents and grandchildren, aunts, uncles, nieces and nephews.
- If married, for how long?
- If divorced or separated or if your client has children from other relationships, does he pay child support; how frequently and how much?

<u>Criminal Record</u>
- All prior arrests, convictions and sentences.
- Bail status on the prior cases, and how many court appearances you made.
- If sentenced to probation or parole, how well did you comply with the conditions?

<u>Other</u>
- Military service: branch, rank, where stationed and type of discharge.
- Immigration status. Ask more than whether your client is here legally or illegally. Did he have a visa or work permit and overstay it? Or enter illegally after being deported previously? Does the client have a green card? Even if the client believes he is a noncitizen, ask if he or his parents were born in the U.S. It is not unheard of for citizens of other countries, especially along our borders, to be deported when in fact they are U.S. citizens because no one realized that the "alien" was born in the U.S. during his parents' brief trip here, making him a citizen.
- Is anyone willing to come to court and either post cash or sign a surety bond?

Form 4-2   Motion to Modify Bail Conditions to Permit Travel

COMMENT:
Paragraph 7 of this form states that you discussed the motion by telephone with the Assistant District Attorney assigned to this case, and he authorized you to represent that he does not oppose the motion. You should seek the prosecutor's consent to the motion but settle for his non-opposition. Some prosecutors believe

that taking no position enables them to avoid responsibility should something go wrong; others simply are unable to agree with anything a defense lawyer proposes

Paragraph 8 of this form states that you spoke with defendant's supervising pre-trial services officer about the motion, and that he informed you that he does not object to the motion. In those jurisdictions where some court official or agency monitors the defendant on pre-trial release, you should approach this official first and seek his consent. Judges may regard the opinion of this official, who is supposedly neutral, works for the Court, and has close interaction with the defendant, more highly than the prosecutor's.

COMMONWEALTH OF PENNSYLVANIA,	)))	
Plaintiff	))	
v.	))	Cr. No. _____
JOHN DOE,	))	
Defendant	)	

MOTION TO PERMIT TRAVEL

AND NOW COMES Defendant, John Doe, by his attorney, Thomas J. Farrell, Esquire, and files this Motion to Permit Travel, and in support thereof, states as follows:

1. Mr. Doe is charged in a two-count information with grand larceny and intimidation of a witness.
2. On [Date], District Justice John Law set fifty thousand dollars ($50,000) cash bail, which defendant posted.
3. A condition of defendant's release was that he not travel outside Allegheny County, Pennsylvania.
4. Since bail was set, defendant has appeared timely at all court dates and has obeyed the other conditions of his release.
5. On Saturday, [Date], defendant's daughter, Ophelia Doe, graduates from Yale University in New Haven Connecticut. The graduation ceremony takes place on Saturday, but the University holds events on campus in New Haven starting on Monday, [Date], for the graduate's parents.
6. Defendant hopes to travel to New Haven by automobile on Sunday, [Date], and return to Allegheny County on Sunday, [Date], with his wife, Livia Doe, should the Court grant this Motion and permit this travel.
7. Defense counsel discussed this motion by telephone on [Date], with the Assistant District Attorney assigned to this case, Lucius Roe, and he authorized defense counsel to represent that he does not oppose this motion.
8. On [Date], defense counsel also spoke with defendant's supervising pre-trial services officer, [Name], concerning this motion and he informed defense counsel that he does not object to the Motion.

WHEREFORE, defendant respectfully requests that the Court grant this motion and permit him to travel to his daughter's graduation.

Respectfully Submitted,

_____
Thomas J. Farrell
Counsel for Defendant

COMMONWEALTH OF PENNSYLVANIA,	)))	
Plaintiff	))	
v.	))	Cr. No. _____
JOHN DOE,	))	
Defendant	)	

ORDER OF COURT

AND NOW, this _____ day of _____, upon consideration of Defendant's Motion to Travel, IT IS ORDERED that Defendant's Motion is GRANTED, and Defendant is permitted to travel to New Haven, Connecticut from [Date] to [Date].

_____
Judge

Chapter 5

EXTRADITION

I. INTERSTATE PROCEDURES

A. Detainers

§5:01 Definition & Process

A detainer is a request to the jurisdiction having custody of an inmate that he be held for prosecution by another jurisdiction. [*Fex v. Michigan,* 507 U.S. 43, 44 (1993).]

Detainers generally are based on outstanding criminal charges, outstanding parole or probation violation charges, or additional sentences already imposed against the prisoner. [*Carchman v. Nash,* 473 U.S. 716, 719 (1985).]

Detainers can be issued by prosecutors and police without judicial approval. [*See United States v. Mauro,* 436 U.S. 340, 358 & n.25 (1978).]

A detainer does not start the process of transferring the inmate. It merely is a notification that he is wanted for trial in another jurisdiction.

To begin the transfer process, the demanding jurisdiction must file one of the following:
*   An extradition warrant.
*   A demand under the Interstate Agreement on Detainers ("IAD").
*   A writ of habeas corpus ad prosequendum.

However, the detainer functions to prevent the inmate from being released until the second jurisdiction can collect him.

§5:02 Effect

Detainers have two principal deleterious effects on sentenced prisoners:
*   A detainer prevents the inmate's early release to parole, community confinement or house arrest programs.
*   The existence of the detainer does not entitle the inmate to credit on whatever sentence the secondary jurisdiction may impose. That sentence will start to run only once the prisoner is produced to the secondary jurisdiction, thus guaranteeing that the two sentences run consecutively.

[*See Carchman v. Nash,* 473 U.S. 716, 730 n.8 (1985) (listing effects of detainers).]

§5:03 Interstate Agreement on Detainers (IAD) Allows Notification

For sentenced prisoners, the IAD may ameliorate some of the adverse effects of a detainer because the IAD obligates prison authorities to notify inmates promptly of any detainers from other jurisdictions. [IAD Article III(c) (the IAD appears as Appendix 2 to Title 18, United States Code).]

The inmate may submit a written request to the prosecuting authority and appropriate court notifying them of his request for a final disposition of the charges and of his place of confinement. [IAD Article III(a).] The inmate delivers the request to his institution's warden, who then must forward it by certified mail, return receipt requested, along with a certificate showing the inmate's sentence and time left to be served. [IAD Article III(b).]

The written request has two consequences:
*   The demanding jurisdiction must try the defendant within 180 days or the charge will be dismissed with prejudice. [IAD Articles III(a) & V(c).] The 180 days begin to run only upon the prosecutor's and court's receipt of the inmate's request and the prison's certificate, not when the inmate sends the request. [*Fex v. Michigan,* 507 U.S. 43.] The filing of defense motions or requests for continuance may toll the 180 days. [Article VI(a).] Once sent to the receiving state, the defendant must be tried before being returned to his place of confinement; "shuttling" the inmate back and forth will result in dismissal of the charge with prejudice. [*See Bozeman,* 533 U.S. 146 (even one day interruption in custody requires dismissal with prejudice).]
*   The request waives extradition. [IAD Article III(e).]

The United States, the District of Columbia, the Virgin Islands, Puerto Rico and 48 states have adopted the IAD. [*See Alabama v. Bozeman,* 533 U.S. 146, 148-49 (2001).]

§5:04 IAD Prosecution-Initiated Request for Temporary Custody

The IAD also contains provisions whereby a prosecutor may initiate a request for temporary custody to resolve charges against an inmate in another state. [IAD Article IV.] Once the defendant is received in the requesting state, trial must commence in 120 days. [IAD Article IV(c).]

A prosecution-initiated request does not eliminate your client's right to an extradition hearing. [IAD Article IV(d).] The inmate retains the rights under the state's extradition laws to a pretransfer hearing and resort to habeas corpus if his extradition is ordered. [*Cuyler v. Adams,* 449 U.S. 433 (1981).]

During the time the defendant is in the receiving jurisdiction, his sentence in the original jurisdiction continues to run. [IAD Article V(f).]

§5:05 Exceptions to the IAD

The IAD has many exceptions.

It applies only to sentenced inmates, not pre-trial detainees, and not to transfers within states or from one federal judicial district to another.

Some courts hold that if the sending state paroles or releases the inmate, even after his transfer to the receiving state, the time periods of the IAD cease to apply. [*Compare Dunaway v. Commonwealth,* 60 S.W.3d 563, 567-68 (Ky 2001) (surveying decisions and claiming that this is the majority rule) *with Snyder v. Sumner,* 960 F.2d 1448, 1453 (9th Cir. 1992) (release from sentence does not end IAD's speedy trial requirements).]

Writs of habeas corpus ad prosequendum are not considered detainers and do not trigger the inmate's rights under the IAD. [*Mauro,* 436 U.S. 340.]

The automatic dismissal with prejudice remedy does not govern if the receiving jurisdiction is the federal courts. [IAD Article IX, §9(1).]

§5:06 Using the IAD for Your Client

Detainers can deprive your client of the opportunity to participate in programs such as work release, furloughs and release to halfway houses as well as prevent his early release on good time or parole. Unless you and your client are certain that lengthy delay will benefit his defense on the outstanding charge, make a prompt written request for disposition under the IAD.

The statute instructs the inmate to send the request for disposition to the warden. [IAD Article III(a).] To trigger the IAD's obligations and time limits, the prosecutor and "the appropriate court of the prosecuting officer's jurisdiction" must receive both the request *and* the prison's certificate as to the sentence and time remaining on it. [*See Fex v. Michigan,* 507 U.S. 43 (time begins to run when prosecutor receives request, not when inmate sends it).]

Receipt of the request without the certificate does not trigger the time limits of the IAD, so you and your client must pursue strict compliance with the IAD's procedures. [*See, e.g., United States v. Jones,* 454 F.3d 642, 646-48 (7th Cir. 2006) (delivering request to warden, who delivered it to U.S. Marshals, who then failed to forward it to prosecutor or court, failed to trigger IAD); *Commonwealth v. Copson,* 444 Mass. 609, 830 N.E.2d 193 (Mass. 2005) (prosecutor and court's receipt of request without certificate of inmate status did not trigger IAD's requirements; surveys cases).]

Forms:
- **Form 5-1** Request for Disposition Under IAD
- **Form 5-2** Certificate of Inmate Status
- **Form 5-3** IAD Offer to Deliver Temporary Custody

[§§5:07-5:09 Reserved]

B. Interstate Extradition

§5:10 The Uniform Criminal Extradition Act (UCEA)

The U.S. Constitution, federal statutes and state statutes all speak to states' responsibilities and defendants' right in cases of interstate extradition. [*See U.S. Constitution,* Article IV, §2, cl.2; 18 U.S.C. §3182.]

Forty-eight states, Puerto Rico and the Virgin Islands have adopted the Uniform Criminal Extradition Act ("UCEA"). [*E.g.,* 42 Pa.C.S.A. §§9121 et seq.; New York Crim. Pro. Law §§570.02 *et seq.*]

§5:11 Extradition Is Mandatory Upon Request

When one state charges a person with a crime, and the person is found in another state, the asylum state *must* extradite the person upon a proper request from the requesting state's Governor. Intent or motive to evade prosecution do not matter, only the change in location.

Although the language in the UCEA states that the defendant must be shown to have escaped or violated the conditions of bail, probation or parole, courts have interpreted that language to be merely illustrative and not comprehensive. [*See People ex rel. Schank v. Gerace,* 231 App. Div. 2d 380, 388, 661 N.Y.S.2d 403 (N.Y. App. Div. 1997).]

Thus, a person can be a fugitive without knowing that charges have been filed, or without knowing that a crime has been committed, or if the person was removed forcibly from the state. [*See, e.g., White v. Armontrout,* 29 F.3d 357, 359 (8th Cir. 1994) (leaving without notice of the charges still makes one a fugitive); *United States v. Gee,* 912 F.2d 414, 418 (10th Cir. 1990) (a person is subject to extradition even though he left with the knowledge and consent of state officials).]

The only exception is that the defendant's presence in the demanding state at the time of the crimes must have been actual and personal, not constructive. [*See Hyatt v. New York,* 188 U.S. 691 (1903).] If the defendant commits a crime in the demanding state without being present there (such as by being a conspirator or accomplice to another's crime), the Governor of the asylum state has discretion to grant or deny the extradition request. [*See, e.g.,* 18 Pa.C.S.A. §9127.]

§5:12   Improper Extradition

Improper extradition, or even intentional bypassing of extradition statutes, does not prevent trial nor void a conviction. [*See United States v. Alvarez-Machain,* 504 U.S. 655 (1992) (international extradition); *Frisbie v. Collins,* 342 U.S. 519 (1952) (interstate extradition).]

§5:13   The Extradition Process

The UCEA requires an asylum state's Governor to issue an extradition arrest warrant upon receipt of a written demand alleging that the accused was present in the demanding state at the time of the crime and thereafter fled, accompanied by an authenticated copy of the indictment, information, arrest warrant and affidavit or judgment of sentence. [*See* 42 Pa.C.S.A. §§9124, 9128.]

Upon arrest, the extraditee must be taken before a judge where he is informed of the demand and the charge and his right to counsel. He may waive his right to oppose extradition (commonly called a "waiver of extradition, *see, e.g.,* 42 Pa.C.S.A. §9146). If he does not waive extradition, the court will fix a reasonable time to apply for a writ of habeas corpus. [*See* 42 Pa.C.S.A. §9131; NY Crim. Pro. L. §570.24.]

If probable cause exists to believe that the defendant committed a crime in another state or escaped or broke the terms of his bail, probation or parole, then the defendant also may be arrested and detained to await the issuance of the extradition warrant. [*See* 42 Pa.C.S.A. §§9134, 9135.] However, this detention may last only for a 30 day period, which a court can extend for another 60 days if the asylum state's Governor has not issued an extradition warrant. [*See* 42 Pa.C.S.A. §§9136, 9138. *See generally Cuyler v. Adams,* 449 U.S. at 443 & n.11; *Commonwealth v. Frias,* 53 Mass. App. Ct. 488, 491-94, 760 N.E.2d 300, 303-06 (Mass. Ct. App. 2002) (overviews of extradition process).]

Once the extradition warrant issues, the demanding state has 30 days to collect the defendant. [18 U.S.C. §3182.] However, the filing of a habeas petition tolls that period. [*Prettyman v. Karnopp,* 192 Neb. 451, 222 N.W.2d 362, 366 (1974).] Release for violations of this 30-day period is discretionary, not mandatory. [*In re Lambert,* 173 Vt. 604, 795 A.2d 1236 (Vt. 2002) (surveying cases).]

§5:14   Habeas Corpus and Review of Extradition Warrant

Once the Governor determines that the demanding state's papers are in order and issues a warrant, review is limited. Extradition proceedings are meant to be summary, reserving defenses to trial in the requesting state. [*See New Mexico ex rel Ortiz v. Reed,* 524 U.S. 151, 153 (1998) (State court could not refuse extradition on the grounds that the defendant fled under duress based on a well-founded belief that the requesting state's parole authorities meant to revoke his parole without due process and then to do him physical harm); 18 Pa.C.S.A. §9141 (courts in asylum state cannot inquire into guilt or innocence except so far as it relates to identity of accused).]

The defendant has the right to apply for a writ of habeas corpus within a reasonable time. [42 Pa.C.S.A. §9131; NY CPL §570.24.] However, habeas review is limited to whether:

- The extradition documents on their face are in order.
- The petitioner has been charged with a crime in the demanding state.
- The petitioner is the person named in the request for extradition.
- The petitioner is a fugitive.

[*Michigan v. Doran,* 439 U.S. 282, 289 (1978).]

On the issue of whether the petitioner is a fugitive, the defendant has the burden of proving beyond a reasonable doubt that he was not present in the demanding state at the time of the crime. [*South Carolina v. Bailey,* 289 U.S. 412, 421-22 (1933) (where there is a conflict in the evidence, extradition must be ordered); *Commonwealth v. Valentin,* 448 Pa. Super. 519, 672 A.2d 338 (1996) (reversing trial court for applying preponderance standard).]

The asylum state may not review the requesting state's probable cause determination. [*Michigan v. Doran,* 439 U.S. 282 (1978); *Commonwealth v. Inadi,* 303 Pa. Super. 409, 411, 449 A.2d 753, 754 (1982).]

Hearsay is admissible, and the exclusionary rules do not apply. [*Inadi,* 303 Pa. Super. at 413, 449 A.2d at 755.]

State statutes generally provide counsel for defendants who lack the financial means to retain a lawyer. [*See, e.g.,* 42 Pa. C.S.A. §9131; NY CPL §570.24.] However, whether an arrest warrant and extradition proceedings mark the start of adversary proceedings and the Sixth Amendment right to counsel is unsettled. [*See generally* LaFave *et al.,* 2 *Criminal Procedure* §6.4(e) & nn.67-72 (surveying split in authority).]

PRACTICE TIP:

> Habeas challenges to extradition rarely succeed. Furthermore, during extradition proceedings:
> * Some states do not credit a defendant with time served toward his sentence. [§5:17.]
> * Bail generally is not available. [§5:18.]
> Therefore, do not hesitate to counsel your client to waive extradition if no strong defenses appear.

§5:15   Federal Habeas Corpus

Since extradition involves federal law, you may seek review in federal court either by filing a petition for a writ of certiorari with the Supreme Court or by filing a petition for a writ of habeas corpus under 28 U.S.C. §2241(c)(3). [*Harden v. Pataki,* 320 F.3d 1289, 1292 n.3 (2d Cir. 2003).]

However, even though 28 U.S.C. §2241 does not explicitly require the exhaustion of state remedies, most federal courts force you to exhaust state remedies out of respect for federal-state comity. [*Whelan v. Noelle,* 966 F. Supp. 992 (D. Or. 1997) (noting that federal courts have discretion to excuse lack of exhaustion in extradition cases for case by case "special circumstances" such as settled state law against the defendant or the inadequacy of state processes, but refusing to do so in the case before it).]

Therefore, your first course is to file a state habeas petition.

§5:16   Try to Prevent Interrogation During Extradition Proceedings

Once extradition is ordered, your client will have little access to counsel and might spend considerable time in the company of the investigating officers.

Do all you can to prevent the officers from interrogating your client:
* State on the record that your client invokes his Fifth and Sixth Amendment right to counsel and will not answer any questions without counsel present.
* Ask the judge to order that no law enforcement officials interrogate your client. The judge may or may not, and the judge's order may or may not have any effect, but your on-the-record statement might provide some legal protection or discourage some questioning.
* Have your client sign a letter invoking his right to counsel.
* Notify the officers that your client has invoked his right to counsel with respect to the charge and will not answer questions.

Instruct your client in strong terms not to discuss the case with the officers and to invoke his right to counsel at every turn. [*Compare Brooks v. State,* 903 So.2d 691 (Miss. 2005) (defendant's right to counsel violated and line-up identification suppressed where police conducted counsel-less line-up after an arrest warrant issued and the defendant extradited when defendant signed statement at the extradition hearing stating that he would not talk without counsel present); *with State v. Taylor,* 354 N.C. 29, 550 S.E.2d 141 (2000) (admitting confession that was product of custodial interrogation over right to counsel objection even though the extradition hearing judge, at the request of defendant's public defender, issued an oral order prohibiting law enforcement officers from speaking to defendant about the matter).]

Form:
* **Form 5-4** Client Letter Invoking Right to Counsel

§5:17 Credit for Time During Extradition Proceedings

At least 40 states credit a defendant with time served toward his sentence for time spent in the asylum state's custody fighting an extradition request. [*See State v. Duran*, 158 N.H. 146, 156, 960 A.2d 697, 706 (NH 2008).] A few states do not grant credit, though; therefore, in considering whether to contest or to attempt to expedite extradition, you must consider the credit rules in the receiving state. [*See Commonwealth v. Beauchamp*, 413 Mass. 60, 62, 595 N.E.2d 307 (1992) (defendant denied credit for more than four years spent in custody in Illinois fighting extradition in state and federal habeas proceedings); *Johnson v. Manson*, 190 Conn. 309, 493 A.2d 846 (1985) (denying equal protection and due process challenges to this interpretation of Connecticut's time credit statutes).]

§5:18 Bail During Extradition Proceedings

The UCEA authorizes courts in the asylum state to release the defendant on bail pending issuance of the asylum state's extradition warrant unless the offense is punishable by death or life imprisonment. [*See* 42 Pa.C.S.A. §9137.]

However, once the Governor issues an extradition warrant and orders extradition, most states do not grant a defendant the right to bail pending resolution of his habeas petition and his return to the demanding state. [*See In re Ford*, 187 Mich. App. 452, 455-59, 468 N.W.2d 260 (Mich. App. 1991) (surveying states and finding that majority rule is not to allow bail); *see generally* Carol Crocca, *Right of Extraditee to Bail After Issuance of Governor's Warrant and Pending Final Disposition of Habeas Corpus Claim*, 13 A.L.R.5th 118.]

§5:19 Defendants Under Criminal Prosecution in Asylum State

If the defendant faces pending charges in the asylum state, the UCEA grants the asylum state's Governor discretion to stay extradition until those charges are tried and the defendant sentenced. [*E.g.,* 18 Pa.C.S.A. §9140.]

A stay may be in your client's interest if a conviction in the demanding state might enhance your client's sentence in the asylum state by triggering habitual or repeat offender penalties, or by serving as an aggravating circumstance in a capital murder prosecution.

If the Governor is inclined to let the asylum state's charges proceed first, ask the extradition judge to incorporate a stay of extradition pending disposition of the local charges into the extradition order. [*See Commonwealth v. Boczkowski,* 577 Pa. 421, 461-65, 846 A.2d 75, 99-101 (2004) (appellate court struck aggravating factor and vacated death sentence where prosecutor in asylum state ignored court-ordered stay and sent defendant to demanding state, where the defendant received conviction that served as aggravating factor in asylum state's subsequent capital prosecution).]

[§§5:20-5:29 Reserved]

C. Federal District Transfers

§5:30 Hearing Procedure

Transfer of a defendant from the federal district of arrest to another district where charges are pending does not involve the extradition statutes.

This transfer is governed by the Federal Rules of Criminal Procedure, and is called a "removal." The defendant is entitled to a hearing to determine that he is the person charged in the arrest warrant. [Fed R Crim Pro, Rule 5(c)(3)(D)(ii).]

Also, if he has not been indicted, the defendant may have a preliminary hearing in the arresting district, although he has the option to defer it to the charging district. [Fed R Crim Pro, Rules 5(c)(3)(C) & 5.1(b). *See generally* Barry Boss & Edward J. Marek, *Federal Criminal Practice* §§5:1–5:16 (2005).]

Usually defendants waive removal hearings because prompt return to the charging district facilitates the client's ability to prepare a defense, obtain local counsel and explore cooperation.

Furthermore, prompt removal enables a defendant detained in the district of arrest to obtain a full bail hearing and review of the release or detention ruling in the charging district. [For the *Melendez-Carrion* bail presumption, *see* §5:31.]

§5:31 Bail Pending Transfer

The defendant can be detained and the issue of release deferred to the charging district because the "first appearance" for bail purposes does not occur until the defendant arrives in the charging district. [*See United States v.*

Melendez-Carrion, 790 F.2d 784, 790 (2d Cir. 1986) (construing bail statute, 18 U.S.C. §3142(f), and noting that evidence about the strength of the case and the defendant's risk of flight probable is more accessible in the prosecuting district).] You should argue for bail nonetheless. Whether to defer the bail determination is a discretionary decision; further, some courts do not follow *Melendez-Carrion*, reasoning that transportation may take weeks and deprive the defendant of a prompt bail determination. [*United States v. Havens*, 487 F.Supp.2d 335 (W.D.N.Y. 2007).]

Even where the court follows *Melendez-Carrion*, its presumption in favor of detention can be overcome:

- Call the prosecutor in the charging district and try to persuade him to agree to release.
- If the district of arrest is your client's home district, present a full case for release on bail because witnesses and suretors will be most available in that district. The presentation might convince the court to release your client. [*See United States v. Barrigar*, 2006 U.S. Dist. LEXIS 23212 (E.D.Mich. 2006) (ordering release and distinguishing *Melendez-Carrion* because the defendant's ties were in the district of arrest, not the charging district).] Even if it does not, the defendant can present the transcript in support of his bail application in the charging district.[*See Melendez-Carrion*, 790 F.2d at 990 (suggesting procedure whereby defendant be allowed to make record in support of bail in the removing district).]

If your client is released, he stands an excellent chance of avoiding detention if he appears voluntarily in the charging district. The government cannot seek review of the release order in the district of arrest. [*See United States v. El-Edwy*, 272 F.3d 149, 152-54 (2d Cir. 2001) (holding that both the government and the defendant must seek any review of a release or detention order in the charging district).] Furthermore, your client's voluntary appearance negates any suggestion that he was a risk of flight.

§5:32   Travel Expenses

If your client is released on bail and is unable to pay his way to the charging district, the magistrate in the removing district can order the government to pay travel and subsistence expenses. [18 U.S.C. §4285. *See* Chapter 20, Trial (including a form motion to pay travel expenses).]

[§§5:33-5:39 Reserved]

II.   FOREIGN COUNTRY PROCEDURES

A. Extradition

§5:40   Requests Are Handled by the Department of Justice

The U.S. Department of Justice handles requests from foreign nations to extradite individuals to face trial in those nations.

If the United States and the requesting nation are signatories to the treaty, the U.S. will pursue extradition requests, even of U.S. citizens. [See 18 U.S.C. §3196 (extradition of US citizens mandatory if treaty demands it; otherwise, within State Department's discretion).]

§5:41   General Procedure

An extradition proceeding commences with the filing of a provisional arrest warrant in federal court. [For general international extradition practice, see Jacques Semmelman & Karen Snell, *Defending the International Extradition Case*, 30 *Champion* 20 (June 2006). See also M. Cherif Bassiouni, *International Extradition: United States Law and Practice* (4th ed. 2002).]

Detention is the rule; bail will be granted only in "special circumstances." [*See* Semmelman & Snell, 30 *Champion* at 21 (special circumstances have been held to include bad health, old age, excessive delay, unavailability in demanding nation of credit for time served, and a substantial chance of acquittal in the demanding nation, among others).]

§5:42   The Extradition Hearing

The prosecution must prove five elements at a hearing before a District Court Judge or a United States Magistrate Judge:

- *The existence of a treaty.*

- *Identity.* Generally the prosecution will use fingerprints, photographs and admissions your client made when arrested.
- *That the crime charged falls within the treaty.* Not all crimes are extraditable. The treaty will specify which crimes are.
- *Dual criminality.* The underlying conduct must constitute a crime *both* in the United States and the requesting nation.
- *Probable cause.* The defendant is entitled to a hearing at which the government must prove probable cause to believe that your client committed the extraditable offense.

[See *Collins v. Loisel*, 259 U.S. 309 (1922); Semelman and Snell, *Defending the International Extradition Case,* 30 *Champion* at 23.]

With regard to the probable cause hearing, the rules of evidence and the exclusionary rule do not apply, and the government often relies entirely on the extradition papers to prove probably cause. [*See, e.g., Afanasjev v. Hurlburt*, 418 F.3d 1159, 1165 (11th Cir. 2005) (hearsay is admissible, and court can rely on unsworn declarations from absent witnesses); *Mainero v. Gregg*, 164 F.3d 1199, 1206-07 (9th Cir. 1999) (accomplices' self-incriminating statements can establish probable cause even though inadmissible in the U.S. under the rule of *Bruton v. United States*, 391 U.S. 123 (1968)).]

§5:43   Defenses

The defense can introduce evidence to explain, but not to contradict the prosecution's case. [*See, e.g., In re Sindona*, 450 F.Supp. 672, 685-90 (S.D.N.Y. 1978) (defining contradictory evidence as that which poses conflicts of credibility or attempts to contradict requesting nation's proofs; explanatory evidence must be of limited scope and have some reasonable chance of negating a showing of probable cause); *In re Extradition of Strunk*, 293 F.Supp.2d 1117 (E.D.Cal. 2003) (noting that the distinction between the two types of evidence often is illusory, and holding that probable cause was not established).]

A political offense exception prohibits extradition for crimes committed incident to waging war. [*See Barapind v. Enomoto*, 400 F.3d 744, 750-51 (9th Cir. 2005) (en banc) (political offense exception applies only if offense occurred during an uprising or other violent political disturbance and the offense was motivated by pursuit of specific political objectives).]

The principle of "specialty" forbids the receiving state from prosecuting the extradited individual for any offense other than that on which extradition was ordered. You may also raise specialty as a defense where your client has been extradited to the United States from a foreign nation. [*See United States v. Puentes,* 50 F.3d 1567 (11th Cir. 1995) (holding that individual defendant, not just the U.S. Department of State, has standing to raise a violation of the specialty doctrine, but ruling that in the particular case before it the indictment did not "materially alter" the offense for which the defendant was extradited from Uruguay); *but see United States v. Valencia-Trujillo*, 573 F.3d 1171 (11th Cir. 2009) (specialty is a treaty-based defense; where defendant's extradition was based on an extradition agreement or the sending nation's laws, which, unlike treaties, lack the force of U.S. law, defendant cannot raise specialty defense in U.S. courts.); *Abbas v. Dep't of Homeland Security*, 2009 U.S. Dist. LEXIS 72410 (W.D. La. July 21, 2009) (surveying split in courts of appeals).]

Even when probable cause is indisputable on some charges, fighting to defeat probable cause on others may serve your client well when he arrives in the requesting jurisdiction. It may limit his prosecution in the requesting jurisdiction to those charges on which probable cause was established. [For an attempt to broaden the defenses to extradition based on a revisionist analysis of extradition's history, *see* John T. Parry, *The Lost History of International Extradition Litigation,* 43 Va. J. Int'l L. 93 (2002).]

§5:44   The Review Process

The review process for extradition cases resembles that for preliminary hearings.

If the prosecution loses, it cannot appeal, but it can refile.

The defense cannot appeal, but it can obtain review by filing a habeas corpus petition, often with the same court that granted the extradition request, and then appealing that decision to the Circuit Court of Appeals. [*See United States v. Doherty*, 786 F.2d 491(2d Cir. 1986) (explaining manner in which parties may seek review and holding that prosecution cannot seek review through a declaratory judgment action).]

§5:45   Unlawful Flight to Avoid Prosecution

Leaving a state to avoid prosecution for a felony, the service of a felony sentence, or to avoid testifying pursuant to subpoena is the federal offense of unlawful flight to avoid prosecution ("UFAP"). [18 U.S.C. §1073.]

Prosecutions to conclusion for this crime are rare. Federal authorities will obtain a UFAP complaint to enlist the assistance of the FBI in apprehending fugitives, but the practice is to surrender the arrestee immediately to state authorities for extradition and to dismiss the federal complaint, avoiding even an initial appearance before a federal magistrate. [*See Fed. R. Crim.* P. 5(a)(2) & *Advisory Committee Notes* to Rule 5.]

An indictment (but not a complaint) for a UFAP violation must have written approval from the Attorney General or one of his deputies or associates. [*See* 18 U.S.C. §1073.]

[§§5:46-5:49 Reserved]

B. Prisoner Transfers

§5:50 Transfer Is According to a Treaty

The United States has treaties with several nations providing for the transfer of inmates serving U.S. sentences, state and federal, back to their home nations to serve of the remainder of their sentence. There can be no transfer without a treaty authorizing it. [18 U.S.C. §4100(a).]

A transfer can have two benefits:

- Your client can serve his sentence nearer to friends and family and in a familiar culture.
- Many foreign nations grant parole more liberally than the U.S., so that your client will serve less time.

The governing statute and regulations are sparse. [See 18 U.S.C. §§4100 et seq. and 28 C.F.R. 527.40–527.46] The best guide to Department of Justice Policy is in the U.S. Attorney's Manual. [U.S. Attorney's Manual, Title Nine, Criminal Resource Manual §§731-740 (available at www.usdoj.gov/usao/eousa/foia_reading_room/usam/title9/title9.htm).]

The inmate must consent, the crime of conviction must be a crime in the prisoner's home nation as well, and no appeals or collateral attacks can be pending. [18 U.S.C. §4100(b)&(c).]

Unless the sentencing court gives explicit permission, incarceration for contempt (either civil or criminal) or the existence of an unpaid fine will prevent transfer. [28 C.F.R. 527.42.]

§5:51 Requesting a Transfer

Your client must await incarceration before he can apply for transfer.

He makes his request to the Bureau of Prisons, which forwards it to the International Prisoner Transfer Unit ("IPTU") of the Office of Enforcement Operations within the Department of Justice's Criminal Division. [*See* U.S. Attorneys' Manual, Criminal Resource Manual §734.]

The IPTU will:

- Seek the prosecutor's input. [U.S. Attorneys' Manual, Criminal Resource Manual §736.]
- Consider information regarding the seriousness of the underlying offenses, whether your client has paid any fines and/or made restitution pursuant to the sentencing court's order, his prior record, the strength of his ties to each country, and the likelihood of rehabilitation. [U.S. Attorneys' Manual, Criminal Resource Manual §734.]

Before transfer is authorized, the prisoner is entitled to the appointment of counsel if he is indigent. [18 U.S.C. §4109.]

The prisoner is also entitled to a hearing before a judge or magistrate at which the judge will verify his understanding and agreement that:

- Only the appropriate courts in the United States may modify or set aside the conviction or sentence, and any proceedings seeking such action may only be brought in such courts.
- The sentence will be carried out according to the laws of the country to which he is to be transferred, and those laws are subject to change.
- If a court in the country to which he is transferred determines that his transfer was not accomplished in accordance with the treaty or laws of that country, he may be returned to the United States for the purpose of completing the sentence if the United States requests his return.
- His consent to transfer, once verified by the verifying officer, is irrevocable.

[18 U.S.C. §4107(b).]

PRACTICE TIP:

You might ask the prosecutor to add his consent to the transfer to the plea agreement. Review the issue carefully with your client. Consent to transfer may require him to abandon his appeals.

III. FORMS

Form 5-1   Request for Disposition Under Interstate Agreement on Detainers

COMMENT:

Prepare six copies if only one jurisdiction within the state involved has an indictment, information or complaint pending.

Additional copies will be necessary for prosecuting officials and clerks of court if detainers have been lodged by other jurisdictions within the state involved.

One copy should be retained by the inmate. One signed copy should be retained by the institution. Signed copies must be sent to the Agreement Administrators of the sending and receiving states, the prosecuting official of the jurisdiction which placed the detainer, and the clerk of the court which has jurisdiction over the matter. The copies for the prosecuting official and the court must be transmitted by certified or registered mail, return receipt requested.

INMATE'S NOTICE OF PLACE OF IMPRISONMENT AND REQUEST FOR DISPOSITION OF INDICTMENTS, INFORMATIONS OR COMPLAINTS

TO: (1) _____ Prosecuting Officer   _____
                                                (Jurisdiction)

(2) Clerk of _____ Court   _____
                                      (Jurisdiction)

And to all other prosecuting officers and courts of jurisdictions listed below in which indictments, informations or complaints are pending.

You are hereby notified that the undersigned, [Inmate's Name & Number] is now imprisoned in [Institution] at [City and State].

I hereby request that final disposition be made of the following indictments, informations or complaints now pending against me:

Failure to take action in accordance with the Interstate Agreement on Detainers (IAD), to which your state is committed by law, will result in the dismissal of the indictments, informations or complaints.

I hereby agree that this request will operate as a request for final disposition of all untried indictments, informations or complaints on the basis of which detainers have been lodged against me from your state. I also agree that this request shall be deemed to be my waiver of extradition to your state for any proceeding contemplated hereby, and a waiver of extradition to your state to serve any sentence there imposed upon me, after completion of my term of imprisonment in this state. I also agree that this request shall constitute a consent by me to the production of my body in any court where my presence may be required in order to effectuate the purposes of the IAD and a further consent to be returned to the institution in which I now am confined.

If jurisdiction over this matter is properly in another agency, court, or officer, please designate below the proper agency, court, or officer and return this form to sender.

_____

The required Certificate of Inmate Status (Form III) and Offer of Temporary Custody (Form IV) are attached.

_____   _____
Inmate's Printed Name & Number   Inmate's Signature

_____
Date

_____   _____
Witness's Printed Name & Title   Witness's Signature

_____
Date

Form 5-2   Certificate of Inmate Status

COMMENT:

For an inmate's request for disposition under Article III, copies of this Form should be attached to all copies of Form II, the inmate's request.

If the request was initiated by a prosecutor under Article IV, a copy of this Form should be sent to the prosecutor upon receipt by the warden of Form V.

Copies of this Form should be sent to all other prosecutors in the same state who have lodged detainers against the inmate. A copy may be given to the inmate.

CERTIFICATE OF INMATE STATUS

_____   _____
(Inmate)   (Number)

_____   _____
(Institution)   (Location)
_____   hereby certifies:
(Custodial authority)

1. The inmate's commitment offense(s): _____
2. The term of commitment under which the inmate is being held: _____
3. The time already served: _____
4. Time remaining to be served on the sentence: _____
5. Good time earned/Good time release date: _____
6. The date of parole eligibility of the inmate: _____
7. The decisions of the state parole agency relating to the inmate: (If additional space is needed, use reverse side.)

_____
8. Maximum expiration date under present sentence: _____
9. Security level/special security requirements: _____
10. Detainers currently on file against this inmate from your state: _____

_____   Dated: _____
Warden

CUSTODIAL AUTHORITY
Name/Title: _____
Institution: _____
Address: _____
City/State : _____
Telephone: _____

Form 5-3   IAD Offer to Deliver Temporary Custody

COMMENT:

Inmate's request: Copies of this Form should be attached to all copies of Form 5-1 (Request for Disposition Under Interstate Agreement on Detainers).

Prosecutor's request: This Form should be completed after the warden has approved the request for temporary custody, expiration of the 30 day period and successful completion of a pretransfer hearing. Copies of this Form should then be sent to all officials who receive(d) copies of Form 5-2 (Certificate of Inmate Status). One copy also should be given to the inmate and one copy should be retained by the institution. Copies mailed to the prosecutor should be sent certified or registered mail, return receipt requested.

OFFER TO DELIVER TEMPORARY CUSTODY

TO: _____ Prosecuting Officer

_____
(Jurisdiction)

And to all other prosecuting officers and courts of jurisdictions listed below from which indictments, informations or complaints are pending.

RE: _____   No. _____
(Inmate)

Pursuant to Article V of the Interstate Agreement on Detainers (IAD), the undersigned hereby offers to deliver temporary custody of the above named inmate to the appropriate authority in your state in order that speedy and efficient prosecution may be had of the indictment, information or complaint which is
___ described the attached inmate's request, or
___ described in your request for custody of _____
                                                                (Date)

The required Certificate of Inmate Status (Form III)
___ is enclosed, or
___ was sent to you with our letter of _____
                                                       (Date)

Indictments, informations or complaints charging the following offenses are also pending against the inmate in your state and you are hereby authorized to transfer the inmate to the custody of appropriate authorities in these jurisdictions for purposes of disposing of these indictments, informations or complaints,

Offense: **County or Other Jurisdiction:**

If you do not intend to bring the inmate to trial, please inform us as soon as possible.
_____ Date: _____
Warden

CUSTODIAL AUTHORITY
Name/Title: _____
Institution: _____
Address: _____
City/State: _____
Telephone: _____

Form 5-4   Client Letter Invoking Right to Counsel

To Whom It May Concern:

I am the defendant in *State v. Jones*. Thomas Farrell, Esquire, of 436 Seventh Avenue, Pittsburgh, PA 15219 and phone number (412) 391-3700 represents me in this matter until otherwise notified.

I hereby invoke my right to counsel under the Fifth and Sixth Amendments of the U.S. Constitution and state law. I do not want to answer any questions without having my lawyer present.

Sincerely,
Robert Jones

(This page intentionally left blank.)

Chapter 6

EXPERTS & INVESTIGATORS

I.   REQUESTING EXPERT & INVESTIGATIVE ASSISTANCE

§6:01   Federal Constitution

The Supreme Court has recognized a due process right to expert assistance at court cost, stating that an indigent defendant who "demonstrates to the trial judge that his sanity at the time of the offense is to be a significant factor at trial ... must [be given free] ... access to a competent psychiatrist who will conduct an appropriate examination and assist in evaluation, preparation, and presentation of the defense." [*Ake v. Oklahoma,* 470 U.S. 68, 83 (1985).] Some courts find authority for the right to reasonably necessary ancillary services in the federal and state rights to counsel. [*See, e.g., People v. Stuckey,* 96 Cal.Rptr.3d 477, 491-92, 175 Cal.App.4th 898, 918 (Cal.App. 3 Dist. 2009).]

Ake requires the state to provide an indigent defendant with any expert services necessary to present an adequate defense. [*Mason v. Mitchell,* 95 F.Supp.2d 744, 774 (N.D.Ohio 2000). *See also State v. Wang,* 92 A.3d 220, 230 & nn. 14 & 15 (CT 2014)(majority of states have held that Ake extends to non-capital cases and experts other than psychiatrists; list cases); *State v. Davis,* 318 S.W.2d 618, 632 (Mo. 2010) ("the majority of federal and state courts that have addressed this issue since Ake have concluded that the reasoning underlying Ake also would apply to other types of experts if the required showing is made that the issue the expert is to address will be a significant factor at trial on a key issue."); *Dubose v. State,* 662 So.2d 1189, 1194 (Ala. 1995) (stating that the principles enunciated in *Ake* apply in a case of nonpsychiatric expert assistance).] You want an independent expert–one who will be part of the defense team and will restrict discussion of his findings to the defense–but the appellate courts are split on whether *Ake* entitles the defense to an independent expert of its own or a competent one who might be accessible to both the defense and prosecution, such as a psychiatric examiner at a state mental hospital. [*See Woodward v. Epps,* 580 F.3d 318 (5th Cir. 2009) (surveying split in authority and holding that examination at state mental hospital is sufficient assistance to develop insanity defense).]

In *McWilliams v. Dunn,* 137 S.Ct. 1790 (2017), the Supreme Court noted the uncertainty about the right to an independent defense expert, but failed to resolve the issue. [*See McWilliams,* 137 S.Ct. at 1804-05 & n.3 (Alito, J., dissenting)(surveys the split in decisions).] The Court did, however, outline the minimum that the constitutional rule of *Ake* requires. First, the *Ake* right is triggered if three prerequisites are met: (1) the defendant is indigent, (2) his mental condition is relevant to guilt or punishment, and (3) there is a serious question as to the defendant's mental condition. [*Id.* at 1794-95, 1798.] If those conditions exist, "a defendant must receive the assistance of a mental health expert who is sufficiently available to the defense and independent from the prosecution to effectively 'assist in evaluation, preparation, and presentation of the defense.'" [*Id.* at 1799.] In *McWilliams,* the Court held that *Ake* assistance includes (1) examination and assistance in (2) evaluation, (3) preparation, and (4) presentation of the defense. *Id.* at 1800. The expert must be available to help the defense interpret medical records and findings and translate them into a defense legal strategy and to assist the defense in constructing and presenting arguments and direct and cross-examination. [*Id.* at 1800-01.] It is difficult to understand how an expert can fulfill these roles unless she works exclusively for the defense.

Most courts include investigators within the meaning of nonpsychiatric experts. [*See generally* Michael J. Yaworsky, *Right of Indigent Defendant in State Criminal Case to Assistance of Investigators,* 81 ALR4th 259 (1991).]

§6:02   State Statutes

Many jurisdictions have statutes providing for the appointment of an expert or investigator for an indigent defendant under certain conditions. These conditions often require the defendant to provide a statement of the circumstances requiring an investigator, a proffer of the evidence you expect to obtain through the investigator's services, and an estimate of the cost. [*See, e.g.,* Vernon's Ann. Texas C.C.P. Art. 26.05, 26.052(f) (request must state "(1) the type of investigation to be conducted; (2) specific facts that suggest the investigation will result in admissible evidence; and (3) an itemized list of anticipated expenses for each investigation").]

You can undertake the investigation before obtaining court approval and hope for reimbursement later. [*See, e.g.,* Texas C.C.P. Art. 26.052(g).] However, the investigator may look to you for payment if the court denies reimbursement.

§6:03   Proof of Need

Courts have insisted that defendants must establish their entitlement to appointments of experts or investigators by demonstrating a particularized, case-specific need for the services so strong that a fair trial cannot be had without the assistance. [*See Moore v. State,* 390 Md. 343, 889 A.2d 325 (Md. 2005) (surveying decisions).

Difficult as it may be to specify what you expect the expert or investigator to find before you have had the benefit of their services, most courts require that a motion for their appointment at court expense include:

- The specific type of expert needed.
- A description of what you expect the expert to conclude.
- An explanation of how such an opinion is critical to the defense, either to develop defense evidence or to assist you in understanding and undermining the prosecution's expert testimony.
- The cost of the services.
- The defendant's inability to pay for such services.

Even a defendant represented by retained counsel may be entitled to court funds for an expert if he currently lacks funds to pay the expert. [*See generally, Guidelines For The Administration Of The Criminal Justice Act*, 3.01 (defendant represented by retained counsel entitled to court funds for expert and investigative services if he lacks funds to pay for those services after paying counsel a reasonable fee, but court can inquire into the fee arrangement to assure that counsel's fee is no more than "customarily paid to qualified practitioners in the community for services in criminal matters of similar duration and complexity"); Stephen B. Bright, "Obtaining Funds for Experts and Investigative Assistance," 21 *The Champion* 31 (June 1997) (surveying case law requirements).]

Examples:

- Federal: *Caldwell v. Mississippi*, 472 U.S. 320, 323 n.1 (1985) ("undeveloped assertions that the requested assistance would be beneficial" insufficient to raise due process right to experts); *Mason v. Mitchell*, 95 F.Supp.2d at 775 (stating that there are three factors in determining whether a Petitioner is entitled to assistance: (1) the effect on Petitioner's interest in the accuracy of the criminal proceeding; (2) the burden on the state if the assistance is provided; and (3) the probable value of the assistance sought and the risk of error in the proceeding if it is not provided).
- Alabama: *Dubose v. State*, 662 So.2d 1189 (Ala. 1995) (defendant entitled to DNA expert at court expense where defendant had no assets and $10,000 fund assembled by family and friends to retain counsel was down to $27; defendant not obligated to draw on family and friends to pay for expert).
- Georgia: *Roseboro v. State*, 365 S.E.2d 115 (Ga. 1988) ("a motion on behalf of an indigent defendant for funds with which to obtain the services of a scientific expert should disclose to the trial court, with a reasonable degree of precision, why certain evidence is critical, what type of scientific testimony is needed, what that expert proposes to do with the evidence, and the anticipated cost for services. Lacking this information, a trial court will find it difficult to assess the need for assistance").
- Texas: *Ex parte Jiminez*, 364 S.W.3d 866, 881-82 (Tex. Crim. App. 2012) (the defendant must explain the defense theory in a written motion supported by affidavits or other evidence "and why expert assistance would be helpful in establishing that theory, or a showing that there was reason to question the State's expert and proof").

PRACTICE TIP:

With regard to the description of what you expect the expert to conclude, you will have to do preliminary research by reading treatises and articles and the case law about the area of expertise. Try to enlist an expert to sketch an opinion pro bono with the hope that the court will appoint and reimburse him to develop and finalize the opinion.

§6:04   Preparing the Motion

In addition to establishing proof of the need for assistance, you may want to include the following in your motion for the appointment of an expert or investigator:

- A detailed curriculum vitae or resume for the witness, to assure the court of his bona fides.
- Citation to other cases in which the witness has testified as an expert or been appointed by the court to assist the defense.

You should cite not only to local statutes and rules, but also to:

- The Sixth Amendment and any state constitutional right to counsel. [*See, e.g., Hinton v. Alabama*, 134 S.Ct. 1081, 1088 (2014) ("Criminal cases will arise where the only reasonable and available defense strategy requires consultation with experts or introduction of expert evidence"; holding that trial counsel was ineffective in that he misinterpreted state statutes to preclude him from applying for appointment of a necessary toolmark and firearms identification expert); *State v. Allen*, 682 So.2d 713, 720-21 (La. 1996) (right to an investigator is part of the right to counsel); *Corenevsky v. Superior Court*, 36 Cal.3d 307, 682 P.2d 360 (Cal. 1984) (federal and state rights to counsel include the right to "reasonably necessary ancillary defense services" such as experts, investigators, a jury selection expert and law clerks).]

- The Due Process and Equal Protection Clauses of the Fifth and Fourteenth Amendments. [*See* Anthony G. Amsterdam, *Trial Manual For The Defense Of Criminal Cases* §§299, 300 (5th ed. 1989).]
- The Sixth Amendment's Compulsory Process Clause, [*See* Anthony G. Amsterdam, and Randy Hertz, *Trial Manual For The Defense Of Criminal Cases* §§5.2, 5.3 (6th ed. 2017).]

Forms:
- **Form 6-1** Motion for Appointment of an Investigator
- **Form 6-2** Motion for Appointment of a Psychiatric Expert

§6:05   Apply Ex Parte

Insist that your application be heard *ex parte* because to do otherwise would reveal defense trial strategy. [*See Ake*, 470 U.S. at 82-83 (assuming, but not deciding, that such motions will be heard *ex parte*); *Williams v. State*, 958 S.W.2d 186, 193-94 (Tex. Crim. App. 1997) (since explaining the need for expert assistance must reveal defense theories, the motion must be heard *ex parte* to protect attorney work-product; suggests that this requirement has constitutional basis); *Moore v. State*, 390 Md. 343, 889 A.2d 325 (Md. 2005) (ordering that such hearings be conducted *ex parte*; surveys several jurisdictions, dividing the camps into those that require an *ex parte* hearing and those that leave it to the trial court's discretion); *but see Sanchez v. Commonwealth*, 41 Va. App. 319, 585 S.E.2d 327 (Va. App. 2003) (proper to deny request to make request for DNA expert in an *ex parte* proceeding and to force defense to proffer in open court what it expected of the witness and how that would assist the defense), *rev'd on other grounds*, 268 Va. 161, 597 S.E.2d 197 (2004).]

In many jurisdictions, statutes authorize hearing such applications ex parte. [*E.g.*, 18 U.S.C. §3006A(e)(1); Vernon's Ann. Texas C.C.P. Art. 26.05, 26.052 (f); Kan.Stat.Ann. §22-4508; S.C.Code Ann. §16-3-26(C); Tenn.Code Ann. §40-14-207(b); Nev.Rev.Stat. Ann. §7.135; N.Y. County Law §722-c.]

Oddly enough, the statute governing federal death penalty cases *forbids* making an *ex parte* request for expert or investigative assistance unless the defense first shows, in an open motion, the need for confidentiality. [18 U.S.C. §3599(f).] To satisfy this statute, a defendant must file and serve a motion seeking authorization for investigative or expert assistance that includes a case-specific statement of the need for confidentiality. This statement must identify the type of services needed and the broad issue or topic for which the services are needed. [*Haight v. Parker*, 2010 U.S. Dist. LEXIS 36158 (W.D. Ky. April. 13, 2010) (surveying cases); *Shields v. Johnson,* 48 F.Supp.2d 719, 721 (S.D. Tex. 1999).] Some courts permit the motion to file confidentially to be filed concurrently with the *ex parte* motion for assistance. [*Shields v. Johnson,* 48 F.Supp.2d 719, 721 (S.D. Tex. 1999).] Others require that the prosecution be permitted to respond to the motion to file *ex parte* before the *ex parte* filing will be allowed. [*Bell v. True,* 356 F.Supp.2d 613, 616 & n.2 (W.D. Va. 2005).]

PRACTICE TIP:

If the court initially denies your motion, renew it when new facts emerge or you find yourself unable to develop evidence due to the lack of an expert. These things may occur:
- When you receive the prosecution's expert report.
- When the expert offers an opinion or test result at trial.
- With respect to a request for investigative assistance, whenever you cannot find and subpoena a defense witness described to you by your client or other witnesses because of the lack of an investigator.

[§§6:06-6:09 Reserved]

II.   INVESTIGATORS

A.   Choosing to Use an Investigator

§6:10   Use a Specialist for Interviewing Witnesses

An adequate defense requires thorough investigation of the facts both to learn what the prosecution witnesses will say and to find and bring to court defense witnesses.

Finding and interviewing witnesses are specialties. You should seek the assistance of a specialist in this area (*i.e.*, a private investigator). [*See* ABA Guidelines for the Appointment and Performance of Defense Counsel in Death Penalty Cases, Guideline 4.1, Comment, note A (stating that the prevailing national standard of practice forbids counsel from shouldering primary responsibility for the investigation).]

§6:11   Advantages of a Private Investigator

Using an investigator has several advantages over attorney-conducted investigation:
- It makes better and more cost-effective use of your time. You can focus on researching the law, drafting pleadings, preparing witnesses and conducting hearings and arguments, while the investigator spends the many hours, at less cost per hour than your customary rate, to find and interview witnesses.
- Factual investigation is a skill that improves with training and experience, something an investigator, who often might be a retired law enforcement officer, has and you do not.
- Investigators may have contacts with law enforcement agencies and access to government and online databases that you could develop only at great time and expense.
- You may need to impeach the witness at trial with an out-of-court statement, and you cannot serve as both the impeaching witness and trial counsel. [*See* ABA Standards Relating to the Defense Function 4-4.3(e); Model Rules of Professional Conduct 3.7(a) (lawyer may not be both advocate and witness at same trial).]

§6:12   Attorney Participation in Investigation

Even if you retain an investigator, you may want to accompany the investigator on certain interviews.

When defending most street crimes, you should get a feel for the scene of the crime. Walk it, photograph it, and observe the lines of sight and whether views are obstructed.

You also may want to participate in interviews of adverse witnesses. This will give you a feel for the witness's confidence, hostility, eloquence, and ability to think on his or her feet.

PRACTICE TIP:

Just as you have a courtroom demeanor which may differ from your bearing in a barroom, so too may the witness. Some witnesses grow hesitant and anxious in court, and others like the spotlight and become more certain and assertive. Also, the chatty witness who opened her home to you may turn hostile on the witness stand; the prosecutor may have reprimanded her for her effusiveness and painted you as a sneak who betrayed her hospitality and led her into damaging statements.

CAUTION:

When accompanying an investigator, do not assume that his law enforcement experience immunizes you from harm. Being a lawyer in a bad neighborhood does not protect you from crime. On the contrary, it announces that you probably carry something worth stealing. Do not try to force your investigator into a situation in which he feels uncomfortable. He may carry a gun and may have been a police officer, but he is physically vulnerable and handicapped by the need to look out for you.

§6:13   Choosing an Investigator

Most investigators are retired law enforcement officers. Try to match the type of investigation to the investigator's background:
- For street crimes, use former narcotics and homicide detectives.
- For financial crimes, use former IRS agents and Postal Inspectors.
- For vehicular homicide and DUI cases, use someone with accident reconstruction training and experience.

Some investigators excel at finding elusive witnesses. Others write good, accurate reports and demonstrate unusually good judgment in deciding what to include and what to omit from a report.

Finding a good investigator can be difficult. Word of mouth is the best reference. Describe your needs to other experienced practitioners and ask for a recommendation.

§6:14 Alternatives to Private Investigators

If you choose not to use an investigator, you still need a witness to your interviews, both to be available to testify to impeach the witness and to vouch that nothing improper happened at the interview.

Use a clerk, associate or paralegal. The critical need is for a person who can pay attention and take good notes.

[§§6:15-6:19 Reserved]

B. Conducting the Investigation

§6:20 Narrow the Scope

Resources and time always have limits, so you must narrow the scope of your investigation. As soon as you can, develop a theory of the defense that will guide your investigation. In most cases, you cannot refute every allegation. You must revise the theory as you discover more facts.

For example, the alibi witnesses may prove unworthy of belief, but the eyewitnesses may admit that their observations were fleeting and their identification of the defendant uncertain. In this situation you might choose to forego the alibi but to emphasize photographs, maps and videotapes of the scene to show the obstacles to a clear view. You might also explore the retention of an expert on the weaknesses of eyewitness identification. [*See* Chapter 9, Pre-Trial Identification.]

Your client is an obligatory starting point, but his desires and statements should not be conclusive. If your client admits the act but claims consent or self-defense, you can put the exploration of an alibi aside for a while. However, defendants frequently mislead their own attorneys, sometimes in perplexing and self-destructive ways. This occurs most often when the material which is helpful for the defense is also embarrassing. For example, many capital defendants had a childhood history of being abused, which could be powerful mitigating evidence at the sentencing phase, but many defendants will defend their parents and deny any abuse even at the cost of their own lives.

Measure the cost and time of the investigation against the possible benefit and the stakes for your client. For example, if your client faces death or life imprisonment, you must explore remote and unlikely leads. However, in a misdemeanor case you might forego such leads to focus on a single defense.

§6:21 Basic Steps

There are a few steps you should consider in every case:
- View the scene.
- Interview all eyewitnesses.
- Obtain 911 tapes.
- Obtain the criminal histories of prosecution witnesses, especially cooperating witnesses.
- Investigate civil filings.
- Interview your client's family, close friends and associates.

With regard to the histories of the prosecution witnesses, the prosecution is required to disclose its witnesses' criminal records. [*Giglio v. United States*, 405 U.S. 150 (1972).] However, most prosecutors will provide only the rap sheet. The rest of the court file may be rich with impeaching material: plea, hearing, trial and sentencing transcripts; victim impact statements; discovery; police reports; letters from the defendant; letters from the prosecutor. [*See Elcock v. Kmart Corp.*, 233 F.3d 734, 752-54 (3d Cir. 2000) (error for trial court to limit cross-examination to fact of witnesses' conviction and to preclude cross into the underlying facts and circumstances).]

Similarly, civil filings such as lawsuits, bankruptcy filings, and divorce actions all may contain evidence of deceit. In many jurisdictions, the courts do not permit filing of civil discovery, and you may have to contact the opposing party's attorney to request a copy. He may be willing to share it without charge, especially if he believed that the witness was a fraud.

The internet is full of resources that enable you to investigate witnesses. For a helpful guide to the possibilities and pitfalls (for example, you should not deceive anyone as to your identity and you should not "friend" any witnesses or victims), see Sean D. O'Brien and Quinn C. O'Brien, *I Know What You Did Last Summer: A User's Guide for Internet Investigations*, 41 THE CHAMPION 18 (June 2017).

Interviews with the client's family and friends can explain the story behind the offense, such as your client's motives and the victim's relationship to him. You want to learn about your client's background to explore any possible mental health defenses or mitigating facts for sentencing. Friends and family can also be a source of rumors and gossip about the other witnesses, and even though much of it may prove useless, some might lead to valuable evidence.

PRACTICE TIPS:

Ask witnesses who else might have knowledge of the events, their opinion on the approachability and credibility of those other potential witnesses, and what talk they have heard about the crime.

Move quickly on that evidence which might disappear in time. For example:

- Police departments typically destroy or record over 911 tapes in 30 to 60 days.
- In a vehicular homicide case, skid and yaw marks will wear and wash away.
- Some offenses occur in a locale such as a bar or street corner that is frequented by individuals who may or may not return.

§6:22   Interview Basics

Choose a time and place during which the witness will be available and unburdened with other responsibilities:

- Transient witnesses with no job and no children should be approached at daybreak. You probably will find them at home, and having just awakened, they will be vulnerable and unlikely to threaten you or think quickly enough to prevaricate.
- Visit unemployed witnesses with children shortly after the children probably left for school.

Rarely should you show up unannounced at a person's workplace. Law enforcement agents do this because the witness feels embarrassed in front of coworkers and customers and eager to cooperate to avoid another visit. However, a witness will not feel the same compulsion to cooperate with a private investigator. More likely, he will just be angry.

Always identify yourself and who you represent accurately. [*See* Model Rule 4.3 ("When the lawyer knows or reasonably should know that the unrepresented person misunderstands the lawyer's role in the matter, the lawyer shall make reasonable efforts to correct the misunderstanding"). *See also Dondi Properties Corp. v. Commerce Sav. & Loan Ass'n,* 121 F.R.D. 284, 290-91 (N.D. Tex. 1988) (en banc) (attorney should identify both himself and his client to witnesses).]

Leave a business card, both as proof that you did identify yourself correctly despite the witness's confusion (many people mistake "investigator with the Federal Public Defender" for "Federal Bureau of Investigation") and so that the witness can contact you later.

Your first objective is to get the witness to start talking. Once witnesses start, they are unlikely to send you away without telling their story, despite the advice of friends, lawyers and police officers.

With hostile witnesses, unannounced visits are a preferred technique. This is because most people find it easier to hang up on a telephone caller than to shut the door in a visitor's face, and the delay between a telephone call scheduling an interview and the interview itself allows others to convince the witness not to speak with you. However, some witnesses, particularly neutral ones whose priority is to avoid inconvenience, might talk on the phone to avoid the inconvenience of a personal visit.

§6:23   Interview Pitches and Techniques

Besides identifying yourself, you should have ready a number of pitches to encourage the witness to talk. For example:

- "I'm only doing my job."
- "We're trying to find out all the facts so we can make a decision whether to work out a plea bargain or go to trial."
- "We want to talk to you in person so we can decide if we can avoid subpoenaing you to trial."
- "If you or a loved one were accused of a crime, you'd want your lawyer to talk to all the witnesses."
- An investigator can find a bond with the witness in the nearly universal dislike of lawyers: "I'm sorry to have to ask you these questions, but the lawyer insisted. You know how pushy lawyers are. He told me to keep calling you until you talk to me or else he'd subpoena you."
- The investigator's tone always should be polite, respectful and non-confrontational. The investigator is not there to convince the witness he is wrong, although he or she might ask the witness to consider limitations on his story: for example, "It was dark, you couldn't see all that happened, could you?"
- Be ready for the witness to ask if your client is guilty or admits his guilt. Answer briefly and directly: "He has pleaded not guilty, and we are trying to determine if there is a valid defense to the charges. I am forbidden by law from telling you anything my client said to me or the lawyers."

- Ask witnesses who else they think might have information about the events: who else witnessed the crime; who knows the other witnesses; what police officers, emergency medical technicians and firefighters responded.
- Always ask a witness how they know what they say if it is not obvious that the information is based on first-hand observations.
- If the witness knows your client or has any reason to have been in contact with him after the offense occurred, ask if the witness has spoken with your client about the case or anything else. Most discovery rules do not entitle you to pre-trial disclosure of your client's statements to civilians. Your client might have called the witness and confessed or threatened the witness.
- Ask the witness if the police or prosecutor interviewed him and if he testified in the grand jury. Explore each interview in depth:
  - Who attended each interview?
  - What did the police ask and what did the witness say?
  - Did they ask you anything that I have not?
  - Did they say if they are going to talk to you again? Learning what the prosecution asked will offer insight into the direction of its investigation and theory of the case.

§6:24   Ethical Constraints

Witness interviews pose some risk of accusations of ethical and even criminal misconduct:

Inducements.

You cannot pay witnesses or offer them anything of value. Lawyers sometimes allow sincere generosity to lead them into misconduct. Buying meals or paying for an apartment for a homeless witness is improper. [*See* ABA Standards Relating to the Defense Function, 4-4.3(b).] Explain the legal prohibitions against such charity and instead try to put the witness in touch with the appropriate social services provider.

However, some jurisdictions permit parties to compensate fact witnesses for their reasonable expenses and lost wages or income for time spent testifying and preparing to testify. [*See ABA Ethics Opinion 96-402* ("The Committee also sees no reason to draw a distinction between (a) compensating a witness for time spent in actually attending a deposition or a trial and (b) compensating the witness for time spent in pretrial interviews with the lawyer in preparation for testifying . . . The Committee is further of the view that the witness may also be compensated for time spent in reviewing and researching records that are germane to his or her testimony, provided, of course, that such compensation is not barred by local law."); *Just in Case Business Lighthouse, LLC v. Murray*, 383 P.3d 1, 6-7 (Colo Ct. Appl 2013); *Roemmich v. Eagle Eye Development, LLC,* 2006 U.S. Dist. LEXIS 94320 (D.N.D. 2006) (in fee-shifting case, upholds award to prevailing party of payments of $125 per hour to fact witness for reviewing documents); *Prasad v. MML Investors Services, Inc.*, 2004 U.S. Dist. LEXIS 9289 (S.D.N.Y. May 27, 2004) (paying witness $125 per hour for preparing to testify was proper; surveys caselaw and disciplinary rules); *State of New York v. Solvent Chemical*, 166 F.R.D. 284, 289 (W.D.N.Y. 1996); *but see In the Matter of the Complaint of PMD Enterprises, Inc.,* 215 F.Supp.2d 519, 530 (D.N.J. 2002) (construing New Jersey law; while compensation for expenses and lost time attending trial are proper, it was improper to pay witness $100 per hour for document review).] Payment made to assuage a witness' hostility or to induce the witness to testify one way or another, even "to tell the truth," are improper. [*See In re Telcar Group, Inc., 363 B.R. 345 (Bankr. E.D.N.Y. 2007) (payments to fact witness contingent on party's success in the litigation were improper); *Golden Door Jewelry Creations, Inc. v. Lloyds Underwriters,* 865 F. Supp. 1516 (S.D. Fla. 1994) (payments contingent on the testimony being truthful and helpful are improper, and testimony was stricken).]

Most cases considering this issue involve civil, not criminal litigation, but those cases often look to the criminal statutes, such as the federal witness bribery statute, 18 U.S.C. §201(b)(3), (d)(generally prohibiting payment of witnesses, but permitting payment "by the party upon whose behalf a witness is called . . ., of the reasonable cost of travel and subsistence incurred and the reasonable value of time lost in attendance at any such trial, hearing, or proceeding"), in reaching their decisions, and the relevant ethical rules, e.g., Rule 3.4, make no distinction between civil and criminal cases. Nonetheless, a practical consideration counsels caution: in criminal cases, unlike in civil cases, your adversary has the power to prosecute you and your client if he believes your payments cross what he sees as the line between reasonable compensation and bribery. Thus, follow the advice of the Board of Governors of the Kentucky Bar Association:

> In the opinion of the Committee, KRPC 3.4(b) allows the lawyer, but does not compel the lawyer, to compensate a witness for reasonable out of pocket expenses and reasonable lost income that will actually

be incurred by the witness while testifying at a trial, hearing, or deposition, or while engaging in necessary preparation with the attorney. The Committee is of opinion that additional payments are imprudent, and may be questioned as being unethical or even illegal. Obviously, no payment may be made for the substance or efficacy of the witness's testimony.

[Kentucky Bar Association Ethics Opinion KBA E-400 (June 1997).]

Moreover, you do not want to pay a witness unnecessarily. Your client, like most criminal defendants, probably has limited funds, and if word leaks that witnesses can demand payment, you may soon find unpaid witnesses even more hostile than usual. On the other hand, some witnesses might deserve compensation, such as a company's former IT director who spends considerable time reconstructing the computer records on which the prosecution rests. Pay if you must, but document carefully that the payment is tied to expenses and hours spent preparing to testify at a rate reflecting the witness' usual wages or consulting fee.

Threats.

You cannot threaten a witness with physical harm, ostracism or economic loss, with one exception. Employers are entitled to their employees' cooperation in investigating a job-related accusation, and if you represent the employer, you can explain that a refusal to be interviewed and to cooperate fully with your investigation may lead to job termination. Be sure to include in your warning that you and your client want only the truth.

Recordings.

Federal law permits a party to a conversation to record it without the interlocutor's consent (meaning that federal agents can record with one party's consent anywhere in the nation). However, states vary in whether they permit recordings with only one party's consent. Surreptitious recordings in violation of state law carry criminal penalties. [E.g., 18 Pa. C. S. A. §5703.]

Lying to Witnesses.

Neither you nor your investigator can lie to or deceive witnesses. [Model Rule 4.1.]

The Witness Who Incriminates Himself and Requests for Counsel.

You have no obligation to warn a witness that his statements may incriminate him or to advise him to obtain counsel. [ABA Standards, 4-4.3(c).] However, if the witness appears confused about whom you represent and your role, you must clarify both. [See §6:22.]

§6:25   Interviewing Your Client's Employees–Warnings

Except where a witness clearly exhibits the mistaken belief that you represent him, you and your investigator have no obligation to inform the witness that his statements can be used against him or of the use to which your client might put the statements.

Special considerations arise, however, when you represent an entity such as a corporation and you interview its agents or employees. The corporation holds the attorney-client privilege, but since the entity can speak only through its employees, the employees' statements to you as the corporation's attorney are privileged and not discoverable, unless the corporation chooses to waive the privilege.

The corporation as the client holds the privilege, not the employee, and the corporation can waive the privilege and reveal the communications without the employee's consent and often to the employee's detriment. Corporations frequently respond to criminal investigations and threats of prosecution by conducting an internal investigation, which in large part consists of interviewing employees, and then offering up the culpable employees for prosecution in order to purchase non-prosecution or leniency for the corporate entity. The interviewed employee may believe, however, that he and his corporate employer share a common interest - defeating any prosecution–and that therefore the attorney hired to defend the corporation also represents him.

Several dire consequences may follow from the employee's belief, if it is found to be correct: (1) The employee can claim the privilege and prevent you or your corporate client from disclosing his statements; (2) he can claim that you operate under conflicting demands of loyalty from two adverse clients–the employee who wants to assert the privilege and the corporation which wants to use the employee's statements to buy its own non-prosecution–and have you disqualified from representing either client; (3) the conflict might subject you to disciplinary action and malpractice suits.

Worried by these potential sanctions, many advise attorneys who represent corporations, particularly in internal investigations but whenever they interview corporate employees, to administer so-called *Upjohn* or *Adnarim* warnings. These should state "that the corporate lawyers do not represent the individual employee; that anything said by the employee to the lawyers will be protected by the company's attorney-client privilege subject to waiver of the privilege in the sole discretion of the company; and that the individual may wish to consult with his own attorney if he has any concerns about his own potential legal exposure." [*See United States v. Ruehle,* 583 F.3d 600, 604 n.3 (9th Cir. 2009).] Some would require a caution to the employees that the corporation might share the statements with law enforcement in a criminal investigation. [*United States v. Nicholas,* 606 F.Supp.2d 1109, 11116 (C.D. Cal.), *rev'd sub nom. United States v. Ruehle,* 583 F.3d 600 (9th Cir. 2009).]

The burden to prove joint representation is on the employee, and it is heavy. "[I]ndividual corporate officers or employees seeking to assert a personal claim of attorney-client privilege must affirmatively show five factors:"

> *First,* they must show they approached counsel for the purpose of seeking legal advice. *Second,* they must demonstrate that when they approached counsel they made it clear that they were seeking legal advice in their individual rather than in their representative capacities. *Third,* they must demonstrate that the counsel saw fit to communicate with them in their individual capacities, knowing that a possible conflict could arise. *Fourth,* they must prove that their conversations with counsel were confidential. And *fifth,* they must show that the substance of their conversations with counsel did not concern matters within the company or the general affairs of the company.

Id. at 1159-60 (adopting the test of *In the Matter of Bevill, Bresler, and Schulman Asset Management Corporation,* 805 F.2d 120, 123 (3d Cir. 1986).

Nonetheless, the consequences of a finding that the employee or witness was misled into believing that the attorney represented him are severe. The attorney might be conflicted out of representing the corporate client; the employee's statements might be suppressed, and the attorney might face disciplinary action. [*See Commonwealth v.Schultz,* 133 A.3d 294 (Pa. Super. Ct. 2016).] Therefore, you must take two precautions at minimum: (1) Inform the witness that you represent the corporation and not the witness; and (2) Do not mislead the witness into thinking that you represent him. [*see Model Rule of Professional Conduct 1.13(f)* (""In dealing with an organization's . . . employees . . ., a lawyer shall explain the identity of the client when the lawyer knows or reasonably should know that the organizations interests are adverse to those of the [employee] . . .")]. Avoid statements along the lines that you may represent both the witness and the corporation if litigation or prosecution results, and avoid giving the employee legal advice. [*See Model Rule of Professional Conduct 4.3* ("The lawyer shall not give legal advice to an unrepresented person . . .")]

§6:26   Use Your Jurisdiction's Freedom of Information ("FOIA") and Right to Know ("RTK") Acts

FOIA and RTK statutes entitle citizens and residents to review and obtain copies of government records. These statutes often exempt criminal investigative records from disclosure, but many records that could be helpful to your case are outside that exemption, even if generated by law enforcement officials. [*E.g., Pennsylvania State Police v. Grove,* No. 25 MAP 2016, 2017 WL 2645401 (PA Sup. Ct. June 20, 2017)(police motor vehicle video recordings of accident subject to disclosure); *Coley v. Philadelphia District Attorney's Office,* 77 A.3d 694, 697-98 (Pa. Commonwealth Court 2013) (immunity agreements with witnesses subject to disclosure).] In white collar cases, agencies that are not within the prosecutor's investigative team and thus not subject to the prosecutor's discovery obligations may possess useful records. Further, if you are involved in a case at the pre-charge stage, you do not have any subpoena power and the prosecutor has no discovery obligations, so FOIA and RTK requests might be the only devices available to compel production of relevant records.

Agencies and jurisdictions vary in how quickly responses are made, so make your requests as early as you can.

[§§6:27-6:29 Reserved]

C. Interference With Investigation

§6:30   Prosecution Interference

Witnesses are free to refuse to talk to you. [*United States v. Agostino,* 132 F.3d 1183, 1191 (7th Cir. 1997).]

However, the prosecution cannot discourage witnesses from speaking to the defense. [*United States v. Leung,* 351 F.Supp.2d 992 (C.D. Cal. 2005) (dismissing indictment where key cooperating witness's plea and cooperation agreement with prosecution forbade him from speaking with the defense); ABA Standards Relating to the Prosecution Function, §3–3.1(d) (stating that a prosecutor should not discourage or obstruct communication between prospective witnesses and defense counsel, and that a prosecutor should not advise a person to decline to give information to the defense investigator).]

PRACTICE TIP:

If you find evidence of interference, ask the court to order that the witnesses be instructed that they are free to speak with the defense. [*See* Anthony G. Amsterdam, & Randy Hertz, Trial Manual for the Defense of Criminal Cases, § 9.14 (6th ed. 2017) (surveying remedies, including joint calls with the prosecutor to the witness, court instructions to the witness, depositions and dismissal of the indictment); Kevin Sali & John Robb, *Fighting Governmental Witness Tampering,* 41 THE CHAMPION 34 (June 2017).]

Ask the court for written directions to be delivered to the witnesses. You do not want the police to deliver oral instructions, tainted with the officer's inflections, tone and gestures.

Some courts also have ordered that the witnesses be produced for discovery depositions where the prosecution interfered with the defense's ability to interview them. [*United States v. Carrigan,* 804 F.2d 599 (10th Cir. 1986) (affirming use of depositions as within trial court's discretion and inherent authority).]

§6:31   Witnesses Represented by Counsel

If a witness is represented by counsel with respect to your case, you should obtain his lawyer's permission before speaking to him. [Model Rule 4.2; *In re Chan,* 271 F.Supp.2d 539 (S.D.N.Y. 2003) (censuring attorney for interviewing co-defendant without counsel's permission); *but see Grievance Committee for the S.D.N.Y. v. Simels,* 48 F.3d 640, 645-47 (2d Cir. 1995) (not improper to interview represented persons so long as they are not co-defendants in same case with defendant).]

Most lawyers will not allow you to speak to their clients regarding their trial testimony, but many will summarize it for you and may even promise answers to particular questions you might pose.

Witnesses, represented and not, may ask you for advice. You must explain that since you are not the witness's lawyer, you cannot give advice. [*See* Model Rule 4.3 ("[d]uring the course of a lawyer's representation of a client, the lawyer should not give advice to an unrepresented person other than the advice to obtain counsel").]

§6:32   Your Witnesses

The boundaries on what you may tell your own witnesses about speaking with the police and prosecutor are similar to those for the prosecutor. [*See* §6:30.]

You can explain the law, such as:

- The parties' attorneys have a duty to try to interview witnesses, but the witness is free to refuse to speak to the prosecution.
- A subpoena can order a witness to appear only at trial or a hearing.
- If the witness chooses to talk, then he or she must tell the truth.

However, you cannot instruct the witness to refuse to speak to the police. And, aside from explaining the few legal principles listed above, you cannot offer legal advice.

If the witness persists with questions about the law, you should:

- Explain the legal impediment to answering these questions. [*See* Model Rule of Professional Conduct 4.3(b).
- Apologize for you inability to answer.
- Suggest that the witness retain his own lawyer.

PRACTICE TIP:

You can explain the interview and trial process to your witnesses and the reasons that the police want an interview. Often, the manner in which you describe the process will predict whether the witness speaks to the police. If you emphasize that the police will take notes and write a report about what the witness says in order to cross-examine him or her if the story at trial differs in any detail, most witnesses will realize that it is not in their interest to be interviewed. [*But see* Colorado Bar Ass'n, Ethics Opinion 65 (March 17, 1984) ("It is deemed unethical conduct for an attorney or his representative to advise or *to imply* to a potential witness that he should not submit to a pre-trial interview by opposing counsel or his representative.") (emphasis added).]

[§§6:33-6:39 Reserved]

D. Discovery Requirements

§6:40   Interview Statements

The rule of thumb is that you or an investigator should document interviews of adverse witnesses, but not those of your witnesses.

To understand this advice and to decide when to deviate from it, you must understand your jurisdiction's discovery, "Jencks Act" [18 U.S.C. §3500], and work product rules.

In most jurisdictions, you must disclose at trial your witness's recorded statement with the following limitations:
*   *It must be your witness.* You have no obligation to disclose statements you took from your opponent's witnesses or witnesses you do not call at trial.
*   *It must be the witness's statement.* Your investigator's notes are not the witness's statement unless the witness signed or initialed them, thereby adopting them, or unless your investigator took word-for-word notes. However, if your investigator testifies to impeach the witness, then you must disclose the investigator's report or notes. The prosecution then may be able to question your investigator about the portions of his interview that were consistent with the witness's trial testimony.

In many courts, however, parties customarily disclose as Jencks material investigators' reports of witness interviews. While the Jencks Act and similar rules do not strictly require this, you depart from this practice at the risk of incurring the judge's wrath.

Even more importantly, if you fail to disclose witness interviews, then the prosecutor may adopt an identical interpretation and refuse to give you agents' reports describing witness interviews that might be your only preview of what prosecution witnesses will say.

§6:41   Recorded Interviews

Generally, do not audio or videotape any interview.
There are two exceptions to this:
*   The witness who confesses to the crime with which your client is charged.
*   The witness who recants.

Prosecutors and judges will be extremely skeptical of such witnesses and will not accept merely your or your investigator's word. Further, such witnesses are likely to recant their recantations and confessions and even deny their statements to you.

§6:42   Investigator's Notes

Attorneys' notes are rarely discoverable because of the work product privilege.

This privilege extends to investigators who are part of the defense team, but the privilege correctly receives less deference for investigators because their notes are less likely to reflect the attorney's thinking. [*See Upjohn v. United States,* 449 U.S. 383, 400-402 (1981) (attorney's notes memorializing a witness's oral statements will rarely be discoverable because they incorporate the attorney's mental impressions); *Bogosian v. Gulf Oil Corp.,* 738 F.2d 587, 594 (3d Cir. 1984) (explaining "core work product" protection afforded mental impressions and opinions of counsel).]

Therefore, when dealing with defense witnesses, you may want the investigator to report orally to you. You may then memorialize the important points in your own notes or memoranda.

[§§6:43-6:49 Reserved]

III. EXPERTS

A. General Points

§6:50   Use Experts Whenever Possible

Your aim is to raise a reasonable doubt, and an expert can help prove that what seemed simple and straightforward actually teems with complexities beyond the jury's unassisted understanding. Of course, your resources are not limitless, and any opinion testimony must fit the theory of the defense.

Your client's truthfulness can save you time and preserve your client's monetary resources for exploring other lines of defense. For example, if the prosecution recovered semen from the victim's person and has submitted it for DNA testing, whether you should retain your own expert depends in large part on whether your client admits that he is the source of the semen.

There are companies that maintain databases of experts. Most lawyers rely on colleagues' word-of-mouth to find an expert. Look to the authors of texts and leading articles in the field as well. Criminal defense list-servs expand your access to the community of lawyers who may help locate an expert.

Another good but neglected resource for criminal defense attorneys, particularly for non-forensic experts, is civil attorneys. Experts appear frequently in many types of civil cases such as commercial disputes, malpractice actions and product liability lawsuits; civil practitioners can direct you quickly to experts such as doctors to defend the legitimacy of your client's prescribing practices in a drug diversion case; to accountants and economists for a financial fraud case; and to environmental scientists in a Clean Air or Clean Water Act case.

Form:
- **Form 6-3** Engagement Letter for Expert or Investigator

§6:51   Choosing and Investigating the Expert

Conduct the same investigation when seeking impeaching material on the prosecution's expert or checking the likely effectiveness of your potential expert:
- Obtain transcripts of the expert's prior testimony.
- Ask lawyers who used or opposed the expert their opinions of the expert's strengths and weaknesses.
- Plumb the expert's professional reputation with peers in his field.
- Review the expert's curriculum vitae for its accuracy.
- Read as many of the expert's publications as you can.
- Run the expert's name through an internet search engine to find stories about the expert, articles in which he is quoted, and interviews and commentary he gave.
- Conduct the same investigation as you would of any witness for criminal record, bankruptcy filings, business ownership interests and UCC filings.

In any case involving forensic evidence, you must investigate both the foundations of the science underlying it and the validity of its application to your case. For example, the prosecution's own expert may have written articles that explain limits on the science for which she advocates in court, limits that fall by the wayside in the race to convict. [*See* Jules Epstein, *When Must Lawyers Learn Science?* (January 21, 2016)(available at http://www.judges.org/when-must-lawyers-learn-science); *Kulbicki v. State*, 53 A.3d 361, 368 (Md. Ct. Spec. App. 2012) (holding that trial counsel was ineffective for failing to find and use report that prosecution's expert wrote four years before his trial testimony which questioned the very basis for his comparative bullet lead analysis testimony), *rev'd Maryland v. Kulbicki*, 136 S. Ct. 2 (2015)(the *Strickland* standard of the Sixth Amendment minimum does not require lawyers to question accepted forensic science).] Reputable organizations, such as the President's Council of Advisors on Science and Technology, regularly issue reports that question accepted forensic "science" and show that the so-called science is junk. [*E.g.*, Executive Office of the President President's Council of Advisors on

Science and Technology, REPORT TO THE PRESIDENT, FORENSIC SCIENCE IN CRIMINAL COURTS: ENSURING SCIENTIFIC VALIDITY OF FEATURE-COMPARISON METHODS (September 2016) (available at www.whitehouse.gov).]

§6:52 Communicating With Your Expert

In the case of a testifying expert, anything the expert considers in reaching his opinion may become fair game for cross-examination. [*See United States v. Zanfordino*, 833 F.Supp. 429, 433 (S.D.N.Y. 1992) (underlying data and materials created and used by expert should be disclosed pre-trial).]

This may include letters and emails to your expert and draft reports.

PRACTICE TIP:

Use the telephone. As convenient as it may be to dash off a letter or email to your expert with a question or comment, you should not. Letters and emails leave a trail that can be erased only with the greatest of efforts, and the effort itself, if discovered, will appear sinister. In contrast, ill-chosen words, worries, speculation about weaknesses in the expert's opinion all disappear into the haze of memory when an expert is questioned about a conversation that was never recorded.

Early on, establish rules with your expert for note-taking and draft-writing because both may become discoverable. Discovery of such documents occurs less frequently in criminal than civil litigation, because the discovery rules impose fewer obligations in criminal cases and because the lack of depositions and interrogatory practice decrease the opportunities for discovery. However, your zeal in pursuing discovery from the prosecution's experts may cause the judge to impose reciprocal obligations on your expert. A *Daubert* hearing also creates a context in which your expert may find himself forced to disclose and answer questions about his notes and drafts. The expert cannot destroy drafts and notes, but neither should he hasten to create them and commit to writing preliminary impressions that he may reconsider.

§6:53 Preparing the Expert Report

Your expert's report should be the product of close collaboration.

You must explain your case theory thoroughly to the expert and modify your theory based upon the expert's conclusions so that the final report fits your theory. Your expert may reach unimpeachable conclusions, but they help little if they are not germane to your defense.

The report must walk the line between covering all the major opinions which the expert will offer, and wallowing in excessive detail. Remember that discovery is stingy in criminal cases, and the trial evidence always will hold surprises. If your expert becomes committed to detailed conclusions or explicitly states reliance on evidentiary details that emerge differently at trial, then he or she is open to damaging cross-examination. You want the report general enough so that the expert can modify the explanations and the particulars of the testimony to accommodate the trial evidence.

Finally, experts, like lawyers, strive to be reasonable. Accordingly, they often share two tactics with lawyers:

- They will concede certain points to emphasize the persuasiveness of their position on the remaining disputed points. You must scrutinize the expert's draft report to guarantee that he or she did not concede more than you want.
- Experts will tend to express their opinions in terms of contingencies. You need to work with the expert to eliminate such contingencies from the report. You and your expert have no obligation to provide a roadmap for a successful cross-examination by outlining how the expert's opinion would differ if certain factual assumptions changed.

§6:54 Disclosing the Expert Report

Reciprocal discovery rules dictate that if your testifying expert prepared a report, then you must produce it to the prosecution. Your failure to produce a required report may cause the court to preclude your expert's testimony. [*E.g., Commonwealth v. McClellan*, 2005 Pa. Super. 376, 887 A.2d 291 (Pa. Super. 2005) (expert precluded where defense failed to disclose report and gave notice that expert would testify only after a month of trial).]

However, jurisdictions differ in whether they require that the expert write a report. [*Compare* Fed. R. Crim. P 16(b)(1)(C) (expert or counsel must prepare and provide prosecution with summary of expert's opinions and the bases for them); Pa. R. Crim. P. 573(C)(2)(b) (court may order defense expert to prepare report stating subject matter of his testimony, substance of the facts to which he will testify and a summary of his opinions and the grounds for each opinion) *with Mulvaney v. Dubin*, 80 A.D.2d 566, 435 N.Y.S.2d 761 (App. Div. 2d Dept.) *rev'd on other grounds*, 55 N.Y.2d 668, 446 N.Y.S.2d 931, 431 N.E.2d 292 (1981) (trial court lacks power to order defense expert to prepare report).]

§6:55 Avoiding Disclosure of the Unfavorable Opinion

Sometimes experts return unfavorable opinions. When that happens, despite your efforts to keep the expert's involvement secret, the prosecutor may learn of it (the expert may need access to items in police custody, such as blood or firearms; your psychiatrist must sign in at the jail to visit and interview your incarcerated client). Once the prosecutor does not receive a report, or when he receives one from a different expert, he may contact the first expert and try to use him as a government witness. This threatens especially severe damage to your case when the expert has spoken with your client.

Generally, defense experts are considered the defense attorney's agents, and the expert's work is protected by the work product privilege, the Sixth Amendment right to the effective assistance of counsel, and, when interviews of the defendant are involved, by the attorney-client privilege. [*E.g., Commonwealth v. Kennedy*, 583 Pa. 208, 876 A.2d 939 (Pa. S. Ct. 2005) (reversing pre-trial order granting prosecution access to the results of DNA analysis run by defendant's expert on work-product grounds); *State v. Dunn*, 571 S.E.2d 650 (N.C. 2002) (Sixth Amendment right to counsel violated when prosecution allowed to subpoena experts retained by defense, but not called to testify); *United States v. Alvarez*, 519 F.2d 1036 (3d Cir. 1975) (permitting prosecution to call psychiatrist retained but not used by defense violated attorney client privilege); *but see Pawlyk v. Wood*, 248 F.3d 815 (9th Cir. 2001) (prosecution could call defense psychiatrist who examined defendant but whom defense did not call to testify); *but see State v. Jones*, 681 S.E.2d 580 (SC 2009) (agreeing that the work-product privilege applied to non-testifying consultative defense expert on "barefoot insole impression" evidence, but finding that where the expert was one of only two available worldwide, the expert would not testify to any defense strategy or reveal any communications with the defendant, and where the expert was to testify only at a pretrial hearing on the admissibility of the evidence, the prosecution had shown substantial need and undue hardship sufficient to overcome the work-product privilege).]

However, these privileges dissolve when the expert is retained for the purpose of offering testimony. Then, since the defense intends that the expert will testify about his work and opinions, the defense waives any privilege.

To avoid prosecution access to an expert that you decide not to use, retain experts in a two-step written process:
- Retain the expert with the understanding that he or she acts as a consultant to assist you in formulating a trial strategy and to advise you on the viability of potential defenses. Prosecutors cannot access the work papers, notes and opinions of consultant experts; it would be identical to invading the defense attorney's strategy sessions with his client and staff. [*See* Fed. R. Civ. P. 26(b)(4) (providing for discovery of testifying expert, but making it near impossible to obtain discovery of consulting nontestifying expert).]
- Do not label the expert as a potential witness unless and until the expert tentatively concludes that he or she can offer a helpful opinion and articulates the opinion with some specificity. [*See generally Pope v. Texas*, 207 S.W.3d 352, 366 (Tex. Crim. App. 2006) ("There is a simple solution: investigate first, consult second, designate third. The designation of a potential expert witness ... is an act similar to crossing the Rubicon in that it may waive many of the protections otherwise provided by the work-product doctrine, although it will not waive any confidential communications under the attorney-client privilege").]

Thus, you must specify two conditions in the expert's engagement letter:
- The expert acts as an agent of defense counsel; therefore, any client communications shared with the expert falls within the attorney client and work product privileges.
- The client is responsible for the expert's fees.

If you must request court funds for an expert, make the request *ex parte.* [*See* §6:05.] Otherwise, the information in your motion (*e.g.,* the expert's identity, the purpose in retaining him/her, the tests you expect to be performed) is public and unprivileged, and the prosecution could use it in questioning its expert or cross-examining the second expert you retain after rejecting the first. [*Pope,* 207 S.W.3d at 363-64 (prosecution allowed to redirect its DNA experts on whether they knew the non-testifying defense expert named in defendant's report and "Motion for Independent Examination of DNA" and whether that expert ever requested any additional testing of the DNA).]

[§§6:56-6:59 Reserved]

B. The *Daubert* Standard

§6:60 The *Daubert* Decision

In 1993 the Supreme Court jettisoned the "general acceptance" standard formulated in *Frye v. United States,* 293 F. 1013 (D.C. Cir. 1923), for a requirement that expert testimony be "relevant" and "reliable" to be admissible under FRE 702. [*Daubert v. Merrell Dow Pharmaceuticals, Inc.,* 509 U.S. 579 (1993).]

While the *Daubert* decision stated that expert testimony would be considered under the more "liberal thrust" of the Federal Rules of Evidence, it commissioned trial judges as "gatekeepers" to ensure that the jury hears only reliable expert testimony. The *Daubert* standard applies not only to scientific experts but to any witness who offers opinion testimony based on specialized knowledge or experience, as permitted by FRE 702. [*Kumho Tire Co., Ltd. v. Carmichael,* 526 U.S. 137 (1999).]

When *Daubert* was decided, many criminal defense attorneys anticipated that it would revolutionize practice in criminal cases. It was thought that *Daubert's* creation of a uniform standard of admissibility for both novel and established expert evidence [*see Daubert,* 509 U.S. at 593 n.11], and its emphasis on standards, empirical testing, and error rates would encourage courts to reexamine many of the generally accepted forensic "sciences" that had never subjected their methods to such scrutiny.

However, for the most part *Daubert* has been a disappointment to the defense bar. "[C]riminal defendants virtually always lose their reliability challenges to government proffers. And ... when criminal defendants' proffers are challenged by the prosecution, the criminal defendants usually lose." [National Academy of Science, *Strengthening Forensic Science in the United States: A Path Forward,* 69-71 (2009); D. Michael Risinger, *Navigating Expert Reliability: Are Criminal Standards of Certainty Being Left on the Dock?* 64 Albany L.Rev. 99 (2000).]

Nonetheless, you should pursue *Daubert* challenges against prosecution experts and be prepared to defend such challenges to your experts whenever possible, both because the challenges sometimes succeed, and because a *Daubert* motion can yield substantial pre-trial discovery.

§6:61   Factors to Determine Reliability

A trial court should consider five factors in deciding whether to admit expert testimony:
* Whether the expert's theory or technique can be (and has been) tested.
* Whether the expert's theory or technique has been subjected to peer review and publication.
* The known or potential rate of error.
* The existence and maintenance of standards controlling the technique's operation.
* Whether the expert's theory or technique has gained general acceptance or only minimal support within the applicable scientific community.

[*Daubert v. Merrell Dow Pharmaceuticals, Inc.,* 509 U.S. 579, 593-594 (1993).]

Some courts additionally consider:
* The relationship of the technique to methods which have been established to be reliable.
* The qualifications of the expert witness testifying based on the methodology.
* The non-judicial uses to which the method has been put.

The test is flexible, not rote; courts have discretion as to which factors to apply in a particular case. [*United States v. Mitchell,* 365 F.3d 215, 235 (3d Cir. 2004); FRE 702, Adv. Committee Notes.]

Reliability is required not only from the expert's methods in general, but in the application of the methods to the facts of this case to reach the expert's conclusion. [*General Electric Co. v. Joiner,* 522 U.S. 136 (1997); *see also Daubert v. Merrell Dow Pharm, Inc.,* 43 F.3d 1311 (9th Cir. 1995).]

Daubert rulings are reviewed under an abuse of discretion standard. [*General Electric Co. v. Joiner,* 522 U.S. 136, 142-43 (1997).] Furthermore, admissibility must be judged in the context of the particular litigation. [*Kumho Tire,* 526 U.S. at 151.] Therefore, one court's conclusions as to admissibility may not bind future courts. [Federal Judicial Center, *Reference Manual on Scientific Evidence* at 27-28 (2d ed. 2000) (available at www.fjc.gov).]

Reliance on unreliable data can render an otherwise qualified expert's opinion inadmissible. When "a trial judge analyzes whether an expert's data is of a type reasonably relied on by experts in the field, he or she should assess whether there are good grounds to rely on this data to draw the conclusion reached by the expert. ... If the data underlying the expert's opinion are so unreliable that no reasonable expert could base an opinion on them, the opinion resting on that data must be excluded." [*Montgomery County v. Microvote Corp.,* 320 F.3d 440, 448 (3d Cir. 2003) (excluding testimony that rested on an attorney's inaccurate summary).]

Likewise, the trial court should not admit opinions that rely on facts contradicted by the record. [*Elcock v. Kmart,* 233 F.3d 734 (3d Cir. 2000) (error to permit economist to base opinion as to plaintiff's lost wages on an annual income of over $12,000 when the plaintiff never earned more than $5,774 a year before her injury).]

§6:62   *Daubert* Hearings

A pre-trial *Daubert* hearing on the admissibility of the prosecution's expert testimony yields substantial benefits:
* You may succeed in excluding or limiting a substantial part of the prosecution's evidence.

- You obtain extensive discovery on the prosecution's evidence and theories.
- You lock-in the expert's testimony.

[*See* Mark A. Morse and Alexandra C. Gaugler, "Daubert Challenges to Experts in Federal Criminal Cases: An Overlooked Defense," 31 *Champion* 20 (July 2007).]

However, hearings are not for the asking. Trial judges have considerable discretion as to when and how to evaluate the admissibility of proffered expert testimony. [*Kumho*, 526 U.S. at 152.]

The ruling must be based on a sufficient factual record, but that record can be developed through judicial notice, consideration of other judicial opinions, affidavits, briefing, discovery, or an *in limine* hearing. No one method is necessary. [*United States v. Downing*, 753 F.2d 1224, 1241 (3d Cir. 1985). *See also Oddi v. Ford Motor Co.*, 234 F.3d 136, 154 (3d Cir. 2000) (refusing a hearing and excluding expert's testimony based on affidavits and a pre-trial deposition).]

The opponent of the evidence has the "burden of production" to indicate how the expert fails in explaining the reliability of his methodology or his conclusions. [*United States v. John*, 597 F.3d 263, 274 (5th Cir. 2010) (absent novel challenges, fingerprint identification evidence is sufficiently reliable to be admitted without a Daubert hearing); *Padillas v. Stork-Gamco, Inc.*, 186 F.3d 412, 418 (3d Cir. 1999); *United States v. Cline*, 188 F.Supp.2d 1287, 1294 (D.Kansas 2002) ("a *Daubert* hearing is unnecessary as the defendant is lodging only a general attack on fingerprint identification testimony and methodology"). *See also Reference Manual on Scientific Evidence* at 28-29 (opponent has a burden of making a prima facie of specific deficiencies in the proposed testimony before a hearing should be held).]

However, this does not require the opponent to proffer its own expert. [*Brooks v. Outboard Marine Corp.*, 234 F.3d 89, 91 (2d Cir. 2000) (expert on causation excluded because he did not examine the motorboat at issue, had failed to talk to witnesses to the accident or to reconstruct the accident).]

§6:63 Presence of the Jury

Generally, *Daubert* hearings, even if conducted mid-trial, should be conducted outside the jury's presence. [*Downing*, 753 F.2d at 1241.] However, the trial court has discretion to conduct the hearing with the jury in the box. [*See Elcock*, 233 F.3d 734, 751 (3d Cir. 2000) (noting that a *Daubert* hearing may take place before the jury).]

Thus, courts have relegated *Daubert* challenges to mid-trial, in-the-jury's-presence hearings where the challenge does not raise significant factual issues and the hearing promises to be a fairly brief cross-examination rather than a matter of presenting outside studies and opposing experts. [*See, e.g., United States v. Alatorre*, 222 F.3d 1098 (9th Cir. 2000) (Customs agent's testimony on the value of marijuana); *United States v. Nichols*, 169 F.3d 1255, 1263 (10th Cir. 1999), *aff'g United States v. McVeigh*, 955 F.Supp. 1278 (D. Colo. 1997) (even though the government consented to a pre-trial hearing, the trial court properly rejected the defense request for such a hearing on admissibility of forensic explosives testimony where the testimony depended on "well-known techniques routinely used by chemists"; voir dire in the jury's presence was sufficient).]

Nonetheless, you have strong arguments why a *Daubert* hearing, at least one presenting a substantial challenge, should take place (1) outside the jury's presence, and (2) pre-trial.

The hearing may entail a probing of the particulars of how the expert arrived at his conclusion, an inquiry that risks "boring or turning off" the jury. Further, once the expert explains his method and underlying hypotheses, the opposing party's experts should have the opportunity to go back to the field or the lab and test the hypotheses and attempt to duplicate the expert's results. [*See Elcock*, 233 F.3d at 747 (giving these reasons for the advisability of pre-trial hearings).] You also may cite the need to prevent the jury from hearing prejudicial and inadmissible foundational evidence. [*United States v. Hermanek*, 289 F.3d 1076, 1095 n.7 (9th Cir. 2002).]

§6:64 The *Daubert* Expert

A *Daubert* expert is one retained to testify to the inadequacies of the opposing party's expert's methods and conclusions.

The trial court must consider such testimony at the *Daubert* hearing and also must allow the jury to hear it on the issue of the weight to be given the expert's testimony even where the *Daubert* challenge fails.

Such an expert need not be one who practices in the opposing expert's field. [*United States v. Velasquez*, 64 F.3d 844 (3d Cir. 1995) (permitting law school professor to testify to the inadequacies of handwriting experts).]

§6:65 Constitutional Issues

Use of unreliable evidence to decide guilt or sentence may violate the Due Process Clause or, in capital cases, the Eighth Amendment's prohibition against cruel and unusual punishment. [*United States v. Matthews*, 773 F.2d 48 (3d Cir.

1985) (due process clause); *Flores v. Johnson*, 210 F.3d 456, 458-64 (5th Cir. 2000) (Garza, J., concurring) (admission of expert psychiatric testimony on future dangerousness where the prosecution psychiatrist did not even interview the defendant may violate Due Process and the Eighth Amendment); *Hellums v. Williams*, 16 Fed. Appx. 905, 2001 U.S. App. LEXIS 17697 (10th Cir. 2001) (affirming district court's grant of habeas relief based on erroneous admission of testimony from psychologist that victim's allegations of sexual abuse were credible).]

Conversely, you should argue that the court's exclusion of your expert violates your client's constitutional right to present a defense. [*See, e.g., Stephenson v. State*, 226 S.W.3d 622, 627-28 (Tex. App. 2007) (exclusion of defense expert testimony on unreliability of eyewitness identification testimony violated right to present a defense and was not harmless error); *Hannon v. State*, 84 P.3d 320, 343-351 (Wy 2004) (exclusion of defense psychiatric testimony to explain that the combination of defendant's low IQ and interrogation techniques likely rendered the confession unreliable violated constitutional right to present a defense).]

[§§6:66-6:69 Reserved]

C. Specific Types of Experts

§6:70   General Points

Nearly every case presents a prosecution expert you must cross-examine or an opportunity to call an expert for the defense. Homicides always have pathologists; chemists are unavoidable in drug-trafficking and driving while intoxicated cases; ballistics experts will appear in every shooting case.

Review the caselaw, law reviews and professional journals for examples of creative defense uses of experts and trends in challenging on *Daubert* grounds certain prosecution experts.

§6:71   Modus Operandi Experts

Prosecutors often call witnesses, usually investigators, to describe how certain criminal schemes work in order in an effort to have the jury fit the defendant's conduct within those models of criminality. [*See generally*, Paul Gianelli, "Modus Operandi Experts," *Criminal Justice 60* (Fall 2005) (listing, *inter alia*, counterfeiting, bookmaking, prostitution, auto theft, telemarketing fraud, organized crime, and drug trafficking cases as ones in which such experts have been used).]

Your principal challenges here are (1) the expert's testimony does not fit the facts of your case, and (2) the testimony does not help the jury by explaining matters beyond its ken, but merely serves as a preliminary summation. A case agent's testimony that purports to give the background or an overview of the investigation may constitute improper lay opinion testimony that conveys hearsay from informants and cooperating witnesses. [*United States v. Flores-De-Jesus*, 569 F.3d 8, 19 (1st Cir. 2009) ("Absent a basis in personal knowledge; however, the overview witness may not offer substantive testimony about the nature of the conspiracy or the involvement of particular defendants. When a law enforcement witness "express[es] opinions as to defendants' culpability based on the totality of information gathered in the course of their investigation[ ]," *Garcia*, 413 F.3d at 211, these conclusory statements often involve impermissible lay opinion testimony, without any basis in personal knowledge, about the role of the defendant in the conspiracy."). *See also United States v. Meises*, 645 F.3d 5 (1st Cir. 2011) (agent testimony identifying the defendants as the buyers in a drug deal was reversible error as it violated both the rules against lay opinion testimony and the Confrontation Clause).]

§6:72   Defense Law Enforcement Experts

Consider calling retired police officers or academics to testify to propositions that might assist the defense (*e.g.*, the practice in drug-trafficking organizations to conceal the nature of the enterprise from low-ranking couriers; street-level drug dealers' stashing of their drugs in tree stumps, abandoned tires, etc.; and a drug cartel's violent methods to support a defense of duress). [*See State v. Nieto*, 761 So.2d 467 (Fla. App. 2000) (professor of international studies permitted to testify to cartel's methods).]

§6:73   Handwriting Experts

Appeals courts all have rejected challenges to the admissibility of forensic document examiners ("FDEs"). [*United States v. Crisp*, 324 F.3d 261, 270 (4th Cir. 2003) (surveying appellate decisions).]

However, trial courts, confronted with the lack of empirical testing to support this expertise, continue to entertain such challenges. A few courts exclude such testimony. [*United States v. Lewis,* 220 F.Supp.2d 548 (S.D. W.Va. 2002); *United States v. Saelee,* 162 F.Supp.2d 1097 (D. Alaska 2001).]

More often, courts will prohibit the document examiner from identifying the defendant as the author of the questioned documents and will limit the FDE to pointing out similarities between the defendant's writing and that on the questioned documents. [*See United States v. Oskowitz,* 294 F.Suppp.2d 379, 384 (E.D.N.Y. 2003) (surveying cases); *United States v. Hidalgo,* 229 F.Supp.2d 961 (D. Ariz. 2002) (thorough survey of the district court cases on all sides); *United States v. Rutherford,* 104 F.Supp.2d 1190 (D. Neb. 2000); *United States v. Hines,* 55 F.Supp.2d 62 (D. Mass. 1999).]

§6:74 Image Authentication Analysts

Image authentication experts claim that just by looking they can distinguish images of real children from digitally created ones. This expertise lacks any empirical support. [*United States v. Fabrizio,* 445 F.Supp.2d 152 (D.Mass. 2006) (excluding such testimony); *but see United States v. Lacey,* 569 F.3d 319, 324 (7th Cir. 2009) (rejecting *Fabrizio* and permitting lay jurors, unaided by expert testimony, to determine on visual inspection whether images were of real children).]

§6:75 Psychiatrists

Besides the obvious use of psychiatrists to support an insanity defense, the defense can use them to undermine the prosecution's case that the defendant had the necessary intent to commit the crime.

The following are examples of areas where psychiatrists might testify about a defendant's intent:
- Stubbornness of tax protestors in believing that their conduct complied with the law. [*United States v. Finley,* 301 F.3d 1000 (9th Cir. 2002).]
- Pseudologia fantastica (a disorder that leads to the making of false confessions). [*United States v. Shay,* 57 F.3d 126 (1st Cir. 1995).]
- Tendency to overlook important visual details (counterfeiting). [*United States v. Rahm,* 993 F.2d 1405 (9th Cir. 1993). *But see United States v. Mezvinsky,* 206 F.Supp.2d 661 (E.D.Pa. 2002) (psychiatrists not permitted to testify that bipolar disorder could have explained how defendant lacked intent to defraud; useful as a catalogue of arguments prosecution will make against such testimony).]
- Ability to cope with communication problems in interrogations (defendant's version of what was said during interrogation differs from agent's version). [*United States v. Vallejo,* 237 F.23d 1008 (9th Cir. 2000), as amended, 246 F.3d 1150 (2001).]

§6:76 Bite Mark Identification Experts

There has been some success in excluding such prosecution evidence of expert analysis of bite marks as unreliable. [*See* Elizabeth L. DeCoux, *The Admission of Unreliable Expert Testimony Offered by the Prosecution: What's Wrong With Daubert and How to Make It Right,* 2007 Utah Law Rev. 131 (2007).]

§6:77 Eyewitness and Confession Experts

There is a strong trend toward admitting defense expert testimony offered to educate the jury on the weaknesses of certain kinds of prosecution evidence, such as:
- Eyewitness identification. [*See Commonwealth v. Walker,* 92 A.3d 766, 783-84 (Pa. 2014) (46 states, the District of Columbia, and all federal circuits that have considered the issue, with the possible exception of the 11th Circuit, permit the admission of eyewitness expert testimony at the discretion of the trial judge); *United States v. Brownlee,* 454 F.3d 131, 141-44 (3d Cir. 2006); *Stephenson v. State,* 226 S.W.3d 622, 628 (Tex. App. 2007).]
- Confessions. [*Hannon v. State,* 84 P.3d 320 (Wy 2004) (surveying jurisdictions); *United States v. Hall,* 93 F.3d 1337 (7th Cir. 1997); but see Commonwealth v. Alicia, 92 A.3d 753 (Pa 2014)(refusing to permit expert testimony on false confessions as an invasion of "jury's role as exclusive arbiter of credibility").]

IV. FORMS

Form 6-1   Motion for Appointment of an Investigator

INTHE UNITED STATES DISTRICT COURT
FOR THE _____ DISTRICT OF _____

UNITED STATES OF AMERICA)	
)	
v.)	CRIMINAL NO.
)	***UNDER SEAL***
JW)	

DEFENDANT'S EX PARTE MOTION TO AUTHORIZE INVESTIGATOR

AND NOW, comes defendant, JW by his attorney, Thomas Farrell, and requests, pursuant to 18 U.S.C. §3006A(e)(1), that the Court authorizes use of an investigator to assist in preparation of this case and in support thereof avers as follows:

Defendant, JW, is charged with violations of the controlled substances statutes, 21 USC §841. He was found to be indigent, and the undersigned counsel was appointed pursuant to 18 U.S.C. §3006A (a)(2)(B) to represent him.

Defendant needs to locate and interview witnesses. I have contacted the investigative firm of Larry Wolf and Associates, and they have indicated that they are willing to investigate this case. Mr. Wolf is a retired City of Pittsburgh Police Officer who worked on many federal task forces. I and other attorneys have used him on other state and federal cases.

Mr. W is indigent, and his counsel is court-appointed under the Criminal Justice Act, 18 U.S.C 3006A. Counsel represents that this work is necessary for effective representation of Mr. W.

Counsel for Mr. W believes that the investigation fees in this case at the present time should not exceed One Thousand Dollars ($1000.00).

WHEREFORE, for the foregoing reasons, the defendant, JW, requests that this Honorable Court appoint Mr. _____'s firm to investigate this matter. A CJA 21 form is attached.

Respectfully submitted,
Thomas J. Farrell

IN THE UNITED STATES DISTRICT COURT
FOR THE _____ DISTRICT OF _____

UNITED STATES OF AMERICA)	
)	
v.)	CRIMINAL NO.
)	***UNDER SEAL***
JW)	

ORDER OF COURT

AND NOW, to-wit, this _____ day of _____, 20__, upon consideration of the foregoing Motion to Authorize Investigator, it is hereby ORDERED, ADJUDGED AND DECREED that said motion is GRANTED;

It is FURTHER ORDERED, pursuant to 18 U.S.C. §3006A(e)(1), that the Clerk's office shall seal this order and motion.

_____
BY THE COURT

Form 6-2   Motion for Appointment of a Psychiatric Expert

IN THE UNITED STATES DISTRICT COURT
FOR THE _____ DISTRICT OF _____

UNITED STATES OF AMERICA	)	
	)	
v.	)	No.
	)	
BW,	)	
	)	
Defendant.	)	

DEFENDANT'S EX PARTE MOTION FOR
THE APPOINTMENT OF A PSYCHIATRIC EXPERT

Defendant BW, by his undersigned attorney, respectfully move this Court pursuant to 18 U.S.C. §3599(f), and 18 U.S.C. §3006A (e)(1) for an order authorizing the expenditure by defendant of reasonable funds to retain and reimburse Dr. P of _____ University Hospital. Dr. P would examine defendant and offer testimony about neurological impairments defendant suffers, in support of the defenses outlined below.

Attached is an affidavit by defense counsel setting forth the need for this appointment.

Respectfully submitted,
Thomas J. Farrell
Attorney for Defendant

IN THE UNITED STATES DISTRICT COURT
FOR THE _____ DISTRICT OF _____

UNITED STATES OF AMERICA	)	
	)	
v.	)	No.
	)	
BW,	)	
Defendant.	)	

AFFIDAVIT

THOMAS J. FARRELL does depose and state:

I am the attorney representing defendant in this case. Defendant is charged in a five-count indictment with, inter alia, capital murder.

Defendant's medical and psychiatric records indicate that defendant suffers from neurological deficits, due in particular to a gunshot wound to the head.

I have contacted Dr. P, chair of the _____ University Hospital's Department of Neurology, to examine defendant. Dr. P is the co-author of "_____," Am. J. Psychiatry _____ (attached). I provided Dr. P with a summary of defendant's medical and psychiatric records and the police reports concerning the homicide.

Dr. P responded with the preliminary assessment contained in the attached letter of [Date]. As the letter indicates, Dr. P believes that defendant likely suffers "brain damage or neurological dysfunction contributing to his violent behavior." Dr. P concludes that further testing and examination of petitioner is necessary to determine his true neurological condition.

Dr. P's examination and testimony may strongly establish two mitigating factors–defendant's extreme mental and emotional disturbance, *see* 21 U.S.C. §848(m)(7), and his inability to conform his conduct to the requirements of the law, 21 U.S.C §848(m)(1). Defendant will be unable to develop and present these penalty phase defenses without the assistance of Dr. P.

Dr. P has agreed to set aside [Dates], to examine defendant. He estimates that the cost of this examination would be approximately [Dollar amount]. Additional funds will be needed if Dr. P is to testify at trial. His customary rate is [Dollar amount] per hour.

I declare under penalty of perjury that the foregoing is true and correct. Executed this _____ day of [Month, Year].

_____
Thomas J. Farrell

Form 6-3   Engagement Letter for Expert or Investigator

_____[Date]

[Address]

Re: Commonwealth v. Doe

Dear [Name]:

This letter will confirm our understanding regarding your retention by the defense in order to conduct investigative work in this case. The nature of the investigation involves utilizing legal and appropriate means to develop information which may assist in the above captioned case.

As we agreed, the purposes for which this engagement have been made and the substance of your review and analysis are confidential. Disclosure of any information relating to the purpose of this engagement and the substance of your work shall not be made unless and only to the extent specifically authorized by this law firm. For purposes of this engagement, you are an agent of this law firm as that term has been construed pursuant to Rule 26 of the Federal Rules of Civil Procedure; *Commonwealth v. Kennedy*, 876 A.2d 939 (Pa. Sup. Ct. 2005); and *Commonwealth v. Noll*, 443 Pa. Super. 602, 662 A.2d 1163 (1995), appeal denied, 543 Pa. 726, 673 A.2d 333 (1996). It is contemplated that your work will receive attorney work product protection to the full extent authorized by law. Furthermore, you recognize that any communications between us or members of this firm and you and your agents are protected by the attorney-client and work product privileges to the full extent authorized by law.

You will not prepare a written report of the results of your work unless specifically requested to do so by this firm. In the event such a report is prepared, it shall become the property of our law firm immediately upon its preparation, whether or not such report is complete, in the same manner and to the same extent as though such report had been prepared by our law firm, as will any other written or recorded material that you generate relating to your work under this agreement. You will not disclose any report or other material, its existence, its contents, or any results of your work or analysis to any other person or entity at any time without our prior written approval. Any and all documents or other information shown or otherwise made available to you in connection with your work shall remain the property of our firm. You will retain custody of such documents only to the extent necessary and for the period necessary to perform assignments pursuant to this engagement.

You will notify this firm immediately and prior to responding to a request by anyone to question you about the existence or results of your work, or to examine, inspect, subpoena, or seize any documents or records relating to your work. You will respond to such a request only at the specific direction of our firm or in compliance with the final order of a court of the highest appellate jurisdiction.

All information received by you and/or generated by you during this engagement and in connection therewith shall be safeguarded and kept strictly confidential so as to protect the attorney-client privilege and work product doctrine that attaches to such information. Any disclosure whatsoever will be made by you only upon express written waiver of the client (regarding attorney-client privilege) and our firm (regarding work product) or upon a court order following all rights of appeal. Unless otherwise authorized, all of the information relating to the client shall be deemed to be confidential client information and you have no authority to disclose any of this information to any third party.

You are retained as an expert consultant in this matter. You are not engaged to testify. If at some point your testimony is required, we will explicitly notify you of that change in status.

As we have discussed, although you are an agent of this firm, your fees and costs are the sole responsibility of Mr. Doe and will be paid by him. It is understood the Client will pay your usual hourly rate and has paid a retainer of $5,000 toward your fees. We request that you send your bills to us at the end of each month, and we will include your bill in our monthly invoice to the client.

If the terms proposed in this letter are acceptable, please indicate your agreement by signing in the space below. A duplicate original is enclosed for your records.

                              Very truly yours,
                              Thomas J. Farrell

Enclosure

ACCEPTED AND APPROVED:

_____
[Name]

Dated: _____

Chapter 7

SEARCH & SEIZURE

I.   GENERAL POINTS

§7:01   Current State of the Law

In recent years, search and seizure law, which is defined primarily by the Fourth Amendment and its state constitutional counterparts, has developed in ways especially unfavorable to defendants.

Courts have fixed reasonableness as the guidepost to search and seizure claims, and when there is a "war"–on drugs, on domestic violence, on gangs, on organized crime, on corporate crime, on pornography, on terrorism–little that the police do to the enemies in that war is adjudged unreasonable.

Nonetheless, the courts continue to protect certain zones of privacy from government intrusion, such as:
- Homes.
- Cars.
- Personal records.
- Medical information.
- Computer files.

What has emerged from this tension between metaphorical war and the yearning for privacy is one of the most complex areas of the criminal law, full of fact-specific rules, exceptions, and exceptions to the exceptions.

§7:02   The Defense Goals

The primary aim in claiming an illegal search and seizure is to suppress the evidence, because in many cases, such as drug or weapons possession charges, suppression will be fatal to the prosecution's case.

However, search and seizure challenges serve another purpose. Most searches are warrantless, and when the police lack a warrant, the prosecution has the burden of introducing evidence to prove that the search was legal. [*Katz v. United States,* 389 U.S. 347, 357 (1967); *United States v. Johnson,* 63 F.3d 242, 245 (3d Cir. 1995).]

In proving probable cause to believe your client committed a crime or to believe that evidence of a crime was in his possession or proximity, the prosecution must reveal some of the evidence it will use at trial to prove its case. Thus, the prosecution's allegations in its written response to the motion to suppress and the testimony at the hearing may serve as your best opportunity for discovery, especially in those jurisdictions without preliminary hearings.

§7:03   Begin With the Federal Constitutional Standards

When confronted with a search issue, particularly in a context with which you are unfamiliar, start with federal constitutional standards.

There are two multi volume treatises that are especially thorough and contemporary:
- Wayne LaFave, *Search and Seizure: A Treatise on the Fourth Amendment* (4th ed. 2004).
- Judge William E. Ringel, *Searches and Seizures, Arrests and Confessions* (2d ed. 2005).

Both treatises suggest state constitutional distinctions. Research these thoroughly, for in many areas of search and seizure law, state courts have extended greater protections to defendants under their state constitutions than the U.S. Supreme Court has under the federal constitution.

[§§7:04-7:09 Reserved]

II.   IDENTIFYING SEARCH AND SEIZURE CLAIMS

A. Establishing a Claim

§7:10   Checklist for Suppression Issues

To determine if you have a suppression issue, ask the following questions:
- Did the police stop or arrest your client? Anything taken from him or anything he said after the stop may be suppressible.
- Did the police take or inspect anything belonging to your client, such as wallets and belongings, bags and briefcases, drugs and guns, books and records and computers?

- Once they seized that item, did the police probe further by opening containers or files, either paper or computer?
- Did the police make any examinations of your client's body or any substance taken from his body, such as hair, blood or urine?
- Did the police search or seize your client's car or any car in which he was present?
- Did the police enter or search your client's home, the areas around his home, his place of business, or any other place with which he had anything more than a transitory connection (whether or not he was present at the time)?
- Did the police intercept or overhear your client's telephone conversations, mail or computer communications?
- Did the police use any extraordinary technology to monitor your client's activities or see into any space where he would have an expectation of privacy?

§7:11   Establishing a Search

A government intrusion constitutes a search when two conditions are present:
- The individual manifested a subjective expectation of privacy in the object of the challenged search.
- Society is willing to recognize that expectation as reasonable.

[*Kyllo v. United States*, 533 U.S. 27, 32 (2001).]

Establishing that the intrusion is a search is critical, for only if it is a search must there be some justification (either probable cause or reasonable suspicion) for it.

The police need no justification to:
- Approach an individual on the street and ask him questions, so long as there is no official compulsion to stop or respond. [*See Florida v. Royer*, 460 U.S. 491, 497 (1983); *Commonwealth v. Polo*, 563 Pa. 218, 224, 759 A.2d 372, 375 (Pa. 2000); *but see People v. Moore*, 6 N.Y.3d 496, 498, 814 N.Y.S.2d 567, 568, 847 N.E.2d 1141, 1142 (2006) (under New York law, a police officer must have "an objective, credible reason, not necessarily indicative of criminality" to make any noncustodial approach to an individual to request information).]
- Look into an open window. [*See United States v. Taylor*, 90 F.3d 903, 908 (4th Cir. 1996).]
- Shine a flashlight into a car from the outside. [*See Texas v. Brown*, 460 U.S. 730, 739-40 (1983).]

§7:12   Seizure of a Person

Seizure of a person occurs when under all the circumstances a reasonable person would have believed that he was not free to leave or to decline the officer's request and terminate the encounter. [*Florida v. Bostick*, 501 U.S. 429, 436 (1991); *Michigan v. Chesternut*, 486 U.S. 567, 573 (1988); *United States v. Mendenhall*, 446 U.S. 544, 554 (1980).]

As a Fourth Amendment matter, there must be some use of force or a show of authority to which the defendant submits. [*California v. Hodari D.*, 499 U.S. 621, 625-26 (1991) (no seizure when defendant fled and threw drugs to the ground upon seeing police approach and yell, "Stop"; seizure occurred when police tackled defendant). *But see Joseph v. State*, 145 P.3d 595, 604-05 (Alaska Ct. App. 2006)(citing decisions from 12 states that have rejected Hodari D. on state law grounds; "when the police, whether by physical force or by show of authority, undertake to restrain the freedom of a citizen, the principles of the exclusionary rule apply equally regardless of whether the police succeed in unlawfully seizing the person or merely attempt to do so.")]

The Supreme Court has listed four examples of circumstances that might indicate a seizure even where the person did not attempt to leave:
- The threatening presence of several officers.
- The display of a weapon by an officer.
- Some physical touching of the person of the citizen.
- The use of language or tone of voice indicating that compliance with the officer's request might be compelled.

[*United States v. Mendenhall*, 446 U.S. 544, 554 (1980).]

§7:13   Seizure of Property

A seizure of property occurs when there is some meaningful interference with an individual's possessory interests in that property. [*United States v. Jacobsen*, 466 U.S. 109, 113 (1984). *See generally Thirty-Sixth Annual Review of Criminal Procedure*, 36 Georgetown L.J. 12 & n.22 (2007) (collecting cases).]

Whether the use of sense-enhancing devices is a search depends on several factors, the most important of which is whether the device enables the police to gather information about the interior of a residence. [*See Kyllo v. United States*, 533 U.S. 27 (2001)(use of thermal imaging device to detect which portions of a residence threw off an unusual amount of heat and hence probably were the sites of marijuana grow rooms was a search requiring a warrant).]

Other factors include:
- Whether the technology is in general public use.
- Whether the technology yields information that otherwise could not be obtained without a physical intrusion into the home.
- The extent and breadth of the information gathered.

[*Kyllo*, 533 U.S. at 37-39.]

The Supreme Court recently resurrected the use of property rights to create Fourth Amendment standing and to define relatively minor intrusions into privacy expectations as searches requiring warrants and probable cause. In *United States v. Jones*, 132 S.Ct. 945 (2012), five justices ruled that placing a magnetic global positioning transponder onto the underside of a car which the driver borrowed interfered with his rights as bailee of the borrowed vehicle, and hence required a warrant. *Jones* signals that you should raise search issues wherever you can find that your client has some property right to exclude others, no matter how minor. For example, employees using employers' computers or apartment building residents in a building's common areas do not have exclusive control of the computer or area, but they do have a property right that entitles them to exclude the general public. A governmental intrusion or interference with that property right might constitute a search requiring probable cause and a warrant under *Jones*. [Compare *United States v. Correa*, 653 F.3d 187 (3d Cir. 2011) (holding, pre-*Jones*, that tenant has no expectation of privacy in building's common area).]

Another five justices in *Jones* ruled that twenty-four hour a day GPS monitoring for 28 days of a car's movements on public thoroughfares amounted to such a serious intrusion as to constitute a search under an expectation of privacy, not a property rights analysis.

Jones left many questions open, but courts have begun to answer some. At least one court has held that attachment of GPS to a vehicle requires a warrant supported by probable cause. [*Keeylen v. State*, 14 N.E.3d 865, 874 (Ind. Ct. App. 2014).]

Until recently, the law analyzed technology by analogy to simpler methods of surveillance: computers were like filing cabinets, global positioning devices ("GPS") like beepers or police surveillance. Legislatures and courts have begun to realize that the ability of such technology to closely monitor an individual's activities, associations and thoughts renders them qualitatively different and necessitates legal restrictions on their use. Thus, a number of courts have used state constitutions to deem the installation of GPS on a car a "search" requiring a warrant [*e.g., United States v. Jones*, 132 S.Ct. 945 (2012); *People v. Weaver*, 12 N.Y.3d 909 N.E.2d 1195 (NY 2009)] and legislatures have imposed restrictions on its use, ranging from a showing of relevance [*e.g.*, Utah Code Ann. §77-23a-15.5(3)(b); Minn Stat. §626A.37(1); Fla Stat. §934.42(2)(b)]; to one of reasonable suspicion [18 P.C.S.A. §5761(c)(4); Tex Code Crim. Pro. Ann. Art 18.21, §14(c)(5)]; to probable cause [S.C. Code Ann. §17-30-140(B)(2); Okla Stat., tit 13, §177.6(A); Haw. Rev. Stat. §803-44.7(b)]. Similarly, searches of computers can expose an enormous amount of personal information; therefore, warrants to search computers should include search protocols to avoid a general rummaging through all the personal information contained in the computer. [*See* §7:95.]

§7:14   Establishing Police Action

The first step in any suppression motion is to establish that there is some police action–a search or seizure–in need of justification.

In addition to the *Mendenhall* and *Kyllo* factors, emphasize the particular facts of your case that make the police action especially intrusive or overbearing, such as:
- The defendant's youth. [*See Kaupp v. Texas*, 538 U.S. 626 (2003) (seizure when 17-year-old awakened at home by father and six officers and taken shoeless and in his underclothes to police station).]
- His state of undress. [*Kaupp.*]
- The number of officers.
- The display of weapons. [*People v. Moore*, 6 N.Y.3d at 499, 847 N.E.2d at 1142 (2006) (display of weapons made encounter at least an investigative stop requiring reasonable suspicion).]
- Blocking the defendant's car. [*People v. Luedemann*, 222 Ill.Dec.2d 530, 559-60, 857 N.E.2d 187, 205 (2006) (reviewing cases).]

- A protracted encounter. [*See United States v. Place*, 462 U.S. 696, 707-710 (1983) (90-minute duration of detention of luggage elevated it from a *Terry* detention to a full-blown seizure requiring probable cause); *United States v. Angulo-Fernandez*, 53 F.3d 1177 (10th Cir. 1995) (officer's continued retention of driver's license and registration may convert consensual encounter to stop requiring reasonable suspicion of illegal activity).]
- The degree to which the police intrude into spaces society recognizes as private. [*Compare California v. Ciraolo*, 476 U.S. 207 (1989) (police unaided observation of defendant's fenced in marijuana field from a helicopter flying above 1000 feet, the navigable airspace as recognized by 14 CFR §91.79, was not a search), *with Commonwealth v. Oglialoro*, 377 Pa. Super. 317, 547 A.2d 387 (Pa. Super. 1988) (illegal search when police flew 50 feet above defendant's pole-barn and observed marijuana plants beneath its translucent roof; distinguishing *Ciraolo*).]

Bring attention as well to the efforts your client made to protect his privacy, such as:

- Password protecting the computer or files within it. [*See United States v. Slanina*, 283 F.3d 670, 676 (5th Cir. 2002), vacated on other grounds, 537 U.S. 802 (2002); *but see United States v. Cotterman*, 709 F.3d 952, 969 (9th Cir. 2013)(en banc)(in the context of a border search of a laptop, the existence of password-protect files on the computer contributed to reasonable suspicion to believe that there was child pornography on the computer; court distinguishes password protecting an entire device – as opposed to files within a device – because it is a basic means of ensuring that the device cannot be accessed by another if lost or stolen).]
- Constructing obstacles to a public view. [*See Commonwealth. v. Lemanski*, 365 Pa. Super. 332, 529 A.2d 1085 (1987) (observation of greenhouse attached to house from point 200 feet away by use of binoculars, when police had to find vantage point within shrubbery along property line, was a search).]

§7:15   Standing

The fact that a search yielded evidence that the prosecution intends to use against your client does not alone give your client "standing" to challenge the search and the admission of the evidence.

Before the court will grant a suppression hearing, the defendant must establish that he or she (and not someone else) had a legitimate expectation of privacy in the place searched or the item seized. [*Rakas v. Illinois*, 439 U.S. 128 (1978) (where passengers in car failed to assert ownership interest in car, rifle or shells found in it, they did not have standing to protest seizure of rifle and shells); *United States v. Padilla,* 508 U.S. 77 (1993) (there is no coconspirator exception to requirement of personal standing).]

Merely having an ownership interest in the property seized does not confer standing. [*Rawlings v. Kentucky*, 448 U.S. 98 (1980) (claiming ownership of drugs in a purse owned by a friend did not entitle petitioner to challenge the search of the purse); *United States v. SDI Future Health, Inc.*, 553 F.3d 1246, 1255-56 (9th Cir. 2009) (managerial control does not alone establish individual owner's standing to challenge search of company premises; must establish the area searched was given over to individual's exclusive use). *But see State v. Bruns*, 172 N.J. 40, 796 A.2d 226, 236 (N.J. 2002) (explaining New Jersey's broader standing rule, based on the state constitution, granting standing whenever the defendant "can demonstrate a proprietary, possessory, or participatory interest in the place searched or items seized").]

Standing presents a delicate problem for a defendant. At trial, you will want to distance the defendant from the drugs or gun or other incriminating evidence that the police seized. However, you will not get a suppression hearing unless you allege sufficient facts to establish standing.

Canny prosecutors will challenge standing with the aim of forcing the defendant to take the witness stand at the suppression hearing and admit that he possessed the incriminating item. While the prosecution cannot use the defendant's admissions in its case in chief at trial, the defendant might be impeached with them if he testifies on his own behalf at trial. [*See* §7:116.]

PRACTICE TIP:

Try to establish standing through witnesses other than your client. For example:

- The arresting officer's testimony that he saw the defendant in possession of the incriminating item or that the defendant stated that he borrowed a car from its rightful owner may be enough to establish standing. [*See United States v. Angulo-Fernandez*, 53 F.3d 1177, 1179 (10th Cir. 1995) (officer's testimony that defendant claimed during the stop that he borrowed the car from the rightful owner and that defendant produced a registration in that name sufficed to establish standing).]

- You might call other people to testify to the defendant's interest in the vehicle or premises. A friend or paramour, if not charged as a co-defendant, might be able to testify that the defendant slept several nights in the apartment, thereby establishing standing. [*Minnesota v. Olson*, 495 U.S. 91 (1990) (overnight guest had standing to challenge search).]

§7:16   Private Searches

The Fourth Amendment and its state counterparts prohibit only governmental intrusions. Therefore, the fruit of searches conducted by private parties can be used despite the unreasonableness of the intrusion. [*United States v. Jacobsen*, 466 U.S. 109, 113 (1984).]

However, the search must comply with Fourth Amendment standards when:

- The individuals act as instruments or agents of the government. [S*ee George v. Edholm*, 752 F.3d 1206, 1215 (9th Cir. 2014) (doctor's actions in performing an invasive rectal search attributable to the state where police gave him false information about the arrestee's medical condition to induce him to perform search); *United States v. Walther*, 652 F.2d 788 (9th Cir. 1981) (airport employee who had history of providing information to the DEA for money and opening packages and searching for drugs held to have acted as government agent; reviews cases); *Commonwealth v. Borecky*, 277 Pa. Super. 244, 249, 419 A.2d 753, 755 (Pa. Super. 1980) (officer had prior knowledge of and acquiesced in informant's search of home)].
- The officers join the private search while in progress. [*United States v. Knoll*, 16 F.3d 1313, 1320 (2d Cir. 1994) (prosecutor instructed individual who had burglarized lawyer's office to search further through documents taken).]

[§§7:17-7:19 Reserved]

B.   Abandonment

§7:20   Relinquishing the Privacy Interest

Actions indicating an intent to relinquish one's privacy interest in an item may amount to abandonment or forfeiture of one's Fourth Amendment interest in the item and the right to contest its seizure and search. For example:

- Leaving a gym bag in a public hallway. [*United States v. Thomas,* 864 F.2d 843 (D.C. Cir. 1989).
- Putting the garbage at the curb. [*California v. Greenwood*, 486 U.S. 35 (1988).]
- Throwing drugs to the ground when chased by the police. [*California v. Hodari D.*, 499 U.S. 621 (1991).]

However, entrusting a bag or item to another person or setting it down temporarily does not amount to abandonment. For example:

- Giving computer disks to another in a sealed envelope marked "confidential and private" was not an abandonment and did not authorize possessor to consent to search of the disk's contents. [*United States v. James*, 353 F.3d 606 (8th Cir. 2003).]
- Giving bag to store clerk and leaving store did not amount to abandonment. [*United States v. Most*, 876 F.2d 191, 197 (D.C. Cir. 1989).]

The government bears the burden of proving abandonment. [*United States v. Cofield*, 272 F.3d 1303, 1306 (11th Cir. 2001).]

Here, too, the Supreme Court's recent re-emphasis on using property rights to delineate Fourth Amendment rights may provide hope where there may have been none under prior law. Thus, putting items in the trash suggests an intent to relinquish one's privacy interests, but so long as the trash remains within the home's curtilage, the property owner retains a right to exclude intruders and a corresponding Fourth Amendment right to object to the warrantless search of the trash. [*United States v. Jackson,* 728 F.3d 367, 373-74 (4th Cir. 2013) (dicta).]

§7:21   Disclaiming an Interest

The police may testify that when they approached your client, he disclaimed any interest in his possessions. [*See United States v. Cofield*, 272 F.3d 1303 (11th Cir. 2001) (when approached, defendant took bags off his shoulders, put them down, began to walk away, and told police, "No, those are not my bags"; held, no seizure occurred).]

Such testimony, if believed, can be fatal to a suppression motion. Explore exactly what the police said and the circumstances:

- Sometimes the police enter an area (*e.g.,* a stopped bus) and ask generally to whom a bag belongs. They will take silence as the occupants' collective denial of any interest in the bag. Ask the police whether they saw your client in the area or on the bus at the time; passengers, including your client, may have disembarked and not yet reboarded, so they may not have heard the question.
- Try to establish that the abandonment resulted from some police illegality. The abandonment then becomes the fruit of the illegal official conduct, and the item would be suppressed. For example, the police detained your client without probable cause or reasonable suspicion before the act which might constitute abandonment. [*E.g., State v. Reichenbach*, 153 Wash.2d 126, 101 P.3d 80 (Wash. 2004) (abandonment involuntary where police stopped car, drew their guns and ordered defendant out with his hands up before he threw drugs to the floor). *See also United States v. Garzon*, 119 F.3d 1446 (10th Cir. 1997) (defendant did not abandon bag when he left it on the bus after illegal police order that all passengers disembark with their bags and parade them before drug-sniffing dog).]

§7:22   Dropsy Cases

Abandonment issues arise often in so-called "dropsy" cases, in which the police claim to observe your client sell or possess drugs or a gun and then throw it to the ground when the police approach. Once the police see the drop and recover the contraband, they have probable cause to arrest your client.

In dropsy cases, a suppression hearing can yield ample discovery. Since the suppression issue is whether the police had articulable and reasonable facts justifying their approach to your client, you will hear the whole prosecution case regarding what the police saw your client do.

However, the prosecution can avoid any inquiry into what the police observed if the court accepts the argument that the approach was not a stop and that your client abandoned any interest in the item, thereby leaving nothing (neither the stop nor the seizure) to suppress.

Your argument must be that the police seized your client when they approached him, and that the seizure caused your client to drop the drugs or gun so that the dropping is the suppressible fruit of the illegal seizure.

Some state courts accept that the approach is a seizure. [*Commonwealth v. Matos*, 543 Pa. 449, 672 A.2d 769 (1996) (police pursuit is a seizure under the Pennsylvania constitution).]

However, the United States Supreme Court says that the approach is not a seizure. [*California v. Hodari D.*, 499 U.S. 621, 625-26 (1991) (no seizure when defendant fled and threw drugs to the ground upon seeing police approach and police yelling, "Stop"; seizure occurred when police tackled defendant).]

Nevertheless, even in federal jurisdictions, you can avoid the *Hodari D.* holding if you can establish that the police did more than approach and yell, "Stop." For example: Did they lay hands on your client before he slipped away? Did they point or fire their guns at him?

[§§7:23-7:29 Reserved]

III.   SEARCH WARRANTS

§7:30   Basic Requirements

To obtain a warrant, law enforcement officers either must submit a written and sworn affidavit or provide sworn oral testimony demonstrating probable cause to believe a crime was committed and requesting to search the place and seize the item as evidence or instrumentalities of the crime or as contraband.

To establish probable cause, the affidavit's four corners must provide a "substantial basis" for the magistrate to find a "fair probability" that evidence of crime will be found at the location to be searched at the time it will be searched. [*United States v. Pavulak*, 700 F.3d 651, 660-62 (3d Cir. 2012).] Conclusory assertions generally will not suffice; the affiant must state facts which will enable the magistrate to discharge his duty to make an independent assessment of probable cause. [*Pavulak*, 700 F.3d at 662-63 (assertions that witnesses had seen defendant "viewing child pornography" of females between 12 and 18 years old did not establish probable cause).]

The warrant itself must specify with particularity the places to be searched and the items to be seized. [U.S. Constitution, Amend. IV.] It is common for the list of items to be seized to appear not on the warrant's face but in an attachment, but if this is the case, the list cannot be sealed and must be served with the warrant. [*United States v. Franz*, 772 F.3d 134 (3d Cir. 2014).]

A warrant will state the times and dates during which it may be executed. A copy and a receipt for the property seized must be left with the person from whom the property was seized. [*See* Fed.R.Cr.P. 41.]

Forms:
- **Form 7-1** Federal Search Warrant Based on Affidavit(s)
- **Form 7-2** Federal Search Warrant Upon Oral Testimony

§7:31   The Good Faith Exception

The United States Supreme Court has held that evidence seized in good faith reliance upon a warrant will not be suppressed. However, the Court noted four situations in which a warrant will not protect a search:

> Suppression therefore remains an appropriate remedy **[1]** if the magistrate or judge in issuing a warrant was misled by information in an affidavit that the affiant knew was false or would have known was false except for his reckless disregard of the truth. *Franks v. Delaware*, 438 U.S. 154 (1978). **[2]** The exception we recognize today will also not apply in cases where the issuing magistrate wholly abandoned his judicial role in the manner condemned in *Lo-Ji Sales, Inc. v. New York*, 442 U.S. 319 (1979); in such circumstances, no reasonably well-trained officer should rely on the warrant. **[3]** Nor would an officer manifest objective good faith in relying on a warrant based on an affidavit "so lacking in indicia of probable cause as to render official belief in its existence entirely unreasonable." *Brown v. Illinois*, 422 U.S. at 610-611 (Powell, J., concurring in part); *see Illinois v. Gates*, supra, 462 U.S. at 263-264 (White, J., concurring in the judgment). **[4]** Finally, depending on the circumstances of the particular case, a warrant may be so facially deficient–i.e., in failing to particularize the place to be searched or the things to be seized–that the executing officers cannot reasonably presume it to be valid. *Cf. Massachusetts v. Sheppard*, 468 U.S., at 988-991.

[*United States v. Leon*, 468 U.S. 897, 923 (1984).]

§7:32   Attacking Warrants

The good faith exception has made attacking searches conducted pursuant to a warrant more difficult. However, courts are willing to find some warrants so deficient that reliance upon them is unreasonable, or to rule that the police unreasonably exceeded the scope of a warrant. [*E.g., United States v. Zimmerman*, 277 F.3d 426 (3d Cir. 2002) (despite postal inspector's boiler plate allegation that "persons with a sexual interest in children may possess child pornography and keep it in their homes for extended periods of time," affidavit was so plainly lacking in probable cause to believe that child pornography would be found in defendant's house that reliance on it was unreasonable).]

Additionally, many state courts refuse to follow the good faith exception. [*E.g., Heien v. North Carolina*, 2014 US. LEXIS 8306, *33 & n.2 (U.S. 2014) (Sotomayor, J., dissenting) (counting 14 states that do not recognize a good faith exception); *Gary v. State*, 262 Ga. 573, 422 S.E.2d 426 (1992); *Commonwealth v. Edmunds*, 526 Pa. 374, 586 A.2d 887 (1991); *State v. Marsala*, 216 Conn. 150, 579 A.2d 58 (1990).]

§7:33   General Warrants, Particularity, and Overbreadth

Besides the necessity for probable cause, the Fourth Amendment requires that a search warrant "particularly describ[e] the place to be searched, and the person or things to be seized." The purpose of this language is to prevent general warrants that authorize law enforcement to rummage through a person's belongings at their unguided discretion. [*Andresen v. Maryland*, 427 U.S. 463, 478 (1976).]

This particularity requirement encompasses two distinct, but intertwined, concepts. "First, the warrant, as supplemented by any attached or incorporated supporting documents, must so clearly describe the place to be searched and the items to be seized and examined that officers can, 'with reasonable effort, ascertain' the place and those items 'to a reasonable degree of certainty.' [Particularity or Specificity] Second, the warrant must, to the extent reasonably possible, be drawn in such a way as to preclude seizures and searches not supported by probable cause." [Overbreadth] [*State v. Mansor*, 381 P.3d 930, 938 (Or. App. 2016). *See also United States v. SDI Future Health, Inc.*, 553 F.3d 1246, 1261, 1263-64 (9th Cir. 2009) (explaining the relationship between overbreadth and particularity/specificity as two aspects of the Fourth Amendment's "particularly" language).]

In other words, a warrant that authorizes search of "a Lenovo computer" lacks particularity because it does not specify the files to be searched. A warrant that lists many files by name or type, many of which lack any nexus to the probable cause established in the affidavit, might be particular, but it is overbroad. Since the two concepts overlap, raise both to avoid a waiver argument. [*See Wheeler v. State*, 135 A.3d 282 (Del. 2016) (suppressing results of a warrant for electronic devices as both overbroad and lacking in particularity); *see* §7:35, *infra*, on particularity and specificity.]

The search warrant affidavit may establish probable cause to believe that your client committed the crime under investigation, but if the warrant authorizes a search for items that lack a probable cause connection to the crime under investigation, it is impermissibly overbroad. [*United States v. SDI Future Health, Inc.*, 553 F.3d, 1263-64 (warrant's paragraphs authorizing seizure of "Documents relating to non-privileged internal memoranda and E-mail; . . . Documents relating to bank accounts, brokerage accounts, trusts; . . . Checking, savings, and money market account records, . . . [and] Documents relating to personnel and payroll records" were overbroad); *Commonwealth v. Grossman*, 521 Pa. 290, 297, 555 A.2d 896, 899-900 (1989) (holding that a warrant authorizing the seizure of "all files" in an insurance fraud investigation of a doctor was overbroad and that all evidence seized as a result of the deficient warrant should have been suppressed); *Commonwealth v. Orie*, 88 A.3d 983, 1008 (Pa. Super. Ct. 2014) ("warrant for the USB flash drive, while supported by probable cause to believe the flash drive contained evidence of criminal activity, was overbroad, in that the warrant sought "any contents contained therein, including all documents, images, recordings, spreadsheets or any other data stored in digital format" without limitation to account for any non-criminal use of the flash drive; also, a warrant for defendant's AOL account that sought all stored communications over a five-month period was overbroad); *Commonwealth v. Santner*, 308 Pa. Super. 67, 69 & n. 2, 76-77, 454 A.2d 24, 25 & n. 2, 28-29 (1982).]

A computer is not typically an instrumentality or evidence of a violent crime. [*See United States v. Turner*, 169 F.3d 84, 88-89 (1st Cir. 1999) ("aggravated assault is neither akin to so-called 'paper trail' crimes like bank or mail fraud, nor to possession of child pornography, wherein the suspect might be expected to retain evidence of the offense itself among personal papers or in a computer hard drive").]

It has become common for prosecutors to seek warrants for computers in all investigations, but since most defendants rarely plan violent crimes on their computers, challenge the warrant as overbroad if no specific allegations connect the computer to the crime. [*See, e.g., Santner*, 308 Pa. Super. At 82, 454 A.2d at 31 (noting that a practice of authorizing the seizure of all of the personal possessions and records of every suspected murderer, rapist or arsonist would be overbroad).]

§7:34   Officers' Experience and Expectations

Officers sometimes try to supply the missing nexus by an averment in the affidavit that in their experience as investigators of such types of crimes, they often find evidence of the crime in such a place–a home, or on a computer, for instance. Courts have become skeptical of such allegations especially when they are boilerplate with little connection to the facts of the case. [*See Zimmerman*, 277 F.3d at 433 n.4.]

You should consider consulting with an investigator or retired officer and determining if such an averment is merely fanciful. If so, consider a *Franks* challenge to the warrant. [*See Hervey v. Estes*, 65 F.3d 784, 789-91 (9th Cir. 1995) (officer's allegations about what his experience told him about the smell of a methamphetamine lab found to be false).]

§7:35   Particularity

Warrants must describe the places to be searched and items to be seized with particularity. "Particularity means that the warrant must make clear to the executing officer exactly what it is that he or she is authorized to search for and seize." [*United States v. SDI Future Health, Inc.*, 553 F.3d at 1260).] "To be sufficiently particular under the Fourth Amendment, a warrant must satisfy three requirements. First, a warrant must identify the specific offense for which the police have established probable cause. . . . Second, a warrant must describe the place to be searched. . . . Finally, the warrant must specify the items to be seized by their relation to designated crimes." [*United States v. Ulbricht*, 858 F.3d 71, 2017 WL 2346566 , *14 (2d Cir. May 31, 2017)(citations omitted).] "[T]he particularity requirement 'makes general searches ... impossible and prevents the seizure of one thing under a warrant describing another. As to what is to be taken, nothing is left to the discretion of the officer executing the warrant.'" [*United States v. Wecht*, 619 F.Supp.2d 213, 226 (W.D. Pa. 2009) (warrant authorizing seizure of "boxes (approximately 20) and contents containing private autopsy files" insufficiently particular).]

Compare the list of items for which the warrant authorizes seizure with the supporting affidavit's assertions about those items to ensure that the warrant was sufficiently particular. "Generic classifications in a warrant are acceptable only when a more precise description is not possible." [*United States v. Kow*, 58 F.3d 423, 427 (9th Cir. 1995).] The warrant should specify the crimes to which the evidence relates in order to avoid a general search. [*See Kow*, 58 F.3d 423 (warrant authorizing seizure of 14 categories of business documents and computers so overbroad that officers were unreasonable in relying upon it because warrant failed to specify crimes of which the items were evidence and affidavit lacked probable cause explaining the nexus between the crimes and the items to be seized).]

Neither the supporting affidavit (unless attached to the warrant as served) nor the searching officer's oral description of the items for which he is searching may remedy a lack of particularity in the warrant itself. [*Groh v. Ramirez*, 540 U.S. 551 (2004) (warrant authorizing search of blue two-story residence so general that officers did not act reasonably in relying on it; faxing more detailed application in support of the warrant to defendant's attorney the day after the search did not remedy lack of particularity); *but see United States v. SDI Health*, 553 F.3d at 1258 (affidavit may cure warrant's lack of particularity if the warrant incorporates it by reference and it accompanies the warrant while agents execute the search, even if it is not physically attached to the warrant); *State v. Mansor*, 381 P.3d 930, 934 n.10 (Or. App. 2016) (characterizing *Groh's* "attachment" requirement as a "broadly functional concept . . . , encompassing not only actual physical connection but also, more broadly, circumstances in which supporting documents are present and available for immediate reference when the warrant is executed.").]

Where the items to be seized "are books and the basis for their seizure is the ideas which they contain," a higher degree of particularity is demanded. [*Stanford v. Texas*, 379 U.S. 476, 485 (1965) (warrant authorizing seizure of books, pictures and other written instruments concerning the Communist Party of Texas failed particularity requirement). *See also United States v. Abrams*, 615 F.2d 541 (1st Cir. 1980) (suggesting that increased particularity also should be required in investigations of largely legitimate businesses; warrant authorizing seizure of records "which show actual medical services performed and fraudulent services claimed to have been performed in a scheme to defraud the United States and to submit false Medicare and Medicaid claims for payments to the United States or its agents; in violation of Title 18, United States Code, Section 1001" was overbroad).]

This increased exactitude applies most often to obscenity investigations. [*See New York v. P.J. Video*, 475 U.S. 868 (1986).] Nevertheless, you should argue for its application when computers are searched as well, because individuals store the most personal and private of writings, photographs, and thoughts. [*See generally* Amy Baron-Evans, *When the Government Seizes and Searches Your Client's Computer*, 27 Champion 18 (June 2003).]

§7:36   Unsealing Search Warrant Affidavits

The probable cause affidavit that the magistrate considered in issuing the warrant is a separate document. Often, it is not served with the warrant; rather, the prosecution obtains an order sealing it at least until an indictment issues.

The law on the target's and the public's right to unseal the affidavit is unsettled:

- Some courts have held that the First and Fourth Amendments erect a presumption in favor of unsealing, and the prosecution has the burden of showing a compelling need to continue the sealing and the absence of any less restrictive means to serve that need. [*See, e.g., In re Search Warrant (Gunn)*, 855 F.2d 569, 574 (8th Cir. 1988) (First Amendment right found); *In re Search Warrants*, 353 F.Supp.2d 584, 587-92 (D. Md. 2004) (basing right to access on Fourth Amendment).]
- Other courts hold that there is no right to access an affidavit, at least pre-indictment. [*E.g., In Matter of EyeCare Physicians of America*, 100 F.3d 514, 517 (7th Cir. 1996) (rejecting any Fourth Amendment right to access pre-indictment).

CAUTION:

The affidavit can be of great value. It often contains a comprehensive picture of the evidence against your client at the time the warrant was issued. However, think twice about moving to unseal the affidavit in any news-worthy investigation. Once the affidavit is unsealed, it becomes a public record, and the media can read and report any damning rumors and hearsay it may contain.

Form:
- **Form 7-3** Motion to Unseal Search Warrant Affidavit

§7:37   Expansion of the Good Faith Exception

The Supreme Court has extended the good faith exception past the limited situation of good faith reliance on a warrant. [*See Davis v. United States*, 131 S. Ct. 2419 (2011).] You must be prepared to argue in every case that the police conduct not only violated the Fourth Amendment, but that exclusion is necessary to deter similar future misconduct. [*E.g., United States v. Gray*, 669 F.3d 556 (5th Cir. 2012) (search warrant for protoscopy to detect and remove baggie of crack failed *Winston v. Lee*, 470 U.S. 753 (1985), compelling need test as there were other available means for obtaining this evidence, but upholds the search under the good faith exception), *vacated and remanded on sentencing issue*, 133 S.Ct. 151 (2012); *United States v. Davis*, 690 F.3d 226 (4th Cir. 2012) (ruling that warrantless extraction and testing of DNA from suspect's clothing was an unreasonable and illegal search, but refusing to apply the exclusionary rule); but see *Davis*, 690 F.3d at 277-81 (Davis, J., dissenting) (evidence indicated that violative police conduct was routine and systematic; therefore, suppression should have been ordered to deter it); *United States v. Edwards*, 666 F.3d 877 (4th Cir. 2011) (search incident to arrest for domestic assault became unreasonable when police, after opening arrestee's pants, shining flashlight down it and seeing baggie containing drugs wrapped around his penis, used sharp knife to cut the bag off; to deter such dangerous tactics, exclusionary rule should be applied).]

Some courts now limit application of the exclusionary rule to those cases in which "a reasonably well trained officer would have known that the search was illegal in light of all the circumstances," [*United States v. Katzin*, 769 F.3d 163, 171 (3d Cir. 2014)(en banc)], or where the officers "should have known" that their actions were unconstitutional [*id.* at 177]. If officers act with " a good faith belief in the lawfulness of their conduct that was objectively reasonable," suppression is unwarranted. [*Id.* at 173.] Certainly, reliance on binding circuit or state authority establishes good faith, but under some decisions, so too does reliance on the consensus of non-binding authority from other jurisdictions. [*Katzin, supra; see also United States v. Aguiar*, 737 F.3d 251 (2d Cir. 2013) (finding good-faith in absence of binding circuit precedent; surveys different approaches to good faith).]

Other courts maintain that only reliance on binding precedent, from the Supreme Court or the controlling appellate court, can establish good faith. [*See State v. Adams*, 409 S.C. 641, 763 S.E.2d 341 (S.C. 2014)(no good faith because the police actions violated South Carolina law); *State v. Mitchell*, 234 Ariz. 410, 418, 323 P.3d 69, 77 (Ariz. 2014)("When applying the *Davis* good-faith exception, courts generally agree that the authority must be binding in the jurisdiction where the police conduct occurred, and that reliance on the prevailing view among other jurisdictions falls outside the scope of *Davis*."); *United States v. Martin*, 712 F.3d 1080 (7th Cir. 2013)(*Davis* and the good faith exception are contrary to the usual rule of exclusion and should be confined to their specific facts until the Supreme court says otherwise); *United States v Sparks*, 711 F.3d 58, 63-64 & nn.3-4 (1st Cir. 2013) (surveying state and federal decisions).]

The good faith exception has been a barrier to obtaining suppression for warrantless searches of cell phones that pre-dated the decision in *Riley v. California*, 134 S.Ct. 2473 (2014), [*E.g., United States v. Garcia*, 2014 U.S. Dist. LEXIS 128207 (N.D. Cal. Sept. 12, 2014)(finding good faith and refusing to suppress because of local officers' reliance on binding state court precedent permitting the search, even thought the case ultimately was prosecuted in federal court; *United States v. Clark*, 2014 U.S. Dist LEXIS 86807 (E.D. Tenn. June 26, 2014(refusing to suppress); *United States v. Spears*, 2014 U.S. Dist. LEXIS 94968 (N.D. Tex. July 14, 2014)(same)] and for GPS installation and monitoring that pre-dated the Supreme Court's decision in *United States v. Jones*, 132 S.Ct. 945 (2012), [*see, e.g., United States v. Katzin*, 769 F.3d at 170 n.5 (surveying federal courts of appeals; with the Katzin decision, five courts of appeals hold that the good faith exception applies to pre-*Jones* GPS monitoring and that suppression is unwarranted)].

This is a complex and evolving area, so you should raise all non-frivolous arguments against application of a good faith exception, even if your jurisdiction's appellate courts have ruled otherwise, until the United States Supreme Court settles the issue. As challenging as the good faith decisions appear, they still place the burden on the prosecution to prove good faith and the objective reasonableness of reliance on warrants or precedent. [*United States v. Ganias*, 755 F.3d 125, 140 (2d Cir. 2014).]

The new good faith standards might expand the scope of cross examination available to the defense on a suppression motion, at least once a Fourth Amendment violation is established. Whether exclusion is appropriate depends on the officer's culpability - whether law enforcement "exhibited 'deliberate,' 'reckless,' or 'grossly negligent' disregard for Fourth Amendment rights . . . ." [*United States v. Franz*, 2014 U.S. App. LEXIS 21030, *19 (3d Cir. Nov. 4, 2014) (quoting *Davis v. United States*, 131 S.Ct. 2419, 2427 (2011)(in denying exclusion, the *Franz* court relied in part on subjective factors such as the officer's consultation with a prosecutor and that it was his first search warrant).]

Thus in *Ganias*, the seizing agents assured the defendant that they would search the seized mirror-images of his computer hard drives only for information relating to the companies identified in the warrant and would "purge" all other files once they completed their review. Despite these assurances, they retained the complete, unpurged hard drives for two and a half years until they obtained another warrant to search further. In ruling that exclusion was appropriate, the appellate court cited to the agents' statements that they "viewed the data as the government's property" and acted intentionally in retaining it. [*Ganias*, 755 F.3d at 140.]

[§§7:38-7:39 Reserved]

IV.   DEALING WITH THE SEARCH

§7:40   Advice During the Search

While it is relatively infrequent, a client may call you while a search of a home or business is underway and ask for your assistance. Do the following:

- *Calm your client down.* Assure him that the less he complains or interferes with the officers, the quicker and less painful the search will be.
- *Tell your client that he should not speak with the officers except to ask for a copy of the warrant and the inventory of what was seized.* Although the probable cause affidavit may be under seal, ask for it in case it is not. [*See* §7:36.]
- *Tell your client to send away the other occupants of the property–employees and family.* This will prevent the agents from interrogating and intimidating them during the search.
- *Have your client obtain as many business cards as he can from the agents and note the agencies involved.* Officers frequently wear windbreakers that announce in large letters their agencies: "FBI," "IRS," "State Police." Knowing which agencies are involved helps predict where the investigation is likely to go: Will it be prosecuted in federal or state court? Will it be only a fraud investigation, or will the investigation include tax violations? (Only the IRS can investigate federal income tax violations.)
- *Ask your client to put the supervising officer on the phone with you.* After introducing yourself and getting the officer's name and agency, politely instruct him that your client is represented and that any communications should go through you.
- *Get as much information as you can from the officer about the reason for the search, its objects, and how long it will take.*
- *Go to the search location, or send an associate or investigator.* Once there, cautiously and politely follow the officers and observe to make sure they do not exceed the warrant's scope and to prevent ransacking and destruction of the property. Remember, however, that you do not have a right to monitor the search and that officers imagine danger in every investigation, so your opportunity to observe lasts only as long as your diplomacy gains their indulgence.
- *Assert privileges.* Locate any attorney-client communications and ask the agents either not to seize those documents, to provide you copies, or to segregate those materials so that you can assert the privilege later. *See* §7-22, *infra.* Make a record of your request and the agents' response.

Whether you or your client should assist in the search by directing the officers to the items they are seeking is a delicate issue:

- If the search is for records routine in nature (i.e., tax records, patient files, financial records, indicia of residency such as credit card and utility bills) your client can prevent the ransacking of his home or business by directing the agents to the proper areas and files.
- If the search seeks items the knowing possession of which incriminates (i.e., large amounts of cash, weapons, pornography, narcotics) your client should not assist because to do so may constitute an admission that your client knowingly possessed the incriminating item.
- Your client should not use passwords to access computer files for the agents. Standard operating procedure is for the officers to copy computer hard drives on the spot and leave the computers.

§7:41   Post-Search Conclusions and Advice

You may draw some conclusions from the police decision to execute a search, particularly one supported by a warrant.

The investigation is mature and prosecution is likely.

To obtain a warrant, the police had to show probable cause to believe that evidence of a crime was to be found at the location, much the same standard to obtain an indictment or a bindover decision at a preliminary hearing. Thus, even putting aside whatever the police found, they likely have enough evidence to prosecute.

Further, a search entails a significant commitment of resources to execute the search and (particularly if voluminous records were taken) to sift through and analyze the items seized. The prosecution would not commit those resources unless it were likely to prosecute.

Finally, a search tips off the target that there is an investigation, so the police usually do not conduct one until after they exhaust covert investigative techniques, such as use of undercover informants, wiretaps, and interviews of witnesses unlikely to report back to the target. (Federal law does provide for a covert search with delayed notification. [18 U.S.C. §3103a.] However, such searches remain relatively rare.)

The police probably have informants.

To obtain a warrant, the police often need inside information about your client. The sources might be friends, associates or coconspirators. Keeping the affidavit of probable cause sealed even after the search's execution also suggests the desire to continue to conceal the existence and identity of undercover informants.

A common investigative technique is for the police to have informants call or contact the target to learn what he is saying about the investigation and what he might be doing to conceal evidence, obstruct the investigation or mount a defense. Informants often wear body wires during these discussions.

Likewise, the police might have a wiretap and will monitor closely the "buzz" among the targets the days after the search.

Therefore, you *must* instruct your client not to discuss the search or the investigation with anyone after the search. Have him report back to you about anyone who calls or contacts him to inquire about the search or investigation in the days after the search.

[§§7:42-7:49 Reserved]

V.   SPECIFIC TYPES OF SEARCHES

A. *Terry* Stops

§7:50   Investigative Stop Allowed on Reasonable Suspicion

Under *Terry v. Ohio*, the police may make an investigative stop, short of a full arrest, when they have reasonable suspicion, based upon "specific and articulable facts ... taken together with rational inferences from those facts," that criminal activity is afoot. [*Terry v. Ohio*, 392 U.S. 1, 21 (1968).]

Since a *Terry* stop is less intrusive than a full arrest, the reasonable suspicion that must support it is less than the probable cause needed for a full arrest.

Along with the stop, the police may conduct a brief pat-down for weapons to protect themselves. For the stop and its accompanying investigative and protective measures to remain reasonable, the police "must employ 'the least intrusive means reasonably available' to effect their legitimate investigative purposes." However, where the situation involves weapons, these means may be as intrusive as drawing firearms and handcuffing the detainee. [*United States v. Newton*, 369 F.3d 659, 674 (2d Cir. 2004) (quoting *Florida v. Royer*, 460 U.S. 491, 500 (1983)).]

While reasonable suspicion is a forgiving standard, it may be lacking when police rely on an anonymous tip of criminal activity. If the tip is truly anonymous, its assertion of criminality must contain indicia of reliability, usually in the way of detail that the police corroborate. [*United States v. Nelson*, 284 F.3d 472, 477 (3d Cir. 2002).]

§7:51   Analyze the Details of the Tip

Pick apart the tip:
*   Were the details, even if they turned out to be accurate, ones that could have been observed by anyone (*e.g.*, that a man meeting the defendant's general description was on a busy corner) in contrast to details that would be known only to someone who had inside knowledge of the criminal activity? [*See Florida v. J.L.,* 529 U.S. 266 (2000) (tip that a young black male standing at a particular bus stop and wearing a plaid shirt was carrying a gun did not establish reasonable suspicion to frisk young black man in plaid shirt found at that bus stop).]
*   Did facts alleged in the tip, particularly predictions, turn out to be false? [*See Alabama v. White*, 496 U.S. 325 (1990) (tip found to be reliable where police independently corroborated significant aspects of informer's predictions).]

§7:52   Analyze the Police Action

You want to convince the court that what happened to your client was a full-blown arrest, not a *Terry* stop, because to arrest, the police must meet the greater burden of showing probable cause to believe a crime was committed and that your client committed it. However, the line between a *Terry* stop and an arrest is not clear, and courts have held that police actions as intrusive as ordering a person out of a car at gunpoint and handcuffing him do not constitute an arrest. [*Compare United States v. Heath,* 259 F.3d 522, 530 (6th Cir. 2001) (police action pulling defendant from car with guns drawn and handcuffing him was reasonable under circumstances of drug investigation and did not convert investigative stop into arrest) *with Longshore v. State,* 399 Md. 486, 924 A.2d 1129 (Md. 2007) (person was under arrest for Fourth Amendment purposes when he was asked to step out of his car and placed in handcuffs, when no special circumstances existed to justify the handcuffs; however, use of handcuffs does not always convert stop into arrest); *United States v. Robertson,* 833 F.2d 777, 781-82 (9th Cir. 1987) (unreasonable for 7 to 10 officers to confront woman at gunpoint, tell her to freeze, and detain her for 5 to 15 minutes because no indication she was armed or dangerous).]

The courts consider the reasonableness of the police action under the totality of the circumstances, including "factors such as the transportation of the detainee to another location, significant restraints on the detainee's freedom of movement involving physical confinement or other coercion preventing the detainee from leaving police custody, and the use of weapons or bodily force." [*United States v. Lopez-Arias,* 344 F.3d 623, 627 (6th Cir. 2003) (defendants under arrest when "they were (1) stopped by four DEA agents brandishing firearms, (2) handcuffed, (3) placed into the backseats of separate DEA vehicles, (4) transported from the scene of the stop, (5) read their Miranda rights, and (6) questioned").]

Other factors are:

- The detention's duration. [*See United States v. Place,* 462 U.S. 696, 707-710 (1983) (90-minute detention of luggage elevated the stop to a full seizure requiring probable cause).]
- The relation of the police action to the reason for the stop. This means that the more dangerous the crime under investigation, the more forcefully the police may act to protect themselves without exceeding the bounds of a *Terry* stop. [*See Heath; Robertson; Newton.*]

A *Terry* stop permits the officers only to conduct a relatively brief patdown for weapons. In contrast, a lawful arrest authorizes a contemporaneous search of the arrestee's person and the area within his immediate control, including any containers, regardless of whether the police have any reason to suspect that evidence or weapons lie within that area or container. [*United States v. Osife,* 398 F.3d 1143 (9th Cir. 2005).]

[§§7:53-7:59 Reserved]

B. Automobile Stops and Searches

§7:60   Automobile Stop Rules

Cars receive scant protection under the Fourth Amendment. "In light of the "automobile exception" to the usual search warrant requirement, it is difficult to pick a worse place to conceal evidence of a crime than an automobile. The Supreme Court has interpreted—and reinterpreted—the automobile exception so expansively that the Court essentially has obviated the requirement that the government obtain a warrant to search a vehicle provided it has probable cause to believe that the vehicle contains evidence of a crime." [*United States v. Donahue,* 764 F.3d 293 (3d Cir. 2014); *see also United States v. Mosley,* 454 F.3d 249, 252 (3d Cir. 2006) ("When one peruses the traffic-stop suppression caselaw, one is struck by how rarely a traffic stop is found to have been illegal. ... Courts give considerable deference to police officers' determinations of reasonable suspicion, ... and the cases are steadily increasing the constitutional latitude of the police to pull over vehicles.").]

The police may stop a car upon reasonable suspicion to believe a traffic offense has been committed. [*Berkemer v. McCarty,* 468 U.S. 420, 439 (1984). *But see Commonwealth v. Gleason,* 567 Pa. 111, 122, 785 A.2d 983, 989 (Pa. 2001) (requiring probable cause to believe driver committed a traffic violation).]

Vehicle stops at sobriety checkpoints or roadblocks constitute Fourth Amendment seizures. [*Michigan Dept. of State Police v. Sitz,* 496 U.S. 444, 450 (1990).] Random, discretionary stops to check automobile registrations and licenses without reasonable suspicion or probable cause violate the Fourth Amendment. [*Delaware v. Prouse,* 440 U.S. 648 (1979); *United States v. Orozco,* No. 15-10385, 2017 WL 2367983 (9th Cir. June 1, 2017).] Checkpoints that have a primary purpose other than the detection of evidence of ordinary criminal wrongdoing and that operate under rules that eliminate the unconstrained exercise of discretion, are permissible without reasonable suspicion under the administrative or special purpose search rules. [*Michigan Dept of State Police v. Sitz,* 496 U.S. 444 (1990)(approving sobriety checkpoints); *United States v. Richardez-Fuerte,* 428 U.S. 543 (1976) (upholding immigration checkpoints); *United States v. Orozco,* — F.3d —, 2017 WL 2367983 (9th Cir. June 1, 2017) (safety inspections of tractor-trailers permissible); *but see City of Indianapolis v. Edmond,* 531 US. 32 (2000)(holding that a suspicion-less drug interdiction checkpoint had as its primary purpose ordinary crime control and therefore violated Fourth Amendment).]

Of course, even administrative stops sometimes yield evidence of a crime. Where, however, the prosecution seeks to justify a suspicionless stop and search as an administrative stop, the defense can invalidate the stop and suppress the evidence if it can show that the stop was a pretext concealing an investigatory police motive. [*Orozco, supra,* *5.] In the case of administrative and special needs searches the usual rule that an officer's subjective intent is irrelevant does not apply [*Id.*].

§7:61   Police Authority to Search

Upon stopping a car, police may:
- Ask for the driver's registration and license and ask identifying questions. [*Berkemer v. McCarty,* 468 U.S. 420, 439 (1984).]
- Shine a flashlight inside and seize whatever they see in plain view. [*See Texas v. Brown,* 460 U.S. 730, 739-40 (1983).]
- Move papers to look at the vehicle identification number; and order the drivers and passengers out of the vehicle. [*Maryland v. Wilson,* 519 U.S. 408 (1997).]

Stopping a vehicle and ordering its occupants out does not, without more, authorize a frisk or pat-down of them. [*United States v. Powell,* No. 08-4696, 2011 U.S. App. LEXIS, 2011 WL 5517347 (4th Cir. Nov. 14, 2011).] The occupant's suspicious behavior, such as furtive movements and refusal to obey the officer's orders, may justify a pat-down of the vehicle's occupants. [*United States v. Moorefield,* 111 F.3d 10, 14-15 (3d Cir. 1997).]

The Supreme Court recently re-wrote the rules on the permissible scope of a search incident to the arrest of a recent occupant of an automobile. Under the rules of *New York v. Belton,* 453 U.S. 454 (1981), and *Thornton v. United States,* 541 U.S. 615 (2004), the arrest of a car's recent occupant justified a search of the entire passenger compartment and any containers found therein, even if the occupant was arrested outside the car, handcuffed and removed from any access to the car. In *Arizona v. Gant,* 129 S.Ct. 1710 (2009), the Supreme Court effectively overruled these cases and held that an officer may "search a vehicle incident to a recent occupant's arrest only when the arrestee is unsecured and within reaching distance of the passenger compartment at the time of the search" or when it is "reasonable to believe evidence relevant to the crime of arrest might be found in the vehicle." [*Gant,* 129 S.Ct. at 1718-19.] Since the police usually will handcuff and secure arrestees so they cannot access the car, the first prong of *Gant*'s search-incident-to-arrest exception, what some courts call the "officer-safety" justification [see *United States v. Polanco,* 634 F.3d 39, 42 (1st Cir. 2011)], seldom will justify auto searches.

The second justification, the "evidence-preservation" justification [*Polanco,* 634 F.3d at 42], seldom will apply when the arrest is for a traffic offense (because the auto is unlikely to conceal evidence relevant to the crime). [*Gant,* 129 S.Ct. at 1719 n.4.] Whether it applies to arrests for other offenses depends on the nature of the offense and whether it is "reasonable"–a much lower standard than probable cause–to believe that evidence of the offense will be found in the car [*Polanco,* 634 F.3d at 43]. Where the offense is a possession of drugs or weapons, the police generally will have reason to search the car and everything in it. [*Wyoming v. Houghton,* 526 U.S. 295 (1999) (upholding search of front seat passenger's purse found on back seat where driver was arrested for having syringe in his breast pocket).]

However, if the police issue the driver a citation for a traffic offense rather than arresting him, they may not search the car or frisk the driver, absent articulable reasonable suspicion that the driver poses a danger. [*Knowles v. Iowa,* 525 U.S. 113 (1998) (improper to search under passenger's seat; marijuana found there suppressed).]

If the stop is for a traffic violation, the resulting detention must be "reasonably related in scope to the circumstances that justified the stop in the first place." Actions or questioning that are unrelated to the stop's justification and that unduly prolong it may render the detention unreasonable and any evidence gained during the period of delay suppressible. [*United States v. Valenzuela,* 494 F.3d 886, 888 (10th Cir. 2007) (but holding that officer's questions as to whether car's occupants had weapons was reasonable measure for officer's safety and brief next question, "May I search?" did not unreasonably prolong the detention).]

If furnished with probable cause to believe that the automobile contains evidence of a crime, the police may forego a warrant and search it and any containers within it that may hold the evidence. [*Maryland v. Dyson,* 527 U.S. 465 (1999) (no exigency required to forego a warrant for a car search); *California v. Acevedo,* 500 U.S. 565 (1991); *United States v. Donahue,* 764 F.3d 293 (3d Cir. 2014)(since fugitives often carry false identification documents, warrantless search of car in which he was arrested permissible)] Delay between seizure of the vehicle and its search is immaterial. [*Donahue,* 764 F.3d at 300-01 (automobile exception permitted warrantless search five days after seizure and impoundment).]

§7:62   Challenge the Reasonable Suspicion or Probable Cause

Faced with the automobile stop and search rules, your best approach to an automobile search is to challenge the reasonable suspicion for the stop or the probable cause to believe the car contained evidence or contraband.

Remember, even if your client is a passenger without any ownership interest in the car, a car stop seizes him as well, and he has standing to suppress anything seized from within the car or from his person as a result of the stop. [*See Brendlin v. California*, 127 S.Ct. 2400 (2007). *See also* §7:15.]

[§§7:63-7:64 Reserved]

C. Search Incident to Arrest

§7:65   Search Incident to Arrest

Upon arrest, police officers lawfully may search the person arrested and "the area 'within his immediate control'–construing that phrase to mean the area from within which he might gain possession of a weapon or destructible evidence." [*Chimel v. California*, 395 U.S. 752, 763 (1969).] Opportunities to suppress seized evidence arise when the police search bags or containers incident to arrest. Courts have begun to apply the rule of *Arizona v. Gant*, 129 S.Ct. 1710 (2009) (*see* §7:61, *supra*), which forbids searches of the "grab area" if the suspect already has been handcuffed and his ability to "grab" eliminated, from automobile searches to other searches-incident-to-arrest. Thus, the *Chimel* rule permits searches only of the arrestee's person and any areas or containers from which it was reasonably possible that the suspect could access a weapon or destructible evidence, whether the item searched was the interior of a car or some other container. [*United States v. Shakir*, 616 F.3d 315 (3rd Cir. 2010).] This rules does not forbid all searches of bags or containers once the arrestee is handcuffed if the arrestee or bystanders arguably could access the bag. [*Shakir, supra* (upholding search of bag dropped right next to arrestee in a hotel lobby when many people milled around; noting that even a handcuffed person can access weapons within his grab area).]

Your task is to demonstrate to the court that your client was secured–by handcuffs, or, better, yet, by removal to a police vehicle–and the bag or container was inaccessible to him or confederates and bystanders once he was arrested.

In *Riley v. California*, 135 S.Ct. 2473, 2490-93 (2014), the Supreme Court held that the heightened privacy interest in digital devices is of such magnitude that the search incident to arrest exception does not apply to them, and "officers must generally secure a warrant before conducting such a search." [*Id.* at 2485.] The *Riley* decision involved both a smartphone and a less sophisticated flip cell phone, but the Court included both in its holding. The same rule is sure to apply to laptops, tablets, and personal digital assistants seized from an arrestee. Case specific facts could justify exceptions, but the only one the Court recognized was the exigent circumstances exception where facts give reason to believe that evidence might be destroyed or persons harmed if the device is not searched immediately and without a warrant. [*Id.*at 2493-94.]

[§§7:66-7:69 Reserved]

D. Inventory Searches

§7:70   Inventory Search Rules

Upon an arrest or seizure, the police may inventory personal effects, cars and seized material if the inventory "is part of a bona fide police routine administrative caretaking function [and] ... not ... a ruse for a general rummaging in order to discover incriminating evidence." [*United States v. Lage*, 183 F.3d 374, 380 (5th Cir. 1999).]

The inventory must be "conducted pursuant to standardized regulations and procedures that are consistent with (1) protecting the property of the vehicle's driver, (2) protecting the police against claims or disputes over lost property, and (3) protecting the police from danger." [*United States v. Lage*, 183 F.3d 374, 380 (5th Cir. 1999). *See South Dakota v. Opperman*, 428 U.S. 364, 369 (1976).]

§7:71   Attacking an Inventory Search

Attack an inventory search on two grounds:
*   Question the officers on the existence and documentation of inventory procedures and the extent to which they are standardized. [*See, e.g., Florida v. Wells*, 495 U.S. 1, 4-5 (1990) (where police had no standard procedure with respect to the opening of closed containers found during inventory searches, marijuana found in a closed suitcase was properly suppressed); *Commonwealth v. Thurman*, 2005 PA Super. 126, 872 A.2d 838

(2005) (town had no legislation authorizing officer to tow and impound vehicle when registration was expired; therefore, drugs found during inventory search of car were suppressed).]
- Question whether the inventory served the purpose of protecting the property or the police. [*See United States v. Best*, 135 F.3d 1223, 1225 (8th Cir. 1998) (searching behind car door panel was not a standard procedure and did not protect recognized interests).]

[§§7:72-7:79 Reserved]

E. Plain View

§7:80   Plain View Search Rules

"Under the plain view doctrine, if the sight of an object gives the police probable cause to believe that it is the instrumentality of a crime, the object may be seized without a warrant if three conditions are met: (1) the police are lawfully in the position from which the object is viewed; (2) the police have lawful access to the object; and (3) the object's incriminating nature is immediately apparent." [*People v. Diaz*, 81 N.Y.2d 106, 110, 595 N.Y.S.2d 940, 943, 612 N.E.2d 298, 301 (1993); *see also Horton v. California*, 496 U.S. 128, 136-37 (1993); *United States v. Murphy*, 69 F.3d 237, 241 (8th Cir. 1995).]

"Immediately apparent" means that the viewing of the object must create probable cause to believe it is contraband without further search of the object. [*Minnesota v. Dickerson*, 508 U.S. 366, 375 (1993); *Arizona v. Hicks*, 480 U.S. 321 (1987) (rejecting position that reasonable suspicion suffices; officers could not move stereo turntable to look at serial number to confirm suspicions).]

In addition, if the police violate the Fourth Amendment to reach their plain view vantage point by violating the Fourth Amendment, the plain view exception does not save the search. [*Horton*, 496 U.S. at 136.]

Some states add the requirement that the view be inadvertent, meaning that the officer did not expect or seek to find the item, a requirement that the United States Supreme Court rejected in *Horton*. [*See, e.g., State v. Cuntapay*, 104 Hawaii 109, 85 P.3d 634 (2004); *Commonwealth v. Balicki*, 436 Mass. 1, 762 N.E.2d 290 (2002).]

§7:81   Attacking a Plain View Search

Challenge plain view in two ways:
- How did the police put themselves in a position to view the item? They may have entered into an area where they had no right to be, such as by looking through photo albums when they are searching for a firearm, or by looking into a car they illegally stopped.
- Was the incriminating nature of the item immediately apparent? If it was not, and the police inspected the item in an intrusive manner or conducted more investigation after seizing the item to determine its incriminating character, the plain view exception does not apply. [*E.g., Minnesota v. Dickerson*, 508 U.S. 366 (when officer felt a hard object in defendant's pocket in a valid *Terry* stop and knew it was not a weapon, he could not remove the object to confirm his suspicion that it was crack cocaine); *Hicks*, 480 U.S. 321 (officer's actions in moving stereo turntable to see its serial number constituted search that needed probable cause; therefore, seizure of a computer, when probable cause of its incriminating nature become apparent only upon seeing the serial number, could not be justified under plain view doctrine).]

[§§7:82-7:89 Reserved]

F. Search of Computers

§7:90   A Computer Is More Than Another Container

Computer searches can present complications, often to your benefit.

In the past, courts analyzed the searches of computers and other digital devices by analogy to non-digital objects, in particular, briefcases, diaries or file cabinets. In 2014, however, the Supreme Court decisively rejected all analogies to physical containers and records in *Riley v. California*, 135 S.Ct. 2473, 2490-93 (2014) (holding that any search of a cell phone or smartphone, even incident to arrest, requires a warrant). "Indeed, a cell phone search would typically expose to the government far *more* than the most exhaustive search of a house: A phone not only contains in digital form many sensitive records previously found in the home; it also contains a broad array of private information never found in a home in any form – unless the phone is." [*Id.* at 2491. *See also United States v. Ganias*, 755 F.3d 125, 135 (2d Cir. 2014)(computer hard drive is "akin to a residence in terms of the scope and quantity of private information it may contain.").]

Because the variety and extent of information, much of it highly personal, commonly stored on computers, "justifies the highest expectation of privacy" [*United States v. Stierhoff*, 477 F.Supp.2d 423, 442 (D.R.I. 2007)], you should argue that searches must meet high standards for precision and specificity. [*See, e.g., id.* (holding that consent to search computer folder labeled "Creative Writing" did not permit IRS agents to open folder labeled "Offshore."); *United States v. Galpin*, 720 F.3d 436, 447 (2d Cir. 2013)("This threat [of over-inclusiveness] demands a heightened sensitivity to the particularity requirement in the context of digital searches.").] The search of each path, directory, folder and file name within the computer or smart phone is an independent search; demand that the police show probable cause and a warrant, or justification for the lack of a warrant, for each intrusion. [*E.g., State v. Mansor*, 381 P.3d 930 (Or. App. 2016) (Holding that warrant authorizing search and seizure of computers without specifying the particular files within was impermissibly overbroad: "we believe that for purposes of the constitutional particularity requirement, personal electronic devices are more akin to the 'place' to be searched than to the 'thing' to be seized and examined. Concomitantly, that requires that the search of that 'place' be limited to the 'thing(s)' – the digital data – for which there is probable cause to search.")]

Pre-*Riley*, many courts treated computers as filing cabinets containing many discrete file folders and documents and demand that the police show probable cause and a warrant, or justification for the lack of a warrant, to search each path, directory, folder and file name within the computer. [*See United States v. Stierhoff*, 477 F.Supp. 423 (D.R.I. 2007); *In re Grand Jury Subpoena*, 846 F.Supp. 11 (S.D.N.Y. 1994).]

Treating a computer as just another container has its disadvantages: warrants to search for a particular item, such as a document or photograph, generally permit search of any place or container within the area that might contain the item. Recognizing that computers are unique in the volume and variety of personal information they may hold, and that "[s]earches of computers therefore often involve a degree of intrusiveness much greater in quantity, if not different in kind, from searches of other containers," [*United States v. Payton*, 573 F.3d 859, 862 (9th Cir. 2009)], some courts have ruled that absent special circumstances, search of a computer without explicit authorization in a warrant violates the Fourth Amendment standard of reasonableness. [*United States v. Payton, supra.*]

§7:91 Challenge Based on the File Name

If the police claim that they encountered incriminating files in plain view while searching for other files, argue that there must be probable cause to believe the folder and file contain contraband or evidence based solely on the name of the file or folder.

Most data files bear extensions that identify them as one type of file or another, and files bearing different extensions will not be found in the same folder. Therefore, a search for e-mails, which bear an "eml" extension, should not wander through those folders containing picture files, identified by a "jpg" or "tiff" extension.

Check carefully what the warrant or the justification for the search authorize: document files often end with the extensions "pdf," "rtf," "wpd," or "doc," so if the officers review files ending in "jpg," they should know they are viewing picture files and exceeding the warrant's scope. [*Compare United States v. Carey*, 172 F.3d 1268, 1273-76 (10th Cir. 1999) (when officer searching computer under warrant for "names, telephone numbers, ledger receipts, addresses, and other documentary evidence pertaining to the sale and distribution of controlled substances," opened JPEG files with sexually suggestive titles and found child pornography, plain view doctrine did not apply and files were suppressed); *with Commonwealth v. Hinds*, 437 Mass. 54, 58-62 & n.2, 768 N.E.2d 1067 (2002) (when officer had consent to search defendant's computer directory for electronic mail extension and saw files with names such as "2BOYS.JPG," the filenames themselves made it immediately apparent they contained child pornography, and the search was upheld under the valid plain view doctrine).]

§7:92 Challenge Based on the Search Method

You can demand precision in executing a search of computer files.

Standard procedure these days is that the authorities seize or mirror-image the network server or the computer hard-drive for review on a later date back at their offices. Federal Rule of Criminal Procedure 41 specifically permits this practice: "Unless otherwise specified, the warrant authorizes a later review of the media or information consistent with the warrant." [Fed. R. Cr. P. 41(e)(2)(B). *See United States v. Ganias*, 755 F.3d 125, 135 (2d Cir. 2014)("In light of the significant burdens on-site review would place on both the individual and the Government, the creation of mirror images for offsite review is constitutionally permissible in most instances, even if whole sale removal of tangible papers would not be.")] This procedure, however, does not entitle the police to retain indefinitely those files on the seized or copied media that fall outside the warrant's scope. If the police hold non-responsive records beyond a reasonable time, they cannot search them when they later develop probably cause, even if they obtain a warrant to do so, because the extended retention violates the Fourth Amendment. [*Ganias*, 755 F.3d at 141.]

The police can and should use a key-word search and other technological search methods without unnecessary review of material for which there is no probable cause, rather than opening each file on the computer and inspecting its contents, as they might do when rummaging through a file cabinet to find documents responsive to a warrant. [*United States v. Carey*, 172 F.3d at 1274-75 (rejecting file cabinet analogy and demanding that the government use more precise search methods); *United States v. Comprehensive Testing Laboratories*, 473 F.3d 915 (9th Cir. 2006) (approving assistance of computer specialist during search and copying apparently relevant files for off-site examination rather than seizure of entire computer; however, agents not required to rely on searching key words suggested by computer's owner) or hard drive).]

To restrict the potential overbreadth of computer warrants, issuing magistrates often will attach prospective conditions or search protocols to the warrants, specifying how the warrant is to be executed. Recently, the Vermont Supreme Court thoroughly reviewed the law in this area and held that the setting of ex ante, prospective conditions to execution of a computer warrant was within a magistrate's authority. [*In re Appeal of Application for Search Warrant*, 2012 VT 102 (VT 2012).] The conditions upheld included the following:

> (2) requiring third parties or specially trained computer personnel to conduct the search behind a 'firewall' and provide to State investigatory agents only 'digital evidence relating to identity theft offenses'; (3) requiring digital evidence relating to the offenses to be segregated and redacted from surrounding non-evidentiary data before being delivered to the case investigators, 'no matter how intermingled it is'; (4) precluding State police personnel who are involved in conducting the search under condition (2) from disclosing their work to prosecutors or investigators; (5) limiting the search protocol to methods designed to uncover only information for which the State has probably cause; (6) precluding the use of specialized 'hashing tools' and 'similar search tools' without specific authorization of the court; (7) allowing only evidence 'relevant to the targeted alleged activities' to be copied to provide to State agents' (8) requiring the State to return 'non-responsive data' and to inform the court of this action; (9) directing police to destroy remaining copies of electronic data absent judicial authorization otherwise; and (10) requiring the State to file a return within the time limit of the warrant [which was 'as long as reasonably necessary' to search the items seized] to indicate precisely what data was obtained, returned and destroyed.

The court struck down a condition that forbade reliance on the plain view doctrine to seize evidence not authorized by the warrant. [*See also United States v. Ulbricht*, 858 F.3d 71, 101 (2d Cir. 2017) (protocols "included opening or 'cursorily reading the first few' pages of files to 'determine their precise contents,' searching for deliberately hidden files, using 'key word searches through all electronic storage areas,' and reviewing file 'directories' to determine what was relevant."). *See* Marcia G. Shein, *Cybercrime and the Fourth Amendment*, THE CHAMPION 36 (July 2016) (Because it is inevitable that non-responsive files will be seized, defense counsel should request that (1) protocols for review be set; (2) some sort of filter team do the review; and (3) that non-pertinent files be returned promptly.)]

Search warrants for computers frequently include search protocols setting time limits for the prosecution to review the seized computer, hard drive or other media and to identify files beyond the warrant's scope and return those files. Typical language states that within some time period after seizure, government agents will "use reasonable efforts to return, delete or destroy any data outside the scope of the warrant unless the government is otherwise permitted by law to retain such data." Insist on enforcement of this protocol by post-seizure motion requiring that the data be turned over to a judge and quicker return of the documents, both to guarantee that the government's intrusion on your client's privacy remains limited and to exert pressure on the prosecution. [*See* Vanessa Blum, "Hacker Case Could Test Limits on Electronic Searches," *The Recorder* (October 5, 2012) (available at http://www.law.com/jsp/ca/PubArticleCA.jsp?id=1202573972635&slreturn=20120921073016) (last visited October 21, 2012).] Excessive delay in reviewing seized electronic data can be grounds for suppression. [*United States v. Ganias*, 755 F.3d at 141 ("[T]he Government violated Ganias's Fourth Amendment rights by seizing and indefinitely retaining non-responsive computer records, and then searching them when it later developed probable cause."); *United States v. Metter*, 860 F.Supp.2d 205 (E.D.N.Y. 2012) (seized electronic evidence suppressed because the government's delay of more than 15 months in reviewing the evidence to determine whether it was within the scope of search warrants was unreasonable under the Fourth Amendment).]

§7:93   Preserve the Evidence

Take steps to preserve the electronic evidence to make sure that the police do not alter it.

Nowadays, the police either make a mirror-image of the computer's hard drive and leave the computer itself, or they make the image rather quickly back at the station and return the computer.

Engage a computer technician to make your own mirror-image of the hard drive before the computer is used again to preserve an image of the files at the time of the search and to compare that image to the files the police present as evidence. [*See generally* Amy Baron-Evans, "When the Government Seizes and Searches Your Client's Computer," 27 *Champion* 18 (June 2003); Carla Rhoden, *Challenging Searches and Seizures of Computers at Home or in the Office: From a Reasonable Expectation of Privacy to Fruit of the Poisonous Tree and Beyond*, 30 Am. J. Crim. L. 107 (2002). For the leading prosecution work on searching computers, *see* U.S. Department of Justice, Computer Crime and Intellectual Property Section, "Searching and Seizing Computers and Obtaining Electronic Evidence in Criminal Investigations" (July 2002) (available at www.usdoj.gov/criminal/cybercrime/s&smanual2002.htm#_IC1b_).]

§7:94   Move for the Return of the Property

When the police seize files, especially computer files, that may have intermingled in them documents covered by the warrant and others beyond the warrant's scope, do one of the following:
*   Move promptly for the return of the property.
*   Demand that the files be sealed and provided to an independent magistrate or special master for review.

[*See United States v. Comprehensive Drug Testing, Inc.*, 473 F.3d 915, 937-40 (9th Cir. 2006) (directing trial courts to follow such a procedure especially when intermingled computer files are seized).]

Form:
*   **Form 7-7** Motion for Return of Property under FRCrP 41 & Supporting Brief
*   **Form 7-8** Motion to Compel Return of Property

§7:95   Plain View and Computer Searches

The plain view exception obviates the need for a warrant only if the evidence and its incriminating character are "immediately apparent" while looking for the authorized objects of the search. A crucial question is whether the police action necessary to "look" at a computer file constitutes a further intrusion of privacy–a search. You should challenge any police action that reveals the name or contents of the file as a further intrusion into your client's reasonable expectation of privacy, thus requiring probable cause and perhaps even a warrant. [*See Arizona v. Hicks*, 480 U.S. 321, 325 (1987) (turning a turntable a few inches to observe the serial number was an independent search requiring its own probable cause).] Thus tapping a keyboard or moving a mouse to disable a screen saver and reveal the last file viewed is a search, and observing the screen is not "plain view." [*United States v. Musgrove*, 845 F.Supp.2d 932 (E.D. Wis. 2011).] Each clicking-open of a directory, file and document also constitutes a separate search requiring separate justification. [*Stierhoff*, 477 F.Supp.2d at 443-444.] Likewise, a hash-value analysis of a computer, in which an examiner copies the hard drive and, using forensic software such as EnCase, applies an algorithm to the drive to produce a string of digits that uniquely identifies the underlying data, constitutes a search requiring a warrant. [*United States v. Crist*, 627 F.Supp.2d 575 (E.D. Pa. 2008); *see generally* Marcia Hoffman, "Arguing for Suppression of 'Hash' Evidence," 33 CHAMPION 20 (May 2009); Orrin S. Kerr, "Searches and Seizures in a Digital World," 119 HARV. L.REV. 531 (2005).]

You must scrutinize the manner in which the agents searched and viewed computer files, and even portions within a single file. For example, in *United States v. Comprehensive Drug Testing, Inc.*, 621 F.3d 1162 (9th Cir. 2010) (en banc), the agent scrolled to the right to view drug test results within an Excel spreadsheet and in so doing, saw the results for players not named in the warrant. Had the agent copied the spreadsheet rows for the ten players named in the warrant and then pasted them into a blank spreadsheet, he would have seen only those drug testing results for which he had a warrant. [*Comprehensive Drug Testing, Inc.*, 621 F.3d at 1181 n.2 *supra* (Bea, J., concurring in part and dissenting in part).]

Finally, insist on the "immediately apparent" prerequisite of the plain view doctrine–the requirement that merely viewing the item provides probable cause to believe.

[§§7:96-7:99 Reserved]

G. Consent Searches

§7:100   Consent Search Rules

According to the police, individuals consent to the search of their bags, cars and apartments alacriously. Consent has obvious allure for police: if upheld, it dispenses with the need to prove any basis for the search, because consent waives the defendant's Fourth Amendment rights. [*Schneckloth v. Bustamonte*, 412 U.S. 218, 235 (1973).]

The prosecution has the burden of showing a voluntary waiver of Fourth Amendment rights under the totality of the circumstances, but the waiver can be made unintentionally and without knowledge of the right to refuse consent. [*Schneckloth* at 227, 235-36.]

Among the relevant circumstances identified by the courts are:
- Knowledge of the constitutional right to refuse consent.
- Age, intelligence, education, and language ability.
- The degree to which the individual cooperates with the police.
- The individual's attitude about the likelihood of the discovery of contraband.
- The length of detention and the nature of questioning, including the use of physical punishment or other coercive police behavior.

[36 Geo. L.J. Ann. Rev. Crim. Proc. 84-89 (2007) (collecting cases). *See also United States v. Givan*, 320 F.3d 452, 459 (3d Cir. 2003) (reciting factors to consider); *United States v. Gonzalez*, 79 F.3d 413, 421 (5th Cir. 1996) (same).]

Consent is not voluntary when it is "no more than acquiescence to a claim of lawful authority." [*Bumper v. North Carolina*, 391 U.S. 543, 548-49 (1968).] *Bumper* held that a police representation that they *have* a warrant vitiates consent. However, subsequent cases have restricted *Bumper*'s holding and held consent voluntary where the police state only that they *will* get a warrant if the defendant does not consent. [*See Commonwealth v. Mack*, 568 Pa. 329, 796 A.2d 967 (2002).]

Evidence that your client refused to consent to a search, sometimes offered to show consciousness of guilt, is objectionable because it impermissibly burdens and penalizes exercise of the defendant's Fourth Amendment rights. [*People v. Pollard*, 307 P.3d 1124, 1129-30 (Colo. Ct. App. 2013) (collecting cases)].

§7:101   Consent by a Third Party

A third party who had some authority over premises or property may consent to a search that affects the defendant. [*Georgia v. Randolph*, 547 U.S. 103 (2006) (consent of one who possesses common authority over premises or possessions is valid as to the absent, nonconsenting person with whom authority is shared, but where the co-occupant is present and expressly refuses to consent to entry, the warrantless search and consent are invalid).]

Officers may rely upon a third party's consent to search where the circumstances reasonably justify a belief that the third party had authority over the premises or item. [*Illinois v. Rodriguez*, 497 U.S. 177, 188 (1990) ("Determination of consent to enter must be judged against an objective standard: would the facts available to the officer at the moment ... 'warrant a man of reasonable caution in the belief that the consenting party had authority over the premises?'").]

§7:102   Challenge Voluntariness

Officers often will attempt to describe the consent in conclusory terms, such as: "I asked him for consent to search the trunk, and he gave consent."

Elicit the exact words, because what the officer describes as consent may be no more than compliance with an order. [*See, e.g., United States v. Weidul*, 325 F.3d 50, 53-53 (1st Cir. 2003) (resident's response of "Okay" to police officer statement, "I'm going to look in here," did not constitute voluntary consent); *United States v. Worley*, 193 F.3d 380 (6th Cir. 1999) (no consent where defendant responded, "You've got the badge, I guess you can," when police officer asked if he could look in his bag); *United States v. Conner*, 127 F.3d 663 (8th Cir. 1997) (when police knocked vigorously at door and yelled, "open up," opening the door was not voluntary consent to entry).]

Pitting your client's word against the officer's usually fails. Instead, use the police and your defense witnesses to elicit other factors, not inconsistent with the officer's description of the verbal exchange, that may undermine voluntariness. For example, your client's fear, immaturity, low intelligence, poor command of the English language, and feeble medical or mental condition.

§7:103   Challenge the Probable Cause or Reasonable Suspicion

An illegal arrest invalidates any consent that follows. [*See Florida v. Royer,* 460 U.S. 491 (1983).]

Therefore, you may attack the probable cause to arrest or reasonable suspicion to stop your client. [*See also United States v. Hotal,* 143 F.3d 1223 (9th Cir. 1998) (written consent did not save search of residence when police entered with an invalid warrant).]

§7:104   Challenge Third Party's Authority Regarding a Computer

With respect to computers, do not assume that because a third party used your client's computer, the third-party had authority to consent to a search.

The third party might have that authority if both freely accessed each other's files. However, if your client password-protected his files or had a separate username and password so that others could not open his files, other users will not have authority to consent to a search of your client's computer files. [*Trulock v. Freeh,* 275 F.3d 391, 403 (4th Cir. 2001) (analogizing computer to a locked locker within a bedroom to which others had access); *see also United States v. Carey,* 172 F.3d 1268 (10th Cir. 1999) (consent to search apartment for cocaine did not encompass search of computer files).]

§7:105   Emphasize the Client's Cooperation

If winning a consent issue seems hopeless, adopt the opposite approach at the suppression hearing and commit the officer to fulsome descriptions of just how freely and enthusiastically your client consented. Use that testimony at trial to argue that your client behaved just as an innocent man would: ignorant of the contraband that was in his car, bag or home. After all, a drug trafficker would not freely consent to a search of the apartment where he had stashed drugs, would he?

H.   Exigent Circumstances

§7:106   Exigent Search of a Home

A home may be searched without a warrant if both probable cause and exigent circumstances exist. [*Steagald v. United States,* 451 U.S. 204, 211 (1981); *United States v. Mallory,* 765 F.3d 373 (3d Cir. 2014).] Courts evaluate the existence of an exigency by an objective standard; the subjective intent of the officer is irrelevant. [*Mallory,* 765 F.3d at 383.] Three types of exigency are recognized: (1) pursuit of a fleeing suspect; (2) a reasonable belief of imminent danger to another; and (3) a reasonable belief that intrusion is necessary to prevent the imminent destruction of evidence. [*Id.; see also Kentucky v. King,* 131 S. Ct. 1849, 1856 (2011).]

You may challenge the search by attacking the reasonableness of the belief that danger or destruction is imminent. Examine, as well, *when* the damaging evidence was seized. Once the danger passes – the suspect and scene are secured – "the police must obtain a warrant for any further search of the premises." [*Mallory,* 765 F.3d at 384 (Once suspect who fled into house with a gun was arrested and handcuffed and all other occupants cleared from the house, warrantless search behind door as suspect was being escorted out violated Fourth Amendment).]

I.   Border Searches

§7:107   Generally Allowed, Without Reasonable Suspicion or Probable Cause

The government may stop, detain and search those crossing the border without either reasonable suspicion or probable cause. [*United States v. Montoya de Hernandez,* 473 U.S. 531, 538 (1985).] The theory is that the government's interest in securing its borders renders any search there reasonable. "This does not mean, however, that at the border anything goes." [*United States v. Cotterman*, 709 F.3d 952, 960 (9th Cir. 2013)(en banc).] If the search reaches an extraordinary level of intrusion, it must be justified by reasonable suspicion. [*E.g., compare United States v. Flores-Montano*, 541 U.S. 149, 152 (2004)(searching the inside of car's gas tank characterized as a routine search that does not require any particular justification) *with Montoya de Hernandez*, 473 U.S. at 541 (reasonable suspicion required for alimentary canal search).]

§7:108   Computers and Smartphones

A controversial issue is whether and to what extent the authorities may search computers and smartphones travelers carry when they cross the border. Routine inspection of the device and its files is permitted without any suspicion [*see United States v. Arnold*, 533 F.3d 1003, 1008 (9th Cir. 2008)], but when the border officials conduct a more intrusive forensic examination that uses sophisticated tools to break into encrypted and password-protected files and to recover deleted files, some courts require a showing of reasonable suspicion to believe the device contains evidence of a crime. [*Cotterman*, 709 F.3d 952; *United States v. Saboonchi*, 990 F.Supp.2d 536 (D. Md. 2014)(While officers need no suspicion to have traveler boot up computer and to look through it, they need reasonable suspicion for a more intrusive forensic examination)].

[§§7:108-7:109 Reserved]

VI.   SUPPRESSION HEARINGS

§7:110   Keep Allegations to a Minimum

Your suppression motions should state as few facts as possible and attribute as little as possible to the defendant or defense witnesses for two reasons:
- The more detail you reveal in your moving papers, the better prepared the prosecutor and officers will be to investigate, to interview and perhaps intimidate your corroborating witnesses, and to mold testimony to refute your position not only at the hearing, but at trial.
- If your client states in a sworn affidavit a version of events that the judge finds demonstrably false, he may consider increasing your client's sentence for the attempted obstruction of justice.

Weighing against these tactical considerations is your need to convince the judge to hold an evidentiary hearing, for judges prefer to dispose of issues on the papers if they can. [*See United States v. McGill*, 11 F.3d 223, 225 (1st Cir. 1993) (commenting on general hostility against holding evidentiary hearings on pre- and post-trial motions, even in criminal cases).]

§7:111   Allege the Necessary Facts

Some courts will grant a hearing simply on the allegation that the police executed a warrantless search or arrest, on the theory that the government has the burden of proving the legality of warrantless searches and seizures. [*United States v. Johnson*, 63 F.3d 242, 245 (3d Cir. 1995) ("As a general rule, the burden of proof is on the defendant who seeks to suppress evidence. ... However, once the defendant has established a basis for his motion, i.e., the search or seizure was conducted without a warrant, the burden shifts to the government to show that the search or seizure was reasonable."); *see United States v. Coward*, 296 F.3d 176, 180 (3d Cir. 2002) (district court erred in placing on defendant burden of showing lack of reasonable suspicion). *But see Rawlings v. Kentucky*, 448 U.S. 98, 104-05 (1980) (defendant has the burden of proving both standing and the ultimate illegality of the search).]

Still, you should be careful to allege sufficient facts to establish your client's standing, especially if you anticipate that the prosecution will contest standing. [*See Rakas v. Illinois*, 439 U.S. 128, 129 n.1 (1978) (rejecting defendant's argument that court should remand for an evidentiary hearing where defendant failed to allege ownership or possession of rifle and ammunition at issue after the prosecution challenged standing). *See generally People v. Mendoza*, 82 N.Y.2d 415, 604 N.Y.S.2d 922 (1993) (extensive discussion of how specific moving papers must be to require an evidentiary suppression hearing).]

One relatively safe strategy is to allege the minimum necessary to get a hearing, such as that the search was warrantless and without probable cause and occurred in an area in which your client had a legitimate expectation of privacy. Then, if the prosecution answers with evidentiary averments that, if accepted, might defeat the motion (i.e., that your client consented to the search), reply with additional allegations tending to disprove or cast doubt on the prosecution's version of events. [*People v. Rodriguez*, 79 N.Y.2d 445, 583 N.Y.S.2d 814 (1992) (lower court should have granted a hearing to suppress a pre-trial identification where counsel, in his affirmation in reply to prosecution's response, denied that defendant knew or had any relationship with witness who claimed in prosecution affidavit to have seen defendant at least four dozen times in the neighborhood); *People v. Lopez*, 263 A.D.2d 434, 695 N.Y.S.2d 76 (NY App. Div. 1999) (holding that lower court should have granted hearing where defendant's reply to prosecution's affidavit supplied missing denial that he participated in drug transaction).]

Forms:
- **Form 7-4** Motion to Suppress & Supporting Brief (Automobile Stop)
- **Form 7-5** Motion to Suppress & Supporting Brief (Search of Apartment)
- **Form 7-6** Motion to Suppress With Citation of Authorities

§7:112   Avoid Client Affidavits

Consider what sort of materials to submit in support of your motion at the pleadings stage.

Try to avoid affidavits signed by your client, and rely instead on your general description of other witnesses' allegations or helpful facts in the discovery and police reports. Some assertions obviously originate with your client, for example, the assertion that he did not consent to a search where the police say he did and there was no other witness to the encounter, but if you can, avoid explicitly citing your client as the source.

Most courts will accept averments from counsel in the motion papers, even though counsel obviously lacks personal knowledge of the facts. [*See also People v. Huggins*, 162 A.D.2d 129, 556 N.Y.S.2d 75 (NY App.Div. 1990) (defendant can obtain a hearing on defense counsel's affirmation citing as sources conversations with the defendant and pre-trial discovery).

However, some courts demand that allegations come from document or witnesses whose testimony would be admissible at trial. [*See United States v. Wardlow*, 951 F.2d 1115, 1116 n.1 (9th Cir. 1991) (affirming denial of hearing based upon local trial court rule to this effect).]

Others strike a middle ground and require sworn allegations of fact, but accept counsel's affirmation on information and belief if counsel states the sources of the information and grounds of the belief. [NY Criminal Procedure Law 710.60[1].]

Many suppression issues do not lend themselves to resolution on documents alone. There is an exception when a supporting affidavit contains sufficient allegations to constitute probable cause for issuance of a warrant, but you still must convince the court that material facts are in dispute or doubt. [*United States v. McGill*, 11 F.3d 223, 225 (1st Cir. 1993).] Moreover, where there is some chance that the court will rule solely on the papers, you must offer sufficient factual allegations and legal argument to preserve your issues for appeal and postconviction attacks.

§7:113   Timing of the Suppression Hearing

Local rules and statutes generally require that the suppression motion be made before trial, *e.g.,* Fed.R.Cr.P. 12(b)(3), 41(f); and most courts hold the hearing before trial begins. You want a hearing before a jury is selected, preferably some days or weeks in advance, both to obtain a transcript of the hearing testimony and to reevaluate the merits of going to trial if you lose the motion. Argue to the court that scheduling the hearing with time before the trial enables the court to manage its calendar more efficiently; the suppression hearing's outcome may obviate a trial and therefore, the court need not set aside the time it would have held open for the trial.

Some jurisdictions have a provision for entering a conditional guilty plea that preserves suppression issues for appeal, *see* Fed. R. Cr. P. 11(a)(2) (requiring the prosecution's agreement and court approval, however, to enter a conditional plea of guilty); while others hold that a guilty plea waives all non-jurisdictional issues, which includes Fourth Amendment challenges to the admission of evidence, without provision for entering a conditional plea. In the latter jurisdictions, you may choose a non-jury trial after losing the suppression hearing, perhaps on stipulated facts, to preserve your issue while also obtaining whatever sentencing benefit the court and prosecution may offer for your client's acceptance of responsibility and willingness to spare the court a full-fledged contested jury trial. This option has merit if your only viable defense was the suppression motion, and the court's ruling depended upon issues of law rather than on findings of fact that are unlikely to be considered on appeal.

§7:114   Conducting the Hearing

Try to expand the scope of inquiry in a suppression motion and hearing back and forward in time.

"Back" means shifting the court's focus from the search to the initial police contact: Did the police have a valid basis for stopping your client? Did they legally enter the residence which they then obtained consent to search?

If the initial Fourth Amendment intrusion lacks a valid legal basis, all that flowed from it will be suppressible. Further, this shift may expand the scope of discovery you can obtain. Stops demand either reasonable suspicion or probable cause. In trying to justify the basis for the stop, the officer might be forced to reveal the details of a prior investigation or tip that brought suspicion upon your client.

Seek a hearing on the probable cause to arrest your client or conduct the search, for two reasons:

- Whether the facts amount to probable cause is a legal issue. Therefore, you may be able to persuade the trial judge to suppress even if he believes the prosecution witnesses, and you may have a shot at reversal on appeal if you lose.
- A suppression hearing focusing on probable cause will yield the maximum in discovery. Often, the prosecution's entire case amounts to nothing more than the probable cause the police had at the time of the arrest or search plus whatever they discovered in the search.

Conversely, even if the issue seems to be whether the initial stop and detention or seizure were justifiable, attempt to move the focus forward in time and examine whether the stop and detention became prolonged or particularly oppressive so that you can argue that either:

- The *Terry* investigative stop blossomed into a full arrest, but without facts supporting probable cause to arrest. [See §7:52.]
- The police behavior was in some way unreasonable. [*E.g., Burchett v. Kiefer*, 310 F.3d 937, 944-45 (6th Cir. 2002) (detaining defendant in car for three hours in 90 degree weather unreasonable), *Farm Labor Org. Comm. v. Ohio State Highway Patrol*, 308 F.3d 523, 544-45 (6th Cir. 2002) (holding green cards for four days unreasonable); *United States v. Onumonu*, 967 F.2d 782, 789-90 (2d Cir. 1991) (four-day detention of suspected drug swallower at border required reasonable suspicion); *United States v. Cagle*, 849 F.2d 924, 927 (5th Cir. 1988) (holding suitcase for 90 minutes so it missed plane was unreasonable).]

Unlike at trial, you should use some exploratory, open-ended questions when examining the officer because if there is damaging evidence of your client's involvement in criminal activity, you want to hear it at the hearing rather than for the first time before a jury.

Courts are split on whether the Confrontation Clause, with its newly potent requirement that witnesses to testimonial hearsay appear and face cross-examination [See §20:120, infra (discussing *Crawford v. Washington*, 541 U.S. 36 (2004))], applies to pretrial suppression hearings. [*See State v. Zamzow*, 892 N.W.2d 637 (WI 2017) (holding that it does); *Curry v. State*, 228 S.W.3d 292, 298 (Tex. App. 2007) (same); *Lieser v. Miller*, 2012 U.S. Dist. LEXIS 108381 (N.D. Ohio Aug. 2, 2012) (collecting split authorities but not deciding the issue).]

§7:115   Examination of Police Officer

COMMENT:

This sample examination of a police officer is in the context of an investigative search on an anonymous tip. Approach the anonymous tip in two ways:

- Elicit all the details about the scene and the alleged perpetrators that an accurate, reliable observer would have noticed–where in the parking lot the car was, description of the car, of the individuals, of the gun or other alleged criminal acts. You should subpoena or request the actual radio transmission or 911 recording.
- Ask the officer about every way in which the scene he met upon his arrival differed from the tip so as to cast doubt on its reliability. If the officer adds details missing from his reports, impeach him with his reports.

Direct Examination:

Q: What did you hear on the radio transmission?

A: They were saying there was a man with a gun. They said three black males. One of them had a gun. It was in a gray car parked in the corner of Pennsylvania and Wertman Avenues, the White Castle parking lot.

Q: Could you describe the area?

A: It's in the precinct, it has a reputation as a high robbery area.

Cross-Examination:

Q: Over your six and a half years working in this precinct, how many robberies were reported as having happened on the corner of Pennsylvania and Wertman?

A: I don't remember.

Q: Prior to this case, have you arrested anyone for a robbery occurring at the corner of Wertman and Pennsylvania Avenues?

A: No.

Q: Do you know whether the corner of Wertman and Pennsylvania had more robberies reported in 2006 than did the corner two blocks over, Pennsylvania and McDaniel?

A: No.

Q: Or more than the corner four blocks over?

A: No.

COMMENT:

You can go on and on with this with little risk because the answers rarely will worsen the description of the area as a "high crime area." The prosecution's response to your written motion to suppress will indicate whether or not the prosecution intends to rely on assertions of frequent criminality. [*See Illinois v. Wardlow,* 528 U.S. 119 (2000) (defendant's presence in area of heavy narcotics traffic plus his unprovoked flight created enough reasonable suspicion to justify a *Terry* stop).]

If you see such a response, request statistics, either from the prosecutor or by subpoenaing records from the precinct or police department.

Q: The car had tinted windows, didn't it?

A. I don't recall if it did or didn't.

Q: Could you see the individuals inside the car as you approached it?

A: I don't recall that.

Q: Could you tell the color of their skin?

A: I don't recall.

Q: So you can't testify today that you noticed that the occupants were black or white?

A: Well, almost everyone in the neighborhood is African-American.

Q: So your answer is no, you cannot say today whether you noticed if they were black or white?

A: I can't say.

Q: But as you testified, nearly everyone in the neighborhood is African-American?

A: Yes.

Q: And all the tip told you about the skin color of the car's occupants was that they were black?

A: Yes.

Q: So not different from most anyone else in the neighborhood?

A: No.

Q: You couldn't tell how many people were in the car from looking at it either?

A: No, I couldn't.

Q: So you didn't notice if there were one, two, three or more individuals in the car?

A: I could see the shapes of individuals in the car, but I didn't notice how many people were in the car.

Q: The radio transmission you received said nothing about the car's windows being tinted, did it?

A: No.

Q: Didn't even say what kind of car it was?

A: A grey one.

Q: Dark or light grey?

A: I don't remember.

Q: Didn't say if it was a Chevy, a Ford, a Mercedes?

A: No.

Q: Old or new model?

A: No.

Q: Four door or coupe?

A: No, only a grey car.

Q: At the time you approached the driver's door, you had not seen any gun in the car?
A: No.
Q: When you approached, the driver's window was rolled up?
A: I don't remember.
Q: You don't remember if you knocked on the window?
A: No.
Q: You did tell my client to get out of the car?
A: I asked him to.
Q: You said words to the effect, "Please get out of the car."
A: Yes.
Q: And he complied?
A: Yes.
Q: No hesitation?
A: No.

COMMENT:

You want to emphasize your client's cooperativeness so as to argue later, if the circumstances permit (*e.g.,* the gun was closer to another occupant) that he did not know that there was a gun or other contraband in the car.

Q: You had your gun in your hand?
A: No, I think my hand was on my holster, but my weapon was still holstered.
Q: So you are saying that the gun was not in your hand, but your hand was on your gun?
A: Yes, but it was still in my holster.
Q: My client was facing you when he exited the car?
A: Yes.
Q: You have any reason to think he could not see your hand on your gun?
A: I couldn't say what he saw or not.
Q: You frisked him then, right?
A: Yes.

COMMENT:

Have the officer describe in detail how and where he touched your client. Be sure to ask whether he or your client said anything. Then, try to elicit details showing that your client was under arrest *before* any evidence justifying an arrest had been found.

Q: You still had not seen any gun, either on my client or in the car?
A: No.
Q: And my client still was being cooperative?
A: Yes.
Q: After you frisked my client, you held him by the front of the car?
A: I don't know if it was the front or the back. I held him on the car.
Q: He was facing the car?
A: Yes, he was.
Q: And you were behind him?
A: Yes.
Q: You told him to put his hands on the car?
A: Yes.
Q: And he did?
A: Yes.
Q: And you had your hand on his back, right?
A: Yeah.
Q: So that he couldn't move at all?
A: Yes.
Q: It's fair to say that at this point he wasn't free to go anywhere?

A: At this point, no.
Q: And you still hadn't seen any gun?
A: No.
Q: And at this point your partner still hadn't said anything about finding a gun in the car?
A: No.

§7:116   Avoid Having the Client Testify

A defendant's suppression hearing testimony cannot be used against him at trial on the issue of guilt on the theory that the need to protect his Fourth Amendment rights renders the testimony compelled and thus unusable under the Fifth Amendment. [*Simmons v. United States*, 390 U.S. 377 (1968).]

However, *Simmons'* protection is limited. Most courts have held that the government may use the defendant's suppression hearing testimony to impeach if the defendant testifies to the contrary at trial. [*See People v. Rosenberg*, 213 Ill.2d 69, 820 N.E.2d 440 (2004); *Reinert v. Larkins*, 379 F.3d 76, 96 n.5 (3d Cir. 2004) (noting that the Supreme Court has not decided the issue, but most courts that have rule that the testimony is admissible for impeachment).]

However, the testimony, which is considered compelled, probably cannot be used to rebut other defense evidence at trial. [*See James v. Illinois*, 493 U.S. 307 (1990) (illegally seized evidence could not be used to refute defense witnesses other than the defendant himself).]

On the other hand, evidence suppressed on Fourth Amendment grounds can be introduced to rebut the *defendant's* trial testimony. [*Walder v. United States*, 347 U.S. 62 (1954).]

Furthermore, the court may penalize the defendant at sentencing for suppression hearing testimony it believes to have been false by increasing his sentence for the apparent obstruction of justice.

PRACTICE TIP:

In very few cases should you call your client to testify at a suppression hearing. For example, where your client's testimony contradicts that of the officers on a consent issue, the judge seldom will credit your client's testimony rather than the officers'.

Standing is one issue that may necessitate your client's testimony, but see if you can replace it with the testimony of other witnesses. [See §7:15.]

[§§7:117-7:119 Reserved]

VII. RETURN OF PROPERTY

§7:120   Property of Little Probative Value

Evidence that fell within the warrant's scope may turn out to have little or no probative value. Sometimes the item may have some value to the prosecution, but your client needs it or a copy to conduct his personal or business affairs. In such cases, your immediate remedy is not a motion to suppress, but a motion to return the property or copies of it. [See Fed.R.Cr.P. 41(e).]

PRACTICE TIP:

Try to negotiate this issue with the prosecutor before filing a motion.

The prosecutor and agents may be eager to return non-probative items cluttering their offices. Further, the standard for return is reasonableness. [*See J.B. Manning Corp. v. United States*, 86 F.3d 926 (9th Cir. 1996).] The prosecutor's refusal to comply with your patient entreaties to negotiate return helps set up a subsequent argument that the prosecution is acting unreasonably.

Where the prosecutor wants to keep documents, but is willing to return copies, she may demand either that you pay for commercial copying or that government agents make the copies. Choose the former if you can afford it, because the government agents will perform the task on their schedules, which usually means very slowly. If you cannot afford commercial copying, suggest that the government permit a student or clerk in your employ to copy the documents under the watch of a government clerk.

Form:
- **Form 7-7** Motion for Return of Property Under FRCrP 41 & Supporting Brief

§7:121   Protecting Privileges

A lawful search, particularly of your client's home, business or computer, may yield evidence that was seized lawfully, but which the government has no right to review, for example, privileged communications, such as those with attorneys or psychotherapists.

Do not try to be too clever and await the prosecutor's review of privileged materials so that you later can argue that the violation of the privilege taints the prosecution and requires dismissal.

Not only will a court hesitate to impose such a severe sanction, but if you do not assert the privilege promptly on your client's behalf and seek the timely return of documents you believe to be privileged, the court may hold that your client waived the privilege. [*See In re Grand Jury (Impounded)*, 133 F.3d 978, 982-83 (3d Cir. 1998) (even though target asserted privilege claim to prosecutor, privilege was waived by his failure to seek judicial relief for nearly four months).] In contrast, if you assert the privilege immediately and obtain a court order that privileged materials be segregated and returned, the prosecution's violation of such an order can result in sanctions as severe as dismissal of the charges. [*State v. Lenarz*, 301 Conn. 417, 22 A.3d 536 (2011) (ordering reversal of the conviction and dismissal with prejudice where the prosecution retained and reviewed privileged communications from defendant's computer).]

If you suspect that the government seized privileged documents, notify the prosecutor as soon as possible and demand that no government agent review the documents. Ask for an opportunity to review the documents yourself to segregate privileged documents.

The government will try to anoint a government agent or lawyer as a "taint team," to review the documents and challenge the defense assertion privilege. Resist this. It achieves exactly what the privilege is meant to prevent, government examination of protected communications.

Instead, if the government will not accept your assertions of privilege, ask the court to give you permission to review the documents and flag those that might be privileged; to review the materials *in camera*; or to appoint a special master to decide whether the assertions of privilege are valid. [*Compare Commonwealth v. Flor*, 136 A.3d 150, 161 (PA 2016) (in the context of a postconviction ineffectiveness claim, Supreme Court ordered court on remand to permit defense counsel to review files and determine what portions were privileged); *In re Grand Jury Subpoenas*, 454 F.3d 511 (6th Cir. 2006) (error to permit government taint team to review allegedly privileged documents); and *United States v. Neill*, 952 F.Supp. 834 (D.D.C. 1997) (special master or in camera inspection is preferable to review by a government taint team) with *United States v. Segal*, 313 F.Supp. 774 (N.D. Ill. 2004) (approving government taint team review).]

If the prosecutor does not return the privileged documents, you must file a prompt motion under Rule 41 or its state equivalent for the return of the privileged documents; otherwise, a court later may find that your inaction waived your client's privilege. [See *In re Grand Jury (Impounded)*, 133 F.3d at 982-83.]

Where the privilege has been breached, the prosecution must return and cannot use the privileged materials, but most courts refuse to suppress evidence derived from information protected by a non-constitutional privilege. [*United States v. Warshak*, 661 F.3d 266, 274 (6th Cir. 2010) ("no court ha[s] applied the fruit-of-the-poisonous-tree doctrine to derivative evidence obtained as a result of improper access to materials covered by a non-constitutional privilege"; attorney-client privilege); *United States v. Squillacote*, 221 F.3d 549, 559 (4th Cir. 2000) (psychotherapist-patient privilege).] If serious governmental misconduct accompanied the privilege breach, a more drastic remedy, such as dismissal, might be available. [*Commonwealth v. Schultz*, 133 A.3d 294 (Pa. Super. Ct. 2016) (dismissing charges because the prosecutor misrepresented his intentions to the court when he elicited in the grand jury testimony about communications protected by the attorney-client privilege); *United States v. White*, 879 F.2d 1509, 1513 (7th Cir. 1989) (if privileged information is obtained through "serious governmental misconduct" and used at trial, dismissal might be appropriate; dicta).]

Form:
- **Form 7-7** Motion for Return of Property under FRCrP 41 & Supporting Brief
- **Form 7-8** Motion to Compel Return of Property
- **Form 7-9** Motion to Impound Privileged Documents for *In Camera* or Special Master Review

VIII. FORMS

Form 7-1   Federal Search Warrant Based on Affidavit(s)

COMMENT:

    The warrant itself does not specify the facts supporting its issuance. In some jurisdictions, the officers serve the affidavit along with the warrant. The practice in others (for example, in federal investigations) is to seal the affidavit to conceal the identities of cooperating witnesses and investigative techniques.

℅ AO 93   (Rev. 12/03) Search Warrant

UNITED STATES DISTRICT COURT

District of _____

In the Matter of the Search of
(Name, address or brief description of person or property to be searched)

SEARCH WARRANT

Case Number:

TO: _____ and any Authorized Officer of the United States

Affidavit(s) having been made before me by _____ who has reason to believe
Affiant

that ☐ on the person of, or ☐ on the premises known as (name, description and/or location)

in the _____ District of _____ there is now
concealed a certain person or property, namely (describe the person or property)

I am satisfied that the affidavit(s) and any record testimony establish probable cause to believe that the person or property so described is now concealed on the person or premises above-described and establish grounds for the issuance of this warrant.

    YOU ARE HEREBY COMMANDED to search on or before _____
Date

(not to exceed 10 days) the person or place named above for the person or property specified, serving this warrant and making the
search ☐ in the daytime — 6:00 AM to 10:00 P.M. ☐ at anytime in the day or night as I find reasonable cause has been established and if the person or property be found there to seize same, leaving a copy of this warrant and receipt for the person or property taken, and prepare a written inventory of the person or property seized and promptly return this warrant to
_____ as required by law.
U.S. Magistrate Judge (Rule 41(f)(4))

_____   at   _____
Date and Time Issued   City and State

_____   _____
Name and Title of Judge   Signature of Judge

RETURN	**Case Number:**	
DATE WARRANT RECEIVED	DATE AND TIME WARRANT EXECUTED	COPY OF WARRANT AND RECEIPT FOR ITEMS LEFT WITH
INVENTORY MADE IN THE PRESENCE OF		
INVENTORY OF PERSON OR PROPERTY TAKEN PURSUANT TO THE WARRANT		

CERTIFICATION

I swear that this inventory is a true and detailed account of the person or property taken by me on the warrant.

_____

Subscribed, sworn to, and returned before me this date.

_____ _____

Signature of Judge   Date

Form 7-2   Federal Search Warrant Upon Oral Testimony

✎AO 93A   (Rev. 12/03) Search Warrant Upon Oral Testimony

UNITED STATES DISTRICT COURT

District of _____

In the Matter of the Search of
(Name, address or brief description of person or property to be searched)

SEARCH WARRANT UPON ORAL TESTIMONY

Case Number: _____

TO: _____ and any Authorized Officer of the United States

Sworn oral testimony has been communicated to me by _____

Affiant

that ☐ on the person of, or ☐ on the premises known as (name, description and/or location)

in the _____ District of _____ there is now
concealed a certain person or property, namely (describe the person or property)

I am satisfied that the circumstances are such as to make it reasonable to dispense with a written affidavit and that there is probable cause to believe that the property or person so described is concealed on the person or premises above described and that grounds for application for issuance of the search warrant exist as communicated orally to me in a sworn statement which has been recorded electronically, stenographically, or in long-hand and upon the return of the warrant, will be transcribed, certified as accurate and attached hereto.

YOU ARE HEREBY COMMANDED to search on or before _____

Date

the person or place named above for the person or property specified, serving this warrant and making the search ☐ in the day-time — 6:00 AM to 10:00 PM   ☐ at anytime in the day or night as I find reasonable cause has been established and if the person or property be found there to seize same, leaving a copy of this warrant and receipt for the person or property taken, and prepare a written inventory of the person or property seized and promptly return this warrant to _____

U.S. Magistrate Judge (Rule 41(f)(4))

as required by law.

_____ at _____

Date and Time Issued   City and State

_____ _____

Name and Title of Judge   Signature of Judge

I certify that on _____ at _____

Date   Time

_____ orally authorized the

Judge

issuance and execution of a search warrant conforming to all the foregoing terms.

_____ _____ _____

Name of affiant   Signature of affiant   Exact time warrant

AO 93A   (Rev. 12/03)   Search Warrant Upon Oral Testimony

RETURN		
DATE WARRANT RECEIVED	DATE AND TIME WARRANT EXECUTED	COPY OF WARRANT AND RECEIPT FOR ITEMS LEFT WITH
INVENTORY MADE IN THE PRESENCE OF		
INVENTORY OF PERSON OR PROPERTY TAKEN PURSUANT TO THE WARRANT		

CERTIFICATION

I swear that this inventory is a true and detailed account of the person or property taken by me on the warrant.

_____

Subscribed, sworn to, and returned before me this date.

_____   _____
Signature of Judge   Date

Form 7-3   Motion to Unseal Search Warrant Affidavit

IN THE UNITED STATES DISTRICT COURT FOR THE

_____ DISTRICT OF _____

In Re Search Warrant Issued on _____,
for 1001 Main St., Pittsburgh, Pennsylvania

MOTION TO UNSEAL SEARCH WARRANT AFFIDAVIT

And now comes John Doe, owner of 1000 medical office, by his attorney, Thomas Farrell, and files this motion to unseal the search warrant affidavit.

On June 1, 2006, agents of the United States Postal Inspection Service executed a search warrant at the medical office located at 1001 Main Street, Pittsburgh, Pennsylvania. They left a copy of the warrant at Misc. No. 0000-000 after seizing all the patient files and billing records of the office.

Dr. John Doe is the owner of the medical office. He operates a physical therapy clinic at that address.

Undersigned counsel telephoned postal Inspector Tom Smith and requested a copy of the affidavit in support of the search warrant executed on June 1, 2006. Agent Smith referred counsel to the Assistant United States Attorney in charge of this investigation, Jane Roe. AUSA Roe said that the search warrant affidavit has been sealed by this Court on the government's application. Ms. Roe said that the affidavit was sealed to protect the government's ongoing investigation, and she refused to move to unseal the affidavit.

Undersigned counsel asked Ms. Roe whether Dr. Doe is a target of the investigation and when, if ever, she expected the grand jury to issue an indictment. Ms. Roe responded that the investigation is in early stages, and any indictment is not likely within the coming year. Further, she said that the investigation concerns health care fraud, but she refused to provide any further details about the investigation.

Rule 41 (g) of the Federal Rules of Criminal Procedure authorizes a party whose property has been seized to move for the return of the property. In order to file an intelligent motion under that rule, Counsel needs access to the allegations in the search for the affidavit.

Courts have held a party aggrieved by a search conducted pursuant to a search warrant has a right under the fourth amendment to obtain the affidavit in support of the warrant so that the party can adjudicate and defend its fourth amendment rights. *In re Search Warrants,* 353 F.Supp.2d 584, 587-92 (D. Md. 2004).

In addition, there is a First Amendment right of access to search warrant affidavits. The government submits its affidavit to courts in support of search warrant applications, and the affidavit becomes a court record. Under the First Amendment, the public has a right to review documents filed with the court. *In re Search Warrant (Gunn),* 855 F.2d 569, 574 (8th Cir. 1988).

There is no countervailing government interest in maintaining the affidavit under seal in this case. This is a fraud investigation, and not an investigation into drug trafficking, organized crime, or violent activity. There is no reason to believe that disclosure of the affidavit will pose a hazard to a witness, and the government has not given undersigned counsel a reason to believe so. Further, Dr. Doe will agree that the affidavit can be produced to him with the names or identifying information of any witnesses or informants redacted.

WHEREFORE, Dr. John Doe respectfully requests that the Court issue an order unsealing the search warrant affidavit in this matter.

Respectfully submitted,

_____

Thomas J. Farrell

Form 7-4   Motion to Suppress & Supporting Brief (Automobile Stop)

IN THE UNITED STATES DISTRICT COURT FOR THE
_____ DISTRICT OF _____

UNITED STATES OF AMERICA,

> Plaintiff,

> v.   CRIMINAL NO.

JOHN DOE,

> Defendant.

MOTION TO SUPPRESS PHYSICAL EVIDENCE AND STATEMENTS

AND NOW COMES the Defendant, John Doe, by his attorney, Thomas Farrell, and files this Motion to Suppress Physical Evidence and Statements:

The Defendant, John Doe, was arraigned on _____, on an indictment charging him with one count of possessing a firearm on _____, after having been convicted of a felony.

City of _____ police officers arrested Mr. Doe on the offense on _____, and charged him locally with aggravated assault and illegal possession of a firearm. Federal authorities played no part in investigating the local offense, but they adopted it from state court and indicted him here.

MOTION TO SUPPRESS PHYSICAL EVIDENCE

On _____, City of _____ police officers stopped Mr. Doe as he was lawfully driving his girlfriend's car. They ordered him out of his car with guns drawn and made him lie down on the ground and handcuffed him. They then searched the car and found a firearm and ammunition. They also searched Mr. Doe and allegedly found pistol cartridges in his left front pocket.

The police did not have a warrant to search or arrest Mr. Doe or his car. Mr. Doe had not been engaging in any illegal activity before he was stopped; therefore, the officers lacked any probable cause or reasonable suspicion to stop or arrest him, and the fruits of the stop and search must be suppressed.

MOTION TO SUPPRESS STATEMENTS

After arresting Mr. Doe and placing him in custody, the officers questioned him about the firearm, and Mr. Doe allegedly made incriminating statements. Mr. Doe had not been advised of his *Miranda* rights before this interrogation. The statements, therefore, should be suppressed as taken in an illegal interrogation.

Further, the statements should be suppressed as the fruit of the Fourth Amendment violation alleged in paragraphs two through four, *supra.*

WHEREFORE, defendant John Doe respectfully requests that the Court suppress Mr. Doe's statements and the evidence seized from him and his girlfriend's car on _____, or, in the alternative, that the Court hold a hearing on defendant's motions.

> Respectfully submitted,

> _____
> Thomas J. Farrell

IN THE UNITED STATES DISTRICT COURT FOR THE
_____ DISTRICT OF _____

UNITED STATES OF AMERICA,

      Plaintiff,

  v.   CRIMINAL NO.

JOHN DOE,

      Defendant.

ORDER OF COURT

AND NOW, this _____ day of _____, 2004, IT IS ORDERED that Defendant John Doe's Motion to Suppress Physical Evidence and Statements is GRANTED; and

IT IS ORDERED that:

(1) The items seized on _____; are suppressed; and

(2) Mr. Doe's post-arrest statements are suppressed.

OR

IT IS ORDERED that a hearing be held on Defendant John Doe's Omnibus Pre-Trial Motion on _____, 2005, at _____.

_____
U.S. District Judge

IN THE UNITED STATES DISTRICT COURT FOR THE
_____ DISTRICT OF _____

UNITED STATES OF AMERICA,

      Plaintiff,

  v.

JOHN DOE,

      Defendant.

MEMORANDUM OF LAW IN SUPPORT OF DEFENDANT'S MOTION TO SUPPRESS PHYSICAL EVIDENCE AND STATEMENTS

AND NOW COMES the Defendant, John Doe, by his attorney, Thomas Farrell, and files this Memorandum of Law in Support of His Motion to Suppress Physical Evidence and Statements:

MOTION TO SUPPRESS PHYSICAL EVIDENCE

When the police make a warrantless stop or seizure, the government bears the burden of proving that the stop or seizure was justified. *United States v. Johnson*, 63 F.3d 242, 245 (3d Cir. 1995). Mr. Doe's car could not be stopped without articulate and reasonable suspicion that the vehicle or occupant violated the law. *Id.* Ordering Mr. Doe out of the car and onto the ground and handcuffing him constituted a full-fledged arrest, not merely an investigatory stop under Fourth Amendment law; this step required probable cause to believe he had committed a crime. *See Washington v. Lambert*, 98 F.3d 1181 (9th Cir. 1996). There was neither probable cause nor reasonable suspicion to stop him or to search him or his car. Therefore, the evidence seized should be suppressed.

MOTION TO SUPPRESS STATEMENTS

Before conducting a custodial interrogation of an arrestee, the police must read the familiar *Miranda* [*v. Arizona*, 384 U.S. 436 (1966)] warnings. Failure to give the warnings mandates suppression. *Dickerson v. United States*, 530 U.S. 428 (2000).

Statements taken pursuant to an arrest that violates the Fourth Amendment must be suppressed as the fruit of the illegal search. *Kaupp v. Texas*, 538 U.S. 626 (2003); *Dunaway v. New York*, 442 U.S. 200 (1979). Since Mr. Doe's statements were the result of custodial interrogation after an invalid arrest and without *Miranda* warnings, they must be suppressed.

CONCLUSION

For the foregoing reasons, Defendant's Motion to Suppress should be granted, or, in the alternative, an evidentiary hearing should be held on the motion.

Respectfully submitted,

_____
Thomas J. Farrell

Form 7-5   Motion to Suppress & Supporting Brief (Search of Apartment)

COMMENT:

This sample Motion and Memorandum involves a third party, and argues, among other things, that the third party neither consented to the search nor had the ability to consent.

Whether the government might assert that the landlord of the building gave the officers the keys to the apartment is not known, and does not matter. A landlord cannot consent to the search of a tenant's apartment. *Stoner v. California*, 376 U.S. 483, 488-89 (1964); *Chapman v. United States*, 365 U.S. 610, 616-17 (1961).

IN THE UNITED STATES DISTRICT COURT
FOR THE _____ DISTRICT OF _____

UNITED STATES OF AMERICA)) v.) CRIMINAL NO.) RICHARD ROE)	

MOTION TO SUPPRESS PHYSICAL EVIDENCE

AND NOW COMES Defendant, RICHARD ROE, by his attorney, Thomas J. Farrell, Esquire, and files the following Motion to Suppress Physical Evidence.

On _____, state police officers and troopers conducted a warrantless search of apartment number ___ at the _____ Apartment Complex in Pittsburgh and seized, among other things, a cardboard box containing 16 kilograms of cocaine from a bedroom closet in that apartment. They placed Defendant Richard Roe under arrest and seized papers and personal items from his person. The officers also conducted a search of the white mini van which Mr. Roe had occupied earlier that day and seized other papers. This Motion seeks to suppress all the above described items.

On _____, the officers had been conducting surveillance of a green Mercedes Benz driven by three African-American gentlemen and the white mini van driven by co-defendant IP. Mr. Roe was a passenger in the van at various times on _____.

As described in the attached Affidavit in Support of Criminal Complaint (Exhibit A), the officers did not observe any illegal activity on the part of the drivers of the Mercedes Benz or the driver or occupant of the white van.

During the day on _____, the officers observed three meetings between the white van and the green Mercedes Benz, at least according to their affidavit. During two of these meetings, they saw the exchange of some item which they could not identify. These exchanges occurred during daylight in public parking lots.

Prior to _____, the officers did not have any information indicating that either of the defendants in this case was engaged in any illegal activity. They also had no evidence that any of the occupants of the green Mercedes Benz were engaged in any drug trafficking activity.

Sometime in the afternoon, before officers approached and searched the green Mercedes Benz, several officers followed defendants P and Roe to the _____ Apartments.

Defendant Roe had been an overnight guest in apartment ___.

While defendant Roe and one JL were inside apartment ___, police officers approached the apartment, knocked and demanded entry. The officers then pushed open the door and entered the apartment before anyone inside could either grant or deny them entry.

The officers then ordered Roe and JL up against the wall, effectively placing them in custody. One of the officers searched the apartment and found the sixteen kilograms of cocaine. The officers then handcuffed Roe and JL and officially placed them under arrest.

Neither JL nor Roe consented to the officers' entrance of the apartment, or to their search of the apartment.

The officers did not have a warrant to enter the apartment nor to search it.

Before they found the cocaine, the officers lacked probable cause or reasonable suspicion to enter the apartment or to place Roe or JL in custody.

Neither Roe nor JL consented to any search of the apartment. Any such consent would have been invalid as it was tainted by the illegal entry into the apartment and the illegal detention of Roe and JL.

Based upon the cocaine that the officers found in the bedroom closet, the officers arrested Roe and searched his person. All of the items found in that search must be suppressed as the fruit of the illegal entrance, custody and search.

Subsequently, based upon the cocaine found in the apartment, the officers searched the white mini van. Any items they found in this mini van must also be suppressed as the fruit of the illegal entrance into the apartment, the illegal detention of Roe and JL, and the illegal search of the apartment.

The government has not informed the defense of any statements made by Roe after the officers entered the apartment. If any were made, the defense moves to suppress them as the fruit of the illegal entrance, custody and search.

Respectfully Submitted,

_____

Thomas J. Farrell

IN THE UNITED STATES DISTRICT COURT
FOR THE _____ DISTRICT OF _____

UNITED STATES OF AMERICA	)	
	)	
v.	)	CRIMINAL NO.
	)	
RICHARD ROE	)	

<u>ORDER OF COURT</u>

AND NOW, this _____ day of _____, 2004, it is ORDERED that the Defendant's Motion to Suppress Physical Evidence is GRANTED, and all items seized in apartment ___ on _____, seized from Defendant Richard Roe and taken from the white mini van are suppressed.

In the alternative, a hearing is set on Defendant's Motion to Suppress for _____.

By the Court:

_____

IN THE UNITED STATES DISTRICT COURT
FOR THE _____ DISTRICT OF _____

UNITED STATES OF AMERICA	)	
	)	
v.	)	CRIMINAL NO.
	)	
RICHARD ROE	)	

MEMORANDUM OF LAW IN SUPPORT OF DEFENDANT
RICHARD ROE'S MOTION TO SUPPRESS EVIDENCE

AND NOW COMES Defendant RICHARD ROE by his attorney, Thomas J. Farrell and files this Memorandum of Law in Support of his Motion to Suppress Evidence based upon the facts alleged in his Motion to Suppress. (Defendant requests leave to supplement this Memorandum should additional facts emerge at the hearing.)

Warrantless searches, especially of residences, are presumptively illegal. *Katz v. United States*, 389 U.S. 347, 357 (1967). "When a prosecutor seeks to rely upon consent to justify the lawfulness of a search, he has the burden of proving that the consent was, in fact, freely and voluntarily given. This burden cannot be discharged by showing no more than acquiescence to a claim of lawful authority." *Bumper v. North Carolina*, 391 U.S. 543, 548-49 (1968). *See also Schneckloth v. Bustamonte*, 412 U.S. 218, 227, 229 (1973); *United States v. Givan*, 320 F.3d 452, 459 (3d Cir. 2003) (reciting factors to consider).

Mr. Roe was an overnight guest at the apartment. Therefore, he has standing to complain of the search. *Minnesota v. Olson*, 495 U.S. 91 (1990).

An illegal entry or an illegal detention taints a subsequent consent so that, absent attenuating circumstances, the consent is invalid. *Florida v. Royer,* 460 U.S. 491, 501 (1983) (illegal detention invalidated consent); *United States v. Vega,* 221 F.3d 789, 801-02 (5th Cir. 2000) (illegal intrusion into apartment tainted subsequent consent to search). Here, the officers exploited two separate Fourth Amendment violations. First, they entered apartment ___ without a warrant and without consent from the occupants. Second, by ordering Roe and JL up against the wall, the officers detained them without any probable cause or even reasonable suspicion to do so. Therefore, all that followed–the seizure of the cocaine, the search of Mr. Roe' person, and the search of the van–violated the Fourth Amendment.

JL, a woman who was found in apartment ___ with Mr. Roe, did not consent to a search of the apartment. Even if the officers claim she did, such a consent would not be valid. Officers may rely upon a third party's consent to search only where the circumstances reasonably justify a belief that the third party had authority over the premises. *Illinois v. Rodriguez*, 497 U.S. 177, 188 (1990) ("Determination of consent to enter must be judged against an objective standard: would the facts available to the officer at the moment ... 'warrant a man of reasonable caution in the belief that the consenting party had authority over the premises?'") There was no basis for such a belief in this case. JL did not rent or reside in the apartment. Until they entered the apartment, the officers never saw JL with Roe or any other resident of the apartment.

Further, the officers illegally entered the apartment and detained JL just as they detained Mr. Roe. A defendant has standing to assert the involuntariness of a third party's consent. *See Bumper v. North Carolina,* 391 U.S. 543 (fruit of search suppressed where defendant's grandmother was coerced into consenting to search).

CONCLUSION

For the foregoing reasons, the Court should grant defendant's motion to suppress, or, in the alternative, hold a hearing on it.

Respectfully submitted,

_____

Thomas J. Farrell, Esquire
Attorney for Defendant
Richard Roe

Form 7-6   Motion to Suppress With Citation of Authorities

UNITED STATES OF AMERICA,

           Plaintiff,

        v.

LD,

           Defendant.

MOTION TO SUPPRESS EVIDENCE SEIZED FROM ____ MCDONALD BUILDING

On _____, _____ police officers executed a search warrant at _____ McDonald Building, _____. The search warrant authorized search of that address and of GD. It did not name LD at all. A copy of the warrant and affidavit are attached to this motion as Exhibit A.

As a result of the search, LD was charged with possession with intent to deliver, simple possession, and conspiracy, in violation of 35 P.S. §§780-113(a)(30) and (a)(16). At a preliminary hearing on _____, in the District Court for _____, the Court dismissed the possession with intent to deliver and conspiracy charges against LD and held the simple possession charge for court. *See* Exhibit B (preliminary hearing transcript). On _____, the Allegheny County District Attorney withdrew the simple possession charge.

As is stated in the Motion to Suppress filed by Co-Defendant GD, the affidavit in support of that warrant was so lacking in probable cause as to make its execution unreasonable. LD incorporates those arguments herein.

LD was an overnight guest at the apartment. Therefore, he has standing to complain of the search. *Minnesota v. Olson*, 495 U.S. 91 (1990).

MOTION TO SUPPRESS EVIDENCE SEIZED FROM THE PERSON OF LD

When the officers entered the apartment, they found LD asleep on a couch in the living room. Exhibit B at 11-12, 23-24. The officers handcuffed and patted down LD and found nothing in his pockets. *Id.* at 25, 29. At this point, they did not have probable cause to arrest LD nor any cause or suspicion to search him any further. However, the officers searched him again and this time found twelve packets of heroin and approximately $500 in cash in his pockets. *Id.* at 30-31. By the time of this second search, GD may have made statements admitting that the drugs in the apartment were his. He did not implicate LD in any of his statements. This second pat down search was conducted in violation of the Fourth Amendment. The heroin and cash found in LD's pocket must be suppressed.

The officers awakened and surrounded LD with guns drawn and handcuffed him. *Id.* at 23, 29. This was a full arrest, and without probable cause. Thus the fruits of that arrest–the heroin found in LD's pockets–must be suppressed.

Under the precedent established in *Michigan v. Summers*, 452 U.S. 692 (1982), the officers might have been justified in detaining, though not arresting, LD while they conducted the search of the apartment. *But see United States v. Reid*, 997 F.2d 1576, 1579 (D.C. Cir. 1993)(*Summers* does not justify search of visitors as opposed to occupants); *Stanford v. State*, 353 Md. 527, 727 A.2d 938, 942-45 (MD 1999)(explaining the different approaches to the occupant issue courts have taken). However, LD's presence and detention during the search did not permit the officers to search his person. *See Ybarra v. Illinois*, 444 U.S. 85, 91 (1979). To do so, they needed reasonable suspicion to believe that LD possessed a weapon, and this they did not have. *See Baker v. Monroe Township*, 50 F.3d 1186, 1194 (3rd Cir. 1995)(emptying one detainee's purse and another's pants pockets during execution of a warrant to search for drugs violated the Fourth Amendment); *Willowby v. City of Philadelphia*, 946 F.Supp. 369, 377 (E.D.Pa. 1996) (searching pockets violated Fourth Amendment).

Even if the first pat-down of LD's pockets were a permissible *Terry* frisk, by the time of the second pat-down, the officers had satisfied themselves that he did not have a weapon. Further, no probable cause to arrest him had developed; to the contrary, by this time, GD had claimed possession of the drugs in the apartment. Therefore, the second pat-down, the one that yielded the heroin, lacked any Fourth Amendment justification.

                      Respectfully submitted,

                      _____

                      Thomas J. Farrell, Esquire
                      Attorney for Defendant
                      LD

Form 7-7   Motion for Return of Property Under FRCrP 41 & Supporting Brief

<u>COMMENT:</u>

The caption includes a reference to a related case. This is the case number at which the warrant was filed.

IN THE UNITED STATES DISTRICT COURT
FOR THE _____ DISTRICT OF _____

IN THE MATTER OF THE SEARCH
AND SEIZURE OF PROPERTY OF
LOCAL, THE AT&T   Case No. _____
CO-LOCATION FACILITY,   (Related to Case No. _____)
PITTSBURGH, PENNSYLVANIA

MOTION FOR RETURN OF PROPERTY PURSUANT TO FED. R. CR. P. 41(E)

AND NOW COMES Local Company, LLC (hereinafter "Local"), by and through its counsel, Thomas J. Farrell, Esquire of Thieman & Farrell, and file this Motion for Return of Property Pursuant to Fed. R. Cr. P. 41(e) and state in support thereof as follows:

On or about _____, a federal search warrant at Mag. No. 00-000M was issued under seal by the Honorable _____, United States Magistrate Judge, for a SUN 1U Computer Server at the AT & T Co-Location Facility.

On or about _____, the aforesaid search warrant was executed and the property was seized.

According to the search warrant, the agents were seeking evidence of violations of the International Emergency Economic Powers Act, 50 U.S.C. §§1701 et seq.

Undersigned counsel has been advised by the United States Attorney's Office that the investigation is continuing and will take at least one year to complete, and perhaps much longer. Local is, at a minimum, a subject of the investigation.

Local has retained undersigned counsel to represent it with respect to the ongoing criminal investigation and, ultimately, with respect to any criminal proceedings should the investigation lead to an indictment.

Federal Rule of Criminal Procedure 41(e) provides that a person aggrieved by the "deprivation of property" may move for the return of the property. Since Rule 41(e) was amended in 1989, it is not necessary to allege that the search and seizure was unlawful and Local does not so allege.[1] Moreover, this motion seeks the return of <u>original</u> property.

Local, through counsel, has sought the return of the SUN 1U Computer Server which was seized from Local. After such return of the property, the server and files contained therein would be marked for copying which are relevant to the ongoing business of Local that would aid in the investigation being conducted by undersigned counsel. It is proposed that an outside copying service would then make a mirror copy of the identified server and files contained therein. The government has refused to agree to this request.

Local needs the server to conduct its business. The server contains many business files that cannot be re-created and that concern ongoing accounts and business transactions.

Any inconvenience to the government from the proposed procedure is minimal. The mirroring/copying of the server would likely consume only one additional day.

No rule gives the government a monopoly on the investigation of a matter. Local is entitled to investigate the facts and circumstances of any alleged criminal activity, just as the government investigates. The procedure suggested by Local is a reasonable accommodation of the government's legitimate law enforcement interests and the rights of Local, which is presumed to be innocent. See Fed.R.Cr.P. 41, 1989 Amendment, Advisory Committee's Notes, second paragraph.

Local submits that the selection of files for copying by the government clearly constitutes work product and, therefore, the government is not entitled to know which files have been selected and copied. Therefore, it is submitted that the government should not be permitted to record which files are selected for copying by Local's counsel.

If the government desires to retain the original property seized, Local submits that the government should bear the expense of providing a new replacement server. This is a matter within the discretion of the court.

Legal authority supporting this Motion is set forth in a Brief in Support of Motion for Copies of Documents Pursuant to Rule 41(e), which accompanies this Motion and is fully incorporated herein by reference.

---

[1] Local expressly reserves its right to file suppression motions related to the search warrants and the execution thereof should the investigation result in an indictment.

WHEREFORE, LOCAL respectfully requests this Honorable Court to grant this Motion for Return of Property Pursuant to Rule 41(e).

Respectfully submitted,

_____

Thomas J. Farrell, Esquire

Dated:

IN THE UNITED STATES DISTRICT COURT
FOR THE _____ DISTRICT OF _____

IN THE MATTER OF THE SEARCH
AND SEIZURE OF PROPERTY OF   MISC. No. 00-
LOCAL, THE AT&T   (Related to 00-000M)
CO-LOCATION FACILITY

[UNDER SEAL]

ORDER OF COURT

AND NOW THIS _____ day of _____, 2003, upon consideration of the Motion for Return of Property Pursuant to Fed. R. Cr. P. 41(e), it is hereby ORDERED, ADJUDGED AND DECREED that the Motion is GRANTED.

It is further ORDERED, ADJUDGED AND DECREED that the government shall return the property seized pursuant to the federal search warrants issued at No. 03-000M on or about November 1, 2003.

It is further ORDERED, ADJUDGED AND DECREED that the government shall make no record of the files marked for copying.

It is further ORDERED, ADJUDGED AND DECREED that an independent copying service agreed to by the government and counsel for Local shall make mirror copies of the server and files contained therein, deliver the copies to the government, and return the originals to Local.

It is further ORDERED, ADJUDGED AND DECREED that the United States government shall bear the expense of providing the copies as set forth above.

By the Court:

_____

IN THE UNITED STATES DISTRICT COURT
FOR THE _____ DISTRICT OF _____

IN THE MATTER OF THE SEARCH
AND SEIZURE OF PROPERTY OF
LOCAL, THE AT&T   Case No. _____
CO-LOCATION FACILITY,   (Related to Case No. _____)
PITTSBURGH, PENNSYLVANIA

BRIEF IN SUPPORT OF MOTION FOR
RETURN OF PROPERTY PURSUANT TO FED. R. CR. P. 41(E)

Local, LLC (hereinafter "Local") is presently the subject of a federal criminal investigation. A location not on the business premises was searched on _____ pursuant to a federal search warrant and its company server was seized. The search warrant provided that the criminal offenses under investigation are violations of the International Emergency Economic Powers Act, 50 U.S.C. §§1701 et seq.

The accompanying Motion seeks court authority for the return of the property seized by the government, specifically the SUN 1U Computer Server. Local submits that the procedure suggested is permitted by law and constitutes a reasonable accommodation of the legitimate interests of both the government and Local.

Federal Rule of Criminal Procedure 41(e), as amended in 1989, provides in part as follows:

> A person aggrieved by an unlawful search and seizure or by the deprivation of property may move the district court for the district in which the property was seized for the return of the property on the ground that such person is entitled to lawful possession of the property. The court shall receive evidence on any issue of fact necessary to the decision of the motion. If the motion is granted, the property shall be returned to the movant, although reasonable accommodation may be imposed to protect access and use of the property in subsequent proceedings.

Where a person seeks to have seized records returned, Rule 41(e), as amended:

> Avoids an all-or-nothing approach whereby the government must either return records and make no copies or keep originals notwithstanding the hardship to their owner. The amended rule recognizes that reasonable accommodations might protect both the law enforcement interests of the United States and the property rights of property owners and holders. In many instances documents and records that are relevant to ongoing or contemplated investigations and prosecutions may be returned to their owner as long as the government preserves a copy for future use. ... The amended rule contemplates judicial action that will respect both possessory and law enforcement interests.

Fed. R. Crim. P. 41, 1989 Amendment, Advisory Committee Notes, ¶6.

Although Rule 41(e) itself sets forth no standard to govern the determination of whether property should be returned to an aggrieved person, the Advisory Committee Notes to the 1989 amendment to Rule 41 makes clear that the Fourth Amendment protects people from unreasonable seizures, and that "reasonableness under all of the circumstances must be the test when a person seeks to obtain the return of property." *Id.* ¶2. If the government "has a need for the property in an investigation or prosecution, its retention of the property generally is reasonable." *Id.* If, however, the government's "legitimate interests can be satisfied even if the property is returned, continued retention of the property would become unreasonable." *Id.*

The Court of Appeals for the Third Circuit has stated that this standard set forth in the Advisory Committee Notes is comparable to the standard that the court used in *United States v. Premises Known as 608 Taylor Ave.*, 584 F.2d 1297 (3d Cir. 1978). *See Virgin Islands v. Edwards*, 903 F.2d 267, 273 (3d Cir. 1990). In *608 Taylor Avenue*, the court noted that the need to retain items seized was not reasonable if the government's interest could be satisfied through alternative means. *See* 584 F.2d at 1304. Thus, "the Third Circuit and Rule 41(e) require that a district court balance the interests of the parties to determine the reasonableness of the government's continued retention of seized property." *United States v. Lamplugh*, 956 F.Supp. 1204, 1206 (M.D. Pa. 1997).[2]

Other courts have followed similar logic.[3] In *Ramsden v. United States*, 2 F.3d 322 (9th Cir. 1993), *cert. denied*, 511 U.S. 1058, 128 L.Ed 2D 349, 114 S. Ct. 1624 (1994), for example, the Court of Appeals for the Ninth Circuit referred to the Advisory Committee Notes to the 1989 Rule 41(e) Amendment and held that the most appropriate outcome in that case was to allow the movant to retain the original documents, but to permit the government to make copies thereof. The *Ramsden* court stated that "the spirit of Rule 41(e) is one of compromise." *Id.* at 327. *See also J.B. Manning Corp. v. United States*, 86 F.3d 926, 928 (9th Cir. 1996) (where documents illegally seized, the government's offer to provide the movants with copies of documents essential to their business was insufficient, and that unless the government could demonstrate that it was unreasonable to do so, all original documents should be returned while copies of any documents necessary for investigation or prosecution could be retained); *United States v. Rotzinger*, 1995 U.S. App. LEXIS 3333, at *7 n.5 (7th Cir. Feb. 9, 1995) (noting that alternatives to the government's retaining property "may include returning original documents to the owner but preserving copies for government use").

In this case, Local is seeking the return of the _original_ property seized. Unlike *Lamplugh*, this case does not involve currency, so the government could easily provide the seized property to movants without injuring any investigatory and prosecutorial interests. See *J.B. Manning Corp.*, 86 F.3d at 928; *Ramsden*, 2 F.3d at 327. Local is willing to provide a mirror copy of the server and files contained therein to the government after receipt of its original property. The inconvenience to the government will be minimal–perhaps an inability to work with the property for a day or two out of the month since the property was seized. Moreover, the government should not be allowed to stymie the return of the property of the putative defendants for merely strategic reasons–the government does not have a monopoly on pre-indictment investigation.

---

[2] With regard to certain financial records that the government was retaining, the court in *Lamplugh* ordered the government to show cause why it should not be ordered to return the originals or provide photocopies of the documents to the defendants at the government's expense. *See* 956 F.Supp. at 1208.

[3] Some courts have held that a motion to return property prior to an indictment requires the movant to show that there is no adequate remedy at law, and that the movant will suffer irreparable harm if the property is not returned. In *Lamplugh*, Judge Vanaskie, following the reasonableness standard set forth by the Third Circuit and the Advisory Committee notes to Rule 41, specifically declined to require a demonstration of irreparable injury if the property is not returned. *See* 956 F.Supp. at 1207. Regardless, in this case the movants are not seeking return of the actual property, but merely copies of the seized documents.

The selection of documents or files by counsel clearly constitutes protected work product. *Sporck v. Peil*, 759 F.2d 312 (3d Cir. 1985). It is work product because disclosure of files selected by counsel would reveal attorney thought processes and possibly defense strategy. Thus, the government should not be permitted to retain a written record of the files selected for copying by the Court.

Since an evaluation of the foregoing considerations indicates that the government's continued retention of Local's property is unreasonable and since a mirror copy of the server and the files contained therein can satisfy the government's interest, the Motion should be granted.

Respectfully submitted,

_____

Thomas J. Farrell, Esquire

Dated:

Form 7-8   Motion to Compel Return of Property

IN THE COURT OF COMMON PLEAS OF
_____COUNTY, PENNSYLVANIA

IN RE:

)

1ST STATEWIDE INVESTIGATING GRAND JURY   )

)

)

)

)

)

MOTION TO COMPEL RETURN OF PROPERTY

The Moving Party ("Moving Party"), by and through its counsel, Thomas J. Farrell, Esquire, and the law firm of Farrell & Reisinger, LLC, respectfully requests that this Court enter an Order directing the Commonwealth to comply with this Court's Order dated _____, and return property seized during the execution of a search warrant on _____, and in support thereof, states as follows:

1. On _____, agents and representatives of the Office of Attorney General (hereafter, "OAG") arrived at the Moving Party with several search warrants.
2. In executing these warrants, the OAG seized, among other things, all computers, external hard drives, and active files from the Moving Party. The OAG informed the Moving Party that the computers would be returned within a few days.
3. On _____, after several weeks passed and several attempts were made by undersigned counsel to obtain information about when the Moving Party's computers and files would be returned, the Moving Party filed an Emergency Motion for Return of Property. A copy of this Motion is attached as Exhibit A. This Court scheduled a hearing on that Motion on _____.
4. After hearing the Motion for Return of Property, this Court issued a sealed Order directing, in relevant part, as follows:

     AND NOW, this ___ day of ____, after in camera hearing on the Motion to Impound Privileged Documents and Motion for Return of Property, IT IS HEREBY ORDERED, DIRECTED AND DECREED as follows:

       2. The Commonwealth will make copies of the ___ files and deliver copies to Thomas J. Farrell, Esq. within a reasonable period of time.

3. The Commonwealth will return the original _____ that were discovered in the documents seized to Attorney Farrell. The Attorney General is authorized to copy such items that may disclose information only relevant to their investigation.

4. The Commonwealth will continue to tag potential documents and correspondence which may be subject to attorney/client and/or work product privilege and deliver them into the custody of Agent _____, who will organize and catalog all items delivered to her and upon completion notify this Court. The Court will then select a third party to review the documents.

5. As of the date of this filing, no physical files or documents have been delivered to or otherwise made available to undersigned counsel or to the Moving Party.

6. On _____, undersigned counsel sent an e-mail to Deputy Attorney General _____ asking when the Moving Party could expect to receive the physical files and documents. This e-mail also asked for an update on the status of the review for privileged documents. A copy of this e-mail is attached as Exhibit B. As of the date of filing, DAG _____ has not responded to this e-mail.

7. Although this Court did not set a specific date by which the Commonwealth must comply with the _____ Order, it directed that the copies be delivered "within a reasonable period of time." Exhibit A.

8. Given that there has been no communication from the Commonwealth regarding these documents or the review for documents that may be subject to privilege since the ___ hearing took place, and that undersigned counsel's attempts to contact the Commonwealth have been unsuccessful, the Moving Party asks this Court to compel the Commonwealth to provide the promised documents without additional delay.

WHEREFORE, the Moving Party respectfully asks this Court to enter an Order compelling the Office of Attorney General to immediately deliver the documents and files at issue in this Court's _____ Order.

Respectfully submitted,

Dated: _____

_____
Thomas J. Farrell (Pa. ID —)
FARRELL & REISINGER, LLC

IN THE COURT OF COMMON PLEAS OF
_____ COUNTY, PENNSYLVANIA

IN RE:)

THE FIRST STATEWIDE   )

)

INVESTIGATING GRAND JURY   )

)

)

)

ORDER OF COURT

AND NOW, to-wit, this _____ day of _____, upon consideration of the foregoing Motion to Compel Return of Property, it is hereby ORDERED that the Commonwealth must immediately comply with this Court's Order of _____.

BY THE COURT:

_____

Form 7-9   **Motion to Impound Privileged Documents for In Camera or Special Master Review**

IN THE COURT OF COMMON PLEAS OF
_____COUNTY, PENNSYLVANIA

IN RE:

)

THE FIRST STATEWIDE   )
)

INVESTIGATING GRAND JURY   )

)

)

**MOTION TO IMPOUND PRIVILEGED DOCUMENTS
FOR IN CAMERA OR SPECIAL MASTER REVIEW**

The Moving Party("the Moving Party"), by and through its counsel, Thomas J. Farrell, Esquire, and the law firm of Farrell & Reisinger, LLC, respectfully moves this Court to impound for in camera or special master review privileged documents and copied hard drives seized during the execution of search warrants on _____, and in support thereof, states as follows:

1. On _____, agents and representatives of the Office of Attorney General (hereafter, "OAG") arrived at the Moving Party with search warrants, Warrant Control No. ___, Warrant Control No. ___, Warrant Control No. ___, and Warrant Control No. ___. Copies of these warrants are included as Exhibit A.

2. Warrants ___ and ___ list the items to be searched for and seized as, "_____."Warrants 5-A2 and 5-B2 list the items to be searched for and seized as, "_____."Exhibit A.

3. Warrants ___ and ___ name the premises to be searched as, "Name. Address." Warrants 5-B and 5-B2 name the premises to be searched as, "Name. Address." Id.

4. The Affidavit supporting these warrants is under seal, unavailable for the Moving Party's review.

5. The premises at ____ house the Moving Party's administrative offices. The Moving Party employs a staff who conduct regular operating business such as managing bills and invoices, benefits administration, and fundraising. The ___ is the residence for several members of the Moving Party and regular payment must be made for utilities and living expenses.

6. In executing these warrants, the OAG seized, among other things, all computers, external hard drives, and files from the Moving Party. A copy of the inventory lists of items seized is attached as Exhibit B.

7. These seized items contain material that is protected by the attorney-client privilege and the psychologist-patient privilege, and mental health records protected under the Illinois Mental Health and Developmental Disabilities Confidentiality Act, 740 ILCS 110/1 *et seq*[4]. These privileged materials should not be reviewed by the OAG or its agents.

8. Undersigned counsel contacted the OAG during the week of____, at which time Deputy Attorney General ___ was out of the office and unavailable. Counsel spoke with DAG _____ on____, and followed up with a letter on that same day asserting privilege and asking the OAG to halt its review of materials that may be privileged. A copy of this letter is attached as Exhibit C.

9. Undersigned counsel followed the ___ letter with an e-mail to DAG ___ on ___, providing additional information about which files may contain privileged information. A copy of that e-mail is attached as Exhibit D, and lists the following:
   a. Files taken from [address] pursuant to search warrant ___;
   b. The following files taken from [address] pursuant to search warrant ___: Items # [list items by number];
   c. The following files taken from [address] pursuant to search warrant ___: Items # [list items by number].

---

[4] The Illinois Mental Health and Developmental Disabilities Confidentiality Act's protections are broad and encompass not only mental health records as such, but also communications revealing that someone was a recipient of mental health services. 740 ILCS 110/2 (defining "communication" to include "information which indicates that a person is a recipient"); *see People v. Gemeny*, 313 Ill. App. 3d 902, 908 (2d Dist. 2000) (Act protects communications for purpose of setting up treatment). "The protection of the Confidentiality Act is broader than the physician-patient privilege, and all communications and records generated in connection with providing mental health services to a recipient are protected unless excepted by law." *People v. Kaiser*, 239 Ill. App. 3d 295, 301 (2d Dist. 1992).

10. Undersigned counsel was retained subsequent to the execution of the search warrants, but the Moving Party has been represented by the law firm of Dewey Cheatham & Howe. Following is a list of attorneys from these firms who have been involved in the representation of the Moving Party, and with whom communications are protected by attorney-client privilege:
    a. John Anderson
    b. Millard Fillmore
    c. Joseph Biden
    d. Theodore Roosevelt
    e. Andrew Jackson (paralegal)
    f. Dolly Madison
11. Brother John Doe, a deceased member of the Order, underwent mental health treatment and counseling at the ___ in the general time frame of ____ and at the ____ and _____ in____.
12. The OAG's continued review of documents, files, and computers jeopardizes the Moving Party's and its members' privilege and legitimate expectation of confidentiality.
13. The use of a "taint attorney" or "taint team" drawn from OAG attorneys and agents that are not connected to the investigation does not suffice to protect the privilege. It does what the privilege is meant to prevent: exposure of confidential information to outside eyes. *See In re Grand Jury Subpoenas*, 454 F.3d 511 (6th Cir. 2006) (error to permit government taint team to review allegedly privileged documents); and *United States v. Neill*, 952 F.Supp. 834 (D.D.C. 1997) (special master or *in camera* inspection is preferable to review by a government taint team).
14. In *Commonwealth v. Jane Orie*, 88 A.3d 983, 1011 (Pa. Super. 2014), the Superior Court did not rule on whether judicial review or taint team review was required, but it did affirm a grand jury supervising judge's decision to remove review from a prosecutorial taint team and refer it to a special master.
15. Thus, instead of taint attorney review, we ask that the Court impound the seized materials identified in paragraphs 10-12 and either conduct its own review or appoint a special master to conduct that review, and then permit the Commonwealth, through its taint attorneys, and the Moving Party, through counsel, to attempt to reach agreement or make challenges to the preliminary determinations of privilege before materials are released to the OAG for its continued investigation.

WHEREFORE, the Moving Party respectfully asks this Court to impound and seal the materials seized during the ____ search of the Moving Party's buildings and residences and either review the materials itself for privilege or appoint a special master to do so.

Respectfully submitted,

Dated: _____

_____
Thomas J. Farrell (Pa. ID----)
FARRELL & REISINGER, LLC

IN THE COURT OF COMMON PLEAS OF
_____COUNTY, PENNSYLVANIA

IN RE:

THE FIRST STATEWIDE   )
)
)
INVESTIGATING GRAND JURY   )
)
)
)

ORDER OF COURT

AND NOW, to-wit, this _____ day of _____, upon consideration of the foreoing Motion to Impound Privileged Documents for *In Camera* or Special Master Review, it is hereby ORDERED that all potentially privileged materials seized as a result of Warrant Control No. ___, Warrant Control No. ___, and Warrant Control No., served and executed on___, will be impounded pending privilege review. These materials will be analyzed by this Court or by an appointed special master. Upon completion of privilege review and approval by this Court, all nonprivileged materials will be released to the Office of Attorney General for use in its investigation.

BY THE COURT:

_____

(This page intentionally left blank.)

Chapter 8

INTERROGATIONS, CONFESSIONS AND OTHER STATEMENTS

I. INTERROGATIONS AND CONFESSIONS

A. General Points

§8:01 Move to Suppress

A confession changes the complexion of a case and your approach to it. "[T]he defendant's own confession is probably the most probative and damaging evidence that can be admitted against him." [*Arizona v. Fulminante*, 499 U.S. 279, 296 (1991) (quoting *Bruton v. United States*, 391 U.S. 123, 139 (1968) (White, J., dissenting)).]

If your client has confessed or made damning admissions, the most likely approaches become a guilty plea or cooperation against a more culpable individual.

To forestall the inevitability of those approaches, you should move to suppress your client's statements. Allege violations of as many of the following rights as you might apply to your client's case:

- The Fourth Amendment prohibition against detaining or arresting your client. [*See* §8:10.]
- The Fifth Amendment's privilege against self-incrimination. [*See* §§8:40 et seq.]
- The *Miranda* rule and the Fifth Amendment right to counsel it creates. [*See* §§8:30 et seq.]
- The Sixth Amendment right to counsel. [*See* §8:32.]
- State right to counsel rules and ethical rules governing attorneys' conduct. [*See* §8:34.]
- The Fifth and Fourteenth Amendment bar to the use of involuntary confessions. [*See* §§8:40 et seq.]
- State rules deeming involuntary confessions unreliable and inadmissible. [*See* §§8:40 et seq.]

§8:02 Working With a Confession

Even if your client has made a confession, do not abandon investigation and preparation of a defense. Your client's own admissions must be investigated and tested.

Especially when your client is immature, infirm, or feeble-minded, the police might extract a confession where there was no guilt. DNA exonerations have exposed the phenomenon of false confessions. [*See* www.williams.edu/Psychology/Faculty/Kassin/research/confessions.htm (collection of articles about false confessions).]

Further, some admissions may contain the seeds of a defense:

- When accused of a rape, your client may have admitted the intercourse, but insisted it was consensual.
- The drug courier may have admitted carrying the package, but asserted that he thought its contents were innocent.
- The accused fraudster may have explained why he believed his representations were not fraudulent, but true.

[§§8:03-8:09 Reserved]

B. The Fourth Amendment

§8:10 Statements Are Suppressed if Arrest Is Illegal

If your client spoke after being arrested, explore whether the arrest was legal. Statements produced following an illegal arrest or detention should be suppressed. [*Dunaway v. New York*, 442 U.S. 200 (1979); *Brown v. Illinois*, 422 U.S. 590 (1975).]

§8:11 Burden Is on Prosecutor

If an arrest or detention is illegal, it is the prosecution's burden to prove that the taint of the illegal arrest had dissipated at the time of the interrogation. This involves an analysis of the following factors:

- The time elapsed between the illegality and the statements.
- Intervening circumstances.
- The flagrancy of the official misconduct.

[*Brown v. Illinois*, 422 U.S. at 603-04. *See United States v. Stark*, 499 F.3d 72 (1st Cir. 2007) (surveying cases and finding *Mirandized* confession, given two days after illegal traffic stop, was admissible).]

[§§8:12-8:19 Reserved]

C. *Miranda*

§8:20   Necessity for *Miranda* Warnings

Before questioning an arrestee, the police must administer the fabled *Miranda* warnings. That is:
* The arrestee has a right to remain silent.
* Any statement the arrestee makes can and will be used in court as evidence against him.
* The arrestee has a right to consult with a lawyer and to have the lawyer with him during interrogation.
* If the arrestee cannot afford a lawyer, he has a right to have a lawyer appointed without cost to represent him or her prior to any interrogation.

Failure to give any of these warnings renders a subsequent statement inadmissible. [*Michigan v. Tucker*, 417 U.S. 433, 445-46 (1974); *Clark v. Smith*, 403 U.S. 946 (1971), *rev'g* 224 Ga. 766, 164 S.E.2d 790 (1968) (conviction summarily reversed where accused had been informed of all *Miranda* rights except the right to court-appointed lawyer in case of indigency).

No precise language is dictated for the four warnings. [*See Florida v. Powell*, 130 S.Ct. 1195 (2010) (warning a custodial suspect that he had a right "to talk to a lawyer before answering any questions" and could invoke that right "at any time ... during the [police] interview" adequately complied with Miranda even though it did not explicitly inform the suspect that he had a right to have an attorney present during questioning).]

Contemporaneous police statements can undo the efficacy of the *Miranda* warnings and render even a precise recitation inadequate. In *People v. Dunbar*, 104 A.D.3d 198, 958 N.Y.S.2d 764 (NY App. Div. 2013), the District Attorney's Office had a program whereby a prosecutor and police officer would confront arrestees immediately before their arraignment and instruct them:
* "If you have an alibi, give me as much information as you can, including the names of any people you were with.
* "If your version of what happened is different from what we've been told, this is your opportunity to tell us your story. If there is something you need us to investigate about this case you have to tell us now so we can look into it.
* "Even if you have already spoken to someone else you do not have to talk to us.
* "This will be your only opportunity to speak with us before you go to court on these charges."

104 A.D.3d at 202, 958 N.Y.S.2d at 768-69. The Court held that this spiel undermined the *Miranda* warnings given immediately after and made the waivers ineffective.

Miranda applies to "custodial interrogation." The defense has the burden of proving that there was custodial interrogation so as to trigger the need for *Miranda* warnings. [*United States v. Bassignani*, 560 F.3d 989, 993 (9th Cir. 2009); *United States v. Davis*, 792 F.2d 1299, 1309 (5th Cir. 1986).]

"Interrogation" encompasses any "words or actions on the part of the police ... that the police should know are reasonably likely to elicit an incriminating response from the suspect." [*Rhode Island v. Innis*, 446 U.S. 291, 301 (1980); *Commonwealth v. DeJesus*, 567 Pa. 415, 431, 787 A.2d 394, 403 (2001) (showing to arrestee statements accomplices had made implicating him in shooting amounted to interrogation); *People v. Ferro*, 63 N.Y.2d 316, 472 N.E.2d 13, 482 N.Y.S.2d 237 (1984) (silently placing furs stolen from murder victim's residence outside suspect's cell was interrogation).] Some courts employ a standard that emphasizes the suspect's reasonable perceptions [*Phillips v. State*, 285 G. 213, 675 S.E.2d 1 (Ga. 2009) (surveying cases)]; others focus on the officer's intent [*State v. Grant*, 286 Conn. 499, 944 A.2d 947 (Conn. 2008) (surveying cases)].

§8:21   Custody for Purposes of *Miranda*

To determine whether a person is in custody under *Miranda*, "a court must examine all of the circumstances surrounding the interrogation, but the ultimate inquiry is simply whether there [was] a formal arrest or restraint on freedom of movement of the degree associated with a formal arrest." [*Stansbury v. California*, 511 U.S. 318, 322 (1994)] The test for custody is an objective one, both from the officer's and the arrestee's perspective. The officer's subjective intent to detain the defendant is not determinative. [*Stansbury v. California*, 511 U.S. 318, 322 (1994) (stating that a court must examine all the circumstances, but the ultimate inquiry is whether there was a formal arrest or restraint on freedom of movement).]

No single factor is dispositive. "The following factors are among those likely to be relevant to deciding that question: (1) the language used to summon the individual; (2) the extent to which the defendant is confronted with evidence of guilt; (3) the physical surroundings of the interrogation; (4) the duration of the detention; and (5) the degree of pressure applied to detain the individual." [*United States v. Kim*, 292 F.3d 969, 974 (9th Cir. 2002). *See United States v.*

Barnes, 713 F.3d 1200 (9th Cir. 2013) (where parolee told to appear for a meeting under threat of revocation of parole, FBI immediately confronted him with evidence of guilt, and the meeting occurred with three officers behind a closed door after the defendant was researched and escorted to an electronic door, defendant was in custody); *United States v. Cavazos,* 668 F.3d 190 (5th Cir. 2012) (affirming lower court's finding that defendant was in custody even though the interrogation occurred in his home and the officers told him it was a "non-custodial interview." Just after 5:30 a.m., Cavazos was awakened from his bed, identified and handcuffed, while more than a dozen officers entered and searched his home; he was separated from his family and interrogated by two federal agents for at least an hour. He was informed he was free to use the bathroom or get a snack, but followed and monitored when he sought to do so; and he was allowed to make a phone call, but only when holding the phone so that the agents could overhear the conversation. An interrogation under such circumstances, and those others discussed above, would lead a reasonable person to believe that he was not "at liberty to terminate the interrogation and leave," *J.D.B.,* 131 S.Ct. at 2402, notwithstanding the fact that the interrogation occurred in his home and he was informed the interrogation was "non-custodial.").]

Objective characteristics of the suspect, so long as obvious to the officer, may bear on the determination of whether a reasonable suspect would believe that he was free to leave. [*J.D.B. v. North Carolina*, 131 S.Ct. 2394 (2011) (court may consider suspect's youth if known or obvious to officer); *id.* at 2415 (Alito, J., dissenting) (noting that lower courts have considered defendant's alienage, education, experience, maturity, and intelligence).]

Handcuffing generally constitutes the sort of custody that requires *Miranda* warnings before interrogation. It signals to a reasonable person "that his detention was no longer likely to be 'temporary and brief,' but 'long term.' ... Under th[os]e circumstances ... a reasonable person ... would believe that his freedom of movement was restrained to the degree associated with a formal arrest." [*State v. Ortiz*, 346 S.W.3d 127, 134 (Tex. App. 2011) (quoting *Berkemer v. McCarty*, 468 U.S. 420, 437 (1984); while handcuffing for officer safety did not escalate *Terry*-detention to full-blown arrest for Fourth Amendment purposes, it did constitute "custody" requiring *Miranda* warnings), *affirmed*, 382 S.W.3d 367 (Tex. Crim. App. 2012). *See also United States v. Cavazos*, 668 F.3d 190, 194 (9th Cir. 2012) (defendant "was awakened from his bed, identified and handcuffed, while more than a dozen officers entered and searched his home; he was separated from his family and interrogated by two federal agents for at least an hour, he was informed he was free to use the bathroom or get a snack, but followed and monitored when he sought to do so; and he was allowed to make a phone call, but only when holding the phone so that the agents could overhear the conversation." Held, interrogation was custodial despite fact that interrogation occurred in his home and he was told it was "non-custodial."); *United States v. Newton*, 369 F.3d 659, 676 (2d Cir. 2004) (defendant handcuffed in his apartment while the officers searched for a gun was in custody for *Miranda* purposes, even though for Fourth Amendment purposes, this was an investigative detention requiring only reasonable suspicion).]

The Supreme Court recently complicated the *Miranda* custody inquiry for the interrogation of prison or jail inmates. Some courts, applying the "free to leave test," automatically assumed that any interrogation of inmates required *Miranda* warnings. [*E.g., Commonwealth v. Cohen*, 53 A.3d 882 (Pa. Super. Ct. 2012).] In *Howes v. Fields*, 132 S.Ct. 1181 (2012), however, the Court ruled that *Miranda* warnings must precede interrogation of inmates only if the circumstances are such that the inmate reasonably would not believe that he was free to terminate the interrogation and leave. [*Howes*, 132 S.Ct. at 1189; *see also State v. Butt*, 284 P.3d 605, 608-611 (UT 2012) (explaining *Howes*).]

PRACTICE TIP:

The Officer's Intent

Stansbury does not foreclose suppression hearing questioning directed at the officer's intent. The court recognized that "instances may arise in which the officer's undisclosed views are relevant." [*Stansbury,* 511 U.S. at 325.]

For example, a dispute might emerge over whether the officer laid hands on the defendant. The officer's belief that the defendant was a prime suspect and his intent to take him into custody makes it more likely that he did, especially if the defendant began to walk away. Your questions represent nothing more than the principle that evidence of a witness's intent is admissible to prove that he acted in conformity with that intent.

Similarly, officers' statements and actions conveying to the defendant that he is a suspect or target of the investigation should be admitted to show that a person knowing of such statements is less likely to believe that he is free to leave. [*State v. Buck*, 181 Md. App. 585, 622-23, 956 A.2d 884, 906 (Md. App. 2008).]

PRACTICE TIP:

Argue That a **Terry** *[v. Ohio] Detention Triggered* **Miranda**

There is a growing trend toward "granting officers greater latitude in using force ... to 'neutralize' potentially dangerous suspects during an investigatory detention," including gunpoint handcuffing. [*United States v. Newton*, 369 F.3d 659, 673 n.4 (2d Cir. 2004).]

While this latitude is consistent with the Fourth Amendment focus on the reasonableness of the officers' actions in neutralizing a threat, it does not diminish the compulsion that a reasonable person would feel in the circumstances, and it is that compulsion, not the officers' reasonable concern for their safety, which is *Miranda*'s concern. [*See Newton*, 369 F.3d at 668-676. *See also State v. Bordeaux*, 38 Kan. App. 2d 757, 764-67, 172 P.d 78, 84-85 (2007) (holding that a *Terry* stop requires the giving of *Miranda* warnings before questioning; surveying state decisions on this point).]

Thus, argue that a detention triggered *Miranda* even in situations where a court might hold that the officer's action was a *Terry* stop and not an arrest under the Fourth Amendment.

§8:22   *Miranda* Waivers

The prosecution has the burden of proving by a preponderance of the evidence a voluntary waiver of the *Miranda* rights. [*Colorado v. Connelly*, 479 U.S. 157, 168-69 (1986).]

An inadvertent failure to administer the warnings does not prevent the police from later warning the defendant and obtaining a waiver and confession. [*Oregon v. Elstad*, 470 U.S. 298 (1985).] However, the police cannot evade *Miranda*'s requirements by deliberately eliciting an unwarned confession first, then administering the warnings and having the accused repeat the statements in the same interrogation session. [*Missouri v. Seibert*, 542 U.S. 600 (2004); *see also Bobby v. Dixon*, 132 S.Ct. 26, 30 (2011) (characterizing *Seibert* as prohibiting a "deliberate question-first, warn-later strategy.").]

Seibert was a plurality decision, and many courts look to Justice Kennedy's concurrence as establishing the definitive standard, a subjective one:

> Under Justice Kennedy's approach, the first question would be whether law enforcement officers used a "deliberate two-step strategy" in "a calculated way to undermine the *Miranda* warning," *id.* at 622, and "to obscure both the practical and legal significance of the admonition when finally given," *id.* at 620. If the answer to that question were "no," then the suppression analysis would be governed by the voluntariness standard set forth in *Elstad. Id.* If the answer were "yes," however, the next question would be whether any curative measures were taken "to ensure that a reasonable person in the suspect's situation would understand the import and effect of the *Miranda* warning and of the *Miranda* waiver." *Id.* Justice Kennedy provided two examples of such curative measures: (1) "a substantial break in time and circumstances between the prewarning statement and the *Miranda* warning ... [because] it allows the accused to distinguish the two contexts and appreciate that the interrogation has taken a new turn"; and (2) "an additional warning that explains the likely inadmissibility of the prewarning custodial statement."

[*United States v. Capers*, 627 F.3d 470, 484 (2d Cir. 2010) (also reviews federal cases).]

Nonetheless, most courts also examine the five objective factors identified by the *Seibert* plurality to determine whether the warn-later strategy undermined the effectiveness of the mid-stream *Miranda* warnings: "the completeness and detail of the questions and answers in the first round of interrogation, the overlapping content of the statements given by the suspect, the [closeness in] timing and setting of the first and the second interrogation sessions, the continuity of police personnel, the degree to which the interrogator's questions treated the second round of interrogation as continuous with the first, and whether the police cautioned that the earlier unwarned statement could not be used in any subsequent prosecution." [*State v. Jarnagin*, 351 Ore. 703, 720 n.12, 277 P.3d 535, 544 (Ore. 2012). *See also Bobby v. Dixon*, 132 S.Ct. at 31-32 (2011).]

PRACTICE TIP:

The *Seibert* decision presents an opportunity to inquire into both the officer's subjective intent and the circumstances surrounding the interrogations. In addition to proving the case for suppression, inquiry into the officer's intent may open more avenues to the defense, such as: the officer's bias, his basis for believing the defendant guilty, and his perception that a confession was necessary to prove the case.

After *Seibert*, the Supreme Court explained that the test expressed in Justice Kennedy's concurrence is the controlling one: whether "the two-step interrogation technique was used in a calculated way to undermine the *Miranda* warnings. [*Bobby v. Dixon*, 132 S.Ct. 26, 31 (2011) (citing *Seibert*, 542 U.S. at 622 (Kennedy, J., concurring)).] This inquiry does include a number of objective factors:

- Whether the first, unwarned confession obtained the entire incriminating story, so that it would be "unnatural" not to "repeat at the second stage what had been said before." [*Bobby,* 132 S.Ct. at 31 (quoting *Seibert,* 542 U.S. at 616-17).]
- Whether the unwarned and subsequent warned interrogation blended into one "continuum" by virtue of proximity in time and location and similarity of circumstances without any intervening changes, such as opportunity to talk to family and attorneys. [*Bobby,* 132 S.Ct. at 32).]

Courts remain reluctant to explore police subjective intent. [*State v. Vondehn,* 348 Ore. 462, 482-83, 236 P.3d 691, 704 (Ore. 2010) (rejecting Justice Kennedy's subjective approach).] They prefer multi-factor tests: "the completeness and detail of the questions and answers in the first round of interrogation, the overlapping content of the statements given by the suspect, the timing and setting of the first and the second interrogation sessions, the continuity of police personnel, the degree to which the interrogator's questions treated the second round of interrogation as continuous with the first, and whether the police cautioned that the earlier unwarned statement could not be used in any subsequent prosecution." [*State v. Jarnagin,* 351 Ore. 703, 720 n.12, 277 P.3d 535 544 n.12 (2012).]

§8:23   *Miranda* Exceptions: Booking and Pedigree Questions

Routine booking and border inspection questions generally do not require *Miranda* warnings. [*Pennsylvania v. Muniz,* 496 U.S. 582, 600-02 (1990); *United States v. Ozuna,* 170 F.3d 654, 657-59 (6th Cir. 1999).]

Miranda warnings are necessary, however, when the question was designed to elicit or was such that the officer should have known it would elicit incriminating information. [*See Muniz,* 496 U.S. at 604 n.14; *United States v. Henley,* 984 F.2d 1040, 1042-43 (9th Cir. 1993) ("should have known" standard regarding ownership of car used in bank robbery); *Alford v. State,* 358 S.W.3d 647, 659 & nn.24-25 (Tex. Crim. App. 2012) (noting confusion in the standard and collecting cases).] The "should have known" standard is an objective one, and under that standard the test is whether a reasonable officer in this setting would have known that the question was likely to elicit an incriminating response. [*See United States v. Williams,* 842 F.3d 1143, 1147-49 (9th Cir. 2016) (sheriff deputy's question about the defendant's gang membership was reasonably likely to elicit an incriminating response in the context of a homicide arrest; therefore, it exceeded the booking exception, and the answer was suppressed).]

To rebut the booking exception to *Miranda,* explore the following two issues:

Does the police conduct conform to usual booking practice?

When booking an arrestee, the police will question him from a form consisting of standard questions restricted to biographical information. If instead the questioning was a protracted interrogation veering from biographical information to the offense, it will not pass muster as routine booking questions.

Viewed against the information the police had about the crime and the information they were lacking, did the biographical questions appear to be aimed at obtaining the missing information?

This issue is demonstrated in a case involving a lengthy police questioning by homicide detectives of a marijuana sale arrestee about his name. [*See Thomas v. United States,* 731 A.2d 415, 432 (D.C. 1999).]

In *Thomas* the police had a description of a shooter that matched the arrestee, and a dying declaration that "Tony" shot the decedent. What the police lacked was confirmation that the suspect's first name was Tony. If it turned out that the name of the man who called himself "David" was really Tony then this would provide a link in the chain of evidence against the suspect. Under these circumstances, the court held that the lengthy questioning of the arrestee about his name constituted custodial interrogation within *Miranda.*

§8:24   *Miranda* Exceptions: Public Safety

The police may dispense with *Miranda* warnings where, under the circumstances confronting the officers, there is "an objectively reasonable need to protect the police or the public from any immediate danger associated with [a] weapon." [*New York v. Quarles,* 467 U.S. 649, 659 n.8 (1984) (where police had been told suspect was armed, they saw him discard something in a grocery store, and upon arresting him, they saw that his shoulder holster was empty, police entitled to ask him where he had discarded gun); *United States v. Fautz,* 812 F.Supp.2d 570, 621-31 & nn.39-49 (D.N.J. 2011) (extensively surveying fact patterns in cases and finding that courts generally permit pre-*Miranda* public safety questioning where there is reason to believe in the presence of a hidden weapon in premises or in an automobile).]

To rebut the public safety exception, examine the circumstances and argue that there were no specific and articulable facts raising a danger to the police or public or that the danger had dissipated with the arrest and handcuffing of the defendant. [*See United States v. Mobley*, 40 F.3d 688 (4th Cir. 1994) (public safety exception did not apply where suspect arrested naked, handcuffed and removed from his house before the police asked him if there was a gun in the house; refusing to recognize an across-the-board public safety exception for the arrest of narcotics suspects).]

§8:25   *Miranda* Violations

A *Miranda* violation has limited effect:
*   The prosecution can use the statements to cross-examine the defendant or in rebuttal of the defendant's testimony. [*Harris v. New York*, 401 U.S. 222 (1971).]
*   Physical evidence to which the statements lead is admissible. [*United States v. Patane*, 542 U.S. 630 (2004); *but see State v. Vondehn*, 348 Or. 462, 236 P.3d 691 (2010) (Oregon joins Vermont, Massachusetts and Ohio to reject *Patane* as a matter of state constitutional law).]

Forms:
*   **Form 8-1** Motion and Supporting Brief to Suppress Statements (Unknowing Waiver)
*   **Form 8-2** Motion and Supporting Brief to Suppress Statements (Custody, Invocation of Right to Remain Silence)
*   **Form 7-4** Motion to Suppress & Supporting Brief (Automobile Stop) [*See* Chapter 7]

[§§8:26-8:29 Reserved]

D. Right to Counsel

§8:30   Fifth Amendment (Before Charge)

Miranda creates a right to counsel triggered by an arrestee's unequivocal and unambiguous post-warning request for counsel. [*Edwards v. Arizona*, 451 U.S. 477 (1981); *see Davis v. United States*, 512 U.S. 452, 458-59 (1994).]

Once a suspect asserts the right to counsel, not only must the interrogation cease, but the suspect may not be approached for further interrogation until counsel is present. If the police subsequently initiate an encounter in the absence of counsel, the suspect's statements are presumed involuntary and inadmissible as substantive evidence at trial, even where the suspect executes a waiver and his statements would be considered voluntary under traditional standards. [*McNeil v. Wisconsin*, 501 U.S. 171, 176-77 (1991) (stating that this procedure is "designed to prevent police from badgering a defendant into waiving his previously asserted *Miranda* rights").]

The Fifth Amendment right to counsel (unlike the Sixth Amendment right) is not offense specific. [*Arizona v. Roberson*, 486 U.S. 675, 682-84 (1988) (arrestee's request for counsel barred questioning by different officers investigating offense other than one of arrest, even though new officers did not know that arrestee had requested counsel).]

Once invoked, the police cannot approach the arrestee about any offense without counsel being present. This is true even when different law enforcement authorities who may be unaware of the suspect's prior invocation of his Fifth Amendment right to counsel reapproach the suspect regarding a different offense. [*Goodwin v. Johnson*, 132 F.3d 162, 179 (5th Cir. 1997).]

The *Edwards* prohibition against further attempts to question an arrestee no longer applies once the defendant has been out of custody for 14 days on the theory that the risk of coercion inherent in custodial interrogation has dissipated by then. [*Maryland v. Shatzer*, 130 S.Ct. 1213 (2010).]

§8:31   Asserting the Fifth Amendment Right to Counsel

If you represent a suspect who has not yet been charged, good practice is to notify the police and prosecuting authority of your representation and to insist that all communications with your client cease.

Language in *Miranda* seems to support this technique. [*See Miranda*, 384 U.S. at 473-74 ("If the individual indicates in any manner, at any time prior to or during questioning, that he wishes to remain silent, the interrogation must cease").]

However, recent decisions refuse to honor such anticipatory invocations. [*See Montejo v. Louisiana*, 556 U.S. 778, 797 ("We have in fact never held that a person can invoke his *Miranda* rights anticipatorily, in a context other than custodial interrogation . . . ." (quoting *McNeil*, 501 U.S. at 182 n.3)).] And most courts have held that the *Miranda* right to counsel applies and the police must honor their invocation only when an individual is in custody and under interrogation. [*See Commonwealth v. DeJesus*, 567 Pa. 415, 430, 787 A.2d 394, 403 (2001) ("a person accused of a crime who has already engaged counsel may, with full knowledge of his rights but in the absence of counsel, effectively waive his right to have counsel present while he is questioned by the police"); *United States v. Grimes*, 142 F.3d 1342, 1348 (11th Cir. 1998) (executing public defender's form notifying police that defendant is represented and serving it on police and district attorney did not trigger right to counsel at a later interview, reasoning that *Miranda* right to counsel cannot be invoked anticipatorily and outside the context of a custodial interrogation); *Alston v. Redman*, 34 F.3d 1237, 1242-51 (3d Cir. 1994) (same); *Sapp v. State*, 690 So.2d 581 (Fla 1997) (same).]

Further, the Supreme Court has held that an attorney's statement that he represents the arrestee does not trigger the right to counsel protections. [*Moran v. Burbine*, 475 U.S. 412 (1986). *But see People v. Bender*, 452 Mich. 594, 597 n.1, 551 N.W.2d 71 (1996) (noting that several states reject *Moran*).]

Whether the Fifth Amendment's protections extend at all to the pre-arrest, pre-charge stage remains undecided. [*See* §8:71, *infra*.] *State v. Borg*, 806 N.W.2d 535 (Minn. 2011), illustrates the hazards if it does not. There, a detective investigating a child molestation mailed the suspect a letter accusing him of the offense and inviting him to comment. The suspect did not answer, and after he was charged, at trial the prosecution used his silence in the face of the allegation as a tacit admission of guilt. The Minnesota Supreme Court affirmed, ruling that outside the context of a criminal case or an arrest, questioning works no compulsion; therefore, the Fifth Amendment's bar on compelled self-incrimination does not apply.

In *Salinas v. Texas,* 133 S.Ct. 2174 (2013), the Supreme Court granted certiorari to decide whether pre-custodial assertion of the privilege or silence could be used in the prosecution's direct case as evidence of guilt, and then avoided the issue, but in a way that provides some direction to practitioners in how to counsel clients. There, a plurality of the Court assumed that the Fifth Amendment did apply to pre-arrest, pre-charge questioning, but it must be invoked and that mere silence does not suffice to invoke it. Therefore, that silence, or the selective answering of some and avoiding other questions, can be used against the individual as substantive evidence of guilt.

Thus, if you represent someone under investigation, you must school him in how to respond to police inquiries. *Salinas* precludes reliance on mere silence or refusal to answer. Pre-*Salinas* case law permitted sloppy invocations [*e.g., Quinn v. United States,* 349 U.S. 155, 164, (1955) ("[N]o ritualistic formula is necessary in order to invoke the privilege")], but the *Salinas* plurality seems to indicate that the individual must refer to the Fifth Amendment privilege with some specificity. [133 S.Ct. at 2179 (witness must "expressly invoke the privilege," citing *Hutcheson v. United States,* 369 U.S. 599, 610-11 (1962), for the proposition that invocation of "due process" is not a proper assertion of the privilege); *but see Commonwealth v. Molina*, 2014 Pa. LEXIS 3035 (Pa. Nov. 20, 2014)(breaking off telephone conversation and refusing to go to police station for further questioning sufficient to invoke privilege against self-incrimination); *Sessoms v. Grounds*, 768 F.3d 882 (9th Cir. 2014)(en banc)(defendant's statements at the beginning of custodial interrogation, but before *Mirandized* ("There wouldn't be any possible way that I could have a—a lawyer present while we do this? . . . Yeah, that's what my dad asked me to ask you guys . . . uh, give me a lawyer"), sufficient to invoke right to counsel and questioning should have ceased); *United States v. Okatan,* 728 F.3d 111 (2d Cir. 2013) ("I want a lawyer" sufficient); *Commonwealth v. Fischere*, 2013 PA Super 191, 70 A.3d 1270, 1277 n.4 (2013) (informing the detective that the witness did not wish to answer any further questions without speaking to an attorney sufficient); *Baumia v. Commonwealth,* 402 S.W.3d 530, 536 (KY 2013) (Defendant's pre-arrest statement, "My father told me not to talk to the f——n' police, see my attorney" sufficient to invoke the privilege; "Although not an ideal statement, Appellant's chosen method of invoking her right to remain silent was effective, as the invocation of the right is afforded a liberal construction and does not require any specific combination of words to garner its protection").] Excessive specificity poses several problems, however: (1) the client is likely to forget or bungle a detailed invocation; (2) too much talking, and the client is likely to keep going and explain *how* the answer would incriminate him, thereby disclosing exactly what the privilege should guard; (3) it might open a dialogue in which the officers try to dissuade him from his invocation; and (4) while unclear on this point, *Salinas* might encourage courts to admit the words in which the defendant invoked, and a statement about "incrimination" sounds, well, incriminating.

Our suggestion is that you give your client a card to read or present that says, "I respectfully refuse to answer based on my Fifth Amendment privilege. Please direct any further questions to my lawyer." *Salinas* indicates that "Fifth Amendment privilege" are the magic words, and that much, without the addition of "incrimination," sounds harmless.

§8:32   Sixth Amendment Post-Charge Right to Counsel

The Sixth Amendment right to counsel attaches with the initiation of adversary proceedings. [*Brewer v. Williams,* 430 U.S. 387, 399 (1977) (right attached upon defendant's arraignment on arrest warrant and complaint).]

It applies only to that charge, and the police are free to question the defendant about other charges, even factually related ones, so long as the charges do not constitute the same offense under double jeopardy. [*Texas v. Cobb*, 532 U.S. 162 (2001). *See Maine v. Moulton*, 474 U.S. 159 (1985).]

Once it attaches, the Sixth Amendment right to counsel prohibits the government from the deliberate elicitation of any statement absent counsel or the waiver of the right to counsel. [*Fellers v. United States*, 540 U.S. 519 (2004).] While the prosecution cannot use the statement in its direct case, it can cross-examine the defendant on the statement. [*Kansas v. Ventris*, 556 U.S. 586 (2009).]

The prohibition extends to non-custodial questioning and forbids the elicitation of statements in circumstances that might fall short of interrogation under the *Miranda* standard. [*Fellers v. United States*, 540 U.S. 519 (2004) (holding that post-indictment statements made in defendant's home when police came to discuss his involvement in methamphetamine distribution violated the Sixth Amendment).]

Thus the Sixth Amendment right forbids the use of undercover informants to elicit statements from a defendant free on bond. [*See Maine v. Moulton*, 474 U.S. 159 (1985).] But the informant can testify to the defendant's incriminating statements if the informant acts only as a "listening post" and makes no attempt to elicit statements about the charged offense. [*Kuhlmann v. Wilson*, 477 U.S. 436 (1986).]

§8:33   Waiver of Sixth Amendment Right to Counsel

The *Miranda* warnings sufficiently apprise a charged defendant of his Fifth and Sixth Amendment right to counsel. Once warned, a defendant, even one who is represented, can waive the right on his own and speak to the police. [*Montejo v. Louisiana*, 556 U.S. 778 (2009); *Patterson v. Illinois*, 487 U.S. 285 (1988).]

Until the decision in *Montejo*, a defendant's request for counsel at an initial appearance triggered a Sixth Amendment right to the assistance of counsel at any questioning, a right which could not be waived in the absence of counsel. *Montejo* overruled the holding in *Michigan v. Jackson*, 475 U.S. 625 (1986), that once a defendant requests counsel in connection with the initiation of formal proceedings, the police cannot obtain a waiver in the absence of counsel. Under *Montejo*, the appointment of counsel or a defendant's request for counsel in connection with formal proceedings does not prevent the authorities from approaching and questioning him. Further, *Montejo* indicates that anticipatory invocations of the right to counsel, or any invocation outside the context of custodial interrogation, are ineffective. [*Montejo*, 556 U.S. at 797; *but see State v. Bevel*, 745 S.E.2d 237 (W.Va. 2013) (rejecting *Montejo* as a matter of state constitutional law; once defendant requests the assistance of counsel at his initial appearance, no waiver is valid unless he initiated the conversation and waiver).]

The Sixth Amendment right to counsel is a broad right to interpose counsel as a medium between the charged defendant and the government, whereas the Fifth Amendment right to counsel is a prophylaxis restricted to only so much as is necessary to dispel the coercive tendencies of custodial interrogation. The broader nature of the Sixth Amendment right empowers you to argue that waiver standards should be stricter than those that govern the Fifth Amendment right, at least in circumstances where the government seeks to circumvent counsel as protective medium. Thus, in *Patterson*, the Supreme Court itself acknowledged that the holding of *Moran v. Burbine*, permitting a *Miranda* waiver to stand where a suspect was not told that his lawyer was trying to reach him during questioning, does not apply to post-charge questioning and that such a waiver would be invalid under the Sixth Amendment. [*Patterson*, 487 U.S. at 296 n.9.] Likewise, at least one court has held that "the broader Sixth Amendment protection of counsel . . . is not vulnerable to a waiver by inference from merely informed silence or from merely the acto of confessing itself after having been given *Miranda* rights." [*In re Darryl P.*, 211 Md. App. 112, 63 A.3d 1142, 1191 (Md. Ct. App. 2013).]

As with the Fifth Amendment right, you have two practical options:

First, you must educate your client to invoke his right to counsel if questioned because the only invocation the courts consistently recognize must come from his lips. Repeat the advice and perhaps rehearse with him:

"Okay, I'm a police officer. I say to you, 'Joe, picking up that charge was pretty bad luck. Seems like you were in the wrong place at the wrong time–Bob is the one who planned the robbery, isn't he?'"

"I don't want to talk about it. I want my lawyer present."

Arm him with a card that he can pull out, recite and hand to a police officer.

Second, you still can write the prosecutor and insist that you be present at any questioning. While it may not trigger the Sixth Amendment right, it does alert the prosecutor to the ethical risks of participating in or directing any questioning. Realize, however, that the ethical rules do not apply to non-lawyer law enforcement officials. [*See Montejo*, 556 U.S. at 790; *but see* §8:34, *infra*, for arguments applying the ethical rules when law enforcement officials work with lawyer prosecutors.]

§8:34   State and Ethical Right to Counsel Rules

Some courts have fashioned a broader right to counsel from state law and the rules of professional conduct, in particular, Model Rule 4.2 ("Communication with Person Represented by Counsel") or its predecessor, DR 7-104(A)(1). [*See People v. West*, 81 N.Y.2d 370, 599 N.Y.S.2d 484, 615 N.E.2d 968 (1993) (under New York state constitution, right to counsel bars police contact even pre-charge with person who is represented with respect to matter at issue as well as upon commencement of formal proceedings, whether or not defendant requested counsel, and cannot be waived in counsel's absence); Richard T. Farrell, *Richardson on Evidence* §§8-256 to 258 (11th ed) (explaining New York rule at length); *State v. Lefthand*, 488 N.W.2d 799 (Minn. 1992) (in-custody interrogation of formally accused person who is represented by counsel should not proceed prior to notification of counsel or presence of counsel, relying on state law and Rule 4.2); *United States v. Hammad*, 858 F.2d 834 (2d Cir. 1988) (violation of DR 7-104(A)(1) in having informant record conversation with represented person pre-indictment could be grounds for suppression).]

Unfortunately, most courts have rejected expansion of the right to counsel, aside from the limited *Miranda* right to counsel, to the stage before adversary proceedings commence. [*See State v. Norgaard*, 201 Mont. 165, 653 P.2d 483 (1984) (notes that other state courts overwhelming reject New York right to counsel rules).]

To avail yourself of arguments based on the rules of professional conduct, you must convince a court that:

- The rule against communications with a represented person applies before the commencement of criminal proceedings. [*See Hammad*, (DR 7-104(A)(1) applies before formal proceedings commence); *State v. Miller*, 600 N.W.2d 457 (Minn. 1999) (same; where corporation's counsel called agent during execution of search warrant, stated that he represented the employees as well and that they should not be interviewed, but agent refused to inform employees of that fact and continued interview, statements should be suppressed); *United States v. Talao*, 222 F.3d 1133, 1139 (9th Cir. 2000) (Model Rule 4.2 applies pre-indictment, at least where the adversary positions have hardened); *compare United States v. Balter*, 91 F.3d 427, 436 (3d Cir. 1997) (claiming that at that time, all federal courts of appeals besides the Second Circuit had held that the rule does not apply before the filing of criminal charges); *United States v. Brown*, 595 F.3d 498, 515-16 (3d Cir. 2010) (prosecutor's use of an informant to question a represented target pre-indictment falls within Rule 4.2's "authorized by law" exception).]

- The rule should apply to non-lawyer agents and informants. [*See* MR 5.3(c)(1) (lawyer responsible for conduct of nonlawyer assistants if lawyer ratifies the conduct); MR 8.4(a) (lawyer may not violate rules of professional conduct "through the acts of another"); *Miller*, 600 N.W.2d at 464 (prosecutor responsible for agent's actions); *United States v. Koerber*, No. 09-CR-302, 2013 U.S. Dist. LEXIS 116442 (Aug. 15, 2013 D. Utah) (prosecutors held responsible for agents' interview where they discussed their desire and intention with the agents to contact and interview defendant and told the agents to proceed with such contact); *United States v. McNaughton*, 848 F.Supp. 1195, 1202 (E.D.Pa. 1994) (FBI agent subject to restrictions of MR 4.2 prohibiting communications under authority of MR 8.4(a) where prosecutor was "aware of and working with" the agent on the case). Attributing the agent's actions to the prosecutor is easier where the agents have consulted with a prosecutor and worked closely with him. The argument lacks force if the police or agents have not even notified the prosecutor's office of the investigation.

- Suppression is an appropriate remedy for violation of a disciplinary rule. [*See Hammad* (may be, in the trial court's discretion); *Miller* (same); *State v. Gilliam*, 748 So.2d 622 (La. App. 1999) (same); *Koerber, supra* (elevating Rule 4.2 violation into a due process violation and ordering suppression); *compare United States v. Lowery*, 166 F.3d 1119 (11th Cir. 1999) (suppression is never an appropriate remedy); *Balter*, 91 F.3d at 436 n.7 (same); *Brown*, 595 F.3d at 516 n.23 (same).]

PRACTICE TIP:

You may be able to use the disciplinary rules to your client's advantage preemptively even in those jurisdictions that reject them as grounds for suppression.

If you know that your client is under investigation, notifying the police and prosecutor of your representation probably does not trigger the Fifth or Sixth Amendment rights to counsel. [*See* §§8:30 & 8:32.] However, the prosecutor who ignores Model Rule 4.2 risks disciplinary sanctions. As zealous as many prosecutors are, few will risk their license on an investigation.

Therefore, a representation letter to the prosecutor may deter the prosecutor from having the police or informants communicate with your client. [For a form Representation Letter, *see* Chapter 1, Entering the Case.]

[§§8:35-8:39 Reserved]

E.   Involuntary Confessions

§8:40   General Points

Before *Miranda*, courts dealt with challenges to the means used to elicit confession by evaluating each confession under the totality of the circumstances to determine if it was so coerced by official pressure as to be considered "involuntary" and its eliciting offensive to the Due Process Clause of the Fourteenth Amendment. [*Miller v. Fenton*, 474 U.S. 104, 109 (1985).]

Miranda was intended to be a prophylactic against pressure tactics, and confessions are seldom found to be involuntary where *Miranda* is obeyed. [*Missouri v. Seibert*, 542 U.S. at 608-609.] However, *Miranda* did not supplant the case law prohibiting involuntary confessions. [*See Withrow v. Williams,* 507 U.S. 680, 693-94 (1993).]

Establishing that a confession was coerced has several advantages over proving a *Miranda* violation: the coerced confession cannot be used in cross-examining the defendant at trial [*Kansas v. Ventris*, 556 U.S. 586, 590 (2009) (citing New *Jersey v. Portash*, 440 U.S. 450, 458-59 (1979)]; and evidence derived from the confession, including physical evidence, must be suppressed as fruits of the poisonous tree [*e.g., Dye v. Commonwealth*, 411 S.W.3d 227 (Ky. 2013); *compare United States v. Patane*, 542 U.S. 630 (2004)].

§8:41   Totality of the Circumstances

The due process clause and the Fifth Amendment forbid not only physical torture, but more subtle psychological devices used to elicit a confession against the accused's will. The question is "whether the behavior of the State's law enforcement officials was such as to overbear [the defendant's] ... will to resist and bring about confessions not freely self-determined." [*Rogers v. Richmond*, 365 U.S. 534, 544 (1961).]

To determine whether a confession is voluntary, the court must assess "the totality of all the surrounding circumstances–both the characteristics of the accused and the details of the interrogation." [*Schneckloth v. Bustamonte*, 412 U.S. 218, 226 (1973).]

Factors to be considered include the "[accused's] lack of education, or his low intelligence, the lack of any advice to the accused of his constitutional rights, the length of detention, the repeated and prolonged nature of the questioning, and the use of physical punishment such as the deprivation of food or sleep." [*Schneckloth*, 412 U.S. at 226. *See also Withrow,* 507 U.S. at 693-94 (listing factors); *Dassey v. Dittmann*, 860 F.3d 933 (7th Cir. 2017) (special attention must be paid to manipulative interrogation techniques, such as false promises, cajoling, and actively misleading, when applied to a young and intellectually challenged arrestee who has no parent present), *rehearing en banc granted, opinion vacated*, — F.3d – (7th Cir. Aug. 4, 2017); *State v. Rettenberger*, 984 P.2d 1009, 1013-14, 999 UT 80 (1999) ("under the totality of circumstances test, courts must consider such external factors as the duration of the interrogation, the persistence of the officers, police trickery, absence of family and counsel, and threats and promises made to the defendant by the officers. ... [C]ourts must also consider such factors as the defendant's mental health, mental deficiency, emotional instability, education, age, and familiarity with the judicial system").]

§8:42   Threats or Appeals to Friendship

Threats to the suspect's family and appeals to special friendship between the interrogating officer and the arrestee have been deemed offensive to due process. [*See Lynum v. Illinois*, 372 U.S. 528 (1963) (invalidating confession after defendant was falsely threatened that her children would be taken away from her and she would lose her government benefits for them if she did not "cooperate"); *Spano v. New York*, 360 U.S. 315 (1959) (invalidating confession to murder where police officer, who was a "childhood friend" of defendant, falsely told defendant that his telephone confession had placed the officer's job at risk and losing his job would create a hardship for the officer's family); *Dye v. Commonwealth*, 411 S.W.3d 227 (Ky. 2013) (misinforming defendant that his crime made him eligible for the death penalty and suggesting that he would be raped in prison rendered confession involuntary).]

§8:43   Weakened Defendants

There must be some action by state officials causally related to the confession. [*See Colorado v. Connelly*, 479 U.S. 157 (1986) (rejecting contention that defendant's unsolicited confession to a police officer was involuntary because his mental illness drove him to confess).]

However, the analysis of involuntariness must consider the effect of the interrogation techniques "as applied to the unique characteristics of a particular suspect." [*Miller v. Fenton*, 474 U.S 104, 109 (1985). *See also State v. Rettenberger*, 984 P.2d at 1014, (*Connelly* does not mandate that courts must determine that police tactics were coercive before examining whether defendant's will was overborne, but merely "stands for the limited proposition that a defendant's mental condition is not in itself sufficient to make a confession involuntary").]

Thus, some decisions anchor the finding of involuntariness to the effect of relatively mild police tactics on weakened defendants. [*See, e.g., Mincey v. Arizona*, 437 U.S. 385 (1978) (defendant subjected to 4-hour interrogation while incapacitated and sedated in intensive-care unit); *Hill v. Anderson*, 300 F.3d 679, 682 (6th Cir. 2002) ("When a suspect suffers from some mental incapacity, such as intoxication or retardation, and the incapacity is known to interrogating officers, a lesser quantum of coercion is necessary to call a confession into question"); *United States v. Haddon*, 927 F.2d 942, 946 (7th Cir.1991) ("when the interrogating officers reasonably should have known that a suspect is under the influence of drugs or alcohol, a lesser quantum of coercion may be sufficient to call into question the voluntariness of the confession").]

§8:44   Misrepresentations

Threats to inform the prosecution and courts of the suspect's refusal to cooperate, or promises to inform them of cooperation, and exaggerations and outright lies about the evidence against the defendant do not render a confession involuntary. [See *Frazier v. Cupp*, 394 U.S. 731 (1969) (confession was voluntary where police lied to defendant that his co-defendant had implicated him in the crime); *see also Miller v. Fenton*, 474 U.S. 104 (1985) (upholding confession obtained after an hour-long interrogation where the police lied about evidence they had against defendant, expressed sympathy toward defendant by indicating suspect was not a criminal and should receive psychiatric help, and where the suspect collapsed in a state of shock immediately after confessing); *United States v. Braxton*, 112 F.3d 777 (4th Cir. 1997) (en banc) (telling defendant that he would get five years if he did not "come clean" did not make statement coerced); *but see United States v. Harrison*, 34 F.3d 886 (9th Cir. 1994) (threatening to inform the prosecutor of a suspect's refusal to cooperate violates her Fifth amendment right to remain silent).]

The Supreme Court has overruled an early case that held that a confession is involuntary if given with "the slightest hope of benefit or remotest fear of injury." *See Arizona v. Fulminante*, 499 U.S. 279, 285 (1991) (overruling *Bram v. United States*, 168 U.S. 532 (1897)). However, a false promise that if the defendant confesses, he will be set free makes the confession involuntary and inadmissible. [*Dassey v. Dittmann*, 860 F.3d 933.]

§8:45   Fabricated Evidence

While police misrepresentations do not doom a confession to inadmissibility, several state courts have held that use of police-fabricated evidence does. [*State v. Patton*, 362 N.J.Super. 16, 826 A.2d 783 (NJ App Div 2003) (confession inadmissible where police played to arrestee fabricated audiotape of a fictitious eyewitness identifying arrestee as shooter; reviewing cases from several jurisdictions); *State v. Farley*, 452 S.E.2d 50, 60 n.13 (W. Va. 1994) (dicta; confession admissible where police misrepresented that defendant failed polygraph, but would have been suppressed had police fabricated a false report of the polygraph results). *But see State v. Whittington*, 809 A.2d 721 (Md 2002) (rejecting such a bright line standard).]

§8:46   Burden of Proof

Federal law imposes on the prosecution the burden of proving that a confession was voluntary by a preponderance of the evidence. [*Missouri v. Seibert*, 542 U.S. 600, 124 S.Ct. 2601, 2608 n.1 (2004).]

Some states, recognizing the probative force of a confession, set the standard at beyond a reasonable doubt. [*See, e.g., State v. Raiford*, 846 So.2d 913, 923 (La. App.), *writ denied*, 847 So.2d 1217 (La. 2003); *People v. Huntley*, 15 N.Y.2d 72, 255 N.Y.S.2d 838, 204 N.E.2d 179 (1965).]

§8:47   The Common Law Rule of Unreliability

A confession's reliability bears no relevance to its admissibility under the due process clause. [*See Rogers v. Richmond*, 365 U.S. 534, 540-41 (1961) (court may not consider confession's veracity in deciding admissibility).]

However, before the law of constitutionally involuntary confessions developed, the common law forbade the admission of a confession rendered under circumstances making it likely to have been unreliable. [*See People v. Schompert*, 19 N.Y.2d 300, 305, 279 N.Y.S.2d 515 (1967).]

The common law may exclude statements made by mentally ill or intoxicated defendants whether or not the police played a role in eliciting the confession. [*People v. Schompert*, 19 N.Y.2d 300, 305, 279 N.Y.S.2d 515 (1967); *People v. Braggs*, 268 Ill. Dec. 861, 335 Ill. App.3d 52, 779 N.E.2d 475 (Ill. App. 2002) (especially in cases of mentally retarded and juvenile defendants, courts must consider reliability and credibility of confession to guard against danger of false confessions), *aff'd as modified*, 209 Ill.2d 492, 810 N.E.2d 472 (2004).] Iowa's revived common-law evidentiary rule excludes statements induced by any threats or promises of leniency. [*State v. Madsen*, 813 N.W.2d 714, 724-28 (Iowa 2012) (officer's statements that there would be an unfavorable news story if defendant did not tell him everything and that there was "an advantage ... to be gained" if he confessed violated state's evidentiary rules and rendered confession inadmissible).]

PRACTICE TIP:

Raise a common law unreliability claim in those instances where you have evidence of your client's inability to make an intelligent statement due to some impairment or where you have independent evidence that your client's statements were false. Argue that the common law rule recognizes the misleading potential of admitting such statements and therefore entitles you to a pre-trial hearing on the issue and a judicial determination of admissibility.

The common law rule applies to statements obtained by private as well as official action. [*State v. Bowe*, 77 Hawaii 51, 881 P.2d 538 (1994); *Trinkle v. State*, 284 N.E. 2d 816, 819-20 (Ind. 1972) (DeBruler, J., concurring).]

PRACTICE TIP:

Some state statutes preclude use of involuntary statements regardless of who elicited the statement. [*See, e.g., Bowe; People v. Grillo*, 176 A.D.2d 346, 574 N.Y.S.2d 583 (NY App. Div. 1991) (applying involuntariness standard of NY Crim. P. Law §60.45 to statements made to private citizens).] If your facts suggest traditional involuntariness, even if it was coerced by a private actor, do not assume the burden of proving the confession's falsity or unreliability unless that helps your case.

§8:48   Procedure for Challenging the Confession

The Due Process Clause requires that the trial judge decide the issue of a confession's voluntariness before the jury hears it. [*Sims v. Georgia*, 385 U.S. 538 (1967); *Jackson v. Denno*, 378 U.S. 368 (1964).]

A hearing will be held only if the defendant alleges in his motion facts which, if true, would render his statements involuntary. The detail required depends on the nature of claim; for example, if the basis for suppression is a *Miranda* violation, a motion or affidavit alleging that the defendant had been arrested, that the police asked him questions, and that they omitted the warnings would suffice. In contrast, a true involuntariness claim requires the defendant to spell out the circumstances which amount to coercion. [*United States v. Mathurin*, 148 F.3d at 69-70 (2d Cir. 1998) (explaining the difference in detail required for each kind of claim).]

Some courts will insist that the allegations come from an affidavit by a person with personal knowledge, usually the defendant. [*United States v. Miller*, 382 F.Supp.2d 350, 361 (N.D.N.Y. 2007).]

The hearing can be pre- or mid-trial, but you should request that it be held pre-trial for several reasons:

- The decision on the suppression issue may dictate whether there is a trial, plea or dismissal.
- You need to know whether the jury will hear the confession to be able to voir dire the jury on it during jury selection and discuss it in opening statements. The practice in most jurisdictions is that the hearing takes place outside the jury's presence (whether the suppression motion is heard pre or mid-trial). Insist on this, arguing that if the jury hears the confession, suppression and a curative charge cannot undo the harm. [*See Bruton v. United States*, 391 U.S. 123 (jury could not be expected to ignore co-defendant's confession).]
- By holding the hearing pre-trial rather than mid-trial, the court saves the jury considerable delay and inconvenience.

Winning an involuntary confession claim has an advantage over prevailing on a *Miranda* violation because a coerced confession cannot be used for any purpose, including cross-examination of your client at trial. [*Mincey v. Arizona*, 437 U.S. 385, 398-402 (1978).]

Even if you lose an involuntariness challenge before the judge, you are entitled to introduce "testimony about the environment in which the police secured [the] confession" to the jury to show that it should not be credited. [*Crane v. Kentucky*, 476 U.S. 683, 691 (1986).] This may include expert testimony on your client's unusual susceptibility to be compliant and adopt suggestions even where untrue and the phenomenon of false confessions. [*See* §8:50.]

§8:49 Preparing an Involuntariness Claim

Look to make a coerced confession claim whenever:
- Your client suffered some mental or emotional disturbance of which the police had knowledge.
- The police made exaggerated promises or threats to your client, in particular, threats of harm to him or his loved ones.
- The interrogation spans an unusually long time.
- The police likely have a special dislike for your client, or feel strong pressure to solve the crime (*e.g.,* child homicide cases, serial rapes and murders, assault or homicide of a police officer, and terrorism cases (a category that, depending on local sentiment, may include everything from bombings to immigration violations).

Mounting an involuntariness claim calls for substantial preparation:
- If your client claims physical abuse, document this as soon as possible by having his injuries photographed and having a medical examination.
- Many police stations and jails sign in detainees. Subpoena those records to show how long your client was interrogated and whether he was removed from the premises for some reason.
- If your client has a disability, obtain medical and psychiatric records. You might want to retain a psychiatrist to interview your client and report on his IQ and other mental conditions.
- Subpoena <u>all</u> officers who participated in the interrogation. The prosecution likely will call only the officer who played "the good guy."

At the suppression hearing, explore the following topics:
- The manner in which the interrogation was carried out (e.g.: How many officers? For how long?).
- Any exculpatory statements your client made. Have the officer flesh out such statements in his report to make sure he will not hedge on them at trial.
- Any threats or promises made to your client.
- Exactly what your client said and how he said it (e.g.: What were the questions? How did your client answer (at length, in monosyllabic words, mumbling, crying)?).

§8:50 Expert Testimony

Courts have begun to admit expert testimony to demonstrate either that a confession was involuntary or that it was false. [*Hannon v. State*, 84 P.3d 320 (Wy. 2004) (error to preclude defendant from calling expert to testify to mental capacity of defendant to voluntarily admit the allegations, but expert could not give opinion on whether defendant was telling the truth in police interview; analogizes to prosecution expert testimony to explain victims' behavior; surveys cases); *State v. Rettenberger*, 984 P.2d 1009, 1999 UT 80 (1999) (court suppressed confession as involuntary based in part on expert testimony that 18-year-old defendant had attention deficit disorder, below average IQ, maturity of 15-year-old, symptoms of depression, anxiety disorder, and dependent personality disorder such that he would tend to agree with police officers to relieve his stress); *United States v. Hall*, 93 F.3d 1337 (7th Cir. 1996); *but see Commonwealth v. Alicia*, 92 A.3d 753 (Pa. 2014) (refusing to permit expert testimony on false confessions as an invasion of "jury's role as exclusive arbiter of credibility").]

For the most part, the cases require that the defense lay a foundation that the client suffers some impairment (i.e., some mental or personality disorder) that makes his situation unusual and in need of expert testimony to explain it. [*See United States v. Adams*, 271 F.3d 1236, 1246 (10th Cir. 2001) (rejecting testimony in case where testimony would not have linked voluntariness and truthfulness of confession to any disorder; distinguishing *Hall* on these grounds).]

If your client's understanding of the *Miranda* warnings is at issue, you also may use expert testimony to show his low intelligence or his unfamiliarity with the language in which the warnings were administered.

EXAMPLE:

A forensic psychologist, after administering a number of tests to the defendant, testified that the defendant had an IQ of 65 and a mental age of 10. He then reviewed the *Miranda* advisement and waiver form with the defendant, asking him to explain what the words meant to him, and concluded that the defendant could read it only with difficulty and could not explain words on the form such as "privilege" and "waiver." In addition, the psychologist read the form to the defendant at the speed reflected on the taped confession and found that the defendant could not keep up at that speed and did not understand. Finally, the witness added that the defendant would "probably portray himself as understanding things that he did not so as to appear normal." [*State v. Raiford*, 846 So.2d 913, 924 (La. App. 2003).]

Note that the psychologist did concede that the defendant could be made to understand the *Miranda* warnings, but not as put to him. An honest expert must make that concession in all but the most extreme cases, and the prosecution will argue that "could understand" meant "did understand" (after all, the police thought he understood). However, the *Raiford* defense avoided a ruling based on such speculation by having the psychologist tie his opinion to the particular facts of the case.

[§§8:51-8:59 Reserved]

F.   Dealing With the Confession at Trial

§8:60   The Unrecorded But Noted Confession

Most law enforcement agencies do not record statements in any way. The agent, officer or his partner takes notes, then types or dictates a report purporting to describe the statement.

You will find such reports fraught with inaccuracies, wishful thinking about what your client said, and unjustified conclusions about what your client meant. Look for examples of sentences and word choices in the report that clearly are not your client's.

To attack the officer's report:

- *Move for production of the officer's handwritten notes and compare differences and note omissions.* This technique works best with details that may not have seemed crucial at the time the notes were taken, but that become decisive at trial. If the officer cannot get the story right between the time of his note-taking and the time of his report-writing, how can the jury trust his recollection on the witness stand to the extent it differs from the notes?
- *Elicit the preconceptions the officer brought to the interview.* This is a risky tactic, because the officer's pre-conceptions are that your client was guilty, and given a chance he will recite the bases for his beliefs, which may include statements by other witnesses and informants and your client's prior criminal record.
- *Emphasize noncompliance with procedures.* If, as in a growing number of jurisdictions [*see* §8:62, *infra*], your jurisdiction has adopted a policy requiring that interrogations be recorded, the officer's noncompliance or evasion of such guidelines is grist for cross-examination. Try to develop the reasons which motivated the adoption of the guidelines: the need to create an accurate record of what was said, the desire to avoid convicting the innocent with coerced false confessions.

§8:61   The Confession Nowhere Noted

Sometimes, an officer will testify to a confession or particularly damning admission that does not appear in any report or notes.

Attack such testimony aggressively to suggest that the officer is mistaken or even lying.

Make the following points, which you can prolong or abbreviate as you see fit:
- The statement purportedly was made months or years ago.
- The officer has participated in scores of arrests and investigations since then. If yours is a routine type of case, have the officer agree that many of them, like this case, have been the same type of case (*e.g.*, drug arrest, assault, domestic dispute, etc.).
- In the course of those investigations, he has interviewed hundreds of arrestees, suspects and witnesses.
- He knows through experience and training that an arrestee's exact words are important evidence.
- He is trained to write reports, and routinely does so, to preserve evidence important to a case.
- He relies on those reports to recall what happened in an investigation that may have occurred some time ago; other officers and prosecutors rely on those reports to investigate and to put together a case; and the law requires that the prosecutor turn over the reports to the defense so that the defendant and his lawyer will know what evidence they are facing and so they can prepare their defense.

If the cross-examination appears productive, you can be as aggressive as you want. Your argument may range from if the officer cared so little about the case that he could not commit the defendant's own words (or so he claims) to writing, the jury should not place any weight on his testimony, to an argument that the whole prosecution case is tainted because if the prosecutor had a strong case there would have been no reason for him to rely on a purported confession that never surfaced until halfway through trial.

§8:62 The Recorded Confession

Although it is still the minority approach, there is a trend toward requiring, either by statute or case law, that all confessions be recorded. [*See, e.g.,* 725 ILCS 5/103-2.1 (homicide cases); Tex. Code Crim. Proc. Ann. art. 38.22, §3, D. C. Code Ann. §5-133.20 (crimes of violence). *See generally People v. Combest,* 4 N.Y. 3d 341, 350 nn.5, 828 N.E. 2d 583, 795 N.Y. S. 2d 481, 487 n.5 (2005) (noting trend); *Commonwealth v. Harrell,* 2013 PA Super. 82, 65 A.3d 420, 449 (2013) (Donohue, J., dissenting) (urging Pennsylvania Supreme Court or Legislature to adopt a recording rule).] The National Association of Criminal Defense Lawyers maintains a compendium on electronic recording at www. nacdl.org/electronicrecordingproject. It includes legislation, court rulings, and commission reports, and identifies those state and local police departments that have adopted a recording practice or policy.

For example:
- The supreme courts of Alaska and Minnesota require recording of custodial questioning. [*Stephan v. State,* 711 P.2d 1156, 1158 (Alaska 1985); *State v. Scales,* 518 N.W.2d 587, 592 (Minn. 1994).]
- Wisconsin requires all custodial interrogations of juveniles to be recorded, when feasible. [*In re Jerrell,* 699 N.W.2d 110, 2005 WI 105 (WI 2005).]
- In Massachusetts, the court must instruct the jury that it may find that the prosecution has not carried its burden of proving a confession's voluntariness and hence admissibility because of the prosecution's failure to record the confession. [*Commonwealth v. DiGiambattista,* 442 Mass. 423, 447-48, 813 N.E. 2d 516, 533-34 (2004).]
- In New York, the District Attorneys Association of the State of New York's Best Practices Committee published "Guidelines for Recording Custodial Interrogations of Suspects" that generally require video recordings of such interrogations. [Available at http://tinyurl.com/7qpqog5; *see generally* Kristine Hamann, "New York Law Enforcement Creates Best Practices to Prevent Wrongful Convictions," 27 CRIMINAL JUSTICE 36 (Fall 2012).]
- By memorandum dated May 12, 2014, the United States Attorney General established a presumption that all federal law enforcement agencies will video-record custodial interviews. [Memorandum from Monty Wilkinson, Director, Executive Office for United States Attorneys, "New Department Policy Concerning Electronic Recording of Statements."]

If the police have audio- or video-taped your client's confession, try two attacks:

Your client's confession is demonstrably false.

If your independent investigation proves that the confession contradicts the forensic evidence, unimpeachable records or the testimony of credible witnesses, you have a strong argument that the police broke your client to the point of agreeing to fantasy.

In this situation, argue that not only should the confession be disbelieved, but the police have shown such a disregard for the truth that the jury should reject the whole of the prosecution's case.

The interviewer put words into your client's mouth.

Demonstrate that the police did not record the events leading to the confession, in which your client first denied guilt and then cajoled and coerced your client into confessing. This works best if you can show a substantial passage of time from the start of the interrogation until the recording began.

Often, the police or a prosecutor will elicit the confession through a series of leading questions, each one suggesting facts already known to the police before your client confessed.

Use two techniques to suggest that your client merely parroted the story the police wanted him to tell, guilty or not:
- First, go through each fact in the confession and show that the police knew it before the interview.
- Second, demonstrate that the police rehearsed the story with your client and put words in his mouth. This works best when the confession was recorded, and the questions are leading ones (as they usually are), to which your client replies with a "yes" or a grunt.

Example:

COMMENT:

Begin by going through each fact in the confession. Finish with questioning along the following lines.

Q. So, my client did not tell you a single fact about how the crime was committed that you did not already know?

A. Well, we didn't know that he was the one that committed the murder.

Q. Before the interview, you did suspect him, right?
A. Yes, that's what our investigation showed.
Q. You arrested and interrogated him because of your suspicions?
A. Yes.
Q. Now, I was asking you about the description of how the murder was committed, not who committed it. So, my client did not tell you a single fact about how the crime was committed that you did not already know?
A. That's right.

COMMENT:

Next, demonstrate that the police rehearsed the story with your client.
Q. Officer, you know what a leading question is, don't you?
A. Yes.
Q. That's a question in which the person asking suggests the answer?
A. Yes.
Q. Just like I'm doing now, right?
A. Yeah.
Q. That's different from a non-leading question, which is one that lets the witness tell his story the way he wants.
A. I don't know what you mean.
Q. Well, on direct examination, the prosecutor asked you several times, "What happened next?" Right?
A. Yes.
Q. And that kind of question let you tell the story in your own words.
A. Yes.
Q. You were in the courtroom when the prosecutor played the videotape of my client's statement, weren't you?
A. Yes.
Q. All the questions asked my client about the killing were leading questions, weren't they?
A. I don't know.
Q. Well, let's look at a couple of them.

COMMENT:

Go through one or two of the questions.
Q. In each one of these questions, you gave my client the answer in your question, didn't you?
A. He didn't have to agree with the question.
Q. You didn't let him tell the story in his own words by asking him, "What happened?"
A. I did before we started the recording.
Q. So you're telling us that when my client told the story in his own words, you didn't record him, but when you recorded him, you chose to put words in his mouth?
OBJECTION: Argumentative. The tape speaks for itself.

COMMENT:

The objection may be correct, but you've made your point and can return to it in closing argument.
Q. So my client made a statement to you before the recording started, is that what you're saying?
A. It was basically the same thing.
Q. But you chose not to record that statement?
A. We had not turned on the recorder yet, that's right.
Q. You had it there in the precinct, didn't you?
A. Sure.
Q. Just didn't turn it on?
A. Right.
Q. Didn't write down what my client said before the recording started either, did you?
A. No. I knew we'd be recording him later.
Q. So the answer is no?
A. That's what I said.

Q. You were interviewing my client for four hours before you started the recording according to your records?

A. Well, we weren't talking to him the whole time.

Q. Sometimes you just let him sit there?

A. Yes.

Q. But most of the time you were talking to him?

A. Yeah, sure.

Q. And the recorded statement lasted only 20 minutes?

A. That's what it said on the video.

Q. So you didn't make any record of what my client said to you in the four hours before the recording?

A. No

Q. We just have the 20 minutes of you giving my client facts and him saying yes or grunting?

A. We have whatever is on the tape.

COMMENT:

You can protract this questioning more or less as you choose. The more evasive the officer is, the better for you. You can be sure that he will insist that your client's pre-recording statement was basically the same, at least by the time he chose to record your client; he would not have recorded otherwise. Most likely, your client initially denied any involvement or knowledge; bring that out as well.]

The outline of your closing argument is:

(1) Before the police began to work on him, your client insisted he was innocent.

(2) The police did not accept that and began to work on him.

(3) Here are the techniques the police used to break down his will.

(4) The police already knew how the crime was committed (list each fact they knew).

(5) The police, as you saw on the tape, fed your client the facts they already knew and got him to agree with them.

(6) He did not agree because those facts were true, but because after so many hours, even your client, with all his mental deficiencies, realized that it was the only way to stop the interrogation and get the police off his back.

(7) The police could have chosen to record the entire interrogation to let you judge, but they did not want you to see my client's insistence on his innocence and the techniques they used to break him down.

(8) Therefore, this so-called confession is just the police story, put into my client's mouth. You cannot trust it or what the police did or told you about what they did.

[*See generally* Andrea D. Lyon and Michael J. Morrissey, "In Case of Confession," The Champion 9 (May 1990).]

§8:63   Corpus Delicti

The corpus delicti rule most often operates to regulate the sufficiency of the evidence. It forbids conviction solely on the defendant's confession and requires that there be independent evidence proving each element of the offense, albeit not identifying the defendant as the perpetrator. [*See, e.g.,* NY Criminal Procedure Law 60.50; *People v. Chico*, 90 N.Y.2d 585, 589-90, 665 N.Y.S.2d 5 (1997); Richard T. Farrell, *Richardson on Evidence*, §3-207 (a); *Commonwealth v. Verticelli*, 550 Pa. 435, 706 A.2d 820 (1998).]

In some jurisdictions, however, the rule also regulates admissibility of statements, and the prosecution must establish a prima facie case with independent evidence before a confession can be admitted. [*See Commonwealth v. Verticelli, supra; State v. Aten*, 130 Wash.2d 640, 927 P.2d 210 (1996) (holding with regard to the strength of the independent evidence "the *corpus delicti* is *not* established when independent evidence supports reasonable and logical inferences of both criminal agency and noncriminal cause").]

§8:64   The "Humane" or Massachusetts Rule

While not required by the federal constitution, some jurisdictions re-submit the issue of voluntariness to the jury and instruct the jury that it must find the confession to have been voluntary before the jury may consider it as evidence. [*Commonwealth v. Watkins*, 425 Mass, 830, 683 N.E.2d 653 (1997) (ruling, however, that the jury need not be unanimous on the issue of voluntariness); *Commonwealth v. Joyner*, 441 Pa. 242, 272 A.2d 454 (1971); *People v. Graham*,

55 N.Y. 2d, 144, 432 N.E. 2d 790, 447 N.Y.S. 2d 918 (1982) (*Miranda* violations also must be submitted to the jury under New York state law).]

[§§8:65-8:69 Reserved]

G.   Use of the Defendant's Silence

§8:70   General Points

A savvy prosecutor will attempt to use your client's silence, in circumstances where an innocent person could be expected to speak, as substantive evidence of guilt in his case in chief or as impeaching evidence during cross-examination of the defendant.

The constitutional limits on the use of the defendant's silence vary, depending on the time period of the silence:

- Pre-arrest silence: Silence admissible on cross-examination; courts split on introduction as substantive evidence. [*See* §8:71.]
- Post-arrest, pre-*Miranda* silence: Silence may be used to impeach; courts split on introduction as substantive evidence. [*See* §8:72.]
- Post-arrest, post-*Miranda* silence: Silence not admissible on direct or cross, but selective responses admissible. [*See* §8:73.]

[*See generally* Christopher Macchiaroli, "To Speak or Not to Speak: Can Pre-Miranda Silence Be Used As Substantive Evidence of Guilt?" 33 CHAMPION 14 (March 2009) (surveying positions of federal courts of appeals and arguing for a rule that forbids substantive use of pre-arrest, pre-*Miranda* use of silence, although conceding that it can be used on cross-examination).]

§8:71   Pre-Arrest Silence

The prosecution may introduce evidence of the defendant's pre-arrest silence upon cross-examination of the defendant. [*Jenkins v. Anderson*, 447 U.S. 231 (1980).]

Whether it may be used as substantive evidence without violating the Fifth Amendment privilege against self-incrimination is unclear. [*See Salinas v. Texas,* 133 S.Ct. 2174 (2013) (granting certiorari on this issue, but failing to decide it) (discussed in §8:31, *supra*); *Commonwealth v. Molina*, 2014 Pa. LEXIS 3035 (Pa. Nov. 20, 2014)(surveying decisions; because of the split among courts, decides that under the Pennsylvania state constitution pre-arrest silence or refusal to cooperate may not be used as substantive evidence of guilt); *State v. Lovejoy*, 2014 ME 48, 89 A.3d 1066 (Maine 2014)(pre-arrest silence and defendant's statement over the phone to detective that he wanted to speak to a lawyer could not be used in prosecution case); *Ouska v. Cahill-Masching*, 246 F.3d 1036, 1047 & n.9 (7th Cir. 2001) (noting split in opinion, but deciding that comment on silence violates the Fifth Amendment); *but see People v. Pollard,* 2013 COA 31, 307 P.3d 1124, 1129-30 (Colo. Ct. App. 2013) (surveying jurisdictions; "courts . . . uniformly hold that the prosecution may not use evidence of a person's refusal to consent to a search to prove his or her guilt through an inference of guilty knowledge or consciousness of guilt," but it can be used for other purposes); *State v. Gauthier,* 174 Wn. App. 257, 265-66, 298 P.3d 126, 131 (2013) (noting that five federal courts of appeals and 15 states forbid use of a defendant's refusal to consent to search as evidence of guilt); *but see State v. Stevens,* 228 Ariz. 411, 267 P.3d 1203, (2012) (refusal to consent cannot be used as substantive evidence of guilt, but can be used for impeachment).]

Even in a jurisdiction that permits the use of such evidence in the prosecution's case in chief, do not abandon the fight. Shift your argument from a constitutional one to an argument that under the circumstances, silence lacks any probative value. While relevance arguments lack force in many contexts, it is likely to resonate with judges here because they sense the unfairness of using against a defendant the silence that is his right. [*See Irwin v. Commonwealth*, 465 Mass. 834, 852-53 & n.31, 992 N.E.2d 275, 288-89 & n.31 (2013) (pre-arrest silence may not be used either for substantive or impeachment purposes because it is not probative); *State v. Thomas*, 766 N.W.2d 263 (Iowa App. 2009) (relying on relevance principles, court reverses conviction for prosecution's use of defendant's refusal to consent to search).]

§8:72   Post-Arrest, Pre-*Miranda* Silence

A post-arrest, pre-*Miranda* silence may be used to impeach. [*See Fletcher v. Weir*, 455 U.S. 603 (1982); *but see Commonwealth v. Kuder,* 2013 PA Super 35, 62 A.3d 1038, 1049-53 (2013) (under Pennsylvania Constitution, post-arrest silence cannot be used for any purpose; reviews different standards applying to pre-arrest and post-arrest silence).]

However, courts disagree on whether the prosecution may introduce the silence as substantive evidence in its case. [*See United States v. Moore*, 104 F.3d 377, 384-90(D.C. Cir. 1997) (prosecution cannot use post-arrest, pre-*Miranda* silence as evidence of guilt); *compare United States v. Frazier*, 408 F.3d 1102, 1111 (8th Cir. 2005) (may be used in case in chief because there is no government compulsion to speak or remain silent, therefore, no Fifth Amendment violation; surveys split in federal courts of appeals).]

§8:73   Post-Arrest, Post-*Miranda* Silence

Since *Miranda* warnings promise that silence is without cost, the Due Process Clause prohibits any use of such silence, even to impeach. [*Wainwright v. Greenfield*, 474 U.S. 284 (1986) (defendant's invocation of silence may not be used to show his sanity); *Doyle v. Ohio*, 426 U.S. 610 (1976) (may not be used to impeach).]

However, the prosecution can introduce evidence of the defendant's picking and choosing which questions to answer and which not to answer. [*United States v. Harris*, 956 F.2d 177, 181 (8th Cir. 1992); *see also United States v. Lopez-Lopez*, 282 F.3d 1, 13 (1st Cir. 2002) (defendant's post-arrest instruction to co-defendant, "Don't answer," admissible at joint trial because it was not silence and it was not a confession implicating the co-defendant).] A defendant's trial testimony that he told his exculpatory story to the police post-arrest also may open the door to impeachment with silence. [*Doyle*, 426 U.S. at 619 n.11; *United States v. Shannon*, 766 F.3d 346 (3d Cir. 2014)(reversing conviction because the defendant's trial testimony was not "blatantly inconsistent" with his post-arrest silence).]

[§§8:74-8:79 Reserved]

II.   OTHER STATEMENTS

A.   The Fifth Amendment

§8:80   Invoking the Fifth Amendment Privilege

The Fifth Amendment provides that "No person ... shall be compelled in any criminal case to be a witness against himself."
"Criminal case" includes preliminary hearings, grand jury hearings, all pre-trial hearings, trial and sentencing. [*See* Wayne R. LaFave, Jerold H. Israel, Nancy J. King, 3 *Criminal Procedure* §8.10(a) (2005).]

The privilege has a broad scope, extending to anything that would provide a link in the chain of evidence needed to prosecute:

> The privilege afforded not only extends to answers that would in themselves support a conviction ... but likewise embraces those which would furnish a link in the chain of evidence needed to prosecute. ... [I]f the witness, upon interposing his claim, were required to prove the hazard ... he would be compelled to surrender the very protection which the privilege is designed to guarantee. To sustain the privilege, it need only be evident from the implications of the question, in the setting in which it is asked, that a responsive answer to the question or an explanation of why it cannot be answered might be dangerous because injurious disclosure could result.

[*Hoffman v. United States*, 341 U.S. 479, 486 -87 (1951).]

Thus, an individual can decline to answer a prosecutor's questions at any criminal hearing on the grounds that the answer may incriminate him, or may provide a link in a chain of inferences that might tend to prove his guilt of a criminal charge. Even the innocent may invoke the privilege if there is reasonable cause to fear prosecution. [*Ohio v. Reiner*, 532 U.S. 17 (2001).]

§8:81   No Adverse Inferences May Be Drawn

No adverse inferences may be drawn from the exercise of the privilege because doing so would penalize its exercise. [*See Griffin v. California*, 380 U.S. 609 (1965) (prosecutor may not comment on defendant's exercise of privilege); *Carter v. Kentucky*, 450 U.S. 288 (1981) (court must instruct jury that it cannot draw any adverse inference from defendant's choice not to testify).]

To the extent possible, a criminal trial jury should not learn that the defendant exercised the privilege outside the courtroom or in another legal proceeding, such as before the grand jury. [*Grunewald v. United States*, 353 U.S. 391, 421 (1957) (defendant could not be cross-examined at trial on his invocation of Fifth Amendment in grand jury).]

§8:82   Civil or Administrative Proceedings

The privilege may be asserted at civil or administrative proceedings "in which the witness reasonably believes that the information sought, or discoverable as a result of his testimony, could be used in a subsequent state or federal criminal proceeding." [*Balsys v. United States*, 524 U.S. 666, 672 (1998).]

This means that he cannot be threatened with contempt for his refusal to answer and that his assertion of the privilege cannot be used against him in a later criminal proceeding. However, an inference can be drawn against him in the civil proceeding. [*See SEC v. Graystone Nash, Inc.*, 25 F.3d 187, 190 (3d Cir. 1994) (inference proper, but not summary judgment unless no other sanction would be fair).]

Furthermore, the prosecution cannot introduce in the criminal case the assertion of the privilege in the civil proceeding, even to cross-examine the defendant. [*Grunewald v. United States*, 353 U.S. 391, 421 (1957).] Even if your client chooses to testify before a grand jury, at earlier proceedings in the case, or at a related civil proceeding, he may still assert the privilege at his criminal trial. [*Pillsbury Co. v. Conboy*, 459 U.S. 248 (1983) (witness could not be compelled to give a deposition to repeat his immunized testimony because new testimony was a new incriminating event); *In re Neff*, 206 F.2d 149, 152 (3d Cir. 1953) ("It is settled by the overwhelming weight of authority that a person who has waived his privilege of silence in one trial or proceeding is not estopped to assert it as to the same matter in a subsequent trial or proceeding.")] However, the prosecution can introduce his earlier testimony unless it was given under a grant of immunity. When criminal proceedings are on the horizon, your client should avoid testifying or personally answering discovery at a civil proceeding that touches on the same issues. [See Chapter 19, Related Civil Litigation.]

[§§8:83-8:89 Reserved]

B.   Exculpatory Statements

§8:90   False Exculpatory Statements

Upon being confronted by the police, many individuals tell a story that exculpates them, but that can be proven false in many of its particulars. Such false exculpatory statements are admissible as evidence of consciousness of guilt, and the prosecution is entitled to an instruction explaining to the jury the inference of guilt that they may draw from the statement.

In some respects, false exculpatory statements are more powerful evidence of guilt than a confession. If you succeed in undermining the officer's credibility by showing his overzealousness in getting a confession, a jury may be willing to doubt that the confession was made. However, juries usually buy the prosecutor's argument that the officer accurately described a false exculpatory statement because if the officer were intent on fabricating evidence of guilt, why did he not go further and create a confession?

Do not underestimate the power of this evidence when considering whether to go to trial or to accept a plea offer.
The best responses to a false exculpatory statement are to:
- Show that your client was confused.
- Show that your client had some motive, aside from concealing his guilt, to lie to the officers. For example, he may have lied about the source of his income because it came from some illegal or improper activity unrelated to the crime at issue, or he may have lied about his whereabouts because he was married and did not want to disclose that he was with a paramour at the time of the crime.

§8:91   Exculpatory Statements

Generally, if you attempt to introduce your client's exculpatory statement, it will be considered inadmissible hearsay. [*People v. Reynoso*, 73 N.Y.2d 816, 818-19, 534 N.E.2d 30, 537 N.Y.S.2d 113 (NY 1988).]

However, there are hearsay exceptions that may allow admissibility. For example:
- The excited utterance exception for a statement made immediately under the influence of a surprising event (*e.g.*, your client blurted, "I didn't know that was there," upon the officers opening his car trunk and finding cocaine). [Fed. R. Evid. 803(2).]

- The present sense impression exception. [Fed. R. Evid. 803(1).]
- The then existing mental, emotional, or physical condition exception. [Fed. R. Evid. 803(3). See *United States v. DiMaria*, 727 F.2d 265 (2d Cir. 1984) (defendant's statement upon arrest that he was just there to buy cheap cigarettes admissible under Rule 803(3) to support defense theory that defendant thought he was buying bootleg rather than stolen cigarettes).]

A protestation of innocence maintained in the face of considerable incentives to admit guilt may also be admitted as evidence of your client's consciousness of innocence. [*United States v. Biaggi*, 909 F.2d 662, 690-91 (2d Cir. 1990) (trial court should have admitted evidence that defendant rejected offer of immunity to maintain that there was no wrongdoing); *State v. Santana-Lopez*, 237 Wis.2d 332, 613 N.W.2d 918 (Wis. App. 2000) (court erred in not admitting testimony that defendant accused of rape offered to police that he would take a DNA test).]

III. FORMS

Form 8-1   Motion and Supporting Brief to Suppress Statements (Unknowing Waiver)

IN THE UNITED STATES DISTRICT COURT FOR
THE _____ DISTRICT OF _____

UNITED STATES OF AMERICA,
         Plaintiff   CASE NO. _____

MM,
         Defendant

DEFENDANT'S PRE-TRIAL MOTIONS

AND NOW COMES Defendant MM, by his attorney, Thomas J. Farrell, and files the following pre-trial motions, further support for which is found in the attached Exhibits and Brief.

MOTION TO SUPPRESS POST-ARREST STATEMENTS

On _____, federal agents appeared at MM's home. He was on the road, driving a truck on a job. His cousin called him on MM's cell phone, told him agents were at his home, and MM turned around and drove back.

Upon his arrival, the agents arrested him in front of his wife and children, handcuffed him and took him away for questioning.

Before beginning their interrogation of MM, the agents provided MM a one-page document in Arabic that appeared to be a *Miranda* waiver form.

Neither agent spoke Arabic. MM does not speak English fluently and has difficulty understanding it.

By the time of MM's arrest, the horrors of September 11 had directed suspicion and hostility, both from the government and private individuals, toward many Americans of Middle Eastern descent, such as MM. MM was understandably terrified.

MM's difficulties with English, his fear, and the agents' inability to explain to him his rights in Arabic prevented MM from making an informed, knowing or voluntary decision to waive his Fifth Amendment privilege against self-incrimination.

Further, the affidavit in support of the arrest warrant plainly failed to establish probable cause to believe that MM had committed a crime and to arrest him. Thus, he was questioned pursuant to an illegal detention, in violation of the Fourth Amendment. *Dunaway v. New York*, 442 U.S. 200 (1979); Exhibit D (affidavit).

Respectfully submitted,

_____
Thomas J. Farrell

IN THE UNITED STATES DISTRICT COURT FOR
THE _____ DISTRICT OF _____

UNITED STATES OF AMERICA,	)	
Plaintiff	)	
	)	
v.	)	CASE NO. _____
	)	
MM,	)	
Defendant.	)	

BRIEF OF DEFENDANT MM IN SUPPORT OF PRE-TRIAL MOTIONS

MM, a refugee from Saddam Hussein's Iraq and a naturalized American citizen, is charged in a one-count indictment with aiding and abetting the production, without lawful authority, of a Pennsylvania commercial driver's license ("CDL") with a hazardous materials endorsement ("HDE"). 18 U.S.C. §1028(a)(1). The government's theory appears to be that MM received his license on _____, from RF, a PennDOT examiner, who solicited bribes for issuing licenses without administering the required tests to a number of individuals brought to him by one EB. Twenty of these individuals, all Iraqi immigrants, have been indicted separately on the same charge as MM. As far as the defense is aware, however, there is no evidence that MM either paid a bribe or dealt with EB.

ARGUMENT

The Court Should Hold an Evidentiary Hearing to Determine Whether the Government Can Establish a Knowing, Voluntary and Intelligent Waiver of *Miranda* Rights and the Voluntariness of the Statement.

A. The Government Must Establish a Knowing, Voluntary and Intelligent Waiver of *Miranda* Rights

The Fifth Amendment to the Constitution ensures a person's right against self-incrimination. Custodial interrogation implicates the Fifth Amendment privilege because of the danger that police officers might exert "informal compulsion" on suspects during questioning. *Miranda v. Arizona*, 384 U.S. 436, 460-461 (1966).

Before the government may introduce a defendant's incriminating statement in its case in chief, it must prove a voluntary, knowing and intelligent waiver of the accused's *Miranda* rights. *Miranda*, 384 U.S. at 475; *Moran v. Burbine*, 475 U.S. 412 (1986). In *Moran v. Burbine*, the Court further refined the concept of a valid waiver:

> First, the relinquishment of the right must have been voluntary in the sense that it was the product of a free and deliberate choice rather than intimidation, coercion, or deception. Second, the waiver must have been made with a full awareness of both the nature of the right being abandoned and the consequences of the decision to abandon it. Only if the "totality of the circumstances surrounding the interrogation" reveals both an uncoerced choice and the requisite level of comprehension may a court properly conclude that the *Miranda* rights have been waived.

Moran v. Burbine, 475 U.S. 412, 421 (1986).

In determining whether an accused validly waived his *Miranda* rights, a court must consider the particular facts and circumstances involved in the case, including the accused's background, experience, intelligence, physical and mental condition, and his conduct. *Moran v. Burbine*, 475 U.S. at 421; *North Carolina v. Butler*, 441 U.S. 369, 373 (1979); *Arizona v. Fulminante*, 499 U.S. 279 (1991). A court may find a proper waiver "[o]nly if the 'totality of the circumstances surrounding the interrogation' reveal both an uncoerced choice and the requisite level of comprehension." *Burbine*, 475 U.S. at 421.

It is not enough for the government simply to prove that the defendant executed a verbal or written waiver. Case law clearly indicates that it is not enough for law enforcement to recite a person's *Miranda* warnings without some explanation of those rights and the consequences of foregoing the same. The government has the burden of introducing sufficient evidence establishing "that under the 'totality of the circumstances,'" the defendant was aware of 'the nature of the right being abandoned and the consequences of the decision to abandon it.'" *United States v. Garibay*, 143 F.3d 534, 536 (9th Cir. 1998) (emphasis added). This burden is 'great' and this court must 'indulge every reasonable presumption' against such waiver. *Id.* at 537 (citations omitted).

Given that the government has the heavy burden of demonstrating defendant's valid waiver, the court should conduct a hearing to determine whether in fact a constitutionally valid waiver of *Miranda* rights did in fact occur. Such a hearing will further enable the court to ascertain the conditions under which defendant's statement was provided.

B. The Government Must Demonstrate the Voluntariness of Defendant's Statement

In addition to the deficient waiver of his *Miranda* rights, defendant also challenges the government to demonstrate the voluntariness of any statements given to the FBI. Although they are closely interrelated, the inquiry regarding the voluntariness of a defendant's confession is not coextensive. *Oregon v. Elstad*, 470 U.S. 298, 306-07 (1985); *see also Lego v. Twomey*, 404 U.S. 477 (1972); 18 U.S.C. §3501 (*Miranda* warnings are but factors to be considered by the trial judge in determining if a confession is voluntary.). "A *Miranda* violation does not *constitute* coercion but rather affords a bright-line, legal presumption of coercion, requiring suppression of all unwarned statements." *Elstad*, 470 U.S. at 306-07 n.1. The government additionally bears the burden of providing voluntariness by a preponderance of the evidence. *Lego v. Twomey*, 404 U.S. 477 (1972).

Again, in assessing the voluntariness of a defendant's statement, no one factor is determinative; rather, the "totality of the circumstances" must be considered. *Crane v. Kentucky*, 476 U.S. 683 (1986); *Mincy v. Arizona*, 437 U.S. 385 (1978); 18 U.S.C. §3501. The factors to be considered include both the characteristics of the accused and the details of the interrogation. *Schneckloth v. Bustamonte*, 412 U.S. 218, 226 (1973); 18 U.S.C. §3501.

"Before [a] confession is received in evidence, the trial judge <u>shall</u>, out of the presence of the jury, determine any issue as to voluntariness." 18 U.S.C. §3501 (emphasis added); *see also Jackson v. Denno*, 378 U.S. at 390-94. Defendant accordingly requests the court to conduct a hearing prior to the trial, wherein the government is held to its burden of establishing the voluntariness of his statements.

Respectfully submitted,

_____
          Thomas J. Farrell

Form 8-2 Motion and Supporting Brief to Suppress Statements (Custody, Invocation of Right to Remain Silent)

IN THE UNITED STATES DISTRICT COURT FOR
THE _____ DISTRICT OF _____

UNITED STATES OF AMERICA,
    Plaintiff,

    v.   CASE NO. _____

JOHN DOE,
      Defendant.

DEFENDANT'S MOTION TO SUPPRESS STATEMENTS

Pursuant to Fed. R. Crim. P. 12(b)(3)(C), defendant John Doe files this motion to suppress statements he allegedly made during the course of the _____ search of his home, 1000 Main Street, Pittsburgh, Pennsylvania on the following grounds and those further stated in the accompanying Memorandum of Law:

1. On _____, nine or more FBI agents entered Mr. Doe's home to execute a search warrant. That warrant is the subject of a separate motion to suppress physical evidence.
2. During the search, Mr. Doe was subject to restraints equivalent to a formal arrest. The agents did not permit Mr. Doe to get dressed, to use the bathroom alone, or to speak with his family or anyone else during the search.
3. The agents questioned Mr. Doe during the search about allegations concerning a mortgage fraud. According to the agents, Mr. Doe made statements in response to their questions.
4. The agents did not warn Mr. Doe of his rights to remain silent and his right to counsel before questioning him, as is required by *Miranda v. Arizona,* 383 U.S. 384 (1966).
5. After approximately one hour of questioning, Mr. Doe stated that he did not want to answer any more questions. Rather than "scrupulously honor" this assertion of his right to remain silent, the agents played an audiotape of Mr. Doe and asked him what he had to say about it. Mr. Doe allegedly made more statements.

WHEREFORE, defendant requests that the Court issue an order suppressing any statements he made on _____ or holding an evidentiary hearing on this motion.

Respectfully submitted,

_____

Thomas J. Farrell
Counsel for Defendant, John Doe

IN THE UNITED STATES DISTRICT COURT FOR
THE _____ DISTRICT OF _____

UNITED STATES OF AMERICA,
      Plaintiff,

v.   CASE NO. _____

JOHN DOE,
         Defendant.

MEMORANDUM OF LAW IN SUPPORT OF DEFENDANT'S MOTION TO SUPPRESS STATEMENTS

Defendant John Doe moves this Court to suppress statements he allegedly made during the course of the _____ search of his home. During the course of the execution of the warrant, Mr. Doe was subjected to custodial interrogation without being advised of his *Miranda* rights; therefore, all his statements should be suppressed. Further, during the course of the questioning, Mr. Doe invoked his right to remain silent, but the FBI agents persisted in the interrogation; therefore, any statement made after that invocation must be suppressed.

STATEMENT OF FACTS

Mr. Doe was awakened at 6:30 a.m. on _____ by a knock on the door of his home. He arose from bed, donned a robe over his underwear, and opened the front door. At least five FBI agents were standing at the front door. Special Agent Jones presented a search warrant and stated that he wished to ask Mr. Doe some questions.

Approximately four agents entered the home and began to question Mr. Doe. They did not advise him of his constitutional rights; nor did they inform him that he was free to go. Mr. Doe's wife and daughter were upstairs, and he was questioned alone. The questioning lasted approximately two hours.

During the course of the interrogation, Mr. Doe was not allowed to return upstairs to dress, shave or brush his teeth. When he needed to use the bathroom, the agents insisted on accompanying him, and the agents who had been blocking the front door followed him and demanded that he leave the bathroom door open. All of these circumstances gave rise to the reasonable belief on Mr. Doe's part that he was not free to leave the house.

After about an hour of questioning, Agent Jones became angry and began to yell at Mr. Doe that he believed him to be lying. At that point, Mr. Doe stated that he did not wish to talk to the agents any further. Rather than honor this invocation of the right to silence, the agents produced an surreptitiously recorded audiotape of a conversation which Mr. Doe had had with one of his employees a week before the search and began to play it for him on a Dictaphone the agents had brought with them. Further questions followed the playing of the tape.

ARGUMENT

I. Agents Questioned Mr. Doe in Circumstances Amounting to Custody Equivalent to Formal Arrest, But Failed to Administer *Miranda* Warnings.

Miranda v. Arizona, 384 U.S. 436 (1966), requires that when an individual is questioned by the police while in custody, he must first be advised of his constitutional rights and his right to counsel. Statements made by a suspect subjected to custodial interrogation without the benefit of *Miranda* warnings are inadmissible in the prosecution's case in chief.

Custody attaches for these purposes when the person interrogated is subjected to a "restraint on his freedom of movement to the degree associated with a formal arrest." *Thompson v. Keohane,* 516 U.S. 99, 112 (1995).

Neither the officer's intent nor the subject's perception are determinative; the test looks to how a reasonable person would have understood the suspect's freedom to leave under all the circumstances. *Stansbury v. California,* 511 U.S. 318 (1994). Factors often considered include the extent to which the defendant is confronted with evidence of guilt, the physical surroundings in which the interrogation was conducted, the duration of the questioning, and the degree of pressure applied to detain the suspect. *United States v. Kim,* 292 F.3d 969, 974 (9th Cir. 2002).

The execution of a warrant does not in and of itself always create a custodial situation. But "officers conducting a lawful search on a person's home are not permitted to use the suspect's detention to their official advantage by attempting to extract self-incriminating statements from the suspect." *United States v. Mittel-Carey,* 456 F.Supp.2d 296, 303 (D. Mass. 2006). Courts look for the presence of the "police-dominated atmosphere" that is the hallmark of custody, and the determination involves a fact-intensive examination of all of the circumstances, including the extent to which the suspect was made aware that he was free to refrain from answering and the nature of the questioning. *United States v. Griffin,* 7 F.3d 1512, 1518-19 (10th Cir. 1993).

Here, while Mr. Doe was in his home, he was stripped of all freedom of movement or personal privacy, and the house was therefore transformed into a place of confinement, not security. Mr. Doe was questioned alone, in the company of four agents, while his family remained upstairs. As the court found in *United States v. Mittel-Carey,* this practice is "indicative of police domination." 456 F.Supp.2d at 3077. Mr. Doe was under the constant supervision and observation of the FBI, and he was not even trusted or granted the privacy or freedom to enter a small bathroom alone. No reasonable person who has been barred by the police from going to the bathroom alone could understand that he was free to exit the home altogether. *See United States v. Madoch,* 149 F.3d 596, 601 (7th Cir. 1998).

Moreover, Mr. Doe was never advised that he was free to refrain from answering questions, and at no point during the questioning was he informed that he could leave at any time. The failure to advise a suspect that he is free to go is a significant indicator of custodial detention. *Griffin,* 7 F.3d at 1518. The questioning began in the early morning hours, and Mr. Doe was not given an opportunity to dress properly. He was questioned alone, separated from his family, and there were never fewer than four FBI agents in his home. Mr. Doe remained under police observation the entire time the nine or more agents searched the house. The detailed factual questions and investigative techniques were clearly designed to elicit incriminating admissions. These are precisely the kinds of facts that have led courts to consider questioning within a suspect's home to be custodial. *See Mittel-Carey,* 493 F.3d at 39; *United States v. Daubmann,* 474 F.Supp.2d 228 (D. Mass. 2007); *United States v. Bullins,* 880 F.Supp. 76 (D.N.H. 1995).

The questioning of Mr. Doe progressed well beyond the type of conversation that might attend a short investigatory stop, *see Griffin,* 7 F.3d at 1518, or the necessary background information incident to a search, *see Bullins,* 880 F.Supp. at 79. The agents came prepared to interrogate Mr. Doe with the facts that they believed demonstrated his wrongdoing; surely the only purpose served by bringing the audiotape and player was to confront Mr. Doe with what the agents assumed was strong evidence of his guilt. The prolonged, detailed, accusatory interview contributes to the inescapable conclusion that no matter who owned the home, it was the FBI that dominated the scene.

Under all of these circumstances, no reasonable person would have felt that he was free to leave; rather, a reasonable person would have believed he was under arrest. Since the FBI conducted a custodial interrogation but failed to provide Mr. Doe with his *Miranda* warnings, all statements made to the agents on June 1, 2007, must be suppressed, as well as the fruits of those statements. *Wong Sun v. United States,* 371 U.S. 471, 488 (1963).

II. The Agents Did Not Honor Mr. Doe's Invocation of His Right to Remain Silent.

According to the FBI's own account of the interrogation, when the agents began pressing Mr. Doe on their assertions about the alleged mortgage fraud scheme, he stated that he no longer wished to be questioned. Instead of honoring that request and terminating the interview, the agents produced an audiotape secretly recorded during the investigation as well as a machine on which it could be played. They told Mr. Doe something to the effect of, "you need to hear this," and played the recording for him. This constituted interrogation which was impermissible after the suspect had invoked his right to remain silent.

Law enforcement agents are required to scrupulously honor a person's invocation of his right to remain silent. "If the individual indicates in any manner, at any time prior to or during questioning, that he wishes to remain silent, the interrogation must cease." *Michigan v. Mosely,* 423 U.S. 96, 100 (1975). This unequivocal prophylactic rule is specifically intended to prevent further questioning designed to encourage the suspect to change his mind. *Campaneria v. Reid,* 891 F.2d 1014, 1021 (2d Cir. 1989). In this case, the playing of the tape resumed the interrogation, and the violation was particularly egregious because it came right on the heels of Mr. Doe's unambiguous request to terminate the interview.

The Supreme Court has explained that interrogation includes "express questioning or its functional equivalent." *Rhode Island v. Innis,* 446 U.S. 293, 300-01 (1998). Interrogation involves "words or actions on the part of the police ... that the police should know are reasonably likely to elicit an incriminating response from the suspect." *Id.* at 301. Confronting a suspect with evidence falls squarely within that definition. *See United States v. Williams,* 227 Fed. Appx. 307, 311 (playing taped conversations and then offering the defendant an opportunity to help himself by cooperating deemed to be interrogation). *See also Commonwealth v. DeJesus*, 567 Pa. 415, 431, 787 A.2d 394, 403 (2001) (showing to arrestee statements accomplices had made implicating him in shooting amounted to interrogation); *People v. Ferro*, 63 N.Y.2d 316, 472 N.E.2d 13, 482 N.Y.S.2d 237 (1984) (silently placing furs stolen from murder victim's residence outside suspect's cell was interrogation). In this case, the FBI did not bring a copy of the incriminating tape and a player to the defendant's home for any purpose other than eliciting an incriminating response from Mr. Doe. The decision to play the tape at the very moment Mr. Doe concluded the interrogation was clearly intended to undermine his decision to stop talking and to extract more admissions from him.

The failure to read Mr. Doe his *Miranda* rights was part of a calculated effort to secure damaging admissions to be used in evidence against him, and the resumption of questioning after he had clearly exercised his right to cut it off was yet another deliberate transgression. All statements made to the agents in response to these tactics on _____ must be suppressed.

CONCLUSION

For the foregoing reasons, all statements made during the _____ interrogation, and any fruits of those statements, should be suppressed.

Respectfully submitted,

_____

Thomas J. Farrell
Counsel for Defendant John Doe

Chapter 9

IDENTIFICATIONPROCEDURES

I.   PRE-TRIAL

A. Procedures and Techniques

§9:01   General Points

Mistaken identification produces more wrongful convictions than any other cause. [*See United States v. Wade*, 388 U.S. 218, 228 (1967) ("The identification of strangers is proverbially untrustworthy," (quoting Felix Frankfurter, *The Case of Sacco and Vanzetti* at 30 (1927))); *United States v. Smithers*, 212 F.3d 306, 312 n.1 (6th Cir. 2000) (citing studies to the effect that half of all wrongful convictions result from mistaken identifications); www.innocenceproject.org/understand/ Eyewitness-Misidentification.php (mistaken identification was a factor in 75% of DNA exonerations for wrongful convictions).]

Many researchers have published articles that can be helpful to the practitioner in the right case. Whether yours is the right case depends on a number of factors, principally, the extent to which the prosecution case relies on identification of your client by a stranger. [*See generally National Research Council. 2014. Identifying the Culprit: Assessing Eyewitness Identification.* (Washington, DC: The National Academies Press 2014); *Dennis v. Sec'y, PA Dep't of Corrections*, 834 F.3d 263, 313-16, 321-332 (3d Cir. 2016)(McKee, C.J., concurring)(extensive review of latest research on identification errors and procedures to improve reliability).]

A witness's misidentification is rarely reviewable on appeal. Commentators and defense lawyers have been hammering on this issue for nearly a century. Recently the legal system has shown openness to effective remedies to misidentification. While there is no sign yet of a greater willingness to suppress identifications reaped from suggestive procedures, law enforcement has become more receptive to using fairer identification procedures, and courts appear more willing to allow defense input into pre-trial identification procedures and to permit expert testimony on the weaknesses of identification testimony.

§9:02   Types of Identification Procedures

The Show-Up

The show-up has long been considered the most suggestive form of identification procedure. [*See Stovall v. Denno*, 388 U.S. 293, 301 (1967) (show-ups "widely condemned").]

In a show-up, the police confront the witness one-on-one with the suspect to determine if the witness can identify the suspect as the perpetrator. Police employ this method when they make an arrest, usually soon after the crime, and need to decide whether to continue to hold the suspect or to look further.

The Photo Array

Displays of photographs can occur in different ways.
The police may:
- Have the witness look through a book of arrest photographs (i.e., "mug shots").
- Arrange the photographs similar to a line-up, trying to select photographs that resemble each other to avoid suggestiveness.

The Line-Up

The police may have several individuals, usually five or six, sit or stand next to each other and have the witness look at them, usually through a one-way mirror.

§9:03   Constitutional Restrictions on Procedures

The United States Constitution places some restrictions on pre-trial identification:
- The Due Process Clause prohibits unduly suggestive identification procedures. [See §9:04.]
- Once adversary proceedings have commenced, the defendant has a Sixth Amendment right to have counsel present at an in-person identification procedure. [See §9:05.]

§9:04   Due Process Protection

The Supreme Court has established the rule that "[a] government identification procedure violates due process when it is 'unnecessarily suggestive' and creates a 'substantial risk of misidentification.'" [*United States v. Emanuele,*

51 F.3d 1123, 1128 (3d Cir. 1995). See the series of cases starting with *Stovall v. Denno*, 388 U.S. 293 (1967), and continuing through *Manson v. Brathwaite*, 432 U.S. 98 (1977).]

The first part of this standard entails inquiry into both whether the procedure was suggestive and "whether there was a justification for the government's failure to resort to a less suggestive identification procedure." [*United States v. Stevens*, 935 F.2d 1380, 1389 (3d Cir. 1991).]

The second part of the standard is whether the procedure was so conducive to mistaken identification or gave rise to such a substantial likelihood of misidentification that admitting the identification would be a denial of due process. [*Stevens*, 935 F.2d at 1389.]

Under both federal law and the law of all states except Massachusetts, New York, and Wisconsin, even if an identification procedure is proven to be unduly suggestive, the government gets a second opportunity to admit both the in-court and out-of-court identifications if it can prove that "under the 'totality of the circumstances' the identification was reliable even though the confrontation procedure was suggestive." [*Neil v. Biggers*, 409 U.S. 188, 199 (1972).]

The court must examine the following factors:

- The opportunity of the witness to view the criminal at the time of the crime.
- The witness's degree of attention.
- The accuracy of the witness's prior description of the criminal.
- The level of certainty demonstrated at the confrontation.
- The time between the crime and the confrontation.

Against these factors is to be weighed the corrupting effect of the suggestive identification itself. [*Manson v. Brathwaite*, 432 U.S. at 114. See also *United States v. Stevens*, 935 F.2d 1380, 1392 (3d Cir. 1991); and *State v. Long*, 721 P.2d 483, 494 n.8 (Utah 1986) (listing other factors bearing on reliability, such as difference in race between the witness and defendant, stress, weapon focus, lighting, and others).]

In Massachusetts and New York, once a pre-trial identification procedure is shown to be unnecessarily suggestive, the pre-trial identification is automatically excluded, and the burden shifts to the prosecution to show an independent source for admitting the in-court identification under the factors set forth in *Neil v. Biggers* and *Manson v. Brathwaite*. [*See Commonwealth v. Johnson*, 420 Mass. 458, 650 N.E.2d 1257 (1995); *People v. Adams*, 53 N.Y.2d 241, 440 N.Y.S.2d 902, 423 N.E.2d 379 (1981).]

Wisconsin excludes any out-of-court show-up identification unless the prosecution shows that it was necessary under the totality of the circumstances. The prosecution also must prove that any in-court identification following the improper showup is based on an independent source. [*State v. Dubose*, 285 Wis.2d 143, 699 N.W.2d 582 (2005).]

The due process standard applies, and a pretrial hearing will be required, only if the suggestivity results from improper government, as opposed to private, conduct. [*Perry v. New Hampshire*, 132 S.Ct. 716, 181 L.Ed.2d 694 (2012); *but see State v. Chen*, 208 N.J. 307, 327, 27 A.3d 930, 943 (2011) (under state law, pretrial hearing on admissibility must be held if the private action was "made under highly suggestive circumstances that could lead to a mistaken identification").] The *Perry* decision offers some comfort, however, in that it emphasizes the importance of eyewitness-specific jury instructions [*see* §§9:70, 9:71, 9:72, *infra*], expert testimony [*see* §§9:60, 9:61, *infra*] and the ability of trial judges to exclude identification testimony under the state equivalents of FRE 403 if its probative value is outweighed by its prejudicial effect or risk of misleading the jury. [*Perry*, 132 S.Ct. at 728-29.]

§9:05   The Right to Counsel

Once adversary judicial proceedings commence, the defendant has a right to counsel at a line-up or other pre-trial identification procedure that requires the defendant's presence. [*United States v. Wade*, 388 U.S. 218 (1967); *Gilbert v. California*, 388 U.S. 263 (1967).]

Adversary judicial proceedings are defined to have begun with "formal charge, preliminary hearing, indictment, information, or arraignment." [*Kirby v. Illinois*, 406 U.S. 682, 689 (1972).]

However, there is no right to counsel at a photo display, whether or not adversary proceedings have commenced. [*United States v. Ash*, 413 U.S. 300, 321 (1973).]

§9:06   Counsel's Function at the Line-Up

Your role at a line-up is to witness, suggest, disagree and criticize. Since you cannot act both as trial counsel and a witness, you should bring an investigator, paralegal or associate to serve as a possible trial witness. You might also try to audio and videotape the line-up and any discussions with the witness leading up to it or have a stenographer present. You might ask the court to order such a memorialization of the line-up. [*See, e.g., People v. Hammond*, 1 Misc.3d 880,

888, 768 N.Y.S.2d 166, 174 (NY Sup. Ct. Westchester Co. 2003) (court refused to order police to use double blind and sequential procedures, but did order that a stenographer and photographer attend the line-up).]

Try to be present and listen to any police discussions with the witness to discourage any suggestions to the witness.

Get the names and identifying information (addresses and phone numbers) of the fillers and all persons present at the line-up. The witness may bring friends for support, who may have planted suggestions in his mind. Those friends may themselves be witnesses to the offense, and their presence at the line-up may taint their testimony. Try to interview everyone present.

Suggest (preferably in letter or motion before the line-up) that the police follow the procedures adopted by the Attorney General of New Jersey and suggested by the Department of Justice. [*See* §§9:10 et seq.]

Comment on the suitability of the fillers. Make sure they resemble your client closely in age, skin color, facial hair, clothing and size. If your client differs in height, ask that the participants be seated.

The police may ask for your agreement that the line-up is a fair one and the fillers suitable. Do not agree. The police will be sure to tell a judge and jury that you agreed to the fairness of the line-up from which your client was selected. You can always find something to criticize. Pick any difference in appearance and make note of it. If the police do not ask, volunteer your objections to the line-up so that they cannot represent later that you acquiesced.

§9:07   Motions to Dictate Line-Up Procedures

If you have time before a line-up and the police or prosecutor will not agree to non-suggestive procedures, seek a court order dictating those procedures. [*See* Lisa Steele, *Trying Identification Cases: An Outline for Raising Eyewitness ID Issues,* 28 Champion 8 (Nov. 2004) (description of issues and motions to raise throughout identification cases).]

Some courts doubt that they have the authority to dictate line-up procedures to the police. [*People v. Hammond,* 1 Misc.3d 880, 888, 768 N.Y.S.2d 166, 174 (NY Sup. Ct. Westchester Co. 2003) (lauding the benefits of double blind and sequential procedures, but refusing to order police to use them).]

However, most courts acknowledge that courts have discretion to order line-ups and particular procedures. [*State v. Delgado,* 188 N.J. 48, 902 A.2d 888 (2006) (ordering that as a condition of an out-of-court identification's admissibility, officers must make a written record detailing the identification procedure, including place and any dialogue between the witness and police); *United States v. Ravich,* 421 F.2d 1196, 1203 (2d Cir. 1970) (within the trial court's discretion); *United States v. Crouch,* 478 F. Supp. 867, 871 (E.D. Cal. 1979) (discussing court's inability to dictate conditions of a line-up, but granting defendant's request for a blank line-up to precede the one in which he will be placed).]

PRACTICE TIP:

Consider asking the police and prosecution to consent to these procedures by preceding your motion with an informal written request to adopt your procedures, or if time does not permit you to await a response, send a cover letter making the request along with a draft motion.

The police refusal to employ recognized non-suggestive procedures, even if not ordered by a court, might create fodder for cross-examination at trial or it might justify you in asking the court to instruct the jury that the prosecution chose to forego more reliable identification procedures and that therefore the less reliable in-court identification should be viewed with caution. [*See Commonwealth v. Sexton,* 485 Pa. 17, 25, 400 A.2d 1289, 1293 (Pa. 1979) (requiring such an instruction where trial court arbitrarily and for no good reason denied defense request for a line-up).]

CAUTION:

Be careful what you ask for. Consider whether your client's chances are better attacking the witness's opportunity to observe, the suggestivity of whatever show-up procedure led to his prosecution, and relying on expert testimony about the inaccuracy of eyewitness identification rather than chancing a carefully arranged line-up in which your client is identified as the perpetrator. A suggestive in-person or photographic show-up at the start of the case also may taint any line-up, no matter how carefully conducted. On the other hand, a non-identification in the line-up may effectively end the case. These line-up procedures might be better left to administrative reforms than defense motions.

Form:
• **Form 9-1** Motion for Double Blind Sequential Line-Up

[§§9:08-9:09 Reserved]

B.   Better Line-Ups

§9:10   General Points; Research Resources

Several jurisdictions have promulgated guidelines for law enforcement use in improving the accuracy of identification procedures. [*See, e.g.*, California Commission on the Fair Administration of Justice, *Report and Recommendations Regarding Eyewitness Identification Procedures* (April 2006); Office of the Attorney General, State of New Jersey, *Attorney General Guidelines for Preparing and Conducting Photo and Live Line-Up Identification Procedures* (April 2001); Wisconsin Attorney General, *Model Policy and Procedure for Eyewitness Identification* (Sept. 12, 2005); U.S. Department of Justice's October 1999 report. [*Eyewitness Evidence: A Guide for Law Enforcement* (available at www.ojp.usdoj.gov/nij/pubs-sum/178240.htm).]

These reports generally recommend (1) the use of double-blind line-ups; (2) limits on statements made to witnesses informing them that the suspect is in the line-up or approving the witness's selection after the line-up is completed; (3) sequential rather that simultaneous line-ups and photo arrays; and (4) the recording of identification procedures.

For the most part, your interests coincide with those of reformers because the reforms are designed to minimize the incidence of false positives and therefore make identification less likely.

§9:11   The "Double-Blind" Line-Up

In a double blind line-up or photo array, neither the witness nor the person administering the line-up knows which person is the suspect or arrestee.

Studies show that even honest officers send unconscious hints to witnesses when the officers know which person is the suspect. Additionally, investigating officers tend to congratulate witnesses when they pick the arrestee or suspect, thereby reinforcing what might have been a hesitant identification. A blind administrator is less likely to reinforce the identification in this manner.

Courts and legislatures have recognized that the scientific evidence on the value of double blind procedures in avoiding false identifications and ensuring accurate identifications is undisputed. [*See Dennis*, 834 F.3d at 313-16; *People v. Hammond*, 1 Misc.3d 880, 885, 768 N.Y.S.2d 166, 171 (N.Y. Sup. Ct. West. Co. 2003). *See* Florida Senate Bill 312, "Eyewitness Identification Reform Act" (eff. Oct. 1, 2017) (requiring double blind lineup procedures); NJ Guidelines, I.A.; California Report and Recommendations 1, 2; Wisconsin Model Policy and Procedure at 3, 6-16 (photo arrays), 17-21 (line-ups).]

§9:12   Instructions to the Witness

The DOJ, New Jersey, California and Wisconsin guidelines include useful instructions for the officers to give to witnesses to avoid suggestiveness and avoid reinforcing tentative identifications, including:
- "The witness should be instructed prior to the photo or live line-up identification procedure that the perpetrator may not be among those in the photo array or live line-up and, therefore, they should not feel compelled to make an identification." [NJ Guidelines, I.B.]
- "If an identification is made, avoid reporting to the witness any information regarding the individual he or she has selected prior to obtaining the witness's statement of certainty." [NJ Guidelines, II.A.4.]
- "Instruct the witness not to discuss the identification procedure or its results with other witnesses involved in the case and discourage contact with the media." [NJ Guidelines, II.A.7.]

The NJ Guidelines also furnish useful guidance on recording identification results:
- Record both identification and nonidentification results in writing, including the witness's own words regarding how sure he or she is.
- Ensure that the results are signed and dated by the witness.
- Ensure that no materials indicating previous identification results are visible to the witness.
- Ensure that the witness does not write on or mark any materials that will be used in other identification procedures.

[NJ Guidelines, II.E. See also *State v. Delgado,* 188 N.J. 48, 902 A.2d 888 (2006) (requiring the recording of identification procedures).]

§9:13   The Blank Line-Up

With a blank line-up procedure, the police show the witness two line-ups:

- One that has the suspect.
- One that does not (the "blank" one).

§9:14   The Sequential Display

Studies show that when viewing a group of photographs or individuals simultaneously, the witness tends to compare the line-up members and pick the person who looks most like the witness's recollection of the perpetrator, whether or not that person is the perpetrator. [See Wisconsin Model Policy and Procedure at 5.]

Presenting photographs or individuals one at a time to the witness and having the witness state after each whether or not the person is the perpetrator avoids such comparisons and forces the witness instead to compare each person to his memory of what the perpetrator looked like.

[§§9:15-9:19 Reserved]

C. Defense-Requested Line-Ups

§9:20   General Points

There may be occasions where the police have not conducted an identification procedure and you want one, perhaps where you exhaustively investigated and corroborated your client's claims of innocence.

CAUTION:

This strategy is risky. If your client is identified at a procedure you arranged, you may have guaranteed his conviction.

If a witness already identified your client in a police-arranged show-up, photo array or line-up, the witness likely will recognize your client from that procedure and identify him whether or not he is innocent.

§9:21   Court Discretion to Order Line-Up

A number of decisions recognize that a court has discretion to order a defense-requested line-up. [*See Moore v. Illinois*, 434 U.S. 220, 230 n.5 (1977) (approving the granting of defense requests, but recognizing that they are committed to the trial court's discretion) (citing *United States v. Ravitch*, 421 F.2d 1196 (2d Cir. 1970)).]

Courts likely will apply the factors set forth in *Ravitch*, the leading case on this topic:

> A pre-trial request by a defendant for a line-up is thus addressed to the sound discretion of the district court and should be carefully considered. Without any attempt at being exhaustive, we think some relevant factors are the length of time between the crime or arrest and the request, the possibility that the defendant may have altered his appearance (as was at least attempted here), the extent of inconvenience to prosecution witnesses, the possibility that revealing the identity of the prosecution witnesses will subject them to intimidation, the propriety of other identification procedures used by the prosecution, and the degree of doubt concerning the identification. We find no abuse of discretion in denying a line-up here.

[*Ravitch*, 421 F.2d at 1203. *See State in Interest of W. C.,* 85 N.J. 218, 426 A.2d 50 (N.J. 1981) (holding that court has discretion to order line-up; surveying jurisdictions and finds that most follow similar rule); *Commonwealth v. Sexton,* 485 Pa. 17, 400 A.2d 1289 (1979) (while the matter is in the court's discretion, court cannot arbitrarily and capriciously deny such a request); *Evans v. Superior Court,* 11 Cal. 3d 617, 522 P.2d 681, 114 Cal. Rptr. 121 (1974) (referring to a *right* to a line-up, but committing the granting of a request to the trial court's discretion in much the same way as other courts that find no due process right); *People v. Mena,* 54 Cal. 4th 146, 160-61, 141 Cal. Rptr. 3d 469, 277 P.3d 160, 169-71 (2012) (surveying cases and explaining that while there is no federal due process right to a defense line-up, such a right arises under the California Constitution).]

Several states have rules authorizing judges to order line-ups or photo arrays at a defendant's request. [*E.g.,* Colo. Crim. P. 41.1(g); Vermont R. Cr. P. 41.1(k). *See People v. Monroe,* 925 P.2d 767 (Colo. 1996) (affirming trial court's discretionary power to order a pre-trial line-up).]

§9:22   When to Request a Line-Up

It is best to make a request for a line-up before there has been a police-conducted identification procedure for two reasons:
*   The court likely will cite the prior procedure as reason to deny a request. [*See, e.g., Commonwealth v. Torrez*, 335 Pa. Super. 612, 485 A.2d 63 (1984).]
*   The witness likely will remember your client from the first identification procedure and will identify him with even more certainty, a fact the prosecution is sure to bring before the jury.

§9:23   Including Another Suspect

If you have identified another suspect, you might request that the court order an identification procedure including that suspect, not your client.

Unfortunately, courts that have considered this issue have ruled that there is no right or authority under either state law or the Constitution to such a procedure. [*People v. Braxton*, 807 P.2d 1214, 1216-17 (Colo. Ct. App. 1990) (state rule entitles defendant only to an identification procedure including himself and the due process clause does not require the prosecution to help the defendant create exculpatory evidence); *State v. Messier*, 146 Vt. 145, 155, 499 A.2d 32, 40 (1985) (basing refusal on language of Vermont rule of criminal procedure).]

PRACTICE TIP:

You might counter the *Braxton* reasoning with an analogy to another area that troubles courts: the use of informants. That is, argue that courts should impose on the prosecution a duty to investigate potentially exculpatory evidence. [See *Commonwealth of N. Mariana Islands v. Bowie*, 243 F.3d 1109 (9th Cir. 2001) (prosecution's obligations extended beyond merely turning over to the defense a letter found in the cell of one of its witnesses that suggested a plan among the witnesses to frame the defendant; the prosecution had an obligation to collect potentially exculpatory evidence by questioning its witnesses and submitting a letter for handwriting analysis).]

Thus, when presented with a serious claim of misidentification, you may argue that the prosecution should be charged with a duty to investigate. However, making this argument requires you to commit to revealing your investigation and the basis for believing that another committed the crime. The prosecution may take you up on your offer, investigate the defense and, to your chagrin, disprove rather than confirm it. Therefore, make sure you are right and consider whether you can trust the prosecutor to view your evidence with an open mind.

Also, the prosecution might not be able to force the suspect to attend a line-up against his will (at least in the absence of probable cause to arrest him). On the other hand, a photo array does not require his consent, if the prosecutor has a photo of him.

If you request that the prosecution put another person in a line-up or photo array, the prosecution's refusal lays the groundwork for the argument at trial that the prosecution is more interested in convicting the first named suspect, your client, rather than finding the truth. [*See Commonwealth v. Sexton,* 485 Pa. at 25 (defendant entitled to a jury instruction along the lines that he "had been denied the opportunity for a more objective identification and for that reason the subsequent less reliable identification could be viewed with caution").]

[§§9:24-9:29 Reserved]

II.   TRIAL

A.   The In-Court Show-Up

§9:30   General Points

One of the most suggestive forms of identification procedures is the in-court identification. [*See Commonwealth v. McGaghey*, 510 Pa. 225, 507 A.2d 357 (1986) (holding that in-court identification at preliminary hearing was so suggestive as to taint identification at trial).]

With an in-court show-up, the witness (after being informed that the prosecutor and police had enough evidence to arrest and charge the defendant, and perhaps after being told of the defendant's criminal history and congratulated on his part in taking the defendant off the streets) is asked to look around and see if anyone in court looks like the person who victimized him.

Especially at a sparsely attended preliminary hearing or other pre-trial hearing, there is little mystery who the witness will pick: not the prosecutor he just met, or the police officer who has shepherded the witness through the process, or the man in the black robe, or even the stranger in a suit with the briefcase and legal pad at the defense table. The witness's gaze inescapably fixes on the shabbily dressed man sitting next to the defense attorney.

§9:31   Moving for an Alternative

There are alternatives, but you must act before the hearing starts.
The law is relatively clear on two points:
*   Whether to grant relief lies in the trial court's discretion.
*   Attempting a ruse to avoid your client's identification (*e.g.*, seating him in the audience and a decoy at counsel table, or disguising him) may be grounds for discipline against you. [*See United States v. Sabater*, 830 F.2d 7, 9 (2d Cir. 1987) (noting that such a ruse violates both DR 7-106(C)(5) and Model Rules 3.3 and 3.4 as an attempt to mislead the court).]

Therefore, ask the court (either orally or in a written motion) for an alternative to avoid a suggestive identification procedure.

There are many appellate opinions acknowledging the suggestivity of the traditional in-court identification and indicating receptivity to alternatives. [*See Moore v. Illinois*, 434 U.S. 220 (1977); *United States v. Rogers,* 126 F.3d 655, 658 (5th Cir. 1997) (holding that it was unduly suggestive to ask witness to identify perpetrator in the courtroom when it was clear who was the defendant).] While most courts have held that the *Biggers* Due Process analysis of undue suggestivity does not apply to in-court identifications [*Galloway v. State*, 122 So.3d 614, 663-64 (Miss. 2013)], the Connecticut Supreme Court has held that first-time in-court identifications are inherently suggestive and implicate due process protections and must be prescreened by the court: "We are hard-pressed to imagine how there could be a more suggestive identification procedure than placing a witness on the stand in open court, confronting the witness with the person the state has accused of committing the crime, and then asking the witness if he can identify the person who committed the crime. If this procedure is not suggestive, then no procedure is suggestive." [*State v. Dickson*, 141 A.3d 810, 822-23 (Conn. 2016), *cert. denied*, No. 16-866, 2017 WL 108128 (U.S. June 19, 2017).]

Your options include:
*   Seek to excuse your client entirely from the hearing. [*People v. James*, 100 A.D.2d 552, 553, 473 N.Y.S.2d 252, 254 (N.Y. App. Div. 2d Dept. 1984) (since right to attend is defendant's, request to be excused from pre-trial hearing should be granted in an identification case).]
*   Ask to seat your client in the audience and a decoy at counsel table during the eyewitness's testimony. [*See Moore*, 434 U.S. at 231 n.5 (approving of this procedure); *United States v. Sebetich*, 776 F.2d 412, 420-21 (3d Cir.1985); *State v. Tatum*, 219 Conn. 721, 729, n.15; 595, A.2d 322, 328 & n.15 (Conn. 1991) (among allowable procedures for lessening suggestiveness of pre-trial identification are pre-hearing line-up or having defendant sit in the audience).] NOTE: This works best if the decoy matches the description that the witness provided the police and you can fill the audience with others who resemble your client.
*   Request that a line-up be conducted in court. [*United States v. Archibald*, 734 F.2d 938, *modified*, 756 F.2d 223 (2d Cir. 1984) (recommending that trial judge use its discretion to grant defense request where identification is a serious issue).]
*   Ask the court to adopt the prescreening procedures established in *Dickson, supra*, unless identification is not an issue or the witness knows the defendant well:

If the trial court determines that the state will not be allowed to conduct a first-time identification in court, the state may request permission to conduct a nonsuggestive identification procedure, namely, at the state's option, an out-of-court lineup or photographic array, and the trial court ordinarily should grant the state's request. If the witness previously has been unable to identify the defendant in a nonsuggestive identification procedure, however, the court should not allow a second nonsuggestive identification procedure unless the state can provide a good reason why a second bite at the apple is warranted. If the eyewitness is able to identify the defendant in a nonsuggestive out-of-court procedure, the state may then ask the eyewitness to identify the defendant in court. If the trial court denies a request for a nonsuggestive procedure, the state declines to conduct one, or the eyewitness is unable to identify the defendant in such a procedure, a one-on-one in-court identification should not be allowed. The prosecutor may still examine the witness, however, about his or her observations of the perpetrator at the time of the crime, but the prosecutor should avoid asking the witness if the defendant resembles the perpetrator. *See United States v. Greene, supra*, 704 F.3d at 304 ("if there is a line between resemblance and identification testimony it is admittedly thin" [internal quotation marks omitted].)

[*State v. Dickson*, 141 A.3d 810, 836–37 (2016).]

PRACTICE TIP:

Consider how to handle the prosecutor and police in making your motion. You may want to ask them to agree to one of these procedures before you ask the court so that if they refuse, at trial you can make it seem that they wanted to hide the truth by avoiding a fair, nonsuggestive identification procedure.

In any event, you should ask the court to direct the prosecutor and police that they should not discuss with the witness the arrangements that have been made in court. Evaluate your judge and consider how best to make the request. That is, should you put it in your motion and proposed order or just add it orally, after the court grants your motion (saying, "Of course, the prosecution and Officer Smith should not discuss with the witness that the defendant will not be at counsel table or anything about these arrangements.").

§9:32   Make Motion Before the Pre-Trial Hearing

Just as with any other in-court demonstration, do not attempt an alternative to the in-court show-up for the first time before a jury.

Any plausibility your argument of misidentification had will disappear once the witness picks your client out of the audience or in an in-court line-up arranged at your insistence. [*See United States v. Matthews*, 20 F.3d 538, 547 (2d Cir. 1994) (explaining the strategic reasons why defense counsel may not choose to conduct a line-up or other non-suggestive in-court identification procedure before the jury).]

Therefore, make your motion at a pre-trial hearing, not at trial.

If there is no identification, you have scored a tremendous victory, whereas you still might be able to explain away the identification at trial (the police might have pointed out the defendant, the witness might have been already prejudiced by an in-person or photographic show-up).

[§§9:33-9:39 Reserved]

B. Motion to Suppress Identification Testimony

§9:40   The *Wade* Hearing

The hearing on a motion to suppress identification testimony is often called a *Wade* Hearing. [*See United States v. Wade*, 388 U. S. 218 (1967). For the standard and factors considered at a *Wade* hearing, see §9:04.]

While a court is not constitutionally required to hold such a hearing outside the hearing of the jury, most courts will. [*See Watkins v. Sowders*, 449 U.S. 341, 345 (1981) (holding that a hearing is not required, but noting that most courts deem it prudent).]

Form:
• **Form 9-2** Motion to Suppress Pre-Trial and In-Court Identification

§9:41   Benefits of a Hearing

Obtaining a pre-trial hearing on a motion to suppress an identification may yield great benefits besides the (unlikely) suppression of the identification.

If you can show that the identification procedure was unduly suggestive, the burden shifts to the prosecution to prove that under the totality of the circumstances, the identification was reliable. Making this showing may compel the prosecution to call the victim as a witness and open him to cross-examination on all the circumstances surrounding his observation of the defendant at the time of the offense and his identification.

§9:42   Examining the Officer at the Hearing

The defense rarely wins *Wade* hearings. Therefore, you should focus your efforts on laying the groundwork for a trial cross-examination or for your own expert witness to testify on the factors that emerged at the hearing.

If the police preserved the array or photographed or videotaped the line-up, the court often will base its findings regarding suggestiveness on the array or line-up itself. Still, you might direct questioning at other conduct that may have amounted to improper suggestions.

Areas to explore at a hearing include:

- Suggestions that may have been made to the witness:
  - Did you or any other officer speak with the witness before the line-up?
  - What did you tell him was going to take place that day?
  - Did you tell him that you had arrested someone?
  - If not, what did you tell him about why he was viewing a line-up?
  - Did anyone accompany the witness?
  - Did you hear them have any conversation about what happened the day of the offense?
  - Did you hear the witness describe the perpetrator to any other officers?
  - What did you say to the witness as you were showing him the line-up?
  - What did he say to you?
  - Did anyone else say anything to him before he made an identification?
  - How much time went by before he made the identification?
  - How do you know that–did you time it? With what? Did you record the time anywhere? Did any other officer?
  - What did you say to the witness after the identification?
  - What did he say?
  - Did you smile at him?
  - Pat him on the back?
  - Did anyone else say anything to him in your presence?

COMMENT:

If the witness testifies, go through the same with him.
- You didn't audiotape your discussion with the witness?
- You do have tape recorders in your precinct?
- And even video recorders?
- You didn't use either, did you?
- Descriptions of the perpetrator.
- Did the witness describe the assailant to you?
- What was that description?

COMMENT:

Go through every physical attribute you can imagine and exhaust everything the witness might have said about the attribute. Do not settle.
- Did he say anything more about the assailant's hair color/hair style?
- So he didn't say anything about the assailant being bald?
- Did you ask?
- And he didn't say anything about the assailant wearing a hat?
- Did he say anything more about the shade of the assailant's skin color? Weight? Height? Age?
- So anything the witness told you about the assailant's description, you put in your report?
- If he told you anything more about the assailant's description [or you can go feature by feature–skin color, age, height, weight, build, facial hair, hair style, clothing, etc.], you would have put it in your report, right?
- Did you put anything in notes that did not make it into the report?
- Did you tell any other officers anything about the description that did not make it into the report?
- As you sit here today, there is nothing you can remember about the description that is not in your report?
- In fact, your memory about what the witness said is based entirely on what's in your report?

§9:43   Examining the Eyewitness at the Hearing

At a pre-trial hearing, you want to ask for as much detail as possible about anything relevant to the identification. You want to hear the good and the bad to know what awaits you at trial.

Areas to explore at a hearing include:
- Any prior acquaintance with the perpetrator.
- Distractions immediately before the event.
- On what the witness focused during the event.
- The duration of the event.
- Everything the witness noticed about the perpetrator.
- The description the witness gave to the police, and all he omitted.
- All the details about any pre-trial identification procedure:
  - What was said to him before and after.
  - His certainty.
  - How long he took to make an identification.
  - Why he picked the person he did.
  - Whether he thought anyone else in the line-up or photo array could be the perpetrator.

[§§9:44-9:49 Reserved]

C. Witness Examination at Trial

§9:50   Attack Credibility

Attack the witness's credibility generally.

While the defense of misidentification alleges mistake rather than falsehood, anything that makes the witness less believable and less attractive to the jury will diminish the jury's sympathy with the witness and its likelihood of giving him the benefit of the doubt.

Therefore, do not hesitate to point out the witness's criminal history or prior inconsistent statements.

Emphasize an inaccurate description. This is a safe area because you will rely on the report the police wrote of the description, probably soon after the event. All the factors the prosecution cites in favor of believing the victim–his desire to see the culprit caught, the focus which the stress of the event brought to him at the time of the crime–also suggest that any description he gave to the possible would be as accurate as possible.

Consider the following types of questions:
- You called the police on your cell phone as soon as the robber turned the corner?
- And the police arrived within five minutes?
- You called them because you wanted to see the robber caught?
- Officer Smith asked you to describe the robber?
- You gave as accurate and complete a description as you could so that the robber would be caught?
- You described the robber as African-American?
- You didn't say whether his complexion was dark, fair or somewhere in between?
- Officer Smith did ask you to describe the robber's complexion, didn't he?
- If you had noticed the robber's complexion, you would have told Officer Smith, right?
- But you didn't?
- Officer Smith left you with his card?
- You never called him to add more information about the robber's appearance than you gave on the night of the robbery?
- You met with Officer Smith to view some photographs on June 1, just one week after the robbery?
- He pulled out a big book for you to look through?
- Before he opened the book, you didn't say, "Just show me photos of dark-skinned African-American men," did you?
- Look at my client. Would you agree that his complexion is noticeably darker than most African-American men?
- Well, he's noticeably darker than any African-American individuals you see in this courtroom, isn't he?
- And you never described the robber to the police as a noticeably dark in skin complexion?

§9:51   Avoid Questioning About Certainty

Unless you have a helpful statement memorialized in a report or prior testimony, avoid questioning on witness certainty.

By the time of trial, whether consciously or not, the witness is invested in his identification and will express it with a certainty that your questioning on this point will only emphasize. Jurors mistakenly tend to defer to a witness's statement of certainty. [*Newsome v. McCabe*, 319 F.3d 301, 305 (7th Cir. 2003).]

§9:52   Be Cautious About Questioning About Duration

Question on the duration of the event only with great caution.

Studies show that witnesses commonly overestimate the duration of stressful events, like a crime. An event that took two seconds becomes twenty, enabling the prosecutor to tick off twenty-seconds of silence to the jury in summation to show how long a time that is.

If you can, try to back into this by questioning about what did not happen during the crime. If you are fortunate, you might exploit a witness's admission that he did not notice a particular feature because of the event's brevity.

Consider the following types of questions:

*   The robber told you to give him your money?
*   You opened your purse to get the money out, right?
*   He snatched the whole purse from you?
*   He didn't give you time to take out your money?
*   That purse was a favorite of yours, wasn't it?
*   Losing the purse may have hurt more than losing the money?
*   You didn't get time to say to him, Hey, I'll take the money out?"
*   Is it fair to say that you didn't get time to say anything before he snatched the purse?
*   And he didn't take time to look through the purse, did he?
*   Just took off and ran, right?
*   As you said on direct, you didn't even have time to notice if he had any facial hair, right?
*   When asked for the money, his face could not have been more than two feet from yours?
*   And when he snatched the purse, he got even closer?
*   If you had a good look at his face from that close, you would have noticed if he had a beard?
*   Or a mustache?

[§§9:53-9:59 Reserved]

D. Expert Testimony at Trial

§9:60   Trend Is to Allow Court Discretion

At this writing, all states but Louisiana and all federal courts of appeals, with the possible exception of the Seventh and Eleventh Circuits [*see United States v. Hall*,165 F.3d 1095 (7th Cir. 1999); *United States v. Smith*, 122 F.3d 1355, 1358 (11th Cir. 1997)], recognize that trial judges have the discretion to admit expert testimony on the weaknesses of eyewitness identification. [*See generally Commonwealth v. Walker*, 92 A.3d 766 (Pa. 2014), *overruling Commonwealth v. Simmons*, 541 Pa. 211, 662 A.2d 621 (Pa. 1995); *State v. Carr*, 331 P.3d 544 (Kansas 2014), *overruling Kansas v. Gaines*, 926 P.2d 641, 646-49 (Kan. 1996); *Bomas v. State*, 412 Md. 392, 407-08 & nn.5-9, 987 A.2d 98, 107 & nn.5-9 (MD 2010) (surveying cases); *but see State v. Henry*, 147 So.3d 1143, 1164 (La. Ct. App. 2014) (noting Louisiana's continued prohibition against expert testimony on eyewitness identification).]

In addition to *Walker* and *Carr, cited supra*, the following cases have allowed expert testimony:

*   *State v. Guilbert*, 306 Conn. 218, 49 A.3d 705 (2012) (overruling *Connecticut v. McClendon*, 248 Conn. 572, 730 A.2d 1107, 1114-17 (Conn. 1999), and holding that the weaknesses of eyewitness testimony are not generally known to jurors and expert testimony on those weaknesses generally should be permitted).
*   *State v. Clopten*, 2009 UT 84, 223 P.3d 1103 (2009) (such expert testimony is reliable and helpful; the application of Utah Rule of Evidence 702 "will result in the liberal and routine admission of eyewitness expert testimony, particularly in cases where, as here, eyewitnesses are identifying a defendant not well known to them").

- *People v. LeGrand,* 8 N.Y.3d 449, 867 N.E.2d 374, 835 N.Y.S.2d 523 (2007) (reversing trial court for exclusion of eyewitness expert testimony on the correlation between confidence and accuracy of identification, the effect of post-event information on accuracy of identification and confidence malleability).
- *United States v. Brownlee,* 454 F.3d 131 (3d Cir. 2006) (reversing conviction for exclusion of eyewitness expert testimony).
- *United States v. Moore,* 786 F.2d 1308, 1312 (5th Cir. 1986) (abuse of discretion to exclude testimony in case involving one identification, by one witness, under stress).
- *Arizona v. Chapple,* 660 P.2d 1208, 1217-25 (Ariz. 1983) (abuse of discretion to exclude testimony of qualified eyewitness expert in case "with identification the one issue on which guilt or innocence of defendant hinged").

Jurisdictions that follow the *Daubert* test seem more amenable to the admission of this testimony than those who still apply the *Frye* test to the admissibility of expert testimony. There is, however, in all jurisdictions a strong trend against any per se rules of inadmissibility in favor of committing the issue to the trial court's discretion to be exercised on a case-by-case basis. [*See Bomas v. State,* 412 Md. 392, 987 A.2d 98 (MD 2010) (admission of expert testimony on eyewitness identification is within trial court's discretion; acknowledging that scientific advances in the field favor more liberal admissibility); *Johnson v. State,* 272 Ga. 254, 256, 526 S.E.2d 549, 552 (Ga. 2000); *People v. LeGrand,* 8 N.Y.3d 449, 867 N.E.2d 374, 835 N.Y.S.2d 523 (2007) (in New York, a *Frye* jurisdiction, admissibility is within the trial court's discretion).]

Decisions upholding the exclusion of expert testimony rely on the unsupported assertion that eyewitness identification experts add nothing to what the jurors' own common sense tells them. [*United States v. Hall,* 165 F.3d 1095 (7th Cir. 1999) (although the trial court has discretion to admit expert testimony, it is disfavored because jurors are already aware of the factors bearing on the reliability of eyewitness identification).] Several recent decisions and studies confront this assertion and prove it wrong. [*See, e.g., Walker,* 92 A.3d at 779-84 (surveying studies and judicial opinions); *People v. Tisdale,* 376 Ill. App. 2d 511, 526, 875 N.E.2d 1221, 1233 (Ill. App. 2007) (jurors mistakenly believe that a witness faced with a weapon is more likely to be accurate in his identification); Elizabeth F. Loftus, Timothy P. O'Toole, Catharine F. Easterly, *Juror Understanding of Eyewitness Testimony: A Survey of 1000 Potential Jurors in the District of Columbia* at 10-11 (witnesses commonly overestimate the duration of stressful events, but jurors tend to accept the erroneous estimate)].

§9:61 Develop Specific Basis for Misidentification

The trend to leaving the issue of the admissibility of expert testimony to the discretion of the trial court places the onus on defense counsel to demonstrate that:
- The issue of identification is central to the case.
- The expert's testimony, rather than being a general lecture on the vagaries of eyewitness identification, relates closely to the specific circumstances of the case and why those circumstances might produce a misidentification.

[*See, e.g., United States v. Brownlee,* 454 F.3d 131, 143 (3d Cir. 2006) ("a defendant who seeks the admission of expert testimony must make an on-the-record detailed proffer to the court, including an explanation of precisely how the expert's testimony is relevant to the eyewitness identifications under consideration. The offer of proof should establish the presence of factors *(e.g.,* stress, or differences in race or age as between the eyewitness and the defendant) which have been found by researchers to impair the accuracy of eyewitness identifications."); *United States v. Mathis,* 264 F.3d 321 (3d Cir. 2001) (testimony should have been admitted to explain influence of viewing an earlier, single photograph of the defendant and of seeing a weapon during the crime); *People v. Williams,* 14 Misc.2d 571, 830 N.Y.S.2d 452 (NY Sup. Ct. Kings Co. 2006) (admitting expert testimony on the issues of (1) cross-racial identification, (2) weapon focus, (3) exposure duration, (4) confidence malleability (i.e., the extent to which police feedback increases a witness's confidence in his identification), (5) mug shot exposure, and (6) lack of double-blind line-ups).]

Therefore, you should plan your discovery, factual investigation and the conduct of your *Wade* hearing to elicit those facts that experts deem conducive to misidentification: fear, focus on a weapon, racial differences between the witness and the defendant, any police confirmation that the witness made the correct identification, exposure duration, the failure to use better out-of-court identification procedures, and the passage of time. [See www.seweb.uci.edu/faculty/loftus/ (Professor Elizabeth Loftus website with CV and articles); www.psychology.iastate.edu/faculty/gwells/ (website of Professor Gary Wells).]

[§§9:62-9:69 Reserved]

E. Jury Instructions

§9:70   Focus on Specific Factors

If identification testimony plays a role in the trial, you should urge the court to instruct the jury on the weaknesses of such testimony. Many courts require such an instruction whenever eyewitness identification is a central issue in the case. [*E.g., State v. Cabagbag,* 127 Haw. 302, 277 P.3d 1027 (2012) (surveying jurisdictions).]

Many jurisdictions employ a weak standard instruction which merely repeats the *Neil v. Bigger* factors. [See §9:04.]

However, there is a trend toward warning a jury in stronger and more specific terms of identification testimony's weaknesses. [*See State v. Ledbetter,* 275 Conn. 534, 579-80, 881 A.2d 290, 318-19 (Conn. 2005).] In *State v. Henderson,* 208 N.J. 208, 27 A.3d 872 (2011), the New Jersey Supreme Court commissioned a special master to hear expert testimony and report on the need for better identification procedures. The principal result of the hearing and decision was a set of very strong, detailed jury instructions to focus jurors on the special concerns raised by identification testimony. [*See* http://www.judiciary.state.nj.us (July 19, 2012).] These instructions can be a model for any case in which eyewitness identification testimony is at issue. [*See Young v. State,* 374 P.3d 395 (Alaska 2016); *Commonwealth v. Gomes,* 22 N.E.3d 897 (Mass. 2015); *State v. Lawson,* 291 P.3d 673 (Or. 2012); *State v. Guilbert,* 306 Conn. 218, 49 A.3d 705, (2012) (following *Henderson*).]

A proposed instruction should focus on factors peculiar to your case, such as the inaccuracy of cross-racial identification. [*See State v. Cromedy,* 158 N.J. 112, 118, 727 A.2d 457 (1999) (charge must warn of unreliability of cross-racial identifications); *Commonwealth v. Bastaldo,* 32 N.E.3d 873 (Mass. 2015)(same).]

Forms:
- **Form 9-3** Basic Jury Instruction
- **Form 9-4** Instruction Based on Cross Racial Identification
- **Form 9-5** Instruction Based on Inadequate Instructions During Line-Up

§9:71   Burden of Proof

Request that the instruction specify that the identification must be proven beyond a reasonable doubt. [*See generally* Jules Epstein, *Tri-State Vagaries: The Varying Responses Of Delaware, New Jersey, And Pennsylvania To The Phenomenon Of Mistaken Identifications,* 12 Widener L. Rev. 327, 2353 & n.14 (2006) (surveying New Jersey, Delaware and Pennsylvania on their jury instructions).]

Form:
- **Form 9-3** Basic Jury Instruction

§9:72   Witness Confidence

Many standard charges instruct the jury to consider the witnesses' confidence in the identification; seek to omit this language.

Studies have singled out witness confidence as an unreliable predictor of an identification's accuracy. [*See Commonwealth v. Santoli,* 424 Mass. 837, 846, 680 N.E.2d 1116, 1121 (1997) (removing confidence language from Massachusetts jury instruction); *Newsome v. McCabe,* 319 F.3d 301, 305 (7th Cir. 2003) ("The basic problem about testimony from memory is that most of our recollections are not verifiable. The only warrant for them is our certitude, and certitude is not a reliable test of certainty. ... [T]he mere fact that we remember something with great confidence is not a powerful warrant for thinking it true. ... Jurors, however, tend to think that witnesses' memories are reliable (because jurors are confident of their own), and this gap between the actual error rate and the jurors' heavy reliance on eyewitness testimony sets the stage for erroneous convictions when (as in Newsome's prosecution) everything depends on uncorroborated eyewitness testimony by people who do not know the accused.").]

III. FORMS

Form 9-1   Motion for Double Blind Sequential Line-Up

UNITED STATES DISTRICT COURT
_____ DISTRICT OF _____

UNITED STATES OF AMERICA,
       Plaintiff,

v.   CASE NO. _____

JOHN DOE,
            Defendant.

DEFENDANT'S MOTION FOR A DOUBLE-BLIND SEQUENTIAL RECORDED LINE-UP

AND NOW COMES defendant John Doe by his attorney, Thomas J. Farrell, Esquire, and files the following Motion for a Double Blind Sequential Line-Up and in support thereof avers as follows:

1. Mr. Doe is charged in a one count indictment with bank robbery, in violation of 18 USC 2113. The indictment alleges that on _____ Mr. Doe robbed one John Smith, a First Bank employee, as he was refilling the cash in a First Bank ATM machine.

2. The ATM camera took a photograph of the robber, but the picture is blurry, and the face of the robber is unrecognizable, even as to race.

3. Mr. Smith had never seen the individual who robbed him before the robbery. The robbery lasted no more than several seconds. During that time, the robber pointed a firearm at Mr. Smith; it can be assumed that Mr. Smith was extremely scared and anxious during the robbery.

4. Mr. Smith gave police a sketchy description of the robber: an African-American male in his 20s, without any description of hairstyle, facial hair, complexion, height or weight. Mr. Smith is Caucasian.

5. Mr. Smith apparently picked Mr. Doe's photograph from a book of mugshots which the Pittsburgh Police showed to him two weeks after the robbery. No line up or photo array or any other out-of-court identification procedure has been conducted in this case.

6. As is detailed in the accompanying memorandum of law, numerous studies, state and federal guidelines and court decisions recognize that in-court identification procedures are unnecessarily suggestive.

7. Many authorities recommend that when conducting an out-of-court line-up, the line-up should be a "double-blind" line-up, in which neither the witness nor the police officer conducting the line-up know whether the defendant or a suspect is one of the individuals in the line-up. This procedure prevents the police officer from giving hints to the witness, whether conscious or unconscious, as to who to pick in the line-up. Further, the knowledge that the suspect is within the line-up motivates the witness to pick someone, most likely the individual who most resembles his memory of the perpetrator, rather than picking the actual individual who committed the crime.

8. In addition, any comments by the police confirming or congratulating the witness's identification tends to imprint the identification on the witness's memory and lends a degree of certainty that the witness did not have (what is called "confidence malleability"). To prevent this, commentators and government authorities recommend that all discussions at the line-up be recorded and that the police make no comments to the witness.

9. Studies also show that a sequential line-up, as opposed to a simultaneous line-up, decreases the likelihood of false identification. In a simultaneous line-up, a number of individuals are shown to the witnesses at the same time. In that case, the individual will tend to pick whomever of the participants most resembles his memory of the perpetrator. In a sequential line-up, the participants are shown to the witness individually and one at a time. This increases the likelihood that the witness's selection will be the perpetrator rather than the best of the lot in the line-up.

10. Videotaping the line-up and any interactions between the police and the witness at the line-up will create an indisputable record of what happened at the line-up as to the identification, the time it took, the witness's certainty, and any comments made by the police or the witness.

WHEREFORE, defendant respectfully requests that the Court enter the attached order directing the police to conduct a double-blind sequential line-up and to make a videotaped and written record of the proceeding.

Respectfully submitted,

_____
Thomas J. Farrell
Counsel for Defendant

UNITED STATES DISTRICT COURT
_____ DISTRICT OF _____

UNITED STATES OF AMERICA,
Plaintiff,

v.

CASE NO. _____

JOHN DOE,
Defendant.

DEFENDANT'S MEMORANDUM OF LAW IN SUPPORT OF MOTION FOR SEQUENTIAL DOUBLE-BLIND RECORDED LINE-UP

Introduction

In this case, the defendant's guilt or innocence of a serious felony charge rises or falls on the eyewitness testimony of a single witness. This motion seeks the use of a line-up procedure which is no more costly or unwieldy than any other line-up, but which has been scientifically proven to reduce the number of false identifications while leaving intact the number of accurate identifications.

Social science research has shown that the use of simultaneous line-ups–where a witness views photographs or persons at the same time–exacerbates the inaccuracies of eyewitness identifications. In contrast, blind and sequential line-up procedures have been shown to heighten the validity and accuracy of eyewitness evidence. Accordingly, numerous jurisdictions have ordered the use of these procedures as well as a recording of line-ups to avoid any suggestions, intentional or inadvertent, as to who the witness should identify; to deter any confirmations of the witness's identification, which may create an exaggerated sense of confidence in the identification; and to ensure that the procedure is conducted fairly. As described below, this Court has the inherent authority to order the use of the procedure we request and should exercise its discretion and ordering a double-blind sequential recorded line-up.

As the attached motion describes, this is a case in which the risk of mistaken identification is especially great. The witness and perpetrator were strangers of different races. The encounter lasted seconds under stressful conditions. There is little corroborating evidence.

Argument

The Risks of Mistaken Identification.

It has long been recognized that mistaken identification produces more wrongful convictions than any other cause. *See United States v. Wade*, 388 U.S. 218, 228 (1967) ("The identification of strangers is proverbially untrustworthy," (quoting Felix Frankfurter, *The Case of Sacco and Vanzetti* at 30 (1927))); *United States v. Brownlee*, 454 F.3d 131, 141-42 (3d Cir. 2006) (eyewitness identification testimony not only is unreliable, but jurors give it undue weight); *United States v. Smithers*, 212 F.3d 306, 312 n.1 (6th Cir. 2000) (citing studies to the effect that half of all wrongful convictions result from mistaken identifications); www.innocenceproject.org/causes/index.php (mistaken identification was a factor in 61 of 70 DNA exonerations for wrongful convictions); United States Department of Justice Office Of Research Programs, Convicted By Juries, Exonerated By Science: Case Studies In The Use Of DNA Evidence To Establish Innocence After Trial (1996) (reporting study of 28 cases of mistaking convictions in which defendants were later cleared by DNA evidence, the majority of which were predicated on mistaken eyewitness identifications). Those risks are especially great where, as here, the victim and perpetrator are strangers of different races. *United States v. Stevens*, 935 F.2d 1380, 1392 (3d Cir. 1991).

Asking the witness to identify the perpetrator in-court is unnecessarily suggestive. *United States v. Rogers,* 126 F.3d 655, 658 (5th Cir. 1997) (holding that it was unduly suggestive to ask witness to identify perpetrator in the courtroom when it was clear who was the defendant); *United States v. Beeler,* 62 F.Supp.2d 136, 141-45 (D.Me. 1999) (prohibiting any in-court identification where witness failed to identify defendant in pre-trial line-up).

Studies have shown that certain pre-trial identification procedures–for example, leading questions, positive feedback from police after making the desired selection from a line-up or photo array, or repetitive viewing of the same suspect–can have a distorting effect on memory. See Loftus & Doyle, *Eyewitness Testimony: Civil And Criminal* §§3.04, 3.06, 3.10-11.1; John C. Brigham & Robert K. Bothwell, *The Ability Of Prospective Jurors To Estimate The Accuracy Of Eyewitness Identifications,* J. Law & Human Behavior 19 (1983); Elizabeth F. Loftus & Catherine E. Ketchum, "The Malleability Of Eyewitness Accounts," in *Evaluating Witness Evidence* (1983); Elizabeth F. Loftus, *Eyewitness Testimony* 150-52 (2d ed. 1996). *See generally* Gary L. Wells *et al., From the Lab to the Police Station: A Successful Application of Eyewitness Research,* 55 Am. Psychologist 581 (June 2000) (summarizing research and its application to identification procedures).

This Court Should Order a Double-Blind Sequential Line-Up and Should Order the Police to Record the Procedure.
A.   Sequential Line-Ups.

Numerous studies show that a sequential line-up, as opposed to a simultaneous one, reduces the risk of false identification with little reduction in the likelihood of accurate identifications. B. L. Cutler & S. D. Penrod, *Improving The Reliability Of Eyewitness Identification: Line-Up Construction And Presentation,* 73 Journal of Applied Psychology 281-290 (1988); R. C. L. Lindsay & G. L. Wells, *Improving Eyewitness Identifications from Line-Ups: Simultaneous Versus Sequential Line-Up Presentations,* 17 Journal of Applied Psychology 556-564 (1985). Accordingly, the states of New Jersey, California and Wisconsin all have recommended the use of sequential line-ups rather than simultaneous ones. California Commission on the Fair Administration of Justice, *Report and Recommendations Regarding Eyewitness Identification Procedures* (April 2006)(available at www.ccfaj.org/reports.html); Office of the Attorney General, State of New Jersey, *Attorney General Guidelines for Preparing and Conducting Photo and Live Line-Up Identification Procedures* (April 2001); Wisconsin Attorney General, *Model Policy and Procedure for Eyewitness Identification* (Sept. 12, 2005) (available at www.doj.state.wi.us/dles/tns/EyewitnessPublic.pdf); U.S. Department of Justice's October 1999 report. [*Eyewitness Evidence: A Guide for Law Enforcement* (available at www.ojp.usdoj.gov/nij/pubs-sum/178240.htm)

B.   The Double-Blind Procedure and Recordings.

It is well documented that police officers' unintentional cues, such as body language, gestures and tone of voice, may negatively impact the reliability of eyewitness identifications. Studies have shown that the margin of error for both sequential and simultaneous line-ups is further reduced when the procedure is performed by an officer who is not involved in the investigation and does not know the identity of the suspect. *See People v. Williams,* 14 Misc.3d 571, 580-83, 830 N.Y.S.2d 452, 460-62 (N.Y. Sup. Ct. Kings Co. 2006); Donald P. Judges, *Two Cheers For The Department Of Justice's Eyewitness Evidence: A Guide For Law Enforcement,* 53 Ark. L. Rev. 231, 253 (2000); Gary L. Wells *et al., From the Lab to the Police Station: A Successful Application of Eyewitness Research,* 55 Am. Psychologist 581 (June 2000). Thus, the states of New Jersey, Wisconsin, and California, as well as numerous municipalities have recommended the use of double-blind identification procedures. *See* NJ Guidelines, I.A.; California Report and Recommendations 1, 2; Wisconsin Model Policy and Procedure at 3, 17-21.

For similar reasons, the Supreme Court of New Jersey has required that all identification procedures be recorded. *State v. Delgado,* 188 N.J. 48, 902 A.2d 888 (2006). The U.S. Department of Justice has recommended the same. U.S. Department of Justice, Office of Justice Programs, *Eyewitness Evidence: A Guide for Law Enforcement* (1999). *See also Newsome v. McCabe,* 319 F.3d 301, 305 (7th Cir. 2003)(noting that despite inaccuracy of identifications based on fleeting events, witnesses often express at trial an unfounded sense of certainty).

C.   The Court's Authority to Dictate the Manner in Which a Line-Up Will Be Conducted

Numerous decisions authorize a trial court to order a line-up in order to prevent the irreparable suggestivity of in court identification procedure. *See, e.g., United States v. Ravitch,* 421 F.2d 1196, 1203 (2d Cir. 1970); *State in Interest of W. C.,* 85 N.J. 218, 426 A.2d 50 (N.J. 1981) (holding that court has discretion to order line-up; surveying jurisdictions and finds that most follow similar rule); *Commonwealth v. Sexton,* 485 Pa. 17, 400 A.2d 1289 (1979) (while the matter is in the court's discretion, court cannot arbitrarily and capriciously deny such a request); *Evans v. Superior Court,* 11 Cal.3d 617, 522 P.2d 681, 114 Cal.Rptr. 121 (1974) (recognizing a right to a line-up, but committing the granting of a request to the trial court's discretion). Likewise, a number of courts have used their authority to order line-ups to dictate that particular procedures be followed, such as a double-blind line-up, a sequential line-up, and the recording of any line-up procedures as well as any discussions between the police and the witness. *State v. Delgado,* 188 N.J.

48, 902 A.2d 888 (2006) (ordering that as a condition of an out-of-court identification's admissibility, officers must make a written record detailing the identification procedure, including place and any dialogue between the witness and police); *In re Investigation of Thomas,* 189 Misc.2d 487, 733 N.Y.S.2d 591 (NY Sup. Ct. Kings Co. 2001) (ordering double blind sequential line-up).

Conclusion

For the reasons stated above, the Court should enter the attached order granting a sequential double-blind line-up to be conducted and recorded as stated in the attached order.

Respectfully submitted,

_____

Thomas J. Farrell
Attorney for Defendant

UNITED STATES DISTRICT COURT
_____ DISTRICT OF _____

UNITED STATES OF AMERICA,
        Plaintiff,

        v.   CASE NO. _____

JOHN DOE,
        Defendant.

ORDER OF COURT

AND NOW, this___ day of July, 2004, upon consideration of defendant's motion for a sequential double-blind recorded line-up, it is ordered that defendant's motion is granted;

Further, it is ordered that a sequential double-blind line-up procedure shall be employed in this case and that the procedure shall be videotaped; and

Further, it is ordered that:

1. The police officer administering the line-up, "the line-up administrator," shall remain with the witness during the duration of the line-up.
2. No police officer present at the line-up shall discuss the identity of the defendant or any other information relevant to the identity of the defendant at any time prior to the viewing of a line-up.
3. Prior to the presentation of a line-up, the line-up administrator shall instruct the witness as follows:

You'll soon be asked to view a group of individuals. As you know, it is just as important to clear innocent persons from suspicion as to identify guilty parties. The individuals you're about to see will be viewed one at a time. They will be presented at random order. The person who committed the crime may or may not be present in this group of individuals. Take as much time as needed in making a decision about each individual before moving to the next one. You understand that all the individuals will be presented, even if an identification is made.

If you can, you should identify the person who committed the crime if he or she is present. Regardless of whether you identify one of the individuals, the police will continue to investigate this incident. This procedure requires you to state, in your own words, how certain you are of any identification. Once you have even made a positive identification or decided that the individual you are observing is not the person who committed the crime, you should tap the two-way glass separating you from the individual being observed three times with your hand. This signal shall indicate to the police officer conducting the line-up that the next individual is to be presented.

4. The line-up administrator shall instruct all those present at the line-up that they may not say or communicate, directly or indirectly, anything to the witness that may influence, intentionally or inadvertently, the witness's selection.
5. The police shall follow these procedures when composing presenting the line-up:
    a. Include only one suspect in each identification procedure.
    b. Include a minimum of five fillers for identification procedure.
6. The witness shall be allowed to view each individual presented before him for as long as he feels is necessary.

7. If an identification is made, the police shall avoid reporting to the witness any information regarding the individual he has selected.
8. If an identification is made, the line-up administrator shall:
   a. Record both identification and non-identification results in writing, including the witness's own words regarding how sure he is.
   b. Ensure results are signed and dated by the witness.
   c. Ensure that no materials indicating previous identification results are visible to the witness.
   d. Ensure that the witness does not write or mark any materials that may be used in other identification procedures.
9. The line-up administrator shall make a written record of the line-up procedures, including:
   a. Names of all persons present at the line-up.
   b. Date and time the identification procedure was conducted.
   c. Both identification and nonidentification results, including the witness's own words regarding how sure he is.
10. The witness shall be instructed not to discuss the identification procedure or its results with the witnesses involved in the case.
11. The entire line-up procedure shall be documented by videotape. This videotape should be a quality that represents a line-up clearly and fairly and captures all discussions between the witness and police. It shall include each individual who participates in the line-up.

_____

U.S. District Judge

Form 9-2   Motion to Suppress Pre-Trial and In-Court Identification

IN THE UNITED STATES DISTRICT COURT FOR THE
_____ DISTRICT OF _____

UNITED STATES OF AMERICA,

            Plaintiff,

     v.   CASE NO. _____

MA,

            Defendant.

DEFENDANT'S PRE-TRIAL MOTION TO SUPPRESS IDENTIFICATION

AND NOW COMES defendant MA by his attorney, Thomas J. Farrell, Esquire, and files the following Pre-Trial Motion to Suppress Identification and in support thereof avers as follows:
1. Assistant United States Attorney NC has informed me that sometime in _____, RO, the corrupt PennDOT employee who is now cooperating with the government, was shown MA's drivers' license. RO identified the photograph on the license as being MA's and claimed that MA had paid a bribe to obtain a commercial driver's license.
2. The government did not show RO an array of photos; nor did it display MA's photo in a non-suggestive setting. There was no need to forego a less suggestive means of attempting to identify MA.
3. If RO met MA at all, it was on _____, when MA allegedly obtained a Pennsylvania CDL, over two years before the identification. Their contact would have been only for a few minutes.
4. I am not aware of any physical description that RO provided of MA.
5. MA is of different race and ethnicity than RO.
6. The defense submits that the out of court identification procedure was so unduly suggestive as to violate MA's due process rights. The defense submits that the Court should preclude any testimony about this identification, as well as any in-court identification of MA. In the alternative, the Court should hold a hearing to determine under the five-part test of *Manson v. Brathwaite*, 432 U.S. 98 (1977), whether the identifications should be suppressed.

            Respectfully submitted,

            _____

            Thomas J. Farrell, Esquire

IN THE UNITED STATES DISTRICT COURT FOR THE
_____ DISTRICT OF _____

UNITED STATES OF AMERICA,
      Plaintiff,

    v.   CASE NO. _____

MA,

      Defendant.

ORDER OF COURT

AND NOW, this _____ day of February, 2002, IT IS ORDERED that a hearing be held on defendant's Motion to Suppress Identification on _____ at _____ _____.

_____
United States District Judge

IN THE UNITED STATES DISTRICT COURT FOR THE
_____ DISTRICT OF _____

UNITED STATES OF AMERICA,

      Plaintiff,

    v.   CASE NO. _____

MA,
      Defendant.

BRIEF IN SUPPORT OF DEFENDANT'S SUPPLEMENTAL PRE-TRIAL MOTION TO SUPPRESS IDENTIFICATION TESTIMONY

AND NOW COMES defendant MA by his attorney, Thomas J. Farrell, Esquire, and files the following Brief in Support of Defendant's Pre-Trial Motion to Suppress Identification and in support thereof avers as follows:

I.   Displaying a Single Photo to RO Was Unnecessarily Suggestive and So Unreliable as to Require Suppression of Any Identification Testimony

"A government identification procedure violates due process when it is 'unnecessarily suggestive' and creates a 'substantial risk of misidentification.' *United States v. Emanuele*, 51 F.3d 1123, 1128 (3d Cir. 1995)." The general inquiry is whether the procedure was unnecessarily suggestive, and if so, whether its corrupting influence outweighs the reliability of the identification testimony. *Manson v. Brathwaite*, 432 U.S. 98, 114 (1977)." *Burkett v. Fulcomer*, 951 F.2d 1431, 1448 (3d Cir. 1991). *See also United States v. Stevens*, 935 F.2d 1380, 1388-92 (3d Cir. 1991). To determine reliability, courts consider "the identification procedure in light of the 'totality of the circumstances.' ... These circumstances may include the witness's original opportunity to observe a defendant and the degree of attention during that observation; the accuracy of the initial description; the witness's degree of certainty when viewing a defendant or his image; and the length of time between the crime and the identification procedure." *Emanuele*, 51 F.3d at 1128. If the photographic identification procedure is found to be so unnecessarily suggestive and unreliable as to create a substantial risk of misidentification, the court should suppress both the out-of-court and any in-court identification. *Emanuele*, 51 F.3d at 1131 (suppressing both out-of-court and in-court identification testimony).

Display of a single photograph is unnecessarily suggestive, at least absent some exigency that would preclude a non-suggestive array or line-up. *Stovall v. Denno*, 388 U.S. 293, 302 (1967); *United States v. Stevens*, 935 F.2d 1380,

1390 (3d Cir. 1991); *see Marsden v. Moore*, 847 F.2d 1536, 1547 (11th Cir. 1988) (collecting cases). Here there was no exigency, as the suspect had been apprehended, the witness was cooperating, and the government did not operate under any time constraints.

The totality of circumstances tilts toward unreliability:

1. *Opportunity to observe and degree of attention.* RO observed MA briefly in the licensing office of PennDOT. If MO was anything like other licensing officials, hardly a glance or a "hello" would have passed between them, much less scrutiny of MA's face.

2. *Accuracy of the initial description.* As far as the defense is aware, RO did not give any description.

3. *Degree of certainty.* I am unaware as to how much certainty RO expressed when shown MA's driver's license in _____. As the Third Circuit Court of Appeals has noted, though, "that factor is not always a valid indicator of the accuracy of recollection." *Stevens*, 935 F.2d at 1392 & n.15.

4. *Passage of time.* A two-year delay seriously undermines reliability. *United States v. Rogers*, 126 F.3d 655, 659 (5th Cir. 1997) (10-month delay raised serious concerns; identification should have been suppressed, but admission harmless error); *Marsden v. Moore*, 847 F.2d at 1546 (passage of two years weighed heavily in decision to suppress).

Another factor to consider is that MA and RO are of different race and ethnicity, a factor known to decrease the accuracy of identifications. *Stevens,* 935 F.2d at 1392.

These circumstances, combined with the highly suggestive photo display, require suppression of any identification testimony, or, in the alternative, a *Wade* hearing to decide its admissibility.

It is true that in this case the government has significant evidence that MA did appear before RO on _____: MA admitted it in his post-arrest statement, and the license application appears to reflect the appearance as well. However, other evidence of guilt is irrelevant to the reliability determination. *Emanuele*, 51 F.3d at 1128. Further, the issue here is not whether MA was in the PennDOT office that day, but whether RO can identify MA as being the individual who, according to RO, entered his office with EB on January 7 and gave RO a cash bribe for a license. RO dealt with scores of applicants every day and thousands since _____. There is great risk in this case that RO will extrapolate from the belief that all Middle Easterners who came into his office for a CDL paid a bribe to the testimony that he recognizes this particular individual, MA, as the person who paid him a bribe on _____, a risk especially great with RO's obvious motive to embellish his testimony to please the government.

Conclusion

For the foregoing reasons, the Court should suppress any identification testimony by RO, or, in the alternative, hold a *Wade* hearing.

Respectfully submitted,

_____

Thomas J. Farrell, Esquire

Form 9-3   Basic Jury Instruction

<u>**COMMENT:**</u>

This instruction is based on the Third Circuit Court of Appeals' Model Jury Instructions, Instruction 4.15, available at www.ca3.uscourts.gov.

Many of the U.S. Courts of Appeals maintain model jury instructions on their websites. [*See also* CAL-CRIM No. 315, available at www.courtinfo.ca.gov/jury/criminaljuryinstructions/.]

In the second question in this form the jury is asked to consider whether the witness is positive in the identification. If the witness did express certainty, you may want to exclude this language on the argument that this "factor is not always a valid indicator of the accuracy of recollection." [*United States v. Stevens*, 935 F.2d at 1392 & n.15; see *Commonwealth v. Santoli*, 424 Mass. 837, 846, 680 N. E. 2d. 1116, 1121 (1997) (removing confidence language from Massachusetts jury instructions).]

GENERAL CHARGE

One of the *(most important)* issues in this case is whether *(name of defendant)* is the same person who committed the crime*(s)* charged in *(Count(s) ___ of)* the indictment. The government, as I have explained, has the burden of proving every element, including identity, beyond a reasonable doubt. Although it is not essential that a witness testifying about the identification *(himself)(herself)* be free from doubt as to the accuracy or correctness of the identification, you must be satisfied beyond a reasonable doubt based on all the evidence in the case that *(name of defendant)* is the person who committed the *crime(s)* charged. If you are not convinced beyond a reasonable doubt that *(name of defendant)* is the person who committed the *crime(s)* charged in *(Count(s) ___ of)* the indictment, you must find *(name of defendant)* not guilty.

Identification testimony is, in essence, the expression of an opinion or belief by the witness. The value of the identification depends on the witness's opportunity to observe the person who committed the crime at the time of the offense and the witness's ability to make a reliable identification at a later time based on those observations.

You must decide whether you believe the witness's testimony and whether you find beyond a reasonable doubt that the identification is correct. You should evaluate the testimony of a witness who makes an identification in the same manner as you would any other witness. In addition, as you evaluate a witness's identification testimony you should consider the following questions as well as any other questions you believe are important *(include only those called for by the facts of the case)*:

(First), you should ask whether the witness was able to observe and had an adequate opportunity to observe the person who committed the crime charged. Many factors affect whether a witness has an adequate opportunity to observe the person committing the crime; the factors include the length of time during which the witness observed the person, the distance between the witness and the person, the lighting conditions, how closely the witness was paying attention to the person, whether the witness was under stress while observing the person who committed the crime, whether the witness knew the person from some prior experience, whether the witness and the person committing the crime were of different races, and any other factors you regard as important.

(Second), you should ask whether the witness is positive in the identification and whether the witness's testimony remained positive and unqualified after cross-examination. If the witness's identification testimony is positive and unqualified, you should ask whether the witness's certainty is well-founded.

(Third), you should ask whether the witness's identification of *(name of defendant)* after the crime was committed was the product of the witness's own recollection. You may take into account both the strength of the later identification and the circumstances under which that identification was made. You may wish to consider how much time passed between the crime and the witness's later identification of the defendant. You may also consider *(whether the witness gave a description of the person who committed the crime) (how the witness's description of the person who committed the crime compares to the defendant.)* (You may also consider whether the witness was able to identify other participants in the crime.) If the identification was made under circumstances that may have influenced the witness, you should examine that identification with great care. Some circumstances which may influence a witness's identification are whether the witness was presented with more than one person or just *(name of defendant)*; whether the witness made the identification while exposed to the suggestive influences of others; and whether the witness identified *(name of defendant)* in conditions that created the impression that *(he) (she)* was involved in the crime.]

[(Fourth), you should ask whether the witness failed to identify *(name of defendant)* at any time, identified someone other than *(name of defendant)* as the person who committed the crime, or changed his or her mind about the identification at any time.]

[The court should also give the following admonition if the witness's opportunity to observe was impaired or if the witness's identification is not positive, was shaken on cross-examination, or was weakened by a prior failure to identify the defendant or by a prior inconsistent identification:

You should receive the identification testimony with caution and scrutinize it with care.]

If after examining all of the evidence, you have a reasonable doubt as to whether *(name of defendant)* is the individual who committed the *crime(s)* charged, you must find *(name of defendant)* not guilty.

Form 9-4   Instruction Based on Cross Racial Identification

COMMENT:

This instruction is based on the New Jersey *Model Jury Charge (Criminal)* "In-court and out-of-court identifications" (1999). [*See State v. Cromedy*, 158 N.J. 112, 727 A.2d 457, 467 (1999) (requiring such a charge).]

[Add to the list of factors the jury may consider:]

The fact that an identifying witness is not of the same race as the perpetrator and/or defendant, and whether that fact might have had an impact on the accuracy of the witness's original perception, and/or the accuracy of the subsequent identification. You should consider that in ordinary human experience, people may have greater difficulty in accurately identifying members of a different race.

Form 9-5   Instruction Based on Inadequate Instructions During Line-Up

In this case, the state has presented evidence that an eyewitness identified the defendant in connection with the crime charged. That identification was the result of an identification procedure in which the individual conducting the procedure either indicated to the witness that a suspect was present in the procedure or failed to warn the witness that the perpetrator may or may not be in the procedure. Studies have shown that indicating to a witness that a suspect is present in an identification procedure or failing to warn the witness that the perpetrator may or may not be in the procedure increases the likelihood that the witness will select one of the individuals in the procedure, even when the perpetrator is not present. Thus, such behavior on the part of the procedure administrator tends to increase the probability of a misidentification. This information is not intended to direct you to give more or less weight to the eyewitness identification evidence offered by the state. It is your duty to determine whether that evidence is to be believed. You may, however, take into account the results of the studies, as just explained to you, in making that determination.

Chapter 10

PRELIMINARY HEARINGS

V.   COMMON ISSUES

VI. FORMS

I. GENERAL POINTS

§10:01 The Right to a Preliminary Hearing

Shortly after the initial appearance, a defendant is entitled to a preliminary hearing or examination at which the prosecution must introduce sufficient evidence to justify holding the case for court (also known as "bind over") [*E.g.,* Fed. R. Cr. P. 5.1(c) (10 days if the defendant is detained; 20 days if the defendant is free on bail).]

The defendant has a Sixth Amendment right to the assistance of counsel at this preliminary hearing. [*Coleman v. Alabama,* 399 U.S. 1 (1970).]

While a preliminary hearing is not constitutionally required, the Fourth Amendment does entitle the defendant to some judicial review of probable cause, which could be non-adversarial, if detained beyond 48 hours. [*County of Riverside v. McLaughlin,* 500 U.S. 44, 56-57 (1991) (an arrested person must receive a probable cause determination within 48 hours unless the prosecution establishes a "bona fide emergency or other extraordinary circumstance").]

There is a statutory right to cross-examine the prosecution's witnesses at the preliminary hearing. [*E.g.,* Fed. R. Cr. P. 5.1(e); Pa. R. Cr. P. 542(c)(2).]

§10:02 Preemption by Grand Jury Indictment

If a charging grand jury is available, a prosecutor can preempt the preliminary hearing by obtaining a grand jury indictment within the time set for a preliminary hearing. [*E.g.,* Fed. R. Cr. P. 5.1(a)(2); 725 Ill. Comp. Stat. 5/103-3.1(b)(2); *Bowens v. Superior Court,* 1 Cal. 4th 36, 2 Cal. Rptr.2d 376, 820 P.2d 600 (1991).]

Therefore, if possible, schedule the preliminary hearing quickly, before the prosecutor can present the case to a grand jury. However, consider a prosecutor's threats that if forced to indict sooner, rather than later, he or she will indict on the highest charge or will charge a mandatory minimum that may be difficult to waive. Look into any office policy and local custom to ascertain if the threats are real.

EXAMPLE:

In federal cases, the Department of Justice has a policy that forbids bargaining away the highest charge if it is "readily provable." [*See United States Attorney Manual* ("USAM") 9-27.300, 9-27.330, 9-27.430.]

While on its face the policy appears to treat pre- and post-indictment plea bargaining identically, in practice, a prosecutor will maintain that any indicted charge is "readily provable" and will be more likely to forego charges that do not appear in an indictment yet.

§10:03 Timing

The magistrate usually sets the preliminary hearing date at the initial appearance or arraignment.

If no date has been issued, file a written demand to set a hearing. Under the law of some states, the right to a hearing will be waived if not invoked. [*E.g., Powell v. State,* 324 Md. 441, 597 A.2d 479 (1991) (defendant must demand preliminary hearing at arraignment or soon after; the failure to hold hearing does not divest trial court of jurisdiction).]

Failure to hold a timely preliminary hearing results in release of the defendant, but not in dismissal of the charges. [*Commonwealth v. Zook,* 532 Pa. 79, 87-88, 615 A.2d 1, 5-6 (1992).]

If you need more time to prepare, seek a short postponement of the preliminary hearing. This will require the defendant to stipulate that the time should be excluded under the speedy trial statute.

Forms:
- **Form 10-1** Demand for Preliminary Hearing
- **Form 10-2** Request for Continuance

§10:04 The Standard of Proof

The standard of proof varies by jurisdiction:
- In some jurisdictions, the standard of proof at the preliminary hearing is probable cause. [*E.g.,* Fed. R. Cr. P. 5.1 (e).]
- In other jurisdictions, the prosecution must establish a "*prima facie*" case, a standard that is somewhat higher than probable cause. [*E.g.,* Pa. R. Cr. P. 543 (*prima facie* case). *See Illinois v. Gates,* 462 U.S. 213, 235 (1983) (probable cause is a lesser standard than a *prima facie* case).]

The *prima facie* standard requires the prosecution not only to establish probable cause to believe that the accused committed the offense, but to present evidence supporting each of the material elements of the charge. [*Commonwealth v. Huggins*, 575 Pa. 395, 401, 836 A.2d 862, 866 (2003).]

However, both standards demand something more than the probable cause needed to search or arrest, because the preliminary hearing serves as a screening device to select those cases in which the evidence is substantial enough to bind the case over for trial and restrain the defendant's liberty, either by bail conditions or detention. [*See Commonwealth v. Teixeira*, 58 N.E.3d 292, 299 n.14 (Mass. 2016) (probable cause standard at a preliminary hearing is more demanding than the probable cause sufficient to arrest); Wayne R. LaFave, Jerrold H. Israel & Nancy J. King, *Criminal Procedure* §14.3(a) (2d ed. 1999).]

If testimony conflicts or the magistrate can draw any of several inferences, the magistrate must accept the prosecution's version. [*E.g., Huggins*, 575 Pa. at 402, 836 A.2d at 866; *Hunter v. District Court*, 190 Colo. 48, 53, 543 P.2d 1265, 1268 (1975).]

§10:05   Making a Record

The preliminary hearing takes place in court before a magistrate or district justice of limited jurisdiction. Often this court is not "of record," meaning that it does not record the proceedings. Therefore, you must retain and schedule your own court reporter to preserve the testimony for later use, such as impeachment at trial.

Whether an indigent defendant has a federal constitutional right to transcribe the preliminary hearing is not a settled question. [*See* Anthony G. Amsterdam, *Trial Manual for the Defense of Criminal Cases*, §139 (5th ed. 1989).] Therefore, court-appointed counsel should consult state law and local rules.

§10:06   Applicability of the Rules of Evidence

Jurisdictions fall into three camps with respect to the applicability of the rules of evidence at preliminary hearings:
* They do not apply at all. [*E.g.,* FRE 1101(d)(3); *Almada v. State*, 994 P.2d 299, 303 (Wyo. 1999).]
* While they do not apply, the bind-over decision cannot be based entirely on hearsay or inadmissible evidence. [*E.g., People v. Horn*, 772 P.2d 108, 109 (Colo. 1989); *Commonwealth v. Jackson*, 2004 PA Super 150, 849 A.2d 1254 (Pa. Super. Ct. 2004); *but see Commonwealth v. Ricker*, 120 A.3d 349 (Pa. Super. 2015) (probable cause determination may be based entirely on hearsay), *appeal granted*, 135 A.3d 175 (Pa. 2016).]
* They generally apply. [*E.g.,* NY Crim. Pro. Law 180.60(8).]

Custom supplements and sometimes supplants these legal rules. Some prosecutors and magistrates routinely rely solely on hearsay, and the only witness will be the investigating officer. Others (usually where the law requires some non-hearsay evidence) seldom use hearsay on crucial points, and in these jurisdictions the victim must testify.

In most jurisdictions, the defendant is not entitled to suppress evidence for constitutional violations such as an illegal search or interrogation. [*State v. Kane*, 218 Conn. 151, 588 A.2d 179 (1991); *but see* 725 ILCS 5/109-3(e) (motions to suppress may be heard at preliminary hearing).]

Other evidentiary rules may apply at preliminary hearings, and you should be ready to exploit them. For example:
* Privileges apply.
* You may invoke the *corpus delecti* rule to require evidence of criminality before a confession can be received. [*See State v. Davis*, 273 P.3d 693, 697 n.2 (Idaho 2011) (surveying split in state courts on this issue); *Commonwealth v. Meder*, 416 Pa. Super. 273, 611 A.2d 213 (1992).] This may mean that even where the defendant has confessed, the prosecution cannot obtain a bind over if the victim does not testify to establish intercourse and lack of consent in a rape case, or lack of authority in a stolen car case.

§10:07   The Arresting Officer

The word and recommendation of the arresting officer carry great weight with most magistrates. District justices are just as often retired police officers as they are lawyers. They work and may share office space with the police. Therefore, before the hearing, you should approach the arresting or investigating officer and pitch your assessment of the case to the officer.

The officer may have his or her own doubts about the victim's story and the value of the case. The officer might be willing to:
* Clue you into helpful concessions that he or she would be willing to make on the stand (*e.g.,* the victim was noticeably intoxicated when he reported the offense).

- Offer to persuade the victim to accept a non-criminal disposition, such as restitution.
- Warn you about pitfalls in certain lines of questioning.

However, it is just as likely that the officer may lobby you to waive the hearing so the matter can be dealt with "downtown." The officer's motivation might range from the weakness of the case to the simple desire to avoid waiting all day in a crowded courtroom for the case to be called. In any event, you seldom should waive the hearing. [*See* §10:42.]

The officer has already done as much harm to the defendant as he or she can by arresting him and filing the complaint. Any frustration by the officer at your refusal to waive the hearing will not worsen the situation appreciably.

§10:08   Cross-Examination

There is a right to cross-examine to test the plausibility of the witness's story and his or her willingness to adhere to it on cross-examination.

Magistrates will allow some leeway in this regard. Most recognize that an assessment of the victim or witness's credibility is essential if they are to discharge their screening function. [*See Wilson v. State*, 59 Wisc.2d 269, 295, 208 N.W.2d 134, 148 (1973) (error to preclude cross-examination of eyewitness as to description he initially gave to police).]

However, magistrates will have little patience for questions trying to show a witness's general untrustworthiness, such as questions regarding the witness's bias or motive or questions about the witness's criminal record or uncharged acts of dishonesty. [For explanations of the difference between permissible and impermissible inquiries, *see People v. Stafford*, 434 Mich. 125, 450 N.W.2d 559 (1990); *State v. Dunn*, 121 Wisc.2d 389, 359 N.W.2d 151 (Wisc. 1984); *Hunter v. District Court*, 190 Colo. 48, 53, 543 P.2d 1265, 1268 (1975).]

Such questions are meaningless in the preliminary hearing context, and it is best to avoid giving the witness practice at fielding the trial cross-examination.

[§10:09 Reserved]

II.   DEFENSE OBJECTIVES

§10:10   Dismissal or a Reduction in Charges

With the prosecution's light evidentiary burden and the relaxation of evidentiary rules at preliminary hearings, a full dismissal is unlikely. Magistrates are disposed to err on the side of letting the case go forward so that the court of general jurisdiction can evaluate the case, especially if the charge is a serious one. They are more likely to entertain arguments that the case is overcharged.

However, charges sometimes are an outright error, and you must assess whether to "go for broke" at the hearing.

Dismissal at the hearing has the obvious advantages of freeing the defendant from detention or bail restrictions, from the uncertainty of pending charges, and the adverse publicity that may result from formal charges.

<u>CAUTION:</u>
The near certainty that this attempt will fail cautions against any sacrifices at the preliminary hearing that will harm the defense case later. Do not:
- Expose defense theories that the prosecutor can investigate and refute.
- Open defense witnesses, especially the defendant, to cross.

Furthermore, dismissal may prove a Pyrrhic victory. Apprised of the weaknesses in his case, the prosecutor may improve it and refile. [*See* §10:49.]

§10:11   Bail Reduction

Even if the defense presentation falls short of convincing the magistrate to dismiss, demonstrating the weaknesses in the case may convince the magistrate to reduce bail to an amount the defendant can make.

Questioning may show that:
- The victim's testimony is suspect.
- Injuries are not so severe.
- The defendant's involvement in the transaction was minimal.

Questions can be directed on all three points. [*See* §§10:30, *et seq.*]

Further along in the proceedings, these same three points might justify a more lenient plea and sentence.

§10:12   Discovery

Formal discovery is sparse in criminal cases. Even if funds are available for investigation, witnesses may be difficult to find and reluctant to be interviewed. Prosecutors often have little time to prepare witnesses before the hearing, and the defense might have its best chance to hear the witnesses' unrehearsed story, verbatim and under oath.

Even if a magistrate severely limits cross-examination, or if the hearing reveals no facts previously unknown, the opportunity to hear the witness live and to record that testimony is invaluable.

You can start to assess whether to:
- Attack the witness's credibility at trial.
- Claim that the witness is honest but mistaken.
- Adopt a theory that accepts this witness's testimony as accurate.
- Avoid trial altogether.

Cold facts about the witness's background are no substitute. Even educated witnesses with clean records may prove to be inarticulate, twitchy or surly. Likewise, the felon who never completed high school may be charming and charismatic.

§10:13   Locking In Testimony

Commit the prosecution's witnesses to a sworn version of events that cannot be changed at trial.

When you obtain a favorable concession or even a version of events that is not as harmful as other possibilities, use short, concrete, specific questions to assure that the answer cannot be changed or explained later. Questioning also should explore explanations both for the purpose of excluding them and learning them before they become a surprise at trial. [*See, e.g.,* §§10:30, *et seq.*]

EXAMPLE:

On a charge against a pharmacist for illegally dispensing medication without a valid prescription, a treating physician may testify that based on the lack of an entry in his chart, he did not prescribe the medication on a particular date.

However, he may have no independent present recollection of whether or not he did prescribe the medication on that date. He should be asked if there is any other reason he can say that he did not prescribe that particular medication for that patient. Perhaps he does not believe in that medication for the condition at issue. Or, the patient might have been taking another medication that would have interacted adversely with the particular medication.

[§§10:14-10:19 Reserved]

III. PREPARATION

§10:20   General Points

A preliminary hearing is not a civil deposition. Although you have some leeway to probe, it will be severely limited.

Therefore, you must begin to think of the likely defense theory and focus questioning on laying the basis for that theory by discovering and locking in testimony helpful to the theory and excluding harmful explanations.

Alternatively, the preliminary hearing may debunk the defense and direct you to explore a different theory.

§10:21   Interview the Client

While you never should rely exclusively on the defendant's version of events, it is a good starting point for developing a defense.

Begin with these points:
- Does the defendant concede that he was at the scene?
- Does he have an excuse or justification for the conduct?

- What is his prior history with the victim or witnesses?

The above information is indispensable for building defenses, such as entrapment or consent, or beginning to explore the witnesses' credibility.

During the hearing, you can present the client's story to the witness in your questions and elicit confirmation or denial. You can then prepare for trial knowing which points you can make through the witness (and perhaps even avoid calling the defendant), and which questions you must avoid.

You also must lower the client's expectations about the hearing. Clients often are angry and indignant and want the charges exposed as false, immediately. You must explain that:

- A preliminary hearing is not a trial.
- Many issues that are foremost with the defendant (*e.g.,* the victim's mendacity, the officer's abusiveness) do not matter at all to the magistrate.
- An overly aggressive cross-examination may frustrate efforts to discover the prosecution's case.
- Defense witnesses generally should not testify.
- The defendant should almost never testify.

§10:22   Obtain All Charging Papers and Police Reports

The prevailing rule is that there is no right to discovery before a preliminary hearing. [*E.g., Almada v. State*, 994 P.2d 299, 303-04 (Wyo. 1999) (upholding lower court quashing of a discovery request and a subpoena on officers for tapes of conversations with an undercover informant in a controlled-buy drug case) ; *but see Commonwealth v. Teixeira*, 58 N.E.3d 292 (Mass. 2016) (magistrate has discretion for the proper administration of the criminal justice system to order discovery before a preliminary hearing).]

Nevertheless, the discovery rules of some jurisdictions may entitle a defendant to prior statements of any witness who testifies at the preliminary hearing. [*E.g.,* Fed. R. Cr. P. 26.2 (g)(1); *LaFortune v. District Court*, 972 P.2d 868, 872-73 (Okl. Crim. App. 1998); *People v. Laws*, 218 Mich. 447, 451–52, 554 N.W.2d 586, 589 (Mich. App. 1996).]

In addition, you may make a demand for exculpatory evidence. [*Brady v. Maryland*, 373 U.S. 83 (1963) (prosecution has a due process obligation to disclose exculpatory evidence); Rule 3.8(d) of the Rules of Professional Responsibility (requiring prosecutors to make timely disclosure of exculpatory evidence to the defense). *See State v. Mitchell*, 200 Conn. 323, 338, 512 A.2d 140, 149 (1986) (recognizing due process right to disclosure of exculpatory evidence at the preliminary hearing); *In the Matter of Attorney C.*, 47 P.3d 1167 (Colo. 2002) (Rule 3.8(d) requires disclosure of exculpatory evidence to the defense in advance of any critical stage of the criminal process, including preliminary hearings).]

There may be no immediate remedy for a refusal to provide discovery. However, the prosecution's failure to provide the defense with the necessary accoutrements for cross-examination can enhance a defense argument at trial that preliminary hearing testimony should not be admissible if the witness becomes unavailable. [*See* §10:44.]

You may also use the hearing as an opportunity to subpoena records from third parties even if you choose not to offer the evidence at the hearing. A subpoena cannot require a witness to come to counsel's office, but you may mark on the subpoena that the witness, if he chooses, can avoid a personal appearance by delivering the subpoenaed records to counsel's office. This is especially effective for business records, which counsel then can use to begin investigation, to share with witnesses and to plea bargain.

Forms:
- **Form 10-3** Discovery Letter
- **Form 10-4** Subpoena for Records

§10:23   Visit the Scene

In some cases, familiarity with the scene is indispensable to understanding whether the crime could have happened as the prosecution describes.

The preliminary hearing offers the defense an opportunity, perhaps the only one, to have the prosecution's witnesses place themselves by their testimony in locations where they could not have observed what they claim to have seen. By the time of trial, the prosecutor probably will have persuaded the witnesses to reconcile these inconsistencies.

Also, specific descriptions of where witnesses were in relation to each other and to key events are unlikely to appear in police reports or other discovery. The hearing is the time to obtain this information, and often you can understand and direct this testimony through questions only if you have viewed and paced the scene.

Bring a camera. You can decide later whether to use the photographs.

§10:24   Interview Defense Witnesses

Defense witnesses can:
* Steer you toward the successful defense and away from the fruitless.
* Assist in disabusing the defendant of an improbable story.
* Alert you to concessions prosecution witnesses are likely to make.

Such interviews serve to develop the defense theory that should be pursued at the hearing.

[§§10:25-10:29 Reserved]

IV.   EXAMPLES OF CROSS-EXAMINATION QUESTIONS

§10:30   General Techniques

Use a "funneling" technique; that is, conceptualize the criminal event as a series of chronologically arranged chapters in a story.

If the direct examination has not done so, establish the setting for each chapter (when, where, and who made up the cast of characters). Then ask general questions with respect to each chapter, funneling down to more specific questions that may be crucial for a defense's viability.

You should know which details are most important based on your interviews of the defendant, view of the scene and any other investigation. The important details are the ones that set up a suppression motion or some trial defense, such as consent, or the ones that show the defendant behaved cooperatively, as if having nothing to hide.

Questions should proceed in a logical, chronological order, rather than jumping back and forth. Proceeding chronologically gives the impression that you are moving it along. If the magistrate sees progress toward an endpoint, he or she is more likely to let you proceed.

However, listen for and explore issues that the witness raises rather than sticking to your own agenda. Look for uncertainties suggested by "I guess" or "I think" or "to the best of my recollection" answers.

If the witness must read a report or statement to refresh recollection, establish that the witness cannot recall important details without reading the statement. If something is not in the statement, the witness does not remember it.

§10:31   Drug Sale

For this example, the defendant has been arrested after surveillance of a drug sale.
Arresting officer is testifying. The cross-examination follows this outline:
* In front of which address were you parked?
* Were you on the driver's side or the passenger's?
* Were you on the same side of the street or across the street from my client?
* Were there parked cars between you and Defendant?
* Did you use binoculars or any other viewing device to observe Defendant?
* Did your partner?
* Were there other officers on surveillance? If yes, who were they?
* Where were they stationed?
* Did they use binoculars to your knowledge?
* At the time you saw Defendant give some item to another individual, how far were you from the Defendant?
* Had you moved from the position from which you first saw Defendant?
* The item you say you saw Defendant give to the individual who approached him–you could not see what it was? [Have the witness describe it in as much detail as possible to prevent harmful elaboration at a suppression hearing or trial.]
* And you could not identify the item the individual gave to Defendant? [Again, seek detail.]
* You say that my client handed the package you thought was crack cocaine to another man?
* Could you please describe that other man?
* Was this a man you had seen before?
* [If so] Where / when / doing what?

- What did you see the man do with the package he got from my client?
- Did you stop that man that night?
- Did any of the other officers?
- Did anyone search him?
- Did you find any crack cocaine on him?
- What was his name?
- His address?

§10:32 Rape Case–Consent Defense

For this example, the defendant has been arrested for rape.

The victim is testifying. In this situation many of your questions will be based on your client's story, and the cross-examination tests the willingness of the witness to concede that story.

Especially when the case is certain to be bound over, do not fear bad answers and the sort of open-ended questions that you would avoid at trial. Learn how bad the case could get, both to evaluate the strength or weakness of any possible defense and to lock in the story so that it cannot get worse at trial.

The cross-examination follows this outline:
- You and defendant had been in the bar drinking?
- For about two hours?
- You were drinking gin and tonic?
- You had about five drinks?
- The two of you were laughing and talking?
- You went alone with defendant to his room?
- When the defendant asked you to go with him, you were with other people? [Identify]
- You did not ask anyone to accompany you?
- After you had sex, defendant gave you a hug?
- And asked you if you were all right?
- After, where did you go?
- Whom did you speak with?
- Did you tell that person what had happened between you and defendant?
- What did you say?
- What did she say?
- You did not tell that person that defendant forced you to have sex with him, did you?
- Why not?
- Did you report the incident to the police after talking to that person?

§10:33 Robbery Case–Possible Identification Defense

For this example, the defendant has been arrested for robbery and you are evaluating a possible identification defense. The victim is testifying.

If identification will be an issue at trial, seeing the defendant at the defense table may taint the witness's identification of the defendant at trial. You should attempt to avoid this taint by either:
- Requesting that the court order a line-up before the hearing.
- Requesting that the defendant sit in the audience rather than at counsel table.

[*See* Chapter 9, Pre-Trial Identifications.]

The cross-examination follows this outline:
- You said on direct examination that the man who robbed you was a black man about five feet, ten inches tall, is that right?
- What was his complexion–dark, fair or somewhere in-between?
- Is there anything else you remember about what the man looked like?

COMMENT:

You must use your judgment at this point. You might choose to survey several points of description (age, weight, build, hair color, cut and length, eye color, facial hair, etc.).

Asking these specific points and getting in response, "I don't remember," makes for a more powerful impeachment if the witness adds detail at trial. On the other hand, many witnesses who would have said "nothing" to the "anything else" question (perhaps believing that they hurt the defense by being uncooperative) will start providing detail if taken through area by area.

Certainly, experience helps in making this judgment, but you might also assess how talkative the witness is in response to direct and some preliminary cross, or you might try an area or two to see whether the witness is the kind who will elaborate.

- Is there anything else you can tell the Court and all of us about the man?
- You aren't able to describe anything you remember about his face?
- Why not?
- Is it because you didn't get a very good look at him?
- Did he speak to you at all?
- What did he say?
- Anything else?
- What did his voice sound like?
- For example, was it deep, high or somewhere in-between?
- Gravelly or clear?
- Did he have any kind of accent? What kind?
- What was he wearing?
- Was there a street light? Where was it? Was it working? Was the man in the shadows?
- You say he had a handgun. Are you familiar with guns?
- Were you looking at the gun during the robbery?
- Do you know the difference between a revolver and a semiautomatic?
- What kind was this?
- What color was the gun?
- If the witness is familiar with guns: Could you tell what make it was?
- What caliber?

§10:34 False Billing

For this example, the defendant is a pharmacist charged with fraudulently billing for drugs dispensed without a valid prescription.

The doctor is testifying.

The cross-examination follows this outline:

- Part of Ms. Smith's medical condition was that she had high cholesterol levels?
- That's a chronic condition–meaning it doesn't go away?
- And it is treated with what you might call maintenance medications–medications that the patient must take every day?
- According to your chart on Ms. Smith, you did prescribe Mevacor for Ms. Smith in the years before 2004?
- Did Ms. Smith sometimes call in to your office to ask that a new prescription be issued?
- Did you always speak to her or did members of your staff?
- Who?
- Would your secretary make a note of the call?
- And leave it for you?
- Did you then call the pharmacy to authorize the medication or did you sometimes authorize a member of your staff to call?
- Could your secretary call in the prescription without obtaining your prior authorization for that particular prescription, at least if it was a maintenance medication?
- Did your secretary then make an entry in the chart on that day for the prescription?
- You say that was the usual practice. Did your secretary sometimes not chart the medication?
- You have no way of knowing how often your secretary failed to chart her call-in to a pharmacy of a maintenance medication?
- Do you carry a cell phone?
- Have you on occasion called in prescriptions to a pharmacy over your cell phone when you're not in your office?

- Of course, you don't have the patient chart with you?
- On those occasions you may not have charted the call-in?
- So looking back at your chart several years later, even if there is no entry on a particular date, the patient may have called on that date?
- And asked for the medication?
- And you or a member of your staff may have called it in to the pharmacy?
- Even though there is no entry?
- And you have no independent recollection apart from what is written in your patient chart of what you may or may not have prescribed or called in to my client's pharmacy for Ms. Smith on June 1, 2004, do you?
- And Ms. Smith did have high cholesterol levels, a condition for which Mevacor would have been an appropriate medication?
- You had prescribed Mevacor for her prior to 2004, right?
- How then can you say with any certainty that you did not prescribe Mevacor for her on June 1, 2004?

COMMENT:

Ask this question as broadly as possible because there might be a reason you don't suspect the following, for example: "She was experiencing adverse reactions to that medication"; "I stopped using that particular medication because I lost faith in its effectiveness"; and "I do have an entry in my chart that the day before, I prescribed Lipitor for her, and I would never prescribe Lipitor and Mevacor to be taken at the same time because they are the same type of drug for the same condition."

§10:35   Aggravated Assault

For this example, the defendant is charged with aggravated assault.

The victim is testifying.

Your objective is to minimize the injuries so that the charge may be reduced to simple assault or bail may be reduced.

Avoid questions that suggest to the authorities investigative steps they have not taken yet but still can (*e.g.,* submit a firearm for fingerprint analysis or interview witnesses).

The cross-examination follows this outline:

- When my client pushed you to the ground, you say that you experienced pain in your back?
- Were you able to get up from the ground of your own power?
- No one assisted you?
- Did you call for an ambulance or did someone else?
- Did anyone tell you to call for an ambulance?
- So you didn't think you needed an ambulance?
- What treatment did the paramedics give you in the ambulance?
- Where did they take you?
- When you arrived at the emergency room, do you remember which doctor you saw?
- What did he do for you?
- How long did you stay in the hospital?
- What was the diagnosis that the doctor gave you at the emergency room?
- What if anything did the doctor prescribe for you by way of medication or follow-up treatment?
- Did the emergency room doctor or nurse instruct you to restrict your activities in any way? Did he put those directions in writing? Do you have it?
- Did you go to work the next day?
- How long did you stay out of work?
- Did your boss require that you provide him with some documentation of your condition from a doctor?
- What did you provide to your boss?
- Who was it from?
- Was that the doctor you were seeing for follow-up care?
- What kind of doctor is he?
- Did anyone give you a prescription or a doctor's order to go see that chiropractor?
- Where are his offices?
- How often did you see the chiropractor?

- What kind of treatment do they perform on you at the chiropractor's office?
- How did you get to his office?
- So you were able to drive on your own?
- While you were at home, were you able to cook and clean on your own?
- Could you lift things?
- Play with your children?
- Were you getting any exercise? What? How often? How does this compare to how much exercise you were getting before you were pushed to the ground?
- Did you have anyone come in and help you?
- Were you on any medications? Which?
- Did the chiropractor doctor instruct you to restrict your activities? Did he put those instructions in writing? Do you have them?
- Has your insurance agreed to pay for your treatment by the chiropractor?

[§§10:36-10:39 Reserved]

V.   COMMON ISSUES

§10:40   The "Fishing Expedition/Discovery" Objection

Both practitioners and judges recognize that discovery is a legitimate defense objective at a preliminary hearing. [See *Coleman v. Alabama*, 399 U.S. 1, 9 (1970) (counsel is needed at the preliminary hearing because she can use questioning skills to discover the prosecution's case).]

Nevertheless, courts uniformly rule that the questions directed purely at discovering the prosecution's case should not be allowed. [*E.g.*, Cal Penal Code §866(b) ("the examination shall not be used for the purpose of discovery").]

As a result of the tension between the rule and the reality, defense counsel must frame questions carefully and be prepared to respond to the objection that the question serves no purpose but discovery.

A question is not objectionable merely because discovery is an incidental result of a question that does have some tendency to test the existence of probable cause. [See *Coleman v. Burnett*, 477 F.2d 1187, 1200 (D.C. Cir. 1973) (recognizing that discovery is an acceptable by-product of the probable cause inquiry, but not a permissible end unto itself); *Poteat v. King*, 487 A.2d 215 (D.C. 1984) (directing magistrate to reopen hearing so defense can cross-examine detective on issues relating to reliability of eyewitness informant and can call informant to testify about those issues).]

EXAMPLE:

You may ask an officer who claims to have observed the defendant sell drugs the description and identities of other participants and bystanders with the following question: Was the buyer stopped, searched, questioned or arrested? [*See* §10:31.]

You may be seeking witnesses, but you also can argue that you are testing the officer's perception and the plausibility of the officer's story.

Other valid responses include:
- "The prosecution covered this area on direct."
- "I'm testing the witness's recollection (or story)."
- "Whether my client confessed, ran, had a gun or had a large amount of cash goes to the issue of whether or not there is probable cause."

PRACTICE TIP:

Do not beg. If you concede that you are trying to get just a little discovery, but you are entitled to it, you are lost. Frame questions that can be argued to have a purpose other than discovery and be prepared to argue that other purpose.

§10:41   To Impeach or Not?

You may be tempted to launch an aggressive cross-examination, attacking the witness with the full cross-examination arsenal (prior inconsistent statements, motive and bias, prior convictions and dishonest acts). However, this is generally a bad idea. First, it will not succeed, and second, it will interfere with your legitimate defense goals of discovery and obtaining concessions from the witness.

If the basis for the impeachment is information that the prosecutor does not possess and is not likely to obtain before trial (a motive to lie, a bias, an inconsistent statement contained in a document not within police or prosecution files) you should almost never reveal the information at the preliminary hearing, unless it is the rare bombshell that could cause the prosecutor to lose all confidence in the case. Such bombshells land in fiction, but almost never in fact.

Consider the following:

Reasons not to impeach:

- It will not affect the bind-over decision. In many jurisdictions, the magistrate should take the prosecution's evidence as true in deciding whether to bind over.
- It reveals lines of cross-examination, surrenders the element of surprise and enables the witness and prosecutor to prepare to respond at trial.
- It consumes some of the limited time the magistrate allotted for the hearing, subtracting from the time that may be used for discovery.
- It antagonizes the witness. Not only will he become uncooperative during the hearing, but he is less likely to submit to an informal defense interview afterwards.

Reasons in favor of impeachment:

- If the witness equivocates or fumbles, the magistrate may consider not binding over or holding the case on a lesser charge. The prosecutor may start to consider a more lenient plea offer.
- Where the inconsistency between a prior statement and the present is drastic, you might need to know the explanation for it sooner rather than later. For example, the victim witness who incriminates the defendant at the hearing initially may have told the police that the defendant had nothing to do with crime, because the defendant threatened the witness. At trial, you would never ask why the change in story, but the "why" question can be asked without much risk at the preliminary hearing.
- If the witness becomes unavailable at trial, the preliminary hearing testimony may be admissible. [*See* §10:44.] If this is a possibility, you may want to conduct the impeachment at the hearing. On the other hand, you can impeach an unavailable declarant by introducing the impeaching material at trial. [FRE 806.] Reading an inconsistent statement into the record does not capture the flavor of a witness squirming and equivocating before a jury, but it does have the advantage of depriving the witness of an opportunity to explain. Further, while you lose the effect that an unsavory witness has on a jury, the prosecution likewise has to make do with a cold transcript read to the jury.

§10:42 Waiver

Do not waive a preliminary hearing except in rare circumstances. The preliminary hearing presents an opportunity to question witnesses and officers before they have had a chance to rehearse, clarify and coordinate their stories. The prosecutor handling a preliminary hearing typically sees the file for the first time that day and may not speak to the witnesses at all before calling them to the stand.

The hearing is less valuable and the waiver more understandable in those jurisdictions (such as the federal courts) where only agents and officers testify, and the testimony consists of hearsay and multiple hearsay. However, even there the hearing provides some discovery. In federal court, having a hearing also forces the prosecution to disclose law enforcement reports that it otherwise would not have to provide until the time of trial. [*See* Fed. R. Crim. P. 26.2 (a), (g)(1) (upon defense motion, the prosecution must disclose witness statements relevant to the subject matter of their testimony at, *inter alia*, preliminary hearings).]

Nevertheless, you may consider waiving the hearing in these situations:

- Absent a waiver, the prosecutor will preempt the hearing by obtaining a grand jury indictment or filing an information that will include more serious charges.
- The prosecution will reduce the charges or offer a more favorable plea than otherwise available in return for the waiver. Make sure to memorialize the agreement, either by having the prosecutor amend the complaint on the record, by stipulating on the record that the case will be bound over only on the lesser charge, or by following it up with a confirming letter.
- The case has a high profile, and the preliminary hearing will disclose to the public inflammatory evidence that will wreck the defendant's chance for a fair trial. The press and public have a First Amendment right of access to preliminary hearings. To close the hearing, the defendant must show a substantial probability of prejudice

and the lack of any reasonable alternative to closure, a standard rarely met. [*Press-Enterprise Co. v. Superior Court*, 478 U.S. 1 (1986).]

- The hearing may alert the prosecution that the crime is more serious than initially believed, and the defendant is undercharged.
- The victim might be amenable to a lenient or even non-criminal disposition, but after testifying and weathering cross-examination, the victim may harden his or her position. This may arise especially where the victim is a domestic partner or friend.
- You know that a crucial prosecution witness is unlikely to appear at trial, and holding the hearing will enable the prosecution to preserve the testimony for trial.

CAUTION:

In indicting jurisdictions, an agreement with a prosecutor for reduced charges or a favorable plea may not be binding, and the grand jury may return a more serious charge, especially if the investigation later reveals that your client's involvement was more extensive than suspected at the time of the preliminary hearing. Nevertheless, putting the prosecutor's representations on the record arms you with some bargaining leverage to persuade the prosecutor or her superiors that seeking higher charges would undermine their office's credibility.

Form:
- **Form 10-5** Letter Confirming Plea Offer

§10:43   Calling Witnesses

Defense Witnesses

You may call witnesses, including the defendant, at the preliminary hearing. [*See, e.g.,* Fed. R. Cr. P. 5.1(e); Pa. R. Cr. P. 542(c) (3).] However, you should not.

Calling witnesses gives the prosecution all that it strives to keep from the defense: free discovery, a chance to lock in testimony, and a fixed story that can now be investigated and refuted. Despite your best efforts, no defense attorney can know the case thoroughly at this early stage, and even a well-rehearsed defendant's story may crumble before unexpected questions on cross and evidence in rebuttal. Finally, defense evidence most likely will make no difference in the outcome.

If the prosecution case already established probable cause, the magistrate will not weigh the credibility of the witnesses and revisit that determination.

Prosecution Witnesses

Calling prosecution witnesses in your case may seem a clever idea, particularly when the prosecution relies on an interviewing officer's hearsay recitation of the witness's story. However, in litigation clever ideas generally turn out to be bad ones.

Prosecutors and magistrates are wary of this technique and will demand an offer of proof before permitting the testimony. [*E.g.,* NY CPL 180.60(7) (witnesses may be called only if court, in its discretion, permits); *Commonwealth v. Wortman*, 929 S.W.2d 199, 200 (Ky. Ct. App. 1996) (although the state rules authorized a defendant to call witnesses at the hearing, the testimony must be relevant to the probable cause determination); *Commonwealth v. Tyler*, 402 Pa. Super. 429, 435, 587 A.2d 326, 329 (1991) (magistrate correct in denying defense request to have informant testify because defense had not interviewed the witness and could not make any proffer).]

If you have not interviewed the witness, you have nothing to proffer. If a witness has been interviewed and an investigator has memorialized the statement (as always should be done with exculpatory statements), it is unwise to disclose the helpful defense evidence in a setting where there is little to gain. If you feel that the witness may change his story, an investigator's testimony at trial will be less convincing than the transcript of the sworn preliminary hearing testimony, so have the witness sign a sworn statement or give an audio or videotaped statement outside the hearing.

Furthermore, if you call the witness on direct, you must proceed with non-leading questions, but the prosecutor can lead the witness and attempt to mold the story to fit his case. Worst of all, if the witness offers some incriminating testimony and then fails to appear at trial, you now have preserved evidence that the jury never would have heard.

CAUTION:

There may be an exception where the witness is willing to recant entirely his or her story to the police. However, be cautious even in this situation. Full recantations are notoriously suspect. Often they achieve nothing, but rather serve to prove the witness's misplaced affection for the defendant, or the defendant's ability to intimidate.

§10:44   Unavailable Witness–Preliminary Testimony Generally Admissible

You should assume that if a preliminary hearing witness becomes unavailable at trial, the hearing testimony will be admissible. [*See, e.g., People v. Samayoa*, 15 Cal.4th 795, 64 Cal.Rptr.2d 400, 938 P.2d 2, 39-40(1997) (10-year-old testimony from preliminary hearing for an unrelated crime admitted at penalty phase of defendant's capital murder trial).]

Admission of this testimony does not violate the Sixth Amendment's Confrontation Clause. [*See Ohio v. Roberts*, 448 U.S. 56 (1980); *State v. Estrella*, 277 Conn. 458, 474–77, 893 A.2d 348, 359-60 (2006); *but see Vasquez v. Jones*, 496 F.3d 564, 577 & n.11 (6th Cir. 2007) (interpreting *Roberts* and its as establishing that the opportunity to cross-examine at a preliminary hearing generally does *not* satisfy the Confrontation Clause except on those infrequent occasions where defense counsel "was not 'significantly limited in any way in the scope or nature of his cross-examination' at the preliminary examination" (quoting *Roberts*, 448 U.S. at 71)).]

Furthermore, it fits within the prior testimony hearsay exception. [*E.g., Commonwealth v. Fink*, 2002 PA Super. 32, 791 A.2d 1235, 1245 (Pa. Super. Ct. 2002); FRE 804 (b)(1).]

§10:45   Unavailable Witness–Prosecution Must Prove Unavailability

The prosecution has the burden of proving the witness's unavailability. [*Cook v. McKune*, 323 F.3d 825, 832 (10th Cir. 2003).]

The prosecution must exercise reasonable diligence in a good faith effort to procure the witness's testimony. [*Cook* at 832-39 (extensive explanation of reasonableness of prosecution efforts; the more important the witness, the greater the efforts required); *State v. Flournoy*, 272 Kan. 784, 36 P.3d 273, 285-86 (2001) (visiting several addresses, speaking with neighbors and relatives to no avail and leaving subpoenas with them sufficient).]

§10:46   Unavailable Witness–Reliability Satisfied by Opportunity to Cross-Examine

Decisions talk about "indicia of reliability" or an adequate opportunity to cross-examine and a similarity of issues as additional requirements before the preliminary hearing testimony will be admitted. However, in practice, courts generally assume that a preliminary hearing meets all those tests, unless the opponent of the testimony can show some case-specific circumstances that interfered with an adequate cross-examination.

Merely arguing that the goals of a preliminary hearing and trial cross-examinations differ will not defeat admissibility. [*See Ohio v. Roberts*, 448 U.S. 56 (1980) (rejecting the dissimilar goals argument); *People v. Zapien*, 4 Cal.4th 929, 975, 17 Cal. Rptr.2d 122, 846 P.2d 704 (1993) (sufficient that the goals of a preliminary hearing cross and a trial cross are similar, even if not identical).]

A strategic decision to ask few or no questions at the hearing will not prevent admissibility at trial. [*See State v. Norman*, 664 N.W.2d 97, 106-07 (2003) (preliminary hearing testimony admitted at trial even though defense counsel chose to ask only three questions at the hearing).]

To bar use of the prior testimony at trial, the defense must show that the preliminary hearing magistrate precluded specific lines of cross-examination that bear on the issues at trial. [*See, e.g., Commonwealth v. Johnson*, 2000 Pa. Super. 194, 758 A.2d 166, 172-73 (Pa. Super. Ct. 2000) (testimony precluded because magistrate precluded cross concerning another possible suspect, stating, "save it for trial); *Russell v. State*, 604 S.W.2d 914, 922-23 (Tex. Crim. App. 1980) (magistrate shown to have a general practice of severely restricting cross; at hearing, counsel proffered several specific questions that the magistrate would not allow); *People v. Simmons*, 36 N.Y.2d 126, 131, 365 N.Y.S.2d 812, 325 N.E.2d 139 (1975) (error to admit hearing testimony because hearing magistrate precluded defense "questions bearing on the correctness of the identification, the extent of the lighting at the scene of the crime, a description of the defendant's clothing and facial features, and the complainant's visual acuity").]

Most courts hold that the unavailability of discovery prior to the preliminary hearing does not prevent an adequate opportunity for cross-examination. [*See* Francis M. Dougherty, *Admissibility or Use in Criminal Trial of Test Given at Preliminary Proceeding by Witness Not Available at Trial*, 38 ALR4th 378, §8 (1985). *But see Commonwealth v. Bazemore*, 531 Pa. 582, 614 A.2d 684 (1992) (rule in Pennsylvania is that lack of discovery concerning "vital impeachment evidence," such as witness's prior inconsistent statements and criminal record, at the hearing precludes admission of the testimony at trial).]

PRACTICE TIP:

Begin to make the record that you did not have a full opportunity to cross-examine. If cross-examination is limited, proffer what would have been asked. State on the record that the defense has not received any witness statements or other discovery (such as disclosure of the witness's criminal record) or any agreement with the prosecution.

§10:47   Unavailable Witness–Impeachment

The defense can introduce at trial extrinsic evidence to impeach the unavailable declarant, such as evidence of favorable treatment, bias, motive, the witness's criminal record and prior inconsistent statements. [*See* FRE 806; Christopher B. Mueller & Laird C. Kirkpatrick, Federal Evidence §510 nn. 8-9 (2004) (most states have an equivalent evidentiary rule); Richard T. Farrell, Prince, Richardson on Evidence §8-111 (11th ed.) (explaining New York rule permitting impeachment of unavailable declarant with inconsistent statements); *e.g., State v. Bryant,* 71 Conn. App. 488, 496, 802 A.2d 224, 229 (2002) (defense should have been permitted to introduce extrinsic evidence that witness's bond reduced and he was released after testifying for prosecution at preliminary hearing).]

§10:48   Review of the Bind-Over Decision

Appeals from preliminary hearing rulings lie with the trial court, either by way of a petition for a writ of habeas corpus or motion to quash or dismiss the information, depending upon the local rules. [*See Commonwealth v. Hess,* 489 Pa. 580, 589, 414 A.2d 1043, 1047 (1980).]

Such a petition or motion must be raised before trial, because a guilty verdict or plea cures any error in the preliminary hearing. [*See, e.g., State v. Webb,* 160 Wisc.2d 622, 467 N.W.2d 108 (Wisc. 1999); *Commonwealth v. Jackson,* 2004 Pa. Super. 150, 849 A.2d 1254 (Pa. Super. Ct. 2004).]

The trial court's denial of the writ or motion is not a final order and is not appealable. However, the prosecution can appeal a court's order granting the writ and dismissing the case. [*See, e.g., Commonwealth v. Jackson.*]

§10:49   Rearrest After Dismissal

Jeopardy does not attach until trial. Therefore, the prosecution can refile charges after dismissal at a preliminary hearing and rearrest the defendant. [*United States ex rel. Rutz v. Levy,* 268 U.S. 390 (1925); *People v. Noline,* 917 P.2d 1256 (Colo. 1996) (surveying law of several states); *Liciaga v. Court of Common Pleas,* 523 Pa. 258, 566 A.2d 246 (1989) (no state or federal double jeopardy bar against refiling).]

A few jurisdictions require the prosecution to submit additional evidence, and some will entertain a motion to preclude rearrest if an improper or harassing motive can be shown. [*See Commonwealth v. Thorpe,* 549 Pa. 343, 701 A.2d 488 (1997) (rearrest prohibited where prosecution arrested defendant three times on same charges, was unprepared for five scheduled preliminary hearings, and failed to make out *prima facie* case at the hearing). *See also* Wayne R. LaFave, Jerrold H. Israel & Nancy J. King, *Criminal Procedure* §14.3(c), p.157 & n.68 (listing new evidence jurisdictions).]

Additionally, the U.S. Department of Justice and local United States Attorney's Offices periodically decide to adopt certain types of crimes for federal prosecution, especially the possession of firearms by convicted felons and drug offenses. In that case, a dismissal may be followed by a federal arrest and prosecution.

There is little you can do to prevent this. The federal government can prosecute even if the defendant is tried and convicted or acquitted in state court. Usually, such federal initiatives are preceded by a press conference announcing them. Be forewarned and advise your client that he should be on his best behavior because the feds might be watching.

After a dismissal, it is generally advisable to send a letter to the prosecutor stating that you continue to represent the defendant so that any further communication must be through you.

PRACTICE TIP:

Although the threat of rearrest is a great disruption to the client's life, it should neither deter you from seeking dismissal, nor lead to waiving the hearing. A dismissal will give pause to most prosecutors. If they cannot prove the case under a probable cause standard, they will worry about convincing a jury beyond a reasonable doubt. The defense can portray a refiling, even if legally permissible, as overreaching. Furthermore, to avoid a second dismissal, prosecutors will tend to "overtry" the second preliminary hearing and introduce more evidence than usual, thereby providing the defense with additional discovery.

Form:
• **Form 10-6** Letter Upon Dismissal

VI.   FORMS

Form 10-1   Demand for Preliminary Hearing

STATE	)
v.	) CASE NO. _____
DEFENDANT	)

Please take notice that pursuant to [*e.g.,* Maryland, Rule 4-213(a)(4)], Defendant, _____, demands a preliminary hearing on or before _____, on the Complaint filed against him at the above case number.

Respectfully submitted,

_____
Defense Counsel

Form 10-2   Request for Continuance

COMMENT: _____
    Call the magistrate's office before requesting an adjournment to learn whether they:
    • Want a motion or will accept the letter.
    • Demand the consent of the prosecutor or arresting officer.
    • Require defense counsel to notify the prosecutor of the new date.

VIA FACSIMILE

The Honorable District Justice _____
Coraopolis, PA

Re: *Commonwealth of Pennsylvania v. Defendant,* CR-000000-00

Your Honor:
    The preliminary hearing in the above-captioned case is scheduled to occur on September 4, 2005, at 1 p.m. I am the attorney for defendant. I was retained just today, September 2, 2005, and need additional time to meet with my client and prepare for the hearing. I request, pursuant to PA Rule of Criminal Procedure 542(E), that the preliminary hearing in this case be postponed to September 18, 2005, or some other date that is convenient for the Court.
    On behalf of defendant, I waive the protections of Rule 600 for the time period from the date of this letter until the date of the preliminary hearing, *see* Rule 600(C)(2). I also note that this time is excluded from the speedy trial calculations pursuant to Rule 600(C)(3).
    I spoke to the arresting officer, Detective Jones of the Moon Township Police today, and he agreed to this continuance.

Sincerely,

_____
Thomas J. Farrell

Form 10-3   Discovery Letter

COMMENT:

Call the magistrate or the district attorney's office, find out who the assistant district attorney (ADA) specifically assigned to the magistrate is, and serve the letter on that ADA.

Assistant District Attorney
400 Courthouse
Pittsburgh, PA

Re: Commonwealth v. Defendant, Cr. No. _____

Dear ADA:

I represent the defendant in the above-captioned matter, which is scheduled for a preliminary hearing before District Justice _____ on _____. This is an informal discovery request. I would appreciate a written response to each requested item, with a response of "none," if that is appropriate, before the day of the hearing. When I mention the "government," I also mean any state or federal law enforcement agents who participated in this or any related investigations.

1. Disclosure of any statements and anything allegedly said by the defendant to any agents of the government or any cooperating witnesses at any time. Disclosure is also requested of the date, time, location and persons present when such oral or written statements were made.

2. Copies of any other reports, notes or memoranda prepared in the course of the investigation and arrest of the defendant.

3. Please preserve and produce any notes and draft reports prepared by any agents or officers. *See United States v. Ramos*, 27 F.3d 65, 68 (3d Cir. 1994).

4. Disclosure of and examination of all physical evidence in the possession or control of the government.

5. You have represented that the defendant does not have any criminal record in any jurisdiction. If this is inaccurate or has changed, please so inform me.

6. The circumstances and results of any identification procedure involving the defendant or any other person, by voice, photograph, or in person.

7. Please state whether the government intends to offer any other crime evidence under FRE 404(b), whether it be alleged other acts of the defendant or any other person pertinent to this case, and if so, please provide the particulars of those acts including date, location of commission and description of the acts, and whether any court proceedings resulted, and if so, in what court and with what result.

8. Any items seized from the defendant upon his arrest.

9. The officers' notes of their interview with the defendant on _____;

10. Please provide or state:
    a. A list of all witnesses' names, addresses and phone numbers;
    b. Whether any government informant has provided any information which led to the arrest or prosecution of the defendant;
    c. Whether any informant or witness has worked for the government in the past;
    d. Whether any informant or witness has a prior criminal record and if so, provide it;
    e. Whether any informant or witness was paid for his or her efforts in this case or any other case and if so, how much;
    f. Whether any informant or witness has any pending cases anywhere, and if so, whether any assistance or consideration was offered or suggested, formally or informally, or is intended by the government to be offered on behalf of the informant with respect to any pending case the informant has;
    g. Whether any informant or witness requested of the government anything of value or any assistance or consideration in any legal matter;
    h. Any agreement promise or suggestion made by the government or its agents to any prospective informant offering assistance to the informant in obtaining leniency in any court, or lack of prosecution or arrest, or any other favorable treatment or consideration for the efforts made in connection with any aspect of this case by the informant.

11. Pursuant to the Constitutional requirements of *Kyles v. Whitley*, 514 U.S. 419 (1995); *United States v. Agurs*, 427 U.S. 97 (1976); *Giles v. Maryland*, 386 U.S. 66 (1967); and *Brady v. Maryland*, 373 U.S. 83 (1963); please provide any exculpatory or favorable evidence or information, or any evidence or statements of anyone which may be favorable to the defendant, which is in the possession or control of the government or its agents, or,

if unknown, can by due diligence become known or acquired by the government, or its agents, including, but not limited to, the following:

a. Copies of any statements or the substance of any oral statements made by any prospective government witness, or by alleged coconspirator, which is exculpatory of or favorable to the defendant, or which is inconsistent with any fact the government alleges with respect to the charges in the Complaint;

b. Copies of any reports of mental illness, drug use, excessive alcoholism, or any medical condition of any prospective government witness or informant which would affect the ability to observe or remember an observed fact;

c. The defense asks that the government memorialize, preserve and produce all proffers, communications with the government and statements made by any cooperating witness or his attorney, whether made formally or informally, *see United States v. Sudikoff*, 36 F.Supp.2d 1196 (C.D.Cal. 1999);

d. Copies of any witness's criminal record;

e. Any government report on any witness's uncharged criminal behavior.

Your prompt attention to this matter is appreciated.

Sincerely,

_____

Thomas J. Farrell

Form 10-4   Subpoena for Records

COMMENT:

Unless local law or rules or a court order specifically provide, subpoenas may not be returnable to an attorney's office. However, the suggestion that the recipient of the subpoena may deliver the subpoena to the attorney's office generally does not offend that rule.

Check local practice and rules.

Court of Common Pleas of Allegheny County, Pennsylvania
THE COMMONWEALTH OF PENNSYLVANIA
ALLEGHENY COUNTY, SS:

Commonwealth of Pennsylvania
         v.   No. Cr. 00000-00
Defendant

SUBPOENA TO ATTEND AND TESTIFY

TO: Custodian of Medical Records
     First Hospital
You are ordered by the Court to come to:
Pittsburgh Magistrates Court at 660 First Avenue, Pittsburgh, Pennsylvania, on September 28, 2005, at 8:30 a.m., to testify on behalf of defendant in the above case and to remain until excused.

And bring with you the following: certified records of treatment for Joe Victim, DOB 1/1/1970, on 7/4/04, in the emergency room or any other department. Note: personal appearance is not required if the records are delivered to counsel at the below address before September 28, 2005.

If you fail to attend or to produce the documents or things required by this subpoena, you may be subject to sanctions authorized by Rule 234.5 of the Pennsylvania Rules of Civil Procedure, including, but not limited to, costs, attorney fees and imprisonment.

Requested by an attorney in compliance with Pa.R.C.P. 234.2(a):

Thomas J. Farrell
1000 Court Street
Pittsburgh, PA
(412) 555-5555
Supreme Court ID # 000000
(Seal of Court)

Form 10-5   Letter Confirming Plea Offer

Assistant United States Attorney
United States Courthouse
Pittsburgh, PA

Re: *United States v. Defendant*

Dear Ms. Smith:

I write to confirm our agreement, made on _____. You agreed that in consideration for my client's agreement to waive his right to a preliminary hearing, you would not seek an indictment for using a firearm in connection with a drug offense, 18 U.S.C. §924(c), an offense that carries a five-year consecutive term to any other sentence. Our decision to waive the hearing was based on that representation.

Sincerely,

_____

Thomas J. Farrell

Form 10-6   Letter Upon Dismissal

Dear Mr. Prosecuting Attorney:

I write to inform you that I continue to represent defendant with respect to your office's investigation even after the dismissal at the preliminary hearing. Therefore, I ask that your office and any law enforcement agents involved in the case and investigation continue to avoid any contact with my client and direct all inquiries to me. *See* Model Rules of Professional Conduct 4.2, 8.4(a) (attorney and his agent may not communicate with represented person).

Further, should you choose to refile charges, my client will surrender and face the charges without the need for a second arrest and detention and the ensuing cost to the government and inconvenience to my client. Please contact my office to arrange his surrender if you decide to refile charges. Please understand that I do not mean to suggest by this letter that a refiling of the charges would be either expected or legally justified.

Sincerely,

_____

Thomas J. Farrell

Chapter 11

FORFEITURE

(This page intentionally left blank.)

I.   BACKGROUND AND THEORIES

§11:01   General Points

In addition to an indictment, a criminal investigation may result in seizure and forfeiture of your client's property, including everything from bank accounts to the automobiles and boats used to ferry contraband, and the house which he may have purchased with some of the proceeds, or from which he dealt the drugs, that landed him in an indictment.

In pursuit of its forfeiture claim, the government may disgorge assets that have been transferred to other individuals. This may include your fees.

Forfeiture proceedings can be civil or criminal. A criminal forfeiture proceeding accompanies the filing of a criminal case and will be adjudicated along with the case. However, a civil forfeiture proceeding may be filed before, or even in the absence of, any criminal proceeding.

The substantive and procedural law of forfeiture is delineated by statutes. Nonetheless, certain common-law doctrines reappear in the statutes and account for some of the challenges that forfeiture actions present:

- The wrongdoer in a civil forfeiture action is the property. For this reason, civil forfeiture actions are *in rem*, against the property, and the property might be forfeitable even though its owner was innocent.
- The property becomes forfeitable and title vests in the government at the time of the crime which gives rise to the forfeiture–the "relation back" doctrine. Thus, innocent transferees may find themselves divested of the property even if they obtained title before the crime was prosecuted or even discovered. [*See Calero-Toledo v. Pearson Yacht Leasing Co.*, 416 U.S. 663 (1974) (explaining the history of forfeitures).]

The Civil Asset Forfeiture Reform Act of 2000 (CAFRA; 106 Pub.L. No. 185, 114 Stat. 202) simplified federal civil forfeiture law to some extent [18 U.S.C. §§981-988]. However, forfeiture remains a complex area of the law.

There are several comprehensive and useful texts on both federal and state forfeiture. [*See* Dee R. Edgeworth, *Asset Forfeiture: Practice and Procedure in State and Federal Courts* (2004) (succinct 250-page volume summarizing both federal and state forfeiture, with useful tables citing the controlling statutes and noting the distinctions from jurisdiction to jurisdiction); Stefan D. Cassella, *Asset Forfeiture Law in the United States* (2006) (one-volume work on federal forfeiture work by U.S. Department of Justice's leading forfeiture expert; while comprehensive and clear, advocates government's position on most issues); Steven L. Kessler, *Civil & Criminal Forfeiture: Federal and State Practice* (2006) (comprehensive three-volume work on federal and state practice with helpful forms and pleadings); and David B. Smith, *Prosecution and Defense, Forfeiture Cases* (2008) (two-volume work focusing on federal law and practice, but including chapters on New York, Florida, and Texas law).]

§11:02   The Four Theories of Forfeiture

There are four theories under which a prosecutor can seek the forfeiture of assets:

(1) The assets are contraband.
(2) The assets are the proceeds of criminal activity or derived from the criminal activity.
(3) The assets were used to commit or facilitate a crime, or they were an "instrumentality" of the offense. [*E.g., Commonwealth v. 1997 Chevrolet*, 160 A.3d 153, 163 (Pa. 2017).]
(4) The assets are "substitute assets" for criminally derived property or instrumentalities; that is, if otherwise forfeitable property has been spent or dissipated, the prosecution can forfeit untainted "substitute" property of similar value. [*See Luis v. United States*, 136 S.Ct. 1083, 1090 (2016); 21 U.S.C. 853(p).]

Contraband

Under the contraband theory, the very possession of the property violates the law. Therefore, the property cannot be claimed or returned. [*See* 18 U.S.C. §983(d)(4) ("Notwithstanding any provision of this subsection, no person may assert an ownership interest under this subsection in contraband or other property that it is illegal to possess").]

Proceeds of Criminal Activity

When the theory of forfeiture is that the property is the proceeds of a crime, litigation will focus on whether the crime has been proven, or, when the proceeds have been sold or transferred to a third party, whether that third party has a statutory defense such as the bona fide purchaser for value or innocent owner defenses. [*See* §§11:20, 11:21.]

What the term "proceeds" means depends on the statute at issue. A Supreme Court plurality ruled that under 18 U.S.C. §1956, "proceeds" meant profits, and in the case of an illegal business, the parties might need to re-create expenses of which the business probably kept few records. [*United States v. Santos*, 553 U.S. 507, 511 (2008); *but see United States v. Baum*, 461 Fed. Appx. 736, (10th Cir. 2012) (limiting *Santos* to illegal gambling businesses and refusing to apply it to a real estate fraud); *United States v. Thornburgh*, 645 F.3d 1197, 1208-09 (10th Cir. 2011) (same; surveys cases); *United States v. Quinones*, 635 F.3d 590 (2d Cir. 2011) (refusing to apply *Santos* to illegal drug-trafficking businesses).] While Congress amended the money laundering statute in 2009 to define "proceeds" to include gross receipts, *see* 18 U.S.C. §1956(c)(9), you might attempt to use *Santos'* reading in connection with state statutes. In contrast, courts have interpreted "proceeds" in the context of 18 U.S.C. §982(a)(2) to mean gross receipts. [*United States v. Peters*, 732 F.3d 93 (2d Cir. 2013).]

Facilitation of a Crime

Disproportionality issues arise most often in facilitation or instrumentality forfeiture cases. [*See* §11:03, *infra*.] Relatively minor crimes (*e.g.*, personal drug use, prostitution, or currency reporting violations) may involve expensive property such as cars or houses or substantial amounts of currency. Prosecutors sometimes attempt to forfeit the car, the house or the legally obtained but undeclared currency, giving rise to defense arguments that the forfeiture violates the Eighth Amendment's Excessive Fines Clause.

Substitute Assets

The Government's forfeiture power is at its ebb with respect to untainted substitute assets. The relation-back doctrine, which vests title in criminal proceeds or instrumentalities in the Government as of the time of the crime, does not apply to untainted assets. [*See Luis v. United States*, 136 S.Ct. 1083, 1090 (2016).] The common law prohibited pretrial freezes of untainted assets [*Luis*, 136 S.Ct. at 1099 (Thomas, J., concurring)], and most courts have interpreted the leading federal forfeiture statute, 21 U.S.C. 853, as prohibiting pretrial restraint of substitute assets [*United States v. Jones*, 844 F.3d 636, 641 (7th Cir. 2016).] A defendant "has a Sixth Amendment right to use her own 'innocent' property to pay a reasonable fee for the assistance of counsel," so a court may not restrain pretrial untainted assets needed to pay counsel. [*Luis*, 136 S.Ct. at 1096.] Courts can, however, freeze before-trial assets that are the proceeds of or traceable to a crime even if the freeze would prevent the defendant from retaining counsel. [*United States v. Monsanto*, 491 U.S. 600 (1989).]

§11:03   Disproportionality

Both statutory law and the Eight Amendment's Excessive Fines Clause forbid forfeitures that are disproportionate to the criminal offense. [*See Commonwealth v. 1997 Chevrolet*, supra (describing the constitutional disproportionality defense at length); 18 U.S.C. §983(g)(2)(3)(The claimant has the burden of proving, in a non-jury hearing, that the forfeiture is grossly disproportionate to the gravity of the offense).]

Initially, success with this argument was had in cases of currency reporting violations where the evidence indicates that the currency was legally derived and intended for legal uses. [*E.g., United States v. Bajakajian*, 524 U.S. 321 (1998) (criminal forfeiture of $357,000 in currency for defendant's failure to report that he was carrying it out of the country violated the Excessive Fines clause); *but see United States v. Jose*, 499 F.3d 105, 109 (1st Cir. 2007) (Congress responded to *Bajakajian* by creating the offense of bulk cash smuggling at 31 U.S.C. §5332; forfeitures for violations of that statute rarely will be excessive).] More recent caselaw indicates that disproportionality challenges may succeed in proceeds and facilitation forfeiture cases. [*E.g., United States v. Beecroft*, 825 F.3d 991, 1000, 1002 (9th Cir. 2016) (holding that forfeiture order that was 100 times the maximum find was disproportionate even in a proceeds case); *United States v. Viloski*, 814 F.3d 104, 109 n.7 (2d Cir. 2016) (proceeds); *Commonwealth v. 1997 Chevrolet*, 160 A.3d 153 (Pa. 2017)(facilitation).]

The abuse of forfeiture statutes has renewed interest, both in the courts and legislatures, in scrutinizing forfeitures for disproportionality. [See S. 642, Fifth Amendment Integrity Restoration Act, 115th Congress (introduced March 15, 2017 by Sen. Rand Paul); http://ij.org/activism/legislation/civil-forfeiture-legislative-highlights (website collecting state-by-state reforms to forfeiture laws; last visited Aug. 18, 2017); *Commonwealth v. 1997 Chevrolet, supra*.] In *1997 Chevrolet*, the Pennsylvania Supreme Court promulgated a test for disproportionality that incorporates many factors, including the effect that loss of property, such as a family home or vehicle, will have on the owner's and his/her family's ability to maintain a livelihood:

> In conclusion, we hold that, for purposes of an Excessive Fines Clause challenge to a civil in rem forfeiture, a court must first assess whether the property sought to be forfeited is an instrumentality of the underlying offense. If the property is not found to be an instrumentality of the criminal conduct, the inquiry is dispositive and ends, and the forfeiture is unconstitutional. If the property is an instrumentality, the inquiry continues

to the proportionality prong and an assessment of whether the value of the property sought to be forfeited is grossly disproportional to the gravity of the underlying offense. If it is grossly disproportional, the forfeiture is unconstitutional. As discussed in detail above, and summarized below, we find various factors to be relevant in resolving an excessive fines challenge to a civil in rem forfeiture. We caution, however that these factors are not meant to be exhaustive, and that additional factors, when relevant, may be considered by a court, depending upon the particular circumstances at issue.

In making the instrumentality determination, a court should consider, inter alia:

(1) whether the property was uniquely important to the success of the illegal activity;
(2) whether the use of the property was deliberate and planned or was merely incidental and fortuitous to the illegal enterprise;
(3) whether the illegal use of the property was an isolated event or repeated;
(4) whether the purpose of acquiring, maintaining or using the property was to carry out the offense;
(5) whether the illegal use of the property was extensive spatially and/or temporally; and
(6) whether the property is divisible with respect to the subject of forfeiture, allowing forfeiture of only that discrete property which has a significant relationship to the underlying offense.

The factors, among others, to be considered in assessing the value of the property are:

(1) the fair market value of the property;
(2) the subjective value of the property taking into account whether the property is a family residence or if the property is essential to the owner's livelihood;
(3) the harm forfeiture would bring to the owner or innocent third parties; and
(4) whether the forfeiture would deprive the property owner of his or her livelihood.

The factors to be considered in gauging the gravity of the offense include:

(1) the nature of the underlying offense;
(2) the relation of the violation of the offense to any other illegal activity and whether the offender fit into the class of persons for whom the offense was designed should be considered;
(3) the maximum authorized penalty as compared to the actual penalty imposed upon the criminal offender;
(4) the regularity of the criminal conduct—whether the illegal acts were isolated or frequent, constituting a pattern of misbehavior;
(5) the actual harm resulting from the crime charged, beyond a generalized harm to society; and
(6) the culpability of the property owner.

Id. at *27.

Federal courts have interpreted the Supreme Court's decision in *Bajakajian* [524 U.S. at 334] to require consideration of four factors in measuring proportionality under the Eighth Amendment's Excessive Fines Clause:

(1) the essence of the crime of the defendant and its relation to other criminal activity, (2) whether the defendant fits into the class of persons for whom the statute was principally designed, (3) the maximum sentence and fine that could have been imposed, and (4) the nature of the harm caused by the defendant's conduct.

[*United States v. Viloski*, 814 F.3d 104, 110 (2d Cir. 2016); *see also United States v. Beecroft*, 825 F.3d 991, 1000 (9th Cir. 2016)(describing a similar four-factor test).] The same courts aacknowledge, however, that the *Bajkakajian* factors are not exclusive, and courts may consider as part of the proportionality determination other considerations, such as whether the forfeiture would deprive the defendant of his future ability to earn a living. [*Viloski*, 814 F.3d at 107, 111-12 (but upholding the forfeiture in that case against disproportionality challenge).]

Another related development in forfeiture law should provide additional relief from excessive forfeiture judgments. In *Honeycutt v. United States*, 137 S.Ct. 1626 (2017), the Supreme Court held that joint and several liability does not apply to proceeds forfeiture under 21 U.S.C. §853. Instead, forfeiture is limited to property personally acquired or used by the defendant, and a forfeiture judgment may not hold the defendant liable for property that other members of the conspiracy acquired. [*See also United States v. Brown*, 137 S.Ct. 2240 (U.S. June 12, 2017)(vacating 661 Fed. Appx. 190 in light of *Honeycutt*), *on remand*, — Fed. Appx. —, 2017 WL 3404979 (3d Cir. Aug. 9, 2017) (*Honeycutt* also applies to forfeitures under 18 U.S.C. § 982).]

Appropriate relief for a disproportionate forfeiture can be elimination or reduction of the forfeiture. [18 U.S.C. §983(g)(4); *United States v. $120,856 in U.S. Currency*, 394 F.Supp.2d 687 (D.V.I. 2005) (on defendant's motion to dismiss, limits government's forfeiture of $120,856 in undeclared currency to $7,500, the maximum fine for defendant's offense of conviction); *United States v. $293,316 in U.S. Currency*, 349 F.Supp.2d 638, 650-51 (E.D.N.Y. 2004) (reducing forfeiture by 50% in smuggled currency case).]

[§§11:04-11:09 Reserved]

II.   COMMENCING A FORFEITURE ACTION

§11:10   Civil Actions

Civil forfeiture actions usually are *in rem* and name the property as the defendant.

The action commences either with the filing of a complaint against the property or with the pre-complaint seizure of the asset.

If the government seizes property before filing a complaint, it must file the complaint or provide written notice to interested parties within a time set by statute or rule. [*E.g.*, 18 U.S.C. §983(a)(1) (absent extension by court order or the filing of an indictment with criminal forfeiture allegations against the property, the government must file a civil complaint or provide written notice within 60 days of the seizure); 18 U.S.C. §983(a)(3) (once a claim is filed, government must file a complaint or obtain an indictment within 90 days or release the property).]

Claimants may have an opportunity to contest the seizure after it takes place, but before the full trial.

The Due Process Clause prohibits the government from seizing real property without prior notice and an opportunity to be heard. [*United States v. James Daniel Good Real Prop.*, 510 U.S. 43 (1993).]

The government can protect its interests by filing a *lis pendens* against the property to prevent its sale. [*United States v. Register*, 182 F.3d 820, 836-37 (11th Cir. 1999).]

To retain possession of seized assets, the government must show probable cause for the retention. [*See Krimstock v. Kelly*, 306 F.3d 40, 67 (2d Cir. 2002) (when the police seized vehicles driven by driving-while-intoxicated arrestees, there must be a prompt post-seizure, but pre-judgment, hearing before a neutral officer to determine whether the City is likely to succeed on the merits of the forfeiture and whether means short of retention of the vehicle can satisfy the City's need to preserve it); *but see United States v. All Funds on Deposit*, 255 F.Supp.2d 56, 72 (E.D.N.Y. 2003) (magistrate's determination of probable cause to issue seizure warrants against bank accounts, the lack of physical seizure of monies, and the owner's ability to resort to hardship provisions of 18 U.S.C. §983(f) obviated need for post-seizure hearing).]

The court's pre-seizure determination of probable cause to issue a seizure warrant usually suffices to establish probable cause for the retention. [*See United States v. All Funds on Deposit*, 255 F.Supp.2d 56 (E.D.N.Y. 2003).]

§11:11   Administrative Actions

When an agency seizes an individual's property, such as contraband at an airport, the agency will issue a notice to the person from whom the property was seized.

If the person does not contest the administrative notice, the property will be forfeited. If the individual gives notice of a claim, the government must initiate a civil forfeiture action to preserve its forfeiture rights. [*See* Edgeworth, *Asset Forfeiture* at 59–64.]

§11:12   Criminal Actions

A criminal forfeiture action commences with the inclusion in the indictment of forfeiture allegations. "The indictment or information need not identify the property subject to forfeiture or specify the amount of any forfeiture money judgment that the government seeks," Fed R. Cr. P. 32.2(a), but the defendant may obtain a bill of particulars identifying the specific property or amount of money. [Notes of Advisory Committee on 2009 Amendments to Rule 32.2.]

Upon the prosecution's application, the court can restrain the defendant's assets to "preserve the availability of [forfeitable] property" while the case is pending. [21 U.S.C. 853(e); *Kaley v. United States*, 134 S.Ct. 1090, 1094 (2014).] The standard is probable cause to believe the property is forfeitable. That showing has two parts: "There must be probable cause to think (1) that the defendant has committed an offense permitting forfeiture, and (2) that the property at issue has the requisite connection to that crime." [*Kaley*, 134 S.Ct. at 1095.] An indictment is conclusive on probable cause as to the first prong, and the defendant is not entitled to a further hearing on it, but the defendant is entitled to a hearing to attempt to rebut the second prong – to show that the assets restrained are not actually proceeds of the charged criminal offense. [*Id.* at 1095 & n.3 (majority op.), 1108 (Roberts, C.J., dissenting).]

Criminal forfeiture is part of the defendant's sentence, and the judgment is *in personam*. [*See United States v. Bennett*, 423 F.3d 271, 275 (3d Cir. 2005); 18 U.S.C. §1963(a); Fed. R. Crim. P. 32.2(b)(3).] However, the court can correct the failure to include the forfeiture order in the sentence at any time. [Fed. R. Crim. P. 32.2(b)(4)(B); *United States v. Grasso*, 376 F.3d Appx 166 (3d Cir. 2010).]

While the underlying crime must be proven beyond a reasonable doubt, proof of the property's forfeitability (i.e., its substantial connection to the crime) need meet only a preponderance standard. [*Libretti v. United States*, 516 U.S. 29, 36 (1995); *United States v. Leahy*, 438 F.3d 328 (3d Cir. 2006) (no Sixth Amendment right to jury or proof beyond a reasonable doubt in criminal forfeiture action even after the decision in *United States v. Booker*, 543 U.S. 220 (2005)).]

However, some states impose a reasonable doubt standard by statute. [*See, e.g.,* Calif. Penal Code §186.5(d).] Other jurisdictions entitle the defendant to a jury determination of whether property is forfeitable. [*E.g.,* Fed. R. Cr. P. 32.2(b)(4).]

A prosecutorial advantage of criminal forfeiture is that the government can obtain a judgment not only against specific property, but against the defendant personally and against any "substitute assets" up to the value of the forfeitable property. [*United States v. Voigt*, 89 F.3d 1050, 1084 (3d Cir. 1996); *United States v. Salvagno*, 2006 WL 2546477 (N.D.N.Y. Aug 28, 2006) (may forfeit substitute assets only up to value of the funds used or derived from offense).]

This enables the prosecution to seize legitimately obtained property when the illegal property has been spent or cannot be located. [*United States v. Vondette*, 352 F.3d 772 (2d Cir. 2003) (government could seize defendant's individual retirement accounts as substitute assets), *vacated and remanded on other grounds*, 543 U.S. 1008 (2005) (vacating sentence on *Booker* grounds).]

The government has no right to substitute assets until it obtains an order of forfeiture upon conviction. Unlike the situation with tainted property such as criminal proceeds or property used to facilitate a crime, its title to the property does not "relate back" to any earlier time [*See* §11:21], and it may not obtain a pre-trial order restraining substitute assets. [*See United States v. Jarvis*, 499 F.3d 1196 (10th Cir. 2007) (surveying courts and joining the Second, Third, Fifth, Eight, and Ninth Circuits in this regard); *but see In re Billman*, 915 F.2d 916 (4th Cir. 1990) (allowing pre-trial restraint); *United States v. Parrett*, 530 F.3d 422 (6th Cir. 2008) (although federal law does not permit the prior restraint of substitute assets, the federal government may avail itself of state law remedies to file notices of lis pendens on substitute assets prior to the entry of judgment of the order of forfeiture).]

CAUTION:

Since an order of criminal forfeiture against the defendant is part of the sentence, it becomes final as to the defendant at sentencing, and the defendant's time to appeal begins to run when the judgment and sentence are entered. [*See Fed. R. Crim. P.* 32.2(b)(3); *United States v. Pelullo*, 178 F.3d 196, 202 (3d Cir. 1999).]

Third-party rights may remain to be adjudicated, but the defendant cannot await that adjudication to appeal. [*See United States v. Christunas*, 126 F.3d 765 (6th Cir. 1997) (dismissing as untimely defendant's appeal that awaited the adjudication of third-party interests).]

§11:13 Filing a Claim

To preserve rights to the property, in a civil or administrative forfeiture action, your client must file a claim in response to the forfeiture within the time period specified by statute. [*See, e.g.,* 18 U.S.C. §983(a)(2)(B) (within 35 days of mailed notice or 30 days of published notice).]

Filing the claim triggers the government's obligation to file a civil complaint, if one has not yet been filed. [18 U.S.C. §983(a)(3)(A), (B) (complaint must be filed within 90 days, or property released).]

The claim must establish your client's ownership interest in the property. [18 U.S.C. §983(a)(2)(C)(ii).]

Most statutes also require that the claimant himself sign the claim. [*E.g.,* 18 U.S.C. §983(a)(2)(C)(iii); *Supplemental Rules for Admiralty or Maritime Claims and Asset Forfeiture Actions*, Rule C(6)(a)(i), Rule G(5)(a)(i)(c).]

Obviously, this filing procedure creates a dilemma for an individual where possession or ownership of the property (*e.g.,* large amounts or cash or firearms) tends to prove guilt. Where there is an ongoing criminal investigation, you should consider filing a motion for a stay. [*See* §11:31.] However, consider the possibility that the prosecution may not know of your client's involvement with the property. In that case, asserting a claim or moving for a stay may alert the prosecution to the need to investigate your client.

In a federal criminal forfeiture action, third parties must assert their rights to the property by filing a petition within thirty days of notice, by publication or receipt of notice, of a preliminary order of forfeiture. [*United States v. Marion*, 562 F.3d 1330 (11th Cir. 2009).] The government may obtain a preliminary order any time after plea or verdict. Thus a third-party petition that awaits the final judgment of forfeiture is untimely and must be dismissed where there was a preliminary order and notice thereof more than 30 days before the filing of the petition. [*Marion, supra.*]

The claimant, not his or her lawyer, must sign the petition and verify it under oath. [*United States v. Commodity Account No. 549-54930*, 219 F.3d 595, 597 (7th Cir. 2000); *Mercado v. U.S. Customs Service*, 873 F.2d 641, 645 (2d Cir. 1989).]

Form:
*   **Form 11-1** Claim

[§§11:14-11:19 Reserved]

III.   THIRD PARTIES

§11:20   Attorneys' Fees

Attorneys' fees are not immune from forfeiture. The prosecution can seize tainted funds even if the forfeiture would leave the defendant unable to retain counsel and can seize from the attorney illegally derived funds paid or transferred for legal fees. [*Caplin & Drysdale, Chartered v. United States*, 491 U.S. 617, 626 (1989); *United States v. Monsanto*, 491 U.S. 600 (1989).]

To defend fees from forfeiture, attorneys must resort to the same bona-fide-purchaser-for-value arguments available to any other person. That is, the attorney provided the services in return for the property and did not know that the property was the proceeds of the illegal activity. [*See* §11:21.]

Unfortunately, your knowledge that your client has been indicted or your pre-indictment investigation of the facts may put you on notice that your client's funds came from illegal sources. [*See Caplin & Drysdale v. United States*, 491 U.S. at 632 n.10 (indictment itself gave attorney, retained after indictment, reason to believe that property is subject to forfeiture, thereby defeating bona-fide purchaser defense); *United States v. Moffitt, Zwerling & Kemler, P.C.*, 83 F.3d 660, 665-66 (4th Cir. 1996) (concluding that defense attorney was not a bona fide purchaser because he was aware that his fee was subject to forfeiture from his objective assessment of the law and the facts of the case).]

The federal money laundering statutes do exempt from criminal prosecution the use of criminally derived property to secure legal representation for a criminal case. [18 U.S.C. §1957(f)(1); *United States v. Velez*, 586 F.3d 875 (11th Cir. 2009).]

Insisting that you be paid with untainted assets does not guarantee that the government will not seize your fees at some point. Every federal court of appeals but the Fourth Circuit has held that substitute assets are not subject to pretrial restraint. [*United States v. Jones*, 844 F.3d 636, 641 (7th Cir. 2016); *United States v. Jarvis*, 499 F.3d 1196, 1204 nn. 7 & 8 (10th Cir. 2007).] Untainted substitute assets cannot be restrained pretrial if so doing would deprive a defendant of money necessary to retain counsel. [*Luis v. United States* 136 S.Ct. 1083 (2016).]

Courts are split, however, on whether the government can use criminal forfeiture statutes to seize substitute assets in a third party's possession after conviction (your other funds). [*Compare United States v. McHan*, 345 F.3d 262, 270-72 (4th Cir. 2003) (yes); *United States v. Loren-Maltese*, 2006 U.S. Dist. LEXIS 11969, 2006 WL 752958 (N.D. Ill. March 21, 2006) (ordering forfeiture of $625,000 in fees and escrow funds paid to defense counsel as a "substitute asset"); *with United States v. Saccoccia*, 354 F.3d 9 (1st Cir. 2003) (no).]

Some states forbid forfeiture of funds designated for payment of attorneys' fees. [*See, e.g., State ex rel Topeka Police Dept. v. $895.00 in U.S. Currency*, 281 Kans. 819, 837, 133 P.3d 91, 103 (2006) (listing Kansas, Illinois and Connecticut as states with statutes exempting attorneys' fees); *Commonwealth v. Hess*, 532 Pa. 607, 617 A.2d 307 (1992) (exempting attorneys' fees as a matter of state constitutional law).]

Also, Department of Justice policy counsels restraint before seeking to forfeit attorneys' fees in order to avoid "hampering [defense attorneys'] ability to represent their clients." [*U. S. Attorneys' Manual* §§9–119.200.] Prosecutors may not seek forfeiture of legitimate attorneys' fees unless the attorney had *actual* knowledge at the time of the payment that the particular asset used to pay the attorney was subject to forfeiture. [*See U. S. Attorney's Manual, Title 9, Criminal Resource Manual* at §§2306–2312.] To prove knowledge, the prosecutor ordinarily must rely on objective facts and circumstances apparent to the attorney, not upon confidential client communications. [*Criminal Resource Manual* at 2307, 2311-12, 2316.]

Some prosecutors will show a willingness to negotiate the attorneys' fees issue and release currency and bank accounts which they seized under a pre-trial seizure order so that the defendant can retain and pay counsel. In federal court, any agreement to exempt an asset from forfeiture so that it can be transferred to an attorney as fees must be approved by the Assistant Attorney General for the Criminal Division. [*USAM* §§9–119.203.]

If the government obtains a pre-trial restraining order against assets, the defendant is entitled to a hearing to lift the order so he can retain counsel if he shows that he is otherwise unable to retain counsel. If the government shows probable cause to believe that the assets are forfeitable, however, the order will stand even if it deprives the defendant of the ability to retain counsel. [*See United States v. Farmer*, 274 F.3d 800 (4th Cir. 2001) (defendant has the burden of showing that he lacks the means to hire an attorney independent of the seized assets and that the seized assets were legitimately derived).]

PRACTICE TIP:

You might consider asking your client to represent in the engagement letter that the funds with which he paid you came from legal sources. Alternatively, you might demand that your fees come from a family member or friend known to have legitimate earnings and savings or from the account of a legitimate business.

§11:21   Bona Fide Purchaser for Value

Under the "relation back" doctrine, title to the forfeitable property vests in the government at the moment of the illegal act giving derivation. [*See United States v. 92 Buena Vista Avenue*, 507 U.S. 111 (1993) (describing both the common law and statutory, 21 U.S.C. §881(h), relation-back doctrines).]

This doctrine can eliminate the property rights of those who purchase after the illegality.

However, forfeiture statutes provide a defense for those who prove that they purchased the property without reason to believe that it was subject to forfeiture. [*See* 21 U.S.C. §853(n)(6)(B) (criminal forfeiture); 18 U.S.C. §983(d)(3)(A).]

Because the bona fide purchaser for value defense applies only to those individuals who provide payment or services in return for the money, it does not protect family members or spouses to whom property was transferred without financial consideration. [*United States v. Infelise*, 938 F. Supp. 1352, 1368 (N.D. Ill. 1996); *see generally,* Stefan D. Cassella, *The Uniform Innocent Owner Defense to Civil Asset Forfeiture*, 89 Kentucky L.J. 653, 692-94 & nn. 171-79 (2001) (heirs, donees and unsecured creditors are not purchasers for value).]

§11:22   Innocent Owners

Landlords who find that their tenants have dealt drugs out of apartments and parents whose children were caught with drugs in mom and dad's car may find themselves defending the forfeiture of their assets.

In a federal civil forfeiture, the owner has the burden of proving that he is an innocent owner, meaning that he did not have knowledge of the illegal use to which his property was put or, that as soon as he learned of the illegal activity, he notified the police. [*See* 18 U.S.C. §983(d)(2).] The state law defense may be broader. [*E.g., Commonwealth v. 1997 Chevrolet,* — *30 (Under 42 Pa.C.S. § 6802(j), innocent owner may prevail by showing either lack of knowledge or lack of consent to property's use as an instrumentality).]

"Willful blindness" cannot support a claim of lack of knowledge. [*See United States v. One 1988 Checo Let 410 Turbo Prop Aircraft*, 282 F.Supp.2d 1379, 1383 (S.D. Fla. 2003).]

However, in a criminal forfeiture action, an innocent owner must prove only that he had a valid ownership interest prior to the crime. [21 U.S.C. §853(n)(6)(A); Edgeworth, *Asset Forfeiture* at 152-53.]

[§§11:23-11:29 Reserved]

IV. COMMON ISSUES

§11:30 Whether to Litigate the Forfeiture Action

A civil forfeiture action proceeds like any other civil action with a Complaint and Answer, document discovery and interrogatories, depositions and summary judgment motions.

If your client is under investigation, the lure of obtaining agent reports and deposing the investigating agents might tempt you to litigate the forfeiture action fully. On the other hand, your client also may be obligated to sign pleadings making detailed factual allegations and to answer interrogatories and depositions under oath.

Recent reform of the federal forfeiture statutes under CAFRA and many state statutes impose the burden of proof on the government. In many cases, though, the circumstantial evidence, as a practical matter, shifts the burden to the claimant to justify the claimant's ownership of the property.

Consider the following factors in deciding whether and to what extent to contest the forfeiture:

- Does your client need the forfeited or seized property to run his business, house, family or pay his attorney? A court can release property, at least until final disposition of the forfeiture action, upon a showing of hardship if the claimant convinces the court that the property will not be dissipated. [*See* 18 U.S.C. §983(f).] This argument works best for residences, offices and business equipment.
- Can your client litigate the forfeiture action without prejudicing his defense in the criminal case? Anything your client represents in contesting the forfeiture can be used against him, but the forfeiture defense might depend on issues unrelated to the criminal action or involve issues which will be undisputed in the criminal case. For example, defense of a facilitation-based forfeiture case may depend on whether there was a "substantial connection between the property and the offense," rather than whether the offense was committed. [18 U.S.C. §983(c)(3).] A stay of the forfeiture action pending completion of the criminal case may be the solution. [*See* §11:31.]
- Will contesting the forfeiture aid in negotiating a favorable criminal plea agreement? Federal and many state policies forbid using forfeiture to coerce a plea. [*See* U. S. Department of Justice, *Asset Forfeiture Policy Manual* at 69–70 (2006): Edgeworth, *Asset Forfeiture* at 230-31.] Therefore, a vigorous defense of the forfeiture should not elicit vindictive terms in the criminal plea offer. To the contrary, the prospect that your client will continue to fight the forfeiture even after a plea may persuade the government to offer favorable terms to settle the forfeiture action. For example, a conviction might result in a restitution order against your client, but your client might find that the assets he may have used to satisfy that order have been seized as the forfeitable proceeds or instrumentalities of the crime. The government has no obligation to apply those assets to restitution. If it does not, your client, in effect, will pay double. [*See* 18 U.S.C. §981(e) (whether to apply forfeited assets to restitution is discretionary); *United States v. Bright*, 353 F.3d 1114 (9th Cir. 2004) (holding that district court lacked authority to order the U. S. Postal Service to apply forfeited assets toward restitution to victims of mail fraud).] However, the prosecution, when faced with the prospect of protracted forfeiture litigation, might agree to apply the assets to restitution in return for an agreement that they are forfeitable.
- Is your client an innocent third party? If so, he can litigate the case vigorously without fear of incrimination. Once a criminal forfeiture judgment has been entered, third parties still can vindicate their interests in the property in an "ancillary proceeding." [*See* 18 U.S.C. §1963(l)(2); Fed. R. Crim. P. 32.2(c)(4).]

Forms:
- **Form 11-2** Answer to Forfeiture Complaint–Federal
- **Form 11-3** Answer to Forfeiture Complaint–State
- **Form 11-4** Forfeiture Plea Agreement Language

§11:31 Stays

The court hearing the civil forfeiture action may stay it during the criminal investigation and prosecution at the request of either the prosecution or the claimant. You may wish a stay to protect your defendant's property rights, while not sacrificing his privilege against self-incrimination. Likewise, the government may seek a stay to avoid disclosing its investigation before it is ready to file charges. [*See* 18 U.S.C. §981(g) (authorizing stays at defense or prosecution request).]

Form:
- **Form 11-5** Motion for Stay

V.   FORMS

Form 11-1   Claim

IN THE UNITED STATES DISTRICT COURT
FOR THE _____ DISTRICT OF _____

UNITED STATES OF AMERICA,	)	
Plaintiff,	)	
v.	)	Civil Action No. _____
REAL PROPERTY KNOWN AND	)	
NUMBERED AS _____	)	
ROAD, FOREST HILLS, PA 00000,	)	
Including all improvements, fixtures	)	
And appurtenances thereto and	)	
therein,	)	
Defendant.	)	

VERIFIED CLAIM OF ABC HOLDINGS, INC.

PLEASE TAKE NOTICE THAT ABC Holdings, Inc., ("Claimant") has an interest in the defendant property, the Real Property Known And Numbered As _____ Road, Forest Hills, Pa 00000, including all improvements, fixtures and Appurtenances thereto and therein.

On _____, Claimant was served with the Verified Complaint for forfeiture and Warrant of Arrest in this action.

Claimant is owner and titleholder of the defendant real property, having purchased the property for $37,000 on _____, which deed was recorded in the Allegheny County Recorder of Deeds Office in Deed Book Volume 66666, Page 60. A true and correct copy of the deed is attached as Exhibit A.

Claimant entered into an installment land contract dated _____, to sell the property to Ms. A. That contract was amended by an addendum dated _____, between ABC Holdings, Inc., and Ms. A. True and correct copies of the installment land contract and addendum are attached as Exhibit B. However, Ms. A violated the terms of the installment-lost-land contract, in particular, paragraph 28, by conducting illegal activities upon the property (according to the Government's allegations). By virtue of that violation, the installment land contract is void, and Ms. A and the Government have no right to the property.

Claimant was without knowledge or any reason to know of any illegal activities that may have been conducted on the property.

Title to the property never passed to Ms. A.

At the request of the United States Government, and in consideration for the Government's promise to reimburse Claimant for all costs and expenses of upkeep, Claimant has paid the taxes, insurance, maintenance and upkeep on the property since in or around _____. That amount totals approximately $5,000.

Claimant is the innocent owner of the property and a bona fide purchaser for value.

WHEREFORE, by virtue of Claimant's interest in the defendant property, Claimant demands restitution and the right to defend this action.

Respectfully submitted,

_____
Counsel for Claimant
Thomas J. Farrell

VERIFICATION

I, J.T., am the president of ABC Holdings, Inc., and I am authorized to make this verification on behalf of the Claimant.

I have read the foregoing Verified Claim. The statements therein are correct to the best of my personal knowledge or information and belief.

I declare under penalty of perjury that the foregoing is true and correct. Executed on July _____, 20__.

_____
J.T.
President, ABC Holdings, Inc.

Form 11-2   Answer to Forfeiture Complaint–Federal

IN THE UNITED STATES DISTRICT COURT
FOR THE _____ DISTRICT OF _____

UNITED STATES OF AMERICA,	)	
Plaintiff,	)	
v.	)	Civil Action No. _____
REAL PROPERTY KNOWN AND	)	
NUMBERED AS _____	)	
ROAD, FOREST HILLS, PA 00000,	)	JURY TRIAL DEMANDED
Including all improvements,	)	
fixtures and appurtenances	)	
thereto and therein,	)	
	)	
Defendant.	)	

VERIFIED AMENDED ANSWER TO COMPLAINT FOR FORFEITURE

AND NOW comes ABC Holdings, Inc., ("Claimant") by and through its counsel, [*Name of attorney*], and files the following Amended Answer to the Verified Complaint for Forfeiture:

Paragraph 1: Admitted.

Paragraph 2 states legal conclusions to which no responsive pleading is required.

Paragraph 3: Admitted.

Paragraph 4: Admitted in part and denied in part. It is admitted that the Defendant Real Property was titled in the name of J.T. by deed date _____. However, the property was conveyed by Mr. T to Claimant by deed dated _____, for the purchase price of $37,000. A true and correct copy of the _____ deed is attached as Exhibit A.

Paragraph 5: Admitted in part and denied in part. It is admitted that Claimant entered into an installment land contract dated _____, with Ms. A. That contract was amended by an addendum dated _____, between Claimant and Ms. A. However, Ms. A violated the terms of the installment land contract, in particular, paragraph 28. By virtue of that violation, the installment land contract is void, and Ms. A and the Government have no right to the property.

The allegations in paragraph 6 of the Complaint contain legal conclusions to which no responsive pleading is required. To the extent that a responsive pleading is required, the allegations in paragraph 6 are denied. The Defendant Real Property is not forfeitable to the United States because as of the time that the property was used to facilitate violations of federal law, if such occurred, the installment land contract was voided, and Ms. A had no interest in or right to the property. Further, Claimant is an innocent owner of the property and a bona fide purchaser for value.

Claimant is without knowledge or belief to admit or deny the allegations in paragraph 7 of the Complaint. Claimant was an innocent owner of the property. Any illegal activities that may have occurred on the property took place without Claimant's knowledge or consent. Further, Claimant had no reason to know of any such illegal activities. To the extent that the allegations of paragraph 7 are true and demonstrate that illegal acts were committed on the property, the installment land contract was voided, and Ms. A was in default, depriving her of any possessory or ownership interest in the property.

The allegations of paragraph 8 are legal conclusions to which no responsive pleading is required. To the extent a responsive pleading is deemed required, the allegations in paragraph 8 are denied.

FIRST DEFENSE

The Government has failed to state a claim upon which relief can be granted.

SECOND DEFENSE
The Claimant is an innocent owner.

THIRD DEFENSE
The Claimant is a bona fide purchaser for value.

FOURTH DEFENSE
The Government's forfeiture claim, being penal in nature, is excessive.

FIFTH DEFENSE
The Government lacks probable cause for the institution of this forfeiture action.

SIXTH DEFENSE
The Claimant's due process rights have been violated by the forfeiture of the property and the institution of this civil action.

WHEREFORE, Claimant respectfully requests that this Honorable Court:

Dismiss Plaintiff's Complaint and enter judgment on behalf of Claimant;

Deny issuance of a Certificate of Probable Cause, pursuant to 28 U.S.C. §2465 and award costs and attorneys' fees to Claimant; and

Provide such other relief as the Court deems just and proper.

COUNTERCLAIMS COUNT I
BREACH OF CONTRACT
Claimant repeats and realleges paragraphs 1-14 as if fully set forth herein.

In or around _____, Claimant learned that federal authorities had executed a search warrant at _____ Road. Claimant had no knowledge of the basis for the warrant or the allegations that supported it or what was seized. Shortly thereafter, a federal grand jury subpoena was served on the offices of Claimant requesting documents relating to _____ Road. Claimant cooperated with the investigation and responded fully to the grand jury subpoena.

3. In or around _____, J.T. (Mr. T), manager of ABC Holdings, had a telephone conversation with Assistant United States Attorney W.H. (Ms. H). Ms. H asked Mr. T to ensure that title was not transferred to Ms. A. Further, Ms. H requested that Claimant not rent the property to anyone else because the Government may attempt to seize the property at anytime. In addition, Ms. H asked Claimant to pay the upkeep on the property: maintenance, utilities, insurance and property taxes. In return, Ms. H promised to reimburse Claimant for its expenses in maintaining the property.

4. On behalf of Claimant, Mr. T agreed to Ms. H's request. Claimant has paid all the upkeep on the property, an amount that now exceeds $5,000 since the forfeiture complaint was filed. Claimant has not rented the property.

The Government has not reimbursed Claimant for the expenses of maintaining the property or the loss of rental income.

WHEREFORE, Claimant respectfully requests that this Court enter a judgment in its favor and against the Government in an amount to be proven at trial.

COUNT TWO
UNJUST ENRICHMENT–QUANTUM MERUIT
Claimant repeats and realleges paragraph 1-19 as if fully set forth herein.

By maintaining the Defendant real property at the Government's request, Claimant conferred substantial benefits upon the Government at the Government's request.

It would be unfair and inequitable to permit the Government to retain these benefits without adequate compensation to Claimant.

WHEREFORE, Claimant respectfully requests that this Court enter a judgment in its favor and against the Government in an amount to be proven at trial.

COUNT THREE
PROMISSORY ESTOPPEL

Claimant repeats and realleges paragraph 1-22 as if fully set forth herein.

8. Claimant relied to its detriment on the Government's promise and misrepresentation that it would reimburse Claimant for maintenance to the Defendant real property.

WHEREFORE, Claimant respectfully requests that this Court enter a judgment in its favor and against the Government in an amount to be proven at trial.

Respectfully submitted,

_____

Counsel for Claimant
Thomas J. Farrell

VERIFICATION

I, J.T., am the president of ABC Holdings, Inc., and I am authorized to make this verification on behalf of the Claimant.

I have read the foregoing Verified Amended Answer. The statements therein are correct to the best of my personal knowledge or information and belief.

I declare under penalty of perjury that the foregoing is true and correct. Executed on August _____, 2004.

_____

J.T.
President, ABC Holdings, Inc.

Form 11-3   Answer to Forfeiture Complaint–State

COMMENT: _____

This is an answer to a complaint for the return of legally owned firearms and cash seized during the search of a home for controlled substances.

IN THE COURT OF COMMON PLEAS _____ COUNTY, _____
CIVIL ACTION–*IN REM*

COMMONWEALTH OF _____	No. _____
Plaintiff	**RESPONSE TO PETITION FOR FORFEITURE AND CONDEMNATION**
v.	
THIRTY-THREE THOUSAND SIX HUNDRED FORTY-ONE DOLLARS ($33,641.00) IN UNITED STATES CURRENCY AND ASSORTED ITEMS OF PERSONAL PROPERTY	Filed on Behalf of Claimant, C.W.
	THOMAS J. FARRELL, ESQ.

IN THE COURT OF COMMON PLEAS _____ COUNTY, _____
CIVIL ACTION–*IN REM*

COMMONWEALTH OF _____
    Plaintiff
            v.   No. _____
THIRTY-THREE THOUSAND SIX
HUNDRED FORTY-ONE DOLLARS

($33,641.00) IN UNITED STATES
CURRENCY AND ASSORTED ITEMS
OF PERSONAL PROPERTY

RESPONSE TO PETITION FOR FORFEITURE AND CONDEMNATION

And now comes Claimant C.W. and makes the following response to the Commonwealth's Petition for Forfeiture and Condemnation:

1. Admitted. Claimant makes a claim only to $30,000 of the $33,641 in currency and to the firearms (which she intends to convey to her father-in-law, L.W., or her daughter, A.W.).
2. Admitted.
3. Admitted.
4. Admitted in part and denied in part. After reasonable investigation, C.W. is without knowledge or information sufficient to form a belief as to the truth or falsity of the allegations in paragraph 4 concerning ownership of the firearms; therefore, those allegations are denied.
5. Admitted.
6. Admitted.
7. Admitted.
8. Admitted.
9. After reasonable investigation, Defendant C.W. is without knowledge or information sufficient to form a belief as to the truth or falsity of the allegations in paragraph 9; therefore, those allegations are denied.
10. Admitted.
11. Admitted.
12. Admitted.
13. After reasonable investigation, Claimant is without knowledge or information sufficient to form a belief as to the truth or falsity of the allegations in paragraph 13; therefore, those allegations are denied.
14. Admitted.
15. Admitted in part and denied in part. The $30,000 in currency and the firearms were in a Fort Knox safe and not in proximity to any controlled substance.
16. Admitted.
17. After reasonable investigation, Claimant is without knowledge or information sufficient to form a belief as to the truth or falsity of the allegations in paragraph 17; therefore, those allegations are denied. Further, Claimant is uncertain to what Petitioner refers to when it speaks of "the circumstances of this case."
18–20. Denied as to the $30,000 in currency and the firearms. That money was accumulated over many years by withdrawing cash from the bank from the substantial legal earnings that the Ws have collected from C.W.'s employment, Tom W's disability and veterans' compensation, distributions from several insurance policies and the settlement of various lawsuits, including the Agent Orange case. The firearms were purchased over many years with legal income and were not used in any drug-trafficking activity.

NEW MATTER

21. The $30,000 in the safe was accumulated over years of saving the Bs' legitimate income, not from selling any illegal controlled substance. Further, none of this money was used or intended to be used in the purchase of any illegal controlled substance. To the contrary, the Ws intended to give that money to their only surviving child, A.W., when she eventually marries.
22. Tom W is a disabled veteran of the Vietnam War. For the last 28 years, Tom W has received non-taxable service-connected benefits from the United States Department of Veteran Affairs, the amount of which has increased over time until it amounts to $2,429 per month for the last 12 months.
23. Tom W. also receives disability benefits from the Social Security Administration–approximately $14,000 per year since 2001.
24. Since March 1, 1986, Claimant C.W. has been employed full-time by Washington County. In the year 2001, her annual wages were $40,375; in 2002, $28,563; in 2003, $16,615; and in 2004, 39,621.
25. In addition, the Ws received a $57,000 life insurance distribution upon their son John's death in 1994. Mr. W received $6,869.33 in 1995 from settlement of the Agent Orange lawsuits, and in 1997, the Ws received a $2,000 distribution from an insurance policy for a gun that was stolen from their home.

26. Tom W suffers from post-traumatic stress disorder and other emotional disorders. He is suspicious of authority and banks. Since 1981, C.W. every month takes $400 from her paycheck, in four $100 bills, and gives them to Tom. He also had her cash approximately $10,000 of the insurance proceeds checks, and Tom stored the $100 bills in the safe.

27. The Ws live a relatively frugal life on their considerable income (over $20,000 of which, the Veterans benefit, is untaxed). Their cars are 11 and 17 years old; their mortgage, but $500 per month. Therefore, they were able to accumulate considerable savings, in both investments and cash, legally.

WHEREFORE, Claimant C.W. respectfully requests that a hearing be held on the petition for forfeiture and that the Court order the return of the $30,000 in currency to her.

Respectfully submitted,

_____
[*Name of Attorney*], Esq.
Attorney for C.W.

VERIFICATION

I, C.W., hereby verify and state that the statements made in the foregoing Response to Petition for Forfeiture and Condemnation are true and correct to the best of my knowledge, information and belief.

The undersigned understands that the statements therein are made subject to the penalties of 18 Pa. C.S.A. §4904 related to unsworn falsification to authorities.

Dated: _____

Form 11-4   Forfeiture Plea Agreement Language

Thomas J. Farrell
436 Seventh Avenue, Suite 1000
Pittsburgh, PA 15219

     Re: *United States of America v.*
             SS
             <u>Criminal No.</u>

Dear Mr. _____:

This letter sets forth the agreement by which your client, SS, will enter a plea of guilty in the above-captioned case. The letter represents the full and complete agreement between Mrs. S and the United States Attorney for the Western District of Pennsylvania. The agreement does not apply to or bind any other federal, state or local prosecuting authority.

Upon entering a plea of guilty, Mrs. S will be sentenced under the Sentencing Guidelines promulgated by the United States Sentencing Commission and the Sentencing Reform Act, 18 U.S.C. §3551, *et seq.* and 28 U.S.C. §981, *et seq.* The facts relevant to sentencing shall be determined initially by the United States Probation Office and finally by the United States District Court.

A. The defendant, SS, agrees to the following:

1. She will waive in open court her constitutional right not to be prosecuted for felonies except by indictment in accordance with Rule 7(b) of the Federal Rules of Criminal Procedure, and consent that the proceedings may be initiated by the United States Attorney through an Information charging criminal felonies and criminal forfeiture allegations, a draft of which is being forwarded for the use of your client with this letter, charging her in Count One (subject to the understanding, below) with conducting the affairs of an enterprise engaged in interstate commerce through a pattern of racketeering activity, in violation of 18 U.S.C. §1962(c); in Count Two with mail fraud in violation of 18 U.S.C. §§1341 and 2; in Count Five with personal income tax evasion in violation of 26 U.S.C. §7201 and 18 U.S.C. §2l; and in Counts Six, Eight and Ten with filing false corporate income tax returns in violation of 26 U.S.C. §7206(1). With

regard to Count One, it is understood that prosecution pursuant to this agreement of charges under 18 U.S.C. §1962 is subject to approval by the Department of Justice, and that in the absence of such approval, at the option of the United States Attorney, a count charging a violation of 18 U.S.C. §371, conspiracy, punishable by up to five years imprisonment and/or a fine of up to $250,000, may be substituted at Count One.

2. She will enter a plea of guilty to all Counts of the Information to be filed as agreed in subparagraph 1, above (hereinafter referred to as "the Information"), pursuant to Rule 11 of the Federal Rules of Criminal Procedure. She will also consent to an order of criminal forfeiture on the forfeiture count, as discussed in Part A, subparagraph 3, below.

3. SS acknowledges that her right, title and interest in the Subject Properties will be the subject of criminal forfeiture as alleged in the information, and herewith voluntarily consents to the District Court entering an order of criminal forfeiture of the Subject Properties, subject to Section B, Subparagraph 1, below, regarding the payment of restitution. She waives any former jeopardy or double jeopardy claims in or as a result of the criminal forfeiture of said property.

4. SS acknowledges that the Subject Properties are also the subject of civil forfeiture actions as listed on Attachment A hereto. Subject to Section B, Subparagraph 1, below, regarding the payment of restitution, she acknowledges that the United States may, at its sole discretion, simultaneously proceed to final forfeiture of all or part of the Subject Properties through the civil forfeiture actions and may sell said assets by interlocutory sale or by final sale. She hereby consents to any such interlocutory or final sale and to the entry of judgments of forfeiture in the civil actions, subject to Section B, Subparagraph 1, below, regarding the payment of restitution. She waives any former jeopardy or double jeopardy claims in or as a result of any civil forfeiture seizures and arrests, any interlocutory or final sales and/or the entry of judgments of forfeiture in the civil actions. She further acknowledges that the Subject Properties are civilly forfeitable to the United States for the reasons outlined in the civil forfeiture actions.

5. Upon the request of the United States and subject to Section B, Subparagraph 1, below, regarding the payment of restitution, SS agrees to execute any documents reasonably requested by the United States to effectuate the criminal and/or civil forfeiture of her interests in the Subject Properties. In her capacity as officer, shareholder and/or partner of _____ Corporation and _____, Ltd., she consents to the criminal and/or civil forfeiture of the Subject Properties.

6. SS represents to the United States that other than the Subject Properties, she has no interest of any kind in any other property that was involved in, or that constitute or are derived from the proceeds of, her violations of 18 U.S.C. §§1341 and/or 1962(c). If it should ever be determined that she, in fact, has retained any right, title or interest in any property not disclosed to the United States ("undisclosed property"), she agrees that such interest shall be immediately forfeited to the United States as substitute assets. The United States District Court shall retain jurisdiction of all disputes concerning application of this clause. She further agrees that the forfeiture of the undisclosed property as authorized herein shall not be deemed an alteration of her sentence.

7. Upon request of the United States, she agrees to provide all information regarding her income, assets and financial status. She agrees to submit to interviews as to these matters, complete a financial statement under oath, and submit to a polygraph examination as may be deemed necessary by the United States Attorney.

B. In consideration of and entirely contingent upon the provisions of Parts A and C of this agreement, the United States Attorney for the Western District of Pennsylvania agrees to the following:

1. In the event that the United States District Court orders the defendant to pay restitution, the United States Attorney will agree to release the United States' forfeiture interests in the Subject Properties in favor of the victims ordered by the District Court. Furthermore, the United States Attorney agrees to release its forfeiture interests in any additional property forfeited under the terms of this agreement in favor of the victims as long as there is a restitution obligation outstanding. Finally, in recognition of the fact that Mrs. Smith and her husband, Thomas Smith, engaged in business which realized some legitimate receipts that were not fruits of unlawful conduct, it is understood and agreed that the total value of money and property to be forfeited pursuant to this agreement will not exceed the total of (1) the amount of loss to victims from offenses for which responsibility is acknowledged by Mrs. S in this agreement, and/or by Mr. S in his plea agreement reached with the United States Attorney for the Western District of Pennsylvania; plus (2) the total amount owed by Mrs. S, and/or Mr. S and/or any business entities operated by them on account of violations of the Internal Revenue Code for which responsibility is acknowledged by Mrs. S in this agreement, and/or by Mr. S in his plea agreement reached with the United States Attorney.

Form 11-5   Motion for Stay

IN THE UNITED STATES DISTRICT COURT
FOR THE _____ DISTRICT OF _____

UNITED STATES OF AMERICA,
     Plaintiff,

v.   No. _____

REAL PROPERTY LOCATED AT
_____ STREET,
     Defendant.

MOTION TO STAY FURTHER PROCEEDINGS

The Claimant, J.D., by his attorney, _____, pursuant to 18 U.S.C. §981(g)(2), moves the court to stay further proceedings in this case until the conclusion of *Commonwealth v. JD*, CC No. 20050111, currently pending in the Court of Common Pleas for Allegheny County. As grounds for this motion, the Claimant asserts that:

1. The above reference to the Allegheny County case is directly related to the plaintiff's forfeiture claim;
2. The Claimant, as owner of the defendant property, has standing to challenge its forfeiture; and
3. The continuation of the forfeiture proceedings, particularly the discovery process, will burden the right of the Claimant against self-incrimination in the Allegheny County criminal case.

Dated this ___ day of _____, _____.

                         _____
                         Attorney

IN THE UNITED STATES DISTRICT COURT
FOR THE _____ DISTRICT OF _____

UNITED STATES OF AMERICA,
     Plaintiff,

v.   No. _____

REAL PROPERTY LOCATED AT
_____ STREET,
     Defendant.

AFFIDAVIT IN SUPPORT OF MOTION TO STAY FURTHER PROCEEDINGS

[*Name of attorney*], being first duly sworn, on oath deposes and says:

1. I am the attorney for the Claimant, J.D., in reference to the above matter;
2. I am aware that J.D. has been criminally charged in state court for matters directly related to the facts underlying this forfeiture action; and
3. Attached to this affidavit is the CCAP printout of the criminal case docket and a copy of the criminal Information filed in that matter.

I declare under penalty of perjury that the foregoing is true and correct. Executed on _____ ___, _____.

                         _____
                         Attorney

Chapter 12

GRAND JURY PRACTICE

(This page intentionally left blank.)

I. GENERAL POINTS

§12:01 Grand Juries Are an Investigative Tool

Clients and even many lawyers find grand juries mysterious. To allay fears and assist your client in making informed decisions, you must explain what the grand jury is and how it works.

While historically, grand juries were supposed to stand between the sovereign and the citizen by screening cases and rejecting those unfit for prosecution, they have become a powerful investigative tool for prosecutors.

Grand jurors are selected from the same pool as regular jurors, but defense attorneys do not play any role in challenging or selecting the jurors. Typically, the grand jury consists of 16 to 23 members who sit for 18 months, but only for a few days each month.

Explain to your client that the grand jury was not impaneled to deal with his case. They hear evidence in any number of investigations underway at the same time. Neither probable cause nor reasonable suspicion is required to initiate a grand jury investigation; it is free to investigate the flimsiest of rumors and suspicions. [*United States v. R. Enters., Inc.*, 498 U.S. 292, 297 (1991).]

Grand juries are *not* impartial bodies. They hear only the evidence the prosecutor chooses to present, much of it hearsay in the form of interviews summarized by law enforcement agents. The jurors receive their instructions in the law from the prosecutor, and spend their recesses bantering with agents and prosecutors and their staff. Grand juries rarely review documents subpoenaed to them. Instead, the prosecutor reads a return, that is, an extremely brief description of what was subpoenaed and what was received (*e.g.,* "all business records of Enron relating to its accounting for profits").

Prosecutors often remind the grand jury that it is not to determine guilt or innocence, only whether there is probable cause to vote an indictment. Grand jurors learn that their days will go quickly and easily if they ask few probing questions and vote to indict whenever requested to do so. It is not uncommon to see grand jurors dozing or reading during testimony.

PRACTICE TIP:

Stress to your client that the grand jury is not there to be charmed or persuaded. His objective is to avoid testifying. If he must testify, then his goal is to get in and out as quickly as possible while saying as little as possible in a business-like fashion.

§12:02 Grand Juries' Proceedings Are Secret

Only the grand jurors, a court reporter, the prosecutor and the witness may be present during the grand jury's proceedings. Matters occurring before the grand jury are secret, and the First Amendment right of public access does not apply. [*Press-Enterprise Co. v. Superior Court*, 478 U.S. 1, 8-9 (1986); *United States v. Index Newspapers, LLC.*, 766 F.3d 1072, 1084 (9th Cir. 2014) (proceedings on motion to quash grand jury subpoena should be closed)]

Some jurisdictions permit witnesses to have their lawyer present; others consign the attorney to a post outside the grand jury room and permit the witness to leave and consult with the lawyer. [*See* §12:100.]

Everyone in the grand jury room except the witness is legally bound to keep its proceedings secret.

Still, leaks occur. Further, in many courthouses, the grand jury room is situated so that the media and representatives of the investigation's targets can stake out the grand jury room, observe who enters, and try to question outside the grand jury room those who appear to be witnesses.

The defense does not receive transcripts of any testimony until after indictment, when the defendant may obtain the transcript of his own testimony in discovery. [*See, e.g.,* Fed. R. Cr. P. 16(b)(1)(A).] The defendant cannot obtain the transcript of a witness's testimony until the witness testifies at trial. [*See* 18 U.S.C. §3500 (the Jencks Act), or the state equivalent. *But see* §12:120 (citing authority that entitles a witness to see a transcript of his testimony).]

The defense will never see the transcripts of the document returns, prosecutor's legal instructions, descriptions of the evidence, or the prosecutor's colloquies with the grand jurors.

Whether a contempt proceeding which relates to a grand jury should be open to the public depends on the circumstances of each case. "Logic may require that a portion of a contempt hearing transcript be accessible to the public where there has been a request to make the hearing public, where the witness does not object, and where the court is satisfied that opening the hearing will not thwart the grand jury's investigation or jeopardize other witnesses or evidence." [*Index Newspapers*, 766 F.3d at 1089.] But those portions of the contempt proceeding that disclose questions asked before the grand jury or other information regarding the grand jury's investigation may be sealed. [*Id.* at 1090.]

Whether an open contempt proceeding benefits your client is a case-specific determination. Your client might want to avoid the public notoriety of being called as a grand jury witness; if so, you can advance the presumption of grand jury secrecy to protect him. [*See Index Newspapers*, 766 F.3d at 1091 n.12 ("There may be circumstances where the disclosure of a witness's identity could compromise the grand jury investigation or put other witnesses in danger. In each case, a court must consider these risks and balance the interests of the government, the grand jury witness, and the public.").]

§12:03   Alternative Functions of Grand Juries

Grand juries operate in two different ways, depending on the jurisdiction and type of case:
• The Charging Grand Jury.
• The Investigating Grand Jury.

Charging Grand Juries

Where the defendant already has been arrested on a preliminary charging document, like a complaint, and the time is short before he must have a preliminary hearing or be released, the grand jury does little investigation and acts mainly to:
• Hear some brief testimony, usually hearsay from the arresting officer.
• Rubber-stamp the prosecutor's charging decision.
• Deprive your client of his statutory right to a preliminary hearing.

With such charging grand juries, there is little you can do unless your client wants to take the risk of testifying. [*See* §12:23.]

Investigating Grand Juries

Investigating grand juries handle more complex matters and follow a more circuitous course.

Such an investigation usually starts with subpoenas for documents. Over the next several months, the prosecutor will:
• First, call minor witnesses, or present their testimony through agents.
• Then proceed to immunized witnesses and cooperators.
• Circle back to determine if previously uncooperative witnesses are willing to testify truthfully now.
• Finish with an agent who summarizes the investigation and covers details that had been missed.

In a matter of any complexity, this process takes months or even years. The expiration of the grand jury's term does not end the investigation. Prosecutors can either extend the grand jury's term for several months or summarize the testimony for a new grand jury.

When it comes time to make a charging decision, the prosecutor will summarize the testimony and the important documents. Before the grand jury votes, the prosecutor briefly describes the legal elements of the charges and how the evidence satisfies each element. Then the prosecutor will ask the grand jury if they have any questions and leave for them an indictment that he has drafted.

The grand jury has no role in drafting the indictment. It merely votes up or down on the version presented by the prosecutor. A majority of those present suffices to return an indictment, and the defense never learns what the vote was.

§12:04   Grand Jury Reference Materials

When dealing with federal grand jury investigations, refer to the *Antitrust Division's Jury Manual*, available at www.usdoj.gov/atr/public/guidelines/4371.htm, and Part 9-11.000 of the *United States Attorney's Manual* (*USAM*).

The Department of Justice also published a *Federal Grand Jury Manual* in 1993, but it has not been updated. It is available for download at www.usdoj.gov/criminal/publicdocs/111prior/crm08.pdf.

Do not expect creative arguments in these publications, because they present the law in the light most favorable to the government. However, they illuminate the prosecutor's perception of the limits on his behavior.

For example, while there is no legal prohibition against calling one sibling to testify against another, the *USAM* prohibits this practice except in delineated circumstances:

> where (i) the witness and the relative participated in a common business enterprise and the testimony to be elicited relates to that enterprise or its activities; (ii) the testimony to be elicited relates to illegal conduct in which there is reason to believe that both the witness and the relative were active participants; or (iii) testimony to be elicited relates to a crime involving overriding prosecutorial concerns.

[*USAM* §§9-23.211.]

You cannot enforce these limitations in court, but you can confront a prosecutor, or his supervisors, with them in an effort to discourage the forbidden action.

There are also excellent treatises that present the law and practical advice from the defense perspective. [*See* Sara S. Beale, William C. Bryson, James E. Felman and Michael J. Elston, *Grand Jury Law and Practice* (2d ed. 2004) (covering state and federal law); The National Lawyers Guild's *Representation of Witnesses Before Federal Grand Juries* (4th ed. 2005).]

[§§12:05-12:09 Reserved]

II. REPRESENTING A CLIENT IN AN INVESTIGATION

A. General Points

§12:10 Three Categories: Target, Subject, Witness

Your first task when there is a grand jury investigation in which your client has been or may be subpoenaed is to ascertain your client's status. The prosecutor's estimation of your client's status will influence both your approach to the investigation and your client's level of anxiety.

In federal practice, the *United States Attorneys' Manual* establishes three categories: target, subject and witness.

A target is someone against whom the prosecutor intends to seek an indictment, a "putative defendant." [*See* USAM §§9-11.121.]

Witnesses generally are those have no culpability and face little risk of indictment.

Subjects fall in-between; they are "persons whose conduct is within the scope of the grand jury's investigation." [*USAM* §§9-11.121.] This means that the investigation may or may not disclose wrongdoing on their part, and the prosecutor has not decided whether to seek charges against that person.

Local prosecutors may not use the *USAM* definitions, but they categorize people in the same way:
- Those they seek to indict.
- Those who are innocent witnesses.
- Those about whom they have not decided and who could end up as defendants or as witnesses, depending not only on the depth of their involvement, the extent to which they profited and the deliberateness of their actions, but also on whether and to what degree they cooperate with the investigation of the more culpable targets.

Do not expect precision in the use of these definitions. Many prosecutors see only targets and witnesses. Others would call nearly everyone a subject, at least until the morning they seek an indictment. Some will not say.

Furthermore, a prosecutor's statement about your client's status does not guarantee that it will not change.

§12:11 Determining Your Client's Status

There is only one way to ascertain your client's status: ask the prosecutor. (His/her name will be at the bottom of any grand jury subpoena, or, if the agents left you or your client a business card, you can ask them for the prosecutor's name.)

Ask the agents first to see whether they have a different opinion. The prosecutor has the final say, but the agents may know more about the investigation at the time you ask. A different assessment from them may augur ill for your client.

Seek as much information as the prosecutor is willing to disclose about the offenses and transactions under investigation. Ask:
- Where your client fits in.
- What the prosecutor thinks your client can say as a cooperating witness.
- Who the targets are.
- How long before indictment will be sought.

Next, contact other attorneys you know who represent witnesses or subjects and see what they are willing to tell you about the investigation, what their clients are saying and what the prosecutor and agents have been saying and asking about your client.

Proceed cautiously, however, in organized crime, drug trafficking and violent crime investigations. Revealing that the prosecution seeks your client's testimony may put him/her at risk of harm.

[§§12:12-12:19 Reserved]

B. Targets

§12:20   The Target Letter

Department of Justice policy discourages subpoenaing grand jury targets to testify. [*See USAM* §§9-11.150.]

When a federal prosecutor does so, the prosecutor must accompany the subpoena with a "target letter" informing the witness that he is a target of the investigation and of the rights he has if he testifies. [*See USAM* Title 9, *Criminal Resource Manual* at 160.]

CAUTION:

Do not overestimate the importance of a target letter. Your client may be a clear target and never receive one.

Some prosecutors send them to all witnesses they subpoena. Others never send one because they never subpoena anyone they would consider a target.

Prosecutors use them mainly to encourage unrepresented targets to retain counsel and begin plea or cooperation discussions. For the most part, prosecutors do not expect targets to testify even if subpoenaed. A lawyer's representation that the target will invoke the privilege against self-incrimination usually is enough to earn discharge from a subpoena's obligations. [*See USAM* §§9-11.154 (where attorney advises prosecutor in writing that his client will invoke the privilege, prosecutor should discharge the witness).]

Likewise, receiving a subpoena without a target letter does not mean that your client is not or will not become a target. Things change, and prosecutors err. The failure to send a target letter or to advise a witness of his status and rights in the grand jury (that is, to invoke the privilege and to consult with counsel) does not prevent either an indictment or the use of the testimony against the witness-defendant at trial. [*United States v. Gomez*, 237 F.3d 238 (3d Cir. 2000). *But see* Wayne R. LaFave, Jerold H. Israel and Nancy J. King, *Criminal Procedure*, §8.10(d) at nn. 77-79, 92-94 (2005) (citing state statutes which create a right to warnings).]

Form:
•   **Form 12-1** Sample Target Letter

§12:21   Representing a Target

If you represent a target, your client should not testify before the grand jury without a grant of immunity, except in those rare circumstances when you believe that your client's testimony can convince the grand jury not to indict. [*See* §12:23.]

Your goals in the pre-indictment representation are to:
•   Convince the prosecutor that he/she does not have a winning case and should not seek an indictment. [*See* §12:31.]
•   Offer your client's cooperation and possible testimony against a more culpable individual in return for immunity or a plea to a less serious charge or a reduced sentence (an option only if there are more culpable individuals). [*See* §§12:52, 12:60, *et seq.*]
•   Negotiate a plea to a less serious charge.
•   Shadow the investigation to discover as much as you can about it and to prepare for defense of the eventual indictment. [*See* §§12:90, *et seq.*]

§12:22   The Target's Testimony in the Grand Jury

In most jurisdictions, a target has no right to testify. [*See*, Beale, *Grand Jury Law and Practice*, §4:19.]

However, some jurisdictions grant a defendant a statutory right to testify in the grand jury if he serves notice that he intends to do so at the time of his initial appearance on a felony complaint. [*See* NY Criminal Procedure Law §190.50(5).] And others encourage prosecutors ordinarily to grant a target's request. [*See USAM* §§9-11.152.]

Occasionally, targets or arrestees choose to testify, and some succeed in convincing a grand jury not to return a true bill. [*See* William Glaberson, "New Trend Before Grand Juries: Meet the Accused," *New York Times* (June 20, 2004) (14 percent of defendants testified before Brooklyn, New York, grand juries, and half succeeded in having the charges dismissed).]

§12:23   Deciding Whether to Allow a Target to Testify

Generally, a target should not testify. No targets testify in federal grand juries because the crimes are complex, the prosecutors prepared and the witness without counsel in the room. Remember, this testimony can and will be used against your client in anyway possible.

In deciding whether your client should testify consider the following factors:

The type of crime.

Testifying works best in simple cases, such as street crimes, that come down to a single issue your client can address, such as:

- Your client's knowledge or intent in a possession case.
- Who struck the first blow in an assault or homicide case.
- Whether a shooting was justified where your client was a police officer.
- Consent in a rape case.

If your client has a longstanding relationship with the alleged victim (*e.g.,* paramours in a rape case, an estranged spouse claiming spousal or child abuse, a neighbor or local merchant with whom your client has been feuding), your client can provide a context and an explanation of which the prosecutor will not.

The evidence contradicting your client's story.

The prosecutor will not tell you what other evidence exists, so you must investigate as much as you can by speaking to the witnesses and the police, if they will talk to you. You probably do not have any reports of any statements that your client made to the police yet, and clients seldom remember exactly what they told the police, so if your client made statements, hesitate to call him as a witness.

Your client should testify only if you can reconcile his story with the independent, unimpeachable evidence, such as the testimony of uninvolved bystanders and business records.

Whether anyone else can tell your client's story.

Testifying makes sense if your client can agree with nearly all the prosecution's significant evidence and can offer insight that no one else has into a single issue.

This usually means the client's own actions or state of mind. For example, if your client is arrested entering a courthouse or airport with a gun in his briefcase, he might be able to explain when he put it there (long ago, you hope) and how he forgot it was there.

Whether you can be present.

You should hesitate to permit your client to testify in those jurisdictions where you cannot be present in the grand jury room.

If you are allowed to be present, you can:

- Prevent the prosecutor from bullying your client.
- Consult with your client before answering to avoid misunderstandings.

[*See* §12:16.]

However, remember that if your client chooses to testify, then he is trying to persuade the jury, and their inherent skepticism will double if they see him confer with you frequently. Should everything go sour, you can advise your client to invoke the privilege or even to refuse to answer any further questions if you are present.

The extent to which prosecutors prepare for grand jury proceedings.

In many jurisdictions, prosecutors have little time to prepare cases before presenting them to the grand jury and less to conduct follow-up investigations. These are the best jurisdictions for a defendant to testify.

However, tread carefully where the prosecutor can devote time and resources to shooting down your client's testimony.

The law and custom on re-submitting cases to the grand jury.

The double jeopardy clause does not forbid a prosecutor from re-submitting a case to the grand jury and seeking an indictment even if the grand jury returns no true bill. [*See United States v. Williams*, 504 U.S. 36, 49 (1992); Beale, *Grand Jury Law and Practice*, §8:6.]

Some offices and jurisdictions require supervisory approval or leave of court to seek an indictment after dismissal. [*See* Beale.] Even where such leave is not required, the custom may be not to submit the case a second time. After all, if the prosecutor could not convince a grand jury to indict, his chances of success with the trial jury are slim.

Prosecutors are more likely to try again if the charge is very serious (*e.g.,* murders, rapes, and serious assaults). Also, if they discover strong evidence contradicting your client, they probably will return to the grand jury with a vengeance, with dire results for your client.

The urgency with which your client must avoid an indictment.

Being indicted serves no defendant well. However, some more than others can ill afford to postpone the fight until trial. It may be more worthwhile for your client to testify if:
- He will not be able to make bail should he be indicted and would lose a job during his incarceration
- He is awaiting sentencing for another offense.

[§§12:24-12:29 Reserved]

C. Subjects

§12:30 Representing a Subject

Subjects are such people as:
- Billing clerks in a doctor's office in a billing fraud investigation.
- The siblings, parents, children or significant others of bank robbers or drug traffickers who received and spent some of the ill-gotten gain.

Representing the subject pre-indictment carries great responsibility because it is during this phase that your client's fate will be decided.

The target's attorney views this phase as a time to marshal resources and prepare for the real fight, which starts when charges are filed. The witness runs little risk unless his duplicity earns him an indictment. In contrast, at the end of this stage, the subject will either be a defendant, facing loss of liberty, reputation and much of his assets, or a bystander to someone else's misery.

Your main task here is to convince the prosecutor that your client should not be charged.

CAUTION:

Your argument is to the prosecutor, not to the grand jury. Do not mistake the grand jury for a trial jury. You cannot expect to go over the prosecutor's head and appeal to the grand jury as an independent decision-maker that might disagree with the prosecutor. Grand juries tend to err on the side of indicting, believing that the trial jury will catch and acquit any unfounded prosecutions under the reasonable doubt standard.

In contrast, prosecutors are held to a higher standard in making a charging decision. They should not seek charges unless they believe that the defendant's guilt can be proven beyond a reasonable doubt by admissible evidence. [*See* ABA Standards for the Prosecution Function, Standard 3-3.9(b); *U.S. Attorneys' Manual*, §§9-27.220 ("The attorney for the government should commence or recommend Federal prosecution if he/she believes that the person's conduct constitutes a Federal offense and that the admissible evidence will probably be sufficient to obtain and sustain a conviction").]

§12:31 Four Principal Strategies

There are four principal strategies to consider when representing a subject:

Sit tight and wait.

Frustrating as it may be, sometimes the best approach is to hunker down and silence your client so that he does not add to the incriminating evidence.

This is advisable where your investigation and discussions with the prosecutor convince you that the prosecutor is slightly short of the evidence needed to indict your client. You do not want to be the one to carry your client across the line to indictment.

Present evidence other than your client's statements.

Your investigation may uncover evidence that exonerates your client.

Share it with the prosecutor only if your trust in the evidence and the prosecutor are such that the evidence will stand up, and the prosecutor will listen to it. An example might be an unassailable alibi (*e.g.,* records show that your client was in prison at the time of the robbery).

Argue that the law and policy do not support an indictment.

You should argue the law only if the prosecutor cannot find evidence that will correct the legal insufficiency. Your argument might be a combination of law, policy and sympathy. For example, you might say that this is a close case under the law, and with your sympathy-eliciting problems that the jury will hear, this is not a case to hazard a stretch in the law.

Such arguments work best when grounded in the particular office's established policies, not in esoteric arguments about what is just. For example:

- Many offices routinely decline to prosecute doctors' billing clerks or business people's secretaries, even if they knowingly participated in the fraud, if they cooperate against their bosses.
- Some offices do not prosecute drug amounts or fraud or theft losses below a particular amount, especially, in the case of larcenies, if the client makes restitution.
- Federal prosecutors frequently will decline to prosecute the offense of structuring (*i.e.,* dividing cash deposits or withdrawals so that they are below $10,000 each in an effort to evade the currency transaction reporting requirements) if the potential defendant otherwise has no criminal record and the money came from a legal source and was not used to fund criminal activity.

Offer to cooperate in the investigation.

Your client's willingness to waive to some extent the Fifth Amendment privilege and to submit to an interview in which he describes his own actions truthfully and provides substantial evidence against more culpable targets and subjects weigh heavily in a prosecutor's decision to forego indictment of your subject-client. [*See, e.g.,* USAM 9-27.230 (willingness to cooperate is an important factor in charging decision) (available at www.usdoj.gov).]

The prosecutor eventually may immunize your client before grand jury or trial testimony, but will not do so until he has a chance to hear and check your client's story.

Usually, the prosecutor will offer some limited immunity, under what is called a proffer or "queen for a day" agreement, but this immunity is of limited value. [*See* §12:61.]

Some lawyers counsel that a client should never speak to a prosecutor without full immunity, but such advice may deprive your client of the one chance, albeit risky, to head off an indictment.

You should hazard this chance only after thoroughly testing your client's story through investigation and office cross-examination and if the prosecutor is one who can be trusted to follow through on a promise that full immunity or a lenient plea is possible with truthful cooperation.

Form:
- **Form 12-2** Immunity Request Form

[§§12:32-12:39 Reserved]

D. Witnesses

§12:40   Representing a Witness

Witnesses are those whom have evidence but no exposure to prosecution. An example is the teller who was held up in a bank robbery.

Your goal in representing witnesses is to make sure they stay witnesses and nothing more.

Usually, this simply means ensuring that your client tells the truth. However, that task may have its complications. For example:

- The client may have sympathies or a relationship with the target and might try to color his testimony to help the target.
- The witness might have his own scandal that he wishes to hide, but that might become relevant to the grand jury's investigation (*e.g.,* drug addiction, or an adulterous affair with an associate of the target).

§12:41   Demanding Immunity

One challenge in representing the witness is deciding whether to demand immunity.

If the prosecutor has told you that your client is purely a witness with no criminal exposure, a demand for immunity might pique the prosecutor's curiosity and cause the investigation to swing to your client's activities. The prosecutor might deny your immunity request and elevate your client's status to that of a subject.

Immunity comes with costs. Only those who can reasonably fear that the answer to a question might incriminate them can stand on the privilege and receive a grant of immunity. The innocent may be entitled to claim the privilege in some circumstances. [*See Ohio v. Reiner*, 532 U.S. 17 (2001) (babysitter who claimed innocence could claim privilege where she spent substantial time alone with child before his death).] Nevertheless, invoking the privilege and receiving immunity signals that your client did something wrong. Despite a grand jury's shroud of secrecy, the public often learns who testified and who was immunized, especially if charges and a trial ensue. Being immunized might bring some infamy to your client that he needs to avoid, depending on his profession and standing in the community.

In jurisdictions such as the federal courts where indictments can rest solely or principally on hearsay, prosecutors frequently use hearsay in the grand jury. Rather than call a pure witness and create a record that can be used to cross-examine the witness at trial, the prosecutor will have an agent summarize an interview in the grand jury.

If the prosecutor insists on having your client-witness testify in such a jurisdiction, it is fair to inquire why. Such insistence may indicate that the prosecutor does not trust your client to stick to the same version of events as he told in an interview when called at trial. Ask if this is so, and why. Do not hesitate to ask if your client is in some kind of trouble. The victim may turn out to have been an insider who set up the theft; the financial institution might be suspected of knowingly laundering the crime's proceeds.

Because it is unusual for a prosecutor to have such a witness testify in person, consider invoking the privilege and insisting on a grant of immunity. Having first-hand knowledge about the events under investigation may mean that your client participated in those events in some way. Even admitting to being at the scene of a crime and witnessing it could prove incriminating. [*See Reiner, supra.*]

§12:42   Representing Multiple Witnesses

There is no prohibition against representing multiple witnesses so long as none of them are targets of the investigation, none incriminates another, and no fatal inconsistencies (as opposed to explicable discrepancies and differences of memory) appear in their testimony. [*See In re Philadelphia County Investigating Grand Jury*, 529 Pa. 471, 605 A.2d 318 (1992) (error to disqualify lawyer representing multiple witnesses unless each is a potential target and the testimony of one might incriminate another); *In re Abrams*, 62 N.Y.2d 183, 465 N.E.2d 1, 476 N.Y.S.2d 494 (1984) (attorney could not be prevented from representing multiple grand jury witnesses on the grounds that he was asserting the privilege on behalf of all and insisting on immunity for each).]

Such multiple representation saves money if a third party, such as an employer, is paying for the representation, and it aids each witness by having his testimony prepared and groomed by an attorney who knows what the other witnesses are saying.

Prosecutors' reactions will vary. They too may benefit from having a single lawyer hear and reconcile the witnesses' stories before the versions reach the government's and grand jury's ears. Should the government hear the discrepancies before they are reconciled, the prosecutor will have to disclose the inconsistencies as *Brady* material. You do not have such an obligation.

CAUTION:

Prosecutors sometimes fear that a single attorney may rally the witnesses to a single version of events that eliminates discrepancies, particularly where the witnesses sympathize with the target. Therefore, be especially careful to question your clients on what they may have told investigators before your representation began. A sudden consistency among what the investigators knew to be previously conflicting accounts may focus suspicion on you as well as on your clients.

Remember that you have a separate obligation of loyalty and confidentiality to each client witness. You can use knowledge gained from other clients to steer your questioning of another, but do not reveal the source of the knowledge.

[§§12:43-12:49 Reserved]

III. DEALING WITH A SUBPOENA

A. Subpoena for Testimony

1. General Points

§12:50   Accept Service and Request an Informal Interview

If you know the subpoena is coming, contact the prosecutor and offer to accept service on your client's behalf both to save your client the embarrassment of having officers show up at his home or place of business and to prevent him from volunteering statements to the officers.

Unless you are certain that your client will invoke the Fifth Amendment in response to all questions, contact the prosecutor and explore whether submission to an interview at a mutually convenient time will satisfy the subpoena. Grand jury appearances are inconvenient. Often your client must wait for considerable periods of time while the grand jury and prosecutor attend to other matters. In most jurisdictions, you cannot be present in the grand jury room while your client testifies.

An informal interview has many advantages:
* You will witness what is asked and can prevent misunderstandings and badgering of your client.
* Even if your client must testify later, the interview will preview the areas of inquiry and the prosecutor's attitude toward your client.

After interviewing your client thoroughly, investigating to the extent you can, and discussing the matter with the prosecutor, unless you are satisfied that your client is a pure witness with no criminal exposure, you should seek some form of immunity to protect your client even in the interview. [*See* §12:52.]

After the interview, ask the prosecutor his opinion of your client's honesty.

§12:51   Office Subpoenas

Agreeing to an interview is not the same as an "office" subpoena.

Absent specific statutory authorization, a prosecutor cannot subpoena a witness to his office for an interview, subpoena the production of documents, or subpoena handwriting and hair samples and the like. [*See United States v. Di Gilio*, 538 F.2d 972, 985 (3d Cir. 1976); *United States v. Swanson*, 155 F. Supp. 2d 992, 1001 (C.D. Ill. 2001) (suppressing hair and saliva samples obtained by "office" subpoena); *People v. Natal*, 75 N.Y. 2d 379, 553 N.Y.S. 2d 650, 553 N.E. 2d 239 (1990) (prosecutor could not issue subpoena to jail ordering jail to produce defendant's clothing to his office).]

If your client receives an office subpoena, call the prosecutor and ask what he wants from your client. Explain, politely, that you will comply with a request for an interview when you and your client are ready.

If the prosecutor claims he will enforce the subpoena, tell him that you know the subpoena is unenforceable as issued and that you will move to quash it.

§12:52   Immunity

The prosecutor can make your client talk by giving him immunity co-extensive with the Fifth Amendment privilege.

Immunity against use of your client's statements ("use immunity") suffices. [*See United States v. Hubbell*, 530 U.S. 27, 38 (2000).] However, some jurisdictions require so-called transactional immunity, which prohibits prosecution of the witness for any transaction about which the witness testifies. [*See* Beale, *Grand Jury Law and Practice*, §7:8.]

Use immunity prohibits use of the testimony to derive investigative leads against your client or for cross-examination at any prosecution other than a perjury trial. [*New Jersey v. Portash*, 440 U.S. 450 (1979).] A refusal to testify after being immunized would warrant prosecution and incarceration for both civil and criminal contempt.

"Letter," or informal immunity, falls short of the constitutional requirement because it does not protect your client against use of statements by other jurisdictions. Where that is not a concern, letter immunity may be sufficient.

No form of immunity protects your client against prosecution for perjury should his grand jury testimony prove intentionally false, and in that prosecution his testimony is admissible. [*United States v. Apfelbaum*, 445 U.S. 115 (1980).]

Forms:
* **Form 12-2** Immunity Request Form

- **Form 12-3** Motion for Order Granting Immunity
- **Form 12-4** Court Order of Use Immunity
- **Form 12-5** Letter Immunity

§12:53　　Subsequent Prosecution of the Immunized Witness

Occasionally, prosecutors try to charge witnesses who testified under grants of immunity.

Most such prosecutions are brought under the perjury statutes because the grant of immunity does not forbid perjury prosecutions.

However, if a prosecutor charges a substantive violation of law related to the matter in which the client testified, you should demand a *Kastigar* hearing. [*See Kastigar v. United States*, 406 U.S. 441 (1972).]

A *Kastigar* hearing is one in which the prosecution must prove that no part of its case is derived from the immunized testimony. This is a significant obstacle because the prohibition against derivative use forbids "any use, direct or indirect" of the immunized testimony. [*United States v. Poindexter*, 951 F.2d 369, 373 (D.C. Cir. 1991) (*quoting United States v. North*, 910 F.2d 843, 860-61 (D.C. Cir. 1990)).]

Forbidden uses include exposing a witness in any way to the immunized testimony, such as:
- Pre-trial preparation.
- Deriving investigative leads from the testimony.
- Planning trial strategy around the testimony.

[*See generally* Beale, *Grand Jury Law and Practice*, §7:20; *United States v. Poindexter*, 951 F.2d 369 (D.C. Cir. 1991).]

[§§12:54-12:59 Reserved]

2.　Interview Protections

§12:60　　General Points

Sometimes prosecutors are uncertain about how to deal with an individual. This is especially true in dealing with subjects.

The prosecutor does not want to grant immunity, because a later investigation may indicate that the person had significant culpability. To decide how to proceed, the prosecutor may invite the individual to be interviewed.

Some lawyers counsel never to submit to an interview without either:
- A formal grant of immunity.
- "Letter" immunity (that is nearly as comprehensive).

Safe as this strategy may seem, it holds its own risk because the prosecutor may put your client aside for now and start asking other witnesses about him. Those witnesses may see their salvation in implicating your client. Thus, your client's uncooperativeness could lead the prosecutor to target him.

The most common arrangements to provide some limited protection in an interview are:
- The "Queen for a Day" Agreement. [*See* §12:61.]
- Plea Negotiation Immunity. [*See* §12:62.]
- Attorney Proffers. [*See* §12:63.]

Forms:
- **Form 12-4** Court Order of Use Immunity
- **Form 12-5** Letter Immunity

§12:61　　The "Queen for a Day" Agreement

This agreement (also known as a "proffer" agreement) is named after a long forgotten television show in which a member of the audience would be crowned queen and showered with gifts and service.

The agreement provides very limited protection. It limits the government only to foregoing use of the defendant's statements in its direct case at trial.

However, the government can use the statements to point it toward independent evidence of the defendant's wrongdoing, for cross-examination, and, most disturbingly, to rebut any inconsistent position the defendant takes at trial. [*See United States v. Barrow*, 400 F.3d 109 (2d Cir. 2005) (statements admitted to rebut defense attorney's opening argument and cross-examination questions raising the defense of mistaken identification even where he did not offer any evidence in support of that defense); *United States v. Krilich*, 159 F.3d 1020, 1024-25 (7th Cir. 1998) (prosecution could use the statements to respond to inferences the defense raised in cross-examination of a prosecution witness, but rebuttal right is not triggered by merely putting on a reasonable doubt defense).]

Some lower courts have held that the rebuttal provisions of the standard proffer agreement are coercive and refused to enforce them. [*See United States v. Duffy*, 133 F.Supp.2d 213 (E.D.N.Y. 2001).] However, most appellate courts have rejected that view, taking the approach that a proffer agreement is a binding agreement to waive the protections of FRE 410. [*See United States v. Velez*, 354 F.3d 190 (2d Cir. 2004); *United States v. Krilich*, 159 F.3d 1020 (7th Cir. 1998). For an explanation of Rule 410, *see* §12:62.]

Form:
- **Form 12-6** "Queen for a Day" Agreement

§12:62   Plea Negotiation Immunity

Rule 410 of the Federal Rules of Evidence and its state law equivalents forbid use against the defendant of statements made during the course of plea negotiations. These rules apply only to statements to an attorney for the government, and not to statements to agents and officers without any prosecutor being present.

This protection goes further than a Queen for a Day Agreement because it protects the defendant against use of the statements on cross-examination or rebuttal. [*United States v. Mezzanatto*, 513 U.S. 196 (1995) (noting that under FRE 410, statements cannot be used on cross or in rebuttal).]

However, the government can make derivative use of the statements; That is, it can investigate leads obtained from the defendant and use the evidence discovered in that investigation against defendant. [*See United States v. Fronk*, 173 F.R.D. 59 (W.D.N.Y. 1997); *United States v. Stein*, 2005 U.S. Dist. LEXIS 11141, Cr. No. 04-269-9 (E.D. Pa. June 8, 2005).]

Furthermore, relying on Rule 410 to shield a subject's statements during a proffer carries a substantial risk. The rule applies only where the interviewee has a subjective intent to engage in plea negotiations, and the belief that the discussion was part of plea negotiations is reasonable under the circumstances. [*United States v. Stein.*]

Some courts have held that a plea must be explicitly discussed for the discussion to fall within the rule. [*See United States v. Morgan*, 91 F.3d 1193, 1195-96 (8th Cir. 1996); *United States v. Hare*, 49 F.3d 447, 450-51 (8th Cir. 1995); *United States v. Penta*, 898 F.2d 815, 817-18 (1st Cir. 1990); *but see United States v. Serna*, 799 F.2d 842, 848 (2d Cir. 1986) (no explicit discussion of a plea required); *Fronk*, 173 F.R.D. at 68-69 (same); *United States v. Ross*, 588 F.Supp.2d 777 (E.D. Mich. 2008) (rejects government's attempt to distinguish between meeting to explore whether defendant had enough information to interest government in starting plea discussions and actual plea discussions; rule applies even when AUSA leaves before interview starts).]

If your client is a subject, not a target, and your objective is to avoid any charges, rather than to negotiate a plea to lesser charge, the rule may not apply. [*See United States v. Cunningham*, 723 F.2d 217, 228 (2d Cir. 1983) (Rule inapplicable because defendant had stipulated that anything he said could be used against him; however, court also stated that "These stipulations confirm that the interview was not a plea bargaining conference but an effort by him to convince the government that he was not guilty of any crime. The rules invoked by him are inapplicable to such an interview."); *Stein* (rule applied where defendant had been informed that he was a target, though not the primary one, of a drug trafficking investigation).]

It helps to have the prosecutor's agreement that Rule 410 applies in order to prevent the government from saying otherwise later, but it is not necessary for the rule to apply. [*See Stein.*]

§12:63   Attorney Proffers

You can attempt to obtain immunity by giving an attorney proffer, rather than one from your client (the Queen for a Day Agreement).

Many prosecutors will insist that you give a proffer in writing before they decide on a grant of immunity.

As your client's agent, your statements are attributable to your client. [*See* FRE 801(a)(1)(E).]

Thus, making an attorney proffer could put you in the miserable position of being a prosecution witness at trial. Therefore, it is imperative that you claim that the statement is protected by FRE 410 or that the statement is hypothetical or made "without prejudice," and, if you can, obtain the prosecutor's agreement to the rule's applicability. Prosecutors seldom will agree in writing; your best result is to have an oral agreement that you then confirm in a letter.

Of course, even the most scrupulous of lawyers make mistakes in describing what their clients might know, and prosecutors realize that. Therefore, they often will seek to reinforce the certainty of your client's position on critical issues by questioning you repeatedly on those points.

Form:
•   **Form 12-7** Proffer Letter

[§§12:64-12:69 Reserved]

B.   Document Production

1.   The Fifth Amendment Privilege

§12:70   General Points

The application of the Fifth Amendment privilege to document subpoenas can be complex, but a few basic rules have emerged:
•   Individuals have a Fifth Amendment privilege.
•   Organizations, such as corporations (even closely held corporations with but a single shareholder), unincorporated associations, partnerships and labor unions, do not. [*See Braswell v. United States*, 487 U.S. 99 (1988); *but see Bellis v. United States*, 417 U.S. 85, 87-88 (1974) (Fifth Amendment privilege does protect a sole proprietorship).]

§12:71   Individuals

The act of selecting and producing documents has testimonial aspects because it communicates that the recipient possesses or has control of the documents, that the documents are authentic, and that the documents produced meet the subpoena's descriptions. [*Fisher*, 425 U.S. at 410; *United States v. Hubbell*, 530 U.S. 27 (2000).]

Therefore, an individual has a right to claim the Fifth Amendment privilege and refuse to produce documents unless he receives "act of production" immunity.

Thus, if your client receives a document subpoena in his individual capacity, he can assert the Fifth Amendment privilege. To overcome the privilege, the government must grant act of production immunity.

If your client must testify to authenticate the documents (which usually is not the case), obtain act of production immunity (unless he is a pure witness with no risk of self-incrimination) and insist that he leave the grand jury room and consult with you after each question so that the prosecutor does not go any farther than questions to authenticate the documents. Instruct your client to assert the Fifth Amendment privilege to any questions beyond the authenticating ones covered by the act of production immunity.

Occasionally, the prosecution cannot access encrypted or password-protected computer hard drives and files and may subpoena your client to provide the password or decrypt the files. Since the act of providing the password or decrypting the files requires the witness to make use of his mind's contents, it is a testimonial act, and the Fifth Amendment applies. Therefore, the prosecution must choose either to immunize the witness or forego the decryption. [*In re Grand Jury Subpoena Duces Tecum Dated March 25, 2011*, 670 F.3d 1335 (11th Cir. 2012).]; *United States v. Kirschner*, 823 F. Supp. 2d 665, 669 (E.D. Mich. 2010) (providing the password is testimonial and protected by the Fifth Amendment); *but see State v. Stahl*, No. 2D14-4283, 2016 WL 7118574 (Fl. Ct. App. Dec. 7, 2016) (providing password not testimonial; therefore, the Fifth Amendment does not protect it); *Commonwealth v. Baust*, 89 Va. Cir. 267 (Va. Cir. Ct. 2014) (providing a password is a testimonial act, but applying a fingerprint to unlock a smartphone is not).]

Form:
•   **Form 12-8** Act of Production Immunity Letter

§12:72   Organizations

When presented with a document subpoena, an entity, even it has but a single shareholder and employee who are the target of the investigation, must designate someone to produce the documents. [*See In re Grand Jury Empaneled on May 9, 2014*, 786 F.3d 255, 262 (3d Cir. 2015) (surveying federal courts of appeals, "all of which have agreed that a corporate custodian may not refuse to comply with a subpoena on Fifth Amendment grounds merely because he or she is also that corporation's sole owner and employee."); *In re Grand Jury*, 836 F.2d 150 (3d Cir. 1987) (small size of the corporation does not absolve it from duty to designate a corporate representative and respond).]

The record custodian's act of producing responsive documents cannot be used against him. [*See United States v. Dean*, 989 F.2d 1205, 1208 & n.3 (D.C. Cir. 1993) ("in a criminal prosecution against the custodian, the Government may not introduce into evidence before the jury the fact that the subpoena was served upon and the corporation's documents were delivered by one particular individual, the custodian." Relies upon *Braswell v. United States*, 487 U.S. 99, 117-18 (1988).).]

In effect, *Braswell* creates a form of self-executing immunity for an entity's custodian's act of production. [*See generally* Sara Sun Beale & James E. Felman, "The Fifth Amendment and the Grand Jury," 22 *Criminal Justice* 4, 7 (Spring 2007) (thorough explanation of self-incrimination issues and immunity issues that may arise with documentary and testimonial subpoenas).]

The Fifth Amendment privilege does not shield the *contents* of voluntarily created business records and most personal records. [*Braswell*, 487 U.S. at 102 ("There is no question but that the contents of subpoenaed business records are not privileged"). *See* Beale, *Grand Jury Law and Practice*, §6:14.]

If your client's Company receives a document subpoena, you must instruct that your client cannot be involved in searching for and selecting the documents to respond to the subpoena. If the entity has no other employees, you and your client must designate some outside person to be the document custodian and to search for the documents. The prosecutor can demand that the custodian testify not only to authenticate the documents, but to describe his efforts to find and select documents. You do not want that testimony to describe conversations with your client.

Furthermore, you do not want to be the custodian or to select the documents. You should review them, but do not participate in the initial search and selection.

[§§12:73-12:79 Reserved]

2. Complying With the Document Subpoena

§12:80   General Points

A grand jury subpoena should not be treated like a civil discovery request.

In civil practice, you generally have two chances to comply with a document request. Sanctions can be imposed only after a motion to compel has been filed.

In contrast, a subpoena is considered a court order, and lawyers go to prison for contempt for failing to produce documents in response to a subpoena, without a second chance to comply. [*See Nilva v. United States*, 352 U.S. 385 (1957) (upholding conviction and sentence of lawyer to one year and a day when he failed to produce documents in response to subpoena).]

Once you learn that there is a grand jury investigation and that your client's documents are likely to be subpoenaed, instruct your client not to destroy any of the documents that may be subpoenaed. Destruction of documents in anticipation of a subpoena constitutes criminal obstruction of justice. [*United States v. Gravely*, 840 F.2d 1156, 1160 (4th Cir. 1988) (upholding conviction for obstruction of justice when documents destroyed eight months before subpoena issued for them; "The documents do not have to be under subpoena, it is sufficient if the defendant is aware that the grand jury will likely seek the documents in its investigation.").]

This means that if you identify documents or classes of documents likely to be subpoenaed, you should instruct your client to preserve those documents despite a regular document destruction policy. After the fact, you can defend an obstruction prosecution on the grounds that the destruction occurred pursuant to such a policy, not from an intent to obstruct justice. [*See Arthur Andersen LLP v. United States*, 125 S.Ct. 2129, 2135 (2005) (although the Court expressed reservations about the merits of the prosecution because the document destruction may have resulted from an established policy, the Court reversed for error in the jury instructions, thus leaving open the possibility that a properly instructed jury could have convicted even where there was a regularly followed document destruction policy in place).]

However, if you can avoid it, you do not want to put your client in a position where all that stands between him and a felony conviction is the jury's willingness to believe his protestations of innocent intent. Clearly, the commencement of a grand jury proceeding is not the time to revive an otherwise dormant document destruction policy.

§12:81   Accept Service

If you know that the subpoena is coming, contact the prosecutor and accept service on behalf of your client.

Your client cannot evade service of a grand jury subpoena. Accepting service by facsimile or mail not only is a courtesy without cost, but it prevents the agents from visiting your client's home or business and possibly interviewing your client or his employees and friends when they serve the subpoena.

§12:82   Negotiate the Scope of the Response

Once you have the subpoena, negotiate the scope of the response.

You risk finding yourself indicted if you treat a subpoena like a civil discovery demand by interpreting the subpoena narrowly, giving clever and evasive responses to what you read as badly-drafted language, or filing objections at the last minute on the grounds of relevance and burden. With only rare exceptions, such as serious privilege issues, courts do not quash or limit subpoenas. [*See United States v. R. Enters., Inc.*, 498 U.S. 292 (1991) (lack of relevance or admissibility are not grounds to quash grand jury subpoena).]

If you file a motion to quash, you have only guaranteed that the prosecutor will extend no courtesies. Your only chance to narrow the subpoena is to negotiate with the prosecutor.

Prosecutors often ask for more than they really want. Frame the negotiation as an attempt to make the production quicker and more fruitful to the government while minimally disruptive to your client.

§12:83   Negotiate Production by Stages

Try to negotiate a "rolling" or staged production.

To make both the prosecutor's and your life easier, suggest that the prosecutor permit you to produce certain classes of documents, usually the ones most likely to yield probative evidence, first, while you guarantee, in writing, to maintain the integrity of the remainder should the prosecutor request them.

This approach has the added benefit of enabling you to monitor the progress of the investigation as the prosecutor requests additional classes of documents.

§12:84   Ask for More Time

The prosecutor probably will ask you to describe the location and volume of the responsive records and the steps that will be taken to produce them.

While subpoenas *duces tecum* command production to the grand jury at a specific time on a specific date, that never happens. Upon agreement with the prosecutor, you will deliver the documents to his office on a mutually convenient date.

Discuss with your client the individual who will search for the documents and authenticate them upon production. You, rather than your client, should communicate directly with that person because the prosecutor can question the person about your client's instructions (to establish obstruction of justice) or his comments about the documents (to discover your client's state of mind and perhaps admissions that he knew of the documents' existence).

§12:85   Track the Documents You Produce

The traditional method is to Bates-stamp the originals and keep a copy of the documents. Send a cover letter with the document production listing the Bates number range.

While stamping and copying may be costly, it is essential. Prosecutors often issue subpoenas to prove the non-existence of exculpatory documents. Many prosecutors do not track productions well. Furthermore, the grand jury's sessions may be separated by lengthy periods of inactivity, and a different prosecutor may assume the investigation.

Thus, you cannot trust that the government will recall the production, and you need your own, reliable and complete record of which documents were produced in response to which subpoena.

§12:86   Offer an Affidavit From the Custodian

Practice varies as to whether the prosecutor will require the testimony of a records custodian to authenticate the documents and to describe the efforts he made to comply with the subpoena.

Offer to avoid the calling of such a witness by providing a sworn affidavit from the custodian attesting to the documents' authenticity and describing, as briefly as you can get away with, the efforts to answer the subpoena.

Otherwise, once the grand jury room door closes behind the witness, he may find himself facing a much wider range of questions than he anticipated.

Form:
- **Form 12-9** Affidavit by Document Custodian

[§§12:87-12:89 Reserved]

IV. THE GRAND JURY PROCEEDING

A. Preparation

1. Investigating the Grand Jury

§12:90 General Points

If you represent a subject or target, you will want to find out as much as possible about the grand jury investigation for several reasons:
- If you are to have any chance of convincing the prosecutor not to indict, you need to know the strength of the prosecutor's evidence.
- Time for investigation after the indictment is returned will be short, so start now.
- Early interviews of witnesses may make the prosecutor less successful in poisoning their minds against your client and shaping their stories to his liking.

Depending on how aggressively you investigate, be prepared for a hostile reaction from the prosecutor. Some prosecutors confuse interviewing witnesses with tampering with them. Therefore, be scrupulous in emphasizing to all witnesses that you want only the truth and in avoiding any mention of benefits to be gained or harms to be avoided by cooperating with your investigation. Phrase your introduction in terms like this:

> The prosecutor has made some serious allegations against our client. To decide how to defend these charges, we have to know what we are facing. We don't want to be misled by rumors and suspicions; we're only looking to find out the truth.

If you can afford it, you should have an investigator speak to the witnesses, or at least have an associate or clerk with you to witness the interview, both to counter any claims of misconduct and to refute the witness should he change his story to harm your client.

§12:91 *Gelbard* Motions

The initiation of a grand jury investigation may enable you to discover whether there has been any wiretapping of your client or a witness.

A witness may refuse to answer questions or produce documents in response to a grand jury subpoena that derives from illegal electronic surveillance. [*Gelbard v. United States,* 408 U.S. 41 (1972); 18 U.S.C. §2515.]

To enforce the holding in *Gelbard*, courts have imposed explicit disclosure obligations on prosecutors:

> When a grand jury witness raises the issue of possible electronic surveillance as the source of a subpoena or questions, the government is bound to affirm or deny the occurrence of such surveillance. An insufficient denial is just cause for refusing to answer questions or produce subpoenaed records.

[*In re Freedman,* 529 F.2d 543, 549 (3d Cir. 1976).]

Upon a grand jury witness's request, the government must disclose the existence of any electronic surveillance, even if legal, and identify the law enforcement agencies contacted to help furnish the response. [*In re Grand Jury*

Matter, 683 F.2d 66, 68 n.2 (3d Cir. 1982) (holding that an *in camera ex parte* response to the Court cannot substitute for an affidavit provided to the witness); 18 U.S.C. §3504.]

Your motion need not be sworn, but courts are divided on how much certainty and detail the motion must contain. [*See United States v. Rubin,* 559 F.2d 975 (5th Cir. 1977) (motion need not be sworn, but it must affirmatively state that there has been illegal electronic surveillance, not that there "may" have been nor that there is "reason to believe" that such occurred); *In re Grand Jury Proceedings,* 773 F.2d 1071, 1072 (9th Cir. 1985) (detail demanded of Government's response varies with the motion's specificity); *see generally* "What Claims Are Sufficient to Require Government, Pursuant to 18 U.S.C.A. §3504, to Affirm or Deny Use of Unlawful Electronic Surveillance," 70 A.L.R. Fed. 67.]

Form:
*   **Form 12-10** *Gelbard* Motion

§12:92   Attempts to Silence Witnesses

Prosecutors and agents often tell witnesses that they cannot disclose the fact that they have received a subpoena, nor can they tell anyone what they produced or what they said in response to a grand jury subpoena.

Often, agents and prosecutors include a legend on the subpoena that, while prefatory, sounds forbidding.

These restrictions generally are improper unless you are in a jurisdiction where a statute specifically imposes an obligation of secrecy on witnesses. [*See* Beale, *Grand Jury Law and Practice,* §5:5 n. 22 (nine states do; Beale counts ten, but errs in counting New York). *See* NY Crim. Pro. Law §190.25(4) (witness can disclose his own testimony).]

Do not heed them if you represent a witness, and when you speak to witnesses, assure them that such restrictions do not have legal force.

Rule 6(e)(2)(A) of the Federal Rules of Criminal Procedure states, "No obligation of secrecy may be imposed on any person except in accordance with Rule 6(e)(2)(B)." The Advisory Committee Notes explain, "This rule does not impose any obligation of secrecy on witnesses." [*See United States v. Sells Engineering, Inc.,* 463 U.S. 418, 425 (1983) ("witnesses are not under the prohibition [of grand jury secrecy] unless they also happen to fit into one of the enumerated classes [in Rule 6(e)]) (*dictum*).]

When Congress chose to prohibit disclosure by a witness, it enacted statutes specifically prohibiting disclosure, such as the statutes forbidding banks from disclosing that they have received subpoenas in money-laundering investigations. [*See* 12 USC §3420(b); 18 U.S.C. §1510(b).]

Witnesses also have a First Amendment right to speak. [*Butterworth v. Smith,* 494 U.S. 624 (1990).] The witness in *Butterworth* was a newspaper reporter who sued in federal court to enjoin enforcement of a state statute that would prevent him from publishing information regarding his grand jury testimony. The Court held that the First Amendment prohibited restrictions on witness disclosure of what happened in the grand jury, at least after the grand jury dissolved. [*But see Hoffmann-Pugh v. Keenan,* 338 F.3d 1136, 1140 (10th Cir. 2003) (upholding against First Amendment challenge Colorado rule which forbade witness from disclosing content of her testimony, but allowed her to comment on her independent knowledge of the underlying facts and also permitted her to ask for leave to disclose).]

Several courts have held that prosecutors may not restrict a witness's ability to talk. [*In re Grand Jury Proceedings,* 814 F.2d 61 (1st Cir. 1987) (prosecutor's letter, which apparently is used throughout the country, directing witness not to disclose existence of subpoena *duces tecum* for 90 days, was misconduct, and prosecutor ordered to send letter correcting this); *United States v. Radetsky,* 535 F.2d 556, 569-70 (10th Cir. 1976) (prosecutor's admonition to grand jury witnesses that they could not disclose their testimony was improper, but no prejudice was shown because defendant obtained grand jury transcripts prior to trial testimony). *See also* Rules of Professional Conduct 3.4(d); *United States v. Leung,* 351 F.Supp.2d 992 (C.D. Cal. 2005) (dismissing indictment where prosecution's plea agreements with cooperating witnesses forbade them from speaking to the defense).]

A court may order nondisclosure for specific reasons. The power to do so where specific articulable facts justify a nondisclosure order implies that without such a showing and court order, witnesses should be free to disclose. Justification for nondisclosure has been found in the following situation:
*   *In re Grand Jury Subpoena Duces Tecum,* 797 F.2d 676, 679-80 (8th Cir. 1986) (court order prohibiting bank from informing labor racketeer target of subpoena for 90 days upheld because order for appropriate time period and target might have escaped, threatened jurors, or influenced witnesses if aware of investigation).
*   *In re Subpoena to Testify Before Grand Jury Directed to Custodian of Records,* 864 F.2d 1559, 1563-64 (11th Cir. 1989) (closure order prohibiting witnesses from disclosing materials prepared for, or testimony given in, grand jury proceedings upheld because it is within district court's authority to protect integrity of grand jury proceedings).

If you learn that witnesses hesitate to talk to you because of a prosecutor's admonitions:
- Request by letter that the prosecutor authorize you to send a letter to the witness explaining that he is free to speak to the defense. You prefer that the letter come from you, because rest assured that should the prosecutor or agent speak to the witness, they will explain the right to speak briefly and then explain to the witness at great length that he also can choose not to speak to you.

If the prosecutor refuses, file a motion requesting that the court order the prosecutor to send the letter. [*See In re Grand Jury*, 814 F.2d 61 (ordering such a remedy).]

Forms:
- **Form 12-11** Sample Subpoena Advising Witness Not to Speak With the Defense
- **Form 12-12** Letter Informing Grand Jury Witness of Ability to Speak With the Defense

[§§12:93-12:99 Reserved]

2. Preparing Your Client

§12:100 Your Role

In 20 states, lawyers may accompany their clients during grand jury testimony. [*See* Beale, *Grand Jury Law and Practice*, §6:27.]

Nonetheless, nearly all those states prohibit counsel from objecting, arguing, questioning witnesses or in any way participating except to advise their clients. [*E.g.*, NY Crim. Pr. L., §190.52(2); Minn. R. Crim. P. 18.04; 42 Pa.C.S.A. §4549(c)(3).] In these states, if there is an objection to be made or a need to ask that a question be clarified, you must whisper the instructions to your client and have him make the objection or request the clarification.

Some courts even attempt to restrict counsel's advice to whether the client should invoke the privilege, although that limitation is difficult to enforce. After all, your discussions with your client are confidential.

In any jurisdiction, do not hesitate to interrupt if the prosecutor becomes abusive.

Those jurisdictions that consign counsel to a post outside the grand jury still permit the witness, by rule or custom, to leave after a question and consult with counsel before answering. [*See In re Lowry*, 713 F.2d 616, 618 n. 4 (11th Cir. 1983) ("normal practice" to permit non-immunized witness to consult).]

Federal prosecutors are instructed to inform witnesses of this right. [*See* USAM §§9-11.260(D).] Nonetheless, some courts have upheld restrictions on how often and to what extent a witness may consult his lawyer on the grounds that too frequent consultation delays and disrupts the grand jury's proceedings. [*See In re Lowry*, 713 F.2d at 617-18; *but see United States v. Mandujano*, 425 U.S. 564, 606-07 n. 23 (1976) (Brennan, J., concurring) (consultation at will cannot be impermissible delay; collecting cases).]

Prepare your client thoroughly so that he can save the opportunity to consult for:
- Those questions you and he have decided in advance are sensitive.
- Unexpected questions.

§12:101 Explaining the Process to Your Client

Your client's preparation to testify must include a description of what happens inside the grand jury room, especially in a jurisdiction that forbids an attorney's attendance.

The prosecutor will fetch your client from an anteroom right outside the grand jury room. The witness walks to the front of a room where he sits at a table or stands in front of the jurors. A court reporter sits nearby.

After the witness is sworn, the prosecutor advises the witness that his testimony is under oath, and should he lie, he faces criminal penalties for perjury or false statements. The prosecutor will tell the witness that he can refuse to answer a question if the answer would tend to incriminate him and that he will be permitted a "reasonable opportunity" to leave and to consult with counsel during the questioning.

The questioning will resemble trial or deposition questioning, but without defense counsel to object or a judge to intervene. However, unless the prosecutor views your client as a hostile witness or is setting a "perjury trap," the questioning will not be as searching and lengthy as trial or deposition testimony. The prosecutor wants to elicit enough to establish a prima facie case against the target and to commit your client to a favorable version of events on the key points, without eliciting details that the defense later can prove to be inaccurate.

When the prosecutor finishes, the grand jurors can ask questions. Some prosecutors will excuse the witness momentarily while they gather and screen the questions; others will permit the jurors to ask as the witness sits there. These questions can be especially dangerous because they often take the form of accusations.

A juror may ask, "Didn't you, or shouldn't you have known it was wrong?"

Tempted as your client may be to try to help the jurors, he should pause, think and exercise great caution in answering their questions. In this situation, he should ask for a chance to consult you (especially if you have not prepared him with an answer beforehand), and you should either tell him to invoke his privilege or tell him to answer something along the following lines, assuming their truth: "I did not think it was wrong at the time." Or, "I don't remember what I thought about it at the time. Now, after the prosecutor told me it was wrong, I guess it was."

§12:102   Preparing Your Client to Testify

Prepare your client as you would for his trial testimony, with some extra precautions because the grand jury holds unique risks:

- At this stage, there are no pleadings to define the scope of the inquiry; rather, it may change day-to-day in scope and targets.
- You have no discovery rights during a grand jury investigation, even to your client's own statements, so you will not know what other evidence the prosecutor has that may contradict your client.
- If your client should err (*e.g.,* misunderstand a question, answer incompletely, or prevaricate), you cannot correct it on redirect or consult with him during a recess.

If your client is cooperative with the investigation, you will be able to sit in on his preparation sessions with the prosecutor. Afterward, ask the prosecutor if he has any concerns about your client's truthfulness and accuracy. Immediately before your client's testimony, ask the prosecutor if he intends to ask your client about any new matters.

Rehearse your client by tossing him as many variations on the prosecutor's questions as you can imagine. Grand jury preparation is much like preparation for a deposition or a cross-examination. Your client should make sure he understands the question and should answer only the question asked, fully enough to be understood, but no more. If he has any doubt as to a question's meaning, he should say he does not understand.

The rules of evidence do not apply to grand jury proceedings, so your client can be asked for hearsay and opinions. Prepare him for such questions and ensure that he explains the extent of his knowledge and the source for it. If he has an imperfect memory about an event, he should preface his answer by explaining the limitations on his knowledge:

- "I don't remember the exact words I said, but I know I went ahead and billed as my boss told me."
- "I don't know exactly when he said it, but Joe told me that after Saturday, we would not have to worry about money anymore."
- Still, your client should decline invitations to speculate or guess. "I don't know *[what Joe was thinking, etc.]*" or "I don't remember" are acceptable answers–if true. Perjury prosecutions have gone to conviction over "I don't recall" answers, so discourage your client's inclination to stonewall the grand jury with a string of "I don't recall" answers.

Prepare your client to invoke any privileges that may be applicable. [*See* §§12:110, *et seq.*]

Thorough preparation enables your client to make optimal use of his right to leave and consult with you. Prosecutors have been upheld in refusing the opportunity to consult after each and every question. [*In re Lowery, supra.*] If your client has been prepared so that he has heard the questions before and knows the answers, he can reserve his opportunity to consult for unforeseen, hostile or confusing questions.

[§§12:103-12:109 Reserved]

B.   Objections and Privileges

§12:110   Objections

The rules of evidence and the Fourth and Fifth Amendment exclusionary rules do not apply in the federal grand jury. [*See United States v. Williams*, 504 U.S. 36, 49 (1992); *United States v. Calandra*, 414 U.S. 338 (1974), *but see* Beale, *Grand Jury Law and Practice*, §6:7 & n.2 (16 states apply the rules of evidence to grand juries).]

Many evidentiary objections are meant to save the witness from being forced to answer misleading, ambiguous or unfair questions, for example, the objections to compound, vague or argumentative questions.

To deal with such questions when you are not there to object, tell your client that should he detect the slightest ambiguity or lack of clarity in a question or should he have the slightest doubt what a question means, he should tell the prosecutor he does not understand the question and ask him to explain it.

If he still has difficulty with the rephrased question, your client should leave to consult with you.

§12:111   Privileges

Although the rules of evidence do not apply, privileges generally do. Thus it is appropriate to invoke the following privileges: the attorney-client confidential communications privilege, the attorney work-product privilege, the spousal communications privilege, the Fifth Amendment privilege against self-incrimination, and the psychotherapist-patient privilege. [*See LaFave Criminal Procedure*, §8.6(b); Beale, *Grand Jury Law and Practice*, §§6:7–6:9; *In re Grand Jury (Duffy)*, 473 F.2d 840 (8th Cir. 1973) (attorney-work-produce doctrine applies).]

However, federal grand juries do not honor state law privileges unless they have become part of the federal common law. [*See In re Grand Jury*, 198 F. Supp. 2d 1113, 1115 (D. Alaska 2002).]

When you anticipate a possible privilege issue, discuss it in advance and attempt to secure an agreement to avoid the topic. If the prosecutor will not agree, seek a protective order.

Occasionally, a prosecutor will not disclose the areas of questioning. In that case, you must prepare your client to invoke the applicable evidentiary privilege. Review with your client the sensitive areas and instruct him to leave the grand jury room to consult with you before answering any question touching on the sensitive area.

CAUTION:

When grand jury proceedings are pending or on the horizon, do not rely on a civil protective order to safeguard your client's document productions, pleadings, interrogatory responses or deposition testimony from a grand jury subpoena. Most courts will permit the government to obtain documents or depositions produced in civil litigation under a protective order. [*See generally* Beale, *Grand Jury Law and Practice,* §6:19 (Fourth, Ninth and Eleventh Circuits have per se rule that civil order must yield to grand jury subpoena; First and Third Circuits hold that civil order must yield unless party can show exceptional circumstances; Second Circuit requires subpoena to defer to protective order unless government can show exceptional circumstances).]

§12:112   The Privilege Against Self-Incrimination

Occasionally, prosecutors will not excuse a witness from appearing despite counsel's representation that the witness will invoke the privilege and refuse to answer questions.

Explanations for the prosecutor's conduct could be several:
* It might be office practice.
* There might be some desire to harass your client.
* The prosecutor might want to have your client on record as claiming that answers would incriminate him to prevent him from testifying on behalf of another defendant.

No matter how sophisticated your client, you must not trust him with when and how to invoke the privilege. Even questions about where your client worked and when may provide incriminating information, particularly if the crime under investigation arose from the business' operations. Further, once a witness starts answering, stopping is difficult.

Even worse, answering some questions, even ones that seem preliminary and relatively harmless, could be construed as a waiver of the privilege when the prosecutor tries to develop the more harmful details that follow from the answer. [*Rogers v. United States*, 340 U.S. 367 (1951) (once witness acknowledged that she was Treasurer of the local Communist Party and once possessed the membership records of the Party, she could not claim the privilege and refuse to identify to whom she transferred the record, even though identification of that person could implicate the witness in a conspiracy).]

Be prepared to argue the breadth of the privilege. The Fifth Amendment privilege against self-incrimination "must be accorded liberal construction in favor of the right it was intended to secure." [*Hoffman v. United States*, 341 U.S. 479, 486 (1951) (ruling that in a gambling investigation, witness should have been allowed to assert the privilege as to his occupation).] The "privilege not only extends to answers that would support a conviction . . but likewise embraces those which would furnish a link in the chain of evidence needed to prosecute the claimant." [*Ohio v. Reiner*, 532 U.S.

17, 20 (2001).]. A witness may be compelled to answer over her claim of privilege only if it is "perfectly clear from a careful consideration of all the circumstances in the case, that the witness is mistaken, and that the answer(s) cannot possibly have such a tendency to incriminate." [*Hoffman*, 341 U.S. at 488.]

Therefore, instruct your client to invoke the privilege in response to every question besides his name and address. If the crime occurred at his home, he should invoke it for his address as well.

Write out the language he will use to invoke the privilege in large type on a card or piece of paper and command him to read it after each question, no matter how phrased. If the prosecutor asks, "Are you going to give the same answer to any other questions about the matter under investigation?" the answer should still be read from the card.

PRACTICE TIP:

Preparation must be thorough even for the witness who will invoke the privilege, especially if the jurisdiction's law does not permit the attorney to attend the testimony and provide advice. Questions which, standing alone, do not seem incriminating might invite answers that become "a link in a chain" of incriminating inferences and even the basis for a claim of waiver. If the crime arises from your client's employment, questions as to where she works are objectionable. She should assert the privilege as to whether she knows any potential co-conspirators, even if it is the child she bore and raised.

Many prosecutors and judges are unfamiliar with the proposition that the Fifth Amendment privilege protects witnesses who assert their innocence, even witnesses as to whom the prosecutor forswears any intent to prosecute. Always carry a copy of *Ohio v Reiner*, 532 U.S. 17 (2001), the most recent U.S. Supreme Court case on this point, to re-affirm that the Fifth Amendment's protections extend to the innocent, or have the citation memorized and at the ready.

Form:
- **Form 12-13** Invocation of Rights Card

[§§12:113-12:119 Reserved]

C. After the Testimony

§12:120   Debriefing Your Client After His Testimony

Once your client finishes, debrief him immediately and thoroughly, before his memory fades, because rarely will you be given a transcript of his testimony. [*See In re Special Proceedings*, 373 F.3d 37, 47 (1st Cir. 2004) (no witness right to transcript, but noting that prosecutor would have provided a transcript of the witness had his lawyer agreed not to share it with anyone else); *Doe v. United States*, 72 F.3d 271 (2d Cir. 1995) (no right to transcript); *but see In re Grand Jury*, 490 F.3d 978 (D.C. Cir. 2007) (witness should be permitted an opportunity to review the transcript in the prosecutor's office, but not be provided a copy); *In re Sealed Motion*, 880 F.2d 1367 (D.C. Cir. 1989) (witness should be provided transcript); *In re Heimerle*, 788 F. Supp. 700, 704 (E.D.N.Y. 1992) (same).]

Ask him to describe everything he was asked, focusing on:
- Who did the prosecutor ask about? Who did he fail to ask about (likely targets who the prosecutor ignores are probably cooperators)?
- Which events?
- Did the prosecutor ask questions that showed he had spoken with other witnesses or had knowledge of events that must have come from sources other than you?
- Did the prosecutor show you any documents?
- Did the grand jury ask any questions?
- What was the prosecutor's tone throughout? Did he seem to believe you? Did the prosecutor's tone change and become challenging in response to any particular answers?

PRACTICE TIP:

If you are able to interview other witnesses after their testimony, interview them in the same manner.
Try to review the transcript of your client's testimony using the following strategy:
- Ask the prosecutor if you and your client can review it in his office. Emphasize that you are not requesting a copy of it; the prosecutor's concern is that it will be shared with a third party. [*See,*

       e.g., In re Special Proceedings, 373 F.3d 37, 47 (1st Cir. 2004) (noting that prosecutor would have provided a transcript of the witness had his lawyer agreed not to share it with anyone else).]

- If he refuses, file a motion to compel its disclosure, especially if there is a chance that your client must return to the grand jury. [*See In re Grand Jury,* 490 F.3d 978 (D.C. Cir. 2007) (outlining reasons for disclosure).

- Denial of the motion to compel is immediately appealable. [*In re Grand Jury,* 490 F.3d 978 (D.C. Cir. 2007).]

§12:121 Declination

If the investigation ends without your client being charged, request from the prosecutor a "declination" letter.

The usual practice is not to provide one, both to preserve grand jury secrecy and also because nothing prevents the investigation from being revived. However, Department of Justice policy leaves the matter entirely to the local United States Attorney's discretion. [*See USAM* §§9-11:155.]

Form:
- **Form 12-14** Letter Requesting a Declination Letter

[§§12:122-12:129 Reserved]

D. Prosecutorial Misconduct

§12:130 General Points

Most courts perceive the grand jury to be an arm of the prosecution and suspect that defense challenges to prosecution conduct are just disguised attempts to pierce the grand jury's veil of secrecy.

Therefore, in most cases, you gain little in the way of strategic advantage or discovery from such challenges. For example, claims that a subpoena lacks any proper purpose will be dismissed upon the prosecutor's conclusory say-so in an affidavit stating that the subpoena was issued for a proper purpose. [*See R. Enterprises*, 498 U.S. 292; *In re Grand Jury Matter*, 770 F.2d 36, 39 (3d Cir. 1985).]

Rule 6(e)(E)(ii) permits disclosure to adjudicate a motion to dismiss for irregularities in the grand jury. However, before they will open the proceedings (even to *in camera* review), courts first will demand that the defense specifically allege facts, based on first-hand knowledge, showing the irregularity. This requires a showing of the very information that the rule of secrecy keeps from the defense. [*See, e.g., United States v. Jensen*, 193 F.Supp.2d 601 (E.D.N.Y. 2002).]

The federal courts have encouraged a hands-off attitude toward the grand jury by rulings to the effect that courts should not oversee grand jury proceedings and should impose sanctions hardly ever. For example:

United States v. Williams, 504 U.S. 36 (1992) (no sanction for failure to present exculpatory evidence in violation of Tenth Circuit precedent and DOJ guidelines; only supervisory power over the grand jury that remains left is for violations of conduct specifically proscribed by Rule, Statute or the Constitution).

Baylson v. Disciplinary Bd., 975 F.2d 102, 109-110 (3d Cir. 1992) (federal court may not adopt a local or supervisory rule that affects grand jury practice, a rule that prosecutors obtain judicial approval for grand jury subpoenas to attorneys).

Nonetheless, the rules of professional responsibility bind prosecutors as they do any other lawyer. [*See* 28 U.S.C. §530B (state rules apply to federal prosecutors).]

Alleging an ethical violation may not warrant dismissal or the suppression of evidence. [*See Williams*, 504 U.S. 36; *United States v. Lowery*, 166 F.3d 1119 (11th Cir. 1999).] However, the threat of disciplinary action, even an implicit one, should deter the misconduct.

Where you have some basis for the challenge, it may persuade the court that the prosecutor is treating you unjustly or force the prosecutor to change his presentation to the grand jury.

§12:131 Presenting Perjured Testimony

While a witness's perjury before the grand jury is not grounds to dismiss an indictment based on such testimony, dismissal may be warranted if the prosecutor knowingly sponsors the perjury. [*United States v. Strouse*, 286 F.3d 767 (5th Cir. 2002).]

§12:132   Subpoenaing a Defense Attorney

The Rules of Professional Conduct in many jurisdictions require court approval before a prosecutor may subpoena an attorney to the grand jury to testify about matters relating to her representation of a client. [See, e.g, Pa. R. Prof. Conduct 3.10.] A failure to adhere to that rule that results in the disclosure of privileged communications may be grounds to suppress the testimony and even dismiss the indictment. If the prosecutor intends to ask the lawyer questions that might reveal privileged communications, she should notify the client and seek a ruling from a supervising judge. [*Commonwealth v. Schultz*, 133 A.3d 294, 327-28 (Pa. Super. Ct. 2016) (dismissing charges where privileged testimony was elicited despite prosecutor's assurance to grand jury judge that he would inquire into areas that might tough upon privileged communications]; *State v. Wong*, 97 Haw. 512, 40 P.3d 914 (2002) (dismissing indictment where prosecutor elicited privileged testimony in the grand jury without obtaining a preliminary ruling).] The subpoenaed attorney has an obligation to assert the privilege and insist on a court ruling before she answers questions that might reveal client confidences and secrets. [ABA Committee on Ethics and Professional Responsibility, Formal Opinion 10-456 (July 14, 2010).]

Since grand jury proceedings take place in secret and without formal notice to the targets, it may be difficult to object and demand a hearing in advance of your client's former attorney's testimony. The former attorney's retention of counsel and interviews with grand jury witnesses or their counsel that reveal that they are being asked about the attorney's conduct might tip you off to prosecutorial pressure on the attorney to testify. If so, write the prosecutor, the former attorney (or her counsel), and any judge who supervises the grand jury to alert them that your client asserts her privilege and that you demand to be heard before any testimony is elicited from former counsel.

Department of Justice rules also require the prosecutor to show that other alternatives have been exhausted, and to obtain authorization from the Assistant Attorney General for the Criminal Division. [*USAM* §§9–13.410.]

Forms
- **Form 12-15** Letter asserting privilege to former attorney's counsel
- **Form 12-16** Letter to grand jury judge asking to be heard before attorney testifies

§12:133   Failure to Present Exculpatory Evidence

The obligation of *Brady v. Maryland* to disclose exculpatory evidence does not apply in the grand jury.

However, you can lay the ground work for accusations of unfairness, post-indictment, by formally requesting that the prosecution present exculpatory evidence.

Write a letter identifying the witness and summarizing the testimony or attaching the documents and citing both the model ethical rules [Rule 3.3(d) (when appearing *ex parte* before a tribunal, attorney must disclose all facts material to its decision)], and DOJ policy [*USAM* §§9–11.233 (requiring that prosecutors present to the jury evidence that directly negates guilt)].

A clever prosecutor might undercut this ploy by offering the evidence in a weak manner, with, of course, his qualifications about its merit. Still, do not underestimate the arrogance of some prosecutors. If you ask, many will refuse automatically and thoughtlessly.

Form:
- **Form 12-15** Letter Requesting the Presentation of Exculpatory Evidence

§12:134   Insufficiency of the Evidence

In most jurisdictions, an allegation that there was insufficient evidence to indict is not a basis for dismissal of an indictment and will not justify disclosure of the grand jury transcripts even to adjudicate the motion. [*But see* NY Crim. Prac. L. 210-30[2] (allegation, upon information and belief, of insufficiency triggers disclosure of minutes to decide motion to dismiss).]

§12:135   Using the Grand Jury to Prepare for Trial

In federal practice, it is improper for the government to use a grand jury subpoena for the sole or dominant purpose of preparing for trial. [*United States v. Salameh*, 152 F.3d 88, 109 (2d Cir. 1998).]

However, subpoenas are presumed to have a legitimate purpose, and the defense has the burden of proving otherwise. Courts will deem a subpoena legitimate so long as one purpose is to investigate new charges against the defendant (even if substantially similar to the pending charges) or to investigate other potential defendants. [*See* Beale, *Grand Jury Law and Practice*, §9:16.]

§12:136   The Perjury Trap

Prosecutors may not subpoena witnesses for the sole reason of establishing a perjury prosecution. [*See People v. Tyler*, 46 N.Y.2d 251, 385 N.E.2d 1224, 413 N.Y.S.2d 295 (1978); Beale, *Grand Jury Law and Practice*, §11:11; *but see United States v. Burke*, 425 F.3d 400, 408 (7th Cir. 2005); *United States v. Regan*, 103 F.3d 1072, 1079 (2d Cir. 1997); *United States v. Chen*, 933 F.2d 793, 797 (9th Cir. 1991) (all refusing to recognize this defense).]

However, the presence of any legitimate purpose to the subpoena defeats this objection. This includes not only the investigation of suspected crimes, but of information that might lead to evidence of suspected crimes. Thus, while many courts acknowledge the defense, no federal court has granted relief on this basis in 50 years. [Robert G. Morvillo & Christopher J. Morvillo, "Untangling the Web: Defending a Perjury Case," 33 *Litigation* 8, 11 (2007); *but see People v. Tyler* (New York State Court of Appeals affirms dismissal of indictment on this basis).]

V.   FORMS

Form 12-1   Sample Target Letter

COMMENT:
This form comes from the *USAM's Criminal Resource Manual* at 160.

Dear _____:
This letter is supplied to a witness scheduled to appear before the federal Grand Jury in order to provide helpful background information about the Grand Jury. The Grand Jury consists of 16 to 23 persons from the District of ___. It is their responsibility to inquire into federal crimes which may have been committed in this District.

As a Grand Jury witness you will be asked to testify and answer questions, and to produce records and documents. Only the members of the Grand Jury, attorneys for the United States and a stenographer are permitted in the Grand Jury room while you testify.

We advise you that the Grand Jury is conducting an investigation of possible violations of federal criminal laws involving, but not necessarily limited to, _____. You are advised that the destruction or alteration of any document required to be produced before the grand jury constitutes serious violation of federal law, including, but not limited to, Obstruction of Justice.

You are advised that you are a target of the Grand Jury's investigation. You may refuse to answer any question if a truthful answer to the question would tend to incriminate you. Anything that you do or say may be used against you in a subsequent legal proceeding. If you have retained counsel, who represents you personally, the Grand Jury will permit you a reasonable opportunity to step outside the Grand Jury room and confer with counsel if you desire.

Cordially,

_____

Form 12-2   Immunity Request Form

COMMENT:

This form comes from the *USAM*'s *Criminal Resource Manual* at 721.

LIMITED OFFICIAL USE

U.S. Department of Justice

Request for Authorization to Apply for Compulsion Order
(18 U.S.C. §§6001-6003; 28 C.F.R. §§0.175-0.178)

Instructions: Prepare and Submit Original and One Copy. Answer Each Question as Accurately and Completely as Possible.

TO: Witness Records Unit   FROM: USA ~
   Criminal Division   United States Attorney
   U. S. Department of Justice   Address
   MAIN Justice
   Washington, DC 20530
   FAX No.   FAX No.

(1) Name of Witness:
(2) District:
(3) Nature of Proceeding:
  [ ] Trial [ ] Grand Jury [ ] Other
(4) Name of Subject(s) or Defendant(s):
(5) Date of Testimony (two weeks lead time required):
(6) Proffer of Anticipated Testimony:
  [ ] None Obtained   [ ] Proffer by Witness [ ] Debriefing of Witness
  [ ] Proffer by Counsel [ ] Pursuant to Plea Agreement
(7) Summary of Case or Proceeding:
(8) Witness's Background and Role in Case or Matter and Summary of Anticipated Testimony or Information:
(9) Witness's Family Relationship, if any, to the Subject(s) or Defendant(s):
(10) Assurances or Promises, if any, to Witness in Return for his Testimony:
(11) Acts of Witness Considered as a Waiver of Fifth Amendment Privilege:
(12) Means Other than Immunity to Obtain this Testimony:
(13) Basis Other than Proffer for Summary of Anticipated Testimony:
(14) Relative Culpability of Witness Compared to Subject(s) or Defendant(s):
(15) Why Immunity is Necessary to the Public Interest (State Facts):
(16) Basis for Belief that Witness Will Assert Fifth Amendment Privilege:
(17) Likelihood that Witness Will Testify if Immunity is Granted:
(18) Prosecution of Witness in This Case or Matter:
  [ ] Yes   [ ] No   [ ] Acquitted   [ ] Convicted   [ ] Plea
  If not indicted, why not? If convicted, has the witness been sentenced?
(19) witness's Privilege Survives Because:
(20) Witness is Presently Incarcerated:
  [ ] Yes   [ ] No
  If yes, give details:
(21) Pending Federal or Local Charges against Witness:
  [ ] Yes   [ ] No
  If yes, give details:
(22) Federal and State Offenses by Witness that His Testimony Could Disclose:
(23) Opposition, if any, to Granting Immunity by State or Local Prosecuting Officials:
(24) Effect, if any, of Granting Immunity to the Witness Upon any Other Federal District:

(25) Conviction of Witness Possible on Evidence Other than His Own Testimony?
    [ ] Yes   [ ] No
    If yes, give details:
(26) Violations (Statutes and Descriptions) by Subject(s) or Defendant(s):
(27) Witness Previously Immunized?
    [ ] Yes   [ ] No
    If yes, give details:
(28) Witnesses for Whom Immunity has been Authorized in this Proceeding:
(29) Date Investigation Began:
(30) Witness Subject to Electronic Surveillance?
    [ ] Yes   [ ] No
    If yes, give details:
(31) Birth Date of Witness:
(32) FBI I.D. No.:
(33) Birthplace:
(34) Social Security No.:
(35) Alias:
(36) Address of Witness:
(37) If Applicant is Department Attorney, has Local United States Attorney been Notified?
    [ ] Yes   [ ] No

_____
AUSA
Assistant U.S. Attorney

_____
USA
United States Attorney

Form 12-3   Motion for Order Granting Immunity

IN THE UNITED STATES DISTRICT COURT
FOR THE _____ DISTRICT OF _____
_____ Division

IN RE: GRAND JURY PROCEEDINGS	)	
UNITED STATES OF AMERICA	)	MISC NO. _____
v.	)	
JOHN DOE NO.	)	

MOTION

Richard Cullen, United States Attorney for the _____ District of _____, hereby moves that this Court issue an Order pursuant to the provisions of Title 18, United States Code, Section 6001, *et. seq.*, compelling _____ to give testimony or provide other information, which he refuses to give or provide on the basis of his privilege against self-incrimination as to all matters about which he may be interrogated before the Grand Jury of the United States presently empanelled within this District, and respectfully alleges as follows:

1. The said _____ has been called to testify or provide other information before said Grand Jury;
2. In the judgment of the undersigned, the testimony or other information from said witness may be necessary to the public interest.
3. In the judgment of the undersigned, said witness _____ has refused to testify or provide other information on the basis of his privilege against self-incrimination.

4. This application is made with the approval of Robert S. Mueller, III, Assistant Attorney General in charge of the Criminal Division of the Department of Justice, pursuant to the authority invested in him by Title 18, United States Code, Section 6003 and Title 28, Code of Federal Regulations, Section 0.175. A copy of the letter from said Assistant Attorney General expressing such approval is attached hereto.

Respectfully submitted,

_____

RICHARD CULLEN
UNITED STATES ATTORNEY

By: _____

Assistant United States Attorney

Form 12-4   Court Order of Use Immunity

IN THE UNITED STATES DISTRICT COURT FOR THE
_____ DISTRICT OF _____
_____ Division

IN RE: GRAND JURY PROCEEDINGS	)	
UNITED STATES OF AMERICA	)	CRIMINAL NO. _____
v.	)	
JOHN DOE	)	

ORDER OF IMMUNITY

The United States of America by its attorney, Richard Cullen, United States Attorney for the _____ District of _____, and _____, Assistant United States Attorney for the _____ District of _____, having moved the Court for an Order requiring _____ to testify pursuant to Title 18, United States Code, Sections 6002 and 6003, in regard to a matter to be presented to the federal Grand Jury, that is *United States v. John Doe* _____, and to provide such information at any other proceeding ancillary to the above-styled matter, and being advised that the request for immunity was approved by the Assistant Attorney General of the Criminal Division, United States Department of Justice on _____, and that the testimony and other information from this witness may be necessary to the public interest, and furthermore, such individual is likely to refuse to testify or provide other information on the basis of his privilege against self-incrimination, it is hereby,

ORDERED, ADJUDGED and DECREED that _____ be required to testify and provide other information in regard to a matter to be presented to the federal Grand Jury, that is *United States v. John Doe* _____, and to provide such information at any other proceeding ancillary to the above-styled matter.

Provided, that the said _____ is hereby granted immunity from the use against him in any criminal case of any testimony or other information compelled under such Order, or any information directly or indirectly derived from such testimony or other information, except that the above does not immunize the said _____ against charges of perjury, giving a false statement or otherwise failing to comply with the Order of the Court.

_____

UNITED STATES DISTRICT JUDGE

Form 12-5   Letter Immunity

Name _____

Re: United States v. John Doe No. 93-040

Dear: _____:

    If you fully comply with the understandings specified below, you will not be prosecuted by this law office for any violation of federal _____ laws or related offenses, except for crimes of violence.

    The understandings are that you shall truthfully disclose all information with respect to the activities of yourself and all others concerning all matters about which this office inquires of you, shall cooperate fully with agents of the _____ and the U.S. Attorney's Office and truthfully testify before the grand jury and/or at any trial or other court proceeding with respect to any matters about which this office may request your testimony.

    It is further understood that this agreement is limited to the U.S. Attorney's Office for the Eastern District of Virginia and cannot bind any other federal, state or local prosecuting authorities, although this office will bring your cooperation to the attention of other prosecuting offices if requested.

    It is further understood that you shall at all times give complete, truthful and accurate information and testimony. Should it be judged by this office that you have given false, incomplete or misleading testimony or information, or have otherwise violated any provision of this Agreement, you shall thereafter be subject to prosecution for any federal criminal violation of which this office has knowledge, including, but not limited to, perjury and/or obstruction of justice. Any such prosecutions may be premised upon any information, statement or testimony provided by you, and such information and leads derived therefrom, may be used against you. Should you refuse to testify at any trial proceeding, grand jury session or otherwise as requested, that shall be considered a breach of this Agreement, and you may be prosecuted for any offense of which this office has knowledge.

    This Agreement covers only offenses committed by you before the date of your cooperation, which is the date you sign this Agreement, and does not immunize you for any offense committed after this date.

    No additional promises, agreements and conditions have been entered into other than those set forth in this letter and none will be entered into unless in writing and signed by all the parties.

                            Sincerely,

                            _____

                            United States Attorney

         By: _____

                            Assistant United States Attorney

AGREED AND CONSENTED TO:

                                            WITNESS:

_____

(Letter recipient)

                                         _____

Form 12-6   "Queen for a Day" Agreement

Dear Mr. Attorney:

This letter sets forth the full and complete terms of the agreement entered into between this office and your client, Richard Roe.

It is agreed that, in exchange for the commitment of the government set forth below, your client will provide complete and truthful information in connection with an investigation into violations of environmental laws by Richard Roe and others during the period from 1993 to the present. In particular, this office and Richard Roe agree that:

    Richard Roe agrees to be fully debriefed concerning his knowledge of the offenses set forth above. The debriefing of Richard Roe will be conducted by this office and agents of the Federal Bureau of Investigation, and/or other law enforcement agencies, as the case may require. Any and all documents or other written material, and any physical evidence of whatever description, which are relevant to the government's investigation and which are in the possession of Richard Roe or under his control, will be furnished to this office or to the debriefing agents. All information provided by Richard Roe shall be truthful, accurate, and complete.

In any prosecution brought against Richard Roe by the office of the United States Attorney for the Western District of Pennsylvania, except in a prosecution for perjury or false statements, the government will not offer in evidence in its case-in-chief any statements made by Richard Roe pursuant to this agreement.

Notwithstanding paragraph 2 above:

> The government may use information derived from said debriefing directly or indirectly for the purpose of obtaining leads to other evidence, which evidence may be used by the office against Richard Roe at any prosecution of Richard Roe by the office;

> The government may use Richard Roe's statements and all evidence obtained directly or indirectly therefrom for the purpose of cross-examination, should Richard Roe testify at any future proceeding, or for the purpose of a rebuttal case against Richard Roe.

> The government may make any use whatsoever of any documents, written material, and physical evidence provided by Richard Roe pursuant to this agreement, including offering such evidence in it case-in-chief, provided that an evidentiary foundation other than Richard Roe's production of such items can be established.

This letter sets forth the full and complete terms and conditions of the agreement between Richard Roe and the government, and there are no other agreements, promises, terms or conditions, expressed or implied.

Very truly yours,

_____

United States Attorney

Form 12-7   Proffer Letter

Assistant U.S. Attorney
400 U.S. Post Office and Courthouse
Pittsburgh, PA 15219

Re: Smith Grand Jury Investigation

Dear _____:

I write to make a proffer of Richard Roe's testimony should he be interviewed or questioned before the Grand Jury. I make this proffer to continue the plea or charging negotiations that you and I have begun by telephone. Therefore, the protections of FRE 410 apply to this letter. Furthermore, since this proffer concerns matter occurring before the Grand Jury, the non-disclosure provisions of Fed. R. Crim. P. 6(e)(2)(B) protect it from disclosure to third parties.

I am enclosing a short biographical sketch which Mr. Roe authored for this matter at my request. I send it as Mr. Roe wrote it because I think Mr. Roe's selection of his achievements and the manner in which he describes them show admirable modesty. The bottom line is that he has been a pillar of the community for 30 years.

[Summarize what your client could say if interviewed. Emphasize how the testimony would help and fit into the prosecution's case against others.]

Please contact me to discuss this matter further.

Sincerely,

_____

Thomas J. Farrell

Enclosure

Form 12-8   Act of Production Immunity Letter

COMMENT:

This immunity letter is limited to immunizing the witness's production and authentication of the documents.

U.S. Department of Justice

United States Attorney
_____ District of _____

[contact number]

Suite ___
_____ _____ Avenue
P.O. Box _____
_____, __ _____-____

[Date]

Re: Grand Jury Subpoena

Dear Mr. Attorney:

Your client, Mr. John Doe, has been served with a subpoena requiring the production of certain items by him to the Grand Jury. As I informed you, Mr. Doe is presently a target of the Grand Jury investigation. You have informed me that Mr. Doe will assert his Fifth Amendment privilege and will refuse to testify before the Grand Jury. Accordingly, I am excusing him from appearing before the Grand Jury but, pursuant to the agreement set forth below, the United States will provide him with "act of production" immunity for the production of the items required by the Grand Jury subpoena.

By this letter, the government agrees to provide Mr. John Doe with "act of production" immunity for his production of the items described in the Grand Jury subpoena of _____. The government agrees that no direct or indirect use will be made from the "testimonial aspects" of Mr. Doe's providing these items to the Grand Jury. This immunity also applies to the limited questions which will be asked of Mr. Doe before the Grand Jury in order to authenticate and identify the items produced.

If this letter conforms with your understanding of our agreement, would you and your client please sign this letter and return it to me. Thank you for your consideration.

Very truly yours,

_____
United States Attorney

By:

[Date]   _____
                                          Assistant U.S. Attorney

[Date]   _____
                                          Attorney

[Date]   _____
                                          Mr. John Doe

Form 12-9   Affidavit by Document Custodian

IN THE UNITED STATES DISTRICT COURT
FOR THE _____ DISTRICT OF_____

IN RE:	)	
	)	AFFIDAVIT OF COMPLIANCE
GRAND JURY INVESTIGATION	)	*WITH SUBPOENA*
	) SS:	
	)	

, being first duly sworn, deposes and says:

1. I am associated with (the "Company") as . In this position I have the responsibility for the Company's compliance with the subpoena *duces tecum* issued to it on , 1992, which calls for the production of certain documents before a Grand Jury of this court.

2. I make this affidavit and produce these documents in my capacity as representative of the Company, not in my personal capacity. Counsel for the Company has informed me that my act of producing and authenticating these documents cannot be used against me in my personal capacity and that the Government has agreed to this limitation on use of this affidavit and any testimony the Government may request from me to authenticate and produce these documents.

3. I personally have conducted or supervised compliance by the Company with the subpoena *duces tecum*. To the best of my knowledge, information and belief, based upon due diligence and reasonable inquiry, the documents enclosed herewith, bearing the numbers constitute all the documents in the possession, custody or control of the Company that fall within the terms of the subpoena *duces tecum*.

4. No documents responsive to the subpoena *duces tecum* have been withheld by the Company pursuant to a claim of privilege or otherwise. To the best of my knowledge, information and belief, based upon due diligence and reasonable inquiry, no one has directed the destruction of any documents responsive to the subpoena *duces tecum* and no such documents have been destroyed.

5. The documents made by the Company and produced in compliance with the subpoena *duces tecum* are memoranda, reports, records or data compilations of acts, events, conditions, opinions or diagnoses that were made at or near the time, by or from information transmitted by, a person with knowledge, and that have been kept in the course of the Company's regularly conducted business activity. It has been the Company's regular practice in that business activity to make those memoranda, reports, records, or data compilations. Neither the source of information, nor the method of circumstances of preparation, indicate a lack of trustworthiness for those memoranda, reports, records or data compilations.

6. I understand that the furnishing of these documents to counsel for the United States in response to the subpoena *duces tecum* and the execution of this Affidavit are at the sole discretion and election of myself and the Company, and are in lieu of personally producing the documents before the Grand Jury which right to appear is expressly waived.

7. I am authorized by the Company to execute this Affidavit and I have reviewed all its terms with counsel for the Company before signing and swearing to it.

FURTHER AFFIANT SAYETH NAUGHT.

AFFIANT
SWORN AND SUBSCRIBED TO before me this ___ day of _____, _____, at _____.

_____
Notary Public
My Commission Expires: _____

Form 12-10 *Gelbard* **Motion**

IN THE UNITED STATES DISTRICT COURT
FOR THE _____ DISTRICT OF _____

IN RE: GRAND JURY PROCEEDINGS)	
)	
Subpoena to Louis Loe)	MISC NO. _____
)	UNDER SEAL
)	

MOTION FOR DISCLOSURE OF ELECTRONIC SURVEILLANCE

And now comes Louis Loe, by his attorney _____, Esq., and files this motion for disclosure of electronic surveillance and states in support thereof:

1. On _____, Mr. Loe received a subpoena ordering him to produce documents and give testimony before a Grand Jury in this district on _____. The subpoena notes that the Assistant United States Attorney supervising this investigation is John Smith

2. On _____, undersigned counsel telephoned Mr. Smith to discuss the subpoena and investigation. Mr. Smith informed me that this investigation involves allegations of tax violations, prostitution and drug-trafficking at the establishment at which Mr. Loe is employed, the _____ Club, a gentlemen's club in Pittsburgh. These are the sorts of allegations that the government sometimes pursues through the use of electronic surveillance. Furthermore, many of the allegations arise from private transactions between exotic dancers and their customers, the kind of situation in which it is unlikely that the individuals with personal knowledge provided the evidence. This, too, suggests that the government may have conducted electronic surveillance at the _____ Club.

3. During my investigation of this matter, a _____ Club employee informed my investigator that "the feds have a recording of a phone call where Loe ordered some dope." *See* Exhibit A (interview report).

4. Mr. Loe was employed at the _____ Club as a doorman from _____ to _____. During that time, he used the following telephone numbers at the Club: [*list*]. He also used cell phone number [*number*] and made calls to the Club from his home telephone number, [*number*].

5. Mr. Smith informed me that Mr. Loe is a subject of the investigation.

6. A Grand Jury witness may refuse to answer questions or produce documents in response to a Grand Jury subpoena that derives from illegal electronic surveillance. *Gelbard v. United States,* 408 U.S. 41 (1972). To enforce the holding in *Gelbard*, the Third Circuit Court of Appeals has imposed explicit disclosure obligations on prosecutors:

> When a grand jury witness raises the issue of possible electronic surveillance as the source of a subpoena or questions, the government is bound to affirm or deny the occurrence of such surveillance. 18 U.S.C. §3504(a)(1). An insufficient denial is just cause for refusing to answer questions or produce subpoenaed records.

In re Freedman, 529 F.2d 543, 549 (3d Cir. 1976). Upon a Grand Jury witness's request, the government must disclose the existence of any electronic surveillance, even if legal, and identify the law enforcement agencies contacted to help furnish the response. *In re Grand Jury Matter,* 683 F.2d 66, 68 n.2 (3d Cir. 1982) (holding that an *in camera ex parte* response to the Court cannot substitute for an affidavit provided to the witness).

7. Based upon the above facts, we assert that Mr. Loe has been the subject of illegal electronic surveillance and that the Grand Jury questioning of him will be derived from that surveillance..

WHEREFORE, Mr. Loe respectfully requests that the Court order the Government to disclose Mr. Loe was intercepted in any electronic surveillance and to identify the law enforcement agencies contacted to help furnish the response.

Respectfully submitted,

_____
Attorney for Louis Loe

Form 12-11   Sample Subpoena Advising Witness Not to Speak With Defense

United States District Court
WESTERN   PENNSYLVANIA
DISTRICT OF

TO:

SUBPOENA TO TESTIFY
BEFORE GRAND JURY

SUBPOENA FOR:

☐ PERSON   ☒ DOCUMENTS OR OBJECT(S)
X

YOU ARE HEREBY COMMANDED to appear and testify before the Grand Jury of the United States District Court at the place, date, and time specified below.

PLACE	ROOM
United States Post Office and Courthouse Seventh Avenue and Grant Street Pittsburgh, Pennsylvania 15219-1955	155
	DATE AND TIME September 27, 2005 9:00 a.m.

YOU ARE ALSO COMMANDED to bring with you the following document(s) or object(s):*

Please see attachment.

PURSUANT TO AN OFFICIAL CRIMINAL INVESTIGATION OF A SUSPECTED FELONY BEING CONDUCTED BY THE PENNSYLVANIA STATE POLICE, YOU ARE HEREBY REQUESTED NOT TO DISCLOSE THE EXISTENCE OF THIS REQUEST. ANY SUCH DISCLOSURE COULD IMPEDE THE INVESTIGATION BEING CONDUCTED AND THEREBY INTERFERE WITH THE ENFORCEMENT OF THE LAW.

IN LIEU OF PERSONAL APPEARANCE THE RECORDS (along with a copy of this subpoena) CAN BE MAILED DIRECTLY TO THE ASSISTANT UNITED STATES ATTORNEY NAMED BELOW.

☐ Please see additional information on reverse

This subpoena shall remain in effect until you are granted leave to depart by the court or by an officer acting on behalf of the court.

CLERK *R.V. Barth, Jr.*	R.V. BARTH, JR.	Date 08/31/05
(BY) DEPUTY CLERK		

This subpoena is issued upon application of the United States of America	NAME OF ASSISTANT U.S. ATTORNEY Assistant U.S. Attorney 400 U.S. Post Office & Courthouse Pittsburgh, Pennsylvania 15219 (412)

*If not applicable, enter "none."

FORM OBD-227
Revised April 2000

Form 12-12   Letter Informing Grand Jury Witness of Ability to Speak With the Defense

[*Date*]

Mr. Attorney, Esquire
111 First Street
Pittsburgh, PA

Re: John Smith Grand Jury Investigation

Dear Mr. Attorney:

I spoke to AUSA _____ today, _____, and he clarified that while there may be language on the subpoena to your client about not notifying or disclosing information to the subject of the investigation, that language is a request, not a mandatory prohibition. Mr. _____ agreed that the government is not prohibiting your client from sharing documents with me or Mr. Smith or discussing matters that are relevant to the investigation with me or Mr. Smith. Whether your client does so, however, is entirely up to him, acting on your advice, of course.

I sent a draft of this letter to Mr. _____ to assure that I made no representations about or discussion with which he did not agree, and he informed me that he has no problem with my representations.

Please advise me whether your client is willing to provide these documents and/or to speak with us.

Sincerely,

_____
Thomas J. Farrell

cc: Mr. John Smith
     AUSA _____

Form 12-13   Invocation of Rights Card

TO BE READ AFTER EVERY QUESTION:

BASED UPON THE ADVICE OF MY ATTORNEY, I INVOKE MY RIGHTS UNDER THE FIFTH AMENDMENT AND MUST REFUSE TO ANSWER THE QUESTION.

Form 12-14   Letter Requesting a Declination Letter

[*Date*]

<u>BY HAND</u>
Mr. Attorney, Esq.
Assistant U.S. Attorney

Re: John Smith and Dale Evans.

Dear Mr. Attorney:

I write with more information regarding the activities of your witnesses [*names*]. I also request that you have your agents return to us all the Company's proprietary information that may be in their possession. Finally, once again, I urge you to close this investigation and issue a letter to that effect to the Company and the individuals you have named as targets, John Smith and DE.

[*Summarize reasons the investigation has proven to be unfounded.*]

Witness One (W1) and Witness Two (W2) form a true den of thieves. Both have stolen from the very entities they have slandered in the course of this investigation; both lied about their thievery; W1 lied to you about a meeting in Russia that never took place; and now W2 offers to make a case against W1. Your office should not stoop to deal with such people, particularly in a matter in which, after three years of numerous interviews, the execution of search warrants and other investigation, there still is no evidence that a crime was committed nor any reasonable likelihood that such evidence will ever be produced. (We maintain that the reason for the lack of evidence is that, in fact, no crime was committed.)

The pendency of this investigation has been disclosed in the Company's 10-Q and 10-K public filings and may have had an impact on the market for its stock and the public's and customer's confidence in the Company. Mr. E has left the Company and is soliciting venture capital for a new business. Both the Company and Mr. Smith and Mr. E need a formal confirmation from your office that this investigation has concluded with no charges. We ask you to issue a declination letter pursuant to the discretion you have to do so under Department of Justice Policy. *See USAM* §§9-11:155.

Sincerely,

_____

Thomas J. Farrell

Form 12-15   Letter Requesting the Presentation of Exculpatory Evidence

[*Date*]

Mr. Assistant U.S. Attorney
Assistant United States Attorney
United States Attorney's Office
400 U.S. Post Office & Courthouse
Pittsburgh, PA 15219

RE: John Smith Investigation

Dear Mr. Assistant U.S. Attorney:

It has recently come to my attention that Lisa Lowe, who I believe to be an important government witness in this investigation, apparently lied under oath recently in the case of *Lowe v. Development Corporation*, (Civil Division No. AR 04-3309).

While under oath at an arbitration in the above case, Ms. Lowe denied having a criminal record (see attached transcript); however, defense counsel found evidence to the contrary. When Ms. Lowe was subsequently confronted at her deposition in that matter, she apparently admitted to the conviction. *See* Defendant's Pre-Trial Statement (attached) and Deposition Transcript (attached).

I ask you to take this exculpatory information into consideration and submit it to the Grand Jury pursuant to *USAM* §§9-11.233 and Rule 3.3 (d) of the Rules of Professional Conduct before deciding whether to seek an indictment against Mr. Smith.

Should you have any questions, please do not hesitate to call.

Sincerely,

_____

Thomas J. Farrell

Enclosure

Form 12-16   Letter Asserting Privilege To Former Attorney's Counsel

[Date]

PRIVILEGED AND CONFIDENTIAL

By U.S. Mail & E-mail
John Doe, Esq.

Re: [Client]

Dear Mr. Doe:

I was pleased to learn that you are representing Marie Roe, Esq., with respect to the Attorney General's investigation. The time of your engagement, coming in the midst of renewed activity by the OAG, causes me concern that the OAG may attempt to interview Ms. Roe or to obtain notes, correspondence, e-mails or other documents from her.

Ms. Roe — as she represented to Mr. Client, the grand jury supervising judge, the OAG and the grand jury — was legal counsel to my client, Mr. Client, during preparation for his appearance in the grand jury, during his interview and appearance before the grand jury on [date], and through and until my retention on [date]. Therefore, we ask and expect that you and Ms. Roe will assert the attorney-client and work product privileges in response to any and all requests from the OAG, the USAO in the W.D. of Pa., and anyone else who may ask.

Please call me if you have any questions about this matter.

Sincerely,

_____

Thomas J. Farrell
Counsel for Client

Form 12-17   Letter To Grand Jury Judge Asking To Be Heard Before Attorney Testifies

[Date]

By E-mail and Overnight Delivery
Honorable ____
Supervising Judge

RE: ____ Statewide Investigating Grand Jury, [___Misc. Dkt____]

Your Honor:

I am counsel for Client, a subject of the grand jury's investigation. It has come to my attention that the Office of the Attorney General may issue a subpoena for testimony from Mr. Client's former attorney, Marie Roe, Esq., as well as for records that pertain to her representation of Mr. Client.

Ms. Roe represented Mr. Farnsworth in preparation for, during and after his appearance before you and the grand jury on [date]. Any testimony about her communications with Mr. Client in connection with her representation of him and any of her notes or other documentation she may have created concerning the representation and her communications with Mr. Client fall within the attorney-client and work-product privileges. I assert both privileges on his behalf against any production to the grand jury, OAG, or any other party.

Please permit me to be heard on Mr. Client's behalf before Ms. Roe testifies or produces any documents to the grand jury.

Sincerely,

_____

Thomas J. Farrell
Attorney for Client

Cc: OAG
     John Doe, Esq.

(This page intentionally left blank.)

Chapter 13

MENTAL HEALTH ISSUES

VI. FORMS

I.   COMPETENCY

§13:01   The Standard for Competency

Due process forbids trying an incompetent defendant. [*See Cooper v. Oklahoma*, 517 U.S. 348, 354 (1996).]
The constitutional test for competence has four parts. To be competent, a defendant must be able to do all of the following:
- Consult with the lawyer with a reasonable degree of rational understanding.
- Otherwise assist in the defense.
- Have a rational understanding of the criminal proceedings.
- Have a factual understanding of the proceedings.

[*United States v. Duhon*, 104 F.Supp.2d 663, 670 (W.D. La. 2000).]

Defendants are presumed competent, and the defendant has the burden to prove otherwise, but the burden on the defendant cannot be more than a preponderance of the evidence. [*Cooper.*]

§13:02   Conducting Your Own Evaluation

When you suspect that your client might suffer from an incapacitating mental illness, start with in-depth interviews of your client to assess whether he can communicate with you and understand not only the charges, but the nature of possible defenses. Make careful notes of your client's reactions and comments.

Also, speak to your client's friends and family to obtain a complete family and social history as well as descriptions of recent bizarre or incoherent behavior. Mental illness runs in families; ask whether relatives were depressed, institutionalized or suicidal.

Obtain as many records as you can: work, school, medical, psychiatric and military. A prerequisite to establishing incompetence to stand trial or insanity is the existence of a mental disorder. A documented history not only assists in meeting this prerequisite, but helps refute claims that your client is malingering. (Realize, though, that genuinely mentally-ill people also malinger, so a finding of malingering, while harmful, should not be dispositive.)

Next, describe your client's behavior and history to a psychiatrist to elicit a preview of likely findings. Even at this early stage, a psychiatrist can advise you on such issues as:
- Whether a psychiatric defense has hope.
- Whether a psychiatric defense may result in lengthy civil commitment.
- Whether to save the psychiatric issues for sentencing mitigation.
- Whether a psychiatric examination might result in the dreaded diagnosis of antisocial personality disorder (i.e., that your client is a dangerous and incorrigible criminal psychopath).

Form:
- **Form 13-1** Motion for Appointment of Psychologist

§13:03   Whether to Raise Your Client's Incompetence

Since much of the incompetence inquiry focuses on the defendant's ability to consult with and assist counsel, whether incompetence will become an issue is very much your choice.

In deciding whether to raise your client's perceived incompetence, there are several strong disadvantages that you must consider:
- The court likely will commit your client to an extended period of custody for an official evaluation. Where the charge probably will not carry a significant jail sentence, an evaluative commitment may well put your client in jail for longer than a guilty plea.
- The prosecution will have access to your psychiatrist's evaluation, and its psychiatrists will be able to examine your client. With this access, the prosecution can begin to build a case that your client is a malingerer and a sociopath. Thus, raising competence may severely undercut an insanity defense, or, in a capital case, a mitigation defense based mental illness or mental retardation.
- Your client's statements to any examining psychiatrist (yours, the court's or the prosecution's) may be admissible against him at trial. [*See* §13:40.]

PRACTICE TIP:

In some jurisdictions, a mental health court is an alternative for less serious offenses. [*See* §13:30.]

§13:04   Providing a Witness to the Client's Competency

Since so much of the competence issue turns on your client's ability to assist and communicate with you, consider whether you should either:
- Withdraw as counsel to serve as a witness to your client's interactions with you.
- Ask the court to appoint another defense attorney to attempt to communicate with your client and to testify as an expert on your client's ability to assist in the defense of a case as complex as yours. [*See United States v. Duhon*, 104 F.Supp.2d 663, 669 & 676 (W.D. La. 2000) (appointing second criminal defense attorney to examine defendant, review case reports and testify as an expert).]

§13:05   Requesting a Court-Ordered Evaluation

You may request that your client be evaluated to determine whether he is competent to stand trial. You may do this at any time after charges are filed and before sentencing. [*See, e.g.,* NY Crim. Pro. Law §730.30 (1); 18 U.S.C. §4241(a).]

The court may order a competence examination if there is reasonable cause to believe that the defendant suffers from a mental disease or defect that renders him incompetent. [18 U.S.C. §4241(a); *United States v. Downs*, 123 F.3d 637, 640 (7th Cir. 1997).]

The prosecutor or the court may also move independently to have your client evaluated for competency when your client's prior mental history and behavior in court or at the time of the offense suggest reasonable cause to doubt his competency. In these circumstances, the court may be obligated to order a competency evaluation. [18 U.S.C. §4241(a); *People v. Garrasi*, 302 A.D.2d 981, 754 N.Y.S.2d 799 (N.Y. App. Div. 2003) (court erred in not ordering a competency hearing sua sponte upon hearing defendant's delusional comments at sentencing).]

§13:06   The Court Evaluation and Hearing

Once the motion is filed, the court may order an evaluation by a psychiatrist or psychologist.

If your client is free on bail, you can and should insist that the evaluation be conducted in an outpatient and noncustodial setting. However, the court can order that the defendant be committed to official custody for a period to determine his competency.

The period should be no longer than necessary. [*Jackson v. Indiana,* 406 U.S. 715, 738 (1972); *see* 18 U.S.C. §4247(b) (no more than 30 days).]

The examining psychiatrist must file a report of his conclusions with the court and provide it to the parties. [*E.g.,* 18 U.S.C. 4241(b).]

After the evaluation and report are completed, the court must hold a hearing to decide the issue of competency. The defense can call its own psychiatrist in addition to the ones chosen by the court. In practice, the court will defer considerably to the psychiatrists it appointed to conduct the examination.

§13:07   Commitment for Treatment

If your client is deemed competent, the case proceeds as any other. However, if the court finds him lacking in competence, the court will commit him for at least one period of treatment to determine if he can be restored to competence.

The commitment "cannot be ... [for] more than the reasonable period of time necessary to determine whether there is a substantial probability that he will attain ... capacity [to stand trial] in the foreseeable future." [*Jackson v. Indiana,* 406 US 715, 738 (1972).] However, that period can be substantial. [18 U.S.C. §4241(d) (commitment for up to four months); NY Crim. Pro. Law §730.40 (1) (up to 90 days on a misdemeanor), §730.50 (1)-(3) (up to one year on a felony for first commitment, which can be followed by court-ordered extensions).]

In addition, if the court finds a substantial probability that your client will attain competency, the court can recommit him again and again, so long as periodic reevaluations occur and the duration of the confinement does not exceed the maximum penalty for the charged offense. [*United States v. Ecker,* 30 F.3d 966 (8th Cir. 1994) (construing 18 U.S.C. §4241(d); three-year delay in determining competence, during which there were seven evaluations, was not unreasonable).]

If after that the period, the court decides that your client will not regain competence in the foreseeable future, the court must dismiss the charge. [18 U.S.C. §4246.]

However, this may not be the end of the defendant's confinement. The government then can commence civil commitment proceedings and institutionalize the defendant if it is shown under the civil commitment standards that he is a danger to himself or others. [*See Jackson*, 406 U.S. at 738; 18 U.S.C. §4246 (if after a hearing the court finds by clear and convincing evidence that the defendant's release creates a substantial risk of bodily injury to another or serious property damage, the court must commit the defendant to the custody of the Attorney General); 50 Pa. Stat. §7406 (prosecution may petition for commitment after finding of incompetence or verdict of not guilty by reason of insanity).]

The order committing your client for an evaluation to determine if there is a reasonable likelihood that he will regain competency is appealable. [*United States v. Ferro*, 321 F.2d 756, 760 (8th Cir. 2003) (order under 18 U.S.C. §4241(d) committing defendant to Attorney General's custody for competence examination is an appealable order under the collateral order doctrine).]

§13:08   Forced Medication of Your Client

The court can order that your client be medicated to render him competent, but orders for the involuntary administration of antipsychotic drugs are disfavored and should be issued rarely and only on a compelling showing. [*United States v. Rivera-Guerrero*, 426 F.3d 1130, 1137-1138 (9th Cir. 2005).]

The government may involuntarily administer antipsychotic drugs to a mentally-ill defendant in order to render him competent to stand trial only if four factors are present:

(1) "important governmental interests are at stake."
(2) involuntary medication will "significantly further" the concomitant state interests of timely prosecution and a fair trial.
(3) "involuntary medication is necessary to further those interests."
(4) "administration of the drugs is *medically appropriate, i.e.,* in the patient's best medical interest in light of his medical condition."

[*Sell v. United States*, 539 U.S. 166, 180-83 (2003).]

Further, with respect to factor two, the prosecution must show by clear and convincing evidence that the drugs are substantially likely to render the defendant competent, but the drugs also are "substantially unlikely to have side effects that will interfere significantly with the defendant's ability to assist counsel in conducting a trial defense." [*United States v. Valenzuela-Puentes*, 479 F.3d 1220 (10th Cir. 2007) (quoting *Sell*, 539 U.S. at 181).]

You should insist on independent medical evaluations before the court considers ordering forced medication. [*See Rivera-Guerrero*, 426 F.3d at 1137 (stating that a court must be provided with a complete and reliable medically-informed record, based in part on independent medical evaluations).]

The independent medical evaluations include "an independent and timely evaluation of the [defendant] by a medical professional, including attention to the type of drugs proposed, their dosage, and the expected duration of a person's exposure, as well as an opportunity for the [defendant] to challenge the evaluation and offer his or her own medical evidence in response." [*Rivera-Guerrero*, 426 F.3d at 1142.]

[§13:09 Reserved]

II.   INSANITY

§13:10   The Definition of Insanity

Most jurisdictions employ the *M'Naghten* test of insanity. That is:

> The defendant is legally insane only if he suffers from a mental disease or defect such that at the time of the commission of the offense he was unable to understand the nature and quality of his acts, or he was unable to understand that what he was doing was wrong.

[*See* 18 U.S.C. §17; *Commonwealth v. Banks*, 513 Pa. 318, 330, 521 A.2d 1 (1987).]

Ten states have eliminated the "cognitive incapacity" alternative of the *M'Naghten* test, allowing an insanity defense only for defendants who are incapable of understanding that their actions were wrong ("moral incapacity"). [*Clark v. Arizona*, 126 S.Ct. 2709, 2720-22 (2006) (describing the states' different approaches and upholding Arizona's moral incapacity only defense as constitutionally permissible).]

Some states supplement *M'Naghten* with an "irresistible impulse" test. [*See, e.g., Morgan v. Commonwealth*, 50 Va.App. 120, 127, 646 S.E.2d 899, 902 (Va. Ct. App.2007) (the irresistible impulse defense is available when the accused's mind has become so impaired by disease that he is totally deprived of the mental power to control or restrain his act); *Neely v. Newton*, 149 F.3d 1074 (10th Cir. 1998) (under New Mexico law, for defendant to be considered "legally insane" the jury must find that the defendant (a) did not know the nature and quality of the act, or (b) did not know that it was wrong, or (c) was incapable of preventing himself from committing it).]

A number of jurisdictions have adopted the Model Penal Code test for criminal insanity form, under which a person is not responsible for his criminal conduct if, at the time of such conduct, as a result of mental disease or defect, he lacked substantial capacity either to appreciate the criminality or wrongfulness of his conduct, or to conform his conduct to the requirements of law. [*See, e.g., Commonwealth v. Urrea*, 443 Mass. 530, 822 N.E.2d 1192 (2005).]

§13:11   Whether to Risk an Insanity Defense

Since prevailing on an insanity defense carries a substantial likelihood of lengthy post-verdict confinement, you should hazard it only where the alternative is lengthy incarceration.

Besides having your psychiatrist evaluate your client's sanity, seek an opinion on whether your client is likely to be found dangerous.

From the time you begin to consider an insanity defense, explore treatment programs for your client so that upon a verdict of not guilty by reason of insanity, you have an argument that he should be released into a treatment program. [*See* 18 U.S.C. §4243(f)(2) (conditional release is mandatory if court finds that with a prescribed treatment program, the defendant will not be a risk).]

§13:12   Providing Notice of an Insanity Defense

If you intend to raise an insanity defense, you must give notice of your intent to do so, and allow the prosecution to have a psychiatrist of its choosing examine your client. [*See* Fed. R.Cr.P. 12.2.]

Form:
• **Form 13-2** Notice of Insanity Defense

§13:13   Guilty But Mentally Ill

Many jurisdictions have supplemented the verdict of not guilty by reason of insanity with "guilty but mentally ill" ("GBMI"). [*E.g.,* 18 Pa. C.S.A. §314.]

GBMI statutes have two purposes:
• To diminish the frequency of insanity acquittals by providing a jury with an alternative for the mentally ill defendant.
• To guarantee treatment for the mentally ill convict.
[*See Commonwealth v. Trill*, 374 Pa.Super. 549, 543 A.2d 1106 (1988).]

Twenty-two states employ this alternative. [*See* Bradford H. Charles, *Pennsylvania's Definitions of Insanity and Mental Illness: A Distinction With a Difference*, 12 Temp. Pol. & Civ. Rts. L. Rev. 265, 268 & n. 22 (2003).]

Constitutional challenges to the verdict (on due process, equal protection, vagueness, and ex post facto grounds) have failed. [Debra T. Landis, *"Guilty But Mentally Ill" Statutes: Validity and Construction*, 71 A.L.R.4th 702 §2[a] (1989).]

Upon a GBMI verdict, the court may impose any sentence authorized for a conviction, including death. [*See Harris v State*, 499 N.E.2d 723 (Ind. 1986).]

PRACTICE TIP:

Be aware of whether your jurisdiction has a GBMI alternative to insanity. Its availability lessens your chances of success with an insanity defense. If you choose to enter a GBMI plea, remember that any sentence is possible. Therefore, do not do so unless you have assurance that the sentencer, recognizing your client's mental illness, will impose a more lenient sentence than upon a straight conviction.

§13:14   Post-Verdict Considerations

A verdict of not guilty by reason of insanity does not entitle the defendant to immediate release. He will be committed pending a hearing at which he must prove that he is not dangerous. [*E.g.,* 18 U.S.C. §4243; *Shannon v. United States*, 512 U.S. 573, 576 (1994).]

If the court finds that the defendant is mentally ill and dangerous, his detention will continue until he no longer presents a substantial risk to the community. [18 U.S.C. §4243(e); *United States v. Murdoch*, 98 F.3d 472, 476 (9th Cir. 1996).]

Courts disagree over whether a jury must be informed of the post-verdict commitment procedures where the defense seeks a verdict of not guilty by reason of insanity. [*Compare Commonwealth v. Mulgrew*, 475 Pa. 271, 380 A.2d 349 (1977) (jury must be informed that the accused will be detained until the court is satisfied that he has recovered his sanity and will not be dangerous to himself or others), *with Shannon v. United States*, 512 U.S. 573 (1994) (court need not inform jury unless the prosecutor misleads the jury into thinking that the defendant's release will follow automatically upon a verdict of not guilty by reason of insanity).]

[§§13:15-13:19 Reserved]

III. OTHER MENTAL HEALTH DEFENSES

§13:20   Negating Mens Rea

Explore other defenses that aim to undermine the mens rea element of the crime. Mental health evidence that negates mens rea has several advantages over an insanity defense or a claim of incompetence to stand trial.

Many jurisdictions impose on the defense the burden to prove insanity and incompetence. However, the prosecution always must prove the mental state that is an element of the offense. Furthermore, you may be able to avoid the requirement that your client submit to examination by a prosecution psychiatrist. [*See* §13:40; *but see Commonwealth v. Connors*, 447 Mass. 313, 318, 850 N.E.2d 1038, 1042 (2006) (authorizing prosecution examination whenever a defense relies on a psychiatric interview with the defendant).]

Also, an acquittal attributable to the prosecution's inability to prove the necessary mens rea may not trigger the civil commitment provisions that follow a finding of incompetence or a verdict of not guilty by reason of insanity.

§13:21   Retardation or Other Illness

A defendant's mental retardation or mental illness may not amount to insanity, but might be severe enough to cast doubt on his ability to form the intent to commit the crime, particularly for specific intent crimes. [*See United States v. Pohlot*, 827 F.2d 889 (3d Cir. 1989) (admissibility of expert testimony to negate mens rea and disprove element of crime survives Insanity Defense Reform Act; extensive discussion of difference between diminished responsibility and negation of mens rea); *United States v. Childress*, 58 F.3d 693, 726-30 (D.C. Cir. 1995) (trial court erred in excluding defense evidence of mental retardation when offered on issue of intent in drug conspiracy case).]

The deficiency need not be so debilitating that it alone disproves the mens rea. Testimony about the defendant's mental state may be one part of a defense. For example, dependent personality disorder may render a defendant unusually susceptible to entrapment or duress, but you still need to show that the government agent initiated the criminal activity and that your client was not predisposed to commit the crime. [*E.g., United States v. Hill*, 655 F.2d 512 (3d Cir. 1981) (allowing such expert testimony).]

Evidence of a defendant's low intelligence or illiteracy may refute the knowledge or willfulness that is an essential element of the offense. [*E.g., United States v. Hayden*, 64 F.3d 126 (3d Cir. 1995) (holding that trial court erred in not allowing such evidence to show that defendant did not understand that he had been charged in an information, making his answers on Firearms Form 4473 false).]

CAUTION:
Insanity and incompetence are difficult defenses to establish and often carry adverse consequences, such as an extended commitment to await the defendant's return to competence or the same period of incarceration as a conviction.

§13:22   Establishing Relevancy of Mental Illness Evidence

Even where your client does not appear to suffer a disabling mental illness, personal tragedies, pressures and personality disorders may bear some causal relationship to the offense. An expert might be able to weave the defendant's personal situation and the crime into a narrative in which the crime fits as the inevitable and irresistible result of tragic circumstances.

This approach enables you to introduce through your expert sympathy-eliciting evidence that otherwise would be inadmissible. For example, your client's history of childhood abuse ordinarily would be irrelevant. However, an expert might rely on it in reaching the conclusion that your client suffered a personality disorder that undermined his ability to have criminal intent.

Your expert must closely tie the mental illness to your client's state of mind on the days of the offense. Courts will exclude mental illness evidence that sounds too vague and general and does not establish that at the time the defendant committed the criminal acts, he did not or could not have the necessary criminal knowledge or intent. [*E.g., United States v. Agnello*, 158 F.Supp.2d 285, 289 (E.D.N.Y. 2001) (evidence of bipolar disorder excluded where there was "no specificity tying the defendant's mental condition to the particular dates the crimes were committed," and over the three and half years of criminal conduct, the defendant's condition may have been under control through medication).]

[§§13:23-13:29 Reserved]

IV.   MENTAL HEALTH COURT

§13:30   The Mental Health Court Procedure

Many jurisdictions have instituted "mental health courts" as an alternative for offenders with serious mental ill-nesses. There are currently approximately 150 jurisdictions that provide such courts. [*See* www.consensusproject.org (website of the Criminal Justice/Mental Health Consensus Project, coordinated by the Council of State Governments Justice Center; provides links to courts in reader's area); Matthew J. D'Emic, "The Promise of Mental Health Courts," 22 *Criminal Justice* 24 (Fall 2007).]

If a defendant volunteers to undergo such a program, a mental health agency will present the court with a mental health service plan tailored to the defendant's needs. The plan will direct the defendant to a course of treatment at government expense with mental health providers and may include housing placements and enrollment in public assistance.

The court will order the defendant to complete the program while the charges are held in abeyance or as a condition of a probation and will hold "reinforcement hearings" to monitor and encourage the defendant's progress. These hearings are held frequently, varying from every two weeks to every 90 days depending on the jurisdiction.

Upon completion of the program, the court may dismiss the charges or discharge the defendant from probation.

§13:31   Qualifying for a Mental Health Court

Mental health courts may restrict access to defendants charged with misdemeanors or nonviolent felonies. [*But see D'Emic, supra* (Brooklyn, NY, mental health court is open to violent felonies if the victim consents).]

Most jurisdictions disqualify defendants with probation violation proceedings pending, defendants with histories of violence and defendants charged with sex offenses, drug trafficking and violent offenses.

Qualifying mental illnesses are schizophrenia, schizoaffective disorder, major depression and bipolar disorder.

§13:32   Whether to Seek a Mental Health Court

Whether a mental health court is a good choice for your client depends on the alternatives and your client's like-lihood of success, which turns on your client's enthusiasm for the program.

Many defendants might prefer a week or month in jail and being done with the case rather than an extended period of court supervision with the risk of serious sanctions for program failure.

Successful completion of the mental health program may result in a sentence of probation or even dismissal of the charges. Some programs require a guilty plea and postponement of sentencing pending completion of the program. This arrangement puts the defendant at risk of a harsh sentence if he fails the program.

Nonetheless, a mental health court diversion might offer your client an alternative rarely seen in the criminal justice system: a chance to turn his life around and leave the system better than he entered it. If the program in your jurisdiction has a reputation for fairness and efficacy, consider it seriously.

[§§13:33-13:39 Reserved]

V. Prosecution's Psychiatric Examination

§13:40 Waiver of the Privilege Against Self-Incrimination Allows a Prosecution Examination

Prosecution psychiatrists are agents of the state, and your client has a Fifth Amendment privilege to refuse to answer questions and a Sixth Amendment right to consult with counsel before answering questions from the psychiatrist. [*Estelle v. Smith*, 451 U.S. 454 (1981).]

However, once a defendant raises a mental state defense and gives notice that he intends to offer his own psychiatric expert to testify on his behalf, he waives to some extent his Fifth Amendment privilege against self-incrimination. The prosecution is entitled to rebut that defense by having its psychiatrist examine the defendant regarding the particular issues raised. [*Buchanan v. Kentucky*, 483 U.S. 402 (1987).]

Most courts permit a prosecution examination whenever the defense intends to introduce expert testimony of the defendant's mental state on any issue, whether it be competency, insanity, diminished capacity, inability to form the required intent, self-defense, or mitigation at sentencing. [*See Commonwealth v. Ostrander*, 441 Mass. 344, 352-55, 805 N.E.2d 497, 505-06 (2004) (the prosecution is entitled to have its psychiatrist examine the defendant where defendant raises mental impairment defenses, the defense of diminished capacity, a battered woman syndrome defense, or gives notice of intent to present evidence of mental condition at sentencing); *Coffey v. Messer*, 945 S.W.2d 944 (Ky. 1997) (defendant who intends to introduce expert evidence of his extreme emotional disturbance can be compelled to submit to prosecution expert exam); *Commonwealth v. Sartin*, 561 Pa. 522, 751 A.2d 1140 (2000) (when defendant intends to introduce psychiatric testimony in mitigation at the sentencing phase, can be ordered to submit to a prosecution psychiatrist's examination).]

A minority of courts distinguish between affirmative defenses (such as insanity, on which the defense has the burden of proof) and attacks on the prosecution's ability to prove the necessary mens rea. Those courts forbid prosecution examinations in the latter case, reasoning that the prosecution is not entitled to access to the defendant to assist it in carrying its burden on an element of the offense. [*United States v. Davis*, 93 F.3d 1286 (6th Cir. 1996).]

§13:41 Rights After Abandonment of a Mental State Defense

It is unclear what use can be made of your client's statements to the prosecution psychiatrist if you abandon a mental state defense. However, all courts agree that in such a case the prosecution cannot have its psychiatrist testify. [*See People v. Diaz*, 3 Misc.3d 686, 694-95, 777 N.Y.S.2d 856, 863-64 (NY Sup. Ct. 2004) (collecting cases).]

Some court rules restrict the use of prosecution psychiatric testimony to rebutting a defense expert. [*See e.g.*, Fed. R. Cr. P. 12.2(c).]

The Fifth Amendment also may contain this restriction. [*See Buchanan v. Kentucky*, 483 U.S. 402, 422-24 (1987) (prosecution use of psychiatric testimony limited to rebutting defense).]

§13:42 Rights During the Psychiatric Examination

There is little case law on the scope of the Fifth Amendment rights a defendant retains during a psychiatric examination, and the derivative uses to which the prosecution can put the examination and statements the defendant makes during it. [*See* Welsh S. White, *Government Psychiatric Examinations and the Death Penalty*, 37 Ariz. L. Rev. 869, 878-83 (1995).]

One issue is whether the defendant may refuse to answer questions about other uncharged criminal conduct, especially if his psychiatrist did not ask about such conduct. Many prosecution psychiatrists argue that they need to know about such incidents to reach an informed conclusion about the defendant's mental infirmities and mental state at the time of the present crime.

Another issue is whether the prosecution may introduce incriminatory statements the defendant makes about uncharged offenses, or follow the statements' leads and develop and introduce other harmful evidence, such as witnesses to the hitherto uncharged and perhaps even unknown criminal conduct.

Generally, the waiver of the Fifth Amendment privilege extends only so far as is necessary to give the prosecution a fair opportunity to rebut the defendant's testimony and evidence. Accordingly, some courts forbid the prosecution from even seeing the psychiatrist's report or discussing the matter with its psychiatrist until the defense confirms that it will introduce psychiatric evidence. [*See Commonwealth v. Sartin*, 561 Pa. 522, 528, 751 A. 2d 1140, 1143 (2000) (waiver is not "categorical"; ordering that results of prosecution expert's be placed under seal and that the results could be released only if and when the defendant confirmed intent to introduce mental state evidence).]

Other courts impose a burden on the government to show that other evidence was not derived from the defendant's statements to the psychiatrist. [*See United States v. Hall*, 152 F.3d at 399. *But see Jordan v. State,* 786 So.2d 987, 1006-1010 (Miss. 2001) (expert report could be used to cross-examine defendant's character witness where defense did not introduce any expert testimony).]

CAUTION:

Keep in mind that pursuing a mental state defense opens a door behind which great danger lurks. A prosecution psychiatrist eager to demonize your client will have the opportunity to interview your client for hours. You must prepare your client thoroughly for this interview with the help of your own psychiatrist. Use your preparation to assess just how bad your client might appear and to decide whether the mental state defense is worth the risk.

§13:43   Limiting the Scope of the Prosecution's Psychiatric Examination

Avail yourself of constitutional and statutory arguments to limit the scope of any prosecution psychiatric examination and its use.

A defendant's introduction of psychiatric evidence waives the Fifth Amendment privilege only to the extent necessary for the prosecution to have a fair opportunity to meet the defendant's evidence. [See §13:40.]

If your client's defense is not insanity or incompetence, but some other mental state defense, argue that the statute authorizes only examinations on those issues. Therefore, the prosecution psychiatrist should limit his inquiry to rebuttal of the defense claim.

CAUTION:

This argument may not preclude much, for the prosecution psychiatrist usually aims to portray the defendant as a malingering sociopath who acted from racism, greed or misogyny, a conclusion usable to refute claims of incompetence, insanity, diminished capacity and mitigation at sentencing.

§13:44   Limiting the Use of the Prosecution's Psychiatric Examination

If you forego expert testimony on your client's mental state, argue that the prosecution has nothing to rebut so it should not be allowed to use the examination of your client in any way, whether in rebuttal or on cross-examination of defense witnesses and even the defendant. [*Gibbs v. Frank*, 387 F.3d 268 (3d Cir. 2004) (Fifth Amendment permits admission of evaluation and statements made during it only to the extent necessary to rebut psychiatric defense, and none was raised where defense did not pursue mental infirmity defense in retrial after appeal); *People v. Pokovich*, 39 Cal.4th 1240, 141 P.3d 267, 48 Cal.Rptr.3d 158 (Cal. 2006) (statements defendant made to psychiatrist during court-ordered competency examination could not be used to cross-examine him).]

Many cases reason that a prosecution examination is necessary to address the unfair imbalance that would arise if the defense could have an expert base opinions on the defendant's version of the offense and effectively introduce the defendant's uncross-examined testimony. [*E.g., State v. Davis*, 254 Wis. 1, 645 N.W.2d 91 (Wis. 2002).]

Any evidence that does not serve as a conduit for the defendant's statements about the offense (i.e., character evidence or even opinion evidence that is not based on interviews with your client) does not create any such imbalance and the need to lower the Fifth Amendment protections. [*Brown v. Butler*, 876 F.2d 427 (5th Cir. 1989).]

§13:45   Limiting the Prosecution's Access to the Psychiatric Examination

Among the forbidden uses for compelled incriminatory evidence is the formulation of prosecution trial strategy, so the prosecutor should not have any access to its psychiatrist's report and opinions until you confirm that you intend to introduce expert psychiatric testimony.

Ask the court to seal the report until you confirm your intentions. [*See Commonwealth v. Sartin*, 561 Pa. 522, 751 A. 2d 1140 (2000).]

To protect against other uses of the prosecution psychiatrist's interviews, ask that the prosecutor record them, preferably on videotape. [*See* Welsh S. White, *Government Psychiatric Examinations and the Death Penalty*, 37 Ariz. L. Rev. 869, 885-86 (1995) (interview should be videotaped and prosecution should have burden of proving that its evidence was not derived from those statements).]

VI. FORMS

Form 13-1 Motion for Appointment of Psychologist

IN THE UNITED STATES DISTRICT COURT
FOR THE _____ DISTRICT OF _____

UNITED STATES OF AMERICA	)	
	)	
v.	)	CRIMINAL NO.
	)	
SDL	)	**-UNDER SEAL-**

MOTION TO APPOINT PSYCHOLOGIST

AND NOW, comes the Defendant, SDL, by his attorney, Thomas J. Farrell, Esquire, and requests that the Court appoint a psychologist to consult with counsel and to assist counsel in the preparation of the above captioned case and avers as follows:

1. The defendant is charged with two (2) Counts in violation of 18 U.S.C. 1341 arising from an alleged attempted fraud upon the September 11th Victim Compensation Fund.
2. SDL is indigent, and his counsel is court-appointed under the Criminal Justice Act, 18 U.S.C 3006A. Counsel represents that a psychological examination is necessary for effective representation of Mr. L. Counsel for Mr. L has reason believe that Mr. L suffers from a mental illness which may bear on his competence to stand trial and/or his sanity at the time of the offense.
3. Dr. JH, a licensed psychologist with experience in forensic examinations, has agreed to perform a psychological examination of Mr. L.
4. Counsel for SDL believes that Dr. H's fees in this case at the present time should not exceed Three Thousand Five Hundred Dollars ($3500.00).

WHEREFORE, for the foregoing reasons, the Defendant, SDL, requests that this Honorable Court appoint Dr. JH to perform a psychological examination.

Respectfully submitted,

_____
Thomas J. Farrell, Esquire
Dated:

IN THE UNITED STATES DISTRICT COURT
FOR THE _____ DISTRICT OF _____

UNITED STATES OF AMERICA	)	
	)	
v.	)	CRIMINAL NO.
	)	
SDL	)	**-UNDER SEAL-**

ORDER OF COURT

AND NOW, to-wit, this _____ day of _____, 2004, upon consideration of the foregoing Motion to Appoint Psychologist, it is hereby ORDERED, ADJUDGED AND DECREED that said motion is GRANTED;

It is FURTHER ORDERED that the fees for the examination shall not exceed $3500 unless approved by further order of court;

It is FURTHER ORDERED that the Clerk's office shall seal this order and motion.

_____
BY THE COURT

Form 13-2   Notice of Insanity Defense

IN THE UNITED STATES DISTRICT COURT
FOR THE _____ DISTRICT OF _____

UNITED STATES OF AMERICA	)	
	)	
v.	)	CRIMINAL NO.
	)	
SDL	)	

DEFENDANT SDL'S NOTICE OF INSANITY DEFENSE AND MENTAL INFIRMITY DEFENSE PURSUANT TO RULE 12.2 OF THE FEDERAL RULES OF CRIMINAL PROCEDURE

AND NOW COMES Defendant, SDL by and through his counsel, Thomas Farrell, Esquire, of the law firm of Reich, Alexander, Reisinger & Farrell, LLC, and hereby puts the Government on Notice of their intent to put on the defense of insanity pursuant to Federal Rule of Criminal Procedure 12.2.

1. The Defense intends to offer at trial the defense of insanity and mental infirmity.
2. The Defense intends to offer at trial evidence that SDL suffers from Delusional Disorder, Mixed Type and Cognitive Disorder Not Otherwise Specified. The Defense intends to offer at trial evidence that SDL currently suffers from this disorder and did so before and on December 22, 2003.
3. The Defense intends to call at trial the following witnesses to establish the defense of insanity and mental infirmity: JGH, Ph.D.
Clinical Psychologist
_____ Street
_____, PA

Respectfully submitted,

_____
Thomas Farrell, Esquire
Dated:

CERTIFICATE OF SERVICE

I, Thomas Farrell, Esquire do hereby certify that a true and correct copy of the within Notice of Insanity Defense and Mental Infirmity Defense Pursuant to Rule 12.2 of the Federal Rules of Criminal Procedure was served via first-class mail, postage pre-paid, on the 20th day of June, 2005, upon the following:
Assistant U. S. Attorney
633 U. S. Post Office and Courthouse
Pittsburgh, PA 15219

Chapter 14

DISCOVERY

V. *BRADY* DISCLOSURES

VI. *DAUBERT* DISCOVERY

VII. FORMS

I.   GENERAL POINTS

§14:01   Discovery Procedure

Discovery usually is a three-step process.

Step one

The prosecution may make an initial, voluntary disclosure, perhaps at the time of arraignment. This will include:
- Copies of the defendant's statements to law enforcement officials, as memorialized in the officials' reports.
- The defendant's criminal history.
- An offer to make documentary evidence available.

Step two

Most courts require the defense to make an informal request or demand for discovery before filing a motion with the court to seek discovery. [*See* Local Rule 16.1.D, W.D.Pa; NY CPL 240.40.]

Some courts and prosecutors' offices provide a standard form for the defense to check what it wants and to serve upon the prosecutor.

Unless the standard form is unusually detailed, or provides a section for you to make additional requests, you should supplement the form with your own discovery letter. And in many cases you may want to supplement your discovery letter with *Brady* requests tailored to the facts of your case and what you anticipate as defenses. [For more on *Brady* requests, *see* §§14:70 et seq.]

Step three

If you do not obtain what you want, you may file a motion for discovery with the court.

The law on discovery is not favorable. However, many courts will exercise their discretion to order or encourage the prosecution to provide additional discovery or to provide discovery of some things (i.e., witness identities and statements) sooner than otherwise obligated to do so.

Among the arguments that appeal to some courts' discretion:
- You cannot competently advise your client on whether to plead guilty without having additional discovery, such as the witnesses' or coconspirators' statements. Having that material sooner rather than later may result in an earlier disposition of the case and conservation of the court's resources.
- This is not the kind of case in which your client poses any danger to the witnesses.
- You need the discovery sooner rather than later because you need to conduct factual investigation and file motions in limine regarding the evidence's admissibility. If you do not receive the material until trial starts, you may need a continuance to investigate.
- Obtaining the materials well in advance of trial will enable the parties to focus the issues, reach stipulations and otherwise expedite the trial. This argument is particularly appropriate if the materials are voluminous.

Forms:
- **Form 14-1** Sample Informal Discovery Request
- **Form 14-2** Discovery Letter
- **Form 14-3** Specific *Brady* Motion

§14:02   Scope of Discovery Rules

Discovery rights are statutory, with few exceptions. [*See Weatherford v. Bursey*, 429 U.S. 545, 559 (1977) (no constitutional right to discovery); *but see* Anthony G. Amsterdam, *Trial Manual for the Defense of Criminal Cases* §270 (5th ed. 1988) (articulating various constitutional theories for a limited right to discovery).]

While statutes differ, they generally entitle the defense at minimum to four classes of disclosure. [*See, e.g.,* Fed. R. Crim. P. 16.] These are:
- The defendant's own statements. [*See* §14:10.]
- The defendant's criminal record.
- Documents seized from the defendant, or which the government intends to use at trial, or which are material to the defense. [*See* §14:20.]
- Expert and scientific reports. [*See* §14:30.]

[§§14:03-14:09 Reserved]

II. DISCOVERY ITEMS

A. The Defendant's Statements

§14:10   Your Client's Statements

You are generally entitled to disclosure of any statement your client made if in the prosecution's possession. However, there are some variations in different jurisdictions. [*See generally* Caroll J. Miller, *What Is Accused's "Statement" Subject To State Court Criminal Discovery*, 57 A.L.R.4th 827 (2005) (surveying state court rulings).] For example:

- Federal courts: Defense is entitled to any statement made to government official if in response to interrogation; defendant also entitled to any written or recorded statement made to anyone if the statement is in the government's possession. [Fed. R. Crim. P. 16 (a)(1).]
- New York: Defense is entitled to any statement made to government official, whether or not in response to interrogation, but no provision for discovery of statements to private actors. [NY Criminal Procedure Law 240.20. *See People v. Mitchell,* 289 A.D.2d 776, 734 N.Y.S.2d 353 (NY App. Div. 2001) (no discovery of letter defendant wrote from jail to neighbor).]
- Pennsylvania: Defense is entitled to any statement made by defendant if in the prosecution's possession, without any limitation as to whom and when made. [Pa. R. Crim. P. 573 (b)(1)(B). *See Commonwealth v. Rodgers,* 500 Pa. 405, 411, 456 A.2d 1352, 1355 (Pa. 1983) (prosecution obligated to disclose statement defendant made to friend before the crime expressing intent to kill victim).]

§14:11   Co-Defendant's Statements

In some jurisdictions, the discovery rules entitle you to discovery of co-defendants' and coconspirators' statements. [*E.g.,* NY CPL 240.20 (1)(a) (prosecution must disclose statements of co-defendants to be tried jointly).]

In other jurisdictions the rules do not allow such discovery. [*E.g., United States v. Roberts,* 811 F.2d 257 (4th Cir. 1987) (en banc); *but see United States v. Allen,* 289 F.Supp.2d 230, 238-39 & n.2 (N.D.N.Y. 2003) (disclosure ordered of nontestifying coconspirators' statements).]

Argue that disclosure is necessary so that you may file and the court may adjudicate other important pre-trial motions. Admitting co-defendants' post-arrest statements against your client:

- Would violate his Sixth Amendment right to confront the witnesses against him. [*See Bruton v. United States,* 391 U.S. 123 (1968).]
- Might necessitate either a severance shortly before trial or a mistrial.

Likewise, coconspirator statements are admissible only if made in furtherance of the conspiracy. [*See* FRE 801 (d) (2)(E).] You need to know the substance of the statements and the circumstances of their utterance to challenge their admissibility, and the court, to decide the issue.

PRACTICE TIP:

Request copies of co-defendants' statements, or at least a description of them, from their counsel. While they are not obligated to share the statements with you, a mutual exchange of such non-privileged information may assist both defendants by enabling them to craft a defense that accommodates both statements or to move pre-trial for a severance.

[§§14:12-14:19 Reserved]

B. Documents

§14:20   The Defense Is Entitled to Certain Documents

Documents are crucial. Not only may they contain the foundation of the prosecution case, but they may lead to impeaching evidence and may identify prosecution and defense witnesses.

Discovery rules generally entitle the defense to documents that:

- Have been seized from the defendant.

- The government intends to introduce at trial.
- Are material to the defense.

[*E.g.*, Fed. R. Crim. P. 16 (a)(1)(E).]

The prosecution's obligation applies to all documents within its possession or control. [*E.g.*, Fed. R. Crim. P. 16(a)(1)(E); *People v. Santorelli*, 95 N.Y.2d 412, 421, 741 N.E.2d 493, 718 N.Y.S.2d 696 (2000).]

This covers more than just what is found in the prosecutor's files. It obligates the prosecutor to:

- Search for relevant documents possessed by other government agencies. [*See, e.g., United States v. Libby*, 429 F.Supp.2d 1, 6-7 (D.D.C. 2006) (agencies "closely aligned" with prosecution or which participated in the investigation); *United States v. Safavian*, 233 F.R.D. 12 (D.D.C. 2005) (all executive branch agencies and departments).]
- Obtain from private parties those documents which the prosecution has a legal right to obtain upon demand. [*United States v. Stoll*, 2011 WL 703875, No. 10-60194-CR (S.D. FL. Feb. 21, 2011) (cooperating witnesses are "under the unique control of the Government"; therefore, Government sanctioned for cooperator's destruction of pertinent files, even though it occurred without the Government's knowledge, with an adverse inference instruction advising the jury that it may infer that the records destroyed would have been favorable to the defendants); *United States v. Stein*, 488 F.Supp.2d 350, 361-62 (S.D.N.Y. 2007) (government obligated to obtain documents from nonparty company where the company's deferred prosecution agreement obligated it to provide documents to the government on demand).]

The defense bears the burden of establishing the requested documents' materiality under that provision. [*United States v. Gordon*, 316 F.3d 1215, 1250 (11th Cir. 2003) ("A general description of the item will not suffice; neither will a conclusory argument that the requested item is material to the defense. ... Rather, the defendant must make a specific request for the item together with an explanation of how it will be helpful to the defense").]

The definition of "materiality" under the discovery rules includes incriminating evidence. [*United States v. Marshall*, 132 F.3d 63 (D.C. Cir. 1998).]

§14:21   Dealing With Voluminous Documents

In document-intensive cases, many prosecutors will provide you access to all the documents they have, but this creates the needle-in-the-haystack quandary of finding the useful among the voluminous.

There are several solutions:

Request that the prosecutor designate which documents it will use

Some courts will order the prosecution to designate well in advance of trial those documents it intends to use or to provide a table of contents or description of classes of documents so you know where to look for the more helpful documents. [*See United States v. Poindexter*, 727 F.Supp. 1470, 1484 (D.D.C. 1989) (ordering government to identify which of thousands of pages of calendars, financial information and diaries it intended to use at trial and to identify all documents on which each witness will rely or to which he will refer). *See also* Barry Tarlow, "Rico Report: When Too Much Discovery Is Not Enough," 26 *Champion* 56 (March 2002).]

Documentary evidence may raise numerous evidentiary issues (*e.g.*, authentication, hearsay, redaction) that could necessitate interrupting a jury trial for hearings, research and rulings. Argue to the court that if you have the documents well before trial, you may be able to reach stipulations about many of the documents and will obtain pre-trial rulings on many of the other issues.

Request access to scanned electronic files

Prosecutors often will image documents and present them electronically at trial. The electronic images are not the original documents, and you can argue to the prosecutor and the court that you should have access to the scanned electronic files sufficiently in advance of trial so that you can decide whether to contest their authenticity and admissibility. [*See United States v. Labovitz*, 1996 U.S. Dist. LEXIS 10498, 1996 WL 417113 (D. Mass. 1996) (conditioning permission for the prosecution to conduct a paperless trial on providing the defense with the CDs and all *Jencks* material at least 30 days before trial).]

Request originals from which a summary was prepared

Prosecutors frequently offer summaries of voluminous documents at trial. The rule requires the proponent of a summary to make the originals from which the summary was prepared "available for examination or copying, or both, by other parties at reasonable time and place." [FRE 1006.]

Some courts have indicated a preference for a hearing outside the jury's presence to determine the admissibility of such summaries. [*See United States v. Abbas*, 504 F.2d 123 (9th Cir. 1974); *United States v. Bartone*, 400 F.2d 459 (6th Cir. 1968).]

Argue for the hearing to take place pre-trial to avoid inconveniencing the jury.

§14:22   Remedies

The remedy for the prosecution's discovery violation depends principally on the harm it causes. Trial courts have broad discretion in fashioning a remedy, but should consider "the reasons why disclosure was not made, the extent of the prejudice, if any, to the opposing party, the feasibility of rectifying that prejudice by a continuance, and any other relevant circumstances." [*United States v. Lee*, 834 F.3d 145, 159 (2d Cir. 2016).] When detected before trial, an order to compel production of the evidence generally suffices. If the violation comes to light mid- or post-trial, a mistrial may be justified if you can prove that the use of the undisclosed evidence unfairly surprised you and interfered with your ability to fashion an intelligent defense strategy to respond to the evidence. [*United States v. Lee*, 573 F.3d 155 (3d Cir. 2009) (government's failure to produce the original of a hotel registration card, which once introduced into evidence was found to contain notations showing that the defendant was present in room when drugs were discovered there, required new trial).] To obtain a dismissal with prejudice, you must show that the prosecution acted in bad faith. [*Commonwealth v. Burke*, 566 Pa. 402, 419, 781 A.2d 1136, 1146 (2001).]

§14:23   Electronic Discovery

These days, one of the first tasks in nearly every civil case is to establish a protocol for the preservation, retrieval and production of electronically stored information.

A Joint Electronic Technology Working Group ("JETWG") established by the Administrative Office of the U.S. Courts and the Attorney General recently published Recommendations for ESI Discovery in federal criminal cases. The guidelines, including an ESI Discovery Production Checklist, are available at http://pdfserver.amlaw.com/legaltechnology/USDOJ_Intro_Recommendations_ESI_Discovery.pdf and www.fd.org/pdf_lib/final%20esi%20protocol.pdf. The Recommendations do not create rights beyond what is found in discovery rules, and they do not apply to state cases, but they provide guidance that may prove persuasive in any case. Embrace and advocate them as advancing the goals that every judge seeks: expedition in the resolution of cases (by making case-dispositive information easily accessible) and ease in presentation of evidence to the fact-finder.

Among the JETWG's Recommendations are:

Meet and Confer

Courts do not want to micromanage discovery disputes. You should first attempt to negotiate the extent and format of electronic discovery with the prosecutor. If your efforts are rebuffed, your reasonableness and attempts to save the court the work should appeal to the court's discretion. Some courts have adopted local orders requiring that the parties confer to discuss electronic discovery, and its format, and cost-sharing or cost-allocation arrangements. [*E.g.*, General Order Regarding Best Practices for Electronic Discovery of Documentary Materials in Criminal Cases (W.D. Okla. Aug. 20, 2009); *see generally* Justin P. Murphy, "E-Discovery in Criminal Matters - Emerging Trends and the Influence of Civil Litigation Principles," 11 The Sedona Conf. J. 257, 263 (2010).]

Request That Everything Be Produced Electronically in a Usable and Searchable Format

Some courts have imported requirements of the civil rules that ESI be produced in either the form in which the material "is ordinarily maintained," or in a "reasonably usable form." [*United States v. O'Keefe*, 537 F.Supp.2d 14, 18-19, 23 (D.D.C. 2008); *United States v. Briggs*, 2011 WL 4017886, 2011 U.S.Dist. LEXIS 101415 (W.D.N.Y. Sept. 8, 2011); Fed. R. Civ. P. 34(b)(2)(E)(ii).] This means that files must be produced either in their original, "native" format, or in a searchable format, such as a "load" file that includes the electronic document's metadata. Scanned PDF images or TIFF images are not searchable; do not accept those formats for ESI. [*See generally* Justin P. Murphy, E-Discovery in Crminal Matters - Emerging Trends & the Influence of Civil Litigation Principles Post-Indictment E-Discovery Jurisprudence, 11 Sedona Conf. J. 257 (2010).]

A recent decision demonstrates that the "reasonably usable" formatting requirement, besides facilitating review, may be necessary to prevent injustice. In *United States v. Stirling*, 11-CR-20792, 2012 WL 1200402 (S.D. FL. June 5, 2012), the government produced to the defendant before trial an exact replica of his laptop computer but did not disclose that the computer held non-visible files of Skype chats which could be found and retrieved only by hiring a computer forensic expert and using a specialized software. The defense learned that the hidden files existed for the first time when the government introduced them in rebuttal to contradict some of the defendant's own testimony. The trial court held that the "reasonably usable" standard of Federal Rule of Civil Procedure 34(b)(2)(E)(ii) should have been followed and that the interests of justice required that a new trial be granted.

When the amount of ESI is overwhelming, suggest that the prosecution follow procedures used and recommended in several cases: the production of indices, a searchable database, and a set of "hot documents" important to the prosecution's case or potentially relevant to the defense. [*United States v. Skilling*, 554 F.3d 529, 576-77 (5th Cir. 2009); Justin P. Murphy, Matthew A.S. Esworthy, "The ESI Tsunami," 27 Criminal Justice 31 (Spring 2012).] The U.S. Attorney General himself advocates that in complex cases, electronic discovery be produced "in a usable format with a comprehensive table of contents." [Eric H. Holder, Jr., "In the Digital Age, Ensuring that the Department Does Justice," 41 Geo. L.J. Ann. Rev. Crim. Proc. iii, xi (2012).]

Consider the Special Documents Birthed in the Electronic Era

Computers and smartphones do more than preserve information in a different format from that of the paper age; they create types of information never before available in criminal cases.

Cops and agents tend to communicate with witnesses, especially cooperating witnesses, by email and text messages. They write the sort of embarrassing things people once spoke. Such messages contain the witnesses' unscripted descriptions of events and their pleas for leniency and the agents' browbeating and assurances of favorable treatment in return for incriminating information. Unlike spoken words, messages transmitted remain on servers and can be retrieved and produced verbatim.

Witnesses texts and emails are "statements" and should be preserved and produced at the appropriate time. [*United States v. Suarez*, No. 09-932, 2010 U.S. Dist. LEXIS 112097 (D.N.J. October 21, 2010) (holding that texts messages are "statements" under the Jencks Act, 18 U.S.C. 3500, and FRCrP 26.2).] In *Suarez*, the prosecution's failure to preserve and produce texts messages between an FBI agent and witness earned an adverse inference jury instruction.

[§§14:24-14:29 Reserved]

C. Expert Reports

§14:30 The Defense Is Entitled to Certain Expert Reports

The defense is entitled upon demand to reports of:
- Physical and mental examinations.
- Scientific tests and reports.
- Expert reports prepared in connection with the case.

[*See* Fed. R. Crim. P. 16 (a)(1)(F); Pa. R. Crim. P. 573 (B)(1)(e); NY Crim. Pro. Law 240.20 (1)(c).]

Testimony from law enforcement officers regarding criminal modus operandi (*e.g.*, the rules and structure of the drug trade, the meaning of code words, the structure of organized crime, the value of the drugs at issue and the inconsistency of possessing such an amount with a claim of personal use) falls within the expert testimony rules, and any reports are discoverable. [*See United States v. Cruz*, 363 F.3d 187 (2d Cir. 2003) (agent's testimony deciphering drug jargon subject to expert testimony discovery rules); *United States v. Figueroa-Lopez*, 125 F.3d 1241, 1246 (9th Cir. 1997) (officer's testimony that defendant's conduct was consistent with that of a drug-trafficker was expert, not lay opinion testimony, and was subject to discovery rules).]

§14:31 Summaries of Qualifications and Opinion

Some discovery rules compel the prosecution to provide a report or summary of the expert's qualifications and opinion and the bases and reasons for the opinion. [Fed. R. Crim. P. 16 (a)(1)(G); Pa. R. Crim. P. 573(a)(2)(B) (discretionary with the court).]

This avoids circumvention of the discovery rules by calling an expert who never prepared a written report. [*See, e.g., People v. Montelbano*, 232 A.D.2d 255, 649 N.Y.S.2d 406, 407 (NY App. Div. 1st Dept. 1996) (where ballistics expert did not prepare written report, no pre-trial notice or disclosure required because NY discovery rules do not compel the writing of a report).]

While the extent of the detail required in such a report is unclear, you should take the position, especially in a jurisdiction that follows the *Daubert* rule [*see* §14:80], that for the court to discharge its gate-keeping role in keeping unreliable evidence from the jury, the report should explain the witnesses' methodology and how he arrived at his results in detail. [*See Travelers v. GE,* 150 F.Supp.2d 360, 365 (D.Conn. 2001) (explaining need for a detailed and reasoned expert report). *See also United States v. Duvall,* 272 F.3d 825, 828-29 (7th Cir. 2001) (prosecution's expert summary should provide not only a list of topics on which the expert would opine, but should describe the opinion which he would offer on the topics).]

§14:32   Underlying Data for Expert's Opinion

Request the underlying data, notes and materials used to create the report or arrive at the opinion. There are two grounds for such a request.

First, you need this information so that you can have your own expert conduct tests and arrive at an independent opinion. [*United States v. Butler,* 988 F.2d 537 (5th Cir. 1993) (defense entitled to samples of alleged cocaine base to test it); *United States v. Yee,* 129 F.R.D. 629 (N.D. Oh. 1990) (defense entitled to underlying data pertaining to validity of DNA testing, its statistical basis and proficiency tests); *see United States v. Barrett,* 703 F.2d 1076 (9th Cir. 1983) (defense entitled to a continuance so that its expert could conduct tests); *United States v. Kelly,* 420 F.2d 26 (2d Cir. 1969) (same).]

Second, the evidentiary rules mandate disclosure of the facts and data underlying an expert's opinion, on either:
- Direct examination. [*See, e.g.,* Pa. R. Evid. 705.]
- Cross-examination. [*See, e.g.,* Fed. R. Evid. 705.]

Disclosure mid-trial not only poses the danger of unfair surprise to the opponent, but it might also necessitate delaying the trial for full disclosure of extensive materials and perhaps re-testing. [*See United States v. Zanfordino,* 833 F.Supp. 429, 433 (S.D.N.Y. 1993) (using FRE 705 as authority to order pre-trial disclosure of underlying materials and data created and used by prosecution expert); Advisory Committee Notes to FRE 705 ("advance knowledge [of the supporting facts and data] ... is essential for effective cross-examination").]

[§§14:33-14:39 Reserved]

D.   Witness Identities and Statements

§14:40   Disclosure Is Within the Trial Court's Discretion

Obtaining witness identities in those jurisdictions where the discovery rules do not entitle you to them is a challenge. Whether to order disclosure of the identities lies wholly in the trial court's discretion. [*United States v. Bejasa,* 904 F.2d 137, 139 (2d Cir. 1990); *but see United States v. W.R. Grace, Inc.,* 493 F.3d 1119, 1128-31 (9th Cir. 2007) (courts lack the authority or discretion to order parties to identify nonexpert witnesses before trial).]

The standards that guide that discretion indicate that a court should grant a request only if the defendant makes a specific showing that disclosure is both material to the preparation of his defense and reasonable in light of the circumstances surrounding his case. [*United States v. Nachamie,* 91 F.Supp.2d 565, 579 (S.D.N.Y. 2000) (citing *United States v. Cannone,* 528 F.2d 296, 300-01 (2d Cir. 1976)).]

The factors that courts often look to in deciding whether to require the production of a witness list are:
- Did the offense alleged in the indictment involve a crime of violence?
- Have the defendants been arrested or convicted for crimes involving violence?
- Will the evidence in the case largely consist of testimony relating to documents (which by their nature are not easily altered)?
- Is there a realistic possibility that supplying the witnesses' names prior to trial will increase the likelihood that the prosecution's witnesses will not appear at trial, or will be unwilling to testify at trial?
- Does the indictment allege offenses occurring over an extended period of time, making preparation of the defendants' defense complex and difficult?
- Do the defendants have limited funds with which to investigate and prepare their defense?

[*United States v. Nachamie,* 91 F.Supp.2d 565, 579 (S.D.N.Y. 2000) (citing *United States v. Turkish,* 458 F. Supp. 874, 881 (S.D.N.Y. 1978)).]

§14:41 Informal Discovery

Often, the best chance to learn witness identities lies in informal discovery; that is, asking the prosecutor, agents or co-defendants' counsel, searching for the names in documents, or pursuing your own factual investigation.

If the case is a document-intensive one, the witness's identities can be gleaned from documents the prosecution must produce in discovery.

EXAMPLE:

In a mortgage fraud scheme, you will discover in the loan files the identities of the sellers, borrowers, loan originator, bank underwriter, home remodeler and appraiser–all the individuals you might need to interview.

§14:42 *Brady* Motion

A *Brady* motion might elicit the identities of witnesses, but it must be more than a general request for exculpatory information. [For more on *Brady* motions, *see* §§14:70 et seq.]

If you can articulate a specific theory of defense that rests on specific witnesses, you can describe those facts in a motion and demand the identities of witnesses who support your theory.

EXAMPLE:

If you have heard that the prosecution showed your client's photograph to eyewitnesses and those witnesses failed to identify him as the perpetrator, you can ask for a report of that event and the witness's identity. [*United States v. Cadet*, 727 F.2d 1453, 1469 (9th Cir. 1984) (government's intent not to call eyewitnesses to crime gave reason to believe that their testimony would be exculpatory, and trial court acted properly in ordering the prosecution to provide the defense with the witnesses' names and addresses).]

This approach often requires that you already have a good idea of what you are looking for. You may obtain such leads through rumors in the community. Furthermore, you can describe exculpatory scenarios in a discovery letter in hopes that the prosecution will take the bait.

Form:
• **Form 14-3** Specific *Brady* Motion

§14:43 Witness Statements

Many jurisdictions forbid production of witness statements until the time of trial. [*See* Chapter 20, Trial.]

Others entitle the defense to obtain the statements with other discovery materials. [E.g., Pa. R. Crim. P. 573(B)(2)(a)(ii) (eyewitness statements discoverable upon motion if court finds that the statements are material to preparation of the defenses and the request is reasonable).]

In either type of jurisdiction, you should request in both your discovery letter and motion that the officers and agents preserve any notes or rough drafts of witness interviews, your client's statements, or other investigative steps. [*See United States v. Ramos*, 27 F.3d 65 (3d Cir. 1994) (requiring preservation of notes and drafts both under the federal Jencks Act (18 U.S.C. §3500) and *Brady*).]

The transition from notes to finished report often excises material helpful to the defense. If the agents discard the notes, the trial court will look to the prosecution's good or bad faith in fashioning a remedy, and the disregard of your request fortifies your bad faith argument.

Form
• **Form 14-3** Specific *Brady* Motion

§14:44 Early Production of Witness Statements

In those jurisdictions which generally forbid court-ordered early production of witness statements, consider measures to elicit their voluntary production. The key evidence–what the witnesses will say–lies in those reports. Their early production could benefit the prosecution, by persuading your client to forego trial and negotiate a guilty plea, and benefit the court by ensuring that the trial will proceed smoothly, without requests for postponement and with an opportunity for the anticipation and resolution of evidentiary issues which the witness testimony may present. For these reasons, many prosecutors' offices adopt an "open file" discovery policy, a policy permitting defense review of the witness reports early in the case.

Besides the policy arguments outlined above, consider proposing a confidentiality agreement or protective order, in which you agree that the reports will not circulate beyond your client and experts and investigators. It may include provisions that those individuals receiving or reviewing the reports must sign the order and agree to its terms. Witnesses often desire confidentiality as long as possible, and prosecutors often fear tampering with witnesses, even in nonviolent cases. This type of agreement serves both those interests.

§14:45   Sharing Discovery With Your Client

Some prosecutors, and even some courts, have policies or rules forbidding defense attorneys from sharing discovery materials and witness statements with their clients. An across-the-board rule that is not founded on the special circumstances in a particular case may offend the Constitution and should be resisted. Included with a defendant's right to the effective assistance of counsel is the right to consult with counsel. [*Geders v. United States*, 425 U.S. 80 (1976).] Thus, "in the usual case when production [of discovery and witness statements] is ordered, a client has the right to see and know what has been produced." [*United States v. Hung*, 667 F.2d 1105, 1108 (4th Cir. 1981). *See also United States v. Bin Laden*, 2001 U.S. Dist. LEXIS 719, *12 (S.D.N.Y. 2001).]

If proven in a particular case, a need to protect witnesses (or the public or classified information) may justify some limitation on the right to consult, including restrictions on defense counsel's sharing of information with his client. [*In re Terrorist Bombings of U.S. Embassies v. Odeh*, 552 F.3d 93, 127 (2d Cir. 2008) ("Ascertaining the permissibility of a particular restriction requires an intensely context-specific inquiry"); *Morgan v. Bennett*, 204 F.3d 360, 365, 367 (2d Cir. 2000); *Hung*, 667 F.2d at 1108.]

That said, there may be good reasons to avoid giving copies of discovery to your client, particularly if he is incarcerated. Cellmates and acquaintances may read the materials and use the case facts to concoct a story and offer themselves to the prosecution as witnesses to your client's admission of facts in the reports. The discovery may reveal embarrassing or imperiling case facts, such as your client's efforts to cooperate against another or the victimization of a child. Some clients indeed may attempt to threaten or tamper with witnesses mentioned in the discovery, and if those efforts are tied to the discovery, you may be implicated in the client's crime.

As the Constitution demands of courts, you, too, must make a case-specific evaluation of the risks. When you have well-founded concerns, you might take it upon yourself to redact names or addresses of witnesses from your client's copies, or you might have your client return the documents after he reads and reviews them in your presence.

[§§14:46-14:49 Reserved]

III.   DISCOVERY TOOLS

§14:50   Omnibus Motion

Many courts prefer that you file all your motions, discovery and otherwise, in one document entitled an "Omnibus Pre-Trial Motion."

Separate the issues with captions for each type of motion and relief requested.

Forms:
- **Form 14-4** Omnibus Pre-Trial Motion
- **Form 14-5** Federal Omnibus Pre-Trial Motion

§14:51   Notice of Prior Bad Acts

Many court rules require the prosecution to give notice of uncharged misconduct evidence it intends to use at trial, if the defense requests such notice. [*E.g.*, FRE 404(b); NY Criminal Procedure Law 240.43 (only if used to impeach the defendant; no notice required if the prosecution intends to use the evidence in its case in chief).]

While these rules often require only general notice of the nature of the prior misconduct, you can elicit more detail by moving to preclude the evidence. The prosecution will then be forced to describe the particulars of the misconduct to defend its admissibility.

The prior bad act disclosure rules frequently omit any particular deadline for disclosure. However, courts have recognized that the disclosure should occur far enough in advance of trial so that the defense can investigate the allegations and file motions to preclude the evidence. [*E.g., United States v. Dawson*, 243 F.Supp.2d 780 (N.D. Ill. 2003) (thirty days before trial); *Nachamie*, 91 F.Supp.2d at 577 (one month before trial).]

§14:52 Subpoenas

Subpoenas have some limited use as discovery devices. However:
- The items subpoenaed must be admissible evidence. [*Bowman Dairy Co. v. United States*, 341 U.S. 214, 221 (1951).]
- Subpoenas are returnable at trial, unless the court orders pre-trial disclosure. [*See* Fed. R. Cr. P. 17 (c).]

Materials that may be subpoenaed may include purely impeaching material, such as witnesses' prior statements to private entities or government agencies not involved in your prosecution. [*See, e.g., United States v. Cuthbertson*, 630 F.2d 139, 144 (3d Cir. 1980).] However, courts will not order production of such impeaching materials before trial. [*United States v. Nixon*, 418 U.S. 683, 701 (1974); *United States v. Nachamie*, 91 F.Supp.2d 565, 578 (S.D.N.Y. 2000).]

The standard for persuading a court to order pre-trial disclosure is not an easy one. The moving party must show that:
- The documents are evidentiary and relevant.
- The documents are not otherwise procurable reasonably in advance of trial by exercise of due diligence.
- The party cannot properly prepare for trial without such production and inspection in advance of trial and the failure to obtain such inspection may tend unreasonably to delay the trial.
- The application is made in good faith and is not intended as a general "fishing expedition."

[*United States v. Nixon*, 418 U.S. 683, 699-700 (1974).]

Nevertheless, a subpoena may yield important pre-trial disclosures. If all you want are the documents, you may serve a subpoena upon the custodian for personal appearance and production of the documents at the time of trial (which does not require a court order) and indicate on the subpoena that personal appearance will not be required if the documents are delivered to your office at some time before trial. Without a court order, that provision is not enforceable, but many recipients will comply with it.

If you seek a subpoena for pre-trial production, and want to avoid revealing to the prosecution which documents you are subpoenaing, accompany the motion for a subpoena with a motion to seal and to issue the subpoena ex parte on the grounds that providing notice to the prosecution will expose and compromise defense trial strategy. [*See United States v. Fox*, 275 F.Supp.2d 1006 (D. Neb. 2003) (notice must be provided unless the defendant alleges and the court find that notice will disclose trial strategy or attorney work product; surveys cases).]

Some courts specify by local rule whether or not they will seal motions for pre-trial subpoenas. [*Compare* NE Crim. R. 17.2(b)(1) (U.S. Dist. Ct., D. Nebraska) ("Except in extraordinary cases where ex parte consideration may be justified, the motion for issuance of the subpoena must be served on opposing counsel.") *with* L. Cr. R. 49(D) (U.S. Dist. Ct. W.D. Pa.) ("The following documents shall be accepted by the Clerk for filing under seal without the necessity of a separate sealing order: . . . (3) Motions for subpoenas for witnesses.").]

Form:
- **Form 14-6** Ex Parte Motion for Subpoena Duces Tecum

§14:53 Bill of Particulars

The defense is entitled to a bill of particulars when the charging instrument is too vague and indefinite for the defendant "to adequately prepare his defense, to avoid surprise during the trial and to protect him[self] against a second prosecution for an inadequately described offense." [*United States v. Addonizio*, 451 F.2d 49, 63-64 (3d Cir. 1972). *See United States v. Bortnovsky*, 820 F.2d 572, 574 (2d Cir.1987).]

The law seldom compels a bill of particulars; the decision to grant one lies in the trial court's discretion. [*See United States v. Walsh*, 194 F.3d 37, 47 (2d Cir. 1999).]

An indictment that relies on general allegations to describe a complex and wide-ranging scheme is most likely to elicit an order granting a bill of particulars. [*See, e.g., United States v. Davidoff*, 845 F.2d 1151 (2d Cir. 1988) (trial court abused its discretion by denying request for bill of particulars where the indictment did not fully identify the acts giving rise to a RICO charge); *Bortnovsky*, 820 F.2d 572 (trial court abused its discretion by denying request for bill of particulars identifying which of numerous insurance claims were fraudulent); 1 Charles Alan Wright, Nancy J. King, Susan R. Klein, Andrew D. Leipold, *Federal Practice and Procedure* §126 (2d ed.1995) (categorizing cases describing indictment sufficiency requirements by crime).]

Form:
- **Form 14-7** Request for Bill of Particulars

[§§14:54-14:59 Reserved]

IV.   DEFENSE DISCOVERY OBLIGATIONS

§14:60   Reciprocal Discovery and Notice of Defenses

A request for discovery will trigger reciprocal discovery obligations.

Also, you might be required to give notice of certain defenses, such as alibi or insanity. [*See* Fed. R. Crim. P. 12.1 (alibi; upon prosecution request), 12.2 (insanity; must give notice regardless of prosecution request).]

Review your discovery rules carefully and produce what is required, no more and no less. A trial judge has the authority to preclude defense evidence for violation of discovery rules. [*Taylor v. Illinois.* 484 U.S. 400 (1988); *United States v. Ulbricht*, 858 F.3d 71 (2d Cir. 2017) (precluding the defense from calling two experts first disclosed mid-trial, where the disclosures also were inadequate in failing to summarize the experts' opinions and their bases, and where the government could show prejudice and the trial court did consider alternative sanctions such as a continuance).] However, judges are reluctant to impose such a harsh sanction. On the other hand, lesser sanctions may flow (such as a continuance for the prosecution to investigate, or monetary sanctions on defense counsel).

When courts impose onerous reciprocal discovery obligations on the defense, they usually do so in the context of a pre-trial order that likewise forces the prosecution to disclose much more of its case than is customarily required (*e.g.,* witness lists, witness statements, or designation of trial exhibits).

When asking for extra disclosure from the prosecution, you must weigh the value of the additional insight into the prosecution case against the cost of disclosing your defense. Consider the following questions:
- Are you in the dark about the prosecution's strategy and likely witnesses or do you have a good idea of what their evidence will be through document discovery, informal discussions with the prosecutor and your own investigation?
- Are your witnesses such that if disclosed pre-trial the prosecution will be able to intimidate them or excavate damaging information about their credibility?
- Does your defense depend on the element of surprise, or, like most defenses, is it the only feasible one in the circumstances, one that any competent prosecutor would anticipate?

Remember that the court cannot force your client to commit to testifying or not, and you cannot be forced to preview his testimony. Where your client has not made any statement to the authorities, and you plan on having him testify, early disclosure of the prosecution's evidence may enable you to mold his testimony and your trial strategy to anticipate and meet the worst of the evidence.

§14:61   No Requirement to Disclose Harmful Evidence

The defense does not have any obligation analogous to the *Brady* doctrine to disclose evidence harmful to its case. You may hide incriminating evidence safely away in your files so long as it is not contraband.

Furthermore, absent a rule commanding it, a trial court cannot order the defense to produce impeaching and rebuttal evidence to the prosecution before trial. [*State v. Kinney*, 262 Neb. 812 (2001) (ordering the defense to produce pre-trial substance of impeaching and rebuttal evidence was reversible error because it gave away defense trial strategy); *United States v. Hicks*, 103 F.3d 837 (9th Cir. 1996) ("A district court that orders the Government and the defendant to exchange witness lists and summaries of anticipated witness testimony in advance of trial has exceeded its authority under Rule 16 of the Federal Rules of Criminal Procedure and has committed error"); *United States v. Cerro*, 775 F.2d 908, 914-15 (7th Cir. 1985) (court did not have power to order defense to produce pre-trial other crimes evidence it intended to use to impeach government witnesses; the government does not have right to discovery of impeaching evidence).]

[§§14:62-14:69 Reserved]

V. *BRADY* DISCLOSURES

§14:70 The Prosecutor's Obligation to Disclose Exculpatory Evidence

The due process clause obligates the prosecution to disclose to the defense any material evidence favorable on the issues of guilt or punishment. [*Brady v. Maryland*, 373 U.S. 83 (1963).]

Evidence is exculpatory if it tends to disprove the defendant's guilt, whether by:

- Showing his innocence.
- Undermining the credibility of government witnesses. [*See Turner v. United States*, — U.S. —, No. 15-1503, slip op. at 10 (US June 22, 2017); *Giglio v. United States*, 405 U.S. 150 (1972); *Alderman v. Zant*, 22 F.3d 1541, 1554 (11th Cir. 1994) (prosecution must disclose promises, understandings and agreements with its witnesses as well as any "facts that might motivate a witness in giving testimony"); *see generally* Michael L. Piccarreta, Jefferson Keenan, "Impeaching a Cooperating Witness," 49 *Federal Lawyer* 16 (2002) (collecting types of information that should be produced about a cooperating witness to include payments, any agreements and promises, criminal record, drug and alcohol use, psychiatric reports, reports about uncharged misconduct, prior inconsistent statements, tax returns (to the extent they show failure to report earnings from cooperation or from illegal sources), polygraph tests or the refusal to take them).]
- Tending to mitigate the punishment. [*See Cone v. Bell*, 556 U.S. 449, 452, 470 (2009) (reversing because while lower courts evaluated materiality of favorable evidence on guilt, they failed to consider its materiality as to the sentence); *United States v. Severson*, 3 F.3d 1005, 1013 (7th Cir. 1993) ("*Brady* applies to sentencing").]

The prosecutor's *Brady* obligation extends beyond searching his own file to producing information possessed by police agencies which participated in the investigation or prosecution. [*Kyles v. Whitley*, 514 U.S. 419, 437 (1995).] The prosecution team will be charged with knowledge of a police officer's criminality where the officer was part of the team, even if the officer concealed that criminal conduct from the prosecutor. [*Arnold v. Sec'y, Dep't of Corrections*, 595 F.3d 1324 (11th Cir. 2010), *aff'g and adopting opinion in* 622 F.Supp.2d 1294 (M.D. Fl. 2009).]

However, *Kyles* does not "impos[e] a duty on the prosecutor's office to learn of information possessed by other government agencies that have no involvement in the investigation or prosecution at issue." [*United States v. Merlino*, 349 F.3d 144, 154 (3d Cir. 2003) (prosecution not obligated to review recordings of incarcerated government witness's telephone calls for exculpatory information where the Bureau of Prisons was not involved in the prosecution).]

At least one court has held that upon defense request, the prosecutor has an obligation to search the personnel files of its government-employed witnesses for exculpatory and impeaching material. [*United States v. Henthorn*, 931 F.2d 29 (9th Cir. 1991).]

The prosecutor's *Brady* obligation to disclose exculpatory information continues after trial to evidence discovered while the direct appeal is pending. [*Fields v. Wharrie*, 672 F.3d 505, 514-15 (7th Cir. 2012).]

§14:71 Materiality

The materiality requirement is a constant obstacle to obtaining *Brady* disclosures. Evidence "is material only if there is a reasonable probability that, had the evidence been disclosed to the defense, the outcome would have been different." [*Kyles v. Whitley*, 514 U.S. 419, 433, 435 (1995).] Most prosecutors, having filed charges and thus concluded that your client is guilty, have difficulty seeing a probability that a piece of evidence will change the outcome.

A lesser materiality standard governs if you can show that the prosecutor knowingly used perjured testimony or failed to correct what he subsequently learned was false testimony: "the falsehood is deemed to be material 'if there is any reasonable likelihood that the false testimony could have affected the judgment of the jury.'" [*Trepal v. Secretary, Florida Department of Corrections*, 684 F.3d 1088, 1108 (11th Cir. 2012).]

There are two arguments that you can use to approach the prosecutor's mindset.

The pre-trial context requires the prosecutor to err on the side of disclosure

The Supreme Court created the *Brady* standard of materiality in the context of appeals, evaluating the significance of the evidence against the totality of the trial evidence. No one can make this evaluation before trial. The prosecutor cannot predict with certainty how his own evidence will go in, much less the defense side of the case, and what impact the undisclosed evidence will have on the case as a whole. Therefore, a prosecutor should err on the side of disclosure. [*See Kyles*, 514 U.S at 437-40 (mindful that only he knows what was not disclosed, a prudent prosecutor should err on the side of disclosing all favorable evidence).]

Further, application of a materiality standard before trial does not serve the finality interest. To the contrary, the interest that criminal adjudications be final, that trial be the "main event," rather than the start of years of post-conviction litigation, militates in favor of having the prosecution disclose all arguably exculpatory evidence regardless of his appraisal of its potency. [*See United States v. Sudikoff*, 36 F.Supp.2d 1196 (C.D.Cal. 1999) (appellate definitions of materiality are not appropriate in the pre-trial discovery context; pre-trial, the prosecution must produce all evidence that might reasonably be considered favorable to the defense or information that might lead to admissible favorable evidence); *United States v. Carter*, 313 F.Supp.2d 921 (E.D. Wisc. 2004) (same).]

Educate the prosecutor about the defense

A second approach is to educate the prosecutor about the defense so that he understands how a piece of evidence fits into an attack on his case.

Although this approach risks surrendering the element of surprise, most defenses are apparent to any intelligent prosecutor.

Most *Brady* inquiries seek information about the prosecutor's own evidence and witnesses, such as cooperating witnesses' uncharged misconduct, their initial exculpation of the defendant, or their lies to the prosecutor about their own culpability. In the usual case, you lack any access to those witnesses and information. You lose little by revealing to the prosecutor that you have heard that such information exists about the prosecutor's own witnesses.

§14:72   Demanding *Brady* Material

Under the federal *Brady* standard, the same test of materiality applies whether the defense made a general, a specific or even no request. [*See Kyles v. Whitley*, 514 U.S. at 433.]

However, some states have held that under their state constitutions a specific *Brady* demand triggers a less demanding standard of materiality. [*People v. Vilardi*, 76 N.Y.2d 67, 556 N.Y.S.2d 518, 555 N.E.2d 915 (1990).]

Nonetheless, in any jurisdiction you should couple comprehensive *Brady* demands with more specific ones. The more specific the demand, the more likely you are to get relief from the prosecutor, the trial court, or an appellate court. Prosecutors often may not realize how a particular piece of evidence might fit into a defense. With a general demand a trial court will accept the prosecutor's assurance that he has searched his file and found nothing exculpatory. However, when ruling on a specific request, the court may demand that the prosecutor answer whether or not he looked for and found that particular item.

Also, articulating a defense theory and explaining how the sought-after evidence fits assists both the trial and reviewing court in understanding that the evidence is material. [*See United States v. Bagley*, 473 U.S. 667, 682-83 (1987) (Blackmun, J., concurring) ("The more specifically the defense requests certain evidence ... the more reasonable it is for the defense to assume from the nondisclosure that the evidence does not exist, and to make pre-trial and trial decisions on the basis of this assumption."); *Pennsylvania v. Ritchie*, 480 U.S. 39, 58 n.15 (1988) ("The degree of specificity of Ritchie's request may have a bearing on the ... assessment ... of the materiality of the nondisclosure"); Robert S. Mahler, "Extracting the Gate Key: Litigating *Brady* Issues," 25 *Champion* 14, 18-19 (May 2001).]

Furthermore, a specific demand may impose on the prosecution a duty to investigate and develop and obtain exculpatory evidence not yet in its possession. [*Commonwealth of N. Mariana Islands v. Bowie*, 243 F.3d 1109 (9th Cir. 2001) (where prosecutor discovered letter suggesting a scheme among the cooperating witnesses to frame the defendant, merely turning over the letter to the defense did not satisfy the prosecution's *Brady* obligations; prosecutor had a duty to determine who authored the letter and to investigate the scheme).]

Avail yourself of this strategy of imposing an investigatory duty on the prosecutor where bits and pieces of information that you cannot complete on your own suggest improper conduct by government witnesses to whom only the government has access, such as incarcerated cooperating witnesses.

EXAMPLE

A friendly witness may have heard from the cooperator's paramour that the cooperator is colluding with others in prison to fabricate a story to incriminate your client and gain himself leniency on his own case and that the cooperator has discussed these plans over recorded jail phone lines. Advising the prosecutor of this information may force him to obtain the recordings and confront the witness.

Form:
• **Form 14-3** Specific *Brady* Motion

§14:73   Timing of *Brady* Disclosures

Prosecutors frequently resist early disclosure of *Brady* impeaching material on the grounds that statutes similar to the Jencks Act [18 U.S.C. §3500] forbid a court from ordering disclosure of a witness's statements prior to trial.

Further, as many opinions state, *Brady* is not a rule of discovery, but one of trial fairness. [*See, e.g., United States v. Causey*, 356 F.Supp.2d 681, 688 (S.D. Tex. 2005).]

A number of courts have ruled, however, that the Jencks Act does not control the timing of *Brady* disclosures. If the material is exculpatory, it must be disclosed sufficiently in advance of trial to be useful to the defense, and the trial court may order prompt pre-trial disclosure. [*E.g., United States v. Gil*, 297 F.3d 93, 105-06 (2d Cir. 2003) (disclosing impeaching report Friday before trial in a five-ream stack of reports did not satisfy *Brady*); *United States v. Coppa*, 267 F.3d 132 (2d Cir. 2001) (immediate disclosure not required, disagreeing with *Shvarts* on this point; but prosecutor must assess materiality of information and disclose to the defense in sufficient time to be of use to the defense); *United States v. Shvarts*, 90 F.Supp.2d 219, 228-29 (E.D.N.Y. 2000) (prosecutor should disclose exculpatory information immediately without regard to its materiality); *United States v. Poindexter*, 727 F.Supp. 1470, 1485 (D.D.C. 1989) (same).]

§14:74   Look to Local Rules and Rules of Professional Conduct

You may be able to sidestep the statutory interpretation analysis and fine constitutional issues by invoking local rules and the rules of professional conduct, both of which often require prosecutors, on pain of disciplinary action, to disclose such material as soon as they become aware of it. [*Turner v. United States*, — U.S. —, No. 15-1503, slip op. at 10 (US June 22, 2017) (approving of prosecution's adoption of a "generous policy of discovery in criminal cases under which it disclose any information a defendant may wish to use"); *id* at 2 (Kagan, J., dissenting) (noting that she and the majority agree that "exculpatory or impeaching evidence . . . ought to be disclosed to defendants as a matter of course"); *United States v. Starusko*, 729 F.2d 256, 261, 264-65 (3d Cir. 1984) (disclosure required at earliest feasible time, relying on ABA Standards for Criminal Justice §3-3.11 (1980) and Model Rules of Professional Conduct Rule 3.8 (1983)); *United States v. Acosta*, 357 F.Supp.2d 1228 (D. Nev. 2005) (relying in part on local rules adopting Model Rule 3.8 to order disclosure 60 days before trial).]

The American Bar Association's Standing Committee on Ethics and Professional Responsibility recently clarified that Rule 3.8(d) of the Model Rules of Professional Conduct imposes duties on prosecutors far beyond the constitutional minimum. In particular:

- Rule 3.8 does not include a materiality requirement. A prosecutor must disclose any information favorable to the defense without regard to its impact or the prosecutor's assessment of its credibility. "Nothing in the rule suggests a de minimis exception to the prosecutor's disclosure duty where, for example, the prosecutor believes that the information has only a minimal tendency to negate the defendant's guilt, or that the favorable evidence is highly unreliable."
- The ethical duty extends beyond admissible evidence to information that may lead to exculpatory evidence.
- Evidence is exculpatory and must be disclosed if it supports any defense, whether or not one of factual innocence, and if it merely lessens the degree of guilt.
- The disclosure must be early and full enough to enable the defendant to conduct a thorough investigation and to evaluate whether or not to plead guilty.
- Supervisory prosecutors must supervise and train their line assistants in this obligation, including ordering subordinates to commit to writing favorable information conveyed orally and implementing procedures so that prosecutors communicate favorable information to the colleague responsible for disclosure.

[09-454 Formal Opinion (July 8, 2009) (available at www.abanet.org/cpr).]

After serious *Brady* violations in a number of high profile cases, including the prosecution of Senator Stevens of Alaska and several W.R. Grace executives, led to mistrials and sanctions, the U.S. Department of Justice promulgated new *Brady* policies that mandate procedures beyond the constitutional minimum:

- Prosecutors must conduct a thorough search of investigative agency case files, informant files, and, in some situations, the files of civil regulatory agencies, to discover and preserve information favorable to the defense.
- Prosecutors and agents have an obligation to memorialize all witness interviews (rather than, as is common, create a summary report at the end of several interviews).
- Information that "is inconsistent with any element of any crime charged against the defendant or that establishes a recognized affirmative defense" or that "casts a substantial doubt upon the accuracy of any evidence . . . or might have a significant bearing on the admissibility of prosecution evidence" must be disclosed "regardless of whether the prosecutor believes such information will make the difference between conviction and acquittal . . ."

- The disclosure obligation extends to "information" regardless of whether it is admissible evidence.
- The information must be disclosed "reasonably promptly after it is discovered."

[United States Attorneys' Manual 9-5.001; US DOJ Criminal Resource Manual 165, "Guidance for Prosecutors Regarding Criminal Discovery" (January 4, 2010, Memorandum from Deputy Attorney General David W. Ogden).] The Ogden Memorandum also instructs prosecutors to comply with local rules concerning the timing of *Brady* disclosures. [*E.g.,* L CrR 16.C (U.S. District Court, W.D.Pa.) (requiring disclosure of exculpatory evidence at arraignment).] In the past, prosecutors often ignored those local timetables.

§14:75   A Production Order Allows Sanctions

Ask the court to enter an order that the prosecutor produce all *Brady* material by a certain time.

An order for pre-trial disclosure empowers the trial court to impose sterner sanctions than it can for tardy disclosure of *Brady* material where no order compelled its pre-trial disclosure. [*United States v. Starusko,* 729 F.2d 256, 261, 263-64 (3d Cir. 1984).]

Sanctions may include continuances, preclusion of evidence, mistrials and new trials. A dismissal without prejudice is appropriate only in the case of willful prosecutorial misconduct and severe prejudice to the defense that cannot otherwise be remedied. [*See Government of the Virgin Islands v. Fahie,* 419 F.3d 249, 254 n.6 (3d Cir. 2005) (noting that while dismissal with prejudice is an available sanction, there are no published federal appellate opinions in which a court has imposed such a sanction); *but see Commonwealth v. Smith,* 532 Pa. 177, 615 A.2d 321 (1992) (imposing dismissal with prejudice where prosecutor deliberately concealed exculpatory evidence both during trial and for two years afterwards because the prosecutor acted with the deliberate intent to subvert the truth-finding process).]

[§§14:76-14:79 Reserved]

VI.   *DAUBERT* DISCOVERY

§14:80   General Points

The federal courts and many states have abandoned the *Frye v. United States,* 293 F. 1013 (D.C. Cir. 1923) "general acceptance" test for expert testimony for a reliability and relevance test. [*Daubert v. Merrell Dow Pharmaceuticals, Inc.,* 509 U.S. 579 (1993).]

Daubert imposes upon trial judges the "gatekeeping" responsibility of evaluating whether "the reasoning or methodology underlying the testimony is scientifically valid and ... whether that reasoning or methodology properly can be applied to the facts at issue." [*Daubert,* 509 U.S. at 593.]

The gatekeeping responsibility extends to all types of expert testimony, whether based on science or experiential expertise. [*Kumho Tire Co. v. Carmichael,* 526 U.S. 137 (1999); Fed. R. Evid. 702.]

Although this rule has not had the same seismic impact in criminal cases as in civil cases, it is still important to consider *Daubert* challenges to any forensic testimony that seems novel or that has been accepted without rigorous testing.

In civil cases, *Daubert* challenges entail exchange of expert reports and depositions often followed by a pre-trial hearing at which not only do the trial experts testify, but the parties call *Daubert* experts whose role is to opine whether the other experts' methods and application to the facts of the case are reliable. [*E.g., United States v. Velasquez,* 64 F.3d 844 (3rd Cir. 1995) (permitting law school professor to testify to the inadequacies of forensic document examiners).]

Depositions are unlikely in a criminal case unless the jurisdiction's discovery rules authorize them. However, you can urge the rest of the civil model upon the court whenever you can convince it that your *Daubert* challenge presents a substantial question (*e.g.,* an exchange of detailed reports that describe the expert's methodology, its basis in science or another area of recognized specialized knowledge, and the applicability of that method to the facts of your case).

§14:81   The *Daubert* Hearing

The trial court should hold the *Daubert* hearing outside the jury's hearing, and has discretion to hold it pre-trial. The suggested method is an in limine hearing:

It would appear that the most efficient procedure that the district court can use in making the reliability determination is an in limine hearing. Such a hearing need not unduly burden the trial courts; in many cases, it will be only a brief foundational hearing either before trial or at trial but out of the hearing of the jury. In the course of the in limine proceeding, the trial court may consider, *inter alia*, offers of proof, affidavits, stipulations, or learned treatises, *see* Fed. R. Evid. 803 (18), in addition to testimonial or other documentary evidence (and, of course, legal argument). In addition, the court may properly consider the testimony presented to other courts that have addressed the same evidentiary issue, and the opinions of those courts on the subject. If a technique has found favor with a significant number of other courts, a district court may exercise its discretion to admit the evidence through judicial notice.

[*United States v. Downing*, 753 F.2d 1224, 1241 (3rd Cir. 1985). *See also Kannankeril v. Terminix Int'l, Inc.*, 128 F.3d 802, 807 (3rd Cir. 1997); *In re Paoli*, 35 F.3d 717, 739 n.4 (3rd Cir. 1994).]

Even if conducted mid-trial, *Daubert* hearings should generally be conducted outside the jury's presence. [*United States v. Hermanek*, 289 F.3d 1076, 1094 n.7 (9th Cir. 2002) (per FRE 104, to keep prejudicial inadmissible foundational evidence from the jury); *Downing*, 753 F.2d at 1241.]

However, the trial court has discretion to conduct the hearing with the jury in the box. [*See Elcock v. Kmart Corp.*, 233 F.3d 734, 751 (3rd Cir. 2000) (noting that a *Daubert* hearing may take place before the jury).]

Courts have relegated *Daubert* challenges to mid-trial, in-the-jury's-presence hearings where the challenge does not raise significant factual issues and the hearing promises to be a fairly brief cross-examination rather than a matter of presenting outside studies and opposing experts. [*E.g,. United States v. Alatorre*, 222 F.3d 1098 (9th Cir. 2000) (Customs agent's testimony on the value of marijuana); *United States v. Nichols*, 169 F.3d 1255, 1263 (10th Cir. 1999), *aff'g United States v. McVeigh*, 955 F.Supp. 1278 (D.Colorado 1997) (even though the government consented to a pre-trial hearing, the trial court properly rejected the defense request for such a hearing on admissibility of forensic explosives testimony where the testimony depended on "well-known techniques routinely used by chemists"; voir dire in the jury's presence was sufficient). *See also* Federal Judicial Center, *Reference Manual on Scientific Evidence* at 28-29 (opponent has a burden of making a prima facie of specific deficiencies in the proposed testimony before a hearing should be held).]

Nonetheless, there are strong arguments that a *Daubert* hearing, at least one presenting a substantial challenge, should take place (1) outside the jury's presence and (2) pre-trial:

- The hearing may entail a probing of the particulars of how the expert arrived at his conclusion, an inquiry that risks "boring or turning off" the jury. [*Elcock*, 233 F.3d at 747.]
- Once the expert explains his method and underlying hypotheses, the opposing party's experts should have the opportunity to go back to the field or the lab and test the hypotheses and attempt to duplicate the expert's results. [*Elcock*, 233 F.3d at 747. *See also In re Diet Drugs*, 2001 U.S. Dist. LEXIS 1174 at *39 (E.D. Pa. 2001) (citing the inability to reproduce the expert's test results as grounds for exclusion).]

A hearing on even a losing *Daubert* motion has great value because you hear a detailed and under oath preview of the prosecution's expert.

VII. FORMS

Form 14-1   Informal Discovery Request

INFORMAL REQUEST FOR DISCOVERY

NOTICE: Discovery materials will not be disclosed until counsel has entered his or her appearance and has given notice to the District Attorney's Office.

DISCOVERY MATERIAL CANNOT BE PROVIDED WITHOUT THE FOLLOWING:

Defendant's Name: _____

CC Number: _____

Next Action and Date: _____   **Judge:** _____
In compliance with the informal request provisions of Pa. R. Crim. P.573-A, demand is made for the following information and materials.

1.   Material evidence favorable to the accused.

2.   Written, oral, or recorded confession or inculpatory statement.
      Taken by whom? _____ .

3.   Defendant's prior criminal record.

4.   Identification of defendant by:
      Line up   One on one confrontation   One-way mirror
      Single photo   Photo array   Other (specify)
      Show up   Stand up   _____

5.   Results or reports of:
      Scientific tests   Expert Opinion   Polygraph mirror
      Physical/mental exam   Other

6.   Tangible objects:
      Documents Photographs   Fingerprints   Other_____

7.   Transcripts and records of electronic surveillance.

8.   Information re: eyewitness to crime.

9.   Written, recorded, or oral statements made by co-defendant: _____

10.   Other evidence (specify) _____

My appearance has been entered as attorney of record in this case and notice has been served upon the District Attorney's Office.

_____   _____
Attorney submitting request (**PLEASE PRINT**)   Date Submitted

_____   _____
Address   Phone

_____   _____
City, State, Zip   Email Address
          Mail: Yes__ No __ *ONLY FOR THOSE OUTSIDE OF CITY LIMITS.*

Form 14-2   Discovery Letter

VIA FACSIMILE and U.S. MAIL

_____, Esquire
United States Attorney's Office
for the Western District of PA
Pittsburgh, PA

Re: United States v. _____, Cr. No. 00-000

Dear Mr. _____:

I represent the defendant in the above-captioned matter. This is an informal discovery request. I would appreciate a written response to each requested item, with a response of "none," if that is appropriate. When I mention the "government," I also mean any state or federal law enforcement agents who participated in this or the related Hazmat investigations.

1. Disclosure of any statements and anything allegedly said by the defendant to any agents of the government or any cooperating witnesses at any time. Disclosure is also requested of the date, time, location and persons present when such oral or written statements were made.

   [**OR:** I assume from the Rule 16 materials produced at the arraignment that my client made no statements or testimonial assertions of any kind to any agents of the government. Please correct this if I am inaccurate.]

2. Please disclose any statements that my client is alleged to have made to any cooperating witnesses at any time. Disclosure is also requested of the date, time, location and persons present when such oral or written statements were made.

3. Please disclose any recorded statements my client made to anyone.

4. Please disclose any electronic surveillance of my client or his co-defendant or of any telephone they used. *See In re Grand Jury Matter*, 683 F.2d 66, 68 n.2 (3rd Cir. 1982); *In re Freedman*, 529 F.2d 543, 549 (3rd Cir. 1976).

5. Copies of any other reports, notes or memoranda prepared in the course of the investigation and arrest of the defendant.

6. Please preserve and produce any notes and draft reports prepared by any agents or officers. *See United States v. Ramos*, 27 F.2d 65, 68 (3rd Cir. 1994).

7. Disclosure of and examination of all physical evidence in the possession or control of the government.

8. You have represented that the defendant does not have any criminal record in any jurisdiction. If this is inaccurate or has changed, please so inform me.

9. The circumstances and results of any identification procedure involving the defendant or any other person, by voice, photograph, or in person.

10. Please state whether the government intends to offer any other crime evidence under FRE 404(b), whether it be alleged other acts of the defendant or any other person pertinent to this case, and if so, please provide the particulars of those acts including date, location of commission and description of the acts, and whether any court proceedings resulted, and if so, in what court and with what result.

11. Any items seized from the defendant upon his arrest on _____;

12. The agents' notes of their interview with the defendant on _____;

13. The FD-395 Advice of Rights form in Arabic referred to on the first page of SA _____'s _____, report, and any other document that the defendant may have signed or written upon on that day;

14. Please disclose any public statement and/or press release made by any government official in the Executive Branch of the United States government concerning this case or the Hazmat investigations.

15. Please disclose:
    a. with regard to any witness the government intends to call at trial to give opinion testimony under FRE 702, the name of the witness and his qualifications;
    b. a report from the expert as to his expected testimony including an explanation of the bases for his testimony and how his conclusions meet the reliability standards of *Daubert v. Merrell Dow*, 509 U.S. 579 (1993); and *Kumho Tire Co. v. Carmichael*, 526 U.S. 137 (1999);
    c. transcripts of any prior opinion testimony offered in any court by the witness;
    d. any draft reports;
    e. copies of all the data which the witness considered in reaching his opinion, including notes, copies of any reports, the authorities, treatises, witnesses and other experts consulted by the witness in forming his opinion, any correspondence from the government, any written or oral reports, tests, testimony, investigations and any other information consulted by the witness in arriving at his opinion; and

     f.   any results or reports of physical or mental examinations, and or scientific tests or experiments which are intended for use at trial or which are material to the preparation of the defense.

16. Please provide or state:

     a.   a list of all witness's names, addresses and phone numbers;

     b.   whether any government informant has provided any information which led to the arrest or prosecution of the defendant;

     c.   whether any informant or witness has worked for the government in the past;

     d.   whether any informant or witness has a prior criminal record and if so, provide it;

     e.   whether any informant or witness was paid for his or her efforts in this case or any other case and if so, how much;

     f.   whether any informant or witness has any pending cases anywhere, and if so, whether any assistance or consideration was offered or suggested, formally or informally, or is intended by the government to be offered on behalf of the informant with respect to any pending case the informant has;

     g.   any pending cases against any witness's immediate family members, *see United States v. Lankford*, 955 F.2d 1545, 1549 (11th Cir. 1992) (error to preclude cross-examination into arrest of witness's sons on state drug charges because, despite lack of any federal agreement to help the sons, witness may have believed and hoped that his cooperation would persuade federal authorities to assist sons or to forego taking the state prosecutions to federal court).

     h.   whether any informant or witness requested of the government anything of value or any assistance or consideration in any legal matter;

     i.   any agreement promise or suggestion made by the government or its agents to any prospective informant offering assistance to the informant in obtaining leniency in any court, or lack of prosecution or arrest, or any other favorable treatment or consideration for the efforts made in connection with any aspect of this case by the informant.

17. Pursuant to the Constitutional requirements of *United States v. Agurs*, 427 U.S. 97 (1927), *Giles v. Maryland*, 386 U.S. 66 (1967), and *Brady v. Maryland*, 373 U.S. 83 (1963), please provide any exculpatory or favorable evidence or information, or any evidence or statements of anyone which may be favorable to the defendant, which is in the possession or control of the government or its agents, or, if unknown, can by due diligence become known or acquired by the government, or its agents, including, but not limited to, the following:

     a.   copies of any statements or the substance of any oral statements made by any prospective government witness, or by alleged coconspirator, which is exculpatory of or favorable to the defendant, or which is inconsistent with any fact the government alleges with respect to the charges in the Complaint or Indictment;

     b.   copies of any reports of mental illness, drug use, excessive alcoholism, or any medical condition of any prospective government witness or informant which would affect the ability to observe or remember an observed fact;

18. The defense asks that the government memorialize, preserve and produce all proffers, communications with the government and statements made by any cooperating witness or his attorney, whether made formally or informally, *see United States v. Sudikoff*, 36 F.Supp.2d 1196 (C.D.Cal. 1999);

     a.   copies of any witness's criminal record;

     b.   any government report on any witness's uncharged criminal behavior

     c.   a list of other individuals to whom Mr. _____ issued drivers' licenses without lawful authority, including the names of the individuals, their ethnicity, and the type of license issued.

     d.   The defendant stated in his _____ interview with the agents that (1) he never met "_____," and that (2) he did not pay a bribe to anyone to obtain a Pennsylvania CDL or hazardous materials certification. I believe that the government has access to "_____" and Mr. _____ as cooperating witnesses. The defense asks the government to investigate and confirm whether or not its witnesses and evidence confirm assertions (1) and (2). *See Commonwealth of the Northern Mariana Islands v. Bowie*, 243 F.3d 1109 (9th Cir. 2001) (government has an affirmative duty to investigate potentially exculpatory evidence when put on notice that it may exist).

Your prompt attention to this matter is appreciated.

                         Sincerely,

                         _____

                         Thomas J. Farrell

Form 14-3   Specific *Brady* Motion

IN THE UNITED STATES DISTRICT COURT
FOR THE _____ DISTRICT OF _____

UNITED STATES OF AMERICA   )
                 v.   )
_____)

SUPPLEMENTAL DISCOVERY MOTION AND MOTION TO JOIN

AND NOW COMES defendant _____ by his attorney, Thomas J. Farrell, Esquire, and files the following Supplemental Discovery Motion:

1. Defendant has filed previously pre-trial motions, including motions for discovery, to dismiss for prosecutorial misconduct, and for a gag order.

2. Defendant moves to join the Motion to Dismiss for Selective Prosecution and the Motion to Dismiss with Prejudice Due to Prosecutorial Misconduct filed by Defendant _____ at Criminal No. 00-000. Mr. _____ is another of the hazmat defendants, and his motions cite additional material in support of the motions to dismiss and to gag. Defendant _____ seeks to incorporate those arguments and materials in his previously filed motion and to move to dismiss for the grounds cited by Mr. _____.

3. I have become aware that there may be certain exculpatory evidence in the possession of the government which has not been disclosed yet. Therefore, on _____, I sent the attached letter to Assistant United States Attorney _____. As the letter notes, I hope to settle this matter informally with Mr. _____; however, since the Court has warned that the trial date may be advanced, I incorporate that request into this Motion.

4. I submit that the following materials should be disclosed pursuant to *Kyles v. Whitley*, 514 U.S. 419 (1995); *United States v. Agurs*, 427 U.S. 97 (1972), and *Brady v. Maryland*, 373 U.S. 83 (1963):

    a. _____'s _____ interview by agents of the State Attorney General's Office in which he denied any wrongdoing. Since this statement means that he did not provide a license to Mr. _____ in any improper fashion, it is exculpatory.

    b. Any notes from Mr. _____'s _____ predisciplinary conference held at the Penn Hills Driver's License Center. Again, since Mr. _____ denied any wrongdoing, this statement would be exculpatory as to Mr. _____. I believe that _____ and _____ of PennDot attended the meeting and may have taken the notes.

    c. A copy of the _____ letter from _____ to _____ of PennDot. This letter identifies two Washington State drivers who obtained Pennsylvania CDLs; Mr. _____ is not among them.

    d. The fax copies of the driver's license photos of _____ that were shown to _____ on _____, and that he identified as being the "_____" that he dealt with. If this "_____" is not _____, then the government's case does not make sense, and the identification is exculpatory. If these driver's licenses belong to Mr. _____, then he has used false names and driver's licenses; that, too is exculpatory.

    e. Reports of any polygraphs that Mr. _____ or Mr. _____ may have taken and statements they made at the time. Both were asked and agreed to take polygraphs.

    f. All reports by PennDot, the Pennsylvania State Police, the Pennsylvania Attorney General's Office and/ or any other state investigative body into Mr. _____'s illegal dealings while a PennDot employee.

WHEREFORE, it is respectfully requested that the Court grant defendant's pre-trial motions and enter an order requiring the government to disclose the materials described in this supplemental motion and in the earlier pre-trial motions.

Respectfully submitted,

_____

Thomas J. Farrell

IN THE UNITED STATES DISTRICT COURT FOR
THE _____ DISTRICT OF _____

UNITED STATES OF AMERICA,
           Plaintiff,
              v.   CASE NO. _____
U,
            Defendant.

ORDER OF COURT

AND NOW this _____ day of _____, 2002, it is ORDERED upon consideration of defendant's pre-trial motions and supplemental pre-trial motions, that:
1. The indictment is dismissed with prejudice;
2. The government shall disclose forthwith the materials described in defendant's pre-trial motion and supplemental *Brady* motion.

_____
U.S. District Judge

Form 14-4   Omnibus Pre-Trial Motion

IN THE COURT OF COMMON PLEAS OF
_____ COUNTY, _____

COMMONWEALTH OF _____, CRIMINAL DIVISION,
        Plaintiff,
  v.
SPOCK, M.D.,
        Defendant.

DEFENDANT'S OMNIBUS PRE-TRIAL MOTION FOR RELIEF WITH CITATIONS TO AUTHORITY

AND NOW COMES the Defendant, Spock, M.D., by and through his attorney, Thomas J. Farrell, and hereby files the following pre-trial motions, stating in support thereof as follows:

INTRODUCTION

1. On or about _____, a Criminal Complaint was filed against defendant, Spock, M.D., based upon the affidavit of Special Agent _____ of the Office of Attorney General. A preliminary hearing was held on _____. At the conclusion of the hearing, the case was held for court.
2. On or about _____, a Criminal Information containing ten counts was filed against the defendant by the Office of Attorney General. The Information contains the following charges:

Count I	Delivery of controlled substances	35 P.S. 780-113(a) (30)
Count II	Delivery of controlled substances outside scope of treatment principles	35 P.S. 780-113(a)(14)
Count III	Solicitation to deliver controlled substances	18 Pa. C.S.A. Section 902(a) 35 P.A. 780-113(a)(30)
Count IV	Insurance fraud	18 Pa. C.S.A. 4117(a)(2)
Count V	Delivery of a controlled substance	35 P.S. 780-113(a)(30)
Count VI	Delivery of controlled substances outside of treatment principles	35 P.S. 780-113(a)(14)
Count VII	Prescribing controlled substances outside scope of treatment principles	35 P.S. 780-113(a)(14)
Count VIII	Receiving stolen property	18 Pa. C.S.A. 3925(a)
Count IX	Insurance fraud	18 Pa. C.S.A. Section 4117(a)(2)
Count X	Prescribing controlled substances outside scope of treatment principles	35 P.S. 780-113(a)(14)

3.   The defendant filed a request for Bill of Particulars and then, on _____, an Amended Request for Bill of Particulars. The Amended Request for Bill of Particulars sought a description of specific acts which constitute the offenses charged as well as the specific times, places and dates upon which the alleged acts occurred.

4.   The Commonwealth filed its Answer to Defendant's Amended Request for Bill of Particulars on _____. In its Answer, the Commonwealth set forth no specific facts but referred the defendant to the Probable Cause Affidavit, the Grand Jury Presentment, testimony at the preliminary hearing and certain documentary discovery either provided already or to be provided.

5.   By Order dated _____, upon consent of the parties, the Court extended the time for the filing of pre-trial motions by the defendant until August 24, 2001.

Motion for Pre-Trial Discovery and Inspection

6.   In compliance with Rule 573(A) of the Rules of Criminal Procedure, the parties, by letters dated _____ and _____, have attempted to resolve all discovery issues.

7.   The defendant makes the following specific discovery requests pursuant to Rule 573 (B)(1) and Rule 573 (B)(2)(a):

   a.   BNIDC Supplemental Report 73 which was not included in the reports provided;

   b.   Copies of tape recordings seized from Dr. Spock's residence by Police Officer _____ as described in BNIDC Supplemental Reports 75 and 78;

   c.   Any and all immunity applications, orders and other related documents for any government witnesses other than _____;

   d.   Disclosure of any payments in any form to any government witness;

   e.   Disclosure of any type of agreement, promise or statement made to a government witness, whether oral or written, formal or informal, offering any type of assistance to the witness in obtaining leniency in any court or leniency regarding any possible prosecution or arrest, or any other favorable treatment or consideration for the witness's assistance to the government in connection with any aspect of any investigation of Dr. Spock involving the witness, whether made by a government prosecutor, law enforcement agent or officer or other official;

   f.   Transcripts of the tape recordings dated _____, and _____ (a transcript of the tape recording dated _____, was provided);

   g.   Identification of all persons referred to as confidential informants in the reports prepared in connection with the investigation of defendant or in reports related in any way to the investigation of the defendant;

   h.   All statements in any form of any and all witnesses *or* confirmation that all such witness statements have been provided;

   i.   Names and addresses of all government witnesses. See Rule 573(B)(2)(a);

   j.   All written or recorded statements of any alleged coconspirator or accomplice of the defendant, whether or not such individual has been charged. See 573(B)(2)(a)(iii);

   k.   Pursuant to the constitutional requirements of *United States v. Agurs*, 427 U.S. 97 (1927), *Giles v. Maryland*, 386 U.S. 66 (1967), and *Brady v. Maryland*, 373 U.S. 83 (1963), any exculpatory or favorable evidence or information, including any evidence or statements of anyone which may be favorable to the defendant, which is in the possession or control of the government or its agents, or, if unknown, which can by due diligence become known or acquired by the government or its agents including, but not limited to, documents related to government interviews of any witness in which that witness provided any favorable information regarding the medical practices of the defendant;

   l.   Criminal history reports regarding all government witnesses *or* confirmation that all such reports have been provided;

   m.   Disclosure of all laboratory reports reflecting the examination, analysis and/or testing performed on any substance allegedly found in the possession of the defendant or dispensed or delivered by the defendant to any person.

8.   In further support of the above requests, it is noted that the defendant has been aware of the investigation since at least _____, when his offices were searched by the investigating law enforcement agencies. The government has already provided significant discovery concerning the witnesses against the defendant, and 12 witnesses have testified at the preliminary hearing. There is no reason at this point for the government to maintain the confidentiality of any witness. Dr. Spock is a medical doctor who poses no threat to the witnesses. Therefore, the defendant submits that the identification of all witnesses, including all confidential informants, and the provision of the statements of all such witnesses is appropriate and will lead to the fair and expeditious resolution of this case.

MOTION FOR DISCLOSURE OF GRAND JURY TESTIMONY

9. Rule 230(B)(2) of the Rules of Criminal Procedure provides that a defendant is entitled to a copy of the grand jury testimony of any witness in a criminal case. Such rule further provides that the testimony may be made available only after the direct testimony of that witness at trial.

10. Because the defendant poses no threat to the government witnesses and because significant disclosure of the identities of witnesses has already been made, and one grand jury transcript (_____) has already been provided to the defense, it is submitted that early disclosure of the grand jury testimony will lead to the fair and orderly trial of this matter and allow adequate preparation of Dr. Spocks's defense. Therefore, the defendant requests early disclosure of all grand jury testimony on a date at least three weeks prior to trial.

11. Rule 230(B)(3) provides that the "court shall order that the transcript of any testimony before an investigating grand jury that is exculpatory to the defendant, or any physical evidence presented to the grand jury that is exculpatory to the defendant, be made available to such defendant." Therefore, the defendant moves for the immediate disclosure of any such exculpatory evidence.

MOTION FOR DISCLOSURE OF INTENTION TO INTRODUCE EVIDENCE PURSUANT TO RULE 404(B) OF THE PENNSYLVANIA RULES OF EVIDENCE

12. Rule 404(b) of the Pennsylvania Rules of Evidence provides that evidence of other crimes, wrongs, or acts may be admissible in a criminal case for certain enumerated purposes.

13. Rule 404(b)(4) provides that "the prosecution shall provide reasonable notice in advance of trial, or during trial if the court excuses pre-trial notice on such good cause shown, of any such evidence it intends to introduce at trial."

14. The defendant hereby requests notice of the government's intent to offer any such Rule 404(b) evidence at trial on a date as far in advance of trial as possible, and as soon as the government has decided to use such evidence, so that defendant may properly address the government's proffer in this regard.

MOTION FOR WRIT OF HABEAS CORPUS AS TO COUNTS I, II, V, AND VI AND TO DISMISS FOR DUPLICITY

15. As shown on the chart set forth in the Introduction, Counts I, II, V, and VI charge Dr. Spock with delivery of controlled substances between either _____ (Counts I, II) or _____ (Counts V, VI) and _____. In other words, rather than charging each delivery as a separate count, the government has chosen to charge these offenses as "continuing offenses." This type of charge is duplicitous and should be dismissed.

16. Successive sales of narcotics have been held to be separate offenses. In fact, in *Commonwealth v. Sabathne*, 227 Pa. Super 331, 323 A.2d 337 (1974), the defendant made two sales of methamphetamine at the same bar within an hour. The court held that the sales were separate offenses and did not merge. *Id.*

17. In this case, it appears that the government is unable to identify specific deliveries and therefore has elected to charge the deliveries as a vague continuing course of conduct. As the Court is doubtless aware, while a conspiracy is always charged as a continuing course of conduct, substantive drug offenses are normally charged as separate counts. The proper unit of prosecution, as made clear by *Sabathne* and by the plain language of the statutes–which refer to "a delivery"–is each alleged separate delivery or distribution.

18. The defendant has discovered only one case which approved the charging of successive Section (a)(30) violations in one count as a continuing offense. *Commonwealth v. Dennis*, 421 Pa. Super 600, 618 A.2d 972 (1992). In *Dennis*, the court approved the charging of deliveries of methamphetamine from August, 1985 to November, 1986 as one violation of Section (a)(30).

19. It is submitted that the *Dennis* case is unpersuasive. First, the *Dennis* court did not analyze the appropriate unit of prosecution in narcotics delivery cases. Rather, the court found that in other types of crimes, primarily child sexual abuse crimes, charging offenses as continuing offenses had been approved. *See, e.g., Commonwealth v. Niemetz*, 282 Pa. Super 431, 440, 422 A.2d 1369, 1373 (1980) (court approved an information charging sex offenses between 1972 and August 1977 on the ground that it would not serve the ends of justice to permit a perpetrator to sexually abuse a child with impunity because the child failed to record the details in a daily diary.) The court further noted that the date of commission is not an element of a drug charge. *Dennis*, 421 Pa. Super at 615, 618 A.2d at 980. The *Dennis* analysis focused primarily upon whether the charge was in

compliance with Rule 225 of the Rules of Criminal Procedure (now numbered as Rule 560(B)(3)). *Dennis* has never been cited by a Pennsylvania court for the proposition that it is appropriate to charge drug deliveries as continuing offenses over a period of years.

20. The charges here fail because they are duplicitous. Duplicity is the joining in a single count of two or more distinct and separate offenses. *Bidner, supra,* 282 Pa. Super. at 109 n.6, 422 A.2d at 852 n.6. The rule against duplicitous informations is set forth in Rule 563(B) of the Rules of Criminal Procedure: "There shall a separate count for each offense charged." The rule is designed to provide proper notice to the defendant of the accusation against him and to ensure that the jury unanimously agrees to convict the defendant of a single offense. A general verdict on a single count which contains multiple offenses may also lead to double jeopardy problems in the event of subsequent prosecution.

21. The *Dennis* court did not address the issue of duplicity because the defendant in that case apparently did not raise it. However, duplicity is the primary problem with charging delivery of controlled substances as a continuing offense over a period of years. For example, suppose that at trial _____ testifies that he sold pills for Dr. Spock in July of 1996, in December of 1996, and in April of 1997, describing to the jury separate transactions on each of those occasions. It is possible that members of the jury could convict Dr. Spock of the count, now charged as a continuing offense, even though they were not unanimous that a transaction had occurred at any one of those times. The government is unfairly attempting to hide its proof problems due to the vague memories of its witnesses and lack of documentation by lumping multiple alleged offenses together in one substantive count. This procedure is extremely prejudicial to the defendant and constitutes a fatal pleading error in the government's information.

22. For the reasons set forth above, the defendant respectfully requests that the writ issue and that Counts I, II, V, and VI be dismissed as duplicitous.

MOTION TO QUASH COUNTS I–VII, IX AND X
FOR VIOLATION OF THE STATUTE OF LIMITATIONS

23. The criminal complaint in this case was filed on or about _____.

24. Pursuant to Title 42, Pa.C.S.A. §5552(b)(2) the statute of limitations for any offense punishable under the Controlled Substance, Drug, Device and Cosmetic Act, 35 P.S. §780-113(f) and for insurance fraud, 18 Pa.C.S.A. §4117, is five years from the date that the crime was committed.

25. Counts I and II of the information charge continuing offenses involving the delivery of controlled substances beginning in _____. Pursuant to the applicable statute of limitations, prosecution for any delivery of controlled substances which occurred prior to _____ is barred by the statute of limitations.

26. Similarly, with respect to Counts III, IV, V, VI, VII, IX, and X, all of which allege criminal conduct beginning in either "_____" or on "_____," the statute of limitations bars prosecution of any conduct which occurred prior to _____. Therefore, those events should also be quashed.

MOTION TO SEVER COUNT VIII

27. Count VIII, the receiving stolen property count, should be severed from the remaining counts pursuant to Pa.R.Crim.P. 563 and 583 as that count is not part of the same act or transaction as the others and evidence of it would not be admissible at the trial of the remaining charges.

28. The Supreme Court has set forth the following three-part test for deciding a motion to sever:

> Where the defendant moves to sever offenses not based on the same act or transaction that have been consolidated in a single indictment or information, or opposes joinder of separate indictments or informations, the court must therefore determine: [1] whether the evidence of each of the offenses would be admissible in a separate trial for the other; [2] whether such evidence is capable of separation by the jury so as to avoid danger of confusion; and, if the answers to these inquiries are in the affirmative, [3] whether the defendant will be unduly prejudiced by the consolidation of offenses.

Commonwealth v. Lark, 518 Pa. 290, 302, 543 A.2d 491, 496-97 (1988). Pursuant to the *Lark* test, a court must first determine if the evidence of each of the offenses would be admissible in a separate trial for the other. Evidence of crimes other than the one in question is not admissible solely to show the defendant's bad character or propensity to commit crime. *Commonwealth v. Newman,* 528 Pa. 393, 598 A.2d 275 (1991); *Lark.* However, evidence of other crimes is admissible to demonstrate (1) motive; (2) intent; (3) absence of mistake or accident; (4) a common scheme, plan or design embracing the commission of two or more crimes so related to each other that proof of one tends to prove the others; or (5) the identity of the person charged with the commission of the crime on trial. Id. Additionally, evidence of other crimes may be admitted where such evidence is part of the history of the case and forms part of the natural development of the facts. *Lark. Commonwealth v. Collins,* 550 Pa. 46, 54-55, 703 A.2d 418, 422-23 (1997).

29. The gun possession has nothing to do with the insurance fraud and drug distribution charges. Mr. _____ is not a patient to whom it is alleged that Dr. Spock distributed drugs illegally; nor is he a patient on whose account false insurance claims were allegedly submitted. The receipt of stolen property does not form part of the same transactions or history or plan as the other charges. Further, neither of the very different charges–fraud and drug distribution involving misuse of a medical license on the one hand and receipt of a stolen firearm on the other–sheds any light on Dr. Spock's intent, motive, identity or absence of mistake.

30. Admission of evidence of each of these different sets of crimes at the trial of the other set would serve only one purpose: to depict Dr. Spock as a lawless person. While the prejudice to Dr. Spock of consolidation would be severe, inconvenience to the Commonwealth from severance would be minimal. The receipt of stolen property trial would take little time, requiring only three prosecution witnesses: Mr. _____, the gun's owner; Mr. _____, for his testimony about Dr. Spock's statements (if this testimony is relevant, a fact the defense disputes); and Agent Edward, the agent who seized the gun. Only Agent _____ might be a witness at both trials, and his testimony on the stolen property charge would be brief. Therefore, the defendant requests that Count VIII be severed from the remaining counts and tried separately.

Respectfully submitted,

_____

Thomas J. Farrell, Esquire

Form 14-5   Federal Omnibus Pre-Trial Motion

IN THE UNITED STATES DISTRICT COURT FOR THE
_____ DISTRICT OF _____

UNITED STATES OF AMERICA,
           Plaintiff,
        v.   CRIMINAL NO.
GD and LD,
           Defendants.

OMNIBUS PRE-TRIAL MOTION WITH CITATION OF AUTHORITIES

AND NOW COMES the Defendant, LD, by his attorney, Thomas Farrell, and files this Omnibus Pre-Trial Motion:

1. The Defendant, LD, was arraigned on _____ on an indictment charging him with three substantive drug distribution counts and a conspiracy to distribute count.

2. GD is named as a co-defendant of his in the above counts. Mr. D is also charged with possession of a firearm and with a drug distribution count unrelated to the conspiracy with LD.

3. In this Omnibus Pre-Trial Motion, LD moves
    a. to suppress the evidence seized from the apartment at _____ Building on _____;
    b. to suppress evidence seized from Mr. D's pants pockets during the search on _____;
    c. to sever Count 7 of the Indictment as improperly joined;
    d. to sever his trial from that of GD;
    e. for discovery;
    f. to join Co-Defendant GD's Pre-Trial Motions.

MOTION TO SEVER COUNT SEVEN OF THE INDICTMENT
AS MISJOINED UNDER RULE 8(B)

11. Count One of the Indictment charges a conspiracy between G and LD to distribute heroin between _____ and _____. There then follow several substantive counts of distribution in that time period.

12. Count Seven charges distribution of heroin by GD alone nearly one year before the formation of the conspiracy, on _____.

13. Rule 8(b) permits joinder of multiple defendants in one indictment. That rule has been interpreted to restrict a multi-defendant indictment to charging offenses that grew out of the same series of transactions or acts involving all the defendants. *See United States v. Velasquez*, 772 F.2d 1348 (7th Cir. 1985). The government may not join a charge against one of the defendants that arises from a transaction that did not involve the co-defendants even if the charge is of the same character as the other charges. *Id. See also United States v. Toney*, 161 F.R.D. 77 (N.D. Iowa 1995).

14. There is no allegation here that Count Seven arises from the same scheme or conspiracy or series of acts as the rest of the Indictment. It charges a drug deal completely unrelated to the alleged conspiracy between Doe and Doe.

15. "If offenses or defendants have been improperly joined, however, severance is required as a matter of law under Rule 8. *United States v. Andrews*, 765 F.2d 1491, 1496 (11th Cir. 1985) ("Misjoinder under Rule 8(b) is prejudicial per se...."), *cert. denied*, 474 U.S. 1064 (1986); *Bledsoe*, 674 F.2d at 654 (misjoinder is inherently prejudicial); *United States v. Vastola*, 670 F. Supp. 1244, 1261 (D.N.J. 1987) (citing *United States v. Somers*, 496 F.2d 723, 729 (3d Cir.), *cert. denied*, 419 U.S. 832, (1974))." *United States v. Giampa*, 904 F.Supp. 235, 264 (D.N.J. 1995).

MOTION TO SEVER THE TRIAL OF LD
FROM THAT OF GD UNDER RULE 14

16. The defendants will present mutually antagonistic and exclusive defenses at trial. Each will assert that the drugs found in _____ on _____, must have belonged to and been intended for distribution solely by the other defendant and that he did not know of the drugs' presence or the co-defendant's plan. Since only the two, along with GD's paramour NT and two children were present in the apartment, and no one, including the government, asserts that Ms. T or the children were aware of the drugs, the acquittal of either co-defendant would necessarily call for the conviction of the other. In these circumstances, the Court should grant the defendants separate trials as relief from the prejudicial joinder. *See Zafiro v. United States,* 506 U.S. 534, 538-39 (1993); *United States v. Voigt*, 89 F.3d 1050, 1094-95 (3rd Cir. 1996).

17. After his arrest, co-defendant GD admitted that the drugs in the apartment were his. He made no mention of LD. Thus the statement exculpates LD. While GD has moved to suppress this statement, LD will insist upon its admission under FRE 804(b)(3), as a statement against penal interest, and under the Due Process clause, *see Chambers v. Mississippi*, 410 U.S. 284 (1973). This further illustrates the mutually antagonistic nature of the defenses and justifies severance.

MOTION FOR DISCOVERY

18. On _____, I sent the discovery letter which is attached as Exhibit A to the Assistant U.S. Attorney in this case. It requests material that is discoverable under Fed.R.Cr.P. 16 and FRE 404(b) as well as *Kyles v. Whitley*, 514 U.S. 419 (1995); *United States v. Agurs*, 427 U.S. 97 (1976), and *Brady v. Maryland*, 373 U.S. 83 (1963). Further, it asks that the government memorialize, preserve and produce all proffers, communications with the government and statements made by any cooperating witness or his attorney, whether made formally or informally, *see United States v. Sudikoff*, 36 F.Supp.2d 1196 (C.D.Cal. 1999), and that the government preserve and produce any notes and draft reports prepared by any agents or officers as required by *United States v. Ramos*, 27 F.2d 65, 68 (3rd Cir. 1994). I have not received any answer and ask that the Court order the government to provide the information and material requested in the letter.

MOTION REQUESTING NOTICE PURSUANT TO RULE 404(B) OF THE FEDERAL RULES OF EVIDENCE

In our _____ discovery letter, we asked for notice of any FRE 404(b) evidence that the government may intend to offer against Mr. D. Exhibit A, paragraph 8. The government's response was that it was thinking about it and would give us reasonable notice if it decided to use such evidence. Exhibit B, para. 8.

We request that the Court set a date by which the government should provide such notice. Once given, the notice very well may necessitate defense motions as to its admissibility, defense investigation into its particulars and veracity, and, if admitted, a mini-trial on it within the trial. None of this can be done in an effective and efficient manner without substantial notice before trial.

MOTION TO JOIN CO-DEFENDANT'S MOTIONS

19. LD seeks to join the following motions filed by co-defendant GD: (1) Motion to Suppress Evidence; (2) Motion to Reveal Identity of Confidential Informant; (3) Motion to Disclose *Brady* Material; and (4) Motion to Produce Evidence which the Government Intends to Use Under FRE 404(b) and 609. LD does not join in GD's Motion to Return his Mercedes Benz or to Suppress Statements.

CONCLUSION

For the foregoing reasons, Defendant's Motions should be granted.

Respectfully submitted,

_____

Thomas J. Farrell
Attorney for LD

IN THE UNITED STATES DISTRICT COURT FOR THE
_____ DISTRICT OF _____

UNITED STATES OF AMERICA,
             Plaintiff,
       v.
GD
and LD,
             Defendants.

ORDER OF COURT

AND NOW, this _____ day of _____, 2002, IT IS ORDERED that Defendant LD's Omnibus Pre-Trial Motion is GRANTED: and
IT IS ORDERED that:
(1) The trial of LD is severed from that of GD;
(2) The discovery requested in LD's Exhibit A to his Motion is granted; and
(3) Defendant LD is permitted to join in Defendant GD's Motion.

_____

U.S. District Judge

Form 14-6   Ex Parte Motion for Subpoena Duces Tecum

IN THE UNITED STATES DISTRICT COURT
FOR THE _____ DISTRICT OF _____

UNITED STATES OF AMERICA,
        Plaintiff,

    v.   Cr. No.

AG,
        Defendant.

MOTION TO FILE APPLICATIONS FOR PRE-TRIAL SUBPOENAS EX PARTE AND UNDER SEAL

AND NOW, comes the Defendant, AG, by and through his attorney WM, Esquire and moves to file an ex parte application for pre-trial subpoenas pursuant to Federal Rule of Criminal Procedure 17(c) and in support thereof sets forth the following:

1) Rule 17(c) authorizes the issuance of pre-trial subpoenas deuces tecum subject to court authorization.

2) In the instant case, pre-trial production of certain records is necessary for preparation of the defense. Further, due to the quantity and nature of the documents, it is imperative that AG be given an immediate, pre-trial return date in order to allow adequate time to prepare his defense and avoid a continuance of trial.

3) In order to satisfy Rule 17(c) requirements for issuance of the pre-trial subpoenas deuces tecum, the moving party is required to satisfy the standards that were originally established in *U.S. v. Iozia,* 13 F.R.D. 335 (S.D.N.Y. 1952) and subsequently adopted by the U. S. Supreme Court in *U.S. v. Nixon*, 418 U.S. 638 (1974).

4) To provide the information necessary to meet the *Nixon* standard would result in disclosure of certain defense trial witnesses. More importantly, it would require a detailed explanation of AG's trial strategy and counsel's work product in order to satisfy the *Nixon* standards of relevance, admissibility and specificity.

5) Rule 16 does not authorize disclosure of this information to the government at this time and under these circumstances.

6) This Court ruled that AG was not entitled to the government's trial strategy, its witness list, or the documents the government intends to offer in it case in chief until the exchange of witness and document exhibit lists shortly before trial.

7) To protect AG's theory of the case, trial strategy, witness identification, and attorney work product, the request for the subpoenas, the documents sought in the pre-trial subpoenas, and the subpoenas themselves must be kept confidential. They would be revealed to the government to the extent AG decides to use the documents as trial exhibits in his case in chief.

8) In order to avoid disclosure of the protected information to the government, AG requests that the motion identifying the subpoenas and the underlying basis for the request be submitted in a separate motion under seal. Additionally, any subpoenas issued pursuant thereto need to be maintained under seal.

9) The records sought are not available to AG by any other procedure.

10) The records sought are not in the government's possession and therefore are not available to AG pursuant to Rule 16.

11) The subpoenas will be directed to third parties unrelated to the government.

12) This request is made in good faith and solely for preparation of AG's defense.

ARGUMENT IN SUPPORT OF DEFENDANT'S MOTION

Rule 17 is divided in three sub-sections. Sub-section (a) establishes the physical form for all criminal subpoenas and describes the information that must be contained in the form. It enables the government and defendants with financial resources to secure ex parte subpoenas for production at trial. Sub-section (b) is applicable only to indigent defendants and places an indigent defendant on the same footing as both a non-indigent defendant and the government when deciding whether to apply for a subpoena for production at trial. It provides an ex parte procedure for the indigent to apply to the court for issuance of subpoenas without the knowledge of the government. Sub-section (b) provides:

Upon a defendant's ex parte application, the court must order that a subpoena be issued for a named witness if the defendant shows an inability to pay the witness's fees and the necessity of the witness's presence for an adequate defense…

Sub-section (c) allows for issuance of a subpoena deuces tecum with a pre-trial production date upon application to the court by the government or either an indigent or non-indigent defendant. Sub-section (c) provides:

A subpoena may order the witness to produce any books, papers, documents, data or other objects the subpoena designates. The court may direct the witness to produce the designated items in court before trial or before they are to be offered in evidence. When the items arrive, the court may permit the parties and their attorneys to inspect all or part of them.

AG seeks to exercise his right under Rule 17 (c) to file an ex parte motion requesting the issuance of third party subpoenas deuces tecum with a pre-trial return date.

Rule 17 (c) does not directly address whether the government or a defendant, with or without financial means, may apply, ex parte, for pre-trial subpoenas deuces tecum seeking pre-trial production. Upon consideration of the underlying policy reasons and the constitutional underpinnings for Rule 17 (c) the courts and commentators generally agree that the Rule does provide for an ex parte proceeding.

The policy reasons supporting the ex parte procedure have been described as a defendant's right to:
1. Pre-trial production of evidence;
2. Protection of his trial strategy;
3. Obtain and use relevant evidence;
4. Withhold disclosure of his theory of the case from the government;
5. Withhold disclosure of his trial strategy from the government; and
6. Withhold disclosure of his witnesses from the government.

Although there are no appellate decisions dealing with the issue of confidentiality under Rule 17 (c), a number of experienced and highly regarded District Court judges have recognized the right of both the government and the defense to seek the confidential, ex parte issuance of subpoenas deuces tecum with a pre-trial return date. *See U.S. v. Beckford*, 964 F. Supp 1010 (E.D. Va. 1997), *U.S. v. Tomison*, 969 F. Supp. 587 (E.D. Cal. 1997), and *U.S. v. Daniels*, 95 F. Supp. 2d 1160 (D. Kan. 2000).

In *United States v. Tomison, supra,* Chief Judge Karlton thoroughly analyzed the issue and approved the defendant's right to file an ex parte motion seeking confidential third party subpoenas deuces tecum. The court found that the defendant could not make the necessary showing of relevance, admissibility and specificity (the *Nixon* standards) without revealing his trial strategy to the government.

The court reasoned that since the Rule contemplates that the court "may" permit inspection of the documents before trial, it follows that the Rule also empowers the court to deny an adverse party the opportunity to inspect the documents.

Since prohibiting a party access to the documents may have the same practical effect as denying it the opportunity to know that such documents were subpoenaed, the Rule's structure appears to anticipate the possibility of an ex parte request. Given that the court may decline to order pre-trial production of the documents altogether, it is possible that the portion of the Rule allowing for participation by the government would never be triggered. Thus it appears the rule may contemplate situations where the defendant has a right to an ex parte hearing as well as situations where the defendant does not. At the very least, the issue is not directly resolved by the text.

U.S. v. Tomison, 969 F. Supp. at 591.

Since the text of the Rule could not resolve the question, the court looked to the legislative history, the constitutional framework within which the Rule operates, and the intended purpose of Rule 17 (c). The court looked to *U.S. v. Nixon, supra*, at 698-99 and *Bowman Dairy Co. v. U.S.*, 341 U.S. 214, 220 (1951) and concluded that Rule 17 (c)'s "chief innovation was to expedite the trial by providing a time and place before trial for the inspection of subpoenaed materials." The court then correctly concluded that to interpret the Rule as excluding an ex parte proceeding would require a defendant to divulge his theory of the case as a prerequisite for pre-trial production and would discourage defendants from using the Rule in the first place. "Thus, requiring a defendant to apply for the subpoena deuces tecum by noticed motion could defeat the Rule's goal of facilitating the speed and efficiency of trial." *Tomison* at 592-93.

The court then turned to the constitutional underpinnings which included a defendant's right, upon demand, to favorable evidence that bears upon either guild or punishment under the Due Process Clause of the Fifth Amendment[1] and the Sixth Amendment right to process for obtaining witnesses in his favor. The court found Rule 17 (c) was intended to implement both the right to obtain evidence and the right to require its production. And where such evidence is in possession of third parties, pre-trial production is absolutely necessary to preserve the defendant's constitutional right to obtain and effectively use such evidence at trial. *Id.* at 593. *(case citations omitted)*. Further, the government has no constitutional or procedural right to discover the defendant's trial strategy, work product or theory of the case.

The court concluded:

> In sum, the fact that a criminal defendant has both the right to the pre-trial production of evidence and a right to protect his trial strategy contraindicates a noticed motion practice requiring disclosure to the government of the defendant's theory of the case as a precondition to obtaining pre-trial subpoenas duces tecum under Rule 17 (c).

Id. at 593. *(citing U. S. v. Reyes*, 162 F.R.D. at 470).

If this court required AG to offer his trial strategy, work product, and theory of the case *to the government*, the court will have placed an unconstitutional limitation on AG's Fifth Amendment right to due process and his Sixth Amendment right to compulsory process. *See Beckford, supra*, at 1027. AG acknowledges that he must disclose these things *to the court* to satisfy the *Nixon* standards.

Throughout the *Tomison* opinion, the court referenced *U. S. v. Beckford, supra. Beckford* involved four defendants charged in a continuing criminal enterprise indictment with multiple murders and violent past conduct. Both the government and the defendants filed ex parte applications for pre-trial subpoena deuces tecum. All of the subpoenas requested by the government and defendants were granted. A portion of the defendants' subpoenas were directed to a state agency seeking statements of witnesses. The court granted the subpoenas based upon the pre-trial record indicating the state agency was not involved in the government's investigation of the charges in the indictment and was therefore an unrelated third party. The state agency notified the U. S. Attorney of the subpoenas and brought to the government's attention that it had also conducted an investigation into the murders. The government filed a motion to quash, alleging that because the state agency was involved in an investigation, it was, therefore, part of the prosecution and not a third party. Upon proof that the agency was involved, the court withdrew those subpoenas, but provided an in-depth analysis of Rule 17 (c) and held that the Rule did provide for both the government and the defendants to make ex parte applications for pre-trial subpoenas deuces tecum. The government could not condemn the ex parte application since it had also utilized the ex parte procedure in its own application for pre-trial subpoenas deuces tecum.

In arriving at this decision in *Beckford*, Judge Payne explained that a fair reading of the text of Rule 17 (c) coupled with the strong public policy against disclosure of a party's trial strategy determined that in a case where the *Nixon* standards must be satisfied, it would be a denial of a defendant's constitutional rights to due process and compulsory process to refuse an ex parte application for a pre-trial subpoena deuces tecum:

> In the absence of ex parte procedure, however, the constitutionally-prohibited "Hobson's choice" would be forced upon all defendants, whether indigent or financially able, with respect to the issuance of rule 17 (c) pre-trial subpoenas duces tecum. That is because, as set forth in Section II, B [of this opinion] a party must file a pre-issuance motion with the Court before a pre-trial subpoena will be issued. And of course, defendants must make the *Nixon* showing of specificity, relevance and admissibility. If the motion could never be made ex parte, the defendant would, in some cases, be forced to reveal his trial strategy, witnesses' identities or his attorney's work-product in order to secure the issuance of a pre-trial subpoena. If Rule 17 (c) were interpreted to force that result, the defendant's "Sixth Amendment right to compulsory process for obtaining [favorable evidence] would mean little indeed. *(citations omitted)* Therefore, the Sixth Amendment supplies justification for interpreting Rule 17 (c) to permit ex parte procedures..."

U.S. v. Beckford, at 1027.

The Courts in *Tomison* and *Beckford* agree that Rule 17 (c) does not implicate Rule 16 since Rule 17 (c) subpoenas are directed to third parties and not the government. To use Rule 17 (c) as a discovery tool would require the subpoenas be directed to the government. The rule 16 discovery argument is a bogus argument often raised by the government

---

[1]   *Brady v. Maryland*, 373 U.S. 83, 83 S.Ct. 1194.

along with a request to challenge the defendant's ability to satisfy the Nixon standards. The courts in *Tomison* and *Beckford* responded to that argument by noting that a District Court Judge is capable of making the decision without the assistance of the government and that such an argument is merely a government attempt to violate Rule 16 and gain discovery of the defense strategy.

> Courts and commentators which have addressed the issue nearly unanimously have recognized that, although the rule "does not clearly require it," the use of a motion as the procedural means for invoking the court's discretion in advance of issuance of a pre-trial subpoena duces tecum is "an orderly and desirable procedure and one frequently followed." *(Cases and commentators omitted)*

U. S. v. Beckford, at 1021.

Both *Tomison* and *Beckford* agree that to secure pre-trial subpoenas deuces tecum, where the *Nixon* standards must be satisfied, an ex parte application is the appropriate method for either the government or the defendant.

Another case in which the issue was raised is *U.S. v. Daniels, supra. Daniels* was a health care fraud and mail fraud case in which the defendant was charged with billing health care providers for services not rendered to the patients. Daniels applied for and received under seal multiple ex parte subpoenas deuces tecum for pre-trial production of a third-party doctor's patient medical records. Upon receipt of the subpoenas, the doctor refused to comply and gave the subpoenas to the government. The government filed a motion to, 1) unseal the defendant's ex parte motion, which contained the defendant's trial strategy, 2) challenge the sufficiency of the defendant's strategy used to satisfy the *Nixon* standards, 3) demand the defense provide notice to the government of any future Rule 17 (c) requests and 4) demand that any documents already subpoenaed by the defense be produced for inspection by the government. The government's argument to unseal the motion centered on allegations that the defendant was using Rule 17 (c) as a discovery tool and that the government wanted to challenge whether the defendant had satisfied the *Nixon* standards in the ex parte application. The court responded that it was intellectually capable of determining if the *Nixon* standards had been satisfied without the government's help and rejected the government's position that the subpoena was nothing more than a Rule 16 discovery. The court answered that the subpoena was directed to a third-party doctor who was not part of the government, and since the documents were not in the government's possession they were unavailable to the defendant under Rule 16. The court then joined the other District Courts that found that Rule 17 (c) did authorize the ex parte application for pre-trial subpoenas deuces tecum and that the government had no right to know the basis for the request since it could comprise the defendant's trial strategy and the identity of the documents subpoenaed.[2]

These decisions uniformly reason that where a defendant must reveal trial strategy, attorney work product, or witness identities in order to make the *Nixon* showing that the documents sought are relevant, admissible, and specific, then that showing must be made ex parte. If the defendant expects to use the documents in his case-in-chief, he will be required to produce them, but he may withhold from production those documents he will not use in his case-in-chief.

WHEREFORE, it is respectfully requested this court grant leave for the defendant to file a Rule 17 (c) motion under seal and that the subpoenas and the motion remain under seal.

Respectfully submitted,

_____

Thomas J. Farrell
Attorney for AG

IN THE UNITED STATES DISTRICT COURT
FOR THE _____ DISTRICT OF _____

UNITED STATES OF AMERICA,
         Plaintiff,

    v.   CR. NO.

AG,
         Defendant.

---

[2] The government had presented its own ex parte motions for pre-trial subpoenas to the court and anticipated filing additional ones as the matter progressed to trial.

EX PARTE REQUEST FOR ISSUANCE OF RULE 17 (C) SUBPOENAS AND SUPPORTING LAW

AND NOW COMES AG, by and through his attorney WM, Esquire, and respectfully requests that Rule 17 (c) pre-trial subpoenas be approved and in support thereof, sets forth the following:

INTRODUCTION

1) The beneficiaries identified in the conspiracy and substantive counts in the superseding indictment were treated by the following physicians:[3]
   a) Dr. RA, Pittsburgh, PA. The beneficiaries were also participants in various pharmaceutical company sponsored drug studies conducted by A Clinical Research, Inc. until barred by the FDA.
   b) Dr. PC, Niles, Ohio,
   c) Dr. EF, Chillicothe, Ohio,
   d) Dr. DW, Akron, Ohio.
2) The indictment charges G with defrauding Pennsylvania and Ohio Medicaid and Highmark of payments for medication billed on behalf of beneficiaries by one of nine specific methods set forth in paragraphs 37 through 43 in the superseding indictment but failed to disclose which was applicable to each beneficiary.
3) The Defendant has reason to believe and therefore avers, that the records sought will support his innocence. If pre-trial access to the third party documents is refused, he would be denied sufficient time to effectively review and utilize the information to prepare his defense.
4) The document request is specific and the documents sought are relevant, admissible, and material to G's defense.
5) The Government has denied it possesses any of the third-party documents sought by the subpoenas.
6) The government's denial that it possesses these third-party records removes any question that this request could possibly be considered a Rule 16 discovery request or a fishing expedition into the government's case.[4]

HIPAA REQUIREMENTS

45 CFR §164.512(e) of the Health Insurance Portability & Accountability Act permits disclosure of protected health information in response to a subpoena if the subpoena is accompanied by a court order issued in a judicial or administrative proceeding directing compliance with the subpoena.

Separate orders are submitted with each subpoena in order to maintain confidentiality of the subpoenas.

THE INVESTIGATION AND CHARGES

[Describe the investigation, the allegations in the indictment, the defense theory and how the documents will support that theory]

ARGUMENT IN SUPPORT OF G'S REQUEST FOR EX PARTE SUBPOENAS

The criteria for the issuance of pre-trial production of evidence pursuant to a Rule 17 (c) subpoena duces tecum was established by the Supreme Court in *U. S. v. Nixon*, 418 U.S. 683 (1974).

A grand jury indicated several former high ranking government officials in the Nixon administration following the Watergate burglary and the ensuing cover-up. Nixon was identified as an unindicted coconspirator but not charged as a defendant. The special prosecutor issued a Rule 17 (c) subpoena to President Nixon for the pre-trial production of White House documents and presidential tape recordings. The President moved to quash the subpoena on multiple grounds, all of which were denied by the district court. The district court ordered Nixon to produce the documents and tapes five months prior to the trial in order to give the prosecution sufficient time to prepare for trial. Nixon appealed to the Supreme Court.

---

[3] The government has not identified the beneficiaries by name as requested in Defendant's discovery motion; however, based upon Defendant's investigation, G believes the patients identified in the subpoenas are the same patients that appear in the indictment.

[4] Rule 16 applies only to records in the government's possession or under its control. In its response to G's pre-trial motions requesting these documents, the government denied possession or control and reaffirmed its lack of possession or control on the record at the June 5 hearing.

The Supreme Court's Rule 17 discussion appears as part III of the Nixon opinion at pages 697-702. The Court began its discussion by reaffirming that a Rule 17 (c) subpoena for documents may be quashed only if their production would be unreasonable or oppressive to the third party but not for any other reason. Citing *Bowman Dairy v. U.S.*, 341 U S 214 (1951). The Court then acknowledged Judge Winfield's formulation in *U.S. v. Iozia*, 13 FRD 335, 338 (SDNY 1952), as the generally accepted criteria for a Rule 17 (c) subpoenas where a defendant issues a subpoena to the government seeking documents in the government's possession. Iozia issued his subpoenas directly to the prosecution, rather than a third party, seeking production of third party documents held by the government that had been withheld from the defense. The district court ordered the government to provide certain subpoenaed documents and in do doing, established the burden a defendant must satisfy in order to force the government to disgorge documents pursuant to Rule 17 (c). The Court noted that Rule 17 was not intended to be an extension of Rule 16 discovery by permitting a defendant to rummage through the prosecution's file, however, the Court refused to issue a bright line rule that protected the government from any subpoenas for documents it withheld from the defense. In authoring the Nixon opinion, Chief Justice Burger recognized that there is a significant difference between subpoenas issued to the government and those issued to a third party.[5] After reviewing the *Iozia* opinion, the Chief Justice described the elements of a moving party's burden to secure pre-trial production of documents from a third party pursuant to the *Iozia* as follows:

Against this background, the special prosecutor, in order to carry his burden, must clear three hurdles: (1) Relevancy; (2) Admissibility; (3) Specificity.

The court recognized the prosecutor was unable to provide the specific contents of the subpoenaed tapes because he had been denied access, but he was able to provide a sufficient likelihood that the tapes contained conversations relevant to the offenses charged to "permit [the court to make] a rational inference that at least part of the conversations relate to the offenses charged in the indictment."[6] The prosecutor's burden was merely to create a *rational inference* of relevance to the charges in the indictment and that such an inference alone would satisfy the requisite specificity and relevance prongs of the three prong burden. The Court recognized the tapes were clearly relevant if they contained statements relating to the burglary and the cover up. As to admissibility, the Court found that although the tapes represented hearsay, it was not a deterrent to production because if the tapes contained evidence of the defendants' guilt, they would be admissible as one or more exceptions to the hearsay rule. The Court also found that it might take significant time for the special prosecutor to analyze and transcribe the tapes and engage in any follow up investigation. To withhold the subpoenas until the time of trial could result in either a delay of the trial or more importantly deny the prosecutor sufficient time to prepare his case. The Supreme Court affirmed the District Court Judge and order pre-trial production.

In the instant case, the subpoenas for the records are not directed to the government but rather to third parties for documents not in the government's possession and therefore not within any perceived limitations of Rule 16. The defense is clearly not attempting to rummage through the government's file since the government's file does not contain the documents.

The government has no basis to quash the subpoenas since they have no proprietary interest or privilege in the subpoenaed documents.[7] As described in *Nixon*, the only basis upon which a third party may move to quash the subpoenas is if the production would be unreasonable or burdensome. The government has no such basis.

The medical records are relevant to the charges in the indictment, since the indictment alleges that the doctors either did not prescribe, prescribed different dosages or discontinued the medication as three of the nine methods of fraudulent conduct alleged in paragraphs 37 through 43 of the indictment.

G's motion more than adequately creates the necessary preliminary showing of a rational inference that the medical records contain relevant information as to the charges in the indictment. The physician-patient records qualify as an exception to the hearsay rule under both the medical records exception and the business records exception to the hearsay rule.

As to specificity, the records sought are of beneficiaries identified in the indictment. Clearly the records are relevant, admissible and critical to the defense. The need for sufficient time to review them in order to prepare his defense is both obvious and undeniable.

The records of the Food and Drug Administration are not in the government's possession as acknowledged at the June 5 argument. Defendant has filed a request under the Freedom of Information Act, however, the agency refused to guarantee when the records would be made available and indicted with its current backlog it could take six to nine months or longer. No definite date was given even through the urgency was conveyed. The FDA will respond more

---

[5]   *U.S. v. Nixon*, 418 U.S. fn 12 at 700.

[6]   *Id.* at 700.

[7]   *U.S. v. Beckford*, 969 F. Supp 1010 (E.D. Va. 1978); *U.S. v. Tomison*, 969 F.Supp. 587 (E.D. Calif. 1997); *U.S. v. Daniels*, 95 F. Supp.2d 1160 (D. Kansas 2000).

quickly to a subpoena. Since the trial is set for only a few months away, a timely production of the records is imperative to the defense. Without ample time to study these records, the defense will not be able to advance its defense and continue the investigation necessary. These records will identify which of the beneficiaries were entered into the Serostim, Oxandrin or other relevant studies and thus verify the prolonged prescription of the drugs including the dates alleged in the indictment as fraudulently billed.

Similarly, the subpoenas to the drug companies will identify the participants and the prescriptions issued in the event the drug companies had not yet submitted the information to the FDA. The FDA and the Drug Company records will individually or jointly identify the participants in the A studies concerning the drugs identified in the indictment. This information will establish the medication was actually prescribed and that the billings were not fraudulent. They are relevant to the charges in the indictment and are admissible as a business record exception to the hearsay rule. The subpoenas are specific as to the documents dealing with the studies performed for the applicable drug companies.

Wherefore, it is respectfully respected this court issue the subpoenas requested.

Respectfully submitted,

_____

Thomas J. Farrell
Attorney for G

IN THE UNITED STATES DISTRICT COURT
FOR THE _____ DISTRICT OF _____

UNITED STATES OF AMERICA,
        Plaintiff,
     v.   CR. NO.
AG,
        Defendant.

ORDER OF COURT

AND NOW, this _____ day of _____, 200__, upon consideration of the Defendant's motion to serve the Rule 17 (c) third party duces tecum pre-trial subpoenas and a review of the submitted subpoenas, it is hereby order as follows:

Third Party	Granted	Granted in Part	Denied
Dr. RA	_____	_____	_____
Dr. PC	_____	_____	_____
Dr. EF	_____	_____	_____
Dr. DW	_____	_____	_____
Pa. Medicaid	_____	_____	_____
Ohio Medicaid	_____	_____	_____
Food & Drug Admin.	_____	_____	_____

_____ J.

Form 14-7   Request for Bill of Particulars

IN THE COURT OF COMMON PLEAS

COMMONWEALTH OF _____   COUNTY BRANCH– _____
        vs.   CRIMINAL NO.
LOUIS LOE

DEFENDANT'S REQUEST FOR A BILL OF PARTICULARS

AND NOW COMES Defendant, Louis Loe, by his attorney Thomas J. Farrell, and files this Request for a Bill of Particulars pursuant to Pa. R. Crim. P. 572. Please provide the following particulars with respect to each count of the Information.

Please list each prescription upon which the Commonwealth will rely as part of the offense charged in each count. For each prescription, please provide:

1) The prescription number;
2) The prescribing doctor's name;
3) The patient's name;
4) The medication prescribed;
5) The amount billed or paid by the insurer;
6) The date of claim for the prescription.

REASONS FOR THE REQUEST

The purposes of a bill of particulars are to enable a defendant to prepare for trial, to avoid surprise, and to enable the defendant to interpose the defenses of double jeopardy and the statute of limitations to this and future prosecutions. *See Commonwealth v. Chambers*, 528 Pa. 558, 580, 599 A.2d 630, 526 (1991); *Commonwealth v. Simione*, 447 Pa. 473, 291 A.2d 764 (1972). Each of these purposes necessitates a bill of particulars in this case.

The defendant is a pharmacist charged with defrauding insurers by billing for unauthorized prescriptions. Counts One and Two of the Information cover a four-year period–the years 1996, 1997, 1998, and 1999–and state simply that the defendant billed the Department of Public Welfare for unauthorized prescriptions during this time period. Counts Three and Four are similar, but cover 2-1/2 years each, from January 1, 1997, until July 31, 1999, and the billings were to Highmark Blue Cross/Blue Shield.

To defend against these charges, the defendant needs to know which specific prescriptions were allegedly unauthorized. The preliminary hearing and materials already provided by the Commonwealth indicate that the "false" prescriptions were for individuals who were in fact the defendant's customers, who had the medical ailments for which these types of medication would have been prescribed, who were patients of the doctors in whose names the "false" prescriptions were filled, and who did receive similar medications from those very doctors. The Commonwealth's theory is that the defendant either provided unauthorized refills or issued, filled and billed for new prescriptions without the doctors' authorization.

Under this set of facts, it will be difficult to distinguish the appropriately filled prescriptions from the inappropriate. To defend this case, defendant must examine each prescription at issue, compare it to his records, and attempt to interview the doctor or patient involved. This cannot be done and the case cannot be defended unless the defense knows each prescription involved.

Further, as the range of dates indicates, some of the prescriptions fall outside the statute of limitations. If the Commonwealth were to prove only those prescriptions that are outside the statute of limitations, the count would have to be dismissed. However, the defendant has no way of knowing this unless he knows which specific prescriptions, billed or paid on which dates, constitute each count.

Finally, if the defendant were to be prosecuted again for activity that occurred in the same broad time period encompassed by each of the counts here, he could not interpose the defense of double jeopardy unless it were shown which activity formed the basis for the counts on which he was prosecuted.

For all these reasons, a bill of particulars is necessary in this case.

Respectfully submitted,

_____
Thomas J. Farrell
Attorney for Defendant, Louis Loe

Chapter 15

MOTION PRACTICE

VIII. CHANGE OF VENUE

IX.   FORMS

I.   GENERAL POINTS

§15:01   Pre-Trial Motions

Pre-trial motions can include motions regarding:
- Suppression of physical evidence, statements and identification testimony. [*See* Chapter 7, Search & Seizure; and Chapter 9, Identification Procedures.]
- Discovery. [*See* Chapter 14, Discovery.]
- Bill of Particulars. [*See* Chapter 14, Discovery.]
- Dismissal for Failure to State an Offense. [*See* §15:20.]
- Dismissal for Multiplicity or Duplicity. [*See* §§15:30 & 31.]
- Dismissal for Violations of the Statute of Limitations. [*See* §15:10.]
- Dismissal for Speedy Trial Violations. [*See* §15:40.]
- Severance of counts and defendants. [*See* §15:50.]
- Change of Venue. [*See* §15:70.]

You may also make a motion in limine for a pre-trial determination of evidentiary issues you expect will arise at trial. Such motions are better left shortly before trial when the issues are focused. [*See* Chapter 20, Trial.]

§15:02   Motion Procedures

Jurisdictions, and sometimes even judges within the same courthouse, vary in the mechanics of how motions are filed, heard and decided.

The practice in most federal jurisdictions is for the movant to file a written motion with a supporting memorandum of law. Local rules or a judge's standing order may dictate the time for a response. If the motion results in a hearing or argument, you may ask for time to brief the issue further after the hearing.

In some courts, movants proceed by serving and filing a "notice of motion" advising the other party that the movant will present a motion for the specified relief on the date set in the motion. The movant obtains the date either from the court's established motion calendar (in which case you must count backwards to ensure that you serve and file the notice sufficiently in advance to provide the required notice) or by contacting the clerk's office or chambers and obtaining a return date from the court's clerk.

In some jurisdictions, the practice may be to serve all papers on the opponent, but to file and present the motion along with supporting affidavits, if needed, and memorandum of law, for the first time at the hearing or argument. In other jurisdictions, you must attach and file those documents with the notice of motion.

Many of these rules do not appear anywhere in writing, and you must either contact local practitioners (public defenders or former assistant district attorneys are good sources) or call the clerk to discern the correct procedure.

Make motions in writing whenever possible, even mid-trial, to assure that you articulate and preserve all relevant legal arguments. Check that the motion is filed in the record; sometimes handing a written motion to the judge or his clerk, especially if done in an off-the-record in-chambers conference, will not guarantee that it gets filed. If the motion is not filed in the record or articulated and transcribed by a court reporter, your motion does not exist for appellate review.

§15:03   Deciding Whether to Forego Motions

Pre-trial case-dispositive motions are rare in criminal cases. Therefore, the first decision is whether to file motions at all.

In some jurisdictions, including the federal courts, filing a motion stops the running of the speedy trial clock. [*E.g.,* 18 U.S.C. §3161(h)(1)(F).]

In such jurisdictions, it may be better to forego motions and rush to trial because:
- Prosecutors occasionally indict cases before they are ready to try them.
- Sometimes prosecutors indict many defendants, hoping that the less culpable will turn state's evidence against the more. In such cases, the defendants may benefit if all decide to waive any motions and demand a prompt trial. This may cause the prosecution to extend very generous plea offers to the less culpable defendants, even without requiring cooperation, so as to pare down the case and concentrate on the others. Even those pleas may not buy the prosecution enough time and witnesses to strengthen its case against the leaders; thus, all may benefit from this strategy.

If you pursue this course, you must be ready to try the case on very short notice.

Even losing motions have benefits, such as:

- Preserving an issue for appeal. In the heat of trial, with an impatient judge and jury, it may be difficult to articulate all the legal bases for an objection – evidentiary rules, state constitutional grounds, and federal constitutional provisions. For example, a hearsay objection does not preserve a Sixth Amendment Confrontation Clause issue. A definitive ruling on a pretrial motion may preserve it. If you need to renew the motion at trial, it is easier to do so by reference to "the arguments raised in my pretrial memorandum of x-date" rather than to repeat all those arguments.
- Forcing the government to show some of its evidence and case theory in its response to your motions.
- Motions that address the sufficiency of the charge, the elements of the offense, or its legality (for example, a void for vagueness challenge) will educate the court to legal issues likely to arise at trial. The motions, even if they lose, may persuade the court to grant you leeway in the presentation of evidence and gain more consideration for case-specific jury instructions built on the legal issues raised in your motion.
- The education you give the court may advance your evidentiary arguments on relevance.
- Many trial prosecutors have little skill or experience with sophisticated legal arguments and briefing. Aggressive motion practice puts the prosecutor on notice that he is in for a battle on terms he may not relish and may elicit a favorable plea offer.

The strategy of waiving motions and proceeding quickly to trial works best when it surprises the prosecutor, and only when all defendants agree on the strategy.

[§§15:04-15:09 Reserved]

II.   STATUTE OF LIMITATIONS

§15:10   Generally Five Years for Felonies

Limitations periods for criminal offenses are set by statute.

Most felonies have a five-year period. [*See, e.g.,* 42 Pa.C.S.A. §5552(b); 18 U.S.C. §3282.] The exceptions are:

- Tax offenses have a six-year period from filing of the return or, if none was filed, from the date on which it should have been filed. [26 U.S.C. §6531.]
- Bank fraud is 10 years. [18 U.S.C. §3293.]
- Homicide has no limitations period. [*See, e.g.,* 42 Pa.C.S.A. §5551.]
- Some states have no statutes of limitations. [*E.g., Vernier v. State,* 721 P.2d 1344, 1348 (Wyo. 1996) (stating that Wyoming has no statute of limitations for any criminal offense).]

The limitations period may be tolled during:

- The victim's minority. [*See, e.g.,* 42 Pa.C.S.A. §5552(c)(3); *see generally* Lauren Kerns, *Incorporating Tolling Provisions Into Sex Crimes Statutes Of Limitations,* 13 Temple Pol. & Civil Rights L. Rev. 325, 329-30 (2003) (all states have such a provision for sex offenses against children, citing cases and statutes).]
- The perpetrator's flight from prosecution. [42 Pa.C.S.A. §5554; 18 U.S.C. §3290.]
- The perpetrator's concealment of the offense. [*E.g., State v. Palmer,* 248 Kan. 681, 683, 810 P.2d 734, 737 (1991); Ind. Code Ann. §35-41-4-2(i)(2) (the limitation period does not include any period in which "the accused person conceals evidence of the offense").]

§15:11   Measuring the Limitations Period

Depending on local legislation and case law, the ending point for the limitations period may come with any of the following:

- The filing of an indictment.
- The filing of a formal accusatory instrument.
- The timely execution of an arrest warrant.

[*See* LaFave, *et al.,* 4 *Criminal Procedure* §18.5(a).]

For most offenses, determining when all its elements have been completed and the limitations period begins to run is simple. For example, it is when the victim was killed, or the money was taken, or the auto crashed.

However, some offenses are considered "continuing" offenses, and the limitations period does not start until the offense ends. The usual example of a continuing offense is conspiracy. [*E.g., Commonwealth v. McSloy*, 2000 Pa. Super. 130, 751 A.2d 666 (Pa. Super. Ct. 2000).]

Conspiracy continues until its objectives are achieved or the last act is taken in furtherance of it, even if these periods extend beyond your client's involvement with the conspiracy (unless your client withdraws from the conspiracy). [*See United States v. Salmonese*, 352 F.3d 608 (2d Cir. 2003) (fraud conspiracy continued until conspirator received profits from the scheme)]. "To withdraw from a conspiracy a defendant must either disavow the unlawful goal of the conspiracy, affirmatively act to defeat the purpose of the conspiracy, or take 'definite, decisive, and positive' steps to show that the [defendant's] disassociation from the conspiracy is sufficient." [*United States v. Lothian*, 976 F.2d 1257, 1261 (9th Cir. 1992) (citations omitted).] Once the defense makes out a prima facie case of withdrawal, the prosecution must prove beyond a reasonable doubt that the defendant did not withdraw. *Lothian*, 976 F.2d at 1261; *United States v. Read*, 658 F.2d 1225, 1232-36 (7th Cir. 1981); *but see United States v. Hamilton*, 538 F.3d 162, 174 (2d Cir. 2008) (The burden of establishing withdrawal lies on the defendant).]

Efforts to conceal a completed conspiracy do not extend the conspiracy's life for purposes of calculating the limitations period's commencement. [*See Grunewald v. United States*, 353 U.S. 391, 399 (1957).]

§15:12 Raising the Issue of the Limitations Period

Courts vary on their approach to when the issue of the statute of limitations may be raised:
- Some require that the issue must be raised pre-trial.
- Others treat the issue as jurisdictional in the sense that it can be raised even for the first time on appeal.
- Others permit it to be waived, but only explicitly and knowingly.

[*See State v. Pearson*, 858 S.W.2d 879 (Tenn. 1993) (surveying the three approaches and the positions of various states).]

A limitations defense may present a factual issue, such as a determination of when a continuing offense ended, and the jury must decide the issue. [*E.g., United States v. Oliva*, 46 F.3d 320, 324-25 (3d Cir. 1995) (limitations issue must be decided by jury under beyond-a-reasonable-doubt standard); *Commonwealth v. Groff*, 378 Pa. Super. 353, 369, 548 A.2d 1237, 1245 (1988) (issue is for the jury if any of the facts are in dispute).]

Since the issue's determination really depends on the facts adduced at trial, you must be sure to renew your motion at the close of the evidence, even if you filed a pre-trial motion.

Form:
- **Form 15-1** Motion to Dismiss on Statute of Limitations

[§§15:13-15:19 Reserved]

III.   FAILURE TO STATE AN OFFENSE

§15:20   Indictment Must Allege Every Necessary Element

An indictment must allege every necessary element of the offense, and failure to do so warrants dismissal. [*United States v. Du Bo*, 186 F.3d 1177 (9th Cir. 1999) (omission of knowingly element from extortion indictment required dismissal; trial and proper jury instruction did not cure error); *United States v. Spinner*, 180 F.3d 514 (3d Cir. 1999) (conviction after guilty plea reversed and indictment dismissed where indictment failed to state that access device fraud affected interstate commerce); *but see State v. Smith*, 996 S.W.2d 845 (Tenn. Crim. App. 1999) (omission of *mens rea* element not error where the indictment referred to statute that sets forth the *mens rea*).]

Generally, an indictment or charging instrument that tracks the statute suffices, as long as the statute states all the elements of the offense. [*Hamling v. United States*, 418 U.S. 87, 117-18 (1974).]

PRACTICE TIP:

Always compare the indictment to the statutory elements of the offense. Omission of an element occurs most frequently when case law has added to the offense an element that the statute does not explicitly mention. [*E.g., United States v. Du Bo*, 186 F.3d 1177 (statute did not mention a *mens rea* requirement, but case law had interpreted the crime as including one).]

§15:21   Defect Can Be Raised at Any Time

Most courts consider an indictment's lack of a necessary element a jurisdictional defect that may be raised at any time. [*See Spinner*, 180 F.3d 514 (setting aside guilty plea where defect raised for first time on appeal, even though inclusion of missing element in second count of indictment provided defendant with notice of the element); *State v. Smith*, 996 S.W.2d 845, 847 (Tenn. Crim. App. 1999).]

PRACTICE TIP:

If you are in a jurisdiction that permits you to raise such a defect at any time, you should not raise such an issue until post-trial motions or on appeal because such defects usually reflect oversights that could be easily corrected by seeking a superseding indictment, not failures of proof. However, the trial judge is likely to frown on such gamesmanship, so do not raise the issue so late that your client is likely to serve a considerable period of incarceration before the appellate court affords relief.

Form:
- **Form 15-2** Motion to Dismiss for Failure to State an Offense, Duplicity

§15:22   Gun Cases

In *District of Columbia v. Heller,* 554 U.S. 570, (2008), the Supreme Court held that the Second Amendment guarantees individuals the right to possess firearms, at least in their homes for self-defense, and in *McDonald v. City of Chicago,* 561 U.S. 742 (2010), the Court extended that right as enforceable against State and local laws. Language in both opinions suggest that the Court is chary of attempts to use the newly-recognized right as a defense to run-of-the-mill gun prosecutions, such as felon-in possession charges. [*See McDonald,* 561 U.S. at 785-86; *Heller,* 554 U.S. at 626.] Some courts have characterized that language as non-binding dicta, others as part of the *Heller* holding, but in any event, all courts have upheld those restrictions listed among *Heller*'s "presumptively lawful regulatory measures." [*United States v. Huet,* 665 F.3d 588, 600 & n.11 (3d Cir. 2012) (upholding conviction for aiding and abetting a felon's possession of a firearm; reviewing cases)]. Nonetheless, the reasoning of both cases, particularly as expressed in *McDonald,* may be read to support constitutional challenges to restrictions on gun possession: the right to bear arms is a "fundamental right" and on an equal footing with other Bill of Rights guarantees. [*McDonald,* slip op at 20, 29, 40; *United States v. Marzzarella,* 614 F.3d 85 (3d Cir. 2010) (Second Amendment claims should be adjudged under the same standards as First Amendment free speech claims).]

Challenges to gun laws have had mixed results. Absolute bans on carrying any type of gun have fallen [*Moore v. Madigan,* 702 F.3d 933 (7th Cir. 2012) (striking down Illinois' absolute ban on carrying a gun in public)], but strict permit requirements have survived. [*Kachalsky v. County of Westchester,* 701 F.3d 81 (2d Cir. 2012) (upholding New York State's handgun licensing scheme which requires an applicant to demonstrate "proper cause" to obtain a license to carry a concealed handgun in public); *Heller v. District of Columbia,* 670 F.3d 1244 (D.C. Cir. 2011) (upholding law requiring registration of firearms and prohibiting possession of assault weapons and the possession of magazines with a capacity of more than ten rounds of ammunition).] Nearly all "status" restrictions on gun possession–laws against possession by felons, the mentally ill, drug users, and those subject to domestic violence restraining orders–have passed constitutional muster. [*See, e.g., Marzzarella, supra; see also United States v. Mahin,* 668 F.3d 119 (4th Cir. 2012) (domestic violence protective order; reviewing cases); *United States v. Dugan,* 657 F.3d 998 (9th Cir. 2011) (upholding the restriction in 18 U.S.C. §922 (g)(3) against gun possession by habitual drug users); *United States v. Yancey,* 621 F.3d 681, 687 (7th Cir. 2010) (per curiam); *United States v. Seay,* 620 F.3d 919, 925 (8th Cir. 2010), cert. denied, 131 S.Ct. 1027 (2011); *but see Binderup v. Attorney General,* 836 F.3d 336 (3d Cir. 2016) (en banc) (holding that state two-year misdemeanors, which were considered felonies for purpose of federal gun possession disability, were not serious enough to strip individuals of their right to possess a firearm).]

One must raise these challenges in this new and changing area of the law until the Supreme Court weighs in on each particular issue.

[§§15:23-15:29 Reserved]

IV. MULTIPLICITY AND DUPLICITY

§15:30   Duplicity

Duplicity is the charging of more than a single offense in a single count of the indictment. [*United States v. Sturdivant*, 244 F.3d 71, 75 (2d Cir. 2001).]

A duplicitous count exposes the defendant to the risk that the jury might convict without being unanimous as to which of the crimes charged within the single count was proven beyond a reasonable doubt. [*Sturdivant* (Single count charging two separate and distinct drug sales held to be duplicitous).]

However, charging several means of committing a single offense in one count does not amount to duplicity. [*See United States v. Crisci*, 273 F.3d 235, 239 (2d Cir. 2001) (indictment charging fraud by both a scheme to defraud and by false statements properly charged two means of committing one offense).]

Generally, you must raise duplicity before trial. However, it may be raised during trial if the defect does not become apparent until during the trial. [*Indictments,* 34 Geo. L.J. Ann. Rev. Crim. Proc. 245, 267 & n.915 (2004) (listing cases).] The circumstance of the defect not being apparent until during trial may occur if the indictment appears to charge a single continuous transaction, but the evidence proves two distinct offenses. [*E.g., Sturdivant*, 244 F.3d at 75.]

The remedies are to either:
*   Demand that the prosecution elect on which offense to proceed.
*   Ask the court to instruct the jury that it must be unanimous as to which offense the defendant committed.
[*United States v. Ramirez-Martinez*, 273 F.3d 903, 915 (9th Cir. 2001).]

Form:
*   **Form 15-3** Duplicity Motion

§15:31   Multiplicity

Multiplicity is charging a single offense in multiple counts of an indictment, a practice that carries the risk of cumulative sentences for one crime.

The remedy is election of which counts will proceed to trial. [*United States v. Johnson*, 130 F.3d 1420, 1424 & 1426 (10th Cir. 1997).]

[§§15:32-15:39 Reserved]

V. SPEEDY TRIAL VIOLATIONS

§15:40   The Speedy Trial Guarantee

The Constitution guarantees a speedy trial. However, that protection applies only to the most egregious delays. Before it will dismiss a case for a constitutional speedy trial violation, the court will evaluate four factors:
*   Length of delay.
*   The reason for the delay.
*   The defendant's assertion of his right.
*   Prejudice to the defendant.
[*Barker v. Wingo*, 407 U.S. 514, 530 (1972).]
State statutes and rules provide greater protection, often requiring a trial within a specified period, with specified exclusions. [*E.g.,* 18 U.S.C. §3161.]
Generally, a defendant must move to dismiss before trial in order to avail himself of those protections.

§15:41   Evaluating Whether to Waive Speedy Trial Protections

In many cases, your preference will be to waive speedy trial protections to gain time to prepare for trial. You must consult carefully with your client in making this decision, especially if he is wasting in jail.

On the other hand, consider foregoing any extensions of the speedy trial period when the prosecution appears unready to proceed to trial. Where extensions are the norm and the statutory period is relatively brief, prosecutors may count on those extensions for time to prepare. Pushing the case to trial quickly may elicit a generous plea offer or may catch the prosecutor without necessary witnesses or evidence.

[§§15:42-15:49 Reserved]

VI.   SEVERANCE AND MISJOINDER

§15:50   General Points

Joinder rules generally permit prosecutors to join related charges against one defendant in a single indictment, as well as charges against multiple defendants when they participated in a conspiracy or their respective crimes arose out of the same course of conduct. [*See* Fed. R. Crim. P. 8.]

Whenever an indictment or information charges multiple counts against your client or joins him with other defendants, you should consider:

- A motion to sever because of misjoinder (*i.e.*, because the counts did not satisfy the requirements of the joinder rule).
- A motion to sever counts or to sever your client's trial from the other defendants on the grounds that the joinder unfairly prejudices your client. However, before you move for severance on the grounds of unfair prejudice, review the charging instrument to see whether the charges and defendants are properly joined. Misjoinder is legal error and thus more likely to earn relief. [*See United States v. Giampa*, 904 F.Supp. 235, 264 (D.N.J. 1995).]

Prosecutors and trial courts have substantial discretion in joining counts and defendants for trial, and judicial economy favors a single, rather than multiple, trial so if the joinder is proper, severance is not usually granted.

On the other hand, since the decision to sever is discretionary and the prosecution cannot appeal it, courts sometimes will exercise that discretion and sever if you can convince the court of the joinder's unfairness or inefficiency.

You should file a severance motion pre-trial, but renew it during trial whenever evidence or argument inflicts the harm predicted in your motion:

- The admission of a co-defendant's statement.
- The admission of inflammatory evidence that pertains only to co-defendants or some charges, and not others.
- Co-counsel arguments and questions pointing the finger at your client.

Renew the motion again at the close of trial to complete your record.

Form:
- **Form 15-4** Motion to Sever

§15:51   Multiple Charges Against a Single Defendant

When the evidence on the multiple charges is substantially the same, such as when they arise from one incident, or when one witness claims to have been victimized several times, you probably want one trial.

Trying each charge separately enables the prosecution to refine its proof and test it before different juries. [*See* Anthony G. Amsterdam, *Trial Manual for the Defense of Criminal Cases*, §263 (5th ed. 1989).]

Furthermore, producing defense witnesses at multiple trials may come at an unaffordable cost to the defense (in the case of expert witnesses) or unbearable inconvenience to the witness (a consideration especially important where the witness must remain sympathetic if his testimony is to be helpful, such as a character witness).

On the other hand, cumulative evidence from unrelated witnesses to separate events corroborates your client's guilt. The jury may believe that the eyewitnesses to robbery one are mistaken. The jury is less likely to believe that the eyewitnesses to robbery one, the different eyewitnesses for robbery two, and yet another set for robbery three all erred.

Form:
- **Form 15-4** Motion to Sever

§15:52   Multiple Defendants and Evidence Issues

The prosecution's intent to offer a co-defendant's confession may create a right to a severance if that confession names and implicates your client. The co-defendant has a right not to testify; therefore, admission of the confession as evidence against your client would violate his Sixth Amendment right to confront the declarant of testimonial hearsay on cross-examination. [*Bruton v. United States*, 391 U.S. 123 (1968).]

With respect to most evidence offered against only one defendant in a multi-defendant trial, judges avoid prejudice to the other defendants by instructing the jury that they are not to consider the evidence in deciding the guilt of the other defendants. However, confessions are considered such powerful evidence that the law recognizes that such a limiting instruction does not work. [*Bruton*, 391 U.S. at 135.]

Thus, when the prosecution seeks the admission of a defendant's confession at a joint trial, it has two choices:

*   Redact the statement effectively to eliminate any references to co-defendants.
*   Sever that defendant's trial from the others.

Not all efforts at redaction are acceptable. "[R]edactions that replace a proper name with an obvious blank, the word 'delete,' a symbol, or similarly notifying the jury that a name has been deleted" violate *Bruton*. [*See Gray v. Maryland*, 523 U.S. 185 (1998) (redaction that replaced references to co-defendant with the word "deleted" ineffective).] In contrast, "the Confrontation Clause is not violated by the admission of a non-testifying codefendant's confession with a proper limiting instruction when ... the confession is redacted to eliminate not only the defendant's name, but any reference to his or her existence." [*Richardson v. Marsh*, 481 U.S. 200, 211 (1987).]

The Supreme Court's re-writing of Confrontation Clause law in *Crawford v. Washington*, 541 U.S. 36 (2004), has reduced the scope of the *Bruton* rule. Many courts had ruled that *Bruton* applied to co-defendants' admissions to non-law enforcement witnesses under circumstances that would not be considered "testimonial" under *Crawford*. [*E.g., United States v. Berrios*, 676 F.3d 118, 128 (3d Cir. 2012) (reviewing law).] However, *Crawford* and subsequent cases have limited the Confrontation Clause's application to "testimonial" hearsay–statements made in response to interrogation, the primary purpose of which is to provide information potentially relevant to a criminal prosecution. [*Davis v. Washington*, 547 U.S. 814, 821-22 (2006); see §20:120, infra.] Thus, a co-defendant's confession to family and friends, or his surreptitiously recorded statements, do not implicate the Confrontation Clause, and thus *Bruton* no longer provides a basis for severance or redaction. [*Berrios*, 676 F.3d at 125-129.]

Remember, too, that *Bruton* never applied to a co-conspirator's statement made during and in furtherance of a conspiracy to which your client belonged. [*Crawford*, 541 U.S. at 56.]

EXAMPLE:

A confession admitting to an unprovoked attack by the defendant and another unnamed person dooms your client's claim that he acted in self-defense. Even if the court instructs the jury to consider a co-defendant's criminal record only to establish his intent or motive, not your client's, the jury may fault your client for associating with such a character.

On the other hand, a co-defendant may succeed in suppressing evidence where your client would lack standing to challenge it, particularly on Fourth Amendment grounds, forcing the prosecution to choose between severance or foregoing use of the evidence at a joint trial.

§15:53   Multiple Defendants and Guilt by Association

Less culpable defendants might prefer to be tried with those against whom the evidence is stronger so that if the jury is inclined to some leniency or doubt, it might compromise and acquit the less culpable. You can emphasize this theme in closing arguments by explaining proof beyond a reasonable doubt with the suggestion that it is the kind of evidence that exists against the co-defendant, but not against your client.

EXAMPLES:

*   "No one identified my client as being one of the gunmen in the bank."
*   "My client doesn't drive the sort of car that befits a drug dealer."

You may prefer a separate trial when your client's association with co-defendants whose lives seem to be an uninterrupted crime spree may lead the jury to damn him as just another miscreant. The prosecution argument that criminals do not invite innocent bystanders to witness their misdeeds has the ring of truth. Were your client tried separately, the judge might preclude evidence about events in which he did not participate.

Your client will have greater success in hiding behind the other defendants where he has a legitimate reason for associating with the co-defendants (*e.g.,* they are family members or childhood friends, or the crimes occurred as part of a business enterprise that was not wholly illegitimate).

§15:54　　Multiple Defendants and Antagonistic Defenses

Few trial experiences hold more misery for defendants and amusement for prosecutors than the spectacle of co-defendants pointing the finger at each other.

Mutually antagonistic defenses or mere finger-pointing among co-defendants does not require severance. [*Zafiro v. United States*, 506 U.S. 534, 539-40 (1993).]

However, severance is required when the "defenses [are] so *irreconcilable* as to involve *fundamental disagreement over core and basic facts* ... such that "the jury unjustifiably [would] infer that this conflict *alone* demonstrate[d] that both [defendants] [were] guilty." [*United States v. Serafino*, 281 F.3d 327, 329-30 (1st Cir. 2002) (citations omitted; emphasis in original). *See also United States v. Mayfield*, 189 F.3d 895 (9th Cir. 1999) (inconsistent defenses do not require severance, but "mutually exclusive" defenses do); *United States v. Copeland*, 336 F.Supp.2d 223 (E.D.N.Y. 2004) (severance where one defendant would call neutral eyewitness to bank robbery exculpating him but implicating co-defendant).]

Raising this issue before trial forces you to disclose a considerable amount of detail about the defenses. To preserve the issue, you should renew your objection at trial whenever the joinder permits the introduction of evidence prejudicial to your client (*e.g.,* when the co-defendant testifies, or elicits his exculpatory post-arrest statements, or during co-counsel's closing argument). [*United States v. Sherlock*, 962 F.2d 1349, 1362 (9th Cir. 1989); *People v. Collins*, 186 Ill.App.3d 35, 43, 133 Ill. Dec. 870, 541 N.E.2d 1308, 1313 (1989) (court should have granted severance after opening statements and testimony of prosecution's first witness; there is a continuing duty to grant severance if prejudice appears during the trial).]

A similar problem arises when one defendant testifies and the other does not. Rather than sever, courts will forbid the testifying defendant's lawyer from commenting on the other defendant's failure to testify. [*See generally State v. Daluz*, 143 A.3d 800 (Me. 2016) (counsel for testifying defendant at joint trial is not permitted to comment on co-defendant's silence; since severance must be addressed pretrial, what happens at trial is not grounds for severance); *Commonwealth v. Russo*, 49 Mass. App. Ct. 579, 731 N.E.2d 108 (2000) (although co-defendant's counsel may not comment on failure of co-defendant to testify, remarks that his client would take the stand held not to be prejudicial comment on co-defendant's silence); *Head v. State*, 256 Ga. App. 624, 626, 569 S.E.2d 548, 551 (2002) (since co-defendant had no right to comment on other defendant's silence, desire to do so was not grounds for severance); *but see De Luna v. United States*, 308 F.2d 140, 141 (5th Cir. 1962) ("If an attorney's duty to his client should require him to draw the jury's attention to the possible inference of guilt from a co-defendant's silence, the trial judge's duty is to order that the defendants be tried separately").]

Even if the nontestifying co-defendant chooses not to attack the testimony, hearing from one defendant makes the jury more likely to draw the forbidden inference that silence conceals guilt.

Still, where the defense is a unified one, you may benefit by having a co-defendant who can recite the defense better than your client. The co-defendant might have a cleaner record than your client or simply be more articulate and presentable. Defenses where one defendant can cover all the defendants might include self-defense or the defense that a fraudulent scheme really was a legitimate and honest, but perhaps misunderstood, business opportunity.

§15:55　　The Quality of Co-Counsel

You must consider whether you can work with the co-defendants' attorneys.

The court likely will apportion peremptory challenges and preclude cumulative cross-examinations. You do not want co-counsel's sloppy cross-examination to rehabilitate a witness you just demolished. Similarly, if the witness goes first, co-counsel could botch a line of cross-examination that the court will not let you repeat in the hope of better results.

On the other hand, working cooperatively with competent co-counsel might augment chances of acquittal. One attorney may undertake the cross of experts, another might focus on legal issues; the defendants hurt most by a witness can bear the burden of attacking the witness, freeing other defendants to argue that they did not need to cross-examine the witness because the witness really did not have anything meaningful to say about that defendant.

Attacks from many points can flummox a prosecutor and frustrate the judge to the point that he will blame the prosecutor for the decision to join the defendants in one trial.

[§§15:56-15:59 Reserved]

VII. PROSECUTORIAL MISCONDUCT

§15:60   Types of Misconduct

Prosecutorial misconduct comes in many varieties, including:
- Selective prosecution. [*Wayte v. United States,* 470 U.S. 598 (1985).]
- Grand jury abuses. [*Bank of Nova Scotia v. United States,* 487 U.S. 250, 256 (1988).]
- Vindictive prosecution. [*Blackledge v. Perry,* 417 U.S. 21 (1974).]
- Discovery violations. [*Kyles v. Whitley,* 514 U.S. 419 (1995).]
- Presentation of false testimony. [*Napue v. Illinois,* 360 U.S. 264 (1959).]
- Improper trial questioning and argument. [*Donnelly v. DeChristoforo,* 416 U.S. 637 (1974).]

[*See generally* Joseph F. Lawless, *Prosecutorial Misconduct* (3d ed. 2003).]

§15:61   Motions to Dismiss for Prosecutorial Misconduct

Motions to dismiss on the basis of prosecutorial misconduct rarely succeed, but litigating the motion carries many benefits worth the trouble:
- It may deter the prosecutor from future abuses.
- The trial judge may scrutinize the prosecutor's actions more closely during trial.
- Repeated motions lay a ground work for a finding of prejudice if later abuses come to light.
- The prosecutor's response may provide discovery into his case. For example, a response to a selective prosecution claim may describe uncharged conduct or investigative findings that made your client worthy of prosecution, at least according to the prosecutor.
- The prosecutor may stake out a position–such as his full compliance with his *Brady* obligations–that you can disprove later.

Form:
- **Form 15-5** Motion to Dismiss, to Gag, and for Change of Venue

[§§15:62-15:69 Reserved]

VIII. CHANGE OF VENUE

§15:70   Due Process Requirements

Due process requires a change of venue in two situations:
- The jury selection demonstrates actual prejudice permeating the venue. [*See* Chapter 20, Trial.]
- In the exceptional case where pre-trial publicity has been "so sustained, so pervasive, so inflammatory, and so inculpatory" that prejudice can be presumed. These will be the exceptional cases, and each case must turn on its own facts. [*Commonwealth v. Sutton,* 485 Pa. 47, 57, 400 A.2d 1305, 1309 (1979); *see also United States v. McVeigh,* 918 F. Supp. 1467 (W.D. Okla. 1996) (granting pre-trial motion to change venue).]

Thus, you should move for a change of venue before jury selection only when pre-trial publicity has so inflamed the community that your client cannot obtain a fair trial in the county or district where he is charged.

When prejudicial pre-trial publicity is alleged, the trial court should consider:

whether the pre-trial publicity revealed the existence of the accused's prior criminal record; whether the publicity referred to confessions, admissions, or reenactments of the crime by the defendant; and whether such information is the product of reports by the police and prosecutorial officers. The presence of one of these elements does not, in itself, warrant a presumption of prejudice. Inquiry must be made to determine whether such publicity has been so extensive, sustained, and pervasive that the community must be deemed to have been saturated with it.

[*Commonwealth v. Lohr*, 275 Pa Super. 212, 220-221, 418 A.2d 688, 692 (1980); s*ee also Commonwealth v. Rucci*, 543 Pa. 261, 283-84, 670 A.2d 1129 (1996).]

§15:71   Providing a Sufficient Factual Basis

Cases in which you can demonstrate presumed prejudice will be those rare cases of exceptional notoriety, involving either crimes that shake the whole community or in which a public figure is charged.

However, do not take an "everyone knows it when they see it" approach to the venue issue. You must lay a careful factual basis for your motion, including:
- Copies of all the newspaper, television, radio and Internet reports on the case.
- A survey of community members.
- If you can afford it, an affidavit and testimony from a sociologist who specializes in change of venue issues.
  [*See ABA Standards Relating to Fair Trial and Free Press* at Std. 8-3.3(c) (2d ed Approved Draft, 1978).]

Experts can be found by reviewing published decisions or contacting attorneys in the cases of great notoriety, such as the Oklahoma City Bombing, the Nairobi Bombings, the Susan Smith and Andrea Yates homicides, and the Robert Blake case. Some of these experts have worked on cases starting with the civil rights and black militant cases of the 1960s through the terrorism and celebrity homicide cases of the 1990s and 2000s. It is a small community, and one expert will lead you to another.

The expert should conduct a content analysis of the media reports to evaluate the extent to which they emphasize the defendant's guilt, inadmissible evidence, or unfairly prejudicial themes. In addition, he will conduct or manage the community survey, which consists of interviewing random community members to determine how widely news of the case has spread, the opinions people have, and how passionately the community feels about it. The expert can compare the community sentiment and extent and nature of the publicity in your case to other cases in which a change of venue has been granted.

Form:
- **Form 15–5** Motion to Dismiss, to Gag, and for Change of Venue

§15:72   Benefits of the Motion

Even if you do not obtain a change of venue, the motion may elicit other needed relief, such as:
- Gag orders on the parties.
- Orders or judicial cautions that the parties should not file discovery in the public court file and should not place inflammatory material in pleadings.

A caution not to place inflammatory material in pleadings can be important because, while most prosecutors heed the disciplinary restrictions on making public statements about the case, they often seek to influence the media's coverage and public sentiment by attaching to publicly filed pleadings reports of confessions, excerpts from wiretaps, medical reports and proffers of informants' testimony.

IX. FORMS

Form 15-1   Motion to Dismiss on Statute of Limitations

IN THE COURT OF COMMON PLEAS OF
_____ COUNTY, _____

COMMONWEALTH OF _____,   )

)

     v.   )

)

JOHN DOE, M.D.   )

**DEFENDANT'S MOTION TO DISMISS COUNTS
I–VII, IX AND X FOR VIOLATION OF THE STATUTE OF LIMITATONS**

AND NOW COMES the Defendant, John Doe, M.D., by and through his attorneys, and hereby files the following pre-trial motions, stating in support thereof as follows:

The criminal complaint in this case was filed on or about _____.

Pursuant to Title 42, Pa.C.S.A. §5552(b)(2), the statute of limitations for any offense punishable under the Controlled Substance, Drug, Device and Cosmetic Act, 35 P.S. §780-113(f) and for insurance fraud, 18 Pa.C.S.A. §4117, is five years from the date that the crime was committed.

Counts I and II of the information charge continuing offenses involving the delivery of controlled substances beginning in _____. Pursuant to the applicable statute of limitations, prosecution for any delivery of controlled substances which occurred prior to _____ is barred by the statute of limitations.

Neither the delivery or controlled substances nor insurance fraud are considered "continuing offenses" for statute of limitations purposes.

Similarly, with respect to Counts III, IV, V, VI, VII, IX, and X, all of which allege criminal conduct beginning in either "_____" or on "_____," the statute of limitations bars prosecution of any conduct which occurred prior to _____. Therefore, those events should also be quashed.

Respectfully submitted,

_____

Thomas J. Farrell, Esq.

Form 15-2   Motion to Dismiss for Failure to State an Offense, Duplicity

IN THE COURT OF COMMON PLEAS OF _____ COUNTY, _____

COMMONWEALTH OF _____,   )

)

         Plaintiff,)   )

         v.   )   CRIMINAL DIVISION

MN   )

         Defendant.   )

**DEFENDANT'S OMNIBUS PRE-TRIAL MOTION
FOR RELIEF WITH CITATIONS TO AUTHORITY**

AND NOW COMES the Defendant, MN, by and through his attorney, _____, Esquire, and hereby files the following pre-trial motions, stating in support thereof as follows:

INTRODUCTION

On _____, a Criminal Complaint was filed against defendant, MN, based upon the affidavit of Detective _____ of the Central Park Police Department. The complaint alleged that Mr. N raped his niece vaginally in _____, when she was 15 years old, and anally in _____, when she was 16 years old. Exhibit A. Mr. N lives out of town and visits his siblings and parents every year, usually during the Fourth of July holiday.

A preliminary hearing was scheduled for _____, before District Justice _____ in Central Park, but postponed over defense objection until _____, because of the niece's unwillingness to testify. On _____, immediately before the hearing started, the Commonwealth amended to allege that the _____ vaginal rape occurred in _____. Exhibit B, _____, Preliminary Hearing Transcript at 4-5.

At the hearing, the niece testified that she did not recall if Mr. N raped her or had any sexual contact with her in _____.[1] Exhibit B at 14. She did testify that in _____, Mr. N helped her get her long-desired naval piercing, then escorted her to a hotel where he took photographs of her naked and then exposed himself and masturbated. There was no testimony about any sexual or improper contact in _____. The niece claimed that in _____, on the morning after playing a drinking game with her and her parents that the niece suggested, Mr. N had anal intercourse with her in her bedroom while her dog slept at the foot of her bed and her father and brother slept in their rooms across the hallway. Exhibit A at 32, 36. At the conclusion of the hearing, the case was held for court on one count of rape, for the _____ incident, despite the lack of evidence of any force or coercion, and several lesser charges.

A Criminal Information containing five counts was filed against the defendant by the Commonwealth of Pennsylvania. Exhibit C. The Information dropped the rape charge but contained the following charges, all alleged to have occurred from _____, (despite the lack of preliminary hearing testimony about anything occurring in _____) to _____:

Count One	Incest	18 Pa. C.S. §4302
Count Two	Terroristic Threats	18 Pa. C.S. §2607(a)(1)
Count Three	Open Lewdness	18 Pa. C.S. §5901
Count Four	Unlawful Contact With Minor	18 Pa. C.S. §6318(2) [sic]

The defendant filed an Informal Discovery Request on _____ and followed up by filing a Formal Request for Discovery on _____.

MOTION FOR BILL OF PARTICULARS

The defense requests the following particulars with respect to each count of the Information:

The dates, times and locations of each act in furtherance of the charged offenses and the nature of such act.

The purposes of the bill of particulars are to enable a defendant to prepare for trial, to avoid surprise, and to enable the defendant to interpose the defenses of double jeopardy and the statute of limitations to this and future prosecutions. *See Commonwealth v. Chambers*, 528 Pa. 558, 580, 599 A.2d 630 (1991); *Commonwealth v. Simione*, 447 Pa. 473, 291 A.2d 764 (1972). Each of these purposes necessitates a bill of particulars in this case.

8. Mr. N is charged with incest, terroristic threats, open lewdness, unlawful contact with a minor and indecent exposure occurring on or about _____ through on or about _____. This alleges a continuous course of events over a one-year period even though the preliminary hearing testimony suggested two isolated episodes, one in _____ and the other in _____, but nothing in _____.

9. To defend against these charges, Mr. N is entitled to know which crime he committed and the specific date that crime was to have allegedly occurred. Under this set of facts, it will be difficult to defend against the charges because Mr. N will have to prepare a defense that covers a one- or two-year span—it is unclear which. This cannot be done and the case cannot be defended against unless the defense knows the specific dates on which alleged offenses are to have occurred.

---

[1] The niece does not suffer from any mental impairments. In fact, the discovery indicates that she is a high school honor student and plans to open a dance studio when she graduates.

10. If Mr. N were to be prosecuted again for activity that occurred in the same broad time period encompassed by each of the counts here, he could not interpose the defense of double jeopardy unless it were shown which activity formed the basis for the counts on which he was prosecuted.

11. For all these reasons, a bill of particulars is necessary in this case.

MOTION TO QUASH/DISMISS COUNT FOUR

12. Count Four of the Information charges Mr. N with unlawful contact with a minor: "The actor intentionally contacted a minor namely, Jane Doe, a minor, age 16 while the actor or the minor was within this Commonwealth for the purpose of engaging in the activity of anal intercourse in violation of Section 6318(2) [sic] of the Pennsylvania Crimes Code, Act of December 6, 1972, 18 Pa.C.S. §6318(2) [sic], as amended." Section 6318 has no subsection (2), but it does have a subsection (a)(2). Subsection (a)(2) prohibits contact with a minor for the purpose of committing the offense of open lewdness.

13. Although the Information does include an open lewdness count, Count Three, Count Four does not refer to that count. Instead, it specifies contact "for the purpose of engaging in the activity of 'anal intercourse.'" This is not a prohibited activity under Section 6318.

14. The information does refer to sexual intercourse at Count One, which could include anal intercourse, but Count One charges incest, a crime under Chapter 43 of the Crimes Code. The unlawful contact statute does not apply to contact for the purpose of committing incest. It enumerates a number of prohibited activities, none of which is incest, and none of which refers to Chapter 43. *See* 18 Pa.C.S.A. §6318(a)(1)(referring to offenses enumerated in Chapter 31); §6318(a)(2)(referring to Section 5901, open lewdness); §6318(a)(3)(referring to Section 5902, prostitution); §6318(a)(4)(referring to Section 5903, criminal obscenity); §6318(a)(5)(referring to Section 6312, sexual abuse of children); §6318(a)(6)(referring to sexual exploitation of children, Section 6320). *See Commonwealth v. Wojdak*, 502 Pa. 359, 368, 466 A.2d 991, 996 (1983) (to make out prima facie case, Commonwealth must introduce evidence supporting the probable existence of each element of the offense charged and that a crime has been committed).

15. The age of consent in the Commonwealth is 16 years and is codified at 18 Pa. C.S. §3122.1. Mr. N has not been charged with statutory sexual assault, 18 Pa. C.S. §3122.1, because the victim was 16 years old at the time of the alleged incident. Anal intercourse with a person 16 years old or older is not a crime if the act is voluntary. A female's consent to sexual intercourse excludes the possibility of a conviction for the offense of rape or unlawful contact with a minor, and makes the act of intercourse criminally cognizable only if the consenting female is under the age of 16. *Commonwealth v. Walker*, 468 Pa. 323, 362 A.2d 227 (1976) (overruled on other grounds).

16. For the reasons set forth above, Count Four of the Information should be dismissed.

MOTION TO QUASH/DISMISS COUNTS ONE THROUGH FIVE

17. As shown on the chart set forth in the Introduction, the Information charges Mr. N with incest, terroristic threats, open lewdness, unlawful contact with a minor and indecent exposure occurring on or about _____ through on or about _____. In other words, rather than charging each offense as a separate count, the Commonwealth has chosen to charge these offenses as "continuing offenses." This type of charge is duplicitous and should be dismissed.

18. In *Commonwealth v. Levy*, 146 Pa. Super. 564, 23 A.2d 97 (1941), the defendant was charged with sodomizing an 11-year-old boy and was convicted of two counts of sodomy. The victim was unable to testify to any fixed dates as to when he first met the defendant and when he was alone in a car with the defendant. *Id.* at 567. The court held the date of the commission of the alleged offense must be "fixed with reasonable certainty," because "where a particular date or day of the week is not of the essence of the offense, the date laid in the indictment is not controlling, but some other reasonably definite date must be established with sufficient particularity to advise the jury and the defendant of the time the Commonwealth alleges the offense was actually committed." *Id.* at 570 (emphasis added).

19. In this case, it appears that the Commonwealth should be able to identify specific offenses and dates on which they occurred, but nonetheless has elected to charge the offenses as a vague continuing course of conduct. This violates the notions of fundamental fairness and due process embedded in our legal system and does not allow a defendant to present a comprehensive defense. Article I, Section 9 of the Pennsylvania Constitution states:

> In all criminal prosecutions the accused hath a right to be heard by himself and his counsel, to demand the nature and cause of the accusation against him ... nor can he be deprived of his life, liberty, or property, unless the judgment of his peers or the law of the land.

It is a long standing tenet of Pennsylvania jurisprudence that "the law of the land" in Article I, Section 9 is synonymous with "due process of law." *Commonwealth v. Devlin*, 460 Pa. 508, 514, 333 A.2d 888 (1975). *See also Commonwealth v. Jackson*, 457 Pa. 79, 319 A.2d 161 (1974); *Craig v. Kline*, 65 Pa. 399, 413, 1870 Pa. LEXIS 244 (1870). Under both the Pennsylvania and United States Constitutions, a defendant is denied due process of law if he or she is substantially denied an opportunity to present a defense. *See Commonwealth v. Jester*, 256 Pa. 441, 100 A. 993 (1917); *Twining v. New Jersey*, 211 U.S. 78, 29 S.Ct. 14, 53 L.Ed. 97 (1908).

20. Although charging child sex abuse crimes as continuing offenses has been approved, the children in those cases were significantly younger than 16, the age of the victim in the present case.[2] *See, e.g., Commonwealth v. Niemetz*, 282 Pa. Super 431, 440, 422 A.2d 1369, 1373 (1980) (court approved an Information charging sex offenses between 1972 and August 1977 on the ground that it would not serve the ends of justice to permit a perpetrator to sexually abuse a child between the ages of 5 and 10 years with impunity because the child failed to record the details in a daily diary); *Commonwealth v. Groff*, 378 Pa. Super. 353, 548 A.2d 1237 (1988) (the victim testified the abuse occurred when appellant lured her into his bedroom while she was wearing a bathing suit, therefore the abuse could have taken place any warm day between August 1983 and September 1985 when she was between the ages of four and six years old). Further, in each of those cases, the defendant had continuous contact with the victim over a long period of time, so that it was understandably difficult for the young victims to specify on which dates the illegal activity occurred. The present situation is quite different. The alleged victim discussed here is mature and intelligent, and her uncle saw her only on isolated occasions, two to three days every year. She and the Commonwealth should be able to specify when the illegal activity occurred. (She probably is uncertain about when and whether she had sexual contact with her uncle because the allegations are fantasy, not an account of true events.)

21. It is not an absolute requirement that the Commonwealth establish an exact date of offenses in all cases; rather, the rights of the accused must be considered against "the nature of the crime and the age and condition of the victim." *Commonwealth v. Devlin*, 460 Pa. 508, 333 A.2d 888 (1975). Here, although four of the five crimes charged in the Information are sex offenses or related, the victim is 16 years old with no indication of any problems, mental or otherwise, that may affect her memory. Therefore, the Commonwealth should have been able to articulate the specific dates on which the alleged offenses occurred rather than simply charge them as a vague continuing course of conduct as they did here. The Commonwealth has created a fundamentally unfair burden for Mr. N to overcome.

22. The charges in Counts One through Five also fail because they are duplicitous. Duplicity is the joining in a single count of two or more distinct and separate offenses. *Commonwealth v. Bidner*, 282 Pa. Super. 100,109 n.6, 422 A.2d at 852 n.6. The rule against duplicitous informations is set forth in Rule 563(B) of the Rules of Criminal Procedure: "There shall a separate count for each offense charged." The rule is designed to provide proper notice to the defendant of the accusation against him and to ensure that the jury unanimously agrees to convict the defendant of a single offense. A general verdict on a single count which contains multiple offenses may also lead to double jeopardy problems in the event of subsequent prosecution.

23. By charging Mr. N with incest, terrorist threats, open lewdness, unlawful contact with a minor and indecent exposure as continuing offenses over a period of years, the Commonwealth has included at least two episodes, the _____ (or _____) hotel episode and the _____ niece's bedroom episode, in each count, thereby making each count duplicitous. For example, suppose that at trial the victim testifies that Mr. N had sexual intercourse with her, exposed his genitals to her or threatened to commit a crime of violence against her with the intent to terrorize her in _____ (or _____) through _____, describing to the jury separate offenses on each of those occasions. It is possible that some members of the jury could believe her as to the _____ or _____ events, but not the _____, and others could disbelieve the _____ or _____ events, but believe the _____ story. The jury then could convict Mr. N of a count, even though they were not unanimous that the offenses had occurred at any one of those numerous times. The Commonwealth is unfairly attempting to hide its proof problems caused by the unreliability of its witness by lumping multiple alleged offenses together in each substantive count. This procedure is extremely prejudicial to the defendant and constitutes a fatal pleading error in the Commonwealth's Information.

24. For the reasons set forth above, the defendant respectfully requests that Counts One through Five be dismissed for failing to specify a date of commission and for duplicity.

Respectfully submitted,

_____

Attorney for MN

---

[2]   The niece turned 17 in _____.

Form 15-3   Duplicity Motion

IN THE COURT OF COMMON PLEAS OF
_____ COUNTY, _____

COMMONWEALTH OF _____,	)	
Plaintiff,	)	
v.	)	DEFENDANT'S MOTION
JOHN DOE, M.D.,	)	TO DISMISS FOR DUPLICITY
Defendant.	)	

INTRODUCTION

1.   On or about _____, a Criminal Complaint was filed against defendant, John Doe, M.D., based upon the affidavit of Special Agent _____ of the Office of Attorney General.

2.   A preliminary hearing was held on _____ before District Justice _____ in _____, Pennsylvania. Twelve witnesses testified for the Commonwealth at the preliminary hearing. At the conclusion of the hearing, the case was held for court.

3.   On or about _____, a Criminal Information containing 10 counts was filed against the defendant by the Office of Attorney General. The Information contains the following charges:

Count I	Delivery of controlled substances	35 P.S. 780-113(a)(30)
Count II	Delivery of controlled substances outside scope of treatment principles	35 P.S. 780-113(a)(14)
Count III	Solicitation to deliver controlled substances	18 Pa. C.S.A. Section 902(a) 35 P.A. 780-113(a)(30)
Count IV	Insurance fraud	18 Pa. C.S.A. 4117(a)(2)
Count V	Delivery of a controlled substance	35 P.S. 780-113(a)(30)
Count VI	Delivery of controlled substances outside of treatment principles	35 P.S. 780-113(a)(14)
Count VII	Prescribing controlled substances outside scope of treatment principles	35 P.S. 780-113(a)(14)
Count VIII	Receiving stolen property	18 Pa. C.S.A. 3925(a)
Count IX	Insurance fraud	18 Pa. C.S.A. Section 4117(a)(2)
Count X	Prescribing controlled substances outside scope of treatment principles	35 P.S. 780-113(a)(14)

MOTION TO DISMISS COUNTS I, II, V, AND VI

4.   Counts I, II, V, and VI charge Dr. Doe with delivery of controlled substances between either _____ (Counts I, II) or _____ (Counts V, VI) and _____. In other words, rather than charging each delivery as a separate count, the government has chosen to charge these offenses as "continuing offenses." This type of charge is duplicitous and should be dismissed.

5.   Successive sales of narcotics have been held to be separate offenses. In fact, in *Commonwealth v. Sabathne*, 227 Pa. Super 331, 323 A.2d 337 (1974), the defendant made two sales of methamphetamine at the same bar within an hour. The court held that the sales were separate offenses and did not merge. *Id.*

In this case, it appears that the government is unable to identify specific deliveries and therefore has elected to charge the deliveries as a vague continuing course of conduct. As the Court is doubtless aware, while a conspiracy is always charged as a continuing course of conduct, substantive drug offenses are normally charged as separate counts. The proper unit of prosecution, as made clear by *Sabathne* and by the plain language of the statutes–which refer to "a delivery"–is each alleged separate delivery or distribution.

The defendant has discovered only one case which approved the charging of successive Section (a)(30) violations in one count as a continuing offense. *Commonwealth v. Dennis*, 421 Pa. Super. 600, 618 A.2d 972 (1992). In *Dennis*, the court approved the charging of deliveries of methamphetamine from August, 1985 to November, 1986 as one violation of Section (a)(30).

It is submitted that the *Dennis* case is unpersuasive. First, the *Dennis* court did not analyze the appropriate unit of prosecution in narcotics delivery cases. Rather, the court found that in other types of crimes, primarily child sexual abuse crimes, charging offenses as continuing offenses had been approved. *See, e.g., Commonwealth v. Niemetz*, 282 Pa. Super 431, 440, 422 A.2d 1369, 1373 (1980) (court approved an Information charging sex offenses between 1972 and August 1977 on the ground that it would not serve the ends of justice to permit a perpetrator to sexually abuse a child with impunity because the child failed to record the details in a daily diary.) The court further noted that the date of commission is not an element of a drug charge. *Dennis*, 421 Pa. Super at 615, 618 A.2d at 980. The *Dennis* analysis focused primarily upon whether the charge was in compliance with Rule 225 of the Rules of Criminal Procedure (now numbered as Rule 560(B)(3)). *Dennis* has never been cited by a Pennsylvania Court for the proposition that it is appropriate to charge drug deliveries as continuing offenses over a period of years.

The charges here fail because they are duplicitous. Duplicity is the joining in a single count of two or more distinct and separate offenses. *Bidner, supra*, 282 Pa. Super. at 109 n.6, 422 A.2d at 852 n.6. The rule against duplicitous informations is set forth in Rule 563(B) of the Rules of Criminal Procedure: "There shall a separate count for each offense charged." The rule is designed to provide proper notice to the defendant of the accusation against him and to ensure that the jury unanimously agrees to convict the defendant of a single offense. A general verdict on a single count which contains multiple offenses may also lead to double jeopardy problems in the event of subsequent prosecution.

The *Dennis* court did not address the issue of duplicity because the defendant in that case apparently did not raise it. However, duplicity is the primary problem with charging delivery of controlled substances as a continuing offense over a period of years. For example, suppose that at trial a witness testifies that he sold pills for Dr. Doe in _____, in _____, and in _____, describing to the jury separate transactions on each of those occasions. It is possible that members of the jury could convict Dr. Doe of the count, now charged as a continuing offense, even though they were not unanimous that a transaction had occurred at any one of those times. The government is unfairly attempting to hide its proof problems due to the vague memories of its witnesses and lack of documentation by lumping multiple alleged offenses together in one substantive count. This procedure is extremely prejudicial to the defendant and constitutes a fatal pleading error in the government's Information.

For the reasons set forth above, the defendant respectfully requests that Counts I, II, V, and VI be dismissed as duplicitous.

Respectfully submitted,

_____

Thomas J. Farrell, Esq.

Form 15-4   Motion to Sever

IN THE UNITED STATES DISTRICT COURT FOR THE
_____ DISTRICT OF _____

UNITED STATES OF AMERICA,	)	
Plaintiff,	)	
v.	)	CRIMINAL NO._____
GARY DOE and LARRY LOE,	)	
Defendant.	)	

MOTION TO SEVER AND TO JOIN WITH CITATION OF AUTHORITIES

AND NOW COMES the Defendant, Larry Loe, by his attorney, _____, and files this Motion to Sever:

The Defendant, Larry Loe, was arraigned on _____, on an indictment charging him with three substantive drug distribution counts and a conspiracy to distribute count.

Gary Doe is named as a co-defendant of Larry Loe in the above counts. Mr. Doe is also charged with possession of a firearm and with a drug distribution count unrelated to the conspiracy with Larry Loe.

In this Pre-Trial Motion, Larry Loe moves
to sever Count 7 of the Indictment as improperly joined;
to sever his trial from that of Gary Doe;
to join Co-Defendant Gary Doe's Pre-Trial Motion.

Motion to Sever Count Seven of the Indictment as Misjoined Under Rule 8(b)

4. Count One of the Indictment charges a conspiracy between Gary Doe and Larry Loe to distribute heroin between _____ and _____. There then follow several substantive counts of distribution in that time period.

5. Count Seven charges distribution of heroin by Gary Doe alone nearly one year before the formation of the conspiracy, on _____.

6. Rule 8(b) permits joinder of multiple defendants in one indictment. That rule has been interpreted to restrict a multi-defendant indictment to charging offenses that grew out of the same series of transactions or acts involving all the defendants. *See United States v. Velasquez*, 772 F.2d 1348 (7th Cir. 1985). The government may not join a charge against one of the defendants that arises from a transaction that did not involve the co-defendants even if the charge is of the same character as the other charges. *Id. See also United States v. Toney*, 161 F.R.D. 77 (N.D. Iowa 1995).

7. There is no allegation discussed here that Count Seven arises from the same scheme, conspiracy or series of acts as the rest of the Indictment. It charges a drug deal completely unrelated to the alleged conspiracy between Larry Loe and Gary Doe.

8. "If offenses or defendants have been improperly joined, however, severance is required as a matter of law under Rule 8. *United States v. Andrews*, 765 F.2d 1491, 1496 (11th Cir. 1985) ("misjoinder under Rule 8(b) is prejudicial per se..."), *cert. denied*, 474 U.S. 1064 (1986); *United States v. Bledsoe*, 674 F.2d at 654 (misjoinder is inherently prejudicial); *United States v. Vastola*, 670 F. Supp. 1244, 1261 (D.N.J. 1987) (citing *United States v. Somers*, 496 F.2d 723, 729 (3d Cir. 1974), *cert. denied*, 419 U.S. 832, 42 L. Ed. 2d 58, 95 S. Ct. 56 (1974))." *United States v. Giampa*, 904 F.Supp. 235, 264 (D.N.J. 1995).

Motion to Sever the Trial of Larry Loe From That of Gary Doe Under Rule 14

9. The defendants will present mutually antagonistic and exclusive defenses at trial. Each will assert that the drugs found in _____ on _____ must have belonged to and been intended for distribution solely by the other defendant, and that he did not know of the drugs' presence or the co-defendant's plan. Since only the two, along with Gary Doe's paramour NT and two children that were present in the apartment, and no one, including the government, assert that Ms. T or the children were aware of the drugs, the acquittal of either co-defendant would necessarily call for the conviction of the other. In these circumstances, the Court should grant the defendants separate trials as relief from the prejudicial joinder. *See Zafiro v. United States*, 506 U.S. 534, 538-39 (1993); *United States v. Voigt*, 89 F.3d 1050, 1094-95 (3d Cir. 1996).

10. After his arrest, Co-defendant Gary Doe admitted that the drugs in the apartment were his. He made no mention of Larry Loe. Thus the statement exculpates Larry Loe. While Gary Doe has moved to suppress this statement, Mr. Loe will insist upon its admission under FRE 804(b)(3), as a statement against penal interest, and under the Due Process Clause. *See Chambers v. Mississippi*, 410 U.S. 284 (1973). This further illustrates the mutually antagonistic nature of the defenses and justifies severance.

Motion to Join Co-Defendant's Motions

11. Larry Loe seeks to join the following motions filed by Co-defendant Gary Doe: (1) Motion to Suppress Evidence; (2) Motion to Reveal Identity of Confidential Informant; (3) Motion to Disclose *Brady* Material; and (4) Motion to Produce Evidence which the Government Intends to Use Under FRE 404(b) and 609. Mr. Loe does not join in Mr. Doe's Motion to return his Mercedes Benz or to suppress statements.

Conclusion

For the foregoing reasons, Defendant's Motions should be granted.

Respectfully submitted,

_____

Thomas J. Farrell

Form 15-5   Motion to Dismiss, to Gag, and for Change of Venue

IN THE UNITED STATES DISTRICT COURT FOR
THE _____ DISTRICT OF _____

UNITED STATES OF AMERICA	)	
Plaintiff,	)	CASE NO. _____
v.	)	
MD	)	DEFENDANT'S
Defendant.	)	PRE-TRIAL MOTIONS

AND NOW COMES Defendant MD, by his attorney, _____, and files the following pre-trial motions, further support for which is found in the attached Exhibits and Brief.

MOTION TO GAG JOHN ASHCROFT

1. On September 11, 2001, this country endured the worst loss of civilian life ever inflicted on it by a hostile foreign force. The people of this country are furious and demand retribution.

On September 25, the day before Mr. D was arrested, the Attorney General suggested that he and the other hazmat defendants were in league with the terrorists who crashed four airplanes into the World Trade Centers, the Pentagon, and the ground at Shanksville, in this District. Mr. Ashcroft claimed that the impending arrest of the hazmat defendants would prevent future terrorist attacks on American citizens. *See* Exhibit A.

Since then, more responsible government officials, including the Director of the FBI, U.S. Attorney _____, and AUSA _____ all have publicly stated that there is no reason to believe that Mr. D or the other hazmat defendants are terrorists. *See* Exhibit B.

On _____, FBI agents showed up at Mr. D's home to arrest him. Correctly believing that Mr. D was a law-abiding American citizen, they had his cousin call him, for he was on the road on a trucking job. Mr. D turned around and drove home to meet the agents at his home in Seattle, Washington.

The government consented to his release on an unsecured bond in the Western District of Washington on _____ and trusted that he would travel to Pittsburgh for his initial appearance. He did. Neither in Seattle nor in Pittsburgh did the government suggest that he was a terrorist or that his prosecution or detention was necessary to protect America from terrorist attacks.

Nevertheless, on _____, Mr. Ashcroft once again suggested publicly that the hazmat defendants were terrorists and that their prosecution was necessary to protect our country. Concurrent with this press conference, DOJ released to the press a list of the 104 individuals charged in this successful campaign. Twenty of them were the hazmat defendants. *See* Exhibit C.

Mr. Ashcroft's statements have created a substantial likelihood of materially prejudicing prospective jurors. For the sake of justice, he must be gagged.

MOTION TO DISMISS THE INDICTMENT
FOR PROSECUTORIAL MISCONDUCT

The grand jury voted on and returned the indictment in this case on _____, just nine days after Mr. Ashcroft's erroneous statements linking the defendant to the September 11 terrorist attacks.

The publicity surrounding the September 11 attacks and Mr. Ashcroft's recklessly false statements affected the grand jury and prevented a fair and impartial review of the evidence. While the publicity about terrorists in general was not attributable to the prosecution, the nation's highest ranking law enforcement official himself directed that publicity, and the hatred attending it, at the hazmat defendants. His remarks violated the Fifth Amendment right to an impartial grand jury and the McDade Act, 28 U.S.C. §530B, and federal regulations, 28 C.F.R. §50.2. They merit dismissal of the indictment.

MOTION FOR DISCLOSURE OF GRAND JURY
TRANSCRIPTS PURSUANT TO RULE 6(e)(3)(C)(ii)

In the alternative, the Court should order disclosure of all grand jury transcripts, including instructions and any colloquy or voir dire, to determine whether the publicity influenced the grand jury.

MOTION PURSUANT TO RULE 17 FOR THE
ISSUANCE OF A SUBPOENA *DUCES TECUM* TO PENNDOT

Rule 17(b) authorizes the issuance of subpoenas without the payment of costs on court order where a defendant is unable to pay costs. Rule 17(c) provides that a subpoena *duces tecum* may require documents to be produced before trial if the court so orders.

We request that a subpoena *duces tecum* be issued to the Pennsylvania Department of Transportation for all records of commercial drivers licenses with hazardous material certifications issued by _____ for the time period–from _____ (when the first license was issued) to _____, and subsequently revoked.

Mr. D has been unable to secure employment since his arrest and cannot afford the costs of a subpoena.

These documents will show if individuals of other than Middle Eastern ancestry improperly obtained licenses from _____. If they did and were not prosecuted, that would be compelling evidence that Mr. D and the other hazmat defendants were singled out for prosecution because of their ethnicity, a violation of equal protection and grounds for dismissal of this case. *See Yick Wo v. Hopkins*, 118 U.S. 356 (1886).

MOTION FOR CHANGE OF VENUE AND
APPOINTMENT OF VENUE CONSULTANT

Mr. Ashcroft's remarks, compounded by the angry publicity arising from the September 11 terrorist attacks and the special effect those attacks had in this district with the crash of Flight 93, have generated inflammatory and inherently prejudicial publicity that may prevent the defendant from getting a fair trial in this district in violation of the Sixth Amendment and Fed.R.Crim.P. 21(a).

Mr. D asks the Court to appoint a venue expert, Professor _____, to assist in conducting a survey of public attitudes in this district and an alternative survey and an analysis of the pre-trial publicity. Professor _____'s CV is attached as Exhibit E.

Respectfully submitted,

_____

Thomas J. Farrell

IN THE UNITED STATES DISTRICT COURT FOR
THE _____ DISTRICT OF _____

UNITED STATES OF AMERICA
               Plaintiff,   CASE NO. _____

         v.

MD
               Defendant.

ORDER OF COURT

AND NOW, this _____ day of _____, 2002, upon consideration of Defendant D's pre-trial motions, IT IS ORDERED THAT:

The Indictment is dismissed;

Professor _____ is appointed to conduct a change of venue analysis;

A subpoena shall issue the PennDOT for records of all commercial driver's licenses issued by _____ between _____ and _____;

The Government shall disclose to the defense the transcripts of all grand jury proceedings in this matter; and

The parties and attorneys in this case, including Attorney General John Ashcroft, shall be bound by the following gag order:

A. None of the lawyers appearing in this case or any persons associated with them, including any persons with supervisory authority over them, will release or authorize the release of information or opinion about this criminal proceeding which a reasonable person would expect to be disseminated by any means of public communication, if there is a reasonable likelihood that such disclosure will interfere with a fair trial of the pending charges or otherwise prejudice the due administration of justice.

B. This duty to refrain from prejudicial disclosures requires all counsel to take reasonable precautions to prevent all persons who have been or are now participants in or associated with the investigations conducted by the prosecution and defense from making any statements or releasing any documents that are not in the public record and that are reasonably expected to be publicly disseminated which would be likely to materially prejudice the fairness of this criminal proceeding.

C. None of the lawyers appearing in this case or any persons associated with them, including any persons having supervisory authority over them, shall release or authorize the release of any extrajudicial statement which a reasonable person would expect to be disseminated by any means of public communication, concerning any of the following matters related to this case:

(1) The prior criminal record (including arrests, indictments, or other charges of crime), or the character or reputation of the defendants.

(2) The existence or contents of any statements given by the defendants to any law enforcement personnel or the refusal or failure of the defendants to make any statements to law enforcement personnel.

(3) The performance of any examinations or tests or any defendant's refusal or failure to submit to any examination, or test.

(4) The identity, testimony, or credibility of all prospective witnesses.

(5) The possibility of a plea of guilty to the offenses charged or a lesser offense.

(6) Any opinion as to the guilt or innocence of the defendants or as to the merits of the case or the quality or quantity of evidence as to any charge in the case.

D. The foregoing shall not be construed to prevent any of the lawyers appearing in this case or any persons associated with them, including any persons having supervisory authority over them, from quoting or referring without comment to public records of the court in the case; from announcing the scheduling or result of any step in the judicial process; from requesting assistance in obtaining evidence; or from announcing, without further comment, that the defendants deny all charges made against them.

E. Before the trial jury is empanelled, none of the lawyers in this case or those associated with them, including those with supervisory powers over them, shall give or authorize any extrajudicial statement or interview relating to the trial or the parties or issues in the trial, which a reasonable person would expect to be disseminated by means of public communication if there is a reasonable likelihood that such dissemination will interfere with a fair trial, except that a lawyer may quote from or refer without comment to public records of the court in the case and may give such explanations of pleadings and hearings as may assist the public in understanding the legal issues being presented and the relationship of any hearing or ruling to the trial process without expressing any opinions as to the merits of the positions and arguments of any party or giving any predictions concerning the expected result.

_____
U.S. District Judge

IN THE UNITED STATES DISTRICT COURT FOR
THE _____ DISTRICT OF _____

UNITED STATES OF AMERICA
          Plaintiff,   CASE NO. _____

    v.

MD
          Defendant.

BRIEF OF DEFENDANT MD IN SUPPORT OF PRE-TRIAL MOTIONS

MD, a refugee from Saddam Hussein's Iraq and a naturalized American citizen, is charged in a one-count indictment with aiding and abetting the production, without lawful authority, of a Pennsylvania commercial driver's license ("CDL") with a hazardous materials endorsement ("HDE"). 18 U.S.C. §1028(a)(1). The government's theory appears to be that Mr. D received his license on _____, from _____, a PennDOT examiner, who solicited bribes for issuing licenses without administering the required tests to a number of individuals brought to him by one _____. Twenty of these individuals, all Iraqi immigrants, have been indicted separately on the same charge as Mr. D. As far as the defense is aware, however, there is no evidence that Mr. D either paid a bribe or dealt with _____.

ARGUMENT

I. The Court Should Issue an Order Prohibiting the Parties and All Department of Justice Employees and Officials From Commenting Publicly on This Case

On September 11, 2001, this country endured the worst loss of civilian life ever inflicted on it by a hostile foreign force. The people of this country are furious and demand retribution.

On _____, the day before Mr. D was arrested, the Attorney General suggested that he and the other Hazmat defendants were in league with the terrorists who crashed four airplanes into the World Trade Centers, the Pentagon, and the ground at Shanksville, in this District. Mr. Ashcroft claimed that the impending arrest of the Hazmat defendants would prevent future terrorist attacks on American citizens:

> ...The danger that darkened the United States of America and the civilized world on September 11 did not pass with the atrocities committed that day. Terrorism is a clear and present danger to Americans today.

> Intelligence information available to the FBI indicates a potential for additional terrorist incidents. I testified before the House Judiciary Committee yesterday regarding the possibility of attacks using crop dusting aircraft.

> Today I can report to you that our investigation has uncovered several individuals, **including individuals who may have links to the hijackers,** who fraudulently have obtained, or attempted to obtain, hazardous material transportation licenses.

See Exhibit A (Testimony of Attorney General John Ashcroft, Senate Committee on the Judiciary, September 25, 2001, available on the Department of Justice website at www.usdoj.gov/ag/speeches/2001/agcrisisremarks9_25.htm).

After his arrest, Mr. D appeared before a Magistrate Judge in the Western District of Washington. The government did not allege that he was a terrorist; rather, it agreed to his release on an unsecured bond so that he could travel to this district to face the charges against him. No allegation of a link to terrorism was made at the bail hearings of any of the other 19 Hazmat defendants, and all eventually were released on bail.

Since Mr. Ashcroft's imprudent remarks, more responsible government officials, including the Director of the FBI, U.S. Attorney _____, and AUSA _____ all have publicly stated that there is no reason to believe that Mr. D or the other Hazmat defendants are terrorists. *See* Exhibit B.

Nevertheless, on _____, Mr. Ashcroft once again suggested publicly that the Hazmat defendants were terrorists and that their prosecution was necessary to protect our country. After crediting the Department of Justice for the absence of terrorist attacks after September 11, Mr. Ashcroft described how DOJ attained its goal:

As I've discussed previously, the Department of Justice is now focused on two important priorities: First, finding those responsible for the horrific acts of September the 11th; and second and more importantly, making sure that we prevent any further terrorist activity. Through dozens of warnings to law enforcement, a delicate campaign and a deliberate campaign of terrorist disruption, tighter security around potential targets, with arrests and detentions, we have avoided further major terrorist attacks, and we've avoided these further major terrorist attacks despite threats and videotape taunting. America's defenses have grown stronger.

We are standing firm in our commitment to protect American lives. The Department of Justice is waging a deliberate campaign of arrest and detention to protect American lives. We're removing suspected terrorists who violate the law from our streets to prevent further terrorist attacks. We believe we have Al Qaeda membership in custody, and we will use every constitutional tool to keep suspected terrorists locked up.

The department has charged 104 individuals on federal criminal charges.

Exhibit C (remarks of Attorney General Ashcroft at Press Conference, November 27, 2001, available on the DOJ website at www.usdoj.gov/ag/speeches/2001/agcrisisremarks11_27.htm).

Concurrent with this press conference, DOJ released to the press a list of the 104 individuals charged in this successful campaign. Twenty of them were the Hazmat defendants, including Mr. D. (Torsten Ove, "Ashcroft List Dominated by Men Swept Up in Local Probe," *Pittsburgh Post-Gazette,* November 29, 2001 (available at www.postgazette.com/headlines/20011129localmen1129p2.asp). Mr. Ashcroft's prepared remarks suggested to readers and listeners that Mr. D's arrest and indictment were part of the "deliberate campaign of terrorist disruption" and that those charges served "to protect American lives ... [and] prevent further terrorist attack....."

The right to a fair and impartial fact-finder is paramount in our criminal justice system. To protect this right, "a trial judge has an affirmative duty to minimize the effects of prejudicial pre-trial publicity." *Gannett Co. v. DePasquale*, 443 U.S. 368, 378 (1978). The protections may include issuance of a gag order against lawyers and litigants where there is a "substantial likelihood of material prejudice" from extrajudicial statements. *United States v. Scarfo*, 263 F.3d 80, 90 (3d Cir. 2001) (quoting *Gentile v. State Bar of Nev.*, 501 U.S. 1030, 1075 (1991)). Gag orders may be issued more freely against lawyers both because the disciplinary rules notify lawyers of similar restrictions on attorney speech, *see* Rule of Professional Conduct 3.6, and because of the risk that the public and potential jurors will place confidence in the accuracy of statements from lawyers familiar with the case. *Scarfo*, 263 F.2d at 90.

The Attorney General's remarks violated Rule 3.6 of both the Pennsylvania and Missouri disciplinary rules as well as 28 C.F.R. §50.2, which forbid even accurate pre-trial comments when they "materially prejudice" a proceeding, Rule 3.6(a), or "may reasonably be expected to influence the outcome of a pending or future trial," 28 C.F.R. §50.2.[3] Among the remarks that both the rule and regulation absolutely prohibit are those which describe the character of the defendant. A statement that the defendant may have engaged in other serious criminal activity (such as terrorism) is a statement about character. *See* FRE 405(b).

Mr. Ashcroft's remarks violated the further requirement of 28 C.F.R. §50.2 that any public remarks "should include only incontrovertible, factual matters, and should not include subjective observations. In addition, where background information or information relating to the circumstances of an arrest or investigation would be highly prejudicial ... such information should not be made public." Section 50.2(b)(3). His remarks linking the Hazmat defendants to the September 11 terrorists were not only controvertible, they were false. It *is* incontrovertible that the remarks were "highly prejudicial."

To prevent Mr. Ashcroft from doing more harm, we ask that the Court enter an order identical to that entered in the Oklahoma bombing case, *see United States v. McVeigh*,[4] 931 F.Supp. 756, 760-61 (D.Colorado 1996).

Mr. Ashcroft's Statements Should be Met With Dismissal of the Indictment, Both as a Remedy for Violation of the Defendant's Right to a Fair and Impartial Grand Jury and as an Exercise of the Court's Supervisory Power to Enforce Violations of 28 U.S.C. §530B

Mr. Ashcroft's September 25 comments were made before the grand jury voted on the indictment on October 5. These comments violated Mr. D's right to an impartial grand jury. The Court should dismiss the indictment, or in the alternative, order disclosure of the transcript of the grand jury instructions, colloquys, and testimony. *See* Point III, *infra*.

The Fifth Amendment demands that the grand jury that votes on an indictment be unbiased. *United States v. Serubo*, 604 F.2d 807, 816 (3d Cir. 1979). "[A]ssociat[ing] the defendants with a disfavored criminal class" offends the Fifth Amendment's mandate, *United States v. Serubo*, 604 F.2d at 818 (La Cosa Nostra), as does the dissemination to the news media of information considered likely to generate public animus against the potential defendants, *United States v. Sweig*, 314 F.Supp. 1148, 1153-54 (S.D.N.Y. 1970) (Frankel, J.). To the extent that Mr. Ashcroft's statements reached the grand jury, they violated Mr. D's right to an unbiased grand jury.

Mr. Ashcroft's remarks violated not only the Constitution, but both federal regulations and statutes. Congress has elevated state ethics rules into federal law. Section 530B of Title 28, the McDade Amendments, requires that federal prosecutors obey state ethical rules. 28 U.S.C. §530B. Section 530B applies to the Attorney General himself. 28 C.F.R. §77.2. DOJ's regulations apply the ethical rules of the state containing the district in which a case is pending, or if no case is pending, the rules of the state of the attorney's licensure. 28 C.F.R. §77.4. Mr. Ashcroft appears to be licensed in Missouri. Missouri and Pennsylvania have identical versions of Rule 3.6.[5] Additionally, as was described above, Mr. Ashcroft's remarks violated the Department of Justice's longstanding regulations on the public release of information, 28 C.F.R. §50.2.

Dismissal is an appropriate remedy for prosecutorial misconduct where it "substantially influenced the grand jury's decision to indict" or "if there is a grave doubt that the decision to indict was free from substantial influence of such violations." *Bank of Nova Scotia v. United States*, 487 U.S. 250, 256 (1988). *See also United States v. Sigma Intern., Inc.*, 244 F.3d 841, 856-58, 870-73 (11th Cir. 2001) (dismissing indictment for improper comments to the grand jury, including statements implying that defendants had engaged in other criminal conduct.), *vacated by* 251 F.3d 1358 (11th Cir. Fla. 2001); *United States v. Lopez*, 4 F.3d 1455 (9th Cir. 1991) (an ethical violation could result in dismissal of

---

[3] Rule 3.6 applies to all lawyers participating in an investigation or litigation. This rule applies to the Attorney General as it is he who has the statutory authority to conduct litigation on behalf of the United States. *United States v. Nixon*, 418 U.S. 683, 694 (1974). 28 C.F.R. §50.2 applies to all Department of Justice personnel.

[4] The defense trusts that Mr. Ashcroft will understand that such an order prohibits further comments associating the Hazmat prosecutions with the government's anti-terrorism efforts.

[5] Missouri's Rules of Professional Conduct are available at www.courtrules.org.

an indictment if the government's conduct "caused substantial prejudice to the defendant and had been flagrant in its disregard for the limits of appropriate professional conduct.") Courts may exercise their supervisory power to dismiss indictments when prosecutors violate specific statutory or regulatory prohibitions. *United States v. Williams*, 504 U.S. 36, 46 & n.6 (1992).

This case presents an extraordinarily strong one for dismissal for three reasons. First, the improper statements came from the top: the Attorney General himself, rather than from a law enforcement agent or an Assistant United States Attorney. Statements from the nation's highest law enforcement officer are likely to be especially influential with grand jurors and prospective jurors. Further, the government can hardly complain that it is unfair to impute this individual's comments to the government itself. Second, after September 11, there can be no more inflammatory remark than linking a person of Middle Eastern descent with the September 11 terrorists, and the Attorney General should know it. Associating a defendant with La Cosa Nostra pales in comparison. Third, Mr. Ashcroft's statements were false. Much prejudicial pre-trial publicity arises from statements that though improper, are true, such as a description of the defendant's confession or his criminal history. There never has been any evidence linking any of the Hazmat defendants to terrorism and as long ago as September 27, Director Mueller of the FBI said so.

Mr. Ashcroft's September 25 statements create "a grave doubt that the decision to indict was free from substantial influence of such violations," *Bank of Nova Scotia v. United States*, 487 U.S. at 256. Given the extraordinary nature of the statements, dismissal is the appropriate remedy.

III. The Court Should Order Disclosure of Grand Jury Transcripts Pursuant to Rule 6(E)(3)(C)(ii)

Rule 6(e)(3)(C)(ii) specifically permits disclosure of grand jury transcripts "when permitted by a court at the request of the defendant, upon a showing that grounds may exist for a motion to dismiss the indictment because of matters occurring before the grand jury." As has been described, Mr. Ashcroft's statements are grounds for a motion to dismiss. To decide this motion, the court and the defense should have the opportunity to review the grand jury transcripts and determine if the grand jurors discussed the publicity with the AUSA or whether they were voir dired regarding their ability to be impartial. *See United States v. Serubo*, 604 F.2d 807.

In *Serubo*, the Court of Appeals ruled that the prosecutor's conduct before the grand jury, including remarks suggesting an association between the target and organized crime, would justify dismissal of the indictment. However, the remarks were made to the first panel to hear evidence in the matter, and it was unclear whether the AUSA read those portions to the second panel, the one that returned the indictment. The Court remanded the case for production of the complete transcripts to the defense to determine this issue as well as whether the prosecutor made other improper remarks or asked other improper questions. *Id.* at 818-19.

Here, as in *Serubo*, there already is evidence of improper conduct that may have influenced the grand jury: Mr. Ashcroft's September 25 remarks. See *United States v. Fischbach & Moore, Inc.*, 576 F.Supp. 1384, 1394 (W.D.Pa. 1983). If the Court does not believe that these remarks alone justify dismissal, the court should permit inspection of the grand jury transcripts.

IV. The Court Should Grant a Subpoena *Duces Tecum* to PennDOT Under Rule 17 to Assist in Prosecution of the Defense's Selective Prosecution Claim

Rule 17(c) authorizes the production of documents prior to where the movant shows "(1) that the documents are evidentiary and relevant; (2) that they are not otherwise procurable reasonably in advance of trial by exercise of due diligence; (3) that the party cannot properly prepare for trial without such production and inspection in advance of trial and that the failure to obtain such inspection may tend unreasonably to delay the trial; and (4) that the application is made in good faith and is not intended as a general "fishing expedition." *United States v. Nixon*, 418 U.S. 683, 699-700 (1974). PennDOT's records should be produced as relevant to adjudicate a selective prosecution claim.

Selecting a defendant for prosecution based upon his ethnicity violates the Fifth Amendment's Equal Protection Clause. *Wayte v. United States*, 470 U.S. 598 (1985); *Yick Wo v. Hopkins*, 18 U.S. 356 (1886). To establish this claim, the defense must obtain evidence that other non-Middle Eastern individuals who obtained CDLs improperly from _____ were not prosecuted. PennDOT would have records to provide a factual basis for this claim.

The Supreme Court's ruling in *United States v. Armstrong*, 517 U.S. 456 (1996), that a defendant making a selective prosecution claim must establish a prima facie case before obtaining discovery on it from the government does not apply here. *Armstrong* dealt with Rule 16 discovery from the prosecution, not the issuance of a Rule 17 subpoena to a third party. The difference is more than one of form. The Supreme Court's concern was to protect the government from needlessly disclosing prosecutorial strategy. The records I seek are PennDOT's, not the prosecution's; since PennDOT is not a prosecutorial agency, its records cannot reveal prosecutorial strategy.

VII. The Court Should Appoint Professor Edward Bronson to Conduct a Venue Analysis

The Sixth Amendment to the United States Constitution guarantees to each defendant the right to a fair and impartial jury. Where there is a reasonable likelihood that pre-trial publicity has prejudiced the pool of potential jurors, the court is required to change the venue to protect the defendant's rights to a fair and impartial trial. *Sheppard v. Maxwell*, 384 U.S. 333, 363 (1966); *Irvin v. Dowd*, 366 U.S. 717 (1961); *Rideau v. Louisiana*, 373 U.S. 723, (1963); Rule 21(a), Federal Rules of Criminal Procedure

The standard for change of venue in a federal prosecution under Rule 21(a) assures a defendant even more protection against prejudicial pre-trial publicity and community passion than the constitutional standard. It does not require "the same certainty which warrants the reversal of a conviction" under the due process standard. *United States v. Marcello*, 280 F.Supp. 510, 513 (E.D.La. 1968), *affirmed,* 423 F.2d 993 (5th Cir. 1970). Under Rule 21 (a), "the well-grounded fear" that the defendant will not receive a fair and impartial trial requires a change of venue. *United States v. Marcello*, 280 F.Supp. at 513. *See also United States v. Mazzei*, 400 F. Supp. 17 (W.D. Pa. 1970) (ordering a transfer of venue under the provisions of Rule 21(a) because of adverse pre-trial publicity received by the defendant who was a former member of the senate of Pennsylvania).

The Criminal Justice Act, 18 U.S.C. §3006A, authorizes the appointment of experts to assist in defense preparation and litigation. In many cases, federal courts have ordered the appointment of venue experts to assist in change of venue motions. *See* National Jury Project, *Jurywork: Systematic Techniques*, Appendix A (2d ed. 2000).

Professor _____ of California State University is an experienced and respected expert who has been appointed in such cases. He has consulted in cases ranging from the challenges to death-qualified juries that culminated in *Grigsby v. Mabry,* 758 F.2d 226 (8th Cir. 1985), *rev'd sub nom Lockhart v. McCree*, 476 U.S. 162 (1986), to the Oklahoma bombing case and the Unabomber case. He currently is working on several cases involving Arab defendants, including the trial of the fifth defendant, _____, in the Embassy bombing case in the Southern District of New York. (His CV is attached as Exhibit E to the Motion).

Professor _____'s method, as he explained it to me, entails a telephone survey of several hundred community members both in the district and an alternative district to determine their attitudes, analysis of those results and a survey and content analysis of the media reports concerning the case. Only after such surveys and analysis can it be determined if a fair trial is possible in this district and whether another district would be any better.

Respectfully submitted,

_____

Attorney

Chapter 16

[RESERVED]

(This page intentionally left blank.)

Chapter 17

PLEA BARGAINING

I.   INTRODUCTION

A. General Points

§17:01   Most Cases End With a Bargain

Most criminal cases end with a plea of guilty rather than a trial.

From the very start, you should explore with your client and the prosecutor the chance of a disposition short of trial. A willingness to bargain bespeaks wisdom, not weakness. [For excellent practical advice on negotiating a plea and advising a client, *see* Vida B. Johnson, "Effective Assistance of Counsel and Guilty Pleas–Seven Rules to Follow," *The Champion* 24 (November 2013).]

§17:02   Two Types of Bargains

Plea agreements and bargains fall into two categories:
*   Charge Bargains: Agreements to plead to certain charges in exchange for a promise to drop or not to bring others. [*See* §§17:10 et seq.]
*   Sentence Bargains: Bargains in which the parties negotiate the particular sentence to be imposed. [*See* §§17:20 et seq.]

[§§17:03-17:09 Reserved]

B. Charge Bargains

§17:10   Definition

A charge bargain is one in which the prosecutor agrees to dismiss or forego certain charges in return for your client's plea to other charges.

§17:11   When Sentences Merge

If the sentences on multiple charges merge for sentencing, this bargain may confer little benefit on your client.

However, if the other charges carry greater penalties or mandatory minimum or consecutive sentences, a charge bargain is a good deal.

Know which offenses are lesser included offenses of others so that you can propose the less severe but appropriate charge to address your client's conduct.

§17:12   Avoid Collateral Consequences

If each of several charges carries the same sentence, bargain for the one that carries fewer collateral or future consequences.

Generally, try to avoid convictions for crimes of violence, sex offenses or drug offenses because these crimes often trigger adverse immigration consequences, disqualifications for benefits programs, sex offender registration and recidivist sentencing provisions on subsequent convictions.

§17:13   Minimize the Counts

Try to minimize the counts of conviction.

Multiple convictions, even in a consolidated indictment or case, may count more in sentencing calculations on future cases. Furthermore, concurrent multiple sentences of probation or supervised release may return to haunt a defendant. Upon a finding of a violation, the judge can unpack the concurrent sentences and run terms of imprisonment on each count consecutively. [*See United States v. Dees*, 467 F.3d 847 (3d Cir. 2006) (court had authority to impose three consecutive sentences of two years imprisonment on a single violation of three concurrent 36-month terms of supervised release).]

This consideration assumes increasing importance where your client's criminal history or lifestyle (*e.g.,* drug addiction, gambling addiction, or prostitution) make a violation likely.

[§§17:14-17:19 Reserved]

C.   Sentence Bargains

§17:20   Definition

A sentence bargain is one in which the parties negotiate the particular sentence to be imposed.

Thus, with a sentence bargain you reach an agreement either with the judge or the prosecutor on the appropriate sentence.

§17:21   Involvement of the Judge Varies

The value of a sentence bargain depends on several factors, including whether the judge participates or accepts the bargain.

The federal courts and most jurisdictions forbid the trial judge from participating in plea bargaining. [*E.g.,* Fed. R. Crim P. 11 (c)(1); *Commonwealth v. Johnson*, 875 A.2d 328, 331-32 (Pa. Super. 2005) (judge's participation in plea bargaining renders plea involuntary).]

However, this is not a constitutional rule. [*See McMahon v. Hodges*, 382 F.3d 284, 289 n.5 (2d Cir. 2004).] Some jurisdictions permit judges to participate and promise a particular sentence in exchange for a plea. [*E.g., State v. Warner*, 762 So.2d 507 (Fl. 2000) (permitting judges to participate in plea bargaining if a party requests it, but judge may not initiate a plea dialogue; surveys approaches in several states).]

If the judge participates and promises the sentence, you can rely on the promise if it is memorialized on the record.

Where the judge does not promise a sentence, the prosecutor might agree to recommend a particular sentence or sentencing range, but the recommendation does not bind the judge, and the defendant cannot withdraw his guilty plea if the court deviates from the recommendation at sentencing. [*See, e.g.,* Fed. R. Cr. P. 11(c)(1)(B),(C)(3)(B).] The value of this agreement depends largely on the judge's practice in deferring to prosecutors' recommendations.

§17:22   Jurisdictions With Sentencing Guidelines

In jurisdictions where sentencing guidelines direct the judge's discretion, the parties might stipulate to the facts that drive the guideline calculations to arrive at a desired sentencing range.

EXAMPLE:

> You might stipulate that your client embezzled a specified amount of money or that he was responsible for only an identified amount of the drugs involved in the conspiracy and no more. While the factual stipulations do not bind the court, they may be controlling as a practical matter because the judge will lack any information to support a departure from the stipulation.

In guideline sentencing regimes, if you do not obtain an agreement to the facts that will form the basis for the guidelines calculations, you must monitor the prosecution's communications with the pre-sentence investigator to guarantee that the prosecutor or the police or victims do not undermine the agreement by feeding the investigator information inconsistent with the agreement. [*State v. Horness*, 600 N.W.2d 294, 300 (Iowa 1999) (where prosecutor had promised to recommend a specific sentence but instead informed the court of a more severe "alternative recommendation" in the presentence report and made "statements implying that the alternative recommendation was more worthy of acceptance," he breached plea agreement). *Compare United States v. Lewis*, 979 F.2d 1372, 1375 (9th Cir. 1992) (where prosecutor upheld his promise to recommend that defendant not be treated as a career offender, no breach where probation officer recommended otherwise); *State v. Yother*, 253 Mont. 128, 137, 831 P.2d 1347, 1352-53 (1992) (where plea agreement bound prosecutor to recommend a certain sentence, there was no violation where the probation officer recommended higher sentence).]

The probation officer acts as the judge's surrogate and is not bound by your agreement with the prosecution, so he can disagree with the parties' stipulations and recommendations. However, the parties control the probation officer's access to information. An honest prosecutor will control his agents and prevent them from circumventing the plea agreement by feeding the probation officer information at odds with it. [*See* §17:25 (Pre-Sentence Investigation).]

If you cannot trust the prosecutor or agents, you should consider drafting a stipulation of facts that the parties will present jointly to the probation officer for use as the only source for the offense description in the pre-sentence report.

In some jurisdictions, the probation department and the judge will accept the prosecutor's stipulations and guideline calculations. In others, however, probation officers display considerable independence and distrust of the parties' eagerness to make a deal that resolves the case short of trial and often will calculate a more severe guideline range and recommend a lengthier sentence than the prosecutor. Judges give the probation officer's calculations and recommendations considerable weight. If you suspect as much, ask that a presentence investigation report be prepared before a plea so your client can weigh the decision to plead fully informed of this key player's likely position. [*See* Fed. R. Crim. P. 32(e)(1) (permitting pre-plea preparation of a presentence report and forbidding its disclosure to the judge until and unless the defendant pleads guilty).]

§17:23   Right to Withdraw Plea

The parties might stipulate to a sentence with the understanding that the judge will permit the defendant to withdraw his guilty plea if the judge should demur at the time of sentencing. [*See, e.g.,* Fed. R. Cr. P. 11 (c)(1)(C), (C)(5)(B).]

§17:24   Have the Prosecutor Take No Position

A prosecutor may agree not to make any recommendation or statement at sentencing, to take no position regarding the sentence, or not to oppose your recommendation. However, there are complications with this type of agreement.

You must discuss the matter with the prosecutor to the extent of advising him or her in some detail what you will say on your client's behalf at sentencing (*i.e.,* what sentence you will request and what you will claim about your client's culpability, background and other mitigating circumstances to justify the sentence).

You need to know whether the prosecutor will perceive any of your statements as ones that invite response (*e.g.,* an agreement to make no recommendation may permit the prosecutor to disagree vociferously with your characterization of your client as the least culpable member of the conspiracy or as a good person who made only this one mistake in his life).

To the extent that you make factual assertions, be certain they are accurate and that the prosecutor does not disagree with them.

You also need to know what the prosecutor will say if the judge asks for his or her position once you request some particular lenient sentence. Most prosecutors will not agree to join in your request, but a firm statement that the prosecution has no comment on your request for probation or the like gives a signal of agreement to the judge.

In some jurisdictions, the probation department and the judge will accept the prosecutor's stipulations and guideline calculations. In others, however, probation officers display considerable independence and distrust of the parties' eagerness to make a deal that resolves the case short of trial and often will calculate a more severe guideline range and recommend a lengthier sentence than the prosecutor. Judges give the probation officer's calculations and recommendations considerable weight. If you suspect as much, ask that a presentence investigation report be prepared before a plea so your client can weigh the decision to plead fully informed of this key player's likely position. [*See* Fed. R. Crim. P. 32(e)(1) (permitting pre-plea preparation of a presentence report and forbidding its disclosure to the judge until and unless the defendant pleads guilty).]

§17:25   Pre-Sentence Investigation

If you have an agreement on a sentence, your client usually is best served by dispensing with a pre-sentence investigation report if possible under the jurisdiction's rules.

At the time of the plea, the judge usually knows nothing about the case aside from what you and the prosecutor tell him. The pre-sentence investigation report might educate him to sordid details that will persuade him to disregard the prosecutor's recommendation or even to renege on a promised sentence. Your client may have the right to withdraw his plea, but that might do him little good.

§17:26   No Arrest Clauses

Many judicial promises contain a "no-arrest" or "no-misconduct" clause. That is, if the client commits a crime or gets arrested between plea and sentencing, the deal is off.

If the judge suggests such a condition, argue for a "no-misconduct" condition because an arrest might not be your client's doing as the police occasionally arrest the innocent. Nonetheless, courts have upheld rescission of plea agreements for violations of no-arrest conditions. [*People v. Outley*, 80 N.Y.2d 702, 707, 610 N.E.2d 356, 594 N.Y.S.2d 683 (1993) (upholding the condition so long as the arrest is not malicious or baseless).]

[§§17:27-17:29 Reserved]

II.   SPECIAL PLEAS

§17:30   The Open Plea

An open plea is one in which your client pleads to the full indictment or information without any agreement with the prosecutor or judge. [*United States v. Booth*, 432 F.3d 542, 543 n.1 (3d Cir. 2005) (providing definition of open plea).]
An open plea may be to your client's advantage where both of two conditions apply:
*   The judge either will not or cannot (because of rule or statute) promise a particular sentence.
*   The prosecutor insists on disadvantageous conditions or stipulations without offsetting concessions.

EXAMPLE:

This arises in federal fraud cases where you contest the loss amount and the prosecutor wants a waiver of appeal. The prosecutor may offer to dismiss some counts for a plea, but where no count carries a mandatory minimum or consecutive sentence, the dismissal may not earn your client much, if anything. [*But see* §17:13 (potential adverse consequences from violation on multiple concurrent sentences of supervised release).]

On an open plea, you might reap the benefits of a plea, seek a more favorable sentence and then appeal the sentence if it is excessive. [*See Booth*, 432 F.3d at 548-49 (counsel ineffective for failing to advise client of open plea option because client could have obtained benefit of acceptance of responsibility reduction without cooperating with the government).]

§17:31   Appeal Waivers

Even after a plea, a defendant can appeal his sentence as illegal or excessive.
However, with the proliferation of appeals from sentences in guideline sentencing regimes, it has become routine for federal prosecutors to insist that as part of the plea agreement, your client waive any right to appeal either the conviction or sentence.
The federal courts uniformly have upheld appeal waivers, while a minority of state courts have disagreed. [*See United States v. Griffin*, 668 F.3d 987 (8th Cir. 2012); Wayne R. LaFave, Jerold H. Israel, Nancy J. King, 5 *Criminal Procedure* §21.2 (b) at nn. 59-60 (2006).]
The waiver also may include any collateral attack rights such as habeas petitions. This provision is more problematic because it forbids your client from attacking the process that resulted in the very agreement with which the government seeks to bind him. Thus many courts will permit defendants to raise issues of ineffective assistance of counsel and the involuntariness of their plea despite explicit waivers of collateral attack rights. [*See Hood v. State*, 111 Nev. 335, 890 P.2d 797, 798 (1995) (upholding waiver of appeal but not waiver of collateral review); *Jones v. United States*, 167 F.3d 1142, 1145 (7th Cir. 1999) (the right to mount a collateral attack survives only with respect to discrete claims that relate directly to the negotiation of the waiver; surveys federal cases).]
A number of state ethics panels have opined that a defense attorney who advises a client to enter into an agreement which limits the client's opportunity to litigate the attorney's ineffectiveness runs afoul of Rule 1.8(h)(1) of the Rules of Professional Conduct. [*See* Pennsylvania Bar Association, Conflicts of Interest and Other Misconduct Related to Waivers of Claims of Ineffective Assistance of Counsel, Formal Opinion 2014-100 (January 2014; revised September 2014); *United States v. Kentucky Bar Association*, 439 S.W.3d 136 (KY 2014)(upholding the Kentucky Bar Association's ethics advisory opinion against a Supremacy Clause challenge); NACDL Ethics Advisory Committee Formal Opinion 12-02 (October 27, 2012) (available at www.nacdl.org/ethicsopinions/12-02) (citing ethics opinions from Alabama, Arizona, Florida, Missouri, North Carolina, Ohio, Tennessee, Texas and Vermont).] Rule 1.8(h)(1) rule reads, "A lawyer shall not make an agreement prospectively limiting the lawyer's liability to a client for malpractice unless the client is independently represented in making the agreement." Some of the ethical authorities also hold that a prosecutor may not ethically propose a waiver of post-conviction rights to challenge the effective assistance of counsel. [*E.g., United States v. Kentucky Bar Association*, 439 S.W.3d 136; Pennsylvania Formal Opinion 2014-100, *supra*.]
There is no easy resolution to this quandary: the plea agreement otherwise may be beneficial, but you should not advise the client to accept the collateral attack waiver, at least to the extent it includes ineffective assistance of counsel claims. The National Association of Criminal Defense Lawyers advises the following:

Because of the inherent conflict under Rules 1.7(a)(2) and 1.8(h)(1), it is NACDL's position that defense counsel has an ethical and constitutional duty to object to and refuse to sign any plea agreement provision that amounts to a waiver of post-conviction remedies. This protects the rights of the client to later challenge the representation of the lawyer. If the government insists on such a provision, defense counsel then must either (1) raise the issue with the district court or (2) seek additional counsel for the defendant who must be fully apprised of the situation to advise the defendant. New defense counsel would have to be privy to everything the defendant and defense counsel know.

[NACDL Ethics Advisory Committee Formal Opinion 12-02 (October 27, 2012) (available at www.nacdl.org/ethicsopinions/12-02).]

In response to these challenges, the U.S. Department of Justice recently changed course and instructed federal prosecutors that they no longer should seek in plea agreements to have a defendant waive claims of ineffective assistance of counsel. [James M. Cole, Deputy Attorney General, Memorandum of All Federal Prosecutors, *Department Policy on Waivers of Claims of Ineffective Assistance of Counsel* (October 14, 2014)].

PRACTICE TIP:

You are justified in accepting an appeal waiver if the plea agreement confers a benefit that you are unlikely to receive without the government's agreement, such as waiver of a mandatory minimum sentence, dismissal of a count that carries a severe collateral consequence or jacks up the sentencing guidelines, or an agreement to forego provable aggravating factors or to stipulate to controverted mitigating factors.

As an alternative, consider pleading to the indictment, even if that means pleading to more counts of conviction than the prosecution would insist upon in a negotiated plea. Indictments often contain duplicative counts that are likely to merge at the time of sentencing.

§17:32   Bench Trial With Stipulated Facts

If your jurisdiction does not provide for conditional guilty pleas and you desire to preserve a meritorious legal issue for appeal, consider a bench trial on stipulated facts.

Judges grant leniency for guilty pleas because they save time and demonstrate the defendant's contrition. If you waive a jury and stipulate to the facts and explain that though your client does not contest his factual guilt, he has a meritorious legal issue which deserves appellate review, you might be able to preserve the issue for appeal as well as obtain the sentencing discount which a guilty plea warrants.

§17:33   No Contest Pleas

Sometimes a defendant realizes that the evidence is stacked against him and he wants to secure the benefits of a guilty plea, but does not want to admit guilt. He may have difficulty facing friends and family, or he actually may be innocent. Other defendants rightfully wish to avoid the collateral estoppel effect that an admission of guilt will have in subsequent civil litigation brought by the victims, regulatory agencies or shareholders.

In such a case, consider either a "no contest" (or "*nolo contendere*") plea or an "*Alford*" plea.

A no contest or *nolo contendere* plea is one in which the defendant does not plead guilty but consents to the entry of a judgment of conviction. [*See* Fed. R. Crim P. 11, Notes of Advisory Committee on 1966 Amendments.]

Alford pleas are named after the Supreme Court case that recognized the constitutionality of such pleas. [*North Carolina v. Alford*, 400 U.S. 25 (1970).] In an *Alford* plea, the defendant pleads guilty but maintains his innocence. [*See United States v. Tunning*, 69 F.3d 107, 110-14 (6th Cir. 1995) (explaining the difference).]

A court is not required to accept either a no contest or an *Alford* plea. [*See* Fed. R. Crim. P. 11(a)(3).] In some jurisdictions, the court cannot accept a no contest plea without the prosecution's consent. Some prosecutors' offices have a policy to oppose no contest pleas except "in the most unusual circumstances." [*See* U. S. Attorneys' Manual. 9-16.010, 9-16.015.]

PRACTICE TIP:

No contest and *Alford* pleas seldom are recommended unless the prosecution concurs and the judge is willing. The prosecution often will declare all deals "off" unless the defendant admits guilt, and the defendant's refusal to admit guilt might trouble the judge and cost the defendant any credit for accepting responsibility. Such a plea is most advantageous where parallel civil litigation looms. "In general, courts accept a plea of *nolo contendere* only in certain types of cases involving nonviolent crimes where civil implications may arise from a guilty plea." [Federal Judicial Center, *Benchbook For U.S. District Court Judges,* §2.01, p.74 n.10 (March 2000 rev.).]

However, you must check the law of your jurisdiction regarding the impact of a *nolo* plea in civil litigation. The majority rule is that it is inadmissible in civil litigation. [*See* Fed. R. Evid. 410 and Advisory Committee Notes.] However, some jurisdictions dissent. [*See Rusheen v. Drews*, 99 Cal.App.4th 279, 120 Cal. Rptr.2d 769, 772-73 (Cal. App. 2002) (under Cal. Penal Code §1016(3) a no contest plea to a felony is admissible as a party admission in civil cases); *Starr Tyme, Inc. v. Cohen*, 659 So.2d 1064, 1066 (Fl. 1995) (no contest plea serves as collateral estoppel in civil litigation).]

Also, even a no contest plea may give rise to a host of collateral consequences in subsequent litigation, such as deportation, revocation of a doctor's registration to distribute controlled substances, civil commitments and imposition of repeat offender sanctions. [*See Crofoot v. United States GPO*, 761 F.2d 661, 665 (Fed. Cir. 1985) (collecting cases).]

§17:34   Conditional Pleas

A guilty plea waives all but nonjurisdictional issues, even hotly litigated pretrial motions. [*See* §24:41.] Some jurisdictions permit, if the prosecution consents, "conditional pleas" in which the parties agree that the defendant may appeal specified pretrial issues. [*See, e.g.*, Fed. R. Cr. P. 11(a)(2); *but see Alvey v. State*, 911 N.E.2d 1248 (Ind. 2009) (conditional plea not permitted even with consent of prosecution in a plea agreement).]

[§§17:35-17:39 Reserved]

III.   WHEN TO ENTER A GUILTY PLEA

§17:40   Reasons for an Early Plea

Fast Track Programs

Some jurisdictions find themselves flooded with certain routine cases, such as immigration violations. To preserve resources, the prosecution will offer a generous plea if the defendant agrees early in the case and foregoes motion practice. Courts generally enforce the agreement because they share an interest in clearing the docket.

However, be careful to satisfy yourself that there is no defense by at least interviewing your client thoroughly. You do not want to accept a plea to illegal entry by a deportable alien when your client, who was born during his parents' vacation in Arizona, is a U.S. citizen.

Multiple Defendants and the Opportunity to Cooperate

Where there are multiple defendants who are capable of cooperating against each other, the best deal goes to the first in the prosecutor's door.

Failure to Make Bail

Counseling and bargaining for the defendant jailed on a relatively minor charge can be one of your most difficult challenges.

Your client's detention may threaten loss of his job and the welfare of his family. The desire to get out may encourage him to plead quickly, but perhaps to a more serious charge than he should.

The prosecutor may dangle the offer of a plea to the most serious charge and a sentence of probation in front of your client. Often, this is a bad choice because the top charge might carry serious collateral consequences and implications for recidivist sentencing upon a subsequent conviction. Further, probation can be onerous, and clients who regularly engage in petty crimes, such as drug use, prostitution, larceny or vandalism are certain to violate it and face a much lengthier term of incarceration.

Such clients are better off postponing a plea until a later court appearance when the prosecutor likely will reduce the charge and offer time served or a brief period of incarceration.

§17:41   Reasons for Pleading Later

Multiple Defendants Who Are Loyal

In multiple defendant cases, prosecutors often anticipate that at least one will break ranks and testify against the others. Where all stick together, and none offers to cooperate, the prosecutor often will sweeten the deal when trial is imminent to avoid a protracted multiple defendant trial in which his case is weaker than he hoped it would be.

This calculation can backfire where your client's confederates start out loyal but then lose heart and offer to give up your client to buy their freedom.

Shaky Witnesses

Size up the witnesses:

- If their health is bad, perhaps they will not survive to testify.
- Are they transient (*e.g.,* homeless, college students, aliens)? If so, they might be lost to the prosecution by the time of trial.
- Do they have criminal histories or drug habits? If so, delay may allow them to accumulate more convictions further undermining their credibility.

The Innocent Client

If your client insists on his innocence (whether unfounded or not) you cannot broach plea possibilities too early for risk of losing his confidence.

Once you have proven yourself to your client by hard work and listening, you can test his assertions and explain the weaknesses of his story and the dangers of going to trial and explore plea bargains.

[§§17:42-17:49 Reserved]

IV. COLLATERAL CONSEQUENCES

§17:50   The Duty to Advise the Client

Before you advise your client on whether or not to plead guilty, you must consider and explain to him the collateral consequences of a guilty plea.

Different courts have different approaches to the consequences of omitting or misinforming a client on such issues. The general rule appears to be that counsel must advise a noncitizen client of a conviction's deportation consequences, but with respect to other consequences, relief lies only if the attorney misinforms the client:

- Federal: *Padilla v. Kentucky,* 559 U.S. 356 (2010) (counsel must inform client of deportation consequences of a conviction); *but see United States v. Nicholson,* 676 F.3d 376, 381-82 (4th Cir. 2012) (distinguishing *Padilla* and holding that if a consequence is collateral–if it is not automatic and beyond the control of the court–failure of either counsel or the court to explain it is not grounds for vacating a plea). *Compare Bauder v. Dep't of Correction,* 619 F.3d 1272, 1275 (11th Cir. 2010) (counsel ineffective for affirmatively misadvising defendant of the civil commitment consequences of a guilty plea), *with United States v. Youngs,* 687 F.3d 56 (2d Cir. 2012) (court is under no obligation to apprise defendant of civil commitment likelihood).]
- California: *See* Cal.Penal Code §1016.5 (West 1993) (requiring that defense counsel advise client of deportation consequences of a conviction).
- Connecticut: Conn.Gen.Stat. §54-1j (1993) (requiring that defense counsel advise client of deportation consequences of a conviction).
- Florida: Fla.R.Crim.P. 3.172(c)(8) (1993) (requiring that defense counsel advise client of deportation consequences of a conviction).
- Georgia: *State v. Patel,* 280 Ga. 181, 183, 626 S.E.2d 121, 123 (Ga. Sup. 2006) (misstating effect of sexual battery conviction on doctor's eligibility to participate in Medicare and Medicaid deprived client of his Sixth Amendment right to counsel justifying withdraw of plea).
- New Mexico: *State v. Paredez,* 136 N.M. 533, 101 P.3d 799, 803-804 (N.M. 2004) (holding as a matter of state law that failure to inform client of immigration consequences of guilty plea was ineffective assistance of counsel).
- Oregon: Or.Rev.Stat. §135.385 (1993) (requiring that defense counsel advise client of deportation consequences of a conviction).
- Washington: Wash. Rev. Code §10.40.200 (1993) (requiring that defense counsel advise client of deportation consequences of a conviction).

Nonetheless, good practice is to research and notify your client of those collateral consequences that might affect him. [Nat'l Legal Aid and Defender Ass'n, Performance Guidelines for Criminal Representation §6.2(a)(3) (1995);

see Vida B. Johnson, "Effective Assistance of Counsel and Guilty Pleas–Seven Rules to Follow," *The Champion* 24 (November 2013); Colleen F. Shanahan, *Significant Entanglements: A Framework for the Civil Consequences of Criminal Convictions,* 49 Am. Crim. L. Rev. 1387 (2012) (argument for extending *Padilla* to other significant consequences of a conviction).] Once the client finishes his sentence, he needs to resume his life, and he deserves to know what impediments his conviction erects to his opportunities. Erroneous advice on these lines may not overturn the conviction, but it could leave you with bitter clients and a bad reputation.

§17:51   Summary of Significant Collateral Consequences

Good starting points to research the collateral consequences of a particular conviction in your jurisdiction and strategies to minimize them are the ABA's National Inventory of the Collateral Consequences of Conviction, available at www.abacollateralconsequences.org., and the website of the Collateral Consequences Resource Center, www.ccresourcecenter.org.

In *United States v. Nesbeth*, the Court described the extent of defense counsel's obligations to advise a client of the collateral consequences of a guilty plea as undecided, but urged all defense attorneys to do so. [15-CR-18, 2016 U.S.Dist. LEXIS 68731 (E.D.N.Y. May 24, 2016).] The *Nesbeth* Court imposed an obligation on both the prosecutor and the probation officer who prepares the presentence report "to assess and apprise the court, prior to sentencing, of the likely collateral consequences facign a convicted defendant." [*Id.* at *47.] To assist in this task, the Court referred the parties to several online resources: Margaret Colgate Love, Jenny Roberts & Cecelia Klingele, Collateral Consequences of Criminal Convictions: Law, Policy and Practice (2013 ed.); NACDL, Collateral Damage: America's Failure to Forgive or Forget in the War on Crime, at 62 (May 2014)(available at https://www.nacdl.org/restoration/roadmapreport/) ; and Department of Justice, Federal Statutes Imposing Collateral Consequences Upon Conviction, available at https://www.justice.gov/sites/default/files/pardon/legacy/2006/11/13/collateral_consequences.pdf. [*United States v. Nesbeth*, 2016 U.S. Dist. LEXIS 68731, at *49 n.65]. The *Nesbeth* Court also ruled that if the parties cannot agree on the collateral consequences, the court should hold a hearing to decide the issue and provide the defendant with accurate information. [*Id.* at *50].

The following are some of the more significant collateral consequences of a conviction.

Immigration consequences.
   [*See* §17:53.]

Voting rights.
   The impact varies from state to state, but many states disenfranchise felons. [*See* www.sentencingproject.org/pubs_05.cfm for a compilation of state laws on felon disenfranchisement.]

Challenges to disenfranchisement laws under the Equal Protection Clause and Section 2 of the Voting Rights Act, 42 U.S.C. 1973(a), have met with varying success. [Compare *Farrakhan v. Gregoire*, 590 F.3d 989 (9th Cir. 2010) (holding that Washington state's felon disenfranchisement law violated the Voting Rights Act), *vacated pending rehearing en banc*, 603 F.3d 1072 (9th Cir. 2010), *with Simmons v. Galvin*, 575 F.3d 24 (1st Cir. 2009) (Voting Rights Act does not apply to felon disenfranchisement laws); *Hayden v. Paterson*, 594 F.3d 150 (2d Cir. 2010) (upholding New York's felon disenfranchisement law against equal protection challenges).]

Employment consequences.
   Conviction of certain offenses may have a grievous effect on your client's present employment or hopes of future employment. You must explore not only your client's present situation, but his aspirations.
   Different occupations value types of convictions differently.

EXAMPLE:
   A conviction for a drug offense or crime of violence may mean most to child care employers, but may not matter much to a bank. However, a bank might turn down a potential employee with a record for theft offenses.

Debarment from government benefits and contracts.
   [*See* State v. Patel, *supra* (doctor convicted of sexual battery prohibited from billing Medicare or Medicaid for ten years).]

Sex offender registration.
[*See* §17:54 and Chapter 23, Probation, Parole, Other Post-Release Supervision.]

Public housing and education loan and assistance eligibility.
A conviction for either drug trafficking or possession disqualifies an individual from receiving federal student assistance loans and from living in federally subsidized housing. [*See* 34 C.F.R. 668.40 (educational loan and assistance disqualification for one year for first conviction of possession, two years for first conviction for distribution); 42 U.S.C. §11901(3); *HUD v. Rucker*, 535 U.S. 125, 136 (2002) (upholding federal law which "requires lease terms that give local public housing authorities the discretion to terminate the lease of a tenant when a member of the household or a guest engages in drug-related activity, regardless of whether the tenant knows, or should have known, of the drug-related activity").]

Public assistance and food stamps.
A drug-related conviction may bar an individual from ever receiving government assistance or food stamps. [21 U.S.C. §862a.] However, many states have opted out of this restriction.

Suspension or revocation of driving privileges.
Not only do DUI convictions routinely warrant license suspension, but any individual convicted of a drug offense, whether or not related to driving, must have her driver's license suspended for at least six months. [23 U.S.C. §159, 23 C.F.R. §192.4.]
The Motor Carrier Safety Improvement Act of 1999 [49 U.S.C. §§31310 *et seq.*] requires states to suspend the commercial driver's licenses for a wide variety of convictions and counts as convictions even acceptance into alternative disposition programs. [*See* 49 C.F.R. 384.226.]

Eligibility for union office.
[*See* 29 U.S.C. §504(a) (persons convicted of certain crimes barred from holding union office for 13 years).]

The right to bear arms.
The Uniform Firearms Act, adopted by many states, makes it a crime for defendants convicted of enumerated crimes to possess firearms.
Check federal law as well. Many states classify as misdemeanors nonviolent crimes punishable by up to five years in prison. Convictions for those crimes do not disqualify a person from possessing a firearm under state law. However, the federal firearms statutes make it a felony, punishable by up to ten years imprisonment, for anyone convicted of a crime punishable by more than one year in prison to possess a firearm. [18 U.S.C. §922(g)(1).]
There is an exception for crimes classified as misdemeanors under state law, but only if the maximum possible sentence (not the sentence actually imposed) is two years or less. [*See* 18 U.S.C. §921(a)(20)(B).]
Therefore, there will be many situations where a person can possess firearms under state law, but not under federal law. Either seek a plea to a different offense or carefully advise your client of the consequences of his plea.

Loss of professional licenses.
This will vary from profession to profession and jurisdiction to jurisdiction. You must check local law and may be required to ask specialists in the field how often the licensing board takes action against persons convicted of certain types of crimes. [For a 50-state survey of employment consequences, *see* Margaret Colgate Love, "Relief From the Collateral Consequences of a Criminal Conviction: A State-by-State Resource Guide," Table #6: Consideration of Criminal Record in Licensing and Employment (August 2007) (available at www.sentencingproject.org).]

PRACTICE TIP:
Prosecutors, especially local ones, may agree that many of these collateral consequences are unfair and may cooperate to avoid them. (Many result from federal law and federal prosecutors may feel beholden to uphold them.) For example, a conspiracy to possess drugs plea may carry the same sentence as a simple possession plea, but not the same suspension and revocation consequences. Check your local and federal statutes to explore such pleas.

§17:52   Waivers of Non-Jurisdictional Defects

A guilty plea waives any right to attack non-jurisdictional defects in the conviction. [*See Tollett v. Henderson*, 411 U.S. 258, 267 (1973) ("When a criminal defendant has solemnly admitted in open court that he is in fact guilty of the offense with which he is charged, he may not thereafter raise independent claims relating to the deprivation of constitutional rights that occurred prior to the entry of the guilty plea. He may only attack the voluntary and intelligent character of the guilty plea.").]

The New York State Court of Appeals recently described the difference between non-jurisdictional defects and the so-called jurisdictional defects which survive a guilty plea:

> The critical distinction is between defects implicating the integrity of the process, which may survive a guilty plea, and less fundamental flaws, such as evidentiary or technical matters, which do not. A defendant may raise, after a guilty plea, certain constitutional claims such as the voluntariness of a plea; speedy trial claims; double jeopardy claims; competence to stand trial; and the constitutionality of a statute under which the defendant was convicted. Claims that are foreclosed by a guilty plea have, for example, included pre-indictment prosecutorial misconduct; selective prosecution; failure to provide [statutory] notice; the statutory right to a speedy trial; the denial of an application for leave to file a late motion to suppress; transactional immunity; the exercise of alleged discriminatory peremptory challenges; an ex post facto challenge to an evidentiary rule change; and alleged unconstitutional statutory presumptions.

[*People v. Hansen*, 95 N.Y.2d 227, 231, 715 N.Y.S.2d 369 (2000) (Holds that challenge to reliance on hearsay in the grand jury also does not survive the guilty plea).]

Waived issues also include any suppression motions raised and adjudicated before the plea, unless the jurisdiction provides for a conditional plea, meaning that the parties stipulate that certain issues are preserved for appeal despite the plea. [*United States v. Rogers*, 387 F.3d 925, 934 (7th Cir. 2004). *See* Fed. R. Crim. P. 11(a)(2) (any pre-trial motion); *see also, e.g.,* Ark. R. Crim. P. 24.3(b) (limited to motions to suppress evidence and custodial statements); Conn. Gen. Stat. Ann. §54-94a (limited to motions to suppress and motions to dismiss); Mont. Code Ann. §46-12-204(3) (any "specified" pre-trial motion); Nev. Rev. Stat. Ann. §174.035(3) (any specified pre-trial motions).]

§17:53   Immigration Consequences

Individuals may have one of several immigration statuses: citizens, permanent or temporary resident aliens, refugees, non-immigrant visa holders or undocumented aliens. For criminal convictions, the important dividing line is between citizens and others. Citizens cannot be deported or excluded from the U.S. while others can be.

The list of deportable offenses is constantly growing. [*See* 8 U.S.C. §§1101(a), (f), 1182, 1227.]

Certain offenses (*e.g.,* trafficking in controlled substances, crimes of violence, sexual abuse of minors, and many fraud and theft offenses) are classified as "aggravated felonies." [8 U.S.C. §1101(a)(43).] A conviction of an aggravated felony results in nearly automatic deportation. [*See* 8 U.S.C. §1228; *United States v. Couto*, 311 F.3d 179, 184 (2d Cir. 2002).]

Ascertain your client's immigration status as soon as possible. Individuals can be citizens without knowing it. The client may:

- Have been born in the U.S. or a territory (Puerto Rico, the U.S. Virgin Islands, Guam, the Northern Mariana Islands) and raised elsewhere. [*See* 8 U.S.C. §§1401, 1402, 1406, 1407.]
- Have acquired citizenship through a parent or grandparent's birth in the U.S. [8 U.S.C. §§1401, 1409.]
- Have acquired citizenship because a parent became a naturalized U.S. citizen while the client was a minor. [8 U.S.C. §§1431, 1433.]

Whether your client is a citizen on any of these grounds may depend on which version of the immigration statutes was in effect at the time of his birth. Ask your client where he was born and where all of his parents and grandparents were born. In case of any uncertainties, consult an immigration expert. [*See also* www.nationalimmigrationproject. org (website of immigration project of the National Lawyers Guild with links to resources on immigration defense and implications of criminal convictions).]

In *Padilla v. Kentucky,* 559 U.S. 356, 130 S.Ct. 1473 (2010), the Supreme Court held that deportation (or, as it is now known, removal) is a "particularly severe penalty" that is "intimately" related to the criminal process and that the Sixth Amendment's guarantee of the effective assistance of counsel requires that defense counsel investigate and advise his non-citizen client of the immigration consequences of a conviction before his client enters a guilty plea.

Some convictions carry clear and certain immigration consequences: a felony drug distribution conviction will result in deportation. Where the consequence is less certain, consult immigration counsel. A helpful guide is available through the Immigrant Defense Project at http://immigrantdefenseproject.org.

After *Padilla,* it is imperative that defense counsel investigate the client's immigration status at the earliest possible stage of the representation and begin to explore the potential consequences of a conviction and methods to minimize those consequences, such as by a plea to a different offense. In some cases, for example, that of a defendant who left a forsaken homeland in childhood with his entire family and who has raised his own family in the United States, trial may be the only plausible alternative, even in the face of strong evidence of guilt.

Whether *Padilla* imposes an obligation to advise clients of other sentencing consequences is unclear. The Court's opinion emphasizes the severity of deportation, but in this, deportation is not unique: convictions of certain offenses may deprive a defendant of his livelihood, his home, his ability to obtain an education, or a pension he earned through a lifetime of travail. As further support for extending its rule, note that the professional standards upon which the Court relied to set the standard of reasonable competence require that counsel advise clients contemplating a plea of consequences other than deportation. [*See* NLADA Guideline 6.2(a); ABA Pleas of Guilty Standard 14-3.2.] Courts have extended *Padilla* to hold counsel ineffective for failing to notify his client that a guilty plea to aggravated stalking might subject him to involuntary civil commitment. [*Bauder v. Dep't of Corrections, State of Florida,* 619 F.3d 1272 (11th Cir. 2010).] Other courts have applied it to require counsel to notify the client that the conviction mandates sex offender registration [*People v. Fonville,* 291 Mich. App. 363, 804 N.W.2d 878, 894-95 (Mich.Ct. App. 2011) (holding that under *Padilla,* defense counsel must advise a defendant that registration as a sex offender is a consequence of the defendant's guilty plea); *Taylor v. State,* 304 Ga. App. 878, 698 S.E.2d 384, 385 (Ga. Ct. App. 2010) (holding that it is constitutionally deficient for counsel not to advise his client that pleading guilty will subject him to sex offender registration requirements); *but see Commonwealth v. Abraham,* 2012 Pa. LEXIS 2850 (Pa. 2012) (mandatory pension forfeiture is a collateral consequence to which *Padilla* does not apply).]

PRACTICE TIP:

You can control deportation consequences to some extent by the terms of a plea bargain or what is stated on the record at the time of the guilty plea colloquy. [*See Valansi v. Ashcroft,* 278 F.3d 203, 217-18 (3d Cir. 2002) (where guilty plea colloquy established that defendant acted with intent to injure, but not an intent to defraud the victim bank, bank embezzlement conviction under 18 U.S.C. §656 was not an aggravated felony); *compare Moore v. Ashcroft,* 251 F.3d 919, 923 (11th Cir. 2001) (holding that all §656 convictions necessarily involve intent to defraud and are aggravated felonies).]

CAUTION:

Do not assume that a deportable offense will escape the notice of immigration officials. Enforcement priorities change, and cooperation between local and federal immigration officials has been increasing. If not detected while in prison, your client's conviction may bar his re-entry at the border or his attempt to gain naturalized citizenship.

Arrest, even without conviction, poses problems for undocumented aliens under the Trump Administration's January 25, 2017, Executive Order "Enhancing Public Safety in the Interior of the United States" (available at whitehouse.gov). That Order prioritizes for removal aliens who lack valid immigration status and who "have been charged with any criminal offense, where such charge has not been resolved; . . . [or] have committed acts that constitute a chargeable criminal offense." [Section 5, (b), (c).] Especially if your client is charged in federal court, his mere arrest may trigger a report to the Department of Homeland Security, detention by Immigration and Customs Enforcement and the commencement of removal proceedings.

§17:54   Sex Offender Registration

Every state must force defendants convicted of certain sex offenses to register with the state police. [*See* 42 U.S.C. §§16901 *et seq.*] The registration period ranges from 15 years to life, depending on the offense of conviction. [42 U.S.C. §16915. *See* www.klaaskids.org (provides information on every state's sex offender registration requirements). *See* Chapter 23, Probation, Parole, Other Post-Release Supervision.]

If a convicted sex offender moves, he must inform the state police in the new area that he is a convicted sex offender who has moved into the area. A sex offender must update his information annually and notify the state police in his new state of residence of his new address within ten (10) days of the move.

One can access information regarding convicted sex offenders either through national or state databases. The National Sex Offender Public Registry [www.nsopr.gov] and the National Alert Registry [www.registeredoffenders-list.org] provide information on convicted sex offenders within every zip code in the United States. Every state has a Megan's Law website which is maintained by state police departments to provide timely information to the public on registered sex offenders residing in the state.

Conviction of a sex offense has other official ramifications:

- Some states do not permit a convicted sex offender to live within one thousand (1,000) feet of any school related premises.
- Some parole boards and/or departments of children and youth services ("CYS") may not allow a convicted sex offender to live with children that are not his own. CYS cannot impose further criminal penalties on your client, but it can investigate the living situation and threaten to remove children because of the threat the sex offender poses.
- In some states, convicted sex offenders are subject to random polygraph tests while on parole.

[§§17:55-17:59 Reserved]

V. COOPERATION; CONSEQUENCES & PROCEDURES

§17:60   Advantages of Cooperation

The best deals await those who cooperate or turn state's evidence against their confederates. Cooperation is the only way your client can avoid imposition of a mandatory minimum sentence in most federal drug cases. [*See* 18 U.S.C. §3553 (e).] If your client's involvement in a conspiracy is marginal, his cooperation may even convince the prosecutor not to charge him.

§17:61   Risks of Cooperation

Cooperation entails serious risks. [*See* Chapter 18, Representing Victims and Witnesses.]

Delve into the possibility of harm and make sure that the prosecutor and agents or police take those risks seriously and are capable of protecting your client.

Besides risk of harm, your client may not be able to live with the knowledge that he betrayed former friends. Take this concern seriously. Explain to your client that his friends put him in this mess by enlisting him as a criminal conspirator and had they the chance, they probably would cooperate against him without hesitation. Still, your client may refuse to turn against his associates. You must respect that decision so long as he makes it knowing the consequences.

The electronic posting of court records, as on the federal PACER system, facilitates public access to all filings, including plea agreements. This access has put cooperators at risk. Other inmates or former criminal associates can study the plea agreement for cooperation language. [*See generally*, The Honorable Steven Merryday, Caren Myers Morrison, Gerald Shargel, and Barbara Sale, *Panel Four: Cooperation and Plea Agreements-Professors & Practitioners*, 79 Fordham L. Rev. 65 (2011) (available at http://ir.lawnet.fordham.edu/flr/vol79/iss1/4).]

The solutions to this problem are several, but all conflict with the public's right to access court records and your need to have a record of your client's cooperation and the prosecution's promises of reward so that they can be enforced. In some jurisdictions, the prosecutor keeps the original of the agreement, without filing it. In others, cooperation language appears either in none or in all plea agreements.

Case-by-case sealing may be inadequate, but it might be all you can do. While the agreement will not appear on the electronic docket, the fact of sealing will, and suspicious and hostile minds will conclude that any sealed plea agreement is one with cooperation provisions. Thus, the United States District Court for the Western District of Pennsylvania, for example, adopted a procedure whereby all plea agreements, whether or not they include cooperation language, and all motions for reduction of sentence, are filed at a separate, sealed miscellaneous docket number.

Effective resolution of these problems requires district, circuit, or nationwide order, and absent that, the most you can do is insist on the sealing or non-filing of documents that reference cooperation, such as orders, plea agreements, prosecution motions and your own sentencing memoranda.

§17:62   The Carrot and Stick to Cooperation

Most prosecutors take a "carrot and stick" approach to cooperators. The carrot is a substantial sentence reduction. The stick is a surrender of rights and plea to a serious charge such that if the cooperator betrays the prosecutor, the prosecutor easily can impose a crushing sentence as punishment.

Thus, you may find your client forced to plead to more serious charges and stipulate to more weighty sentencing guidelines if he cooperates than on a straight plea.

Prosecutors do this not only to enlarge their "stick," but to persuade a jury that the cooperator is not to be treated so leniently that the jury finds offense. Further, the prosecutor will want to use the cooperator's stipulation to the scope of the conspiracy and the amount of drugs or money involved to set a high benchmark for the rest of the defendants. The prosecutor will claim that the reduction for your client's cooperation will make up for the plea to more serious charges, but this is not always the case.

Some prosecutors specify the degree of the sentence reduction that they will recommend in the plea agreement while others leave the extent of the reduction entirely up to the judge. In the latter case, a rule of thumb often develops among local judges to reduce sentences by a relatively uniform percentage for cooperation (*e.g.,* one-half, one-third, or two-thirds). Ask experienced practitioners and the local public defender to determine the local metric.

§17:63   Prosecutor's Discretion to Assess the Value of the Cooperation

Most cooperation agreements vest in the prosecutor, not the judge, nearly unreviewable discretion to assess the truth and value of the defendant-witness's cooperation and to decide whether to ask the judge for a sentence reduction.

However, courts have authority to review whether this discretion is exercised in good faith. Examples of bad faith include:

- Refusing a reduction based on the defendant's religion, ethnicity or political beliefs, or refusing to ask for a reduction based on conditions or conduct of which the government already was aware at the time of the agreement. [*United States v. Roe*, 445 F.3d 202, 207-08 (2d Cir. 2006).]
- Basing a refusal on a belief that the guideline sentence before a reduction is sufficiently lenient. [*United States v. Floyd*, 428 F.3d 513, 517-18 (3d Cir. 2005).]
- Refusing because the defendant provides truthful information that the government does not want to hear. [*United States v. Knights*, 968 F.2d 1483, 1488 (2d Cir. 1992).]

If the defendant had no cooperation agreement, he has a remedy for the prosecution's refusal to seek a reduced sentence only if the prosecutor acts from an unconstitutional motive, such as race or religion. [*Wade v. United States*, 504 U.S. 181, 185-86 (1992).]

§17:64   Practical Protections

Prepare for the Interview

Prosecutors want to interview a defendant and evaluate the truthfulness and utility of his information before they make any promise. The most useful cooperators are those who unhesitatingly fess up to their own culpability and who have detailed first-hand knowledge of wrongdoing because they personally participated in it.

You must carefully prepare for that interview both by interrogating your client to see that he is forthcoming about both his own and others' crimes (those charged and those uncharged) and by previewing your client's information, in your own words, for the prosecutor to see if it will satisfy him.

Evaluate Queen-for-a-Day Agreements

Prosecutors will demand that your client waive the protections that FRE 410 and its state counterparts offer against the evidentiary use of statements made during plea negotiations, often in a so-called "Queen-for-a-Day" agreement.

This authorizes the use of the statements to cross-examine or rebut any defense your client later may offer if he goes to trial. [*See* Chapter 12, Grand Jury Practice.]

Cooperating and giving a proffer generally rule out any chance of success at trial, so choose the cooperator's path only if you are relatively certain that it will be fruitful and your client does not have a more attractive option.

Give an Attorney Proffer Before Prosecutor Meets Your Client

Consider giving a written proffer, signed by you rather than by your client, and seeing if the prosecutor will agree to a cooperation agreement or immunity on that basis, without speaking with your client.

Preface the letter with a few lines claiming for it the protections of FRE 410. Otherwise, the statements can be used against your client as agent-admissions under FRE 801 (d)(2)(C). [*See* §17:33.]

Prosecutors often reject this option because they want to size up the defendant in person and grill him before agreeing to anything.

Attend the Debriefing Session

Attend at least the first few debriefing sessions to assure that they proceed smoothly, to avoid misunderstandings, and to serve as a witness to what is said.

The prosecutor and police will seek vengeance against your client if they come to believe that he misled them or withheld evidence in the debriefings. Not infrequently, though, they simply misunderstood, mis-transcribed, or forgot what your client said or they just did not ask for the missing information.

Make an Accurate Record

To assure an accurate record while keeping yourself from becoming a trial witness, consider bringing an audiotape recorder or stenographer to the session. The stenographer is the better choice because the sounds of you, your client and the agents yukking it up might prove to be embarrassing.

If the prosecutor refuses these options, be cautious about what you include in your notes, for it later may become discoverable to the defendant against whom your client testifies. [*See United States v. Paxson*, 861 F.2d 730, 735-36 (D.C. Cir. 1988) (denying defense access to witness's lawyer's notes of federal agents' debriefing of witness); *United States v. Arias*, 373 F. Supp. 2d 311 (S.D.N.Y. 2005) (same); *but see In re Grand Jury*, 282 F.3d 156 (2d Cir. 2002) (quashing grand jury subpoena for defense attorney notes as protected work-product, but suggesting that result might be different if the subpoena were a trial subpoena and the government could show substantial need).]

[§§17:65-17:69 Reserved]

VI. ALTERNATIVE DISPOSITIONS

§17:70   Diversion Programs for Minor Offenses

Many jurisdictions have diversion programs for relatively minor offenses and defendants who have little or no criminal history. Under these programs, charges are filed but then adjourned by agreement while the defendant undergoes a period of pre-disposition probation.

The probation may include reporting, restitution and a treatment program, such as a safe-driving program for DUI arrestees. Although rare, the court or probation office may impose a requirement that the defendant consent to (random) searches of his home as a condition of diversion. [*See Commonwealth v. Lebo*, 713 A.2d 1158 (Pa. Super. Ct. 1998) (defendant charged with indecent assault and corruption of minors required to consent to random searches of his home for pornography).]

If the defendant completes the probation successfully, the charges are dismissed. The diversion program also might provide for expungement of the defendant's record. [*See* §17:120.]

Forms:
- **Form 17-1** ARD Application
- **Form 17-2** Diversion Motion
- **Form 17-3** Diversion Agreement
- **Form 17-4** Diversion Order
- **Form 17-5** Diversion Restitution Schedule

§17:71   Disadvantages of Diversion Programs

An alternative disposition is not exoneration. Some programs require that the defendant acknowledge guilt and this acknowledgement might become admissible against the defendant in later civil actions or at the criminal trial, should the defendant flunk out of the diversion program and charges be reinstated. Other programs require that the defendant enter a guilty plea before he may be admitted into the program, and upon unsuccessful discharge, he is subject to sentencing in accordance with his guilty plea–with the added strike that he botched one chance at leniency. [*See, e.g., Williams v. Commonwealth*, 354 S.W.3d 158 (KY Court of Appeals 2011) (construing KY Revised Statutes §§533.250, 533.256).]

Disposition by pre-trial diversion usually precludes the defendant from suing for wrongful prosecution or arrest. [*See Gilles v. Davis*, 427 F.3d 197, 208-210 (3d Cir. 2005) (acceptance and completion of Pennsylvania accelerated rehabilitation disposition program ("ARD") precludes malicious prosecution and civil rights actions attacking arrest because ARD is not a favorable termination; notes similar rulings from Second and Fifth Circuits).]

The diversion might count as a conviction for license suspension purposes or immigration purposes. [*See* 49 C.F.R. 384.226 (CDL suspension); *Acosta v. Ashcroft*, 341 F.3d 218, 223 (3d Cir. 2003) (dismissal after completing Pennsylvania's probation without verdict program, 35 Pa.C.S.A. §780-117, counts as a deportable drug conviction under immigration law).]

Even where the program results in expungement, the prosecutor's office may keep a record of your client's participation so that he will not have diversion available for his next arrest.

In some cases, a summary offense or violation, such as disorderly conduct, might be a better disposition than diversion. Not only does it impose fewer conditions of supervision, your client still may resort to diversion on a subsequent charge.

§17:72   Creative Agreements

In the right case, you might have options other than a plea agreement, cooperation or diversion.

If the defendant and alleged victim have an ongoing relationship, a mediation program might be an option.

You might be able to convince the victim and the prosecutor to forego charges and agree to a protection from abuse order or the local equivalent (applicable when the defendant and victim are family members or have an intimate relationship), in return for restitution, or for submitting to counseling.

Many jurisdictions have instituted a wide range of "problem-solving courts," including drug and mental health courts for offenders who have substance abuse or mental health problems, domestic violence courts, sex offender courts, and even courts designed to treat the problems of veterans. [*See* www.nycourts.gov/courts/problem_solving/ (website of New York State's Problem-Solving Courts); www.nadcp.org (website of National Association of Drug Court Professionals).] Such programs offer a form of intensive probation with mental health or substance abuse treatment and frequent court appearances with the incentive of dismissal or a non-custodial sentence if the defendant successfully completes the program. [*See* Chapter 13, Mental Health Issues; Chapter 23, Probation, Parole, Other Post-Release Supervision.]

Drug courts fall into two models: (1) the diversionary programs, in which an adjudication of guilt is postponed pending the defendant's completion of the program; or (2) the post-adjudication model, in which the defendant first pleads guilty and then sentencing is suspended or deferred pending the defendant's success (or lack of it) in the program. [*See* GAO, Report to Congressional Committees: Adult Drug Court (February 2005) (available at www.gao.gov/ new.items/ d05219.pdf); *e.g., People v. Kimmel*, 24 Misc.3d 1052, 882 N.Y.S.2d 895 (NY City Court 2009) (defendant pleaded guilty and agreed to alternative sentences of five years probation if he successfully completed drug court treatment or one to three years in state prison if he failed).]

CAUTION:

While drug courts offer an opportunity for your client to address the underlying problems that perhaps contributed to a criminal lifestyle, they also may trap him into a long sentence, particularly the programs of the post-adjudicative type. Once your client has pleaded guilty and then failed a drug treatment program, he has little leverage to obtain a favorable sentence. Some courts do not defer sentencing, but impose alternative sentences: one of probation for successful completion, and another of substantial incarceration if the defendant flunks the program. [*E.g., People v. Kimmel*, 24 Misc. 3d 1052, 882 N.Y.S.2d 895 (NY City Court 2009) (denying defendant a hearing on whether his termination from program was due to his knowing and voluntary actions; "Treatment courts operate on the principle that there is both a carrot and a stick. The upside of successfully completing the treatment court program is usually a reduced sentence, typically a sentence of probation, along with, in some cases, a dismissal or reduction of the charge; the downside is the enhanced sentence, i.e., incarceration").]

An entrance requirement for treatment courts often is a contract in which the defendant agrees to waive privacy rights in his treatment records and the right to demand a hearing on whether he successfully completed the program. [*E.g., Kimmel*. For an overview of the constitutional challenges you might raise to a program's invasion of your client's privacy and the absence of procedural due process for the determination that a defendant has failed a program, *see* Trent Oram and Kara Gleckler, "An Analysis of the Constitutional Issues Implicated in Drug Courts," 42 Idaho L.Rev. 471 (2006).]

[§§17:73-17:79 Reserved]

VII. PREPARING YOUR CLIENT

§17:80   It Is Your Client's Decision

The decision whether or not to plead guilty belongs to your client. [*Jones v. Barnes*, 463 U.S. 745, 751 (1983).] The law places the final decision in your client's hands, for he is the one who must live with the decision.

You must communicate to your client all plea offers. [*See* ABA Standards for Criminal Justice: Pleas of Guilty, Standard 14-3.2(a) (3d ed. 1999).]

Nonetheless, he is entitled to your advice and even your persuasion regarding what you adjudge to be in his best interests. Many criminal defendants reached this unfortunate point in their lives as a result of poor judgment, and they need help in making a rational decision.

In *Missouri v. Frye*, 132 S.Ct. 1399 (2012), and *Lafler v. Cooper*, 132 S.Ct. 1376 (2012), the Supreme Court held that the right to the effective assistance of counsel extended to plea bargaining and that an adequately defended trial did not preclude a claim for ineffective assistance in pretrial plea bargaining. In *Frye*, defense counsel failed to convey to his client a favorable written plea offer before it expired, and the defendant later pleaded guilty under a less generous deal. In *Lafler*, counsel incorrectly advised his client that under the facts–the client shot the victim in the buttocks and hip–he could not be convicted of assault with intent to commit murder. In reliance on that incorrect advice, the defendant rejected the offer and went to trial, where he was convicted and received a much more severe sentence than was offered.

Lafler and *Frye* did not teach criminal defense lawyers anything new: it was common knowledge that you have an obligation to convey plea offers to your client in a timely fashion, and your advice on whether to accept a deal must rest on adequate investigation of the facts and an accurate understanding of the law. And most courts already accepted that failure to discharge those duties competently could constitute the ineffective assistance of counsel. But the decisions have generated initiatives among some trial judges to police the effectiveness of plea-bargaining and circumvent postconviction claims of ineffective assistance of counsel by inquiring at pleas and before trial whether there have been any other plea offers.

Well-intentioned as those initiatives may be, they hold some dangers for defense counsel. You do not want the trial judge to hear that initially the prosecution offered a harsher deal, for example, by insisting that the sentencing guideline loss was much greater. The judge may come to believe that your client got a windfall and should not receive any further leniency at sentence. Telling a judge before trial that your client would have entertained a deal, but did not receive the one he wanted may suggest to the judge that your client is guilty but is trying to game the system; on the other hand, a judge hearing that your client always insisted on trial and never would permit plea discussions may feel he needs to teach your client a lesson for his defiance. The point is that any detailed discussion of plea bargaining may provide the judge with insights into your relationship with your client, your estimation of the appropriate sentence, and your client's attitude that you may wish to keep from the judge. Therefore, if you can honestly do so, answer the judge with a terse assurance that there was no better offer than the one you took and that you conveyed all offers to your client. Resist answering inquiries about the particulars of prior offers or why they were rejected with the objection that such questions intrude on the attorney-client relationship.

The manner and stage at which judges conduct *Lafler/Frye* colloquies can be problematic. Some judges will address the client directly and ask if he is or was aware of the offer. As with guilty pleas, you must prepare your client for the judge's questions, because the judge might describe the offer in a way that sounds foreign to the client, and the client might mistake the judge's inquiry for a suggestion that the client erred in rejecting the offer.

Prosecutors may make an offer at an earlier stage, such as an offer to forego a mandatory-minimum sentence in exchange for waiving a preliminary hearing or suppression hearing, and some judges might inquire about the offer, its communication and rejection at the hearing. Giving advice at those early stages is always difficult because you likely lack sufficient information about the case and evidence to assess the worth of the offer. Often, holding the hearing is a necessary step in evaluating the case. Further, many offers really are not–prosecutors tend to say things such as they will "consider" waiving the mandatory-minimum sentence in exchange for your waiver. If the judge insists on a colloquy, use the opportunity to flesh out the offer–your advice might be different if the prosecutor will commit on the record to waiving a mandatory-minimum, especially when the facts suggest an uphill battle (for example, a drug courier case where consent or border search issues paint the chances for suppression as bleak).

You can have more productive discussions with judges and prosecutors about these colloquy practices outside the pressures of a court appearance. Judges are not likely to change their practice on the spot. Instead, use bar conferences and meetings to discuss this issue with your colleagues, judges and prosecutors.

§17:81 Know Your Case

Often, there is no correct decision, even for the most rational of clients.

No one can calculate with certainty the chances of acquittal, because much depends on factors you cannot assess until the end of the trial, such as the jury's composition and the witnesses' appeal. Add to this the paucity of discovery in criminal cases, and any estimation as to probability of acquittal becomes little more than guess-work.

However, you can sharpen your estimation by the more you know about the case through discovery, motion practice, discussions with the prosecutor, and witness interviews.

Talk to as many of the witnesses as you can, both yours and the prosecutor's, for this is the only way you can size up how they will perform on the witness stand.

§17:82 Know Your Client

Even if you could calculate accurately the probability of acquittal and the likely sentence on a plea versus that after a trial conviction, there still often is no clear answer as to whether a plea or a trial is the correct decision.

With a ten percent chance of acquittal, a plea to a likely five year sentence is a better choice than facing 15 years after trial. But is a plea to 15 years the better option than 25 years after trial with the same ten percent chance of acquittal?

The answer depends on many factors such as your client's appetite for risk, his age, his ability to endure a stressful trial, his prior experience with prison, and his family situation. You can help him through this decision only if you are able to address his personal issues.

§17:83 Gain Your Client's Trust

Never counsel a client to plead guilty until you have investigated the case and any defenses.

If your client gives you a lead or suggestion, work it. Explore all possible legal defenses, even the somewhat unusual ones your client concocts, at least to the extent of explaining why the law does not support his argument.

Your client may suspect that a plea is the easy way out for you. Show him that you are advising this course not after loafing through the case, but after you did all you could on his behalf.

§17:84 Play Out the Trial

Avoid making the issue your belief in the client's guilt or innocence.

Your value to the client is to draw on your experience with trials, juries and judges and to predict the verdict that will result from the evidence.

Phrase discussions in this way:

> The judge has decided that the jury will hear that you have a prior drug-trafficking conviction. Once the jury hears that, they will not believe that you did not know what was in the trunk of the car you were paid $500 to drive across town. Maybe you really did not know, but a jury will never believe it.

Do not say:

> You and I know that you knew what was in the trunk.

Play out your client's and other defense witnesses' testimony and cross-examine it just as the prosecutor would.

Refer to the standard jury instructions on credibility to refute your client's unrealistic expectations about tearing apart witnesses. The jury will be told that they can convict on the uncorroborated testimony of an accomplice or of a child victim-witness (if that is the law in your jurisdiction); that they should try to reconcile all the evidence; and that a witnesses' one lie or mistake does not mandate rejection of the remainder of his testimony.

Assure your client that should he choose to go to trial, you will use all of those tactics (*e.g.,* impeachment with prior inconsistent statements, motive to lie, and prior convictions). However, warn him that even when used skillfully, those tactics often fail in the face of cumulative and corroborating evidence.

§17:85   Enlist the Help of Family and Friends

Your client may fear disappointing his friends and family by admitting guilt.

However, those same friends and family might have a degree of objectivity that your client lacks. Their assurances that they will respect your client even if he pleads guilty, their concern for his well-being and their entreaties that he give up the fight so that he can do his time and return home as soon as possible may carry the day.

You probably do not share your client's background. The opinion of peers and mentors may matter more to him than your opinion.

You might even consider putting him in touch with convicts who have experienced similar situations. [*See* Kevin Doyle, "Heart of the Deal: Ten Suggestions for Plea Bargaining," 23 *The Champion* 68 (November 1999) (suggests having death row inmates persuade capital defendants that a life sentence is preferable to sitting on death row).]

§17:86   Give Your Client Time and Attention

No client should be rushed into a guilty plea. Let your client rant and discuss with him all of his concerns. Do not press him for an immediate answer unless absolutely necessary, which will be extremely rare no matter what the prosecutor says.

About the only time the decision must be immediate is when the prosecution needs immediate help to prevent another crime or apprehend a coconspirator. Even then, while the decision to cooperate to that limited extent must be immediate, your client need not commit to a plea, or at least to all of its terms at that time.

Let your client go home and think about it, discuss it with loved ones, and call you with questions.

§17:87   Be Cognizant of Your Own Interests

Much as we like to believe that we consider only our clients' interests, in truth, we may shade our advice to serve our own interests.

You might be coming off two back-to-back trials and want to see your family. Conversely, perhaps you have not been in trial for some time and yearn for the fray.

Trials often are bad business propositions, particularly if you have a flat fee arrangement with the client or he is out of money. On the other hand, the publicity of a trial, win or lose, may attract future clients.

You must look inside and honestly measure the tug of such concerns so that you can offer your client unbiased advice. There will be other days to earn a reputation, sharpen skills, enjoy a deserved rest or fatten your bank balance.

For your client, the day he decides on plea or trial may be the most consequential of his life.

§17:88   Preparing Your Client for the Plea

The change of plea hearing may be the trial judge's only opportunity to size up your client face-to-face before sentencing. Instruct your client to be attentive, well-dressed, respectful, articulate and contrite. A plea is not the time for the defendant to attempt to minimize his wrongdoing.

Rehearse with your client the questions the judge will ask him. While the rights as described by the judge seem routine to you, a person hearing them for the first time may find the judge's explanations confusing.

Sit in the courtroom or draw a diagram. Act it out.

Ascertain how much the judge expects your client to say when asked to admit his guilt.

Some judges have the prosecutor summarize the evidence and then ask the defendant whether he agrees. A "yes" or "no" suffices. Others merely recite the charge and ask the defendant if he did it, again expecting a simple "yes" or "no". In these courtrooms, you should discuss with the prosecutor in advance of the plea what he will say. You do not want your client nitpicking the prosecutor's statements and annoying the judge. On the other hand, you need to avoid having your client admit unnecessary or untrue aggravating circumstances. You also must warn your client not to quibble with inconsequential assertions.

Other judges turn to the defendant and ask him to state, in his own words, what he did to make him guilty of the charge. This requires extensive preparation. Your client should state the facts underlying his guilt succinctly, without excuses. Too many excuses may talk the judge out of accepting the plea. Caution your client against statements such as, "I know <u>now</u> that what I did was wrong." This suggests he acted with innocent intent at the time of the offense. The judge wants to hear acceptance of responsibility, not excuses.

On the other hand, an articulate and remorseful description of his misconduct can impress the judge and start him thinking that your client deserves another chance.

§17:89 Taking the Plea

Explain to your client the mechanics of entering a guilty plea.

The judge will ask your client six categories of questions to ensure that the plea is entered knowingly and voluntarily:
- Questions concerning his mental competence.
- Questions concerning his satisfaction with his legal representation.
- Questions to ensure that he understands the legal rights he surrenders by pleading guilty, including trial and appellate rights.
- Questions to ascertain his understanding of the penalties for conviction.
- Questions about the existence of any plea agreement and any other threats or promises.
- Questions to assure the court that there is a factual basis for the defendant's guilt.

These questions can be quite exhaustive.

Some courts have the defendant review and sign a written advice of rights form.

Forms:
- **Form 17-6** Sample Plea Agreement (Federal)
- **Form 17-7** Sample Plea Agreement (Federal) With Cooperation and Stipulated Factual Basis
- **Form 17-8** Written Plea Colloquy
- **Form 17-9** Script for Federal Plea Colloquy

[§§17:90-17:99 Reserved]

VIII. POST-PLEA PROCEEDINGS

A. Enforcing Plea Agreements

§17:100 Agreements Are Interpreted by Contract Principles

Courts interpret plea agreements according to contract principles. [*Santobello v. New York*, 404 U.S. 257, 262-63 (1971).]

Ambiguities are construed against the government, both because the prosecutor usually drafted the agreement and because the prosecution has superior bargaining power. [*See United States v. Gebbie*, 294 F.3d 540, 552 (3d Cir. 2002) (stating that ambiguities will be construed against the Government because of the Government's advantage in bargaining power); *Allen v. Thomas*, 161 F.3d 667, 671 (11th Cir. 1998) (will construe ambiguous agreement against the government even where defense attorneys drafted the plea agreement).]

Courts will not tolerate a prosecutor's clever attempts to evade his obligations under the plea agreement. [*E.g., United States v. Mitchell*, 136 F.3d 1192, 1193-94 (8th Cir. 1998) (prosecutor breached agreement when he promised to recommend concurrent sentence but then told court he had "no specific recommendation"); *Dunn v. Colleran*, 247 F.3d 450, 459-61 (3d Cir. 2001) (prosecutor had promised to recommend a sentence in the range of 36-60 months, but then referred to this as an initial recommendation, expressed personal reservations about the agreement, and asked for a "lengthy" sentence).]

§17:101 Making a Record

Generally, make a record either by getting a written plea agreement or by laying its terms out on the record at the time of the plea.

Do not rely on any silent or in-chambers promises or agreements. If the judge or prosecutor makes any assurances, either make sure they are memorialized in a writing that becomes an exhibit at the plea or repeat them for the record at the time of the plea. Courts will not enforce unarticulated agreements or side agreements not found in a written agreement. [*See United States v. Wells,* 211 F.3 988, 996 (6th Cir. 2000); *In re Altro,* 180 F.3d 372, 375-77 (2d Cir. 1999) (where there was a written plea agreement, defendant could not rely on government's promise that he would not be required to testify before the grand jury).]

If the plea agreement is not in writing, you should explain its terms in a letter to your client. Even where you carefully and patiently explain the terms orally, hope may distort a client's understanding. For example, he may misunderstand recommendations as ironclad promises. The U.S. Supreme Court decisions in *Lafler* and *Frye* emphasize the importance of communicating plea offers clearly and promptly to clients; follow through with a writing, to avoid misunderstandings and to give the client something to refer to when he has questions.

§17:102   Off-the-Record Agreements

Although you generally want a record of the agreement, there are some circumstances in which you do *not* want to put a prosecutor's or judge's assurances or promises in the record.

A prosecutor may agree to forego mention of other crimes of which the defendant is suspected. Notifying the court of this promise would defeat its very purpose. Or the prosecutor may assure you that after a guilty plea he will not ask the agents to pursue certain investigations (*e.g.,* an investigation into your client's failure to pay taxes on the money he stole). The prosecutor knows that such an assurance is legally unenforceable; he is asking you to rely on his or her good faith. Articulating the assurance for the court evinces your distrust and guarantees that the prosecutor will disavow the assurance.

Even in jurisdictions where the rules prohibit judicial participation in plea bargaining, many judges will permit you to ask them, pre-plea and in chambers, what sentence they are likely to impose. Many judges will give you relatively explicit assurances. However, they will disclaim any such assurance if you repeat it on the record. Furthermore, your attempts to recite the promise on the record often will anger the judge by suggesting to him that you do not play by the rules. Most likely, the judge will clarify that his statements were not promises, and he will prove it by imposing a sentence different (and inevitably harsher) than the one he mentioned in chambers.

You must realize and inform your client that such side agreements are not enforceable. You are at the mercy of the prosecutor's and judge's good faith; therefore, you must evaluate their trustworthiness. Furthermore, the prosecutor may lack the power to deliver on his assurance. That is, the police or IRS already might have started an investigation unbeknownst to the prosecutor, or the agency or another jurisdiction might investigate without informing him first. For example, in the past, prosecutors could assure that they would not inform immigration officials of your client's conviction, and that assurance carried some weight. Now, immigration and the jails check inmates' immigration status and commence post-sentence deportation proceedings independent of any prosecution effort.

You are taking a chance on probabilities, and the best you can do is to elicit as many facts as possible by asking the prosecutor whether any other agency or jurisdiction expressed interest in the case. Advise your client accordingly. Your only alternative is to have your client disclose all the crimes and violations that he might have committed, notify the appropriate agencies and jurisdictions, and obtain their positions on the likelihood of enforcement actions against your client. Obviously, this course of action invites more problems than it solves.

[§§17:103-17:109 Reserved]

B.   Motions to Withdraw Guilty Pleas

§17:110   Withdrawing Plea Before Sentencing

A defendant may seek to withdraw his guilty plea at any time before sentencing upon showing "any fair and just reason." [Fed. R. Crim. P. 11 (d)(2)(B).]

As permissive as this standard may sound, in practice courts treat a guilty plea as a "grave and solemn act" from which they will release the defendant only if he proves good reason to do so. [*United States v. Hyde,* 520 U.S. 670, 677 (1997); *United States v. Bennett,* 332 F.3d 1094, 1099 (7th Cir. 2003) (burden on defendant to prove fair and just reason and to overcome presumption of verity given to statements made at the guilty plea colloquy).]

Four factors guide the court's discretion in deciding whether to grant a motion to withdraw:

- Whether defendant established a fair and just reason to withdraw his plea.
- Whether defendant asserts his legal innocence of the charge.
- The length of time between the guilty plea and the motion to withdraw.
- If the defendant established a fair and just reason for withdrawal, whether the government would be prejudiced.

[*United States v. Fitzhugh*, 78 F.3d 1326, 1328 (8th Cir. 1996).]

The court foremost considers the veracity and force behind the reason the defendant gives for his change of heart. [*See United States v. Parilla-Tirado*, 22 F.3d 368, 371 (1st Cir. 1994). *See People v. Alexander*, 97 N.Y.2d 482, 486-88, 743 N.Y.S.2d 45, 769 N.E.2d 802 (2002) (defendant's emotional distress at time of plea and domestic violence victim's unwillingness to press the charges are insufficient reasons to permit withdrawal).]

§17:111 Withdrawing Plea After Sentencing

After sentencing, a defendant can withdraw his plea only if he shows that his plea was unknowing and involuntary. [*Commonwealth v. Muhammad*, 2002 Pa. Super. 55, 794 A.2d 378, 383 (2002).]

A motion to withdraw frequently calls into question the competence of defense counsel's advice to plead guilty. That is, a guilty plea may be invalidated if the counsel's deficient performance undermines the voluntary and intelligent nature of defendant's decision to plead guilty. [*See United States v. Arteca*, 411 F.3d 315, 320 (2d Cir. 2005).]

Your client deserves to be represented by conflict-free counsel on the motion, so if he insists on proceeding with it, you should ask the court to appoint new counsel. [*See United States v. Davis*, 239 F.3d 283, 287-88 (2d Cir. 2001) (courts generally should appoint new counsel for nonfrivolous motions to withdraw pleas); *see Hines v. Miller*, 318 F.3d 157, 166-169 (2d Cir. 2003) (Winter, J., dissenting) (collecting cases from federal circuits and states that require the appointment of new counsel).]

§17:112 Discussing the Withdrawal With the Client

Treat a client's desire to withdraw his guilty plea with great patience and deliberation. Do not immediately file the motion.

Usually, withdrawal spells nothing but trouble for the client. If the judge denies the motion, the client may lose any benefit the judge was prepared to grant him for his apparent, but now disavowed, acceptance of responsibility.

Making the motion generally requires the defendant to lay out in detail his theory of defense. The prosecution cannot introduce any of that information at trial or cross-examine the defendant on his factual assertions. [*See* Fed. R. Crim. P. 11 (f); FRE 410 (prohibiting use at trial of fact of withdrawn plea or any assertions made during it).] Nevertheless, the defense has lost the element of surprise and the prosecutor can craft his presentation to defeat the defense.

Moreover, the prosecutor may reinstate any charges he agreed to dismiss or forego as part of any plea agreement, and he is not bound by any sentencing stipulations to which he may have agreed. [*United States v. Lewis*, 138 F.3d 840, 842-43 (10th Cir. 1998) (denying defendant's motion to vacate his conviction without vacating the plea agreement under which it was entered).]

Explain all these disadvantages to your client. However, if the client insists on proceeding, seek to withdraw and have conflict-free counsel appointed to give him a fighting chance of having his motion granted.

[§§17:113-17:119 Reserved]

C. Expungements

§17:120 Authority for Expungements

Many jurisdictions entitle a defendant to have his record expunged or sealed and records relating to his arrest, including files, mug shots and fingerprints, destroyed if he is acquitted or the charge dismissed. [*See E.g.*, S.C. Code Ann. §17-1-40, NY Crim. Pr. Law 160.50.]

Some jurisdictions also permit expungement after a first conviction for minor offenses. [*E.g.* S.C. Code Ann. §22-5-910.]

Many states have statutes specifying that expungement is appropriate after a first minor drug possession marijuana arrest and conviction or pre-trial diversion. [*E.g.*, S.C. Code Ann. §44-53-450; 35 Pa.C.S.A. §780-117; 18 U.S.C. §3607(a).]

Where there is no statute, some courts find inherent judicial authority to order expungement. [*United States v. Crowell*, 374 F.3d 790, 793-94 (9th Cir. 2004) (inherent authority to order expungement in cases of unlawful arrest, conviction, or acquittal, but not in cases of convictions); *compare Doe v. United States*, 833 F.3d 192 (2d Cir. 2016) (federal courts lack jurisdiction to expunge records of conviction, but recognizing the continued validity of *United States v. Schnitzer*, 567 F.2d 536 (2d Cir. 1977), which ruled that federal courts do have ancillary jurisdiction to expunge arrest records in dismissed casees); *Camfield v. City of Oklahoma City*, 248 F.3d 1214, 1234 (10th Cir. 2001) (power of courts to order expungement extends to convictions, but denying request); *State v. Schultz*, 676 N.W.2d 337, 345 (Minn. Ct. App. 2004) (ordering expungement of conviction that occurred when defendant was 18 years old and had psychological difficulties because the record caused him difficulties in obtaining employment and housing). *See generally* Vitauts M. Gulbis, "Judicial Expunction of Criminal Record of Convicted Adult," 11 A.L.R.4th 956 (surveying jurisdictions' varying approaches).]

> **Forms:**
> * **Form 17-10** Expungement Order (Pennsylvania)
> * **Form 17-11** Partial Expungement Motion (Pennsylvania)

§17:121   Effect of Expungement

An expungement clears the client's record, thereby avoiding more severe sentences on a future conviction and bars to employment. [*E.g.,* NY Crim. Pro. L. 160.60 ("Except where specifically required or permitted by statute or upon specific authorization of a superior court, no such person shall be required to divulge information pertaining to the arrest or prosecution").]

Many expungement statutes are not self-executing. The defendant must obtain a court order commanding it and see that a certified copy is sent to the appropriate state agency and to any local law enforcement agencies and jails involved in the offense.

An expungement aims to restore the defendant to the status he enjoyed before his arrest. Therefore, some state statutes explicitly authorize individuals who have won expungement to represent to employers, licensing boards and the world at large that they never have been arrested. [*See generally,* Margaret C. Love, "The Debt That Can Never Be Paid: A Report Card on the Collateral Consequences of Conviction," 21 *Criminal Justice*, 16, 20 (Fall 2006); *see* Margaret Colgate Love, "Relief From the Collateral Consequences of a Criminal Conviction: A State-By-State Resource Guide," Table #5: Judicial Expungement, Sealing and Set-Aside (April 2007) (available at www.sentencingproject.org.]

To make sure that the record was actually expunged, after several months, ask the appropriate state agency for a copy of the defendant's arrest record. You should check federal records, too, to ensure that the FBI followed the expungement order. Your client must make the request by sending his fingerprints and a certified check or money order for $18 payable to the Treasury of the United States, to the FBI. [*See https://www.fbi.gov/about-us/cjis/identity-history-summary-checks/identity-history-summary-checks/order (last visited Feb. 3, 2016)*].

Expungements can be partial. If the more serious charges are dismissed and your client is convicted only of a lesser charge, such as disorderly conduct, you may be able to expunge the arrest records and charge records for the more serious offenses. [*Commonwealth v. Rodland*, 871 A.2d 216, 918-19 (Pa. Super. Ct. 2005).]

[§§17:122-17:129 Reserved]

D. Pardons

§17:130   Procedure

Nearly all states and the federal government grant the executive branch the power to commute sentences and pardon offenders.

The pardon process and eligibility differ from jurisdiction to jurisdiction; you must consult your local statutes. [E.g., Cal. Const. Art. 5, §8; Cal. Penal Code §§4800-4813, 4852 (setting procedures for pardon applications and forbidding grant of pardons to those "twice convicted of a felony except on recommendation of the Supreme Court, four justices concurring"); Pa. Const. Art IV, §9 (a) (limiting Governor's pardon and commutation powers to those cases where a majority of the Board of Pardons recommends such action and requiring a unanimous recommendation to commute or pardon a life-imprisoned or death-sentenced inmate); 28 C.F.R. §§1.1-1.11 (procedures for federal pardon application, including restricting eligibility to those who have been five years out of prison).] For a state-by-state survey of pardon and clemency procedures and news, *see* www.pardonpower.com. Standard pardon and commutation application forms are available on several websites: www.cjpf.org/clemency/clemencystates.html (Criminal Justice Policy Foundation); www.usdoj.gov/pardon/forms.htm (U.S. Department of Justice, Office of the Pardon Attorney (federal clemency and pardon application forms)).

§17:131   Effect

While commutation alters the sentence, a pardon erases the fact of conviction and restores the individual to his pre-conviction status for nearly all collateral purposes. [*See* Margaret C. Love, "The Debt That Can Never Be Paid: A Report Card on the Collateral Consequences of Conviction," 21 *Criminal Justice*, 16, 17-18 (Fall 2006).]

Use of the pardon power has waned over the last few years, but a move is afoot to revive it in recognition of the enduring severity of collateral consequences. [Margaret C. Love, "Reviving the Benign Prerogative of Pardoning, 32 *Litigation* 25 (Winter 2006).]

IX.   FORMS

Form 17-1   ARD Application

APPLICATION FOR PRE-TRIAL DIVERSION PROGRAM

Answers must be complete. Use X marks where appropriate.

1. NAME _____ PHONE NO. _____
   ADDRESS _____
              (Street)   (City)   (State)   (ZIP)
   LENGTH OF RESIDENCE AT PRESENT ADDRESS _____
2. AGE ___
3. DATE OF BIRTH _____
4. PLACE OF BIRTH _____
5. SEX: ___ F ___ M
6. SOCIAL SECURITY NO. _____
7. MARITAL STATUS: ___ Never Married ___ Married ___ Widow/Widower
         ___ Separated ___ Divorced
8. NO. OF DEPENDENTS: ___ 1 ___ 2 ___ 3 ___ 4 ___ 5 ___ 6 and over
9. PRESENT LIVING ARRANGEMENTS: ___ Alone ___ With Parent(s) ___ With Spouse
         ___ With Relative(s) ___ With Friend(s)
10. EDUCATION: ___ Less than 8th Grade ___ Less than 12th Grade
          ___ High School Education ___ Other ___ College ___ Graduate School
          IF LESS THAN 12TH GRADE GIVE REASON FOR LEAVING SCHOOL: _____
    _____
11. VOCATIONAL TRAINING COMPLETED: ___ Yes ___ No; Type _____
12. MILITARY SERVICE ___ Yes ___ No; Branch _____
          Type of Discharge _____
          Date of Discharge _____
13. NEAREST CONTACT (Person who would usually know your whereabouts):
          NAME _____ PHONE NO. _____
          ADDRESS _____
               (Street)   (City)   (State)   (ZIP)
          RELATION TO DEFENDANT _____
14. DEFENSE ATTORNEY:
          ADDRESS _____
               (Street)   (City)   (State)   (ZIP)

15. PRESENT EMPLOYER _____ PHONE NO. _____
    ADDRESS _____
           (Street)   (City)   (State)   (ZIP)
    DATE EMPLOYED _____ OCCUPATION _____ SALARY _____

16. EMPLOYMENT HISTORY (Begin with Last Previous Place of Employment)*
    NAME OF EMPLOYER _____ PHONE NO. _____
    ADDRESS _____
           (Street)   (City)   (State)   (ZIP)
    DATES EMPLOYED: From _____ to _____ Occupation _____
    REASON LEFT _____
    NAME OF EMPLOYER _____ PHONE NO. _____
    ADDRESS _____
           (Street)   (City)   (State)   (ZIP)
    DATES EMPLOYED: From _____ to _____ Occupation _____
    REASON LEFT _____

    NAME OF EMPLOYER _____ PHONE NO. _____
    ADDRESS _____
           (Street)   (City)   (State)   (ZIP)
    DATES EMPLOYED: From _____ to _____ Occupation _____
    REASON LEFT _____

    NAME OF EMPLOYER _____ PHONE NO. _____
    ADDRESS _____
           (Street)   (City)   (State)   (ZIP)
    DATES EMPLOYED: From _____ to _____ Occupation _____
    REASON LEFT _____

*List employment for past six years. If you need additional space, use blank sheet of paper.

17. SOURCE OF INCOME ___ Employment (self)   ___ Employment (spouse)
    ___ Unemployment Compensation (amount $_____)
    ___ Public Assistance (amount $_____)   ___ Parents   ___ Relatives   ___ Friends
    ___ Other

18. PRIOR OFFENSE RECORDS: ___ NONE ___ JUVENILE ___ ADULT
    DETAILED CRIMINAL HISTORY (Begin with first arrest)
    <u>DATE</u>   <u>PLACE</u>   <u>CHARGE(S)</u>   <u>DISPOSITION</u>
    _____
    _____
    _____

    I hereby apply for status as a participant in the Pre-Trial Diversion Program and request that the U. S. Attorney temporarily delay further prosecution of me in order to permit consideration of this application.

    I understand that as a condition of my participation in the Pre-Trial Diversion Program I may be required to agree to make restitution to the victim(s) of the actions for which I am accepting responsibility and that any such restitution will be according to a schedule or plan approved by my Pre-Trial Supervisor.

    I further understand that as a condition of my participation in the Pre-Trial Diversion Program, I may be required to agree to perform a specified number of hours of community service for an organization designated by my Pre-Trial Diversion Supervisor and according to a plan approved by my Supervisor.

    I understand that the final decision to commence criminal proceedings or to divert my case from prosecution rests with the United States Attorney.

    I authorize the Pre-Trial Services Agency of the United States District Court for the Western District of Pennsylvania to conduct an investigation to determine my suitability for this program. I understand that any information given by me or authorized by me to be furnished the Pre-Trial Services Agency in connection with this investigation will be kept confidential.

A false answer to any question in this Application will be grounds for recommendation against placement into this program or removal after placement in the program, in which case the United States Attorney will resume prosecution on the original charges.

_____
Applicant's Signature

_____
Date

Form 17-2   Diversion Motion

IN THE UNITED STATES DISTRICT COURT
FOR THE _____ DISTRICT OF _____

UNITED STATES OF AMERICA	)	
v.	)	CRIMINAL NO.
TM	)	

MOTION TO SET CASE OFF COURT CALENDAR

AND NOW comes the United States of America, by its attorneys, Mary Beth Buchanan, United States Attorney for the Western District of Pennsylvania, and _____, Assistant United States Attorney for said District, and, pursuant to Rule 45 of the Federal Rules of Criminal Procedure and Title 18, United States Code, Section 3161(h)(2) (1975), respectfully moves the Court to issue an Order setting the above-captioned case, as to defendant, TM, off the Court calendar pending further motion of either of the parties. In further support of this Motion, the United States avers as follows:

1. Defendant TM has entered into a written agreement with the United States which provides for the deferring of prosecution for a period of twelve (12) months for the purpose of allowing the defendant to demonstrate good conduct and thereby avoid further prosecution of this case. A true and correct copy of said Agreement is attached hereto and marked Exhibit "A".

2. With the approval of the Court, this case may be removed from the Court calendar and returned to the Clerk of Court pending further motion by either of the parties hereto.

WHEREFORE, the United States of America respectfully requests that the Court issue an Order setting the above-captioned case, as to defendant, TM, off the Court calendar pending further motion of either of the parties.

United States Attorney

Assistant U. S. Attorney

Consented to this ___ day of
_____, 200__.

_____
Defendant

_____
Counsel for Defendant

Form 17-3   Diversion Agreement

UNITED STATES OF AMERICA
    v.
TM

_____
Address

_____
City and State

_____
File No.

_____
Telephone No.

AGREEMENT FOR PRE-TRIAL DIVERSION

It appearing that you have committed an offense against the United States from on or about _____, to on or about _____, in violation of Title 18, United States Code, Section 371, in that you are charged with Conspiracy, as set forth in the Indictment attached hereto as Appendix "A".

Upon your accepting responsibility for your behavior and by your signature of this Agreement*, it appearing, after an investigation of the offense, and of your background, that the interest of the United States and your own interest and the interest of justice will be served by the following procedure; therefore on the authority of the Attorney General of the United States, by _____, United States Attorney for the Western District of Pennsylvania, prosecution in this District for this offense shall be deferred for the period of twelve months from this date, provided you abide by the following conditions and requirements of the Pre-Trial Diversion program set out below.

Should you violate the conditions of this supervision, the United States Attorney may revoke or modify any conditions of this pre-trial diversion program or change the period of supervision which shall in no case exceed twelve months. The United States Attorney may release you from supervision at any time. The United States Attorney may, at any time within the period of your supervision, re-initiate prosecution for this offense should you violate the conditions of this supervision. The United States Attorney may re-initiate prosecution for this offense for a reasonable period of time after the period of your supervision has ended for violations that occurred during the period of supervision. If the prosecution is resumed, the United States Attorney will furnish you with notice specifying the conditions of your program which you have violated.

If, upon completion of your period of supervision, a pre-trial diversion report is received to the effect that you have complied with all the rules, regulations and conditions mentioned herein, no further criminal prosecution for the offense set out on page 1 of this Agreement will be pursued in this District, and the Indictment at Criminal No. ____ will be discharged.

Neither this agreement nor any other document filed with the United States Attorney as a result of your participation in the Pre-Trial Diversion Program will be used against you except for impeachment purposes, in connection with any criminal prosecution for the above-described offense.

CONDITIONS OF PRE-TRIAL DIVERSION

(1) You shall not violate any law (federal, state or local). You shall immediately contact your pre-trial diversion supervisor if arrested and/or questioned by any law enforcement officer.
(2) You shall attend school or work regularly at a lawful occupation. When out of work or unable to attend school, you shall notify your program supervisor at once. You shall consult your supervisor prior to job or school changes.
(3) You shall continue to live at the residence address approved by your program supervisor. If you intend to move your residence, you shall inform your supervisor so that the appropriate transfer of program responsibility can be made.
(4) You shall follow the program conditions described below in (7).
(5) You shall report to your program supervisor as directed and keep your supervisor informed of your whereabouts.
(6) You shall strive to achieve the desired goals of the program.

(7) <u>Special Program and/or Condition</u>–
    A. You agree to make restitution in the amount of $300.00 directly to the victims in the case set forth on the Restitution Schedule, and for this purpose you agree to arrange for payment to the victim in a manner and according to a plan or schedule acceptable to your Pre-Trial Diversion Coordinator or Program Supervisor.
    B. You agree to assist law enforcement agencies in investigating violations of federal law during the period from _____ through _____ allegedly committed by the other individuals named in the indictment, hereinafter "the investigation".
    C. You agree to be fully debriefed by personnel of the United States Attorney's Office and Agents from the United States Secret Service.
    D. You agree to provide all information and evidence within your knowledge or control concerning the investigation. All such information will be full, complete, accurate, and truthful. The determination by the United States Attorney as to the completeness, accuracy, and truthfulness of the information and evidence provided shall be final and conclusive.
    E. You agree to submit to a polygraph examination administered by an agent of the federal government if requested to do so by the United States Attorney.
    F. You will, when requested, testify in grand jury, pre-trial, trial, sentencing and post-conviction proceedings in this district and elsewhere.

ACKNOWLEDGEMENT, WAIVER AND ACCEPTANCE

I assert and certify that I am aware of the fact that the Sixth Amendment to the Constitution of the United States provides that in all criminal prosecutions the accused shall enjoy the right to a speedy and public trial.

I am also aware that the Speedy Trial Act, Title 18, United States Code, Section 3161(c)(1) (1975) provides that the trial of a criminal case shall take place within seventy (70) days of the arraignment, _____ in my case, unless delayed as provided by law. I understand that the period of time required for the preparation of the Pre-Trial Services Report concerning my application for consideration for the Pre-Trial Diversion Program and the period of time during which I shall participate in the Pre-Trial Diversion Program are excludable for purposes of the seventy (70) day rule.

I also am aware that Rule 48(b) of the Federal Rules of Criminal Procedure provides that the Court may dismiss an indictment, information or complaint for unnecessary delay in presenting a charge to the Grand Jury, filing an indictment or information or in bringing a defendant to trial.

I hereby request that the United States Attorney for the Western District of Pennsylvania defer any prosecution of me for violation of Title 18, United States Code, Section 371, for the period of twelve months, and to induce her to defer such prosecution, I agree and consent that any delay from the date of prosecution, as provided for in the terms expressed herein, shall be deemed to be a necessary delay at my request, and I waive any defense to such prosecution on the ground that such delay operated to deny my rights under Section 3161(c)(1) of the Speedy Trial Act, Rule 48(b) of the Federal Rules of Criminal Procedure and the Sixth Amendment to the Constitution of the United States to a speedy trial, or to bar the prosecution by reason of the running of the statute of limitations for a period of twelve months, which is the period of this Agreement.

I hereby state that the above has been read and explained to me. I understand the conditions of my pre-trial diversion and agree that I will comply with them.

_____   _____
Defendant   Date

_____   _____
Counsel for Defendant   Date

_____   _____
Assistant U. S. Attorney   Date

_____   _____
Pre-Trial Diversion Coordinator   Date
or Program Supervisor

*Any statement made by you in this Agreement will not be admissible on the issue of guilt in any subsequent criminal proceeding.

Form 17-4   Diversion Order

IN THE UNITED STATES DISTRICT COURT
FOR THE _____ DISTRICT OF _____

UNITED STATES OF AMERICA	)	
v.	)	CRIMINAL NO.
TM	)	

ORDER

AND NOW, to wit, this _____ day of October, 2005, upon consideration of the Motion to Set Case Off Court Calendar, heretofore filed by the United States of American, IT IS HEREBY ORDERED that said Motion is GRANTED.

IT IS FURTHER observed by the Court that the prosecution of defendant, TM, has been deferred for a period of twelve (12) months by the United States Attorney pursuant to a written agreement with the defendant, for the purpose of allowing the defendant to demonstrate good conduct and thereby avoid further prosecution of this case, and that said action of the United states Attorney meets with the approval of this Court.

IT IS FURTHER ORDERED that the case at Criminal No. ___ as to defendant, TM, is hereby set off the calendar of the Court, and IT IS ORDERED that said case is hereby returned to the Clerk of Court pending further motion of the United States Attorney or the defendant, TM.

_____
United States District Judge

cc: Defense Counsel
      United States Attorney
      Pre-Trial Services

Form 17-5   Diversion Restitution Schedule

CASE: United States v. TM
                     Criminal No.

VICTIM(s)

Name:
Address:

AMOUNT OF OBLIGATION:

As a condition of the Pre-Trial Diversion Program to which I have been admitted by Agreement dated _____ , I acknowledge my obligation and agree to make restitution to the victims identified in the amount of $300.00, the present outstanding balance of my obligation, through monthly payments of $25.00, payable at the beginning of every month beginning on _____. Payments will be made by cash, check or money order directly to the victims listed above.

In the event I am unable to make any scheduled payment on time, I will so advise my Pre-Trial Diversion Supervisor in advance in order to make arrangements to satisfy my obligation in a manner acceptable to my Program Supervisor.

I understand that failure to make a good faith effort to pay restitution to the victim(s) according to the schedule to which I have agreed may constitute a violation of the conditions of my Pre-Trial Diversion Agreement, constitute cause for the United States Attorney to terminate the Agreement, and lead to my prosecution for the offenses for which I have been indicted.

_____	_____
Pre-Trial Diversion Supervisor	Date
_____	_____
Defendant	Date

NOTE: THIS SCHEDULE/PLAN IS NOT TO BE ALTERED. IF CHANGES ARE MADE, A NEW SCHEDULE/PLAN IDENTIFIED AS NO. 2, NO. 3, ETC. MUST BE COMPLETED REFLECTING THE NEW SCHEDULE OF PAYMENT OR PLAN FOR PAYMENT OF THE PRESENT OUTSTANDING BALANCE OF THE OBLIGATION. LATE PAYMENT MAY BE AUTHORIZED IF DOCUMENTED BY A NOTATION IN THE CASELOG OF THE PRE-TRIAL SERVICES OFFICE. USE OF LOAN AGREEMENT(S) BETWEEN SUBJECT AND VICTIM(S) IS ACCEPTABLE WHERE APPROPRIATE.

Form 17-6   Sample Plea Agreement (Federal)

COMMENT:

This form includes many of the options that may be chosen in a particular case. Not all will apply to each case.

Re: United States of America v. _____
Criminal No.

Dear:

This letter sets forth the agreement by which your client, _____, will enter a plea of guilty in the above-captioned case. The letter represents the full and complete agreement between and the United States Attorney for the Western District of Pennsylvania. The agreement does not apply to or bind any other federal, state, or local prosecuting authority.

Upon entering a plea of guilty, _____ will be sentenced under the Sentencing Guidelines promulgated by the United States Sentencing Commission and the Sentencing Reform Act, 18 U.S.C. §3551, *et seq.* and 28 U.S.C. §981, *et seq.* The facts relevant to sentencing shall be determined initially by the United States Probation Office and finally by the United States District Court.

A. The defendant, _____, agrees to the following:

1. He will enter a plea of guilty to Count(s) of the Indictment/Information at Criminal No. ____, charging him with violating _____, pursuant to Rule 11 of the Federal Rules of Criminal Procedure.

2. He acknowledges his responsibility for the conduct charged in Count(s) _____ of the Indictment/Information at Criminal No. _____ and stipulates that the conduct charged in that/those count(s) may be considered by the Probation Office or by the District Court in imposing sentence.

3. He will assist law enforcement agencies in investigating violations of _____ during the period from _____ to _____ [allegedly committed by _____] [and others] hereinafter "the investigation." [Such assistance will include but is not limited to **[DESCRIBE THE TYPE OF ASSISTANCE, IF KNOWN, E.G. (undercover introductions) (wearing a body recording device) (tape recording telephone conversation) (immediately reporting criminal activity by _____ and others to federal/ state/local law enforcement authorities).]**

4. He will be fully debriefed by personnel of the United States Attorney's Office and/or Special Agents of the _____ and/or representatives of other federal, state or local law enforcement agencies as may be determined by the United States Attorney.

5. He will provide all information and evidence within his knowledge or control concerning the investigation. All such information will be full, complete, accurate and truthful. The determination of the United States Attorney as to the completeness, accuracy, and truthfulness of the information and evidence provided shall be final and conclusive.

6. He will provide all documents and/or physical evidence within his possession concerning the investigation, including but not limited to **[DESCRIBE THE DOCUMENTS OR PHYSICAL EVIDENCE IF KNOWN].**

7. He will submit to a polygraph examination administered by an agent of the federal government if requested to do so by the United States Attorney.

8. He will, when requested, testify in grand jury, pre-trial, trial, sentencing and post-conviction proceedings in this district and elsewhere.

9. He will pay [mandatory] restitution under the Victim-Witness Protection Act, 18 U.S.C. §§3663, [3663A] and 3664, to the victims and/or other persons or parties authorized by law in such amounts, at such times, and according to such terms as the court shall direct. [The amount of restitution may not necessarily be the same as the amount of loss for the purpose of determining the offense level under the Sentencing Guidelines.] [Although the court will determine the recipients, amounts, times, and terms of restitution payments, the parties agree to make the recommendations set forth in Part C of this agreement.]

10. He will immediately notify the court and the United States Attorney of any improvement in his economic circumstances that might increase his ability to pay restitution and that occurs from the date of this agreement until the completion of his sentence, including any term of supervised release.

11. He will voluntarily forfeit to the United States all property subject to forfeiture under U.S.C. § ___ [including but not limited to the following: _____.]

12. He acknowledges that the above-described property. **[DESCRIBE THE BASIS FOR THE FORFEITURE, E.G., CONSTITUTES PROCEEDS OF THE OFFENSE OF _____.]**

13. He acknowledges that the above-described property is presently the subject of a Civil Forfeiture Action filed by the United States at Civil Action No. _____. He hereby consents to the entry of judgment of forfeiture in the civil action and waives any former jeopardy or double jeopardy claims in or as a result of the civil forfeiture action.

14. He acknowledges that the above-described property is presently the subject of a Criminal Forfeiture action at the above-captioned criminal case number and he herewith voluntarily consents to the District Court entering an order of forfeiture of said property to the United States.

15. He agrees that the United States is not limited to forfeiture of the property described above. If the United States determines that property of the defendant identified for forfeiture cannot be located upon the exercise of due diligence; has been transferred or sold to, or deposited with, a third party; has been placed beyond the jurisdiction of the Court; has substantially diminished in value; or has been commingled with other property which cannot be divided without difficulty; then the United States shall, at its option, be entitled to forfeiture of any other property (substitute assets) of the defendant up to the value of any property described above. The district court shall retain jurisdiction to settle any disputes arising from application of this clause. The defendant agrees that forfeiture of substitute assets as authorized herein and pursuant to 21 U.S.C. §853(p) shall not be deemed an alteration of the defendant's sentence. Forfeiture of the defendant's assets shall not be treated as satisfaction of any fine, restitution, cost of imprisonment, or any other penalty the district court may impose upon the defendant in addition to forfeiture.

16. Upon request of the United States, he agrees to provide all information regarding his income, assets and financial status. He agrees to [submit to interviews as to these matters/complete a financial statement under oath/submit to a polygraph examination].

17. If the Court imposes a fine or restitution as part of a sentence of incarceration, _____ agrees to participate in the United States Bureau of Prisons' Inmate Financial Responsibility Program, through which 50% of his prison salary will be applied to pay the fine or restitution.

18. At the time _____ enters his plea of guilty, he will deposit a special assessment of $_____ in the form of cash, or check or money order payable to "Clerk, U.S. District Court". In the event that sentence is not ultimately imposed, the special assessment deposit will be returned.

19. He will not object to the introduction in evidence by the United States of the report prepared by _____ of the **[E.G., INTERNAL REVENUE SERVICE, CRIMINAL INVESTIGATION DIVISION]**, which will, <u>inter alia</u>, serve as the factual basis for the guilty plea.

20. He stipulates to the release of the report prepared by _____ of the **[E.G., INTERNAL REVENUE SERVICE, CRIMINAL INVESTIGATION DIVISION]**, together with any and all accompanying exhibits to the **[E.G., EXAMINATION DIVISION OF THE INTERNAL REVENUE SERVICE]**. He understands that the information contained in the report will be utilized by the _____ in order to determine his civil liability.

B. In consideration of and entirely contingent upon the provisions of Parts A and C of this agreement, the United States Attorney for the Western District of Pennsylvania agrees to the following:

1. After the imposition of sentence, the United States Attorney will move to dismiss the remaining Count(s) of the Indictment/Information at Criminal No. _____, without prejudice to its/their reinstatement if, at any time, _____ is permitted to withdraw his plea of guilty. In that event, _____ waives any double jeopardy, statute of limitations, speedy trial, or similar objections to the reinstatement of the counts dismissed pursuant to this agreement.

2. Pursuant to Section 1B1.8 of the Sentencing Guidelines, the United States Attorney will not use against _____ any information or evidence provided by him in the course of his assistance in the investigation.

3. In his/her discretion, the United States Attorney may apply for a formal grant of use immunity under Title 18, United States Code, Sections 6002 and 6003, in connection with _____'s testimony before a federal grand jury or in a court proceeding.

4. Prior to sentencing, the United States Attorney will orally or in writing advise the court of his evaluation of the nature, extent, completeness, accuracy, truthfulness and value of the assistance and testimony of _____. This evaluation is committed to the sound discretion of the United States Attorney.

5. The United States Attorney retains the right of allocution at the time of sentencing to advise the sentencing court of the full nature and extent of the involvement of _____ in the offense(s) charged in the Indictment/Information and of any other matters relevant to the imposition of a fair and just sentence.

6. The United States Attorney will make no recommendation as to the specific sentence that the Court should impose, but will provide the United States Probation Office and the District Court with any and all information pertaining to sentencing, including but not limited to all relevant conduct. The United States Attorney also reserves the right to make legal and factual argument as to the provisions of the Sentencing Guidelines, including those provisions concerning the guideline range or upward or downward departures from the guideline range. The United States Attorney will not make any recommendation as to what sentence should be imposed within the guideline range or whether the Court should exercise its discretionary authority to depart upward or downward from the guideline range.

7. The United States Attorney will take no position as to whether the base offense level shall be adjusted under Section ___ of Chapter 2 of the Sentencing Guidelines.

8. The United States Attorney will take no position as to whether the offense level of _____ will be increased under the following section(s) of the Sentencing Guidelines:
   a) 3A1.1 (Vulnerable Victim);
   b) 3A1.2 (Official Victim);
   c) 3A1.3 (Restraint of Victim);
   d) 3B1.1 (Aggravating Role);
   e) 3B1.3 (Abuse of Position of Trust or Special Skill);
   f) 3C1.1 (Willfully Obstructing or Impeding Proceedings);
   g) 3C1.2 (Reckless Endangerment During Flight);
   h) 3D1.1–3D1.5 (Multiple Counts);
   i) 4B1.1 (Career Offender);
   j) 4B1.3 (Criminal Livelihood).

9. Prior to sentencing, the United States Attorney will, orally or in writing, recommend to the court that the base offense level be/not be adjusted under Section _____ of Chapter 2 of the Sentencing Guidelines.

10. Prior to sentencing, the United States Attorney will, orally or in writing, recommend to the court that the offense level of _____ not be increased under the following section(s) of the Sentencing Guidelines:
   a) 3A1.1 (Vulnerable Victim);
   b) 3A1.2 (Official Victim);
   c) 3A1.3 (Restraint of Victim);
   d) 3B1.1 (Aggravating Role);
   e) 3B1.3 (Abuse of Position of Trust or Special Skill);
   f) 3C1.1 (Willfully Obstructing or Impeding Proceedings);
   g) 3C1.2 (Reckless Endangerment During Flight);
   h) 3D1.1–3D1.5 (Multiple Counts);
   i) 4B1.1 (Career Offender);
   j) 4B1.3 (Criminal Livelihood).
   This recommendation is not binding on the District Court.

11. Prior to sentencing, the United States Attorney will, orally or in writing, recommend to the court that _____ be given a sentence at the high/medium/low point of the applicable guideline range. This recommendation is not binding on the court.

12. Prior to sentencing, the United States Attorney will, orally or in writing, recommend that, pursuant to Section 3B1.2 of the Sentencing Guidelines, the court reduce the offense level by ____ level(s) on the ground that the defendant played a minor/minimal role in the offense(s). This recommendation is not binding on the court.

13. Prior to sentencing, the United States Attorney will, orally or in writing, recommend that, pursuant to Section 3E1.1 of the Sentencing Guidelines, the court reduce the offense level by two levels for acceptance of responsibility on the ground(s) that:
   a) Voluntarily terminated or withdrew from criminal conduct or association;
   b) Voluntarily paid restitution prior to adjudication of guilt;

    c)   Voluntarily and truthfully admitted to authorities his involvement in the offense and related conduct;

    d)   Voluntarily surrendered to authorities promptly after the commission of the offense(s);

    e)   Voluntarily assisted authorities in the recovery of the fruits and instrumentalities of the offense(s);

    f)   Voluntarily resigned from the office or position held during the commission of the offense;

    g)   Timely manifested acceptance of responsibility.

14. Prior to sentencing, the United States Attorney will, orally or in writing, recommend that, pursuant to Section 3E1.1 of the Sentencing Guidelines, the court reduce the offense level by three levels for acceptance of responsibility, on the grounds that the offense level prior to application of Section 3E1.1 is 16 or greater, and:

    a)   Timely provided complete information to the government concerning his own involvement in the offense;

    b)   Timely notified authorities of his intention to enter a plea of guilty, thereby permitting the government to avoid preparing for trial and permitting the court to allocate its resources efficiently.

15. Prior to sentencing, the United States Attorney will, orally or in writing, recommend that, pursuant to Section 5K1.1 of the Sentencing Guidelines, the court impose a sentence below the applicable guideline range on the ground that _____ provided substantial assistance in the investigation or prosecution of another person. This recommendation is not binding on the court.

16. Prior to sentencing, the United States Attorney will, orally or in writing, recommend that, pursuant to Title 18, United States Code, Section 3553(e), the court impose a sentence below the applicable mandatory minimum sentence, on the ground that _____ provided substantial assistance in the investigation or prosecution of another person. This recommendation is not binding on the court.

17. Prior to sentencing, the United States Attorney will, orally or in writing, recommend that, pursuant to Section 5K2.0 of the Sentencing Guidelines, the court impose a sentence below the applicable guideline range on the ground that [**DESCRIBE IN DETAIL THE REASONS FOR THE DEPARTURE**]. This recommendation is not binding on the court.

18. Within one year of the imposition of sentence, the United States Attorney will review the timeliness, nature, extent, completeness, accuracy, truthfulness of the assistance and testimony of _____. If the United States Attorney determines _____ has provided substantial assistance in the investigation or prosecution of other persons, the United States Attorney may, in his/her discretion, file a motion under Rule 35(b), Federal Rules of Criminal Procedure, advising the District Court of the assistance to law enforcement authorities. _____ has no right to compel, require or expect that the United States Attorney will file such a motion, however, and the decision to reduce the sentence of _____ below the applicable guideline range or any mandatory minimum sentence is solely in the discretion of the District Court.

19. At the time of sentencing, if his cooperation has been completed, or within one year of the imposition of sentence, the United States Attorney will review the timeliness, nature, extent, completeness, accuracy, and truthfulness of the assistance and testimony of _____. If the United States Attorney determines _____ has provided substantial assistance in the investigation or prosecution of other persons, the United States Attorney may, in his/her discretion, file a motion pursuant to §5K1.1 of the Sentencing Guidelines [and 18 U.S.C. §3553(e)] or under Rule 35(b), Federal Rules of Criminal Procedure, advising the District Court of the assistance to law enforcement authorities. _____ has no right to compel, require or expect that the United States Attorney will file such a motion, however, and the decision to reduce the sentence of _____ below the applicable guideline range or any mandatory minimum sentence is solely in the discretion of the District Court.

20. The United States Attorney will take any position he/she deems appropriate in the course of any appeals from the sentence or in response to any post-sentence motions.

21. Should there be a request by _____, the United States Attorney will submit to the United States Marshals Service an application for acceptance of _____, together with members of his immediate family, into the Witness Protection Program. The decision to accept _____ into said program is solely within the discretion of the United States Marshals Service.

22. In the event that a term of imprisonment is imposed upon _____, the United States Attorney will recommend to the United States Bureau of Prisons that _____ be placed in a secure institution, so as to afford him all reasonable personal security. The decision to accept _____ into said program, together with the place of confinement, is solely within the discretion of the United States Bureau of Prisons.

C. _____ and the United States Attorney further understand and agree to the following:

   1. The maximum penalty that may be imposed upon _____ is:

  a) A term of imprisonment of ___ years;

  b) A fine of $_____;

  c) A term of supervised release of ____ years;

  d) A special assessment under 18 U.S.C. §3013 of $____;

  e) [Mandatory] restitution under the Victim-Witness Protection Act, 18 U.S.C. §§3663, [3663A] and 3664.

2. The district court shall determine the victims and/or other persons or parties authorized by law who will receive restitution. The court shall also determine the amount of restitution for which _____ is liable and the times and terms of payment. Subject to the final authority of the court, the parties agree to the following recommendations:

  a) [_____ and his co-defendants][is/are] liable for a total of $_____ in restitution [to _____].

  b) The total amount of restitution shall be apportioned among the defendants so that _____ is liable for _____.

  c) [In light of _____'s present financial circumstances,] restitution should be paid [to _____] in the amounts indicated according to the [attached schedule/following schedule:].

  d) [In light of _____'s present financial circumstances,] restitution should be paid [to_____] in amounts of per month, together with such lump sum payments necessary to reach the total amount of _____ prior to the completion of _____'s sentence, including any term of supervised release.

  e) In light of _____'s present financial circumstances and subject to any improvement in those circumstances, he should be directed to make nominal periodic payments as follows: _____.

3. The parties stipulate that _____. This stipulation represents the parties' best understanding on the basis of the information available as of the date of this agreement. The stipulation is not binding on the District Court and does not preclude either party from bringing to the attention of the United States Probation Office or the District Court any information not within his knowledge at the time this agreement is executed.

4. The attached stipulation of fact represents the parties' best understanding of the facts on the basis of information available as of the date of this agreement. The stipulation is not binding on the District Court, and has no bearing on any fact not expressly set forth in the stipulation. The stipulation does not preclude either party from bringing to the attention of the United States Probation Office or the District Court any information not within his knowledge at the time this agreement is executed.

5. The parties agree that the attached stipulation is a complete and accurate account of the offense conduct, including all relevant conduct, and therefore that under Section ____ of the Sentencing Guidelines, the base offense level is _____. The parties further agree that the base offense level of _____ should be raised/lowered by ___ levels under Section ___ of Chapter 2 of the Guidelines.

6. The parties further agree that the adjusted base offense level should be raised by a total of ____ level(s) under the following Section(s) of the Guidelines:

  a) 3A1.1 (Vulnerable Victim);

  b) 3A1.2 (Official Victim);

  c) 3A1.3 (Restraint of Victim);

  d) 3B1.1 (Aggravating Role);

  e) 3B1.3 (Abuse of Position of Trust or Special Skill);

  f) 3C1.1 (Willfully Obstructing or Impeding Proceedings);

  g) 3C1.2 (Reckless Endangerment During Flight);

  h) 4B1.1 (Career Offender);

  i) 4B1.3 (Criminal Livelihood).

7. The parties also agree that the adjusted base offense level should be lowered by a total of _____ level(s) under the following Section(s) of the Guidelines:

  a) 3B1.2 (Mitigating Role);

  b) 3E1.1 (Acceptance of Responsibility).

8. Thus, the parties agree that _____'s overall offense level under the Sentencing Guidelines is _____. If _____ is sentenced on the basis of an offense level of _____, he and the United States Attorney waive their respective rights to appeal the sentence under Title 18, United States Code, Section 3742.

9. The parties agree that the appropriate sentence in this case is a term of imprisonment of _____ years, a fine of _____, a term of supervised release of _____, a special assessment of _____, and

restitution of _____. This sentence is within the guideline range/is a departure from the guideline range for the following reasons: _____. If the district court imposes this sentence, the defendant and the United States Attorney waive their respective rights to appeal the sentence under Title 18, United States Code, Section 3742.

10. Under Rule 11(e)(1)(B) of the Federal Rules of Criminal Procedure, and Section 6B1.2(b) of the Sentencing Guidelines, the district court is not bound by the agreed upon-sentence. Even if the court does not accept the sentence, the other provisions of this agreement remain in full force and effect.

11. Under Sections 6B1.2(c) and 6B1.3 of the Sentencing Guidelines, the district court is not bound by the agreed-upon sentence. If, however, the court rejects the sentence, the court must allow _____ to withdraw his plea of guilty.

12. The parties understand that, pursuant to Title 21, United States Code, Section 862, the district court may, in its discretion, order that the defendant be ineligible [permanently/for a period of ___ year(s)] for all Federal benefits as defined in Section 862(d).

13. If, at any time, the United States Attorney determines that _____ has provided any information or evidence that is not full, complete, accurate, and truthful, or that _____ has not provided assistance or testimony upon request, the obligations of the United States Attorney under this agreement are terminated. In that event, the government may prosecute _____ on charges it has agreed to dismiss or has dismissed, and it may use against _____ information and/or evidence obtained from him. The government may also prosecute _____ for perjury or obstruction of justice. Any plea of guilty previously entered will stand, however, and _____ will not have the right to withdraw the plea of guilty by virtue of his breach of this agreement.

14. The parties agree that the willful failure to pay any fine imposed by the court may be treated as a breach of this plea agreement. _____ acknowledges that the willful failure to pay any fine may subject him to additional criminal and civil penalties under Title 18, United States Code, Section 3611 *et seq.*

15. This agreement does not preclude the government from pursuing any civil or administrative remedies against _____ or his property.

16. _____ waives any former jeopardy or double jeopardy claims [he/she] may have in or as a result of any related civil or administrative actions.

17. The parties agree that, although charges are to be dismissed pursuant to this agreement, _____ is not a prevailing party for the purpose of seeking attorney fees or other litigation expenses under Pub. L. No. 105-119, Section 617 (Nov. 26, 1997) (known as the Hyde Amendment). _____ waives any right to recover attorney fees or other litigation expenses under the Hyde Amendment.

18. The parties agree that _____'s plea of guilty is conditioned upon his preservation for appeal of the following issue(s): _____. If _____ takes a timely appeal from the judgment of conviction and sentence to the United States Court of Appeals for the Third Circuit and prevails upon the above-stated issue(s), he may, upon remand, withdraw his plea of guilty. If _____ does not take a timely appeal or does not prevail upon the above-stated issue(s), his plea shall stand.

This letter sets forth the full and complete terms and conditions of the agreement between _____ and the United States Attorney for the Western District of Pennsylvania, and there are no other agreements, promises, terms or conditions, express or implied.

Very truly yours,

United States Attorney

I have received this letter from my attorney, _____, Esquire, have read it and discussed it with him, and I hereby accept it and acknowledge that it fully sets forth my agreement with the Office of the United States Attorney for the Western District of Pennsylvania. I affirm that there have been no additional promises or representations made to me by any agents or officials of the United States in connection with this matter.

_____

_____

Date

Witnessed by:

_____

Counsel for

Form 17-7   Sample Plea Agreement (Federal) With Cooperation and Stipulated Factual Basic

**UNITED STATES DISTRICT COURT
FOR THE DISTRICT OF COLUMBIA**

UNITED STATES OF AMERICA	:	**Criminal Number:**
	:	
	:	**VIOLATIONS:**
	:	
	:	**Count One:**
	:	**18 U.S.C. § 371**
v.	:	**(Conspiracy)**
	:	
JACK A. ABRAMOFF,	:	**Count Two:**
	:	**18 U.S.C. §§ 1341, 1346 and 2**
Defendant.	:	**(Honest Services Mail Fraud)**
	:	
	:	**Count Three:**
	:	**26 U.S.C. § 7201**
	:	**(Tax Evasion)**

PLEA AGREEMENT

Pursuant to Rule 11 of the Federal Rules of Criminal Procedure, the United States of America and the defendant, JACK A. ABRAMOFF, agree as follows:

1.   The defendant is entering into this agreement and is pleading guilty freely and voluntarily without promise or benefit of any kind, other than contained herein, and without threats, force, intimidation, or coercion of any kind.

2.   The defendant knowingly, voluntarily and truthfully admits the facts contained in the attached Factual Basis for Plea.

3.   The defendant agrees to waive indictment and plead guilty to the offenses charged in the attached Information which are:

A.   one count of conspiracy to violate the following federal laws in violation of 18 U.S.C. § 371:

       (1)   honest services wire and mail fraud, in violation of Title 18 U.S.C. §§ 1341, 1343 and 1346;

       (2)   mail and wire fraud, in violation of 18 U.S.C. §§ 1341 and 1343;

       (3)   bribery and honest services fraud of public officials, in violation of 18 U.S.C. §§ 201(b), 1341, 1343 and 1346;

       (4)   post-employment restrictions for former Congressional staff members, in violation of 18 U.S.C. § 207(e);

    B.   one count of honest services mail fraud, in violation of 18 U.S.C. §§ 1341, 1346 and 2; and

    C.   one count of evasion of federal income tax, in violation of 26 U.S.C. § 7201.

The defendant admits that he is guilty of these crimes, and the defendant understands that he will be adjudicated guilty of these offenses if the Court accepts his guilty plea.

    4. The defendant understands the nature of the offenses to which he is pleading guilty, and the elements thereof, including the penalties provided by law. The maximum penalty for violating the law specified in the Information is:

    A.   Count 1 (Conspiracy): five years of imprisonment, a fine of $250,000 or not more than the greater of twice the gross gain or twice the gross loss, and a mandatory special assessment of $100;

    B.   Count 2 (Honest Services Mail Fraud): twenty years of imprisonment, a fine of $250,000 or not more than the greater of twice the gross gain or twice the gross loss, and a mandatory special assessment of $100;

2

C.   Count 3 (Tax Evasion): five years of imprisonment, a fine of $250,000 or

not more than the greater of twice the gross gain or twice the gross loss, the

costs of prosecution, and a mandatory special assessment of $100;

The parties understand that the statutory maximum term of imprisonment for the three offenses

charged in the Information is 30 years. The defendant understands that the Court may impose a

term of supervised release to follow any incarceration, in accordance with 18 U.S.C. § 3583. The

authorized term of supervised release for each of the counts is not more than three years. The

defendant also understands that the Court will impose restitution, and may impose costs of

incarceration, supervision and prosecution.

5. The defendant understands and agrees that restitution to victims in the offense described

in Count 1 of the Information is mandatory. The loss to the victims as a result of crimes charged in

Count 1 of the Information is estimated to be approximately $25,000,000. The defendant agrees not

to transfer or otherwise encumber his assets except with notice to, and consent of, the undersigned

representatives of the United States until such time as this agreement is filed with the Court, at

which point the defendant must seek leave of Court to transfer or otherwise encumber his assets.

The parties agree that the defendant will not be required to obtain the consent of the United States

for property transfers necessary to pay ordinary living expenses, ordinary business expenses and

attorneys fees. The defendant agrees as part of this agreement that he will provide to the United

States detailed and accurate information identifying all of his income, assets, expenses and

liabilities within 45 days of the date of this agreement in a format requested by the United States

and will truthfully answer all questions relative to his finances. Thereafter, the defendant will

3

provide on a monthly basis or as otherwise requested a report of all financial transactions valued at $2,500 or more, including all income, expenditures and transfers of funds or property.

6. This agreement does not resolve the defendant's civil tax liability for any years and does not bind the Internal Revenue Service in any way regarding its efforts to examine or collect defendant's civil tax liabilities. The defendant agrees that he will cooperate fully with the Internal Revenue Service in determining any tax liabilities (civil or criminal) of any entities or persons for any years relating to this prosecution, including but not limited to his personal tax liabilities for the years 2000 through 2003, and in paying all appropriate tax liabilities, penalties and interest. To this end, the defendant specifically agrees to file complete and accurate amended individual income tax returns, Forms 1040X, for tax years 2000 through 2003, as soon as possible upon the signing of this plea agreement, and in any event, no later than the time of the defendant's sentencing. If for any reason complete and accurate returns, prepared in accordance with the revenue agent's report dated November 28, 2005, are not filed by the time of defendant's sentencing, the United States will no longer be bound by the terms of paragraph 11(c) below. The defendant further agrees to waive the statute of limitations with respect to the assessment and collection of his taxes due and owing for these tax years. The defendant also agrees to provide the Internal Revenue Service with all requested documents and information for purposes of any civil audits, examinations, collections, or other proceedings, and to waive any rights regarding disclosure to the Internal Revenue Service Examination and Collection Divisions of all documents obtained and reports produced during the criminal investigation, including but not limited to tax return related information and information obtained from the defendant pursuant to grand jury subpoena. Nothing in this agreement shall limit the Internal Revenue Service in its assessment and collection of any taxes, penalties and interest

4

due from the defendant or other parties. The defendant agrees to waive venue for any tax charges

for purpose of this plea agreement and any rights he may have under 18 U.S.C. § 3237(b).

7. The defendant also agrees to pay restitution to the Internal Revenue Service pursuant to

18 U.S.C. § 3663(a)(3). The defendant further agrees that, pursuant to 18 U.S.C. § 3663(a)(3) and

this agreement, the Court will order as restitution the amount of the criminal tax computation which

the defendant agrees is $1,724,054, and which will be applied to the defendant's civil tax liability

for the years 2001 through 2003, as later determined by the Internal Revenue Service.

8. If the Court accepts the defendant's plea of guilty and the defendant fulfills each of the

terms and conditions of this agreement, the United States agrees that it will not further prosecute

the defendant for crimes described in the factual basis attached as Exhibit A or disclosed by the

defendant in debriefing sessions with the United States on or before January 3, 2006. Nothing in

this agreement is intended to provide any limitation of liability arising out of any acts of violence.

9. The defendant understands and agrees that federal sentencing law requires the Court to

impose a sentence which is reasonable and that the Court must consider the advisory U.S.

Sentencing Guidelines in effect at the time of the sentencing in determining a reasonable sentence.

Defendant also understands that sentencing is within the discretion of the Court and that the Court

is not bound by this agreement. Defendant understands that facts that determine the offense level

will be found by the Court at sentencing and that in making those determinations the Court may

consider any reliable evidence, including hearsay, as well as provisions or stipulations in this plea

agreement. Both parties agree to recommend that the sentencing guidelines should apply pursuant

to United States v. Booker and the final Sentencing Guidelines offense level as calculated herein

provides for a reasonable sentence. Defendant further understands the obligation of the United

5

States to provide all relevant information regarding the defendant, including charged and uncharged criminal offenses, to the United States Probation Office. The United States agrees to recommend that any sentence imposed in this case run concurrently to any sentence imposed in <u>United States v. Jack A. Abramoff</u>, No. 05 CR 60204 (SDFL) ("SDFL Case"). Moreover, the United States agrees to recommend that the conduct at issue in the SDFL Case is not relevant conduct for sentencing purposes in the instant plea provided that the defendant is found guilty in the SDFL Case by plea or otherwise. Defendant also states that he has had ample opportunity to discuss, and has in fact discussed, the impact of the sentencing guidelines and the statutory maximum sentence with his attorney and is satisfied with his attorney's advice in this case.

10. Except to the extent it would be inconsistent with other provisions of this agreement, the United States and the defendant reserve, at the time of sentencing, the right of allocution, that is the right to describe fully, both orally and in writing, to the Court the nature, seriousness and impact of the defendant's misconduct related to the charges against him or to any factor lawfully pertinent to the sentence in this case. The United States will also advise the court of the nature, extent and timing of the defendant's cooperation. The defendant further understands and agrees that in exercising this right, the United States may solicit and make known the views of the law enforcement agencies which investigated this matter.

11. The defendant and the United States agree that the following United States Sentencing Guidelines ("U.S.S.G.") apply based upon the facts of this case:

a. The parties agree that the 2003 Sentencing Guidelines Manual governs the guideline calculations in this case. All references in this agreement to the U.S.S.G. refer to that manual.

6

           b. The parties agree that the total offense level applicable to the defendant's offense conduct is Level 31. This level is calculated as follows:

I. Fraud Offenses:

Base Offense level § 2B1.1	6
§ 2B1.1(b)(1)(L) loss of more than $20,000,000	22
§ 3B1.1(c) organizer or leader	2
§ 3B1.3 abuse of trust	2
	32

II. Corruption Offenses:

Base Offense level § 2C1.1	10
§ 2C1.1(b)(1) more than one bribe	2
§ 2C1.1(b)(2)(b) involving a high level public official	8
§ 3B1.1(a) organizer or leader or was involving more than five participants or was otherwise extensive	4
	24

III. Tax Offense

Base Offense Level § 2T4.1 tax loss of more than $1,000,000 but less than $2,500,000	22
§ 2T1.1(b)(1) failure to identify the source of income from criminal activity	2
§ 2T1.1(b)(2) sophisticated means	2
	26

IV. Treatment of Multiple Counts/Objects

§3D1.4 (2 total) $\underline{2}$
                                                      34

VII. Expected Adjustment under § 3E1.1 $\underline{-3}$

TOTAL   31 (108-135 months)

       c. As indicated above, the United States agrees that it will recommend that the Court reduce by three levels the sentencing guideline applicable to the defendant's offense, pursuant to U.S.S.G § 3E1.1, based upon the defendant's recognition and affirmative and timely acceptance of personal responsibility. The United States, however, will not be required to make these recommendations if any of the following occurs: (1) defendant fails or refuses to make a full, accurate and complete disclosure to this office or the probation office of the circumstances surrounding the relevant offense conduct and his present financial condition; (2) defendant is found to have misrepresented facts to the United States prior to entering this plea agreement; (3) defendant commits any misconduct after entering into this plea agreement, including but not limited to, committing a state or federal offense, violating any term of release, or making false statements or misrepresentations to any governmental entity or official; or (4) defendant fails to comply with any terms of this plea agreement.

       d. The defendant understands that his Criminal History Category will be determined by the Court after the completion of a Pre-Sentence Investigation by the U.S. Probation Office. The defendant acknowledges that the United States has not promised or agreed that the defendant will or will not fall within any particular criminal history category and that such determinations could affect his guideline range and/or offense level as well as his final sentence. The parties understand

8

that the order in which the pleas are entered or sentences are imposed in the SDFL Case and the instant matter could result in the imposition of an additional criminal history category and an increased period of incarceration. Consequently, if a plea or sentence in the SDFL Case results in a criminal history category greater than I, and the defendant has fully complied with all provisions in this agreement, the United States agrees to recommend a downward departure based on U.S.S.G. Section 4A1.3(b).

12. The defendant and the United States agree that neither party will seek or advocate for or suggest in any way an adjustment to or a departure from the sentencing guidelines other than those explicitly set forth in this agreement or for a sentence outside of the range determined to be applicable under the advisory Sentencing Guidelines, provided that those guidelines are calculated as set forth above. In the event that the defendant breaches any term of the plea agreement, the United States may move for upward departures based on any grounds the United States deems appropriate.

13. The parties agree that U.S.S.G. § 5E1.2 provides that the Court shall impose a fine for a guideline offense at level 31 of $15,000 to $150,000, unless the Court finds that the defendant is unable to pay a fine. The defendant understands that the Court must order that the defendant make restitution to victims of these offenses for the full amount of the loss.

14. The defendant agrees to fully cooperate in this and any other case or investigation with attorneys for the United States of America, and federal and state law enforcement agencies by providing truthful and complete information, evidence and testimony, if required, concerning any matter. The defendant understands that if he makes material false statements intentionally to law enforcement, commits perjury, suborns perjury, or obstructs justice, he may be found to have

9

breached this agreement and nothing in this agreement precludes the United States of America or any other law enforcement authority from prosecuting him fully for those crimes or any other crimes of which he may be guilty and from using any of his sworn or unsworn statements against him. The defendant understands that this plea agreement is explicitly dependent upon his providing completely truthful testimony in any trial or other proceeding, whether called as a witness by the United States, the defense or the Court.

15. Further, in the event that the United States determines in its exclusive discretion that the defendant has fully complied with this agreement and provided "substantial assistance" to law enforcement officers in the investigation and prosecution of others, the United States agrees it will file a motion for a downward departure pursuant to Section 5K1.1 and 18 U.S.C. § 3553(e) of the United States Sentencing Guidelines or Rule 35 of the Federal Rules of Criminal Procedure, respectively. Such assistance by the defendant shall include his cooperation in providing truthful and complete testimony before any grand jury and at any trial as requested by the United States and in interviews by investigators. If the United States files a motion either under § 5K1.1 of the guidelines or Rule 35, both parties will have the right to present facts regarding Abramoff's cooperation in any judicial district and to argue for the extent of the departure that is appropriate based on the defendant's cooperation. However, the defendant further understands that the decision whether to depart, and the extent of any departure for substantial assistance is the exclusive province of the Court.

16. The United States cannot and does not make any promise or representation as to what sentence the defendant will receive or what fines or restitution the defendant may be ordered to pay. The defendant understands that the sentence in this case will be determined solely by the Court,

10

with the assistance of the United States Probation Office and that the Court may impose the maximum sentence permitted by the law. The Court is not obligated to follow the recommendations of either party at the time of sentencing. The defendant will not be permitted to withdraw his plea regardless of the sentence recommended by the Probation Office or the sentence imposed by the Court.

17. The defendant, knowing and understanding all of the facts set out herein, including the maximum possible penalty that could be imposed, and knowing and understanding his right to appeal the sentence as provided in 18 U.S.C. § 3742, hereby expressly waives the right to appeal any sentence within the maximum provided in the statutes of conviction or the manner in which that sentence was determined and imposed, including on the grounds set forth in 18 U.S.C. § 3742, in exchange for the concessions made by the United States in this plea agreement. This agreement does not affect the rights or obligations of the United States as set forth in 18 U.S.C. § 3742(b). If the United States appeals the defendant's sentence, the defendant will be entitled to appeal his sentence as set forth in 18 U.S.C. § 3742(a) as to any aspects of his sentence inconsistent with the sentencing provisions of this agreement.

18. If the defendant fails to comply with any of the terms and conditions set forth in this agreement, the United States may fully prosecute the defendant on all criminal charges that can be brought against the defendant. With respect to such a prosecution:

a. The defendant shall assert no claim under the United States Constitution, any statute, Rule 410 of the Federal Rules of Evidence, Rule 11(e)(6) of the Federal Rules of Criminal Procedure, or any other federal rule, that the defendant's statements pursuant to this agreement or any leads derived therefrom should be suppressed or are inadmissible;

11

b. The defendant waives any right to claim that evidence presented in such prosecution is tainted by virtue of the statements the defendant has made; and

c. The defendant waives any and all defenses based on the statute of limitations with respect to any such prosecution that is not time-barred on the date that this agreement is signed by the parties.

19. If a dispute arises as to whether defendant has knowingly committed any material breach of this agreement, and the United States chooses to exercise its rights under Paragraph 18, at the defendant's request, the matter shall be submitted to the Court for its determination in an appropriate proceeding. At such proceeding, the defendant's disclosures and documents shall be admissible and the United States shall have the burden to establish the defendant's breach by a preponderance of the evidence.

20. The parties agree that if the Court does not accept the defendant's plea of guilty, then this agreement shall be null and void.

21. The defendant understands that this agreement is binding only upon the Public Integrity Section and the Fraud Section of the Criminal Division, and the Tax Division of the United States Department of Justice. This agreement does not bind any other prosecutor's office or agency. It does not bar or compromise any civil claim that has been or may be made against the defendant.

22. This agreement and the attached Factual Basis for Plea constitute the entire agreement between the United States and the defendant. No other promises, agreements, or representations exist or have been made to the defendant or the defendant's attorneys by the Department of Justice

in connection with this case. This agreement may be amended only by a writing signed by all

parties.

FOR THE DEFENDANT
Dated: _____1/3/06_____

_____
JACK A. ABRAMOFF
Defendant

_____
ABBE DAVID LOWELL, ESQ.
Counsel for Defendant

13

FOR THE UNITED STATES

Dated: 1/3/06

NOEL L. HILLMAN
Chief, Public Integrity Section

Mary K. Butler
M. Kendall Day
Trial Attorneys
Criminal Division
U.S. Department of Justice

PAUL E. PELLETIER
Acting Chief, Fraud Section

Guy D. Singer
Nathaniel B. Edmonds
Trial Attorneys
Criminal Division
U.S. Department of Justice

BRUCE M. SALAD
Chief, Southern Criminal Enforcement
Section

Stephanie D. Evans
Trial Attorney
Tax Division
U.S. Department of Justice

ATTACHMENT A

FACTUAL BASIS FOR THE PLEA
OF JACK A. ABRAMOFF

This statement is submitted to provide a factual basis for my plea of guilty to the charges filed against me.

1. From 1994 to 2004, Abramoff was a Washington, D.C. lobbyist. In 1994, Abramoff joined a law and lobbying firm ("Firm A"). In January 2001, Abramoff joined a second law and lobbying firm ("Firm B").

2. At all relevant times, Abramoff solicited and obtained business with groups and companies throughout the United States, including Native American tribal governments operating, and interested in operating, gambling casinos. Abramoff sought to further his clients' interests by lobbying public officials, including Members of the United States Congress. Abramoff also sought to further his clients' interests by recommending vendors for grass roots work, public relations services and election campaign support. Typically, Abramoff communicated with his clients by interstate electronic mail, interstate telephone calls, and private or commercial interstate mail carriers.

3. From March 2000 through 2001, Michael Scanlon ("Scanlon") worked for Firm A and Firm B in Washington, D.C. as a public relations specialist engaged in providing public relations services to clients throughout the United States. At these firms, Scanlon worked on many matters, often together with, and at the direction of, Abramoff. Abramoff was influential in Scanlon being hired by both firms.

4. In or about January 2001, Scanlon established a business called Capital Campaign Strategies LLC which had its principal offices in Washington, D.C. Capital Campaign

1

Strategies LLC was formed to provide grass roots work, public relations services, and election campaign support. Scanlon also formed other companies that were used primarily to receive money for the services and work performed by others (collectively referred to as "CCS"). The services that CCS provided frequently involved use of interstate mail and telephone calls. Payments were often made by interstate wire transfer or checks that foreseeably caused interstate funds transfers between banks.

5.   In May 2003, Abramoff established a business called GrassRoots Interactive ("GRI"), which had its principal offices in Silver Spring, Maryland. Abramoff represented that GRI would provide grass roots work, public relations services, and election campaign support.

6.   In July 1999, Abramoff established a private foundation called Capital Athletic Foundation ("CAF") for which he sought and received federal tax-exempt status, in part to provide funding for a non-profit school. In November 2001, Abramoff organized a solely owned entity, Kaygold, LLC. Abramoff used these entities in part to receive funds for his personal benefit, to conceal the destination of the funds, and, with respect to CAF, to evade income taxes. Payments were often made by interstate wire transfer or checks involving interstate funds transfers.

Fraud Based on Violations of Abramoff's Duty of Honest Services

7.   Abramoff was hired by at least four Native American tribes with gaming operations to provide professional services and develop programs to limit market competition or to assist in opening casinos. In 2001, Abramoff and Scanlon agreed that Abramoff would encourage his existing and potential clients to obtain grass roots and public relations

2

services as a critical part of the lobbying program and strategy that Abramoff had been hired to provide. Abramoff promoted and recommended primarily CCS to provide this grass roots and public relations work. The prices CCS charged for its services were significantly in excess of CCS's costs.

8. Abramoff and Scanlon knew and agreed that Abramoff would receive fifty percent of the net profits received by CCS from those clients. Most of the payments from clients under the contracts with CCS were made to CCS. Scanlon then paid Abramoff his share of the net profits to various organizations that Abramoff controlled. The transfer of funds to Abramoff foreseeably involved the interstate transfer of funds.

9. Abramoff and Scanlon understood that the payments to Abramoff would not be disclosed to Abramoff's and Scanlon's four clients. Abramoff and Scanlon understood that disclosure of the profit-sharing arrangement to the clients would likely jeopardize the contracts for services and/or the profit margins of both Abramoff's law firm and CCS because disclosure could encourage the clients to seek competitive proposals from other vendors. Abramoff knew that his clients could receive the same services at significantly reduced prices because the quoted prices incorporated the undisclosed fees Scanlon paid to Abramoff of approximately fifty percent of CCS's net profits.

Abramoff promoted himself as having knowledge superior to his clients regarding lobbying and grass roots activity. Abramoff encouraged his clients to trust his judgment in these matters. Abramoff knew his clients did in fact trust and rely upon him in these matters. Abramoff further knew he had a duty to disclose all relevant facts to his lobbying clients, including conflicts of interest and any financial interest in fees paid to others.

3

Mississippi Tribe

11.   In 1995, Abramoff was hired by a Native American Indian tribal client based in Mississippi ("Mississippi Tribe") to hire him to provide lobbying services on various issues. Abramoff used his knowledge of lobbying and grass roots work, which was superior to the Mississippi Tribe's knowledge of these areas, to secure the trust and confidence of the Mississippi Tribe.

12.   In early 2001, Abramoff recommended and advised the Mississippi Tribe to hire CCS, while concealing the fact that Abramoff would receive approximately fifty percent of the net profits from the Mississippi Tribe's payments to Scanlon.

13.   From June 2001 until April 2004, the Mississippi Tribe paid Scanlon and related entities approximately $14,765,000. Abramoff and Scanlon concealed from the Mississippi Tribe that approximately fifty percent of the profit, approximately $6,364,000 including money not passed through CCS, was paid to Abramoff pursuant to their undisclosed arrangement.

Louisiana Tribe

14.   In March 2001, Abramoff and Scanlon successfully solicited a Native American Indian tribal client based in Louisiana ("Louisiana Tribe") to hire them to provide lobbying and grass roots services to the tribe. Abramoff used his knowledge of lobbying and grass roots work, which was superior to the Louisiana Tribe's knowledge of these areas, to secure the trust and confidence of the Louisiana Tribe.

15.   In March 2001, after CCS had been paid for the first project, Abramoff advised the Louisiana Tribe to rehire CCS, while concealing the fact that Abramoff would receive fifty percent of the profits from the Louisana Tribe's payments to CCS.

4

16.   From March 2001 to May 2003, the Louisiana Tribe paid CCS and related entities approximately $30,510,000. Abramoff and Scanlon concealed from the Louisiana Tribe that approximately fifty percent of the profit, approximately $11,450,000, was paid to Abramoff pursuant to their undisclosed arrangement.

Michigan Tribe

17.   In January 2002, Abramoff and Scanlon successfully solicited a Native American Indian tribal client based in Michigan ("Michigan Tribe") to hire them to provide lobbying and grass roots services. Abramoff used his knowledge of lobbying and grass roots work, which was superior to the Michigan Tribe's knowledge of these areas, to secure the trust and confidence of the Michigan Tribe.

18.   In June 2002, Abramoff advised the Michigan Tribe to expand its contract with CCS, while concealing the fact that Abramoff would receive approximately fifty percent of the profits from the Michigan Tribe's payments to CCS.

19.   From June 2002 to October 2003, the Michigan Tribe paid Scanlon and related entities approximately $3,500,000. Abramoff and Scanlon concealed from the Michigan Tribe that approximately fifty percent of the profit, approximately $540,000, was paid to Abramoff pursuant to their undisclosed arrangement.

Texas Tribe #1

20.   In February 2002, Abramoff and Scanlon successfully solicited a Native American Indian tribal client based in Texas ("Texas Tribe #1") to hire them to provide lobbying and grass roots services designed to reopen Texas Tribe #1's gaming operations that had been closed by Texas authorities because Texas Tribe #1 did not have federal or state authority to operate a casino. Specifically, Abramoff and Scanlon represented that they would

5

work first to open the casino as a Class II gaming facility and then work to expand Texas Tribe #1's casino as a more lucrative Class III facility. Abramoff and Scanlon further proposed that, in return for their work, Texas Tribe #1 would pay CCS $4,200,000 in fees and make additional and substantial political campaign contributions at the direction of Abramoff and Scanlon. Abramoff falsely represented that he would work for free to represent Texas Tribe #1, all the while concealing from the Texas Tribe #1 that approximately fifty percent of CCS's net profits, approximately $1,850,000, was paid to Abramoff pursuant to his undisclosed arrangement with Scanlon.

21.   At no time did Abramoff, Scanlon, or others working with them disclose to Texas Tribe #1 that, beginning in 2001, Abramoff, Firm B, and Scanlon had collected millions of dollars in fees from the Louisiana Tribe to oppose all gaming in the Texas legislature. Abramoff's conduct prevented consideration by Firm B of whether to disclose his representation of Texas Tribe #1 pursuant to the Lobbying Disclosure Act.

22.   After being retained by Texas Tribe #1 in early 2002 to reopen its casino through federal legislation, Abramoff continued representing the Louisiana Tribe for millions of dollars in fees. Pursuant to this representation of the Louisiana Tribe, Abramoff failed to disclose to Texas Tribe #1 that he opposed legislation in the 2003 Texas state legislative session that would have provided a basis to reopen Texas Tribe #1's casino under state law. Abramoff knew that Texas Tribe #1 supported and promoted this legislation while he worked to prevent its passage for the benefit of his other client, the Louisiana Tribe.

<u>Wireless Company</u>

23.   From January 2001 until April 2004, Abramoff was employed by Firm B. As an employee of Firm B, Abramoff had a duty to act in Firm B's best interests and not to divert lobbying fees owed to Firm B.

24.   In 2001, Abramoff was hired by a wireless telephone company ("Wireless Company") to undertake a lobbying effort to assist Wireless Company in securing a license to install wireless telephone infrastructure for the United States House of Representatives. In 2001 and early 2002, Abramoff and his Firm B colleagues lobbied for the Wireless Company without any formal retainer agreement. Rather than make lobbying payments to Firm B, Abramoff directed Wireless Company to make payments totaling at least $50,000 to CAF.

25.   At no time did Abramoff inform his employer, Firm B, of the $50,000 in payments to CAF, of which Firm B was entitled to a portion.

<u>Fraud Based on Abramoff's Affirmative Misrepresentations</u>

<u>Michigan Tribe</u>

26.   From June 2002 to November 2002, Abramoff and a former lobbying colleague, who was also a former congressional staffer ("Staffer A") successfully solicited the Michigan Tribe for a $25,000 payment to CAF. Instead of using the funds for CAF, Abramoff used this money for his personal and professional benefit to partially pay for a golfing trip to Scotland for himself, public officials, members of his staff and others.

Distilled Beverages Company

27.   On or about June 6, 2002, Abramoff and Staffer A successfully solicited one of Firm B's clients, a distilled beverages company, for a $25,000 payment to CAF. Instead of using the funds for CAF, Abramoff used this money for his personal and professional benefit to partially pay for a golfing trip to Scotland for himself, public officials, members of his staff and others.

New Mexico Tribe

28.   In February 2002, Abramoff and others successfully solicited a Native American Indian tribal client based in New Mexico ("New Mexico Tribe") to hire them to provide lobbying and grass roots services to the tribe.

29.   In March 2002, the New Mexico Tribe paid Scanlon and related entities approximately $2,750,000. Abramoff and Scanlon materially understated to the New Mexico Tribe the size of CCS's profit margins and concealed from the New Mexico Tribe that CCS's profit margin was approximately eighty percent and that approximately fifty percent of the net profit, $1,175,000, was paid to Abramoff pursuant to the undisclosed arrangement. At no time prior to March 2004 did Abramoff or others inform Firm B or the New Mexico Tribe of the undisclosed payments.

Manufacturing and Services Company

30.   On May 2, 2003, Abramoff sent a business proposal to a manufacturing and services company ("Company A") to handle its lobbying effort regarding a tax issue. In addition to his services, Abramoff recommended that Company A hire GRI, while concealing from Company A his interest in GRI. In his proposal, Abramoff falsely advised that GRI

8

had no relationship with Abramoff's law and lobbying firm, even though GRI was controlled by Abramoff and paid the vast majority of its profits to Abramoff or entities he controlled. Additionally, Abramoff represented to Company A that he was negotiating on their behalf with GRI to try to save Company A money, when in fact he was simply setting a high price on services that he controlled and from which he would profit.

31. In May and June 2003, Company A paid GRI, directly and through Firm B's bank account, approximately $1,841,429. Abramoff and entities he controlled received approximately $1,655,695 from GRI.

Corruption of Public Officials

32. Beginning as early as January 2000, Abramoff, Scanlon and others engaged in a course of conduct through which one or both of them offered and provided a stream of things of value to public officials in exchange for a series of official acts and influence and agreements to provide official action and influence. These things of value included, but are not limited to, foreign and domestic travel, golf fees, frequent meals, entertainment, election support for candidates for government office, employment for relatives of officials, and campaign contributions. As one part of this course of conduct, things of value were offered to and given to a Member of the United States Congress ("Representative #1") and members of Representative #1's staff, including, but not limited to:

     a.   All-expenses-paid trips, including a trip to the Commonwealth of the Northern Marianas Islands ("CNMI") in 2000, a trip to the Super Bowl in Tampa, Florida in 2001, and a golf trip to Scotland in 2002;

9

b.   Numerous tickets for entertainment, including concerts and sporting events;

c.   Fundraising events, including providing box suites and food at various sport and concert venues and at a restaurant in the Washington, D.C. area owned by Abramoff;

d.   Campaign contributions to campaign committees and to political action committees and organizations, including, but not limited to, the following:

       i. $4,000 in contributions to Representative #1's campaign committee in 2000; and

       ii.   A $10,000 contribution to the National Republican Campaign Committee ("NRCC") in 2000 at Representative #1's request;

e.   Regular meals and drinks at an upscale restaurant owned by Abramoff in Washington, D.C.; and

f.   Frequent golf and related expenses at courses in the Washington, D.C area.

33.   As part of this course of conduct, Abramoff, Scanlon and others provided things of value to public officials in exchange for a series of official acts and influence, and agreements to provide official acts and influence, including, but not limited to, agreements to support and pass legislation, agreements to place statements in the Congressional Record, agreements to contact personnel in United States Executive Branch agencies and offices to influence decisions of those agencies and offices, meetings with Abramoff and CCS's clients, and awarding contracts for services with CCS and Abramoff's law firms. As one part of this course of conduct, Representative #1 and members of his staff agreed to use and did use their official positions and influence, including, but not limited to, the following:

10

a.   Travel by a senior staff member of Representative #1 with others in January 2000 to CNMI for the purpose of assisting Abramoff, his firm and others in obtaining and maintaining lobbying clients;

b.   Representative #1's agreement in March 2000 to place a statement drafted by Scanlon into the Congressional Record that was critical of the then-owner of a Florida gaming company, and was calculated to pressure the then-owner to sell on terms favorable to Abramoff and his partners;

c.   Representative #1's agreement in October 2000 with Scanlon to insert a statement into the Congressional Record which praised the new owner of the Florida gaming company, Abramoff's business partner;

d.   Representative #1's agreement in approximately August 2001 to use his position as Chairman of a Committee of the House to endorse and support a client of Abramoff as the provider of wireless telephone infrastructure to the House of Representatives;

e.   Representative #1's agreement in approximately March 2002 that, as the Co-Chairman of a Conference Committee of House and Senate Members of Congress, he would introduce and seek passage of legislation that would lift an existing federal ban against commercial gaming in order to benefit a client of Abramoff and CCS, Texas Tribe #1;

f.   Representative #1's agreement in approximately June 2002 that, as the Co-Chairman of a Conference Committee of House and Senate Members of Congress, he would introduce and seek passage of legislation that would lift an

11

existing federal ban against commercial gaming for another Native American Tribe in Texas ("Texas Tribe #2") at Abramoff's request;

g.   Representative #1 met in August 2002 with representatives of Texas Tribe #1 to assure them that they were effectively represented by Abramoff and that he continued to agree to work to pass the legislation they wanted;

h.   Representative #1's agreement in December 2002 to seek support from a Member of another Committee of the House of Representatives for passage of legislation to lift the federal gaming ban for Texas Tribe #1;

i.   Representative #1 met in 2002 with a Native American Tribal client of CCS and Abramoff from California ("California Tribe") to discuss Representative #1's agreement to assist in passing legislation regarding taxation of certain payments received by members of the California Tribe, and to assist in an issue relating to a post office of interest to the California Tribe;

j.   Representative #1 agreed to meet with some of Abramoff's clients and others in Russia while Representative #1 was there on official business in August 2003 to, among other things, influence the process of obtaining a visa for travel to the United States for the relative of one of Abramoff's clients; and

k.   Representative #1 at various times, directly and indirectly, contacted public officials at additional government agencies and offices on behalf of clients of Abramoff and CCS in an effort to influence decisions and actions by those officials.

34.   As one part of the same course of conduct outlined in paragraphs 32 and 33 above, in

June 2002, Abramoff informed Representative #1 that Texas Tribe #1 was raising funds

to pay for a golfing trip to Scotland that Representative #1 and members of his staff were

to, and did, attend. In August 2002, Texas Tribe #2, at the request of Abramoff and

Texas Tribe #1, sent a $50,000 check made out to CAF via private interstate mail

delivery to Abramoff at 1101 Pennsylvania Ave, N.W., Washington, D.C.

35.   As one part of the same conduct outlined in paragraphs 32 and 33 above, beginning at

least in 1999 through January 2001, Abramoff and others sought Staffer A's agreement to

perform a series of official acts, including assisting in stopping legislation regarding

internet gambling and opposing postal rate increases. With the intent to influence those

official acts, Abramoff provided things of value including, but not limited to, from June

2000 through February 2001, ten equal monthly payments totaling $50,000 through a

non-profit entity to the wife of Staffer A. The total amount paid to the wife of Staffer A

was obtained from clients that would and did benefit from Staffer A's official actions

regarding the legislation on internet gambling or opposing postal rate increases.

36.   As one part of the same course of conduct outlined in paragraphs 32 and 33 above,

beginning in March 2002, Abramoff and a former staffer to Representative #1 ("Staffer

B") contacted Representative #1, officials employed by the Office of Representative #1,

and officials employed by a House Committee ("Committee") of which Representative

#1 was the chairman. These contacts occurred within one year of Staffer B having served

as the Chief of Staff for Representative #1 and Staff Director of the Committee.

Abramoff intended that Staffer B communicate with Representative #1, his staff, and the

Committee staff for the purpose of influencing official action on behalf of Abramoff's and Staffer B's clients, including Texas Tribe #1 and Wireless Company.

Tax Evasion Offense

37. During the calendar year 2002, Abramoff had and received a substantial amount of income from the conduct discussed in paragraphs 1 through 31. In order to conceal this income from the Internal Revenue Service and others, Abramoff used entities exempt from taxation under Title 26, United States Code Section 501(c), including a private foundation he created and a public policy organization for which he served as a director, to receive income and to make expenditures for his own personal benefit. To further conceal this income, Abramoff and others created, or caused to be created, false invoices and false entries to financial records, which made it appear as if the funds had been received and expended for tax-exempt purposes. In fact, Abramoff and others knew that these activities constituted a misuse of these tax-exempt entities. Through these activities, Abramoff and others intended to and did benefit Abramoff, the entities he controlled or financially supported, and the public policy organization.

38. On or about October 15, 2003, Abramoff signed and filed a false and fraudulent joint U.S. Individual Income Tax Return, Form 1040, which underreported Abramoff's total income for 2002. Specifically, Abramoff willfully and intentionally failed to report the income received from the illegal schemes described in paragraphs 1 to 32 above resulting in the evasion of approximately $628,557 in individual income taxes for the 2002 tax year.

39.   Abramoff signed and filed false and fraudulent Returns of Private Foundations, Forms 990PF, which misrepresented the receipt of diverted funds as charitable donations and mischaracterized personal and business expenditures as being used for a tax exempt purpose.

40.   Furthermore, Abramoff caused false Returns of Organizations Exempt from Income Tax, Forms 990, to be filed by a public policy organization, which misrepresented the receipt of diverted funds as charitable donations and mischaracterized personal and business expenditures of Abramoff as being used for a tax exempt purpose.

41.   Abramoff engaged in similar evasive conduct for the tax years 2001 and 2003. Due to this and other evasive conduct, Abramoff attempted to evade approximately $1,724,054 in individual income taxes for the 2001 through 2003 tax years.

       The preceding statement is a summary, made for the purpose of providing the Court with a factual basis for my guilty plea to the charges against me. It does not include all of the facts known to me concerning criminal activity in which I or others engaged. I make this statement knowingly and voluntarily and because I am in fact guilty of the crimes charged.

DATE: 1/3/06

JACK A. ABRAMOFF
Defendant

ABBE DAVID LOWELL, ESQ.
Attorney for Defendant

15

CREM. DIV. FORM 33
Rev. January, 1994

IN THE COURT OF COMMON PLEAS OF ALLEGHENY COUNTY, PENNSYLVANIA
CRIMINAL DIVISION

COMMONWEALTH OF PENNSYLVANIA   )
)
            vs.   )   CC NO. _____
)
_____)

GUILTY PLEA
EXPLANATION OF DEFENDANT'S RIGHTS

You or your attorney have indicated to the officers of this Court that you wish to plead guilty or nolo contendere to certain specific criminal charges which the Commonwealth of Pennsylvania has brought against you.

In order to have your plea accepted by this Court here today, you must waive your right to confront the prosection witnesses against you and agree to permit an Assistant District Attorney to summarize the Commonwealth's evidence against you. You must agree to stipulate to the authenticity and accuracy of any Crime Laboratory reports presented by the Commonwealth and to the chain of custody of any of the Commonwealth's evidence involved in your case.

You must fully understand that your plea must be voluntary and no clemency is being promised in exchange for your plea, with the exception of any plea bargain or arrangement previously agreed to between your attorney and the Assistant District Attorney assigned to your case.

By pleading guilty to any charge you are admitting that you committed that offense. By pleading nolo contendere you are stating that you do not contest the charges against you. In either case, the Commonwealth would not have to prove each and every element of the crimes with which you are charged as would be required in a jury or non-jury trial.

Please be advised that you must fully understand that the Constitution of the United States of America and the Constitution of the Commonwealth of Pennsylvania give to you an absolute right to have a trial by jury.

If you intend to waive your Constitutional right to a trial by jury, please answer all the questions on this form. Most of the questions are designed to be answered "yes" or "no." Where general

1

information is requested, please answer the question as fully as possible.

If you do not understand the question, you should say so in writing on this form. You should also tell your lawyer and the judge who hears your case so they can explain it to you. You must fully understand all of your rights before your plea can be accepted by the judge.

You should initial each page at the bottom after you have read, understood and completed your answers to the questions on that page. When you have finished all of the questions, you must sign the form at the end.

1. What is your full name? _____

2. How old are you today? _____

3. How far did you go in school? _____

4. Can you read, write and understand the English language? ____

5. Do you understand that because you have been charged with more than one offense the court may impose a separate, or consecutive, sentence for each offense? _____

6. Have you discussed with your attorney the elements of each charged offense? _____

7. Have you discussed with your attorney the factual basis of each charged offense? _____

8. Have you discussed with your attorney how the facts in your case prove the elements of each charged offense? _____

9. Do you understand that both the Constitution of the United States of America and the Constitution of the Commonwealth of Pennsylvania give you an absolute right to a trial by jury? _____

10. Do you understand that if you want a jury trial, you would take part in the selection of the jury along with your attorney and with the Assistant District Attorney assigned to prosecute your case? _____

11. Do you understand that you and your attorney and the Assistant District Attorney assigned to prosecute your case would select a jury from a panel of jurors randomly picked by computer from the voter registration lists and other legally approved lists of citizens of Allegheny County? _____

12. Do you understand that both the defense and prosecution would have the right to "challenge" members of the jury panel and that this means you and the prosecution would have the right to keep certain persons on the jury panel from being a member of the jury in your case? _____

13. Both you and the prosecution would have as many challenges "for cause" as the court would approve. "For cause" means a good reason why the challenged person could not be an impartial juror in your case. Do you fully understand this? _____

14. Both you and the prosecution would each also have a number of "peremptory challenges". A "peremptory challenge" is one in which no reason has to be given to prevent a prospective juror from being a member of your jury. If you are charged with felonies, both you and the prosecution each have seven "peremptory challenges." If you are charged only with misdemeanors, both you and the prosection each have five "peremptory challenges." Do you fully understand this? _____

15. All twelve members of the jury finally selected would have to be satisfied that the Commonwealth had proven your guilt beyond a reasonable doubt on each charge; that is, the vote of all twelve must be guilty before you could be found guilty? Do you fully understand this? _____

16. You also may choose to be tried before a judge without a jury in what is called a "non-jury" trial and that the judge, in addition to ruling on legal questions and defining the law as in jury trials would also sit as a trier of fact, much like a jury does in a jury trial; and it would be the judge who determines from the evidence presented whether the Commonwealth has proven you guilty beyond a reasonable doubt. Do you fully understand this? _____

17. In either the jury trial or non-jury trial before a judge, you enter the courtroom clothed with the presumption of innocence and that presumption remains with you until such time, if ever, that a jury in a jury trial or judge in a non-jury trial, would find you guilty beyond a reasonable doubt. Do you fully understand this? _____

18. In either a jury trial or in a non-jury trial before a judge, it is the burden of the Commonwealth to prove you guilty "beyond a reasonable doubt," and to do this the Commonwealth must prove each and every element of the crime or crimes with which you are charged "beyond a reasonable doubt" to the satisfaction of all twelve jurors in a jury trial or to the satisfaction of the judge in a non-jury trial. Do you fully understand this? _____

3

19. A reasonable doubt is an honest doubt arising from the evidence presented or from the lack of evidence and it is the kind of doubt that would cause a reasonable, prudent person to pause or to hesitate before acting in a matter of the highest personal importance. Do you fully understand this? _____

20. In either a jury trial or a non-jury trial before a judge, you have the absolute right to remain silent and need not present any evidence in your own behalf and there is no burden placed on you to prove your own innocence or, for that matter to prove anything since the burden is always on the Commonwealth to prove you guilty beyond a reasonable doubt. Do you fully understand this? _____

21. However, in either a jury trial or a non-jury trial before a judge, you have the right, if you so desire, to testify and to have witnesses testify on your behalf and you would have the right to present any relevant evidence which you would tend or help to prove your innocence and to challenge the evidence and testimony presented by the prosecution. You also would have the right either yourself or through your attorney to cross-examine or question any witnesses presented by the Commonwealth in order to test their credibility and the truthfulness of their testimony. Do you fully understand this? _____

22. By pleading guilty or nolo contendere you are giving up all of these rights described in the previous questions. Do you fully understand this? _____

23. When you plead guilty or nolo contendere, the Commonwealth would not have to prove each and every element of the crime or crimes with which you are charged by the presentation of witnesses and/or other evidence but the Assistant District Attorney could simply present a summary of the evidence against you. Do you fully understand this? _____

24. By pleading guilty, you are admitting you committed the crime or by pleading nolo contendere, you are stating that you do not challenge or dispute the charges against you. Do you fully understand this? _____

25. By pleading guilty or nolo contendere, you give up the right not only to file pretrial motions, but also you abandon or give up any pretrial motions already filed and not yet decided and any pretrial motions in which decisions were already made. Do you fully understand this? _____

26. Do you understand that by pleading guilty or nolo contendere, you also give up the right to present or assert any defenses on your behalf? _____

4

27. If you were convicted after a jury trial or non-jury trial before a judge, you could appeal the verdict to a higher court and raise any errors that were committed in the trial court and this could result in a new trial or a dismissal. By pleading guilty you are giving up this right. Do you fully understand this? _____

28. Do you fully understand that if you were convicted after a jury trial or a non-jury trial before a judge, you could challenge in this Court and in the appellate courts whether the Commonwealth had presented enough evidence to prove you guilty beyond a reasonable doubt? _____

29. By pleading guilty or nolo contendere, you give up certain rights of appeal; in a jury trial or a non-jury trial before a judge, you would have the right to appeal any errors that might arise in your case to the Superior Court of Pennsylvania. However, when you plead guilty or nolo contendere, you limit the grounds for those appeals to four specific reasons:

     1.   that this Court did not have jurisdiction in your case. With rare exception, this Court only has jurisdiction where the crime was committed in Allegheny County;

     2.   that the sentence or probation imposed by this Court is illegal;

     3.   that your plea was not knowingly, intelligently, and voluntarily made; and

     4.   the incompetence or ineffectiveness of the attorney who represents you.

All other grounds for appeal are given up. Do you fully understand this? _____

30. Do you understand that you have the right to file a motion seeking to withdraw your guilty plea or your nolo contendere plea at any time prior to the date of sentencing? _____

31. Do you understand that you must be sentenced within sixty (60) days of the date of the entry of your plea of guilty or your plea of nolo contendere? _____

32. Do you understand you have the right within ten (10) days after you have been sentenced to file a motion seeking to withdraw your guilty plea or your plea of nolo contendere? _____

5

33. If you were to file a motion seeking to withdraw your plea of guilty or plea of nolo contendere, either prior to sentencing or within ten (10) days after sentencing, that motion must be filed in writing. If you would fail to do so within these time periods, you would forever give up those rights. Do you fully understand this? _____

34. In order to appeal your conviction that results for your plea of guilty or nolo contendere, you must file in writing your motion seeking to withdraw your plea, either prior to sentencing or within ten (10) days after sentencing and state one or more of the four (4) grounds listed below as the basis for a motion seeking to withdraw your plea:

a) Your plea was not knowingly, intelligent and voluntary;

b) that your crime was not committed within the jurisdiction of this Court, i.e., not committed within Allegheny County;

c) that the sentence of this Court is illegal; and/or,

d) that your attorney was ineffective and incompetent.

If you do not file this motion within the proscribed time limits, you will have given up this right. Do you fully understand this? _____

35. If your motion seeking to withdraw your plea of guilty or nolo contendere, which is filed prior to sentencing, is denied you would have ten (10) days from the date of sentencing to file with this Court a post-sentencing motion challenging the denial of your motion to withdraw your plea of guilty or your plea of nolo contendere. Do you fully understand this? _____

36. Following the imposition of sentence upon you for your entry of either a plea of guilty or a plea of nolo contendere, you have the right to file post-sentencing motions with this Court which include:

a) a motion challenging the validity of a plea of guilty or nolo contendere;

b) a motion challenging the denial of a motion seeking a plea of guilty or nolo contendere;

c) a motion to modify sentence.

Do you fully understand these rights? _____

6

37. If you would file any post-sentencing motions, those motions must be decided by this Court within one hundred twenty (120) days of the date of the filing of said motions, or within one hundred fifty (150) days of the filing of those motions if you sought and were granted a thirty (30) days extension, which extension only you can request? Do you fully understand this?
     _____

38. If your post-sentencing motions are not decided within one hundred twenty (120) days of the date of filing, or within one hundred fifty (150) days of the date of filing, if you sought and received a thirty (30) day extension, then said motions are deemed to have been denied by operation of law and cannot be reconsidered by this Court. Do you fully understand this?
     _____

39. If this Court would deny your post-sentencing motion within either the one hundred twenty (120) or one hundred fifty (150) day time periods, you would have the right to file with this Court a motion to reconsider the denials of your post-sentencing motions; however, any motion to reconsider the denial of post-sentencing motions must be filed by you and decided by this Court within either the one hundred twenty (120) or one hundred fifty (150) day time limits. If such a motion to reconsider the denial of post-sentencing motion is not filed by you or, if filed, not decided by this Court within the one hundred twenty (120) or one hundred fifty (150) day time limits, then any appellate rights that you have begin to run from the last day of either time limit. Do you fully understand this? _____

40. Should your post-sentencing motion be denied by this Court or by operation of law, you will receive, either from this Court or from the Clerk of Courts, an order of court advising you of your appellate rights, the right to assistance of counsel, if indigent, the right to proceed in forma pauperis, and, the qualified right to bail. Any appeal to the Superior Court must be filed within thirty (30) days of the denial of your post-sentencing motion. Do you fully understand? _____

41. If you wish to file any of these motions with this Court or an appeal to the Superior Court of Pennsylvania and cannot afford an attorney to assist you do so, this Court will appoint an attorney to assist you to do so, this Court will appoint an attorney for you at no cost to you. Do you fully understand this? _____

42. When you plead guilty or nolo contendere, and your plea is accepted by this Court, all that remains is for the judge to sentence you on the charges to which you are pleading; but if your plea is rejected, your case will be sent back for reassignment to another courtroom and another judge for trial.

7

Do you fully understand this? _____

43. If there is a mandatory minimum sentence applicable and this mandatory sentence is sought by the Commonwealth, then this Court has no discretion to impose a lesser sentence and must impose at least the minimum sentence that is required by law. Do you fully understand this? _____

44. Are you aware that if the offenses with which you are charged do not require a mandatory sentence under the statutory law of Pennsylvania, this Court is not bound by the sentencing guidelines and may deviate from the guidelines; however, if the Court does so, both the District Attorney and you would have a right to appeal such deviation? _____

45. Do you understand that if you are entering a plea of guilty or a plea of nolo contendere to the charge of Violation of the Controlled Substance, Drug, Device and Cosmetic Act, that independent of any sentence this Court might impose, the Department of Transportation has the right, upon receipt of notice of this conviction, to impose an additional penalty upon you, in the form of the suspension of your driver's license for a period of time ranging anywhere from ninety (90) days to two (2) years. _____

46. Do you understand that if you are entering a plea of guilty or a plea of nolo contendere to the charge of Violation Vehicle Code: Driving Under Influence of Alcohol, a controlled Substance or both, that independent of any sentence this Court might impose, the Department of Transportation has the right, upon receipt of notice of this conviction, to impose an additional penalty upon you, in the form of the suspension of your driver's license for a period of one (1) year. _____

47. Do you understand that any term of imprisonment imposed as a result of your plea may be imposed separately, or consecutively, with any other state or federal term of imprisonment you are currently serving? _____

48. Do you understand that the conviction that will result from your plea may serve as a violation of any term of state or federal probation or parole? _____

49. Do you understand that a violation of your state or federal probation or parole could result in the imposition of a further separate, or consecutive, term of imprisonment? _____

50. Your plea must be voluntary and your rights must be voluntarily, knowingly and intelligently waived. If anyone has promised you anything other than the terms of a plea bargain, your plea will be rejected. If anyone has forced you or

8

attempted to force you in any way to plead guilty or nolo contendere, your plea will be rejected. Do you fully understand this? _____

51. Has anybody forced you to enter this plea? _____

52. Are you doing this of your own free will? _____

53. Have any threats been made to you to enter a plea? _____

54. Do you understand that if there is a plea bargain in this case the terms of the plea bargain will be stated on the record before the judge and that you will be bound by the terms of the plea bargain as they appear of record? _____

55. Do you understand that this Court is not bound by any plea bargain entered into by you and the District Attorney? _____

56. If the Court rejects the plea bargain after hearing a summary of the evidence, you would then have a right to withdraw your plea and your case would be reassigned to another judge before whom you would have the option of entering a straight plea with no plea bargain involved or have your case heard by that judge in a non-jury trial and, of course, you would still have the right to a trial by jury if you so desire. Do you fully understand this? _____

57. Are you satisfied with the legal advice and legal representation of your attorney? _____

58. Have you had ample opportunity to consult with your attorney before entering your plea, and are you satisfied that your attorney knows all of the facts of your case and has had enough time within which to check any questions of fact or law which either you or your attorney may have about the case? _____

59. Has your attorney gone over with you the meaning of the terms of this document? _____

60. Have you ever had any physical or mental illness that would affect your ability to understand these rights or affect the voluntary nature of your plea? _____

61. Are you presently taking any medication which might affect your thinking or your free will? _____

62. Have you had any narcotics or alcohol in the last forty-eight (48) hours? _____

63. A.   If you are entering a plea of guilty you admit that you committed the crime(s) with which you are charged and to

9

which you are pleading guilty. Do you fully understand this? _____

B.   If you are entering a plea of nolo contendere, do you admit that you are not challenging the charges against you? _____

64. Do you understand your rights? _____

      I AFFIRM THAT I HAVE READ THE ABOVE DOCUMENT IN ITS ENTIRETY, I UNDERSTAND ITS FULL MEANING, AND I AM STILL NEVERTHELESS WILLING TO ENTER A PLEA TO THE OFFENSES SPECIFIED. I FURTHER AFFIRM THAT MY SIGNATURE AND INITIALS ON EACH PAGE OF THIS DOCUMENT ARE TRUE AND CORRECT.

DATE: _____   _____
                                    Signature of Defendant

CERTIFICATION OF DEFENSE COUNSEL

I certify that:

(1)   I am an attorney admitted to the Supreme Court of Pennsylvania.
(2)   I represent the defendant herein.
(3)   I know no reason why the defendant cannot fully understand everything that is being said and done here today.
(4)   The defendant read the above form in my presence and appeared to fully understand it; I have gone over the form completely with the defendant, explained all of the items on the form and answered any questions he or she had.
(5)   I see no reason why the defendant cannot and is not knowingly intelligently and voluntarily giving up his or her rights to trial and pleading guilty.
(6)   I made no promises to the defendant other than any that appear of record in this case.

DATE: _____   _____
                                    Attorney for Defendant

Form 17-9   Script for Federal Plea Colloquy

COMMENT:

This is the colloquy followed by U.S. District Judge Koss of the District of Indiana and posted on the court's website. [*See* www.iand.uscourts.gov/.]

Other federal judges also post their plea questions. [*See, e.g.,* www.pawd.uscourts.gov/Documents/Public/ Reference/Lancaster.pdf (colloquy of U. S. District Judge Lancaster of the Western District of Pennsylvania).]

GUILTY PLEA COLLOQUY

[THE JUDGE WILL HAVE ANY INTERPRETER SWORN]
[THE JUDGE WILL ANNOUNCE THE CASE]

You are [*Mr./Ms. defendant*]? I am [*name of magistrate judge*], a United States Magistrate Judge. On [*date of Indictment/Information*], [*the judge will say one of the following:*] (the United States Grand Jury for the Northern District of Iowa returned a ___-count Indictment against you) (*or*) (the United States Attorney filed a ___- count Information against you). You previously appeared in court and pled not guilty to the Indictment/Information. I have been advised that you now wish to change your plea(s) and enter (a plea) (pleas) of guilty to [*the Indictment/Information* (*or*) *Count(s) of the Indictment/Information*].

[*Mr./Ms. defense counsel*], is that your understanding?

[IF APPROPRIATE, THE JUDGE WILL REVIEW ANY CONSENT BY THE DEFENDANT TO ALLOW THE GOVERNMENT TO PROSECUTE THIS CASE BY INFORMATION INSTEAD OF INDICTMENT]

1.   CONSENT TO PLEAD GUILTY BEFORE MAGISTRATE JUDGE

[*Mr./Ms. defendant*], this case is assigned to a district court judge. I am a magistrate judge. You have the right under the United States Constitution to have a district court judge preside over any guilty plea hearing. I can preside over your guilty plea hearing, but only with your voluntary consent. You have signed a form stating that you consent to have me preside over your plea hearing. Is that what you would like me to do?

[*Mr./Ms. defense counsel*], do you believe your client's consent is knowing and voluntary?

Very well, I will accept the defendant's consent and go ahead with the guilty plea hearing.

[NOTE TO THE JUDGE–THERE IS [A] [NO] PLEA AGREEMENT]

2.   THE OATH

[*Mr./Ms. defendant*], I will be asking you a number of questions, and you will have to be under oath when you answer them. Would you please raise your right hand so I can place you under oath?

[THE JUDGE WILL PLACE THE DEFENDANT UNDER OATH]

You may put your hand down. [*Mr./Ms. defendant*], you are now under oath. You should tell the truth because if you do not, you could be prosecuted by the Government for perjury or for making a false statement. In any such prosecution, the Government could use against you any statements you make here under oath.

You have pled not guilty to (this charge)/(these charges). Even though you have come here today to change your plea(s) [*and apparently have signed a plea agreement*], you do not have to plead guilty. If at any time during this hearing you change your mind and decide you don't want to plead guilty, just tell me, and I will recess the hearing and schedule your case for trial.

Do you understand?

3.   INSURING MENTAL CAPACITY

I now have to ask you some personal questions to make sure you don't have any mental or physical problems that would make it hard for you to understand what we're going to talk about today.

Would you state your full name? How old are you? How far did you go in school? [*The judge will ask the following questions in appropriate cases: Are you a U.S. citizen? Have you ever been a U.S. Citizen?* **If the answer is "no**," *the judge will ask the following question: Of what country are you a citizen?*]

[*As appropriate, the judge will ask one of the following two questions*: (1) Is it fair for me to assume that you can read and write the English Language? (2) Do you [*read and write*] [*read, write, speak, and/or understand*] the English Language?

[*In appropriate cases, the judge will ask the following questions*: What is your native language? *The judge then will ask the following two questions in appropriate cases*: (1) Do you understand the English language? (2) Do you understand what the interpreter is saying to you?]

If you have problems understanding anything that comes up during this hearing, will you let me know so I can better explain it to you?

Have you ever suffered from or had any problems with **alcohol or drug abuse**? [*If "yes," then the judge will say the following*:] The purpose of my question is to find out whether your abuse of drugs and/or alcohol in the past would make it hard for you to understand what's happening at this hearing today. With that in mind, would you generally describe for me your history of using drugs and/or alcohol? [*After the defendant answers, the judge will say the following*:] Do you think your past abuse of drugs and/or alcohol abuse might affect your ability to understand what's happening at this hearing today?

Have you ever suffered from depression, anxiety, or any other **mental illness**? [*If "yes," then the judge will say the following*:] The purpose of my question is to find out whether any mental illness would make it hard for you to understand what's happening at this hearing today. With that in mind, would you generally describe your mental health history to me? [*After the defendant answers, the judge will say the following*:] Do you think your mental health problems (*in the past*) might affect your ability to understand what's happening at this hearing today?

Here today, are you under the influence of **alcohol, drugs, or medication**? Have you recently used any **legal or illegal drugs** or any **prescription or non-prescription medication**? Has any medication been prescribed for you that you are not taking?

[*Other than what we have talked about,*] Do you know of anything that might affect your ability to understand what's happening at this hearing or your ability to make good judgments today?

[*Mr./Ms. defense counsel*], do you think your client is competent to proceed with a plea hearing today?

I AGREE, AND SO FIND.

4. RIGHT TO A LAWYER

[*Mr./Ms. defendant*], you have the right to a lawyer to help and represent you during every stage of this case. If at any time you can't afford a lawyer, you're entitled to a free one.

[*The judge will ask the following question only if the defendant is not represented by the Federal Public Defender.*] [*Mr./Ms. defense counsel*], are you retained or appointed?

[*Mr./Ms. defendant*], are you satisfied with the representation you have received from [*Mr./Ms. defense counsel*]?

5. INDICTMENT/INFORMATION

[*Mr./Ms. defendant*], in the Indictment/Information in this case, the (Grand Jury)/(United States Attorney) charges that you [*here, the judge will summarize the charge(s) in the Indictment/Information*].

Do you understand what the (Grand Jury)/(United States Attorney) is saying you did wrong?

Have you talked with [*Mr./Ms. defense counsel*] about the evidence in your case?

Have you had the chance to talk with [*Mr./Ms. defense counsel*] as much as you want about (this charge)/ (these charges)?

[*Mr./Ms. defense counsel*], do you think your client understands the charge(s) against him/her?

6. PENALTIES

[*Mr./Ms. defendant*], under the statutes that apply to the charge(s) against you,

on count I, the district court judge could:

send you to prison for up to _____ years, impose a fine of up to $_____, and sentence you to a term of supervised release of up to _____ years. [*If applicable: There also is a mandatory minimum prison term of_____years and a mandatory minimum term of supervised release of_____years.*]

[(*Repeat for any other counts; e.g.,* On count 2, the district court judge could:

send you to prison for up to _____ years, impose a fine of up to $_____, and sentence you to a term of supervised release of up to _____ years. [*If applicable: There also is a mandatory minimum prison term of_____ years and a mandatory minimum term of supervised release of _____ years.*]

The judge also will impose, and you will have to pay, a special assessment of $100 (*for each count on which you plead guilty, for a total of $ _____*). (S)he also has the power to order **forfeiture** and **restitution**, if applicable.

[*If the offense involves **FRAUD** or other intentionally deceptive practices, the judge will say the following:*] The court could order you to provide notice of your conviction to victims of the offense.

Do you understand the statutory penalties?

You should understand you will be in custody for all of any [*jail or*] prison sentence you receive, reduced only by any credit for good time you may earn. You can earn a reduction in your prison sentence for "good time" of up to about 15% of your sentence[, *but only if your sentence is longer than one year*]. [*The judge will give examples, if appropriate.*] You should understand you never will see a parole board or be paroled out of prison before completing your sentence; parole has been abolished in federal court.

[*If the defendant **is a U.S. citizen**, the judge will say the following:*]

After you have served your prison sentence, you will be placed on supervised release, during which your conduct will be monitored by a probation officer. There are a number of standard conditions of supervised release, some of which are that you cannot commit any federal, state, or local crimes, and you cannot possess firearms, ammunition, or illegal controlled substances. The district court judge could impose additional special conditions. If you violate any of the conditions of your supervised release, the district court judge could revoke your supervised release, and require you to serve in prison all or part of the time you otherwise would have been on supervised release, possibly without credit for time served. [*The judge will give examples, if appropriate.*]

> [*The judge may, in appropriate cases, read the following paragraph.*] If, while on supervised release, you are found to be in possession of a controlled substance or a firearm, or if you refuse to comply with drug testing imposed as a condition of supervised release, the judge may revoke your supervised release and require you to go to prison for some period of time.]

[*If the defendant **is not a U.S. citizen**, the judge will say the following:*]

If you were a U.S. citizen, after you served your prison sentence, you would be placed on supervised release and monitored by a probation officer. Because you are not a U.S. citizen, you likely would be deported immediately after serving any jail or prison sentence you are given on (this charge)/(these charges). After that, it is unlikely you would ever be permitted to reenter the United States legally. If you are deported, then while you are on supervised release you will not be under the supervision of a probation officer, but it would be a violation of your supervised release to reenter the United States during your period of supervised release. If you reenter the United States while you are on supervised release, the district court judge likely would revoke your supervised release, and require you to serve in prison all or part of the time you otherwise would have been on supervised release. That prison term would be in addition to any sentence you would receive if you were convicted on an (*another*) illegal reentry charge.

Do you have any questions about good time or supervised release?

7.   COLLATERAL CONSEQUENCES

[*If the defendant **is a U.S. citizen**, the judge will say the following:*]

As a result of your conviction, you also will be deprived of the right to vote, to serve on a jury, to hold public office, and to possess firearms and ammunition.

Do you understand this?

[*If this is a **SEX CRIME**, the judge will say the following:*]

A conviction on this offense likely will require that you register as a sex offender under the laws of the state where you live. Such registration may be required of you for the rest of your life. (*The judge will say the following if the defendant will not be in custody following his/her plea*: In fact, you should check with your local authorities to see if you are required, as a result of this plea, to register immediately as a sex offender under the laws of the state where you live.)

Do you understand this?

8. **RIGHT TO A JURY TRIAL:**

[*Mr./Ms. defendant*], if you plead guilty, you will be giving up your one chance for a jury trial on (this charge)/ (these charges). Before I can let you do that, I must explain your trial rights to you so you'll know what you'll be giving up by pleading guilty.

You have the right to a speedy, public jury trial before a jury of 12 people selected from a cross-section of this community. You and [*Mr./Ms. defense counsel*] would help choose the people who would serve on your jury.

Your jurors would promise under oath to try your case fairly and justly, based only on what is submitted into evidence at trial and the instructions given to them by the district court judge. They would be told by the judge that you are presumed innocent, and that the presumption of innocence remains with you unless and until, at the end of your trial, the prosecution has convinced the jury of your guilt beyond a reasonable doubt. Any verdict by the jury would have to be unanimous, which means all 12 jurors would have to agree on the verdict.

> Do you understand you would be presumed innocent at your trial, and could not be convicted by the jury unless the prosecution proved your guilt beyond a reasonable doubt?
> Do you understand any verdict in your trial would have to be unanimous?

The prosecution would have to call its witnesses to testify under oath here in court. You would be able to see and hear their testimony, and they would be able to see you while they are testifying. [*Mr./Ms. defense counsel*] could confront the prosecution's witnesses, and cross-examine them.

You would not have to put on a defense at your trial, but if you wanted to, you could present any relevant evidence to the jury. You could make witnesses come to court by having subpoenas served on them. These subpoenas could be served anywhere in the United States, and would require your witnesses to come to this court for your trial. If you couldn't afford to pay the costs and fees necessary to serve the subpoenas or get your witnesses to court, I would make the Government pay those costs and fees.

You would not have to testify or say anything at your trial. If you decided not to testify at trial, [*Mr./Ms. prosecutor*] would not say anything about it to the jury. In fact, the judge would, if you asked him/her to, tell the jurors that you have a constitutional right not to testify. (S)he also would tell them that if you choose not to testify, they must not hold it against you. Of course, you could testify at your trial, if you wanted to, but you wouldn't have to.

You would have the right to appeal, and the right to a free lawyer to help you with your appeal if you couldn't afford one.

> Do you understand the rights I've just described to you?

9. **WAIVER OF RIGHT TO JURY TRIAL BY PLEADING GUILTY**

If you plead guilty, you will be giving up your right to a jury trial. You also will be giving up the right to file pre-trial motions, including motions for discovery, motions challenging the Indictment/Information, and motions to suppress evidence.

If you plead guilty, you will have no trial. You will be adjudged guilty based on your plea, just as if a jury had returned a guilty verdict against you.

> Do you understand that if you plead guilty, the next hearing in this case will be your sentencing hearing, and it likely will be the last hearing in your case?
> Do you understand that if you plead guilty, you won't have a jury trial or any other trial?

10. **U.S. SENTENCING GUIDELINES AND SENTENCING HEARING**

If you plead guilty here today, I will order a **presentence investigation report**, which will be prepared by a probation officer. [*The judge may introduce the probation officer if (s)he is present in the courtroom.*] The probation officer will interview you within the next few days, and then will conduct a thorough investigation of your background, which will include an investigation of the facts of this case. (S)he then will prepare a draft presentence investigation report, and will send a copy of the draft report to [*Mr./Ms. prosecutor*] and [*Mr./Ms. defense counsel*]. You should go over the report carefully. [*If you can't read the report in English, you should have it read to you in* (*Spanish*) (*your native language*).] Be sure to point out to [*Mr./Ms. defense counsel*] any mistakes or omissions in the report so (s)he can let the probation officer know about them. The probation officer will be happy to correct or amend the report if warranted. The report will be the most important document at the sentencing hearing, so you will want it to be as accurate as possible.

After the report has been finalized, it will be sent to the district court judge, and copies of the report will be sent to [*Mr./Ms. prosecutor*] and [*Mr./Ms. defense counsel*]. Then you will have a sentencing hearing.

At the sentencing hearing, you and [*Mr./Ms. prosecutor*] can present witnesses and exhibits on any sentencing issue. Then, you will be given a chance to talk to the judge directly and to tell him/her anything you want.

At the end of the hearing, the judge will determine the appropriate sentencing range for you under the U.S. Sentencing Guidelines, which are issued by the United States Sentencing Commission. (S)he then will tell you what your sentence will be, which in most cases **must** be within the range established by the Guidelines. The judge does have the power in certain **special** circumstances to sentence you either above or below the Guideline range [*or below the statutory mandatory minimum sentence*].

[*In cooperation cases, the judge will say the following*: For example, the district court judge could sentence you below the bottom of the Guideline range (*or below the mandatory minimum*) if you provide substantial assistance to the Government and [*Mr./Ms. prosecutor*] asks him/her to sentence you below the bottom of the range (*or below the mandatory minimum*). However, even if you provide substantial assistance to the Government, there is no guarantee you will receive a sentence that is below the bottom of the Guideline range (*or below the mandatory minimum*).]

[(*In non-cooperation cases, the judge will say the following:* However, in this case, there is almost no chance the judge would sentence you below the bottom of the Guideline range (*or below the mandatory minimum*), so you should not expect that to happen.]

In most cases, whatever happens at the sentencing hearing, you will not be allowed to withdraw your guilty plea(s), even if you don't like the sentence the judge gives you. However, both you and [*Mr./Ms. prosecutor*] may have the right to appeal from what happens at the sentencing hearing.

Do you understand how your sentencing hearing would be conducted?

[*If there is no plea agreement, the judge will ask the following questions, and then skip to paragraph 12. If there is a plea agreement, the judge will skip these questions, and go to paragraph 11.*]

[*Mr./Ms. defendant*], have you talked with [*Mr./Ms. defense counsel*] about how the Guidelines might work in your case?

Do you think you generally understand what (s)he has told you about the Guidelines?

[*The judge will ask defense counsel, and then the prosecutor, for any preliminary calculations as to the Guideline range, and then will say the following:*]

[*Mr./Ms. defendant*], you should understand that the district court judge has the responsibility for determining your actual Guideline sentence, and will do so at your sentencing hearing. His/her determinations may be different from the predictions of the lawyers. These predictions are not binding on him/her.

Do you understand the sentence the district court judge gives you may be different from what you're hoping for or what [*Mr./Ms. defense counsel*] has predicted?

11. PLEA AGREEMENT [*If there is a plea agreement, the judge will do the following, but if there is no plea agreement, the judge will skip to paragraph 12, below.*]

[*The judge will have the prosecutor offer the plea agreement.*]

[*The judge will ensure the written plea agreement is in front of the defendant and the defendant's lawyer.*]

[*The judge will make certain that the initials and signature on the plea agreement were placed there by the defendant, and then tell the defendant the following:*]

Do you understand that by initialing and signing the plea agreement, you are agreeing to be bound by its terms, and agreeing that the factual representations in the plea agreement are true and accurate?

Have you read the entire plea agreement? Do you understand all of its terms?

To satisfy myself that you understand what the plea agreement means, I'm going to ask you a few questions about the agreement.

[*The judge will talk about some of the terms of the plea agreement. While doing this, the judge will review any Guideline stipulation in the plea agreement, and then ask defense counsel, and then the prosecutor, for any preliminary calculations as to the Guideline range, and then will say the following:*]

[*Mr./Ms. defendant*], you should understand that the district court judge has the responsibility for determining your actual Guideline sentence, and will do so at your sentencing hearing. His/her determinations may be different from the predictions of the lawyers, and may even be different from what is stipulated in the plea agreement. Stipulations and predictions are not binding on him/her.

Do you understand the sentence the district court judge gives you may be different from what you're hoping for or what [*Mr./Ms. defense counsel*] has predicted?

[*If applicable, the judge will talk about two possible exceptions to the prohibition on withdrawing a guilty plea– (a) an agreement not to bring, or to dismiss, certain charges or counts (11(c)(1)(A)), or (b) an agreement to a specific sentence or sentencing range (11(c)(1)(C)).*]

[*If applicable, the judge will talk about how substantial assistance might operate in this case.*]

[*The judge will review factual basis language in the plea agreement.*]

[*The judge will ask the following:*]

[*Mr./Ms. prosecutor*], does the plea agreement have any provisions waiving the right to appeal or to collaterally attack the sentence? Have I accurately described the important terms of the plea agreement?

[*Mr./Ms. defense counsel*], do you believe your client understands the plea agreement?

[*Mr./Ms. defendant*], do you have any questions about the plea agreement?

12. ELEMENTS AND FACTUAL BASIS

[*Mr./Ms. defendant*], before I can let you plead guilty, I must make sure you know what the prosecution would have to prove at trial to convict you on (this charge)/(these charges), and I also have to determine that the evidence in this case supports a finding that you are, in fact, guilty of the charge(s).

[*The judge will discuss the elements and the required factual basis, and any Apprendi issues.*]

[*Mr./Ms. prosecutor*], did I correctly explain the elements of the charge(s) to the defendant? Do you believe I have established an adequate factual basis for (a guilty plea) (guilty pleas) to the charge(s)?

[*Mr./Ms. defense counsel*], do you think your client understands the elements of the charge(s) against him/ her? Have you had full access to the Government's discovery materials? Do you believe they support a factual basis for (a guilty plea)/(guilty pleas) to the charge(s)? Do you know of any possible defenses to the charge(s) that you haven't discussed with your client?

13. ENSURING VOLUNTARINESS OF PLEA

[*Mr./Ms. defendant*], has anyone made any promises to you to get you to plead guilty [*, other than what's in the plea agreement*]?

Has anyone forced or pressured you to plead guilty?

Has anyone threatened you to get you to plead guilty?

[*Mr./Ms. defense counsel*], do you believe (a guilty plea)/(guilty pleas) by your client to the charge(s) against him/her would be voluntary?

14. [*The judge will ask the lawyers the following question:*] **ARE THERE ANY FURTHER QUESTIONS YOU THINK I SHOULD ASK, [*Mr./Ms. defense counsel*]? [*Mr./Ms. prosecutor*]?**

15. [*Mr./Ms. defendant*], **DO YOU HAVE ANY QUESTIONS ABOUT ANYTHING? DO YOU STILL WANT TO PLEAD GUILTY?**

16. [*Mr./Ms. defendant*], **FORMALLY AND FOR THE RECORD,** how do you plead to Count I of the Indictment/Information–guilty or not guilty? (*Etc.* for any other counts)

The record should reflect that the defendant has pled guilty to [*the one Count]/[Counts _____*] of the Indictment/Information.

17. I find that:

The defendant is competent;

(S)he fully understands the charge(s) against him/her;

There is a factual basis for his/her plea(s);

(S)he knows the maximum punishment that could be imposed on the charge(s); and (S)he knows his/her jury rights and has voluntarily waived those rights.

I further find that:

The defendant's decision to plead guilty was voluntary, knowing, and not the result of any force, pressure, threats, or promises [*, other than the promises made by the Government in the plea agreement*].

Therefore, I find the defendant should be adjudged guilty based on his/her plea(s) of guilty.

18. Report and Recommendation

I am now signing and will file my Report and Recommendation, recommending that the defendant's guilty plea(s) be accepted. I also am serving copies of the Report and Recommendation on the lawyers for the parties. [**THE JUDGE WILL PROVIDE LAWYERS WITH A COPY OF THE REPORT AND RECOMMENDATION**.] The parties are advised they have 10 days from today's date, not counting weekends and holidays, to file objections to the Report and Recommendation. If a party fails to make a timely objection, the party will have waived the right to make the objection. After reviewing any objections, the district court judge may accept the Report and Recommendation, and the defendant's plea(s) of guilty, by simply entering a written order doing so. [**The judge will tell the defendant about any scheduled sentencing date**–*e.g.,* "**Judge Bennett has scheduled a sentencing hearing in this case for (date and time).**"]

    19. I hereby **ORDER A PRESENTENCE INVESTIGATION REPORT**. The parties should pay careful attention to the deadlines relating to the preparation of the report.

    20. [*The judge will take care of any detention issues and, if appropriate, remand the defendant to the custody of the U.S. Marshal.*]

    21. [*The judge will ask the lawyers the following question:*] **IS THERE ANYTHING FURTHER THAT NEEDS TO BE DONE TO CONCLUDE THIS HEARING [***Mr./Ms. defense counsel***]? [***Mr./Ms. prosecutor***]?**

    22. [*The judge will address the defendant, if appropriate.*]

    We are in recess.

Form 17-10   Expungement Order (Pennsylvania)

IN THE COURT OF COMMON PLEAS OF _____ COUNTY, _____
CRIMINAL DIVISION

COMMONWEALTH OF _____

       v.

_____

CC. No.:_____
CHARGE: _____
DATE OF ARREST:_____
DISPOSITION:_____
DATE OF BIRTH:_____
SOCIAL SECURITY No.:_____

EXPUNGEMENT ORDER OF COURT

    AND NOW, to wit, this _____ day of _____, 20___, the within petition having been presented in open Court, upon consideration thereof, and on motion of _____, Attorney for petitioner, the same is ordered filed, the prayer thereof is granted, and

    IT IS HEREBY ORDERED, ADJUDGED AND DECREED that the Clerk of Courts shall serve a certified copy of this Order upon the following persons, keepers of records, pertaining to the above captioned criminal proceedings:

1. District Attorney
2. Bail Agency
3. District Magistrate
4. Arresting Agency
5. Court Reporter
6. Bureau of Criminal Identification
7. Pa. State Police
8. Federal Bureau of Investigation

    IT IS ORDERED, ADJUDGED AND DECREED that the aforementioned keepers of criminal records shall expunge and destroy the official and unofficial arrest and other documents pertaining to the arrest or prosecution or both of the above named defendant in the above captioned criminal proceedings, and that each shall request the return of such records which its agency made available to State or Federal agencies and immediately upon receipt thereof shall destroy such records, with the exception of District Attorney's records concerning ARD, which shall be used solely for the purpose of determining subsequent eligibility for ARD and that said keepers of such criminal records shall file with this Court an Affidavit stating that the mandates of this Order have been fulfilled.

    IT IS ORDERED, ADJUDGED AND DECREED that the Clerk of Courts shall expunge the Indices of the official and unofficial arrest and other documents pertaining to the arrest or prosecution or both of the above-named defendant in the above captioned criminal proceedings, and shall seal and impound the aforesaid Affidavits together with the

Indictment, the Complaint and the original and all copies of this Order, and no person or agency shall be permitted to examine such documents.

BY THE COURT;

_____
Judge

AFFIDAVIT OF EXPUNGEMENT

This is to certify that the official arrest and criminal records and other documents filed pertaining to the particular arrest or prosecution or both of the above named defendant in the above captioned criminal proceedings, which are in custody of and in control of this Office, have been expunged and destroyed.

_____
Certifying Officer

Form 17-11   Partial Expungement Motion (Pennsylvania)

IN THE COURT OF COMMON PLEAS OF _____ COUNTY

COMMONWEALTH OF PENNSYLVANIA	)	CRIMINAL DIVISION
v.	)	CR-
JB	)	PETITION FOR EXPUNGEMENT

Filed on behalf of JB
Counsel of Record for this Party:
Thomas J. Farrell, Esquire

IN THE COURT OF COMMON PLEAS OF _____ COUNTY

COMMONWEALTH OF PENNSYLVANIA	)	
v.	)	CRIMINAL DIVISION
JB	)	CR-

PETITION FOR EXPUNGEMENT

AND NOW, comes the Petitioner, JB, by and through his attorney, Thomas J. Farrell, Esquire who make the within Petition for Expungement and in support thereof, aver the following:

The Petitioner is JB, who resides at _____.
The Petitioner's social security number is _____. His date of birth is _____.
The Petitioner was arrested on _____ at OTN No. _____. He was charged with one (1) count of Simple Assault, one (1) count of Criminal Conspiracy, one (1) count of Criminal Mischief, one (1) count of Theft by Unlawful Taking or Disposition, and one (1) count of Disorderly Conduct.
All charges except for the one (1) count of Disorderly Conduct were withdrawn on _____. A copy of the certified disposition sheet is attached as Exhibit A.
The Petitioner was arrested, fingerprinted and photographed in connection with these charges and the record of the arrest will unfairly reflect upon Petitioner and may adversely affect his employment opportunities.

WHEREFORE, Petitioner, JB, respectfully requests that this Honorable Court grant this Petition for Expungement and order that all keepers of criminal records as set forth in the Expungement Order of Court expunge and destroy all documents pertaining to the arrest and prosecution of the Petitioner.

Respectfully Submitted,

_____
Thomas J. Farrell, Esquire

VERIFICATION

I, Thomas J. Farrell, Esquire, counsel for Petitioner, JB, hereby swear or affirm that Petitioner's signature could not be obtained in time for this filing, and I have been authorized to sign on behalf of Petitioner. I hereby swear or affirm that the facts contained in the foregoing Petition for Expungement are true and correct to the best of my knowledge, information and belief. I understand that the statements made herein are made subject to the penalties of 18 PA.C.S.A. Section 4904 relating to unsworn falsification to authorities.

Thomas J. Farrell

Date

IN THE COURT OF COMMON PLEAS OF _____ COUNTY

COMMONWEALTH OF PENNSYLVANIA	)	
v.	)	CRIMINAL DIVISION
JB	)	CR-

PRELIMINARY ORDER OF COURT

AND NOW, this _____ day of _____, 2005, it is hereby ORDERED that a hearing on the within Petition to Expunge Records of Criminal Proceeding shall be heard by the Court on _____ day of _____ , 2005 at _____.

By the Court:

_____ J.

COMMONWEALTH OF PENNSYLVANIA	)	
v.	)	CRIMINAL DIVISION
JB	)	CR-

AFFIDAVIT OF EXPUNGEMENT

This is to certify that the official arrest and criminal records and other documents filed pertaining to the particular arrest or prosecution or both of the above named Defendant in the above-captioned criminal proceedings, which are in custody of and in control of this Office, have been expunged and destroyed.

_____

Date   Certifying Officer

Chapter 18

REPRESENTING VICTIMS AND WITNESSES

VI. RESTITUTION AND OTHER COMPENSATION
A. Restitution

B. Compensation and Rewards

VII. FORMS

I.   GENERAL POINTS

§18:01   The Role of a Defense Lawyer

Criminal defense lawyers are sometimes called upon to represent witnesses and victims in criminal prosecutions. This often entails assisting the prosecution, a role that is uncomfortable to many defense lawyers.

However, the role makes sense. Defense lawyers know the process and the players in it and can guide victims and witnesses through it. We know which cases prosecutors and agents are likely to prosecute and how vigorously.

Prosecutors represent the interests of the citizenry at large, and those interests often diverge from a victim's. For example, imprisonment might be the best deterrent, but it does nothing to make a victim financially whole. Also, for a prosecutor the case is one among many to be processed and probably compromised, but not to the victim. Finally, prosecutors sometimes treat witnesses as a tool in their case, rather than as individuals to whom the process is an inconvenience and embarrassment.

Recent victims' rights statutes obligate prosecutors to protect victims and to notify them of court proceedings and enable victims to be heard at important proceedings such as bail hearings, pleas and sentencing. [*See* §18:03.] These statutes sometimes place the prosecutor in a conflict between the interests of the public and the government on one side and the victim on the other. The solution is independent counsel for the victim. [*See* Walker A. Matthews, *Proposed Victims' Rights Amendment; Ethical Considerations for the Prudent Prosecutor*, 11 Geo. J. L. Ethics 735, 750-51 (1998).]

Vigorous advocacy for the victim also might benefit the defendant. Sanctions such as full and immediate restitution and agreement to civil protective orders further the victim's interests, and the defendant might have incentive to pursue them if they are presented as alternatives to prosecution or incarceration.

§18:02   Ensure Your Client Is Just a Witness

Your first task in representing a witness or victim is to guarantee that your client is nothing more than that. Even individuals or entities who seem to be victims might turn out to be targets of prosecution.

EXAMPLES:

- Your client-company's purchasing agent may have solicited bribes from vendors and then increased the cost to your client, but perhaps your client passed the cost along to the government on a public contract when it first learned of the bribes.
- Your client may have been invested in some scam and then enlisted other investors in the hope of recouping his losses.
- Your client might be the bank teller or armored car guard held up at gunpoint, but it may come out that he tipped the robbers off as to when the bank or car was flush with cash and later shared in the theft proceeds.

Two basic steps should tip you off as to whether to doubt your client's innocent status in the investigation:

- Interview your client thoroughly. Do not take anything for granted. Inquire whether your client knew the perpetrators. Seek details about what your client did after the crime. To whom did your client report the crime; what exactly did your client tell them; did he omit anything; why?
- Ask the prosecutor and investigating agents as many questions as your imagination might suggest about the investigation and where your client stands. Ask what they think about your client and his information and look for any hesitancy in endorsing the truth of what your client says. Do they seem to be holding back information? Some reticence is understandable because they may not want to influence your client's testimony with other witnesses' stories, or they may have promised other witnesses confidentiality. However, an inexplicable refusal to share information or unanticipated questions, such as where your client got the money to buy an expensive car, might justify questioning your client more closely and warning him carefully that he should share all he knows with you.

§18:03   Victims' Statutory Rights

Most jurisdictions have victims' rights statutes as well as restitution statutes. These generally grant victims the right to notice of court proceedings and to be heard at them and recognize that victims may retain independent counsel to appear and represent their interests.

The following are examples of such statutes [*see United States v. Degenhardt*, 405 F.Supp.2d 1341, 1350 & n.48 (D. Utah 2005) (surveying state statutes)]:

- Federal: 18 U.S.C. §3771 (granting victims right to be reasonably protected from accused, to notice of court proceedings, to be heard at any proceeding involving release, plea sentencing or parole, to confer with the prosecutor, to full restitution, and to seek the advice of counsel; authorizes victims to file motions with the trial court and petitions of mandamus in the court of appeals to enforce these rights).
- Alabama: Ala. Code §15-23-72 (allowing victims to be heard at any sentencing proceeding).
- Alaska: Alaska Stat. §12.55.023(b) (allowing for sworn victim impact testimony or an unsworn victim presentation at sentencing).
- Arizona: Ariz. Rev. Stat. Ann. §13-702(E) (requiring the court to consider victim impact testimony at an aggravation or mitigation proceeding).
- California: Cal. Penal Code §1191.1 (permitting victim to appear and reasonably present views concerning the crime, the person responsible, and the need for restitution); Cal. Penal Code §679.02(a)(3).
- Connecticut: Conn. Gen. Stat. Ann. §54-91c.(b) (permitting testimony of victim concerning the facts of the case, the appropriateness of any penalty and the extent of any injuries, financial losses, and loss of earnings directly resulting from the crime).
- Florida: Fla. Stat. Ann. §921.143(2)(a) (permitting victim impact testimony at sentencing, limited to the facts of the case, the extent of any harm, and "any matter relevant to an appropriate disposition of the case").
- Georgia: Ga. Code Ann. §17-10-1.2(a) (permitting victim impact testimony in the discretion of the sentencing judge, with limitations as to subject matter).
- Hawaii: Haw. Rev. Stat. Ann. §706-604(3) (permitting victim impact testimony at sentencing).
- Indiana: Ind. Code Ann. §35-35-3-5(b) (same).
- Iowa: Iowa Code Ann. §915.21 (same).
- Louisiana: La. Rev. Stat. Ann. §46:1844K (same).
- Maine: Me. Rev. Stat. Ann. tit. 17-A, §1174 (same).
- Massachusetts: Mass. Ann. Laws ch. 279, §4B (same).
- Michigan: Mch. Comp. Laws Ann. §780.765 (same).
- Minnesota: Minn. Stat. Ann. §611A.038(a) (same–subject to "reasonable limitations as to time and length").
- Nevada: Nev. Rev. Stat. Ann. §176.015(3) (permitting testimony of a victim concerning the crime, the person responsible, the impact of the crime on the victim, and the need for restitution).
- New Jersey: N.J. Stat. Ann. §39:4-50.11 (permitting victims to submit an oral statement to be considered in deciding sentencing terms).
- New Mexico: N.M. Stat. Ann. §31-26-4(G) (permitting victim impact testimony at sentencing).
- Ohio: Ohio Rev. Code Ann. §2929.19 (same).
- Rhode Island: R.I. Gen. Laws §12-28-3(a)(11) (permitting victim impact testimony at sentencing where the defendant was found guilty following a trial).
- South Carolina: S.C. Code Ann. §16-3-1550(F) (permitting victim impact testimony at sentencing).
- South Dakota: S.D. Codified Laws §23A-28C-1(8) (same).
- Utah: Utah Code Ann. §77-38-4(7) (same).
- Vermont: VT. Stat. Ann. tit. 13, §5321 (same).
- Washington: Wash. Rev. Code Ann. §9.94A.500(1) (permitting victims to make "arguments" at sentencing).
- West Virginia: W. VA. Code §61-11A-2(b) (permitting victim impact testimony at sentencing).
- Wisconsin: Wis. Stat. Ann. §972.14(3)(a) (same).
- Wyoming: Wyo. Stat. Ann. §7-21-102 (same).

§18:04   Private Prosecutions

Some jurisdictions permit individuals to file private criminal complaints, at least for relatively minor offenses. The individual can then either prosecute the case himself or have a private attorney handle the prosecution. [*See* Herbert B. Chermside, *Power of Private Citizen to Institute Criminal Proceedings Without Authorization or Approval by Prosecuting Attorney*, 66 A.L.R.3d 772.]

This is different than the procedure whereby the state hires a private lawyer as a special prosecutor when the public prosecutor is disqualified for some reason.

Some jurisdictions authorize victims to hire private attorneys to prosecute even serious crimes. [*See* Michael T. McCormack, *The Need for Private Prosecutors: An Analysis of Massachusetts and New Hampshire Law*, 37 Suffolk Univ. L.Rev. 497, 502 & n.43 (2004) (surveying states that allow limited participation by private prosecutors to include Alabama, California, Colorado, Florida, Georgia, Idaho, Illinois, Kansas, Kentucky, Louisiana, Maine, Minnesota, Mississippi, New Hampshire, New Jersey, New Mexico, North Carolina, Oklahoma, Pennsylvania, South Carolina, South Dakota, Tennessee, Texas, Utah, Virginia, U.S. Virgin Islands, Washington, and West Virginia).]

Be cautious about entering into such an engagement. Some courts and disciplinary authorities consider the representation of both a victim and the government's interest a serious conflict of interest. [*E.g., Young v. United States (Ex rel. Vuitton)*, 481 U.S. 787 (1987) (prohibiting use of privately hired prosecutors in federal criminal trials).] Also, your client must understand that prosecuting a criminal case is a very time-intensive endeavor, and he must be prepared to pay accordingly.

§18:05 Protect the Prosecution

Part of your role is to lend your client an objectivity that he might lack because he has been victimized.

If you client chooses to attend trial as a spectator, gently caution your client to avoid outbursts that might endanger the success of the prosecution. Instruct your client not to speak with the media and forbid him from any public display during the trial that might undermine the defendant's right to a fair trial. [*E.g., Musladin v. Lamarque*, 427 F.3d 653 (9th Cir. 2005) (reversing conviction where homicide victim's family wore buttons displaying victim's picture in courtroom during trial), *rev'd sub nom. Carey v. Musladin*, 127 S.Ct. 649 (2006) (holding that under the habeas standard of deference, it could not be said that the state court's actions in permitting the buttons violated clearly established federal law, but left the issue "an open question," reviewing cases from federal and state jurisdictions); *Mask v. State*, 314 Ark. 25, 869 S.W.2d 1 (1993) (reversing conviction where victim permitted to sit at prosecution table during trial); *but see People v. Ramer*, 17 Cal. App.4th 672, 679, 21 Cal. Rptr.2d 480 (5th Dist. 1993), *review denied, op. withdrawn by order of court, People v. Ramer*, 24 Cal.Rptr.2d 237, 860 P.2d 1183 (1993) (no error in permitting victim to sit at prosecution table).]

[§§18:06-18:09 Reserved]

II. INITIAL STEPS

§18:10 Explain the Process

One of the most helpful services you can perform for a victim or witness is to explain how the criminal process works and its timetable. Do not assume any knowledge on your client's part, no matter how sophisticated. Explain the process from start to finish, with emphasis on your client's role at each step:

The pre-charging investigation. Officers will interview your client. They usually do not record the interview, and there will not be a court reporter. Your client should share all he knows about the offense. Explain to your client that if charges result and the case goes to trial, the defendant may receive a report of the interview in discovery, and your client can be cross-examined on inconsistencies between the interview and his testimony.

The arrest, initial appearance and setting of bail. Your client does not need to attend any of these appearances. However, he may want to. Warn him that most defendants obtain release on bail, no matter how obviously guilty.

Preliminary Hearing or Grand Jury. Emphasize to your client just how preliminary these hearings are. Defendants always lose at the preliminary hearing or indictment stage, but this does not mean that the case will end soon.

Formal arraignment, pre-trial conferences and discovery and motion practice. Explain that there will be a number of court appearances dealing with legal issues, and that, for the most part, these will not affect your client.

Informal investigation by the defense. The defense may attempt to interview any potential witnesses. You client will have to decide whether or not to cooperate with such efforts [*See* §18:24 (defense access to your client).]

Plea bargaining. If you client is a victim, the prosecutor should consult your client before agreeing to any plea bargain. [*See* §§18:03 (victims' statutory rights), 18:60 (crime victim compensation funds).]

However, your client should understand that plea bargaining is not an open, on-the-record process. It takes place in informal discussions on the phone, in offices, and in courthouse hallways without you or your client having an opportunity to attend.

Trial. Explain the mechanics of a trial: the sequence of jury selection, openings, examinations and closings. Also explain witness sequestration and the inevitable postponements, delays and waiting. Explain that the defendant cannot be forced to testify, so the jury and your client may never hear his story.

The presentence investigation. After conviction, but before sentence, your client can provide the presentencing investigator with information on the impact of the crime and any restitution. This will be reported in a report which the parties, but not the public, will review and upon which the judge will rely at sentencing. [*See* §18:50.]

Sentencing. [*See* §§18:40 et seq.]

§18:11   Deciding Whether to Go to the Police

Your client has been victimized. Should he or she go to the police?
Two threshold issues should be addressed:
- Make sure your client has absolutely no risk of criminal exposure. [*See* §18:02 (ensure your client is just a witness).]
- Advise your client how a criminal prosecution may harm him or her even if he or she was uninvolved in the defendant's wrongdoing. For example, your client may be the estranged spouse who depends on the wrongdoer for support. Incarceration will end that support, so you do not want anger toward the defendant to cloud your client's judgment. Also, innocent spouses may find that jointly held properties acquired after the offense are not safe from forfeiture because the forfeiture statutes exempt only bona fide purchasers for value, and spouses and family members usually are not considered purchasers for value no matter their bona fides otherwise. [*See* Chapter 11, Forfeiture.]

Even if these concerns do not apply, turning over the matter to the prosecuting authorities still may not be in your client's best interests:

Criminal remedies are quite modest. Prosecutors and judges often compromise restitution awards to avoid protracted hearings on the issue.

Criminal prosecutions are public, and the defense is entitled to investigate witnesses' and victims' backgrounds and cross-examine them vigorously in an attempt to undermine their credibility. The victim's involvement might become especially traumatic in sex crime cases, but public exposure of even a business' victimization by an employee might become embarrassing.

Taking the case to the criminal authorities might diminish the chances of obtaining restitution. A person charged with a crime will dedicate what financial resources he has to defending his liberty, leaving little to make a victim whole. A private civil action might address the victim's needs more appropriately, especially in the case of an economic crime.

Consider the prosecuting authorities' policies on civil settlements. Many local prosecutors will dismiss a charge if the restitution satisfies the victim.

Other jurisdictions, in particular federal prosecutors, have a policy that defendants should not be able to buy their way out of prosecution. Once the office commits to prosecuting, it will not dismiss charges in exchange for restitution.

CAUTION:

Do not threaten a prosecution in order to elicit a financial settlement. Using a threat of prosecution to induce restitution may constitute the crime of extortion under the laws of your jurisdiction, even if the accusation is well-founded. [*E.g., State v. Greenspan*, 92 N.C. App. 563, 568, 374 S.E.2d 884, 887 (N.C. App. 1989) ("Even if the victim were guilty, this would not entitle defendant to demand money in exchange for refraining from initiating criminal proceedings. The majority of jurisdictions that have considered the matter have held that the victim's guilt of the crime of which he is accused is no defense to a charge of extortion.").]

§18:12   Package the Case for Prosecution

If your client decides to contact the police, there are steps you can take to see that the case is prosecuted vigorously.

To increase the likelihood that the police and prosecutor will pursue your client's case vigorously, do as much of their job for them as you can:
- Interview witnesses, including the perpetrator, and record them or dictate memoranda capturing the interview.
- Do a records check on the perpetrator, including criminal records, bankruptcy, judgments, UCC filings. Trace his assets.
- Collect and index the important documents.
- Organize all this in a binder with a summary explaining how the enclosed evidence establishes the elements of the offense you want to see prosecuted.
- Calculate the possible sentences under the applicable sentencing statutes and guidelines. Prosecutors are more likely to take a case if it will result in a serious sentence.

[§§18:13-18:19 Reserved]

III. PROTECTING YOUR CLIENT

§18:20 Police Protection and Bail Recommendation

Spell out in great detail to the police and prosecutor all concerns your client has about the threat the defendant might pose to your client's safety as early in the process as possible so that they can address those concerns in their bail recommendation.

Ask them for an after-hours contact person should your client be threatened or harassed. They have an obligation to listen and accommodate your client's concerns. [18 U.S.C. §3771(f)(2)(C) (Attorney General must establish disciplinary sanctions for prosecutors who shirk their responsibility under the CVRA).]

Some victims' rights statutes confer on the victim the right for the victim to address the court in person at a bail hearing. [*See Kenna v. U.S. District Court*, 435 F.3d 1011, 1014 (9th Cir. 2006) (dicta); *but see United States v. Marcello*, 370 F.Supp.2d 745, 750 (N.D. Ill. 2005) (court can restrict victim to providing written statement).]

If your client wants to appear and make a statement, prepare the statement yourself, and prepare your client for any questions the judge or the defense may ask. Try to keep your client focused on the proceeding's purpose, which is to determine detention or conditions of release, not issues such as restitution or punishment.

Form:
- **Form 18-5** Victim Notification

§18:21 Motions to Quash

The parties may subpoena your client to testify in a trial that your client wants to avoid.

Prosecutors usually try to avoid side issues that might confuse the jury or distract it from the defendant's guilt. In contrast, defendants might try to subpoena witnesses to create just such diversions or to fix blame on the witness.

If you perceive that your client is being called for some irrelevant purpose, move to quash the subpoena.

File a motion to quash sufficiently in advance of the time for your client's testimony that the judge will have time to consider it, but not with so much notice that the party will have time to concoct new reasons for your client's testimony. Even a judge busy with a trial will indulge such a motion if he or she senses that the party is trying to muddy and protract the trial with collateral issues.

If your client does not want to testify, it is best to keep the party from speaking with your client and to avoid previewing your client's testimony. No one wants to call a witness not knowing what he or she will say. If you have some basis for it, suggest to the party's lawyer that your client has harmful testimony to offer that might come out during trial if called.

Document subpoenas must specifically identify the documents to be produced, and, absent a court order, the subpoena cannot order production any time prior to the testimony.

Forms:
- **Form 18-1** Motion to Quash Subpoena for Testimony
- **Form 18-2** Motion to Quash Document Subpoena

§18:22   Whistleblowers

If your client provides information against an employer, especially concerning fraud on the government, whistleblower statutes may protect him from retaliation and even entitle him to remuneration. [*E.g.,* 18 U.S.C. §1513(d) (interfering with the employment of a witness who provides truthful information about any federal offense is a felony punishable by up to ten years); *Field v. Electric Co.,* 388 Pa. Super. 400, 419-22, 565 A.2d 1170 (Pa. Super. Ct. 1989) (at-will employee has action for wrongful discharge where he is fired for complying with legal requirement to reporting exposure to excess radiation to Nuclear Regulatory Commission).]

§18:23   Serve as Liaison With the Police and Prosecutor

Many witnesses become frustrated by the criminal justice system: they show up for hearings that have been cancelled, and they suffer prolonged waits for those hearings and trials which do take place.

Ask the police and prosecutor to contact you when anything significant occurs in the investigation or case so you can communicate it to your client (*e.g.,* the arrest of the defendant, court hearings and postponements, trial, plea and sentencing dates). Show that your client is interested and available.

Serve as a liaison with your client. If you demonstrate that you can produce your client promptly and on short notice, the prosecutor is more likely to give you a specific time and date for your client's appearance rather than making him sit around through days of other witnesses' testimony.

§18:24   Defense Access to Your Client

Usually, if your client is either a victim or a prosecution witness, you should not permit the defense to speak to him or her.

The defense will interview your client as you would a government witness if you were defending the case. That is, it will focus on exculpatory statements and memorialize inconsistencies in a report slanted to make your client seem as unreliable as possible. The interview will be used to make your client look bad on the witness stand and in the eyes of the prosecutor.

In contrast, you may want to preview, in your words, your client's testimony for the defense. Prosecutors can be niggardly in sharing their evidence, especially witness statements. You might describe your client's expected testimony in order to persuade the defense lawyer to strike a deal in the case rather than going to trial. Afterwards, you should report back to your client on the discussion.

Sharing information with the lawyers also preserves your reputation for fairness and camaraderie with fellow defense lawyers.

Remember that what your client has told only you is protected by the attorney-client privilege. However, what he has told the prosecution, even in your presence, is not privileged.

Contact the defense attorney and instruct him to direct all subpoenas and requests for interviews to you. Warn your client that the defense lawyer or a defense investigator may contact him. Assure him that such efforts are not illegal, but tell your client that should anyone contact him, he should say nothing other than to tell them to contact you.

Unless the law of your jurisdiction or a court order specifies otherwise, subpoenas (from either the defense or prosecution) cannot command your client to appear or produce documents anytime before the trial or hearing date. If your client receives a subpoena commanding pre-trial production of documents or his appearance at a lawyer's office not at a hearing or trial, call the lawyer and explain that unless the court orders such early production or appearance, your client will not comply. Send a letter memorializing the conversation. If the lawyer persists, move to quash. [*See* §18:21.]

On the other hand, you may choose to produce documents to the defense before trial to avoid your client's appearance or delay at trial.

§18:25   Post-Release Protection

After a case is concluded and the defendant imprisoned, you should see that your client is protected upon the defendant's release.

The prison may have an obligation to provide notice of release or escape, and you can make your client's position known to the parole board. [*See* 18 Pa. Stat. §11.214(b), (g) (Department of Corrections has obligation to notify victim of pending release decision and allow victim to submit comments to parole board if the victim notified the Department that he wanted an opportunity to provide such comment).]

The inmate's release date usually is available online. [*E.g.*, www.bop.gov. (Federal Bureau of Prisons website).]

[§§18:26-18:29 Reserved]

IV. THE COOPERATING WITNESS

§18:30   The Defense Lawyer's Policy

All witnesses friendly to the prosecution could be considered cooperating witnesses.

However, among defense lawyers, a "cooperator" (also known as an "informant," "snitch," or "rat") generally means a witness with criminal culpability who seeks to minimize his punishment by assisting in the prosecution of another person. Some defense lawyers legitimately refuse to represent witnesses who sell their testimony for leniency for their own wrongdoing, reasoning that the system of rewarding cooperating witnesses and informants undermines the integrity of the adversary system and encourages convictions on perjured testimony. [*See* Barry Tarlow, "The Moral Conundrum of Representing the Rat," *The Champion* 64 (March 2006); *United States v. Singleton*, 144 F.3d 1343 (10th Cir. 1997) (holding that rewarding cooperators with lenient sentences violates the federal witness bribery statute), *rev'd en banc,* 165 F.3d 1297 (10th Cir. 1999).]

However, under mandatory minimum and guideline sentencing regimes, many defendants find that they have little chance of avoiding lengthy sentences other than by cooperating against others. Thus, even lawyers adamant against representing snitches acknowledge that clients must be warned of the lawyer's personal policy in the initial engagement agreement and offered the option of seeking other counsel. [*See* Tarlow, *supra*; Model Rule 1.2(c) (a "lawyer may limit the objectives of the representation if the client consents after consultation").]

When you do represent cooperating defendant-witnesses, your objective will be to get as much as you from the prosecution while giving as little as you can.

§18:31   Preview Your Client's Story

Before you have your client tell his story, you want to summarize it for the prosecutor in your words to determine whether:
- It jibes with the prosecutor's view of the truth.
- It has value to the prosecutor.

Your client's story may sound perfectly truthful to you, but might conflict with another cooperator's story or hard evidence of which you are not aware. If you walk your client in to tell a story that will not be believed, you are weakening the chance of defending the case at trial.

Most prosecutors do not want to trap your client into telling an untruthful story because it wastes considerable prosecutorial time and resources.

Even if your client is telling the truth, the story may be of no value to the prosecutor. Your client may have information about an illegal transaction that cannot be corroborated or in which the prosecutor has no interest (*e.g.,* the coconspirator may have admitted the transaction already, or it may be so insignificant in the scheme of things that the prosecutor has no interest in pursuing it).

§18:32   Rehearse Your Client Thoroughly

Good rehearsal puts your client in the right frame of mind, and guarantees that he is truthful.

Cooperating entails a very different attitude toward the prosecution than the normal adversary stance (an attitude that many defendants and defense lawyers find distasteful).

Prosecutors usually first want the cooperator to demonstrate his credibility and remorse by freely admitting his own wrongdoing. The cooperator should not answer questions like a defendant on cross, interpreting the questions narrowly and answering only what is asked and nothing more; rather, he should volunteer information and try to be helpful.

You must be careful, however, that your client does not admit serious crimes for which he has not been prosecuted unless you have some advance assurance, preferably in a written agreement or through a formal order of immunity, that the information will not be used against your client. [See Chapter 12, Grand Jury Practice.] For example, if your client is cooperating in a relatively mundane drug case, admitting a murder would be unwise. The prosecutor could not forego prosecuting such a serious offense.

Nonetheless, the prosecutor and agents have no right to humiliate cooperators. You should insist that they treat your client respectfully. Your client must admit that he did wrong, but he does not have to grovel. There is no need for a prosecutor to parade your client through acknowledging all whom he has harmed and betrayed and the miserable person he has become.

§18:33   Attend Early Debriefings

You must attend the first few meetings between your client and the agents and prosecutor both to serve as a witness to your client's forthrightness and to avoid misunderstandings.

Later, when the prosecution is evaluating the extent and honesty of your client's cooperation to determine what sentence to recommend, disputes may arise as to whether your client withheld information. Your memory and notes can protect your client from such accusations.

Be cautious about what you commit to paper. The defense may subpoena your notes or file memoranda. The attorney-client privilege does not protect the notes because the meeting is not confidential. The work-product privilege may shield them from disclosure in most, but not all cases. [*See United States v. Paxson*, 861 F.2d 730, 735-36 (D.C. Cir. 1988) (denying defense access to witness's lawyer's notes of federal agents' debriefing of witness); *United States v. Arias*, 373 F. Supp. 2d 311 (S.D.N.Y. 2005) (same); *but see In re Grand Jury*, 282 F.3d 156 (2d Cir. 2002) (quashing grand jury subpoena for defense attorney notes as protected work-product, but suggesting that result might be different if the subpoena were a trial subpoena and the government could show substantial need).]

In your notes, emphasize those statements that help your client both by underscoring the value of his cooperation and by avoiding equivocations which the defense or prosecutors who doubt his sincerity later may use against him. Include instances in which your client stated definite and reliable facts about the other targets of the investigation, but downplay your client's reluctance to admit his own proven wrongdoing.

Early meetings can be testy because your client and the agents do not trust each other. You may need to calm down both your client and the agents. Explain to your client why the agents are asking particular questions. If you realize that your client is prevaricating, you may need to ask for a break and talk to your client alone, either to get him on the right track or to end the meeting before he hurts himself.

§18:34   Limit the Extent of Your Client's Cooperation

Sane clients do not want to cooperate indefinitely. Public testimony exposes them and their families to humiliation, ostracism and physical danger. Eventually, they want to stop testifying, setting up drug deals or wearing recording devices in undercover investigations and get on with their lives.

Try to persuade the prosecution to forego your client's testimony and limit his use to investigative leads, information for sealed search warrant affidavits and grand jury testimony rather than undercover work and trial testimony.

On the other hand, those cooperators who give the most at most risk (*e.g.*, wearing body wires in several investigations, testifying at multiple trials) receive the greatest reward in terms of sentence and charge reductions. Unfortunately, you may find that the agents and prosecutor are reluctant to consider the cooperation completed because of its very productivity.

Be aware that some cooperators come to see themselves as pseudo-cops and enjoy acting in an undercover capacity and "making cases." Agents often encourage them in this fantasy to the benefit of the agent's career.

You do not want any part of this. Not only does it lead to entrapping the otherwise innocent, but cooperators inevitably use this relationship as cover for their own crimes, from evading taxes on the bounties they receive to drug-trafficking and murder. [*See Orena v. United States*, 956 F.Supp. 1071 (E.D.N.Y. 1997) and *United States v. Salemme*, 91 F.Supp.2d 1411 (D. Mass. 1999) (two notorious cases in Boston and New York City, where FBI handlers for high-ranking organized crime snitches fed them information which enabled them to murder rivals).]

§18:35   Obtain Early Assurances From the Prosecution

A cooperation agreement may reserve to the prosecution the right to evaluate the truthfulness, completeness and helpfulness of your client's cooperation before making a decision to ask the court to reduce your client's sentence.

Nevertheless, by signing the agreement the prosecutor has signaled that as of the time of the agreement, your client has cooperated satisfactorily and done enough to earn a sentence reduction. [*See United States v. Roe*, 445 F.3d 202, 207-08 (2d Cir. 2006) (courts will review government's decision not to award cooperation more closely where there is a formal cooperation agreement; "We have made clear, however, that the government may not base its dissatisfaction with a defendant's performance of an agreement on facts known to the government at the time the agreement is executed. Not only would it be unfair for the government to rely upon ... known, pre-agreement circumstances as reasons for not moving [under §3553(e)], it would have been fraudulent to have induced a defendant's plea with a promise that the government already knew it was not going to keep.").]

Generally, once signed to a cooperation agreement, your client will get his sentence reduction unless he does something to bollix it, such as committing another crime or refusing to testify. Thus you want the agreement sooner rather later because once you have an agreement, the prosecutor must justify a refusal to award your client.

The downside of an early agreement is that it commits your client to testify and to plead guilty to specified charges. Your client cannot be forced to plead guilty if he withdraws from the agreement, but the plea agreement will require him to waive many rights, such as the right to challenge the admission of the many statements he made during his cooperation and the right to challenge the timeliness of the prosecution under the statute of limitations. [*See* Chapter 17, Plea Bargaining, and Chapter 12, Grand Jury Practice).]

Form:
- **Form 17-7** Sample Plea Agreement (Federal) With Cooperation and Stipulated Factual Basis [In Chapter 17]

[§§18:36-18:39 Reserved]

V. REPRESENTING THE VICTIM AT SENTENCING

§18:40   Three Rights at Sentencing

Your client has three rights at sentencing:
- To be heard. [*See* §18:41.]
- To see that conditions are imposed to protect the witness from the defendant. [*See* §§18:20 et seq.]
- To restitution. [*See* §§18:50 et seq.]

Most sentencing decisions are made well before the actual sentencing hearings, on the basis of the presentence report and objections and other materials which the parties submit to the judge.

Therefore, to protect your client's rights, you must confer frequently with the probation officer and prosecutor before sentencing and make written submissions to them and the court stating your client's position.

§18:41   The Right to Be Heard

A crime victim has a right to be heard. [*See* 18 U.S.C. §3771(a)(4).]

Your client has a right not only to submit written victim impact statements, but to address the court orally at sentencing and perhaps other proceedings if the statute permits. [*See Kenna v. District Court*, 435 F.3d 1011 (9th Cir. 2006) (right to address court at all proceedings bearing on release, plea and sentencing); *State v. Casey*, 44 P.3d 756 (Utah 2002) (victims had right to address the court before it accepted plea); *but see United States v. Marcello*, 370 F.Supp.2d 745, 748 (N.D. Ill. 2005) (victim has right only to submit written statement).]

This may include the right to argue for sentencing enhancements that the prosecution has agreed to forego. [*See United States v. Degenhardt*, 405 F.Supp.2d 1341, 1343 & n.7 (D. Utah 2005) (claiming that the Crime Victims' Rights Act of 2004, 18 U.S.C. §3771 (d)(1) overrules *United States v. Fortier*, 242 F.3d 1224 (10th Cir. 2001) (finding "an absence of authority" on the issue of whether counsel for victims can participate in a sentencing hearing, and raising "misgivings" about the practice where the government had agreed not to argue for the very issues the victims' counsel did).]

If your client is denied the right to be heard, you may petition the appellate court for a writ of mandamus ordering the trial court to afford the right. In federal cases, the court of appeals must decide the petition within 72 hours. [18 U.S.C. §3773(d)(3).]

§18:42   Oppose No Contest Pleas

A criminal conviction by plea or verdict may have collateral estoppel effect in civil litigation arising from the same transactions; at the minimum, a plea constitutes strong evidence that that the defendant under oath admitted the essential elements of the offense. However, a conviction by plea of nolo contendere does not have such an effect. [*See State v. Salas,* 92 Conn. App. 541, 885 A.2d 1258 (Conn. App. 2005) (explaining difference between no contest plea and guilty plea); Fed.R.Evid. 410 (evidence of a nolo contendere plea inadmissible against criminal defendant in subsequent civil trial); *but see Rusheen v. Drews,* 99 Cal.App.4th 279, 120 Cal. Rptr.2d 769, 772-73 (Cal. App. 2002) (under Cal. Penal Code §1016(3) a no contest plea to a felony is admissible as a party admission in civil cases); *Starr Tyme, Inc. v. Cohen,* 659 So.2d 1064, 1066 (Fl. 1995) (under Florida law, no contest plea serves as collateral estoppel in civil litigation).]

Therefore, you should oppose the acceptance of a no contest plea, both by conferring with the prosecutor and appearing in court to voice your objections to the judge.

[§§18:43-18:49 Reserved]

VI.　RESTITUTION AND OTHER COMPENSATION

A.　Restitution

§18:50　　Assist in the Recommendations

A crime victim has a right to restitution. [*See* 18 U.S.C. §3771(a)(6).]

Furthermore, both the probation officer and prosecutor have an obligation to provide the victim an opportunity to state his position on loss and restitution. [*See* 18 U.S.C. §3664(d)(2).]

Nevertheless, you should take the initiative. Remember, the prosecutor's goal often is more to end the case then to protract it with investigation and litigation over damages. Calculate the loss, including all consequential damages and interest. [*See Ex parte Fletcher,* 849 So.2d 900, 907 (Ala. 2001) (surveying state and federal jurisdictions and finding that most do allow prejudgment interest in restitution orders); *see generally* George Blum, Measure and Elements of Restitution to Which Victim Is Entitled Under State Criminal Statute, 15 A.L.R. 5th 391, §45j (1993).]

Prosecutors often seize and forfeit all assets derived from or traceable to the crime. [*See* Chapter 11, Forfeiture.] The prosecution is not obligated to apply those seized assets to restitution, but usually will. [*See* Department of Justice, *U.S. Attorney's Manual, Criminal Resource Manual* 2290; 18 U.S.C. §981(e)(6) (providing authority to restore property to victims).]

You can facilitate such restoration by responding promptly and fully to any requests for loss information and persistently making your client's position known.

After you have calculated the loss, confer frequently with the probation officer and the prosecutor to participate in shaping their final recommendations.

Your client may also have a right to submit a separate affidavit or victim impact statement on loss. [*See* 18 U.S.C. §3664(d)(2).] The Department of Justice maintains a website which outlines victim impact statements and offers advice in completing them. [www.ovc.gov/publications/infores/is.htm (website of Department of Justice, Office for Victims of Crime).]

Form:
- **Form 18-3** Victim Impact Statement

§18:51　　Review the Presentence Report

Attempt to review the presentence report or at least its recommendation regarding restitution. The court will rely on the report in arriving at a restitution figure, so you want to know its bottom line. If the presentence report is unsatisfactory, you may want to object to its calculation of the loss the defendant caused your client.

Many jurisdictions treat the presentence report as confidential and forbid the parties from disclosing it to others. [*See, e.g.,* 42 Pa. C.S.A. §§9733, 9734.] Whether a victim or his representative has a right to review the presentence report and object to its recommendations is an unsettled issue. [*See* Hon. Paul G. Cassell, *Recognizing Victims in the Federal Rules of Criminal Procedure: Proposed Amendments in Light of the Crime Victims' Rights Act,* 2005 B.Y.U. L. Rev. 835, 891-903 (noting conflicting federal and state laws and decisions and advocating that victims have the right to review and object to the presentence report); *but see In re Kenna,* 453 F.3d 1136, 1137 (9th Cir. 2006) (victim has no right to disclosure of presentence report).]

You can sidestep this issue by asking the probation officer and prosecutor to share with you not the report itself but part of its contents (*e.g.,* the calculations and conclusion on restitution and the defendant's ability to pay). [*See Hunter v. Farmers Ins. Co. of Oregon*, 135 Or. App. 125, 141, 898 P.2d 201, 210 (Or. App. 1995) (construing Or. Rev. Stat §137.077(4) to permit prosecutors to share information and seek input from victims to assist in sentencing).]

§18:52 Converting to a Civil Judgment

Most defendants do not have the ability to pay full restitution immediately. The sentence may permit them to pay it over time, often as a condition of probation, parole or supervised release.

The criminal judgment may expire with the end of the supervision term, but some criminal statutes authorize the victim to convert the criminal judgment into a civil judgment and execute it accordingly. [18 U.S.C. §3664(m)(1)(B); Cal. Penal Code §1214(b) (only in felony cases can criminal order of restitution be converted to a civil judgment).]

It is the victim named in the restitution order, not the prosecutor, who must request that the clerk enter a judgment based on the restitution order. You must see that it gets recorded and entered as a lien on the defendant's property. [*See* 18 U.S.C. §3664(m)(1)(B).]

The restitution order requires the defendant to notify the court and prosecutor of any change in circumstances that might affect his ability to pay restitution and likewise requires the prosecutor to notify the victim of the change. [18 U.S.C. §3664(k).] The victim then can file a motion to adjust the payment schedule. [18 U.S.C. §3664(k)(n).]

§18:53 Civil Remedies–Unjust Enrichment

Besides benefiting from a restitution order or from the government's release of forfeited assets to the victim for restitution, you can sue on your client's behalf under fraud or conversion theories. While these theories and remedies may not yield anything more than what your client will receive in criminal restitution, filing an action protects your client's position should the criminal prosecution falter.

Consider adding an unjust enrichment claim against any friends, relatives or business associates who shared or benefited from the proceeds of the crime. An unjust enrichment claim does not require proof that the defendant knowingly participated in the crime. Proof that it would be unfair for him to retain the unearned benefit of another's wrongdoing suffices. [*See Dominiack Mechanical, Inc. v. Dunbar*, 757 N.E.2d 186, 190-91 (Ind. App. 2001) (where defendants attended party paid for with funds embezzled, without defendants' knowledge, from plaintiff corporation, defendants were not liable for conversion, but could be liable under unjust enrichment theory).]

> **Form:**
> • **Form 18-4** Unjust Enrichment Civil Complaint

[§§18:54-18:59 Reserved]

B. Compensation and Rewards

§18:60 Crime Victim Compensation Funds

Many jurisdictions have statutes and funds to compensate violent crime victims from the public fisc. [*See generally* Andrea G. Nadel, *Statutes Providing for Governmental Compensation for Victims of Crime*, 20 A.L.R.4th 63; 42 U.S.C. §10602 (providing federal funding for state victim compensation programs); *see, e.g.,* NY McKinney's Executive Law §§621-634 (limited to compensation for physical injuries).]

While most such awards are modest, you should explore this option and apply for such funds, especially where the perpetrator lacks the money or insurance to make restitution.

Compensation statutes may require that the victim be innocent of any wrongdoing herself, including any prior criminal record, and lack any familial relationship to the wrongdoer and that the victim fully cooperate in any prosecution, [*In re Rodgers*, 61 Ohio Misc.2d 242, 577 N.E.2d 162 (OH Ct. Cl. 1988) (compensation denied where victim's failure to appear in grand jury to testify caused termination of investigation).]

However, funds might be available even where no conviction results. [NY McKinney's Exec. Law §627 (3).]

The statute also may provide for recovery of attorney's fees to litigate the claim. [*See* 20 A.L.R.4th 63, §13.]

§18:61   Rewards

Determine whether your client is entitled to any rewards. Some law enforcement agencies offer rewards for those whose information leads to successful prosecutions or the recovery of stolen funds. [*E.g.*, 26 C.F.R. §301.7623-1, IRS Publication 733, IRS Form 211 (IRS pays rewards of up to 15 percent of tax recovered for information leading to detection and punishment of tax cheats).]

However, warn your client that he must pay income tax on the reward. [*See* IRS Form 211.]

§18:62   Qui Tam Actions

Federal law and an increasing number of state statutes authorize individuals with firsthand knowledge of fraud against the government to bring a "qui tam" action for damages on the government's behalf, and to share in the recovery. [*E.g.,* 31 U.S.C. §3730(b); 740 Ill. Comp. Stat. Ann. §§175/1 *et seq.*; Cal. Gov't Code §§2650-12655.]

Before filing a *qui tam* action, consult an attorney with experience in such actions. These actions have unique procedural requirements. [*See* www.taf.org (website listing *qui tam* practitioners).]

VII. FORMS

Form 18-1   Motion to Quash Subpoena for Testimony

UNITED STATES DISTRICT COURT

DISTRICT OF _____

UNITED STATES OF AMERICA	)	
v.	)	CRIM. NO.
RC and	)	
JL	)	

MOTION BY JG AND LL TO QUASH SUBPOENA ISSUED BY DEFENDANT RC

And now come nonparties JG and LL, by their counsel Thomas J. Farrell, and, pursuant to Fed. R. Crim. P. 17(c) and for reasons stated more fully in the accompanying Memorandum of Law, move to quash the subpoena issued to them by defendant RC.

Respectfully submitted,

_____
Thomas J. Farrell, Esquire
Counsel for JG and LL

UNITED STATES DISTRICT COURT

DISTRICT OF _____

UNITED STATES OF AMERICA	)	
v.	)	CRIM. NO.
RC and	)	
JL	)	

**NON-PARTY JG AND LL'S MEMORANDUM OF LAW IN SUPPORT OF
MOTION TO QUASH SUBPOENA**

Pursuant to Rule 17(c) of the Federal Rules of Criminal Procedure, JG and LL, non-parties in the above-captioned case, by their attorney, Thomas J. Farrell, submit this Memorandum of Law in support of their Motion to Quash.

STATEMENT OF FACTS

The trial testimony to date has been that John Day approached defendant RC to win his assistance in placing a group of four local subcontractors on the bidding list for the Supercoliseum project. According to Day, RC agreed to help in return for payments amounting to two percent of the contract amount awarded to the local subcontractors. RC did not include the prime contractor, _____ Partners, Inc. in this scheme because he viewed it as composed of outsiders, M Corporation of Pennsylvania and _____ Limited of France, who could not be "trusted" with the corrupt scheme. *See also* Superseding Indictment, ¶¶ 24-26.

The issue before the jury trial is whether the defendants solicited and accepted bribes from subcontractors for obtaining work and payment on the _____ construction project between _____ and _____. The Government does not allege any extortion with respect to contracts that followed, such as the intercity connection contracts.

On _____, counsel for defendant RC faxed a subpoena requesting the testimony of JG and LL, two M Corporation employees, as well as any M Corporation documents relating to JD, GH, JN, and "all persons and entities who lobbied for or consulted with _____ Partners, Inc. and related entities in connection with securing the "Master Agreement" *and later contracts (including the "intercity connections")* for the _____ project in Massachusetts" (emphasis added). Undersigned counsel, Thomas Farrell, agreed to accept service by facsimile on behalf of Messrs. JG and LL. HJ, counsel for RC, explained that he wished to elicit testimony, first, to establish that JG and LL and M Corporation had no dealings with the defendants (a point which we understand is uncontested); and, second, to establish that M Corporation paid GH and JN for lobbying and consulting services.[1] According to Mr. J, testimony that M Corporation retained prominent persons as consultants (if it did) would make it unnecessary for the local subcontractors to pay the defendants (through Mr. D). Mr. J explained that he does not suspect JG, LL or M Corporation of any wrongdoing. [2]

I explained that I do not represent the M Corporation and that the records described are all corporate records, not the personal records of either JG or LL. I understand that John Doe, Esquire, has been in contact with Mr. J about the M Corporation and that the M Corporation may move separately to quash the subpoena for records. Mr. J later extended the date for the expected testimony to _____.

ARGUMENT

I. The Court Has Authority to Quash a Subpoena Ad Testificandum

Rule 17(c) authorizes a trial court to quash or modify a subpoena if compliance would be "unreasonable or oppressive." Although the rule mentions the authority to quash in the subsection, (c), which deals with the production of documents, courts have recognized their authority to quash subpoenas ad testificandum. *See United States v. Campbell*, 874 F.2d 838, 851 (1st Cir. 1989); *United States v. Santiago-Lugo*, 904 F.Supp. 43 (D.P.R. 1995) (recognizing authority to quashing subpoena requiring witness to come to attorney's office for interview); *see also United States v. Dean*, 55 F.3d 640, 642-43 (D.C. Cir. 1995)(quashing private party subpoena).

The Sixth Amendment right to compulsory process is not absolute. *Campbell,* 874 F.2d at 851. "[A] defendant may compel the presence of a witness only if he can "make some plausible showing of how their testimony would be both material and favorable to his defense." *Id.* Given the fact-intensive nature of criminal trials, the district court must be afforded great latitude in weighing factors such as timeliness, materiality, relevancy, competency, practicality, and utility, as a means of determining whether a subpoena request is well founded. *United States. v. Nivica*, 887 F.2d 1110, 1118 (1st Cir. 1989).

II. M Corporation's Retention of Lobbyists and Consultants Is Irrelevant and Likely to Confuse the Issues in This Case

JG's and LL's testimony should be precluded because it has no "logical connection with the consequential facts of [this] case." *See United States. v. Cortez,* Opinion and Order Denying Motion to Recuse, docket no. 266-1 at 18 (defining relevance of potential testimony). As Mr. J recently stated in his motion to sever, "RC's defense on the extortion charge is quite simple: he did not get any money from the Supercoliseum contracts, period." Defendant's Motion for Severance of Counts, dkt 278, at 5. Whether M Corporation may have had consultants working for it on the

---

[1] Mr. H had a consulting contract with M Corporation, but the contract started after the _____ contract at issue in this case was awarded and had nothing to do with that contract. M Corporation did not pay Mr. D for any lobbying or consulting efforts and never paid any monies to Mr. N.

[2] Nor does the Government. Several years ago, the FBI and Assistant United States Attorney interviewed JG and LL concerning the _____ project and investigation. They did not request any form of immunity; they were interviewed only as potential witnesses. The Government never called them to any of the grand juries involved in this matter.

Supercoliseum contract, much less on separate contracts such as the intercity connections, sheds no light on whether RC received kickbacks from the local subcontractors.

RC's proffer in some respects resembles an attempt to introduce reverse 404(b) evidence along the lines that M Corporation paid other people; therefore, RC did not accept payments. While defendants may avail themselves of FRE 404(b) to introduce prior similar acts evidence either to show they did not commit the crime charged or that another did, the evidence must have relevance to the crime charged. *See, e.g., United States v. Williams,* 458 F.3d 312 (3d Cir. 2006) (discussing defense use of reverse 404(b) evidence and explaining that even under the Third and Second Circuit tests, which allow defendants more leeway than the prosecution in introducing 404(b) evidence, the evidence must meet the test of proving something other than propensity); *see DiBenedetto v. Hall,* 272 F.3d 1, 8-9 (1st Cir. 2001) (implicitly recognizing admissibility of third party crimes evidence to exculpate defendant, but affirming decision to exclude the evidence as too speculative). Further, a trial judge has discretion under FRE 403 to exclude such evidence if it would confuse the jury and distract it from the consequential issues at trial. *United States v. Aboumoussalen,* 726 F.2d 906, 912 (2d Cir. 1984) (affirming exclusion under FRE 403 of defense evidence that met FRE 404(b)'s standard).

RC's road from the evidence he wants to introduce to the consequential fact in this case, whether the subcontractors paid him bribes, is paved with speculation, not logical connections. His reasoning appears to run thus: M Corporation paid consultants for their influence with MACA. This influence benefited M Corporation. That benefit flowed to the subcontractors, and the subcontractors knew that M Corporation had such influential consultants and that they would benefit fully from M's efforts. Therefore, according to the defense, the subcontractors would not have paid JD to pay the defendants.

There are many problems along this road, but a principal one is that by the time Mr. D and the local contractors finish their testimony, there will be no dispute that the local subcontractors did pay Mr. D. Thus the proposition for which RC wishes to call JG and LL–that the local subcontractors would not have paid anyone for influence because they believed M Corporation had all the influence needed–will be out of the case. *See United States v. Cortez,* Order, dkt no. 289, at 1 (rulings on admissibility of specific evidence should be made "in the context of the specific factual scenario developed at trial.") Issues remain as to whether Mr. D turned the money over to RC and RC's intent in taking the money, but testimony about M Corporation's consultants has no bearing on those issues.

RC's attempt to divert the jury from his actions and those of the subcontractors to those of M Corporation has no role in this trial. Paying consultants for their supposed influence is a routine and legal business practice. This practice, however, lacks the directness and, some would say, the efficacy of a *quid pro quo* bribe. That the prime contractor hired consultants has nothing to do with whether a few subcontractors paid cash bribes to a public official for specific results. Allowing into a bribery or "color of official right" extortion case all the lawful lobbying and consulting efforts made by entities other than the defendants would serve no purpose other than distracting the jury from the issue of whether the defendants accepted payments for a specific *quid pro quo.* This red herring deserves release. *See United States v. Lopez,* 71 F.3d 954, 963-64 (1st Cir. 1995) ("Here, the trial judge looked about for big fish, saw none, and let the red herrings go."), *aff'g in relevant part,* 851 F.Supp. 57, 59-60 (D.P.R. 1994) (excluding testimony about third party conduct).

III. FRE 404(b) and FRE 403 Forbid Testimony About C's "Prior Good Acts" in Not Approaching M Corporation for Kickbacks

RC's theory in subpoenaing JG and LL to testify that they had no contact with the defendant seems to be to show that since RC forewent the chance to extort the prime contractor, he was not likely to have extorted the local subcontractors. The rules do not permit such good propensity evidence; moreover, the evidence does not fit the facts of this case and thus seems likely to engender jury confusion.

While defendants are entitled to introduce FRE 404(b) evidence, the rule's restriction against the use of such evidence to prove propensity still applies, however. *United States v. Williams,* 458 F.3d 312; *United States v. Marlinga,* No. 04-80372, 2006 U.S. Dist. LEXIS 66053 at *19-20 (D. Mich. Sept. 15, 2006) (attached). In *Marlinga,* the court refused to admit evidence that the defendant, a prosecutor on trial for taking bribes to fix cases, had been offered and refused bribes in two other unrelated cases. The court held that this was pure propensity evidence offered to suggest that the defendant was not inclined to accept bribes. Further, the court noted that the fact that the defendant refused bribes on some occasions lacked relevance; it did "not make it more likely that he refused the bribes allegedly offered in this case." *Id.*

Likewise, evidence that neither defendant here ever approached M Corporation for improper payments has no bearing on whether they accepted kickbacks from the local subcontractors. Not only does this proffer violate the rule against propensity evidence, *see Marlinga, supra;* but it especially lacks probative value given the facts of this case. The evidence has been not that the defendants solicited bribes, but that JD approached them and offered kickbacks, and only from the local subcontractors. Mr. D explained why M Corporation and SMSP were excluded from the scheme, an explanation that no one disputes: as outsiders to Boston, they could not be trusted to honor and conceal the illegal scheme.

CONCLUSION

For the foregoing reasons, and "[t]o kept the jury focused on the heart of this case," *United States v. RC,* Defendant RC's Motion to Sever at 7, dkt 278, this Court should grant the Motion to Quash.

Respectfully submitted,

_____

Thomas J. Farrell, Esquire
Counsel for JG and LL

Form 18-2   Motion to Quash Document Subpoena

IN THE UNITED STATES DISTRICT COURT
FOR THE DISTRICT OF _____

UNITED STATES OF AMERICA,
     Plaintiff,

v.

RC, and
JL,
     Defendants.

MOTION OF NON-PARTY M CORPORATION TO QUASH SUBPOENA FOR DOCUMENTS AND TESTIMONY OF RECORDS CUSTODIAN, AND SUPPORTING MEMORANDUM OF LAW

Defendant RC ("Defendant," or "RC") issued a subpoena to the Custodian of Records of M Corporation ("M Corporation," or, "the Company"), a non-party in this case, requesting "all records and documents" related to three named and an undefined number of unnamed individuals and entities who "lobbied or consulted" with the Company's Massachusetts joint venture, _____ Partners, Inc. ("_____"). Pursuant to Federal Rule of Criminal Procedure 17(c)(2), M Corporation respectfully submits this Motion to Quash Defendant's subpoena and Supporting Memorandum of Law, on the grounds that the large universe of records sought here is irrelevant and inadmissible, that Defendants' request for them lacks the requisite specificity under controlling case law, and because the search M Corporation would have to perform, through over 700 boxes of records which, in some cases, may be as many as ten years old, is overly broad, burdensome and unconscionable.

STATEMENT OF THE FACTS

On or about _____, Defendant issued a Rule 17 Subpoena to a current and a former M Corporation employee, as well as to a Custodian of Records from the Company. The subpoena required M Corporation's production of

All records and documents (in all forms, *e.g.,* paper, electronic, etc.), including e-mails, memos, correspondence, invoices, contracts, phone messages, payments, disbursements, advances, and the like, regarding the following individuals and entities:

1. JD
2. GH
3. JN
4. All persons and entities who lobbied for or consulted with _____ and related entities in connection with securing the 'Master Agreement' and later contracts (including the 'intercity connections') for the _____ project in Massachusetts.

Defendant RC's attempt here to involve M Corporation in this trial can only be one thing: an attempt to obfuscate the testimony that has already been given, at the cost in time and effort of an entity which no one has alleged was involved in the criminal schemes at issue in this case. The defendants and the local contractors who apparently made the corrupt payments alleged in the Indictment feared that M Corporation would rather conduct itself in a lawful manner, and not "go along" with the payment of kickbacks. As important, M Corporation only engaged one of the persons listed in the subpoena, GH, as a consultant, and only then, not until after the _____ Master Contract was awarded.

Nevertheless, Defendant RC has subpoenaed voluminous documents contained in all types of media and a records custodian to authenticate them, which C believes may show that M Corporation employed or contracted with "persons and entities" for "lobby[ing]" and "consult[ing]" on behalf of _____ and other "related" entities. The subpoena has no further restrictions or limitations, including by person, entity, or time period. The request for such documents is also not limited to the _____ contract, which according to the superseding Indictment, is the only one at issue in this case; rather, the document requests extend to other contracts the Company has had in Massachusetts, presumably from about _____ to the present.

Following acceptance of service for the subpoena, and in an effort to accommodate the defense, the Company surveyed its collection of retained documents which might be responsive hereto. Of about 2,136 boxes of documents the Company has stored in Massachusetts, at least 570 are believed to contain documents related to the NCWT _____ project. Another 134 boxes are believed to include documents relating to the various NCWT "Inter-City Connections" [sic], i.e., "Inter-Connect" contracts. On information and belief, the boxes are organized only chronologically, and the documents and their order have been disturbed since the files were established during subsequent proceedings unrelated to the issues in this trial. On further information and belief, the review of just the documents in Massachusetts which would have to be reviewed for responsiveness would take weeks if not months of full-time work, as there is no precise index of the documents stored in Massachusetts. Additional responsive documents may also exist at the Company's Pittsburgh, Pennsylvania corporate headquarters and records storage facility, although this facility was flooded during September of 2004 by Hurricane Ivan and many records were lost or became disorganized at that time.

ARGUMENT

This Court Should Quash Defendant's Subpoena Because It Does Not Seek Relevant, Admissible Evidence, It Fails to Request Documents With Adequate Specificity, And It Would Require M Corporation to Engage in an Unduly Burdensome, Expensive, and Costly Fishing Expedition by Having to Review at Least 704 Boxes For Responsive Items

A court may quash a subpoena if compliance would be "unreasonable or oppressive." Fed. R. Crim. Proc. 17(c)(2). Rule 17(c) is not a discovery device and is only intended to expedite trial by allowing inspection of evidence before trial. *United States v. Nixon*, 418 U.S. 683, 698-99 (1974). A Rule 17(c) subpoena thus requires the moving party to show:

> (1) that the documents are evidentiary and relevant [sic]; (2) that they are not otherwise procurable reasonably in advance of trial by exercise of due diligence; (3) that the party cannot property prepare for trial without such production and inspection in advance of trial and that the failure to obtain such inspection may tend unreasonably to delay the trial; and (4) that the application is made in good faith and is not intended as a general 'fishing expedition.'

Id. at 699-700. In other words, the party seeking documents "must clear three hurdles: (1) relevancy; (2) admissibility; (and] (3) specificity." *Id. at* 700.

A district court has great latitude in determining what evidence must be provided in a challenge to a Rule 17 subpoena. The decision of a court on a motion to quash is within the sound discretion of the district court, and will not be disturbed on appeal absent a clear abuse of discretion. *United States v. Concemi*, 957 F.2d 942, 949 (1st Cir. 1992); *see also, United States v. Lieberman,* 608 F.2d 889, 904 (1st Cir. 1979), *cert. denied,* 479 U.S. 869 (1984) ("[A] ruling quashing a subpoena is appealable after conviction, [however] the trial court has so much discretion in this area that reversal is unlikely.")

A.   Defendant's Subpoena Fails the *Nixon* Relevance and Admissibility Requirements

Defendant cannot show that the requested documents are relevant and admissible. A criminal defendant's belief that documents contain relevant information is insufficient to justify a subpoena for those documents. *See United States v. Concemi*, 957 F.2d 942, at 949-50 ("Mere speculation as to the content of documents is hardly a showing of relevance.") Instead, the party seeking documents must show a sufficient likelihood that each of the requested documents contain relevant, admissible evidence. *See Nixon*, 418 U.S. at 700; *see also, United States v. LaRouche Campaign,* 841 F.2d 1176, 1179-80 (1st Cir. 1988) (Only relevant, admissible evidence subject to disclosure under Rule 17).

Conversely, a defendant cannot request a subpoena for documents without showing what the documents likely contain. *Concemi*, 957 F.2d at 949-50. There, a defendant served a subpoena on a bank requesting personnel files, meeting minutes, financial statements, bank policies, and other documents. The court found that the defendant's simple belief that the documents would contradict government witnesses was "[m]ere speculation" that failed to show relevance to the criminal charges. The appellate panel affirmed the district court's partial grant of a motion to quash the subpoena.

Defendant's subpoena here is unfocused and contains broad, catch-all requests. The individual requests, moreover, are duplicative and unspecified. On its face, the subpoena shows C has no specific knowledge of what the documents he seeks will demonstrate. While the trial counsel and court are in the best position to evaluate relevance on an up-to-the-minute basis, the Company submits that Defendant's requests are far afield from what should be rightly qualify as admissible evidence at trial. Documents and other evidence unrelated to the charges in a criminal case are of course irrelevant and are not subject to disclosure. *Lieberman*, 608 F.2d at 904. (Subpoena requesting accounting work papers from an earlier time (1970) where the charges related to fraudulent accounting credits in 1972, quashed in part.)

To show that M Corporation had consultants and lobbyists "in connection with securing the 'Master Agreement ... and later contracts can only have three possible purposes: to involve and embarrass the Company in the trial of an illegal scheme in which the Government and apparently, the local contractors all agree, it had no part; to deflect attention from the relevant evidence of the case, by injecting tangential issues not related to the defendants' guilt or innocence; or, to simply create confusion before the jury. None are proper purposes at trial. M Corporation had no consulting contracts with two of the three persons named in the subpoena, and Mr. H's contract with the Company started well after the Master Agreement was awarded. Similarly, the Inter-Connect contracts (referred to in the subpoena as the "Inter-City Connections") were all awarded in or after 1998–well after the conspiracy alleged in the indictment had run. M Corporation surmises, rather, that Defendant C subpoenaed the Company documents in an effort to have the jury believe no kickbacks for him were necessary to secure the Master Agreement, because the M Corporation could be expected to win the Master Agreement Contract Award, as it received the subsequent Inter-Connect contract awards. Clearly the subcontractors who made the corrupt payments did not believe so; even if they did, the conclusion that no kickbacks were necessary does not necessarily follow from the proposition that the M Corporation was influential in Massachusetts, especially at a later time than as is charged in the Indictment. The absence of logic in Defendant's relevancy argument should render the documents subpoenaed from the Company inadmissible.

This Court should quash Defendant's subpoena here in full. M Corporation used consultants in all manner and ways for its construction projects, including for specialized designs, for subcontracting purposes, and for projects only marginally related to the Master Agreement, over the course of nearly ten years of doing business. Such documents could not be relevant or admissible here–but they would be responsive under the clear language of Defendant's subpoena.

B. Defendant's Subpoena Fails the *Nixon* Specificity Requirement

For the same reasons that the subpoena fails to satisfy the relevance and admissibility prongs of the *Nixon* test, Defendant's subpoena also fails the specificity prong of the *Nixon* test. Defendant's subpoena here attempts to use Rule 17(c) as a discovery device in order to engage in a "fishing expedition" into the M Corporation's files. *Nixon*, 418 U.S. at 698-700. Courts have consistently found that broad document requests in subpoenas fail to comply with the *Nixon* specificity requirement. Even where information appears highly relevant and is arguably admissible, Courts have ruled that subpoena requests for "all records, documents, reports, telephone logs, etc." in an investigation do not overcome the *Nixon* specificity hurdle. *United States v. Morris*, 287 F.3d 985, 991 (10th Cir. 2002). Similarly, a subpoena's request for "a broad array and large number of documents," including "entire files, all correspondence, and all related records" indicates an improper "fishing expedition," and should not be granted. *United States v. Jackson*, 155 F.R.D. 664, 668 (D. Kan. 1994). Here, Defendant Cortez has subpoenaed "all records and documents ... in all forms ... [regarding] all persons and entities" over a ten-year period. Such a request exemplifies overbreadth.

As with the *Nixon* relevancy requirement, the specificity requirement also cannot be satisfied with speculation. *See United States v. Hardy*, 224 F.3d 752, 755 (8th Cir. 2000) (Speculation about what radio transmissions might contain "failed to establish with sufficient specificity the evidentiary nature of the requested materials.") Even where the defendant can "state[] why he wants to listen to the transmissions, [where] he cannot set forth what the subpoenaed materials contain .... they should not be ordered to be produced." *Id.*

RC has not and cannot possibly assert with specificity why all of these documents are relevant, especially without guessing. Defendant here requests a broad range of documents, including Defendant's request for such a broad array of documents is an improper "fishing expedition" that cannot satisfy the specificity prong of the *Nixon* test. *See Morris*, 287 F.3d at 991; *Hardy*, 224 F.3d at 755; *Jackson*, 155 F.R.D. at 668. This Court should thus quash the subpoena on this independent but equally dispositive ground as well.

C.   **<u>Courts May Consider the Burden on the Producing Party in Ruling on a Motion to Quash a Rule 17 Subpoena</u>**

As with other discovery, courts may consider the burden on the non-party record holder in determining whether a subpoena requesting the production of documents should be quashed, especially where the subpoenas reach is broad, there is limited time for compliance, and some of the documents are inaccessible. *See Concemi*, 957 F.2d 942, 949 (Upholding district court's determination to quash subpoena almost in its entirety). Here, the Company is being asked to comb through more than 700 cartons of documents, at a minimum, during a short trial, with little notice and at its own cost, trouble, and disruption to its ongoing business. To require such a review at this late juncture—or at all—is oppressive and burdensome, and the Company should not be required to engage in it.

CONCLUSION

Because Defendant's subpoena fails to request relevant, admissible evidence, lacks specificity as to requested documents, and would work a severe hardship on the Company, this Court should grant this Motion to Quash Defendant Cortez's subpoena to M Corporation in its entirety.

Form 18-3   Victim Impact Statement

As a victim of crime, you have the opportunity to submit a victim impact statement. The statement is important to us in the Federal Justice System because it reflects what effect this crime has had.

To assist you in preparing your statement, below is a Victim Impact Statement Form. Once returned to us, it will be forwarded to the United States Probation Department and will become part of the presentence investigation reviewed by the judge before the sentencing of the defendant. Your statement will become a formal part of the court record and as such can be seen by the defendant and his or her attorney.

If you have any questions about the Victim Impact Statement or if you need assistance in completing it, please call GM, Victim/Witness Specialist at (412) 555-5555. We have enclosed a self addressed return envelope and encourage you to complete and return your statement within the next fifteen (15) days.

VICTIM IMPACT STATEMENT

NAME:

UNITED STATES v. BT and ST, CASE NO. _____

How has your company/business been affected by this crime?
<u>See attached</u> _____

_____

Please continue your statement on an additional sheet of paper if needed.

Have you or anyone on your company's behalf initiated civil action against any party as a result of this offense?
Yes ___   No <u> x </u>
If yes, please state the case name, docket number and court of jurisdiction:

VICTIM FINANCIAL STATEMENT

Please list your financial losses from this crime.
Mercy's exact loss is undetermined as of yet, but includes at least the amounts listed in Paragraph 25, Racketeering Act Nos. 3-5, 7, and 9-14 of the Information in this case, the combined total of which is $345,470.69.

Was any income lost as a result of this crime?
Yes <u> x </u>   No ___
If yes, state reason(s) for the loss of income and estimate the total dollar amount lost. Indicate how your loss was calculated.
Please see immediately preceding paragraph.

Have you been assessed any additional taxes, penalties or interest by the Federal Government as a result of this case?
Yes ___   No _x_

If yes, explain

I declare under penalty of law that the above information is true and correct.
NAME: DATE:
SIGNATURE:

ATTACHED STATEMENT

_____ Hospital is a private, non-profit healthcare ministry sponsored by the _____ Order of the Catholic Church. It is unconscionable that anyone would victimize this organization and the important work that it does for the residents of Pittsburgh. The Order and its hospital are grateful to see justice, one of the core values upon which the Order was founded and by which it continues to operate, prevail.

According to the Information filed by the Office of the United States Attorney in this matter, Defendant in this case defrauded Mercy Hospital in an amount totaling at least $345,470.69. The Information further indicates, at Paragraph 25, Racketeering Act Nos 3-5, 7 and 9-14, that the Defendant did scheme and conspire with one or more employees of Mercy Hospital, to procure approval for Mercy's payment of the false and fraudulent billings to Enlightened Roads Construction.

These bad acts have injured _____ Hospital above and beyond the financial loss, which may far exceed the amount listed in the Information. The bad acts to which the Defendant has pled undermine _____ Hospital's trust in its employees and its contractors, who purvey goods and services to the Hospital, for the ultimate benefit of its sick patients. The Court should consider not only the monetary loss suffered by this charity and the hospital it operates, but also the erosion of the bond of trust _____ previously had with its workers and service providers.

Form 18-4   Unjust Enrichment Civil Complaint

IN THE COURT OF COMMON PLEAS OF _____ COUNTY,
_____ CIVIL DIVISION

_____ BANK Plaintiff	
v.	JURY TRIAL DEMANDED
TH and MH Defendants	

COMPLAINT IN CIVIL ACTION

AND NOW, comes the Plaintiff, _____ Bank, by and through its attorney, and files the within Complaint in Civil Action, the following of which is a statement:

1. Plaintiff, _____ Bank, is a corporation organized under the laws of the United States of America having its principal place of business at _____.
2. Plaintiff is engaged in the business of banking, serving as a source of financing for financial institutions throughout the Commonwealths of Pennsylvania, West Virginia and Delaware.
3. Defendants, TH and MH were husband wife from _____ until _____.
4. TH resides at _____, Pittsburgh, Pennsylvania and is a citizen of the Commonwealth of Pennsylvania.
5. MH resides at _____, Pittsburgh, Pennsylvania and is a citizen of the Commonwealth of Pennsylvania.

COUNT I–CONVERSION–TH

6. Plaintiff hereby incorporates by reference Paragraphs 1 through 5 of this Complaint as if the same were more fully set forth at length herein.

7. Between _____ and _____, Defendant, TH was employed by Plaintiff at its principal place of business and was responsible for the review and signoff of the reconciliation of the Demand Deposit Suspense Account and performing other depository services in regard to the customer accounts maintained at the Bank.

8. Between _____ and _____, in an ongoing course of conduct, Defendant TH unlawfully and without authority entered false and fraudulent entries into the Plaintiff's accounting system.

9. Between _____ and _____, in an ongoing course of conduct, Defendant, TH. unlawfully and without authority created and then presented false and misleading documentation to the Plaintiff's accounting department in an effort to deceive the Plaintiff and to induce it into issuing at least six checks in various amounts made payable to financial institutions at which Defendant TH personally owed money.

10. Defendant, TH, in an ongoing course of conduct, unlawfully and without authority arranged for these financial institutions to apply the monies of The Plaintiff to pay off his personal debts to these financial institutions and/or to return some of the monies back to him personally.

11. Defendant, TH, acting individually and/or jointly with Defendant, MH, deposited the funds that were sent back to them into their personal checking accounts.

12. Defendant, TH, acting individually and/or jointly with Defendant, MH, spent these funds for personal items such as weddings, honeymoons, vacations, jewelry, yoga studio expenses, meals, cars, etc. that were enjoyed by both Defendants.

13. The total net amount of the monies unlawfully converted by Defendant TH and/or Defendant MH, individually and/or jointly, totals at least $314,755.31.

14. After the aforementioned conduct came to light, Plaintiff incurred expenses in an amount in excess of $63,924.74 in investigating the illegal conversion of funds by Defendant TH and/or Defendant MH.

WHEREFORE, Plaintiff, _____ Bank, demands judgment against Defendant, TH, in excess of $25,000.00 plus interest and costs of suit.

COUNT II–FRAUD–TH

15. This Plaintiff hereby incorporates by reference Paragraphs 1 Through 14 of this Complaint as if the same were more fully set forth at length herein.

16. Defendant, TH, defrauded Plaintiff, _____ Bank, by failing to disclose that he had unlawfully, fraudulently and without authority entered false and misleading entries into the Plaintiff's accounting system, created and presented false and misleading documentation to the Plaintiff's accounting department in order to have checks issued to financial institutions where Defendants, TH and MH, were indebted, and arranged for these third party financial institutions to apply the Plaintiff's monies to the debts Defendant owed them and/or to send some of the monies back to Defendant so he could spend it on personal items for both Defendants.

17. Defendant TH's failure to disclose the above-referenced actions taken by himself and MH, individually and/or jointly, constitutes fraudulent conduct which was intended to and did deceive Plaintiff, _____ Bank.

18. Plaintiff relied upon Defendant TH's silence and his failure to inform it of the unauthorized conduct taken by himself and/or Defendant MH, individually and/or jointly, and were induced into a sense of security created by the actions of Defendant TH and Defendant MH.

19. Defendant TH's fraudulent misrepresentations and omissions were material and caused Plaintiff to incur damages in an amount in excess of $314,755,31 plus $63,924.74 in expenses related to the investigation of the fraudulent conduct.

20. On April 14, 2005, Defendant, TH, plead guilty in U.S. Federal District Court to one count of bank fraud, 18 U.S.C. §1344 in connection with the above acts. A copy of the judgment against Defendant, TH is attached as Exhibit A.

WHEREFORE, Plaintiff, _____ Bank demands judgment against Defendant in excess of $25,000.00 plus interest and costs of suit.

COUNT III–CIVIL CONSPIRACY–TH

21. This Plaintiff hereby incorporates by reference Paragraphs 1 through 20 of this Complaint as if the same were more fully set forth at length herein.

22. Defendant, TH, unlawfully conspired and agreed with Defendant, MH, that they would unlawfully, fraudulently, Intentionally and without authority obtain control over Plaintiff's funds by having financial institutions apply

Plaintiff's monies to the debts they owed to those financial institutions and/or send some of the monies back to him directly so he could spend it on personal items for both Defendants.

23. Defendant TH's above referenced conduct constitutes an illegal conspiracy with MH to unlawfully, fraudulently and without authority, make false and fraudulent accounting entries and convert the proceeds of Plaintiff's bank account and defraud Plaintiff by failing to disclose the said actions.

24. As a direct and proximate result of the Defendant's conspiracy and wrongful conduct, Plaintiff suffered the damages described herein.

WHEREFORE, Plaintiff, _____ Bank demands judgment against Defendant, TH, in excess of $25,000 plus interest and costs of suit.

COUNT IV–CIVIL CONSPIRACY–MH

25. Plaintiff hereby incorporates by reference Paragraphs 1 through 24 of this Complaint as if the same were more fully set forth at length herein.

26. Defendant, MH, unlawfully conspired and agreed with Defendant, TH that they would unlawfully, fraudulently, intentionally and without authority obtain control over Plaintiff's funds by having financial institutions apply Plaintiff's monies to the debts they owed to those financial institutions and/or send some of the monies back to them directly so they could spend it on personal items for both Defendants.

27. Defendant MH's above-referenced conduct constitutes an illegal conspiracy with TH to unlawfully, fraudulently and without authority, make false and fraudulent accounting entries and convert the proceeds of Plaintiff's bank account and defraud Plaintiff by failing to disclose the said actions.

28. As a direct and proximate result of the Defendant's conspiracy and wrongful conduct, Plaintiff suffered the damages described herein.

WHEREFORE, Plaintiff, _____ Bank demands judgment against Defendant, MH, in excess of $25,000.00 plus interest and costs of suit.

COUNT V–UNJUST ENRICHMENT TH

29. Plaintiff hereby incorporates by reference Paragraphs 1 through 28 of this Complaint as if the same were more fully set forth at length herein,

30. As a result of the aforementioned actions of the Defendants, $314,755.31 was stolen and wrongfully diverted from its proper and legal uses.

31. The stolen proceeds were used to purchase weddings and honeymoons, vacations, jewelry, home renovations, cars and other personal and real property that was used, possessed and/or enjoyed by defendants.

32. Defendant, TH, failed to give consideration for the benefits enjoyed and personal and real property that he used and possessed.

33. Defendant, TH, has been unjustly enriched as a result of the benefits enjoyed and personal and real property that he obtained through the use of the stolen proceeds.

34. Defendant, TH, is presently in possession of personal and real property that was purchased with the stolen proceeds.

35. It is unconscionable and inequitable for Defendant, TH, to retain any personal or real property in her possession or continue to enjoy any benefits arising from the use of the converted funds.

WHEREFORE, _____ Bank demands that judgment be entered in its favor and Defendant TH be ordered to surrender to Plaintiff all property in her possession that was purchased with the aforementioned stolen and converted funds, and reimburse Plaintiff the value of any property disposed of or benefits improperly enjoyed.

COUNT VI–UNJUST ENRICHMENT–MH

35. This Plaintiff hereby incorporates by reference Paragraphs 1 through 34 of this Complaint as if the same were more fully set forth at length herein.

37. As a result of the aforementioned actions of the defendants, $314,755.31 was stolen and wrongfully diverted from its proper and legal uses.

38. The stolen proceeds were used to purchase weddings, honeymoons, vacations, jewelry, home renovations, cars and other personal and real property that was used, possessed and/or enjoyed by defendants.

39. Defendant MH failed to give consideration for the benefits enjoyed and personal and real property that she used and possessed.
40. Defendant MH has been unjustly enriched as a result of the benefits enjoyed and personal and real property that she obtained through the use of the stolen proceeds.
41. Defendant MH is presently in possession of personal and real property that was purchased with the stolen proceeds.
42. It is unconscionable and inequitable for defendant MH to retain any personal or real property in her possession or continue to enjoy any benefits arising from the use of the converted funds.

WHEREFORE, _____ Bank demands that judgment be entered in its favor and Defendant MH be ordered to surrender to Plaintiff all property in her possession that was purchased with the aforementioned stolen and converted funds, and reimburse Plaintiff the value of any property disposed of or benefits improperly enjoyed.

COUNT VII–PUNITIVE DAMAGES–TH

43. Plaintiff hereby incorporates by reference Paragraphs 1 through 42 of This Complaint as if the same were more fully set forth at length herein.
44. The conduct of Defendants, TH and MH, as more fully set forth above, was outrageous, malicious, willful and in blatant disregard for the rights of Plaintiff.
45. As a result of said conduct, Defendants TH and MH, are liable to Plaintiff for punitive damages.

WHEREFORE, Plaintiff, _____ Bank demands judgment against Defendant TH in excess of $25,000.00 plus interest and costs of suit.

COUNT VIII–PUNITIVE DAMAGES–MH

46. This Plaintiff hereby incorporates by reference Paragraphs 1 through 45 of this Complaint as if the same were more fully set forth at length herein.
47. The conduct of Defendants, TH and MH, as more fully set forth above, was outrageous, malicious, willful and in blatant disregard for the rights of Plaintiff.
48. As a result of said conduct, Defendants TH and MH are liable to Plaintiff for punitive damages.

WHEREFORE. Plaintiff, _____ Bank, demands judgment against Defendant MH in excess of $25,000.00 plus interest and costs of suit.

WHEREFORE, Plaintiff, _____ Bank, demands judgment against Defendants TH and MH for an amount in excess of the jurisdictional amount for compulsory arbitration along with such other relief as to this court may appear just and proper.

Respectfully submitted,
_____ Bank

VERIFICATION

I verify that the facts set forth in this complaint are true and correct to the best of my knowledge, information, and belief. I understand that false statements herein are made subject To the penalties of 18 Pa. C. S. §4904, referring to unsworn falsifications to authorities.

I am authorized to make this verification on behalf of the First Bank of Pittsburgh because of my position as Managing Director.

Date:

_____
Managing Director, General Counsel & Corporate Secretary

Form 18-5   Victim Notification

 United States Postal Inspection Service

[Date]

[Name]
[Address]

Re: Case Number: _____ , Investigation of investment fraud

Dear _____:

      The United States Postal Inspection Service is committed to protecting the nation's mail system from criminal misuse. Pursuant to federal law, victims are entitled to certain rights which include notification of the status of the investigation. This letter is to inform you that you have been identified as a possible victim of alleged mail fraud.

      We would like to make you aware of the victim services that may be available to you and to resolve any questions you may have regarding the criminal justice process throughout this investigation. Additional information is outlined in the enclosed PUB 308, Know Your Rights: A Guide for Victims and Witnesses of Crime. The enclosed brochures provide information about the USPIS Victim Witness Assistance Program, resources and instructions for accessing the Victim Notification System (VNS). VNS is designed to provide you with information regarding the status of your case.

      This case is currently under investigation. This can be a lengthy process and we request your continued patience while we conduct a thorough investigation.

      As a crime victim, you have the following rights under 18 United States Code § 3771: (1) The right to be reasonably protected from the accused; (2) The right to reasonable, accurate, and timely notice of any public court proceeding, or any parole proceeding, involving the crime or of any release or escape of the accused; (3) The right not to be excluded from any such public court proceeding, unless the court, after receiving clear and convincing evidence, determines that testimony by the victim would be materially altered if the victim heard other testimony at that proceeding; (4) The right to be reasonably heard at any public proceeding in the district court involving release, plea, sentencing, or any parole proceeding; (5) The reasonable right to confer with the attorney for the Government in the case; (6) The right to full and timely restitution as provided in law; (7) The right to proceedings free from unreasonable delay; (8) The right to be treated with fairness and with respect for the victim's dignity and privacy.

      We will make our best efforts to ensure you are accorded the rights described. Most of these rights pertain to events occurring after the arrest or indictment of an individual for the crime, and it will become the responsibility of the prosecuting United States Attorney's Office to ensure you are accorded those rights. You may also seek the advice of a private attorney with respect to these rights.

      It is important to note that at the investigative and/or prosecutive stage this agency makes no express nor implied representations of wrongdoing on the part of the individual or company investigated. These individuals and/or entities and anyone associated with them are innocent until proven guilty in a court of law. This letter should not be considered a reflection, either way, of the honesty or integrity of the individuals or companies involved or anyone in privity with them.

      The Victim Notification System (VNS) is designed to provide you with direct information regarding the case as it proceeds through the criminal justice system. You may obtain current information about this matter on the Internet at WWW.Notify.USDOJ.GOV or from the VNS Call Center at 1-866-DOJ-4YOU (1-866-365-4968) (TDD/TTY: 1-866-228-4619) (International: 1-502-213-2767). In addition, you may use the Call Center or Internet to update your contact information and/or change your decision about participation in the notification program. If you update your information to include a current email address, VNS will send information to that address. In order to continue to receive notifications, it is your responsibility to keep your contact information current.

You will need the following Victim Identification Number (VIN) '_____' and Personal Identification Number (PIN) '____' anytime you contact the Call Center and the first time you log on to VNS on the Internet. In addition, the first time you access the VNS Internet site, you will be prompted to enter your last name (or business name) as currently contained in VNS. The name you should enter is _____.

The Victim Witness Assistance Program of the U. S. Postal Inspection Service is available to assist *victims and* witnesses during the investigative stages of the federal criminal justice process. This assistance can include working with you to resolve any questions or problems you may have as a result of the crime, and providing information on available resources including counseling and consumer protection agencies.

If you have questions about our Victim Witness Assistance Program, please contact me.

Sincerely,

Basic Bill of Rights for Victims

pennsylvania
COMMISSION ON CRIME
AND DELINQUENCY

Pennsylvania Commission on Crime and Delinquency 3101 N. Front Street, Harrisburg, PA 17110

For further information on additional victims' rights, please contact either the district attorney in your jurisdiction or the PCCD's Victims' Services Program at 1-800-692-7292.

Victims of crime have the following rights:

To receive basic information concerning the services available for victims of crime.

To be notified of certain significant actions and proceedings within the criminal and juvenile justice systems pertaining to their case. This includes all of the following:
- Access to information regarding whether the juvenile was detained or released following arrest and whether a petition alleging delinquency has been filed.
- Immediate notification of a juvenile's preadjudication escape from a detention center or shelter facility and of the juvenile's subsequent apprehension.
- Access to information regarding the grant or denial of bail to an adult.
- Immediate notification of an adult offender's pretrial escape from a local correctional facility and of the offender's subsequent apprehension.

To be accompanied at all criminal and all juvenile proceedings by a family member, a victim advocate or other person providing assistance or support.

In cases involving a personal injury crime or burglary, to submit prior comment to the prosecutor's office or juvenile probation office, as appropriate to the circumstances of the case, on the potential reduction or dropping of any charge or changing of a plea in a criminal or delinquency proceeding or diversion of any case, including an informal adjustment or consent decree.

To have the opportunity to offer prior comment on the sentencing of a defendant or the disposition of a delinquent child, to include the submission of a written and oral victim impact statement detailing the physical, psychological and economic effects of the crime on the victim and the victim's family. The written statement shall be included in any predisposition or presentence report submitted to the court. Victim impact statements shall be considered by a court when determining the disposition of a juvenile or sentence of an adult.

To have notice and to provide prior comment on a judicial recommendation that the defendant participate in a motivational boot camp.

Upon request of the victim of a personal injury crime, to have the opportunity to submit written comment or present oral testimony at a disposition review hearing, which comment or testimony shall be considered by the court when reviewing the disposition of the juvenile.

To be restored, to the extent possible, to the precrime economic status through the provision of restitution, compensation and the expeditious return of property which is seized as evidence in the case when in the judgement of the prosecutor the evidence is no longer needed for prosecution of the case.

In personal injury crimes where the adult is sentenced to a **State** correctional facility, to be:
- Given the opportunity to provide prior comment on and to receive State postsentencing release decisions, including work release, furlough, parole, pardon or community treatment center placement.
- Given the opportunity to receive notice of and to provide prior comment on a recommendation sought by the Department of Corrections that the offender participate in a motivational boot camp.
- Provided immediate notice of an escape of the adult and of subsequent apprehension.

Upon the request of the victim of a personal injury crime, to be notified of the termination of the courts' jurisdiction.

To have assistance in the preparation of, submission of and follow-up on crime victim compensation claims to the Office of Victims' Services.

In personal injury crimes where the adult is sentenced to a **local** correctional facility to:
- Receive notice of the date of the release of the adult, including work release, furlough, parole, release from boot camp or community treatment center placement; and
- Be provided with immediate notice of an escape of the adult and of subsequent apprehension.

If, upon the request of the victim of a personal injury crime committed by a juvenile, the juvenile is ordered to residential placement, a shelter facility or a detention center, to:
- Receive prior notice of the date of the release of the juvenile, including temporary leave or home pass.
- Be provided with immediate notice of an escape of the juvenile, including failure to return from temporary leave or home pass; and immediate notice of reapprehension of the juvenile.
- Be provided with notice of transfer of a juvenile who has been adjudicated delinquent from a placement facility that is contrary to a previous court order or placement plan approved at a disposition review hearing and to have the opportunity to express a written objection prior to the release or transfer of the juvenile.

To receive immediate notice of the release of an adult on bail, if the adult is subject to a protection from abuse order and is committed to a local correctional facility for a violation of the order, or for a personal injury crime against a victim protected by the order.

To receive notice if an adult is committed to a mental health facility from a State correctional institution and notice of the discharge, transfer or escape of the adult from the mental health facility.

To be notified of the details of the final disposition of the case of a juvenile.

Additional Statutory Rights

To be present at executions providing the victim has registered with and been selected by the Victim Advocate, Office of the Victim Advocate.

To be present at trials, including murder trials, and the right not to be excluded from the trial if the victim will be providing input at sentencing.

Questions regarding Victims Compensation?

What expenses are not covered?
The fund will not reimburse victims for:
-Pain and suffering
-Stolen or damaged property except loss of medical devices as a result of the crime.

How will the claim be considered?
After all of the information contained in the application is verified the victim/claimant will be notified if he/she is eligible for compensation. The time that it takes to arrive at this decision varies considerably, depending upon the complexity of the claim. The victim/claimant will be mailed a copy of the decision. If the claim is denied, the reason will be explained to the victim/claimant, along with the appeal procedure.

What if the expenses can be paid by another source?
The Crime Victims Compensation Fund is regarded as *"the payer of last resort."* Other sources **must** be utilized before payment can be considered.

What is meant by other source?
Payment will be reduced by the amount of any other source. They include but are not limited to: health or life insurance, awards from civil lawsuits or insurance, Medical Assistance, Medicare, disability insurance, Workers' Compensation, or Social Security.

Must there be an arrest or conviction of the assailant before compensation will be paid?
No. It is not necessary for the alleged offender to be prosecuted for a claim to be filed. However, the victim/claimant must cooperate with law enforcement authorities in the investigation and prosecution of the offender if one is known.

Victims Compensation 1-800-233-2339

What is an emergency award?
In special circumstances an emergency award of up to $1,500 may be considered.

Are Motor Vehicle/Watercraft Crimes eligible for compensation?
Yes. These are limited to DUI, Aggravated Assault while DUI, Homicide by Vehicle while DUI, Hit and Run, and Homicide by Vehicle and acts that would constitute a crime under the Crimes Code, such as reckless endangerment.

How is the program funded?
Passed by the Pennsylvania Legislature in 1976, the Pennsylvania Crime Victims Act created a fund and established eligibility guidelines for providing certain benefits to crime victims. This fund consists of fines and penalties assessed against persons convicted of crimes. No general tax revenues of the state are used, therefore, persons convicted of crime support a program to benefit their victims.

The victim/claimant may be eligible if....

The crime occurred in Pennsylvania OR to a Pennsylvania resident who was injured or killed in a foreign country or by an act of international terrorism.

The crime was reported to the proper authorities or a Protection from Abuse Order was filed within 72 hours unless good cause is shown, or the victim is a minor and meets specific criteria.

The victim has cooperated with law enforcement, the courts, and the Victims Compensation Assistance Program.

The claim is filed within two years after the crime. **There are exceptions when the victim is a child.**

The minimum loss requirement of $100 of any combination of eligible benefits is met. If the victim is age 60 or over, no minimum loss is required.

The victim/claimant may be **ineligible** if the victim was engaged in illegal activity that caused the crime.

What other services are available?

The Direct Victim Services Unit is available to support local advocates with onsite compensation assistance in incidents of mass violence including: crisis intervention, emotional support, assistance in completing a compensation form, and providing referrals. For help with answering questions concerning eligibility or additional services provided by the Unit, contact the Victims Compensation Assistance Program.

To request a claim form:

Victims Compensation
Assistance Program
Office of Victims' Services
Pennsylvania Commission
on Crime and Delinquency
P.O. Box 1167
Harrisburg, Pennsylvania
17108-1167

Toll Free (800) 233-2339
or
(717) 783-5153
Fax (717) 787-4306

www.pccd.state.pa.us

08/06 qxd

Compensation Resource Guide for Victim Services and Allied Professionals

pennsylvania
COMMISSION ON CRIME
AND DELINQUENCY

What expenses may be paid?

The Victims Compensation Assistance Program is committed to helping victims and their families ease the financial burden crime imposes upon them. This brochure provides information on the benefits available, and the rights of victims. This brochure is not the final authority on the law, nor does it create additional rights or entitlements not found in law.

A maximum award of $35,000 may be paid with limits on specific benefits. The award may exceed $35,000 in certain circumstances.

Available Benefits Include:
Medical Expenses
Medical, dental and other expenses related to the injury.
This includes:
- physical therapy
- medications
- ambulance
- home health care
- replacement services
- childcare
- medical equipment/supplies
- transportation costs to medical and counseling appointments, or pharmacy visits

Counseling
Victims of crime may be reimbursed for counseling expenses related to the crime incident. Individuals eligible for counseling include:
- the direct victim
- specific relatives of the direct victim
- person residing with the direct victim
- person engaged to the direct victim
- person who witnesses a violent crime
- person who discovers homicide victim
- person responsible for the direct victims welfare

Loss of Earnings
A victim/claimant who is unable to work due to a physical or emotional disability related to a crime may be eligible for compensation.

The following individuals may also be eligible for loss of earnings:
-a family member who provides home health care or replacement services
-persons who meet specific criteria related to homicide crimes

Loss of Support
Payments may be made for financial dependents of a homicide victim.

Stolen Benefit Cash
If Social Security, pension/retirement, disability or court-ordered child/spousal support is the victim's main source of income, and cash has been stolen or taken through fraud, he/she may be compensated, within certain limits.

Relocation Expenses
Temporary or permanent relocation expenses may be covered for the victim and individuals residing in their household when it is required for the immediate protection of their safety and health. A medical provider, law enforcement, or human service provider must verify the victim's need to relocate.

Funeral Expenses
The person who pays or assumes responsibility to pay the funeral bill for a deceased victim, may be compensated for those expenses, within certain limits.

Crime-Scene Cleanup
If the victim/claimant paid for the costs of cleaning the crime scene of a personal living space, compensation may be awarded. Crime-scene cleanup includes the removal of blood or bodily fluid caused by the crime or other dirt or debris caused by processing the crime-scene.

Chapter 19

RELATED CIVIL LITIGATION

VIII. FORMS

I.   GENERAL POINTS

§19:01   Civil Litigation After Criminal Proceedings

Many civil proceedings await the outcome of a criminal case to use its result (*e.g.*, proceedings to debar the client or to revoke or suspend a professional license based on the conviction; victims' lawsuits; shareholder derivative suits).

If the defendant is convicted, the plaintiffs will exploit the conviction's res judicata effect. [*See SEC v. Bilzerian*, 29 F.3d 689, 693-94 (D.C. Cir. 1994) (criminal conviction for securities fraud given preclusive effect in SEC action); *Gilberg v. Barbieri*, 53 N.Y.2d 285, 423 N.E.2d 807, 441 N.Y.S.2d 49 (1981) (civil plaintiff can use conviction for its preclusive effect even though plaintiff was not a party to the criminal case, but court refuses to give preclusive effect to petty offense conviction); *but see SEC v. Monarch Funding Corp.*, 192 F.3d 295, 305-06 (2d Cir. 1999) (presumption against affording criminal sentencing findings preclusive effect in civil litigation).]

If the defendant wins an acquittal, the plaintiff must prove the civil case like any other, but the defendant cannot rely on the acquittal as a defense. [*See Commonwealth v. Reynolds*, 876 A.2d 1088, 1093 (Pa. Cwlth 2005) (acquittal has no preclusive effect in subsequent civil litigation).]

However, even after an acquittal, the defendant still might be able to assert the Fifth Amendment privilege against self-incrimination if a criminal prosecution is possible on different charges or by a different jurisdiction. Under the separate sovereign doctrine, the double jeopardy clause of the U.S. Constitution does not bar successive prosecution by a separate state or jurisdiction: either the federal government after a state prosecution or vice versa. [*See Heath v. Alabama*, 474 U.S. 82, 93-94 (1985); *but see United States v. Wilson*, 413 F.3d 382, 390 (3d Cir. 2005) (urging the Supreme Court to revisit the separate sovereign doctrine).]

A defendant protected from prosecution in one state or federal jurisdiction by a final judgment of acquittal or conviction still may invoke the privilege in a prosecution based upon the same conduct in a different state or federal jurisdiction. [*Murphy v. Waterfront Commission*, 378 U.S. 52 (1964).]

On the other hand, many states have statutes barring prosecution after a different sovereign has prosecuted the same transaction. [*E.g., Booth v. Clary*, 83 N.Y.2d 675, 680, 635 N.E.2d 279, 613 N.Y.S.2d 110 (1994) (reviewing New York's statutory double jeopardy provisions and holding that U.S. court-martial conviction precluded New York criminal prosecution).]

§19:02   Civil Litigation Before or During Criminal Proceedings

Especially with financial crimes, civil lawsuits may precede or accompany a criminal investigation. [*See United States v. Kordel*, 397 U.S. 1, 11-12 (1970) (noting that parallel proceedings are an accepted practice).]

Prosecutions sometimes grow out of civil lawsuits, especially those brought by the government, such as consumer fraud cases brought by a state attorney general or securities fraud actions brought by the SEC or a state equivalent, but also from private lawsuits alleging fraud. Upon discovery of facts suggesting both criminal and regulatory violations, the government may initiate simultaneous civil or regulatory and criminal investigations. The regulatory agencies may file suit first to seek equitable relief and protect the public from further wrongdoing.

Related civil litigation poses both dangers and opportunities.

Answering pleadings and discovery may cause the client to incriminate himself. The client can invoke the privilege to refuse to answer in the civil matter, but the opponent is entitled to ask the fact-finder to draw a negative inference against the client in the civil case. A complete refusal to respond to the civil suit may lead to a default judgment that could have serious permanent consequences for the client's finances and career.

However, if the client does not have the burden of production and proof in the civil matter, you might use the civil matter to obtain discovery that you would not be entitled to in the criminal case.

While avoidance or mitigation of any criminal prosecution generally will be your client's priority, take steps to advise and safeguard the client from ruinous civil consequences, to the extent possible. An example is the defense of concurrent criminal and civil false claims investigations. Any intentional false claim on the government can be both a crime [*e.g.*, 18 U.S.C. §287] and a civil violation punishable by treble damages and significant civil monetary penalties [*e.g.*, 31 U.S.C. §3730 *et seq.*]. Agreement by the criminal prosecutor to immunize your client and use her solely as a witness does not necessarily protect the client from civil suit. Under the recent Yates Memorandum, even where there is a corporate wrongdoer, federal civil prosecutors are encouraged to sue the individual employees, regardless of their inability to pay the large judgments often obtained in False Claims Act cases. [Deputy Attorney General Sally Quillian Yates, "Individual Accountability for Corporate Wrongdoing," September 15, 2015, available at https://www.justice.gov/archives/dag/file/769036/download.]

As a precaution, then, whenever your client is interviewed as part of a joint criminal/civil investigation, you should request separate proffer agreements from both the civil and criminal prosecutors so that your client's words, though precluded from use to build a prosecution, cannot be used to make a civil case against him.

Form:
- **Form 19 -7** Civil Proffer Agreement

§19:03 Criminal Prosecutors' Misuse of Civil Proceedings

Courts are willing to set limits to a criminal prosecutor's use of civil proceedings and discovery to further the criminal prosecution. [*See United States v. Carriles*, 486 F. Supp. 2d 599 (W.D. Tex. 2007), rev'd 541 F.3d 344 (5th Cir. 2008); *United States v. Stringer*, 408 F. Supp. 2d 1083, 1092 (D. Oregon 2006) rev'd, 521 F.3d 1189 (9th Cir. 2008); *United States v. Scrushy*, 366 F. Supp. 2d 1134, 1137 (N.D. Ala. 2005).]

In *Scrushy*, the court suppressed statements made in the SEC proceeding because behind the scenes, criminal prosecutors manipulated interviews to gather evidence for their investigation. Likewise, in *Carriles*, the district court held that the government deceived the defendant into submitting to a futile naturalization interview as a pretext to secure a criminal indictment; consequently, the court suppressed the statements and dismissed the perjury and false statements indictment.

In *Stringer*, the district court dismissed the indictment on due process and Fifth Amendment grounds where the criminal prosecutors worked with the SEC attorneys to conceal their investigation and interest in prosecuting the defendants. The court also determined that the SEC attorneys affirmatively misled the defendants' civil attorneys as to the lack of any coordination with any prosecutor's office. [*Stringer*, 408 F. Supp 2d at 1092.] However, on appeal, the Court of Appeals reversed the dismissal and suppression rulings and decided that referring the defendant's counsel to SEC Form 1662, which states that information provided to the SEC could be shared with other agencies including prosecutors, was sufficient and adequate disclosure. Likewise, the Court of Appeals reversed the district court in *Carriles* in part because it found that the government did not make affirmative misrepresentations and did warn the defendant that his statements could be used against him. [*Carriles*, 541 F.3d at 356-57.]

The reversals in *Carriles* and *Stringer* suggest that courts see nothing wrong in parallel proceedings and criminal use of evidence gathered in civil investigations and proceedings unless the civil proceeding is not *bona fide* or the government affirmatively misrepresents the existence of a parallel criminal investigation. [*United States v. La Forgia*, 2012 U.S. Dist. LEXIS 71019, 2012 WL 1869035 (SD. Ala. May 22, 2012); *United States v. Stein*, 2008 U.S. Dist. LEXIS 74030 (S.D.N.Y. Sept. 10, 2008); Patricia M. Sulzbach & Christopher B. Clare, *Navigating the Government's Use of Parallel Proceedings*, 41 LITIGATION 1 (Fall 2014).]

PRACTICE TIP:

Ask the civil prosecutors or plaintiffs' counsel pointed and specific questions about any communication with criminal investigators and prosecutors:
- Are you working in conjunction with any criminal prosecutor?
- Have you communicated with any criminal prosecutor's office about this matter?
- Has any prosecutor or law enforcement officer informed you that my client is a target or subject of any criminal investigation?

Consider a *Brady* request for any communications regarding communications between the civil agency and criminal investigators and prosecutors. [*See Stringer*, 408 F. Supp. 2d at 1092 (such communications formed the basis for the suppression of statements and dismissal of the indictment). For *Brady* requests, *see* Chapter 14, Discovery.]

[§§19:04-19:09 Reserved]

II. ORGANIZATIONS AND MULTIPLE DEFENDANTS

§19:10 Need for Individual Counsel

Counsel for an organizational party or for multiple individual defendants in civil litigation who becomes aware of a possible criminal investigation into the same conduct should consider recommending that the employees or individuals retain their own counsel. This is because the criminal investigation may create a conflict between the entity and its employees or even its owners and directors and among individuals. [*See United States v. Stringer*, 408 F.Supp.2d 1083, 1090-92 (D. Oregon 2006) (counsel who represented both corporation and ex-officer in SEC investigation should have been disqualified when she argued that corporation should not be sanctioned because accounting irregularities were the fault of the ex-officer and, after withdrawing from representing ex-officer, assisted Department of Justice in building criminal case against ex-officer).]

In civil litigation, the plaintiff's interest usually lies in proving the entity's liability because the entity has the deep pocket. Thus the entity and its employees share an interest in avoiding liability rather than apportioning blame, especially since under the doctrine of respondeat superior any employee's wrongdoing fastens liability on the company.

However, finger-pointing starts when a criminal investigation looms. Prosecutors will tempt entities with the prospect of avoiding prosecution if the entity helps to prove the guilt of its employees or officers. [*See* U. S. Department of Justice, Criminal Resource Manual §162, III.A. 4, 6 ("Federal Prosecution of Business Organizations," instructing prosecutors to consider corporation's willingness to cooperate in investigation and prosecution of its agents in deciding whether to charge the corporation).]

Of course, being told that they must obtain separate counsel signals to the employees that their interests have diverged from those of the company and perhaps from each other's. This divergence could harm all defendants in their ability to defend both the civil case and the criminal investigation.

§19:11   Joint Defense Agreements

One way to maintain unity among the defendants when each has separate counsel is a joint defense agreement.

Joint defense agreements do not prohibit their signatories from later turning against each other, but by obligating them to maintain the confidentiality of information learned through the joint defense, the agreement makes later betrayals difficult because the turncoat must prove to the prosecution and the court that the information he offers in his cooperation is not derived from privileged joint defense information.

Therefore, parties who have the most to gain from cooperation with prosecutors should avoid joint defense agreements (*i.e.*, less culpable employees; and companies who hope to avoid prosecution by serving up their wayward employees, officers and directors to the prosecution).

The more culpable individuals, with the most to lose, generally should embrace joint defense agreements and suggest them early in the process, before the other parties reassess the disadvantages of jointly defending the case.

Form:
- **Form 1-3** Joint Defense Agreement (in Chapter 1)

§19:12   Advancing Counsel Fees

The company or employer should consider advancing counsel fees for employees, even if not required to do so by law or bylaws. [*See United States v. Stein*, 435 F.Supp.2d 330 (S.D.N.Y. 2006) (finding nothing improper in company advancing fees and holding that government discouragement of it violates employees' Sixth Amendment right to counsel).]

Advancing fees demonstrates that the company has not abandoned its employees and has avoided unduly antagonizing them.

Furthermore, the company can ensure that its employees have competent counsel who will fight the case vigorously, and this might help the company demonstrate to prosecutors that there was no wrongdoing on anyone's part.

Finally, while each attorney, no matter who pays him, owes his duties of loyalty and confidentiality to his client, the company's counsel can coordinate the selection of counsel to insure that the lawyers selected work well together.

Agreements to advance fees often are unwritten to avoid government discovery of their terms. Any written agreement should emphasize that the agreement does not require the witness or client to tell anything but the truth.

State corporate law may forbid indemnification in cases where a court determines that the acts giving rise to indemnification constituted knowing unlawful misconduct, or even recklessness. [*E.g.*, 15 Pa.C.S.A. §§1741, 1746.] Even where there is an adjudication of criminal guilt, the adjudication may not be dispositive on the issue of whether the defendant had "no reasonable cause to believe the person's conduct was unlawful," and in the absence of such reasonable cause, indemnification still may be permissible. [*E.g.*, 15 Pa.C.S.A. §1741; 8 DelC. §145(a).]

Forms:
- **Form 19-1** Agreement to Indemnify Legal Fees
- **Form 19-2** Letter Regarding Agreement to Pay Legal Fees

[§§19:13-19:19 Reserved]

III. COORDINATION BETWEEN CIVIL LITIGANTS AND CRIMINAL INVESTIGATORS

§19:20   Civil Parties and Prosecution Can Share Information

Generally, there is no bar to the sharing of information and discovery materials between civil parties and the prosecution. [*See United States v. Kordel*, 397 U.S. 1, 11-12 (1970) (permitting government to introduce civil interrogatory answers in criminal cases). *See* SEC Form 1662 (warning that SEC regularly shares information and discovery materials with Department of Justice). *But see* §19:21 (prosecution cannot share grand jury material).]

Revealing privileged information to federal regulators and prosecutors outside the grand jury setting renders it available to private civil litigants. Most courts have rejected the enforceability of "selective waiver," whereby a party under investigation discloses privileged material to the government with an agreement that the privilege remains in effect as to any other parties. Rather, the rule is waived as to one, waived as to all. [*See In re Qwest Communications Int'l, Inc.*, 450 F.3d 1179 (10th Cir. 2006); *but see Regents of University of California v. Superior Court*, 165 Cal. App.4th 672, 81 Cal.Rptr.3d186 (Cal. App. 2008) (no waiver because disclosure under pressure of federal investigation amounts to coerced, not voluntary, disclosure); *Diversified Indus. v. Meredith*, 572 F.2d 596 (8th Cir. 1977).]

Federal Rule of Evidence 502(d) seems to suggest that if you can obtain a federal court order restricting the disclosure and waiver of privileged information to the litigation pending before the court, that order should prevent a finding of waiver as to use of the information in any other federal or state proceeding: "A Federal court may order that the privilege or protection is not waived by disclosure connected with the litigation pending before the court-in which event the disclosure is also not a waiver in any other Federal or State proceeding."

There is little case law, though, on the effect of this Rule on the selective waiver doctrine, and some rulings hold that it was not intended to protect the privilege from intentional waivers, such as you might make in an effort to negotiate a settlement with investigative authorities. Instead, the Rule is restricted to inadvertent disclosures to enable parties to respond to discovery demands promptly and to review later for privilege and claw-back any privileged documents unintentionally produced. [*See Potomac Electric Power Co. v. United States*, 107 Fed. Cl. 725, 731-32 (U.S. Ct. Claims 2012).] Thus, if you feel that you must disclose privileged materials to negotiate a settlement or persuade a prosecutor not to charge your client, obtain first a protective or confidentiality order signed by the court, but proceed with the knowledge that the order might not overcome waiver claims in litigation brought by third-parties.

Forms:
- **Form 19-3** SEC Form 1662
- **Form 19-5** Protective Order

§19:21   Prosecution Can Not Share Grand Jury Material

A government prosecutor is barred, absent judicial approval (seldom given), from sharing grand jury material with government civil attorneys. [*See* Fed.R.Crim.P. 6(e)(2); *United States v. Sells Eng'g, Inc.,* 463 U.S. 418, 435 (1983).]

Furthermore, a criminal prosecutor may not conduct a grand jury investigation or issue grand jury subpoenas solely for the purpose of preparing a civil case. [*See In re Grand Jury Subpoena*, 175 F.3d 332, 337-38 (4th Cir. 1999) (quashing grand jury subpoena issued for sole purpose of obtaining evidence for parallel civil proceeding).]

However, proving such improper purpose is a very difficult burden to meet. [*See* Sara Sun Beale, *et al., Grand Jury Law and Practice*, §10:3 (2005) (such claims "do not provide a fertile ground for challenges to the grand jury proceedings").]

[§§19:22-19:29 Reserved]

IV.   TAX INVESTIGATIONS

§19:30   Previously Policy Was No Concurrent Investigations

It long had been the practice of the Internal Revenue Service that it did not conduct simultaneous civil audits and criminal investigations.

Thus, once a civil revenue agent learned of or recommended the commencement of a criminal investigation, the civil agent ceased his work. [*See United States v. Peters*, 153 F.3d 445, 451-55 (7th Cir. 1998) (describing IRS policy that civil auditor was to cease audit and make criminal referral upon detecting indications of fraud); *SEC v. Dresser Industries, Inc.,* 628 F.2d 1368, 1379, n.26 (D.C. Cir. 1980) (same).]

This saved taxpayers from unknowingly waiving privileges against self-incrimination and producing incriminating documents, something that might occur during the civil audit where the taxpayer has the burden of disclosing information and justifying his position by documenting his business expenses.

§19:31   Current Policy Is to Coordinate Investigations

The IRS has switched course and now encourages revenue agents to search for evidence of criminal fraud, to refer the matter to the criminal investigation division and then to continue the civil audit and coordinate efforts with the Criminal Investigation Division ("CID") agents. [*Internal Revenue Manual* §38.3.1.8.; *see* John J. Tigue & Jeremy H. Timkin, "IRS: Quick Simultaneous Enforcement Over Long-Time Practices," 5/19/05 New York Law Journal 3 (reporting remarks of IRS Commissioner Mark W. Everson, Remarks at National Press Club on March 15, 2005, available at www.irs.gov/newsroom/article/0,,id=136835,00.html).]

PRACTICE TIP:

Ask the revenue agent point-blank whether a referral has been made to CID and whether a CID special agent (*i.e.*, an IRS criminal investigator) is involved. While the revenue agent has no duty to volunteer that information, lying or evading your question may cause a court to suppress any document and statements obtained by the revenue agent in any criminal prosecution. [*See United States v. Tweel*, 550 F.2d 297, 300 (5th Cir. 1977); *United States v. Peters*, 153 F.3d at 453.]

[§§19:32-19:39 Reserved]

V.   RESPONDING TO CIVIL DISCOVERY AND PLEADINGS

§19:40   Steps for Avoiding the Civil Action

If your client faces a criminal investigation and is served with a civil complaint relating to the same matter, you could defend it like any other civil case and subject your client to probing discovery that may elicit incriminating statements and documents that will expose any possible defense to the criminal charges.

However, there are better choices. Follow these five steps:
*   Answer with a general denial.
*   Answer by proxy.
*   Seek a protective order.
*   Move for a stay.
*   Invoke the Fifth Amendment.

Employ these tactics consecutively. Your aim is to avoid reaching trial or judgment in the civil action until your client's criminal status and fate are decided, while squeezing what discovery you can from the civil opponent.

Along the way, negotiate with your opponent for more time. Both the opposing party and the court will realize that the criminal prosecution might relieve them of the burdens of trying and proving the case.

§19:41   Enter a General Denial

You might buy some time for your client by answering a complaint or a summary judgment motion with general denials that do not commit your client to a specific factual position that can be used against him in a criminal prosecution. However, this tactic has some dangers:

- Some jurisdictions' pleading rules require specific denials.
- General denials of incontrovertible facts might result in frivolous pleading sanctions. [*See* Fed. R. Civ. P. 11.]
- If your client later attempts to claim the Fifth Amendment privilege within the same civil case, it might be argued that he waived the privilege by answering the complaint on the merits. However, he can assert the privilege and refuse to answer questions in a criminal grand jury or trial because the waiver holds only for the particular proceeding in which the testimony was given, not later proceedings. [*See Slutzker v. Johnson*, 393 F.3d 373, 388-889 (3d Cir. 2004) (witness's testimony at coroner's inquest did not waive privilege and permit compulsion of her testimony at trial for same homicide); *United States v. Gary*, 74 F.3d 304, 312 (1st Cir. 1996) (witness's testimony at first trial was not waiver for second trial). *But see OSRecovery, Inc. v. One Groupe Intern., Inc.*, 262 F. Supp. 2d 302, 311-12 (S.D. N.Y. 2003) (by submitting affidavit, witness waived privilege and could be compelled to answer deposition questions).]

In any event, this tactic buys only limited time because your client cannot make the same response to specific discovery requests.

Eventually, when your client claims the Fifth Amendment privilege, the opposing party might have the answer or summary judgment affidavit stricken because of the subsequent invocation of the privilege. [*See In re Vitamins Antitrust Litigation*, 120 F.Supp.2d 58, 67-68 (D.D.C. 2000) (striking affidavit and drawing adverse inference against party where he invoked privilege in response to deposition questions about subject covered by affidavit).]

§19:42   Answer by Proxy

If your client is a business-owner and the civil action is against his company, not him personally, you might choose another officer or agent of the company to sign the answer and discovery responses or affidavits. [*SEC v. First Jersey Securities, Inc.*, 843 F.2d 74 (2d Cir. 1988) (corporation has no privilege, so must appoint agent to answer discovery when those officers or employees with knowledge have valid personal privilege).]

However:

- This tactic is no help once the opposing party seeks to depose your client personally.
- You must be careful that your individual client does not confer with the agent answering the discovery because the agent can be asked about that in his deposition and thereby might become a witness to your client's admissions.

§19:43   Seek a Protective Order

Sometimes, the civil plaintiff has no interest in assisting the criminal prosecutors. Instead, the plaintiff wants his case heard as soon as possible.

Such a plaintiff might agree to a protective order forbidding the disclosure of any discovery materials to anyone, including criminal investigators, prosecutors and grand juries.

However, be wary of trusting civil protective orders to safeguard discovery materials and deposition transcripts and civil settlements from grand jury subpoenas. Such orders may give way to criminal subpoenas. [*See In re Grand Jury*, 286 F.3d 153, 157-58 (3d Cir. 2002) (absent exceptional circumstances, grand jury subpoena overrides protective order; surveys cases). *But see Martindell v. ITT Corp.*, 594 F.2d 291, 298 (2d Cir. 1979) (protective order takes priority over grand jury subpoena).]

The recent enactment of Rule 502 of the Federal Rules of Evidence strengthens the case for the enforceability of protective orders, at least those that shield privileged materials. Subsection (d) states, "A Federal court may order that the privilege or protection is not waived by disclosure connected with the litigation pending before the court–in which event the disclosure is also not a waiver in any other Federal or State proceeding." This rule covers only attorney-client communications and attorney work-product, not other confidential information, and it requires a court order; the parties' agreement, unless incorporated into an order, is insufficient.

Also, remember that you may not know which court in which jurisdiction will decide whether to honor the protective order because while you can make an educated guess, you cannot control where the criminal prosecution will be filed.

§19:44   Move to Stay the Civil Action

Defending a civil case in the midst of a criminal investigation is perilous:
- If the defendant actively defends the civil matter he may incriminate himself, expose his defense to the criminal charges, and open his records and his witnesses to extensive civil discovery.
- If he does not defend he may be subject to impoverishing damages and injunctive relief without a fair adjudication of his liability.

Unfortunately, this dilemma does not confer any right to a stay of the civil action. [*Keating v. Office of Thrift Supervision*, 45 F.3d 322, 324 (9th Cir. 1995).]

Courts have broad discretion in deciding whether or not to stay the civil case. In exercising that discretion, courts generally consider several factors, such as:
- The extent to which the issues in the criminal case overlap with those presented in the civil case.
- The status of the case, including whether the defendants have been indicted.
- The private interests of the plaintiffs in proceeding expeditiously weighed against the prejudice to plaintiffs caused by the delay.
- The private interests of and burden on the defendants.
- The interests of the courts.
- The public interest.

[*Trustees of the Plumbers and Pipefitters National Pensions Fund v. TransWorld Mechanical, Inc.*, 886 F.Supp. 1134, 1139 (S.D.N.Y. 1995). *See also Keating*, 45 F.3d at 324-25; *Microfinancial, Inc. v. Premier Holidays Int'l, Inc.*, 385 F.3d 72, 78 (1st Cir. 2004) (listing similar factors and adding "(vi) the good faith of the litigants (or the absence of it) and (vii) the status of the cases").]

The strongest case for granting a stay is where a party under criminal indictment is required to defend a civil proceeding involving the same matter. [*Volmar Distributors Inc. v. New York Post Co., Inc.*, 152 F.R.D. 36, 39 (S.D.N.Y. 1993); *see In re Homestore.com, Inc. Securities Litigation*, 347 F.Supp.2d 814, 820-21 (C.D. Cal. 2004) (denying stay because defendant had not been indicted and no certainty when he would be); *American Express Business Finance Corp. v. RW Professional Leasing Services Corp.*, 225 F.Supp.2d 263, 265 (E.D.N.Y. 2002) (noting that stays generally will be granted post-indictment); *but see SEC v. Healthsouth Corp.*, 261 F.Supp.2d 1298, 1326 (N.D. Ala. 2003) (staying SEC civil action pre-indictment).]

PRACTICE TIP:

If your client has not yet been charged, mollify concerns that the stay might be indefinite by asking that it be for a limited period, such as 90 or 120 days, with the opportunity to revisit the issue at the end of that time. [*See Britt v. International Bus Servs.*, 255 A.D.2d 143, 144, 679 N.Y.S.2d 616 (S.C. of N.Y.) (NY App. Div. 1st Dept. 1998) (reviewing standards for stay and granting stay where witness would invoke the Fifth Amendment privilege and his testimony was crucial, even though no criminal prosecution had commenced; plaintiff can move to vacate stay if criminal proceedings do not commence within a reasonable period of time).]

If the civil court will not stay the action in all respects, seek a limited stay of certain aspects of discovery or motion practice, a stay of answers to admissions, of your client's personal deposition, or of the time to respond to a summary judgment motion. [*See Gordon v. FDIC*, 427 F.2d 578, 580–81 (D.C. Cir. 1970) (a stay of answering admissions should be available where a general stay would not); *Brock v. Tolkow*, 109 F.R.D. 116, 120-21 (E.D.N.Y. 1985) (staying discovery in order to protect the defendant from the need to invoke the Fifth Amendment privilege, but otherwise allowing civil case to proceed); but see *SEC v. Caramadre*, 2010 U.S. Dist. LEXIS 59896 (D.R.I. June 10, 2010) (party's need to invoke privilege against self-incrimination in civil proceeding is not reason for a stay).]

Form:
- **Form 19-4** Motion to Stay Civil Proceedings

§19:45   Invoke the Fifth

Refusing to answer on the grounds of self-incrimination is the safest course with respect to criminal liability, but it can be deadly to the civil case and bring about other negative consequences. Therefore, try to forestall the invocation of the privilege until you have no other choice.

The damage to the civil case is that the trier of fact can draw adverse inferences against the party who invokes the privilege. [*Keating v. Office of Thrift Supervision*, 45 F.3d 322, 326 (9th Cir. 1995).]

However, the trial court should not enter judgment against your client until it has considered and found to be inadequate other remedies. [*See McMullen v. Bay Ship Management*, 335 F.3d 215, 219 (3d Cir. 2003) (plaintiff's action should not be dismissed for his invocation of privilege at his deposition); *Steiner v. Minnesota Life Co.*, 85 P. 3d 135, 136 (Colo. 2004) (physician's claim for disability benefits should not be dismissed for his refusal to answer questions about his drug use; surveys cases and finds trend against dismissal for invoking the Fifth).]

Some ancillary negative effects of invoking the Fifth Amendment are:

*   Some regulatory agencies will revoke your client's license or bar him from working in the industry for invoking the Fifth; his employer may even fire him.
*   Where your client seeks the benefits of insurance coverage, he might lose it because refusing to answer the insurer's discovery questions will be considered a breach of the cooperation clause. [*See Dyno-Bite, Inc. v. Travelers Cos.*, 80 A.D.2d 471, 476, 439 N.Y.S.2d 558, (NY App. Div. 4th Dept. 1981) (corporate officers' invocation of privilege violated fire insurance policy's cooperation clause and voided coverage).]

Further, unlike taking the Fifth before a grand jury, your client's assertion that answers might incriminate him will be public and could bring career-ending infamy and suspicion if he is a community leader, politician or renowned businessman. It also might incite other private plaintiffs to file suit against your client because they perceive him as defenseless.

[§§19:46-19:49 Reserved]

VI.   TACTICS AND TIPS

§19:50   Using Civil Discovery to Your Client's Advantage

Civil discovery is more generous than criminal. Where criminal charges have not yet been filed, you are entitled to no discovery of the investigation. Discovery in the civil lawsuit might provide you with precious insights to the prosecutor's evidence against you.

Prosecutors know this and they can intervene in the civil action to seek a stay if it risks disclosing too much of their investigation. [*See SEC v. Chestman*, 861 F.2d 49, 50 (2d Cir. 1988); *SEC v. Mutuals.com, Inc.*, 2004 U.S. Dist. LEXIS 13718 (N.D. Tex 2004) (both permitting intervention and granting stays).]

Courts readily grant such stays, especially where it appears that the criminal defendant or target filed the civil action as plaintiff for the very purpose of obtaining such discovery. [*See United States v. Mellon Bank, N.A.*, 545 F.2d 869, 872-73 (3d Cir. 1976) (similarity of issues left open the possibility that defendant might exploit civil discovery for purpose of his criminal case; granted stay of civil proceedings).]

PRACTICE TIP:

Where your client is the defendant, do not move for a stay until you must, until incriminating discovery is demanded of your client. Even the plaintiff's initial disclosures and document discovery can yield valuable insights and much more than you will see for a long time in the criminal case. [*See* Fed. R. Civ. P. 26(a)(1).]

§19:51   Using a Civil Settlement to Encourage Dismissal

Your priority in responding to a civil action on behalf of a criminal defendant or suspect is to prevent the civil case from worsening your client's position in the criminal matter. However, do not automatically advise that your client cocoon himself in the privilege and abandon any defense to the civil action.

Defending the civil action to some extent may position your client to settle the civil case. Sometimes a civil settlement will persuade the prosecutor that no prosecution is necessary. Generally this is not the case as most prosecuting authorities maintain that their policy is to treat civil and criminal matters independently and that they will not allow a defendant to buy his way out of a prosecution by compensating the victim. However, if the victim is made whole, both the victim and prosecutor may lose enthusiasm for the prosecution.

Some jurisdictions have a formal procedure whereby they will dismiss a prosecution for a financial crime, such as a theft, fraud or embezzlement if the defendant makes the victim whole. [*E.g.*, Pa. R. Crim. P. 585.] Further, even in jurisdictions without such a policy, compensating the victim may persuade the prosecutor that scarce prosecutorial resources are best used for other cases.

If you get to sentencing, early and full restitution might persuade the court to impose a lenient sentence.

§19:52   Avoid Admissions or Preclusive Findings

Be careful to specify in any civil settlement that your client is not admitting liability. Statements made by you or your client in the course of settlement negotiations and the fact of the settlement itself may be admissible in subsequent criminal litigation despite the seemingly clear language of FRE 408 and its state equivalents excluding such evidence. [*See, e.g., United States v. Prewitt*, 34 F.3d 436, 439 (7th Cir. 1994); (holding that Rule 408 applies only to evidence offered in civil cases); *but see United States v. Davis*, 596 F.3d 852, 860 & n.6 (D.C. Cir. 2010) (holding that "The 2006 amendment to Rule 408, . . . made clear that the rule applied to both civil and criminal proceedings," but noting that the Courts of Appeals are split on this); *United States v. Bailey*, 327 F.3d 1131, 1143-47 (10th Cir. 2003) (Rule 408 applies in both criminal and civil cases) *United States v. Logan*, 250 F.3d 350, 366-67 (6th Cir. 2001).]

The 2006 Amendments to Rule 408 adopt the position that Rule 408 precludes the use in criminal cases of admissions made in civil settlement negotiations, but with a twist: "Except when offered in a criminal case and the negotiations related to a claim by a public office or agency in the exercise of regulatory, investigative, or enforcement authority." [FRE 408(a)(2).] Thus, statements made to settle a civil case brought by a private party are inadmissible, either on guilt or for impeachment, in a criminal case, but statements made in an official civil enforcement action or investigation may be admitted.

CAUTION:

The Amendment's language is opaque. Rather than explicitly state that the rule forbids use of private civil settlement negotiations in criminal prosecutions, it implies as much by creating an exception to the rule of inadmissibility for statements made to regulatory officials. [*See United States v. Roti*, 484 F.3d 934, 936-37 (7th Cir. 2007) (describing the structure of the Amendment).] Thus, some courts have continued to follow the *Prewitt* rule and hold that Rule 408 has no force in a subsequent criminal prosecution. [*E.g., McAuliffe v. United States*, 2009 U.S. Dist. LEXIS 568511, 2009 WL 1928547 (S.D.Oh. 2009).] Rule 408 authorizes the investigated party and the government agency to enter into an agreement that statements and negotiations shall not be admitted in a criminal action. [Rule 408, Committee Notes on Rules – 2006 Amendments ("The individual can seek to protect against subsequent disclosure through negotiation and agreement with the civil regulator or an attorney for the government.")]. You should seek such an agreement if trying to reach a civil settlement and you have any inkling that a criminal proceeding is possible. [*See* Form 19-6.]

Civil settlements, even if your client prevails on the merits, do not have preclusive effect in subsequent criminal prosecutions on the same transaction. However, findings in a civil case against a governmental agency might be afforded preclusive effect in a subsequent criminal prosecution by the same government. [*United States v. Rogers*, 960 F.2d 1501, 1507-09 (10th Cir. 1992) (findings in defendant's favor in SEC injunctive action should have been given preclusive effect in criminal case and would result in dismissal of counts of the indictment).]

Form:
•   **Form 19-6** Rule 408 Letter Agreement

§19:53   Avoid Testifying in Civil Proceedings

When criminal proceedings are on the horizon, your client should avoid testifying or personally answering discovery at a civil proceeding that touches on the same issues. [*See* Chapter 8, Interrogations, Confessions, and Other Statements.]

Prepare your client carefully. He should testify only if his story withstands your investigation and preparatory cross-examination and if it does not provide the criminal prosecutors with evidence they would not obtain otherwise. Be aware, however, that by testifying, your client has committed himself to that story as his defense in the criminal case. He no longer can count on the prosecution's inability to prove anything he admits in his story.

PRACTICE TIP:
•   Find someone else who can testify to the same matters or seek a stay of the civil proceeding until the criminal case ends. [*See* §19:42.]

- If your client must sign the answer to a complaint or a discovery response, make the answer as general a denial as the jurisdiction's rules permit. [*See* §19:41.]
- If your client must testify at the civil proceeding (*e.g.,* to avoid a license revocation or a crushing judgment), object to questions first on the ground of relevance. If sustained, this objection removes the need to invoke the privilege.

VII. SETTLING THE PARALLEL CIVIL CASE

§19:60   Cold Comfort Letters

As a matter of policy, the Department of Justice will not agree to language in a civil settlement that might preclude criminal prosecution. As a matter of practice, however, DOJ and United States Attorneys' Offices will state for the record whether they have any open or pending criminal investigations and whether they have any present intent to initiate a criminal investigation.

Seek to have such assurances memorialized in a so-called "cold comfort" letter. If new facts come to the Government's attention, such a letter will not preclude a criminal investigation, but the response to your request for one will educate you as to whether or not an investigation is under way, and the issuance of one may prevent the bad faith filing of criminal charges that were underway while you were settling the civil matter. [*Fresenius Medical Care v. United States*, 526 F.3d 372 (8th Cir. 2008) (cold comfort letter did not preclude investigation on new facts, implying that absent the new facts, the cold comfort letter would have been grounds to quash administrative subpoena).]

VIII. FORMS

Form 19-1   Agreement to Indemnify Legal Fees

SEPARATION AGREEMENT AND GENERAL RELEASE

This Separation Agreement and General Release ("Agreement") is hereby made and entered into this ___ day of April, 2005, between JHG ("G") and M Company, together with its parents, subsidiaries, divisions, affiliates, related companies, predecessors and successors ("M COMPANY").

WHEREAS, G and M COMPANY have agreed to end their employment relationship; and

WHEREAS, in furtherance thereof, G and M COMPANY desire to set forth the terms and conditions relating to G's separation from M COMPANY.

NOW THEREFORE, the parties, intending to be legally bound, and in consideration of the mutual promises and undertakings set forth herein, do hereby agree as follows:

No Other Representations. G represents and warrants that no promise or inducement has been offered or made except as herein set forth and that she is entering into and executing this Agreement without reliance on any statement or representation not set forth within this Agreement by any other party hereto, or any person(s) acting on any party's behalf.

Non-Assignment of Rights. G represents and warrants that she has not sold, assigned, transferred, conveyed or otherwise disposed of to any third party, by operation of law or otherwise, any action, cause of action, debt, obligation, contract, agreement, covenant, guarantee, judgment, damage, claim, counterclaim, liability or demand of any nature whatsoever relating to any matter covered in this Agreement.

Non-Admission of Liability by M Company. G understands and agrees that this Agreement does not and shall not be deemed or construed as an admission of liability or responsibility by M COMPANY for any purpose. Specifically, but without limiting the foregoing, G understands and agrees that this Agreement shall not constitute an admission that any allegation made by G in connection with the charge of discrimination filed with the Equal Employment Opportunity Commission, Charge No. 00000 (cross-filed with the Pennsylvania Human Relations Commission ("PHRA") as _____) (the "EEOC Charge"), or otherwise concerning M COMPANY is true or that any action by M COMPANY relating to G was in any way wrongful or unlawful. G further agrees that nothing contained in this Agreement can be used by G or any other past, present or future employee in any way as precedent for future dealings with M COMPANY, or any of its parents, subsidiaries, divisions, affiliates, related companies, successors, officers, directors, attorneys, agents or employees.

Resignation and Separation Date. G's employment with M COMPANY will terminate effective April ___, 2005 (the "Separation Date"). As of the Separation Date, G will be relieved of all of her titles, duties, responsibilities and authority as an employee of M Company and participation in all M COMPANY benefit plans shall cease. Should G elect continued benefit coverage pursuant to COBRA, she understands and agrees that M COMPANY shall have no obligation to provide any compensation towards the payment of any required premiums, beyond the payments M COMPANY has agreed to provide pursuant to this Agreement. G also understands and agrees that as of the Separation Date any other agreements between G and M COMPANY shall be terminated.

No Future Employment with M Company. G understands and agrees that: (a) her employment relationship with M COMPANY will be terminated as of the Separation Date; (b) she has no intention of applying and will not apply for or otherwise seek reemployment or reinstatement with M COMPANY, or any of its parents, subsidiaries, divisions, affiliates, related companies or successors; and (c) M COMPANY, its parents, subsidiaries, divisions, affiliates, related companies or successors have no obligation to reinstate, rehire, reemploy, recall or hire her at any time in the future.

Separation Payments. In consideration for G entering into this Agreement and fully abiding by and complying with its terms, and assuming G has not revoked the Agreement as described in Paragraph 23 below, and further subject to the provisions of Paragraphs 10 and 19 below, M COMPANY agrees to provide G with the following payments, to which G acknowledges she is not otherwise entitled, totaling $425,000.00. Said payments shall be paid to G as follows:

(a) _Compensation_. M COMPANY agrees to pay G:

(i) Salary continuation payments in the amount of $_____, less applicable withholdings, in twenty equal monthly installments. Said payments shall be made in accordance with M COMPANY's normal payroll schedule and shall begin on the next regularly-scheduled pay date following the expiration of the revocation period described in Paragraph 24 below;

(ii) Additional payments in the amount of $_____, in consideration for the restrictive covenants described in Paragraphs 15 and 16 below, for which no taxes will be withheld, but for which a Form 1099 will be issued. Said payments shall be made in accordance with M COMPANY's normal payroll schedule and shall begin on the next regularly-scheduled pay date following the expiration of the revocation period described in Paragraph 23 below;

(b) _Attorneys' Fees_. M COMPANY agrees to pay G'S counsel a lump sum payment of $38,000 for past fees incurred by G, for which a 1099 Form will be issued to counsel. M Company agrees that it shall pay for G's expenses and reasonable legal fees and legal expenses in connection with any litigation, investigation or governmental proceedings related to M Company;

(c) _Indemnification of M Company by G_. G represents and warrants that she shall indemnify and hold M COMPANY harmless from any liability, including, but not limited to, any taxes, penalties or other amounts imposed upon M COMPANY by any governmental authority, and any costs or fees incurred by M COMPANY to defend any claims, as a result of G'S proposed tax treatment of the payments described above. G understands and agrees that as a nonexclusive remedy for any amounts M COMPANY is owed under this Paragraph, M COMPANY has the right at its election to set off any such amounts it otherwise owes to G under this Agreement.

No Other Compensation or Benefits Owing. G understands and agrees that, except as otherwise provided for in this Agreement, G is not and will not be due any other compensation or benefits including, but not limited to, any other compensation or benefits pursuant to any prior agreement between G and M COMPANY.

Release by G. In consideration of the compensation, benefits and agreements provided for pursuant to this Agreement, the sufficiency of which is hereby acknowledged, G, for herself and for any person who may claim by or through her, releases and forever discharges M COMPANY, and its past, present and future parents, subsidiaries, divisions, affiliates, related companies, predecessors, successors, officers, directors, attorneys, agents, and employees (the "Releasees"), from any and all claims or causes of action that G had, has or may have, known or unknown, relating to the EEOC Charge or G's employment with and/or separation from M COMPANY, up until the date of this Agreement, including, but not limited to, any claims arising under Title VII of the Civil Rights Act of 1964, as amended, Section 1981 of the Civil Rights Act of 1866, as amended, the Civil Rights Act of 1991, as amended, the Family and Medical Leave Act, the Age Discrimination in Employment Act, as amended by the Older Workers Benefit Protection Act of 1990 ("ADEA"), the Americans with Disabilities Act, the Employee Retirement Income Security Act, the Pennsylvania Human Rights Act; claims under any other federal, state or local statute, regulation or ordinance; claims for discrimination or harassment of any kind, breach of contract or public policy, wrongful or retaliatory discharge, defamation or other personal or business injury of any kind; claims for breach of any prior agreement between G and M COMPANY or for any compensation or benefits provided for pursuant to any such agreement; and any and all other claims to any form of legal or equitable relief or damages; any other claims for compensation or benefits, accrued or otherwise; or any claims for attorneys' fees or costs.

In consideration of the agreements provided for pursuant to this Agreement, the sufficiency of which is hereby acknowledged, M COMPANY, for itself and its past, present and future parents, subsidiaries, divisions, affiliates, related companies, predecessors, successors, officers, directors, attorneys, agents, and employees and any person or entity who may claim by or through it, releases and forever discharges G, and her past, present and future affiliates, related companies, attorneys, agents, and employees (the "Releasees"), from any and all claims or causes of action that M COMPANY had, has or may have, known or unknown, relating to G's employment with and/or separation from M COMPANY, up until the date of this Agreement; claims for breach of contract, defamation or other injury of any kind; claims for breach of any prior agreement between M COMPANY and G; and any and all other claims to any form of legal or equitable relief or damages; any other claims for compensation or benefits, accrued or otherwise; or any claims for attorneys' fees or costs.

Exclusion for Certain Claims. G and M COMPANY understand and agree that the release set forth in Paragraph 8 shall not apply to any claims, including any claims under ADEA, arising after the effective date of this Agreement, nor shall anything herein prevent any party from instituting any action to enforce the terms of this Agreement. Moreover, the release set forth in Paragraph 8 shall not apply to any claims relating to vested employee benefits pursuant to any Pension or Welfare Benefit Plan under which G was, or is, a participant or beneficiary.

Dismissal of the EEOC Charge. G shall withdraw dismiss the EEOC Charge (including any charge complaint cross-filed with the PHRC) with prejudice within 24 hours of the expiration of the revocation period described in Paragraph 24 below. G shall provide notice to M COMPANY of said dismissal within 24 hours thereafter. Notwithstanding any other provision in this Agreement to the contrary, G understands and agrees that M COMPANY shall have no obligation to provide any payments under Paragraph 6 above, until M COMPANY has been provided with satisfactory notice that G has requested withdrawal of the EEOC Charge (and any charge complaint cross-filed with the PHRC) has been dismissed with prejudice.

Disclosure of Any Material Information. As of the date G signs this Agreement, G represents and warrants that she has disclosed to M COMPANY any information in her possession concerning any conduct involving M COMPANY that she has any reason to believe may be unlawful, violates any M COMPANY policy or would otherwise reflect poorly on M COMPANY in any respect.

Duty to Cooperate. G understands and agrees that she, and any counsel retained directly by G, shall cooperate fully with M COMPANY and/or its counsel with respect to any matter, including, but not limited to, any litigation, investigation, governmental proceeding or internal M COMPANY review, which relates to any matter with which G was involved or concerning which M COMPANY reasonably determines G may have responsive or relevant information. G further understands and agrees that such cooperation includes, but is not limited to, any interview of G by M COMPANY and/or its counsel, full disclosure of any responsive or relevant information and truthfully testifying and/or answering questions in connection with any such litigation, investigation, proceeding or internal M COMPANY review. G understands and agrees that she shall render any such cooperation in a timely manner and at such times and places as may be mutually agreeable to by G and M COMPANY; provided, however, that M COMPANY will endeavor to reasonably limit the amount of time related to any internal M COMPANY review. M COMPANY shall reimburse G for any of her reasonable costs and expenses incurred in connection with her compliance with the obligations of this Paragraph 12 (including travel expenses and telecommunication charges, but excluding any legal fees for counsel directly retained by G or any costs or expenses associated with any such direct retention of counsel). G understands and agrees that she shall immediately notify M COMPANY if she is contacted for an interview or if she receives a subpoena or request for information in any matter related to or concerning her employment with M COMPANY. G and M COMPANY further understand and agree that G's duty of cooperation as described herein, and her obligations concerning confidential information described in Paragraph 15 below, shall not prevent her from complying with any lawfully-issued subpoena or any request for information or an interview from a governmental agency; provided, however, that G shall notify M COMPANY within 24 hours of her receipt of any such subpoena or request and in any event shall not respond to any such subpoena or request prior to her notification of M COMPANY of same. Provided, further, that G also agrees to advise M COMPANY within 24 hours of any request for information or an interview that she may receive related to or concerning her employment at M COMPANY.

Announcement and Responses to Inquiries. M COMPANY and G agree to cooperate in drafting an internal M COMPANY announcement and a public announcement of G's separation from M COMPANY and a statement to be issued in responding to any inquiries concerning G's departure and tenure at M COMPANY. M COMPANY agrees to provide positive references and positive recommendation letters for Ms. G. The form of the positive recommendation letter is attached hereto as Exhibit A. _____ or the then-acting President of M COMPANY (if _____ is no longer employed by M COMPANY) shall provide the positive references for Ms. G upon request.

<u>Non-Disparagement</u>. The parties agree not to engage in any form of conduct or to make any statements or representations that disparage or otherwise impair the reputation, goodwill or commercial interests of G or M COMPANY, or her or its respective past, present and future parents, subsidiaries, divisions, affiliates, related companies, successors, officers, directors, attorneys, agents and employees. This paragraph does not forbid G from answering questions truthfully in response to any subpoena lawfully issued on behalf of a private party or government agency or any government agency request for information.

<u>Confidential Information</u>. G represents and warrants that she shall not at any time, directly or indirectly, disclose, communicate or divulge to any individual or entity, or use for the benefit of any individual or entity, any knowledge or information with respect to the conduct or details of M COMPANY's business which G, acting reasonably, believes or should believe to be of a confidential nature and the disclosure of which would not to be in M COMPANY's interest. Information of a confidential nature shall specifically include, without limitation, client lists, pricing information, software, trade secrets, business methods and know how, employee and contractor lists, and contact information, and information about costs, markets, sales, products and technical and business processes. G further understands and agrees all work performed by her for M COMPANY is the sole property of M COMPANY and that M COMPANY is the sole owner of all the results and proceeds of her services for M COMPANY. This paragraph does not forbid G from answering questions truthfully in response to any subpoena lawfully issued on behalf of a private party or government agency or any government agency request for information. Should a subpoena or government request seek the disclosure of information that G believes may be M COMPANY confidential information, G shall notify M COMPANY, and it will be M COMPANY'S obligation to object promptly to the request or subpoena. Absent M COMPANY'S prompt objection, G may produce the information.

<u>Non-Competition and Non-Solicitation</u>.

(a) <u>Non-Competition</u>. G represents and warrants that for a period of eighteen months following the Separation Date, she will not, directly or indirectly, whether as an employee, owner, partner, consultant, agent, director, officer, shareholder or in any other capacity, engage in or be employed by any Prohibited Business. For purposes of this Agreement, a Prohibited Business means the medical transcription processing services and dictation business in the geographic territory in which G had regular and continuous business dealings while employed by M COMPANY.

(b) <u>Non-Solicitation</u>. G represents and warrants that for a period of eighteen months after the Separation Date she will not, except with the express prior written consent of M COMPANY, directly or indirectly, whether as employee, owner, partner, consultant, agent, director, officer, shareholder or in any other capacity, for her own account or for the benefit of any individual or entity, (i) solicit any customer of M COMPANY in any manner which would result in such customer terminating their relationship with M COMPANY; or (ii) hire or engage, or solicit or induce any individual or entity which is an employee or contractor of M COMPANY to leave the Company or to otherwise terminate their relationship with M COMPANY.

<u>Remedies Related to Paragraphs 15 and 16</u>. G understands and agrees that a breach of Paragraphs 15 or 16 of this Agreement will result immediate and irreparable injury to M COMPANY. G, therefore, agrees that in the event of a breach of Paragraphs 15 or 16 of this Agreement, in addition to any other remedy that M COMPANY may have under this Agreement or applicable law, M COMPANY shall be entitled to an injunction, temporary restraining order or other equitable relief restraining G from such breach. Nothing herein shall be construed as prohibiting M COMPANY from pursuing any other remedies for such breach or threatened breach.

<u>Confidentiality of Agreement</u>. The parties understand and agree that the terms of this Agreement are confidential and shall be accorded the utmost confidentiality and that these matters will not be disclosed to any third party except for the parties' respective spouse and financial or legal advisor(s), and, in the case of disclosure to any advisor(s), only to the extent necessary to perform services, or except as disclosure of such matters may be required by law; provided, however, that G may disclose Paragraphs 16-20 of this Agreement to a prospective employer.

<u>Remedies Related to Paragraph 18</u>. G understands and agrees that a breach of Paragraph 18 of this Agreement will result in immediate and irreparable injury to M COMPANY. G, therefore, agrees that in the event of a breach of Paragraph 18 of this Agreement, in addition to any other remedy that M COMPANY may have under this Agreement or applicable law, M COMPANY shall be entitled to the following liquidated damages consisting of: (a) a forfeiture of any amounts still due and owing to G under the terms of this Agreement; and (b) $25,000.00. Nothing herein shall be construed as prohibiting M COMPANY from pursuing any other remedies for such breach.

<u>General</u>.

(a) <u>Severability</u>. If any provision of this Agreement is found by a court of competent jurisdiction to be unenforceable, in whole or in part, then that provision will be eliminated, modified or restricted in whatever manner is necessary to make the remaining provisions enforceable to the maximum extent allowable by law.

(b) <u>Successors</u>. This Agreement shall be binding upon, enforceable by, and inure to the benefit of G, M COMPANY and each Releasee, and G's and M COMPANY's respective personal or legal representatives, executors, administrators, successors, heirs, distributees, devisees and legatees, and to any successor or assign of each Releasee, but neither this Agreement, nor any rights, payments, or obligations arising hereunder may be assigned, pledged, transferred, or hypothecated by G or M COMPANY.

(c) <u>Controlling Law</u>. This Agreement shall be construed and enforced under the laws of and before the courts of the State of New Jersey.

(d) <u>Waiver</u>. No claim or right arising out of a breach or default under this Agreement can be discharged by a waiver of that claim or right unless the waiver is in writing signed by the party hereto to be bound by such waiver. A waiver by any party hereto of a breach or default by another party of any provision of this Agreement shall not be deemed a waiver of future compliance therewith and such provision shall remain in full force and effect.

(e) <u>Notices</u>. All notices, requests, demands and other communications regarding this Agreement shall be in writing and delivered in person or sent by Registered or Certified U.S. Mail, Postage Prepaid, Return Receipt Requested, and properly addressed as follows:

To M COMPANY: M Company Inc.
                  Attention: General Counsel
To G: JG

<u>Entire Agreement/Amendment</u>. Except as otherwise indicated herein, the parties hereto agree that this Agreement constitutes the entire agreement between G and M COMPANY, and that this Agreement supersedes any and all prior and/or contemporaneous written and/or oral agreements relating to G's employment with M COMPANY and termination therefrom. G understands and agrees that this Agreement may not be modified except by written document, signed by the parties hereto.

<u>Knowing and Voluntary Action</u>. G acknowledges that she received this Agreement on April ___, 2005 and has consulted an attorney before signing this Agreement. G further represents and warrants that she has read this Agreement; has been given a period of at least twenty one (21) days to consider the Agreement; understands its meaning and application; and is signing of G's own free will with the intent of being bound by it. If G elects to sign this Agreement prior to the expiration of twenty-one (21) days, she has done so voluntarily and knowingly.

<u>Revocation of Agreement</u>. G further acknowledges that she may revoke this Agreement at any time within a period of seven (7) days following the date she signs the Agreement. Notice of revocation shall be made in writing, sent via Registered or Certified U.S. Mail, Postage Prepaid, Return Receipt Requested and properly addressed to M COMPANY in accordance with Paragraph 20(e) above. Such revocation must be received by M COMPANY by the close of business of the first day following the end of the seven-day revocation period. This Agreement shall not become effective until after the time period for revocation has expired.

IN WITNESS WHEREOF, the parties have executed and agreed to this Agreement consisting of 10 pages.
JG

_____

Date: April ___, 20__

M COMPANY INC.
By: _____
Title: _____
Date: April ___, 20__

Form 19-2   Letter Regarding Agreement to Pay Legal Fees

September 1, 20__
Mr. _____
Pittsburgh, PA 15219
Re: AC and X Company

Dear Mr. _____:

On behalf of our client, AC, we acknowledge X Company's agreement to pay the fees and costs Ms. C has incurred in my representation of her from _____, 20__, through and including the date of her interview and her possible testimony at the arbitration proceeding between X Company and Y Company. X Company will pay those fees and costs incurred in counseling her and in corresponding and meeting with federal investigators and prosecutors pursuant to the West Virginia Grand Jury Investigation now taking place.

As of _____, 20__, her fees and costs totaled $_____. Ms. C has contended throughout our representation of her that X Company should pay her legal fees incurred arising out of her employment, as it has done for all other X Company employees who are witnesses, and not subjects or targets, in the Government's Investigation.

You should understand that Ms. C will answer X Company's questions fully and truthfully to the best of her recollection and ability. Her testimony will not be affected or influenced in any way by X Company's payment of her legal fees as described above.

As you requested, we will submit copies of our bills for your review, with any attorney-client privilege or work product doctrine-protected information contained therein redacted.

Very truly yours,
Thomas J. Farrell

Form 19-3   SEC Form 1662

COMMENT:

This SEC form for people who have been requested to supply information either voluntarily or pursuant to a subpoena warns that the SEC regularly shares information and discovery materials with the Department of Justice.

SEC FORM 1662

SECURITIES AND EXCHANGE COMMISSION
Washington, D.C. 20549

Supplemental Information for Persons Requested to Supply Information Voluntarily or Directed to Supply Information Pursuant to a Commission Subpoena

False Statements and Documents

Section 1001 of Title 18 of the United States Code provides as follows:

Whoever, in any matter within the jurisdiction of any department or agency of the United States knowingly and willfully falsifies, conceals or covers up by any trick, scheme, or device a material fact, or makes any false, fictitious or fraudulent statements or representations, or makes or uses any false writing or document knowing the same to contain any false, fictitious or fraudulent statement or entry, shall be fined under this title or imprisoned not more than five years, or both.

Testimony

If your testimony is taken, you should be aware of the following:

1. *Record.* Your testimony will be transcribed by a reporter. If you desire to go off the record, please indicate this to the Commission employee taking your testimony, who will determine whether to grant your request. The reporter will not go off the record at your, or your counsel's, direction.

2. *Counsel.* You have the right to be accompanied, represented and advised by counsel of your choice. Your counsel may advise you before, during and after your testimony; question you briefly at the conclusion of your testimony to clarify any of the answers you give during testimony; and make summary notes during your testimony solely for your use. If you are accompanied by counsel, you may consult privately.

If you are not accompanied by counsel, please advise the Commission employee taking your testimony whenever during your testimony you desire to be accompanied, represented and advised by counsel. Your testimony will be adjourned to afford you the opportunity to arrange to do so.

You may be represented by counsel who also represents other persons involved in the Commission's investigation. This multiple representation, however, presents a potential conflict of interest if one client's interests are or may be adverse to another's. If you are represented by counsel who also represents other persons involved in the investigation, the Commission will assume that you and counsel have discussed and resolved all issues concerning possible conflicts of interest. The choice of counsel, and the responsibility for that choice, is yours.

3. *Transcript Availability.* Rule 6 of the Commission's Rules Relating to Investigations, 17 CFR 203.6, states:

> A person who has submitted documentary evidence or testimony in a formal investigative proceeding shall be entitled, upon written request, to procure a copy of his documentary evidence or a transcript of his testimony on payment of the appropriate fees, provided, however, that in a nonpublic formal investigative proceeding the Commission may for good cause deny such request. In any event, any witness, upon proper identification, shall have the right to inspect the official transcript of the witness's own testimony.

If you wish to purchase a copy of the transcript of your testimony, the reporter will provide you with a copy of the appropriate form. Persons requested to supply information voluntarily will be allowed the rights provided by this rule.

4. *Perjury.* Section 1621 of Title 18 of the United States Code provides as follows:

> Whoever ... having taken an oath before a competent tribunal, officer, or person, in any case in which a law of the United States authorizes an oath to be administered, that he will testify, declare, depose, or certify truly ... willfully and contrary to such oath states or subscribes any material matter which he does not believe to be true ... is guilty of perjury and shall, except as otherwise expressly provided by law, be fined under this title or imprisoned not more than five years or both...

5. *Fifth Amendment and Voluntary Testimony.* Information you give may be used against you in any federal, state, local or foreign administrative, civil or criminal proceeding brought by the Commission or any other agency. You may refuse, in accordance with the rights guaranteed to you by the Fifth Amendment to the Constitution of the United States, to give any information that may tend to incriminate you or subject you to fine, penalty or forfeiture. If your testimony is not pursuant to subpoena, your appearance to testify is voluntary, you need not answer any question, and you may leave whenever you wish. Your cooperation is, however, appreciated.

6. *Formal Order Availability.* If the Commission has issued a formal order of investigation, it will be shown to you during your testimony, at your request. If you desire a copy of the formal order, please make your request in writing.

Submissions and Settlements

Rule 5(c) of the Commission's Rules on Informal and Other Procedures, 17 CFR 202.5(c), states:

> Persons who become involved in ... investigations may, on their own initiative, submit a written statement to the Commission setting forth their interests and position in regard to the subject matter of the investigation. Upon request, the staff, in its discretion, may advise such persons of the general nature of the investigation, including the indicated violations as they pertain to them, and the amount of time that may be available for preparing and submitting a statement prior to the presentation of a staff recommendation to the Commission for the commencement of an administrative or injunction proceeding. Submissions by interested persons should be forwarded to the appropriate Division Director, Regional Director, or District Administrator with a copy to the staff members conducting the investigation and should be clearly referenced to the specific investigation to which they relate. In the event a recommendation for the commencement of an enforcement proceeding is presented by the staff, any submissions by interested persons will be forwarded to the Commission in conjunction with the staff memorandum.

The staff of the Commission routinely seeks to introduce submissions made pursuant to Rule 5(c) as evidence in Commission enforcement proceedings, when the staff deems appropriate.

Rule 5(f) of the Commission's Rules on Informal and Other Procedures, 17 CFR 202.5(f), states:

> In the course of the Commission's investigations, civil lawsuits, and administrative proceedings, the staff, with appropriate authorization, may discuss with persons involved the disposition of such matters by consent, by settlement, or in some other manner. It is the policy of the Commission, however, that the disposition of any such matter may not, expressly or impliedly, extend to any criminal charges that have been, or may be, brought against any such person or any recommendation with respect thereto. Accordingly, any person involved in an enforcement matter before the Commission who consents, or agrees to consent, to any judgment or order does so solely for the purpose of resolving the claims against him in that investigative, civil, or administrative matter and not for the purpose of resolving any criminal charges that have been, or might be, brought against him. This policy reflects the fact that neither the Commission nor its staff has the authority or responsibility for instituting, conducting, settling, or otherwise disposing of criminal proceedings. That authority and responsibility are vested in the Attorney General and representatives of the Department of Justice.

Freedom of Information Act

The Freedom of Information Act, 5 U.S.C. 552 (the "FOIA"), generally provides for disclosure of information to the public. Rule 83 of the Commission's Rules on Information and Requests, 17 CFR 200.83, provides a procedure by which a person can make a written request that information submitted to the Commission not be disclosed under the FOIA. That rule states that no determination as to the validity of such a request will be made until a request for disclosure of the information under the FOIA is received. Accordingly, no response to a request that information not be disclosed under the FOIA is necessary or will be given until a request for disclosure under the FOIA is received. If you desire an acknowledgment of receipt of your written request that information not be disclosed under the FOIA, please provide a duplicate request, together with a stamped, self-addressed envelope.

Authority for Solicitation of Information

Persons Directed to Supply Information Pursuant to Subpoena. The authority for requiring production of information is set forth in the subpoena. Disclosure of the information to the Commission is mandatory, subject to the valid assertion of any legal right or privilege you might have.

Persons Requested to Supply Information Voluntarily. One or more of the following provisions authorizes the Commission to solicit the information requested: Sections 19 and/or 20 of the Securities Act of 1933; Section 21 of the Securities Exchange Act of 1934; Section 321 of the Trust Indenture Act of 1939; Section 42 of the Investment Company Act of 1940; Section 209 of the Investment Advisers Act of 1940; and 17 CFR 202.5. Disclosure of the requested information to the Commission is voluntary on your part.

Effect of Not Supplying Information

Persons Directed to Supply Information Pursuant to Subpoena. If you fail to comply with the subpoena, the Commission may seek a court order requiring you to do so. If such an order is obtained and you thereafter fail to supply the information, you may be subject to civil and/or criminal sanctions for contempt of court. In addition, if the subpoena was issued pursuant to the Securities Exchange Act of 1934, the Investment Company Act of 1940, and/or the Investment Advisers Act of 1940, and if you, without just cause, fail or refuse to attend and testify, or to answer any lawful inquiry, or to produce books, papers, correspondence, memoranda, and other records in compliance with the subpoena, you may be found guilty of a misdemeanor and fined not more than $1,000 or imprisoned for a term of not more than one year, or both.

Persons Requested to Supply Information Voluntarily. There are no direct sanctions and thus no direct effects for failing to provide all or any part of the requested information.

Principal Uses of Information

The Commission's principal purpose in soliciting the information is to gather facts in order to determine whether any person has violated, is violating, or is about to violate any provision of the federal securities laws or rules for which the Commission has enforcement authority, such as rules of securities exchanges and the rules of the Municipal Securities Rulemaking Board. Facts developed may, however, constitute violations of other laws or rules. Information provided may be used in Commission and other agency enforcement proceedings. Unless the Commission or its staff explicitly agrees to the contrary in writing, you should not assume that the Commission or its staff acquiesces in, accedes to, or concurs or agrees with, any position, condition, request, reservation of right, understanding, or any other statement that purports, or may be deemed, to be or to reflect a limitation upon the Commission's receipt, use, disposition, transfer, or retention, in accordance with applicable law, of information provided.

Routine Uses of Information

The Commission often makes its files available to other governmental agencies, particularly United States Attorneys and state prosecutors. There is a likelihood that information supplied by you will be made available to such agencies where appropriate. Whether or not the Commission makes its files available to other governmental agencies is, in general, a confidential matter between the Commission and such other governmental agencies.

Set forth below is a list of the routine uses which may be made of the information furnished.

1. To coordinate law enforcement activities between the SEC and other federal, state, local or foreign law enforcement agencies, securities self-regulatory organizations, and foreign securities authorities.
2. By SEC personnel for purposes of investigating possible violations of, or to conduct investigations authorized by, the federal securities laws.

3. Where there is an indication of a violation or potential violation of law, whether civil, criminal or regulatory in nature, and whether arising by general statute or particular program statute, or by regulation, rule or order issued pursuant thereto, the relevant records in the system of records may be referred to the appropriate agency, whether federal, state, or local, a foreign governmental authority or foreign securities authority, or a securities self-regulatory organization charged with the responsibility of investigating or prosecuting such violation or charged with enforcing or implementing the statute or rule, regulation or order issued pursuant thereto.

4. In any proceeding where the federal securities laws are in issue or in which the Commission, or past or present members of its staff, is a party or otherwise involved in an official capacity.

5. To a federal, state, local or foreign governmental authority or foreign securities authority maintaining civil, criminal or other relevant enforcement information or other pertinent information, such as current licenses, if necessary to obtain information relevant to an agency decision concerning the hiring or retention of an employee, the issuance of a security clearance, the letting of a contract, or the issuance of a license, grant or other benefit.

6. To a federal, state, local or foreign governmental authority or foreign securities authority, in response to its request, in connection with the hiring or retention of an employee, the issuance of a security clearance, the reporting of an investigation of an employee, the letting of a contract, or the issuance of a license, grant or other benefit by the requesting agency, to the extent that the information is relevant and necessary to the requesting agency's decision on the matter.

7. In connection with proceedings by the Commission pursuant to Rule 102(e) of its Rules of Practice, 17 CFR 201.102(e).

8. When considered appropriate, records in this system may be disclosed to a bar association, the American Institute of Certified Public Accountants, a state accountancy board or other federal, state, local or foreign licensing or oversight authority, foreign securities authority, or professional association or self-regulatory authority performing similar functions, for possible disciplinary or other action.

9. In connection with investigations or disciplinary proceedings by a state securities regulatory authority, a foreign securities authority, or by a self-regulatory organization involving one or more of its members.

10. As a data source for management information for production of summary descriptive statistics and analytical studies in support of the function for which the records are collected and maintained or for related personnel management functions or manpower studies, and to respond to general requests for statistical information (without personal identification of individuals) under the Freedom of Information Act or to locate specific individuals for personnel research or other personnel management functions.

11. In connection with their regulatory and enforcement responsibilities mandated by the federal securities laws (as defined in Section 3(a)(47) of the Securities Exchange Act of 1934, 15 U.S.C. 78c(a)(47)), or state or foreign laws regulating securities or other related matters, records may be disclosed to national securities associations that are registered with the Commission, the Municipal Securities Rulemaking Board, the Securities Investor Protection Corporation, the federal banking authorities, including but not limited to, the Board of Governors of the Federal Reserve System, the Comptroller of the Currency, and the Federal Deposit Insurance Corporation, state securities regulatory or law enforcement agencies or organizations, or regulatory law enforcement agencies of a foreign government, or foreign securities authority.

12. To any trustee, receiver, master, special counsel, or other individual or entity that is appointed by a court of competent jurisdiction or as a result of an agreement between the parties in connection with litigation or administrative proceedings involving allegations of violations of the federal securities laws (as defined in Section 3(a)(47) of the Securities Exchange Act of 1934, 15 U.S.C. 78c(a)(47)) or the Commission's Rules of Practice, 17 CFR 202.100–900, or otherwise, where such trustee, receiver, master, special counsel or other individual or entity is specifically designated to perform particular functions with respect to, or as a result of, the pending action or proceeding or in connection with the administration and enforcement by the Commission of the federal securities laws or the Commission's Rules of Practice.

13. To any persons during the course of any inquiry or investigation conducted by the Commission's staff, or in connection with civil litigation, if the staff has reason to believe that the person to whom the record is disclosed may have further information about the matters related therein, and those matters appeared to be relevant at the time to the subject matter of the inquiry.

14. To any person with whom the Commission contracts to reproduce, by typing, photocopy or other means, any record within this system for use by the Commission and its staff in connection with their official duties or to any person who is utilized by the Commission to perform clerical or stenographic functions relating to the official business of the Commission.

15. Inclusion in reports published by the Commission pursuant to authority granted in the federal securities laws (as defined in Section 3(a)(47) of the Securities Exchange Act of 1934, 15 U.S.C. 78c(a)(47)).

16. To members of advisory committees that are created by the Commission or by the Congress to render advice and recommendations to the Commission or to the Congress, to be used solely in connection with their official designated functions.

17. To any person who is or has agreed to be subject to the Commission's Rules of Conduct, 17 CFR 200.735-1 to 735-18, and who assists in the investigation by the Commission of possible violations of federal securities laws (as defined in Section 3(a)(47) of the Securities Exchange Act of 1934, 15 U.S.C. 78c(a)(47)), in the preparation or conduct of enforcement actions brought by the Commission for such violations, or otherwise in connection with the Commission's enforcement or regulatory functions under the federal securities laws.

18. Disclosure may be made to a Congressional office from the record of an individual in response to an inquiry from the Congressional office made at the request of that individual.

19. To respond to inquiries from Members of Congress, the press and the public which relate to specific matters that the Commission has investigated and to matters under the Commission's jurisdiction.

20. To prepare and publish information relating to violations of the federal securities laws as provided in 15 U.S.C. 78c(a)(47)), as amended.

21. To respond to subpoenas in any litigation or other proceeding.

22. To a trustee in bankruptcy.

23. To any governmental agency, governmental or private collection agent, consumer reporting agency or commercial reporting agency, governmental or private employer of a debtor, or any other person, for collection, including collection by administrative offset, federal salary offset, tax refund offset, or administrative wage garnishment, of amounts owed as a result of Commission civil or administrative proceedings.

Small Business Owners: The SEC always welcomes comments on how it can better assist small businesses. If you have comments about the SEC's enforcement of the securities laws, please contact the Office of Chief Counsel in the SEC's Division of Enforcement at 202-942-4530 or the SEC's Small Business Ombudsman at 202-942-2950. If you would prefer to comment to someone outside of the SEC, you can contact the Small Business Regulatory Enforcement Ombudsman at www.sba.gov/ombudsman or toll free at 888-REG-FAIR. The Ombudsman's office receives comments from small businesses and annually evaluates federal agency enforcement activities for their responsiveness to the special needs of small business.

Form 19-4   Motion to Stay Civil Proceedings

IN THE COURT OF COMMON PLEAS FOR ALLEGHENY COUNTY

COMMONWEALTH OF PENNSYLVANIA,
BY D. MICHAEL FISHER, ATTORNEY GENERAL,
      Plaintiff,

   v.

JOHN DOE, Individually and d/b/a
MORTGAGE BROKER FINANCIAL SERVICES, INC., a
Pennsylvania corporation

**MOTION OF DEFENDANTS TO STAY CIVIL PROCEEDINGS IN THE COURT
OF COMMON PLEAS OF PENNSYLVANIA DUE TO THE PENDENCY OF
PARALLEL CRIMINAL PROCEEDING IN THE UNITED STATES
DISTRICT COURT FOR THE WESTERN DISTRICT OF PENNSYLVANIA**

AND NOW COMES the Defendants, John Doe and Mortgage Broker Financial Services, Inc. (the "Brokerage Defendants"), by and through his attorneys, the law firm of Thomas Farrell & Associates, and respectfully file this Motion for Stay.

On or about _____, the Commonwealth of Pennsylvania, ex rel, the Attorney General of the Commonwealth, filed its Original Complaint in Equity in this Court, alleging that defendant, a mortgage broker, submitted fraudulent mortgage applications to plaintiff. On _____, agents of the United States Postal Inspection Service executed a search warrant at defendant's offices and served grand jury subpoenas upon several of defendant's employees. Assistant

United States Attorney John Smith has informed counsel for defendant that the grand jury is investigating allegations that defendant committed bank fraud by submitting fraudulent loan applications to plaintiffs and that defendant is the target of the investigation.

1. The Commonwealth filed an Amended Complaint on _____. The Amended Complaint now asserts 219 allegations and 13 separate counts for allegedly unfair, deceptive and unlawful trade practices pursuant to 73 P.S. §201-3, the Pennsylvania Consumer Protection Law, and violations under other Pennsylvania statutes.

2. Count XII of the Amended Complaint (Civil Conspiracy) alleges a civil conspiracy to market home improvement, mortgages and secondary mortgage loans to consumers through a pattern of deception, fraud and deceit, including: the use of falsely inflated income statements; inflated appraisals; improper notarizations; misrepresentations to consumers and financial institutions through hidden and excessive fees; and substandard and incomplete home improvement services.

3. Appended to the Amended Complaint are lists of consumers the Commonwealth alleges transacted business with the Defendants and upon which the Commonwealth bases the allegations made in its Amended Complaint against the Defendants.

4. The United States Attorney's Office for the Western District of Pennsylvania has launched a criminal investigation into these same consumer transactions which are the subject matter of this civil action. A Grand Jury has been impaneled in the United States District Court of the Western District of Pennsylvania and is conducting criminal proceedings into these same transactions.

5. On or about _____, the U.S. Attorney's Office and the United States Postal Inspection Service served a search warrant and raided the offices and premises of the Mortgage Broker, a home improvement company and an appraisal company. The documents, records, agreements, etc. sought and seized from Mortgage Broker Defendants relate directly to the consumer transactions upon which the Commonwealth bases its Original and Amended Complaints. At the same time the Defendants were being served with the search warrants, numerous subpoenas were served by the U.S. Attorney's Office requiring the testimony of some of Mortgage Broker's employees before the Grand Jury impaneled in the United States District Court for the Western District of Pennsylvania. The criminal investigation is directly parallel to the matter which forms the gravamen of the Commonwealth's case before this court. Doe and Mortgage Broker have been informed that they are targets of this criminal probe.

6. Defendants' ability to properly defend themselves in this civil action and in the criminal investigations and Grand Jury proceedings is gravely undermined:

    a. Because of the parallel criminal proceedings which have been launched against the Brokerage Defendants, they are placed in the untenable position of choosing between their Fifth Amendment right to avoid self incrimination in the criminal matter and in this civil proceeding and their ability to aggressively defend themselves in this action by setting forth their defenses and facts necessary to support their positions; and

    b. Because the scope of civil discovery in this matter is so broad in comparison with the criminal investigation, the Brokerage Defendants are exposed to the substantial, and perhaps inevitable, risk that this case will furnish fodder to the federal prosecutors in the criminal proceedings, thus expanding the discovery in the criminal proceedings well beyond that permitted and contemplated by the Federal Rules of Civil Procedure.

7. By virtue of the existence of the parallel federal criminal investigation and Grand Jury proceedings, the Brokerage Defendants will lose valuable rights secured under both the United States and Pennsylvania Constitutions and will be placed in jeopardy of being rendered defenseless and forced to essentially forfeit this action if it is not stayed until the criminal investigations and proceedings are resolved.

    The public interest will be served through the granting of a stay of this action until such time as the parallel criminal matter has been resolved.

8. The interest of justice and judicial economy will be served by staying this action until the criminal investigation and proceedings are resolved.

    Plaintiff will not be prejudiced by a stay of this action.

WHEREFORE, Brokerage Defendants request that this Honorable Court ADJUGE, ORDER and DECREE that the above entitled action is stayed indefinitely until such time as the Brokerage Defendants are able to defend themselves in this action without jeopardy to their constitutionally protected rights; and Brokerage Defendants are relieved from answering any Amended Complaint that the Commonwealth has filed until such time as this Court has ruled on the merits of this Motion.

Respectfully submitted,

_____

Thomas J. Farrell, Esquire

IN THE COURT OF COMMON PLEAS FOR ALLEGHENY COUNTY

COMMONWEALTH OF PENNSYLVANIA,
BY D. MICHAEL FISHER, ATTORNEY GENERAL,
       Plaintiff,

    v.

JOHN DOE, Individually and d/b/a
MORTGAGE BROKER FINANCIAL SERVICES, INC., a
Pennsylvania corporation

MEMORANDUM OF LAW IN SUPPORT OF DEFENDANTS' MOTION FOR A STAY

I. THE COURT HAS THE INHERENT DISCRETION TO ENTER A STAY IN THIS MATTER

It is well established that a "witness in a ... civil ... proceeding may decline to answer questions when to do so would involve substantial risks of self-incrimination." *United States v. Parente*, 449 F. Supp. 905, 907, 908 (D. Conn. 1978). "Although the proceeding in which the privilege is asserted need not be criminal, the information for which the privilege is claimed must harbor the potential of exposing the speaker to a criminal or quasi-criminal charge." *In re Daley*, 549 F.2d 469, 478 (7th Cir. 1977). As the Court in *United States v. Powe*, 591 F.2d 833, 845, n.36 (D.C. Cir. 1978) noted, the privilege operates where the information sought to be extracted presents "a realistic threat of incrimination..." as distinguished from a 'merely imaginary possibility.'" In the present case, it is clear that given the parallel criminal investigation being conducted by the United States Postal Inspection Authority that Defendants face a very "realistic threat of incrimination" by responding to any discovery or even by filing an Answer.

On the other hand, "proceeding with discovery would force these Defendants into the uncomfortable position of having to choose between waiving their Fifth Amendment privilege or effectively forfeiting the civil suit. On the one hand, if either [Defendant] invokes his Constitutional privilege during civil discovery, not only does this prevent him from adequately defending his position, but it may subject him to an adverse inference from his refusal to testify." *Volmer Distributors, Inc. v. The New York Post*, 152 F.R.D. 36, 39 (S.D.N.Y. 1993). *See also Baxter v. Palmigiano*, 425 U.S. 308, 318 (1976) ("the Fifth Amendment does not forbid adverse inferences against parties to civil actions when they refuse to testify..."). Lastly, if the Defendants fail to invoke a Fifth Amendment privilege, they waive the protections of any such claim and any evidence adduced in the civil proceeding could be used against them in a criminal proceeding. *See Judge Milton Pollack, Parallel Civil and Criminal Proceedings*, 129 F.R.D. 201, 203 (S.D.N.Y. 1989).

The Defendants will suffer significant prejudice if the current action is not stayed for a reasonable amount of time. The alleged actions and transactions in this Complaint are identical to the facts being investigated by the United States Attorney's Office for the Western District of Pennsylvania and the U.S. Postal Inspection Service. If this civil action filed against Defendants is not stayed and if a protective order is not entered protecting him from answering or subjecting himself to discovery, Doe will be faced with the untenable choice of either giving up his Fifth Amendment protections or to effectively forfeit a defense in this action. Moreover, the Brokerage Defendants will be forced to reveal their defenses to any criminal charges, in the event such charges are filed, which would constitute irreparable harm. As such, the request for stay in this particular case is appropriate.

Under the federal discovery rules, any party to a civil action is entitled to all information relevant to the subject matter of the action before the court unless such information is privileged. *See* Federal Rules of Civil Procedure, Rule 26(b)(1). Even if the Rules of Civil Procedure did not contain specific protections for Constitutionally mandated privileges, the Fifth Amendment nevertheless shields a party who fears that complying with discovery would expose him or her to a risk of self-incrimination. The fact that the privilege is raised in a civil proceeding rather than a criminal prosecution does not deprive a party of its protection. *See Wehling v. Columbia Broadcasting System*, 608 F.2d 1084, 1086 (5th Cir. 1979); *Lefkowitz v. Cunningham*, 431 U.S. 801, 805 (1977). Thus, under either the United States Constitution or the Federal Rules of Civil Procedure, these Defendants are under no obligation or compulsion to file an Answer or provide discovery. Nevertheless, it goes without saying that refusing to respond, without the protection of a stay order, would subject Defendant to serious adverse consequences. Accordingly, even if not constitutionally required, a stay is preferable to penalizing a party with dismissal or adverse consequences simply because of a rational exercise of constitutional protections. *See Wehling v. Columbia Broadcasting System*, 608 F.2d 1084, 1088 (CX.A. Tex. 1979) (the Supreme Court has disapproved the procedures which require a party to surrender one Constitutional right in order to assert another); *United States of America v. U.S. Currency*, 626 F.2d 11, 16 (6th Cir. 1980) (citing *Shaffer v. U.S.*, 528 F.2d 920, 922 (4th Cir. 1975) (when faced with such a *Hobson* choice, the Court..." may examine the possible approaches and, perhaps with the cooperation of the parties, select the means which 'strikes a fair balance ... and ... accommodates both parties'"). Accordingly, a stay is a proper balancing of these conflicting considerations.

"It is clearly within the power of a District Court to balance 'competing interests' and decide that judicial economy would best be served by a stay of civil proceedings." *United States of America v. Mellon Bank,* 545 F.2d 869, 873 (3d Cir. 1976); *See, Texaco, Inc. v. Borda,* 383 F.2d 607, 609 (3d Cir. 1967). It is well settled that a court has the discretionary authority to stay a case if the interests of justice are required. *See United States v. Kordel,* 397 U.S. 1, 12 n.27 (1970); *Kashi v. Gratsos,* 790 F.2d 1050, 1057 (2d Cir. 1986); *Trustees of Plumbers and Pipefitters Nat. Pension Fund v. TransWorld Mechanical, Inc.,* 886 F. Supp. 1134, 1138 (S.D.N.Y. 1995). Courts are afforded this discretion because the denial of a stay could impair a party's Fifth Amendment privilege against self-incrimination, extend criminal discovery beyond the limits set forth in the Federal Rules of Criminal Procedure, expose the defense's theory to the prosecution in advance of trial or otherwise prejudice the criminal case. *See Plumbers and Pipefitters, Inc.,* 886 F. Supp. at 1138; *SEC v. Dresser Industries,* 628 F.2d 1368, 1376 (D.C. Cir. 1980); *Volmar Distributors,* 152 F.R.D. at 39 (S.D.N.Y. 1993). Depending on the particular facts of a case, the Court may decide to stay civil proceedings, postpone civil discovery or impose protective orders. *Dresser Industries,* 628 F.2d, 1375. In this particular case, a stay is the appropriate resolution, as requested by Defendants.

II. STANDARDS FOR A STAY

One of the seminal cases discussing such stays, *Volmar Distributors,* set forth the standards for granting such a stay:
When deciding whether to grant a stay, courts consider five factors: (1) the private interests of the plaintiffs in proceeding expeditiously with the civil litigation as balanced against the prejudice to the plaintiffs if delayed; (2) the private interests of and burden on the defendant; (3) the interests of the courts; (4) the interests of persons not parties to the civil litigation; and (5) the public interest. *Arden Way Associates v. Boesky,* 660 F.Supp. 1494, 1497 (S.D.N.Y. 1987); *Twenty-First Century Corp. v. La Bianca,* 801 F.Supp. 1007, 1010 (E.D.N.Y. 1992).

Balancing these factors is a case-by-case determination, with the basic goal being to avoid prejudice. The strongest case for granting a stay is where a party under criminal indictment is required to defend a civil proceeding involving the same matter. *Dresser Industries,* 628 F.2d at 1375-76; *Tolkow,* 109 F.R.D. at 119; *see* Judge Milton Pollack, Parallel Civil and Criminal Proceedings, 129 F.R.D. 201, 203 S.D.N.Y. 1989) (hereinafter Parallel Proceedings). "The most important factor at the threshold is the degree to which the civil issues overlap with the criminal issues." While the Constitution does not mandate a stay in such circumstances, *Dresser Industries,* 628 F.2d at 1375, denying a stay might undermine a defendant's Fifth Amendment privilege against self-incrimination. *Id.* at 1376; *Tolkow,* 109 F.R.D. at 121. Refusing to grant a stay might also expand the rights of criminal discovery beyond the limits of Rule 16(b) of the Federal Rules of Criminal Procedure, expose the basis of the defense to the prosecution in advance of trial, or otherwise prejudice the case. *Dresser Industries,* 628 F.2d at 1376. *Volmar Distributors,* 152 F.R.D. at 39.

Such a test has also been endorsed in the Third Circuit. *See, e.g., Walsh Securities, Inc. v. Cristo Property Management, Ltd.,* 7 F.Supp. 2d 523 (E.D.N.J. 1998). See also *Plumbers and Pipefitters v. TransWorld Mechanical,* 886 F.Supp. at 1139.

Applying the above-noted test to the facts of the instant case, it is clear that a stay is warranted.

a.   Similarity of the Matters

The most important factor at the threshold is the degree to which the civil issues overlap with the criminal investigation. *See Volmar v. New York Post,* 152 F.R.D. at 39. As was noted in *Brock,* "a stay of civil proceedings is most likely to be granted where the civil and criminal actions involve the same subject matter ... and is even more appropriate where both actions are brought by the government." *Brock v. Tolkow,* 109 F.R.D. 116, 119 (E.D.N.Y. 1985). In the present case, although the government is not bringing both cases, the *Plaintiff* is, in effect, bringing both cases. The Plaintiff has filed the current action and the Plaintiff has specifically referred and encouraged the current criminal investigation by the federal authorities. Accordingly, as was noted in the *Brock* decision, a single party is responsible for both the criminal and civil inquiries. More importantly, the subject matter of the inquiries is identical and, in fact, the criminal investigation is premised solely upon the allegations raised by the Plaintiffs as set forth in the current civil case. As was noted in *Walsh Securities,* the similarity of issues between the civil and criminal matters is critical in determining whether or not to grant a stay, "There is no dispute that the civil and criminal cases here involve many of the same issues arising out of [certain real estate transactions] ... the government is investigating whether any of the real estate transactions were fraudulent. This is essentially the same allegation made by *Walsh* in its civil complaint. Therefore, this factor weighs in favor of a stay." *Walsh Securities*, 7 F. Supp. 2d at 527. Here, as in *Walsh*, the same allegations are raised in both the civil and criminal matters; accordingly, the similarity of issues weighs in favor of a stay.

b. Stage of the Parallel Criminal Proceeding

While it is true that the strongest cases for stay are made where an indictment has been returned, each case must be evaluated individually. *Volmar Distributors*, 152 F.R.D. at 38. The fact that an indictment has not yet been returned, while it may be a factor counseling against the stay of a civil proceeding, does not make consideration of the stay motion any less appropriate. As was noted in *Brock*, several of the reported cases dealing with this issue have involved pre-indictment criminal inquiries. *Brock*, 109 F.R.D. at 120. *See also U.S. v. Kordel*, 397 U.S. 1 (1970); *SEC v. Dresser Industries*, 628 F.2d 1368 (D.C. Cir. 1980). It is "still possible" to obtain a stay, even though an indictment or information has not yet been returned, if the government is conducting a parallel criminal investigation. *See Walsh Securities*, where the Court found that although the case was still at a pre-indictment stage, the action presented a strong case for a stay. *Walsh Securities*, 7 F.Supp. 2d at 527-528.

c. The Interests of Plaintiffs

It is true that inconvenience and delay to Plaintiffs will be an unfortunate result of any stay. However, the inconvenience to Plaintiffs is "outweighed by the Defendants' significant Fifth Amendment concerns, particularly where a stay will not inordinately prolong the civil case and where the criminal prosecution could provide some benefit to the civil case and advance public interest." *Plumbers and Pipefitters*, 886 F.Supp. at 1141. *See also Brock*, 109 F.R.D. at 121 (Constitutional rights against self-incrimination are more important consideration than inconvenience and delay); *Paul Harrigan and Sons v. Enterprise Animal Oil Co.*, 14 F.R.D. 333, 335 (E.D. Pa. 1953) ("While this will, undoubtedly, cause inconvenience to the plaintiff, protection of the defendant's constitutional rights is the more important consideration"); *Wehling*, 608 F.2d at 1089 ("permitting such inconvenience seems preferable at this point to requiring defendant to choose between his silence and his lawsuit"); *Dienstag v. Bronsen*, 49 F.R.D. 327, 329 (S.D.N.Y. 1970) ("While this will undoubtedly cause inconvenience and delay to plaintiffs, protection of defendants' constitutional rights against self-incrimination is the more important consideration.")

Indeed, in the *Dienstag* case noted above, the stay was granted even though the Plaintiffs argued aggressively that the civil case was independent of the pending criminal case. *Id.* Counsel for the Plaintiffs in *Dienstag* informed the Court that: "I have never even spoken on the telephone to any member of the prosecutor's staff concerning this matter and have had no requests of any kind for cooperation from the Government. I do not intend to make available to the Government any deposition taken in the action ... There is therefore no reason to fear that the deposition sought will be of assistance in the prosecution of the criminal action." *Id.* at 328. In complete contrast, in the instant case, the Plaintiffs have not only referred this matter to the Federal Government but are cooperating with them on a regular basis. Indeed, government investigators knew the identity of the attorneys who were representing the Defendants even before any pleadings by the Defendants were filed of record.

There is no basis to believe any loss of evidence will result from a delay, *see Plumbers and Pipefitters*, 886 F.Supp. at 1140, nor is there any reason to believe that assets will be dissipated by any delay. "In this case, however, there are no allegations that any of the principals are leaving the country or otherwise attempting to gain an unfair advantage by seeking a stay." *Walsh Securities*, 7 F. Supp. 2d at 528. Indeed, Plaintiffs in this case could even benefit from a stay, pending resolution of the criminal matter because, under the Federal Sentencing Guidelines, victim restitution is a requirement for Federal criminal prosecutions. Accordingly, the absence of any prejudice to the Plaintiffs weighs heavily in favor of a stay in the instant matter.

d. Defendants' Interests

Defendants have a significant interest in both proving their innocence with respect to any criminal investigation and aggressively defending the present suit. Nevertheless, Defendants should not be required to make the *Hobson* choice precipitated by Plaintiffs' efforts to pursue civil recovery while encouraging criminal prosecution. As was noted in *Brock*, 109 F.R.D. 120-121, "Concededly, it does not offend the Constitution if a defendant in a civil case is asked questions the answers to which might incriminate him. But even if the defendant's dilemma does not violate the Fifth Amendment or due process, it certainly undercuts the protections of those provisions, and a court can exercise its discretion to enable a Defendant to avoid this unpalatable choice when to do so would not seriously hamper the public interest." *Brock*, 109 F.R.D. at 120-21.

Indeed, courts have considered that even where a plaintiff raises a Fifth Amendment claim to gain an unequal advantage against the opposing party, thereby using the Fifth Amendment privilege shield as a sword, dismissal is not favored. Rather, a court should fashion appropriate remedies including a stay. *See, e.g., Wehling*, 608 F.2d 1089. By analogy, the Plaintiff should not be permitted to gain a tactical advantage by both initiating a case and encouraging a criminal prosecution where, as here, the Defendants are both defendants in a civil action and targets in a criminal case, both of which were precipitated by Plaintiff. Staying all answers, interrogatory and deposition discovery for a reasonable period of time avoids placing the Defendants in an untenable choice. *See Walsh Securities*, 7.F.Supp. 2d at 528.

e. Interests of the Court

A stay for a reasonable period of time in the instant matter will not work any prejudice to the Plaintiff, but, on the other hand, will not only protect Defendants' Constitutional rights, but importantly could significantly benefit the Court and its docket. This is so for a number of reasons:

The outcome of the criminal investigation could encourage settlement. *Plumbers and Pipefitters*, 886 F.Supp. at 1140; *Volmar Distributors*, 152 F.R.D. at 42.

Developments in the criminal investigation could moot, clarify or otherwise affect the civil proceeding. *United States v. Mellon Bank*, 545 F.2d at 873.

The nature of information that comes out in the criminal investigation may streamline later discovery or eliminate altogether the need for certain depositions. *Volmar* 152 F.R.D. at 42.

It could reduce Motions coming before the court in the civil case: "However, the Court also has an interest in resolving individual cases efficiently. Without a stay, interrogatory and deposition discovery would likely cause inefficiency, because several defendants will be forced to assert Fifth Amendment privileges. Not only would this burden the Magistrate Judge and this Court with deciding a constant stream of privilege issues, but if some defendants were forced to assert the privilege while others were not, it would be difficult or impossible to fairly apportion liability because of the differing factual records among defendants." *Walsh Securities*, 7 F.Supp. 2d at 528-29.

In short, a reasonable stay in the current matter will clarify issues, promote judicial economy and encourage settlement or reduced litigation attendant the civil claim.

f. The Public Interest

There will be no harm to the public interest in granting a stay in the current action. The current action does not involve a need to reign in fiduciaries or otherwise protect the public welfare. *See, e.g., Brock*, 109 F.R.D. at 120; *United States v. Kordel*, 397 U.S. at 11-12 (1970) (involving the distribution of mislabeled drugs); *Dresser Industries*, 628 F.2d at 1389-90 (dissemination of misleading information to the investigative public). Unlike such cases, the current action is simply a monetary dispute between two parties and it is not a case of immediate or seeming harm to the public. *See Volmar*, 152 F.R.D. at 40. In fact, as noted by the District Court for the District of New Jersey, in the *Walsh Securities* matter:

> "...A stay in this case would benefit the public by allowing the Government to conduct a complete, unimpeded investigation into potential criminal activity. In this case, there is no tangible harm to the public from these alleged frauds that could not be remedied by the criminal investigation. Therefore, the public interest weighs in favor of a stay." 7 F. Supp. 2d at 529.

Likewise, in the present case, the public interest would benefited by a stay.

CONCLUSION

Extensive case law supports the discretion of this Honorable Court to grant a stay in the current matter. Indeed, the reasons for granting a stay in the present matter are perhaps even more compelling than the reported case law as a single private party has both filed the civil action and encouraged the criminal investigation. While it is certainly the right of any citizen to request a criminal investigation, no Plaintiff should be entitled to a tactical advantage gained by both filing suit and fanning the flames of a criminal investigation. Accordingly, a stay in the current matter for a reasonable period of time is necessary and appropriate. Plaintiffs remain free to petition the Court at any time to lift the stay should circumstances change. *See Brock v. Tolkow*, 109 F.R.D. at 120. The stay should be granted.

Respectfully submitted,

_____

Thomas J. Farrell, Esquire

Form 19-5   Protective Order

IN THE UNITED STATES DISTRICT COURT
FOR THE WESTERN DISTRICT OF PENNSYLVANIA

UNITED STATES OF AMERICA, ex rel Jones

	Plaintiff,	)	
		)	Electronically Filed
v.		)	
		)	
ABC Corporation,		)	
	Defendant.	)	

PROTECTIVE ORDER

Upon consideration of the motion by the United States and ABC Corporation, and finding good cause exists for issuance of a protective order, IT IS HEREBY ORDERED that all persons and entities subject to this order – including without limitation the parties to this action, their representatives, agents, experts and consultants, successors in interest, and all other interested persons with actual or constructive knowledge of this order – shall adhere to the following terms, upon penalty of contempt:

1. ABC shall designate materials and information produced pursuant to this order by marking on the documents substantially the following words "Privileged – Subject To Protective And Nonwaiver Order Under Fed. R. Evid. 502(d)."

2. All statements and testimony provided by ABC pursuant to this order shall be similarly designated subject to this order.

3. This order shall extend to all materials, including notes and transcripts, derived from material provided pursuant to paragraphs 1 and 2.

4. The United States shall not disclose to any third-party materials or information subject to this order.

5. The materials and information disclosed subject to this order shall be used for the purpose of evaluating whether the United States will intervene in the False Claims Act litigation and/or in the prosecution of the False Claims Act litigation. However, if the United States does not intervene in the prosecution of the False Claims Act litigation, relators shall not use any of the information produced subject to this order as evidence in the case in chief, unless the information has been otherwise lawfully obtained. Nothing in this order prohibits a party from pursuing a motion in the False Claims Act litigation for relief from this use limitation for purposes of addressing false testimony or preventing other manifest injustice in the False Claims Act litigation.

6. ABC's production of the materials and testimony which it agrees to produce pursuant to this order shall not constitute a waiver of any privilege or protection with respect to (a) those materials or testimony, (B) any other communications, materials or testimony relating to the subject matter, or (C) any other communications, materials or testimony relating to the parties who sent or received or are named those materials or testimony. This order is, and shall be construed as, in order under Rule 502 (d) of the Federal Rules of Evidence ordering that privilege or protection is not waived by disclosure connected with the litigation pending before this court. Accordingly, as is explicitly set forth in Rule 502 (d), production pursuant to this order is not a waiver of any privilege or protection in a other federal or state proceeding. Without limiting the foregoing, the existence of this order shall not in any way impair or affect ABC's legal right to assert privilege claims for the materials or testimony produced in any other actions, shall not effect a waiver, and shall not be used to argue that any waiver of privilege or work-product protection has occurred by virtue of any production of materials or testimony pursuant to this order in this case before this court or in any other litigation or proceeding.

7. No person to whom disclosure of materials or information subject to this order is made, shall have the right to use or disclose material subject to this order except as specifically provided here in. No person or entity shall gain access to materials or information subject to this order by way of affiliating themselves with one of the persons or parties to whom disclosure may be made for the purpose of obtaining such documents or information.

8. All recipients of materials or information provided pursuant to this order shall use best efforts at all times to preserve the privilege and confidentiality of all documents and information subject to this order.

9. The parties shall maintain information and documents subject to this order in a safe and secure manner that restricts access by persons who do not require access to the information or documents and restricts access by persons who are not authorized under this order to access such information.

10. The obligation to protect the confidentiality of any document or information subject to this order shall continue indefinitely both during and after the False Claims Act litigation, subject to future order of court.

11. The party shall not file documents or information subject to this order, except under seal, unless this court otherwise orders.

12. Should information subject to this order be requested by a third-party, including regulatory or governmental authority, the recipient of the request shall provide ABC with written notice of that request no more than five days following receipt of the request, and in all events before the time of production called for by the request, and give a reasonable opportunity for ABC to seek protection against disclosure. Parties shall cooperate in efforts to protect documents and information subject to this order against disclosure.

13. This order may be pleaded as a full and complete defense to, and may be used as a basis for temporary or permanent injunction against, any act or attempted act in breach of this order. The existence of this order shall not be used by the parties or their counsel in any litigation or otherwise except to enforce the terms of this order or to prove the continued existence of any privilege. Neither this order nor the exchange of documents or information subject to this order shall constitute waiver of any applicable privilege in any dispute between the parties.

14. Any dispute or controversy between the parties arising out of or relating to this order shall be finally and fully determined by this court if the parties are unable to resolve it amicably. The parties shall adhere to and maintain the terms of confidentiality provided for herein in the event of and throughout the pendency of any such dispute or controversy.

15. Inadvertent production of any information, document or thing without it being designated in accordance with this order shall not itself be deemed a waiver of any claim of confidentiality as to such matter, and the same may thereafter be designated as provided in this order.

16. This court shall retain jurisdiction over all persons subject to this order to the extent necessary to enforce the obligations arising hereunder or to impose sanctions for any content thereof.

BY THE COURT:

Dated: _____

_____
Judge

Form 19-6   Rule 408 Letter Agreement.

[Date]

VIA HAND DELIVERY
Joe Smith, Esquire
U.S Attorney's Office,
Western District of Pennsylvania

Re: Settlement Discussions in Investigation of ABC Products, Inc.; XYZ Importing, LLC; ABC Manufacturing, Inc.; John Doe and Richard Roe

Dear Mr. Smith:

I write this letter on behalf of ABC Products, Inc.; the related companies listed above, and their owners, John Doe and Richard Roe, to memorialize our understanding about our settlement discussions, in particular the meeting to occur tomorrow, [date].

The United States has served civil investigative demands on the companies in contemplation of possible civil actions for damages, and we dispute those claims. Tomorrow, the attorneys for the companies and their owners will meet with Government representatives in an effort to negotiate a compromise and settlement of those potential claims.

We are aware that representatives of the United States Attorney's Office for the Western District's Criminal Division may attend our meeting. The Government and we, on behalf of our clients, agree that the protections of FRE 408 extend to prevent evidentiary use of statements made in our settlement discussions in either a civil or criminal matter. Specifically, the United States and our clients agree that evidence of conduct or statements made during the compromise negotiations about the claim and the fact of the compromise negotiations will not be admissible to prove or disprove the validity or amount of the civil claim or guilt or innocence in a related criminal prosecution or to impeach by a prior inconsistent statement or contradiction in a civil or criminal case.

Very truly yours,

Thomas J. Farrell
Counsel for ABC Products, Inc.

_____
Joe Smith, AUSA
For the Government

Form 19-7   Civil Proffer Agreement

With respect to the meeting of _____ ("Client") and his attorney, Thomas J. Farrell, Esq., with Assistant United States Attorney _____ of the Office of the United States Attorney for the Southern District of New York (the "Office") to be held at the Office of the United States Attorney for the Southern District of New York on [date] ("the meeting"), the following understandings exist:

(1) The Client has agreed to provide this Office with information, and to respond to questions, so that the Office may evaluate Client's information and responses in making decisions regarding prosecuting its civil enforcement case.

(2) In any civil enforcement action brought against Client by this Office, except as provided below, the Office will not offer in evidence on its case-in-chief any statements made by Client at the meeting, except if, at any time following the meeting, Client becomes a fugitive from justice.

(3) Notwithstanding item (2) above, the Office may use information derived directly or indirectly from the meeting in a civil complaint or in civil discovery.

(4) The statements made by Client at the meeting are not made in compromising or attempting to compromise a claim, and are not part of compromise negotiations, and that Rule 408 of the Federal Rules of Evidence is inapplicable. It is the intent of this Agreement to waive all rights to claim that Rule 408 applies.

(5) If this Office receives a request from another United States Attorney's office for access to information obtained pursuant to this Proffer Agreement, this Office may furnish such information but will do so only on the condition that the requesting office honor the provisions of this Agreement. This agreement does not place any restriction on the disclosure and use of such information in connection with regulatory or administrative proceedings, including debarment proceedings.

(6) It is further understood that this Agreement is limited to the statements made by Client at the meeting and does not apply to any oral, written or recorded statements made by Client at any other time. No understandings, promises, agreements and/or conditions have been entered into with respect to the meeting other than those set forth in this Agreement and none will be entered into unless in writing and signed by all parties.

(7) The understandings set forth in paragraphs 1 through 6 above extend to the continuation of this meeting on the dates that appear below.

(8) Client and Attorney acknowledge that they have fully discussed and understand every paragraph and clause in this Agreement and the consequences thereof.

[Dated]
[Signed]

(This page intentionally left blank.)

Chapter 20

TRIAL

VIII. FORMS

I.   BEFORE TRIAL

A.   Motions in Limine

§20:01   General Points

Motions in limine are motions filed shortly before trial to address evidentiary issues likely to arise during trial.

On the defense side, the relief sought usually is to preclude certain kinds of evidence such as similar bad act evidence [*see* FRE 404(b)]; or to limit the scope of testimony, such as the extent to which a police officer can interpret coded conversations.

You also can seek a ruling on the permissibility of lines of cross-examination or the admissibility of certain defense evidence. Such motions can be brief, two or three pages, perhaps with copies of the leading cases attached.

Raising evidentiary issues in a pre-trial motion enables you and the judge, removed from the bustle of trial and pressure of a waiting jury, to discuss issues more thoughtfully and thoroughly. Definitive pre-trial rulings can spare you the embarrassment of rehashing losing arguments in front of the jury and the judge the time and tedium of hearing them.

Motions in limine can also be a useful discovery device. In responding, the prosecutor probably will describe the evidence and how it fits into the prosecution's theory of the case in much more detail than was done in any pre-trial notice or disclosure.

Forms:
- **Form 20-1** Motion in Limine to Preclude Defendant's Other Bad Acts
- **Form 20-2** Motion in Limine to Permit Evidence of Consciousness of Innocence

§20:02   Effect on Need to Renew Objection at Trial

The rules in many jurisdictions eliminate the need to renew an objection or offer of proof at trial when the court has made a definitive ruling *in limine*. [*See* FRE 103.]

There is a risk in relying on this rule. Often, the prudent course is to renew the objection or re-offer the evidence. There are two reasons for this.

The ruling must be "definitive."

This means that there must be "no suggestion that it [the trial court] would reconsider the matter at trial." [*Walden v. Georgia-Pacific Corp.*, 126 F.3d 506, 518 (3rd Cir. 1997). *See also Wilson v. Williams*, 182 F.3d 562, 565 (7th Cir. 1999) (en banc) (a definitive ruling is one that is not conditional, contingent or tentative; it "does not invite reconsideration").]

A court's statement as to its inclination or how it is prepared to rule is not definitive, and necessitates renewing the objection at trial.

In the midst of trial, remembering how the court phrased its pre-trial thoughts is a risky task. To be safe, you should obtain clarification as to the precise scope of the court's in limine ruling. Courts often hedge pre-trial rulings with the warning that the final ruling may depend on the context of the case as it develops. Such a ruling is not "definitive."

Also look for any suggestion that the court might change its mind or revisit the issue depending on how the trial unfolds. In this situation, your failure to object at trial might be considered a waiver of the issue for appeal. Rulings that require a balancing of probative versus prejudicial effect, such as rulings under FRE 403, seldom will be definitive before the evidence is offered. [*Walden*, 126 F.3d at 518 n.10.]

A definitive ruling may be limited.

A definitive ruling extends only so far as the legal theories which the party advances or the court cites for the ruling. [*See Walden*, 126 F.3d at 518-19.]

There often are several bases on which evidence may be objectionable or admissible. A definitive ruling does not preserve for appeal different arguments against the evidence or arguments as to other, proper uses to which it could be put. [*E.g. Wilson v. Williams*, 182 F.3d 562 (civil rights plaintiff's motion in limine to prevent cross-examination of him on his conviction for murdering a police officer held not to preserve objection to defense counsel's repeated references to him in argument as "cop-killer" because in limine ruling did not address all possible uses of the evidence).]

Should you think of new legal arguments or should the trial evidence develop in such a way as to strengthen the argument you lost in limine, you must renew and expand your argument to preserve the additional grounds for appeal.

Emphasize how it has grown stronger and specify how all the abuses you conjured in your pre-trial arguments have come to pass (*e.g.,* the prosecution has used evidence for more than a limited purpose).

Conversely, if you won the pre-trial motion and the prosecutor tries to reopen the issue at trial, emphasize how you relied on the ruling to form trial strategy and how reconsideration will upset the parties' settled expectations as to how the trial would proceed, thereby subverting your trial strategy and prolonging the trial because of the need to research and make new arguments and perhaps to find and introduce new evidence.

§20:03   When to Avoid or When to Use a Motion in Limine

Know the judge's tendencies when left to his or her discretion.

It is not always in the defense interest to give a judge time and law to rule on evidentiary points. An example is a judge who tends to give the defendant considerable leeway in cross-examining cooperating witnesses. Considerable case law exists that might justify the judge in narrowly circumscribing your cross. With extra time to consider the issue the judge might feel that he or she can safely exercise discretion against you. Further, many cross-examinations develop a momentum and drama of their own. If your cross seems to uncover the witness's true character and engages the jury, the judge is unlikely to interfere mid-cross.

In contrast, a pre-trial motion is advisable when you are attempting some out-of-the-ordinary evidentiary maneuver, such as the introduction of reverse 404(b) evidence (evidence of a witness's or third party's other bad acts to show that he, not the defendant, was the wrongdoer). [*See* §20:210.]

With a pre-trial motion the judge might indulge in the luxury of reading and following the law. When raised mid trial, the knee-jerk rejection of the unfamiliar is likely.

§20:04   Prosecution Motions In Limine to Preclude a Defense

A growing trend among prosecutors, particularly in federal court, is to use pretrial motions in limine to preclude affirmative defenses. In response to such motions, courts demand that the defendant proffer sufficient evidence pretrial to make out a prima facie defense before they will permit the defense to introduce any evidence of the defense at trial. [*See United States v. Alicea*, 837 F.2d 103 (2d Cir. 1988) (defendants required to present evidence of duress defense at pretrial hearing on prosecution motion in limine; holds that preclusion of that defense at trial did not deprive the defendants of their right to testify); *United States v. Brodhead*, 714 F.Supp. 593, 595-96 (D. Mass. 1989) (necessity defense; surveying cases).] Other courts disapprove of the use of motions in limine to challenge entire defenses and restrict the motions to discrete legal and factual issues. Under the latter approach, the defense is allowed to introduce the evidence at trial, and the trial judge decides if it is sufficient to merit a jury charge on the defense. "Nor should [the trial court] allow the motion to be used to discover evidence which the defendant has not been required to disclose in the normal course of discovery." [*Commonwealth v. O'Malley*, 439 N.E.2d 832, 837-38 (Mass App. Ct. 1982) (motions in limine should be restricted to challenges to specific items of evidence or discrete issues; trial judge should allow introduction of evidence at trial). *See also Commonwealth v. Hood*, 452 N.E.2d 188, 197 & n. 5 (Mass. Sup. Ct. 1983).] Under either approach, the trial court should not weigh the evidence; if the evidence, however weak or doubtful, supports the essential elements of the defense, the trial court must allow the defense to present it. [*United States v. Hill*, 893 F.Supp. 1044, 1045-46 (N.D. Florida 1994). *See also United States v. Taylor*, 686 F.3d 182, 194 (3d Cir. 2012) ("The tests for precluding a defendant from offering a defense and for denying an instruction on a particular defense are the same: whether the evidence presented (or proffered) is legally sufficient to support the defense"; affirming preclusion of witnesses that would have supported justification defense).]

[§§20:05-20:09 Reserved]

B.   Theory of Defense

§20:10   The Theory Should Shift the Focus

Your theory of defense should be more than just the legal pigeonhole into which your defense fits (*e.g.,* self-defense, alibi, or reasonable doubt).

Instead, the theory must be a narrative or argument that accounts for the indisputable evidence and leads the jury to conclude that the just result is to acquit your client. [For a thorough analysis of forming and using case theories, *see generally* Ty Alper, Anthony G. Amsterdam, et al., *Stories Told and Untold: Lawyering Theory Analysis of the First Rodney King Assault Trial*, 12 Clinical L. Rev. 1 (2005).]

Ideally, the theory should not sound apologetic, but should resonate in themes and stories of injustice shared by the community.

Your theory often should shift the focus to the prosecution's case and its witnesses, and should tell a story of how that case cheats the jury by depriving it of the evidence needed to decide the case fairly (such as forensic evidence) or insults the jurors' common sense or sense of fair play by asking them to rely on tainted and biased witnesses, such as uncorroborated accomplices or informants. [*See* Larry S. Pozner & Roger J. Dodd, *Cross-Examination: Science and Techniques*, §§2.01, 2.14, 2.16 (2d ed. 2005) ("us" versus "them" theories).]

§20:11   The Theory Guides the Trial

Start formulating your theory when you first meet your client, and refine and even discard it in favor of another as informal and formal discovery yield more facts and pre-trial hearings show strengths and weaknesses in your theory.

The theory guides your pre-trial preparation, but also your trial questioning and arguments. Your aim during trial is not to score as many points as you can, but to make those which advance your theory.

The theory generates and rests on themes, which are phrases or words that you harp on in questions and argument (*e.g.,* "mere presence / merely present"). [*See* Larry S. Pozner & Roger J. Dodd, *Cross-Examination: Science and Techniques*, §2.06 (2d ed. 2005) (theory broken down into themes and theme lines).]

The theory should be all-encompassing and consistent. While inconsistent defenses are theoretically possible, they do not work in criminal cases.

EXAMPLE:

If your defense in a drug conspiracy case is that your client unknowingly accompanied a friend to the deal (or, in the words of the typical jury instruction, "mere presence") you usually should not attack the credibility of an informant who damns the alleged coconspirators, but never met your client until the day of the arrest. Rather, you should gently elicit from the informant concessions about your client's non-involvement:

    Q.   Leading up to January 22, you had three meetings with various individuals about the deal that took place on that day?

    Q.   And we've heard played 17 telephone conversations you had with those individuals?

    Q.   And other brief ones that weren't recorded?

    Q.   My client was not present at any of those meetings?

    Q.   Or on any of those calls?

    Q.   In fact, no one even mentioned his name?

    Q.   You never met my client before January 22.

    Q.   On January 22, he did nothing?

    Q.   And said nothing?

    Q.   You didn't see him with any drugs?

    Q.   Or scales?

    Q.   Or beepers?

    Q.   And certainly not with a weapon?

[§§20:12-20:19 Reserved]

C.   Change of Venue

§20:20   General Points

Inflammatory and prejudicial pre-trial publicity may lead you to request that your client's trial be held in a different venue than that in which the crime occurred.

An alternative remedy available in some jurisdictions is to import jurors from another county. [*See* Pa. R. Crim. P. 584.]

You may obtain a change of venue upon a showing of either presumed or actual prejudice:

•   Actual prejudice exists when, during jury selection, the prospective jurors evince an abiding and eradicable inability to be fair.

- Presumptive prejudice entitles you to a change of venue before jury selection because inflammatory and inculpatory publicity has so saturated the jury pool in the venue that selection of a fair jury is impossible. [*United States v. Sherwood*, 98 F.3d 402, 410 (9th Cir. 1996); *Commonwealth v. Sutton*, 485 Pa. 47, 57, 400 A.2d. 1305, 1309 (1979).]

§20:21   Establishing Presumptive Prejudice

Prejudice is rarely presumed "because 'saturation' defines conditions found only in extreme situations." [*United States v. Sherwood*, 98 F.3d 402, 410 (9th Cir. 1996). *See also Skilling v. United States*, 130 S.Ct. 2896, 2915 (2010) ("A presumption of prejudice, our decisions indicate, attends only the extreme case"; size of the community, delay between events and trial, and lack of publicity about a confession or any "smoking gun" evidence eliminated presumption); *Murphy v. Florida*, 421 U.S. 794, 800 (1976) (to hold that the mere existence of any preconceived notion is sufficient to rebut the presumption of a prospective juror's impartiality would be to establish an impossible standard); *Flamer v. Delaware,* 68 F.3d 736, 754 (3d Cir.1995) ("It is the rare case in which adverse pre-trial publicity will create a presumption of prejudice that overrides the jurors' assurances that they can be impartial"); *Commonwealth v. Sutton*, 485 Pa. 47, 57, 400 A.2d. 1305, 1309 (1979) (where the standard for presumptive prejudice is met, defendant need not show a nexus between the publicity and actual jury prejudice).]

According to the ABA Standards Relating to Fair Trial and Free Press at Std. 8-3.3(c) (2d ed. 1980):

> A motion for change of venue ... shall be granted whenever it is determined that because of the dissemination of potentially prejudicial material, there is a substantial likelihood that in the absence of such relief, a fair trial cannot be had. This determination may be based on such evidence as qualified public opinion surveys or opinion testimony offered by individuals, or in the court's owns evaluation of the nature, frequency, and timing of the material involved. A showing of actual prejudice shall not be required.

[*See Commonwealth v. Cohen*, 489 Pa. 167, 413 A.2d 1066, 1073 (1980) (adopting the ABA standards); *United States v. Lindh*, 212 F.Supp.2d 541 (E.D. Va. 2002) (discussing use of experts to conduct and interpret survey interview questionnaires and content analysis of new reports, but denying motion for change of venue).]

The trial court should weigh the nature of the publicity, such as whether it revealed the defendant's criminal record, a confession or inadmissible evidence; its frequency and duration; and source (that generated by official sources being considered more influential and poisonous). [*See Commonwealth v. Rucci,* 543 Pa. 261, 283-84, 670 A.2d. 1129 (1996); *Commonwealth v. Gorby,* 527 Pa. 98, 588 A.2d. 902 (1991).]

PRACTICE TIP:

To present the best argument for a pre-trial change of venue, if you can afford it, retain a jury consultant to collect the media reports about your case and to survey citizens in your jurisdiction and report that the publicity has been pervasive and persuasive, citing the ABA standards. The consultant then can report his findings in an affidavit to support your request for a change of venue and an evidentiary hearing on the issue.

The consultant also can assist you in deciding whether a change of venue is in your best interest by comparing your venue's jury pool to the alternatives. The prejudicial publicity might have spread statewide, and your venue's jury pool might be more pro-defense than other counties. Without a consultant, your evaluation of these factors is hunch and guess.

Even a failing change-of-venue motion may yield benefit. Evidence of prejudicial pretrial publicity will force the trial judge to conduct a more searching voir dire into the jurors' abilities to be fair and unbiased. [See *Skilling*, 130 S.Ct. at 2918-23 (majority found that jury was impartial after selection process consisting of 77-page questionnaire and individualized voir dire), 2942-63 (Sotomayor, J., dissenting) (selection should have been even more thorough).]

[§§20:22-20:29 Reserved]

D.   Jury Trial Versus Non-Jury

§20:30   The Client Can Waive Trial by Jury

Your client can choose to waive the right to trial by jury and proceed before a judge alone, although many jurisdictions give the prosecution the right to veto that choice. [*E.g.* Fed. R. Crim. P. 23(a)(2); Pa. R. Crim. P 620.]

Since this entails waiver of a substantial constitutional right, the decision ultimately is the client's. [*See Jones v. Barnes,* 463 U.S. 745, 751, 753 n.6 (1983).]

However, the client will usually follow your advice.

§20:31   Factors to Consider

Consider the following factors when deciding whether or not to waive the right to a jury trial:

The judge's reputation and track record in bench trials

If bench trials are rare, this may be difficult to determine, and you must rely on the judge's reputation as being more or less pro-law enforcement. However, some courts encourage bench trials to expedite clearing their dockets, and in those courts judges will have extensive histories. The judges most likely to acquit have the most jury waivers.

The nature of the defense

Legal defenses play better with judges, while jurors lend a more sympathetic ear to defenses that attack the prosecutor or the propriety of the prosecution.

Juries occasionally "nullify" (i.e., acquit when the evidence warrants a conviction but the prosecution seems unjust or excessive; or the defendant is likable; or the prosecution, police, or victim offends the jury). Judges don't nullify.

Judges might compartmentalize evidence against multiple defendants more accurately than juries.

With a judge, avoid using oft-heard but unlikely defenses such as: "I was standing outside the liquor/convenience store when this fellow ran out and stuck a bag in my hand; I took $500 to carry a bag one block, but had no idea of its contents." One or two jurors might buy it, especially if your client can tell it earnestly, but not a judge.

Credibility issues

Judges are unlikely to disbelieve police officers.

On the other hand, a judge more likely than a jury will find the testimony of a sympathetic but confused witness insufficient to convict.

Excluded evidence

If you succeed in suppressing evidence, the judge will know it, but a jury will not.

Further, if your client has raped or killed before, the jury may never hear it even if the defendant testifies, but a judge certainly will know it and cannot help but consider it.

The penalty for non-waiver

In those jurisdictions where bench trials are common, a judge might penalize the defendant with a harsher sentence if he refuses to waive jury trial.

The need to preserve legal issues

A guilty plea generally waives all pre-trial legal issues. [*See* Chapter 17, Plea Bargaining.] If you have one that you believe has a substantial chance of success on appeal, you might need to go to trial to preserve it. A bench trial might enable you to preserve the issue and gain your client some credit for not contesting factual guilt.

The slow guilty plea

You may have no plausible defense, but your client just will not plead guilty. A bench trial might avoid a lengthy trial that only will aggravate the judge and earn a severe sentence.

[§§20:32-20:39 Reserved]

E. Final Trial Preparation

§20:40   Last-Month Checklist

By the last month before trial, the discovery has answers, the motions rulings, and the plea offers their rejections. At that point, serious preparation begins.

Do the following in the last month:

- Serve subpoenas on all your witnesses. [See §20:44.] Accompany the subpoena with an "on call" letter that trades an assurance that the witness need not come until needed for current contact information.
- Lock in expert witnesses' availability.
- If your client or witnesses must travel some distance to court and your client cannot pay for a bus or plane, file motions for the government to pay travel expenses.
- Double check the date and time of jury selection and any pre-trial conferences start.
- Assemble your trial binder or folder. [*See* §20:41.]
- Check and record in your trial binder important contact information for witnesses, both phone numbers (work, home, cell, and, if the witness is transient, a close friend or relative who can reach the witness), and addresses.
- Have your client, or his family if he is incarcerated, obtain appropriate clothing for trial. [See §20:42.]
- Research and prepare any motions in limine. [*See* §20:03.] Anticipate and rehearse responses to any your opponent might file.
- Visit the courtroom and familiarize yourself with its layout and any special document display or other technologies. Determine the best locations for whiteboards and other exhibit enlargements.
- Finalize your selection of documents, both those that will be substantive exhibits and those prior statements you will use to impeach. Enlarge or enter into document display databases choice exhibits.
- Review the judge's pre-trial or standing orders on the conduct of counsel during trial. If you have any questions, call and ask his clerk.
- Familiarize yourself with the judge's jury selection procedures. [*See* §§20:51.]
- Conduct mock trials and focus group studies. Decide on any ideal and bad juror profiles.
- Decide, with your client, whether he will testify. Prepare him repeatedly for direct and cross.
- Re-check discovery requests to ensure you are not owed anything.
- Get the witness statements (called "*Jencks*" material in federal cases) as soon as you can and review it with your client. [See §20:43.]
- Save preparation of most witnesses for the last two weeks before trial, or even nights or weekends during trial so that you will have the *Jencks* material during the preparation and so that the rehearsal remains fresh in their minds. Ideally, you will rehearse the witnesses earlier in the month to explore whether their testimony will necessitate further investigation or subpoenas, as would be the case if you discover that what you thought was a statement based on first-hand observation actually is a recitation of hearsay from another witness. You then would do final rehearsal in the last days before the witness is to testify.
- If a reliable alibi emerges, file any required alibi notices if you did not do so during discovery. [See Chapter 14, Discovery.]
- Talk through the case, your arguments and witness examinations, with colleagues and yourself.
- See if the prosecutor will share with you his witness list. Attempt to get a proffer as to their testimony.
- Get your shoes shined, your hair cut and your suits and shirts, blouses and dresses cleaned and pressed. Dress conservatively and neatly, not flashily or shabbily. Even if your client is, and appears, indigent, the jury expects you to be successful enough to afford a decent wardrobe and respectful enough to wear it to court.

Forms:
- **Form 20-3** Motion to Pay Defendant's Travel Expenses
- **Form 20-4** On Call Letter

§20:41   Trial Folder or Binder

Assemble a trial binder or folders early in your preparation.
Whether you use a binder or folders, the system should be organized for easy and rapid consultation during trial.
The binder or folders should have separate sections for the following:
- To do list.
- Witness and exhibit list.
- Voir dire questions.
- Pleadings.
- Witness contact information.

- Examination outline for each witness. This section must include an outline of the witness's examination and a summary of the witness's prior statements with verbatim reproduction of crucial portions. The examination outline should list exhibits that the witness will introduce or upon which he will be questioned.
- Opening and closing arguments.
- Jury instructions.
- Legal argument on evidentiary and substantive issues.

Do not integrate your exhibits with this binder. You should have separate exhibit binders or folders because opening the trial binder or shuffling folders to remove exhibits during trial will cause your trial binder to fall into disarray.

Pre-mark exhibits, and have at least an original and three copies: one for the judge, one for the prosecutor, and one for your use during witness examinations. Some judges encourage the parties to assemble complete exhibit binders, one for each juror.

Many courtrooms have document display technologies that enable you to place the document on a device that will transmit it to television monitors placed before the jury, witness, judge and counsel. Some software programs can scan the documents into a database and generate barcodes for each exhibit so that the image can be retrieved and projected on the monitors. You also can create PowerPoint slides or Adobe Acrobat images of your documents to retrieve and display.

PRACTICE TIPS:

Do not overuse document display technologies at risk of the exhibits losing their impact and the jury ignoring the oral presentation.

Walk through the sections of your trial and exhibit binders before trial so you know where to find things and where to return them. This review also helps you rehearse the trial presentation as an integrated unit.

§20:42   Prepare Your Client

Remind your client that in a way, he is always on the stand because the jury is always watching. While in court, waiting in the hallway, or walking or riding to the courthouse, he must act politely, respectfully, and soberly: no scowling at witnesses; no vulgarity, even in private conversations in the hallway; no excessive laughter. Tell him that he never knows if a juror is standing behind him.

If the client is older, he should have a suit, preferably dark, although light brown or blue might be acceptable in warm months and climes, with white or light blue shirts. If the client is a professional, he must wear a tie.

Clients who appear to be under 30 can wear sweaters and pants, but not jeans. They must have belts.

Women must wear dresses, skirts or slacks and blouses or sweaters or suits. Emphasize that displays of cleavage, bare backs, midriffs, and bare shoulders are verboten.

Clothing should cover all tattoos, and the only visible piercings should be in the ears, with small earrings. Consider tongue piercings to be visible.

Make all this explicit if you have any doubt about your client's taste.

§20:43   Obtaining Witness Statements From the Prosecutor

A statute or rule may set some late date for production of the statements. [*See, e.g.,* 18 U.S.C. §3500(a) (after witness direct examination); NY Crim. Pro. L. §240.45(1)(a) (after opening statements).]

Some jurisdictions entitle the defense to early disclosure of witness statements. [E.g., Pa. R. Crim. P. 573(B)(2) (a)(ii) (eyewitness statements discoverable on motion made 14 days after arraignment).]

However, the prosecutor often will provide witness statements early to avoid mid-trial delays. Friday before a Monday start is typical, but you might see them earlier in a complex case.

As part of his right to consult with his counsel, your client has the right to review the *Jencks* and discovery material with you. [*United States v. Hung,* 667 F.2d 1105, 1008 (4th Cir. 1981).]

The court can order, however, that you not share the material with your client if necessary to protect a strong countervailing interest. [*See Morgan v. Bennett,* 204 F.3d 360, 367 (2d Cir. 2000) (defense counsel ordered not to reveal identity of testifying witness where the witness had been threatened).]

Also, many prosecutors require you to sign an agreement not to photocopy the witness statements, and to return them when trial ends. Never leave the statements with a client in jail, unless redacted as to civilian witness names and addresses. Should the witnesses be threatened or harmed, you will be blamed.

§20:44   Trial Subpoenas

Trial subpoenas are available either at the court clerk's office or online, to be downloaded. [*See* www.uscourts. gov/forms/uscforms.cfm (federal criminal trial subpoena, form AO-89).]

You fill them out; no judge's signature is needed unless you are asking the witness to produce documents before trial.

The subpoena must be returnable the day of trial, not before. However, if you seek only documents or tangible items and not the custodian's testimony, you can suggest (but not demand) on the face of the subpoena or an attached letter that you will consider the subpoena satisfied and will not require the witness to attend if the items are produced to your office.

You must serve the subpoena much like original process, which usually means personal delivery to the witness.

Along with the subpoena, you must tender to the witness the statutory witness fee and travel expenses. You might call the witness before trial and get his assurances, which you should memorialize in a cover letter, that he will honor a subpoena delivered by facsimile or mail or sent to his lawyer. Know your local rules, practice and the judge's predilections on this point: will the judge delay the trial to procure the witness's attendance based on the witness's promise to honor less than perfect service?

§20:45   Time Limits in Criminal Cases

With increasing frequency, trial judges set time limits for the argument and the presentation of witness testimony in civil cases. [*See, e.g., In re Baldwin*, 700 F.3d 122, 129 (3d Cir. 2012).] While relatively rare in criminal cases, some trial judges have imposed time limits especially where the parties' projections of the case's length and complexity exasperate the judge. [*E.g., United States v. Cousar*, 2007 U.S.Dist. LEXIS 92064 (W.D.Pa. Dec. 16, 2007) (in case where the prosecution estimated five weeks to present its case, and each defendant, two days for each one's case, the trial judge limited the prosecution to 40 hours inclusive of opening and closing, direct of its witnesses, and cross of the defense witnesses, and the defense to 12 hours each). *See generally United States v. Hildebrand*, 928 F.Supp. 841 (N.D. Iowa 1996) and *United States v. Reaves*, 636 F.Supp. 1575 (E.D.Ky. 1986), for extensive discussions of the wisdom and permissibility of time limits in criminal cases.]

Weigh such limits against the relative likelihood of harm to you and the prosecutor. Since the prosecution has the burden of proof, and many prosecutors are accustomed to a "kitchen-sink" approach, you may stand to benefit from time limits. On the other hand, the prosecution can eat into your time if its witnesses turn intransigent on cross.

Time limits must be reasonable and must reflect "an informed analysis based on a review of the parties' proposed witness lists and proferred testimony and allocates trial time evenhandedly." [*In re Baldwin*, 700 F.3d at 129.] Your consent to such time limits should not discourage you from requesting additional time. Explain the need for it if events necessitate. The paucity of pretrial discovery in a criminal case as compared to a civil case makes surprises during trial, and the need to respond to them, much more common in criminal litigation.

[§§20:46-20:49 Reserved]

II.   JURY SELECTION

A. How It Works

§20:50   The Venire

A jury commissioner compiles a list of prospective jurors from the voter registration lists supplemented by motor vehicle license lists. Prospective jurors receive a summons ordering them to appear for service on a set date. Members of certain professions, usually law enforcement and firefighters, may be excused, but most other individuals must serve despite hardship. The jurors who appear comprise the "venire," which, if there is more than one courtroom holding trials in that term, will be split into "panels" for jury selection in each courtroom. [*See* Anthony G. Amsterdam, *Trial Manual For The Defense Of Criminal Cases* §§320-323 (5th ed. 1989) (describing methods of assembling jury pools); Federal Defenders of San Diego, Inc., *Defending A Federal Criminal Case* 8.03 (2001); 28 U.S.C. §§1861 *et seq.*]

Jurors serve for a set period. Some courts permit jurors to return home and await a call if needed.

In some jurisdictions, if a juror is chosen for a trial, that completes his or her service. In other jurisdictions, a juror might continue serving until the period of service ends.

§20:51   Jury Selection Procedures

When it comes time to pick your jury, the clerk will bring the panel of prospective jurors into the courtroom and seat them in the gallery. The clerk then calls out names at random, sometimes by picking cards from a wheel or box.

At this point, jury selection procedures vary widely not only from jurisdiction to jurisdiction but judge to judge. Two systems predominate, but each has many variations. These systems are:
- The "struck jury."
- The "jury box" system.

[*See United States v. Blouin*, 666 F.2d 796 (2d Cir. 1981) (describing the two systems and some of their variations); Wayne R. LaFave, Jerold H. Israel, Nancy J. King, 5 *Criminal Procedure* §22.3(d)(2006) (describing systems).]

§20:52   The Struck Jury System

In the struck jury system, the clerk calls a number of names equal to the amount of jurors and alternates required, plus the total of the parties' allotted peremptory challenges.

For example, in a federal trial where the prosecution has six peremptories, the defense ten and each side one for two alternates, the clerk will call at least 32 names (twelve trial jurors plus ten defense peremptories plus six prosecution plus two alternates plus two alternate peremptories). [*See United States v. Delgado*, 350 F.3d 520 (6th Cir. 2003) (describing this method of jury selection); Federal Defenders of San Diego, Inc., *Defending A Federal Criminal Case* 8.14.01 (2001) (calling this the "Arizona" system).]

Voir dire questions then are put to the panel as a whole, asking whether any of the jurors know the parties, have heard about the case, have served as jurors before, have been the victims of a crime or have testified in a trial, have had close friends or relatives prosecuted for a crime, would suffer hardship by serving, or hold firm beliefs on topics pertinent to the case, such as the credibility of law enforcement officers or informants or the evils of drugs or guns. [*See* Pa. R. Crim. P. 632; United States District Court for the Western District of Pennsylvania, Local Rules of Court, LCrR 24.2, for typical questions.]

Some judges will question the individual jurors openly as they answer the questions. Others will call the jurors one-by-one to sidebar as they raise their hands. Still others will note which jurors raise their hands in response to which questions, and then question each juror individually on the set of questions later.

Practices vary as well in how challenges are exercised, with many combinations of the following options:
- Some judges have the parties state their challenges, for cause and peremptory or one or the other, aloud in front of the jury. Others entertain challenges at sidebar or in chambers, orally, or with the peremptories checked off on a list of the jurors. (The for-cause challenges must be oral so the parties can state reasons and the court can rule.)
- Some courts will ask the parties to exercise their challenges for cause first, and then go back and exercise peremptories. Others have the parties go juror by juror, raising whatever challenges, for-cause or peremptory, they have.
- Some require that the parties go through the jurors in order, seats one through twelve and then the alternates; others permit random challenges.
- Practices also vary on the effect of waiving a challenge for cause in a round and the order in which they must be made. Most judges deem the challenge lost; others will permit the side to save the challenge for later rounds.
- Judges vary on whether they permit "backstrikes," that is, whether a party with remaining peremptories can return to a juror who has been accepted and strike that juror. [*See United States v. Williams*, 986 F.2d 86 (4th Cir. 1993) (explaining the backstrike system, and holding that trial court did not have to permit backstrike for out-of-town attorney who was unfamiliar with local method and passed over juror in the mistaken belief he could challenge the juror later); *State v. Taylor*, 669 So.2d 364, 376-77 (La. 1996) (describing backstrike system in detail).]
- Peremptories may be exercised either blindly or openly. In the blind system, each side makes its challenges on a list while the other side simultaneously records its challenges on a copy of the list. It is possible that each side will challenge the same jurors. [*See United States v. Warren*, 25 F.3d 890 (9th Cir. 1994) (describing blind strike system and upholding it against challenge).] In an open system, the parties alternate in announcing their challenges openly or in writing, with many variations as to the amount of turns and number of challenges per turn. The open system also enables the parties to guess at the pattern and logic of the challenges.

§20:53   The Jury Box System

In the "jury box" system, the court fills the twelve to sixteen seats in the jury box and conducts full voir dire of the jurors in the box. The parties then exercise challenges for cause and peremptory challenges. New jurors fill the seats from which jurors are stricken. The same variations apply in exercising challenges as with the struck jury system.

This system has the great disadvantage that since the remaining jurors in the gallery are not questioned until seated in the box, you do not know whether they will be better or worse than the ones on whom you use your challenges.

§20:54   Picking the Jury; Tactics and Tips

The following tips relate to voir dire and the use of peremptories. [For more, see §§20:70 et seq. For a discussion of the tactical approaches to voir dire and the exercise of peremptories, see David Berg, *The Trial Lawyer* Chapters 3 and 4 (2006).]

Learn the local system before the day of jury selection

If possible, sit through a selection in the particular judge's courtroom. Otherwise, grill a local practitioner on the judge's method and the possible permutations. Call the judge's clerk before trial and ask.

Diagram the selection

Keeping track of which juror gave which answer and how the name and information on your paper corresponds to the face in front of you can be impossible without a diagram.

At the minimum, draw on a page laid out landscape style the 12 to 16 seats in the jury box. Place post-it notes in each box to record the juror's name, number and answers so you can discard the note and replace it when the juror is struck.

Pull and stack the notes according to whether the juror was struck for cause or peremptorily and by which party. The notes become your reference material if you later make a *Batson* challenge or request additional peremptories because the court mistakenly denied your for-cause challenge.

Request variations in procedure before trial and attempt to secure the prosecutor's consent

The trial judge has great latitude over the method of jury selection; therefore, arguments that one or another method offends constitutional rights will flounder.

However, some selection methods disadvantage both parties (*e.g.,* the blind strike method or the practice of exercising strikes aloud in the jurors' presence), and the prosecutor might join in your request to vary the practice.

Cite to the practices of other judges in other cases. The closer to home the cited judge and the more esteemed he or she is for both wisdom and efficiency, the more likely your request will prevail.

Count carefully

Keep track not only of the number of peremptories left to you, but how far into the panel the peremptories will carry you.

For example, if ten jurors have been selected, and the parties have one peremptory each left, there is no sense in striking juror number 15 if the next challenge is yours because you will never reach that number.

Bluff

There will be a number of jurors whose answers trouble both sides (*e.g.,* the juror whose one brother is a police officer and the other a defense lawyer; or the well-educated and apparently liberal juror who has been the victim of multiple crimes).

Where backstrikes are allowed, you might want to pass over that juror in the hope that the prosecutor will strike him, thereby saving you a peremptory, but knowing that you can return to the juror and strike him if the prosecutor does not.

Ask for follow-up voir dire where there has been delay between selection and opening

In some jurisdictions, the jurors are sent home for several weeks or a month between selection and the start of trial. During the interim, there is a risk that jurors will read about the case, that people will approach them to urge one verdict or another, or that they might even serve on another jury.

Request voir dire on these topics. [*See Linnell v. State*, 935 S.W.2d 426 (Tex. Crim. App. 1996) (discussing need for voir dire on interim jury service to exercise challenges intelligently); *United States v. Capua*, 656 F.2d 1033, 1036 (5th Cir. 1981) (supplemental voir dire is necessary where there has been significant delay between jury selection and the commencement of trial; 39 days is significant delay).]

Form:
* **Form 20-5** Jury Selection Table

[§§20:55-20:59 Reserved]

B. Questionnaires

§20:60   Advantages of Questionnaires

Questionnaires can accommodate both the judge's interest in abbreviating voir dire and yours in eliciting as much information as you can about the prospective jurors. The jurors can complete them while the judge busies himself with other tasks, and the anonymity of completing a form might evoke more candor from the jurors. [*See* LaFave, 5 *Criminal Procedure* §22.3(c) & n.87 (noting trend toward increasing use of questionnaires and arguments in its favor); Hon. Barbara M.G. Lynn, "From the Bench: A Case for Jury Questionnaires," 33 *Litigation* 3 (Summer 2007) (federal district court judge expresses strong preference for jury questionnaires); Marc A. Raspanti and Michael A. Morse, "Why Isn't Every White Collar Defense Lawyer Using a Jury Questionnaire?" 31 *Champion* 32 (Oct. 2007) (includes sample questionnaire).]

Especially in complex or high-profile cases, where exposure to pre-trial publicity or the hardship of sitting through a lengthy trial might disqualify many jurors, the court might mail the questionnaires to the potential jurors long before trial and provide you with the responses in sufficient time to review them carefully.

Form:
•   **Form 20-6** Juror Questionnaire

§20:61   Requesting a Questionnaire

Consider a joint questionnaire with the prosecutor; the court will be more likely to accept it.

If the questionnaire is not joint, evaluate how extensive your proposal should be. With some judges, arguing for many questions may increase the chance that the judge will grant some. Other judges will look at a 100-item questionnaire and conclude that you are unreasonable and discard the entire list in favor of the judge's usual questions.

You should propose the questionnaire far enough before trial for the court to review the questions. Ask that the jury pool receive the questionnaire a day or two before selection starts, or at the latest, the morning of jury selection, in order for the jurors to have enough time to answer the questions carefully.

Consider carefully the logistics of distributing and reviewing the questionnaires. There must be enough copies, along with pencils or pens, for all panel members. If you cannot arrange quick copying of the responses so that the defense, court and prosecution each have copies, have them printed as tripartite carbons, so each party and the judge has a copy. You need to have time and a place to review the responses with your client. [*See generally* Raspanti and Morse, *supra* (outlining logistical issues for defense).]

[§§20:62-20:69 Reserved]

C. Voir Dire

§20:70   Trends and General Points

The trend in the federal courts and many state courts is to abbreviate jury selection by limiting the number and range of questions and denying attorney-conducted voir dire. [See *United States v. Lawes*, 292 F.3d 123, 128-29 (2d Cir. 2002); *Commonwealth v. Ellison*, 588 Pa. 1, 10-15, 902 A.2d 419, 425-28 (Pa. 2006); *but see* Barry Tarlow, "Rico Report," 26 *Champion* 50 (Dec. 2002) (reviewing older cases that mandate broader leeway in voir dire).]

Many judges do all the questioning themselves and ask a rather narrow range of questions. Further, judges often will work hard to rehabilitate jurors who indicate some bias, thereby defeating challenges for cause and forcing you to use peremptory challenges.

If possible, you want to question jurors yourself, both because you will ask more informative questions and so that you can develop some rapport with the jurors.

Some courts permit attorneys to do some or all of the voir dire; in others the best for which you can hope is that you be allowed to ask follow-up questions when jurors give problematic answers.

§20:71   Juror Profiles and Focus Groups

Before trial, brainstorm on juror profiles, both positive and negative. Try to make the profile as specific as possible and focus on the sort of information you are likely to learn during voir dire.

Stereotypes, such as a preference for African-American jurors or young people, rarely help much and might mire you in a reverse-*Batson* accusation. [*See* §20:91.]

You might want jurors who are Democrats versus Republicans or reformed Jews rather than conservative, but unless the case involves a political or religious donnybrook, the judge likely will not permit you to inquire into such areas.

Conduct mock trials or present a summary of your case to focus groups to assist in forming a juror profile and in evaluating jurors' receptivity to defense themes. How extensive and thorough this process will be depends on your resources. It can range from a full mock trial to several randomly selected panels, with the assistance of professional consultants, to the distribution of a written summary of the case to your friends, neighbors and office staff. [David Berg, *The Trial Lawyer* at 47-61; Federal Defenders of San Diego, Inc., *Defending A Federal Criminal Case* §§8.11.01–8.11.06 (2001).]

§20:72   Investigate Prospective Jurors

In some jurisdictions, you are entitled to a list of the prospective jurors in advance of the jury selection date. [*See* LaFave, et al., 5 *Criminal Procedure* §22.3(b) (listing jurisdictions).]

Consider investigating the backgrounds of the prospective jurors. Do internet searches on their backgrounds, and interview neighbors about their attitudes to decide whether you want them on your jury. [*See Johnson v. McCullough,* 306 S.W.3d 551 (Mo. 2010) (new trial ordered after discovering, post-verdict, that juror had lied during voir dire, but noting that in the future, trial counsel may be charged with investigating jurors' litigation history through online databases); *Sluss v. Commonwealth,* 381 S.W.3d 215 (KY 2013) (hearing ordered where two juror had friended the victim's mother on Facebook but one denied having a Facebook account and another denied knowing the victim's family, but suggests that lawyers are chargeable with information publicly available on social media sites); Amsterdam, *Trial Manual For The Defense Of Criminal Cases* §325 (1989) (suggesting such investigation).] In doing internet searches, be careful to avoid any search that puts you in communication with the potential juror, such as Facebook "friend requests," attempts to connect via LinkedIn.com, or "following" a juror's Twitter account. [*See* Eric P. Robinson, Virtual Voir Dire: The Law and Ethics of Investigating Jurors Online, 36 Am. J. Trial Advoc. 597 (2013); John G. Browning, "As Voir Dire Becomes Voir Google, Where Are the Ethical Lines Drawn?" The Jury Expert (May 31, 2013) (available at http://www. thejuryexpert.com/2013/05/as-voir-dire-becomes-voir-google); Leslie Davis, "Friend or Foe? Social Media, the Jury and You," The Jury Expert (September 2011) (available at http://www.thejuryexpert.com/wp-content/uploads/Ellis. pdf); N.Y. Cnty. Lawyers Ass'n Comm. on Prof'l Ethics, Formal Op. 743 (May 18, 2011).]

§20:73   Have Your Client Present

Your client has a right to be present during voir dire, including any follow-up questioning that occurs at sidebar or in-chambers. [*Cohen v. Senkowski,* 290 F.3d 485, 489-90 (2d Cir. 2002); *People v. Antommarchi,* 80 N.Y.2d 247, 604 N.E.2d 95, 590 N.Y.S.2d 33 (NY 1992); *but see United States v. Reyes,* 764 F.3d 1184 (9th Cir. 2014)(defendant does not have a constitutional right to be present during jury selection sidebars to question witness about a personal matter and for counsel to exercise challenges, but under Fed. R. Crim. P. 43, he did have a right to be present during the questioning of the prospective juror); *United States v. Greer,* 285 F.3d 158, 167-69 (2d Cir. 2000) (neither defendant nor his counsel have right to be present during judge's in camera questioning of juror limited to hardship); *Antommarchi,* 80 N.Y.2d at 250 (defendant does not have a right to be present during questioning about "juror qualifications such as physical impairments, family obligations and work commitments").]

Failure to object to your client's absence waives this right. [*State v. W.A.,* 184 N.J. 45, 875 A.2d 882 (N.J. 2005) (surveying federal and state cases and finding that only New York forbids finding a waiver from silence).]

Insist on having your client present because your client may sense a juror's empathy or hostility where you do not. Moreover, any time your client spends in close proximity to the jurors, making eye contact, nodding in agreement and generally showing interest in what the jurors say humanizes your client and may make a vote for conviction more difficult.

Explain the entire voir dire process to your client, and instruct him on how to act in the juror's presence. As hard as it may be to believe, some defendants will snicker, sneer, leer and stare at jurors.

§20:74   Goals and Questions

The brevity of voir dire, the high standards for disqualifying jurors and the quotas set on peremptories limit your ability to select an ideal jury.

Your goals should be to:

- Eliminate bad jurors.
- Pick a few jurors who will champion your cause during deliberations.

The bad jurors generally are those who tend to defer to authority and law enforcement, or who appear to bear some hostility toward your client. The good ones usually will be those who distrust authority, the quirky ones likely to disagree with the other jurors, and those likely to sympathize either with your defense or your defendant.

If the judge permits attorney-conducted voir dire, ask open-ended questions to draw the jurors out and learn as much as you can about them and their attitudes.

Long leading questions that ask the jurors to commit to some legal position have little value and are likely to draw successful objections (*e.g.,* "You promise me that despite hearing about my client's previous drug selling conviction, you will find him not guilty if you have a reasonable doubt that he sold drugs on the date charged in the indictment"). [*See* Berg, *The Trial Lawyer* at 87-90; Randi McGinn, "Addressing the Ten Scariest Criminal Issues in Voir Dire," 29 *Champion* 26 (August 2005) (both advocating use of open-ended questions and disdaining commitment questions).]

§20:75   Individual Voir Dire

Consider requesting individual voir dire where one juror's answers given in open court might prejudice the other jurors against your client.

Answers likely to hurt include statements that the juror has suffered grievously because of a crime similar to the charge against your client or that the juror has reliable knowledge about the kinds of experts you intend to present and finds them untrustworthy.

On the other hand, some people feel that open voir dire in such a situation can be beneficial because you can start a dialogue with the other jurors and elicit a commitment from the remaining jurors that they will keep an open mind. [*See* Randi McGinn, "Addressing the Ten Scariest Criminal Issues in Voir Dire," 29 *Champion* 26 (August 2005).] However, this works only if the judge permits broad-ranging attorney-conducted voir dire. Few do.

If the judge previously denied your request for individual voir dire, renew it after a potentially prejudicial answer. [*See State v. Anderson*, 355 N.C. 136, 558 S.E.2d 87, 96 (NC 2002) (finding defense waived its demand for individual voir dire by not renewing it after prejudicial answers).]

§20:76   Sample Topics

Whether you or the judge conducts voir dire, consider the following topics of inquiry with the jurors for voir dire or for a jury questionnaire:
- In a drug case, feelings toward the drug problem and personal experiences with family members and friends who have had drug problems.
- Beliefs in the credibility of police officers.
- In a gun case, attitudes toward firearms.
- Attitudes toward victims' rights and memberships in any such organizations.
- Attitudes towards particular defenses or personal experiences that might bear on them, such as misidentification (*e.g.,* "Have you ever had the experience of waving at someone you thought you knew, and then realizing it was the wrong person?") or self-defense.
- Reactions to the defendant's decision not to testify.
- Bad evidence you know the jury will hear (*e.g.,* your client's prior record, or the emotional nature of the crime). The prosecution's uncertainty that it will introduce the evidence is not adequate grounds to preclude voir dire on the prospective jurors' ability to follow the court's instructions about the evidence. [*People v. Miller*, 28 N.Y.3d 355, 358, 68 N.E.2d 61, 45 N.Y.S.3d 336 (NY December 22, 2016) ("the trial court abused its discretion when it entirely precluded questioning on the issue of involuntary confessions and refused to make its own inquiry of the potential jurors on the issue. Defense counsel's request to question prospective jurors about their ability to follow the law and disregard an involuntary confession went to the heart of determining whether those jurors could be impartial and afford defendant a fair trial.")]
- Prior or interim jury service. Courts will permit questions on the juror's prior service, including questions about the nature of the charge and whether a verdict was reached. Some courts will ask what the verdict was, others will not. This question may be especially important where the jurors come from a venire empanelled earlier in the same term of court because the jurors might have served on a similar case in the courthouse, perhaps before the same judge, with the same prosecutor and testifying police officers, earlier in the term. You

are entitled to ask about that prior service and how it might affect the juror's consideration of the evidence in your case. [*See United States v. Mobley,* 656 F.2d 988, 989 (5th Cir. 1981).]

Tailor the list to the issues in your case, and you will more likely have your requests granted.

Form:
• **Form 20-7** Proposed Voir Dire Questions by the Court

§20:77   Jury Deselection

One strategy in vogue for dealing with abbreviated jury selection is the technique of jury "deselection," in which you use your limited time to unearth and eliminate those potential jurors whose life experiences or attitudes predispose them against your defense. This technique requires you to find those issues most likely to derail your defense, either by brainstorming or questioning colleagues, laypeople, or, if you have the resources, mock jurors. These types of issues may include, for example, your client's criminal record, philandering, promiscuity, or confession, if admissible; the fact that the victim is a child; your client's wealth or poverty; the fact that the case involves repulsive facts; or your need to question a police officer's credibility. Encourage jurors to express biases against you, your client, or your case; find out if other jurors share them; and then see if you can have those jurors pledge that they will not surrender those deeply held beliefs no matter what they are told about the law and evidence. If you get that far, you have winnable cause challenges; if not, you still have a good sense of who you need to strike with peremptories. [*See generally* Lisa A. Blue & Robert B. Hirschhorn, "Goals and Practical Tips for Voir Dire," 26 Am. J. Trial Advoc. 233 (2002), for a discussion of this method.]

§20:78   Shackling of Defendant

"No physical restraints may be imposed on a criminal defendant during trial unless the [trial court] finds on the record that they are a necessary last resort." [*United States v. Haynes,* 729 F.3d 178, 190 (2d Cir. 2013).] The court cannot defer the determination of necessity to someone else, such as court security officers, and the court must impose no greater restraints than are necessary and take steps to minimize the prejudice to the defendant. [*Id.* at 189] Limitations on the use of restraints find their source in the constitutional requirement of due process. [*Deck v. Missouri,* 544 U.S. 622, 629 (2005); *Illinois v. Allen,* 397 U.S. 337, 344 (1970).]

[§20:79 Reserved]

D. Challenges for Cause

§20:80   No Limit to Challenges for Cause

The parties are entitled to strike any juror who cannot be fair and impartial and decide the case on the law and evidence given in court.

There is no limit to the number of challenges for cause.

§20:81   Court's Discretion

The juror's assurances that he can be fair and impartial cannot be dispositive of the accused's rights. [*Murphy v. Florida,* 421 U.S. 794, 800 (1976).]

Furthermore, doubts regarding bias should be resolved against the juror. [*United States v. Gonzalez,* 214 F.3d 1109, 1114 (9th Cir. 2000) (error to deny challenge of juror who persistently answered "I'll try" when asked if she could be fair).]

The trial court's determination, based upon voir dire, that the juror can follow the law and decide the case solely on the trial evidence is a factual finding to which an appellate court will defer [*Wainwright v. Witt,* 469 U.S. 412, 428 (1985)] , but the issue of whether the juror should be disqualified for implied bias because of her close relationship to the parties is one of law. [*See Commonwealth v. Kelly,* 134 A.3d 59, 62 (Pa. Super. Ct. 2016); *Gonzales v. Thomas,* 99 F.3d 978, 987 (10th Cir. 1996).]

Sometimes bias will be implied or presumed from the juror's close relationship to the circumstances of the case or familiarity with prejudicial information about the defendant. [*See United States v. Gonzalez,* 214 F.3d at 1112-13 & n.4 (surveying cases where the courts have implied bias, such as where juror worked for same bank as was robbed, though not at same branch; or heroin distribution case where juror's sons were themselves heroin addicts who had served lengthy prison sentences); *United States v. Cerrato-Reyes,* 176 F.3d 1253, 1261 (10th Cir. 1999) ("Implied bias may be demonstrated by showing that the juror is an actual employee of the prosecuting agency, that 'the juror is a close relative of one of the participants in the trial or the criminal transaction, or that the juror was a witness or somehow involved in the criminal transaction...' "(quoting *Smith v. Phillips,* 455 U.S. 209, 222 (1982) (O'Connor, J., concurring)); *Kelly,* 134 A.3d 59 (bias presumed where prospective juror was a police officer who had worked on other cases with the two assistant district attorneys prosecuting the case).]

When deciding a claim of implied bias, the court must assess "whether an average person in the position of the juror in controversy would be prejudiced." [*Cerrato-Reyes,* 176 F.3d at 1260-61.]

The issue of whether the juror should be disqualified for implied bias is one of law. [*See Gonzales v. Thomas,* 99 F.3d 978, 987 (10th Cir. 1996).]

§20:82   The Defense Dilemma When a Challenge Is Denied

Federal law and that of some other jurisdictions put defendants in a dilemma. That is, if the defense uses a peremptory to strike a juror as to whom the court erroneously denied the defense's valid challenge for cause, the erroneous denial of the challenge for cause is not preserved for appeal because the biased juror did not sit. [*United States v. Martinez-Salazar,* 528 U.S. 304 (2000). *But see Busby v. State,* 894 So.2d 88, 101-03 (FL 2004) (disagreeing with *Martinez-Salazar* and holding that if the defendant peremptorily strikes the objectionable juror, exhausts his peremptory challenges and can identify remaining jurors he would have challenged were he not forced to waste peremptories to correct the erroneous for-cause challenge denials, then he has shown prejudice entitling him to reversal on appeal; surveys all states' positions); *Shane v. Commonwealth,* 243 S.W.3d 336 (Ky 2007) (rejecting *Martinez-Salazar* and holding that under state law improper denial of defense challenge for cause which forces defense to use a peremptory challenge is reversible error without need to show any further prejudice).]

Unfair as it may seem, your choice is clear. You cannot permit the biased juror to sit, so you must strike him (unless you later develop information that convinces you that despite the valid challenge for cause, the juror will be favorable–for example, an employee of the police department which investigated the case whose experiences have taught her to mistrust the police).

Ask the court to grant you an extra peremptory to remedy the loss of the one used on the biased juror. [*See Martinez-Salazar,* 528 U.S. at 317-18 (Souter, J., concurring) ("This case does not present the issue whether it is reversible error to refuse to afford a defendant a peremptory challenge beyond the maximum otherwise allowed, when he has used a peremptory challenge to cure an erroneous denial of a challenge for cause and when he shows that he would otherwise use his full complement of peremptory challenges for the noncurative purposes that are the focus of the peremptory right").]

Many jurisdictions permit you to raise the improper denial of a for-cause challenge even if you eliminated the juror with a peremptory, but only if you then exhaust your peremptory challenges and point to jurors you would have stricken had you not been forced to use a peremptory on the biased juror. [*See People v. Ervin,* 22 Cal.4th 48, 71, 91 Cal.Rptr.2d 623, 990 P.2d 506 (2000) (defendant's failure to exhaust peremptories barred claim that challenges for cause improperly denied); *Busby,* 894 So.2d at 92 (same).]

[§§20:83-20:89 Reserved]

E.   Peremptory Challenges

§20:90   Equal Protection Clause Prohibitions

The Equal Protection clause forbids both the prosecution [*Batson v. Kentucky,* 476 U.S. 79 (1986)] and the defense [*Georgia v. McCollum,* 505 U.S. 42 (1992)] from exercising peremptories on the basis of a juror's:
- Race.
- Gender. [*See J.E.B. v. Alabama ex rel. T.B.,* 511 U.S. 127 (1994).]
- Ethnicity. [*United States v. Somerstein,* 959 F.Supp. 592, 595 (E.D.N.Y. 1997) (interpreting "race" as including ancestry and ethnic origin).]
- Religion. [*Highler v. State,* 854 N.E.2d 823, 829-30 & n.2 (Ind. 2006) (surveying cases and finding that most extend *Batson* to challenges based on religious activity or affiliation); *State v. Fuller,* 182 N.J. 174, 862 A.2d 1130 (NJ 2004) (New Jersey prohibits striking jurors based solely on their religious affiliation).]

§20:91　Making an Equal Protection (*Batson*) Challenge

A challenge to the use of a peremptory challenge on Equal Protection grounds triggers a three-part inquiry according to *Batson*:

- A trial court must decide whether the party challenging the strike has made a prima facie showing that the circumstances give rise to an inference that a member of the venire was struck because of his or her race.
- If the party making the *Batson* challenge establishes a prima facie case, the trial court must require the non-moving party to proffer a race-neutral explanation for striking the potential juror.
- If the non-moving party proffers a race-neutral explanation, the trial court must determine whether the moving party has carried his or her burden of proving that the strike was motivated by purposeful discrimination.

[*Galarza v. Keane*, 252 F.3d 630, 636 (2d Cir. 2001).]

Making the prima facie case often depends on the sheer number of strikes aimed at minority group members. Disposition of the *Batson* claim frequently turns on whether the court deems the explanation pretextual rather than genuine. [For a compendium of *Batson* case law, *see* LaFave, et al., 5 *Criminal Procedure* §22.3(d) at nn.185-231.]

At the third stage of the *Batson* inquiry, you are entitled to test the prosecutor's explanations for their genuineness. Compare the answers and attitudes that the prosecutor cites as reason to strike black jurors to the answers and attitudes of white jurors. [*See Miller-El v. Dretke*, 545 U.S. 231 (2005) (illustration of how prosecutor's explanations can be dissected and prove to be pretextual); *People v. Payne*, 88 N.Y.2d 172, 185, 643 N.Y.S.2d 949, 666 N.E.2d 542 (1996) (affirming finding that defense counsel's explanations were pretextual because other jurors not struck gave similar answers and were equally unforthcoming in giving information).]

Most problematic are explanations based on impressions of the juror's demeanor and conduct. The observations must be specific to withstand the charge that they are pretextual. [*See People v. Ying*, 236 A.D. 2d 630, 654 N.Y.S. 2d 389 (N Y App. Div. 2d Dept. 1997) (finding failure to make eye contact justification pretextual because prosecutor asked only two meaningless questions of the juror and based her decision on a "feeling").] Demand specific evidence from the prosecution and be prepared to refute it.

While making a *Batson* claim does not require evidence that the prosecutor or his office had a practice or policy of striking minority-group jurors in cases other than yours, you can supplement your claim with such evidence. [*See Wilson v. Beard*, 426 F.3d 653 (3d Cir. 2005) (granting *Batson* claim in part based on after-discovered training videotape in which assistant district attorneys were taught to strike African-American jurors).]

§20:92　Defending an Equal Protection (*McCollum*) Challenge

If the peremptory was yours, be sure to articulate specific observations in its defense.

Whenever you have an inkling that the prosecutor will raise a *McCollum* claim to your use of peremptories, detail your reasons as specifically as possible and make them as peculiar to that juror and your defense as you can.

Ask that your explanations, if you must give them, be given *in camera* and *ex parte* because they may reveal defense strategy and confidential communications with your client. [*See McCollum*, 505 U.S. at 58 ("In the rare case in which the [defense] explanation for a challenge would entail confidential communications or reveal trial strategy, an *in camera* discussion can be arranged").]

§20:93　Jury Pool Fair Cross Section

Batson Equal Protection challenges are distinguished from challenges to the jurisdiction's method of assembling jury pools on the basis that the method violates the Sixth Amendment right to a jury drawn from a fair cross section of the community. [*See Duren v. Missouri*, 439 U.S. 357 (1979).]

You must raise a fair cross section claim before trial and must show that:

- The group alleged to be excluded is a distinctive group in the community.
- The representation of this group in venires from which juries are selected is not fair and reasonable in relation to the number of such persons in the community.
- This underrepresentation is due to systematic exclusion of the group during the jury-selection process.

[*Duren*, 439 U.S. at 364. *See* Amsterdam, *Trial Manual For The Defense Of Criminal Cases* §324 and *Defending A Federal Criminal Case* §§8.05, 8.06 for approaches to Sixth Amendment challenges.]

[§§20:94-20:99 Reserved]

III. BEGINNING THE TRIAL

§20:100 Closure of the Courtroom

The Sixth Amendment requires that trials be open to the public.

Before public access to a courtroom in a criminal case may be restricted:

- The party seeking to close the hearing must advance an overriding interest that is likely to be prejudiced.
- The closure must be no broader than necessary to protect that interest.
- The trial court must consider reasonable alternatives to closing the proceeding.
- The court must make findings adequate to support the closure.

[*Waller v. Georgia,* 467 U.S. 39, 48 (1984); *Presley v. Georgia,* 130 S.Ct. 721, 725 (2010) ("Trial courts are obligated to take every reasonable measure to accommodate public attendance at criminal trials"; the burden is on the trial court to find that there was no reasonable alternative to closure, not on the defense to propose alternatives).]

Prosecutors sometimes seek closure when an undercover officer testifies.

There must be a specific showing of danger to the officer. If your client's family members are in attendance, argue that the prosecution must show that there is a need to exclude on a person-by-person basis. [*See Sevencan v. Herbert,* 342 F.3d 69, 74-75 (2d Cir. 2003); *People v. Nieves,* 90 N.Y.2d 426, 660 N.Y.S.2d 858 (1997) (although exclusion might have proper as to other members of the public, it was not as to defendant's family; heightened standard for exclusion of family).]

Merely living in proximity to the officer's area of operation does not suffice. [*Vidal v. Williams,* 31 F.3d 67 (2d Cir. 1994) (exclusion improper where no evidence that defendant's parents were inclined to harm a police officer).]

Improper closure of the courtroom is a structural error, mandating reversal without the need to show any prejudice. [*Johnson v. United States,* 520 U.S. 461, 468-69 (1997); *United States v. Gonzalez-Lopez,* 548 U.S. 140, 148-49 (2006); *Judd v. Haley,* 250 F.3d 1308, 1315 (11th Cir. 2001) (once violation of right to public trial is shown, no prejudice needs to be shown; rather, "[t]he mere demonstration that his right to a public trial was violated entitles [him] to relief"). Some courts attempt to avoid this harsh result by conducting what they call a "triviality analysis," in which they emphasize the brief duration of enclosure, the limitation of the exclusion to only certain individuals (typically the defendant's family or friends), and perhaps the inadvertent nature of the closure. [*E.g., United States v. Perry,* 479 F.3d 885 (D.C. Cir. 2007).] The United States Supreme Court has never approved such a limitation of the right to public trial. One method to avoid a finding of triviality is to object vigorously. [*See United States v. Greene,* 2011 U.S. App. LEXIS 12332 (3d Cir. June 17, 2011) (non-precedential) (finding triviality in part because defense counsel did not bring the exclusion by court security personnel to the trial court's attention by objecting).]

§20:101 The Prosecution's Opening Statement

The prosecutor always opens first.

Take careful notes, primarily for two purposes:

- Note witnesses or areas of proof the prosecutor omits or downplays. Such statements may signal that a witness recanted or proved unreliable or that evidence failed to appear.
- Record any promises about what the proof will show so you can harp on whichever promises are broken in your closing argument.

A prosecution opening should not argue the law, should not express the prosecutor's personal opinion of guilt and should not be inflammatory. For these reasons, courts have reversed convictions where prosecutors displayed Powerpoint slides with the word "Guilty" superimposed on the defendant's picture. [*State v. Rivera,* 437 N.J. Super. 434, 99 A.3d 847 (NJ App. Div. 2014); *Watters v. State,* 313 P.3d 243 (Nev. Sup. Ct. 2014); *In re Glasmann,* 286 P.3d 673 (Wash. Sup. Ct. 2012).]

PRACTICE TIP:

Use a motion *in limine* to preclude prosecutor's reference to certain evidence. Even if the judge is inclined to rule against you and admit some bit of prosecution evidence, you might prevail upon the judge to withhold final ruling until he or she hears the context of the trial evidence. Since there has been no final decision, the prosecutor should not be permitted to discuss the evidence in opening on the chance that it might not be admitted.

§20:102 The Defense's Opening Statement

After the prosecution opens, the defense has an opportunity to make an opening statement.

You can reserve your opening until after the presentation of the prosecution's case and before you present your evidence, but you seldom should wait. The jury may have made up its mind by then, especially if it has not had the benefit of hearing your theory of defense.

An exception to this rule is where local voir dire practices enable you to preview your defense in questioning the prospective jurors.

Consider the following concepts when preparing your opening statement:

- *Tell a story*. Your narrative may present an alternative version of events, but often the story will be about the process that led to the prosecution and its unfairness. For example, even if your defense is reasonable doubt, attack some aspect of the prosecution's evidence and explain why it is unfair for the prosecution to ask the jury to convict on such evidence.
- *Plant your themes*. Begin to seed the catch-phrases that will characterize your defense. Informants "sell their testimony"; the prosecutor "holds the jailhouse key." Your client was "in the wrong place at the wrong time." The alleged victim "started the fight and my client ended it, so the complainant ran to the police."
- *Eliminate explanations about the trial process*. Do not tell the jury that what you say is not evidence. If you say this, why should they listen?
- *Make explicit concessions with great caution*. Conceding the indisputable may start the jury thinking that you are helpful, reasonable and trustworthy and that there really might be something to the defense. However, the prosecution can use your concessions as your client's admissions, both for this trial and any retrial. [*United States v. McKeon*, 738 F.2d 26 (2d Cir. 1984).] Miserly pre-trial discovery and the prosecutor's restrictive view of his *Brady* obligations may prevent you from foreseeing areas where the prosecution's evidence might fail. Better to focus your opening on the points you will contest and omit mention of points you must concede rather than make an explicit concession.
- *Be brief*. You should be able to deliver your opening without notes. The opening is the time to introduce themes, the theory of your defense and make an impression of confidence in your case. Speaking to the jurors face-to-face, without notes or a podium separating you, shows confidence and builds rapport. You are conversing with them, not preaching to them.
- *Humanize your client*. Always call your client by name (not "the defendant") and mention the facts that might engender sympathy and respect. Discuss his job and the good he has done. Point out his wife and mother. If he has never been arrested before, if he rose from poor roots, say it.
- *Rarely should you promise that your client will testify*. The defendant's testimony is the main event at any trial. Promise it, and the jury will expect it. You will pay if you dash those expectations.
- *Argue*. The textbook rule is that an opening should not be argument, but a preview of the evidence. Ignore this rule as much as you can. Model your opening as an abbreviated version of your closing argument. Use a quiet voice and matter-of-fact presentation to gain leeway–do not raise your voice or use many adjectives. Save the stories and rhetorical flourishes for closing. Speak softly but firmly and confidently, without excessive gestures. If objections are sustained, preface your remarks with, "The evidence will show that..." or "We/I will introduce evidence showing that..."
- *End positively*. State at the end of your opening that the evidence will not prove the prosecution's case and that the only fair verdict will be not guilty.

[§§20:103-20:109 Reserved]

IV. THE PROSECUTION CASE

A. Objections

§20:110 Object Immediately

Object immediately to improper questions or questions that are likely to elicit improper answers. Do this for two reasons:
- To preserve the issue for appeal.

- To prevent the jury from hearing the objectionable answer.

This usually means objecting after prosecutor ends his question but before the witness answers. Sometimes, though, you may need to interrupt before the prosecutor finishes his question. While many judges consider it bad form to interrupt a questioner, you may need to object if the question clearly suggests to the jury the objectionable information.

Likewise, you may need to interrupt a witness mid-answer when he wanders into improper areas in response to an otherwise proper question. Often, witnesses will speak of "we" or "they" when answering; use of such pronouns may enable the witness to testify to actions of which he does not have personal knowledge, or, worse, to attribute to your client actions that other defendants took. Consider interrupting as soon as you hear the offense pronoun: "I object to 'they'; the witness should specify who exited the car."

At times it may be advisable to object to a question early to prevent the witness from volunteering the objectionable information before the next question. This arises when a foundational question is technically proper, but it may elicit more than a "yes" or "no" answer. A prime example is the question, "Did you speak with anyone?" The witness often will launch into the conversation itself, which probably is inadmissible hearsay, rather than limit himself to identifying the person with whom he conversed and awaiting the next question.

PRACTICE TIP:

Consider foregoing objections to questions, particularly on direct examination, that are improper in form but easily corrected: leading questions, vague or confusing questions, questions without a proper foundation. Sometimes, form objections rattle a prosecutor; usually, however, the prosecutor will reframe the question or lay the foundation in such a way that the evidence is elicited in a more understandable and compelling manner.

§20:111   The Form for Objections

Most judges discourage "speaking" objections in favor of one that states only the evidentiary objection (*e.g.,* "hearsay," or "Rule 403").

Similarly, objections that sound like mini-summations annoy jurors, too.

However, try to state your objection in a manner that fully describes the legal basis and conveys to the jury that you are not being obstructionist, but that the prosecutor is acting unfairly. For example: "Objection, he is violating your pre-trial ruling" or "I object under Rule 403; he is trying to confuse the jury."

§20:112   Use Sidebars When Necessary

Judges and jurors loathe sidebars. Nevertheless, you should request one when necessary to avoid disclosing objectionable and unduly prejudicial information to the jury.

For example, the only previous encounter the witness may have had with your client might have been your client's inadmissible prior arrest or crime. Explaining in front of the jury why the prosecutor's question, "How did you know the defendant?" should not be allowed would disclose the very information you need to exclude.

PRACTICE TIP:

Use recesses and the time at the start and end of the trial day to anticipate objectionable material and get rulings or supplement the basis for objections you made earlier. Request that the prosecutor make proffers of the anticipated testimony at these junctures not only so that you can raise possible objections and either elicit a ruling in limine or alert the judge of an issue that might arise during the testimony, but so that you can be ready to object should the testimony head toward improper areas.

§20:113   Electronic Evidence

Courts have rejected efforts to create unique rules of authentication for electronic communications, such as e-mails and text messages. Instead, parties can authenticate such messages in the usual ways: by the witness or defendant's admission that he or she authored the records and by circumstantial evidence, such as facts contained within the message, that are unique to particular individuals.

Note, however, that the realities of electronic communications will create some twists and opportunities in the application of these rules. E-mails using a particular account can be sent from many different computers, and often more than one person uses the same phone. Therefore, "the mere fact that an e-mail bears a particular e-mail address is inadequate to authenticate the identity of the author; typically, courts demand additional evidence." [*Commonwealth v. Koch*, 39 A.3d 996, 1004 (Pa. Super. 2011) (reviewing decisions from several states and excluding the evidence) appeal granted, 44 A.3d 1147 (Pa. Sup. Ct. 2012).] Text messages are a little different, because the messages correspond to the phone associated with the number from or to which they transmitted. However, if there is evidence from witnesses or in the messages themselves that numerous people use that same phone, the fact that the messages came from the defendant's phone may not be enough to authenticate them as being the defendant's message. [*See Koch*, 39 A.3d at 1003, 1005 (excluding evidence because some of the text messages referred to the phone's owner in the third person and thus did not come from her).]

Often, the issue of authentication will overlap with the issue of admissibility under the hearsay rules. Unless it can be shown that the defendant authored or received the particular message, the message will not be admissible either as an admission or as notice to the defendant. [*Koch*, 39 A.3d at 1006.]

The absence of electronic evidence can create authentication problems that otherwise would not exist. In *United States v. Cross*, the prosecution cited an informant's identification of the defendant in a photo array as part of the probable cause for the defendant's arrest. The prosecution produced the array for the first time in the middle of a suppression hearing, and the police offered an implausible explanation for its tardy discovery and production. The photo array had been created using Microsoft Word. In finding that the photo-array identification never happened and that there was no probable cause, the court relied in part on the prosecution's failure to produce the array's electronic metadata, which would have contained the creation and last modified dates for the document. [*United States v. Cross*, 2009 U.S. Dist. LEXIS 92133, 2009 WL 3233267 (E.D.N.Y. Oct. 2, 2009).]

[§§20:114-20:119 Reserved]

B.   The Hearsay/Relevance Argument

§20:120   The *Crawford* and *Davis* Analysis

The introduction of hearsay evidence deprives the defense of its principal weapon, cross-examination of the declarant.

While the hearsay rules and their exceptions are familiar to all trial attorneys, in the last several years, the United States Supreme Court has revitalized the constitutional aspect of the prohibition against hearsay in two decisions:

- *Crawford v. Washington*, 541 U.S. 36 (2004).
- *Davis v. Washington*, 126 S. Ct. 2266 (2006).

Crawford overruled *Ohio v. Roberts*, 448 U.S. 56 (1980), which had held that to pass Confrontation Clause muster, the admissibility of hearsay evidence must be grounded in a firmly rooted hearsay exception or bear particularized guarantees of trustworthiness.

The *Crawford* Court discarded the "firmly rooted" and reliability tests and, in their place, erected a rule against admitting for its truth any "testimonial" statements unless the declarant was available for cross-examination. [*Crawford*, 541 U.S. at 53-54.]

Davis then provided the following partial definition of "testimonial":

> Without attempting to produce an exhaustive classification of all conceivable statements—or even all conceivable statements in response to police interrogation—as either testimonial or nontestimonial, it suffices to decide the present cases to hold as follows: Statements are nontestimonial when made in the course of police interrogation under circumstances objectively indicating that the primary purpose of the interrogation is to enable police assistance to meet an ongoing emergency. They are testimonial when the circumstances objectively indicate that there is no such ongoing emergency, and that the primary purpose of the interrogation is to establish or prove past events potentially relevant to later criminal prosecution.

[*Davis*, 126 S.Ct. at 2273-74.]

The primary purpose test is an objective one which looks to the "circumstances of an encounter and the statement and actions of the parties to it." [*Michigan v. Bryant*, 131 S.Ct. 1143, 1156 (2011).] Neither the interrogator's nor the declarant's intent controls; the inquiry aims to ascertain the primary purpose of the interrogation as a whole. [*Bryant*, 131 S.Ct. at 1161-62.]

Applying that test to the two cases decided within the opinion, the *Davis* Court ruled that statements made in a 911 call with the primary purpose of enabling the police to respond to and meet an ongoing emergency were nontestimonial and admissible, while statements about past events made to police responding to the scene after any emergency or threat had dissipated were testimonial and barred by the Confrontation Clause.

Crawford and *Davis* do not bar all hearsay. Being based on a historical analysis, *Crawford* does not affect those hearsay exceptions accepted by the Founders, such as the business records rule and the exception for coconspirator statements. [*Crawford*, 541 U.S. at 56.] Further, "when the declarant appears for cross-examination at trial, the Confrontation Clause places no constraints at all on the use of his prior testimonial statements." [*Crawford*, 541 U.S. at 59 n.9.]

Although *Crawford* and *Davis* involved statements to law enforcement, the Confrontation Clause applies to statements made to private individuals and even to statements volunteered or memorialized absent any questioning. [*Melendez-Diaz v. Massachusetts*, 557 U.S. 307 (2009); *see Davis*, 126 S.Ct. at 2274 n.1 (suggesting that volunteered statements, even letters to private parties, might be testimonial if the intent was to memorialize past events for a criminal prosecution); Christopher B. Mueller & Laird C. Kirkpatrick, *Federal Evidence* §8:27 (3d ed. 2007) (while most courts have ruled that statements to friends and family are nontestimonial, in some circumstances, where the declarant expects the statements to initiate or aid a criminal investigation, such statements have been deemed testimonial and subject to the Confrontation Clause).]

While some courts had held that the *Roberts* test still applied to nontestimonial hearsay [*E.g., United States v. Thomas*, 453 F.3d 838, 844 & n.2 (7th Cir. 2006); *United States v. Hinton*, 423 F.3d 355, 358 n.1 (3d Cir. 2005) ("The admission of non-testimonial hearsay is still governed by *Roberts*")], that view is being abandoned in light of the Supreme Court's statements that the Confrontation Clause has no room for a *Roberts* reliability analysis. [*See Whorton v. Bockting*, 127 S.Ct. 1173, 1183 (2007) (referring to "*Crawford's* elimination of Confrontation Clause protection against the admission of unreliable out-of-court nontestimonial statements. Under *Roberts*, an out-of-court nontestimonial statement not subject to prior cross-examination could not be admitted without a judicial determination regarding reliability. Under *Crawford*, on the other hand, the Confrontation Clause has no application to such statements and therefore permits their admission even if they lack indicia of reliability"); *United States v. Berrios*, 676 F.3d 118, 125-26 (3d Cir. 2012); *United States v. Feliz*, 467 F.3d 227, 231 (2d Cir. 2006).]

States courts are free to apply the *Roberts* test or an equivalent as a matter of state law where *Davis/Crawford* do not apply. [*See State v. Rodriguez*, 295 Wisc.2d 801, 722 N.W.2d 136, 148 (Wis. App. 2006) (applying *Roberts* as a matter of state law).] In addition, "the Due Process Clauses of the Fifth and Fourteenth Amendments may constitute a further bar to admission of, for example, unreliable evidence." [*Michigan v. Bryant*, 131 S.Ct. at 1162 n.13.]

While *Crawford's* implications are being sorted out, you should add a Confrontation Clause citation wherever plausible to your hearsay objections.

§20:121   Background of the Investigation

Prosecutors often will ask a police witness to describe what an eyewitness or informant told him on the theory that it explains why the officer did what he did.

Admission of the informant's statements for their truth violates both the hearsay rule [*see United States v. Silva*, 380 F.3d 101 (7th Cir. 2004)] and the Confrontation Clause of the Sixth Amendment [*see United States v. Cromer*, 389 F.3d 662 (6th Cir. 2004) (informant's statements are testimonial under the *Crawford* test)]. Watch out for background testimony that implicitly contains hearsay. [*Wheeler v. State*, 36 A.3d 310 (Del. 2012) (detective's testimony that after speaking with three witnesses who were unavailable to testify at trial he had no reason to believe that any suspect other than defendant was involved in shooting, was inadmissible indirect hearsay, and its admission also violated the Confrontation Clause); *United States v. Meises*, 645 F.3d 5, 22 (1st Cir. 2011) (testimony by police officer that targets of the investigation changed after he spoke with co-conspirator violated defendant's rights under the Confrontation Clause).]

Background or overview testimony, especially when it comes from the case agent or detective, also may violate the limits on opinion testimony. [*See* §6:71, *supra*.]

Unless you suggest in your cross or opening statement that the police improperly targeted your client for investigation, the officers' reasons and state of mind are irrelevant. [*See United States v. Reyes*, 18 F.3d 65 (2d Cir. 1994).]

Include a Rule 403 argument in your objection. That is, even if instructed to consider the evidence only to explain the officer's actions, not for the truth of the matter asserted, the jury is likely to accept the evidence for its truth. [*Reyes*, 18 F.3d at 70 (excluding evidence on FRE 403 grounds).]

Background of the investigation evidence also may include evidence of the defendant's uncharged misconduct; for example, to explain why the police followed or stopped the defendant. [*E.g., People v. Resek*, 3 N.Y.3d 385, 821 N.E.2d 108 (2004) (in drug possession cases, error to admit evidence that the police arrested the defendant because they were responding to a report that he was driving a stolen car).] Object both under Rule 404(b) and 403 and their state equivalents. Where the evidence introduces the defendant's uncharged crimes, its prejudice is especially weighty in comparison to the often scant probative value it has in completing the narrative of the investigation. You may further diminish that probative value by offering to stipulate to the proposition for which the evidence is offered, such as a stipulation that police stop was lawful. [*E.g., Resek,* 3 N.Y.3d at 390 (suggesting the same); *but see People v. Morris,* 2013 NY Slip. 06633 (NYCA October 15, 2013) (rejecting such a stipulation where it did not cover all the uses to which the uncharged misconduct evidence would be put).]

If the judge admits the evidence for a limited explanatory purpose, listen closely to the prosecutor's summation and be ready to renew your objection, for the prosecutor is sure to use the evidence as substantive evidence of guilt. [*See Silva,* 380 F.3d at 1020 (noting such misuse of the evidence); *United States v. Lopez,* 340 F.3d 169, 175-76 (3d Cir. 2003) (same; "The use of such statements for that purpose [background] had been subject to widespread abuse. ... If the hearsay rule is to have any force, ... courts cannot accept without scrutiny an offering party's representation that an out-of-court statement is being introduced for a material non-hearsay purpose").]

§20:122　Victim State of Mind

The prosecution often will attempt to introduce hearsay to the effect that the victim stated that the defendant threatened her in the past and will attempt to evade the hearsay rule with the argument that it is admissible to show the victim's state of mind.

Whether the victim feared the defendant is usually irrelevant. [*E.g., Commonwealth v. Green,* 2013 PA Super 249 (Pa. Super. Ct. 2013) (murder victim's statement that she was afraid of defendant and needed to get away from him was hearsay; although it did fit under the state of mind exception, it was inadmissible because the victim's state of mind was not relevant).]

The only times when such evidence might be relevant are to issues such as explaining why the victim retracted some of her statements on the witness stand or why she took certain actions, such as why she did not go to the police. [*E.g., Commonwealth v. Luster,* 2013 PA Super 204 (Pa. Super. Ct. 2013) (murder victim's statement in phone call that defendant trying to kill her admissible under state of mind exception to explain why she left his car; second call to same effect admissible as well, this time as an excited utterance).]

Generally, the only relevant evidence is whether the defendant in fact threatened the victim with harm, or did harm the victim, in the past.

The evidence has relevance only if it is offered to prove the truth of the matter asserted (i.e., that the defendant did threaten or harm the victim) so it should be excluded. [*See, e.g., Commonwealth v. Levanduski,* 2006 PA Super 204 (Pa. Super. Ct. 2006) (letter written by homicide victim about his suspicions that defendant, who was his wife, and her paramour might kill him was inadmissible hearsay; review of relevance and hearsay issues arising with victim state of mind evidence).]

§20:123　Expert Testimony

Many experts, especially forensic psychiatrists, recite at length statements from nontestifying witnesses as the bases for their opinions.

Since the statements have no relevance, either to the jury or the expert, unless they are true, the recitations should be barred under the Confrontation Clause. [*See People v. Goldstein,* 6 N.Y.3d 119, 843 N.E.2d 727, 810 N.Y.S.2d 100 (2005) (conviction reversed where prosecution psychiatrist testified to several episodes evidencing defendant's hostility to women, which were described to psychiatrist by nontestifying witnesses).]

§20:124　Test Results

In *Melendez-Diaz v. Massachusetts,* 557 U.S. 307 (2009), the Supreme Court held that the Confrontation Clause makes no exception for laboratory analysis and other scientific tests: if the analysis is "made under circumstances which would lead an objective witness reasonably to believe that the statement would be available for use at a later trial," then the witness who performed the test or analysis must testify or the evidence will be excluded. [*Melendez-Diaz v. Massachusetts,* Slip op at 5-6 (quoting *Crawford,* 541 U.S. at 52).] *Melendez-Diaz* ruled inadmissible a certificate of analysis offered to prove that seized substances were cocaine, a procedure authorized by Massachusetts statute, but the practice it forbids has been common with many forensic tests, such as chain of custody affidavits [*City of Las Vegas v. Walsh,* 121 Nev. 899, 124 P.3d 203, 207-08 (Nev. 2005) (nurse's affidavit pursuant to statute establishing chain of custody for blood sample testimonial)], autopsy reports [*Rollins v. State*, 392 Md. 455, 489, 897 A.2d 821, 841 (2006) (admitting routine and descriptive findings about the decedent's physical condition but excluding contested conclusions or opinions about cause and manner of death)], breathalyzer reports [*See Commonwealth v. Walther*, 189 S.W.3d 570, 575 (Ky. 2006) (exempted breathalyzer performance, maintenance and calibration records from *Crawford*)], and DNA tests [*See, e.g., People v. Geier*, 41 Cal.4th 555, 61 Cal.Rptr.3d 580 (Cal. 2007) (noting split among courts but holding that DNA test results were not testimonial and hence not subject to *Crawford*); *compare People v. John*, 27 N.Y.3d 294, 52 N.E.3d 1114 (2016) (DNA tests are testimonial, and Confrontation Clause is violated when the results are introduced by an analyst who did not witness, perform, or supervise the analysis, but also holding that not all the involved analysts must testify; surveying similar decisions from other jurisdictions)]. The *Melendez-Diaz* opinion's rejection of reliability and practicality justifications for the admission of such tests exposes them all to challenge. [*See* 557 U.S. at 319 n.6 ("We would reach the same conclusion if all analysts always possessed the scientific acumen of Mme. Curie and the veracity of Mother Theresa.").] Further, the prosecution may not circumvent the Confrontation Clause's demands by having one analyst testify as to the testimonial statements of others. [*Melendez-Diaz*, 557 U.S. at 332 (Kennedy, J., dissenting).]

The Court approved "notice and demand" statutes and rules which require the defense to give pretrial notice that it wants the analyst produced at trial, but expressed skepticism about the validity of statutes which switch the burden to the defense to show good cause for the analyst's presence. [557 U.S. at 326-27] Defense counsel should insist on the analyst's presence, absent the danger that he will introduce damaging testimony that will not be heard otherwise (a remote danger in the case of analysts who know nothing about the crime's particulars). The analyst might have left his employment and the prosecution might not be able to produce him; further, as the majority opinion in *Melendez-Diaz* recites, forensic analysis has proven to be incompetent, mistaken and outright fraudulent. [557 U.S. at 318-19, describing the findings in National Research Council of the National Academies, Strengthening Forensic Science in the United States: A Path Forward (2009); *see also* Nick Bunkley, "Detroit Police Lab Is Closed After Audit Finds Serious Errors in Many Cases," *New York Times*, September 25, 2008).]

You should be prepared for prosecution arguments that tests, or at least certain steps in the analysis, were not prepared in anticipation of litigation and therefore do not fall within the *Crawford-Davis* definition of testimonial statements subject to the Confrontation Clause. [*See Melendez-Diaz*, 557 U.S. at 311 n.1 ("Documents prepared in the regular course of equipment maintenance may well qualify as nontestimonial records"); Carolyn Zabrycki, Comment, Toward a Definition of "Testimonial"; How Autopsy Reports Do Not Embody the Qualities of a Testimonial Statement, 96 Cal. L.Rev. 1093, 1124-26 (2008) (many autopsies are performed when no crime is suspected); Joe Bourne, Prosecutorial Use of Forensic Science at Trial: When Is a Lab Report Testimonial?, 93 Minn. L. Rev. 1058, 1087-88 (2009) (suggesting that courts must look at the particular circumstances under which an autopsy was performed to determine whether statements were testimonial: was foul play suspected? Had a suspect been identified?); *People v. Rawlins*, 10 N.Y.3d 136, 884 N.E.2d 1019 (2008) (pre-*Melendez-Diaz* decision holding that technicians' reports establishing DNA profile for sperm taken from a rape kit were not testimonial); *United States v. Feliz*, 467 F.3d 227 (2d Cir. 2006) (pre-*Melendez-Diaz* decision holding that autopsy reports are not testimonial and may be admitted without calling the author); *compare State v. Johnson*, 756 N.W.2d 883 (Minn. App. 2008) (holding that autopsy report was testimonial because any medical examiner preparing such a report would reasonably expect that it may later be used at trial; medical examiner could not testify to report he did not prepare).] Forensic analysts and examiners, who often derive a considerable portion of their income from prosecutors' offices, may strive to convince a Court that helping to prove a crime was the last thing on their minds as they performed their tests. Answer this with inquiry about and emphasis on the objective circumstances, for *Davis* holds that the standard for assessing a statement's testimonial nature is an objective one: do "circumstances objectively indicate . . . that the primary purpose of the interrogation is to establish or prove past events potentially relevant to later criminal prosecution?" [*Davis*, 547 U.S. 813, 822 (2006).]

[§§20:125-20:129 Reserved]

C. Prior Bad Acts

§20:130 Admission Leads to a Conviction

Admission of evidence that your client has committed similar crimes in the past almost guarantees a conviction.

Such evidence is inadmissible to show propensity to commit the crime, but might be admitted for other purposes, so long as its prejudicial value does not outweigh its probative value. [*See* FRE 404(b).]

Some jurisdictions treat the rule as one of inclusion. [*United States v. Sriyuth,* 98 F.3d 739, 745 (3d Cir. 1996).] Others presume inadmissibility. [*People v. Resek,* 3 N.Y.3d 385, 390, 821 N.E.2d 108, 787 N.Y.S.2d 683 (2004).]

In either case, trial judges know that improper admission of prior bad acts is an error especially likely to result in reversal on appeal.

§20:131   Tactics to Avoid Admission

Always demand notice of prior bad acts and file a motion in limine regarding them.

Force the government to articulate specifically what the evidence proves besides the defendant's propensity. The government "must clearly articulate how that evidence fits into a chain of logical inferences, no link of which can be the inference that because the defendant committed drug offenses before, he therefore is more likely to have committed this one." [*United States v. Sampson,* 980 F.2d 883, 887 (3d Cir. 1992); *see also United States v. Smith,* 725 F.3d 340 (3d Cir. 2013) (in gun possession and assault case, error to admit evidence that defendant sold drugs on the street corner two years earlier to further argument that he drew a gun on undercover officers to protect his drug turf, not in self-defense; a necessary link in the admissibility argument was the assertion that having dealt drugs in the past, he likely was doing so again).]

You often will find propensity resides somewhere in the chain.

Argue as well that the jury is likely to consider the evidence for propensity or the defendant's bad character, both improper purposes, especially if the prior act was even more sordid than the crime on trial.

Finally, argue that proving the prior act will embroil the court in a trial within a trial. This argument works best where the prior act did not result in a conviction. However, even where there was a conviction, the certified record of conviction often does not show the underlying facts that prove intent or whatever proposition for which the prosecutor wants to use the evidence. The conviction might not include a finding on the facts; therefore, the prosecutor must call witnesses, and you are entitled to defend the allegations, just like another trial.

Form:
- **Form 20-1** Motion in Limine to Preclude Defendant's Other Bad Acts

§20:132   Prosecutorial Misconduct in the Presentation of Its Case

With disturbing frequency, prosecutors elicit evidence they know to be false. [*E.g., Dow v. Virga,* 729 F.3d 1041 (9th Cir. 2013) (detective testified that during a lineup, the defendant himself requested that each of the participants wear a bandage under his right eye at the location in which the defendant had a small scar, when the truth was that the defendant's attorney made that request; habeas granted on this issue).] If the witness testifies falsely, the prosecutor is obligated to correct it as soon as the false testimony appears. [*Napue v. Illinois,* 360 U.S. 264, 269 (1959).]

Identifying a *Napue* error during trial has two advantages that *Brady* errors do not. First, if the defendant knows of exculpatory information, there is no *Brady* violation. To the contrary, a *Napue* error occurs when the prosecutor presents evidence that is false, even when the defendant knows of the falsity. Second, *Napue* error is less likely to be found harmless. A *Napue* violation "results in the reversal of a conviction if the false testimony could in any reasonable likelihood have affected the judgment of the jury." [*Dow,* 729 F.3d at 1047 (quoting *Napue,* 360 U.S. at 271).]

[§§20:133-20:139 Reserved]

D.   Cross-Examination

1.   General Points

§20:140   Cross-Examination Is Part of the Defense

In many criminal cases, you must present your defense through cross-examination of the prosecution's witnesses.

Often, you are limited in the evidence you can present in your case by your client's or witnesses' other convictions or misconduct. The prosecution case, if believed and all pro-prosecution inferences are accepted, will convict your client. At the minimum, you must poke holes in it during its presentation.

Volumes have been written about cross-examination, and many practitioners find it a mysterious gift granted or withheld by providence. It is best approached by learning and hewing to a few rules. [*See* Larry S. Pozner & Roger J.Dodd,

Cross-Examination: Science & Techniques (2004) (providing a summary of cross-examination methods and systems). *See also* David Berg, *The Trial Lawyer* (2006); Ralph Adam Fine, *The How-to-Win Trial Manual* 195-231 (2005).]

Approach cross not as an end in itself, but as part of your theory of defense. The theory should guide your preparation and the on-the-spot decisions you make during trial.

For example, if a witness's trial testimony contradicts a sworn prior statement, but the trial testimony helps your defense and the prior statement undermines it, forego the impeachment.

§20:141 Goals

The general goals of cross-examination are to:
- Elicit favorable evidence.
- Have the witness acknowledge the limits of his harmful testimony.
- Give the jury reasons to disbelieve the witness.

§20:142 Tactics

The following rules should be practiced so that they become second nature:

Ask short simple questions–one fact per question.

You control the witness better by avoiding compound questions, omitting assumptions within your questions, and simplifying your language.

By building one simple question upon another you progress toward a goal, or at least make the jury think you are.

Simple questions are also easier to remember if you need to repeat the question or recall it for summation.

Use concrete language rather than subjective judgmental terms.

Terms such as "important" "good" or "need" invite the witness to quibble and explain, and the use of such words generally undermines your ability to control a witness.

There are instances in which the witness might look foolish to deny that a certain fact or action was "important" (*e.g.,* "Officer, your partner was bleeding to death. You would agree it was important to get him to the hospital? So you didn't notice...").

Hesitate to ask a question if there is a substantial risk that the answer might hurt your client.

Conventional wisdom is that you should never ask a question to which you do not know the answer. This does not strictly apply in criminal case for two reasons:
- The paucity of discovery will leave you in the dark about many areas.
- In many criminal cases, by the time direct is done, you are way behind and must take risks to rescue any chance of acquittal.

Take steps to minimize your risks:
- Set up questions at the preliminary and suppression hearings (*e.g.,* at a probable cause hearing it is relevant to ask if, in the course of the investigation, anyone ever mentioned your client as being involved in the conspiracy; this is a question you may want to repeat at trial if the answer is "no").
- Put the specific question in a *Brady* request. [See Chapter 14, Discovery.]
- Ask the prosecutor informally.
- Ask your client (*e.g.,* "Did this witness ever see you before? Have you talked to her since you were arrested?").

Ultimately, however, you may be forced to rely on the calculation that if the witness was not asked the question on direct (assuming it would be a proper question on direct; some, such as about the defendant's prior uncharged crimes or absence of them, would not be), the answer probably helps you more than the prosecutor. [*See, e.g.,* Berg, *The Trial Lawyer* at 177-92.]

Do not read or memorize your questions.

You should know your case and the points you want to make with the witness well enough that an outline, a list of key points or a timeline should suffice to guide you.

In preparing to cross, talk through your questions–with an associate, friend, or yourself–and possible answers and your follow-up questions.

Reading or memorizing questions interferes with listening and responding to the witness. The witness may give good answers that you can build upon or might attempt to avoid the question in a way that invites questions which will highlight his evasiveness. You will miss these opportunities if you are reading or searching your memory for the next words in your memorized script.

An exception is when you intend to impeach a witness with a prior inconsistent statement. You should write down in your outline the precise prior statement so that you do not misstate the witness's words, thereby inviting objections and evasion.

Be polite.

Courtesy empowers.

Do not argue with the witness, cut him off mid-sentence, yell, bully, or demand yes or no answers. The judge will intervene on the witness's side.

Make sure the witness answers your question, and control the witness (without bullying him).

Your purpose is not to prove to everyone your dominance and superiority, but to guarantee that the witness helps rather than hurts your case.

Prosecution witnesses have two goals on their agenda: making themselves look good and helping to convict your client. Allowed too much freedom, they will turn questions to those purposes. [*See* §20:151.]

[§§20:143-20:149 Reserved]

2. The Difficult Witness

§20:150 Be Persistent

Even when your questions are short, simple and leading, some difficult witnesses (victims, police officers, experts) still may avoid answering questions.

Do not accept this; get your answer.

By persisting in your question, you show the difficult witness for what he is: someone whose goal in testifying is not to play by the rules and tell the truth, but to sell his side of the case.

§20:151 Tactics

The law bestows a powerful tool for controlling witnesses: the witness must answer the question you asked, not the one he wishes were asked. Use the following techniques to ensure you maintain control and show the difficult witness for the cheat that he is:

Repeat the question word for word.

Where the witness has been particularly recalcitrant, you might preface the repetition with, "My question was..." or write out the question on an easel.

Repeat the question, this time framed as a negative.

Q: The light was green?

A: I just couldn't believe how fast your client was driving, etc.

Q: Are you telling us that my client did **not** have a green light?

Repeat the question, this time with the answer the witness is trying to evade.

"So the answer to my question is, 'No, your report nowhere states that Mr. Farrell said he threw the gun under the car'?"

Apologize for the misunderstanding, and restate the question.

"I am sorry, you seem to have misunderstood my question. My question was... Do you understand that question? And the answer is...?"

A more severe form of this is simply to ask, "Did you understand my last question?" The witness's expression will make clear that he has no idea what the question was. Repeat it. He will answer sheepishly. No one likes to look stupid. If he says, "Yes," ask him to answer the question or repeat it. He won't be able to do either, meaning that the "Yes" was dishonest.

When the witness is done, point out that he answered a different question, one of his own creation.
"I didn't ask you [your opinion about the informant or whatever else the witness is addressing]. ... My question was..."

Use more drastic methods.
If the witness persists in nonresponsiveness, you can experiment with more drastic methods:
- Write out the question, and go word by word through it, asking the witness which words he does not understand.
- Let the witness finish his speech, and then say, "Are you finished? Do you have anything else to add? Now can you answer my question, please?"
- Put up a hand as if to say, "Halt."

CAUTION:

Do not object and seek the judge's help.

At best, the judge will tell you to rephrase the question. At worst, the judge will admonish you to let the witness finish his answer.

Instead, resort to the questioning tactics described above. The judge might instruct the witness sua sponte to answer the question. This you welcome because it indicates to the jury that the witness is so evasive that the judge must step in even without invitation.

[§§20:152-20:159 Reserved]

3. Impeachment

§20:160 General Points

Often, your cross will need to render a witness less believable, either generally or on a particular point.
There are five acceptable methods of attacking a witness's credibility:
- Attacking the witness's general character for truthfulness.
- Showing that, prior to trial, the witness has made statements inconsistent with his testimony.
- Showing that the witness is biased.
- Showing that the witness has an impaired capacity to perceive, recall, or relate the event about which he is testifying.
- Contradicting the substance of the witness's testimony.

[*United States v. Lindemann*, 85 F.3d 1232, 1243 (7th Cir. 1996). *See also* Packel & Poulin, *Pennsylvania Evidence* §607-1 (2nd ed. 1999).]

Most jurisdictions permit any party, including the party calling a witness, to impeach the witness. [FRE 607; *United States v. Universal Rehabilitation Services, Inc.*, 205 F.3d 657 (3rd Cir. 2000) (en banc); *Commonwealth v. Kimbell*, 759 A.2d 1273 (Pa. 2000).]

This is the reasoning you use to justify drawing the sting of your own witness's prior convictions or inconsistent statements on direct. [Richard T. Farrell, *Prince, Richardson on Evidence* §6-421 (11th ed. & 2006 Supp.).]

§20:161 Prior Inconsistent Statements

Showing that the witness told a different story on a prior occasion or that he omitted incriminating facts to which he now attests is a standard form of impeachment.

Ideally, you want to impeach with a statement that exculpates where the testimony inculpates; that was made thoughtfully and close to the events described; and that was preserved either by a stenographer or recording.

Follow these steps in a prior inconsistent statement impeachment:
- Commit the witness to the testimony which you want to impeach, using language that characterizes it as the story of the day.
  Example:
  "Your testimony here today is that the man who robbed you had a full beard?"
- Emphasize the witness's certainty to spread the impact of the impeachment.
  Example:
  "You are as certain that the man had a beard as you are about the rest of your testimony?"

- Direct the witness to the time, place, and circumstances of the prior statement. Your purpose is twofold. First, you insinuate to the witness that you know all about the prior statement, and he cannot wiggle away from it. Second, assuming the prior statement helps your case, you build up its accuracy.
  Example:
  "The police came to your store within ten minutes of when the robber fled?"
  "His face was fresh in your mind?"
  "You wanted the police to find this guy."
  "You gave Officer Jones as full and accurate a description of him as you could."
  "You wanted it to be dead-on right so that Officer Jones would recognize this guy when he saw him?"
  "And you told Officer Jones that the robber had a full beard?"

- Draw out the impeachment, breaking it into as many short questions as possible. This creates anticipation in both the jury and the witness. The jury will think it is a matter of importance, and the witness, knowing what is to come, might begin to equivocate and evade. This is what you want, because a prior inconsistent statement cross is a safe one. No matter what the witness says, eventually he must admit the questions you ask. His failure to do so or his attempts to explain himself will only make him look dishonest.

§20:162   Introducing the Prior Statement

If the witness admits that he made the prior statement, the impeachment ends. However, if he denies or does not remember making it, introduce extrinsic evidence of the statement itself. [*Commonwealth v. Scarfo*, 416 Pa. Super. 329, 394, 611 A.2d 242, 274 (Pa. Super. 1992) (extrinsic evidence of prior inconsistent statement admissible if the witness either denies or forgets making the prior statement).]

If the witness wrote the statement, have him authenticate the writing.

If it was prior testimony, ask your opponent to stipulate that the questions and answers you read accurately reflect the prior testimony given on the prior occasion.

Impeachment with an oral statement requires that you call the person to whom the witness made the statement, unless you can persuade the witness to accept it, perhaps by refreshing his recollection with a written report memorializing the statement. [*See* §20:164.]

Most jurisdictions have abandoned the so-called Rule in the Queen's Case, which required that before you even asked a witness about a written prior statement, he be shown it. [*See* FRE 613, Advisory Committee Notes.]

Many courts, however, require that you confront the witness with a prior written or oral inconsistent statement before you may introduce extrinsic evidence of it. [*E.g., United States v. Sutton*, 41 F.3d 1257, 1260 (8th Cir. 1994); Pa. R. Evid. 613(b)(1).]

Other courts merely require that the witness have the opportunity to explain the statement at *some* time during the trial, which can be satisfied by the ability of the party calling the witness to recall him on rebuttal. [*See United States v. McCall*, 85 F.3d 1193, 1196-96 (6th Cir. 1996).]

However, you run the risk that if the witness becomes unavailable before you offer the extrinsic evidence, it cannot be admitted. [*See Wammock v. Celotex Corp.*, 793 F.3d 1518, 1522-24 (11th Cir. 1996) (suggesting that the questioner can shift the risk of the witness's unavailability to the witness's proponent by advising counsel that he will introduce the extrinsic evidence in the questioner's case).]

In any event, you usually want to confront the witness on the stand so that you can emphasize the inconsistency and give the witness the opportunity to equivocate about it, thereby further undermining his own credibility.

§20:163   Prior Consistent Statements

Prosecutors take the position that if you impeach the witness with one prior statement, you have opened the door to the admission on redirect of all the other consistent statements the witness may have made at the same time.

Resist the "door opening" assertion with the argument that only statements that are necessary to explain fairly the inconsistent statement should be admitted. [*See United States v. Collicott*, 92 F.3d 973, 980-82 (9th Cir. 1996) (explaining limits of the door-opening rationale).]

Argue to the judge that the prosecution must meet the stringent requirements for the admission of a prior consistent statement. That is, it must both:

- Rebut the improper influence or motive or other reason that allegedly gave rise to the recent fabrication.
- Have been uttered before the improper influence or motive existed.

[*Tome v. United States*, 513 U.S. 150 (1995).]

Impeachment with a prior inconsistent statement does not give rise to an inference of improper influence or motive. It merely suggests that the witness is not to be trusted because he told different stories on different occasions. [*See United States v. Bishop*, 264 F.3d 535, 548 (5th Cir. 2001) ("Rule 801(d)(1)(B) cannot be construed to allow the admission of what would otherwise be hearsay every time a law enforcement officer's credibility or memory is challenged; otherwise, cross-examination would always transform hearsay notes into admissible evidence").]

§20:164   Refreshing Recollection

If the witness's prior inconsistent statement lies in a report authored by another person, such as a police report of what an eyewitness said, you might have to call the police officer to admit the extrinsic evidence of the statement.

To avoid this, attempt to have the witness adopt the statement by refreshing his recollection with it. Memory may be refreshed with writings authored by a person other than the witness and even by nonwritings. [*See generally* 4 *Weinstein's Federal Evidence* §612.03[3] (2nd ed. 2000). Pa. R. Evid. 612, Comment.]

Often, the witness will lead the way into this technique by expressing his disagreement with the prior statement in words such as, "I don't remember saying the guy had a beard." If he does not give you this lead, repeat the answer, rephrased as a statement about memory.

EXAMPLE:

"I didn't say the guy had a beard."

"So you don't remember telling Officer Jones that the robber had a beard?"

"No."

Let me show you Officer Jones' report from that night. Take a look at what I have marked as Defense Exhibit M and read the third paragraph to yourself. Does that refresh your recollection about what you told Officer Jones?" (If the judge is a stickler for the proper foundation, you first must ask, "Would seeing Officer Jones' report of what you told him that night refresh your recollection about whether you told him that the guy had a beard?")

"I guess I told him the guy had a beard."

Note: Even if the witness still refuses to admit that he remembers or made the prior statement, by this point, the jury knows that Officer Jones' report says the witness said, "Beard."

§20:165   Prior Bad Acts and Criminal Convictions

FRE 609 or its state equivalent allows you to impeach a witness with the fact that he had been convicted of a felony or a crime showing dishonesty.

Prosecutors usually elicit the fact of convictions during the direct testimony. Your aim is to delve into the sordid facts underlying the conviction. The details give the jury a better sense of the witness's character and dishonesty and also generate more questions likely to cause the witness to squirm. He probably has been well-prepared to admit his conviction, but often will deny or minimize questions about the bad deeds themselves.

Some judges forbid inquiry into the underlying facts on the reasoning that Rule 609 permits admission only of the fact of conviction. This is an accurate reading of Rule 609, but cite the judge instead to the rule dealing with acts of dishonesty, whether charged or not, FRE 608. [*See Elcock v. Kmart Corporation*, 233 F.3d 734 (3rd Cir. 2000) (trial court should have permitted the defense to inquire into how much money the witness embezzled and over how long a time period, rather than confining the cross to the fact that the witness had been convicted of embezzlement); *United States v. Hurst*, 951 F.2d 1490, 1500-01 (6th Cir. 1991) (permitting cross to show that witness's obstruction of justice conviction was for attempting to bribe a police officer to file a false report; acknowledges that the statutory name of the offense "is rarely informative and often misinformative" as to the nature of the conduct.)]

[§§20:166-20:169 Reserved]

4. Deals With the Prosecution

§20:170 Emphasize the Prosecutor's Role

Many witnesses will have made a written deal either for immunity or a plea to lesser charges or the promise of some good word from the prosecutor at sentencing.

Defendants have a Sixth Amendment right to inquire into the meaning of the agreement to establish the witness's incentive to earn a reduction by satisfying the prosecution. [*United States v. Schoenberg*, 396 F.3d 1036 (9th Cir. 2005) (trial judge erred by precluding defense questions that under the cooperation agreement, the prosecutor, not the judge or jury, determined the truth of the witness's testimony).]

In as much detail as you can, elicit the severity and possible penalties on any pending charges the witness faces and expectations of leniency that the witness may harbor, whether the prosecutor explicitly promised leniency or the witness just hopes for it.

Emphasize that the prosecutor is the one who controls how much leniency the witness can expect. Establish:

- The maximum and, if there is one, the mandatory minimum prison sentence the witness faces on his guilty plea. If the prosecutor agreed to accept a plea to less than all the charges in the indictment, establish the sentences carried by the charges that the prosecutor agreed to dismiss.
- The probable sentencing guideline range, if there is one.
- That the witness has a written agreement with the same prosecutor who brought the charges against the defendant.
- That the defendant and prosecutor signed the agreement, not the judge, not the jury.
- That under the agreement, only the prosecutor can ask for a reduced sentence.
- *[If applicable]* If the prosecutor does not ask for a reduced sentence, the witness must get a mandatory minimum sentence of so many years.
- That the judge cannot give any less than the mandatory minimum unless the prosecutor asks.
- That whether to request a sentence reduction and a charge dismissal is in the prosecutor's sole discretion; the prosecutor decides, not the judge, and not the jury.
- That the agreement says that the witness must give full and truthful testimony, but under the agreement, the prosecutor judges if the testimony is full and truthful.
- That the prosecutor, and only the prosecutor, decides whether the witness has fulfilled his obligations under the agreement and whether the witness gets what was promised.

§20:171 Focus on the Witness's Understanding of the Deal

Most courts will permit the prosecution to elicit on direct examination the fact of an agreement and to introduce a written plea agreement on direct, whether or not the defense intends to attack the witness's credibility. [*United States v. Universal Rehabilitation Services, Inc.*, 205 F.3d 657 (3rd Cir. 2000) (en banc) (prosecutor permitted to elicit terms of grant of immunity on witness's direct).]

Some courts, however, limit the prosecutor to reading it and do not permit the jury to have the agreement during deliberations, unless the defense introduced it. [*Commonwealth v. Bricker*, 525 Pa. 362, 380, 581 A.2d 147, 155-56 (1990).]

Your cross should focus on the witness's perceptions and expectations, not the prosecutor's explicit promises.

The witness knows that the prosecutor's sentencing recommendation carries great weight and that the prosecutor will condition that recommendation on hearing a version of events that helps convict your client. Whether imbued by the prosecutor, officers, his own lawyer or fellow inmates, the witness expects that if he delivers damning testimony, the prosecutor will do what he can to lessen the witness's sentence.

§20:172 Establish the Sentence the Witness Faces

Fear of any sentence can motivate a witness to testify falsely. However, the greater the possible or likely sentence, the greater the fear and the motive to fabricate and embellish.

Therefore, you should develop with the witness (1) the maximum possible sentence he faces on each charge of which he was convicted; and (2) the specific sentencing range under any sentencing guidelines.

The judge or prosecutor's fear that the sentence will educate the jury about the sentence the defendant faces is not a basis for precluding cross into the witness's likely sentence. [*United States v. Chandler*, 326 F.3d 210, 222 (3d Cir. 2003).]

PRACTICE TIPS:

(1) Do not overdo sentencing guidelines calculations. They are tedious, and you will lose the jury's interest. Further, the witness probably will quibble with you. He may not agree with the calculations, and his counsel may not have discussed the guidelines with him in any depth, especially where the fact of the client's cooperation will trump any guideline sentence. Even where you are dead-on accurate about the calculations, the judge is likely to tell you to move on, because the relevant issue is not what the guidelines are, but what the witness believes he faces under them.

(2) You do not need to tell the jury, either in your questions or closing argument, that if convicted, your client faces the same sentence as the cooperating accomplice or coconspirator. This is the prohibited use of that evidence, and the judge will reprimand you and attempt to make you look sneaky in front of the jury. Further, most jurors do not care. A ten-year mandatory minimum sentence for "muling" a kilogram of heroin may seem outrageous to you, but many jurors will deem it quite lenient. Finally, the jurors are intelligent enough to figure out for themselves that if the co-defendant faces 20 years for pleading to count three of the indictment, your client faces the same sentence if convicted.

§20:173 Prosecutor's Denial of a Deal

Whenever a witness faces a pending prosecution or the possibility of one, you should inquire whether the witness expects or hopes that the prosecutor in your trial will inform the prosecutor in the witness's case of the witness's assistance and request some consideration for the witness, whether or not there is an explicit deal between the prosecutor in your case and the witness. Some judges, however, will limit cross-examination to any explicit agreements or promises of leniency from the prosecution. Thus, if the prosecutor denies any promise or agreement, the judge will preclude questioning the witness about that topic.

This is wrong to the point of violating a defendant's Sixth Amendment confrontation right. [*See Davis v. Alaska,* 415 U.S. 308, 316-17 (1974) ("the exposure of a witness's motivation in testifying is a proper and important function of the constitutionally protected right of cross-examination"); *United States v. Risha,* 445 F.3d 298 (3d Cir. 2006) (where federal and state authorities worked together on an investigation, the federal government could be charged with constructive knowledge of promises made to the witness by state authorities, and federal prosecutors had an obligation to disclose those promises to the defense).]

The witness's motive to lie arises from the witness's subjective belief or hope that his performance as a prosecution witness will earn him leniency on a pending or threatened prosecution. [*See United States v. Landerman,* 109 F.3d 1053, 1062-64 (5th Cir. 1997) (noting that the "right of cross-examination is so important that the defendant is allowed to 'search' for a deal between the government and the witness, even if there is no hard evidence that such a deal exists. What tells, of course, is not the actual existence of a deal but the witness's subjective belief or disbelief that a deal exists."); *United States v. Alexius,* 76 F.3d 642, 646 (5th Cir. 1996) (finding Sixth Amendment violation where the district court refused to allow defendant to cross-examine witness on subject of pending federal and state drug charges, even though witness testified, outside of presence of jury, that he had received no promise of leniency from the government and no specific hope for leniency).]

Witnesses routinely hold onto such hopes even where the prosecutor explicitly states to them that he will not intervene on their behalf in a pending case, such as one in another jurisdiction.

[§§20:174-20:179 Reserved]

5. Cross-Examining the Prosecution Expert

§20:180 Preparing to Cross-Examine the Expert

Experts appear in nearly every criminal case and range from the experiential-based, such as police officers who explain the tools and jargon of the drug trade to jurors, to technical and highly-trained scientists, such as pathologists explaining cause of death or biochemists drawing conclusions from DNA evidence.

Examining the expert can seem daunting. The expert enjoys a specialized education, training and experience that you cannot hope to duplicate in the brief time you have to prepare for trial, and many experts testify frequently and enjoy embarrassing lawyers.

To prepare, at the minimum you must:

- Study the expert's report.
- Scrutinize his curriculum vitae and investigate the bona fides of the education, achievements, publications and appointments he claims.
- Read anything he has published pertinent to his testimony and any transcripts of prior testimony you can find.
- Speak with other lawyers who have examined him.
- Consult with an expert in the same field whom you retain.

Modest goals usually work best. First, determine how much the expert's opinion affects your defense. For example, in most homicide cases, the cause and manner of death are indisputable–*e.g.,* homicide by gunshot to the head–and the defense lies elsewhere, such as in an alibi or misidentification. You might ask no questions of the pathologist in such a case.

Second, find points on which the expert can help you and stress those in your cross-examination rather than attacking the expert and his opinion.

Third, attack the underpinnings of the expert's testimony without debating the expert's analysis: the evidence and witnesses upon which he relies.

[For a comprehensive and methodical, but brief, outline of approaches to cross-examination of expert testimony, see James S. McKay, "What All Experts Have in Common: A Five-Step Analytic Approach to Dealing With Expert Testimony," *Champion* 28 (July 2006).]

§20:181   Challenge the Factual Basis for the Opinion

An expert's conclusion is only as good as the data on which it rests, as reflected in the saw, "Garbage in, garbage out." Most experts lack any personal knowledge of the case facts and must rely on summaries provided by the prosecutor or assumptions that the prosecution's evidence is true.

A cross along these lines either can ask the witness to accept contrary facts developed in your case or can ask the expert to assume that the prosecution's evidence is wrong. If the fact matters to the expert's analysis, he should agree that his conclusion may change.

An attack on the facts fed to the expert avoids a frontal assault on the expert's qualifications or method. Some experts do not hesitate to denigrate the data and witnesses upon which they were forced to rely; it enables them to blame others if the jury or judge disagrees with their opinion.

CAUTION:

Such a cross-examination still requires that you familiarize yourself with the area of expertise and its methods, for you must learn which facts or variables can alter a conclusion and which are inconsequential.

§20:182   Limit the Damage From the Opinion

A good expert will limit his opinion to the bounds of his expertise. Often, you may find that you can accept the expert's opinion because it does not address the ultimate issues in the case.

For example, a fingerprint expert cannot testify as to when your client's fingerprints were left on a firearm, a box, or in the car. The handwriting expert cannot state whether or not a person gave your client permission to sign his or her name.

You should seek to limit the extent of a prosecution expert's opinion through motions in limine, requests for proffers, and objections. It is best to prevent improper expert testimony before it occurs. Many limits arise from case law. For example:

- Watch for attempts to slip in specialized expert opinion testimony through the ruse that it is mere lay opinion testimony. A lay witness' opinion "must be the product of reasoning processes familiar to the average person in everyday life" [*United States v. Garcia,* 413 F.3d 201, 214 (2d Cir. 2005)], and cannot be "based on scientific, technical, or other specialized knowledge" [FRE 701; *e.g., United States v. Haynes,* 729 F.3d 178, 195-96 (2d Cir. 2013) (border agent's testimony as to why a car's fuel gauge would read empty if drugs were hidden in the fuel tank was improper lay opinion testimony because it stemmed from his knowledge of how a fuel tank operates gained through his special experience as an agent inspecting vehicles)]. This ruse is improper because it evades the pre-trial notice and disclosure requirements for expert testimony and the reliability-screening that *Daubert* and its progeny prescribe for expert testimony. [*Haynes, supra.*]
- The expert cannot express an opinion on the issue of the defendant's mental state at the time of the crime. [FRE 704(b); *see Haynes,* 729 F.3d at 196.]

- Law enforcement witnesses should not be permitted to act as a summary prosecution witness, with the effect of bolstering other witness' testimony and impinging on the jury's function. [*United States v. Groysman*, 766 F.3d 147 (2d Cir. 2014)(agent's testimony opining on defendant's role in charged conspiracy was reversible error); *United States v. Garcia*, 413 F.3d 201, 210 (2d Cir. 2005)(testimony by case agent that defendant was a partner in receiving cocaine wrongfully admitted because it told the jury what result to reach); *Haynes, supra* (improper for agent to summarize the government's and conclude that the defendant must have known there were drugs in the car); *United States v. Dukagjini*, 326 F.3d 45, 55 (2d Cir. 2002). *See* §6:71, *supra*.]

§20:183   Attacking the Opinion

In some cases the opinion is so harmful that you must attack it head-on. Such an attack requires thorough preparation, preferably with the assistance of your own expert in the field.

You have several alternatives:

- The expert's science is sound, but he and his assistants do not follow proper procedures–either as stated by the expert, as explained in accepted texts, or as explained by your own testifying expert–in analyzing the evidence and reaching their conclusions.
- The expert's science or area of expertise is unsound: it lacks a basis in empirical testing and otherwise fails the *Daubert* standard of reliability or the *Frye* standard of general acceptance.

You should not undertake the latter attack for the first time at trial. Raise it first in a pre-trial motion to exclude the opinion.

§20:184   Attack the Expert

Do not overlook the same cross-examination techniques that work with the lay witness:

- Impeachment with prior inconsistent statements (such as testimony in prior cases or statements in the expert's report).
- Convictions or other bad acts [*e.g., Elcock v. Kmart Corporation*, 233 F.3d 734 (3rd Cir. 2000) (expert had been convicted of fraud on the government)]; evasiveness; and bias.

One act of dishonesty endemic among experts is resume puffery. Investigate every degree and educational institution that the expert claimed to attend or to which he claimed an appointment. It is not uncommon for experts to fail to complete the final steps toward obtaining their Ph.D. or other higher degree, or to claim faculty membership when they only gave an invited lecture or two.

Some impressive sounding professional memberships may be open to anyone who pays a fee, regardless of their training or accomplishments or lack thereof. Jurors enjoy seeing lawyers deflate pompous experts by pointing out that an eleven-year-old would be granted membership upon completion of the cereal-box-top application and payment of the fee.

Experts tend to ramble, even in response to the simplest question. Ask the witness some concrete, simply-phrased and brief questions and repeat them until you get an answer to the question you asked, not the question the expert wants to answer. [For techniques, see §20:151.] A few exchanges like this enable you to argue persuasively in your closing argument that the expert is a hired gun whose interest was not in truth or educating the jury, but in helping the side that paid him.

Cross-examinations about an expert's bias may seem unimaginative, but they impress juries. An expert who always testifies for the prosecution will not seem impartial. Further, even expert fees that you consider modest will sound outrageous to jurors. Develop the basis for questions about fees step-by-step, for the very facts that the expert believes show that he earned his fee–the tremendous amount of out-of-court time he put into his one hour of testimony–suggest to the jury that he is milking this case for his own enrichment:

- Are you being paid by the time you spent on this case, or a flat fee?
- How much per hour is your rate?
- You use your office at the University to do your work on this case?
- You don't pay any rent for that office, do you?
- And the secretary who typed your report is the same one the university provides to you?
- The university pays her, not you?
- Did you have the assistance of any students on this case?
- Are you billing for them?
- Do you pay them or does the university?
- So the $300 per hour you are charging on this case is pure profit to you–by that I mean you have no overhead expenses like staff or rent or supplies?

- As of today, how many hours have you billed on this case?
- How many hours do you ultimately anticipate billing for?
- So the prosecutor owes you $15,000 for your work on this case?
- Don't you have some worry that he may not pay you the $15,000 if your testimony does not help his case?

[§§20:185-20:189 Reserved]

V.   THE DEFENSE CASE

A.   Before Presenting the Case

§20:190   Motion for Judgment of Acquittal

When the prosecutor rests, move for a judgment of acquittal, a ruling that even taking the prosecutor's evidence as true and drawing all favorable inferences in his favor, the evidence fails to prove the charge. [*See, e.g.,* Fed. R. Crim. P. 29.]

Your grounds will depend on any specific defenses in your case, but you always should specify as many deficiencies as you can imagine in the proof of the elements of the offense. This objection might preserve appellate issues that you overlook in the heat of trial.

Most courts hold that if you present a defense after the trial court denies your motion, then appellate review of the denial will include consideration of whatever evidence you introduce in your case. [*See State v. Perkins*, 271 Conn. 218, 237 n.23, 856 A.2d 917, 932 n. 23 (2004) (all federal circuits and at least 31 states follow this rule; only seven states do not).] Thus if the trial court erroneously denies your motion at the end of the prosecution's case and your evidence supplies proof on the missing element, the appeals court can uphold the conviction based upon your evidence.

Some courts also hold that while the presentation of evidence does not waive the issue, if you then fail to renew your motion at the end of all the evidence, you waive the right to appellate review of the motion you made at the end of the prosecution's case. [*United States v. Maldonado-Garcia,* 446 F.3d 227, 230 (1st Cir. 2006).]

Therefore, be sure to renew your motion once all the evidence (prosecution, defense, and rebuttal) closes.

If a judge grants a judgment of acquittal before a verdict, double jeopardy precludes a government appeal or retrial. [*United States v. Martin Linen Supply,* 430 U.S. 564 (1977).]

In contrast, the government may appeal a post-conviction judgment of acquittal. [*Smith v. Massachusetts,* 543 U.S. 462, 467 (2005).]

Knowing this, some judges will try to withhold ruling on a pre-verdict grant of a judgment of acquittal until after the verdict. Likewise, judges may entertain a second judgment of acquittal more seriously after the verdict if the jury disappoints them and fails to acquit.

§20:191   Preparing Your Witnesses

Many shorter preparation sessions often work better than a few lengthy ones.

Review with great specificity how a trial works: where your client will sit, where the witness stand is in relation to everything else. If possible, go to a courtroom or have the witness watch a trial.

Do more than review areas of examination. Practice direct and cross-examination with the witness. Consider whether the prosecutor will treat the witness gently and attempt to elicit concessions and helpful testimony or whether the prosecutor will attack the witness's credibility and prepare the witness for both kinds of questioning.

Witnesses can be asked about preparation, so prepare them for these questions and remind them that above all you want them to testify truthfully. Therefore, when asked, the witness can answer that your preparation emphasized that he should tell the truth.

Instruct witnesses to take their time in answering, perhaps a breath after the question is done and before they begin to answer. This enables them to think, you to object, and prevents the prosecutor from developing a rapid-fire rhythm.

Tell the witness that whenever he hears an objection he must not answer until the judge tells him to go ahead and answer the question.

If he does not remember the question exactly, he should say so, and the question will be read back or repeated.

Instruct witnesses to listen closely to questions and answer only the question asked, not what the witness anticipates the next question to be or what the witness suspects is the intent behind the question. In normal conversation, we all try to help our interlocutor by anticipating and helping him get to where he is going, often by answering mid-question. Tell the witness that trial testimony is not like that. The witness should wait until the questioner completes his question and then answer only the question asked. The witness should not volunteer information, although he or she should say enough in the answer so that the answer is fully understandable.

Many witnesses and clients need instructions on grooming and behavior. Make sure to instruct the witness on proper attire for trial. [*See* §20:42.]

Tell the witness not to suck on mints or chew gum.

[§§20:192-20:199 Reserved]

B. Defenses

§20:200 SODDI ("Some Other Dude Did It")

This defense has the advantage of diverting the focus from your client to the absent real perpetrator, who is not there to defend himself.

It also enables you to put the police investigation on trial by appealing to a narrative that resonates with many jurors: the lazy bureaucrats ignored clues pointing elsewhere once they arrested your hapless client.

This defense does not require your client to testify because he had nothing to do with the crime and would know nothing about who did.

You have a constitutional right to present such a defense. [*See Holmes v. South Carolina,* 547 U.S. 319, 327-29 (2006) (exclusion of evidence of third-party guilt violated Sixth Amendment Compulsory Process clause and Fourteenth Amendment Due Process)], but the risk of jury confusion requires that you have some evidence to support the "alternative perpetrator" theory other than the defendant's or even the case agent's beliefs:

> In order to elicit testimony implicating an alternative perpetrator, a defendant "must show that his proffered evidence on the alleged alternative perpetrator is sufficient, on its own or in combination with other evidence in the record, to show a nexus between the crime charged and the asserted alternative perpetrator." *Wade v. Mantello,* 333 F.3d 51, 61-62 (2d Cir. 2003) (internal quotation marks omitted). Thus, to avoid a "grave risk of jury confusion," a defendant must offer more than "unsupported speculation that another person may have done the crime." *Id.* at 62 (internal quotation marks omitted). An "agent's state of mind as the investigation progressed is ordinarily of little or no relevance to the question of the defendant['s] guilt." *United States v. Johnson,* 529 F.3d 493, 501 (2d Cir. 2008).

[*United States v. Ulbricht,* 858 F.3d 71, 119 (2d Cir. 2017). *See also United States v. McVeigh,* 153 F.3d 1166, 1191 (10th Cir.1998).]

You can build this defense with evidence of other bad acts on the alleged perpetrator's part (the so-called "reverse [FRE] 404(b) evidence"). [*See* §20:210.]

§20:201 Consciousness of Innocence

Where your defense is lack of intent or lack of knowledge, you can turn evidence of non-action or even harmful evidence into helpful by arguing that it shows that your client believed he had done no wrong.

For example:
- Your client freely consented to search of his backpack and agreed to talk about who gave him the package stowed within because he had no idea it contained drugs.
- Your client did not flee or turned down a generous plea offer because he believed in his innocence.

[*See United States v. Biaggi,* 909 F.2d 662, 690-91 (2d Cir. 1990) (court should have admitted evidence that defendant rejected offer of immunity).]

Form:
- **Form 20-2** Motion in Limine to Permit Evidence of Consciousness of Innocence

§20:202 Good Faith

Where the charge requires fraudulent intent, you might defend with evidence and argument that your client acted with a sincere belief in the honesty of his enterprise and the truth of his representations. [*See* Leonard Sand, et al., *Modern Federal Jury Instructions*, ¶8.01.]

This works best where your client can testify to efforts and sacrifices he made for the good of the putative victims.

§20:203 Advice of Counsel

The basis of this defense is that before undertaking his business enterprise, your client consulted counsel to determine the legality of his actions and followed his lawyer's advice.

If the lawyer will testify, this defense can be powerful. However, to work it requires that the defendant fully disclosed all relevant facts and that he faithfully followed his attorney's advice. [*See* Leonard Sand, et al., *Modern Federal Jury Instructions*, ¶8.04.]

The prosecution will try to scare the lawyer into thinking that he is at risk of prosecution, and the lawyer might hedge and claim that he did not know the full scope of your client's plans.

§20:204 Agency

Some courts have carved out a defense for drug sale or delivery charges where the defendant acted as the agent of the buyer, with only the intent to assist the buyer in obtaining drugs for the buyer's personal use. [*See Commonwealth v. Murphy*, 577 Pa. 275, 291-93, 844 A.2d 1228 (2004) (noting continued validity of agency defense on charge of delivering controlled substances).]

Courts have become increasingly skeptical of this defense. [*See* Scott W. Parker, *An Argument For Preserving The Agency Defense As Applied To Prosecutions For Unlawful Sale, Delivery, And Possession Of Drugs*, 66 Fordham L. Rev. 2649 (1998) (noting trend against this defense, but advocating its renewal).]

It works best if you can prove that your client had a relationship with the buyer and did not benefit from the transaction, so that you can argue that your client's motive was friendship, not pecuniary gain.

Similarly, some courts recognize a "sharing" defense to a charge of distribution, or possession with intent to distribute: joint and simultaneous possession by a few individuals with intent to share the drugs among themselves and distribute the drugs no further. [*See State v. Morrison*, 188 N.J. 2, 902 A.2d 860 (2006); *United States v. Swiderski*, 548 F.2d 445 (2d Cir. 1977).]

§20:205 Alibi

Alibis (evidence that your client was somewhere else at the time of the crime) almost never achieve their promise.

Your client usually wants to rely on friends, lovers and family, all of whom the jury will recognize as biased, and none of whom have any corroboration or specificity for their tales.

Although the prosecution bears the burden of disproving an alibi and still must prove guilt beyond a reasonable doubt, juries tend to switch the burden to the defense upon hearing an alibi. If they believe the alibi, they will acquit, and if not, conviction is probable.

Use an alibi if you can corroborate it with records from a disinterested source, for example, a work time clock, a highway electronic toll record, or an ATM receipt for a withdrawal on your client's account.

§20:206 Affirmative Defenses

Affirmative defenses are those which do not negate the elements of the offense: insanity, self-defense, justification, duress and entrapment.

While in theory a defendant can present alternative defenses by denying guilt and offering an affirmative defense, this tactic usually is self-defeating.

Try to avoid affirmative defenses, for two reasons:

- Courts can impose the burden of proof on the defense for affirmative defenses. [*See Dixon v. United States*, 126 S.Ct. 2437 (2006) (defendant has burden of proving duress by a preponderance of the evidence); *United States v. Al-Rekabi*, 454 F.3d 1113, 1122 (10th Cir. 2006) (defendant has burden of proving necessity by a preponderance of the evidence).] Even if the law does not impose such a burden, as a practical matter the jury may reject the defense unless you persuade them of its truth. Jurors often reason that since your client has admitted the crime, now he seeks an excuse for his guilt. Accordingly, it must be compelling to work.

- An affirmative defense often open the door to otherwise inadmissible evidence in rebuttal. In particular, the defense opens the door to evidence of prior similar bad acts by your client.

§20:207   Affirmative Defenses – Entrapment

The defendant must proffer "some evidence" from which a reasonable jury could find that the government induced him to commit the particular crime charged in order to obtain a jury instruction on entrapment. The prosecution has the burden of proving predisposition and disproving inducement beyond a reasonable doubt.

The prosecution frequently moves *in limine* to preclude this defense, which forces the defense to make a pretrial proffer of its evidence. When the court proceeds in this manner, it must accept the defendant's evidence as true and may not weigh against it the government's evidence. [*United States v. Mayfield*, 771 F.3d 417 (7th Cir. 2014)(en banc).]

Predisposition must be measured as of the time the government agent or informant began his campaign of inducement. Eager participation, once induced, does not prove predisposition. Further, only if they are of very similar nature do prior crimes indicate predisposition. [*See, e.g., Mayfield* (prior armed robbery conviction did not show predisposition to commit the type of crime charged, a robbery of a drug stash house.).]

A defendant with a criminal record may point to his efforts to reform his life to defeat a government claim of predisposition. [*Id.*]

[§§20:208-20:209 Reserved]

C.   Defense Evidence

§20:210   Reverse Rule 404(b)

Consider introducing evidence of government witness's or a third party's prior bad acts to show that he, not your client, was the wrongdoer. [*See United States v. Montelongo*, 420 F.3d 1169 (10th Cir. 2005) (error to prevent defendants from introducing evidence that government witness previously had planted drug in another person's truck without that person's knowledge); *United States v. Stevens*, 935 F.2d 1380, 1405-06 (3d Cir. 1991) (court should have permitted evidence of similar robberies in which witness failed to identify defendant to suggest that another person committed robberies with which defendant was charged); *United States v. Aboumoussalen*, 726 F.2d 906, 911 (2d Cir. 1984) (trial court should have permitted defense to call witnesses to testify that person who gave the defendant the attaché case that contained heroin had previously duped another person to carry contraband unknowingly).]

Reverse 404(b) evidence – evidence offered by the defense about a third party – should be admitted more freely than the prosecution's 404(b) offers because when the individual involved in prior wrongs is not the defendant, one of the rule's primary concerns – to remove from the jury the temptation to convict on an improper basis – is absent. [*Norwood v. State*, 95 A.2d 588, 597-98 (Del. 2014). *See also Aboumoussallem*, 726 F.2d at 911 ("We believe the standard of admissibility when a criminal defendant offers similar acts evidence as a shield need not be as restrictive as when a prosecutor uses such evidence as a sword.")] In this analysis, the prerequisites to admission are that the evidence be relevant and that its probative value not be substantially outweighed by potential prejudice, undue delay or confusion of the issues. [*Norwood*, 95 A.3d at 598.] Among these, prepare most to fight the last: trial courts fear that other uncharged other acts evidence will involve the fact-finder in a mini-trial on the act's commission and the actor's culpability for it. [*See United States v. Battle*, 2014 U.S. App. LEXIS 24127 (8th Cir. Dec. 22, 2014); *Allen v. State*, 2014 Md. LEXIS 809 (MD Nov. 26, 2014)(excluding evidence for this reason).]

Arm yourself with a memorandum in limine, the text of the rule, a written proffer and caselaw to defend admission of such evidence.

The trial judge is likely to bristle at the idea of admitting specific acts to prove character because the general rule is that character is provable only by reputation or opinion evidence, *not* by general acts. Argue that your evidence fits within the specific exception to that general rule.

Prepare to prove the prior act efficiently. The judge might attempt to preclude the evidence under Rule 403 or its equivalent as confusing to the jury and wasteful of trial time. You must be able to describe precisely how many witnesses you need to call and how long their testimony will last.

Make a detailed proffer of the evidence to preserve the issue for appeal. While the judge and prosecutor may know what you mean when you mention calling Officer Smith to testify to the June 2, 2006, incident (perhaps by virtue of off-the-record discussions), the appellate court will have no idea. Have a written proffer that describes who the witnesses are, what they will say, and what arguments you will make based on the testimony, stating it as powerfully as you can. Have the proffer marked as and admitted as an exhibit.

§20:211 Prior Convictions or Inconsistent Statements

If your client has prior convictions or has made flatly inconsistent statements, you should elicit the statements on direct. The law permits this under the rule that a party can impeach its own witness. [*See People v. Guy*, 223 A.D.2d 723, 637 N.Y.S.2d 445 (NY App. Div. 2d Dept. 1996). *See* Farrell, *Richardson on Evidence*, §6-421.]

Prepare your client to admit the convictions, and any inconsistent statements, in a straightforward and calm manner. Warn him against stories of how, though innocent, he was forced to plead guilty. With inconsistent statements, he should admit the prior statement and then explain the inconsistency in answers to your subsequent questions asking for an explanation.

PRACTICE TIP:

The approach recommended here of raising these matters on direct is the conventional wisdom. Some practitioners disagree, reasoning that the introduction or "sponsorship" of this information during your examination overemphasizes it. [Robert H. Klonoff & Paul L. Colby, *Sponsorship Strategy* 85-88 (1990).] However, the approach of not dealing with the issue on direct overlooks the manner in which the evidence will unfold on cross. The prosecutor will develop it with some drama, and your witness is likely to become uncomfortable and might start to equivocate and minimize his prior convictions or inconsistent statements. Most important, the jury might feel that you attempted to deceive them by portraying the witness as a nice young man with a consistent story whereas he is a convicted felon who has told a number of conflicting stories.

§20:212 Character Evidence

You may consider introducing evidence of your client's good character to show that it is inconsistent with the charge (*e.g.,* his character for honesty in a fraud case, or peacefulness where violence is charged).

On direct the character witness can offer only an opinion or describe the party's reputation in the community (some jurisdictions limit the character witness to reputation). The witness cannot testify on direct as to the most convincing form of character evidence: tales of the defendant's good deeds evincing the character trait. [FRE 405(a).]

Furthermore, introducing character witnesses permits the prosecution to introduce negative character witnesses–individuals who will testify that the defendant's reputation is one of dishonesty, violence or whatever heinous trait rebuts your witnesses' testimony. [*See* FRE 404(a).] Such evidence otherwise would not come in.

Therefore, character witnesses usually hurt more than help. They open the door to harmful and otherwise inadmissible evidence, they lack knowledge of the events on trial, and they are forbidden from recounting what the jury really wants to hear–anecdotes about the defendant's good deeds.

Unless the witness is extraordinary (*e.g.,* an esteemed and beloved community leader who knows the defendant well), and there is nothing harmful behind the doors that the testimony will open, avoid character witnesses.

On the other hand, in a minority of jurisdictions, introduction of character evidence entitles the defense to an instruction that character evidence, standing alone, is sufficient to raise a reasonable doubt. [*E.g., Commonwealth v. Neely*, 522 Pa. 236, 561 A.2d 1 (1989).]

If you are in such a jurisdiction, you should call character witnesses absent strong countervailing considerations.

PRACTICE TIP:

Where you put on a character witness, use several questions to lay the foundation for the witness's opinion and reputation testimony by having the witness recount in detail all the (charitable, you hope) organizations and events from which he knows your client. This foundation suggests your client's many good deeds without reciting them.

Prepare the witness to launch into those good acts if the prosecutor gives any opening. The prosecutor inevitably will ask the witness if his opinion would change had he known that your client committed one or another malefaction. Your witness should answer that, first, he cannot believe your client would do such a thing, and, second, that no, it would not because it is so out of character that it must be an isolated instance.

§20:213 Consider an Offer of Proof

Where objections are sustained to your questions or evidence, consider making a proffer as to what the answer or evidence would have been to preserve the issue if your intended evidence was not clear from the context.

Ask to do it immediately, because the judge may reconsider once he or she hears the evidence fully described. The judge is less likely to do so if you make the proffer hours later, when the witness is off the stand.

[§§20:214-20:219 Reserved]

D. The Defendant as a Witness

§20:220 Whether the Defendant Should Testify

Your client should testify only if he must.

The decision whether or not to testify is the client's, and you may not override it, but you are obligated to give the client your best advice on the wisdom of testifying:

> [D]efense counsel bears the primary responsibility for advising the defendant of his right to testify or not to testify ... Although counsel should always advise the defendant about the benefits and hazards of testifying and of not testifying, and may strongly advise the course that counsel thinks best, counsel must inform the defendant that the ultimate decision whether to take the stand belongs to the defendant, and counsel must abide by the defendant's decision on this matter.

[*Bennett v. United States*, 663 F.3d 71, 84 (2d Cir. 2011).]

If you believe that you have created reasonable doubt in the prosecutor's case, advise your client not to testify. If the defendant testifies and the jury disbelieves him, they will convict regardless of the shortcomings in the prosecution case. A defendant's testimony becomes the main event at trial, and the jury will decide the case on whether or not they believe the defendant.

The testimony also might enable the prosecutor to introduce otherwise inadmissible evidence to impeach your client, such as your client's convictions or prior inconsistent statements. Be mindful that the judge will allow the prosecutor considerable leeway on cross-examination. [*See United States v. Raper*, 676 F.2d 841, 846 (D.C. Cir. 1982) ("When a defendant in a criminal trial takes the stand the scope of cross-examination is very broad"; defendant could not take stand for a limited purpose and limit cross to that issue).]

In some jurisdictions, the defense is entitled to a pre-trial ruling as to which convictions can be the subject of cross-examination. [*People v. Hayes*, 97 N.Y.2d 203, 207, 738 N.Y.S.2d 663 (2002).]

In those jurisdictions, the defense may be able to contest on appeal a pre-trial ruling permitting the prosecution to impeach him with prior convictions even where the defendant does not testify at trial, whereas the federal rule is that to preserve an objection to his impeachment with a prior conviction, the defendant must testify. [*Luce v. United States*, 469 U.S. 38 (1984).]

Even if your jurisdiction's law does not entitle your client to a pre-trial ruling, ask for one. Renew your request at the end of the prosecution's case and before you call your client. By then, the judge should have a good idea of how your client's testimony fits into the case.

Certain defenses (*e.g.*, self-defense and good faith) need the defendant's testimony to work. If your client is articulate and likable, without prior conviction or known acts of dishonesty, and can explain his actions plausible, he should testify.

If your client is going to testify, prepare him very carefully, and subject him to close, grueling cross-examination. Articulate clients, particularly fraudsters, believe that they can talk themselves out of any situation. However, they are accustomed to misdirecting questions with evasive patter and glib retorts, and this routine wilts quickly before a cross-examiner who insists that they answer hard questions directly. If your client can give a straight answer to the hard questions, he should testify. If not, find another defense.

PRACTICE TIPS:

In preparing your client, focus on the following:
1. *Demeanor*. The defendant must show the same poise and courtesy in answering the prosecutor as he displays on direct. Most defendants view the prosecutor as a dishonest bully, and the day they

testify is when they finally get to put him in his place. Jurors don't think the same way. To them, most prosecutors seem like nice young men or women whom the judge obviously likes. The defendant must show the prosecutor respect; answer calmly; and, above all, avoid anger. Questions on cross naturally will be leading, so answers do not need to be as lengthy as on direct, but when an explanation is needed, the client should give it – but only after first answering the question.

Some prosecutors, on the other hand, make a point of treating the defendant with respect at every pretrial court proceeding and during trial. This may lull some defendants into being too cooperative and conceding points too freely. Anticipate both approaches and prepare your client for both.

2. *"Why" Questions.* Prosecutors sometimes violate the conventional wisdom that one should never ask "why" on cross-examination. Many times, though, defendants have no good answer to the question. For example, your client may claim that he went along with the drug deal because he feared the confidential informant. You may have prepared him with good reasons to justify that fear, but the prosecutor is likely to ask, "Why didn't you call the police?" The worst possible answer is befuddled silence.

3. *Unsuccessful Objections.* You may be confident that you can exclude bad extrinsic evidence or that the judge will forbid the prosecutor from asking your client to comment on the credibility of other witnesses. [See, e.g., §20-231, infra.] Even when you are correct on the law, you often will lose those arguments, and the judge will force your client to answer. Prepare him in advance to have an answer. The best answer is to refuse to agree that the other witness is lying. Instead, the defendant should repeat his version of events. "Lying" implies intent, and the defendant cannot know the other witness' intent. The most the defendant should say is that the witness is "wrong."

4. *Don't open doors.* Even good answers should be narrow and to the point. Your client might be tempted to exaggerate. For example, the answer to the question, "Did you ever sell cocaine to John Doe?" might become "I never had anything to do with cocaine." This opens the door to questions about his uncharged distribution to other people and his personal drug use, none of which may have been disclosed in discovery (because the prosecutor did not intend to use it in his direct case) and much of which you might be ignorant.

5. *Preview your client.* After spending so much time with your client, you may have convinced yourself that he is likeable and credible. Conversely, he might wear on you so that tics that few others notice light a murderous fire in you. You need laypeople who do not know him or the case to listen to him, size him up, generally, and his story and manner of telling it, in particular. Be careful to preserve confidentiality if you expose your client to outsiders. Engage them as consultants to assist in your defense and have them sign confidentiality agreements.

§20:221   Potential Perjury–The Lawyer's Dilemma

You cannot call a witness who you know will lie. Not only would it be unethical, but it might be criminal.

However, your client can overrule you and insist upon testifying. This creates a dilemma that vexes lawyers, courts and commentators. [*See* Stephen Gillers, *Monroe Freedman's Solution to the Criminal Defense Lawyer's Trilemma Is Wrong as a Matter of Policy and Constitutional Law,* 34 Hofstra L. Rev. 821 (2006).]

§20:222   Potential Perjury–Representing the Client

The following concepts are useful in interpreting the lawyer's ethical obligation and still upholding the obligation to provide a defense.

Do not create a problem where none exists.

Your obligation to decline the testimony arises only when you *know* that it will be perjury. [Model Rule 3.3(a)(3).]

You rarely reach that level unless your client outright admits that he intends to lie on the stand. [*State v. McDowell,* 681 N.W.2d 500, 510 (Wis. 2004) ("absent the most extraordinary circumstances, criminal defense counsel, as a matter of law, cannot know that a client is going to testify falsely absent the client's admission of the intent to do so"); *United States v. Midgett,* 342 F.3d 321 (4th Cir. 2003) (while client's story was "far-fetched" and contrary to other witnesses' testimony, he consistently maintained to attorney it was true; defense counsel found ineffective for refusing to present it); *but see People v. Calhoun,* 351 Ill.App.3d 1072, 815 N.E.2d (Ill. App. 4th Dist. 2004) (surveying jurisdictions and finding most do not follow a standard as high as the *McDowell* standard, but rather a "firm factual basis" standard).]

This knowledge requirement will eliminate any ethical problem for you in almost all cases. It is not an evasion of the prohibition against presenting perjury; to the contrary, your duty is to present and argue your client's story. Determining guilt or innocence, truth or falsity, is the jury's obligation. [*See United States v. Litchfield*, 959 F.2d 1514, 1517 (10th Cir. 1992) (in rejecting defense counsel's advice that the defendant would commit perjury, court stated that the lawyer was not in the best position to decide what is true and not true, and further, that counsel should let the jury arrive at its own conclusions).]

Assess the issue practically rather than ethically.

If your client's story conflicts with indisputable evidence or lacks internal consistency and verisimilitude, it probably will fail to convince the jury.

Point this out to him and urge him to modify his testimony or to forego testifying altogether. Clients frequently prove more receptive to advice based on the probability of success rather than on ethics.

Work with your client

Begin working on your client's testimony well before trial so you have advance notice of what he will say, giving you time to bring him around to the truth or a believable facsimile of it, or to withdraw if the high standard for knowing the story is perjury is met.

The story might be true.

Do not ignore the possibility that the story you disbelieve, or even which your client declares to be false actually is true.

Many criminal defendants have mental illnesses that may cause them to confuse fact and fiction, and others might conceal and distort the truth out of ignorance or shame. [*See* J. Vincent Aprile, "Client Perjury: When Do You Know the Client is Lying?"14 *Criminal Justice* 15 (Fall 2004).]

For example, your client might deny his abuse and victimization at the hands of a spouse or parent even though those facts might support a duress defense or mitigation at sentencing.

§20:223   Potential Perjury–Protecting Yourself

The following steps are useful in protecting yourself if you are convinced that your client will commit perjury.

Presume your client is wired.

If the client tells you that he intends to present false evidence, proceed as if your client is wearing a wire and the prosecutor is listening to everything you say.

Choose your words carefully; using the word "truth" often and insisting that whatever story your client tells, it must be the truth. Take careful notes and dictate detailed post-meeting memos.

Seek counsel for yourself.

It is important to choose on the basis of credentials: a professor of legal ethics, a retired judge, a former disciplinary board member or counsel or an attorney who practices frequently before the disciplinary board.

This person is your lawyer, not the client's. Maintain the confidentiality of your communications with this advisor.

Move to withdraw.

If you are convinced that your client will commit perjury and you cannot dissuade him, move to withdraw but try not to reveal the substance of your client's testimony.

Tell the court as little as you can. Try to couch your motion in terms of an ethical dispute creating a conflict or interest or a breakdown in communication. [*Commonwealth v. Mitchell,* 438 Mass. 535, 550 n.7, 781 N.E.2d 1250 n.7 (2003) (should not reveal substance of the testimony because it is a confidential communication); *People v. Calhoun,* 351 Ill.App.2d at 1087 (same).]

Many judges will not press for more detail. However, you must research thoroughly your jurisdiction's ethical rules and should seek outside advice. Some jurisdictions hold that the attorney *must* reveal the substance of the contemplated perjury to the court because statements of intent to commit a future crime are not privileged. [*See Nix v. Whiteside,* 475 U.S. 157, 168 (1986) (interpreting both the Model Code of Professional Responsibility and the Model Rules of Professional Conduct as requiring disclosure) (but note: states deviate substantially in their wording and interpretation of the model rules on this point; therefore, the Supreme Court's interpretation of the ABA version of the rules is not binding);

ABA Committee on Ethics and Professional Responsibility, Formal Opinion 87-353 (stating that it is mandatory for a lawyer who knows the client has committed perjury to disclose this knowledge to the tribunal).]

Ask that the presentation be made ex parte and in camera to avoid revealing the situation to the prosecution.

If new counsel is appointed, you cannot disclose to the new attorney the reasons for your withdrawal or your client's story unless the client explicitly consents or the court orders you to do so.

Present the testimony as narrative.

After exhausting all other options, either present the testimony as narrative or disclose the perjury to the court, whatever your research and advisor deem to be required.

If you reach this point, your goal is to protect yourself while doing the minimum damage to your client.

[§§20:224-20:229 Reserved]

E.   The Prosecutor's Cross-Examination

§20:230   General Points

Prosecutors work from a disadvantage on cross.

Defense lawyers present fewer witnesses than prosecutors do, and as a result, the prosecutor will have fewer opportunities to hone his cross-examination skills. If a defense witness has a long criminal record, we will not call him. However, prosecutors often must call victims, informants and coconspirators who carry baggage containing long criminal records and promises of favorable treatment.

Most defense witnesses, except in white-collar cases, usually do not leave the same trail of prior reports and testimony that prosecution witnesses do as gist for a prior inconsistent statements cross.

Prosecutors often resort to several routine techniques. You can defeat some with valid evidentiary objections. Others you must seek to neutralize by preparing your client for them.

§20:231   Comments on the Credibility of Other Witnesses

A common but improper tactic is for the prosecutor to ask a defense witness to comment on the credibility of another witness, usually a police officer.

EXAMPLE:

Q. So you say you never had the gun that is Government Exhibit 1 in your hands on June 5?
A. That's right.
Q. You heard Officer Smith's testimony yesterday, didn't you?
A. Yes.
Q. And you heard him testify that he saw you with the gun in your hands, pointing it at Mr. Lewis, on June 5, you heard that, didn't you?
A. Yes.
Q. So you're telling this jury that Officer Smith was lying when he gave that testimony yesterday?
A. If that's what he said, he must have been.
Q. And you're telling the truth?
A. Yes.

This cross hurts for several reasons:

• It enables the prosecutor to repeat, sometimes at length, the testimony of his witnesses.

• It puts the defendant in the distasteful position of calling reputable witnesses "liars." Most people, including jurors, find that accusation distasteful and will hold the accusation against the defendant.

• It is nearly impossible to give a direct answer to any of these questions. Nearly any answer sounds evasive (*e.g.,* "I don't know," "I can't say, I just know what I said," "I don't know if they're lying or if they're mistaken"). Any answer invites safe, follow up questions that mostly consist of repeating the prosecution witnesses' damaging testimony and getting the defendant either to assert that the witnesses were mistaken or that the witnesses are lying. Jurors do not like evasive witnesses. Getting a witness to answer evasively, even on minor points, is one of the most devastating of cross-examination techniques.

Most courts flatly prohibit this tactic, and will rule as follows: "Counsel should not ask one witness to comment on the veracity of testimony of another witness." [*United States v. Sullivan*, 85 F.3d 743, 746 (1st Cir. 1996); *see also United States v. Harris*, 471 F.3d 507, 511-12 (3d Cir. 2006) (surveying cases). *But see State v. Johnson*, 273 Wis.2d 626, 681 N.W.2d 901 (Wis. 2004) (ruling that such questioning is permissible to highlight inconsistencies in the testimony and to permit witness to explain them).]

Such questioning infringes "on the jury's right to make credibility determinations." [*United States v. Boyd*, 54 F.3d 868, 871 (D.C. Cir. 1995); *Commonwealth v. McClure*, 144 A.3d 970, 977 (Pa. Super. Ct. 2016).]

Also, the question is argumentative and improperly suggests to the jury that the only way to acquit the defendant is to find that the prosecution's witnesses lied. [*See State v. Singh*, 259 Conn. 693, 793 A.2d 226 (Conn. 2000) (reviewing federal and state cases); *Liggett v. People*, 135 P.3d 725 (Colo. 2006) (prohibiting such questioning also because witness's belief is irrelevant and whether another witness is lying is beyond defendant's competence; question unfairly excludes alternative explanations for discrepancies in testimony); *Commonwealth v. Yockey*, 158 A.3d 1246, 1255-56 (Pa. Super. Ct. 2017)]

However, some courts draw a distinction between asking the defendant if another witness is lying and asking if another witness is mistaken, and those courts allow the latter. [*Harris*, 471 F.3d at 512 (dicta).]

§20:232 Admission That Witness Did Not Notify Police

Another common technique is to elicit from a witness an admission that he did not notify the police or prosecutor of his exculpatory story prior to trial. This is done with a question like, "Why didn't you tell the police before?"

When the witness is the defendant, use of this technique is restricted to those instances in which the defendant did make a statement to the police or grand jury, but omitted the exculpatory story or some of its details. [*See United States v. Harris*, 956 F.2d 177, 181 (8th Cir. 1992).]

If the defendant chose not to speak at all prior to trial, drawing any attention to the defendant's pre-trial silence might impinge on his Fifth Amendment privilege against self-incrimination. [*See* Chapter 8, Interrogations.]

You must prepare your witness with a response for cross-examination, because this technique usually is not objectionable. Furthermore, many prosecutors will ask the question in an open-ended fashion, inviting the witness to answer with why he did not speak to the police. While such a style is risky for the questioner, even more damaging is a witness who, given the chance, cannot answer a "why" question.

You will find many possible answers, which vary in helpfulness from believable but apologetic to those that throw into doubt the integrity of the prosecution:

- Distrust of the police, especially based on past experience. This rings true especially for minority group members from disadvantaged neighborhoods.
- The witness in fact may have contacted the police, but they did not have any interest in speaking to him.
- The witness was interviewed, but noticed that the police stopped writing whenever she said anything helpful to the defendant, so she realized they had no interest in the truth.
- Counsel advised the witness that the police could not be trusted and that he should save the story for trial.

§20:233 Impeachment by Contradiction

Under this doctrine, "once a witness (especially a defendant–witness) testifies as to any specific fact on direct testimony, the trial judge has broad discretion to admit extrinsic evidence tending to contradict a specific statement even if such statement concerns a collateral matter in the case." [*United States v. Benedetto*, 571 F.2d 1246, 1250 (2nd Cir. 1978).]

This doctrine trumps other rules of inadmissibility, including:

- The prohibition against the use of illegally seized evidence. [*See Walter v. United States*, 347 U.S. 62 (1954) (where defendant testified that he had never had narcotics in his possession, prosecution could introduce heroin suppressed in a previous investigation of defendant).]
- Rule 404(b)'s prohibition on the use of evidence of other crimes. [*See United States v. Morla-Trinidad*, 100 F.3d 1, 4-5 (1st Cir. 1996).]

This doctrine also permits the introduction of extrinsic evidence to contradict answers given on cross-examination if the cross-examination questions were reasonably suggested by the direct examination. [*See United States v. Havens*, 446 U.S. 620, 627 (1980).]

You might prevent this technique by objecting to the initial cross-examination questions as being irrelevant, and then to any offer of extrinsic contradicting evidence as collateral, irrelevant, and likely to confuse the jury under FRE 403. Many defendants can be counted on to lie about all manner of things, but, you should argue, the prosecutor should not introduce extraneous topics solely to set up the contradiction.

The best antidote to this cross-examination is preparation. Train your client to answer questions directly and not to volunteer self-serving information or to exaggerate his moral purity on either direct or cross. Get to know your client and unearth before trial the skeletons about which he would lie to avoid their exhumation (*e.g.,* other crimes, infidelities, petty deceits on friends and family and embarrassing scams). Thus you will realize where the prosecutor might be heading with certain questions and be ready to object. If you fail, your client will be prepared to admit the truth.

Argue to the jury in closing that the prosecutor took cheap shots, but your client owned up to the peccadilloes, honest man that he is.

§20:234   Consultation With Defense Counsel

The trial court can forbid your client from consulting with you during brief recesses. [*Perry v. Leake,* 488 U.S. 272, 283-84 (1988).]

However, a ban on overnight consultation, even while the defendant is mid-cross, violates the Sixth Amendment right to counsel. [*United States v. Sandoval-Mendoza,* 472 F.3d 645, 650-52 (9th Cir. 2006).]

§20:235   Cross-Examination on Character Evidence

On cross-examination, a witness who has provided good character evidence on direct [see §20:212] can be asked if he or she knows of specific bad acts that the party committed, if they are relevant to the character trait, and whether knowledge of those acts would change the witness's opinion or testimony as to reputation. [FRE 405(a).]

The cross can include questions about both:
* Arrests. [*E.g., Michelson v. United States*, 339 U.S. 465, 481-86 (1948).]
* Uncharged acts. [*E.g., United States v. Holt,* 170 F.3d 698 (7th Cir. 1999) (defendant charged with illegal transfer of automatic weapon; witnesses who testified to his character as an honest and law-abiding citizen properly cross-examined as to allegations that he was behind on child support and allegations of sexual harassment at his workplace).]

However, some states forbid the prosecution from cross-examination about arrests and uncharged conduct. [*Commonwealth v. Morgan,* 559 Pa. 248, 739 A.2d 1033 (1999); Pa.R.Evid. 405(a).]

Since the asking of the question alone suggests to the jury that your client has a hitherto undisclosed sordid past, check your jurisdiction's rules and move in limine to preclude cross-examination on these forbidden areas.

There are some limits on the prosecutor's cross of a character witness. The questioner must have a good faith basis (which can be pretty weak) that the facts implied in his question are true. More important as a practical matter, most courts forbid questions that assume the defendant's guilt of the very charges for which he is on trial. [*United States v. Shwayder,* 312 F.3d 1109, 1120-21 (9th Cir. 2002) (collecting cases); *United States v. Oshatz,* 912 F.2d 267 (2nd Cir. 1990). *See generally* Stephen A. Saltzburg, Guilt Assuming Hypotheticals: Basic Character Evidence Rules, 20 Criminal Justice 47 (Winter 2006). *But see United States v. Kellogg,* 510 F.3d 188 (3d Cir. 2007) (holding, in contrast to most other circuits, that guilt-assuming hypothetical questions may be used of defense opinion character witnesses, though not of reputation character witnesses).]

[§§20:236-20:239 Reserved]

VI.   CLOSING ARGUMENTS AND MOTIONS FOR MISTRIAL

§20:240   Sequence of Closing Arguments

Prosecutors always have the final argument, but practice varies as to whether the prosecutor goes first and then has rebuttal after the defense or whether the defense starts and the prosecution follows.

§20:241   Time Limits

Some judges set time limits for closing arguments. Many will ask the parties to estimate how much time they need, then hold you to it. Whether the court sets a time limit or not, keep your argument brief. Jurors raised in today's video and sound-bite culture cannot tolerate listening to one person speak for much more than 30 minutes. Think of how often you dozed, daydreamed and doodled during college lectures, religious sermons and sports banquet speeches and how you resented those who let their eloquence carry them into an hour of talking.

Remember that your time estimates usually fall short. You may have practiced your argument, but the need to slow down for the jury and to elaborate on some points will extend its duration.

§20:242   Prosecution Closing Argument

Listen carefully. Where does the prosecutor fudge on the promises he made in his opening statement? Where does he misstate the evidence or draw unwarranted inferences?

If the prosecutor follows you, anticipate what he will say and build in responses in your argument.

If the prosecutor goes first, you still should anticipate and attempt to preempt his rebuttal.

Do not feel beholden to the courtroom etiquette that frowns upon objections during your opponent's closing. Instead, guide your objections by the law. You *must* object to improper arguments, especially those that appeal to passion, comment on the defendant's silence, or reference the prosecutor's personal beliefs or matters not in evidence, and request an immediate curative instruction. [*See* §20:243.]

Contemporaneous objection is necessary to halt the misconduct immediately, preserve the issue for appeal and to notify the jury that the prosecutor is misbehaving. *See Maleske v. State,* 89 P.3d 1116, 1119 (OK Crim. App. 2003) ("Regarding the portions of this argument to which defense counsel did not object, we find no plain error occurred. ... We find, however, that the trial court erred by overruling defense counsel's objection once it was made and by allowing the prosecutor to continue this line of improper argument."); *Carruthers v. State*, 272 Ga. 306, 310 & n.16, 528 S.E.2d 217, 222 & n.16 (Ga. 2000) (if defense objects to closing argument, reversal is required if the argument was objectionable and might have contributed to the verdict; otherwise, defense must show a reasonable probability that it had an effect on the trial's outcome).]

If you wait until after the prosecution ends, you also run the risk that the judge will reinforce the prejudicial point. For example, it is not helpful if the judge says, "Remember when the prosecutor referred to the defendant's prior child molestation conviction? Ignore it."

However, hesitate to object to what you believe are misstatements of the evidence:
- Your recollection might be the mistaken one.
- Most judges will express annoyance and simply remind the jury that their recollection controls; seldom will the judge correct the prosecutor.
- The melee that will ensue between you and the prosecutor might revive jurors' interest.
- In this situation your breach of etiquette indeed might backfire. Your discourtesy will embolden the prosecutor to interrupt your closing with similar objections.

§20:243   Improper Prosecution Closing Argument

For the most part, improper comments in a prosecutor's summation must be so egregious as to render the trial fundamentally unfair to warrant a mistrial or reversal on appeal. You must object to preserve the issue.

A judge's admonition and instruction to the jury cure most improper arguments. The admonition has value not only to cure the prejudice, but to demonstrate to the jury that the prosecutor cannot be trusted to argue fairly.

The following types of improper argument are most likely to draw a trial court's ire (embarrassing the prosecutor and making you look good). They are also the most likely to attract appellate scrutiny. [For an excellent compendium of improper arguments, *see* Bennett L. Gershman, *Prosecutorial Misconduct*, Chapter 11 (2d ed. 2005).]

Appeals to passion.

This can take many forms, such as:
- Sympathy for the victim. [*Moore v. Morton*, 255 F.3d 99, 117-18 (3d Cir. 2001) (improper in rape case to argue, "if you don't believe ... [M.A.] and you think she's lying, then you've probably perpetrated a worse assault on her").]

- Name-calling. [*United v. Cannon*, 88 F.3d 1495 (8th Cir. 1996) (calling African-American defendants "bad people" reversible error); *Commonwealth v. Johnson*, 516 Pa. 527, 531, 533 A.2d 994, 996 (1987) (Referring to the defendant as an "executioner" improper).]
- Invocations of wars on crime and the need to protect the community. [*United States v. Arrieta-Agressot*, 3 F.3d 525 (1st Cir. 1993) (urging jurors to view drug-trafficking case as part of war on drugs and defendants as enemy soldiers improper); *Commonwealth v. DeJesus*, 580 Pa. 303, 321-331, 860 A.2d 101, 113-19 (2004) (prohibiting "send a message" arguments).]
- Predictions that dire consequences will flow from an acquittal. [*See United States v. Weatherspoon*, 410 F.3d 1142, 1149 (9th Cir. 2005) ("Convicting Mr. Weatherspoon is gonna make you comfortable knowing there's not convicted felons on the street with loaded handguns, that there's not convicted felons carrying around semiautomatic. ... You can feel comfortable knowing there's a convicted felon that's been found guilty of possessing a loaded firearm, a fully loaded semiautomatic weapon. ... [T]he law of being a felon in possession of a firearm, that protects a lot of people out there too. ... [F]inding this man guilty is gonna protect other individuals in this community" all improper).]
- Overly dramatic Powerpoint displays. Slides that superimpose the word "Guilty" over a picture of the defendant have led to reversal on the reasoning that they are inflammatory and suggest that the prosecutor holds a personal opinion as to the defendant's guilt. [*State v. Hecht*, 319 P.3d 836 (Wash Ct. App. 2014).]
- Also forbidden is the argument that the defendant's marital infidelity proves him or her to be dishonest. *United States v. Repak*, 852 F.3d 230, 259 (3d Cir. 2017).

Comment on the defendant's silence.

The prosecutor cannot ask the jury to reach an adverse inference from the defendant's failure to testify at trial. Doing so penalizes the defendant for standing on his Fifth Amendment privilege against self-incrimination. [*Griffin v. California*, 380 U.S. 609 (1965).]

Watch for more subtle comments on the defendant's silence such as:

- References to the defendant's post-arrest silence. [*United States v. Mooney*, 315 F.3d 54, 61 (1st Cir. 2002) (improper to mention that after his arrest, defendant chose not to talk to the police).]
- Comments on his failure to show remorse for his actions. [*See Lesko v. Lehman*, 925 F.2d 1527, 1544-45 (3d Cir. 1991) (commenting on defendant's failure to apologize for his crimes improper).]
- Comment on the defendant's consultation with or retention of counsel after the offense. [*State v. Marshall*, 123 N.J. 1, 124, 586 A.2d 85, 148 (NJ 1991) ("we are fully in accord with the decisions of the federal Courts of Appeals holding that a prosecutor's statement suggesting that retention of counsel is inconsistent with innocence impermissibly infringes on a defendant's constitutional right to counsel"; collecting cases).]

However, the prosecutor can highlight the defense failure to introduce evidence to support a particular argument or the absence of evidence contradicting the prosecution's witnesses. [*See United States v. Brennan*, 326 F.3d 176 (3d Cir. 2003) (prosecutor's argument that nothing in the evidence contradicted prosecution's description of transaction with the defendant was proper); *but see United States v. Skandier*, 758 F.2d 43 (1st Cir. 1985) (reversible error to state baldly that prosecution case is unrebutted or to pose to jury questions such as, "How can defense counsel explain...?").]

Citation to religious authority.

[*See State v. Ceballos*, 266 Conn. 364, 382-93 & nn.31-37, 832 A.2d 14 (Conn. 2003) (extensive review of caselaw and commentary; improper for prosecutor in sex abuse case to contrast victim's fear that God would punish her for lying with defendant's lack of concern for God's laws and to refer to "Satan's daughter"); *Commonwealth v. Chambers*, 528 Pa. 558, 599 A.2d 630 (1991) (invocation of the Bible at sentencing phase of capital trial results in automatic reversal and possible disciplinary action).]

Reference to matters not in evidence or to the prosecutor's personal beliefs; vouching for witnesses.

[*See State v. Mussey*, 893 A.2d 701 (NH 2006) (arguments that police would not lie because in doing so they risk their careers are improper; surveys decisions).]

Reliance on racial or ethnic stereotypes.

Besides the obvious racial and ethnic slurs, watch for:

- Comparisons drawn between the fair victim and the swarthy perpetrator. [*State v. Shabazz*, 98 Haw. 358, 48 P.3d 605 (Ct. App. 2002) (reference to complainant as "young local woman" "trapped" and "surrounded" by "six African-American males" reversible error).]

- Comments on the defendant's status as an illegal alien. [*See United States v. Cruz-Padilla*, 227 F.3d 1064, 1068-69 (8thCir. 2000) (in drug-trafficking case, improper to argue, "He is here under fraudulent and illegal circumstances, and as such, he is basically from day to day living a lie. So lying and deceiving to Mr. Cruz-Padilla is not something that is hard to do or out of the ordinary").]
- Arguments that intra-racial eyewitness identifications are more reliable. [*People v. Alexander*, 94 N.Y.2d 382, 727 N.E.2d 109, 705 N.Y.S.2d 551 (1999) (treating this primarily as improper vouching because there was no evidence introduced to show that intra-racial identifications are in fact more reliable).]
- Arguments based on the defendant's sexual orientation. [*People v. Garcia*, 229 Cal. App.4th 302, 177 Cal. Rptr.3d 231 (Cal App 4th Div. 2014)(Defendant was charged with sexually abusing a female child. The prosecutor implied in questions and argued in summation that because the defendant was a lesbian, she was more likely to abuse a female child. The court reversed, holding that sexual orientation is absolutely inadmissible for any purpose and is not relevant to motive or intent.)]

Misuse of evidence admitted for limited purposes.

[*E.g., Weatherspoon*, 410 F.3d at 1149 n.5 (while defendant's status as convicted felon was admissible as element of offense in felon in possession case, prosecutor improperly harped on it in context of arguing that jury needed to protect community from convicted felons carrying guns).]

Misstating the evidence.

Prosecution misstatements of the evidence violate the defendant's right not to be convicted except on the basis of evidence adduced at trial. [*United States v. Mageno*, 762 F.3d 933, 943 (9th Cir. 2014).] While prosecutors properly may ask the jury to draw reasonable inferences from the evidence, they may not flatly misstate it [*Id.*] The failure to preface assertions with "I submit" or to warn the jury that its recollection controls or that the statement to come represents a suggested inference from the evidence aggravates the error. [*Id.* (reversing drug conspiracy conviction where defendant's role was to translate for her godson during drug negotiations. The godson admitted on cross-examination that he was deported years ago for dealing drugs, but he never was asked if the defendant knew he was deported, much less the reason. The prosecution improperly argued that the defendant knew the godson was deported for prior drug activity and that the godson testified that she knew it).]

§20:244   Defense Closing Argument

View your closing argument as an opportunity to make inferences and draw conclusions from the evidence, apply the law to it, and equip the jurors with arguments to make on your behalf. You cannot and should not bludgeon the jury into seeing the correctness of your case.

Forego boilerplate.

The jury wants a framework for analyzing and weighing the evidence. Do not lecture them on the purpose of closing argument or the evolution of our legal system since the nobles confronted King John at Runnymede.

Explicit flag-waving usually achieves little for the defense. It is the government (i.e., the prosecution) that wages war, and most good citizens consider it their duty to follow the government until the enemy (i.e., your client) is defeated.

Your appeals should be to the values embodied in our legal system. That is, the presumption of innocence and the requirement of proof beyond a reasonable and their corollaries: the need for corroboration and trustworthy witnesses.

Tell a story.

This may seem difficult where you want to emphasize the prosecution's failure to meet its burden of proof and where you want to avoid taking on any burden of proof yourself. Usually, by the time you rest, you may have succeeded in poking large holes in the prosecution's proof, but will not have proven anything affirmative. Your story, then, is about the recklessness of the prosecution and the perfidy of its witnesses.

Emphasize reasonable doubt.

Standard jury instructions usually repeat over and over that the elements of the offense must be proven beyond a reasonable doubt. However, when it comes to explaining what a reasonable doubt is, most judges say little more than, "A reasonable doubt is the kind of doubt that would cause you to hesitate in one of the most important decisions of your life." Then the judge will explain at length what a reasonable doubt is *not*: it is not doubt founded on speculation or sympathy or any possible doubt.

List the defects in the prosecution's case and explain that each alone is reason to doubt–reasonable doubt.

You also can explain what proof beyond a reasonable doubt would look like and contrast the weak proof upon which the prosecution relies. This technique resonates in this day of police procedural novels and television shows which exaggerate the efficiency and availability of DNA evidence and other forensic techniques.

Tell a story or offer an analogy that explains what a reasonable doubt is and immediately apply it to your case. For example, you might emphasize the weight of the reasonable doubt burden by informing the jury that it is heavier than the burden the government bears when it is trying to sever a parent's rights to see his child, clear and convincing evidence. Then ask the jury whether it would rely upon the prosecution's drug-addicted snitch to decide who is a fit parent, much less whether your client is guilty of a serious crime.

Use physical exhibits and demonstrative aids.

Presenting blow-ups or electronic visual displays of the evidence or testimony, if a transcript is available, enhances the persuasiveness of your argument. It breaks the monotony, and jurors tend to remember better what they are shown rather than just what is described to them. Pointing to a document or verbatim testimony to support your points proves that you can back up your argument and builds credibility.

Once upon a time, enlargements had to be prepared well in advance of arguments and placed on large posterboards. Most courtrooms now have video monitors on which you can display exhibits without special preparation. Prepare nonetheless–technical glitches, your resulting embarrassment and the judge and jury's impatience may sabotage the best of arguments.

Avoid improper argument.

You should convey strong belief in the righteousness of your cause, but the same rules apply to you as to the prosecutor:

- Do not misstate the evidence.
- Do not cite to your personal beliefs.
- Do not appeal to religious doctrine or prejudice.
- Do not attempt to inflame the jury.

Of course, the prosecutor cannot appeal if your arguments improperly move the jury to acquittal, but he can object, and the judge might admonish you in front of the jury, signaling to them that you are trying to break the rules and that you cannot be trusted. Further, under the doctrine of invited response, the judge might permit the prosecutor to respond to your improprieties with his own. [*See United States v. Young*, 470 U.S. 1, 12-13 (1985).]

Finally, remember we live in the day of cynicism and understatement. Tears, yelling, and getting down on your knees are both bad argument and bad theater.

§20:245   Motions for Mistrial

Generally, a defendant's successful motion for a mistrial waives the Double Jeopardy protection against retrial. [*United States v. Doyle*, 121 F.3d 1078, 1084 (7th Cir. 1997).]

There is an exception to this rule for those cases where the prosecutor's conduct "was intended to provoke the defendant into moving for a mistrial." [*Oregon v. Kennedy*, 456 U.S. 667, 679 (1982).]

The key question is whether the prosecutor deliberately introduced the error in order to provoke the defendant into moving for a mistrial, and thereby rescuing a trial going badly. [*United States v. Higgins*, 75 F.3d 332, 333 (7th Cir. 1996).]

If that is the case, the Constitution treats matters as if the mistrial had been declared on the prosecutor's initiative, and bars retrial. [*United States v. Gilmore*, 454 F.3d 725, 729 (7th Cir. 2006).]

To preserve any claim of error in the court's grant of a mistrial, you must object. [*Camden v. Circuit Court*, 892 F.2d 610, 615 (7th Cir. 1989) (a defendant who fails to object to a mistrial gives his or her implied consent to it).]

Should the court deny your motion to preclude retrial on double jeopardy grounds, you can appeal immediately, without awaiting retrial and conviction. [*Abney v. United States*, 431 U.S. 651, 662 (1977) (holding that denials of motions to dismiss claiming double jeopardy grounds are immediately appealable).]

[§§20:246-20:249 Reserved]

VII. JURY INSTRUCTIONS, READ-BACKS, AND VERDICT

§20:250   The Timing of the Instructions

Practices differ as to whether the judge instructs the jury before or after the parties present closing arguments. Some judges give part of the charge before argument and then finish after the attorneys close.

Opinions vary on which approach benefits the defense. Having the charge before closings gives the jury a framework to guide their listening to the arguments. You can echo the instructions in your argument and emphasize how the reasonable doubt charge applies to the evidence, or how the evidence fails to establish a particular element of the offense. The jury then is less likely to rely on an overall sense that the defendant is a bad person or did something wrong, but instead will demand proof and argument that the evidence established the elements beyond a reasonable doubt.

Instructing before closings does have some disadvantages. In jurisdictions where the defense closes first, you lose the advantage of primacy. The jury might be dozing by the time you begin. Also, since the instructions have been completed before closing argument, the last words that jury hears are the prosecutor's, urging them to convict.

Structure your argument differently depending on the timing of the judge's charge. Where the judge goes first, abbreviate your explanations of the law and quickly transition from the judge's charge to an application of the instructions to your case.

§20:251   General Jury Instructions

Always request jury instructions on credibility that support your defense.

Many jurisdictions require that, where applicable, the judge must instruct the jury on:
- The unreliability of testimony from:
    - Informants.
    - Accomplices.
    - Drug addicts.
    - Interested witnesses such as those who stand to receive a sentence reduction.
- The special considerations that might apply to:
    - Eyewitness identification testimony.
    - Prior inconsistent statements.
    - Testimony from witnesses with prior convictions.

Weave these instructions into your closing argument so that the judge reinforces both your argument and your credibility.

Most jurisdictions entitle both the defense and prosecution to a "missing witness" charge where its adversary fails to call an apparently favorable witness who was within the opponent's power to produce. Challenge a prosecution request for such a charge on the grounds that it undermines the presumption of innocence and violates Due Process by casting the burden of proof on the defendant. [*See State v. Hill*, 199 N.J. 545, 974 A.2d 403 (2009) (forbidding such a charge against the defense in New Jersey and noting that while most jurisdictions permit it, a growing minority do not).]

§20:252   Theory of Defense Charge

Always submit a brief theory of defense charge telling the jury that if it accepts your contentions or theory, it must acquit.

"[A] criminal defendant is entitled to have instructions presented relating to any theory of defense for which there is any foundation in the evidence, no matter how weak or incredible, that evidence may be." [*United States v. Durham*, 825 F.2d 716, 718-19 (2d Cir. 1987) (in arson case, error to refuse defense instruction that defendants must be acquitted if they intended only to dupe undercover agents and never intended to burn down bar for hire). *See also United States v. Brown*, 287 F.3d 965, 974 (10th Cir. 2002) (error to refuse charge on lesser included offense of involuntary manslaughter in murder case where evidence supported claim if impact self-defense).]

Merely stating the general principles of law is not sufficient. "[I]t is of some value to a defendant to have the trial judge clearly indicate to the jury what his theory of the case is, and that that theory, if believed, justifies acquittal." [*United States v. Pedroza*, 750 F.2d 187, 205 (2d Cir. 1984) (in kidnapping case, court should have instructed jury that if defendants believed that the child-victim's father voluntarily turned him over to defendants, they must be acquitted).]

Having the judge summarize your defense and instruct the jury that if it accepts the defense it must acquit reinforces your closing argument.

To increase the likelihood that the judge will give the instruction, tailor the charge to the facts of your case, avoid argumentation and adhere accurately to the law.

Be brief. Otherwise, the judge might reject the charge as inaccurate and as subsumed within his general instructions.

Form:
• **Form 20-8** Theory of Defense Charge

§20:253   Juror Misconduct

Occasionally, you may learn before the verdict of juror misconduct, such as premature deliberations, or of improper extraneous influences on the jury. "Faced with a credible allegation of juror misconduct during trial, a court has an obligation to investigate and, if necessary, correct the problem." [*United States v. Haynes*, 729 F.3d 178, 191 (2d Cir. 2013) (when alternate informed defense counsel that prior to deliberations, some of the jurors said that the defendant "might be guilty, [because] she's here," court erred in failing to inquire of the alternate juror).]

You must raise these concerns as soon as possible with the judge to preserve the issue. [*See Government of Virgin Islands v. Weatherwax*, 20 F.3d 572, 578-79 (3d Cir. 1994) (finding counsel ineffective for failing to raise the issue promptly); *People v. Friedgood;* 58 N.Y. 2d 467, 448 N.E. 2d 1317, 462 N.Y.S. 2d 406 (1983) (denying hearing into misconduct where trial counsel irresponsibly delayed raising issue).]

Seek individual voir dire of the jurors to determine whether the misconduct or influence was prejudicial. [*See United States v. Resko*, 3F.3d 684, 691-93 (3d Cir. 1993) (strong preference for individual rather than in banc voir dire, at least once the misconduct is shown to have taken place); *Tunstall v. Hopkins*, 306 F.3d 601, 610 (8th Cir. 2002) (jurors should be polled individually to see if they were exposed).]

Courts apply different standards of prejudice. Some courts presume prejudice. [*E.g., Tunstall*, 306 F.3d at 611 (collecting cases).] Others require that extraneous information must "substantially prejudice" the defendant before a mistrial will be granted (or a new trial on appeal) [*United States v. Fumo*, 655 F.3d 288 (3d Cir. 2011) (affirming denial of mistrial for juror's Facebook posts during deliberations)], although those courts, too, will presume prejudice if the extraneous information "is of a considerably serious nature," [*United States v. Lloyd*, 269 F.3d 228, 238 (3d Cir. 2001)], or if it is through a direct third-party contact rather than a media report. [*United States v. Urban*, 404 F.3d 754, 777 n.9 (3d Cir. 2005).]

"The factors ... looked to in determining whether there was substantial prejudice include whether (1) "the extraneous information ... relate[s] to one of the elements of the case that was decided against the party moving for a new trial"; (2) the extent of the jury's exposure to the extraneous information; (3) the time at which the jury receives the extraneous information; (4) the length of the jury's deliberations and the structure of the verdict; (5) the existence of instructions from the court that the jury should consider only evidence developed in the case; and (6) whether there is "a heavy volume of incriminating evidence." [*Fumo*, 655 F.3d at 307 (citations omitted).]

§20:254   Allegations of Juror Bias or Refusal to Deliberate

Occasionally, juror notes mid-deliberation will suggest that one or a few jurors hold biases or refuse to deliberate. This becomes a delicate issue both for you and the judge: the notes may indicate that the allegedly-disruptive juror is on your side, but sometimes you cannot tell. The judge will not, and should not, inquire into the jurors' views. Absent compelling evidence that the juror is biased against you (e.g., a note stating that the juror hates the defendant because of his race or other inappropriate reason), you should assume that the juror is holding out for you, resist efforts to question him or replace him, and insist either that deliberations continue or a mistrial be declared.

The standards for replacing the juror are high, and you should insist on them. There must be "substantial evidence of juror misconduct–including credible allegations of jury nullification or of a refusal to deliberate ..." [*United States v. Kemp*, 500 F.3d 257, 302 (3d Cir. 2007).] Upon such allegations, the trial court has discretion to investigate by questioning the jurors. The inquiry must avoid touching on the merits of the deliberations, and the trial judge must warn the jurors that in responding to questions they must not reveal the substance or method of their deliberations. [*Id.* at 302.]

In deciding whether to discharge the juror, the "'court may not dismiss a juror during deliberations if the request for discharge stems from doubts the juror harbors about the sufficiency of the government's evidence.'" [*Id.* at 303 (quoting *United States v. Brown*, 823 F.2d 591, 596 (D.C. Cir. 1987)).] On the other hand, refusal to apply the law or to follow the court's instructions, or a bias not based on the evidence, are appropriate grounds for dismissal. [*Id.*]

The ultimate standard, though, is equivalent to the reasonable doubt standard: discharge is appropriate only "when there is no reasonable possibility that the allegation of misconduct stems from the juror's view of the evidence." [*Kemp*, 500 F.3d at 304. *See, e.g., United States v. Symington*, 195 F.3d 1080 (9th Cir. 1999).] Other courts articulate an even more stringent "any possibility" standard. [*E.g., United States v. Thomas*, 116 F.3d 606, 622 (2d Cir. 1997).]

§20:255 Requests for Read-Backs

The judge's discretion.

Whether to allow a read back is in the judge's discretion. However, the judge must exercise discretion. [*United States v. Zarintash*, 736 F.2d 66, 70 (3d Cir. 1984) (judge should consider whether readback will excessively prolong trial and whether it will emphasize unduly one portion of the evidence).]

The judge cannot issue a blanket prohibition against readbacks. [*United States v. Criollo*, 962 F.2d 141 (2d Cir. 1992) (trial judge interrupted defense counsel's summation when counsel suggested jury request readback if it had doubt about what testimony said to tell jury there would be no readbacks; reversed even absent jury request for a readback).]

Lengthy read-backs.

Especially where the readback may be lengthy, some courts favor sending the jury a transcript of the testimony rather than having an oral recitation in the courtroom. The jury should be instructed to consider the evidence as a whole and not give undue emphasis to any single portion of the testimony. [*United States v. Escotto*, 121 F.3d 81 84-85 (2d Cir. 1997).]

The danger in a readback is that it will emphasize the prosecution's side of the case. "The parameters concerning the extent that testimony should be read to the jury are to be set by the jury's request. Hence the court, if it deems it appropriate, may permit the jury to hear only a portion of a witness's testimony." [*Miller v. Larkins*, 111 F.Supp.2d 575, 585 (E.D.Pa. 2000).]

Argue that if the jury requests a prosecution witness's testimony on a topic, the readback should include direct and your cross to answer the jury fairly.

The trial court's discretion includes the authority to deny a readback when it would be excessively time-consuming or when it would unduly emphasize one portion of the evidence over others. [*United States v. Binder*, 769 F.2d 595 (9th Cir. 1985) (error to replay videotape of child-victim's testimony for jury because unduly emphasized that evidence); *State v. Lane*, 582 N.W.2d 256, 259-60 (Minn. 1998) (affirming trial court's denial of readback on rationale that it would improperly highlight certain testimony at expense of others and the trial was brief and jury should be able to recall the testimony).]

Exploit the judge's interest in expediency. The fewer pages and passages designated, the briefer the readback, but the lawyers' haggling might consume more time than the brevity saves. Decide quickly what you want read and propose a readback that fairly includes the sections that both you and the prosecutor want the jury to hear.

Often, however, an extensive readback holds little benefit for the defense, such as when the jury requests only the direct of a prosecution witness or when the cross's value lay in tone of voice and expression, not the information conveyed. (The court reporter will read the testimony in a speedy drone.) In that case, stall. Ask that the jury be more specific. As time passes, the jury might send another note abandoning its request.

The client's presence.

Whenever there is a readback, make sure your client is present. He has a right to be there. [*See* W.R. Habeeb, Giving, in Accused's Absence, Additional Instruction to Jury After Submission of Felony Case, 94 A.L.R.2d 270 (right to be present during answering jury questions, readbacks and supplemental instructions).]

The client's attentive presence will remind the jurors of the importance of their decision.

§20:256 The "Dynamite" Charge

If the jury indicates difficulty in reaching a unanimous verdict, the judge may give a charge admonishing them to try, and asking the minority jurors to reconsider.

This type of charge is called an "Allen" charge [*see Allen v. United States*, 164 U.S. 492 (1896)] or a "dynamite" charge for its effect in blasting a jury into unanimity.

The charge must be evaluated carefully to see that it does not coerce the jurors to the extent of demanding a verdict. Courts consider the coercive effect in light of all the facts and circumstances. [*See Spears v. Greiner*, 459 F.3d 200, 205-07 (2d Cir. 2006).]

However, in federal cases, inquiry into the jury's numerical division "requires automatic reversal even when the judge does not determine which side the majority favors and defense counsel raises no objection." [Annual Review of Criminal Procedure, 34 Geo. L. J. 517, 531-32 (2005); *Brasfield v. United States*, 272 U.S. 448 (1926). *See also Sanders v. Lamarque*, 357 F.3d 943, 947-50 (9th Cir. 2004) (reversible error when judge removed sole dissenting juror upon disclosure that 25 years before the trial she lived in an area with gang activity when juror's answers showed that she was not biased); *but see Commonwealth v. Greer*, 597 Pa. 373, 951 A.2d 346 (2008) (Pennsylvania does not follow the federal supervisory rule and permits inquiry into the jury's numerical division).] Further, where the judge knows which jurors are holdouts, and the jurors know that the judge knows their identities, an *Allen* charge is coercive and improper because it appears directed specifically directed at them. [*United States v. Williams*, 547 F.3d 1187, 1205-07 (9th Cir. 2008).]

PRACTICE TIPS:

- Object.

Among the circumstances the court considers in assessing coerciveness is the presence or absence of a contemporaneous defense objection, because it indicates whether the coercive effect was immediately apparent. [*Greiner*, 459 F.3d at 206.]

- Insist on balance in the charge.

"[A] necessary component of any *Allen*-type charge requires the trial judge to admonish the jurors not to surrender their own conscientiously held beliefs." [*Smalls v. Batista*, 191 F.3d 272, 279 (2d Cir. 1999); *see also United States v. Haynes*, 729 F.3d 178, 194 (2d Cir. 2013) (charge improper for not suggesting that failure to reach a verdict was permissible and for statement that the court believed the jury would arrive at a just verdict after the weekend); *United States v. Eastern Medical Billings, Inc.*, 230 F.3d 600, 613 (3d Cir. 2000) (instruction imbalanced to the extent of requiring reversal where it never instructed majority jurors to reexamine their views, but told minority to consider whether their views were reasonable in light of their failure to persuade the majority).]

- Object to any reference to extraneous factors.

[*See United States v. Jackson*, 443 F.3d 293, 297 (3d Cir. 2006) (time and expense an improper consideration).]

- Note the time between the charge and a guilty verdict.

If the time between the supplemental charge and the verdict is brief, make sure to note the brevity of the interval. One of the factors in assessing coerciveness is how quickly the jury returned a verdict after hearing the charge, with rapidity suggesting coercion. [*See Lowenfield v. Phelps*, 484 U.S. 231, 240 (1988).]

§20:257 Supplemental Instructions During Deliberations

Supplemental instructions during deliberations that introduce a new theory of liability or materially modify the original instructions are improper because they deprive the defense of the opportunity to address the instructions in closing argument. [*Commonwealth v. Melvin*, 2014 PA Super 181 (Pa. Super. Court 2014)(Instructing jury during deliberations on a new theory of criminal liability - accomplice liability - violated Pa. R. Cr. P. 647(A), which is identical to Fed Rule 30); *United States v. Smith*, 789 F.2d 196, 202 (3d Cir. 1986).] To preserve the issue, defense counsel must request (and be denied) opportunity to offer additional argument to the jury to address the supplemental charge after being informed that it would be given. [*Melvin, supra*.] In addition, the defense must show prejudice in the form of explaining how he was misled in formulating closing arguments. [*United States v. Eisen*, 974 F.2d 246, 256 (2d Cir. 1992).]

§20:258 The Verdict

A general verdict (i.e., guilty or not guilty for each count) is the norm in criminal cases.

Special verdicts or special interrogatories, which ask the jury to make specific findings on dispositive issues, tend to direct the jury to the findings it must make to convict, and you should object to them. [*United States v. Wilson*, 629 F.2d 439 (6th Cir. 1980) (reversing for use of special interrogatories on the elements of insanity defense); *see United*

States v. Fanfan, 458 F.3d 7, 13 (1st Cir. 2006) ("special interrogatories or special verdicts pose risks in criminal cases; for example, they can be asked in a form that suggests through progressive steps a particular outcome"; dicta).]

If the jury convicts, be sure to ask the clerk to poll each juror and ask if the verdict as stated is his or her verdict. While usually a meaningless exercise, juror recantation does happen.

VIII. FORMS

Form 20-1   Motion in Limine to Preclude Defendant's Other Bad Acts

IN THE UNITED STATES DISTRICT COURT
FOR THE _____ DISTRICT OF _____

UNITED STATES OF AMERICA	)	
	)	
V.	)	CRIMINAL NO.
	)	
JF	)	

DEFENDANT'S MOTION IN LIMINE REGARDING EVIDENCE THE GOVERMENT INTENDS TO INTRODUCE AT TRIAL PURSUANT TO FEDERAL RULE OF EVIDENCE 404(B) AND SUPPORTING MEMORANDUM OF LAW

AND NOW, comes the Defendant, JF ("F"), by his attorney, Thomas Farrell, Esquire, and files this Motion in Limine Regarding Evidence the Government Intends to Introduce at Trial Pursuant to Federal Rule of Evidence 404(b) and Supporting Memorandum of Law and in support thereof, avers as follows:

In its Notice, filed on _____, the government identifies several prior bad acts which it proposes to introduce at trial on Count Two. As to the bad acts, identified in Paragraphs 1, 2, 3, and 4 of the Government's Notice, F objects to the proposed admission of evidence tending to prove that on October 20, 1995; October 29, 1996; October 30, 1996; and May 28, 2002; he possessed deliverable amounts of a controlled substance, and when arrested on October 20, 1995, October 29, 1996, October 30, 1996, and June 8, 2002, he gave police false names, that is, names other than his own. All this evidence should be excluded under FRE 403 and 404(b) for the following reasons.

PRIOR BAD ACTS
A. The October 20, 1995, October 29, 1996, and October 30, 1996 Incidents

Evidence of F's prior convictions or the nature of the underlying crimes is not relevant to any issue in the case. These convictions merely go to his propensity to commit crime and should be excluded. *United States v. Sampson,* 980 F.2d 883 (3d Cir. 1992). There is no "genuine need" for the admission of any of the defendant's convictions or the nature of the underlying offenses. *United States v. Scarfo,* 850 F.2d 1015 (3d Cir. 1988). Here, the risk is great that F's prior convictions and/or "bad acts" will arouse the jury against him unnecessarily and will influence the jury to convict him on improper grounds. *Id.*

The Third Circuit has held that "Federal Rule of Evidence 404(b) generally prohibits evidence of extrinsic acts that are intended to show a defendant's propensity for crime or to suggest pejorative inferences that may reflect upon a defendant's character." *Government of Virgin Islands v. Harris,* 938 F.2d 401 (3d Cir. 1991). "When such evidence inadvertently reaches the attention of the jury, it is most difficult, if not impossible, to assume continued integrity of the presumption of innocence. A drop of ink cannot be removed from a glass of milk." *Government of Virgin Islands v. Toto,* 529 F.2d 278, 283 (3d Cir. 1976).

Here any introduction of evidence of F's past crimes or "bad acts," especially because they are similar in nature to the crime charged in Count Two of the Indictment, would prejudice F's case before the jury and they may be inclined to convict him based on the prejudicial information.

In order for the government to offer evidence of prior "bad acts," especially those involving prior drug offenses, "it must clearly articulate how that evidence fits into a chain of logical inferences, no link of which can be the inference that because the defendant committed drug offenses before, he therefore is more likely to have committed this one." *United States v. Sampson,* 980 F.2d 883, 887 (3d Cir. 1992). In its Notice, the government fails to articulate how the evidence of F's prior narcotics transactions fits into a chain of logical events. This evidence does not tend to show anything other than F's character and propensity to commit the crime charged in Count Two of the Indictment.

The government asserts that F's prior narcotics transactions show his access to large quantities of cocaine. However, this case does not involve large quantities of cocaine. In Count Two of the Indictment, F is charged with possessing 21 grams of cocaine base. Twenty-one grams of cocaine base is the amount possessed by street-level buyers and sellers, not by large-scale drug traffickers.

While evidence of prior "bad acts" sometimes can be admitted to show opportunity to commit a crime under FRE 404(b), *see, e.g., United States v. McGlory,* 968 F.2d 309, 338-39 (3d Cir. 1992); whether F had access to large quantities of cocaine is irrelevant to the present case. This case deals with quantities of cocaine that are routinely available on the streets of any city. In a large-scale distribution case, such evidence tends to prove guilt because few individuals have access to multi-kilogram quantities of cocaine; that the defendant on trial once did in the past tends to show he might have the same access now. This is not such a case.

The government's purpose in admitting this evidence is improper because it could be inferred that not only may F be guilty of the charge of possession, but he may be a drug trafficker as well. Such an inference offends both Rules 404(b) and 403. In *United States v. Schwartz,* 790 F.2d 1059, 1062 (3d Cir. 1986) (per curiam), unfair prejudice arose from the fact that the testimony of prior sales suggested the defendant was a large scale supplier of cocaine to high school students, while the indictment only charged the defendant with "giving away a small quantity of cocaine in a social setting." The Court of Appeals held that the relevance of this evidence to any issue other than "character/propensity" was marginal while "the prejudice to the defendant was very great" and reversed the conviction. *Id.*

Finally, the government intends to offer F's prior narcotics transactions to rebut his defense that he did not know that there was cocaine in his pocket. F will not be asserting the defense that he did not know there was cocaine in his pocket. In this case, the cocaine was found on the street, where F allegedly threw it. The defense will be that F did not possess cocaine, not the improbable defense that he had the bags in his pocket but did not know they were there or did not know what they were.

Further, the 1995 and 1996 events are too old to have any probative value. On June 8, 2002, F was 23 years old. On October 20, 1995, F was 16, and on October 29 and 30, 1996, he was 17. Nearly eight and nine years have lapsed between F's prior arrests for possession and the conduct at issue in the trial on Count Two. This time lapse renders the 1995 and 1996 evidence stale and meaningless.

In *United States v. Aguilar-Aranceta,* 58 F.3d 796 (1st Cir. 1995), the court reversed the defendant's conviction for possession with intent to distribute because the district erred in admitting four-year-old conviction for possession of cocaine. In its FRE 403 analysis, the court reasoned that the probative value of the defendant's prior drug conviction was low because the passage of four years made it too remote in time. While the court conceded that, since the prior conviction and the prosecution at issue both involved the mailing of a package from Colombia to the defendant's same post office box, the prior conviction was probative on the issue of knowledge, the court held its admission was error under FRE 403. *Id.* at 801. *See also United States v. Lynn,* 856 F.2d 430 (1st Cir. 1988) (noting that six-year period between the prior conviction and the instant offense significantly diminished the probative value of the prior conviction).

The evidence of the 1995 and 1996 arrests for possession do not tend to make any more likely the ultimate matter of proof, that is, that on June 8, 2002, F possessed the "crack" in question. If evidence of F's dated behavior does, in some marginal way, make his alleged June 8, 2002 possession of "crack" more likely, then the prejudicial effect of its admission in the trial on Count Two far outweighs its probative value and it should be inadmissible. Fed. R. Evid. 403.

WHEREFORE, the Defendant, JF, respectfully requests that the Court grant the within in Motion in Limine to the Government's Notice of Evidence it Intends to Introduce at Trial Pursuant to Federal Rule of Evidence 404(b), and bar the evidence relating to F's conduct in October 1995, October 1996, and May 2002.

Respectfully submitted,

_____

Thomas J. Farrell

Form 20-2   Motion in Limine to Permit Evidence of Consciousness of Innocence

Motion in Limine

IN THE COURT OF COMMON PLEAS OF _____ COUNTY, PENNSYLVANIA
COMMONWEALTH OF _____,

      Plaintiff.

    v.

EP,

      Defendant.

CRIMINAL DIVISION

NO. CC–

MEMORANDUM OF LAW IN SUPPORT OF DEFENDANT'S MOTION IN LIMINE TO PERMIT EVIDENCE OF CONSCIOUSNESS OF INNOCENCE

**Filed on behalf of Defendant,
EP**

**Counsel of record for this party:
THOMAS J. FARRELL, ESQUIRE**

MEMORANDUM OF LAW IN SUPPORT OF DEFENDANT'S MOTION IN LIMINE TO PERMIT EVIDENCE OF CONSCIOUSNESS OF INNOCENCE AND TO PERMIT CROSS-EXAMINATION ON WITNESS'S PENDING CHARGES

AND NOW COMES Defendant, EP, by and through his attorney, Thomas J. Farrell, and files the following Memorandum of Law and Motion in Limine.

Consciousness of Innocence

The defense intends to introduce evidence that Mr. P remained in the neighborhood and stuck to his usual routine in the days after the _____ shooting to show his consciousness of innocence.

A defendant in a criminal case has a fundamental right "to present evidence provided that the evidence is relevant and not subject to exclusion under one of our established evidentiary rules. Evidence is relevant if it tends to prove or disprove some material fact or tends to make a fact at issue more or less probable." *Commonwealth v. McGowan*, 535 Pa. 292, 294-95, 635 A.2d 113, 115 (1993); *see Holmes v. South Carolina*, 126 S.Ct. 1727 (2006); *Chambers v. Mississippi*, 410 U.S. 284 (1973).

While the case law in Pennsylvania on evidence of consciousness of innocence is sparse, what little there is acknowledges that a defendant is entitled to present and argue to the jury evidence that suggests a consciousness of innocence. *See Commonwealth v. Wyoda*, 44 Pa. Super. 552 (1910); *Commonwealth v. Shoemaker*, 8 Pa. D&C 668 (CCP Center County 1926).

Numerous federal courts, however, have ruled that evidence of the defendant's failure to flee is admissible, and defense counsel may argue to the jury that it tends to prove innocence, although these courts have not required trial courts to instruct the jury specifically on the significance of such evidence. *See, e.g., United States v. McQuarry*, 726 F.2d 401 (8th Cir. 1984); *United States v. Telfaire*, 469 F.2d 552, 558 (DC Cir. 1971); *United States v. Scott*, 446 F.2d 509 (9th Cir. 1972). *See generally* Weinstein's FEDERAL EVIDENCE, §401.08 [4] at p.401-59 (2nd Ed. 1997) (evidence of consciousness of innocence should be admitted).

BIAS

Defendant submits that the Court should grant him wide latitude in cross-examining the prosecution's cooperating witnesses who have pending charges on (1) the nature of pending charges, both related and unrelated to the present offense; (2) the penalties faced on those charges; (3) any probationary sentence the witness is under; and (4) the witness's past criminal history.

Criminal defendants have a constitutional right under the Sixth Amendment to the United States Constitution and Article I, Section 9 of the Pennsylvania Constitution to cross-examine prosecution witnesses for possible bias. *Commonwealth v. Evans,* 512 A.2d 626 (1986). Consequently, wide latitude must be afforded the defense in probing a cooperating witness's bias: "the better course in instances such as the present is to favor the defendant's ability to fully and freely challenge the testimony and evidence of the prosecution with whatever tools are at his disposal, so long as that use can be justified by an offer of relevance to the proceedings." *Commonwealth v. Borders,* 522 Pa. 161, 165, 560 A.2d 758, 760 (1989) (reversing conviction for precluding cross of victim on juvenile adjudications that occurred after the victim made a pre-trial identification of the accused).

In *Evans,* the Court reversed a conviction where the trial court permitted cross-examination of the prosecution's accomplice-witness on the crime he committed with the defendant, but forbade cross on an unrelated pending case. Although both the witness and the prosecution denied that any favorable treatment had been promised for the testimony, the Supreme Court held that the defense must be allowed to question the witness on pending cases:

Even if the prosecutor has made no promises, either on the present case or on other pending criminal matters, the witness may hope for favorable treatment from the prosecutor if the witness presently testifies in a way that is helpful to the prosecution. And if that possibility exists, the jury should know about it.

Evans, 511 Pa. at 224-25, 512 A.2d at 631-32.

In *Commonwealth v. Wilson,* 619 A.2d 1063 (Pa. Super. 1993) it was reversible error to disallow cross-examination of a prosecution witness with regard to fact that pursuant to a plea agreement a three-year mandatory sentence was waived by the prosecution. Defendant was also charged with a drug offense which carried a three-year mandatory jail sentence. The court rejected the Commonwealth's argument that to permit such cross-examination would impermissibly allow the jury to learn the sentence faced by the defendant. The court reasoned that the ancillary effect brought about by eliciting the testimony could not bar constitutionally permissible confrontation to demonstrate bias or motive. *Id.* at 1065.

The appellate courts have extended the right to cross-examine cooperating witnesses for bias to instances in which the pending cases are in other jurisdictions, *e.g., Commonwealth v. Rickabaugh,* 706 A.2d 826, 839-40 (Pa. Super. 1997)(cross should have been permitted on hopes for favorable treatment in New Jersey case); to charges which no longer are pending, but have resulted in sentence by the time of trial, *Commonwealth v. Nolen,* 535 Pa. 77, 634 A.2d 192 (1993); and to charges for which the witness is serving a sentence of probation; *Commonwealth v. Simmon,* 521 Pa. 218, 555 A.2d 860 (1989). Further, when the witness has pending charges, the witness's past criminal history also may be elicited on the issue of bias, for the extent of that history bears on the severity of the sentence the witness faces and hopes to avoid by his cooperation. *Borders,* 522 Pa. at 163, 560 A.2d at 759.

Respectfully submitted,

_____

Thomas J. Farrell, Esquire
Attorney for EP

Form 20-3   Motion to Pay Defendant's Travel Expenses

IN THE UNITED STATES DISTRICT COURT FOR
THE _____ DISTRICT OF _____

UNITED STATES OF AMERICA,
                Plaintiff,

          v.   CASE NO. _____

M,

                Defendant.

MOTION FOR THE COURT TO ORDER PAYMENT FOR NON-CUSTODIAL TRANSPORTATION PURSUANT TO 18 U.S.C. §4285

AND NOW COMES the defendant M by his attorney, Thomas J. Farrell, Esquire, and respectfully asks this Honorable Court to order the United States Marshal Service to arrange Mr. M's non-custodial transportation from his home in Seattle, Washington to Pittsburgh, Pennsylvania for the purpose of attending the trial scheduled for _____ at 9 a.m. and to provide subsistence expenses as authorized under 18 U.S.C. §4285.

1. Mr. M's trial is scheduled for _____ at 9 a.m. Mr. M is currently residing in Seattle, Washington.
2. Title, 18 U.S.C. §4285 provides:

Any judge or magistrate of the United States, when ordering a person released under Chapter 207 on a condition of his subsequent appearance before that court, any division of that court, or any court of the United States in another judicial district in which criminal proceedings are pending, may, when the interests of justice would be served thereby and the United States judge or magistrate is satisfied, after appropriate inquiry, that the defendant is financially unable to provide the necessary transportation to appear before the required court on his own, direct the United States marshal to arrange for such transportation to the place where his appearance is required, and in addition may direct, the United States Marshal to furnish that person with an amount of money for subsistence expenses to his destination, not to exceed the amount authorized as per diem allowance for travel under section 5702 of title 5, United States Code. When so ordered, such expenses shall be paid by the marshal out of funds authorized by the Attorney General for such expenses.

18 U.S.C. §4285.

3. Mr. M has previously been found to be indigent by United States Magistrate Judges both in the Western Districts of Washington and of Pennsylvania, who appointed CJA counsel to represent him at his Rule 40 hearing and in this case. Mr. M remains unemployed, without any income aside from public assistance, and does not have the income to pay for transportation to Pittsburgh in addition to his lodging while in Pittsburgh and his return home.

WHEREFORE, Defendant M moves the court to order the United States Marshal Service to arrange for transportation to Pittsburgh, Pennsylvania so that Mr. M may be present in Pittsburgh on _____, the Friday before trial, for trial preparation, and at trial, and further order the United States Marshal to furnish Mr. M with an amount of money for subsistence expenses to his destination, not to exceed the amount authorized as per diem allowance for travel under §5702 of Title 5, United States Code.

DATED: _____

Respectfully submitted,

_____
Thomas J. Farrell, Esquire

IN THE UNITED STATES DISTRICT COURT FOR
THE _____ DISTRICT OF _____

UNITED STATES OF AMERICA,
    Plaintiff,
      v.   CASE NO. _____
M
    Defendant.

ORDER OF COURT

AND NOW, to-wit, this _____ day of February 2002, upon consideration of the foregoing Motion for the Court to order payment for non-custodial transportation pursuant to 18 U.S.C. §4285, it is hereby ORDERED, ADJUDGED, AND DECREED that the United States Marshal Service shall arrange for non-custodial transportation from Seattle, Washington, to Pittsburgh, Pennsylvania, so that Mr. M may be present by Friday, _____, for trial preparation and trial, and it is further ORDERED that the United States Marshal shall furnish Mr. Mustafa with an amount of money for subsistence expenses to Pittsburgh, Pennsylvania, not to exceed the amount authorized as per diem allowance for travel under §5702 of Title 5, United States Code. Costs to be borne by the government.

cc: United States Marshal

_____
U.S. District Judge

Form 20-4   On Call Letter

On Call Letter

March 17, 20___

Dear Witness:

Enclosed is a subpoena to appear in the United States District Court.

The trial of the above case is expected to begin on _____ at **9:00 a.m.**

DO NOT COME ON THAT DATE, but remain on call until notified of the exact date. We will either write or telephone you to notify you of the exact time your service will be necessary.

When you do appear, please check in with me outside Courtroom 7, on the third floor of the U.S. Post office and Courthouse, Seventh Avenue and Grant Street, Pittsburgh, Pennsylvania. Witnesses are <u>not</u> permitted in the courtroom until called to testify.

Please fill in the enclosed form and return it to this office in the enclosed self-addressed envelope as soon as possible so we can notify you of exact date and time.

Very truly yours,

Enclosures

United States of America v. _____
Criminal No. _____

Name: _____
Address: _____
_____
_____
Home Telephone: _____
Place of Employment: _____
_____
Business Telephone: _____
I will be available at the above addresses and telephone numbers for the trial of the above case.
Signature: _____
Date: _____

Form 20-5   Jury Selection Table

JURY SELECTION TABLE

Form 20-6   Juror Questionnaire

IN THE UNITED STATES DISTRICT COURT
FOR THE _____ DISTRICT OF _____

UNITED STATES OF AMERICA	)	
	)	
v.	)	CRIMINAL NO.
TB,	)	(18 U.S.C. §§2,
JB,	)	844(h)(1),
SD,	)	844(m) and 1341)
WR	)	

JUROR QUESTIONNAIRE

You are being considered for jury duty in a criminal case. The United States has charged certain defendants with participating in an alleged arson and others with an alleged mail fraud. The defendants have pleaded not guilty to the charges and are presumed to be innocent.

The information which you give in response to this questionnaire will be used only by the Court and authorized parties to select a fair and impartial jury. After a jury has been selected, all copies of your response to this questionnaire will be returned to the Clerk of Court and kept in confidence. Any person having access to this questionnaire is under court order to maintain the confidentiality of any information learned in the course of reviewing these questionnaires.

Please answer each question as completely and as accurately as you reasonably can. If you cannot answer a question in the space provided, you may use the reverse side of the page. Your complete written answers will save a great deal of time for everyone involved in the jury selection process.

What is needed is your very best, honest effort to answer the questions contained in the questionnaire. The only right answers are complete and honest responses to all questions. Because the answers must be your own, you should fill out the questionnaire without consulting any other prospective juror.

After you have completed, signed and turned in the questionnaire, you may leave. You will be notified by the clerk's office when to report for jury duty. You should not discuss this questionnaire or your answers with family members, friends, or other prospective jurors. You should not make, or attempt to make, any investigation regarding the incident.

Thank you for your cooperation.

_____
United States District Judge

Juror Number _____

Name: _____
Sex: Male ___ Female ___
Home Address: _____
How long have you lived at this address? _____
List any other addresses at which you have lived in the past five years: _____
_____
_____

1. Date of Birth: _____
2. What is your race?
___ White
___ African American
___ Hispanic
___ Asian
___ Other (Please state) _____
3. Present Occupation: _____
4. Name and Address of Employer: _____

5. Describe your current job (what do you do): _____
_____
_____

6. List all of your previous jobs: _____
_____
_____

7. What is the highest level of education you completed? _____
8. Are you currently a student? Yes ___ No ___
    a. If so, what school? _____
9. Do you have any special training or skills? If so, what are they? _____
_____
_____

10. List any profession licenses you hold or have held: _____
_____

11. Present Marital Status: Single ___ Married ___ Separated ___ Divorced ___ Widowed ___
12. Spouse's Present Occupation: _____
_____

13. Spouse's previous occupations: _____
_____
_____

14. What is your spouse's highest level of education completed? _____
15. Do you have any children? _____
16. For each child or stepchild 18 years or older, please complete the following:
    a. Child's name: _____
    Age: ___ Sex: ___
    School attending: _____
    Current Employment: _____

    b. Child's name: _____
    Age: ___ Sex: ___
    School attending: _____
    Current Employment: _____

    c. Child's name: _____
    Age: ___ Sex: ___
    School attending: _____
    Current Employment: _____

    d. Child's name: _____
    Age: ___ Sex: ___
    School attending: _____
    Current Employment: _____
17. What is/was your father's occupation? _____
18. What is/was your mother's occupation? _____
19. Have you ever served in the military? Yes ___ No ___
    a. If yes, what branch? _____
    b. What was your rank at discharge? _____
    c. Dates of Service: _____
20. Was your spouse in the military? Yes ___ No ___
    a. If yes, what branch? _____
    b. What was his/her rank at discharge? _____
    c. Dates of Service: _____
21. Have you ever worked in public or private law enforcement? Yes ___ No ___
    If yes, please answer the following:

     a.   Agency: _____

     b.   Job Title: _____

     c.   Dates of service: _____

     d.   Your current status: _____

23. Has a family member or close friend worked in public or private law enforcement? Yes ___ No ___
     If yes, provide the following information:

     a.   Family member/friend's name: _____

     b.   Nature of relationship: _____

     c.   Agency: _____

     d.   Job title: _____

     e.   Dates of service: _____

     f.   Current status: _____

24. Have you ever had an experience with a law enforcement officer in which you felt you were treated either fairly or unfairly? Yes ___ No ___

     a.   If yes, please explain: _____

25. Has a member of your family or close friend ever had an experience with a law enforcement officer in which you felt they were treated either fairly or unfairly? Yes ___ No ___

     a.   If yes, please explain: _____

26. Have you ever been involved in a lawsuit? Yes ___ No ___

     a.   How many lawsuits have you been involved in? _____

     b.   Were you the plaintiff? Yes ___ No ___

     c.   Were you the defendant? Yes ___ No ___

     d.   What was the nature and outcome of the lawsuit(s) (*e.g.,* car accident, suit to collect money, etc.)?

         _____

     e.   Were you satisfied with the outcome? Yes ___ No ___

     f.   Did the legal system work to your satisfaction? Yes ___ No ___

     g.   If no, why not? _____

27. Have you served as a juror in the past? Yes ___ No ___

     a.   If yes, how many times have you served as a juror? _____

     b.   How long ago? _____

     c.   How many cases were criminal? _____ Civil? _____

     d.   How many were in state court? _____ Federal court? _____

     e.   If criminal, describe the charges: _____

     f.   Did you reach a verdict? Yes ___ No ___

     g.   Were you the jury foreperson? Yes ___ No ___

     h.   Did the jury decide the punishment? Yes ___ No ___

     i.   Based on your experience as a juror, do you feel that the legal system worked to your satisfaction? Why or why not? _____

28. Have you served as a grand juror? Yes ___ No ___

     a.   Was the grand jury state? ___ or federal? ___

     b.   Were you the grand jury foreperson? Yes ___ No ___

     c.   How did you feel about your grand jury service?

29. Has your spouse ever served as a juror? Yes ___ No ___

     a.   If yes, was this jury service in a criminal case? ___ Civil? ___ Grand jury? ___

30. Have you or has anyone close to you ever worked for or been associated with a District Attorney's Office or a United States Attorney's Office? Yes ___ No ___

31. A Public Defender's Office? Yes ___ No ___

     a.   If yes, explain: _____

32. Have you ever worked for any other type of lawyer or in a law office? Yes ___ No ___

     a.   If yes, what were your responsibilities? _____

     b.   What kind of practice (criminal/civil/corporate) did the lawyer/law office engage in? ___

     _____

33. Has your spouse worked for any other type of lawyer or in a law office? Yes ___ No ___

     a.   If yes, what were his/her responsibilities? _____

b. What kind of practice (criminal/civil/corporate) did the lawyer/law office engage in? ___

_____

Regarding your health and your family's health, do you have:

34. Hearing difficulties? Yes ___ No ___
35. Vision problems? Yes ___ No ___
36. Someone sick to care for? Yes ___ No ___
37. Regular doctor appointments? Yes ___ No ___
38. Small children to care for? Yes ___ No ___
39. Some other problem which will make it difficult for you to serve for 3-4 weeks? Yes ___ No ___
40. Have you, a family member or close friend been the victim of a crime? Yes ___ No ___
   a. If yes, please describe the circumstances: _____
41. Have you ever been arrested or charged with a crime? Yes ___ No ___
   a. If yes, what was the charge? _____
   b. What was the outcome of the case? _____
42. Has a family member or close friend even been arrested or charged with a crime? Yes ___ No ___
   a. If yes, what was the charge? _____
   b. What was the outcome of the case? _____
43. How often do you watch television news? _____
44. What newspapers, periodicals, and magazines do you regularly read? _____
45. Do you follow criminal cases, or criminal trials, or crime stories in the news? Yes ___ No ___
   a. If yes, what cases have you followed recently? _____
46. Please list the names of all organizations to which you belong including clubs, unions, societies, fraternal organizations and professional organizations: _____
47. If you hold an office or official positioning any organization, please state the organization and the position:
   _____
48. If you do volunteer work, please indicate the organization(s) for which you work and describe the services which you provide: _____
49. What are you hobbies, favorite recreations, or pastimes? _____
50. Have you ever run for or held public office? Yes ___ No ___
51. Have you seen, read or heard anything about the June 23 and June 30, 2002, fires at the Isabella Fire Hall? Yes ___ No ___
52. Is there any additional information not asked in this questionnaire that you feel the judge or the lawyers should know about before you are considered for jury service? Yes ___ No ___
   a. If yes, please explain: _____

I certify that I have answered all of the questions in this Juror Questionnaire myself and to the best of my ability and that I will not discuss this questionnaire with anyone else unless directed by the court.

_____
Signature

_____
Date

Form 20-7   Proposed Voir Dire Questions by the Court

IN THE UNITED STATES DISTRICT COURT
FOR THE _____ DISTRICT OF _____

UNITED STATES OF AMERICA	)	
Plaintiff,	)	
v.	)	CRIMINAL NO.
TB,	)	
JB,	)	
SD,	)	
WR,	)	
Defendants.	)	

QUESTIONS BY THE COURT

Defendant, SD, by his attorney, Thomas J. Farrell, requests that the Court ask the following questions of the prospective jurors:

1. During this trial I shall instruct the jury that the government has the burden of proving the defendant guilty beyond a reasonable doubt. Do you have any doubt or reservation about following my instruction?

2. During this trial, I shall also instruct the jury that the Defendant in a criminal case does not have to testify or present any evidence on his behalf and that his failure to do so is not to be considered evidence against him or of his guilt. Do you have any doubt or reservation about following that instruction?

3. The jury in this case will be instructed that a Defendant in a criminal case is presumed innocent and that presumption of innocence remains with him throughout the entire trial. Do you have any doubt or reservation about following that instruction?

4. Would you be inclined to believe the testimony of a witness called by the prosecution over the testimony of a witness called by the defense simply because the prosecution called the witness?

5. One or more witnesses in this case may be law enforcement officers. If I were to instruct you that the testimony of a law enforcement officer is not to be given greater weight that the testimony of another witness simply because of his or her job as a law enforcement officer, would you be able to follow that instruction?

6. This case involves an allegation of arson, the burning of a building to recover the insurance proceeds. Do you have any feelings or experiences that would influence your ability to consider the evidence in this case? How so?

7. Would you tend to disbelieve the testimony of a defendant, if he chooses to testify, simply because he is a defendant?

8. Are you or anyone in your family a member of any organization which takes a position either pro- or anti-police or law-enforcement?

9. This case is being prosecuted by the federal government. Have you ever had any experiences with or opinions about the federal government, including the Federal Bureau of Investigation, the United States Attorney's Office, or the United States Department of Justice, that you think may affect your ability to be fair and impartial to either the defense or prosecution in this case?

10. Potential prosecution witnesses in this case are employed by the Pennsylvania State Police and Selective Insurance Company. Have you ever had any experiences with or opinions about with the Pennsylvania State Police or any insurance company that you think may affect your ability to be fair and impartial to either the defense or prosecution in this case?

11. Are you a member of any victim rights organization? Which one?

12. If you have worked as a firefighter or ever applied for employment as a firefighter, would you have any difficulty in putting aside your personal experience and deciding this case on the evidence and the court's instructions on the law?

13. Our law requires that each case be decided solely on the evidence introduced in court during the course of trial. Would you be able to do this?

14. Our law also requires that you must accept and apply the law as the judge instructs you even though you might not agree with it personally. Would you be able to do this?

15. Do you know of any matter which you feel you should call to the Court's attention which may have some bearing on your qualifications as a juror or which you feel may prevent you from rendering a fair and impartial verdict based solely upon the evidence and the Court's instructions as to the law?

16. Is there anything about the nature of the charges which would prevent you from being a fair and impartial juror in this case?

17. Do you believe that you could be a fair and impartial juror in this case?

18. The defendant need not testify in this trial and no inference can be drawn from his failure to testify. Will you follow that law and not hold it against the defendant if he does not testify?

19. Do you have such feelings about the United States Government, the criminal justice system or the prosecution of criminal cases that those feelings would affect your ability to return a fair and impartial verdict in this case?

20. Do you have any beliefs, opinions, scruples or matters of conscience that would prevent you from following the instructions of the Court and returning a verdict in a criminal case, either guilty or not guilty?

21. Do you have any health, hearing or vision impairment, or is there any reason, personal, business or otherwise, that would prevent you from rendering a fair and impartial verdict in this case based on the evidence and the court's instructions on the law?

22. Do you know of any reason why you could not render a fair and impartial verdict in this case?

Respectfully submitted,

_____

Thomas J. Farrell

Form 20-8   Theory of Defense Charge

You are instructed that the defendant's position is that he was not involved in the narcotics conspiracy. It is his position that the government witnesses must have falsely testified against him for reasons of their own, such as to obtain their own freedom from imprisonment by providing a target for prosecution other than themselves.

(From *United States v. Alfonso-Perez*, 535 F.2d 1362, 1365 (2d Cir. 1976).)

Chapter 21

POST-TRIAL MOTIONS

(This page intentionally left blank.)

I.   GENERAL POINTS

§21:01   Purpose of Post-Trial Motions

Before and during trial you may have:
- Filed pre-trial motions to suppress.
- Filed a motion to dismiss.
- Lodged every meritorious objection at trial.
- Moved for a judgment of acquittal at the end of the prosecution's case and then again at the close of all the evidence.
- Submitted pro-defense requests to charge.

Despite all your efforts before and at trial, the jury may convict your client. However, a post-trial motion still might bear fruit in several situations:
- To argue more fully legal defenses. [See §21:11.]
- To preserve issues that may not have been raised sufficiently at trial. [See §21:12.]
- To address after-discovered evidence. [See §§21:14 et seq.]
- Where you are new to the case, to raise the ineffectiveness of trial counsel. [See §21:17.]

§21:02   Basis and Timing

There is no constitutional right to file post-trial motions. Both the grounds and the timing for such motions are based on statutes and rules.

Therefore, you must consult your local rules on the filing deadlines. Deadlines vary greatly from jurisdiction to jurisdiction, and you should expect strict enforcement of these deadlines. [*E.g.,* 725 IL Comp. Stat. 5/116-1, 116-2 (30 days after verdict for a new trial motion or for a motion in arrest of judgment); Fed. R. Cr. P. 33(b)(2) (new trial motion on any grounds but newly discovered evidence must be filed seven days after verdict; for newly discovered evidence, within three years of verdict or plea); NY Crim. Proc. Law §330.30 (anytime between verdict and sentence).]

Generally, the time to file will lie between trial and sentencing because, with few exceptions, the "adjudicatory power of the criminal court end[s] with the imposition of sentence." [*People v. Stevens*, 91 N.Y.2d 270, 277, 669 N.Y.S. 2d 962, 692 N.D. 2d 985 (1998).]

However, some jurisdictions explicitly authorize the filing of post-sentence motions. [*E.g.,* Pa. R. Crim. P. 720.]

If you discover new evidence of a constitutional violation or your client's innocence while the case is on appeal, you still can file a motion for a new trial and request a hearing in the district court and request that the appellate court remand the case for that purpose. [*See United States v. Cronic*, 466 U.S. 648, 667 n.42 (1984) (trial court has jurisdiction to entertain a new trial motion and either deny the motion on its merits, or certify its intention to grant the motion to the Court of Appeals, which could then entertain a motion to remand the case).]

§21:03   Preparing and Filing the Motion

Because post-trial motions are based on local statutes and rule [see §21:02], you must consult local rules for procedural requirements for filing the motion.

The motion may (and frequently does) include several different grounds.

Along with filing your motion, order the trial transcript and ask the court for leave to amend your motion upon receipt of the transcript.

Forms:
- **Form 21-1** Motion for Post-Sentence Relief
- **Form 21-2** Supplemental Motion for Post-Sentence Relief
- **Form 21-3** Second Supplemental Motion for Post-Sentence Relief

[§§21:04-21:09 Reserved]

II. SPECIFIC MOTIONS AND GROUNDS

§21:10   New Trial in the Interest of Justice

Some post-trial motion rules empower the trial judge with broad discretion to grant a new trial "if the interest of justice so requires." [Fed. R. Crim. P. 33(a). *See also* Pa. R. Crim. P. 704(B) (motion for extraordinary relief before sentencing may include new trial "in the interests of justice"); *but see People v. Colon*, 65 N.Y.2d 888, 482 N.E.2d 1218, 493 N.Y.S.2d 302 (1985) (New York's rule, Crim. Pro. L. §330.20, strips trial court of authority to order new trial in interests of justice or because verdict is against weight of evidence; rule limits grounds to legal errors which would require appellate reversal, juror misconduct, or newly discovered evidence).]

On an "interests of justice" motion, the trial court sits as a "thirteenth juror" and can order a new trial on the ground that the verdict, although based on legally sufficient evidence, was against the weight of the evidence. [*See, e.g., Tibbs v. Florida*, 457 U.S. 31, 40-45 (1982) (describing the new trial standard, and holding that double jeopardy permits appellate review of the grant of a new trial and retrial if grant is reversed).]

In so ruling, the court may consider its own evaluation of the witnesses' credibility and the evidence's persuasiveness. [*See* Charles A. Wright, Nancy J. King, Susan R. Klein, & Sarah N. Welling, 3 *Federal Practice And Procedure* §553 (2006).]

The defendant has a heavy burden to compel the exercise of that discretion. The trend is toward narrowing the permissible circumstances in which the trial judge can overturn the verdict to those situations where "an innocent person may have been convicted." [*United States v. Canova*, 412 F.3d 331, 349 (2d Cir. 2005); *see People v. Lemmon*, 576 N.W.2d 129, 136, 456 Mich. 625, 640 (Mich. 1998) (surveying jurisdictions and describing trend away from "thirteenth juror" standard to one of a "serious miscarriage of justice").]

§21:11   Judgment of Acquittal Notwithstanding the Verdict

On two occasions prior to the verdict you may have moved for a judgment of acquittal on the grounds that the evidence was legally insufficient to support an acquittal:

- At the end of the prosecution's case.
- At the close of all the evidence.

However, your mid-trial motions probably were oral and rather perfunctory. Courts tend to err on the side of letting the case go to the jury even when the judge doubts the evidence's sufficiency, thinking that a verdict of acquittal might save the judge from facing the issue.

A post-trial motion for a judgment of acquittal notwithstanding the verdict might win where:

- The judge had doubts.
- The defense was technical.

Renewing your motion post-trial may be well suited to address legal issues that a jury was unlikely to appreciate.

EXAMPLE:

There is little jury appeal to defenses that the evidence showed multiple criminal conspiracies rather than the one charged in the indictment, or that your client committed the crime after the statute of limitations expired. Even with proper jury instructions, the jury may overlook such defenses. The trial judge, on the other hand, might consider the motion more carefully after the verdict. [*E.g., United States v. Eppolito*, 436 F.Supp.2d 532, 569-73 (E.D.N.Y. 2006) (while finding overwhelming evidence that defendants, two retired police officers, committed several organized crime murders, enters judgment of acquittal after the trial verdict of conviction because the statute of limitations had expired).]

You should raise these issues at trial and argue them to the judge in a motion for judgment of acquittal. However, you inevitably will deemphasize them in your closing argument in favor of arguing that the evidence does not prove guilt.

You also should consider a motion for a judgment of acquittal notwithstanding the verdict where your defense had more technical and legal merit than emotional.

EXAMPLE:

The evidence might have failed to prove that the value of the goods stolen met the statutory standard for grand, as opposed to petit, larceny. Or the evidence may have proven that your client lied, but his fraud was not intended to further the particular fraudulent scheme charged in the indictment.

A trial judge, looking at the evidence after trial and perhaps with the benefit of a transcript, might appreciate the nuances that did not bear emphasizing during trial and before the jury.

Form:
- **Form 21-4** Motion for Judgment of Acquittal

§21:12   Renewed Legal Issues

Post-trial, you can renew and more fully brief legal motions and objections.

When raising these issues post-trial you must show prejudice to justify a new trial. [*See, e.g.,* NY Crim. Proc. Law §330.20; Amsterdam, *Trial Manual For The Defense Of Criminal Cases*, §457(D) (5th ed. 1989).]

The rule in most jurisdictions is that you cannot litigate in post-trial motions issues that you failed to raise at the appropriate time before or during trial. [*E.g., Cronan ex. rel. State v. Cronan*, 774 A.2d 866, 877-78 (RI 2001) (claims that private prosecution violated due process, separation of powers and equal protection all waived because raised for the first time in post-trial motions).]

Nevertheless, a trial court might ignore your failure to raise the legal issue earlier, either granting your motion or rejecting the claim on the merits, thereby preserving your ability to have appellate review of the issue.

§21:13   Motion for Arrest of Judgment

Many jurisdictions authorize you to raise certain narrow issues post-trial in a "motion for arrest of judgment." Typically, these issues go to the very power of the court to try the case, such as:
- Lack of jurisdiction.
- Failure of the charging document (not the evidence) to state an offense.

[Fed.R.Crim.P. 34; Wayne R. LaFave, Jerrold H. Israel and Nancy J. King, 5 *Criminal Procedure* §24.11(c) (2005).]

§21:14   Newly Discovered Evidence–Grounds

Obtaining a new trial on the grounds of newly discovered evidence requires a five-part showing:
- The evidence is newly discovered and was unknown to the defendant at the time of trial.
- The failure to detect the evidence was not due to a lack of diligence by the defendant.
- The evidence is not merely cumulative or impeaching.
- The evidence is material.
- The evidence if introduced at a new trial would probably produce an acquittal.

[*United States v. Wall*, 389 F.3d 457, 467 (5th Cir. 2004) (explaining the so-called *Berry* standard, derived from *Berry v. State*, 10 Ga. 511 (1851)).]

The requirement that the evidence not be "merely impeaching" admits of some flexibility: if the newly-discovered impeaching evidence is so powerful that it "destroy[s] critical trial evidence," or "throw[s] severe doubt on the truthfulness of the critical inculpatory evidence that had been introduced at the trial," it can be the basis for a new trial. [*United States v. Quiles*, 618 F.3d 383 (3d Cir. 2010).]

If the new evidence is a prosecution witness's recantation, many jurisdictions demand that the trial court evaluate the recanting witness's credibility before granting relief. [*Armstrong v. State*, 642 So.2d 730, 735 (Fl. 1994) (trial judge has duty to deny new trial where he is not satisfied that recanting testimony is true); *compare State v. Clark*, 330 Mont. 8, 125 P.3d 1099 (Mont. 2005) (reviewing various standards and rejecting requirement that trial judge make factual findings on veracity of recantation in favor of a focus on whether there is a reasonable probability that the new evidence would produce a different outcome, taking into account the suspect nature of recantations). *See generally* Tim A. Thomas, *Standard for Granting or Denying a New Trial in State Criminal Cases on Basis of Recanted Testimony–Modern Cases*, 77 A.L.R.4th 1031 (surveying different standards).]

More success lies with after-discovered evidence of juror or prosecution misconduct. For example, the prosecutor may have suppressed *Brady* material. To prove a *Brady* violation you must show not only that the prosecutor failed to produce the evidence, but that it is reasonably probable that the outcome would have been different had you received the material in time to use it at trial.

You must raise the issue within a relatively short time after you either discover or should have discovered the evidence. [*E.g.,* 42 Pa. C.S.A., §9545(b)(2) (must raise claim within 60 days after discovering the evidence). *Compare* Fed. R. Crim. P. 33(b)(1) (three years from verdict to raise after-discovered evidence claim).]

§21:15   Newly Discovered Evidence–Sources for New Evidence

There are several sources for new evidence:

Cooperating Witnesses' Sentencing

Cooperators with pending charges usually postpone their sentencing until after their trial testimony and then request lenient treatment as a reward.

If the witness denied that the prosecutor promised any assistance on the witness's pending cases, follow the cooperator's sentencing. A light sentence might suggest that the prosecutor did intervene with the judge or prosecutor. Look at the court file or transcript if available. Either of those may note that the leniency was in exchange for the cooperation in your trial.

Jurors

The jurors might have engaged in misconduct during trial, or court staff or third parties might have tampered with them.

You probably will not discover this until after trial, when the jury has been discharged and you can interview them. [*See* §21:19.]

Accomplices' or Coconspirators' Trials

Not only might you hear of new evidence during related trials, but the prosecutor might embrace theories of culpability and facts inconsistent from that which he advanced at your client's trial.

Advancing inconsistent theories of prosecution might amount to a due process violation, or, the prosecutor's or his witness's new factual assertions might constitute new evidence. [*See Smith v. Groose*, 205 F.3d 1045, 1052 (8th Cir. 2000) (holding that use of inherently contradictory factual theories at separate trials of two defendants for same criminal event violated due process; reviews cases); *see also Bradshaw v. Stumpf*, 545 U.S. 175, 187 (2005) (suggesting but not deciding that inconsistent prosecution theories might be due process basis for vacating sentence); *United States v. Salerno*, 937 F.2d 797, 810-12 (2d Cir. 1991) (trial court should have permitted defense to introduce into evidence prosecutor's opening and closing statements from another defendant's trial), *rev'd on other grounds*, 505 U.S. 317 (1992).]

DNA Testing

Recently, many jurisdictions have enacted statutes affording defendants resources to have post-trial DNA testing performed and a new trial obtained if the results exonerate the defendant.

Usually, the defendant must show that the perpetrator's identity was an issue at trial and that the testing technology was not available at the time of trial. [*E.g.*, 725 IL Comp. Stat. 5/116-3. 42 Pa. C.S.A., §9543.1. *See generally* Marjorie A. Shields, *DNA Evidence as Newly Discovered Evidence Which Will Warrant Grant of New Trial or Other Postconvicton Relief in a Criminal Case*, 125 A.L.R.5th 497.]

Some DNA testing statutes lack *any* time restriction on when such a motion may be made. [*See People v. Pitts*, 4 N.Y.3d 303, 795 N.Y.S.2d 151, 828 N.E.2d 67 (2005).]

§21:16   Newly Discovered Evidence–Focus on Innocence

Defense attorneys sometimes hear rumors of new evidence after trial.

For example, a prosecution witness recants, a fellow inmate claims he heard the witnesses conspiring to frame your client, or your client's associates direct you to someone who allegedly confessed to the crime. Judges tend to be skeptical of these things, but you should still explore them because sometimes they are true.

Surprisingly, whether the conviction of the actually innocent violates the constitution in the absence of governmental misconduct is open to debate. [*See Herrera v. Collins*, 506 U.S. 390, 428 (1993) (Scalia, J., concurring); Spero T. Lappas, "The Embarrassment of Innocence," 30 *Champion* 12 (Aug. 2006); *but see Ex parte Brown*, 205 S.W.3d 538 (Tex. Crim. App. 2006) (recognizing that conviction of the demonstrably innocent, here by recantation, violates Due Process).]

Focus on proving innocence first and a legal theory second. If you can convince a judge, or the prosecutor, that your client is innocent, a way will be found to grant relief.

PRACTICE TIP:

The relief may be vacatur of the conviction upon a plea to a lesser charge, or a reduction of sentence. This type of a proposal may seem nonsensical when your client is innocent, but do not reject it out of hand. If your client already has a criminal record or may in fact be guilty of a lesser offense, such a resolution might be his quickest way out of jail.

§21:17   Ineffective Assistance of Counsel

Many jurisdictions forbid defendants from raising ineffective assistance of counsel claims on direct appeal. In those jurisdictions, the defendant is limited to collateral attacks. [*See, e.g., Massaro v. United States*, 538 U.S. 500 (2003) (claims of ineffective assistance of counsel in federal court should be raised in habeas proceeding under 28 U.S.C. §2255); *Commonwealth v. Grant*, 572 Pa. 48, 813 A.2d 726 (2002) (ineffectiveness claims should be raised in postconviction collateral proceedings; surveys other states and finds most follow this rule).]

This raises a tactical quandary: if the sentence is no more than several years, the defendant may serve it in full by the time he exhausts direct appeals and obtains a ruling on collateral attack.

The solution may be a post-trial motion. The trial judge can hold an evidentiary hearing to hear about the investigations trial counsel failed to pursue and evidence he overlooked and create a record ready for appellate review. [*See Commonwealth v. Bomar*, 573 Pa. 426, 463-66, 826 A.2d 831 (2003) (reviewing ineffectiveness claim on direct appeal where evidentiary hearing held on post-trial motions; surveys other jurisdictions and finds most permit review on direct appeal where trial court held a hearing).]

A former client's filing of an ineffectiveness claim does not relieve you of your responsibility to respect client confidences. The Rules of Professional Conduct require you to assert the privilege as to any prosecution attempt to obtain information concerning your representation, and it is the prosecutor's burden to convince a court that by raising the ineffectiveness claim, your ex-client waived the privilege as to specific, relevant communications or information. [*See* Rule 1.6, cmts 18; ABA Committee on Ethics and Professional Responsibility, Formal Opinion 10-456 (July 14, 2010).] You should not discuss the representation with the prosecutor outside any court proceeding; any disclosure must be with the client's consent or under court order. Therefore, speak only in settings supervised by the court, such as hearings or, if so ordered, in pleadings on notice to both sides. [Formal Opinion 10-456.] An ineffectiveness claim does not give you license to disclose your client's admissions of wrongdoing or otherwise to tar him in order to defend yourself. [*Id.*]

CAUTION:

Some jurisdictions continue to follow the rule that new counsel must file ineffectiveness claim as soon as one assumes the representation. [*Ex parte Ingram*, 675 So.2d 863 (Alabama 1996).]

PRACTICE TIP:

Do not rush into filing a post-trial ineffectiveness motion. Gathering the information you need (obtaining records, finding and interviewing witnesses the trial lawyer missed) might take substantial time. If you cannot do this effectively, save the ineffectiveness claim for a post conviction proceeding. Otherwise, your loss on an incomplete motion might preclude your client from raising the issue later.

§21:18   Juror Misconduct–Grounds for New Trial

Jurors do things they should not in the course of a trial. For example, they may:
- Spend a weekend at a religious retreat with a testifying police officer. [*Jenkins v. State*, 375 Md. 284, 825 A.2d 1008 (Md. 2003) (new trial ordered even though juror and witness did not discuss case).]
- Conduct experiments. [*Doan v. Brigano*, 237 F.3d 722 (6th Cir. 2001) (juror's at-home experiment on visibility of a bruise in dim light, which she then reported to other jurors, was constitutional violation and trumped state rule against impeaching verdicts with jurors' testimony).
- Review extraneous information. [*See United States v. Scull*, 321 F.3d 1270, 1280 (10th Cir. 2003) (exposure to extraneous information creates presumption of prejudice in federal cases); *United States v. Schwartz*, 283 F.3d 76, 88-89, 98-100 (2d Cir. 2002) (jurors learned that co-defendant in his guilty plea allocution implicated the defendant on trial).]
- Begin deliberations before the close of the evidence. [*United States v. Resko*, 3 F.3d 684, 688 (3d Cir.1993).]
- Make comments showing their prejudice and prejudgment. [*See People v. Rivera*, 304 A.D.2d 841, 759 N.Y.S.2d 361 (NY App. Div. 2003) (where uncontradicted post-trial hearing testimony established that a juror stated before and during trial "I know that n****r is guilty," defendant was entitled to a new trial).]

- Sleep. [*People v. Evans*, 710 P.2d 1167 (Colo. App. 1985) (court should have granted new trial where juror slept through defense counsel's closing argument).]
- Lie during voir dire. [*Dyer v. Calderon*, 151 F.3d 970 (9th Cir. 1998) (new trial ordered where juror lied in voir dire when she denied that any member of her family had been a victim of a crime even though her brother had been murdered in circumstances similar to the homicide on trial); *Florida v. Goodman*, 2013 WL 2127070 (Fl. Cir. Ct. May 3, 2013) (new trial ordered in DUI case where juror failed to disclose that his ex-wife had been convicted of DUI); *Sluss v. Commonwealth*, 381 S.W.3d 215 (KY 2013) (hearing ordered where two jurors had friended the victim's mother on Facebook, but one denied having a Facebook account and another denied knowing the victim's family, but suggests that lawyers are chargeable with information publicly available on social media sites); *but see Johnson v. McCullough*, 306 S.W.3d 551 (Mo. 2010) (new trial ordered after discovering, post-verdict, that juror had lied during voir dire, but noting that in the future, trial counsel may be charged with investigating jurors' litigation history through online databases).]

All these examples can be grounds for a new trial, but you must discover them.

You must characterize your claim as one that "extraneous prejudicial information" or an "outside influence" entered into the jury's deliberations and verdict, for FRE 606(b) and the hoary "Mansfield rule" forbid impeaching a verdict with jurors' description of the deliberation process:

> Upon an inquiry into the validity of a verdict or indictment, a juror may not testify as to any matter or statement occurring during the course of the jury's deliberations or to the effect of anything upon that or any other juror's mind or emotions as influencing the juror to assent to or dissent from the verdict or indictment or concerning the juror's mental processes in connection therewith. But a juror may testify about (1) whether extraneous prejudicial information was improperly brought to the jury's attention, (2) whether any outside influence was improperly brought to bear upon any juror, or (3) whether there was a mistake in entering the verdict onto the verdict form. A juror's affidavit or evidence of any statement by the juror may not be received on a matter about which the juror would be precluded from testifying.

[FRE 606(b); *see also Tanner v. United States,* 483 U.S. 107 (1987) (reading FRE 606(b) to preclude testimony about jurors' drug and alcohol use during trial).]

The distinction between matters inherent in the deliberations or verdict and outside influence is not a clear one, and some courts have shown an openness to overturning verdicts where jurors engaged in reenactments or their own research, or where their comments exhibited racial or ethnic bias. [*See, e.g.,* Richard T. Farrell, PRINCE, RICHARDSON ON EVIDENCE §6-112(b) (11th ed. 1995) (collecting New York cases which permit relief for reenactments and outside influences); *United States v. Benally,* 546 F.3d 1230 (10th Cir. 2008) (attempting to explain the difference between outside influence cases and matters inherent in the deliberations).]

In *Pena-Rodriguez v. Colorado,* — S.Ct. —, 2017 WL 855760 (US March 6, 2017), the Supreme Court created a constitutional exception to the Mansfield no-impeachment rule. There the Court held "that where a juror makes a clear statement that indicates he or she relied on racial stereotypes or [racial] animus to convict a criminal defendant, the Sixth Amendment requires that the no-impeachment rule give way in order to permit the trial court to consider the evidence of the juror's statement and any resulting denial of the jury trial guarantee." [2017 WL 855760, *14.] The statement must be more than an "offhand comment"; it "must tend to show that racial animus was a significant motivating factor in the juror's vote to convict." [*Id.; see also United States v. Villar,* 586 F.3d 76, 87 (1st Cir. 2009) ("While the issue is difficult and close, we believe that the rule against juror impeachment cannot be applied so inflexibly as to bar juror testimony in those rare and grave cases where claims of racial or ethnic bias during jury deliberations implicate a defendant's right to due process and an impartial jury"); *Fleshner v. Pepose Vision Inst., PC,* 304 S.W.3d 81 (Mo. 2010) (ordering an evidentiary hearing in a civil case to investigate a juror's alleged anti-Semitic remarks about a witness; holding that a single juror's statements evincing ethnic or religious bias or prejudice during deliberations deprives the parties of their right to a fair and impartial jury and equal protection, even if it had no impact on the other jurors, on due process and equal protection grounds).]

While *Pena-Rodriguez* rests on the historical "imperative to purge racial prejudice from the administration of justice" [*Id.* at *11], it suggests that its rule includes at least ethnicity, for the offensive prejudice in *Pena-Rodriguez* was against a Mexican defendant. The dissent warned that the decision also would apply to "any suspect classification – such as national origin or religion," as well as bias based on sex or the exercise of First Amendment rights. [Id. at 27 (Alito, J., dissenting)].

Pena-Rodriguez' future application remains to be seen. Certainly, if your case fits one of its categories, litigate under that precedent, but other decisions also might foreshadow a trend to granting hearings whenever you can make a colorable showing of any serious juror misconduct. [*See Fleshner,* 304 S.W.3d at 88 ("[w]hile the rule against impeachment of a jury verdict is strong and necessary, it is not written in stone, nor is it a door incapable of being opened" (quoting *After Hour Welding, Inc., v. Laneil Management Co.,* 324 N.W.2d 686, 689 (WI 1982)).]

Juror non-disclosure or dissembling during voir dire appears to be on the increase, perhaps because jurors now boast of it on the Internet and social media, making it more easily discoverable. This claim has the advantage that its proof does not entail inquiry into what occurred in the jury room.

The standard for deciding non-disclosure claims is unsettled. Some jurisdictions use a test that considers whether the undisclosed information would have been valuable in exercising peremptory challenges:

1. Was the undisclosed information material and relevant to jury service in the case?
2. Was the undisclosed information concealed during voir dire?
3. Was the failure to discover the undisclosed information attributable to the defendant's lack of diligence?

[*De La Rosa v. Zequeira,* 659 So.2d 239 (Fla. 1995).] "Material" information under the Florida test includes information "so substantial that, if the facts were known, the defense likely would peremptorily exclude the juror from the jury." [*McCauslin v. O'Conner,* 985 So.2d 558, 561 (Fla. 5th DCA 2008).] Other courts limit relief to where a truthful response "would have provided a valid basis for a challenge for cause," once the party shows that "the juror failed to answer honestly a material voir dire question." [*Sampson v. United States,* 724 F.3d 150, 164-65 (1st Cir. 2013).]

Whether relief may be had for unintentional nondisclosure, and if so, under these or some other standard, also is unsettled. [*See generally* Robert G. Loewy, *When Jurors Lie: Differing Standards for New Trials,* 22 AM. J. CRIM. L. 733 (1995).]

§21:19   Juror Misconduct–Investigating the Conduct

Some jurisdictions permit you to interview jurors after the verdict; others do not or require that you obtain leave of court first. [*See generally* Kevin F. O'Malley, Jay E. Grenig, & Hon. William C. Lee, *Federal Jury Practice & Instructions* §9:8 & n.4 (2006) (collecting local federal rules); *see United States v. Schwarz,* 283 F.3d 76, 98 (2d Cir. 2002) (defense counsel should give notice to opposing counsel and the Court before conducting post-verdict interviews of jurors, but no notice required where juror initiated the contact); *United States v. Logan,* 250 F.3d 350, 377-81 (6th Cir. 2001) (upholding district court's denial of permission to interview jurors unless trial counsel first could allege factual basis for believing there was the sort of misconduct or external improper influence that would warrant a new trial).]

You must consult your rules; otherwise, you risk a contempt citation.

Pena-Rodriguez [*see* §21:18] does not vitiate ethics and local court rules that limit post-verdict contact with jurors. In that case, jurors initiated contact with defense counsel, who then sought and received permission from the court to contact them again and obtain affidavits. [2017 WL 855760, *14]. Again, however, the dissent points the way forward: such "no contact" rules should yield to "the imperative to purge racial prejudice from the administration of justice," or so it can be argued. [*Id.* at 28 & n.15].

Even where such investigation is permissible, judges, out of concern for jurors' privacy or the finality of a verdict, might discourage jurors from speaking with the attorneys after trial. [*E.g., United States v. Self,* 681 F.3d 190, 199-200 (3d Cir. 2012) (affirming district court order forbidding defense counsel from interviewing alternate juror who told courtroom deputy that several jurors said that they went along with the verdict even though they did not agree with it).]

Interview jurors alone and in a location away from the courthouse. Temporal and spatial distance from the trial and the fellow jurors increases the chance that the jurors will speak candidly about their colleagues and courtroom personnel.

Be non-threatening. It might be best to use a young lawyer or law student, who gives the impression that his or her motive is to learn about the trial experience.

Do not focus the interview. Let the juror speak about the whole experience, even though the juror will consume much time trying to impress on you the correctness of his or her verdict. Nearly everything the juror says could be helpful. For example, a description of what evidence and argument the juror found persuasive might help if a retrial is gained on other grounds. Further, even though courts may disavow reliance on the jurors' description of the deliberative process, a juror's statement that evidence later found inadmissible turned him to conviction might dissuade an appellate court from finding admission of that evidence harmless. [*See, e.g., Romine v. Head,* 253 F.3d 1349, 1370 (11th Cir. 2001) (relying on jurors' post-verdict testimony to determine that prosecutor's citation to Bible in closing argument was not harmless).]

§21:20   Juror Misconduct–Proof

You need proof of the juror's statement, and in a swearing contest between you or a single investigator and the juror, you lose.

Courts will not hold an evidentiary hearing on an allegation of juror misconduct absent clear and specific affidavits showing "strong, substantial and incontrovertible evidence" of misconduct or exposure to improper influences. [*Schwarz*, 283 F.3d 76, 98 (2d Cir. 2002).]

Talkative jurors turn forgetful in a courtroom once they realize that their remarks will undo their verdict. Therefore, two people (a lawyer and an investigator, or two investigators) should interview each juror.

Try to get the juror to sign a handwritten affidavit prepared on the spot by including in it all the juror says, submerging the trial error in the narrative of the juror's whole experience.

III. FORMS

Form 21-1   Motion for Post-Sentence Relief

IN THE COURT OF COMMON PLEAS
OF _____ COUNTY, _____

Commonwealth of _____,	)	
Plaintiff,	)	CRIMINAL DIVISION
v.	)	NO.
RB,	)	
Defendant.	)	

MOTION FOR POST-SENTENCE RELIEF

AND NOW COMES the Defendant, RB, by and through his attorney, Thomas J. Farrell and files this Motion for Post-Sentence Relief pursuant to Pa.R.Crim.P. 720:

INTRODUCTION

1. At the September 6, 2001, sentencing in this case, Defendant requested an extension of time to file post-sentence motions, and the Court granted an extension of 90 days. However, defense counsel files this preliminary motion to preserve the defendant's rights under Pa.R.Crim.P. 720, as defense counsel is uncertain whether the ten-day time limit of Rule 720 may be extended. This motion is preliminary; defendant intends to supplement and refine it, perhaps adding and eliminating bases for relief, upon review of the transcript and further research and investigation. Therefore, defendant asks that the Court grant him 90 days from completion of the trial and penalty phase transcripts to supplement this post-sentence motion.

**MOTION TO SUPPRESS EVIDENCE OBTAINED AS A RESULT OF
THE SEARCH OF DEFENDANT'S HOME ON APRIL 28, 2000**

2. The affidavit of probable cause failed to supply any cause to believe that evidence of homicide would be found in Mr. B's home.

3. Therefore, all the evidence seized from the house must be suppressed pursuant to the Fourth Amendment of the U.S. Constitution and Article I, Section 8 of the Pennsylvania Constitution.

4. The prosecution's psychiatrist in large part based his opinions on evidence derived from the hard drive of Mr. B's computer. Therefore, this opinion constituted the fruit of the poisonous search, and it, too, should be stricken from the record.

MOTION FOR CHANGE OR VENUE OR VENIRE

5. The pervasive and prejudicial pre-trial publicity that attended this case deprived the defendant of a fair and impartial jury in violation of the Due Process Clause of the 14th Amendment of the U.S. Constitution and Article I, Section 9 of the Pennsylvania Constitution.

6. Therefore, despite trial counsel's insistence on a trial and jury drawn from Allegheny County, the Court should have changed the venue of the trial or asked the Supreme Court to assign a venire from another county. Pa. R. Crim. P. 584; 42 Pa. C.S.A. §8702.

MOTION FOR A NEW TRIAL AND PENALTY HEARING BASED UPON INEFFECTIVE ASSISTANCE OF COUNSEL

7. Trial counsel was ineffective at the guilt phase of defendant's capital trial by failing to move for a change of venue and venire and by failing to life qualify the jury, as authorized by *Morgan v. Illinois*, 504 U.S. 719 (1992).

8. Trial counsel failed to present an adequate mitigating case at the penalty phase of the trial.

9. These errors deprived the defendant of his right to the effective assistance of counsel under Sixth and Fourteenth Amendments of the U.S. Constitution and Article I, Section 9 of the Pennsylvania Constitution.

MOTION TO SUPPRESS TAPE RECORDED CALLS

10. The prosecution introduced at trial an audio tape-recording of a _____ telephone conversation between the defendant, in jail, and his parents, at home. The introduction of this recording violated both the federal, 18 U.S.C. §§2510 et seq., and Pennsylvania wiretap statutes, 18 Pa. C.S. §5704.

CONCLUSION

11. None of the foregoing allegations are intended to be exhaustive. All may be supplemented or corrected upon review of the transcript. These motions require both the transcript and an evidentiary hearing for their adjudication.

12. The defense is uncertain whether the Court intended that the extension be measured from _____ or from the date on which the trial transcript is completed (I ordered it on _____). Since the trial of this case was both lengthy and complex and review of those transcripts is necessary preparation for new counsel to file post-trial motions, I ask that the Court set a date 90 days from the completion of the transcripts for supplementation of this motion and hold it in abeyance until then.

WHEREFORE, Defendant respectfully requests that this Honorable Court enter an order holding this motion in abeyance and granting the defendant ninety (90) days from the completion of the trial transcript to file a supplemental post-sentence motion.

Respectfully submitted,

_____
Thomas J. Farrell, Esquire
Dated: _____

Form 21-2   Supplemental Motion for Post-Sentence Relief

IN THE COURT OF COMMON PLEAS
OF _____ COUNTY, _____

COMMONWEALTH OF _____,
               Plaintiff,   CRIMINAL DIVISION
      v.   Nos.:
RB,
            Defendant.

SUPPLEMENTAL MOTION FOR POST-SENTENCE RELIEF

AND NOW COMES the Defendant, RB, by and through his attorney, Thomas J. Farrell and files this Supplemental Motion For Post-Sentence Relief pursuant to Pa.R.Crim.P. 720:

1. At the _____, sentencing in this case, Defendant requested an extension of time to file post-sentence motions, and the Court granted Defendant 90 days from the completion of the trial transcript to file this Motion. The transcript was completed and received on _____. Defendant requests that the Court grant this motion and order a new trial, or a new sentencing hearing, as indicated in each of the following bases for relief. In addition to this Supplemental Motion, defendant relies on the attached Memorandum of Law and its Exhibits as well as the trial transcript in this case. This motion requires a hearing, and the defendant requests that the Court schedule one.

2. The Court should have changed venue on its own motion to preserve the defendant's fundamental right to a trial by a fair and impartial jury. The relief requested is a new guilt phase trial (and penalty phase trial, if it comes to that).

3. Defendant was denied an impartial capital sentencing jury by the Court's erroneous exclusion for cause of jurors who expressed reservations regarding the death penalty in violation of the Sixth, Eighth, and Fourteenth Amendments of the United States Constitution and Article I, Sections 9 and 13 of the Pennsylvania Constitution. The relief requested is a new penalty phase trial.

4. The _____ search of Defendant's home and the seizure of his computer and personal papers violated both the Fourth Amendment of the United States Constitution and Article I, Section 8 of the Pennsylvania Constitution. The relief requested is a new guilt phase trial (and penalty phase trial, if it comes to that).

5. The recording of Defendant's _____ telephone conversation with his parents was obtained in violation of the Pennsylvania Wiretapping and Electronic Surveillance Statute as no written notice was given to any of the parties to the conversation, as required by title 18 Pa.C.S.A. Section 5704 (14). The relief requested is a new guilt phase trial (and penalty phase trial, if it comes to that).

6. The prosecution relied on testimony that the Commonwealth knew to be untrue to admit the March 2 tape, in violation of Defendant's due process rights guaranteed by the Fourteenth Amendment of the United States Constitution. The relief requested is a new guilt phase trial (and penalty phase trial, if it comes to that).

7. The prosecution's failure to provide the inmate handbook to the defense, evidence which was exculpatory to the accused, constituted a violation of its obligations under *Brady v. Maryland*. The relief requested is a new guilt phase trial (and penalty phase trial, if it comes to that).

8. Dr. W elicited incriminating statements from Defendant in violation of his privilege against self-incrimination and his right to counsel under both the United States and Pennsylvania Constitutions by misleading him as to Dr. W's role and the purpose of the interview and exceeding the scope of a proper rebuttal psychiatric examination. The relief requested is a new guilt phase trial (and penalty phase trial, if it comes to that).

9. The Commonwealth, through Dr. W, improperly commented on Mr. B' lack of remorse in violation of the Fifth Amendment and Due Process Clause of the United States Constitution and Article I, Section 9 of the Pennsylvania Constitution. The relief requested is a new guilt phase trial (and penalty phase trial, if it comes to that).

10. It was error to permit Dr. W to testify that he "entertained" the diagnosis of anti-social personality disorder and to describe the prejudicial information he examined to entertain that diagnosis. The relief requested is a new guilt phase trial (and penalty phase trial, if it comes to that).

11. Dr. W's numerous judgments on the credibility and motivations of Defendant and defense witnesses exceeded the scope of Rule 702 and invaded the jury's role, an exclusive province in determining the credibility of witnesses. The relief requested is a new guilt phase trial (and penalty phase trial, if it comes to that).

12. The Court's pre-trial rulings and jury instructions precluded the jury from considering the recognized *M'Naughton* defense of delusional insanity. The relief requested is a new guilt phase trial (and penalty phase trial, if it comes to that).

13. Since the evidence raised an inference of the Defendant's future dangerousness, the Court's failure to permit the defense to introduce evidence of the Defendant's parole ineligibility and to instruct the jury that Pennsylvania law does not permit a defendant convicted of first degree murder to be released on parole violated the Defendant's due process rights. The relief requested is a new penalty phase trial.

14. The court's failure to give a jury instruction required by *Simmons v. South Carolina* and to permit the introduction of evidence of the Defendant's ineligibility for parole violated the Defendant's Eighth Amendment rights. The relief requested is a new penalty phase trial.

15. The Commonwealth failed to charge the element of grave risk of death or multiple murders in any of the informations, in violation of the principle of *Ring v. Arizona* that aggravating factors must be treated procedurally as elements of the offense. The relief requested is a new penalty phase trial.

16. Sentencing a mentally ill person to death violates the Eighth Amendment. The relief requested here is vacatur of the death sentence and imposition of a life sentence.

WHEREFORE, Defendant respectfully requests that this Honorable Court enter an order scheduling a hearing on Defendant's motions.

Respectfully submitted,

_____

Thomas J. Farrell, Esquire
Dated:

Form 21-3   Second Supplemental Motion for Post-Sentence Relief

IN THE COURT OF COMMON PLEAS
OF _____ COUNTY, _____

COMMONWEALTH OF _____ ,
               Plaintiff,   CRIMINAL DIVISION
       v.   Nos.:

RB,
               Defendant.

SECOND SUPPLEMENTAL MOTION FOR POST-SENTENCE RELIEF

AND NOW COMES the Defendant, RB, by and through his attorney, Thomas J. Farrell and files this Second Supplemental Motion for Post-Sentence Relief pursuant to Pa.R.Crim.P. 720:

1. Defendant filed his Supplemental Motion for Post-Sentence Relief along with a supporting Memorandum of Law and Exhibits on _____. On _____, the Commonwealth filed a Response in which it raised the issue of trial counsel's waiver of many of the issues raised in the Supplemental Motion. The Commonwealth based this argument on the Supreme Court's May 30, 2003, decision in *Commonwealth v. Freeman*, No. 234 Capital Appeal Docket (Pa. 2003), which eliminated Pennsylvania's relaxed waiver rule.

2. The defense does not concede that these issues were waived. This case is not yet on appeal; it is on post-sentence motions, and, therefore, the Court may address these issues in the context of this post-sentence motion for a new trial. Rule 302 of the Pennsylvania Rules of Appellate Procedure, which was the basis for the Court's ruling in *Commonwealth v. Freeman*, states, "Issues not raised in the lower court are waived and cannot be raised for the first time on appeal." We still are in the lower court; this rule does not apply to post-sentence motions.

3. In the event that the Commonwealth is correct and trial counsel waived the following issues, trial counsel was ineffective for failing to raise them:

    a. Trial counsel should have requested a change of venire or venue. *See* Memorandum of Law in Support of Defendant's Supplemental Motion for Post-Sentence Relief ("Defendant's Memorandum") at 5-9.

    b. Trial counsel should have objected to the exclusion for cause of prospective jurors M, G, S, and H. *Id.* at 10-19.

    c. Trial counsel should have moved to suppress the _____, search of defendant's home and the seizure of his computer and personal papers. *Id.* at 19-25.

    d. Trial counsel should have obtained and introduced into evidence the Allegheny County Jail Inmate handbook to demonstrate that no written notice was given to any of the parties to the conversation, as required by title 18 Pa.C.S.A. Section 5704 (14) of the Pennsylvania Wiretapping and Electronic Surveillance Statute. *Id.* at 25-32.

    e. Trial counsel should have objected on Fifth and Fourteenth Amendment grounds to the admission of Dr. W's testimony to the extent that that testimony was based on his interviews of defendant. *Id.* at 34-41.

    f. Trial counsel should have objected to Dr. W's testimony about defendant's lack of remorse. *Id.* at 41-42.

    g. Trial counsel should have objected to Dr. W's testimony about antisocial personality disorder. *Id.* at 43-46.

h. Trial counsel should have objected to Dr. W testimony impugning the honesty of defendant and his parents. *Id.* at 46-47.

i. Trial counsel should have objected to the Court's insanity charge to the jury and requested one on the recognized *M'Naghten* defense of delusional insanity. *Id.* at 47-51.

j. Trial counsel should have requested the Court to instruct the jury at the sentencing phase that Pennsylvania law does not permit a defendant convicted of first-degree murder to be released on parole. *Id.* at 51-62.

k. Trial counsel should have moved to preclude a death sentence on the grounds that the Commonwealth failed to charge the element of grave risk of death or multiple murders in any of the informations, in violation of the principle of *Ring v. Arizona* that aggravating factors must be treated procedurally as elements of the offense. *Id.* at 62-64.

l. Trial counsel should have moved to preclude a death sentence on the grounds that sentencing a mentally ill person to death violates the Eighth Amendment. *Id.* at 64-65.

4. All these issues have merit, as is described at length in Defendant's Supplemental Motion for Post-Sentence Relief and his Memorandum of Law in support of his Supplemental Motion for Post-Sentence Relief pursuant to Pa. R. Crim. P. 720. None of these decisions were reasonable strategic decisions made after thorough investigation, see *Wiggins v. Smith*, 539 U.S. 510 (2003) (citing *Strickland v. Washington*, 466 U.S. 668, 670-71 (1984)), nor did they have some reasonable basis designed to effectuate defendant's interests, see *Commonwealth v. Bomar*, No. 276 Capital Appeal Docket (Pa. May 30, 2003).

5. Further, with respect to the change of venue issue, this Court conducted its own investigation and test jury selections. Even when that investigation and those tests and the Court's careful opinion demonstrated to trial counsel that prejudicial pre-trial publicity had saturated Allegheny County to the extent that defendant could not have a fair trial here, the defense, without conducting further investigation, chose to waive the change of venue or venire issue.

6. In addition, defendant submits as Exhibit A in support of his Supplemental Motion and this Second Supplemental Motion the declaration of Professor EB. Professor B's declaration establishes that had defense counsel conducted adequate investigation and consulted with a competent jury selection consultant, they would have realized that nothing was to be gained and much lost by a trial before an Allegheny County jury, and would have requested a change of venue or venire. See B Declaration, ¶¶195-226; ABA, "Guidelines for the Appointment and Performance of Defense Counsel in Death Penalty Cases," Guideline 10.10.2 (C) (Rev. ed. 2003) ("Counsel should consider seeking expert assistance in the jury selection process."); *Wiggins*, slip op. at 9-10 (Courts should determine adequacy of counsel's performance by looking to ABA standards).

7. The ineffective assistance of counsel issue requires a hearing.

8. The defendant relies upon and incorporates into this Second Supplemental Motion his Supplemental Motion for Post-Sentence Relief and its supporting Memorandum of Law; the Reply Memorandum of Law filed this same day; and the Declaration of Prof. EB and its exhibits, filed this same day.

WHEREFORE, Defendant respectfully requests that this Honorable Court enter an order scheduling a hearing on Defendant's motions.

Respectfully submitted,

_____

Thomas J. Farrell, Esquire

Form 21-4   Motion for Judgment of Acquittal

IN THE UNITED STATES DISTRICT COURT

FOR THE _____ DISTRICT OF _____

UNITED STATES OF AMERICA	)
	)
	) CRIMINAL NO.
v.	)
	)
	)
SD	)

DEFENDANT D'S MOTION AND MEMORANDUM OF LAW FOR JUDGMENT OF ACQUITTAL PURSUANT TO FEDERAL RULE OF CRIMINAL PROCEDURE 29

AND NOW COMES the defendant, SD ("D"), by his attorney, Thomas J. Farrell, Esquire, and respectfully requests the Court to enter a judgment of acquittal pursuant to Federal Rule of Criminal Procedure 29:

On _____, D was found guilty of violating 18 U.S.C. 1341, a charge that arose from arsons at the _____ Social Hall committed on _____ and _____.

At the end of the government's case, D moved for a judgment of acquittal. Specifically, D argued that the indictment charged a mail fraud scheme by means of false representations, *see United States v. Frankel*, 721 F.2d 917 (3d Cir. 1983), and that since the only representations made by D and alleged in the indictment occurred after the mailing, as a matter of law, the evidence could not prove D's knowing participation in the scheme charged in the indictment, *see United States v. Pflaumer*, 721 F.2d 917 (3d Cir. 1983); *United States v. Pearlstein*, 576 F.2d 531 (3d Cir. 1978) (to stand, a mail fraud conviction must be of the scheme charged in the indictment and not some other scheme to defraud).

The Court denied the motion, primarily for the reason that the evidence could support a conviction on an aiding and abetting theory.

The scheme described in the indictment alleges that beginning on or about _____, defendants B and B planned to burn down the _____ social hall to obtain insurance money. According to the indictment, the defendants, including D, then made false representations to the insurance company to further the scheme. The crime was completed on _____, when the proof of loss was mailed. *See* Indictment, paragraphs 8-13; *Pflaumer, supra.*

The indictment does not charge that the claim mailed on _____ itself contained any false representations, nor did the government argue that the claim made false representations.

The only evidence of D's knowing participation in the scheme before the _____ mailing was his _____ statement to PK. However, this cannot suffice for the following reasons:

- During D's trial, the Government never proved D knew who set the fires at the _____.
- The only pre-mailing false representation charged in the indictment and proven at trial was TB's statement to K on the _____ videotape to the effect that B did not know who set the _____ fire. See Indictment paragraph 8. However, D gave his statement to K *before* the videotaped B statement; therefore, since B had not yet spoken, D could not have known of B's false representation at the time K interviewed D.

Further, the government's evidence never proved that D ever knew who set the _____ social hall fires.

The evidence the Government produced at trial did not prove D had any involvement with Defendant Thomas Earl Baker's ("Baker"), false statement charged in Paragraph 8 of Count Three of the Indictment. Instead, the evidence at trial only showed D lied to Selective Insurance Company about his knowledge of other people, namely the other named Defendants in this case, commenting about wanting to burn down the IVFD Social Hall prior to June 25-26, 2002.

The Government produced no evidence at trial that D knew who set the fire on June 25-26, 2002 when he was interviewed by a Selective Insurance Company investigator on July 2, 2002. Therefore, the Government could not produce any evidence that D knew that Baker's statement, that he had no information regarding the identity of any persons who may have set the fire on June 25-26, 2002, was false. *See Pearlstein*, 576 F.2d at 543-44 (reversing mail fraud convictions for lack of evidence that defendant knew that the co-defendants' claims were false); *Id.* at 541 ("But evidence of mere ongoing friendships, even where the defendants might have known that their friends were engaged in criminal activity, will not support a finding that the defendants knew or should have known of their friends' specific fraudulent intentions.")

Therefore, D requests that the Court enter a judgment of acquittal on the grounds that the evidence failed as a matter of law to prove his knowing participation before September 5, 2002, in the scheme alleged in the indictment.

Further, If D's guilt was proven at all at trial, it was his guilt of a scheme to defraud that was at variance with the scheme to defraud charged in the Indictment. The scheme to defraud as charged in the Indictment consisted of D, along with the other three named defendants in this case, of setting the IVFD Social Hall on fire with the specific intent to defrauding Selective Insurance Company, and then lying to the Selective Insurance Company in interviews and statements under oath about who set the fire. D's false statements at most formed part of a scheme to protect his brother-in-law, a scheme substantially different from that charged in the Indictment. *See Pearlstein*, 576 F.2d 545 & n.7; *United States v. Klein*, 515 F.2d 751, 754-55 (3d Cir. 1975) (to convict defendant of conspiracy to commit mail fraud in an arson-based insurance fraud case, it was "essential for the government to prove his knowledge of a plot to defraud the insurers. Mere knowledge of arson would be insufficient to support a guilty verdict in this case.") This variance involves elements of a crime distinct from the crime with which the Indictment originally charged. *See United States v. Asher*, 854 F.2d 1483, 1497 (3rd Cir. 1998).

WHEREFORE, for the foregoing reasons, the defendant, SD, requests that this Honorable Court enter a Judgment for Acquittal Pursuant to Federal Rule of Criminal Procedure 29.

DATED: _____

Respectfully submitted,

_____

Thomas J. Farrell

Chapter 22

SENTENCING

I. GENERAL POINTS

§22:01 Importance of Sentencing

With approximately 90% of federal and 70% of state criminal cases ending in conviction, sentencing may be the most important proceeding in a criminal case. [*See* United States Sentencing Commission, *Sourcebook of Federal Sentencing Statistics* (available at www.ussc.gov); Administrative Office of U.S. Courts, *Federal Judicial Caseload Statistic*, Table D-4, Defendants Disposed of, by Type of Disposition and Offense (March 31, 2007) (available at www.uscourts.gov/); U.S. Department of Justice, Bureau of Justice Statistics, *Felony Defendants in Large Urban Counties,* Appendix Table G (2002).]

From the start of your representation, everything you do should position your clients for sentencing. Interview your clients and their families with an ear for good works, difficulties overcome, and disorders that could mitigate the offense. Limit the prosecution's damning evidence and extract helpful concessions in pre-trial motions and hearings. Negotiate for a favorable plea and sentencing range, all with an eye on the likely sentence such a plea will evoke.

Sentencing litigation requires much more than throwing the client upon the court's mercy and expecting to reap the benefits of your earlier efforts. Some of the legal issues you face are as complex as any in the criminal justice system, and the strategic decisions demand your best advocacy.

§22:02 Sentencing in Capital Cases

Death penalty cases not only are the most serious, but a specialized and complex body of law applies to those cases. [*See, e.g., ABA Guidelines for the Appointment and Performance of Defense Counsel in Death Penalty Cases.*]

Many jurisdictions require counsel to undergo specialized training and demonstrate competency before undertaking a capital case. No one should represent a defendant in a capital case without that training and associating with an experienced death penalty lawyer.

[§§22:03-22:09 Reserved]

II. SENTENCING SCHEMES

§22:10 Determinate Versus Indeterminate Sentencing Schemes

Indeterminate sentencing schemes

Most states employ indeterminate sentencing schemes.

Under an indeterminate sentencing scheme, the judge imposes a sentence as a range of years or months with a mandatory and minimum term (*e.g.,* three to nine years) and a parole board decides the defendant's release date within that range based upon parole guidelines and the defendant's behavior and rehabilitative progress during incarceration.

Determinate sentencing schemes

The federal government and some states have turned to determinate sentencing.

In determinate sentencing the judge announces a specific sentence. Most jurisdictions couple this system with the abolition of parole, so that the defendant serves his full term, minus a modest reduction for good behavior or "good time." [*Mistretta v. United States,* 488 U.S. 361, 367 (989) (explaining federal system); Wayne LaFave, *et al.,* 5 *Criminal Procedure* §26.1(c) (2006).]

However, judges then tack on a term of "supervised release," a form of post-incarceration probation, so that the defendant still remains subject to state control and incarceration if he violates the conditions. [*E.g.,* 18 U.S.C. §3583; Minn. Stat. Ann. §244.05 (inmate may be released on good time equal to up to one-third his sentence, but remains on supervised release for that period).]

§22:11 Sentencing Guideline Schemes

Many jurisdictions leave the sentence in a particular case to the judge's discretion. This allows the judge to individualize the sentence to the defendant's background and needs and to the particular circumstances of the crime. However, it also means that sentences for nearly identical crimes might vary from judge to judge.

Largely to eliminate unwarranted disparity in sentencing, but also to impose some legislative control over judicial discretion, many jurisdictions, including the federal government, have enacted numerous mandatory minimum statutes and sentencing guideline schemes for felony offenses (misdemeanor sentences usually are left unregulated). [*See* Richard S. Frase, *State Sentencing Guidelines: Diversity, Consensus and Unresolved Policy Issues,* 105 Colum.L.Rev. 1190, 1196-1203 (2005) (listing and describing features of all state and federal guideline systems).]

In a series of decisions, the Supreme Court ruled that under the Sixth Amendment, any fact that increases the penalty for a crime, either by increasing the statutory maximum sentence, or by triggering or increasing a mandatory minimum sentence, other than the fact of a prior conviction, must be submitted to a jury, and proved beyond a reasonable doubt. [*Apprendi v. New Jersey,* 530 US. 466, 490 (2000) (increases to statutory maximum); *Alleyne v. United States,* 133 S.Ct. 2151 (2013) (mandatory minimum sentences).]

Guidelines schemes assign point values to the offense of conviction and points to the defendant's criminal history to arrive at a recommended sentencing range within a statutory range [*See* United States Sentencing Commission, *Guidelines Manual* (2013).] Until the decisions in *Blakely v. Washington,* 542 U.S. 296 (2004), and *United States v. Booker,* 543 U.S. 220 (2005), guideline schemes limited "departures" outside the guideline range to extraordinary situations. [*See Koon v. United States,* 518 U.S. 81 (1996) (explaining circumstances in which departures were permitted).]

Booker invalidated those mandatory guidelines schemes that lack a requirement of jury fact-finding under a "beyond a reasonable departure" standard. [*See* §22:12.] Now, sentencing courts may vary from guideline ranges on any reasonable ground. [*See Kimbrough v. United States,* 522 U.S. 85, 128 S.Ct. 558 (2007) (courts may deviate from guidelines based on policy disagreements with the guidelines).]

§22:12 Establishing Facts in Mandatory Schemes

Some jurisdictions, such as the federal system, attempt to enact "real offense" sentencing in which the conduct surrounding the commission of the offense (*e.g.,* the amount of drugs or theft, the defendant's role in the offense, or the abuse of a trust relationship) earn point increases or, less often, reductions.

Real offense sentencing tries to neutralize the prosecutorial control over sentencing which stems from the ability to choose the charge of conviction. This means, however, that the defendant's sentence could depend on facts of which he was not convicted.

Therefore, the Supreme Court has ruled that increasing a sentence under a mandatory guideline scheme requires that the sentence-enhancing facts either be admitted by the defendant or found by the jury beyond a reasonable doubt. [*United States v. Booker*, 543 U.S. 220, 244 (2005).] In 2013, the Supreme Court ruled that the Sixth Amendment, as interpreted in *Booker*, also requires that any fact that triggers a mandatory minimum sentence, other than the fact of a prior conviction, also must be submitted to a jury and decided beyond a reasonable doubt. [*Alleyne v. United States,* 133 S.Ct. 2151 (2013).] Prior to *Alleyne,* many courts exempted mandatory minimum sentences from *Apprendi's* and *Booker's* coverage in reliance on *Harris v. United States,* 536 U.S. 545 (2002), and *McMillan v. Pennsylvania,* 477 U.S. 79 (1986), but *Alleyne* overruled those cases. Thus, its impact may be widespread. [*E.g., Commonwealth v. Watley,* 2013 PA Super 303 (Pa. Super. Ct. 2013) (*Alleyne* rendered unconstitutional 42 Pa. C.S.A. §9712.1, which specified that a mandatory minimum sentence of five years must be imposed upon a post-conviction finding by the court under a preponderance of the evidence standard that the defendant possessed a firearm in connection with a controlled substance offense).]

However, the jury-trial right and reasonable doubt standard do not apply if the guidelines are only advisory. [*Booker*, 543 U.S. at 255-265.]

The *Booker* decision resulted in a federal guideline system in which sentencing judges must calculate the guideline range but consider it as only one of several factors specified by statute. The other factors are the traditional penalogical goals of deterrence, incapacitation, rehabilitation and the need to promote respect for the law. [*See* 18 U.S.C. §3553(a); *United States v. Cooper,* 437 F.3d 324, 329-30 (3d Cir. 2006) (court should consider each of the statutory factors).]

Booker and its predecessor [*Blakely v. Washington,* 542 U.S. 296 (2004)] invalidated aspects of several state guideline systems as well. [*See Commonwealth v. Kleinicke,* 2006 Pa. Super 48, 895 A.2d 562, 583 n.21 (2006) (Bender, J., dissenting) (collecting decisions).]

Some states have responded to *Blakely* and *Booker* "by calling upon the jury–either at trial or in a separate sentencing proceeding–to find any fact necessary to the imposition of an elevated sentence." [*Cunningham v. California,* 127 S.Ct. 856, 876 & n.17 (2007) (surveying states); *see* Marc L. Miller, *A Map of Sentencing and a Compass for Judges: Sentencing Information Systems, Transparency, and the Next Generation of Reform,* 105 Colum.L.Rev. 1351, 1366-67 & n.41 (2005) (article comparing state sentencing guideline schemes, and providing links to state sentencing commission information); Richard S. Frase, *State Sentencing Guidelines: Diversity, Consensus, and Unresolved Policy Issues*, 105 Colum. L. Rev. 1190 (2005) (reviewing state guideline systems).]

§22:13   Working With a Guideline System

Handling a sentencing in a guideline system requires that you thoroughly review the jurisdiction's guideline manual or regulations and case law.

The systems appear daunting, but are actually more tedious than complex. Most include introductory provisions which outline the methodology to follow in calculating a sentence. [*See, e.g.,* Lucien B. Campbell & Henry J. Bemporad, *An Introduction to Federal Guideline Sentencing* (9th ed. 2006) (available at www.ussc.gov/training/intro9.pdf).]

Public defenders' offices often offer half- or full-day training programs on the guidelines.

Determine how much deference your jurisdiction and your judge give to the guidelines. Even within advisory schemes, some judges afford the guidelines substantial respect as expressing the considered judgment of the legislature or sentencing commission, while other judges pay them little heed. [*See Rita v. United States,* __ U.S. __, 127 S.Ct. 2456 (2007) (appellate court may, but is not required to, presume a within-guidelines sentence to be reasonable); *compare Gall v. United States,* __ U.S. __, 128 S.Ct. 586 (2007) (appellate court may not presume that an outside-guidelines sentence is unreasonable).]

Where the guidelines weigh heavily, focus on litigating the facts that drive the calculations and researching the legal interpretive issues. Some appellate courts demand that the sentencing court demonstrate on the record a consideration of the guidelines and other specified sentencing factors. [*See Gall v. United States,* __ U.S. __, 128 S.Ct. 586, 596-97 (2007).] In that situation, facilitate the court's task by reciting the factors in your sentencing memorandum and demonstrating how the application of each applies and yields a mitigated sentence in your case.

Where the guidelines merit only passing reference, emphasize your client's character and prospects for rehabilitation. [*See* §§22:90 et seq.]

In any system, use the following tactics:

Humanize your client.

Even where judges defer to guidelines, a sympathetic depiction of your client will influence the exercise of the judge's and even the prosecutor's discretion. [*See* §22:40.]

Attack all upward adjustments.

Complex real offense systems, which attempt to account for myriad factors, spawn the prospect of protracted litigation, and you can exploit the fear of such protraction. Attack upward adjustments on legal and factual grounds and push the prosecutor to stipulate to facts which will lower the guideline range.

A point off here and there may not mean much to the prosecutor and may save him a lengthy hearing and appeal, but it will mean months or even years less in prison for your client. Begging does not work; you *must* support your arguments to the prosecutor to forego upward adjustments or not to oppose downward ones with references to case law and the case facts, because the prosecutor must justify the guideline stipulations to the judge, but more importantly, to her supervisors.

Start negotiations early.

Early and thorough plea negotiations are particularly important in real offense systems because the best deals can be made early in the case before the investigation has uncovered aggravating circumstances and the prosecutor's position has hardened.

Develop downward departures.

Even the strictest guideline regimes permit downward departures to sentences below the guideline range for extraordinary mitigating circumstances. These circumstances usually lie in your client's psychiatric and personal history and how they contributed to the offense. [*E.g., United States v. Brown,* 985 F.2d 478 (9th Cir. 1993) (downward departure where history of abuse contributed to commission of offense).]

Always develop these and advocate for a departure. Even if unsuccessful, presentation of these mitigating facts might influence the exercise of what discretion the judge has within a sentencing range and might persuade the prosecutor to ease off the search for upward adjustments.

§22:14   Departures and Variances From the Federal Guidelines

In federal sentencing guideline parlance, a "departure" differs somewhat from a "variance." A court "departs" when it deviates from the guidelines for some extraordinary circumstance not contemplated by the guidelines. The departure methodology presumes that the guideline range is reasonable in the usual case, but some specific reason, often authorized by caselaw precedent or the guidelines themselves, justifies a different sentence in this case.

In contrast, a "variance" need not be founded on some extraordinary or uncontemplated circumstance; a court can vary on any reasonable basis, including an individualized assessment of the defendant and the crime, policy reasons, or a determination that a non-guideline sentence better accommodates the statutory purposes of sentencing. [*See United States v. Ausburn,* 502 F.3d 313 (3d Cir. 2007); *United States v. Anati,* 457 F.3d 233, 236-37 (2d Cir. 2006) (explaining the differences and overlap between departures and variances).]

With the considerable overlap between the two concepts, you will find yourself repeating the same arguments as reasons for both departure and variance (for example, your client's family needs, his extraordinary acceptance of responsibility and efforts to rehabilitate). However, the redundancy may spell success. Your departure argument says to the judge, "You should depart because other judges have for similar reasons, and it sets or furthers a good precedent." The variance argument works at a different level: "The specific needs of this case and defendant call for a lesser sentence; the court need not evaluate whether it is setting or following a rule of general application, because the variance here addresses only the application of sentencing discretion to this case and this defendant."

Raise both legal and policy arguments for a sentence below the guideline range.

The Supreme Court's recent decisions hold (at least) two lessons for practitioners in those sentencing guideline jurisdictions where the judge, not a jury, makes findings on sentencing factors:

- First, any indication that the sentencing judge is treating the guidelines as presumptively correct invites a Sixth Amendment challenge under the *Booker* line of cases. [*See Gall,* 128 S.Ct. at 595-97 (sentencing court may not presume that guideline range is reasonable or that sentences outside the range are unreasonable); *id.* at 602-03 (Scalia, J., concurring) (door is open for as-applied Sixth Amendment challenges to sentences in individual cases).]
- Second, since these decisions have returned authority to sentencing courts to disagree with the application of guidelines to individual cases and even with the policy choices behind particular guidelines, defense counsel now has the opportunity and the obligation to use the client's good works, disabilities, family needs, prospects for rehabilitation–just about anything in his individual situation–as well as policy arguments and empirical studies to advocate for a lesser sentence. [*See Gall,* 128 S.Ct. at 596-97 ("As a matter of administration and to secure nationwide consistency, the Guidelines should be the starting point and the initial benchmark. The Guidelines are not the only consideration, however. Accordingly, after giving both parties an opportunity to argue for whatever sentence they deem appropriate, the district judge should then consider all of the §3553(a) factors [need to promote respect for the law, deterrence, incapacitation, and the defendant's need for effective correctional programs] to determine whether they support the sentence requested by a party. In so doing, he may not presume that the Guidelines range is reasonable."); *Kimbrough,* 128 S.Ct. 558 (sentencing court may deviate from particular guideline on policy grounds); *Rita,* 127 S.Ct. at 2468 (sentencing judge should address all nonfrivolous arguments for a non-guideline sentence).]

The Office of Defender Services of the Administrative Office of the U.S. Courts collects legal and policy arguments and caselaw and empirical studies on recidivism and other sentencing issues useful for defense advocacy on its Sentencing Resource Page at www.fd.org.

There is a growing receptivity toward sentencing consideration for the many harsh collateral consequences that accompany a conviction, especially for a drug offense. [*See, e.g., United States v. Thavaraga,* 740 F.3d 253 (2d Cir. 2014)(affirming downward departure from 20 years to 9 years because defendant faced likely deportation when his incarceration ended); *United States v. Nesbeth,* 188 F.Supp.3d 170 (E.D.N.Y. 2016)(downward departure from range of 33 to 41 months to one-year probation in light of many collateral consequences that faced defendant convicted of drug offenses)]. Even in a non-guideline regime, you should inform the court of the collateral consequences of the conviction to convince the court that even a non-custodial sentence imposes substantial punishment.

<u>**PRACTICE TIP:**</u>

The considerable leeway defendants now enjoy to argue for variances and departures changes the calculation as to whether to enter into sentencing stipulations and appeal-waivers. Federal prosecutors routinely demand appeal waivers, stipulations as to guideline factors such as loss amount and drug weight, and even waivers of the right to argue for variances or departures below the guideline range. Once agreed, such waivers and stipulations are enforceable. [*See* §17:31 (appeal waivers); *United States v. Williams*, 510 F.3d 416 (3d Cir. 2007) (enforcing against defendant an agreement not to argue for a departure or variance).]

Enter into such stipulations and waivers only if you obtain something of value unlikely to be granted without the prosecution's cooperation: a stipulation to a lower-than-provable loss amount; waiver of a mandatory-minimum sentence; or a government motion to reduce the sentence for your client's cooperation in the prosecution of another.

[§§22:15-22:19 Reserved]

III. SENTENCING ALTERNATIVES

§22:20 General Points

Where your client has little criminal history, poses little threat to the public and the crime does not spark public outrage, the court may be amenable to an alternative sanction that is more onerous than probation but less than incarceration.

Alternative sanctions permit your client to work and pursue educational or rehabilitative programs while saving the cost of incarceration.

Some counties use alternative programs frequently in cases where statutes may forbid straight probation, such as repeat driving-while-impaired offenders.

Many of these programs pose considerable burdens and multiple opportunities for your client to fail. Consider whether the offense is one in which the judge routinely imposes straight probation or a fine. Suggest alternatives only where your client needs them to avoid incarceration.

§22:21 Possible Alternatives

Boot camp.

The judge may order or recommend that in lieu of serving his full term, the defendant serve a reduced term in a boot camp, where he will be subject to military-style discipline and training, including drug treatment and counseling in the development of life skills.

This sentence is most appropriate for young healthy offenders who seem in need of guidance to develop self-discipline.

Weekend or intermittent incarceration.

This prevents your client from missing work and losing his job.

House arrest or community confinement.

With house arrest, judges often will order electronic monitoring. Your client must wear a transmitting device, usually around his ankle, which will trigger a notification to the probation office if he leaves his home or a specified radius. The device can be turned off during the hours approved for work, school, church attendance or the like.

The appropriateness of this alternative depends on your client's personal situation. For example, a defendant who lives in a two-bedroom apartment with three toddlers and in-laws might prefer a short term of incarceration.

Intensive supervision.

Intensive supervision programs may require a combination of more frequent visits to the probation officer, drug testing, consent to random searches, community service, curfews and electronic monitoring. Besides home arrest ankle bracelets, some probation departments can fit your client with a global positioning system ("GPS") to monitor whether he remains within the county or other limited geographical area.

Technology is available that can monitor whether your client consumes any alcohol. Where alcoholism might have contributed to the crime, the judge might order this. Your client may have to pay for its cost.

Community Service.

Judges like this for affluent offenders who are not in need of rehabilitative programs.

[§§22:22-22:29 Reserved]

IV.   THE PRESENTENCE INVESTIGATION REPORT (PSIR)

§22:30   General Points

Most guilty pleas are rapid and rote and do not provide much information to the judge about your clients, their merits and their foibles.

Most jurisdictions authorize an adjournment between plea or trial and sentencing for court officers (usually representatives of the probation department) to conduct presentence investigations of your clients and report to the judge and parties.

Judges use presentence investigation reports ("PSIRs") to arrive at appropriate sentences, and the correctional authorities rely upon them to determine defendants' security classifications and institutional placements.

§22:31   What the Report Covers

The preparation of the PSIR does not involve much investigation other than interviewing the prosecutor and the defendant and gathering records. Presentence investigators usually do not canvass the neighborhood to ascertain the defendant's reputation and good or bad deeds.

The PSIR will cover the following areas:

The underlying facts of the offense.

The investigator usually relies upon the prosecutor or case agent for this, but might ask for your client's version. [*See* §22:32.]

Your client's health and medical and psychiatric background.

The investigator will have your client sign releases for records, but will not know of special needs unless you tell the investigator. Included in the topics will be illegal drug use.

Family background.

The investigator will start with your client's description, but may contact a sibling or parent to confirm the information.

Educational and employment history.

Be accurate. The investigator will seek corroboration.

Assets, income and expenses.

This becomes important where a fine or forfeiture is likely or where the crime calls for restitution.

Criminal record.

Educational, treatment and rehabilitative programs available for the defendant.

PSIRs often fall short in this respect, but seek recommendations that might help keep your client from recidivating (*e.g.,* job training, drug and alcohol treatment, anger management classes and counseling for gamblers).

Sentencing guideline calculations.

The presentence report usually produces an initial calculation that will hold unless the parties object.

Sentencing recommendation.

The probation officer often will recommend a specific sentence to the judge. Unlike the rest of the report, the recommendation often remains secret from the parties. [*See, e. g.,* Fed. R. Crim. P. 32(d)(1)(2); ABA Standards for Criminal Justice; Sentencing, Standard 18–5.4 (3d ed. 1994); *Commonwealth v. Goggins*, 2000 Pa. Super. 69, 748 A.2d 721, 728-29 (Pa. Super. 2000) (all listing recommended PSIR contents).]

Forms:
- **Form 22-1** U.S. Probation Department Presentence Interview Worksheet
- **Form 22-2** Probation Department Financial Disclosure Forms

§22:32   Waiving the PSIR

In most misdemeanor cases, you will have an agreement or at least a relatively certain expectation of the sentence, and there is only one institution in which to serve custodial sentences (the county jail) so a presentence report serves little purpose and may not be required.

With a felony conviction a presentence investigation is usually mandatory. However, the applicable rule or statute might leave some room for the parties and trial judge to waive it. [*E.g.*, Fed. R. Crim. P. 32 (c)(1)(A)(ii) (PSIR required unless judge finds sufficient information in record to exercise sentencing discretion); Wayne LaFave, *et al.*, 5 *Criminal Procedure* §26.5(b) nn. 35-38 (surveying states' different approaches to need for PSIR).]

Waive a presentence investigation and report where you have a favorable sentence guarantee from the judge or prosecutor. Where the judge can sentence-bargain, a presentence investigation may provide the judge an out from a favorable promise. [*E.g., People v. Hicks*, 98 N.Y. 2d 185, 774 N.E.2d 205, 746 N.Y.S. 2d 441 (2002) (court could reject agreement and impose higher-than-agreed sentence where defendant lied in presentence interview and denied guilt).]

Where the judge does not participate in bargaining and the prosecutor can make only non-binding recommendations, the trial judge likely will follow the recommendation, reasoning that the prosecutor and you know best your client's conduct and background and the proper dose of punishment.

Remember, at the time of plea the judge has heard nothing more than the brief plea colloquy, which merely sketches the offense conduct and says nearly nothing about your client's background. The presentence investigator might excavate sordid details of the crime and your client's background, which might justify a more severe sentence.

§22:33   The Presentence Interview

Attend the presentence interview unless your attendance would so offend the investigator as to result in a hostile interview.

The weight of authority is that a presentence interview is not a critical stage of the proceedings at which the defendant has a right to counsel. These rulings are premised on the belief that the investigator acts as an arm of the court, not an adversary. [*See United States v. Tyler*, 281 F.3d 84, 968 n.15 (3d Cir. 2002) (collecting cases); *but see State v. Everybodytalksabout*, 166 P.3d 693 (WA 2007) (holding that presentence interview is a critical stage, at least if prosecution seeks to use the statements at a retrial).] However, many jurisdictions permit an attorney to attend, either by rule or custom. [*See, e. g.,* Fed. R. Crim. P. 32 (c) (2).] In jurisdictions which recognize that the presentence interview is a critical stage with an attendant Sixth Amendment right to counsel, failure to request that you be present may waive any Sixth Amendment objection.

If you are met with resistance, explain that you are there principally to facilitate the interview and to avoid misunderstandings. And, for the most part, that should be your role. Also, take extensive notes of your client's remarks.

Whether you attend or not, clients should not answer questions about either their criminal history or about the offense conduct. Clients often deny guilt of crimes to which they pleaded guilty, and sometimes in good faith assert that a case that resulted in a conviction and time served was "dismissed." These inaccuracies can lead the presentence investigator to characterize your client as dishonest. Further, clients may inform the investigator about crimes that never would have been discovered (*e.g.,* crimes in other states or convictions in local courts or before the minor judiciary). When asked, you and your client must answer honestly. Therefore, the best strategy is an across-the-board refusal to address the topic.

A defendant retains his Fifth Amendment privilege against self-incrimination between conviction and sentencing, and even on appeal. [*Mitchell v. United States*, 526 U.S. 314 (1999).] While a guilty plea waives the privilege for the elements of the offense necessary to establish the conviction, the privilege survives for aggravating factors or other crimes beyond the plea. [*Mitchell, supra; Bank One of Cleveland v. Abbe*, 916 F.2d 1067, 1075 (6th Cir. 1990).] If your client went to trial, the privilege stands in full, and it continues through appeal. [*E.g., Martin v. Flanagan*, 259 Conn. 487, 496 n.4, 789 A.2d 979, 984 n.4 (Conn. 2002) (collecting cases).] Admissions in the presentence interview can be used at a retrial after a successful appeal. Thus, it is crucial that your client not make statements about the offense if he went to trial, or about any conduct beyond the plea.

Statements about the crime of conviction may similarly entangle clients. The client might add otherwise unknown damning facts or dishonestly minimize guilt. If the investigator demands a statement on the threat that silence will lose the client credit for accepting responsibility for his crime, provide a written one that you author in consultation with your client.

Questions about drug use should be handled on a case-by-case basis, depending on your client, the nature of the crime and the judge. Some judges consider drug use mitigating, and reference in the presentence report to your client's drug use may facilitate entry into treatment programs which could reduce his sentence. [*See* 18 U.S.C. §3621(e) (up to 12 months early release for completing 500-hour residential drug abuse program, "RDAP"); Alan Ellis & J. Michael Henderson, *Federal Prison Guidebook*, Ch. 13 (2008 ed.) (describing RDAP).]

Drug dealers who sell to support their habit seem less culpable than those who sell from greed. However, drug use is criminal conduct, and it may disturb some judges, especially if your client was on probation or parole while using drugs.

Many probation officers demand that your client give a urine sample at the interview. Warn your client to clean himself up or to confess to his drug use so he is not caught in a lie. If you know that the sample will be positive, notify the probation officer in advance.

PRACTICE TIP:

If your client does make admissions during the presentence interview and the prosecution seeks to use them during a retrial, you still may have winning arguments under the rules or statutes providing for the confidentiality of presentence interviews and reports that the statements should not be admissible, at least in the prosecution's direct case. [*States v. Maestas*, 63 P.3d 621, 626-29 (UT 2002) (reversing for admission of report during prosecution's direct case).]

Forms:
• **Form 22-1** U.S. Probation Department Presentence Interview Worksheet
• **Form 22-2** Probation Department Financial Disclosure Forms

§22:34   Providing Information to the Investigator

Submit information about your client, his version of the offense and any mitigating factors as soon as possible to increase the likelihood that the probation officer will include the information in the report. The officer's endorsement of the information cloaks it with a credibility that your post-report sentencing memorandum will not have. Give specifics and supporting documentation to which the officer can refer.

If you do not have an agreement on the sentencing guidelines range, present the probation officer with factual statements, references to the trial record or law enforcement reports and law that will support a favorable guideline calculation.

Think in terms of making the probation officer's job easier and his or her calculations defensible. The PSIR's initial calculation carries inertial heft, so that a favorable one imposes a substantial burden on the prosecution.

With respect to your client's personal background, designate a family member to be ambassador to the presentence investigator. This should be someone responsible and sympathetic to your client, who can assemble pertinent information, share it with the investigator and support it with corroborating details and documents.

§22:35   Risk Assessment Tools

A number of states have begun to permit or even mandate that sentencing judges use evidence-based risk assessment tools at sentencing. [*See States v. Loomis*, 881 N.W.2d 749, 760 nn. 23 & 24 (WI 2016).] Using proprietary algorithms developed by private companies, these tools consider static information (such as criminal history) and some dynamic variables (such as criminal associates and substance abuse) to score a defendant's risk of recidivisim. [*See Loomis*, 881 N.W.2d at 761]. The private developers treat the tools as proprietary trade secrets and do not disclose how the risk scores are determined or how the factors are weighed. [*Id.*]

In some jurisdictions, risk assessment tools have been used primarily to reduce incarceration rates by identifying those defendants more properly channeled into probation or other rehabilitative programs. [American Bar Association, Criminal Justice Section, *State Policy Implementation Project* at 18-19 (available at http://www.americanbar.org/content/dam/aba/administrative/criminal_justice/spip_handouts.authcheckdam.pdf)]. The tools' developers , and some states' statutes, caution that the tool should be used to assist corrections authorities in making placement decisions, managing offenders, and planning treatment, and not to determine the severity of a sentence or whether an offender should be incarcerated. [*Loomis*, 881 N.W.2d at 754-55, 767-68]. Nonetheless, there is a risk that a sentencing judge will misuse use these tools to justify increased incarceration for a defendant scored as a risk of re-offending.

These tools pose a number of other concerns. Since the developers refuse to disclose the basis for their calculations, a court's reliance on the tools threatens a defendant's due process right to have an opportunity to explain or deny the information on which his sentence is based. [*See Gardner v. Florida*, 430 U.S. 349, 351 (1977); *Loomis*, 881 N.W.2d at 760-64.] In addition, there have been attacks on the tools' predictive accuracy and findings that the risk assessment tools disproportionately classify minority offenders as having a higher risk of recidivism. [*Loomis*, 881 N.W.2d at 763-64; *see* Pennsylvania Commission on Sentencing, Risk/Needs Assessment Project, Interim Report 7: Validation of Risk Scale, Appendix D (noting that Pennsylvania tool has an accuracy rate of only 58.8%)(available at http://pcs.la.psu.edu/publications-and-research/research-and-evaluation-reports/risk-assessment/phase-i-reports/interim-report-7-validation-of-risk-scale/view)]. In light of these concerns, the Wisconsin Supreme Court warned sentencing judges that they should restrict use of these tools to one factor in the evaluation of matters such as "(1) diverting low-risk prison-bound offenders to a non-prison alternative; (2) assessing whether an offender can be supervised safely and effectively in the community; and (3) imposing terms and conditions of probation, supervision, and responses to violations." [881 N.W.2d at 767.] The tool "should not be used as an a aggravating or mitigating factor in determining the severity of an offender's sanction." [*Id.* at 768.]

Another objection to the use of some risk assessment tools is that some assign points to a defendant's prior arrests, even if they did not result in conviction. Mere arrests cannot be considered to enhance a sentence. [*Townsend v. Burke*, 334 U.S. 736 (1948).]

§22:36   Challenging the PSIR

It is important to challenge inaccuracies in the PSIR and to ask the judge to order inaccurate allegations be redacted from the PSIR because:
- The trial judge will rely upon the factual assertions in the PSIR unless you challenge them.
- Prison officials rely heavily on the PSPIR to arrive at a security classification. Inaccuracies about your client's drug use, risk of flight or history of violence may result in placement in a higher security prison or more restrictive conditions of confinement even if the inaccuracies do not affect the sentence.

Obtain the report far enough in advance of sentencing to review it with your client, investigate its inaccuracies, research any legal issues on merger, concurrency of sentences and guidelines calculations and file written objections. On many issues, such as the facts underlying prior convictions, family history, and drug use, your client is an essential starting point for any challenges.

Your client has a right to receive the report in sufficient time to review and challenge it. [*See generally* Wayne LaFave, *et al., 5 Criminal Procedure* §§26.4(d), 26.5(c) (reviewing statutory and constitutional arguments for early disclosure).] This right may be established either by:
- Rule. [*See United States v. Nappi*, 243 F.3d 758 (3d Cir. 2001) (under Fed. R. Crim. P. 32, any information upon which the court relies at sentencing must be disclosed in sufficient time for counsel to comment on it, correct mistakes and prepare a meaningful response).]
- Due Process. [*Gardner v. Florida,* 430 U.S. 349 (1977) (due Process violated by sentencing defendant to death based in part on confidential information in PSIR that was not disclosed to defendant or his attorney).]

If you receive materials late, request a continuance and justify the request with an explanation of what investigation and research you need to do. [*Nappi*, 243 F.3d at 770-72 (finding late disclosure of state PSIR at federal sentencing harmless because defendant did not assert how he could have been helped by more time and notice).]

The court cannot rely upon unsupported conclusory assertions from the prosecution which work their way into the report. [*See United States v. Elwood*, 999 F. 2d 814, 817-18 (5th Cir. 1993) (where there was no evidence at trial about the defendant's leadership role, probation officer and court could not rely on prosecutions' bald allegation that defendant deserved upward adjustment for leadership role).]

Object in writing well before sentencing and with specificity; where possible. Refer to trial evidence or witness statements that support your position or give specific reasons why the information underlying the report is unreliable. [*E.g., United States v. Brown*, 314 F.3d 1216, 1226 (10th Cir. 2003) (allegation that report "contains many inaccuracies, unsupported assumptions and ... a whole lot of fluff that is just not true" insufficient to trigger any obligation on district court to make specific findings or to hold a hearing).]

Object even if an inaccuracy does not affect your client's sentencing range because it might worsen your client's security classification. For example, if the presentence report indicates that a prior conviction for simple assault rested upon sexually abusive conduct, the defendant will receive a "public safety factor," which disqualifies him from minimum security prison, even if never convicted for the sexually abusive conduct. [*See* U.S. BOP *Program Statement 5100.08*, Chapter 5, p.8.]

Forms:
- **Form 22-3** Position of Defendant With Respect to Sentencing Factors
- **Form 22-4** Motion and Order to Redact Presentence Investigation Report

[§§22:36-22:39 Reserved]

V.   ADVOCATING FOR YOUR CLIENT

§22:40   Humanize Your Client

The criminal justice system dehumanizes defendants before disposing of them. Your job is to introduce your client to the judge and prosecutor as a person with hopes and dreams, friends and family, strengths and weaknesses. Judges and prosecutors have more difficulty sending to prison those individuals they could know as friends.

The presentence report rarely achieves this. Even in the section that describes your client's upbringing and family, it reads as a list of incomplete facts raising more questions than it answers.

Use three devices to humanize your client:
*   The sentencing memorandum. [*See* §22:41.]
*   Letters from friends and family. [*See* §22:42.]
*   The sentencing hearing. [*See* §§22:90 et seq.]

The least important of these is the sentencing hearing, because most judges already have decided what sentence they will impose by the time they take the bench at sentencing.

§22:41   The Sentencing Memorandum

Provide the judge with a sentencing memorandum that reads as a narrative humanizing the client, explaining his offense and suggesting how he, with the court's help, will avoid recidivating.

Aim at three purposes in the narrative:

Show that your client is more than just his worst day.

Your client's crime represents the worst he has to offer; he is more and better than that.

Tell the court about the good works he has done for his family and community and how he prevailed over various hardships or how disappointments oppressed him.

Support this section with citations to letters from friends, family, community leaders and persons whom your client has assisted.

Explain why he came to this.

Explanations about how circumstances, personality disorders, need or mental illness led your client into wrong-doing mitigate his culpability.

Rarely will your explanation amount to an irresistible cause for your client's offense. Rather, use the force of narrative to make your client's crime sound like the inevitable denouement of his personal situation.

For example, where your client suffers from depression, you often will find that he committed his offense in a clumsy manner almost designed to result in arrest. Depression does not cause tax evasion, drug-trafficking or bank-robbing. However, people who are depressed, whose attempts to achieve prosperity flounder, often engage in riskier and riskier behavior in a disguised call for help. Look to medical and psychiatric reports and letters from therapists as well as family members to support this argument.

Argue that steps short of lengthy incarceration will prevent him from re-offending and protect the public.

Your client can build a foundation for this argument by seeking post-arrest counseling and treatment for his disorders and addictions.

Judges also consider cooperation against other offenders, or attempts to do so, as strong evidence that your client has severed his criminal ties and started down a law-abiding path. You might consider a specific sentencing alternative here (*e.g.,* boot camp, intensive probation supervision, an inpatient drug or alcohol program). [*See* §22:21.]

Forms:
*   **Form 22-3** Position of Defendant With Respect to Sentencing Factors
*   **Form 22-4** Motion and Order to Redact Presentence Investigation Report
*   **Form 22-5** Sentencing Memorandum

§22:42   Letters

Heartfelt letters from friends, coworkers and family are crucial.

Judges treat a lawyer's words with appropriate skepticism. They are more impressed by simple words from righteous community members who know of the defendant's errors but still support him publicly.

The rules of evidence do not apply at sentencing. [*See* §22:80.] Therefore, you can introduce the letters as a factual basis for your arguments. Prosecutors rarely object to their admission.

Urge people to send the letters to you well in advance of sentencing so you can screen them and bundle them to present to the judge before he has made up his mind and so that you can cite to them in your sentencing memorandum.

Letters work better than live witnesses at sentencing because judges rarely change their minds the day of sentencing and they appreciate having the leisure to review the letters in chambers.

Explain the following guidelines to your client, an ambassador to the community, or the letter writers themselves:
- Ensure that the authors know the purpose of the letter: to request leniency of a judge for one convicted of a crime.
- The author should introduce himself and describe how and how long he has known the defendant.
- Offer an opinion about the defendant's character and, if known, his reputation in the community.
- Do not contest the defendant's guilt.
- Recite anecdotes demonstrating the defendant's character.
- Ask the judge for mercy, not a specific sentence. An exception would be an immediate family member who can express a compelling reason to have the defendant home to attend to family needs.

Make sure that the writers know what the crime of conviction is, at least in general terms; retractions caused by learning the crime's severity look very bad.

In addition, you might consider sending a sample letter to educate supporters as to the proper form.

Form:
- **Form 22-6** Sample Sentencing Letter

§22:43   Videos and Photographs

Some defense attorneys have adopted the use of "day in the life" videos and photographs often used by plaintiffs in personal injury cases. Before sentencing you can send the judge, perhaps in conjunction with letters or your sentencing memorandum, a CD or DVD showing, for example:
- The earnest efforts your client makes to get through each day–feeding her children, getting them to school, rushing off to a job, attending job training, mental health or drug rehabilitation sessions.
- Statements and stories by friends and relatives about good deeds the defendant did for them, his struggles to remain sober, his remorse about the offense, how he has taken solid steps to change since his offense.
- Narratives in lieu of letters by individuals who come across more articulate and heartfelt in oral statements.
- Family photographs showing the defendant in his human roles as parent, friend, son or daughter.

Any of these may assist in delivering the message, prior to the day of sentencing, that your client is a multi-dimensional human being with a strong support system, not just the bad actor in a crime drama.

[§§22:44-22:49 Reserved]

VI.   CONSECUTIVE VS. CONCURRENT SENTENCES

A.   Single Jurisdiction

§22:50   General Points

Sentencing defendants for multiple convictions can be perplexing.

You may need to learn the practices of the respective departments of correction or bureau of prisons, because often the corrections officials have more say than the sentencing judges over how time will be calculated and credited.

You cannot defer this issue to those officials because the consequences for your client can be severe: doubling of a sentence.

§22:51　Single Case

Whether convictions on multiple counts in the same case should merge for the purpose of sentencing depends on whether the legislature intended that the same conduct be punishable under two different statutes. Offenses are separate only if each includes an element that the other does not. [*Blockburger v. United States*, 284 U.S. 299 (1932).]

Generally, where one offense is a lesser included of the other it is presumed that the legislature did not intend cumulative punishment or sentences, and only one sentence can be imposed. [*See Rutledge v. United States,* 517 U.S. 292, 304 (1996) (conspiracy was a lesser included offense of participating in a continuing criminal enterprise; conspiracy conviction had to be vacated even though sentences were fully concurrent); *but see Missouri v. Hunter,* 459 U.S. 659 (1983) (where legislature so intended, cumulative punishments could be imposed for identical conduct that violated two statutes, here, "armed criminal action" and robbery).]

However, other jurisdictions follow a single transaction test. That is, if the offenses all arise from a single transaction, the sentences must be concurrent. [*See, e.g.,* NY Penal Law 70.25; *People v. Hamilton,* 4 N.Y.3d 654, 830 N.E.2d 306, 797 N.Y.S.2d 408 (2005) (criminal possession of weapon and manslaughter sentences from same incident must run concurrent).]

In some situations merger is mandatory, or explicit legislation orders consecutive sentences. [*E.g.,* NY Penal Law §70.25 (2-b) (sentence for violent felony committed while defendant on bail shall run consecutive to any sentence on the pending charge); 18 U.S.C. §924(a)(4) (sentence for carrying or using a firearm during a crime or violence or a drug offense must run consecutive to any other sentence).]

Otherwise, sentencing statutes leave the issue to the sentencing court's discretion, but with a default rule to govern if the sentencing court does not articulate whether the sentence is to be consecutive or concurrent. [*E.g.,* 18 U. S.C. §3584(a) (sentences imposed in same proceeding presumed to be concurrent). *See generally* Wayne LaFave, *et al., 5 Criminal Procedure* §26.3 (f) & nn.50-55 (surveying states' different approaches).]

Unless you are certain that silence results in full concurrency, you must ask the court to specify that the sentences be concurrent.

§22:52　Multiple Cases

Often, a different statutory rule applies when the defendant receives sentences on different cases at different times. Consult the sentencing statutes in your jurisdiction:

- Some create a presumption that sentences run concurrent in the judge's silence. [*E.g.* Calif. Penal Code §669; NY Penal Law §70.25.]
- Others presume consecutive sentences. [*E.g.,* 18 U.S.C. §18 U.S.C. §3584 (a).]

[*See generally,* Erin E. Goffette, *Note, Sovereignty in Sentencing: Concurrent and Consecutive Sentencing of a Defendant Subject to Simultaneous State and Federal Jurisdiction,* 37 Valparaiso Univ. L. Rev. 1035, 1050-51 & nn.67-70 (2003) (collecting state statutes); Wayne LaFave, *et al., 5 Criminal Procedure* §26.3 (f) & nn.50-55 (surveying states' different approaches).]

The sentencing judge can specify that the sentences be concurrent. [U.S.S.G. §5G1.3(c) (the sentence may run concurrently, partially concurrently, or consecutively to the prior undischarged term).]

However, sentencing judges may have no authority to run sentences concurrently where one involves a probation or parole violation. In such a case, sentencing statutes may mandate consecutive sentences, and the judge may lack control because a parole board will order that the parole violation sentence be consecutive. [*E.g., Griffin v. Pennsylvania Department of Corrections,* 862 A.2d 152, 155-56 (Pa Cmwlth 2004).]

If charges in a single indictment or information are severed for trial and result in two or more separate sentencings, the correctional officials may presume an intent to run the sentences consecutively in the court's silence. [*See BOP Sentence Computation Guide,* PS 5880.028 at p. 1- 32 (February 14, 1997) (available at www.bop.gov/DataSource/execute/dsPolicyLoc) (interprets 18 U.S.C. §3584(a), which states, "Multiple terms of imprisonment imposed at different times run consecutively unless the court orders that the terms are to run concurrently," to apply to sentences arising out of different trials imposed at different times, "even if the trials arose out of the same indictment").]

Make sure the judge explicitly orders that the second sentence runs concurrent to the first.

Form:
- **Form 22-7** Motion and Order for Adjustment to Award Credit for Time Served

[§§22:53-22:59 Reserved]

B. Different Jurisdictions

§22:60   Obstacles to Concurrent Sentencing

Difficulties often arise in coordinating sentences when clients are in custody in one jurisdiction, and another seeks to adjudicate its case.

To produce the defendant, the second jurisdiction issues a writ of habeas corpus ad prosequendum, which results in his presence in the secondary jurisdiction until the case is finished. However, under the concept of "primary custody," the defendant legally remains in the primary jurisdiction's custody that whole time and is "loaned" to the secondary jurisdiction. [*Ruggiano v. Reish*, 307 F.3d 121, 125n.1 (3d Cir. 2002).]

Under the primary jurisdiction rule, the second jurisdiction's sentence does not start to run until the defendant is received in the jurisdiction's custody, and any time credit is attributed to the jurisdiction which first took custody.

This is not necessarily the first jurisdiction to impose sentence. If the secondary jurisdiction imposes its sentence first, two obstacles forbid the defendant from starting to earn credit toward his sentence:

- The sentence will not begin until he enters the secondary jurisdiction's custody, because he still is under the primary jurisdiction's custody. [*Ruggiano v. Reish*, 307 F.3d 121, 125n.1 (3d Cir. 2002) (where a defendant is in state custody for a state sentence, his federal sentence does not start to run until he is released from state custody and enters federal custody).]
- The primary jurisdiction has not yet convicted the defendant nor imposed a sentence. Therefore, there is nothing to which the secondary jurisdiction can run its sentence concurrent if it so desires. [*See generally* Savvas Diacosavas, *Vertical Conflicts in Sentencing Practices: Custody, Credit and Concurrency*, 57 N.Y.U. Ann. Survey of Am. Law 207 (2000) (explaining problems created by primary jurisdiction rules).]

It may seem that the solution is for the secondary jurisdiction to await the outcome in the primary jurisdiction before sentencing the defendant, but this solution often fails where the secondary jurisdiction is federal.

Federal and state authorities work in task forces, especially in gun, drug and robbery cases, to target those offenders they consider problems. The offender may suffer a state arrest, and while the defendant is detained on that case, a federal indictment issues for other, more serious conduct. Federal cases usually move more rapidly to conclusion than state cases, and defendants have a motive to reach federal sentencing before conviction on the pending unrelated state case because a state conviction may increase the defendant's criminal history score and sentence under the federal sentencing guidelines [*see* U.S.S.G. §4A1.2] and might even convert him to a "career offender," thereby doubling his likely federal sentence [*see* U.S.S.G. §4B1.1 (enhanced sentence on third felony conviction for crime of violence or drug offense)].

In the primary state custody situation, you often find both the federal and state judges agreeable to running the sentences concurrently, to be served in federal custody. The federal sentence likely will be lengthier, and the state is eager to shift the costs of incarceration to the federal authorities.

There are three approaches to this problem:

- Get the client released to the secondary jurisdiction. [See §22:61.]
- Have the federal judge specify that the federal sentence is to run concurrent to the state sentence and will be served in state custody. [See §22:62.]
- Ask the second sentencing jurisdiction to reduce its sentence. [See §22:63.]

§22:61   Release to the Secondary Jurisdiction

One solution to the problem of getting concurrent sentencing when different jurisdictions are involved is to get your client released to the secondary jurisdiction's custody.

For example, where the primary jurisdiction is state and the secondary federal, have a federal detention order entered, and then ask the state judge and prosecutor to agree to release your client from state custody. In this case, federal custody becomes the primary custody. The state judge then imposes sentence last and directs that the state sentence be served concurrently to the federal one and in federal custody.

This solution requires the cooperation of the state prosecutor and judge. It helps considerably to have the federal prosecutor assure them that the defendant will not be released from federal custody and will face a substantial federal sentence.

§22:62   Obtain a Concurrent Sentence From the Federal Judge

Another solution to the problem of getting concurrent sentencing when different jurisdictions are involved is to have the federal judge specify at sentencing and on the judgment that the federal sentence is to run concurrent to the state sentence and will be served in state custody.

A federal sentencing judge has authority to specify that a federal sentence be served concurrent to a yet-to-be-imposed state sentence. [*Setser v. United States*, 132 S.Ct. 1463 (2012).]

You *must* persuade the federal judge to specify concurrency. If the judge says nothing, the federal sentence will run consecutive to the state sentence. [*United States v. Chea*, 231 F.3d 531, 535 (9th Cir. 2000); *Romandine*, 206 F.3d at 737-38.]

Some states have similar statutes, and those statutes may give the sentencing judge the binding authority which the federal system reserves to the Bureau of Prisons. [*E.g.*, Calif. Penal Code §2900(b)(2) (sentencing judge may designate that California sentence is concurrent and to be served in foreign jurisdiction's custody).]

You *must* ask the judge to include the language, "to be served in state [identify state] custody." That language is not superfluous. Some jurisdictions and prison officials may not award credit unless they see that language. [*See, e.g., Griffin v. Pennsylvania Dept of Corrections*, 862 A.2d 152 (Pa. Cwlth 2004) (Parole Board refused to consider federal sentence concurrent to state sentence and award credit for backtime where federal judge stated sentence was concurrent to state sentence, but failed to state that it should be served in state custody).]

Call the respective corrections departments or bureau of prisons to ask them how they will calculate your client's sentence and credit time served. The institutions realize that this area is complex, and they wish to avoid both frustrating the intentions of sentencing judges and inviting the prisoner habeas actions that come when credit is lost or sentences are served consecutively. [*See United States v. Smith*, 101 F.Supp.2d 332, 347 (W.D.Pa. 2000) ("the BOP itself considers the interaction of federal and state sentences where the state has primary jurisdiction to be probably the single most confusing and least understood sentencing issue in the Federal system.").]

The institutions are usually willing to advise how to structure a sentence and phrase the commitment order to see that the judge's intention is fulfilled.

PRACTICE TIP:

Do not make assumptions about which custody your client prefers.

Defendants charged with non-violent, white collar offenses usually prefer federal custody because they will serve their time in a lower security facility occupied by similar individuals, not by violent criminals.

However, if your client is charged with a street crime he might prefer a state institution because he is likely to be closer to his family, and he might have friends and associates in prison who can ease his transition.

Form:
• **Form 22-7** Motion and Order for Adjustment to Award Credit for Time Served

§22:63   Ask the Second Jurisdiction to Reduce its Sentence

Another remedy is for the sentencing judge to impose a much reduced sentence in recognition that he cannot save the defendant from serving some extended consecutive term.

For example, the federal sentencing guidelines authorize a downward departure when a sentence to which the federal sentence should have been concurrent has been discharged. [U.S.S.G §5K2.13 (Policy statement); *see Ruggiano v. Reish*, 307 F.3d 121 (3d Cir. 2002) (authorizing federal court to reduce or "adjust" sentence on this basis).]

This may be the only remedy where the defendant faces a state parole violation. The parole board will not take action until the federal sentence is imposed, and the law and policy of most boards is always to impose a revocation sentence consecutive to a new sentence.

[§§22:64-22:69 Reserved]

VII. CREDIT FOR TIME SERVED

§22:70   General Points

Your client should receive credit toward his sentence for the time he spent in pre-trial detention. The right is statutory, not constitutional.

However, obtaining credit is complex where your client had several cases underway at the same time. The credit belongs to the case on which he was first detained; he cannot receive multiple credits toward several different cases at the same time. [18 U.S.C. §3585(b); 42 Pa. C.S.A. §9760(4).]

Your client generally will not receive credit toward his sentence for time spent under house arrest or in a community confinement center or halfway house. [*See, e.g., Reno v. Koray*, 515 U.S. 50 (1995) (no credit if the house arrest or halfway house was a condition of release); *Commonwealth v. Kyle*, 582 Pa. 624, 874 A.2d 12 (2005) (forbidding credit spent on bail under home electronic monitoring); *Detar v. Pa. Bd. of Prob. & Parole*, 890 A.2d 27 (Pa Cwlth 2006) (defendant not entitled to credit for time he spent in inpatient drug rehabilitation center as a condition of parole).]

You should ask the judge to spell out with as much specificity as possible the credit to which your client is entitled, *e.g.*, "Credit for time served since his arrest on xx/xx/xx to the present date." Prisons and corrections departments frequently refuse to give credit if the sentencing order, or forms that accompany it, is at all vague, *e.g.*, one that merely states, "Credit for time served," without specifying the dates.

If your judge is amenable, a sentence of "time served" is preferable to a sentence specifying a term of days, months or years. A term sentence might entail the defendant's return to incarceration while corrections calculates credit and release dates, whereas a "time served" sentence avoids the wait for calculations and, absent detainers, mandates the defendant's immediate release.

Form:
- **Form 22-7** Motion and Order for Adjustment to Award Credit for Time Served

§22:71   The Determination of Credit

Whether to award credit often lies with the Bureau of Prisons or Department of Corrections, not the sentencing judge.

Credit may be awarded if the judge ordered detention, but recommended a community treatment center, and the sheriff or marshals, in their discretion, honored the recommendation. [*See* U.S. Bureau of Prisons Program Statement 5880.28, page 1-14F.]

You can ask the sentencing judge to depart or reduce the sentence to account for lengthy periods of time your client spent under restrictive pre-trial house arrest. [*United States v. Romualdi*, 101 F.3d 971, 977 (3d Cir.1996) ("it may be proper to depart because of the ... home detention [a defendant] had already served." (quoting *United States v. Miller*, 991 F.2d 552, 554 (9th Cir.1993)).]

Carefully consider the interplay between the concurrent sentencing rules and the rules for time credits. Even where you seem to achieve concurrency between sentences in two different jurisdictions, your client may serve extra time because the time in presentence custody may count only toward one jurisdiction's sentence. In that case, argue to the judge that since corrections will not award your client credit for the many months he spent under restrictive and punitive conditions, the court should reduce his sentence to account for this time period. [*See, e.g.*, U.S.S.G. §5G1.3 (b)(1) (court can reduce a sentence for time served that will not be credited to the federal sentence by the Bureau of Prisons).]

Under federal law, such reductions are not subject to the restrictions on reducing a sentence under a so-called "departure" rationale. The judge must state clearly that the sentence is being adjusted under U.S.S.G. §5G1.3(b)(1), and the judgment and commitment order must cite that section. [*Ruggiano*, 307 F.3d 121.]

Consult with corrections and prison officials to guarantee that your clients receive the credits they deserve. [*See United States v. Wilson*, 503 U.S. 329 (1992) (Bureau of Prisons, not sentencing judge, has the authority to award credit for time served).]

In the federal system, review Program Statement 5880.28, the Sentence Computation Manual. [www.bop.gov.]

CAUTION:

Prison officials may take months to calculate credit for foreign pre-trial detention, especially if it was in another country. In the meantime, your client might serve more time than the judge would have ordered. You might do better asking the judge to sentence the client to "time served."

[§§22:72-22:79 Reserved]

VIII. SENTENCING HEARINGS

A. Evidence

§22:80   Rules of Evidence Do Not Apply

The rules of evidence do not apply at noncapital sentencings. Courts can consider all manner of evidence from whatever source. [*See* Fed. R. Evid. 1101(d)(3) (rules of evidence do not apply to sentencing); 18 U.S.C. §3661 ("No limitation shall be placed on the information concerning the background, character, and conduct of a person convicted of an offense which a court of the United States may receive and consider for the purpose of imposing an appropriate sentence."); *United States v. Simmons*, 164 F.3d 76 (2d Cir. 1998) (FRE 410, which prohibits use at trial of factual admissions made during a later-withdrawn guilty plea, does not apply to sentencings).]

However, due process forbids basing a sentence on unreliable information. [*Townsend v. Burke*, 334 U.S. 736, 741 (1948) (holding that sentence based on materially false information violates the Due Process Clause).] This Due Process principle prohibits use of the bare fact of an arrest record without more to aggravate a sentence. [*United States v. Berry*, 553 F.3d 273, 282 (3d Cir. 2009).] Some courts have observed that since residents of high crime areas, black Americans, and Latinos are overrepresented in arrest records, reliance on those records also exacerbates racial and economic disparities in our criminal justice system. [*United States v. Mateo-Medina*, 845 F.3d 546 (3d Cir. 2017).] If the prosecution or presentence officer adduces reliable evidence to establish the facts underlying those arrests, even if from police reports, the court can rely on the underlying conduct. To prevent this, the defense must contest the accuracy of those underlying facts. [*Berry*, 553 F.3d at 284 ("Nevertheless, appellate courts do permit consideration of the underlying conduct where reliable evidence of that conduct is proffered or where the PSR adequately details the underlying facts without objection from the defendant.")]

The defendant has an affirmative duty to show that the alleged misinformation is materially inaccurate. [*State v. Harper*, 334 Mont. 138, 144 P.3d 826, 829 (MT 2006); *United States v. Fatico*, 579 F.2d 707, 711-714 (2d Cir. 1978) (extensive discussion of application of Due Process clause to sentencing).]

§22:81   Confrontation Clause Does Not Apply

Courts uniformly have rejected application of the decision in *Crawford v. Washington,* 541 U.S. 36 (2004), and the Confrontation Clause to sentencing proceedings. [*See, e.g., United States v. Martinez*, 413 F.3d 239, 242 (2d Cir. 2005); *see United States v. Fanfan,* 468 F.3d 7, 15 (1st Cir. 2006).]

The court can consider reliable hearsay evidence. Therefore, the prosecution can rely on hearsay and avoid cross-examination of its witnesses.

§22:82   Fourth and Fifth Amendment Violations

Sentencers can consider illegally seized evidence at sentencing. [*See United States v. Brimah,* 214 F.3d 854, 858-59 & n.4 (7th Cir. 2000) (surveying cases; might be an exception where police act with purpose of obtaining evidence to enhance sentence).]

However, they cannot consider evidence obtained in violation of the Fifth Amendment privilege against self-incrimination. [*See Mitchell v. United States*, 526 U.S. 314 (1999).]

Thus, the sentencing judge or jury cannot hold against a defendant his post-arrest silence nor his refusal to turn state's evidence against other offenders. [*See Roberts v. United States,* 445 U.S. 552 (1980); *Commonwealth. v. Freeman*, 573 Pa. 532, 574, 827 A.2d 385, 410 (2003) (error to permit cross-examination of defendant at sentencing on his failure to tell the police his present story).]

Nor can the court draw an adverse inference from his silence at the sentencing or during a presentence interview. [*Mitchell v. United States*, 526 U.S. 314 (1999).]

However, the defendant's silence can result in a finding that he has failed to carry his burden of proving an entitlement to certain sentence reductions. [*See United States v. Warren*, 338 F.3d 258 (3d Cir. 2003) (upholding denial to defendant of safety valve reduction because defendant failed to disclose all information concerning the offenses that were part of the same course of conduct as the offense of conviction).]

§22:83 Acquitted Conduct

The sentencing court can consider acquitted conduct to increase a sentence. [*United States v. Watts*, 519 U.S. 148 (1997); *United States v. Dorcely*, 454 F.3d 366 (D.C. Cir. 2006) (affirming that *Watts* remains good law after *Booker*).]

However, you may argue that the court should consider the fact of acquittal in deciding how much weight to give the conduct. Many trial courts find the use of acquitted conduct to increase a sentence disturbing and exercise their discretion to reject an increase. [*See United States v. Ibanga*, 454 F.Supp.2d 532 (E.D. Va. 2006) (collecting cases and noting that all appellate courts have rejected constitutional challenges to use of acquitted conduct, but a number of trial courts have refused to base sentencing enhancements on acquitted conduct for nonconstitutional reasons); *United States v. Coleman*, 370 F. Supp.2d 661, 668 (S.D. Ohio 2005) (acquitted conduct should always be considered using a reasonable doubt standard); *United States v. Huerta-Rodriguez*, 355 F. Supp. 2d 1019, 1028 (D. Neb. 2005) (stating that it can never be reasonable to base any significant increase in a defendant's sentence on facts that have not been proved beyond a reasonable doubt); *United States v. Pimental,* 367 F. Supp.2d 143 (D. Mass. 2005) (stating that it makes no sense to conclude that the Sixth Amendment is violated whenever facts essential to sentencing have been determined by a judge rather than a jury and also conclude that the fruits of the jury's efforts can be ignored with impunity by the judge in sentencing).]

§22:84 Polygraphs

Most jurisdictions forbid prosecution use of polygraph results at sentencing, while some allow the defense leeway to do so. [*See Height v. State*, 604 S.E.2d 796, 799 (Ga. 2004); *Paxton v. Ward,* 199 F.3d 1197, 1211-1216 (10th Cir. 1999) (prosecution may not apply a per se bar on polygraph evidence so as to abridge a capital defendant's right to present mitigating evidence in seeking imposition of a sentence less than death); *Rupe v. Wood*, 93 F.3d 1434, 1439-1441 (9th Cir. 1996) (trial court's refusal to admit polygraph results in penalty phase pursuant to general rule of inadmissibility violated capital defendant's right to present mitigating evidence).]

Other jurisdictions do not allow polygraph results at sentencing. [*See People v. Szabo*, 447 N.E.2d 193, 210 (Ill. 1983) (favorable polygraph evidence could not be considered by the jury in the penalty phase of capital murder trial); *State v. Pierce*, 138 S.W.3d 820, 826 (Tenn. 2004) (polygraph examination results, testimony on such results, or testimony regarding a defendants willingness or refusal to submit to a polygraph examination is not admissible during either capital or non-capital sentencing hearings); *People v. Maury*, 30 Cal.4th 342, 68 P.3d 1, 133 Cal.Rptr.2d 561 (2003) (inadmissible).]

[§§22:85-22:89 Reserved]

B. Preparing for the Hearing

§22:90 General Points

At sentencing, try to present a narrative about your client that explains how and why he arrived at the point in his life where he committed his crime, how he will avoid wrongdoing again, and why the judge should feel confident that the punishment you propose addresses the goals of rehabilitating your client, deterring his and others' wrongdoing and protecting the public.

Deliver all certificates and letters and sentencing memoranda to the judge and prosecutor at least one week before sentencing.

§22:91 Submit Certificates and Letters

As early in your representation as possible, you should address what steps your client can take to mend the error of his ways and convince a judge that he has been rehabilitated.

Good intentions prove nothing. It is best to present evidence of steps your client has taken to put his life in order through drug treatment programs and gainful employment. [*See United States v. Sally,* 116 F.3d 76 (3d Cir. 1997) (post-offense rehabilitation could be basis for downward departure below sentencing guideline range).]

Document your client's changes with certificates and letters from treatment and counseling programs and an employer.

§22:92   Have Friends and Character Witnesses Ready

For the most part the judge has made up his mind by the day of the sentencing hearing and does not want to hear lengthy testimony, but a few well-chosen witnesses can have impact.

Three types are best:

A very close friend or spouse.

This person should attest to the goodness in your client, his remorse and suffering for his offense, and the rehabilitative steps he has taken to reform and make amends.

This person also might write the court and testify about any special needs only your client can meet (*e.g.*, a particularly ill or disabled family member for whom your client cares on a regular basis). [*E.g., United States v. Sclamo,* 997 F.2d 970 (9th Cir. 1993); *United States v. Gaskill,* 991 F.2d 82 (3d Cir. 1993) (downward departures granted where defendant provided indispensable care for troubled or disabled family members).]

Individuals who can describe the difference your client has made in their lives through especially charitable or noble deeds. [*See United States v. Cooper,* 394 F.3d 172 (3d Cir. 2005) (downward departure granted for defendant's charitable works).]

Ministers, public servants and community leaders who know your client and can attest to his good character.

These witnesses show that a person of high repute thinks so highly of you client that he will risk his reputation by testifying publicly for him.

To be useful, such people must enjoy the judge's respect, must know the defendant well, and must be informed about the nature of the crime and any sordid details which the prosecutor might disclose at a sentencing hearing.

Prepare all the witnesses for the usual character witness cross-examination along the lines, "Would you have the same opinion of defendant's character if you knew that he pleaded guilty of stealing from a charity or to selling drugs to children?"

§22:93   Seek the Prosecutor's and Probation Officer's Input

Usually, the prosecutor seeks prison time and views treatment programs as attempts to avoid just punishment. It does not hurt to explore the prosecutor's likely reaction to your arguments and proposals.

For example, explain that your client suffered from depression, which ran in his family, and began to self-medicate through drugs. You must disclose information about witnesses and character letters anyway. Discuss how your client has pursued treatment with success and your proposal that probation be imposed to include continued treatment.

Prosecutors like to think of themselves as both righteous and reasonable. Yours might be the one time the prosecutor acted reasonably, thus enabling him to believe in his fairness when he righteously seeks the maximum for the next defendant.

§22:94   Prepare Social Workers and Therapists to Testify

Psychologists and mitigation specialists can describe how your client's misfortunes led to his misdeeds.

However, this testimony does not help much unless you can demonstrate the steps your client has taken to reform and the workable plan he has for the future.

§22:95   Make Restitution

Early and full restitution to the victims impresses courts and might deflate the victims' anger and opposition to any leniency. [*See, e.g., United States v. Lieberman,* 971 F.2d 989 (3d Cir. 1992) (early and extraordinary restitution could be basis for downward departure from sentencing guideline range).]

§22:96   Check for Special Sentence Thresholds

Your jurisdiction may have peculiar rules that trigger substantial changes in the length or nature of your client's sentence at specific sentence lengths.

For example, in the federal system, inmates are eligible for good-time release only if their sentence *exceeds* one year, meaning that a defendant sentenced to a year and a day serves less time than a defendant sentenced to eleven months. [18 U.S.C. §3624(b). *See also* 61 Pa. Stat. §331.26 (if maximum sentence on indeterminate sentence range is less than two years, defendant serves sentence in county, not state custody, and sentencing judge, not parole board, makes parole decisions, which generally facilitates early release).]

Besides thoroughly reviewing the sentencing statutes, consult an experienced practitioner or the presentence investigator about peculiar sentence options and pitfalls.

§22:97   Your Client's Testimony

"Grovel or keep quiet" is the best advice to your client.

Defendants have a right to address the court at sentencing. [*See Green v. United States,* 365 U.S. 301 (1961).] The court must invite the defendant to allocute, but the remedy for a failure to ask is unclear. Some courts hold the error waived if defense counsel does not object. If the court affords the opportunity upon objection after the sentence is announced, most courts will pronounce the error harmless so long as the record shows that the sentencing court carefully considered the statements. [*See generally West Valley City v. Waljasper,* 2012 UT App 252, 286 P.3d 948 (UT 2012) (good survey of the cases on point).]

However, clients often hurt themselves more than help. Clients want to tell the judge that they really are good people and that the offense was atypical of them, that other forces (*e.g.,* a bad marriage, depression, drug and drink, or evil friends) led them to commit this crime. Do not let the client say any of this. It usually alienates judges by sounding like excuse-making.

Let other witnesses (family, friends, therapists) describe the good side of your client and explain what led him to commit his crime. The main things that judges want to hear from defendants are remorse, shame and a resolution that they will do whatever it takes to avoid relapse. Your client succeeds if he makes a brief and sincere-sounding apology to the victims and the court.

Do not underestimate how difficult this will be for your client. Articulate, educated clients are most at risk of saying the wrong thing. They suffer from self-images that cannot accept that they have become felons. Therefore, they will try to rationalize their conduct or blame others, such as the prosecutor. If they have lived the sort of dual lives that many criminals do, lives of attending church and charitable projects while at the same time molesting children or cheating on their taxes, they are practiced at denial and rationalization and will have great difficulty, no matter how much you rehearse them, in sounding remorseful.

Defendants convicted of street crimes have the best chance to persuade the court because the judge does not expect much from them. If they can sound thoughtful and articulate in expressing remorse for the harm they have done to the victims, the disappointment caused to their families and their desire to make things and themselves right, the judge might deduct a few months from the sentence.

PRACTICE TIP:

Have your client write out what he will say and rehearse it in front of you. Your client can and often should read his statement to the court instead of improvising.

[§§22:98-22:99 Reserved]

IX.   SPECIAL SITUATIONS

§22:100   Fines and Restitution

Sentences often carry monetary penalties along with probation or incarceration, such as fines, an order of restitution to the victims, court costs, or assessments.

The court might waive a fine if you convince the judge that your client lacks the means to pay. You have the burden of persuasion on this issue, and the best approach is to present financial information to the presentence investigator for inclusion in the presentence report demonstrating that your client lacks the means to pay.

The court may impose restitution to be paid over time, while your client is on probation, during a prison term, or during post-incarceration parole or supervised release. [*E.g.,* 18 U.S.C. §3664(f)(3)(B).] The prison may deduct from the inmate's prison earnings and account to pay the fine and restitution. [*See* 28 C.F.R. §545.11.]

Even if an order of restitution in the full amount is mandatory, a showing of inability to pay will buy your client a payment schedule. [18 U.S.C. §3664(f)(2),(3).] Some courts make payment of the fine or restitution a condition of probation or parole and defer the terms of a payment schedule to the supervising probation or parole officer. Check your jurisdiction's caselaw to see if the court has authority to defer the setting of a schedule.

Failure to pay court-ordered restitution or fines can be punished by incarceration for contempt of the court's order or by a violation of probation, parole or supervised release. However, your client can avoid punishment if he demonstrates an inability to pay and a good faith effort to pay. [*Bearden v. Georgia,* 461 U.S. 660 (1983).]

Once your client finishes the term of parole, probation or supervised release, the court may lose the power to incarcerate for the failure to satisfy fine or restitution obligations. However, the obligation remains in effect, just like a civil debt, and suit can be brought against your client to enforce it. [*F.D.I.C. v. Dover*, 453 F.3d 710, 716-717 (6th Cir. 2006) (obligation to pay fine or restitution does not end with expiration of supervision; can be enforced as any other judgment); *see* 18 U.S.C. §3664(m)(1)(B); Cal. Penal Code §1214(b) (only in felony cases can criminal order of restitution be converted to a civil judgment).]

Bankruptcy does not discharge a criminal fine or restitution obligation. [18 U.S.C. §3613(e).]

Of course, your client may be judgment proof by the time supervision ends, and few creditors pursue a debt after that time.

The jurisdiction's statutes define the obligation's duration. [*See, e.g.,* 18 U.S.C. §3613(b)&(f) (liability to pay fine or restitution terminates 20 years after judgment or release from imprisonment or death).]

Fines do not bear interest, but a restitution order may carry prejudgment interest in order to allow the victim to recoup the time-value of his loss and to make him whole. [*United States v. Fumo*, 655 F.3d 288 (3d Cir. 2011).]

§22:101 Sex Offender Registration

Federal law requires states to impose registration requirements on convicted sex offenders, and every state does. [*See Smith v. Doe*, 538 U.S. 84, 90 (2003) (describing 42 U.S.C. §14071 and upholding state registration statute against Ex Post Facto challenge because court did not consider it to be punishment). Note: effective July 27, 2009, The Adam Walsh Act, Pub. L. 109-248, will repeal the current registry law (42 U.S.C. §14047-73) and create a new sex offender registry law at 42 U.S.C. §§16901-16962.]. However, a state cannot include within its sex offender registration laws a requirement that offenders no longer under parole or court supervision consent to searches of their computers or other devices with Internet capability. [*Doe v. Prosecutor, Marion County*, 566 F.Supp.2d 862 (S.D. Ind. 2008) (issuing declaratory judgment that Indiana's statute violated the Fourth Amendment).]

Registration requirements apply even to those adjudicated as juveniles, so long as they were over 14 years old at the time of the offense and the offense of conviction is equivalent to what is defined as aggravated sexual abuse under federal law–genital or anal penetration or any oral-genital or oral-anal contact by use of force, or threat of serious bodily injury, or with one rendered unconscious or drugged involuntarily or under 12 years old. [42 U.S.C. §16911(8) (referring to definition of "aggravated sexual abuse" in 18 U.S.C. §2241).]

The Department of Justice created an Office of Sex Offender Sentencing, Monitoring, Apprehending, Registering and Tracking as part of the Sex Offender Registration and Notification Act ("SORNA"). This office provides guidance to the states and Indian jurisdictions and tracks legislative and case law developments on its website, www.ojp.usdoj.gov/smart. Its perspective is pro-prosecution, but the website is a starting point to track the latest developments and the prosecution's official position, which sometimes may be more lenient than your individual prosecutor's. The U.S. Department of Justice has promulgated guidelines for the implementation of SORNA, available at www.ojp.usdoj.gov/smart, and regulations are codified at 28 C.F.R. Part 72.

The SORNA and Adam Walsh Acts set minimum requirements for all U.S. jurisdictions, enforced by the federal threat to withdraw criminal justice funding if states fail to implement them. However, many states have even more severe registration requirements. For example, some states impose registration on defendants convicted for prostitution-related offenses, public urination, and consensual sex between teenagers. [*See* Human Rights Watch, No Easy Answers at nn. 108-122 (available at www.hrw.org).]

If your client has been convicted of a sex offense the prosecution may seek to have him classified as a "sexually violent predator" (SVP) either at or shortly after his sentencing. A finding that your client is an SVP imposes more onerous restrictions, such as police-conducted door-to-door community notification, frequent verification of registration and counseling requirements. [*See, e.g.,* 42 Pa. C. S. A. §9795.1 *et. seq.*, 42 U.S.C. §§14071, 14072.]

Violations of these conditions are punishable criminal offenses. [18 U.S.C. §2250(a) (felony punishable by up to ten years imprisonment).]

Before your client enters a plea, you must check carefully the list of offenses that qualify for sexually violent predator treatment. The list grows with each legislative session.

SVP statutes generally have four prerequisites to finding that your client is an SVP: (1) conviction of a qualifying offense; (2) assessment by a court-appointed expert and a hearing before the court; (3) a mental abnormality or personality disorder that (4) makes the defendant likely to engage in a violent sexually predatory offense, as defined in the statute. [*See, e.g.,* 42 Pa.C.S.A. §9795.4, 42 U.S.C. §14071(a)(3)(C).]

The SVP assessment occurs before sentencing, and the hearing usually takes place on the day of sentencing, immediately before the court imposes sentence. Since your client still has a Fifth Amendment privilege and the SVP expert's assessment is likely to ask whether your client has engaged in other sexual conduct criminal in nature, you generally should not permit the evaluator to interview your client. Most evaluators base their assessment and testimony entirely on court records.

NOTE:

This SVP assessment is not the same as statutes that authorize civil commitment upon a finding that a convict suffers from a mental abnormality such that he cannot control himself from the likelihood of committing sex crimes. These statutes impose onerous and indefinite civil commitment. [*See* §22:103.]

PRACTICE TIP:

Usually you do not want your client to be interviewed. The rare case where you will allow an interview is when your own investigation and psychiatric assessment can provide assurances that your client's conduct was an aberrational event unlikely to reoccur.

Consider a slew of legal challenges to registration requirements:

1. Argue that the requirements do not apply retroactively. Your argument is two-fold: (1) the Legislature did not intend that the particular provision of the statute have retroactive interpretation. [*See, e.g., Carr v. United States*, 130 S.Ct. 2229 (2010) (the federal offense of a state offender failing to register, 18 U.S.C. §2250, applies only to an offender who traveled in interstate commerce after July 26, 2006, SORNA's effective date); and (2) the particular provision constitutes criminal punishment and its retroactive application violates the Constitution's Ex Post Facto Clause; *but see Smith v. Doe*, 538 U.S. 84, 90 (2003) (upholding state registration statute against Ex Post Facto challenge because court did not consider it to be punishment).] Having a statute declared unconstitutional presents a formidable challenge, and federal regulations expressly state that SORNA's requirements "apply to all sex offenders, including sex offenders convicted of the offense for which registration is required prior to the enactment of that Act." [28 C.F.R. 72.3.] Focus on an argument from legislative intent where you can.

2. Argue that under the Sixth Amendment as interpreted by *Apprendi v. New Jersey*, and its progeny, registration requirements amount to criminal punishment and must be found by a jury beyond a reasonable doubt.

[For a collection of federal constitutional challenges to registration statutes, *see* Corey Rayburn Yung, "One of These Laws Is Not Like the Others: Why the Federal Sex Offender Registration and Notification Act Raises New Constitutional Questions," 46 *Harvard Journal on Legislation* 369 (Summer 2009) (advocating Ex Post Facto, Due Process, and Commerce Clause challenges to SORNA).]

§22:102   Persistent and Habitual Offender Sentences

"Three-strike" statutes have become common. These statutes authorize lengthy sentences for recidivists even when the current charge is relatively minor. [*E.g., Ewing v. California*, 538 U.S. 11, App A (2003) (appendix to Justice Breyer's dissenting opinion compiling statutory provisions in every state enhancing sentences for thieves with prior felony convictions).]

Some repeat offender statutes are construed so that even if the prior conviction occurs in the same case, with no arrest intervening between the charges, the statute applies and the defendant's sentence is enhanced. [*Compare Commonwealth v. Shiffler*, 583 Pa. 478, 879 A.2d 185, 195-96 (Pa. 2005) (no enhanced sentence where statute required that at time of commission of present offense, defendant previously have been convicted of other offenses) *with Commonwealth v. Bell*, 2006 PA Super 131; 901 A.2d 1033 (Pa. Super. Ct. 2006) (sentence enhanced where statute required that at time of sentencing on present offense, defendant must previously have been convicted of other offenses); *Deal v. United States*, 508 U.S. 129 (1993) (no requirement that there be an intervening sentence, case or arrest for consecutive sentences under 18 U.S.C. §924(c)(1), carrying and using a firearm in relation to a crime of violence).]

Courts admit that imposing enhanced and consecutive sentences for multiple counts in the same case does not further the presumed purpose of punishing more severely individuals who failed to learn their lesson from a prior sentence, but they approach the issue as a matter of statutory interpretation and impose the sentence commanded by the statute's language.

Once the defendant is shown to be the person who suffered the prior conviction, the conviction is presumed to be valid. [*See Parke v. Raley*, 506 U.S. 20 (1992); *State v. McCann*, 200 Ariz. 27, 21 P.3d 845 (2001) (surveying states that follow this rule).] Generally, a prior conviction is proven by introducing a certified copy of the judgment of conviction. Reliance on non-judicial records, such as the criminal history record maintained by the National Crime Information Center ("NCIC"), should be challenged. [*See United States v. Bryant*, 571 F.3d 14 (1st Cir. 2009) (noting mixed decisions by courts as to whether the NCIC record suffices to prove a prior for determining whether the defendant should receive an enhanced "career offender" sentence; remanding for a determination of reliability where defendant challenged the presentence report and denied that the prior conviction was his).]

To attack the prior you must offer credible and specific evidence that the prior was not obtained constitutionally. [*State v. McCann*, 200 Ariz. 27, 21 P.3d 845 (2001).]

Federal courts have prohibited collateral attacks on priors unless the prior conviction was uncounseled and the defendant did not waive his right to counsel. [*Custis v. United States*, 511 U.S. 485 (1994).]

The "uncounseled" exception arises only where there was a failure to appoint counsel for an indigent in violation of *Gideon v. Wainwright*, 372 U.S. 335 (1963). It has not been extended to ineffective assistance of counsel claims.

Some states have followed suit and prohibit any challenges at sentencing to prior convictions unless the prior was uncounseled. [*See, e.g., State v. Hahn*, 238 Wis.2d 889, 618 N.W.2d 528 (2000). *People v. Allen*, 21 Cal.4th 424, 87 Cal.Rptr. 682, 981 P.2d 525 (1999) (will allow challenges to guilty pleas as not knowingly and voluntarily entered, but will not permit ineffective assistance of counsel claims).]

However, sentencing statutes may authorize challenges to the priors at the sentencing hearing. [*E.g.,* NY CPL 400.15(7)(b), 400.21 (7)(b) (may challenge prior as unconstitutionally entered); Cal. Veh. Code §41403 (in aggravated DUI case, may challenge prior DUI as unconstitutionally obtained).]

Therefore, you must analyze each statute's language carefully before advising your client to plead guilty to multiple counts. If you must litigate the issue, start with the statutory language and then wrap yourself in the rule of lenity and the "recidivist philosophy." [*See Commonwealth v. Dickerson*, 404 Pa. Super. 249, 258, 590 A.2d 766, 771 (Pa. Super. 1991) ("If the heavier penalty prescribed for the second violation ... is visited upon the one who has not had the benefit of the reproof of a first conviction, then the purpose of the statute is lost." (quoting *Morgan v. Commonwealth*, 170 Ky. 400, 186 S.W. 132 (1916)).]

If you are challenging a prior conviction, try to bring a collateral attack in the court where the conviction was entered. Statutes of limitations for collateral attacks or requirements that the defendant still be in custody from the prior conviction may preclude bringing such an action. File the petition as soon as possible and attempt to win a favorable ruling before sentencing. Do not wait until the verdict or guilty plea to begin the challenge.

If the law of your jurisdiction permits a challenge to priors on more than just *Gideon* grounds, realize that the prior will be presumed valid, and you must allege specific and credible reasons why it was unconstitutional. [*State v. McCann,* 200 Ariz. 27, 21 P.3d 845 (2001).]

In *Apprendi v. New Jersey*, 530 U.S. 466 (2000), the United States Supreme Court held that any finding which increases the statutory maximum for an offense constitutes an element of the offense must be submitted to the jury under the beyond a reasonable doubt standard. Since then, the *Apprendi* holding has been extended to guideline sentencing schemes and sentencing factors increase the mandatory minimum sentence for an offense.

An exception is the existence of prior convictions, which often constitutes the triggering factor for the application of habitual or three strikes sentencing statutes. Nonetheless, *Apprendi* has vitality here, too. The sentencing judge's authority is limited to identifying the prior conviction. It may not "make a disputed determination about what the defendant and state judge must have understood as the factual basis of the prior plea, or what the jury in a prior trial must have accepted as the theory of the crime." [*Descamps v. United States,* 133 S.Ct. 2276, 2288 (2013); *see People v. Wilson*, 219 Cal. App. 4th 500, 162 Cal. Rptr.3d 43 (Cal. Ct. App. Sept. 5, 2013) (improper for sentencing court to make a finding that defendant had "personally afflicted" great bodily injury on the victims from his prior drunk driving offenses, which was necessary to make each offense a separate strike).]

§22:103 Dangerous and Sexually Violent Predator Statutes

Many states have civil commitment statutes triggered by conviction for certain violent or sexual offenses or acquittals by reason of insanity.

Under these statutes, if an offender is proven to suffer from a mental illness or personality disorder such that he is likely to offend again, he may be committed to a mental institution for a period of time or until he is safe to be released. [*E.g.,* Calif. Welf. & Inst. Code §6600 *et seq.*]

Arrest and commitment under these statutes do not occur until your client has completed his criminal prison term and is about to be released. [*E.g., Burgess v. Watters,* 467 F.3d 676 (7th Cir. 2006) (explaining procedures under Wisconsin statute).]

These statutes have been construed as civil, not criminal in nature and thus lack many of the protections afforded in criminal proceedings. [*E.g., Kansas v. Hendricks,* 521 U.S. 346, 370-71 (1997) (upholding Kansas' statute against Due Process challenge); *Allen v. Illinois,* 478 U.S. 364 (1986) (Fifth Amendment privilege against self-incrimination does not apply at SVP proceedings; therefore, defendant could be compelled to submit to psychiatric evaluation); *State v. Harris,* 881 So.2d 1079 (Fl. 2004) (state does not violate plea agreement for certain prison time followed by probation where it commences civil commitment when defendant due for release from prison).]

Due process requires that the conditions and duration of confinement bear some reasonable relation to the purposes of incapacitation and treatment for which persons are committed. [*See Kansas v. Crane,* 534 U.S. 407 (2002) (offends due process to commit person without any finding that person lacked ability to control behavior; there must be proof of a serious difficulty in controlling behavior, but not an absolute lack of control).]

However, conditions like pedophilia and anti-social personality disorder are notoriously resistant to treatment. Therefore, a commitment can result in lifetime incarceration in some prison mental institution under the control of the corrections department. [*Allen v. Illinois,* 478 U.S. 364, 377 (1986) (Stevens, J., dissenting) (noting that Illinois statute sometimes resulted in commitment for much longer than maximum term of incarceration under the criminal statute).]

PRACTICE TIP:

Dangerous offender commitment hearings take place after the criminal process rather than as part of it. Therefore, your ability to assist your client is limited. Ideally, you should avoid conviction for one of the triggering sexually violent offenses. If that cannot be done, try to avoid inclusion in the record or presentence report of any diagnosis that might form a basis for commitment, such as pedophilia, sexual paraphilia or anti-social personality disorder.

§22:104 Stipulation to Deportation

Many offenses are grounds for deportation. [*See* Chapter 17, Plea Bargaining.]

However, defendants must serve their full sentence before Immigration and Customs Enforcement will deport them.

Where clients have no interest in fighting deportation, they might stipulate to deportation in exchange for a reduced sentence. [8 U.S.C. §1228 (c)(5); *see United States v. Ramirez-Marquez,* 372 F.3d 935, 938 (8th Cir. 2005) (departure warranted where defendant had a "colorable, non-frivolous defense to deportation and showed a waiver of that defense would substantially assist the administration of justice").]

Some federal districts have a "fast-track" program for aliens convicted of illegal entry into the United States in which minimal prison time is exchanged for a stipulation for deportation.

Form:
• **Form 22-8** Stipulation to Deportation

[§§22:105-22:109 Reserved]

X. AFTER THE SENTENCE

§22:110 Preparing Your Client for Incarceration

Nearly as important as the term of incarceration is its place. Even within the same jurisdiction, prisons differ markedly in risk and programs. You want your client in the lowest security level possible because discipline will be less severe, restrictions fewer, and the inmates less dangerous.

Some systems, like the federal Bureau of Prisons, have an elaborate designation process. The presentence report is the basis for the calculations, so ensure that it is accurate with respect to its descriptions of your client's acts of violence, drug addictions, and gang affiliations.

Self-reporting to prison demonstrates your client's trustworthiness and will lower his security classification. Your client must pay for his own travel, but it is worth the cost. It also frees your client from waiting in a dingy local jail until the designation process is completed, and from the roundabout plane and bus routes marshals and sheriffs take to bring inmates from multiple jails to prisons. Such travels have stops at local jails where your client will be locked down and where the risk of losing his personal belongings increases. Argue that your client be allowed to self-report whenever he has been free on bail through his sentencing. Most prosecutors and judges will agree to this because it saves the government the cost of transporting the defendant.

Ask the judge to recommend a place of incarceration. Prison officials usually try to accommodate the judge.

Detailed information is available on the internet and in several publications about the nature of various prisons, their regulations and programs and visiting privileges. [*See, e.g.,* www.bop.gov (federal Bureau of Prisons website); www.cor.state.pa.us (Pennsylvania Department of Corrections website); Alan Ellis & J. Michael Henderson, *Federal Prison Guidebook* (2008).]

Prison officials may not allow clients to bring books and legal papers to prison. Clients should arrange to have someone mail those documents to the prison once the client is designated.

Arranging for visitors can take considerable time, so you and clients should start that process as soon as possible. Immediate family members and spouses have greater privileges. Ensure that the presentence report lists spouses. Common-law spouses and paramours generally do not enjoy the same privileges. [*See* U.S. Program Statement 5267.08 (Visiting Regulations).]

Federal prisons limit inmates to a maximum of ten visitors. Potential visitors must complete a form authorizing the prison to conduct a criminal history and background check. [*See* Form BP-A629, available at www.bop.gov/DataSource/execute/dsFormLoc; U.S. *BOP* Program Statement 5267.08, Section 18.]

Remind your client that the prison will monitor his non-legal mail and telephone calls. If he is appealing his conviction he must avoid discussing the facts of his case in letters and calls.

§22:111   Sentence Reduction Motions

In some jurisdictions, judges frequently grant motions to reduce sentence or to parole the defendant shortly after the sentence is imposed. [*See, e.g., Pa. R. Crim. P.* 720(B)(1)(a)(v).]

The judge may have intended to scare the defendant or might be willing to reconsider once the public focus has blurred. Consider filing one whenever you believe that there might be arguments for a lesser sentence to which, for one reason or another, the court did not give adequate weight.

The federal system has eliminated sentence reduction motions except those filed by the prosecution in consideration for the defendant's post-conviction cooperation against another offender. [*See* Fed. R. Crim. P. 35.]

XI. FORMS

Form 22-1   U.S. Probation Department Presentence Interview Worksheet

PROB 1
(Rev. 4/01)

UNITED STATES DISTRICT COURT
Federal Probation System

WORKSHEET FOR PRESENTENCE REPORT
(See Publication 107 for Instruction)

---

1. FACESHEET DATA

Defendant's Court Name:

Defendant's True Name:

Docket No.:	District:
Judge/Magistrate:	Sentencing Date:
USPO:	Arrest Date:
Assistant U.S. Attorney (Name, address, telephone)	Defense Counsel (Name, address, telephone)

DEFENDANT'S IDENTIFICATION

Defendant's Names: (List every name the defendant has used, e.g., name given at birth, name given at adoption, nickname, alias, names used as a result of marriage, etc.)

Date of Birth:	Age:	Place of Birth:

Race: ☐ White ☐ Black ☐ American Indian/Alaskan Native   Hispanic Origin:
☐ Asian or Pacific Islander ☐ Unknown   ☐ Hispanic ☐ Not Hispanic ☐ Unknown

Sex:	Country of Citizenship:	Immigration Status:
No. of Dependents:	Education:	SSN:
FBI No.:	U.S. Marshal's No.:	Other ID No.:

Defendant's Legal Address: _____
(Number and Street)   (Apartment)
(City)   (State)   (Zip)

Defendant's Current Address: _____
(Number and Street)   (Apartment)
(City)   (State)   (Zip)

Referral Date: _____

Interview Date: _____

PROB 1
(Rev. 4/01)

2. OFFENSE DATA (Presentence Report Part A)

CHARGES AND CONVICTIONS	RELEASE STATUS
Date Information/Indictment Filed: _____	Check the Appropriate Box(es):

CHARGES AND CONVICTIONS

Date Information/Indictment Filed: _____

Date of Conviction: _____

Count No.(s): _____

Conviction by (Check one):

☐ Guilty Plea/Plea of Nolo Contendere
☐ Court Trial Verdict
☐ Jury Trial Verdict

RELEASE STATUS

Check the Appropriate Box(es):

☐ In federal custody since _____
☐ In non-federal custody since _____
Released on _____
☐ Unsecured personal recognizance
☐ $ _____ personal recognizance bond since _____

☐ $ _____ cash security since _____
☐ $ _____ corporate security since _____
☐ $ _____ property bond since _____
☐ Pretrial services supervision

COUNTS OF CONVICTION

Count Nos.	Offense and Statutes	Offense Classification	Minimum/Maximum Statutory Penalty

DETAINERS

☐ No Detainers

Agency or Court	Type of Detainer	Case Number

CODEFENDANTS

☐ No Codefendants

Codefendant(s) Name(s): _____

_____

RELATED CASES (Co-offenders)

☐ No Related Cases

Docket No.	Defendant(s) Name(s)

2

PROB 1
(Rev. 4/01)

PLEA AGREEMENT

Check One:

☐ Written   ☐ Accepted

☐ Oral   ☐ Deferred

☐ No Agreement   ☐ Binding

Substantial Assistance Motion:

☐ No   ☐ Yes

Notes:

OFFENSE CONDUCT

VICTIM IMPACT

☐ No Loss

Victim's Name	Financial Loss	Victim's Address	Victim's Phone
	$		
Loss to All Victims:	$		

Describe any social, psychological, or medical impact upon the victim of the offense behavior.

ACCEPTANCE OF RESPONSIBILITY

Defendant's statement regarding offense:

PROB 1
(Rev. 4/01)

3. DEFENDANT'S CRIMINAL HISTORY (Presentence Report Part B)

☐ None

Date of Arrest, Prosecution, Referral, or Detention	Charge/ Conviction	Court City/County/State Action No.	Date Sentenced or Case Disposed	Sentence	Defendant Represented by or Waived Counsel (Y) or (N)	

PENDING CHARGES AND SUPERVISION STATUS

☐ The defendant has no pending charges.

Charge(s)	Court	Docket/Action No.	Next Appearance Date

☐ The defendant is not currently under supervision.
(division, probation, supervised release, or parole supervision)

☐ The defendant is currently under criminal justice sentence. Type of Supervision:

☐ Diversion   ☐ Probation   ☐ Supervised Release

☐ Parole   ☐ Escape Status   ☐ In Custody

Jurisdiction(s): _____

Supervising Officer's Name and Telephone Number: _____

_____

4

PROB 1
(Rev. 4/01)

4. OFFENDER CHARACTERISTICS (Presentence Report Part D)

DEFENDANT

Residential History: (List every town or city where the defendant has lived.)

PARENTS AND SIBLINGS

(List the defendant's biological parents. If defendant was reared by persons other than his natural parents, add the surrogate parent's names immediately below the space allocated to Father and Mother. After the parents, list all siblings, living or dead.)

Name	Relationship and Age		Present Address and Telephone Number	Occupation
	Father			
Current Name: Maiden Name:	Mother			

Notes regarding family history; identify any significant problems:

PROB 1
(Rev. 4/01)

MARITAL STATUS

☐ The defendant is presently single and has no marital history.

Spouse or Domestic Partner	Date and Place of Marriage	Status	Date of Separation	Date of Divorce	Court Where Divorce was Granted	Number of Children

Employment status of current spouse:

CHILDREN

☐ The defendant has never had any children.

Child's Name	Name of Other Parent of this Child	Age	Custody/ Support	Child's Address and Telephone Number (If different from defendant)

Note health problems, criminal history, substance abuse, or any other significant information.

✎PROB 1
(Rev. 4/01)

DEFENDANT'S PHYSICAL CONDITION		
PHYSICAL DESCRIPTION		
Height:	Weight:	Eye Color:
Hair Color:	Tattoos:	Scars:

PHYSICAL HEALTH

☐ The defendant is healthy and has no history of health problems.

List the date(s) and nature(s) of any serious or chronic illnesses and medical conditions.

List all current prescriptions.

Provide the name, address, and telephone number of the defendant's physician.

MENTAL AND EMOTIONAL HEALTH

☐ The defendant has no history of mental or emotional problems, and no history of treatment for such problems.

Describe any past or present mental, emotional, or gambling problems. Include the diagnosis of any problems (if known) and the dates of any treatment. List the name and address of the treatment provider.

PROB 1
(Rev. 4/01)

SUBSTANCE ABUSE

☐ The defendant has no history of alcohol or drug use and no history of treatment for substance abuse.

Which of the following substances has the defendant used?

☐ Alcohol   ☐ Heroin/Opiates

☐ Marijuana   ☐ Barbiturates

☐ Cocaine   ☐ Hallucinogens

☐ Crack   ☐ Inhalants

☐ Amphetamine/   ☐ Other: _____
    Methamphetamine

When was alcohol or any controlled substance last used? _____

Which substance does the defendant prefer? _____

Which substance has caused the defendant the most problems? _____

Urine test results:

Describe in detail the defendant's history of substance abuse and treatment.
(Overdose, daily cost to support habit, frequency and quantity of use, treatment programs and dates)

8

🖎PROB 1
(Rev. 4/01)

EDUCATION AND VOCATIONAL SKILLS

Highest grade completed: _____

SCHOLASTIC HISTORY

Name and Location of School (List most recent school first)	Dates Attended	Degree, Diploma, or Certificate Received

Does the defendant have any specialized training or skill(s)?

☐ Yes   ☐ No   If yes, what training or skill(s)?

_____

_____

Does the defendant have any professional license(s)?

☐ Yes   ☐ No   If yes, what license(s)?

_____

_____

☐ None   **MILITARY**

Branch of Service:	Service Number:	Entered:	Discharged:	Type of Discharge:
Highest Rank:	Rank at Separation:	Decorations and Awards:		VA Claim Number:

Summarize the defendant's military service. Describe any courts martial or non-judicial punishments. Describe any foreign or combat service. Describe any special training or skills acquired in the service. Describe previous VA claims.

✎PROB 1
(Rev. 4/01)

EMPLOYMENT

Defendant's usual occupation: _____

Defendant's employment status:

At the time of the offense, the defendant was (select the appropriate number from the categories below) _____

At present, the defendant is (select the appropriate number from the categories below) _____

1. Employed full-time	2. Employed part-time
3. Unemployed temporarily, looking for work	4. Unemployed seasonal worker
5. Unemployed due to disability	6. Unemployed, history of extensive unemployment
7. Incarcerated or confined	8. Student
9. Homemaker	10. Retired

11. Other (Specify): _____

FINANCIAL CONDITION/ABILITY TO PAY

☐ Refer to Form 48A

☐ Defendant has few assets and liabilities.

EMPLOYMENT HISTORY
(Describe the defendant's employment history for the last ten years)

Dates	Name and Address of Employer	Job, Monthly Wage, Reason for Leaving
From: To Present	Phone No.:	
From: To:		
From: To:		
From: To:		

10

PROB 1
(Rev. 4/01)

EMPLOYMENT HISTORY (Continued)		
From: To:		
From: To:		
From: To:		
From: To:		
From: To:		
From: To:		
Summarize any employment history over 10 years old:		

✎PROB 1
(Rev. 4/01)

NOTES:

12

Form 22-2   Probation Department Financial Disclosure Forms

COMMENT:

Defendants must complete these forms during the presentence investigation.

PROB 48
(Rev. 9/00)

Last Name	First Name	Middle Name	Social Security Number

Instructions for Completing Net Worth Statement

Having been convicted in the United States District Court, you are required to prepare and file with the probation officer an affidavit fully describing your financial resources, including a complete listing of all assets you own or control as of this date and any assets you have transferred or sold since your arrest. Amendments were made to 18 U.S.C. §§ 3663(a)(1)(B)(i), 3664(d)(3), and 3664(f)(2), and Rule 32(b)(4)(F) to clarify that the assets owned, jointly owned, or controlled by a defendant, and liabilities are all relevant to the court's decision regarding the ability to pay. Your Net Worth Statement should include assets or debts that are yours alone (I-Individual), assets or debts that are jointly (J-Joint) held by you and a spouse or significant other, assets or debts that are held by a spouse or significant other (S-Spouse or Significant Other) that you enjoy the benefits of or make occasional contributions toward, and assets or debts that are held by a dependent (D-Dependent) that you enjoy the benefits of or make occasional contributions toward.

If you are placed on probation or supervised release (or other types of supervision), you may be periodically required to provide updated information fully describing your financial resources and those of your dependents, as described above, to keep a probation officer informed concerning compliance with any condition of supervision, including the payment of any criminal monetary penalties imposed by the court (see 18 U.S.C. § 3603).

Please complete the Net Worth Statement in its entirety. You must answer "None" to any item that is not applicable to your financial condition. Attach additional pages if you need more space for any item. All entries must be accompanied by supporting documentation (see Request for Net Worth Statement Financial Records (Prob. 48A)). Initial and date each page (including any attached pages). Also, sign, date, and attach the Declaration of Defendant or Offender Net Worth & Cash Flow Statements (Prob. 48D).

✎PROB 48
(Rev. 9/00)   Page 2 of _____

Last Name -

NET WORTH STATEMENT

NOTE: I = Individual   J = Joint   S = Spouse/Significant Other   D = Dependent

ASSETS

BANK ACCOUNTS (Include all personal and businesses checking and savings accounts, credit unions, money markets, certificates of deposit, IRA and KEOGH accounts, Thrift Savings, 401K, etc.)

Section A

I/J S/D	Name of Institution	Address	Type of Account	Account Number	Personal or Commercial	Balance

SECURITIES (Include all stocks in public corporations, stocks in businesses you own or have an interest in, bonds, mutual funds, U.S. Government securities, etc.)

Section B

I/J S/D	Name and Kind of Security	Location of Security	Number of Units	Fair Market Value

MONEY OWED TO YOU BY OTHERS (Include all money owed to you by any person or entity.)

Section C

I/J S/D	Name and Address of Debtor	Amount Owed to You	Reason Owed to You	Date Money Loaned	Relationship to Debtor (if any)	Monthly Payment or Date Full Payment Expected	Is Debt Collectible ?

Initials _____   Date _____

PROB 48
(Rev. 9/00)

Last Name -

Section D

LIFE INSURANCE (Include type of policy [whole life, variable, or term], face amount [the stated amount of coverage] and cash surrender value [the value of the investment portion of a whole life or variable policy.])

I/J S/D	Name and Address of Company and Name of Beneficiary	Policy Number	Type of Policy	Face Amount	Cash Surrender Value	Amount Borrowed	Amount You Can Borrow

Section E

SAFE DEPOSIT BOXES OR STORAGE SPACE FACILITY (Include all safe deposit boxes or storage space you rent or places you have access to in which others are holding assets or items belonging to you.)

I/J S/D	Name and Address of Box or Facility Location	Box Number or Space	Contents	Fair Market Value

Section F

MOTOR VEHICLES (Include all cars, trucks, mobile homes, motorcycles, all terrain vehicles, boats, airplanes, etc.)

I/J S/D	Year, Make & License Number/Vehicle Identification Number	Mileage	Loan/Lease Balance (if any)	Date Loan/Lease Will be Paid Off or Ends	Monthly Payment	Fair Market Value

Section G

REAL ESTATE (Include property, parcels, lots, timeshares, and developed land with buildings.)

I/J S/D	Real Estate Address (include county and state)/ Mortgage Company or Lien Holder	Purchase Date	Purchase Price	Mortgage Balance (if any)	Date Mortgage Will be Paid Off	Monthly Payment	Fair Market Value

Section H

MORTGAGE LOANS OWED TO YOU (Include name, address, and relationship [if any] to the mortgagee [the party that bought the real estate you sold and is making payments to you].)

I/J S/D	Mortgagee (name & address)/ Relationship to Mortgagee	Mortgage Balance	Date Mortgage Will be Paid Off	Balloon Payment? If Yes, Date?	Monthly Payment	Is Debt Collectible?

Initials _____ Date _____

PROB 48
(Rev. 9/00)

Last Name -

OTHER ASSETS (Include any cash on hand, jewelry, art, paintings, coin collections, stamp collections, collectibles, antiques, copyrights, patents, etc.)

Section I

I/J S/D	Description	Loan Balance (if any)	Date Loan Will be Paid Off	Monthly Payment	Where is Asset Located?	Fair Market Value

ANTICIPATED ASSETS (Include any assets you expect to receive or control from lawsuits for compensation or damages, profit sharing, pension plans, inheritance, wills, or as an executor or administrator of any succession or estate.)

I/J S/D	Amount Received or Expected to Receive	Date Expected to Receive	Reason You Expect This	Name and Address of Person or Company That Can Verify This (e.g., attorney, financial institution, executor)

Section J

TRUST ASSETS (Include all trusts in which you are a grantor or donor [the person who establishes the trust], the trustee or fiduciary [who controls the trust assets and income or the beneficiary who has or will receive benefits from the trust].)

I/J S/D	Name of Trust/ Taxpayer ID#	Value of Trust	Your Annual Income From Trust	Your Interest in Trust Assets

BUSINESS HOLDINGS (Include all businesses in which you have an ownership interest or with which you had an affiliation within the last three years; e.g., self-employed sole proprietor, officer, shareholder, board member, partner, associate, etc.) Complete Section N (attach additional pages, if necessary).

Section K

I/J S/D	Name and Address of Business/ Taxpayer I.D.#	Type of Business Entity	Industry of Business	Date Business Started	Capital Investment to Start	Your Ownership Interest Percentage	Sale Price or Fair Market Value of Your Interest

Initials _____ Date _____

✎ PROB 48
(Rev. 9/00)

Last Name -

Section L

INCOME TAX RETURNS

Type of Income Tax Return Filed	Last Filing Year	Years of Last 5 Income Tax Returns You Will Submit to the Probation Officer
Individual (Form 1040)		
Partnership/Limited Liability Company (Form 1065)		
Corporation (Form 1120)		
S Corporation (Form 1120S)		

Section M

TRANSFER OF ASSETS (Include any assets you have transferred or sold since the date of your arrest with a cost or fair market value of more than $500.00. Also list any assets that someone else is holding on your behalf.)

I/J S/D	Description of Asset/ Reason Transferred/Sold	Date of Transfer/Sale	Original Cost	Amount You Received, if Any	Name of Purchaser or Person Holding the Asset	Sale Price or Fair Market Value at Transfer

Section N

NAMES OF SHAREHOLDERS OR PARTNERS (Include all shareholders, officers, and/or partners, indicating each respective ownership interest.)

Name of Business	Names of Shareholders/Partners	Ownership Interest Percentage

Initials _____ Date _____

✎PROB 48
(Rev. 9/00)

Page 6 of _____

Last Name -				
	ASSETS YOU WILL LIQUIDATE (Include all assets you intend to liquidate to satisfy any criminal monetary penalties that may be imposed.)			
Section O	**Asset Description**	**Estimated Value of Asset**	**Date You Will Liquidate**	**Current Location of Asset (if real property, county and state)**
Section P	**PROSPECT OF INCREASE IN ASSETS** (Give a general statement of the prospective increase of the value of any asset you own.)			

Initials _____ Date _____

PROB 48
(Rev. 9/00)

Last Name -

LIABILITIES

CHARGE ACCOUNTS AND LINES OF CREDIT (Include all bank credit cards, lines of credit, revolving charge accounts, etc.)

Section A

I/J S/D	Type of Account or Card	Name and Address of Creditor	Credit Limit	Amount Owed	Credit Available	Minimum Monthly Payment

OTHER DEBTS (Include mortgage loans, notes payable, delinquent taxes, and child support.)

Section B

I/J S/D	Owed To	Address	Relationship (if any)	Amount Owed	Reason Owed	Monthly Payment

PARTY TO CIVIL SUIT (Include any civil lawsuits you have ever been a party to.)

Section C

I/J S/D	Name of Plaintiff in the Case	Court of Jurisdiction and County	Case Number	Date of Suit Filed	Date of Judgment	Judgment Amount/ Unpaid Balance

BANKRUPTCY FILINGS (Include information requested for any Chapter 7, 11, or 13 bankruptcy filings you have ever been a party to as an individual or as a business entity.

Section D

I/J S/D	Type of Bankruptcy (Voluntary or Involuntary)/ Name and Address of Trustee	Bankruptcy Case Number	Bankruptcy Court of Jurisdiction	County and State of Discharge	Date Filed	Date of Discharge

Signature _____ Date _____

PROB 48A
(9/00)

REQUEST FOR NET WORTH STATEMENT FINANCIAL RECORDS

DEFENDANT'S FULL NAME	DOCKET NUMBER

All entries on the Net Worth Statement must be accompanied by supporting documentation. Provide the probation officer with all records listed below that are applicable to your financial statements, along with your completed Net Worth Statement by the close of business _____ .

ASSETS

Section A - Bank Accounts

♦ Most recent bank account statements (e.g., checking, savings, credit union, money market, brokerage, Certificate of Deposit, or savings bonds) for a three-month period, along with canceled checks.

Section B - Securities

♦ Most recent securities account statements (e.g., brokerage, annuities, life insurance, IRA, KEOGH, 401K, or thrift savings account) for a three-month period.

Section C - Notes & Accounts Receivable

♦ Copy of signed note receivable.

Section D - Life Insurance

♦ Copy of all life insurance policies (e.g., whole life, variable life, term).

Section E - Safe Deposit Boxes or Storage Facilities

♦ Copy of most recent rental invoice for all safe deposit boxes or storage facility rentals within the past year, including receipts or verification of content value.

Section F - Motor Vehicles

♦ Copy of vehicle registration and title for all vehicles owned or leased.

Section G - Real Estate

♦ Copy of purchase agreement, deeds, and escrow statement for all real property.

Section H - Mortgage Loans Owed To You

♦ Copy of the sales agreement and escrow statement for all real property.

Section I - Other Assets

♦ Copy of purchase invoice and appraisal (if already previously obtained), and documentation to verify the fair market value of the asset.

Section J - Anticipated Assets

♦ Copy of documentation to verify future receipt of anticipated asset, (e.g., claim or lawsuit filings, profit sharing plan and current statement, pension plan and current statement, inheritance documents, copy of all trusts, trust income tax returns), and most recent accounting reflecting the value of your interest and income from the trust.

Section K - Business Holdings

♦ In addition to providing the information requested in Section K and completing Section N, provide copies of all income tax returns for each business you had an ownership interest in (e.g., shareholder, partner, proprietor) or an affiliation with (e.g., officer, director, board member, agent, associate) within the last five years. Also provide all financial statements for each business, prepared by you or your accountant, within the past five years.

Business Accounts Receivable

♦ Copy of current month's billing statements that verify business accounts receivable.

Business Accounts Payable

♦ Copy of current month's vendor invoices that verify business accounts payable.

Section L - Income Tax Returns

♦ Copy of the five most recent years' income tax returns filed for: Individual (Form 1040), Partnership (Form 1065), Corporation (Form 1120), S Corporation (Form 1120S), and Limited Liability Company (Form 1065). Be sure to include all related schedules and forms. Provide a written explanation for any returns not filed.

Section M - Transfer of Assets

♦ Copy of the bill of sale, documentation of funds received from sale (e.g., a personal or business check, cashiers check or money order), copy of vehicle registration and title of sold vehicle, and escrow closing statements for any real estate sold since the date of your arrest.

Section N - Names of Shareholders or Partners

♦ Copy of Articles of Incorporation for all corporations you own or have an interest in. Copy of partnership agreement for all partnerships you have an ownership interest in.

✎ PROB 48A
(9/00)

REQUEST FOR NET WORTH STATEMENT FINANCIAL RECORDS (cont.)

LIABILITIES	OTHER RECORDS REQUESTED
Section A - Charge Accounts ♦ Copy of most current billing statement for all charge accounts (e.g., credit cards, revolving charge cards, and department store cards) and lines of credit (e.g., bank line of credit). **Section B - Other Debts** ♦ Copy of all notes payable, mortgage loans, current statement of delinquent taxes due, and statements documenting child support/ alimony obligations and payment history. **Section C - Party to Civil Suit** ♦ Copy of all civil suit filings and judgments. **Section D - Bankruptcy Filings** ♦ Copy of all bankruptcy filings including petition, financial statements submitted, final judgment and order of discharge.	

ADDITIONAL INSTRUCTIONS:

A personal interview has been scheduled for you with:

_____ on _____
U.S. Probation Officer   Date

at _____   Office Location _____
         Time

                                    Telephone _____

✎PROB 48B
(9/00)

Last Name	First Name	Middle Name	Social Security Number

Instructions for Completing Monthly Cash Flow Statement

Having been convicted in the United States District Court, you are required to prepare and file with the probation officer a statement fully describing your financial resources, including a complete listing of all monthly cash inflows and outflows.

If you are placed on probation or supervised release (or other types of supervision), you may be periodically required to provide updated information fully describing your financial resources and those of your spouse, significant others, or dependents, as described above, to keep a probation officer informed concerning compliance with any condition of supervision, including the payment of any criminal monetary penalties imposed by the court (see 18 U.S.C. § 3603).

Amendments were made to 18 U.S.C. §§ 3663 (a)(1)(B)(i), 3664(d)(3), and 3664(f)(2), and Rule 32(b)(4)(F) to clarify that the assets owned, jointly owned, or controlled by a defendant; liabilities, and the financial needs and earning ability of a defendant and a defendant's dependents are all relevant to the court's decision regarding a defendant's ability to pay. Your Cash Flow Statement should include assets or debts that are yours alone (I-Individual), assets or debts that are jointly (J-Joint) held by you and a spouse or significant other, assets or debts that are held by a spouse or significant other (S-Spouse or Significant Other) that you enjoy the benefits of or make occasional contributions toward, and assets or debts that are held by a dependent (D-Dependent) living in your home that you enjoy the benefits of or make occasional contributions toward.

Please complete the Monthly Cash Flow Statement in its entirety. You must answer "None" to any item that is not applicable to your financial condition. Attach additional pages if you need more space for any item. All entries must be accompanied by supporting documentation (see Request for Cash Flow Statement Financial Records (Prob. 48C)). Initial and date each page (including any attached pages) and sign and date the last page of the Cash Flow Statement.

✎ PROB 48B
(9/00)

Page 2 of _____

Last Name -		
MONTHLY CASH FLOW STATEMENT		
Monthly Cash Inflows		
Defendant	Gross	Net
Your Salary/Wages (List both monthly gross earnings and take-home pay after payroll deductions.)		
Your Cash Advances (List all payroll advances or other advances from work.)		
Your Cash Bonuses (List all payments from work in addition to your salary that are not an advance.)		
Commissions (List all non-employee earnings as an independent contractor.)		
Business Income (List both monthly gross income and net income after deducting expenses.)		
Interest (List all interest earned each month.)		
Dividends (List all dividends earned each month.)		
Rental Income (List all monthly income received from real estate properties owned.)		
Trust Income (List all trust income earned each month.)		
Alimony/Child Support (List all alimony or child support payments received each month.)		
Social Security (List all payments received from Social Security.)		
Other Government Benefits (List all amounts received from the government not yet reported (e.g., Aid to Families with Dependent Children.)		
Pensions/Annuities (List all funds received from pensions and annuities each month.)		
Allowances-Housing/Auto/Travel (List all funds received from housing allowances, auto allowances, travel allowances, and any other kind of allowance.)		
Gratuities/Tips (List all gratuities and tips received each month from any and all sources.)		
Spouse/Significant Other Salary/Wages (List all gross and net monthly salary and wages received by your spouse or significant other.)		
Other Joint Spousal Income (List any monthly income jointly earned with your spouse or significant other [e.g., any income from spouse or income from a business owned or operated by the spouse that you have a joint ownership interest in or control]).		
Income of Other In-House (List all monthly income of others living in the household or the monthly amount actually paid for household bills by these persons.)		
Gifts from Family (List all amounts received as gifts from family members each month.)		
Gifts from Others (List all gifts received from any sources not yet reported.)		
Loans from Your Business (List all loan amounts received each month from all businesses owned or controlled by you.)		
Mortgage Loans (List all amounts received each month from mortgage loans owed to you.)		
Other Loans (List all other loan amounts received each month not yet reported.)		
Other (specify) (List all other amounts received each month not yet reported.)		
TOTALS		

PROB 48B
(9/00)

Last Name -	
Necessary Monthly Cash Outflows	
	Amount
Rent or Mortgage (List monthly rental payment or mortgage payment.)	
Groceries (List the total monthly amount paid for groceries and number of people in your household.)　　#	
Utilities (List the monthly amount paid for electric, heating oil/gas, water/sewer, telephone, and basic cable.)	
Electric	
Heating Oil/Gas	
Water/Sewer	
Telephone	
Basic Cable (no premium channels)	
Transportation (List monthly amount paid for gasoline, motor oil, necessary auto repairs, or the cost of public transportation.)	
Insurance (List the monthly amount paid for auto, health, homeowner/rental, and life insurance.)	
Auto	
Health	
Homeowner/Rental	
Life	
Clothing (List the monthly amount actually paid for clothing.)	
Loan Payments (List all monthly amounts paid toward verified loans, other than loans to family members, which are non-allowable expenses.)	
Credit Card Payments (List all monthly credit card or charge card payments.)	
Medical (List all monthly payments for necessary medical care or treatment.)	
Alimony/Child Support (List all alimony or child support payments made each month.)	
Co-payments (List the total monthly payments made for electronic monitoring and drug and mental health treatment.)	
Other (specify) (List all other necessary monthly amounts paid each month not yet reported.)	
Other Factors That May Affect Monthly Cash Flow (Describe)	
TOTAL	

NET MONTHLY CASH FLOW: $ (CASH INFLOWS LESS NECESSARY CASH OUTFLOWS)

MONTHLY CRIMINAL MONETARY PENALTY PAYMENT: $

PROSPECT OF INCREASE IN CASH INFLOWS (Give a general statement of the prospective increase of the value of any cash inflows reported.)

Signature _____   Date _____

✎PROB 48EZ
(Rev. 9/00)

Last Name	First Name	Middle Name	Social Security Number

Instructions for Completing Net Worth Short Form Statement

Having been convicted in the United States District Court, you are required to prepare and file with the probation officer an affidavit fully describing your financial resources, including a complete listing of all assets you own or control as of this date and any assets you have transferred or sold since your arrest. Amendments were made to 18 U.S.C. §§ 3663(a)(1)(B)(i), 3664(d)(3), and 3664(f)(2), and Rule 32(b)(4)(F) to clarify that the assets owned, jointly owned, or controlled by a defendant, and liabilities are all relevant to the court's decision regarding the ability to pay. Your Net Worth Statement should include assets or debts that are yours alone (I-Individual), assets or debts that are jointly (J-Joint) held by you and a spouse or significant other, assets or debts that are held by a spouse or significant other (S-Spouse or Significant Other) that you enjoy the benefits of or make occasional contributions toward, and assets or debts that are held by a dependent (D-Dependent) that you enjoy the benefits of or make occasional contributions toward. The court may require relating to such other factors as the court deems appropriate (see 18 U.S.C. § 3664(d)(3)).

If you are placed on probation or supervised release (or other types of supervision), you may be periodically required to provide updated information fully describing your financial resources and those of your dependents, as described above, to keep a probation officer informed concerning compliance with any condition of supervision, including the payment of any criminal monetary penalties imposed by the court (see 18 U.S.C. § 3603).

Please complete the Net Worth Short Form Statement in its entirety. You must answer "None" to any item that is not applicable to your financial condition. Attach additional pages if you need more space for any item. All entries must be accompanied by supporting documentation (see Request for Net Worth Statement Financial Records (Prob. 48A)). Sign and date Page 2 (including any attached pages). Also, sign, date, and attach the Declaration of Defendant or Offender Net Worth & Cash Flow Statements (Prob. 48D).

✎PROB 48EZ   Page 2
(Rev. 9/00)

NET WORTH SHORT FORM STATEMENT

NOTE: I = Individual   J = Joint   S = Spouse/Significant Other   D = Dependent

ASSETS

Include below all cash on hand, bank accounts, securities, money owed to you by others, life insurance, safe deposit boxes or storage facilities, motor vehicles, real estate, mortgage loans owed to you, other assets, anticipated assets, and business holdings.

I/J S/D	Type of Asset (e.g., cash, bank account)	Location of Asset (e.g., bank, including account number)	Fair Market or Actual Value

Include below all assets transferred or sold since your arrest with a cost or fair market value of more than $500.00, or assets that someone else is holding on your behalf.

I/J S/D	Type of Asset	Date Sold or Transferred	Fair Market or Actual Value

Identify below any assets you will liquidate to satisfy any criminal monetary penalty that may be imposed, and/or describe the prospect of increase in assets.

I/J S/D	Type of Asset	Fair Market or Actual Value

LIABILITIES

Include below all charge accounts and lines of credit, mortgage balances, other debts, civil suits, and bankruptcy filings.

I/J S/D	Type of Debt (e.g., credit card)	Debt Owed to (e.g., name, account number)	Balance Outstanding

Signature _____   Date _____

Form 22-3   Position of Defendant With Respect to Sentencing Factors

IN THE UNITED STATES DISTRICT COURT
FOR THE _____ DISTRICT OF _____

UNITED STATES OF AMERICA,
v.
CS,
DEFENDANT.

POSITION OF THE DEFENDANT WITH RESPECT TO SENTENCING FACTORS

AND NOW, comes the Defendant, CS, by counsel, and respectfully sets forth the following Position of the Defendant With Respect to Sentencing Factors.

BACKGROUND

The body of the Pre-Sentence Investigation Report (PSIR) is generally accurate regarding the facts and circumstances surrounding this incident and the Defendant has no substantive objections to the Report.

Indeed, as the PSIR suggests, the Defendant respectfully submits that by the time of sentence he will have qualified for treatment under the Safety Valve, Title 18, U.S.C. §3553(f)(1-5) and the parallel Guideline provision, U.S.S.G. Section 5CI.2. As Paragraph 55 and 56 of the PSIR further indicates, application of the Safety Valve thus renders the five-year mandatory minimum sentence inapplicable. The additional application of Title 18, U.S.C. §3553(f)(1-5), by operation of Section 2D 1. 1 (b)(6) of the Guidelines, also reduces the Defendant's offense level by two points, as Paragraph 22 of the PSIR correctly notes, rendering Snead's proper sentencing guideline range at 57-71 months.

SUBSTANCE ABUSE TREATMENT

As the PSIR also correctly notes at Paragraphs 33, 43 and 44, CS continues to suffer a substantial substance problem requiring professional attention and it is specifically recommended that the Court recommend that Snead be permitted to participate in the 500-hour residential substance abuse treatment program offered through the Bureau of Prisons in accordance with Title 18, United States Code §3621(b) & (e).

FACILITY RECOMMENDATION

In order that CS be able to maintain as firm a bond with his family as possible, it is respectfully requested that the Court recommend that the Defendant be permitted to serve his term of incarceration at FCI Morgantown. FCI Morgantown is a facility with a residential inpatient substance abuse treatment program near enough to the Defendant's family members so that he can maintain the extremely strong family bonds that he has with his family.

SELF REPORT

Finally, the Defendant respectfully requests that the Court permit him to self-report if a term of incarceration is in fact imposed. A male Defendant who is permitted to self-report receives a three-point reduction in his security score under Bureau of Prisons Policy and is thus available to participate in a variety of programs within the Bureau of Prisons system that would otherwise be available.

As the PSIR points out, the Defendant has only the mildest of criminal records, has complied with all conditions of pre-trial release and has close family ties to the area. As such, he simply poses no risk of not reporting to his place of incarceration.

In light of the foregoing, it is respectfully requested that an appropriate sentence enter.

Respectfully Submitted,

_____
Attorney for the Defendant

Form 22-4   Motion and Order to Redact Presentence Investigation Report

IN THE UNITED STATES DISTRICT COURT

FOR THE _____ DISTRICT OF _____

UNITED STATES OF AMERICA)

  v.   ) CRIMINAL NO:

JL   ) ELECTRONICALLY FILED

DEFENDANT JL'S MOTION TO REDACT PRESENTENCE INVESTIGATION REPORT

AND NOW comes the Defendant, JL, by and through his attorney, JKR, Esquire, and files the following Motion to Redact Presentence Report, and in support thereof, avers as follows:

1. On _____, JL, pleaded guilty to Count One of a Three Count Indictment charging him with possession with intent to distribute five (5) grams or more of a mixture and substance containing a detectable amount of cocaine base, in a form commonly known as crack in violation of 21 U.S.C. §§841(a)(1) and (b)(1)(B)(iii). The plea was entered in accordance with a plea agreement which was negotiated between the Government and Mr. L's prior counsel.

2. On or about _____, a Presentence Investigation Report ("PSIR") was prepared for Mr. L by United States Probation Officer RL. Mr. L's PSIR lists his prior criminal history. Specifically, Mr. L's PSIR lists a conviction for Disorderly Conduct on or about _____, for conduct that occurred on or about _____. Mr. L was originally charged with two (2) counts of Unlawful Restraint, two (2) counts of Conspiracy to Commit Indecent Assault and one (1) count of Corruption of Minors. All counts were dismissed with the exception of the Corruption of Minors which was moved to non-traffic court and ultimately reduced to Disorderly Conduct.

3. Neither Mr. L nor the Government filed any Objections to the PSIR.

4. On _____, the Court sentenced Mr. L to 84 months imprisonment (imposing a mandatory minimum sentence) and committed him to the custody of the United States Bureau of Prisons ("BOP"). Furthermore, this Court recommended that Mr. L serve his term of incarceration at a facility where he may participate in the 500-hour intensive drug treatment program in or near Pittsburgh, Pennsylvania.

5. In the Statement of Reasons, this Court adopted the PSIR without change.

6. Upon entering the BOP, Mr. L was subject to an Initial Classification and received a Public Safety Factor of Sex Offender ("PSF") due to the underlying conduct of his conviction for Disorderly Conduct on or about _____. See Exhibit A. Attached as Exhibit A is a true and correct copy of the Administrative Remedy Attempt at Informal Resolution: Response.

7. Pursuant to BOP Program Statement 5100.08, Chapter 5, page 8, Security Designation and Custody Classification Manual,

   Sex Offender. A male or female inmate whose behavior in the current term of confinement or prior history includes one or more of the following elements shall be housed in at least a Low security level institution, unless the PSF has been waived. A conviction is not required for application of this PSF if the presentence investigation report (PSR), or other official documentation, clearly indicates the following behavior occurred in the current term of confinement or prior criminal history. If the case was dismissed or nolle prosequi, application of this PSF cannot be entered. However, in the case where an inmate was charged with an offense that included one of the following elements, that as a result of a plea bargain was not convicted, application of this PSF should be entered.

8. Therefore, because Mr. L was charged, but not convicted, of Conspiracy to Commit Indecent Assault and Corruption of Minors, the BOP has classified him with a PSF of Sex Offender. Due to the Sex Offender classification, Mr. L has been incarcerated at FCI Cumberland in its medium security facility, not its minimum security satellite camp.

9. Without a PSF of Sex Offender, Mr. L would be eligible to be housed at a minimum security camp for the remainder of his incarceration and have the opportunity to participate in the 500-hour residential drug abuse program.

WHEREFORE, it is respectfully requested that this Court redact Paragraph 26 of Mr. L's PSIR omitting the description of the events leading up to Mr. L's plea of guilty to Disorderly Conduct on _____, so that he may be reclassified by the BOP without a PSF of Sex Offender and be eligible to be housed at a minimum security camp, whether it be at FCI Cumberland or wherever the BOP deems appropriate.

Respectfully submitted,

_____

IN THE UNITED STATES DISTRICT COURT
FOR THE _____ DISTRICT OF _____

UNITED STATES OF AMERICA	)	
v.	)	CRIMINAL NO:
JL	)	ELECTRONICALLY FILED

ORDER

AND NOW this _____ day of _____ 2006, it is upon consideration of JLs Motion to Redact Presentence Investigation Report, it is hereby ORDERED, ADJUDGED and DECREED that said Motion is GRANTED. Paragraph 26 of Mr. L's PSIR is to be redacted to omit the description of the events leading up to Mr. L's plea of guilty to Disorderly Conduct on _____, so that he may be reclassified by the BOP without a PSF of Sex Offender and be eligible to be housed at a minimum security camp, whether it be at FCI Cumberland or wherever the BOP deems appropriate.

By the Court:
_____ J.

Form 22-5   Sentencing Memorandum

IN THE UNITED STATES DISTRICT COURT
FOR THE _____ DISTRICT OF _____

UNITED STATES OF AMERICA
  v.   CRIMINAL NO.
CB

DEFENDANT'S SENTENCING MEMORANDUM

Defendant, CB, through his attorney, Thomas J. Farrell, Esquire, files this Sentencing Memorandum in support of his Position With Respect to Sentencing Factors.

A.   Post-*Booker* Sentencing Procedure.

Under the Probation Office's calculation, the PSIR yields an imprisonment sentencing range of 41 to 51 months, based upon an offense level of 22 and no criminal history points. This calculation is only the first step in the process of post-*Booker* sentencing, recently summarized in *Rita v. United States,* 127 S.Ct. 2456 (2007). The Court summarized this process as follows:

> The sentencing judge, as a matter of process, will normally begin by considering the presentence report and its interpretation of the Guidelines. 18 U.S.C. §3552(a); Fed. Rule Crim. Proc. 32. He may hear arguments by prosecution or defense that the Guidelines sentence should not apply, perhaps because (as the Guidelines themselves foresee) the case at hand falls outside the "heartland" to which the Commission intends individual Guidelines apply, USSG §5K2.O, perhaps because the Guidelines sentence itself fails properly to reflect §3553(a) considerations, or perhaps because the case warrants a different sentence regardless. See Rule 32(f). Thus, the sentencing court subjects the defendant's sentence to the adversarial testing contemplated by federal sentencing procedure. See Rules 32(f), (h), (i)(C) and (i)(D); see also *Burns v. United States*, 501 U.S. 129, 136 (1991)(recognizing importance of notice and meaningful opportunity to be heard at sentencing).

The United States Supreme Court clearly established in *Rita* that, in determining the merits of any argument by either the prosecution or defense that the Guidelines sentence should not apply, the sentencing court may not apply any presumption of reasonableness to the Sentencing Guideline range. *Id. See also Gall v. United States,* 128 S.Ct. 586 (2007) (appellate court may not presume that an outside-guidelines sentence is unreasonable). Therefore, district courts need not impose sentences greater than they believe necessary out of fear of reversal.

The United States Supreme Court recognized throughout its opinion in *Rita* that a sentencing court has broad discretion in sentencing and the guidelines are truly advisory. The Supreme Court explained that the sentencing court may disagree with or reject policy judgments of the Sentencing Commission and the Guidelines, stating the judge must address arguments that the Guidelines "reflect unsound judgment, or, for example that they do not generally treat certain defendant characteristics in a proper way." *Id.* The Supreme Court further explained that the district court may even "disregard" the Guidelines in exercising its broad discretion at sentencing. *See id.*; *Kimbrough v. United States,* 128 S.Ct. 558 (2007)(courts may deviate from guidelines based on policy disagreements with the Sentencing Commission).

The Court emphasized in *Rita* that the sentencing court does not have a subordinate role to the Sentencing Commission, but instead can reach its own judgments, stating "[t]he upshot is that the sentencing statutes envision both the sentencing judge and the Commission as carrying out the same basic 3553(a) objectives, the one at retail, the other at wholesale." If this Court determines, after considering the §3553(a) factors related to this case, that Mr. B is deserving of a sentence lower that the Guideline range, Mr. B respectfully requests this Court to exercise its discretion and impose a lower sentence.

A sentence that varies from the Guidelines, even if for disagreement with the Guidelines' policy choices, will not be presumed unreasonable. *Gall v. United States,* 128 S.Ct. 586 (2007) (appellate court may not presume that an outside-guidelines sentence is unreasonable); *Kimbrough v. United States,* 128 S.Ct. 558 (2007) (courts may deviate from guidelines based on policy disagreements with the guidelines).

B.   Application of the Section 3553(a) Factors to Mr. B.1

With the broader discretion this Court has post-*Booker,* Mr. Biller is hopeful that the Probation Department and the Court will agree that the factors discussed below justify exercising the Court's discretion to
- reduce the term of incarceration, or
- take advantage of the "kinds of sentences available" to impose home confinement for part of the sentence, or
- do both.

1.   The nature and circumstances of the offense and the history characteristics of the defendant.

Mr. B served the public faithfully for ___ years at the United States Forest Service. Since then, has become a successful businessman and landlord through his hard work and hands-on efforts, not through passive investments, *see, e.g.,* letters of DG and VM, providing employment to many individuals who otherwise would have been unemployed. Mr. B is now ___ years old. He has been married for ___ years and raised two successful children. Mr. B lives modestly in the house he and his wife bought in _____, furnished with items bought at yard sales. *See* letter of CP; PSIR ¶119.

As the attachments to this position paper show, many individuals have stepped forward to submit letters on Mr. B's behalf.

Mr. B began the offense conduct at issue here in part as a response to a desire to protect the assets he accumulated through hard work from claims of creditors. Just as this Court sees many victims in fraud cases who fell prey to schemes that were too good to be true, Mr. B swallowed a tax evasion scheme when he should have known better. Mr. B understands that he stands before this Court to be sentenced for a serious tax offenses, and prays that this Court will view that conduct as the exception, not the rule to his character.

The letters submitted from Mr. B's employees, friends and tenants militate in favor of a below-guidelines sentence. Employees RC and BB describe how Mr. B opened a machine shop to give jobs to the laid-off employees of _____. and tell how Mr. B accommodated his family needs. Writes Mr. BB, "It would be a shame to send him to jail when there is so many people depending on him. Mr. B is a good family man, Husband, Father, and Grandfather." Along the same lines, RD writes, "When my last place of employment closed without notice, Mr. B after learning of this matter, offered me a job at his machine shop. Myself and three other employees have jobs because of Mr. B's kindness and concerns for others." VM describes how Mr. B accommodated her medical problems and the therapy schedule for her foster child. DG, a former factory worker, describes how Mr. B gave him the opportunity to prove himself in sales and construction and how Mr. B gave him time off to deal with child support issues, and how Mr. B accommodated tenants, providing them with lodging while repairs were made. *See also* letters from employees TG ("There is no one who reaches out to lend a helping hand quicker than he does. ... He has helped my family on more than occasion."); EP (Tells of how Mr. B employed him even though Mr. P had neither a high school diploma nor a GED; "He is also the only Boss that I've known that will talk to you about problems or help you work through them, not yell at you."), TU (Mr. B will help drive employees to work in bad weather), NT, and RS.

Seventy-year-old DS, who lives in a trailer she used to rent from Mr. B, describes how Mr. B forgave her rent and drove her to doctors' appointments and chemotherapy appointments. She states, "Many lives would be affected, if he is sentenced to prison." CP, a friend of Mr. B's daughter, describes how when she overdrew her bank account by $5,000, Mr. B co-signed a loan for her and solved the crisis. RC, now an economist at _____ University in _____, relates that Mr. B permitted Mr. C to live rent-free with Mr. B's family during Mr. C's undergraduate education. Real estate agent JD writes that Mr. B lowered lease payments or extended due dates to help struggling business tenants in Harvard Square. *See also* letters from CC, Sr. ("He has helped MANY people when they needed him. Some of these people still need him. He is their only means of support.") and LG. As Dr. CM states, "Fines and penalties perhaps, but it just doesn't seem right or make any sense to me to put a good man like Mr. B behind bars."

These letters justify departures on several bases: extraordinary charitable works, *see United States v. Cooper,* 394 F.3d 172 (3rd Cir. 2005) (in securities fraud and tax evasion case, with sentence range of 14-21 months, four-level downward sentencing departure for "good works" and sentence of probation was warranted for defendant's "exceptional" good works who did not simply donate money to charity but also organized and ran youth football team in depressed area, mentored its members, and helped several members attend better high schools or go to college, which qualified as exceptional because they entail "hands on personal sacrifices which have a dramatic and positive impact on the lives of others"); *United States v. Woods,* 159 F.3d 1132, 1136-37 (8th Cir. 1998) (defendant's exceptional charitable efforts`bringing two troubled young women in her home, paying for them to attend private high school–and also assisting elderly friend to move from nursing home to apartment–justified one level departure); and the adverse impact Mr. B's incarceration would have on the tenants and employees who depend on him, *see United States v. Milikowsky,* 65 F.3d 4 (2d Cir. 1995) (The high probability that business run by an antitrust offender would go under if she were incarcerated and the resulting hardship on 100 employees of those business justified downward departure of one level from 11 to 10 authorizing probation; *United States v. Olbres,* 99 F.3d 28 (1st Cir. 1996) (guidelines do not prohibit departure on grounds that incarceration of defendant will cause job losses to his employees; case remanded to determine if extent of loss outside the heartland of such cases); *but see United States v. Lawrence,* 1997 U.S. App. LEXIS 23849 (4th Cir. Va. Sept. 11, 1997) (non-precedential opinion rejecting *Milikowsky*).

If not a departure, a variance would be proper. The Court of Appeals deems a guideline sentence presumptively reasonable in part because the guideline calculation process yields an "individualized determination," *see United States v. Johnson,* 445 F.3d 339, 344 (4th Cir. 2006); however, "departures or variances are available when that range does not accurately capture the particular circumstances of an individual defendant." Such is the case here. Very few tax defendants had amended their returns and paid in full taxes due before they are charged, and very few have the record of honest hard work and good deeds Mr. B presents.

2. Purposes of Sentencing.

18 USC 3553 (a) (2) identifies four purposes a sentence should serve. The sentence imposed should reflect the seriousness of the crime, promote respect for the law, and provide just punishment; afford adequate deterrence to criminal conduct; protect the public from further crimes of the defendant; and provide the defendant with needed educational or the occasional training, medical care, or treatment in the most effective manner.

Mr. B understands that this Court will impose a prison sentence in this case. The advisory guideline sentence of 41 to 51 months or even 27 to 33 months, represents a term "greater than necessary" to serve those sentencing purposes. 18 USC 3553 (a). Mr. B is hopeful that this court will find that a lesser sentence is "sufficient but not greater than necessary" to serve the purposes of sentencing. 18 USC 3553(a).

a. Deterrence and respect for the law.

Only a brief term of incarceration is needed to achieve the purposes of deterrence and promotion of respect for the law. Mr. B already has shown his respect for the law by submitting amended tax returns and paying his back taxes. Thanks to his conviction, he has been branded as a felon, with all the disabilities–loss of voting rights, gun possession rights–that accompany that status. Mr. B faces an added penalty that will serve as a deterrent both to him and the public: the interest and fraud penalties on the $331,226 in taxes he paid. *See United States v. Adelson,* 441 F.Supp.2d 506, 514 (S.D.N.Y. 2006) ("In the case of financial fraud, however, an important kind of retribution may be achieved through the imposition of financial burdens.")

A brief period of incarceration, along with the fines Mr. B faces here and in civil tax proceedings, suffices to deter any other potential offenders. As the *Adelson* court stated, "[T]here is considerable evidence that even relatively short sentences can have a strong deterrent effect on prospective "white collar" offenders." *Id.* A Guidelines sentence–three and a half to four years of incarceration–will cost the taxpayers more money and inflict considerably more suffering on Mr. B, but it will not give the Court or Government any more bang for its buck:

> [Studies show] no significant difference in recidivism between white-collar offenders sentenced to prison and similar offenders who did not receive a prison sentence. This finding is consistent with the research on specific deterrence and conventional crime. Based on their review of the literature, these researchers stated, "[a]t least since the 1970s, criminologists have consistently shown that those who are sentenced to prison have, at best, about the same rates of recidivism as nonimprisoned offenders, and in some cases, a much higher rate. They speculated that perhaps the criminal process itself–charge, trial, conviction, and sentencing–has the greatest impact on the offender, and the period of imprisonment adds little by way of deterrence. "Whatever specific deterrence is gained," they argue, "may be produced before the imprisonment sanction is imposed.

Elizabeth Szockyj, *Imprisoning White Collar Criminals?* 23 S. Ill. U. L.J. 485, 495 (1999).

b. Protection of the public.

Mr. B lived ___ years as a law-abiding and productive citizen and public servant before the commission of this crime. The public has no reason to fear any further crimes from him. Besides the assurances offered from Mr. B's background, the Court can take added comfort in knowing that the Sentencing Commission's own statistical evidence supports the assertion that Mr. B will not re-offend. The Commission notes that offenders over age fifty have a recidivism rate of only 9.5%. *See,* U.S.S.C., *Measuring Recidivism: The Criminal History Computation of the Federal Sentencing Guidelines* at 12 (2004) (available at www.ussc.gov/publicat/Recidivism_General.pdf). The Commission also found lower recidivism rates for defendants with a history of stable employment (19.6% versus 32.4%), who are well-educated (8.8% among college graduates), and first-time offenders with no history of illicit drug use in the year preceding arrest (10.8%). *Id.* at 29. These statistics, coupled with Mr. B's payment of his taxes and his background, provide powerful support that he is unlikely to re-offend. They suggest a sentence at the bottom of or below the guidelines. *See United States v. Nellum,* 2005 U.S. Dist. LEXIS 1568 (N.D. Ind. Feb. 3, 2005) (relying on *Measuring Recidivism* to justify below-guidelines variance).

3. Kinds of sentences available.

While the guidelines range is 41 to 51 months, the sentencing statutes under which Mr. B was convicted have no mandatory minimum sentences. The court has discretion to impose incarceration, a fine, or both.

Therefore, this Court may impose a period of incarceration below the range suggested by the sentencing guidelines and may also add a period of home confinement on top of the incarceration sentence, if additional punishment is necessary to serve the purposes of sentencing. Home confinement for a defendant in his mid-60s who does not pose a threat to the public may be equally efficient, and less costly than incarceration. Home confinement serves the purposes of sentencing: the public will be protected and Mr. B will be deterred from future criminal conduct. It also promotes respect for the law, reflects the seriousness of the offense, and is just punishment for Mr. B's crimes.

A shortened incarceration sentence, followed by a period of home confinement, would enable the court to structure a fair and just sentence that serves the purposes of sentencing, which are discussed above, is tailored to the circumstances of this case, and satisfies the statutory mandate to impose a sentence that is "sufficient, but not greater than necessary," to serve the purposes of sentencing.

For all these reasons, Mr. B respectfully asked the court to impose a structured sentence which provides for a shortened term of imprisonment followed by a period of home confinement.

Thomas J. Farrell, Esq.

Form 22-6   Sample Sentencing Letter

Re: United States v. AB

Your Honor:

I am writing to you on behalf of my wonderful sister-in-law, A. She will appear before you for sentencing on _____, for her involvement in my brother's trafficking in methamphetamine.

Ann came from a large family with a lot of personal challenges, and the only thing she ever knew she could count on was her family and God. Her mother suffered from bipolar disorder, and A and several of her brothers and sisters were placed in _____ Orphans Home here in _____, Pennsylvania, during one of her mother's lengthy illnesses. These eight kids learned to stay together and always look out for one another, not just for treats and for fun, but for food and love and security.

A had huge responsibilities as a teenager and handled them all with a sweetness and a smile. As the second oldest child, she bore much of the responsibility for raising and caring for her six younger siblings. She overcame every personal challenge. She was elected homecoming queen of her local high school in her senior year. That year, she married my brother before he went off to fight in the Vietnam War.

It was only the natural progression of her sweetness and loyalty to her family that led her to be part of any bad choices made by my brother. I know that A believed and still believes that this is just one more challenge that God has given to them to keep them together. They made it through the death of a child (who was also bipolar), which is statistically nearly impossible. They made it through Vietnam, and the numerous mental and physical health issues which my brother developed. And they still have given a great deal of money and time to numerous nieces and nephews on both sides of the family when these youngsters had no one else to turn to.

A started the annual food drive in _____ for the US Post Office; she has taken Communion to shut-ins two times a week for the last 15 years for _____ Church. She was a CCD teacher for 20 years, taught religion classes, was a Eucharistic minister for many years, and was very active in her children's activities as they grew up.

I ask you to please be lenient with A at her sentencing. This situation has cost her dearly already. She may lose her job of 20-plus years, and she has seen and felt the hurt that her husband and their daughter and all of the rest of the family have suffered. I assure you that this is punishment enough for this selfless woman.

As you look upon the face of A, please just see a woman who is standing by her husband (again), as marriage vows dictate, so that a solution could be found. She never gives up on anyone or on any issue in which she believes. I know she believed that she could help her husband through this latest curse also. Unfortunately, the law intervened before she and her God could help him.

If by chance, you are to be lenient on my brother, please consider the fact that A needs to be able to drive to take him into all of his doctor appointments. He goes to various doctors three times every week. I talked to her often and that seems to be the busiest part of her days. She's taking care of him and taking him to the doctors. He seems to be going all the time.

Thank you for your time and consideration.

Sincerely yours,

Form 22-7   Motion and Order for Adjustment to Award Credit for Time Served

IN THE UNITED STATES DISTRICT COURT
FOR THE _____ DISTRICT OF _____

UNITED STATES OF AMERICA	)	
v.	)	CRIMINAL NO.
JSF	)	

MOTION TO AMEND JUDGMENT, OR IN THE ALTERNATIVE TO VACATE JUDGMENT AND FOR RE-SENTENCING

AND NOW COMES Defendant JSF by his attorney, Thomas J. Farrell, and files this Motion:

I.   The Sentences on Counts One and Two Should Be Ordered To Run Concurrently

1.   As the Court is aware, Mr. F received two separate sentences for each count of a severed two-count indictment. On November 12, 2004, he was sentenced to 85 months on Count One of the indictment, and on September 6, 2005, he was sentenced to 360 months on Count Two of the Indictment.

2.   The Court's intent appears to have been to run Mr. F's sentence on Count II concurrent to his sentence on Count I. Although that issue was not addressed at the time of sentencing on Count II1, the Court did express

on the record an intent to give Mr. F credit toward the Count II sentence for all the time he had served in pre-trial detention, a result possible only if the sentence on Count I runs concurrent to the sentence on Count II.

3. Section 3584(a) of Title 18 states, "Multiple terms of imprisonment imposed at different times run <u>consecutively unless</u> the <u>court orders</u> that <u>the terms are</u> to <u>run concurrently</u>." (emphasis added). While this section does not explicitly address the rather rare case of sentences imposed at different times within the same indictment, the Bureau of Prisons interprets this section to mandate consecutive sentences in such situation unless the court orders otherwise: "Sentences that are imposed on the same date, or on different dates, based on convictions arising out of different trials, are considered to have been imposed at different times <u>even if the trials arose out of the same indictment</u>." BOP Sentence Computation Guide, PS 5880.028 at p. 1- 32 (February 14, 1997) (available at www.bop.gov/DataSource/execute/dsPolicyLoc).

4. The Judgment does not address whether Count II will run concurrent to Count I. Under BOP interpretation of §3584(a), the sentences will run <u>consecutively</u>. <u>See</u> paragraph 2, <u>supra</u>. Therefore, we ask that the Court either amend the judgment or vacate the Judgment to specify that the sentences are concurrent.

II. <u>The Court Should Amend the Judgment to State That Mr. F's Sentence Runs Concurrent to and Should Be Served in State Custody</u>

5. Additionally, I learned yesterday that Mr. F has been sent to a state correctional institution, when I received a letter from him from SCI Waynesburg. Apparently, when Mr. F was arrested back on _____, and charged in state court, his parole officer lodged a detainer with respect to Mr. F's _____ sentence in Allegheny County at Criminal No. CC9616266. <u>See</u> PSIR ¶2, ¶32. When the federal indictment was returned and the state charges were dropped, the detainer remained in place, and Mr. F continued to be a state detainee. The federal government "borrowed" Mr. F for prosecution under a writ of habeas corpus ad prosequendum, meaning that despite the Court's and counsels' assumptions at sentencing that he would receive credit for the three years he has been in custody awaiting final resolution of his federal charges, Mr. F has not and will not receive credit for that time nor for any time going forward because where a defendant is in state custody for a state sentence, his federal sentence does not even start to run until he is released from state custody and enters federal custody. *Barden v. Keohane*, 921 F.2d 476, 480 (3d Cir. 1990). *See, also, Ruggiano v. Reish*, 307 F.3d 121, 125n.1 (3d Cir. 2002). The Bureau of Prisons can remedy this by designating the state institution to be the place where the federal sentence is to be served, *see Barden*, 921 F.2d at 480; and BOP will do so if the judgment states that the federal sentence is to be served concurrently with the state sentence and in state custody:

> The court may, for a prisoner who is serving a non-federal undischarged term of imprisonment while "on loan" to the federal government under the jurisdiction of a federal writ of habeas corpus ad prosequendum, impose the federal sentence to run concurrently with, or consecutively to, the other undischarged term of imprisonment. Upon receipt of the judgment and commitment from the U. S. Marshals' Service that orders the federal sentence to be served concurrently with the non-federal sentence, the RISA shall, in accordance with 18 U.S.C. §3621(b), designate the non-federal facility as the place to serve the federal sentence and complete the other procedures required by the Program Statement on Designation of State Institution for Service of Federal Sentence, for executing this type of concurrent sentence. On occasion, a federal court will order the federal sentence to run concurrently with or consecutively to a not yet imposed term of imprisonment. Case law supports a court's discretion to enter such an order and the federal sentence shall be enforced in the manner prescribed by the court. If the just imposed federal sentence is ordered to run concurrently with a non-existent term of imprisonment, then the RISA shall designate the non-federal place as the place to serve the federal sentence as of the date that the federal sentence was imposed. If the federal sentence is silent, or ordered to run consecutively to the non-existent term of imprisonment, then the federal sentence shall not be placed into operation until the U.S. Marshals' Service or the Bureau of Prisons gains exclusive custody of the prisoner.

BOP Sentence Computation Guide, p.1-32 to 1-33.2 *See also United States v. Fuentes*, 107 F.3d 1515, 1519 n.6 (11th Cir. 1997) ("district courts now have authority to impose sentences concurrent to undischarged state sentences").

6. The court should amend its judgment to state that it is adjusting Mr. F's sentence to be fully concurrent with his state sentence back to _____, the date on which he was detained in federal court.

III. The Court Should Amend the Judgment to Give Mr. F Credit For Time Served in Custody Since His Arrest

7. The Court stated in its Judgment: "Defendant, who has been in federal custody since _____, may be given credit for prior custody pursuant to 18 U.S.C., §3585(b)." Similarly, when we raised the issue of whether Mr. F would receive credit for the time he spent in custody since _____, when the federal order of detention was entered, <u>see</u> PSIR, §2, the Court stated orally during the sentencing that Mr. F should receive credit for that time and that the defense could return to the Court to ensure that the Court's statement would have effect.

8. As is discussed above, Mr. F spent his entire time awaiting trial on a writ of habeas corpus ad prosequendum, meaning that contrary to the Court's Judgment, he <u>never</u> was in <u>federal</u> custody and that BOP will not credit him with any of that time toward his federal sentence under 18 U.S.C. §3585(b). *See Ruggiano v. Reish*, 307 F.3d 121, 125 n.1 (3d Cir. 2002). In *Ruggiano*, the defendant was writted into federal court while he was two months into serving a state sentence. He spent another 12 months in custody until he was sentenced on the federal charge and paroled from his state sentence into federal custody. At sentencing, the trial court stated, "The defendant is hereby committed to the custody of the United States Bureau of Prisons to be imprisoned for a term of 112 months. Sentence imposed to run concurrent with State sentence. Defendant to receive credit for time served." *Id. At* 125. The Bureau of Prisons refused to give the defendant credit for the 14 months served, however, reasoning that it has the sole prerogative to determine credits toward a sentence and that Section 3584(b) of Title 18 prohibited credit for the 14 months because it was time spent in custody in fulfillment of his state sentence. *Id. At* 126. The Court of Appeals disagreed with BOP, ruling that under U.S.S.G. §5G1.3(c), a sentencing court has the power and discretion to run a federal sentence fully and retroactively concurrent to time spent serving a state sentence and finding that the district court in *Ruggiano* intended its sentence to be fully and retroactively concurrent with the state sentence. However, to avoid confusion over the terms "credit" or "departure," the Court of Appeals recommended that the sentencing court should use the term "adjust" and "state something to the effect of 'I hereby adjust the defendant's federal sentence under §5G1.3(c) so as to be fully concurrent with his state sentence,' in order to avoid much of the confusion that this case, and many others, have presented." *Id.* At 133.

9. Here, the Court clearly intended to shorten the length of Mr. F's sentence by the three years he spent in custody since September 19, 2002. This is the type of Section 5C1.3 "adjustment" that the *Ruggiano* court found to be within a sentencing court's power. *See Ruggiano*, 307 F.3d at 132 (relying on *United States v. Dorsey*, 166 F.3d 558, 564 (3d Cir. 1999)). Therefore, to give effect to its intent, the Court should amend its judgment to state, "The Court adjusts the defendant's sentence at Count Two under §5G1.3(c) so as to be fully concurrent with his state sentence back to _____."

10. These calculation issues, which both the BOP and at one judge in this district have called "probably the single most confusing and least understood sentencing issue in the Federal system," *see United States v. Smith*, 101 F.Supp.2d 313, 347 (W.D.Pa. 2000) (Lee, J.) (but finding merit in an ineffective assistance of counsel petition based on trial counsel's failure to resolve this issue at sentencing and urging the government to resolve the issue amicably with the defense), can result in Mr. F serving an additional 11 years or more: lack of credit for the three years he served awaiting trial plus the 8 years on count one plus the balance of the time to be served on his state sentence.

11. The judgment was docketed on _____. The defendant has only 10 days, until _____, to file a Notice of Appeal. *See*, Fed. R. App. 4(b)(1)(A)(i) (notice must be filed in 10 days); 26(a)(2) (exclude weekends and legal holidays when period is under 11 days). Rule 4(b)(4) permits the district court to extend the time for filing a notice of appeal for "30 days from the expiration of the time otherwise prescribed by this Rule 4(b)." I will seek the government's consent to this Motion. However, if it is not forthcoming, I ask that Court to grant a 30-day extension of the time to file a Notice of Appeal.

WHEREFORE, the defendant requests that the Court amend its judgment as stated in the attached order or vacate the judgment and resentence him to correct this error under Fed.R.Crim.P. 35(a).

Respectfully submitted,
Thomas J. Farrell, Esquire

IN THE UNITED STATES DISTRICT COURT
FOR THE _____ DISTRICT OF _____

UNITED STATES OF AMERICA) v.) JSF)	CRIMINAL NO.

ORDER OF COURT

AND NOW, this _____ day of _____, 2005, it is ORDERED that page two of the Judgment, "Imprisonment," is amended to state:

Pursuant to 18 U.S.C. §3584(a) and (b) and U.S.S.G., §5G1.3(c), the sentence at Count II of 360 months of imprisonment shall be fully concurrent to the sentence at Count I. Defendant's sentence shall run concurrent to any state sentence and should be served in state custody, beginning September 19, 2002.

By the Court:

_____

Form 22-8   Stipulation to Deportation

IN THE UNITED STATES DISTRICT COURT
FOR THE _____ DISTRICT OF _____

UNITED STATES OF AMERICA,
           Petitioners,
    v.
VSB,
           Respondent.

STIPULATION OF DEPORTATION PURSUANT TO 8 U.S.C. §1228(C)

AND NOW COMES Defendant, VSB, and his attorney, Thomas J. Farrell and stipulates as follows:

1. Defendant agrees that he is not a citizen of the United States, and that he is a native of India and a citizen of Italy.
2. Defendant agrees that when he is sentenced in the instant criminal proceeding, he will be convicted in this court for the offense of wire fraud involving a loss of more than $10,000, in violation of 18 U.S.C. §1343, an aggravated felony as defined in Section 101(a)(43) of the Immigration and Nationality (8 U.S.C. §1101(a)(43)).
3. Defendant acknowledges that his rights in this proceeding with respect to his deportability from the United States have been fully explained to him by his attorney.
4. Defendant understands and knowingly waives his right to a hearing before this court, or before an immigration judge, or any other authority under the Immigration and Nationality Act, on the question of his deportability from the United States. In this regard, defendant understands and knowingly waives his rights to examine the evidence against him, to present evidence on his own behalf, and to cross-examine witnesses presented by the government.
5. Defendant waives the 30-day notice provision of 8 U.S.C. §1228(c).
6. Defendant agrees that all factual allegations contained in the government's Factual Allegations in Support of Request for Judicial Order of Deportation are true and correct.
7. Defendant concedes that he is deportable from the United States as charged in the government's notice of intent to request an order of judicial deportation.
8. Defendant agrees and stipulates to accept a deportation order by the sentencing judge, knowing that this will result in his immediate deportation from the United States upon completion of any period of incarceration. Defendant agrees that the order be issued for his deportation to Italy.
9. Defendant knowingly waives any and all rights to appeal, reopen, or challenge in any way the deportation order of the sentencing judge.

VSB
Defendant

Thomas J. Farrell
Attorney for Defendant

IN THE UNITED STATES DISTRICT COURT
FOR THE _____ DISTRICT OF _____

UNITED STATES OF AMERICA,
             Petitioners,

    v.

VSB,

           Respondent.

FACTUAL ALLEGATIONS IN SUPPORT OF REQUEST FOR JUDICIAL ORDER OF DEPORTATION

The United States Attorney Charges:
1. The defendant, VSB, is not a citizen or national of the United States.
2. Defendant is a native of India and a citizen of Italy.
3. Defendant entered the United States on or near _____.
4. At that time, Defendant entered as an alien on a visa for his prosecution.
5. At the time of sentencing in this criminal proceeding, Defendant will be convicted in this court for the offense of wire fraud involving a loss of more than $10,000, committed on or about _____, in violation of 18 U.S.C. §1343.

Wherefore, at his sentencing, Defendant will be subject to deportation under Section 241(a)(2)(A)(iii) of the Immigration and Nationality Act, as amended (Act), (8 U.S.C. §1251(a)(2)(A)(iii), in that at any time after entry, Defendant will have been convicted of an aggravated felony as defined in Section 101(a)(43) of the Act, 8 U.S.C. §1101(a)(43).

Accordingly, pursuant to Section 242A(d) of the Act, 8 U.S.C. §1228(c) the Government requests that this Court, after imposing sentence, order that the defendant be deported from the United States so that promptly upon his release from confinement herein, the Immigration and Naturalization Service may execute said deportation order according to applicable laws and regulations.

United States Attorney
Dated: _____

CONCURRENCE OF IMMIGRATION AND NATURALIZATION SERVICE
Based upon the factual allegations stated above, on behalf of the Commissioner of the Immigration and Naturalization Service, I concur in the request by the Government herein that a judicial order of deportation be issued.

Name

Title/Office
Dated: _____

(This page intentionally left blank.)

Chapter 23

PROBATION, PAROLE & OTHER POST-RELEASE SUPERVISION

I.　GENERAL POINTS

A.　Probation and Supervised Release

§23:01　The Different Ways to Be Placed on Probation

A defendant may be placed on probation in one of three manners:
- The imposition of sentence is suspended, and the defendant placed on probation.
- Sentence is imposed, but the execution of sentence is suspended, and the defendant placed on probation. [*See* Neil P. Cohen, *The Law of Probation and Parole* §27:16 (2d ed. 1999).]
- The court sentences the defendant to probation. [*E.g.,* 18 U.S.C. §3561 (establishing probation as a separate sentence).]

These differences matter.

When the court suspends imposition of sentence, the court may re-sentence the defendant to any period of incarceration up to the statutory maximum should the defendant violate the conditions of probation.

When suspending the execution of the sentence, the court first will announce a period of incarceration, then suspend its execution or service while the defendant serves the term of probation. Should probation be revoked, the court will order the defendant to serve the jail-time that it suspended.

If the sentence is probation, the court may impose any sentence allowed by the applicable statutory maximum or sentencing guidelines upon violation and revocation of probation.

§23:02　Supervised Release

The federal Sentencing Reform Act of 1984 created another form of supervision that has the worst features of probation and parole: supervised release. [18 U.S.C. §3583(a).]

Unlike parole, supervised release does not reduce a defendant's period of incarceration. Unlike probation, supervised release does not replace imprisonment.

There is no parole for federal sentences. A defendant must serve his full term, minus a fifteen percent reduction for good time. However, once released, he must serve a period of supervised release, usually ranging from three to five years. [18 U.S.C. §3583(b).]

Should the defendant violate the conditions of that release, he can be incarcerated again. [18 U.S.C. §3583(e).]

A number of states have followed the lead of the federal government and allow for the imposition of a term of post-release supervision to follow a determinate sentence. [*E.g.,* New York Penal Law §70.45.]

[§§23:03-23:09 Reserved]

B.　Applying for Parole

§23:10　Hearing Is by an Administrative Board

Parole is not a sentence. It is an early release from incarceration on conditions.

Usually it is an administrative board rather than a judge that paroles a defendant.

For example, in Pennsylvania, the sentencing court retains parole authority over any sentence less than two years. This difference is more than procedural. The sentencing judge has much more discretion than the parole board over the duration of the sentence and the conditions of parole. [*See* 61 Pa. Stat. §314 (explaining judge's authority).] Further, whereas the board must award credit for "street" time on a revocation for a technical violation [*see* §23:55], a court need not. [*Commonwealth v. Fair*, 345 Pa. Super. 61, 64, 497 A.2d 643, 645 (1985).]

Attorneys rarely attend parole hearings. [*See* Neil P. Cohen, *The Law of Probation and Parole* §6:21 (2d ed. 1999).]

If you are retained to assist at a parole hearing, you best serve your client by gathering information that might be inaccessible to your incarcerated client (such as statements from victims that they have no objection to release or a promise of employment upon release) and preparing him to make an effective presentation about his rehabilitation and hopes and goals, and to answer the board's questions.

Form:
- **Form 23-1** Petition for Parole (to a Court)

§23:11   Admissions of Guilt

Inmates convicted after trial face a quandary upon applying for parole. Many parole boards will not accept that a convict has been rehabilitated and worthy of parole unless he admits guilt of his offense.

Parole boards seem to favor this requirement when the defendant has been convicted of a sex offense. [*E.g., McKune v. Lile*, 536 U.S. 24 (2002) (putting convicts to choice of admitting sex offense, which admissions could be used against them, as condition of entering sex offender rehabilitation program, or being transferred to higher security prison was not kind of compulsion covered by the Fifth Amendment).]

Courts may also condition entry into probation on admissions of guilt necessary to qualify for rehabilitative programs. [*See, e.g., State v. Hernandez*, 231 Ariz. 353, 295 P.3d 451 (2013) (denying probation to a defendant who refused to admit guilt to probation officer during presentence interview); *Dzul v. State*, 118 Nev. 681, 56 P.3d 875 (Nev. 2002) (upholding trial court refusal to admit defendant to probation because of his refusal to admit guilt of the offense in psychosexual interview); *Newman v. Beard*, 617 F.3d 775 (3d Cir. 2010) (denying parole to sex offenders who did not complete the sex offenders treatment program, completion of which required an admission of guilt, did not violate the First Amendment or Due Process).]

Parole boards and courts may condition release on admissions of guilt if they immunize the inmate from subsequent use of his statements in a criminal prosecution. [*Minnesota v. Murphy*, 465 U.S. 420, 426 (1984) ("a State may validly insist on answers to even incriminating questions and hence sensibly administer its probation system, as long as it recognizes that the required answers may not be used in a criminal proceeding and thus eliminates the threat of incrimination"); *State v. Spaeth*, 2012 WI 95, 343 Wis. 2d 220, 819 N.W.2d 769 (2012) (while statements made in a polygraph compelled as a condition of probation could be used to violate the defendant's probation, they could not be used in a subsequent criminal prosecution because they are compelled incrimination under the Fifth Amendment).]

[§§23:12-23:19 Reserved]

II.   CONDITIONS OF PROBATION AND PAROLE

A. Standard Conditions

§23:20   The Imposition of Conditions

Courts and parole boards have a list of standard conditions with which every probationer or parolee must comply. The list of standard conditions can be found in statute, rule, sentencing guidelines or in the forms customarily used in the jurisdiction. [*E.g.,* 18 U.S.C. §3583(d).]

Some courts read the conditions at the time of sentence. Others merely refer to the standard conditions and have the defendant review and sign them at the first meeting with the defendant's probation or parole officer. [*See State v. Statts*, 144 Ariz. 72, 78, 695 P.2d 1110, 1116 (1985) (written conditions added and signed later are enforceable).]

If the judge imposes special conditions, he or she must announce them at the sentencing so that the defense has an opportunity to object. [*See United States v. Sepulveda-Contreras*, 466 F.3d 166 (1st Cir. 2006) (court violated defendant's constitutional and statutory rights to be present at sentencing by adding to the written judgment conditions not announced at the sentencing).]

Jurisdictions differ in whether you must lodge any objections to conditions of probation at sentencing, or at the time of a violation hearing, so check your rules. Your safest course is to challenge the conditions at the time they are imposed. Your challenge may succeed, thus relieving your client of attempting to satisfy an onerous condition.

Review the conditions with your client to ensure that he understands them. If you find that the probation officer interprets them differently than you or your client do, return to the court for clarification.

Form:
* **Form 23-2** Standard Probation/Parole Conditions for Washington County, Pennsylvania

§23:21   Limits on Conditions

Conditions of release may not extend beyond the period of probation, parole or supervised release. [*E.g., State v. Welwood*, 258 Conn. 425, 433-35, 780 A.2d 924, 930-31 (2001); *People v. Dodson*, 48 N.Y.2d 36, 421 N.Y.S.2d 47, 396 N.E.2d 194 (1979).]

Thus the court or parole board cannot order a probationer or parolee *never* to have contact with a victim (unless the defendant is on life-time supervision).

§23:22 Restitution as a Condition

The payment of restitution or a fine is frequently a condition of probation or supervised release.

When your client lacks the means to make full payment immediately, the court will spread payments over the term of supervision to accommodate your client's ability to pay. Your client cannot be imprisoned for his indigency so long as he makes a good faith effort to pay. [*Bearden v. Georgia*, 461 U.S. 660 (1983).]

Many statutes authorize victims in federal cases to reduce a restitution order to a civil judgment and to continue attempts to collect it, as with any other judgment. [*E.g.*, 18 U.S.C. §3664(m)(1)(B).]

Restitution obligations are not dischargeable in bankruptcy. [*Kelly v. Robinson*, 479 U.S. 36 (1986).]

However, since the court's supervision has ended, the defendant no longer can be incarcerated for failure to pay the judgment. [*See State v. Griffin*, 83 Haw. 105, 108-09 & n.4, 924 P.2d 1211, 1214-15 & n.4 (1996) (probationer could not be ordered to execute a promissory note in the amount of restitution order because the note would be enforceable beyond the five-year probation term; however the restitution order could be converted to civil judgment and a levy entered against defendant's property after probation ended).]

§23:23 Searches

Probationers are subject to warrantless searches of their homes and person upon reasonable suspicion to believe that they are violating a condition of release, and any evidence found is admissible at a later criminal prosecution. [*United States v. Knights*, 534 U.S. 112 (2001) (probationer).]

Searches of parolees need neither a warrant nor any suspicion, at least according to the Fourth Amendment. [*Samson v. California*, 547 U.S. 843 (2006) (police officer who knew that defendant was a parolee could approach him on the street and search his person without any cause or suspicion; while stating that parolees have a lesser expectation of privacy than probationers, does not decide whether probationers are subject to suspicionless searches); *but see In re the Interest of J.E.*, 937 A.2d 421, 427 (Pa. 2007) (rejects *Samson* as a matter of state law because state statute authorizing warrantless searches of juvenile probationers requires reasonable suspicion).]

Since *Samson* rested, at least in part, upon the language of the California parole agreement, which explicitly diminished the parolee's expectation of privacy, look to state law and the language of the parole agreement or instructions to argue that some degree of reasonable suspicion is necessary before a parolee may be searched. [*See Watson v. Cielslak*, 2009 U.S. Dist LEXIS 122706 (S.D.N.Y. December 3, 2009) (under New York parole agreement, search of a parolee must be reasonably related to the performance of the parole officer's duties).]

What is reasonable for Fourth Amendment purposes may depend upon local parole regulations and policies governing the authority of parole and other law enforcement officers to conduct warrantless searches of parolees. [*See United States v. Freeman*, 479 F.3d 743, 746 (10th Cir. 2007) (firearm suppressed in federal prosecution because, contrary to Kansas parole department policies, non-parole officers conducted warrantless and suspicionless search of parolee's home).]

Such conditions apply only while the offender remains subject to probation, parole or other court supervision. Thus, a state cannot include within its sex offender registration laws a requirement that offenders no longer under parole or court supervision consent to searches of their computers or other devices with Internet capability. [*Doe v. Prosecutor, Marion County*, 566 F.Supp.2d 862 (S.D. Ind. 2008) (issuing declaratory judgment that Indiana's statute violated the Fourth Amendment).]

§23:24 Drug Testing

Drug testing is a standard condition of release. [*E.g.*, 18 U.S.C. §3563(a)(5) (drug-testing should be ordered for all probationers unless they show that they are at low-risk for illegal drug use).]

§23:25 DNA Samples

Federal or state statutes may require inmates, probationers and parolees convicted of certain offenses to allow DNA to be taken and placed in databases. [*See* 42 U.S.C. §14135a ("DNA Act"; individuals convicted of qualifying federal offenses must give DNA samples for inclusion in the Combined DNA Index System (CODIS) during their incarceration or as a condition of probation, parole or supervised release).] Law enforcement officials then will compare the DNA to that taken from victims and crime scenes.

According to the Supreme Court, the Fourth Amendment permits DNA collection, even from those arrested and not yet convicted. [*Maryland v. King,* 133 S.Ct. 1958 (2013); *State v. O'Hagen,* 189 N.J. 140, 150, 914 A.2d 267, 273 (2007) (noting that "[t]hus far, each appellate court that has addressed the constitutionality of a state or federal DNA testing statute has found the statute constitutional" and upholding New Jersey's statute).] At least one federal court of appeals has held that the government can retain a convict's DNA in a database even after he ends his term of supervision. [*United States v. Kriesel,* 720 F.3d 1137 (9th Cir. 2013); *but see id.* at 1148-63 (Reinhardt, J., dissenting); *United States v. Weikert,* 504 F.3d 1 (1st Cir. 2007) (upholding the practice of collecting and analyzing the DNA of those currently on supervision, but withholding decision on whether the DNA profile could be retained after the individual completed supervision).]

PRACTICE TIP:

Before mounting a Fourth Amendment challenge to such a condition, check the governing statute to verify that your client has been convicted of a qualifying offense. [*See, e.g., United States v. Cooper,* 396 F.3d 308 (3d Cir. 2005) (possession of stolen bank funds was not a qualifying offense under the federal act).]

[§§23:26-23:29 Reserved]

B. Special Conditions

§23:30 Creative Conditions

Courts and parole boards often impose "special" conditions of supervision in addition to the standard conditions.

While statutes or regulations may offer a menu of special conditions from which to choose, some courts and boards will create imaginative and oppressive conditions, such as:

- Prohibitions on political activity. [*E.g., United States v. Peete,* 919 F.2d 1168, 1181 (6th Cir. 1990) (elected official convicted of attempting to extort bribe lawfully prohibited from seeking or serving in elected public office during probation).]
- Bans on internet use. [*United States v. Silvious,* 512 F.3d 364 (7th Cir. 2008) ("a total ban on the use of computers with access to the Internet is in most cases an overbroad condition of supervised release"); *United States v. Cabot,* 325 F.3d 384, 386 (2d Cir. 2003) (condition prohibiting defendant who pleaded guilty to producing child pornography from possessing or using a computer or any other device with ability to access internet without prior approval of probation officer inflicted greater deprivation of liberty than necessary).]
- Bans on certain types of employment. [*See United States v. Coon,* 187 F.3d 888 (8th Cir. 1999) (prohibition against self-employment upheld).]
- Limits on procreation. [*See* LaFave *et al,* 5 *Criminal Procedure* §26.9(a) (challenges to prohibitions against bearing children have met mixed results); Rebecca L. Miles, *Criminal Consequences for Making Babies: Probation Conditions that Restrict Procreation,* 59 Wash. & Lee L.Rev. 1545 (2002) (most such conditions are struck down, with a few exceptions).]

Courts have upheld bans on internet usage for particularly severe child pornography convictions. [*E.g., United States v. Angle,* 598 F.3d 352, 361 (7th Cir. 2010) (ban on personal use of internet during unspecified term of supervised release upheld for "one of the worst child predators" the trial judge claimed to have seen in 25 years; case involved not only viewing but producing child pornography and committing acts of actual child sexual abuse). A two-part test generally applies:

First, we must examine the scope of the supervised release condition, including both its duration and its substantive breadth–here, the degree to which access to computers and the internet is restricted. . . *[W]e* cannot divorce the amount of time a special condition lasts from the question of whether that particular special condition is reasonably related to the considerations laid out in §3553(a). Second, we must consider the severity of the defendant's criminal conduct and the facts underlying the conviction, with a particular focus on whether the defendant used a computer or the internet to solicit or otherwise personally endanger children.

[*United States v. Miller,* 594 F.3d 172, 187 (3d Cir. 2010) (holding that lifetime ban on internet usage was unreasonable).]

§23:31   Seek Clarification of Unreasonable Conditions

If the court announces a condition that seems questionable, impractical in compliance or unreasonable, seek clarification and narrowing of the condition.

For example:

- Does a prohibition on the use of alcohol mean all alcohol or just its excessive consumption?
- Does the bar against associating with convicted felons apply to immediate family members? [*E.g., United States v. Jacques*, 321 F.3d 255, 266 (2d Cir. 2003) (vacating and remanding a condition of probation requiring that the defendant not associate with known felons where defendant's common-law husband was a convicted felon, but it was not clear that the trial court knew this).]

§23:32   Propose Alternatives

Propose alternatives when conditions have some validity but seem overbroad.

Be creative. For example, judges impose restrictions on computer and internet usage for defendants convicted of identity theft or child abuse or pornography charges. However, these days, computer use is nearly indispensable to many jobs, to socializing, and to be an informed member of society. Therefore, investigate and propose filtering software or programs to monitor your client's computer usage. [*See United States v. Freeman*, 316 F.3d 386, 392 (3d Cir. 2003) ("There is no need to cut off Freeman's access to email or benign internet usage when a more focused restriction, limited to pornography sites and images, can be enforced by unannounced inspections of material stored on Freeman's hard drive or removable disks"); *United States v. Lifshitz*, 369 F.3d 173 (2d Cir. 2004); *In re Stevens*, 119 Cal. App.4th 1228, 15 Cal.Rptr.3d 168 (Cal.App. 2d Dist. 2004); Marc M. Harrold, *Computer Searches of Probationers*, 75 Miss. L.J. 273, 343-45 (2005) (all detailing available computer monitoring programs).]

§23:33   Attacking Conditions

If you cannot reach an acceptable compromise on the conditions, consider three lines of attack on conditions of release.

Check whether the statutory scheme authorizes this condition.

Standard and suggested conditions will appear in a statute, but courts often are free to impose other reasonable conditions, which the probation department generally suggests.

The court will realize that non-standard conditions are more susceptible to attack.

Question whether the condition is reasonably related to the authorized purposes of sentencing.

Many jurisdictions limit conditions to those reasonably related to the circumstances of the defendant's crime and personal characteristics and the need for rehabilitation, deterrence and protection of the public. [*See United States v. Murray*, 692 F.3d 273, 280 (3d Cir. 2012) (purpose of supervised release is to integrate the offender back into the community, not to punish; therefore, court should not consider need of supervised release conditions "to reflect the seriousness of the offense, to promote respect for the law, and to provide just punishment for the offense"); *United States v. Holm*, 326 F.3d 872, 876 (7th Cir. 2003) (interpreting 18 U.S.C. §3583(d) to impose such a limit on supervised release conditions); LaFave, et al, 5 *Criminal Procedure* §26.1(d), p.833 ("In order to be valid, probation conditions must be reasonably related to the offense involved, the rehabilitation of the defendant, the protection of the public, or another legitimate punitive purpose.").]

Such conditions must restrict the defendant's freedom no more than necessary to achieve their goals. [*See United States v. Murray*, 692 F.3d at 281; 18 U.S.C. §3583(d)(2).]

Some jurisdictions follow the so-called "California Rule" of Model Penal Code §301.1, which provides that a condition of probation does not serve the statutory ends of probation and is invalid if it:

(1) Has no relationship to the crime of which the offender was convicted; and

(2) Relates to conduct which is not itself criminal; and

(3) Requires or forbids conduct which is not reasonably related to future criminality.

[Neil P. Cohen, *The Law of Probation and Parole* §7:15 (2d ed. 1999).]

For example, people certainly commit crimes while intoxicated, but a prohibition against any alcohol use might be unreasonable where your client does not have a history of alcoholism and did not commit the crime while drunk. [*E.g. Biller v. State*, 618 So.2d 734 (Fl. 1993) (may not all prohibit alcohol use where not related to the crime); *United*

States v. Bello, 310 F.3d 56, 61-62 (2d Cir. 2002) (probation condition barring television viewing during home detention unreasonable because it is unrelated to defendant's crime and does not further sentencing goals).]

Consider constitutional challenges.

Does the condition restrict your client's First Amendment speech or association rights, subject him to unreasonable searches, or force him to incriminate himself? [*E.g., Murray*, 692 F.3d at 282 (imposing a condition forbidding possession of sexually explicit material involving adults on offender convicted of sexually assaulting a child raised First Amendment concerns).]

The Due Process clause requires fair notice as to what behavior the condition prohibits. [*Grayned v. City of Rockford*, 408 US. 104 (1972). *See, e.g., United States v. Cabot*, 325 F.3d 384 (2d Cir. 2003) (blanket prohibition on possessing "pornography" is unconstitutionally vague because a probationer could not reasonably understand it); *Jones v. State*, 41 P.3d 1247 (Wy. 2002) (prohibition against associating with "disreputable characters" too vague to enforce); *State v. Cote*, 539 A.2d 628 (Me. 1988) (requirement that the defendant cooperate in the investigation of drug trafficking unconstitutionally vague).]

While constitutional challenges rarely succeed standing alone, the precept that courts should avoid constitutional difficulties may persuade the sentencing judge to delete a troublesome condition or to make it less restrictive.

[§§23:34-23:39 Reserved]

III. COMMUNICATIONS WITH PAROLE OR PROBATION OFFICER

§23:40   Requirement to Answer Truthfully

A standard condition of release requires probationers and parolees to answer truthfully any question put to them by their parole or probation officer.

If the answer will incriminate the defendant in other criminal activity, he must claim the privilege and refuse to answer; answering waives the privilege. [*See United States v. Nace*, 418 F.3d 945, 948 (8th Cir. 2005) (court cannot violate probation for a legitimate exercise of the Fifth Amendment privilege).]

The officer is not required to warn the defendant that he has a privilege not to answer because a probationer or parolee is not in the kind of custody that triggers the *Miranda* rule. [*Dzul v. State*, 118 Nev. 681, 56 P.3d 875 (2002).]

An exception exists to the requirement that the probationer claim the privilege where it is clear that invocation of the privilege and refusal to answer will itself subject the probationer or parolee to revocation of release. [*State v. Gaither*, 196 Or. App. 131, 100 P.3d 768 (2004) (holding that revocation under these circumstances violated Fifth Amendment privilege and that statements made were coerced and thus inadmissible); *United States v. Saechao*, 418 F.3d 1073 (9th Cir. 2005) (same).]

§23:41   Representation Before Revocation Proceedings Have Begun

If you are consulted in such a situation before revocation proceedings commence, attempt to negotiate an explicit understanding with the probation officer as to what questions your client will answer and what protections he has for his answers.

Consider speaking with the counselor or psychiatrist in charge of any psychosexual rehabilitation program to determine what statements the counselor believes your client must make, and how comprehensive the statements must be to satisfy the program's rehabilitative ends:
- The offense of conviction only?
- Any other incidents of sexual misconduct?

False exculpatory statements are not protected and always will prompt revocation, so interview your client thoroughly and discourage any such statements.

§23:42   Representation After Revocation Proceedings Have Begun

If you enter such a case after revocation proceedings begin, you must establish the facts of your client's situation precisely:
- What he was required to answer?

- How comprehensive his answers were required to be?
- What he said or claimed in response to those requests?
- What was said or threatened to him?

You must carefully eliminate any other basis for revoking your client's release, such as a failure to cooperate in other ways, other misconduct, or misstatements to the officer.

While the caselaw generally is not favorable, courts are uncomfortable with revoking release solely on the assertion of the privilege or a refusal to answer questions, so you want to frame the issue as a revocation solely for assertion of the privilege. [*E.g., Doe v. Sauer*, 186 F.3d 903, 906 (8th Cir. 1999) (parole may be denied to "a prisoner who, by invoking his privilege against self-incrimination, refuses to make statements necessary for his rehabilitation, as long as its denial is based on the prisoner's refusal to participate in his rehabilitation and not his invocation of his privilege").]

[§§23:43-23:49 Reserved]

IV.   REVOCATION OF PROBATION OR PAROLE

§23:50   Revocation Requires Two Hearings

Due process entitles a probationer or parolee to two hearings before a release may be revoked. [*Morrissey v. Brewer*, 408 U.S. 474 (1972) (parole); *Gagnon v. Scarpelli*, 411 U.S. 778 (1973) (extending the *Morrissey* holding to probation revocation proceedings).]

In *Commonwealth v. Ferguson*, 2000 PA Super 312, 761 A.2d 613, 617-18 (Pa. Super. 2000), this two-step revocation process was summarized as follows:

> At the preliminary [*Gagnon* I] hearing, a probationer or parolee is entitled to notice of the alleged violations of probation or parole, an opportunity to appear and to present evidence in his/her own behalf, a conditional right to confront adverse witnesses, an independent decisionmaker, and a written report of the hearing." *Gagnon v. Scarpelli, supra*, at 786, citing *Morrissey v. Brewer*, supra, 408 U.S. at 487. Thus, the *Gagnon* I hearing is similar to the preliminary hearing afforded all offenders before a Common Pleas Court trial: the Commonwealth must show probable cause that the violation was committed.

> The *Gagnon* II hearing entails, or may entail, two decisions: first, a "consideration of whether the facts determined warrant revocation." *Morrissey v. Brewer*, 408 U.S. at 488. "The first step in a *Gagnon* II revocation decision ... involves a wholly retrospective factual question: whether the parolee [or probationer] has in fact acted in violation of one or more conditions of his/her parole [or probation]." *Gagnon v. Scarpelli*, supra 411 U.S. at 784, citing *Morrissey v. Brewer*, supra, 408 U.S. at 479-80. It is this fact that must be demonstrated by evidence containing "probative value." *Commonwealth v. Kates*, supra, 452 Pa. at 118-19, 305 A.2d at 710. "Only if it is determined that the parolee [or probationer] did violate the conditions does the second question arise: should the parolee [or probationer] be recommitted to prison or should other steps be taken to protect society and improve chances of rehabilitation?" *Gagnon v. Scarpelli, supra*, 411 U.S. at 784, 93 S.Ct. at 1761, citing *Morrissey v. Brewer*, supra, 408 U.S. at 479-80, 92 S.Ct. 2593. Thus, the *Gagnon* II hearing is more complete than the *Gagnon* I hearing in affording the probationer additional due process safeguards, specifically:

> (a) written notice of the claimed violations of [probation or] parole; (b) disclosure to the [probationer or] parolee of evidence against him; (c) opportunity to be heard in person and to present witnesses and documentary evidence; (d) the right to confront and cross-examine adverse witnesses (unless the hearing officer specifically finds good cause for not allowing confrontation); (e) a "neutral and detached" hearing body such as a traditional parole board, members of which need not be judicial officers or lawyers; and (f) a written statement by the factfinders as to the evidence relied on and reasons for revoking [probation or] parole.

[*Commonwealth v. Ferguson*, 761 A.2d 613, 617-18 (Pa. Super. 2000).]

§23:51   Evidence, Discovery & Burden of Proof

The court and board may hear and rely on hearsay as long as it bears some indicia of reliability and there is good cause for foregoing live testimony. However, the defendant has a right to cross-examine any witnesses who appear. [*See* Neil P. Cohen, *The Law of Probation and Parole* §20:11 (2d ed. 1999); Daniel F. Piar, *A Uniform Code of Procedure for Revocation of Probation*, 31 Am. J. Crim. L. 117, 153-60 (2003).]

As a matter of federal constitutional law, the exclusionary rule does not apply to revocation proceedings [*Pa. Bd. of Probation & Parole v. Scott*, 524 U.S. 357 (1998)], but a number of courts have found authority in their state constitutions to extend the exclusionary rule to revocation proceedings. [*E.g., Commonwealth v. Arter*, 151 A.3d 149 (Pa. 2016) (surveying states).]

Some jurisdictions permit pre-hearing discovery, but usually it is more limited than that before a criminal trial. [Daniel F. Piar, *A Uniform Code of Procedure for Revocation of Probation*, 31 Am. J. Crim. L. at 160-64.]

The prosecution's burden to prove a violation is by a preponderance of the evidence. [*See State v. Davis*, 229 Conn. 285, 641 A.2d 370, 376-77 (Conn. 1994) (collecting cases).]

Since the defendant already has been sentenced, there is no right to bail, but the courts in its discretion may allow the defendant to remain free pending the final revocation hearing.

§23:52   Timing for Hearing

A revocation hearing must be held without unreasonable delay after arrest. [*See Morrissey v. Brewer*, 408 U.S. 471, 485, 488 (1972).]

This time limitation is not a strict one. For example, so long as a violation warrant or summons issues before the expiration of the term, the court may hold a hearing and revoke even after the term of probation, parole or supervised release ends. [*E.g.,* 18 U.S.C. §3583(i) (supervised release); *United States v. Sczubelek*, 402 F.3d 175, 180-81 (3d Cir. 2005) (noting that the concept of "delayed revocation" applies equally to supervised release, probation and parole; surveys federal courts and finds unanimity on this issue). *See generally* Neil P. Cohen, *The Law of Probation and Parole* §§18:12, 18:13 (2d ed. 1999).]

Some jurisdictions even permit the filing of a revocation warrant after the supervision period expires for conduct that occurred during the period. [*Commonwealth v. Hackman*, 623 A.2d 350, 351-52 (Pa. Super. 1993).]

The delay becomes a factor for the court to consider in deciding whether to permit the revocation hearing to proceed. [*Commonwealth v. Ruff*, 272 Pa. Super. 50, 55-56, 414 A.2d 663, 666 (Pa. Super. 1979).]

§23:53   Strategy at Hearing

Talk to the probation or parole officer.

Discuss both the facts underlying the violation and your client's progress on supervision with the supervising officer before the hearing. While discovery rights are limited, the probation or parole officer might be willing to share information with you.

Lobby the officer for a favorable recommendation. Probation and parole officers occupy a role midway between a police officer and a social worker. While they serve a crime-control function, they also have responsibility for assisting the offender in transitioning to law-abiding and productive behavior. Therefore, they might be willing to give your client a second (or third or fourth) chance.

Research the law.

Carefully check any re-sentencing statutes or guidelines to avoid pleading your client guilty to a violation that carries mandatory incarceration.

Examples are violations for possessing controlled substances or firearms. [*E.g.,* 18 U.S.C. §§3565(b) (probation); 3583 (g) (supervised release).]

Suggest a postponement.

If your client is not in custody, suggest a postponement of the hearing while your client enters a program or a return to supervision, perhaps with additional conditions of supervision. Several months of gainful employment and negative drug tests may convince the court to restore him to probation or supervised release.

Emphasize rehabilitative progress.

Violation hearings are difficult to win and resemble sentencing hearings more than guilt or innocence trials. Your best approach often is to admit the violation and try to build a case that your client was making rehabilitative progress (*e.g.,* working, supporting his family, and attending drug treatment) and deserves another chance.

The supervising probation or parole officer might be somewhat supportive, because he or she has invested time and effort into your client's rehabilitation and would like to claim some success. Although some officers perceive themselves more as law enforcement officers than social workers, office directives often obligate them to make some effort to assist in the defendant's rehabilitation by establishing a rehabilitative plan, referring the defendant to appropriate programs and monitoring and assisting the defendant's progress.

You might inquire of the probation officer the plan he or she formed for the defendant and the steps that both the officer and the defendant took to fulfill that plan and steps they might explore in the future to return the defendant to the rehabilitative track. [*See, e.g.,* Michael L. Desuatels, "Defending a Supervised Release Case for Drug Use: the U.S Probation's Department's Own Manual Could Help You," 30 *The Champion* 24 (March 2006) (Probation Department Monograph 109 commands officers to conduct an initial assessment, formulate a supervision plan, get addicted offenders into treatment programs and periodically evaluate and update the plan to account for the probationer's progress or lack thereof).]

Focus on the explicit terms of the supervision.

Conditions of supervision must "be sufficiently clear to enable individuals on supervised release to freely choose between compliance and violation.... Conditions of supervised release must provide a defendant with adequate notice of what he may and may not do...." [*United States v. Bagdy,* 2014 U.S. App. LEXIS 16102, *8-9 (3d Cir. 2014).] A violation must be based on failure to comply with an explicit and specific condition of supervision, not on general bad faith. [*Id.* (where restitution condition stated that defendant must pay ten-percent of his gross monthly income, defendant did not violate supervision where he paid one-third of $435,000 inheritance toward restitution and dissipated rest).]

§23:54   Re-Sentencing for Probation Violations

Upon finding a violation, a court may reinstate the defendant to probation, extend the term of probation, or revoke probation and sentence the defendant to a term of imprisonment.

The manner in which the court imposed probation becomes important. If the court suspended imposition of sentence or if probation was an independent sentence, the court can impose any other sentence that could have been imposed initially. [18 U.S.C. §3565.]

Policy statements to the United States Sentencing Guidelines set the sentence upon a finding that the defendant violated federal supervised release or probation. The severity of the sentence depends on whether the violation is a new crime and whether the new crime is one of violence or drug distribution. [*See* U.S.S.G. §§7B1.3, 7B1.4.]

Violations for possession of a controlled substance or possession of a firearm mandate imprisonment. Otherwise, the court can restore the defendant to supervision. [18 U.S.C. §§3565(a)(1) (court may continue defendant on probation, extend the term, and modify conditions); 3583(e)(2) (may extend term of supervised release and modify, reduce or enlarge conditions).]

PRACTICE TIP:

Be ready to suggest alternatives to the stark choices of restoring your client to parole or probation or incarcerating him, such as:

- An extension of the term of supervision (especially if the violation is for failure to pay a fine or restitution).
- Closer supervision with more frequent reporting.
- House arrest during non-working hours with electronic monitoring.

§23:55   Re-Sentencing for Parole Violations

Upon finding a violation, the board can commit the defendant to serve the balance of his original sentence, but no more. [*See Commonwealth v. Sharpe,* 445 Pa. Super. 419, 665 A.2d 1194 (1995); *Commonwealth v. Bischof,* 420 Pa. Super. 115, 616 A.2d 6 (1992).]

This is the one advantage of parole over probation. Many jurisdictions have guidelines that set presumptive sentences for particular violations. [*E.g.,* 37 Pa. Code. §§75.2–75.4.]

Even where the judge ran the original sentences on multiple counts concurrently, the judge can impose consecutive terms of imprisonment for supervised release violations. [*United States v. Dees*, 467 F.3d 847 (3d Cir. 2006).]

Your struggle will be to gain your client credit for "street time" (i.e., the time he spent at liberty on parole). The general rule is that upon a "technical violation" (a violation for anything but a new conviction) your client is entitled to credit for street time. However, upon a "substantive violation" (a new conviction) your client loses his street time and may be forced to serve the full balance of his sentence in custody. [61 Pa.Stat. §331.21a(a).]

Jurisdictions vary widely on street time credit and revocation, and you must consult local law and regulations. [*See* Neil P. Cohen, *The Law of Probation and Parole* §28:3 (2d ed. 1999).]

Determine your jurisdiction's rule on street time and if winning the violation hearing seems unlikely, try to plead your client to a technical violation that will obviate a hearing on the substantive violation, but carry a less severe penalty.

§23:56   Violation Sentences and Sentences for Underlying Convictions

Where your client faces both a sentence for a new conviction and resentencing for a parole or probation violation, your challenge is to avoid the sentences running consecutively. This will be difficult, because parole boards and re-sentencing judges generally add the violation sentence onto any new sentence. [*See Commonwealth v. Ferrer*, 319 Pa. Super. 152, 465 A.2d 1275 (1983) (parole violation sentences must run consecutively to any other sentence).]

Since parole boards act nearly automatically in this regard, your best bet usually is to have your client start the violation sentence and then ask the judge on the new case to make the new sentence at least partly concurrent to the violation sentence.

When attempting this, you must ensure that your client has started to serve the violation sentence at the time the new sentence is imposed. Sometimes this is not an easy task. Even if your client is resentenced first, he will not start that sentence unless he is in that jurisdiction's custody at the time that the sentence is imposed. If your client is produced for a prosecution on writ of habeas corpus ad prosequendum, he is not actually in the receiving jurisdiction's custody. Rather, the jurisdiction "borrows" him for the prosecution, and once the prosecution is done, returns him to the other jurisdiction. You may need to get him released from the underlying custody and agree that he will be detained and sentenced first by the jurisdiction to whose sentence you want the second sentence to run concurrent.

[§§23:57-23:59 Reserved]

V.   EARLY TERMINATION OF PROBATION

§23:60   Motions for Early Termination

Your client's good conduct and fidelity to his obligations may earn him early termination of his supervision.

In some jurisdictions, statutes explicitly authorize early termination after a set period of good conduct. [*E.g.,* 18 U.S.C. §§3564(c) (probation), 3583(e)(1) (supervised release).]

Where the statute is silent, assume that a motion is permissible.

§23:61   Preparing for the Motion

Set up a motion to terminate probation with three steps:
(1) Make sure your client has paid all fines, restitution and costs.
(2) Obtain the supervising probation officer's consent. If your client has behaved, the officer usually will be glad to discharge him so the officer can devote his or her energies to those in need of supervision.
    Note the officer's consent in your motion. You are unlikely to win unless the officer consents.
(3) Ascertain the minimum period of supervision your judge demands before he or she will grant a motion to terminate supervision. The probation officer should be able to tell you this.

Form:
•   **Form 23-3** Motion to Terminate Probation

VI. FORMS

Form 23-1 Petition for Parole (to a Court)

IN THE COURT OF COMMON PLEAS OF _____ COUNTY, _____

COMMONWEALTH OF _____,
 	
      v.
 	
MRF
      Defendant.
	CRIMINAL DIVISION
	
	CC No:
	
	PETITION FOR RELEASE ON PAROLE
	
	Filed on behalf of Defendant,
	Counsel of Record for this Party:
	THOMAS J. FARRELL, ESQUIRE

IN THE COURT OF COMMON PLEAS OF _____ COUNTY, _____

COMMONWEALTH OF _____,
 	
      v.
 	
MRF
      Defendant.
	)
	)
	)
	)
	)
	)
	)
	)
		CRIMINAL DIVISION
		
		CC No:

NOTICE OF PRESENTMENT

TO:
Deputy Attorney General
Pennsylvania Office of Attorney General
564 Forbes Avenue
Manor Complex
Pittsburgh, PA 15219

You are hereby notified that the within Petition for Release on Parole will be presented to the Honorable _____ at the Washington County Courthouse on _____ at 9:15 a.m. or as soon thereafter as suits the convenience of the Court.

_____
THOMAS J. FARRELL, ESQUIRE

IN THE COURT OF COMMON PLEAS OF _____ COUNTY, _____

COMMONWEALTH OF _____,
 	
      v.
 	
MRF
      Defendant.
	)
	)
	)
	)
	)
	)
	)
	)
		CRIMINAL DIVISION
		
		CC No:

PETITION FOR PAROLE

AND NOW comes Defendant, MRF, by and through his attorney, Thomas J. Farrell, Esquire, and hereby petitions this Honorable Court for release on parole from his 23-month sentence now being served at the Washington County Jail, and represents:

1. On _____, the Washington County Adult Probation Office lodged a detainer against MRF alleging that he had violated the conditions of parole imposed by this Court on _____.

2. The detainer followed MRF's indictment in the United States District Court for the Western District of Pennsylvania on a charge of illegally possessing firearms. On _____, Magistrate-Judge _____ ordered MRF's release on the condition that he post a $175,000 property bond (which he has done) and that he be subject to GPS monitoring and that he not leave Washington County. See Exhibit A, attached.

3. On _____, after a hearing, the Court revoked MRF's parole finding that he had engaged in gambling and had possessed firearms in violation of his parole conditions. The Court stated that it would consider MRF's reparole only after he served five months of imprisonment. (It is not clear if that is measured from _____, or _____.)

4. We ask that the Court re-parole MRF as of the time he has served five months. In support, we ask the Court to consider the attached character letters, Exhibit B, from the following persons:

[LIST]

5. These letters attest to MRF's good character, his good works and the toll that his incarceration has taken on him, his family and his business.

6. By telephone call on _____, I informed Deputy Attorney General MA that we would be presenting this petition on _____. Mr. A said that he did not know what the position of his office would be on this petition, but he would inform me and the Court by _____.

7. MRF has had no misconducts while in the Washington County Jail.

8. MRF has never failed to appear for a court appearance in this or any other matter.

9. I have consulted with the Warden of the Washington County Jail and the Deputy Attorney General, and they have the following positions on this petition:

Warden, Washington County Jail:

No Objection: _____

Objection: _____

Deputy Attorney General:

No Objection: _____

Objection: _____

WHEREFORE, we respectfully request that this Court re-parole MRF and permit him to serve the remaining 18 months of his 23 month sentence on parole.

Respectfully submitted,

_____

Thomas J. Farrell, Esquire

CERTIFICATE OF SERVICE

I, Thomas J. Farrell, Esquire, hereby certify that a true and correct copy of the within Petition for Parole was served by Federal Express upon the following this _____ day of _____:

Deputy Attorney General
Pennsylvania Office of Attorney General

_____

Thomas J. Farrell, Esquire

IN THE COURT OF COMMON PLEAS OF _____ COUNTY, _____

COMMONWEALTH OF _____,	)))
v.	))
MRF	))
Defendant.	)

CRIMINAL DIVISION

CC No:

ORDER

AND NOW this _____ day of _____, upon consideration of MRF's Petition for Furlough, it is hereby ORDERED that MRF be paroled from the Washington County Jail to serve the remainder of his 23-month sentence on parole under the supervision of Washington County Adult Probation.

By the Court:

_____ J.

Form 23-2   Standard Probation/Parole Conditions for Washington County, Pennsylvania

WASHINGTON COUNTY ADULT PROBATION & PAROLE OFFICE

I have read (or had read to me) these conditions and I will comply with them and any special conditions (such as evaluation or treatment) that the Court or my PO imposes. If I comply, I will be discharged from supervision when my term expires. If I fail to comply, my case may be revoked and I may be arrested and detained pending the revocation hearing. If I am enrolled in the ARD program and fail to comply, my PO may petition the District Attorney's Office to have my ARD status revoked.

CLIENT: _____   DATE:_____
WITNESS: _____   DATE:_____

CONDITIONS OF PROBATION/PAROLE/IPP/ARD

1. Report to your PO (probation/parole officer) as directed and permitted a PO to visit you at your residence and submit for the searches of your residence, vehicle, property, and/or your person (including drug/alcohol testing).

2. Do not violate any criminal laws or ordinances. Notify your PO within 72 hours of any new arrest or citation or any other contact with law enforcement.

3. Notify your PO within 72 hours of any significant change in employment. You must show your pay stubs to your PO to verify your employment and work hours. If unemployed, you must seek work as instructed by your PO.

4. You must reside at the address you report to your PO and may not move without approval from your PO. In an emergency, notify your PO within 24 hours of the reason for the move and your new address. Upon request, you must list all persons staying at or visiting your residence.

5. Your PO must give permission whenever you plan to stay overnight away from your listed address. You may not leave Pennsylvania without a written travel permit from your PO.

6. Do not possess a firearm or other dangerous weapon. You will be in violation if there are any firearms or other dangerous weapons in your residence, on your person, or in your vehicle.

7. Do not display assaultive, threatening, or harassing behavior.

8. Do not unlawfully possess or use any controlled substance. Do not abuse any prescribed medication. Notify your PO of any medications you're taking upon request or upon your analysis or other drugs/alcohol testing.

9. Do not possess, purchase, or use alcoholic beverages. Do not enter bars or taverns.

10. Avoid unlawful and disreputable places and people. Avoid any specific persons, places, groups, or locations if so instructed by your PO.

11. It is your responsibility to make payments as scheduled to the clerk of courts. You may request a payment extension if you are unable to pay the scheduled amount but you must show that you have made a good-faith effort to comply. You will be charged with contempt of court if you did not fulfill your payment obligations.

12. The Ignition Interlock law (act 63 of 2000) may apply to you. See the Ignition Interlock Restricted License FAQ sheet for details. Notify your PO if you did not receive the FAQ sheet.

YOUR RIGHTS: if you believe that your PO has violated your rights, you may make a written report to the PLO's supervisor. You must be specific about when and where the violation occurred and the details. Anonymous complaints will not be considered. You will receive written notice of your rights regarding any arrests or revocation proceedings.

Form 23-3   Motion to Terminate Probation

United States of America

     v.

                                    Cr. No. 00-000

John Doe,

     Defendant

DEFENDANT'S MOTION FOR EARLY TERMINATION OF PROBATION

And now comes defendant, John Doe, by his attorney, Thomas J. Farrell, Esquire, and files this motion for early termination of probation and alleges in support thereof the following:

On _____, 20__, this Court sentenced defendant to a term of five years probation on a conviction for one count of tax evasion, in violation of 26 U.S.C. §7201.

Defendant has served three years of his probationary term and has obeyed all conditions of probation. In addition, defendant paid in full the $_____ in taxes, penalty and interest he owed to the Internal Revenue Service. Defendant has been employed full-time as a mortuary assistant and has paid regular child support and alimony to his ex-wife, Jane Doe. Defendant has filed and paid his federal and state income tax returns.

The undersigned consulted by telephone on February 20, 20__, with Mr. Doe's supervising probation officer _____, and she informed me that she has no opposition to the early termination of defendant's probation.

WHEREFORE, defendant respectfully requests that the Court terminate defendant's term of probation and discharge him from any further supervision.

                                Respectfully submitted,

                                _____

                                Thomas J. Farrell,
                                Counsel for Defendant

Chapter 24

APPEALS

I. GENERAL POINTS

§24:01   The Importance of the Factual Record

Success on appeal starts at trial. Not only does failure to object relegate the appellant to an unforgiving "plain error" review, but it signals that trial counsel did not consider the issue significant.

Well-argued objections and fully developed factual records achieve several tactical objectives. The appeals court will not feel that its judicial compatriot below was ambushed. If the record demonstrates persistent objections and requests, the appeals court might blame the prosecution for pursuing a tenuous legal strategy or for failing to respond to your discovery requests.

A developed factual record also positions you to argue that your issue is a narrow, fact-specific one. Sweeping legal arguments rarely prevail on appeal. The words of Professor Anthony Amsterdam, one of our times' foremost appellate advocates, on strategy for winning habeas corpus petitions apply with equal strength to defense arguments on appeal:

> Thus, winning a habeas case for the petitioner has become in no small part a matter of developing a bolt-hole theory of the case: a narrow argument through which your individual client can be slipped away to freedom, with a door somewhere in the passageway that can be slammed shut in the faces of all other prisoners seeking to follow. ... Unless the judge is satisfied that s/he can give relief in this case with no (or very little) prospect that other accused or convicted persons will escape punishment, the judges will simply not rule your way.

[Anthony G. Amsterdam, "Foreword" to Randy Hertz & James S. Liebman, *Federal Habeas Corpus Practice and Procedure* (5th ed. 2005).]

§24:02   Time to Appeal

Time limits on filing the notice of appeal are brief and strictly enforced. [*See* Fed. R. App. P. 4(b)(1)(A) (14 days).] Check your rules, but err on the side of caution.

The sentence is the judgment in a criminal case, and the time to appeal usually runs from the imposition of sentence. However, some questions can arise. Motions for reconsideration extend the time to appeal only if the motion was made properly and timely. [*See United States v. Comprehensive Drug Testing, Inc.,* 513 F.3d 1085, 1097-99 (9th Cir. 2008).]

The time for a defendant to appeal a criminal forfeiture judgment starts when the sentence is docketed, even though considerable ancillary litigation over third party rights may lie ahead. [*See United States v. Christunas,* 126 F.3d 765 (6th Cir. 1997) (dismissing as untimely defendant's appeal that awaited the adjudication of third party interests).]

Err on the side of caution. Since a simple notice of appeal preserves your client's rights, there is no reason not to file one promptly. [*See* §24:04.]

§24:03   Continued Representation

Filing the notice may obligate you to continue as counsel on appeal. [*See* Local Appellate Rules, United States Court of Appeals for the Third Circuit, LAR Misc. 109.1 ("Trial counsel in criminal cases, whether retained or appointed, are expected to continue on appeal absent extraordinary circumstances."); Eleventh Cir. Rule 46-1(g)(1) (Retained counsel must continue on appeal until successor counsel is appointed and cannot withdraw absent order of court).]

If your client has not resolved to retain you for the appeal, have the clerk of court file a notice on your client's behalf or assist your client in filing a notice pro se.

§24:04   The Notice of Appeal

In most jurisdictions, a simple one-page notice of appeal suffices to start the appeal process.

The notice need not specify the issues on appeal. However, local practice may authorize the trial judge to demand of the appellant a statement of issues on appeal. [*See, e.g., Pa. R. App. P.* 1925(b).]

The rules of appellate procedure might foreclose appeal of any issue not specified in the statement of issues. [*Commonwealth v. Lord,* 553 Pa. 415, 719 A.2d 306 (1998) (issues not specified in 1925(b) statement cannot be raised on appeal); *but see Pa. R. App. P. 1925(c)(3)* (complete failure to file a 1925b) statement is per se ineffective assistance of counsel and results in remand for the filing of a Statement nunc pro tunc); *Commonwealth v. Burton,* 973 A.2d 428 (Pa. Super 2009) (extends 1925(c)(3)'s reinstatement of appellate rights to untimely filed 1925 statements).]

You are not obligated to develop your argument fully in such a statement, but cite enough law to preserve the legal basis for your appeal. Make the statement over-inclusive to foreclose prosecution waiver arguments. You are free to omit issues later.

Soon after you file the notice and the appellate court dockets the appeal, the appellate court will inundate you with forms that you must complete, such as appearance forms and information statements. As trivial and routine as they seem, appellate courts take these forms and the rest of their idiosyncratic rules very seriously and impose sanctions for their violation. Read them carefully and complete them with care.

Forms:
- **Form 24-1** Notice of Appeal
- **Form 24-2** Motion for Extension of Time
- **Form 24-3** Case Opening Scheduling Notice
- **Form 24-4** Calendaring Notice

§24:05   The Decision to Appeal

You have an obligation to consult with the client on whether to appeal or not, and to give your best advice, but ultimately, your client chooses. [*Roe v. Flores-Ortega,* 528 U.S. 470, 477 (2000).]

Once your client expresses an intent to appeal, it is your duty to file a notice of appeal.

In most cases, choosing to appeal carries little risk: generally, a sentence cannot be increased upon conviction at retrial after appeal. [*See* § 24:90, *infra*] In at least two situations, however, a defense appeal may prove harmful:

1. A sentencing appeal may elicit the prosecution's cross-appeal on other sentencing issues that went the defendant's way.
2. If a plea agreement included an appeal waiver and the prosecution's sentencing under a guideline or mandatory minimum sentencing scheme, the appeal might be construed as a breach of the plea agreement and might release the prosecution to seek a higher sentence on remand. [*United States v. Erwin,* 765 F.3d 219, 236 (3d Cir. 2014)("We hold that, like any defendant who breaches a plea agreement in advance of sentencing, a defendant who breaches his plea agreement by appealing thereby subjects himself to the agreement's breach provision. The breach provision in this case permits the Government to withdraw its motion for a downward departure. To that end, we will vacate and remand Erwin's judgment of sentence."]

However, the decision regarding which issues to raise and which to jettison on appeal belongs to counsel's professional judgment. [*Jones v. Barnes,* 463 U.S. 745 (1983) (counsel should winnow issues on appeal).]

In choosing issues, look for the following:
- Issues of law that receive de novo review on appeal.
- Clearly preserved issues.
- Harmful issues. Think of how the issue affected the trial's outcome. Did it undermine the cross-examination of a crucial prosecution witness? Did the ruling lead to the admission of damning evidence? Can you show that the issue of guilt or innocence was a close one–by review of the evidence, the length of the jury's deliberations and the nature of its questions, by the acquittal on some counts–and that this ruling contributed to the conviction? Avoid issues that are cumulative (*e.g.*, a precluded line of cross-examination where other lines effectively impeached the witness or the preclusion of defense evidence that merely corroborated other evidence).
- Issues that ride a trend in the law. Sense that the law is unsettled and trial courts and litigants need guidance. In such cases it is more likely that the trial court relied on an outdated view of the law. This will vary from month to month and court to court.

PRACTICE TIP:
Since deadlines to file a notice of appeal are short, and the failure to file irrevocably waives the right to appeal, you must obtain a certain decision from your client as soon as possible. Begin to discuss the issue with your client before sentencing. Once he decides, document the decision in your file.

§24:06   The *Anders* Brief

In those cases in which you cannot find any nonfrivolous issue to raise on appeal, you may move to withdraw, but this should be rare: you should make any conceivable argument on your client's behalf. [*See* ABA Crminal Justice

Standards, The Defense Function Standard 4-8.3 (a) ("Appellate counsel should not seek to withdraw from a case solely on the basis of his or her own determination that the appeal lacks merit.")]

If you do move to withdraw, you must accompany the motion to withdraw with an "*Anders*" brief. [*See Anders v. California*, 386 U.S. 738 (1967) (explaining counsel's obligations when there are no nonfrivolous issues).]

An *Anders* brief must describe anything in the record that might arguably support an appeal so that the appellate court can review whether you discharged your duty to your client. You must provide the brief to your client in sufficient time for him to supplement it.

Anders set a constitutional minimum, and many states require more from counsel seeking to withdraw on what she believes to be a frivolous appeal. For example, Pennsylvania requires:

> Prior to withdrawing as counsel on a direct appeal under Anders, counsel must file a brief that meets the requirements established by our Supreme Court in Santiago. The brief must:
>
> (1) provide a summary of the procedural history and facts, with citations to the record;
>
> (2) refer to anything in the record that counsel believes arguably supports the appeal;
>
> (3) set forth counsel's conclusion that the appeal is frivolous; and
>
> (4) state counsel's reasons for concluding that the appeal is frivolous. Counsel should articulate the relevant facts of record, controlling case law, and/or statutes on point that have led to the conclusion that the appeal is frivolous.
>
> Counsel also must provide a copy of the Anders brief to his client. Attending the brief must be a letter that advises the client of his right to: (1) retain new counsel to pursue the appeal; (2) proceed pro se on appeal; or (3) raise any points that the appellant deems worthy of the court['s] attention in addition to the points raised by counsel in the Anders brief.

Commonwealth v. Orellana, 2014 Pa. Super 33, 86 A.3d 877, 879-80 (Pa. Super. 2014)(citing *Commonwealth v. Santiago*, 602 Pa. 159, 978 A.2d 349, 361 (Pa. 2009) and *Commonwealth v. Nischan*, 2007 PA Super 199, 928 A.2d 349, 353 (Pa. Super. 2007).]

Other states, following the ABA standards, forbid no-merit briefs altogether. [*See generally* Martha C. Warner, Anders in the Fifty States: Some Appellants' Equal Protection is More Equal Than Others', 23 Fla. St. U.L. Rev. 625 (1996).]

PRACTICE TIP:
_____

Shun *Anders* briefs. When your client went to trial, almost never will an *Anders* brief be justifiable. However, you may be forced to file one when your client dislikes the sentence after a guilty plea, or if your client wants to appeal a second time after a remand on a narrow issue.

Forms:
- **Form 24-5** Motion to Withdraw From Appeal (*Anders*)
- **Form 24-6** *Anders* Brief

§24:07   Communicate With Your Client

Especially if you were not the trial lawyer, you should discuss the appeal and your client's expectations for it thoroughly. Many defendants bring unrealistic expectations to the appeal: they believe it will be a forum to relitigate guilt, to attack lying witnesses, or to criticize their trial lawyer.

Proceed with caution, however, before you rely on your client's recollection of what happened at trial or how trial decisions were made. Listen closely, for sometimes clients have insights, but sometimes they have obsessions that distort and exaggerate their recollection.

Further, you may learn other ways you can assist and satisfy your client: he may have issues with the Department of Corrections or Bureau of Prisons you can resolve, or he may seek the return of non-incriminating evidence subpoenaed or seized from him, a wish you often can fulfill with a telephone call.

[§§24:08-24:09 Reserved]

II.   INTERLOCUTORY APPEALS

§24:10   Collateral Orders

Interlocutory appeals by the defense are rarely permitted. The principal exception arises under the "collateral order" doctrine.

An immediate appeal lies from a collateral order only if:

- The trial court's order had fully disposed of the question and did not leave the matter "open, unfinished or inconclusive."
- The decision was not simply a "step toward final disposition of the merits of the case (which would) be merged in final judgment" but instead resolved an issue completely collateral to the cause of action asserted.
- The decision had involved an important right which would be "lost, probably irreparably," if review had to await final judgment.

[*Abney v. United States,* 431 U.S. 651, 658-59 (1977) (denial of double jeopardy motion is appealable as a collateral order); *United States v. McDade*, 28 F.3d 283, 288 (3d Cir. 1994) ("A district court order entered prior to final judgment is immediately appealable if it (1) conclusively determines the disputed question, (2) resolves an important issue completely separate from the merits of the case, and (3) is effectively unreviewable on appeal from a final judgment"); Pa. R. App. P. 313(b) (a collateral order is one that is "separable from and collateral to the main cause of action where the right involved is too important to be denied review and the question presented is such that if review is postponed until final judgment in the case, the claim will be irreparably lost").]

A collateral order was held appealable from the following trial court orders:

- An order that defendant be forcibly medicated to render him competent to stand trial. *Sell v. United States*, 539 U.S. 166, 176 (2003).
- A pretrial order denying the media access to the names of prospective jurors. *United States v. Wecht*, 537 F.3d 222, 228 (3d Cir. 2008).
- An order under the DNA Act, 42 U.SC. §§33701 et seq., that a defendant submit a DNA sample. *United States v. Pool*, 621 F.3d 1213, 1217 (9th Cir. 2010), vacated, appeal dismissed as moot, 659 F.3d 761 (9th Cir. 2011); *United States v. Mitchell*, 652 F.3d 387 (3d Cir. July 25, 2011) (en banc).
- Orders overruling claims of privilege and requiring disclosure. [*Commonwealth v. Williams*, 86 A.3d 771 (Pa. 2014)(order permitting defense discovery of interview notes for which prosecution claimed work product protection was immediately appealable); *Commonwealth v. Kennedy*, 583 Pa. 208, 876 A.2d 939 (2005) (discovery order compelling the defense to disclose the opinion of a non-testifying defense expert appealable because the order threatened the attorney-client and work product privileges).]

However, the following collateral orders were held not appealable:

- Order removing defense counsel. [*Flanagan v. United States,* 465 U.S. 259 (1984); *but see State v. Chambliss*, 128 Ohio St.3d 507, 947 N.E.2d 651 (2011) (holding that under the Supreme Court's subsequent decision in *United States v. Gonzalez-Lopez*, 548 US. 140 (2006), which held that the erroneous disqualification of defense counsel is structural error, the disqualification of counsel is an appealable interlocutory order).]
- Denial of motion to quash search warrant for blood and saliva. [*In re Solomon*, 465 F.3d 114, 122 (3d Cir. 2006).]

PRACTICE TIP:

While the failure to take an interlocutory appeal generally does not waive the issue upon appeal from a final judgment, your failure to appeal when the error and harm first occurred may limit the relief available in some instances. [*E.g., Rivera-Domenech v. Calvesbert Law Offices PSC*, 402 F.3d 246, 249 & n.2 (1st Cir. 2005) (attorney's failure to appeal refusal of trial court to hold hearing on his motion to withdraw limited relief available where attorney then continued to represent client through trial).]

§24:11   Writs of Mandamus or Prohibition

An interlocutory appeal may also be raised by writs of mandamus or prohibition.

A writ may be useful when a trial court orders discovery that would infringe on the attorney-client privilege, at least where the issue is a novel and important one. [*See Pritchard v. County of Erie*, 473 F.3d 413, 416-17 (2d Cir. 2007) (issuing writ where discovery order would have infringed on privilege between a government attorney and government official; issue was a novel and important one).]

An appellate court also might grant a pre-trial writ to recuse the trial judge if the defendant can show a clear entitlement to relief and irreparable harm. [*In re Vazquez-Botet*, 464 F.3d 54, 57 (1st Cir. 2006) (denies writ because right to relief was not clear, though suggests there might be a different outcome on appeal after judgment).]

To obtain a writ of mandamus, the petitioner must show:

- The presence of a novel and significant question of law.
- The inadequacy of other available remedies.
- The presence of a legal issue whose resolution will aid in the administration of justice.

[*United States v. Amante*, 418 F.3d 220, 222 (2d Cir. 2005) (granting prosecution's motion for a writ to prohibit trial court from bifurcating elements of felon-in-possession charge); *see also Davis v. Brown*, 87 N.Y. 2d 626, 641 N.Y.S. 2d 819, 664 N.E. 2d 884 (1996) (write of prohibition issued where double jeopardy prohibited retrial).]

However, successful resort to a writ of mandamus or prohibition is rare. "Mandamus is an extraordinary remedy, the touchstones of which are usurpation of power, clear abuse of discretion and the presence of an issue of first impression." [*Amante*, 418 F.3d at 222 (2d Cir. 2005).]

[§§24:12-24:19 Reserved]

III. PRESERVING AND WAIVING APPEAL

A. Preserving Issues

1. When to Raise Objection

§24:20   Objection Must Be Timely

Trial lawyers play a crucial role in assuring the success of an appeal. Appellate courts will not review legal error absent a seasonable objection in the trial court.

Being seasonable means that the objection must draw the error to the trial court's attention in time to correct it. [*See* Richard T. Farrell, *Richardson on Evidence* §1-201 (11th ed. 1995).]

With trial objections, this usually means an objection before the witness answers or a motion to strike immediately after the offending answer.

Objections to procedural improprieties in sentencing must be made at the sentencing to be preserved. [*United States v. Flores-Mejia*, 759 F.3d 253 (3d Cir. 2014) (en banc).] Many sentencing judges will follow the imposition of sentence with a question to the lawyers asking if they have anything else to bring to the court's attention. This is the time to raise any other objections to the manner and nature or length of the sentence. [*See, e.g., United States v. Hunter*, 809 F.3d 677, 682-83 (D.C. Cir. 2016).] The Sixth Circuit Court of Appeals has fashioned a supervisory rule to the effect that sentencing judges "after pronouncing the defendant's sentence but before adjourning the sentencing hearing, [must] ask the parties whether they have any objections to the sentence just pronounced that have not previously been raised. If the district court fails to provide the parties with this opportunity, they will not have forfeited their objections and thus will not be required to demonstrate plain error on appeal." [*United States v. Wettstain*, 618 F.3d 577, 592 (6th Cir. 2010) (quoting *United States v. Bostic*, 371 F.2d 865, 872-73(6th Cir. 2004).] Other courts of appeals have rejected the *Bostic* rule and place the burden on defense counsel to raise objections before the sentencing proceeding is adjourned. [*United States v. Flores-Mejia*, 759 F.3d 253, 258 n.8 (3d Cir. 2014) (en banc); *United States v. Vanderwerfhorst*, 576 F.3d 929, 933 (9th Cir. 2009).]

Trial counsel should comply with any court rules on the timeliness of pre-trial and post-trial motions, but making a motion as soon as possible, even if untimely, is far superior to mentioning the issue for the first time on appeal. Trial courts often will decide the issue on the merits rather than deny it for untimeliness. This might preserve the substantive issue for appeal.

"[R]aising an argument for the first time in a motion for reconsideration results in waiver of that argument for purposes of appeal." [*United States v. Franz*, 772 F.3d 134, 150 (3d Cir. 2014) (motion for reconsideration that raised for the first time arguments under Fed. R. Crim. P. 41 and due process based upon the failure to serve a warrant at the time of its execution failed to preserve those issues where the suppression motion challenged the warrant only for lack of probable cause and particularity).]

§24:21   Motions in Limine

Motions in limine can assist in guaranteeing the adequate preservation of issues. In limine motions are especially helpful where you wish to preserve multiple bases for an objection, such as state law, state constitution, and federal constitutional grounds.

Even if you file a motion in limine, the safer course is to renew the objection at trial, but you can refer the court to your motion, thereby saving yourself from remembering and reciting a lengthy litany of legal arguments mid-trial. [*See* Chapter 20, Trial.]

Where the trial court denies a motion in limine to preclude certain government questions on cross-examination or evidence in rebuttal, you face the dilemma of whether to introduce the evidence yourself and thereby waive appellate review of the issue or to forego mentioning the evidence and risk the greater impact it will have when introduced for the first time on cross or rebuttal. [*See* §24:40 (discussing *Ohler v. United States*, 529 U.S. 753 (2000)).]

§24:22   Recess Objections

Sometimes a judge does not want to hear you mid-trial. In that case, try to renew your objection at a recess, or even submit it handwritten at the earliest possible time.

Insist on your right to make your record. Do not fall into the trap some judges set of entertaining argument off-the-record in chambers. If the court reporter did not take it down, or if it is not in writing filed of record, it does not exist for the appellate court.

If you try and the judge prevents you, the appeals court may afford you *de novo* review of all the legal arguments that were precluded. [*See United States v. Schray*, 383 F.3d 430, 431 n.1 (6th Cir. 2004) (where court does not give the defendant in opportunity to object, issue would receive full review on appeal).] *See also* Fed. R. Cr. P. 51 ("If a party does not have an opportunity to object to a ruling or order, the absence of an objection does not later prejudice that party.")]

[§§24:23-24:29 Reserved]

2. Objection Requirements

§24:30   Objection Must State the Basis

To preserve legal issues, the objection either must specify its legal basis or the basis must be apparent from the context, and the basis you specify must be correct. [*See, e.g., United States v. O'Brien*, 435 F.3d 36, 39-40 (1st Cir. 2006) (objection to prosecution cross-examination of defendant on his failure to tell police that his brother, not he, committed crime on the grounds that "he was under no obligation to speak to the FBI" insufficient to preserve Due Process bar to impeaching defendant with post-*Miranda* silence under *Doyle v. Ohio,* 426 U.S. 610 (1976)); *United States v. Musa*, 45 F.3d 922, 924 n.5 (5th Cir. 1995) (argument in motion to suppress that search of car was illegal because there was no consent and inventory rules not followed failed to preserve claim that there was no probable cause to stop and search car); *Burgess v. Premier Corp.*, 727 F.2d 826, 835 (9th Cir. 1984) (objection to question as "improper" did not preserve hearsay issue); *but see United States v. Shannon*, 766 F.3d 346, 355-56 (3d Cir. 2014)(reference to "Fifth Amendment" in objection during defendant's cross-examination sufficient to preserve issue of impeaching use of defendant's silence when it was clear from the record that the court and prosecution knew the basis for the objection).] If you are uncertain whether you sufficiently stated the basis for a meaningful objection, at the first opportunity, raise the issue anew to reiterate and explain. The trial judge may acknowledge he understood it, thereby proving that the basis was apparent from the context and the issue preserved. [*See, e.g., Shannon, supra* (relying in part on discussion during later sidebar to conclude that the trial court knew the objection's basis).]

This rule becomes most important if you later seek federal habeas corpus review of the conviction. The federal habeas court will review only federal issues, and to preserve a federal issue, you must alert the state court to the federal nature of the claim. [*See Duncan v. Henry,* 513 U.S. 364, 365-66 (1995) (argument that erroneously admitted testimony was "irrelevant and inflammatory," leading to a "miscarriage of justice" did not preserve federal due process claim).]

Gone are the days, if they ever existed, when defense counsel can surreptitiously plant issues for appeal "A fleeting reference or vague allusion to an issue will not suffice to preserve it for appeal." [*United States v. Dupree*, 617 F.3d 724, 728 (3d Cir. 2010).] You must articulate your theory of objection or suppression, and when citing a case, particularly in papers, explain for which of the many propositions encompassed by the decision you cite it.

Raising an issue in general fashion will not work to avoid waiver on appeal, at least in the context of pretrial suppression motions. You must articulate a legal rule or standard and specify the facts on which it depends. For example, a motion to suppress for "lack of probable cause" will not preserve any specific suppression argument for appeal. Further, arguing one reason for that lack of probable cause, such as arresting officers' inability to discern that currency is counterfeit, does not preserve other arguments, such as a lack of probable cause to believe that the arrestee knew the currency was counterfeit. [*United States v. Joseph*, 730 F.3d 336 (3d Cir. 2013) (defining and explaining the difference between "issues" and "arguments").]

A different rule applies on those happy occasions when you prevailed in the trial court and defend its decision as the appellee. You may advocate affirmance for any reason supported by the record, whether argued below or not. [*Dupree*, 617 F.3d at 728 n.2.]

Especially where your client faces a lengthy sentence, or a death sentence, cite a federal constitutional basis for your objections and arguments. It can save his life decades after trial.

§24:31   Evidence Objections Must Include an Offer of Proof

Where the trial court excludes evidence, you must make an "offer of proof" describing what the evidence would have been unless its substance is apparent from the context and questions. [FRE 103.]

The offer should describe the nature and content of the evidence and its purpose and relevance to the case. [*See* Christopher B. Mueller & Laird C. Kirkpatrick, *Federal Evidence* §14 (2d ed. 2006).]

You also should explain the legal basis for its admissibility if not obvious, such as whether it falls within a particular hearsay exception and why.

§24:32   Objections to Jury Instructions

Objections to jury instructions may demand special caution. Do not assume that the court's rejection of your proposed charge preserves a claim of error in the charge as given. You must object specifically to the court's charge as inadequate. [*People v. Hoke,* 62 N.Y.2d 1022, 123-24, 468 N.E.2d 677, 479 N.Y.S.2d 495 (1984).]

The objection must be made before the jury retires to deliberate. [Fed. R. Crim. P. 30(d).]

§24:33   Plain Error

Some jurisdictions permit "plain error" review. With this approach, claims not preserved in the trial court can be raised on appeal, but the appellant bears a much heavier burden of showing that any error was "clear" or "obvious"; it affected the outcome of the trial court proceedings," and it "seriously affected the fairness, integrity or public reputation of judicial proceedings." [*United States v. Olano*, 507 U.S. 725, 733-36 (1993); Fed. R. Crim. P. 52(b).]

§24:34   Get a Ruling

Only adverse rulings are appealable–not compromises, and not suggestions to withdraw or re-phrase questions. During the heat of trial, you may choose to make such compromises and follow suggestions for many good reasons, such as to save what capital you have with the judge for more important issues, or perhaps you realize you can make your point or introduce your evidence in some alternative fashion.

Be aware, however, that unless the judge makes a clear adverse ruling, you have nothing to appeal. If the point is an important one you may wish to pursue on appeal, get the ruling. Judges frequently defer ruling on issues in the hope that the issue will work itself out or that the party simply will forget the matter. Make note of such pretermissions and pursue a final and definitive ruling.

[§§24:35-24:39 Reserved]

B.   Waiving Appeal

§24:40   Impeaching One's Own Witness

The Supreme Court has ruled that a party who first introduces in his case evidence to which he objected waives his right to appeal the court's definitive pre-trial ruling admitting the evidence over his objection. [*Ohler v. United States*, 529 U.S. 753 (2000).]

This ruling penalizes the trial tactic known as "drawing the sting" (i.e., impeaching one's own witness to minimize the effect of cross-examination on the same point).

The tactic remains legitimate, but know that if you admit impeaching or otherwise adverse evidence to which you objected, the objection is waived as an issue for appeal.

However, several state courts refuse to follow *Ohler*. [*See McGill v. DIA Airport Parking, LLC*, 395 P.3d 1153 (Col. Ct. App. 2016) (rejecting *Ohler* for the reasons stated in Justice Souter's dissent and as inconsistent with the truth-seeking purposes of the rules of evidence); *State v. Swanson*, 707 N.W. 2d 645, 654 (Minn. 2006) ("we hold that a defendant who testifies about his conviction on direct examination after denial of a motion in limine to exclude those convictions, has not forfeited the opportunity to appeal the admissibility of those convictions"); *Pineda v. State*, 120 Nev. 204, 209 & nn. 7-8, 88 P.3d 827, 831 & nn.7-8 (Nev. 2004) (refusing to follow *Ohler* and surveying split in state courts).]

§24:41   Guilty Pleas

In most jurisdictions, a guilty plea waives all but "jurisdictional" issues. Some jurisdictions permit "conditional" guilty pleas, in which the parties agree to preserve certain issues for appeal, for example, suppression issues litigated in a hearing. [*E.g.,* Fed. R. Crim. P. (a)(2).]

The rules typically require the prosecution's consent to a conditional guilty plea.

Prosecutors increasingly demand waivers of the right to appeal and even of the right to mount post-conviction collateral attacks as a condition of concessions in plea agreements. Most courts have upheld such waivers so long as they are knowing and voluntary. [*See, e.g., United States v. Khattak*, 273 F.3d 557, 563 (3d Cir. 2001); *People v. Hidalgo*, 91 N.Y.2d 733, 698 N.E.2d 46, 675 N.Y.S.2d 327 (1998) (unrestricted waiver includes right to appeal sentence even though sentence not specifically mentioned).] Recently, though, state ethical authorities have questioned the ethics of waivers that include the right to attack counsel's ineffective assistance; accordingly, the Department of Justice has instructed its prosecutors no longer to seek waivers of that issue. [*See* § 17:31, *supra.*]

The appeal waiver may be ignored in the "unusual circumstance of 'an error amounting to a miscarriage of justice.'" [*United States v. Castro*, 704 F.3d 125, 136 (3d Cir. 2013).] "Courts apply the 'miscarriage of justice' exception sparingly and without undue generosity . . . ." [*Id.*] The complete absence of proof on one element of the offense warrants application of that exception, although mere insufficiency of the evidence does not. [*Castro,* 704 F.3d at 138 (a miscarriage of justice occurs only where the record "is devoid of evidence pointing to guilt–a stricter than usual standard").]

If a defendant takes an appeal in breach of a plea agreement's appeal-waiver provisions, the appellate court may vacate the sentence and free the prosecution to seek a greater sentence on remand. [*United States v. Erwin*, 765 F.3d 219 (3d Cir. 2014) (on resentencing, the prosecution would be relieved of its obligation under the plea agreement to file a motion for a downward departure); *see* §24:05, *supra.*]

PRACTICE TIP:

Whether to agree to an appeal waiver depends on your options: trial or an open plea. Where the prosecutor offers significant concessions, such as the elimination of a mandatory minimum sentence, the waiver is usually worthwhile. [*See* Chapter 17, Plea Bargaining.]

[§§24:42-24:49 Reserved]

IV.   THE APPELLATE COURT BRIEF AND ARGUMENT

A.   The Record and Brief

§24:50   Grounds For Appeal

Pick your two or three best issues for appeal, and no more. The multiplication of issues suggests that no single one merits relief.

As Judge Aldisert of the Third Circuit Court of Appeals has stated:

> When I read an appellant's brief that contains ten or twelve points, a presumption arises that there is no merit to any of them. I do not say that it is an irrebutable presumption, but it is a presumption that reduces the effectiveness of appellate advocacy.

[*United States v. Hart,* 693 F.2d 286, 287 n. 1 (3d Cir. 1982).]

However, remember that any issue you fail to raise on appeal is lost forever. Collateral review rules generally prohibit raising issues that could have been raised on direct appeal, but were not.

Exceptions to this advice lie in death penalty and life sentence cases. The weighty stakes in those cases require that your raise anything with arguable merit. Your client has a decade or more of appeals and state and federal collateral attacks ahead of him. It is difficult to predict which claims will prevail, so preserve as many as possible.

Insufficiency-of-the-evidence arguments rarely prevail, but you might have reason to raise one even where your chances of success are remote. Your insufficiency argument may foreclose harmless error claims on other errors, and the suggestion that your client indeed might have been innocent also might render the appellate court more receptive to ordering a new trial on other issues. Finally, most claims just result in remands for retrial; an insufficiency win is equivalent to an acquittal and precludes retrial on double jeopardy grounds. [*Burks v. United States,* 437 U.S. 1, 18 (1978).]

PRACTICE TIP:

Do not discuss errors for which you do not request relief. The appeals court has no interest in hearing your gripes about the trial court's conduct unless they bear directly on a claim on appeal. Likewise, errors that had no arguable effect on the verdict, such as most objections to cumulative evidence or the form of questions, should be discarded on appeal.

§24:51   The Record on Appeal and the Appendix

Begin to assemble the record on appeal immediately after filing your notice of appeal.

Most appellate courts require the appellant to ensure that the record is complete. This involves ordering transcripts of all hearings and conferences at which issues pertinent to your appeal may have been discussed and seeing that all motions and supporting legal memoranda have been docketed.

Most appellate courts do not review the entire record. Rather, the appellant assembles an appendix of those portions needed for the appeal. Appellate rules will specify certain documents that must be included (*e.g.,* the indictment, the clerk's docket sheet, the judgment and commitment order, and any order from which you appeal). Aside from those, you have discretion what to include and what not to.

Confer with the prosecution because omitting an important portion of the record which the prosecutor adds in a supplementary appendix harms your credibility and focuses the appellate court's attention on the omitted material. Failure to agree might also compel you to serve a statement of issues on the prosecution. [*See* Fed. R. App. P. 30.]

Include any written motions and memoranda of law filed in the trial court on your appellate issues. These will help demonstrate that you preserved the issues properly in the lower court.

If the record needs to be supplemented or corrected, first seek the prosecution's stipulation to the correction. Often, the prosecutor will agree because he or she will need to make use of the same materials. If that fails, file a motion with the trial court. As a last resort, file a motion with the appellate court. [*See* Fed. R. App. P. 10(e); Pa. R. App. P. 1926.]

Once you have assembled an appendix, cite to the appendix to support every factual assertion in your brief. Add a parenthetical after the citation if you need to identify the document or testimony which you cite (*e.g.,* A0001 (testimony of Officer Farrell); A0027 (indictment)).

Form:
•   **Form 24-7** Certified Record Order

§24:52   Standards of Review

Lawyers sometimes lend only perfunctory attention to arguing the standard of review on appeal. This is unwise, for the standard of review often dictates the result.

The three principle standards of review, in order of most deferential to the trial court to the least, are:
•   Clearly erroneous review of factual findings.
•   Abuse of discretion review, which often applies to evidentiary rulings.
•   De novo or plenary review.

If the issue seems to be a factual one or a matter within the trial court's discretion, try to re-phrase it as one that turns on the definition of a legal rule or the application of the rule to the facts. Fact-finding deserves deference, but the application of the law to facts often is a matter for plenary appellate review:

Where ... the relevant legal principle can be given meaning only through its application to the particular circumstances of a case, the Court has been reluctant to give the trier of fact's conclusions presumptive force and, in so doing, strip a federal appellate court of its primary function as an expositor of law.

[*Miller v. Fenton,* 474 U.S. 104, 114 (1985) (even on federal habeas, reviewing court should not defer to trial court determination that a confession was "voluntary"). *See also Thompson v. Keohane,* 516 U.S. 99 (1995) (reviewing fact/law distinction and standards of review and ruling that whether a suspect is in custody for *Miranda* purposes merits de novo review).]

Try to shoehorn your issue into this category of "mixed questions of fact and law." The appellate court will defer to the trial court's findings as to the underlying facts. Your argument is that the proper conclusion from those facts is a matter for de novo review. [*See generally* Steven A. Childress, *Standards of Review Primer: Federal Civil Appeals,* 229 F.R.D. 267, 275-76 (2005) (explaining various approaches to mixed question standard of review); *United States v. Mallory,* 765 F.3d 373, 383 (3d Cir. 2014) (whether exigent circumstances justified a warrantless search is a mixed question, and the court of appeals "will review the district court's findings of fact for clear error, but will review its conclusion that those facts establish a legal exigency de novo.")]

Likewise, courts routinely categorize evidentiary rulings as reversible only for an abuse of discretion, but "when ... a ruling on the admissibility of evidence ... turns on an interpretation of a Federal Rule of Evidence, ... review is plenary." [*Barker v. Deere & Co.,* 60 F.3d 158, 161 (3d Cir. 1995).]

§24:53   The Form of the Brief

Appellate courts strictly enforce their requirements on length and form of a brief. Review the rules carefully because each court has its own idiosyncrasies.

Do not try to evade the rules, such as by consigning arguments to footnotes or using a smaller typeface. Courts will reject your brief for errors in form.

If you need more pages, file a motion asking for leave to exceed the page limit. However, be aware that courts demand a compelling reason to grant such a motion.

The usual rules of good legal writing apply, with emphasis on two points:

Your audience is a very sophisticated one.

The judges know the law, and often you will be discussing decisions authored by the very judges reading your brief.

Focus on the cases from your jurisdiction, and, if possible, your panel. Be certain to describe the cases accurately, and if unfavorable, distinguish them respectfully rather than ignore or denigrate them.

Your audience is very busy.

Appellate judges face a torrent of poorly written drivel every day. Make your brief as short as possible and to the point. Avoid string-cites of cases; focus on the few important ones.

Appellate judges are not jurors, and they abhor the written equivalent of a screaming summation. Avoid italics, boldfaced text, exclamation points, too many adjectives, and *ad hominem* attacks on the attorneys, witnesses or especially the trial judge. Use simple declarative sentences, bereft of legalese.

Tell a story in the statement of facts. The facts and the narrative (not an adjectival characterization of the facts) should suggest that the officers' or the prosecutor's or the lower courts' actions or rulings wronged your client. A precise but compelling statement of the facts motivates the court to rule your way and starts the court to thinking that it can fashion a ruling in your favor tied to the peculiar facts of your case, not to some sweeping principle of law that may wreak havoc in other cases. [*See* §24:01.]

Form:
*   **Form 24-8** Sample Appellant Brief

§24:54   Extensions of Time

Appellate courts are hostile to requests for an extension of time to file a brief. However, if you need an extension to file a good brief, ask.

File your request as far as possible in advance of the brief's due date. Seek your opponent's consent. Explain with specificity the reasons, the most acceptable being the complexity of the case or the demands of other cases.

When seeking an extension for complexity, briefly describe the length of the record, the number, complexity or novelty of the issues; or whatever else makes the appeal complex.

If your reason is the press of other cases, give their captions, case number and court. Appellate courts are more likely to defer to the demands of other cases in their court.

Check with other practitioners or even the appellate court clerk to determine the length of extension the court will entertain and whether the court grants more than one extension. Most appellate courts do not.

If at the last minute, you realize your brief will be late by a day or two, you have three options:
- You can call the Clerk's office to ask for a brief extension orally. Most will not give it, but they may advise you on what to do.
- You can risk filing the brief late along with a motion to file it out of time, explaining the reasons.
- You might file a draft of the brief along with a motion to refile the final version out of time.

Seek the advice of either the clerk or a practitioner or former clerk in that particular court as to which course is preferred.

Form:
- **Form 24–2** Motion for an Extension of Time

[§§24:55-24:59 Reserved]

B.   Oral Argument

§24:60   Suggest a Narrow Ruling

Oral argument is your last and best chance to convince the court. Think of your task as assisting the court to fashion a ruling in your favor:
- What precedents must they distinguish?
- Which facts might trouble or persuade them?
- What jurisprudential trends are furthered and which obstructed by a ruling your way?
- How can the court phrase a ruling so that it guides courts in the future without causing too many problems?
- How and why did this error matter to your case–why isn't it harmless?

In most cases, this means suggesting a ruling that is as narrow as possible, because appellate courts are not eager to create rules that help criminal defendants win cases.

You do not want to rehash your written argument. Think of new angles on your argument or arguments you wished you had included but did not.

Nonetheless, you must know your brief and record because many judges will ask to rehash even that which you believe your papers thoroughly covered. Prepare and practice brief summaries of your main points and of the leading precedents.

§24:61   Ten Practical Tips

Over 65 years ago, an Olympian of the appellate bar, John W. Davis, gave a lecture entitled, "The Argument of an Appeal," which listed a Decalogue for appellate argument. Much in the list endures as sound advice:

1. *Change places, in your imagination of course, with the Court.*
   Consider the predilections of your particular panel, but also imagine what they would want to know and how they can reach a decision in your favor.

2. *State first the nature of the case and briefly its prior history.*

3. *State the facts.*
   Even on an appeal, the facts drive the outcome. Obey three rules in stating facts:
   - Chronology.
   - Candor (admit the good with the bad).
   - Clarity (meaning not only simplicity, but a statement of facts "so framed and delivered as to show forth the essential merits, in just and in right, of your client's cause.")

4. *State next the applicable rules of law on which you rely.*

5. *Always "go for the jugular vein."*
   In other words, focus.

6. *Rejoice when the court asks questions.*
   Answer the question. A question is almost always good news. It tells you what is on the judge's mind and what concerns you must allay to obtain a favorable ruling. Or the question might represent the judge's efforts to make points with or against other judges through your answer. Answering questions adequately should be a higher priority than covering the points in your outline. However, try to anticipate questions and how you will transition your answer back to the points you want to emphasize.
   Be ready for the easy questions. Judges sometimes throw you easy questions in the hope that you will provide a clear and definite answer that they can use to persuade their reluctant colleagues that what appears to be an obstacle to a decision in your favor really is nonexistent. Such a question might be one that calls for a citation to a leading decisive case.

7. *Read sparingly and only from necessity.*

8. *Avoid personalities.*

9. *Know your record from cover to cover.*

10. *Sit down.*
   When you have made your point, stop.
   On the other hand, a particularly engaged panel will keep you past your allotted time. If they are still asking, keep answering. Then ask for a chance to conclude, notwithstanding the red light.

§24:62   Research the Judges

Scout your judges and panel before argument.
Many intermediate appellate courts employ "panels." The full court does not hear a case, but only three or five members. The court usually will notify you of the panel's composition a month or two before argument.
Read what the judges have written on issues similar to yours, or just on criminal cases, especially in the last year.
If you can, attend an argument involving the panel members. At the least, ask practitioners about how prepared they are, how aggressive their questioning is, and what their idiosyncrasies are.

§24:63   The Active Bench

Some appellate courts pride themselves on their preparation and quickly will interrupt your prepared remarks to interrogate you. Investigate whether your court is considered an "active bench" and prepare accordingly. While thorough knowledge of the record, the briefs and the pertinent precedents should characterize preparation for any argument, consider the following steps for an active bench:
- Memorize a concise summary of your main argument and deliver it at the start of your argument so that you can complete it before the questions start and return to it if interrupted.
- Active judges, especially those hostile to your position, frequently attempt to elicit concessions that undermine your position. Spend time before the argument considering where possible concessions lead and ways to hedge any concessions so that they do not prove fatal.
- Impatient judges might interrupt your lengthy answers to their colleagues' questions; therefore, you must practice formulating pithy answers that lead with your conclusion and add explanation if time permits.
- To transition back to your argument after answering lengthy questions, reduce your argument to several points that you outline on index cards. Shuffle them and work on transitioning from one to the next in any order.

[*See* Timothy S. Bishop, "Oral Arguments in the Roberts Court," 35 *Litigation* 6 (Winter 2009).]

[§§24:64-24:69 Reserved]

C. Harmless Error

§24:70   Address Harmless Error in the Reply Brief

Even if you win on the law, the appellate court may deny you relief if the error was harmless. [*See generally* Wayne R. LaFave, Jerold H. Israel, Nancy J. King, *5 Criminal Procedure* §27.6 (2007) (a description of harmless error review).]

Generally, harmless error is not an issue you want to address explicitly in your opening brief. You should indicate that the error was substantial (*i.e.*, that the excluded or admitted evidence made a difference or the improper ruling affected the decisive issues in the case). Save a direct discussion of harmless error for your reply brief, and discuss it if the prosecution raises harmless error in its responsive brief.

There are three arguments to make regarding harmless error:
- It was not harmless: the point at issue decided the case. [§24:71.]
- Even if it was not outcome-determinative, the error was structural and not subject to harmless error review. [§24:72.]
- The cumulative effect of several errors mandates reversal. [§24:73.]

Prosecutors frequently cite a split verdict – acquittal on some counts – as evidence that error was harmless. "Whether a split verdict supports or undermines a finding of harmless error depends on the circumstances of the case." [*United States v. Franz*, 772 F.3d 134, 153 (3d Cir. 2014) (finding error harmless where jury acquitted on those counts as to which the trial court told it to disregard the improper evidence, but surveying other opinions that rejected a split verdict as showing harmlessness).]

Form:
- **Form 24-9** Excerpts From Reply Brief on Harmless Error

§24:71   The Point at Issue Decided the Case

Most harmless error arguments require you to review the evidence thoroughly and discuss how thin it was, However, you also can point to external indications that the case was close:
- Lengthy deliberations.
- A hung jury the first time the case was tried.
- Acquittal on the majority of counts.
- A co-defendant's acquittal.

However, partial acquittals cut both ways. If your argument is that the evidence was prejudicial, the appellate court is likely to cite the jury's ability to parse a verdict count by count as evidence that the prejudicial evidence did not overwhelm the jury's ability for sober and careful consideration of the evidence.

§24:72   The Error Was Structural

A structural error is one that undermines the integrity of the process to the point that no harmless error review is appropriate. [*E.g.*, *United States v. Gonzalez-Lopez*, 548 U.S. 140, 149 (2006) (erroneous deprivation of counsel of choice is structural error and harmless error review is not appropriate; lists as other structural errors, the denial of the right of self-representation, the denial of the right to public trial, and the denial of the right to trial by jury by the giving of a defective reasonable-doubt instruction). *See also Vasquez v. Hillery*, 474 U.S. 254, 260-64 (1986) (racial discrimination in selection of grand jury is structural error).]

This category is very narrow, and courts are wary of expanding it. [*See generally Weaver v. Massachusetts*, — U.S. —, 2017 WL 2674153 (U.S. June 22, 2017) (reviews the structural error doctrine and holds that while denial of the right to a public trial automatically requires reversal on direct review as structural error, prejudice must be shown if the claim is raised as part of an ineffective assistance of counsel claims on collateral review).] However, if you can characterize the error in your case as structural you can avoid harmless error review.

§24:73   The Cumulative Effect of Several Errors

A cumulative-error analysis aggregates all the errors that individually have been found to be harmless, and analyzes whether their cumulative effect is such that they can no longer be determined to be harmless. [*United States v. Rivera*, 900 F.2d 1462, 1470 (10th Cir. 1990) (en banc).]

However, non-erroneous adverse rulings do not count. [*Rivera*, 900 F. 2d at 1471. *See* generally *Annual Review of Criminal Procedure, "Appeals"*, 34 Geo. L. J. 784, 822-238 & N. 2555 (2005) (collecting cases that have adopted the cumulative error analysis).]

[§§24:74-24:79 Reserved]

V.   DISCRETIONARY APPEALS

§24:80   Second Level Appeal Is Discretionary

A criminal defendant's first level appeal, to the intermediate appellate court, is of right.

However, whether the jurisdiction's highest court will review the intermediate court's decision is usually discretionary. You must petition the highest court for allowance of appeal, for allocatur, or for certiorari to accept the appeal.

In deciding whether to grant your petition and hear the appeal, the Supreme Court will consider the importance of the issue to the legal system, but the decision will depend primarily on whether the decision below reflects a split among the lower level courts or deviates from Supreme Court precedent. [*See* U.S. Sup. Ct. R. 10; Pa. Sup. Ct. IOP 5.]

Here the standard of review reasserts its importance. The Supreme Court is unlikely to accept issues that fell within the trial court's discretion or that amount to factual findings.

§24:81   Continued Representation

Appellate counsel generally must continue the representation and file the petition for discretionary review.

However, counsel can refuse to file a petition for discretionary review, despite the client's wishes, where the petition would be frivolous. [*See Austin v. United States*, 513 U.S. 5 (1994) (even court-appointed counsel can be sanctioned for filing frivolous certiorari petition); 3d Cir. LAR 109.2(b) (appointed counsel is obligated to file certiorari petition unless he files motion to withdraw on grounds that it is frivolous).]

VI.   REMANDS

§24:90   Resentencing

When a habitual or repeat offender sentence is reversed on appeal for insufficient evidence, on remand for resentencing the prosecution may again attempt to prove that the defendant meets the criteria for such sentencing without violating Double Jeopardy or Due Process rules against vindictive sentencing. [*State v. Collins*, 985 So.2d 985 (Fl. 2008).]

If a conviction is set aside on appeal, and the defendant convicted again on remand and resentenced, the Double Jeopardy Clause requires that he receive credit for time served on the original conviction. [*Jones v. Thomas*, 491 U.S. 376, 378, 382 (1989).]

The Due Process Clause sets limits, albeit flexible, on a trial court's authority to increase a defendant's sentence after a successful appeal. "Due process of law, then, requires that vindictiveness against a defendant for having successfully attacked his first conviction must play no part in the sentence he receives after a new trial. In order to assure the absence of such a motivation, we have concluded that whenever a judge imposes a more severe sentence upon a defendant after a new trial, the reasons for him doing so must affirmatively appear. . . . Otherwise, a presumption arises that a greater sentence has been imposed for a vindictive purpose — a presumption that must be rebutted by "'objective information . . . justifying the increased sentence." [*Alabama v. Smith*, 490 U.S. 794, 798-99 (1989)(permitting greater sentence to be imposed following trial after successful appeal of a guilty plea)(citing *North Carolina v. Pearce*, 395 U.S. 711, 725-26 (1969), and *Texas v. McCullough*, 475 U.S. 134, 142 (1986)).] Generally, the justification must be newly discovered evidence or the defendant's conduct since the first conviction, but it can be new evidence about events that pre-dated the first trial. [*See generally* Sentencing, Annual Review of Criminal Procedure, 43 Geo. L.J. Ann. Rev. Crim. Proc. 745, 812-814 & nn. 2233-2235 (2014).]

An appeal may result in the vacatur of certain counts of conviction but survival of others. On remand for resentencing, the trial court may increase the sentence on the surviving counts to reconstruct the "sentencing package" it originally imposed. [*United States v. Fowler*, 749 F.3d 1010 (11th Cir. 2014); *see also Pepper v. United States*, 131 S.Ct. 1229,

1251 (2011) (explaining that because "[a] criminal sentence is a package of sanctions that the district court utilizes to effectuate its sentencing intent," which "may be undermined by altering one portion of the calculus, an appellate court when reversing one part of a defendant's sentence may vacate the entire sentence so that, on remand, the trial court can reconfigure the sentencing plan to satisfy the sentencing factors in 18 U.S.C. § 3553(a)").]

VII. FORMS

Form 24-1   Notice of Appeal

IN THE UNITED STATES DISTRICT COURT
FOR THE _____ DISTRICT OF _____

UNITED STATES OF AMERICA   )
                        v.   )   CRIMINAL NO. 00-0000
JF   )   NOTICE OF APPEAL

NOTICE OF APPEAL

Notice is hereby given that Defendant JF hereby appeals to the United States Court of Appeals for the Third Circuit from the judgment entered in this action on the _____ day of _____, and amended on the _____ day of _____.

Respectfully submitted,

_____
Thomas J. Farrell
Attorney for Defendant, JF

Pa. I.D. #00000
Address
Phone

Form 24-2   Motion for an Extension of Time

IN THE UNITED STATES COURT OF APPEALS
FOR THE THIRD CIRCUIT

UNITED STATES OF AMERICA
v.
JF

Appeal From Judgment of Conviction Entered by the United States District Court for the Western District of Pennsylvania (Conti, J.) at Criminal No. 00-000-1

MOTION FOR AN EXTENSION OF TIME TO FILE APPELLANT'S BRIEF

AND NOW comes Appellant, JF, by his attorney, Thomas J. Farrell, and respectfully requests an extension of time to file Appellant's brief.

As the court is aware, appellant's brief is due on _____, 20__. For the reasons set forth below, appellant requests an extension of time 32 days, until _____, 20__, to submit its brief.

1. Undersigned counsel is also counsel of record on *United States versus Smith*, No. 00-0000 (Third Circuit). The brief in *Smith* is due on _____, 20__. Undersigned counsel is also counsel record in *United States versus Doe*, No. 06–0001 (Third Circuit). The brief in *Doe* is due on _____, 20__.

2.   Accordingly, in order to allow the appellant sufficient time within which to provide a full and thorough brief, appellate request that the court grant an extension of time until _____, 20__, to file the appellant's brief.

3.   The appellant does not seek this extension of time for purposes of delay.

Opposing counsel has consented to appellant's request for an extension of time in this case.

WHEREFORE, Pursuant to Third Circuit Local Rule 31, counsel for appellant respectfully Request an Extension from _____, 20__, to _____, 20__, by which to file its brief.

Respectfully submitted,

_____

Thomas J. Farrell
Counsel for Appellant

Form 24-3   **Case Opening Scheduling Notice**

UNITED STATES COURT OF APPEALS
FOR THE FIRST CIRCUIT

No. 07-1398

UNITED STATES

Appellee

v.

MARCOS MORELL-CORRADA

Defendant - Appellant

CASE OPENING SCHEDULING NOTICE

Issued: 3/6/07

The above-captioned appeal was docketed in this court today pursuant to Rule 12 of the Federal Rules of Appellate Procedure. This case number and caption should be placed on all papers subsequently submitted to this court, unless the court orders that the caption be amended.

Appellant must complete and return the following documents to the clerk's office within fourteen days of the date of this notice:

*   **Appearance Form**(Enclosed)
*   **Docketing Statement**(Enclosed)
*   **Transcript Report/Order Form**(The district court should have provided you with a Transcript Report/Order Form upon filing a notice of appeal. Please carefully read the instructions for completing and filing the form.)

Additional copies of these forms are available on the court's website, **www.cal.uscourts.gov** , or at the clerk's office. Failure to comply with the deadline set by the court may result in dismissal of the appeal for lack of diligent prosecution. See 1st Cir. R. 3.0, 10.0, 45.0.

If less than the entire transcript is ordered, appellant must file and serve on all other parties a statement of the issues in accordance with Fed. R. App. P. 10(a)(3)(A). In addition, if the parties are unable to agree as to the contents of the joint appendix, then appellant must file and serve a statement of the issues and designation of the contents of the appendix. Fed. R. App. P. 30(b)(1); 1st Cir. R. 30.0(b). Upon confirmation by the circuit clerk that the record is complete either because no hearing was held, no transcript is necessary, or the transcript is on file, the clerk's office will set the briefing schedule and forward a scheduling notice to the parties.

Within 7 days of filing the notice of appeal, appellant must pay the filing fee* to the district clerk. An indigent appellant who seeks to appeal in forma pauperis must file a motion and financial affidavit in the district court in compliance with Fed. R. App. P. 24. Unless this court is provided with notice of paying the filing fee to the clerk of the district court or filing a motion seeking in forma pauperis status on or before fourteen days of the date of this notice, this appeal may be dismissed for lack of prosecution. 1st Cir. R. 3.0(b).

The enclosed appearance form should be completed and returned immediately by at least one attorney for each side and by any attorney that wishes to file pleadings in this court. 1st Cir. R. 12.0(a) and 46.0(a)(2). An attorney who has not been admitted to the Bar of the First Circuit Court of Appeals must submit an application and fee for admission with the appearance form.

Dockets, opinions, rules, forms, attorney admission applications, and the court calendar can be obtained from the court's website, **www.ca1.uscourts.gov**.

If you wish to inquire about your case by telephone, please contact the case manager at the direct extension listed below.

                              Richard Cushing Donovan, Clerk

cc: Mary K. Butler, Esq.
            Matthew C. Solomon, Esq.
            Francisco Rebello-Casalduc, Esq.
            Octavio M. Rivera Bujosa, Esq.
            Rafael F. Castro-Lang, Esq.
            PHV Thomas J. Farrell, Esq.
            Steven C. Lausell, Esq.
            Luis A. Oliver, Esq.
            Efrem M. Grail, Esq.
            Humberto Guzman-Rodriguez, Esq.
            Maria H. Sandoval, Esq.
            Juan R. Acevedo Cruz, Esq.

UNITED STATES COURT OF APPEALS
FOR THE FIRST CIRCUIT

_____

APPEARANCE FORM
(Please type or print all answers)

Case No.:

Case Name (short):

FAILURE TO FILL OUT COMPLETELY MAY RESULT IN THE REJECTION OF THIS FORM AND COULD AFFECT THE PROGRESS OF THE APPEAL

THE CLERK WILL ENTER MY APPEARANCE AS COUNSEL ON BEHALF OF:

_____ as the

(Specify name of person or entity represented.)

If you represent a litigant who was a party below, but who is not a party on appeal, do not designate yourself as counsel for the appellant or the appellee.

[ ] appellant(s)   [ ] appellee(s)   [ ] amicus curiae

[ ] petitioner(s)   [ ] respondent(s)   [ ] intervenor(s)

                           [ ] not a party on appeal

_____

(Signature)

Name & Address:

_____

_____

_____

_____

Telephone:_____   **Court of Appeals Bar Number:**_____

Fax: _____   E-Mail: _____

Has this case or any related case previously been on appeal?

Yes _____   Court of Appeals No. _____

No _____

[ ]   IF YOU WILL NOT BE PARTICIPATING IN THIS CASE, PLEASE CHECK HERE
AND RETURN, AND GIVE US THE NAME AND ADDRESS OF ANOTHER
ATTORNEY, IF ANY, WHO WILL PROVIDE APPELLATE REPRESENTATION.

_____

_____

NOTE: Must be signed by an Attorney admitted to practice before the United States
Court of Appeals for the First Circuit pursuant to 1st Cir. R. 46.0(a)(2). If you are
applying for admission, please return this appearance form **with** your application for
admission, including the admission fee.

If your name has changed since you were admitted to the First Circuit Bar PLEASE show
the name under which you were admitted.

**COUNSEL MUST COMPLETE & RETURN THIS APPEARANCE FORM
IN ORDER TO FILE PLEADINGS IN THIS COURT**

UNITED STATES COURT OF APPEALS
FOR THE FIRST CIRCUIT
(617-748-9057)

NOTICE TO APPLICANT FOR ADMISSION

An attorney who is qualified for admission must file an application with the Clerk of the United States Court of Appeals. Admission may be accomplished in person any morning that the Court is in session. The applicant must appear at the office of the clerk by 8:30 a.m. on the day he or she plans to be admitted, but the Court does not sit every day. Please check for the actual dates of session.

Admission may be accomplished by mail if the attorney represents a party to an appeal presently before the Court. For admission by mail, the application form must note the name and docket number of the case, and attach the admission fee. The applicant should mail the application to the United States Court of Appeals, United States Courthouse, 1 Courthouse Way, Suite 2500, Boston, MA 02210.

The payment of the attorney admission fee - - including both the $150.00 attorney admission fee due under 28 U.S.C. § 1913 and the $50.00 local fee due under 1st Cir. R. 46.0(a)(1) - - should be made with one check, in the amount of $200.00, made payable to "Clerk, United States Court." The Clerk's Office does not accept cash or credit card payments. The admission fee is waived if the attorney appears as (1) counsel for the United States or an officer or agency thereof, or (2) counsel appointed under the Criminal Justice Act in an appeal presently before the Court. However, if you are counsel for the U.S. or agency thereof, or are appointed under the Criminal Justice Act and would like a certificate of admission there is a fifteen ($15.00) dollar charge.

Once admitted, the attorney will be assigned a First Circuit Court of Appeals Bar Number which must be used on any pleading filed with the Court.

RICHARD CUSHING DONOVAN, CLERK
United States Court of Appeals
for the First Circuit

UNITED STATES COURT OF APPEALS
FOR THE FIRST CIRCUIT
(617-748-9057)

APPLICATION FOR ADMISSION TO PRACTICE
(Please type or print all answers)

Name ....
                 Last , First, Middle

Firm or Business Name ....

Firm Address...

City...State...Zip............................

Telephone ....

Fax.. E-mail ....

Name one court before which you have been admitted to practice, and in which you are in good standing, and give the date of your admission to the court.

Name of Court...Date of Admission...

Have you ever changed your name or been known by any name other than that appearing on the application? If so, please elaborate.

....

Have you ever been disbarred or suspended from practice before any court, department, bureau, or commission of the United States or of any state, or have you ever received any reprimand from any such court, department, bureau, or commission pertaining to your conduct or fitness as a member of the bar? If so, attach a separate statement.

If you are filing an appearance subject to admission, please indicate the Appeals Court docket number and name of the case in which you wish to appear.

Case No................................... Case Caption..

CERTIFICATION AND OATH

I certify that the foregoing answers are true, and further,

I do solemnly swear (or affirm) that I will conduct myself as an attorney and counselor of this court, uprightly and according to law; and that I will support the Constitution of the United States.

....
     (Date)   (Signature of Applicant)

Counsel are referred to Fed.R.App.P. 12(b) and 1st Cir. R. 12.0

Rev.4/02

OFFICE OF THE CLERK
UNITED STATES COURT OF APPEALS
FOR THE FIRST CIRCUIT

RICHARD CUSHING DONOVAN
CLERK

JOHN JOSEPH MOAKLEY
UNITED STATES COURTHOUSE
1 COURTHOUSE WAY, SUITE 2500
BOSTON, MA 02210
(617) 748-9057

Transcript Notice

The Judicial Council of the First Circuit requires court reporters to file transcripts within 60 days or suffer a 10% discount penalty. If the transcript is not filed within 90 days, a 20% discount is applicable. See Judicial Council Order dated 12/15/05, available on the First Circuit website, <www.ca1.uscourts.gov>, on the Forms & Notices page, under Transcript Information.

It is the court reporter's obligation to take a fee reduction if one is applicable. This court will issue a Fee Reduction Notice, copied to counsel, if it appears that the 60-day period has expired without the filing of the transcript and we have received no certification from the court reporter that a fee reduction was taken. Although this court will continue to monitor the filing of transcripts, no further Fee Reduction Notice will typically issue.

The discount policy is mandatory. The grant of a court reporter's request for an extension of time does not waive the mandatory fee reduction. Rather, to obtain a waiver of the discount the court reporter must file a separate motion. Absent a waiver of the fee reduction granted by the clerk, the court reporter is obligated to take the fee reduction.

Form 24-4   **Calendaring Notice**

UNITED STATES COURT OF APPEALS
FOR THE FIRST CIRCUIT

NOTICE TO COUNSEL AND *PRO SE* LITIGANTS

Since this case will be governed by the Federal Rules of Appellate Procedure and the First Circuit Local Rules, you should familiarize yourself with both sets of rules. Your attention is called specifically to the requirements listed below.

TRANSCRIPT REPORT/ORDER FORM: Appellant must *immediately* order any necessary transcript from the court reporter, using the form specified in 1st Cir. R. 10.0(b). Within 14 days after the appeal is docketed, appellant must file a copy of the transcript report/order form with the circuit clerk.

TIMELINESS: A brief is timely if it is mailed by First-Class mail, hand-delivered to the clerk, or given to a commercial carrier for three day delivery on the due date set in the schedule or order. All other papers must be received by the clerk's office within the time fixed for filing. Fed. R. App. P. 25(a)(2).

SEALED MATERIAL: To avoid the need to seal the entire brief or appendix, counsel shall place sealed or confidential material in a separate, sealed volume of the brief or appendix. 1st Cir. R. 11.0.

REFERENCES TO THE RECORD REQUIRED IN BRIEFS: To enable the court to verify the documentary bases of the parties' arguments, factual assertions must be supported by accurate references to the appendix or to the record. Counsel should ensure that transcripts cited in the briefs have been filed and made a part of the record on appeal. The appellant is responsible for preparing the appendix.

MOTIONS TO ENLARGE FILING DATES OR LENGTH OF BRIEFS: Motions for extensions of time to file briefs or to file briefs in excess of applicable length limitations are discouraged. Any such request must be made by a motion filed well in advance of the date the brief is due and must set forth the additional time or length requested and detailed reasons for the request.

CERTIFICATE OF SERVICE: The Court will not consider any motion, brief, or document that has not been served on all parties. Therefore, all documents submitted for filing must contain a statement, preferably attached to the document's last page, indicating: the date of service; the manner of service and the names and addresses of the persons served. Fed. R. App. P. 25.

COMPUTER GENERATED DISK: A represented party must submit one copy of its brief, petition for rehearing, and any paper exceeding 10 pages in length on a 3 1/2" disk, or Windows-based CD or DVD, in WordPerfect for Windows, 5.1 or greater. 1st Cir. R. 32.0.

CORPORATE DISCLOSURE STATEMENT: Counsel representing corporations in proceedings before the Court must include a corporate disclosure statement in the first document filed with the Court, and **again** in front of the table of contents in a party's principal brief. Fed. R. App. P. 26.1.

UNITED STATES COURT OF APPEALS
FOR THE FIRST CIRCUIT

No. 07-1205

UNITED STATES

Appellee

v.

RENE VAZQUEZ-BOTET

Defendant - Appellant

Calendaring Notice
Entered: 1/22/08

This case is presently scheduled to be called for oral
argument <u>Wednesday, March 5, 2008 at 9:30 a.m. in Old San Juan, PR.</u>

By no later than <u>February 8, 2008</u> counsel for each
party should advise this office, **by completing and returning the
enclosed designation form,** of the name of the person who will be
presenting oral argument. If counsel presenting oral argument
has not yet entered an appearance, counsel must file an appearance
and motion in accordance with 1st Cir. R. 12.0(a) with
the designation form.

There will be no continuance except for grave cause.

All counsel presenting oral argument must arrive at least
15 minutes before court convenes. Arguing counsel should proceed
directly to the courtroom and check-in with the courtroom deputy.

On occasion, cases scheduled for oral argument
are removed from the calendar before the scheduled date. The
oral argument calendar is frequently prepared before the judges
have completed their review of the briefs. Therefore, if the
panel ultimately concludes that argument is not warranted in a
particular case, that case will be removed from the argument
calendar. In such circumstances, the Clerk's Office will
endeavor to notify counsel as promptly as possible.

Richard Cushing Donovan, Clerk

Kristie Trimarco
Courtroom Deputy
617-748-9069

cc: Edgar R. Vega-Pabon, Esq.
       Howard M. Srebnick, Esq.

UNITED STATES COURT OF APPEALS
FOR THE FIRST CIRCUIT

Designation of Attorney Presenting Oral Argument

**Counsel who intend to present oral argument to the court must complete this form
and return it to the clerk's office no later than <u>February 8, 2008.</u>**

Counsel presenting oral argument <u>must</u> be admitted to practice before this court and <u>must</u> have entered an appearance in the case. Counsel who have not entered an appearance <u>must</u> file an appearance and a motion for leave pursuant to Loc. R. 12.0(a) with this designation by the due date above.

Appeal No._____   Date of Argument: <u>Wednesday, March 5, 2008</u>
                                Location: <u>Old San Juan, PR</u>

Case Name:_____

_____

Name and appellate designation of the party(ies) you will be arguing on behalf of:

_____

Attorney Name:_____   First Circuit Bar No._____

Phone Number:_____   Fax Number:_____

Email:_____

Check the box that applies:

☐   I have already filed an appearance in this matter.

☐   I have attached my appearance form and a motion in accordance with Loc. R. 12.0(a).

Signature:_____   Date:_____

PLEASE NOTE: Only arguing counsel will be notified by phone when the opinion is released.

Form 24-5   Motion to Withdraw From Appeal (*Anders*)

IN THE UNITED STATES COURT OF APPEALS
FOR THE THIRD CIRCUIT

UNITED STATES OF AMERICA   )
               v.   )   Docket No.: 00-0000
RN   )
               Appellant.   )

MOTION FOR LEAVE OF COURT TO WITHDRAW AS COUNSEL FOR RN

This is a motion by counsel to withdraw appearance on behalf of Appellant, RN ("N"), in the above referenced matter. This motion is intended to be in conformity with *Anders v. California*, 386 U.S. 738, 87 S. Ct. 1396 (1967) and *United States v. Marvin*, 211 F.3d 778 (3d Cir. 2000). *See* Local Appellate Rule 109.2.

Thomas J. Farrell, Esquire moves to withdraw his appearance on behalf of the Appellant, RN, and avers as follows:

1. The reasons in support of the motion are discussed more fully in the accompanying brief.
2. Appellant received a sentence calling in part for 103 months of imprisonment to be served concurrently with a related state conviction involving drugs. The federal offense involved possession of a firearm by a convicted felon in violation of 18 U.S.C. §922(g). He also possessed the firearm in connection with a drug violation leading to the state conviction. Appellant had a substantial criminal history.
3. Counsel is well aware of his duties as an advocate in this Court. Counsel served as Appellant's trial attorney. Thus, not only has counsel reviewed the record seeking possible errors, but he has added perspective because of his personal involvement. It is particularly painful (and a career first) for this attorney to represent that he is unable to find *any* appellate issues of arguable merit.
4. Counsel claims no infallibility on this point. However, after a thorough review of his case file, the record including the trial transcript, and legal precedents, counsel has not found anything which would permit a principled argument that Appellant's sentence was infected by legal error or "unreasonable."
5. This is not a case in which the sentencing Judge mechanistically applied the United States Sentencing Guidelines and imposed a maximum sentence as "advised" due to Appellant's Guideline range suggested by the Presentence Investigation Report. Essentially, all aspects of the sentence, including the weight of Appellant's criminal history, involved the exercise of the Court's reasonable sentencing discretion. The sentence was within the statutory maximum and, in practical effect, below the maximum levels established by the Sentencing Guidelines.
6. Appellant pleaded guilty. No objections were raised to the sentencing Judge's fact-finding procedures or to any specific factual determinations. The Judge considered all contentions raised on behalf of Appellant and ruled favorably to him on several crucial matters. The Judge also specifically considered other factors relevant under the Sentencing Reform Act. The Guidelines were treated as advisory. In fact, the final sentence departed downward from the Guidelines and was structured to give Appellant the full benefit of concurrency with his previously-imposed state sentence.
7. Some of the Judge's rulings potentially saved Appellant from the risk of serving approximately ten (10) more years of imprisonment. In no sense was Appellant's sentencing a one-sided proceeding.
8. Nothing in the record contradicts the discretionary nature of the sentence or supports contentions of error or unreasonableness.

WHEREFORE, it is respectfully requested that this Honorable Court permit Thomas J. Farrell, Esquire to withdraw his appearance on behalf of Appellant, RN, as Appellant's legal counsel in these proceedings and any other related proceedings.

Respectfully submitted,

_____
Thomas J. Farrell, Esquire
PA I.D. No.: 00000
Dated:

VERIFICATION

I, Thomas J. Farrell, Esquire, Petitioner herein, hereby swear or affirm that the facts contained in the foregoing Motion to Withdraw as Counsel for RN are true and correct to the best of my knowledge, information and belief. I understand that the statements made herein are made subject to the penalties of 18 Pa.C.S.A. §4904 relating to unsworn falsification to authorities.

_____
Thomas J. Farrell, Esquire
Date:

IN THE COURT UNITED STATES COURT OF APPEALS
FOR THE THIRD CIRCUIT

UNITED STATES,	)	
v.	)	Docket No.:
RN,	)	
Appellant.	)	

ORDER OF COURT

AND NOW, to-wit, this _____ day of _____, 2005, upon consideration of the within Motion to Withdraw as Counsel for Appellant, RN, it is hereby ORDERED, ADJUDGED and DECREED as follows:

1. Thomas J. Farrell, Esquire, is hereby withdrawn as legal counsel for Appellant in these and any other related proceedings; and
2. The Clerk of Courts is directed to mark the records accordingly.

BY THE COURT:

_____

CERTIFICATE OF SERVICE

I, Thomas J. Farrell, Esquire, hereby certify that a true and correct copy of the within Motion to Withdraw as Counsel for RN was served via first class mail, postage prepaid to the following this _____ day of _____, 2005:

RN
DOC # 0000

_____
Thomas J. Farrell, Esquire

Form 24-6   *Anders* Brief

IN THE UNITED STATES COURT OF APPEALS
FOR THE THIRD CIRCUIT

UNITED STATES OF AMERICA
v.
RN

Appeal from Judgment of Conviction and Sentence Entered by the United States District Court for the Western District of Pennsylvania (McVerry, J.) at Criminal No. 00-000

BRIEF OF APPELLANT

RN

ANDERS BRIEF

THOMAS J. FARRELL
Pa. I.D. No.
Attorney for Appellant

TABLE OF CONTENTS

STATEMENT OF RELATED CASES

There are no related cases.

STATEMENT OF SUBJECT MATTER AND APPELLATE JURISDICTION

The District Court had jurisdiction over this federal criminal prosecution by virtue of 18 U.S.C. §3231
Section 1291 of Title 28 confers jurisdiction on this Court to hear this appeal, because the appeal comes from a final judgment of conviction and sentence entered on _____. Appellant filed a timely notice of appeal on _____.

STATEMENT OF ISSUES AND STANDARDS OF REVIEW

Whether there is any principled basis to argue that the sentencing Court committed legal error or acted unreasonably in sentencing Appellant to imprisonment for 120 months, less 17 months credit for time served in state custody. *Anders v. California*, 386 U.S. 738 (1967); *United States v. Marvin*, 211 F.3d 778 (2000).

The sentence was not specifically challenged in the lower Court. This Court, however, may review sentences for reasonableness under *United States v. Booker*, and exercise plenary review over application of the Guidelines. *United States v. Marin-Castaneda*, 134 F.3d 551, 554 (3d Cir. 1998).

STATEMENT OF THE CASE

Procedural History

A one-count indictment returned in the Western District of Pennsylvania charged RN ("Appellant" or "N") with unlawful possession of a firearm by a felon, in violation of 18 U.S.C. §922(g). (A 000023)

On _____, N pleaded guilty with a plea agreement. (A 000024-26) At that time, N was represented by the Federal Public Defender's Office. The plea agreement did not limit the Court's sentencing options.

On _____, the sentencing Judge imposed a sentence of 120 months, less 17 months credit for time served in state custody. (A000003) The statutory maximum for a violation of 18 U.S.C. §922 (g) (1) is 120 months.

This appeal followed.

STATEMENT OF FACTS

[Omitted]

The State Court Proceedings

Initially, local authorities in Allegheny County, Pennsylvania, charged N in a seven (7) count Criminal Information, including weapons charges, but a federal grand jury then indicted him for unlawful possession of a firearm by a felon, in violation of 18 U.S.C. §922(g)(1). (PSIR paragraph 56) Thus, the local weapons charges were *nol prossed*, but the remainder of the state case was pursued. (Second Addendum to PSIR)

N thereafter was convicted on state drug and other charges after a trial by jury, and was sentenced to the mandatory minimum term of imprisonment: five (5) to ten (10) years. (A000032)

The Federal Sentencing

In the calculations under the Sentencing Guidelines, N was assessed with a two (2) point enhancement under U.S.S.G. §2K2.1(b)(4) because the firearm at issue was stolen, and a four (4) level enhancement under U.S.S.G. §2K2.1(b)(5), because he possessed the firearm in connection with another felony offense, namely, the distribution of crack cocaine. (PSIR paragraph 17) These enhancements were contested. (A000044-A000045)

In Tentative Findings and Rulings, the sentencing Court rejected various objections raised by N to the sentencing factors (A000011) and concluded that the normal sentencing range would be 130 to 162 months, based upon an offense level of 27 and a criminal history category of VI. Utilizing an offense level 27 and a criminal history category of VI, the Guideline calculation exceeded the statutory maximum of not more than (10) years under 18 U.S.C. §922(g)(1). (A000013) Therefore, the statutory maximum controlled.

On January 12, 2005, the Supreme Court, in *United States v. Booker*, 125 S.Ct. 738, in effect made the Guidelines advisory. The sentencing in this case took place three and a half weeks later, on February 18, 2005. Defense counsel again addressed the two (2) level enhancement under U.S.S.G. §2K2.1(b)(4) (A000044-A000045), and both parties addressed the four (4) level enhancement under U.S.S.G. §2K2.1(b)(5). (A000044, A000050)

The sentencing Judge adopted his tentative findings as the final findings and rulings. (A000042) He stated his intention to impose a sentence of 120 months (the statutory maximum under 18 U.S.C. §922(g) (1)) to run concurrently with the five (5) to (10) year sentence previously imposed by the state court judge for the drug aspects; however, the sentencing Court adjusted N's sentence pursuant to U.S.S.G. §5G1.3(c) by 17 months due to N's continuous incarceration since the date of the offense, September 9, 2003. The final result is a federal sentence of 103 months.

Nixon filed his Notice of Appeal the same day. (A000001).

SUMMARY OF ARGUMENT

The sentencing Court exercised discretion when it imposed a sentence of 120 months (less 17 months for credit for time served) to be served concurrently with a related state sentence upon Appellant for his violation of 18 U.S.C. §922(g). While the sentencing Judge consulted the United States Sentencing Guidelines in reaching the final sentence, he departed from the Guidelines. Absent the statutory maximum that was applicable in this case, N's Guideline range suggested a sentence of 130 to 162 months.

Notwithstanding that the Guidelines suggested *more* than ten (10) years of imprisonment, the sentencing Court structured the sentence so that Appellant would serve no more than ten (10) years on his state and federal convictions *combined* and would be assured of full credit for his 17 months in state/federal pre-sentencing confinement.

Moreover, the sentencing Court had discretion to consider Appellant's extensive criminal history, evidence of his proneness to assaultive/resistant conduct, and his failure to benefit from prior sentences involving probation and parole.

After thoroughly examining all aspects of the present case, including the record, the case file, and legal precedents, counsel represents to this Court that he is unable to find *any* appellate issues of arguable merit.

ARGUMENT

This is not a case in which the Guidelines called for a ten (10) year sentence and the sentencing Court perfunctorily imposed it. The discretionary nature of the sentencing Court's decision is underscored by reference to the intricate procedural problems confronting the defense.

N's arrest by local police involved possession of cocaine base, more commonly known as crack, with intent to distribute. At the time, he also was carrying a firearm and had a prior felony record. Initially, he was charged in state court for both the drugs and firearms. Federal authorities filed a charge for convicted felon in possession of a firearm. The state firearms charge then was dismissed, but the state retained control over the rest of the case.

While represented by other counsel, N pleaded guilty to the federal count. He continued to dispute the drug possession and was convicted by a state court jury. The state conviction was obtained on virtually the same evidence relative to the federal charge.[1] The state court imposed the mandatory minimum sentence of five (5) to ten (10) years.

The statutory maximum sentence on the federal case was ten (10) years. Due to N's criminal history, the Sentencing Guidelines provided for a prison sentence in excess of ten (10) years. Therefore, N was likely to receive ten (10) years of imprisonment on the federal charge of felon in possession.

However, N actually was in greater jeopardy. Unless the sentencing court made several favorable rulings in his favor, N could serve approximately 20 years. The main objective of the defense was to avoid a sentence of such length. To accomplish that objective, it was necessary to seek and obtain several favorable discretionary rulings by the sentencing Judge.

Under state law, N must serve five (5) to ten (10) years (unless his state conviction is reversed). Because he was initially a state prisoner, the state sentence must be served before the federal custody commences. Similarly, the state sentence also had to be imposed before the federal sentence or there would have been no possibility of having the sentences run concurrently. (A concurrent federal sentence must be "hooked" onto some previously imposed sentence.) Finally, N had been in state custody for approximately 17 months and it was not clear whether the federal Bureau of Prisons would grant credit for that time.

There were strong factors mitigating against any leniency whatsoever. Because of his extensive prior record, N's criminal history was at Level VI. Even if some of his prior convictions were subject to attack (they do not seem to be), the applicable Guideline range still would have exceeded ten (10) years. N's criminal record suggested proneness towards violence and particularly physical resistance in his dealings with police officers or guards.

N already had received considerable leniency in the way the federal government charged him. Had the Government also assumed control over the drug portion of the case and/or charged him to the maximum for carrying a firearm in connection with a drug transaction, the federal sentence could have exceeded 20 years. *See* 18 U.S.C. §924(c) and U.S.S.G. §4B1.1. The serious nature of N's violation and prior record certainly were relevant in the exercise of sentencing discretion. A lot of good things had to happen for N to avoid a much longer sentence.

The sentencing Judge responded to several crucial requests on behalf of N. He delayed sentencing pending the Supreme Court's decision in *United States v. Booker*, 125 S. Ct. 738 (2005). This enabled the state proceedings to be nearly concluded before federal sentencing. He granted another motion to delay federal sentencing until after the state sentence was imposed. He made the federal sentence run concurrently with the state sentence. Finally, he reduced N's ten (10) year sentence by 17 months to assure that N received full credit for his time in state custody.

All of these decisions eliminated the more than theoretical risk that N would serve all or most of ten (10) years in state prison and in addition serve all or most of his federal sentence.

The Court did reject two defense contentions. However, both contentions were addressed to the sentencing Court's discretion and the Court resolved these as discretionary matters and not because of any compulsion from the Guidelines. The defense contested six (6) points in enhancements: four (4) points because the firearm was possessed in connection with the drug transaction, and two (2) points because the firearm was stolen and/or its serial number obliterated.

1.

First, since N had been convicted for the drugs and received a mandatory state sentence, the sentencing court was urged to avoid what amounted to "double impact." This was an appeal to the Court to exercise sentencing leniency and not raised as a point of law. The Guidelines appear to require the enhancement. U.S.S.G. §2K2.1(b)(5). (The state *conviction* did not necessarily increase the federal Guideline calculations. It was the underlying facts which had the impact.) The Court's rejection of N's point was strictly discretionary.

2.

Likewise, the Guidelines and rulings of this Court make the history of a stolen weapon and/or obliteration of its serial identification number matters of strict liability, regardless of whether the individual knows of such facts. *United*

---

[1] In view of the jury conviction in state court on the same evidence, and the need for favorable rulings from the sentencing Court, no request was made for additional fact-finding regarding the drug possession.

States v. Mobley, 956 F.2d 450 (3d Cir. 1992). The sentencing Court was invited to exercise discretion because such factors really did not make N's conduct any more or less serious in this case. (A000045) The Court chose not to rule favorably to N on this point.

3.

Had the sentencing Judge rejected the above contentions because he felt bound by the Guidelines, counsel could present those issues here, regardless of how dubious they seem. However, the Judge made it clear that he was imposing the enhancements "knowing that I don't have to" (A000047), but because he concluded they were appropriate.

Although non-Guideline sentences are still reviewed for "reasonableness" no principled arguments appear that N's sentence, which took into account both the seriousness of his conduct and his criminal history was unreasonable. *See United States v. Abdel-Karim*, 124 Fed. Appx. 461, 2005 U.S. App. LEXIS 4877 (7th Cir. 2005). In *United States v. Hadash*, 2005 U.S. App. LEXIS 9718, *4-*5 (8th Cir. May 27, 2005), a case in which the government appealed a downward departure by the district court, the Eighth Circuit delineated instructions for reviewing a sentence for reasonableness, 1) review the factual findings for clear error, 2) determine if the correct Guideline range was applied, 3) determine whether the sentence was reasonable in light of §3553(a) factors. In the instant case, the sentencing Court met the above requirements and additionally afforded considerable leniency in several ways including the reduction of Nixon's sentence by 17 months.

The record of the proceedings specifically shows that no objections were raised to the sentencing Judge's fact finding procedures or to any specific factual determinations.[2] The Judge considered all contentions raised on behalf of N and ruled favorably to him on several crucial matters. The Judge also specifically considered other factors relevant under the Sentencing Reform Act. The Judge made specific reference to N's prior criminal history and the lack of responsiveness to non-custodial sentences. (A000055) The Guidelines clearly were treated as advisory. In fact, the final sentence departed downward from the Guidelines and was structured to give N the full benefit of concurrency with his previously-imposed state sentence.

Counsel is not aware of precedent finding legal error or unreasonableness when a sentencing court imposes a sentence within the statutory and Guideline maximums and 1) departs downward in some respects but not as far as requested by the defense and, 2) clearly states the reasons supporting the sentence, including the nature of a defendant's criminal record. *See United States v. Edwards*, 400 F.3d 591 (8th Cir. 2005) (on *Anders* appeal from revocation of supervised release, in light of defendant's criminal history and nature of violation and fact that defendant received sentence at low end of recommended range, "we cannot say that in this instance such a sentence was unreasonable.")

Although *Booker* has increased a defendant's ability to challenge the reasonableness of a sentence, it does not appear that pre-*Booker* authority regarding appellate review of discretionary sentences is changed very much where, as here, the record shows that the sentencing Court sentenced the defendant within the statutory and Guideline limits after considering all factors which might have mitigated the sentence and, specifically, responded to all requests by the defense. *See United States v. Fessler*, 453 F.2d 953 (3d Cir. 1972) (Pre-Guidelines case in which defendant's sentence was upheld because it was within maximum statutory limit and sentencing Court took into consideration the presentence report, as well as other factors, such as defendant's cooperation with law enforcement and the economic hardship to defendant's family).

CONCLUSION

There simply seems to be no basis for claiming legal error or abuse of discretion. Considering the nature of the events and that a gun was involved, Appellant's prior record, the advisory Guidelines and other factors, counsel is unable to find anything to argue. The sentence here did not exceed the statutory maximum and is consistent with the United States Sentencing Guidelines. Actually, the sentence is lower than what was possible under a different application of the Guidelines or a different structuring of the sentence.

Would counsel have preferred that the sentencing judge impose a lower sentence? Certainly. However, the sentencing court had the power to structure a sentence of greater length and counsel is unable to cite legal reasons why the sentence was "erroneous" or should be characterized as "unreasonable."

Counsel takes no pleasure in writing a brief that sounds more like it came from the Government. That seems to be required by *Anders* and *Marvin*. Counsel's search for positions which would benefit the client began at the district court level. Options were few and the final choices of strategy essentially precluded later relief in this Court. Appellant asked the sentencing Court to exercise sentencing discretion and the Court did so. Not all of the discretion operated

---

[2] Because of the compelling nature of the evidence available to the government and for tactical reasons, the defense elected not to demand more formal evidentiary proceedings.

favorably to N. It is much easier to urge legal error when the sentencing judge interprets the Guidelines than when the case involves an exercise of sentencing discretion. This case essentially involved exercises of discretion.[3]

Therefore, counsel respectfully requests that this Honorable Court permit Thomas J. Farrell, Esquire to withdraw his appearance on behalf of Appellant, RN, as Appellant's legal counsel in these proceedings and any other related proceedings.

Respectfully Submitted,

_____

CERTIFICATE OF BAR MEMBERSHIP

Counsel for Appellant, Thomas J. Farrell, Pa. Id. No. 00000, is a member in good standing of the bar of the Third Circuit Court of Appeals since 1988.

_____
Thomas J. Farrell
Dated:

CERTIFICATE OF VERIFICATION

I hereby certify that the text of the E-Brief and Hard Copies of Brief of Appellant are identical.

_____
Thomas J. Farrell
Dated:

CERTIFICATE OF VERIFICATION

I hereby certify that a virus check was performed on the E-Brief and Hard Copies of Brief of Appellant using Norton AntiVirus Professional 2004.

_____
Thomas J. Farrell
Dated:

CERTIFICATE OF SERVICE

I hereby certify that two copies of the within brief and appendix has been served by mail and by electronic transmission to and upon the following:

_____
_____

I hereby certify that one copy of the within brief and appendix has been served by mail to and upon the following:
RN
DOC # 00000
Allegheny County Jail
912 Second Avenue
Pittsburgh, PA 15219

_____
Thomas J. Farrell
Dated: June 13, 2005

---

[3] Counsel believes that there would be many more potential negatives than positives for Nixon if this case were remanded for new sentencing. That is besides the main point that counsel perceives no arguable basis for relief.

Form 24-7   Certified Record Order

COMMONWEALTH OF PENNSYLVANIA

Superior Court of Pennsylvania
Western District

Karen Reid Bramblett, Esq.
Prothonotary
Eleanor R. Valecko
Deputy Prothonotary

February 1, 2007

310 Grant Street. Suite 600
Pittsburgh. PA 15219-2297
412-565-7592
www.superior.court.state.pa.us

Thomas Farrell, Esq.
Reich Alexander Reisinger & Farrell
1000 Koppers Building 436 7th Avenue
Pittsburgh, PA 15219

In The Superior Court of Pennsylvania

Comm. v. Brown, Oscar	Superior Court Docket No. 1317 WDA 2006
	Trial Court Docket Nos No. CC 2005-4588, 2005-02628

Order

The trial court record has been filed in this office in the above-captioned matter.

It is your responsibility to review the record inventory list and make sure that the certified record forwarded to this court contains those documents necessary to the issues raised on appeal; failure to do so may result in waiver. Pa.R.A.P.1926,1931 (d); *Bennyhoff v. Pappert*, 790 A.2d 313 (Pa.Super.2001); *Commonwealth v. Wint*, 730 A.2d 965 (Pa.Super.1999).

Pursuant to Pa.R.A.P. 2185(a) briefs for the appellant must be filed on or before March 13, 2007.

Upon failure to timely file briefs for the appellant, the court will, on its own motion and without further notice, dismiss the appeal. If the briefs are filed late but before the appeal is dismissed counsel shall not be permitted to argue but shall be available to answer any questions the court may ask.

Pursuant to Pa.R.A.P. 2111(B), copies of the trial court opinion must be appended to the appellant's brief. Briefs will not be accepted for filing unless you comply with this request.

Seven (7) copies of briefs, together with seven (7) copies of the reproduced record, if applicable, must be filed and opposing parties must be served.

If this is a cross appeal, your attention is directed to Pa.R.A.P. 2136 to determine which party is considered the appellant for the purpose of establishing the briefing schedule.

Per Curiam

KSJ

Form 24-8   Sample Appellant Brief

IN THE UNITED STATES COURT OF APPEALS
FOR THE THIRD CIRCUIT

UNITED STATES OF AMERICA

v.

JF

Appeal from Judgment of Conviction Entered by the United States District Court
for the Western District of Pennsylvania (Conti, J.) at Criminal No. 00-000-1

BRIEF OF APPELLANT

JF

Thomas J. Farrell
Pa. I.D. No. 48976
1000 Koppers Building
436 7th Avenue
Pittsburgh, PA 15219
(412) 391-3700
Attorney for Appellant

TABLE OF CONTENTS

TABLE OF AUTHORITIES

Cases

Affronti v. United States, 145 F.2d 3, 7 (8th Cir. 1944)

Christmas v. Sanders, 759 F.2d 1284, 1288 (7th Cir. 1985)

Ellicott v. Pearl, 35 U.S. (Pet.) 412, 439 (1836)

Gelbin v. New York N.H. & H.R.R., 62 F.2d 500, 502 (2d Cir. 1933)
Government of Virgin Islands v. Pinney, 967 F.2d 912 (3rd Cir. 1992)
Pursell v. Horn, 187 F.Supp.2d 260, 356 (W.D. Pa. 2002) (Smith, J.)
Tome v. United States, 513 U.S. 150 (1995)
United States v. Bao, 189 F.3d 860 (9th Cir. 1999)
United States v. Bishop, 264 F.3d 535, 548 (5th Cir. 2001)
United States v. Nelson, 735 F.2d 1070, 1072 (8th Cir. 1984)
United States v. Reyes, 18 F.3d 65 (2nd Cir. 1994)
Statutes
18 U.S.C. §922(g)
18 U.S.C. §3231
21 U.S.C. §841(a)(1)
21 U.S.C. §841 (b)(1)(B)(iii)
28 U.S.C. §1291
FRE 401
FRE 403
FRE 801(d)(1)(B)
FRE 803(3)
Other Authorities
Edward D. Ohlbaum, *The Hobgoblin of the Federal Rules of Evidence: An Analysis of Rule 801(d)(1)(B), Prior Consistent Statements and a New Proposal*, 1987 BYU L. Rev. 231   20, 21, 24

STATEMENT OF RELATED CASES

STATEMENT OF SUBJECT MATTER AND APPELLATE JURISDICTION

The District Court had jurisdiction over this federal criminal prosecution by virtue of 18 U.S.C. §3231.

Section 1291 of Title 28 confers jurisdiction on this Court to hear this appeal because the appeal comes from a final judgment of conviction entered on _____. The District Court amended its judgment of conviction on _____. F filed a timely notice of appeal on _____. (A 000001, A 000037)

STATEMENT OF ISSUES AND STANDARDS OF REVIEW

Whether the District Court erred by admitting hearsay as a prior consistent statement where no allegation of recent fabrication or an improper motive had been made.

This issue was raised and preserved by defense counsel in both Defendant's Motion in Limine and Memorandum of Law and by objections at trial. (A 000215) The standard of review for evidentiary issues is abuse of discretion. *Government of Virgin Islands v. Pinney*, 967 F.2d 912 (3rd Cir. 1992). However, this Court reviews *de novo* the application of an evidentiary rule to the facts.

STATEMENT OF THE CASE

F was arrested on _____ and lodged into state custody on a state parole detainer. A federal grand jury issued a two (2) count Indictment against F on _____, charging him at Count One with possession of a firearm in violation of 18 U.S.C. §922(g) for events that occurred on _____ (A000039), and at Count Two with possession with the intent to distribute five (5) grams or more of a crack cocaine, in violation of 21 U.S.C. §§841(a)(1) and 841 (b)(1)(B)(iii), for events that occurred on _____. (A 000040)

A suppression hearing was held on _____, as to the legality of a vehicle stop of F on _____, the encounter with F on _____, and the evidence obtained as a result of both of those incidents. (A 000043) On _____, the District Court found that the officers' observations of F on _____, gave them a reasonable articulable suspicion that criminal activity was afoot sufficient to justify an investigatory stop and the crack cocaine recovered after the pursuit of F was not "fruit of the poisonous tree," and thus, admissible. (A 000049)

On _____, the District Court also granted a motion by F severing Counts One and Two. (A 000020-21)

On _____, a jury trial found F guilty at Count One. (A 000025) The District Court sentenced F to 85 months on Count One on _____. (A 000031)

On _____, the jury trial on Count Two ended in a mistrial. (A 000031) At the conclusion of F's retrial on Count Two, on _____, the jury returned a verdict of guilty. (A 000034)

On _____, the District Court sentenced F to a term of imprisonment of 360 months. (A 00003, A 000475) On _____, the District Court amended its sentence of _____, by ordering the 360 month term of imprisonment at Count Two to be fully concurrent with the 85 month sentence at Count One. (A 000011) Furthermore, the District Court ordered F's sentence for Count Two to run concurrent to any state sentences he is currently serving and to be served in state custody. (A 000011)

This appeal followed.

STATEMENT OF FACTS

[Omitted]

SUMMARY OF ARGUMENT

The district court violated FRE 801(d)(1)(B) by admitting hearsay as a prior consistent statement where no allegation of recent fabrication or an improper motive had been made. For a statement to be admissible under FRE 801(d)(1)(B), the statement must meet two conditions: (1) It must rebut the improper influence or motive or other reason that allegedly gave rise to the recent fabrication; and (2) it must have been uttered before the improper influence or motive existed.

The district court allowed the government to present evidence of a conversation between the two police officers, M and K, regarding the seizure of evidence that occurred prior to the arrest of F under FRE 801(d)(1)(B). The statements were not prior consistent statements as defined under FRE 801(d)(1)(B) and were used by the government to bolster the testimony of M whose credibility had been placed in question by the defense during its cross-examination.

The government furthered argued, in the alternative, that even if M's statements to K did not meet the requirements of a prior consistent statement under FRE 801(d)(1)(B), they should nonetheless be admitted under the state of mind exception to hearsay under FRE 803(3) to show the officer's plan and background investigation. However, the government did not use K's testimony as background, but as substantive evidence, as shown in the government's closing argument at trial.

ARGUMENT

I.   The District Court Violated Federal Rule of Evidence 801(d)(1)(B) by Allowing the Introduction of Inadmissible Hearsay Evidence

[Omitted]

A.   K's Testimony Was Inadmissible as a Prior Consistent Statement Because the Defense Had Not Raised an Allegation of Improper Motive or Recent Fabrication

B.   K's Testimony Was Not Admissible to Show the Officers' Plan or the Background of the Investigation

CONCLUSION

For the reasons stated above, the case should be remanded for a new trial directing the district court to preclude the use of M's _____ statement to K at the abandoned lot regarding the alleged recovery of the crack cocaine.

Respectfully Submitted,

_____

Thomas J. Farrell
Pa. I.D. No.

CERTIFICATE OF BAR MEMBERSHIP

Counsel for Appellant, Thomas J. Farrell, Pa. Id. No. 48976, is a member in good standing of the bar of the Third Circuit Court of Appeals since 2002.

_____

Thomas J. Farrell
Dated:

CERTIFICATE OF COMPLIANCE WITH FED.R.APP.P. 32(A)(7)(B)

I hereby certify that the brief contains 4,351 words and therefore complies with the type-volume limitation of Fed. R. App. P. 32(a)(7)(B).

_____

Thomas J. Farrell
Dated:

CERTIFICATE OF VERIFICATION

I hereby certify that the text of the E-Brief and Hard Copies of Brief of Appellant are identical.

_____

Thomas J. Farrell
Dated:

CERTIFICATE OF VERIFICATION

I hereby certify that a virus check was performed on the E-Brief and Hard Copies of Brief of Appellant using Norton AntiVirus Professional 2004.

_____

Thomas J. Farrell
Dated:

CERTIFICATE OF SERVICE

I hereby certify that two copies of the within brief and appendix have been served by mail and by electronic transmission to and upon the following:

Assistant U.S. Attorney
United States Attorney's Office
for the Western District of PA
400 U.S. Post Office & Courthouse
Pittsburgh, PA 15219

_____

Thomas J. Farrell
Dated:

Form 24-9   Excerpts From Reply Brief on Harmless Error

IN THE SUPERIOR COURT OF _____
_____ DISTRICT

APPELLATE DOCKET NO.

COMMONWEALTH OF _____
    Appellee

v.

OB
    Appellant

Appeal from the Order of the Honorable _____ of the _____ County Court of Common Pleas, Entered _____ In CC Nos. (Consolidated)

REPLY BRIEF OF APPELLANT, OB

Counsel for Appellant, OB:
Thomas J. Farrell, Esquire
Dated:

TABLE OF CONTENTS

TABLE OF CITATIONS

Cases
Commonwealth v. Dillon, 528 Pa. 417, 598 A.2d 963 (1991)
Commonwealth v. Nolen, 535 Pa. 77 634 A.2d 192 (1993)
Commonwealth v. Ray, 2000 Pa. Super. 126, 751 A. 2d 233 (2000)
Commonwealth v. Rittle, 285 Pa. Super. 522, 425 A. 2d 168 (1980)
Commonwealth v. Gray, 2005 Pa. Super 22, 867 A.2d 560 (2005)
DePetris v. Kuykendall, 239 F.3d 1057 (9th Cir. 2001)
United States v. Burks, 470 F.2d 434(D.C. Cir. 1972)
United States v. James, 169 F.3d 1210 (9th Cir. 1999)

Statutes:
18 Pa.C.S. §6106
Pa. R. Evid. 404(a)(2)(i)
Pa. R. Evid. 405(b)(2)
18 Pa.C.S. §2503(b)

SUMMARY OF ARGUMENT

Appellant, OB, submits this Reply Brief to address three points raised in the Commonwealth's Brief.
[sections omitted]
Finally, the Commonwealth asserts that the trial court's error in precluding the victim character evidence was harmless because it would have been cumulative to the co-defendant's testimony, which the trial court allowed the jury to hear. We submit that this argument is without merit because the co-defendant's testimony was tainted with credibility issues, and the exclusion of additional untainted testimony was substantially prejudicial to the defendant's theory of self-defense.

IV. The Error Was Not Harmless Because the Co-Defendant's Testimony Was No Substitute for the Excluded Independent Unbiased Testimony About the Victim's Violent Acts.

With respect to harmless error, the Commonwealth relies upon *Commonwealth v. Nolen*, 535 Pa. 77, 85, 634 A.2d 192, 196 (1993), which characterizes an error as harmless only if any prejudice from it was de minimus or the evidence was cumulative of "other, untainted evidence."

The Commonwealth attempts to argue that the excluded evidence was cumulative of the co-defendant's testimony, but that testimony surely does not meet the criteria of "other, untainted evidence." There is no more tainted evidence in a criminal case than a defendant's testimony, and the trial court jury instructions so informed the jury. The jury was instructed, in pertinent part, as follows:

> In making your credibility evaluation you should consider testimony of OB as a defendant even though the case regarding him is not before you. You should not disbelieve Mr. B simply because he is a defendant. *However, in weighing his credibility against any other witness, you should consider that he has a vital interest in the outcome of this case.* You can take his interest in the outcome of the case into account, just as you would the interest of any other witness in making up your minds what weight his testimony deserves.

(RR 428a) (emphasis added).

Since a defendant's testimony, particularly about self-defense, is inherently suspect, independent evidence corroborating it must be admitted. *See United States v. James,* 169 F.3d 1210, 1214 (9th Cir. 1999); *see also DePetris v. Kuykendall,* 239 F.3d 1057, 1063 (9th Cir. 2001) (holding that exclusion of such corroborating testimony on the issue of self defense or imperfect self-defense violates the due process right to present a valid defense). "Extrinsic proof that the decedent did in fact commit a violent act serves to corroborate the defendant's testimony as to what he heard, and is therefore relevant to the question whether the defendant did, in fact, fear injury at the hands of the decedent." *Burks,* 470 F.2d at 435 n.5.

Mr. B sought to introduce independent eyewitness testimony regarding a specific incident of M's violent conduct to corroborate his co-defendant's testimony that M had violent gun-carrying tendencies. Testimony from the responding police officer and tavern owner, who bore no relationship to the defendants and who would have had no personal interest in the outcome of the this trial, was not cumulative to the co-defendant's testimony because this testimony, unlike the co-defendant's, would not be tainted with credibility problems. The trial court's improper exclusion of these witnesses at trial was seriously prejudicial to Mr. B's defense. The prejudice was substantial because this evidence was vital to the defendant's strategy to not testify at trial, and yet offer a theory of self-defense to show that M, while in a heated argument with B on the night of the shooting, may have been the aggressor.

Further, the testimony from the _____ Tavern owner and arresting officer would not have been cumulative because B did not testify as to the _____ incident. He testified merely that he knew M to carry a weapon and he believed that M was not afraid to use it. (R3 19a) This vague testimony was no substitute for specific testimony from unbiased witnesses.

The _____ testimony would have established both the likelihood of a belief that M was violent and the probability that he was the initial aggressor. Perhaps the belief that M was reaching for a gun was unreasonable, but evidence of an unreasonable belief in the need to defend himself would have earned B to convict him of the lesser offense of voluntary manslaughter rather than first-degree murder. *See* 18 Pa.C.S. §2503(b).

Finally, it is the prosecution's burden to prove that the trial court's error in the exclusion of evidence was harmless beyond a reasonable doubt. *Nolen, supra.* This was not met here. The evidence would justify a verdict of acquittal based upon self-defense, or a lesser conviction for voluntary manslaughter based upon imperfect self-defense.

CONCLUSION

For the reasons stated above and those stated in Appellant's opening brief, the Court should vacate the convictions and enter judgments of acquittal.

Respectfully Submitted,

_____

Thomas J. Farrell
Counsel for
Defendant/Appellant
OB
Date:

INDEX

References are to sections and form numbers.

J

S

Search and Seizure
Generally, §7:01
Abandonment, §§7:20–7:22
Advice during search, §7:40
Automobile stops and searches, §§7:60–7:62; Form 7–4
Border, §§7:107, 7:108
Computer searches. *See* **Computer Searches**
Consent searches. *See* **Consent Searches**
Consent to, §4:55
Constitutional standards, §7:03
Defense goals, §7:02
Establishing a search, §7:11
Exigent circumstances, §7:106
GPS tracking and, §7:13
Incident to arrest, §7:65
Inventory searches, §§7:71, 7:70
Person, seizure of, §7:12
Plain view searches, §§7:81, 7:80
Police action, establishing, §7:14
Police authority to perform, §7:61
Post-search conclusions and advice, §7:41
Private searches, §7:16
Probation and parole conditions, §23:23
Property, seizure of, §7:13
Return of property, §§7:120, 7:121; Form 7–7
Standing to challenge, §7:15
Suppression checklist, §7:10
Suppression hearings. *See* **Suppression Hearings**
Terry stops, §§7:50–7:52
Warrants. *See* **Search Warrants**
Search Warrants
Affidavits
based on, Form 7–1
unsealing, §7:36; Form 7–3
Attacking, §7:32
Good faith exception for, §7:31
Identification of items seized, §7:35
Officers' experience and expectations, §7:34
Oral testimony, based on, Form 7–2
Overly broad warrants, §7:33
Particularity requirement of, §7:35
Requirements, §7:30
Scope of, §7:31
SEC Forms
1662, Form 19–3
Selection of jury. *See* **Jury Selection**
Self-Reporting to Prison
Generally, §4:86
Sentence Bargains
Conditional pleas, §17:34
Defined, §17:20

Guidelines, jurisdictions with, §17:22
Judge, involvement of, §17:21
No arrest clauses, §17:26
Pre-sentence investigations, §17:25
Probation officer powers, §17:22
Prosecutor's position, §17:24
Types of bargains, §17:02
Withdrawal of plea, §17:23
Sentencing
Advocating for your client, §§22:40–22:42
Alternatives to, §§22:21, 22:20
Bargains. *See* **Sentence Bargains**
Capital cases, §22:02
Consecutive *vs.* concurrent sentences
multiple jurisdictions, §§22:60–22:63
single jurisdiction, §§22:50–22:52
Credit for time served, §§22:70, 22:71; Form 22–7
Dangerous predators, §22:103
Deportation, §22:104; Form 22–8
Determinate schemes, §22:10
Factors, position of defendant with respect to, Form 22–3
Facts in a mandatory scheme, §22:12
Financial disclosure forms, Form 22–2
Fines, §22:100
Guidelines, §§22:11, 22:13
Habitual offenders, §22:102
Hearings
evidence, §§22:80–22:84
preparation for, §§22:90–22:97
Importance of, §22:01
Incarceration, preparation for, §22:110
Indeterminate schemes, §22:10
Interview worksheet, Form 22–1
Letter, sample, Form 22–6
Letters, §22:42
Memorandum, §22:41; Form 22–5
Persistent offenders, §22:102
Presentence investigation reports, §§22:30–22:35; Form 22–4
Probation and parole revocation, §§23:54–23:56
Reduction motions, §22:111
Representing victims at, §§18:40–18:42
Resentencing, §24:90
Restitution, §§22:100, 22:95
Sex offender registration, §22:101
Sexually violent predators, §22:103
Settlements
Client's advantage, using to, §19:51
Severance and Misjoinder
Generally, §15:50; Form 15–4
Co-counsel, quality of, §15:55
Multiple charges against single defendant, §15:51
Multiple defendants

Read-back requests, §20:255
Relevance of evidence, §§20:120–20:124
"Some other dude did it" defense, §20:200
Subpoenas, §20:44
Theory of defense charge, §20:252; Form 20–8
Venue changes
    generally, §20:20
    motion practice, §§15:70–15:72; Form 15–5
    presumptive prejudice, establishing, §20:21
Verdicts, §20:258
Witnesses and testimony. *See* **Witnesses and Testimony**
Witness statements, obtaining, §20:43

U

Uniform Criminal Extradition Act (UCEA). *See* **Extradition (Interstate)**
Unjust Enrichment
    Restitution, §18:53; Form 18–4
Unsecured Bail Bonds
    Generally, §4:20

V

Venire
    Jury selection, §20:50
Venue Changes
    Generally, §20:20
    Motion practice, §§15:70–15:72; Form 15–5
    Presumptive prejudice, establishing, §20:21
Verdicts
    Trials, §20:258
Victims
    Attorneys and. *See* **Attorneys**
    Compensation, §18:60
    Impact statements, Form 18–3
    Notification of, Form 18–5
    Qui tam actions, §18:62
    Restitution, §§18:50–18:53
    Rewards, §18:61
    Rights, §18:03
Violent Crimes
    Bail and pretrial release, §4:70
Voir Dire
    Generally, §20:70
    Focus groups, §20:71
    Goals, §20:74
    Individual voir dire, §20:75
    Investigations, §20:72
    Juror profiles, §20:71
    Presence of client, §20:73
    Sample questions, Form 20–7
    Topics, §20:76

W

Wade **Hearings**
    Identification testimony, §9:40
Waiver
    Appeals, §§24:40, 24:41
    Extradition waivers, §4:52
    Jury trials, §20:30
    Miranda, §8:22
    Plea bargaining, §§17:31, 17:52
    Preliminary hearings, §10:42
    Psychiatric examinations, §13:40
    Right to counsel, §8:33
Whistleblowers Protection
    Generally, §18:22
Witnesses and Testimony
    Avoiding testimony in civil proceedings, §19:53
    Client as witness, §18:02
    Competency, §13:04
    Cooperating witnesses
        assurances from prosecution, §18:35
        defense lawyer's policy, §18:30
        early debriefing, attending, §18:33
        limiting extent of, §18:34
        preview of client's story, §18:31
        rehearsing, §18:32
    Cross-examination. *See* **Cross-Examination**
    Defendant as, §§20:220–20:223
    Discovery of witness identities, §§14:40–14:42
    Experts. *See* **Experts**
    Grand juries. *See* **Grand Juries**
    Identification procedures (trial), §§9:50–9:52
    Interference with, §§6:32, 6:31
    Investigator, choosing, §6:10
    Obtaining statements from, §20:43
    Preliminary hearings
        calling, §10:43
        interviewing, §10:24
        unavailable witnesses, §§10:44–10:47
    Preparation of defense witnesses, §20:191
    Prior consistent statements, §20:163
    Prior inconsistent statements
        cross-examination, §20:161
        defense evidence, §20:211
    Privileges
        attorney-client privilege. *See* **Attorney-Client Privilege**
    Fifth Amendment. *See* **Fifth Amendment**
        grand juries. *See* **Grand Juries**
    Refreshing recollection, §20:164
    Suppression hearings. *See* **Suppression Hearings**
Witness Instructions
    Lineups, §9:12